THE
LONE
RANGER

THE
RADIO
YEARS
1938 – 1942

by
Terry Salomonson and Martin Grams, Jr.

OTR Publishing

Published in the United States of America by:
OTR Publishing, LLC
PO Box 52
Whiteford, MD 21160
www.MartinGrams.biz

Printed in the United States.

Typesetting and layout by Allan Duffin

ISBN 9798324106379

Table of Contents

Introduction

THEY SAY REMBRANDTS DO NOT ARRIVE ready-made, as proven with the publication of the first volume in this series, spanning the years of 1933 through 1937 and demonstrating in immaculate detail that *The Lone Ranger* program was not created overnight – it evolved over time. Month by month, the wholesome trademarks that became part and parcel of the program changed in subtle ways from a laughing-at-danger rendition to one humble and virtuous. By 1938, the characters of The Lone Ranger and Tonto had matured to the personas we are familiar with today. The Lone Ranger was no longer gunning down Mexicans and gypsies, but rather assisting meek cattle ranchers against overwhelming odds, ending their campaigns for justice with an eruption of action and musical crescendo.

Rumors, myths, and misconceptions run rampant on the Internet with little regard to examining historical documents for accuracy. Anyone with access to a keyboard can describe what they think might have happened as if it were fact, but few document what *really* happened. No better example can be found than that of *The Lone Ranger* radio program, inaccurately documented on numerous Internet websites by fanboys who write romantically with suggestions that *The Lone Ranger* was a national sensation from day one, unaware the program was rarely heard outside of Michigan during those first few months of 1933.

Truth be told, radio during its early years was considered a throw-away medium. No sooner did the broadcast conclude when the cast tossed their scripts into a box in the corner of the room and returned a couple days later to rehearse for the next *Lone Ranger* adventure.

Over a number of years, through network connections, coverage expanded from the East Coast to the West. All of this was covered extensively in the first volume of this massive *Lone Ranger* project. With this second volume, we will explore how the coverage was expanded to areas that could not connect to network affiliates via phone lines, thanks to H. Allen Campbell, who possessed the foresight to record the radio broadcasts on transcription discs for syndication.

Historical hindsight applied, it was not until 1938 that *The Lone Ranger* radio program truly became a national sensation through those transcription discs, aided by a silver screen cliffhanger serial produced and released by Republic Pictures, and an explosion of licensed toys that made even Santa Claus consider delivering presents via stagecoach instead of sleigh that Christmas.

What will also be evident is how Trendle was short-sighted when it came to merchandising. His vision never extended beyond his corner office, or the contracts he negotiated, underestimating the value of premiums and collectibles until the royalty checks started to pour in during the first few months of 1938 – especially with rentals of the transcription discs. The reason why, today, we have thousands of radio broadcasts to enjoy in recorded form is not due to preservation methods. It was a business decision that led to the program's unintended preservation on 16-inch electrical transcription discs. These business decisions will be explored, and in the process set the facts straight regarding the romance behind the merchandising.

When the transcription discs began to be distributed in March of 1938, the radio program grew in popularity not because of the program's content, but because of the extended coverage. The movie serial chapters added more fuel as radio stations across the country sought out rental fees for the program, hoping to cash in on what appeared to be a craze so popular that Hollywood had beaten local radio stations to the punch.

No adequate study of the radio program prior to 1938 has, so far as we know, ever been made. It was a difficult challenge, to be sure, but an important one. The publication of our first volume, spanning the years 1933 to 1937, debunked a number of oft-reported inaccuracies, with scans of archival documents to back up the true facts. Anyone with an I.Q. higher than room temperature can decipher the truth when reviewing scans and reprints of historical documents. Sadly, with valuable space limited to 800 pages per volume, it is a darn shame that information regarding *The Lone Ranger* is sacrificed for archival scans to combat the ever-growing problem of Internet falsehoods.

Among the misconceptions is a frequent claim that recordings of radio broadcasts from 1933-1937 are "lost," but that term indicates a possible chance for transcriptions to be found in a warehouse or military hangar crated next to the Lost Ark of the Covenant. Since recordings of *The Lone Ranger* were not authorized on a regular basis until early 1938, recordings pre-1938 are extremely rare and should not be considered "lost," but rather "non-existent." The authors of this book made sure to apply proper terminology throughout the book to ensure the accuracy of the facts contained within this volume, and to avoid the same pitfall others have fallen into with their publications, blogs, and websites.

The first five years of the series (1933-37) were chosen deliberately for the first book because those were the years that *The Lone Ranger* was not recorded. This book picks up where that initial volume left off, now spanning the years 1938 to 1942, beginning with Trendle's decision to start recording the radio broadcasts on a regular basis. It was during these years that the origin of The Lone Ranger was fully established, through multiple parties, and evolved with each retelling.

It was during this time period that Shirley Temple confessed *The Lone Ranger* was her favorite radio show. General MacArthur's small son swore he never missed a *Lone Ranger* broadcast. First

Lady Eleanor Roosevelt, the wife of the U.S. President, wrote of her grandson in her column: "The other evening I offered to read aloud to Buzz until bedtime, but there is a program on the air called *The Lone Ranger* which seems to be entirely satisfactory."

The western program was a favorite in the household of actress Helen Hayes. Verification can be found when the actress's daughter, Mary MacArthur, celebrated her tenth birthday in February of 1940 and she received a phone call from Earle Graser, The Lone Ranger himself, wishing her a happy birthday. The phone call was arranged by her mother.

During World War II, the Army used the phrases "Hi-Yo Silver" and "Get 'em up, Scout" as passwords. Out in the Libyan desert, "Hi-Yo Silver" was the battle cry of a British tank corps as the firing began.

J. Edgar Hoover was quoted in *Time* magazine as saying that *The Lone Ranger* "is one of the greatest forces for juvenile good in the country."

At a race track, a horse who broke from the crowd and ran part of the distance was hailed "Hi-Yo Silver."

A couple of debutantes from Chicago attended a fox hunt in England. The host of the young ladies asked, "What is that jolly cry you Yanks use to start a horse?" In unison the girls shouted, "Hi-Yo Silver, away!"

By 1939, it was estimated that Fran Striker had created 10,000 different characters on *The Lone Ranger* program, while Striker himself was also a consultant for the filmed rendition at Republic Pictures. The radio program was not without critics, however, and Fran Striker deliberately read every fan letter. One letter from a mother protested the use of the phrase "You dirty rat." Her son, feeling that The Lone Ranger would say nothing that was not in the best of form, had used the phrase in addressing his mother. Striker made sure the phrase was never again heard on the radio program.

In another letter, this one from Hollywood, a writer objected to a program in which marijuana traffic had been dealt with. Despite the fact that the illicit traffickers had ended up behind the eight ball, or that the subject of "loco weed" had appeared on the radio program multiple times prior, the subject of dope (featured in a number of radio adventures in the 1930s) was thus permanently banned from the show.

Perhaps no letter was more moving than the one Fran Striker received on a rainy Tuesday morning: "Dear Lone Ranger, it might interest you to know that one of your Lone Ranger Scouts is riding now the long, long trail. He wears that beautiful Ranger pin of blue and silver just as his own hands placed it in a new blue-and-silver tie just a few days ago. Your Lone Ranger program was the very last program he listened to over the radio just before he died."

According to one account, a hundred thousand kids in ten-gallon hats in Baltimore – along with plenty of adults – paraded through downtown streets when *The Lone Ranger* made his debut on WBAL.

The main theme of this volume is the commercial recognition of a radio program originally conceived for adults and by 1938 evolved into a national phenomenon for both adults and children. It is our hope, as historians and researchers, that this book (and the additional volumes that follow) helps clarify the correct broadcast dates and script titles, having consulted the radio scripts for proper spelling of script titles and character names, and clarifying when George W. Trendle's operation made clerical errors in the numbering sequence on the disc labels. (Some of our research verified collectors had incorrect broadcast dates for some recordings. Yikes!)

Attention is given to operations outside the radio studio, namely the two cliffhanger serials, the expansion of licensed properties, and the facts as they happened when star Earle Graser was suddenly killed in an accident and was almost immediately replaced by Brace Beemer. Throughout decades of research, no rock was left unturned. Where a seemingly simple question led to considerable discussion and frustration when hitting dead ends, and inconsequential matters left unsettled, part of the conflicting evidence is outlined accordingly – and literally.

Mass marketing of the character of The Lone Ranger established the franchise as a brand name – influencing impressionistic young children to dress up like The Lone Ranger or Tonto and play cowboys and Indians. Perhaps no larger influence can be found than the introduction of young Dan Reid to *The Lone Ranger* saga, in December of 1942, a juvenile sidekick who would ride alongside The Lone Ranger and Tonto on many of their adventures.

Assistance in the preparation of this volume includes D.A. Berryhill, Michael Biel, Rodney Bowcock, Roy Bright, Bob Burnham, Gene Carpenter, Ned Comstock, Travis Conner, Bob Daniel, Ted Davenport, Sean Dougherty, Allan Duffin, Ryan Ellett, Karen Fishman of the Library of Congress, John Gassman, Larry Gassman, John Gunnison, Michael Hayde, Jay Hickerson, Doug Hopkinson, Walden Hughes, Ed Hulse, Everett Humphrey, Reginald M. Jones, Jr., Sammy Jones, Patrick Kerwin of the Library of Congress, Karen Lerner, Gary Lowe, Bobb Lynes, Bill McMahon, Jim Nixon, Daniel O'Neill, Ben Ohmart, numerous photographs from Rick Payne, Rick Rieve, Karl Schadow, Fran Striker, Jr., Janet Striker, Lara Szypszak of the Library of Congress, Mark Tepper, Bob Tevis, Steven Thompson, Kerrie Williams of the Library of Congress, and the impressive photo collection of Larry Zdeb.

Where the first book emphasized the origin of the radio program, and the early adventures that were never recorded, this book emphasizes the merchandise aspect of *The Lone Ranger* beginning in 1938 as the program entered a new phase. Along the way we will explore the legend and lore as it pertains to the mysterious, masked man. Wherever danger threatened, pioneers could always count on The Lone Ranger, on top of the magnificent horse named Silver, riding the Western Range with his faithful Indian friend, Tonto, ever at his side. These are the breathless tales of adventure with a hero whose famous exploits made him beloved to radio and movie audiences everywhere.

Terry Salomonson and Martin Grams, Jr.
March 2024

Chapter One
The Radio Transcriptions

THE ORIGINAL IMAGE OF THE WILD WEST contains a number of elements – one of which was the confrontation between nature and civilization. Civilization is what threatens nature, which constitutes the essence of America as a radical European ideal that brings civilization into the west, and so destroys it. As an example, the plough that broke the plains is the end of the buffalo and the Indian. In terms of literary pedigree, the invented cowboy was a late romantic creation. But in terms of social content, he had a double function: he represented the ideal of expansion and progress, the closing of the frontier, and the coming of the big corporations. Such is what happened in the corporation at Detroit when, in late 1937, H. Allen Campbell convinced George W. Trendle to expand coverage of *The Lone Ranger* program across the blazing frontier.

For reflective insight, *The Lone Ranger* radio program was originally written for grownups, but plain enough for youngsters. By the time the program expanded via transcription in early 1938, the adventures were formatted to please both. (For the purpose of merchandise and licensing, the program was aimed toward youngsters.)

Today, over 2,000 recordings of *The Lone Ranger* radio program exist courtesy of the transcription business. This fact is irrefutable: Trendle and his business partners never funded the recording of transcriptions until early 1938 and then not for preservation. It was solely a business decision. While *The Lone Ranger* program originated from the studios in Detroit, Michigan, the episodes were recorded by NBC in Chicago, via line feed. Regrettably, the misconception continues to circulate that every radio broadcast dating back to 1933 exists and that some hidden treasure trove or stockpile of "lost" episodes remain guarded jealously by a hoarder. Depending on which rendition you hear, that hoarder was either a private collector or a dealer who will not release the recordings without payment of an astronomical ransom. One rendition claims that hundreds of transcription discs were sitting in the basement of a private collector but were destroyed by flood or fire.

Newspaper advertisement in California for *The Lone Ranger*, sponsored by Weber's Bakery (makers of Weber's Bread), October 1937.

Newspaper advertisement in Binghamton, New York, for *The Lone Ranger*, sponsored by the Cobakco Bakery, November 1937.

Newspaper advertisement from Detroit, Michigan,
December 17, 1937.

The story began in late 1937, when H. Allen Campbell sat in the office of Tucker Wayne & Company, in Atlanta, Georgia. The advertising agency represented American Bakeries, makers of Merita Bread, which was sold through seven states in the south: Alabama, Florida, Georgia, Louisiana, North Carolina, South Carolina, and Tennessee. (Southern Virginia would be added soon after). Campbell was trying to sell *The Lone Ranger* as a marketing strategy for the company but his competition in the sale was a popular transcribed series.

"Where do you come up with these prices?" Wayne wanted to know. "I can buy this other show for a third of what you have quoted me."

"Buy it if you like," said Campbell, with his Southern drawl, relaxed and confident. "I mean – I'm givin' you something that shows results – in New York, in Detroit, in Chicago. I don't know what this other show's goin' to do."

"I know you've got a good show," Wayne admitted.

"I don't care what price this other one will quotcha. The price I'm quotin' is our price, take it or leave it."

Campbell was grinning and Wayne laughed.

"You're sure a tough character," said Wayne.

Ultimately, an agreement was drawn up and contracts signed by both parties. The technical problem, however, was how to get *The Lone Ranger* into those southern states without a fourth performance. The cast and crew were already performing *The Lone Ranger* three times each night to accommodate schedules over the Michigan Radio Network, Don Lee Network, and the Mutual Broadcasting System. The answer was electrical transcription. For the technicians of WXYZ, electrical transcription was unexplored technology, but Campbell knew that if others could sell programs that way, so could WXYZ. The sponsor wanted flexibility of having the program aired on various stations at different times across the seven states to accommodate local programming schedules, something Campbell and Trendle could only provide through transcription. *The Lone Ranger* program would air at 4:45 p.m. over WIOD in Miami, Florida, while the same program would air at 6:30 p.m. over WGST in Atlanta, Georgia. *

Back in Detroit, Campbell suggested and then insisted that *The Lone Ranger* expand to regions via transcription discs. As a ten percent stockholder of The Lone Ranger, Inc., Campbell was risking not just his reputation, but his investment as well.

Inter-office memos indicate Trendle eventually relented but insisted that an experiment be made to test the waters in advance and verify transcriptions could, in fact, work out sufficiently. Also, a stockpile of transcription discs would be needed as a safety cushion – at least, three weeks' worth of episodes in advance before making them available nationally. By some accounts, the program was kept four weeks ahead. Safety cushion aside, it also appears that throughout 1938 and 1939 radio stations were provided with six special discs as buildup for characters on the new outlets, all before being supplied with consecutive transcriptions. These would be the transcription discs labeled numbers one through six.

---

* Soon after sponsorship began, The Lone Ranger Safety Club proved a handy index to the popularity of the radio program in the eight Southeastern states where it functioned. American Bakeries jumped from a gross of $4 million dollars a year to $37 million dollars a year as a direct result of sponsoring *The Lone Ranger*.

George W. Trendle at his desk.

Cast of *The Green Hornet* in a promotional photo.

To test the waters, the broadcast of December 17, 1937, was recorded off the air in Chicago. Playback capability would then be used as an inside joke. During *The Green Hornet* broadcast of January 13, 1938, The Green Hornet paid a late-night visit to the house of Judge Woodbury, known for being strict in his courtroom and in need of a motivational push to set a trap and expose a crooked attorney. The Green Hornet climbed through the window of the judge's bedroom. As the announcer described…

ANNOUNCER: The slick black car of The Green Hornet with its super-powered motor was parked in the drive of Judge Woodbury's home a few minutes later. The Judge was listening to *The Lone Ranger*, one of his favorite radio programs, half dozing in his chair.

Striker's notes on the script indicated playing back a recording of *The Lone Ranger*. This was the December 17 test recording. With success evident, George W. Trendle went into the transcription business. The first few broadcasts to be recorded were sporadic beginning with the broadcast of January 17, 1938.

It should be noted that in some instances, to accommodate scheduling conflicts, recordings of *The Lone Ranger* were made prior to December 1937, but only at local stations across the country such as WOR in New York. These were never done on any type of regular basis and only allowed under two provisions: Trendle had to approve the request in advance and the discs were to be destroyed after playback. At the time of this book's publication, a few recordings exist with WOR labels, from April and September of 1937.

Beginning with the January 10, 1938, issue of *Radio Daily*, this would be the first quarter-page advertisement promoting the transcription discs would appear in print.

The earliest announcement of transcription discs available to radio stations came on Monday, January 10, 1938, when King-Trendle released a public statement that *The Lone Ranger* would be riding cross-country. Coinciding with the Republic serial released in theaters in February, King-Trendle announced it would market transcriptions of the radio series for February 1 assignments. "The strong growth of the series since it premiered four years previous showed promise and broke all records for mail response for WXYZ," claimed the report. The discs would be available for broadcast starting February 15. *

As director Jim Jewell recounted to author Dick Osgood, the contract was signed on a Friday and the first recorded shows were to be in the mail three days later. Recording the shows as they aired live, piped through to Chicago, proved a challenge when three episodes were needed prior to commencement. "Allen Campbell sold *The Lone Ranger* to seven stations in the south without telling me about it," Jewell recalled. "I was informed on Friday that we were to send three half-hour transcribed shows out of WXYZ to these stations that following Monday, in addition to all the other work we were doing." Jim Jewell's recollection demonstrated how characteristic it was of "the downtown office" to issue a command with no thought as to what was involved.

Al Hindle, who was head of RCA in Chicago, was a friend of Jewell's. Arrangements were made with Hindle to open a line between Detroit and Chicago and the three radio dramas would be performed on Saturday and/or Sunday, the same dramas featured through the week prior for live feeds. "The troupe of actors – and God love 'em, God bless 'em – just said 'All right, Jim, it's going to take us two days to do this and we won't have time to eat or sleep and let's get to work,'" Jewell recalled. "So this is literally what happened. We piped those first three shows over from Detroit and they were recorded by RCA in Chicago. And we met the deadline for Monday. The records were mailed out on time. And nobody ever said thank you."

Careful review of the radio scripts to the transcription numbers verify that the assigned transcription disc numbers are out of sequence. The first six recordings were not consecutive. Recording #3, for example, was episode #777, broadcast on January 19, 1938. Recording #4 was episode #763, broadcast December 17, 1937. The transcription discs had their own numbering system, played back chronologically, based on the numbering sequence on the disc labels. It would not be until the last week of February 1938 that the disc labels corresponded consecutively with the live broadcasts. Beginning with recording #7, the radio broadcasts were recorded in chronological order, beginning with the broadcast of January 31, 1938.

The first stations to broadcast *The Lone Ranger* through transcription discs did so on the evening of February 21, 1938. The Schulze Baking Company (also referenced interchangeably with Interstate Bakeries due to a merger at the time) footed the bill over WCKY in Cincinnati, KOIL in Omaha, KSO-KRNT in Des Moines (inclusive of WMT, Waterloo), and WCBS in Springfield, Illinois, while the V-Bev Beverage Company was responsible for the program over WCAE in Pittsburgh, WAAD in Boston, and WEAN in Providence. *Variety* reported the set-up was "due to the fact expense and staging efforts entailed would run too high; time variations too great, since cast now

---

* Regardless of what is reported in printed reference guides, *The Green Hornet* was not the second program originating out of WXYZ to be transcribed. That honor was reserved for *Ann Worth, Housewife*.

enacts nightly skit three times to catch other outlets on hookup." This meant the Michigan and Mutual broadcasts were four weeks ahead of the seven stations referred to above; each station provided with six discs in advance."

When Schulze began sponsoring *The Lone Ranger* program over KRNT, they thought to do a little showmanship of their own by asking their truck drivers to adopt the wide-brimmed sombrero, red kerchief and other ranger frills on their routes. This gimmick backfired. Reporting in for work (about 4:30 a.m.) the first morning, one of the men was picked up by a squad car and was not released until the baking company identified him and explained the 'get up.'

TUNE IN
"The Lone Ranger"
Over These Stations

TOWN	STATION	DAYS	TIME
Cincinnati Ohio	WCKY	Tuesday Thursday Sunday	7:30 P.M. 4:30 P.M.
Des Moines Iowa	KRNT	Sunday Wednesday Friday	6:30 P.M.
Omaha Nebr.	KOIL	Monday Wednesday Friday	6:30 P.M.
Springfield Illinois	WCBS	Monday Wednesday Friday	7:30 P.M.

SCHULZE BAKING COMPANY

© 1938, The Lone Ranger, Inc.

This Week
with
"THE LONE RANGER"

Tell Your Mother to Order the Official

Dolly Madison CAKES

LONE RANGER CAKES

At Your Grocer's

You've never tasted cakes more tempting, more delicious. In many different flavors. Inexpensive. Ask for DOLLY MADISON CAKES—the cakes that make the Lone Ranger radio programs possible.

In Cincinnati, Schulze was promoting Butter-Nut Bread and Dolly Madison Cakes during the commercial breaks, and also requested their driver-salesmen to wear 10-gallon cowboy hats, red bandanas and large badges publicizing the program, on their daily rounds. The men also placed wall and window signs in 3,500 bread outlets in Greater Cincinnati, in addition to 7,000 pennants calling attention to *The Lone Ranger* broadcasts. The bread packages were banded with a special red label, giving the time of the program on WCKY. Bread wrappers also provided program information. The entire campaign, with explanations of premiums to be given later, was outlined at a meeting of the driver-salesmen at the Sinton Hotel prior to the first broadcast. For two weeks, every loaf of Butter-Nut Bread sold out in Cincinnati.

Next, Campbell called on the General Baking Company in Kansas City, Missouri. Through the office of B.B.D.&O., *The Lone Ranger* was sold for broadcast on eight stations – but not without hesitation over the price.

"Look," said Campbell. "What do you want to do – have your competitor buy this show? I mean – they'd grab it!" Kansas City bought the program. (See Appendix D for a list of stations.)

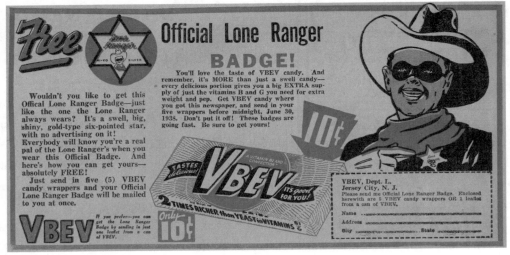

1938 full page ad for Friday, November 24 edition of the *Kansas City Journal*.

In the middle of March, a deal was made whereby the NBC Thesaurus division in Chicago would handle the sale of *The Lone Ranger* transcription discs in certain areas of the United States and all foreign countries where Campbell had less negotiable leverage. Maurie Wetzel, Thesaurus chief in Chicago, spent the last week of March on a general sales trip through the south and southwest peddling *The Lone Ranger* platters along with the rest of the Thesaurus service.

The transcription disc rentals were profitable enough to warrant expansion. In early April 1938, an arrangement was made by Campbell to pipe *The Green Hornet* into WGN for sponsorship twice weekly for Healthairs, Inc., promoting their V-Bev beverage. *The Green Hornet* was broadcast Tuesday and Thursday, fitting in between the three shows of *The Lone Ranger* program. Campbell figured on selling *The Green Hornet* to regional advertisers on the same basis as *The Lone Ranger* set up. *The Green Hornet* started as a sustainer at WGN, then switched to its V-Bev sponsorship on May 3. (There is indication that Campbell wanted to transcribe *The Green Hornet* for shipping to the West Coast in late February as a sustainer for a few weeks, for a build up before adding a network sponsor, but Trendle insisted they wait to see the sales results of *The Lone Ranger* first.) Recording of *The Green Hornet* program commenced on the evening of May 24, 1938.

Naturally, expansion through transcription discs meant expansion of The Lone Ranger Safety Club. Plans for the organization of a large safety club with all the boys and girls in Des Moines were announced by the sponsors of *The Lone Ranger*, the Schulze Baking Company, beginning on the broadcast of Wednesday, May 4. The program was heard on Wednesdays, Fridays and Sundays at 5:30 pm over KRNT. Application blanks were included in *The Lone Ranger News*, copies of which were available at most grocery stores in Des Moines.

In March of 1938, tying in with the present State campaign to cut highway accidents, WFIL in Philadelphia organized the Lone Ranger Safety Club for kids, with the half-hour show airing once a week every Sunday morning. Overseen by Dave Tyson, who handled the production and direction of children's programs under the tag "Daddy Dave," Lone Ranger troops were formed in each section of the city, with the station awarding a charter to each group and badge to each "trooper." Troop leaders assembled at the radio station during broadcasts for weekly "pow-wows." A bronze plaque was given every Sunday to the troop who contributed most towards highway safety during the prior seven days.

BRIT REID, EDITOR-THE GREEN HORNET SENTINEL
COPYRIGHT 1939 –GREEN HORNET INC.

Al Hodge as Britt Reid, alias "The Green Hornet."

THE SHADOW OF SECRET JUSTICE
COPYRIGHT 1939-GREEN HORNET INC.

On Sunday, March 20, 1938, at the conclusion of *The Lone Ranger* adventure heard over KRNT (a station of the Iowa Network), the following announcement was made: "Go to your grocer tomorrow or to any Schulze truck driver, say 'Hi-Yo, Silver,' and you will get an exact replica of the black mask worn by The Lone Ranger." By noon on Monday, the entire supply of 20,000 masks was completely exhausted. An announcement was made during the following Wednesday night's broadcast apologizing for not having a large enough quantity and letting youngsters know more were on the way. An additional 30,000 were ordered from the manufacturer, delivered a week and a half later, and all 30,000 were gone within three days.

Officials of the Schulze Baking Company knew that WCKY used double street car cards to publicize the program on the street cars, signs on the backs of taxicab covers, and a massive mailing of postcards which not only told of the radio program, but also told the grocers how much they were losing by not stocking Butter-Nut Bread.

On April 20, 1938, Emil Reinhardt of Oakland, California, who handled radio advertising on the Pacific Coast, reported 76,000 members of the Kilpatrick Lone Ranger Safety Club in the San Francisco area, which included members from the following counties: Alameda, San Francisco, San Mateo, Santa Clara, Solano, Sonoma, Stanislaus, Contra Costa, and Marin, with members also scattered throughout the remainder of Northern California.

On April 23, 1938, John J. Corrigan, Program Director of WCBS, Inc. (Wider Coverage Better

Service, located in Springfield, Illinois), wrote to Charles Hicks (Sales Promotion Department of the King-Trendle Broadcasting Corp.), providing an update regarding the recent promotion of *The Lone Ranger* under sponsorship of the Schulze Baking Company. "So great was the response and the calls for the *Lone Ranger* masks that the offer had to be discontinued after one week of presentation. We are calling upon the sponsor who will explain this element more in a separate letter. Meanwhile, we have not yet begun the Safety Club campaign. It will probably get under way about April 25."

On April 25, 1938, E.B. Craney of KGIR in Butte, Montana, reported that on the broadcast of April 13, an announcement was made preceding *The Lone Ranger*, offering 50 *Lone Ranger* premiums to the first 50 people writing in letters. A total of 270 letters from that single announcement was received.

According to a letter from James V. Bonner, Sales Promotion Manager for the Colonial Network, dated May 12, 1938, addressed to Charles Hicks, the broadcast

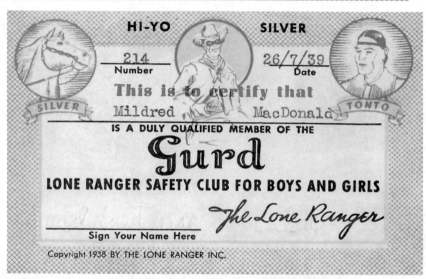

THIS IS TO CERTIFY THAT

Burton Clendenn

IS A CHARTER MEMBER

OF THE

LONE RANGER SAFETY CLUB

1939

Sponsored by

The Bakers of TOWN TALK BREAD

Hi-Yo Silver

NO _____ DATE _Dec. 5. 39_

This is to certify that

Jack Hooker, Jr.

is a duly qualified member of the

BESTYETT

LONE RANGER SAFETY CLUB FOR BOYS AND GIRLS

The Lone Ranger

© 1939, T. L. R., Inc.

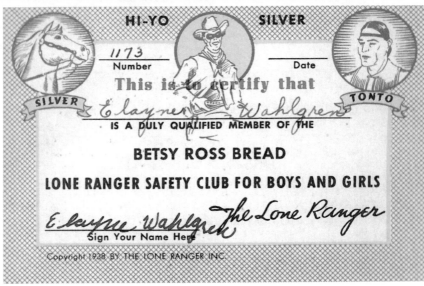

HI-YO SILVER

_1173_
Number   Date

SILVER   TONTO

This is to certify that

Elayne Wahlgren

IS A DULY QUALIFIED MEMBER OF THE

BETSY ROSS BREAD

LONE RANGER SAFETY CLUB FOR BOYS AND GIRLS

Elayne Wahlgren   _The Lone Ranger_
Sign Your Name Here

Copyright 1938 BY THE LONE RANGER INC.

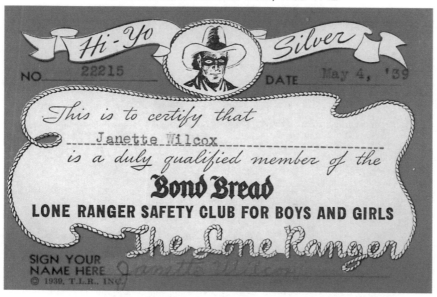

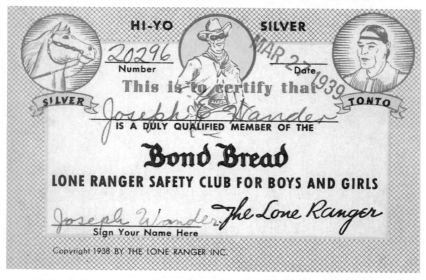

Advertisement in the February 1, 1940, issue of a Corsicana, Texas, newspaper.

The New
LONE RANGER SAFETY CLUB
SPONSORED BY MERITA BREAD AND CAKE

HEADQUARTERS "HI-YO SILVER"

Dear Safety Ranger:

Here is your official badge of membership in the New Lone Ranger Safety Club. Take good care of it and wear it always, because it reminds you and other folks to follow the rules of safety. Now, how would you like to have your own local chapter of the Lone Ranger Safety Club? Yes, a real Safety Club of your own, for yourself and your schoolmates!

Just think of all you can do for Safety when you and your friends band together in an official chapter of the Safety Club. It will be a real help to your own community's safety campaign. What's more, you and your fellow club-mates can have loads of fun, with picnics, hikes, sporting events, parades and all sorts of club activities.

Below is a picture of the handsome charter that the Merita folks and I have reserved for your chapter of the club, absolutely free. Now, here is what you do to form your club and obtain the charter, which bears the official gold seal of the Safety Club.

Show this letter to your school-teacher, and tell her you would like to have a chapter of the club in your classroom at school. There should be ten or more members in the chapter, and of course each one of them <u>must</u> be a member of the <u>new</u> Lone Ranger Safety Club. <u>Ask your teacher to write to the Lone Ranger, care of Merita Bread, Atlanta, Ga., to ask for an official charter for your club.</u> If any of the boys or girls who will be in your club have not yet joined the <u>new</u> Lone Ranger Safety Club, your teacher should ask me to send her enough safety club cards so that all of them can join right away, when I send the charter to her.

School-teachers all over the South have been organizing their classes as chapters of my safety club, and I know your teacher will be delighted to get the charter for you. The reason I suggest that she help you obtain the charter and form the club is that she can be a big help to you in showing

how you can get the club started and how you can best make it work for the safety of your school and your community. On the very next school day, get together with the fellows and girls who will belong to your chapter of the club and talk to teacher about sending for the charter. Be sure to show her this letter, so she can send for the charter and club cards right away.

RQFJ S JYSUFO "JQ-OV, EQCWYU!"

Your friend,

Lone Ranger

THE LONE RANGER

Copyright, 1942, The Lone Ranger, Inc.

TUNE IN *"THE LONE RANGER"* THREE TIMES A WEEK OVER A STATION NEAR YOU

When Safety Club cards were mailed out to fans of the radio program, letters like these were often included.

LONE RANGER SAFETY CLUB
SPONSORED BY MERITA BREAD AND CAKE

Dear Safety Ranger:

Here's your Lone Ranger Lucky Coin. Isn't it a beauty? Surely you'll want to take good care of it and be sure that you never lose it.

Now don't forget that your loyalty to Merita makes it possible for me not only to bring you my radio programs, but also to carry on the work of the new Lone Ranger Safety Club, and to offer you all these fine free gifts too. Each of these surprises is a reward for your loyalty. So, be sure to enjoy Merita Bread and Cakes at your house always, and tell all your friends that when they eat Merita Products, they help to support the new Lone Ranger Safety Club.

And say, there are still more good things in store for you. Here is a picture of the next one. It's the official Lone Ranger Safety Club Badge... an emblem of honor you'll be proud to wear. Don't fail to send for one. It's a fine star-shaped, gold-colored badge with red and blue lettering which shows you are an official Safety Ranger. And it's easy for you to get one.

Just write on a postcard, the words "Please send my Safety Club Badge" and then print your name and complete address plainly, so I'll know where to send the badge. Then, at the bottom of the postcard, write the word "MERITA" in the secret code of our club. Send for yours right away. Mail the postcard to The Lone Ranger, care of Merita Bread, Atlanta, Ga.

UYKYKAYU, KYUQFS AUYSP STP HSLYE KSLY VNU HCNA DVEEQACY.

Your friend,

Lone Ranger

THE LONE RANGER

P. S. Do you want to have your own neighborhood chapter of The Lone Ranger Safety Club? After you send for the badge. I'll tell you how to form a club and get the handsome club charter.

TUNE IN *"THE LONE RANGER"* THREE TIMES A WEEK OVER A STATION NEAR YOU

HEADQUARTERS

LONE RANGER SAFETY CLUB
SPONSORED BY MERITA BREAD AND CAKE

Dear Safety Ranger:

It's a real pleasure to send you your Tonto Headdress and I look forward to sending you the other rewards for your loyalty that the Merita Bakers want you to enjoy.

Now, I know you want to help me get more members, because the more boys and girls we have in our new club, the more accidents we can prevent. Also, I'm sure you want your friends to belong, so you can exchange messages in my new Secret Code and work together for Safety. So Merita has a gift you'll want to get right away.

This gift is a beautiful, bright, shining silvered Lone Ranger Lucky Coin. One side shows our club emblem, and the other shows Silver's Lucky Horseshoe. It's a good luck token you'll want to treasure always. Here's how to

get it _free._ With this letter are three safety club cards. Get three of your friends to fill out the cards so they can join the club. Then, put the filled-out cards in an envelope with a slip of paper showing your name and complete address printed plainly, and the words, "Please send my Lucky Coin." Address the envelope to The Lone Ranger, care of Merita Bread, Atlanta, Ga.

SEL KVFJYU FV AY ENUY FJY AUYSP OVN YSF QE KYUQFS.

Your friend,

Lone Ranger

THE LONE RANGER

P. S. More surprises ahead! After you send for the coin, I'll tell you how to get a free official Safety Club badge and a handsome charter for your own safety club.

Copyright, 1942, The Lone Ranger, Inc.

HEADQUARTERS

LONE RANGER SAFETY CLUB
SPONSORED BY MERITA BREAD AND CAKE

Dear Safety Ranger:

Welcome to my new club! I'm happy to enroll you officially as a fully qualified Safety Ranger, and I'll depend on you to help me promote safety. By doing so, you render yourself, your parents and your community a valuable service.

Our club is really <u>new</u> in every way. There are new rules, a brand new Secret Code, and many surprises in store for you as an active member. The new rules are shown on the enclosed Pledge Certificate. Sign it and put it on your wall or mirror, so you can learn the rules by heart and observe them every day. Your Official Membership Card is enclosed, too. Sign it and take good care of it. Don't show it to anyone not a member of the new club (except Mother or Dad) because on the back is my new Secret Code, which members use to exchange messages.

Nearly 400,000 boys and girls joined my original Safety Club, sponsored by the Merita folks, and they've done splendid safety work. Our new rules are even finer than the old ones, because they help prevent accidents not only on the street, but at home and at school, too. Since everything is new, it's important for all members of the original club to join the New Lone Ranger Safety Club. I'll count on you to see that your friends join it.

<u>You'll Surely want all the big surprises which are in store for members of the new club.</u> Here's the first one—the Lone Ranger Mask, like I wear. You can get one <u>free.</u> Just send me the names of three housewives who promise

to try Merita Bread. Simply write their names on a postcard and say, "Please send my Lone Ranger Mask." <u>Print your name and complete address plainly,</u> so I'll know where to send the mask. Address the card to The Lone Ranger, care of Merita Bread, Atlanta, Ga. Don't delay. Send for your mask right away.

CYF'E OVN STP Q RVUL FVBYFJYU IVU ESIYFO SCRSOE.

Your friend,

Lone Ranger
THE LONE RANGER

P. S. <u>LOOK! After you send for your mask, I'll tell you how to get other grand gifts, like the Tonto Headdress, the Lone Ranger Lucky Coin, official Safety Club Badge, and a Charter for your own Safety Club.</u>

Copyright, 1942, The Lone Ranger, Inc.

of April 8, 1938, featured an offer of a picture of The Lone Ranger. Listeners were encouraged to write in for a free photograph and the offer was used consistently until the broadcast of April 18, when the V-Bev Beverage Company offered *The Lone Ranger and the Secret Killer* (Big Little Book) in return for an insert from a V-Bev carton. The photograph offer was repeated in early May. *

"The program has, in the short time it has been on the air, grown to be one of our most popular features," wrote Bonner, "and the mail count reveals an unusually high return for a program in this area." From April 11 to May 9, the mail count for radio station WAAB in Boston came to 6,387, not representative of the entire Colonial Network. Raymond Spector, of the agency named after him, provided early indication back in February when he remarked in a letter: "As you know, we introduced V-Bev in a highly competitive market simultaneously with the commencement of this program. Today, its sales are on a par with products that have been on the market for years and are most extensively advertised."

On May 17, 1938, James S. Jennison of radio station WEAN in Providence, Rhode Island, part of the Yankee Network, reported: "On three programs of *The Lone Ranger* we made an offer of the picture, which would be sent to the first 5,000 responding and enclosing a three-cent stamp to cover postage. We received 5,842 responses. This response is very large indeed comparing it to similar offers made in recent years. It seems that New England reticence keeps the radio population of this area from replying in large volume to giveaway propositions, so that any offer which brings nearly 6,000 requests can be attributed definitely to a very great popularity of the program involved."

If trade papers can be believed, one grocer remarked: "I've never seen advertising that has everybody talking about it like your *Lone Ranger* program. Many of my customers say *The Lone Ranger* is as important in their homes as breakfast, lunch or dinner." Another remarked, "I found out long ago that I could make more bread and cake profits by featuring Merita products. They always have been best in quality and freshness and most in demand because of that. But now, more people know Merita's goodness than ever, thanks to *The Lone Ranger*, and the demand for Merita is growing greater all the time."

All of this is just a sample of the positive results George W. Trendle reserved for his filing cabinets, verifying the popularity of the programs. Some of these accolades would be reprinted in press books, created with the intent of convincing other potential sponsors to carry the program on local radio stations.

The December 23, 1940, issue of *The Greenville News* reported: *The Lone Ranger* premieres this afternoon from 5:15 to 5:45 pm over WFBC. TLR risks death and danger to save a man from hanging for a crime he did not commit. Long been on the trail of the Sagebrush Gang, which left an innocent victim to take the blame for their crimes, The Lone Ranger and Tonto save the day. Directions for securing applications to join the Lone Ranger Safety Club will be given during the broadcast. Sponsored by Merita bread, with the co-operation of their dealers in this area.

* By 1939, more than half a million Lone Ranger masks and two million photographs of The Lone Ranger were supposedly given away. In 1941, another giveaway was conducted in connection with *The Lone Ranger* program by ad-man Raymond Spector, of the Raymond Spector Company, in which a limited number of announcements produced over 60,000 requests from listeners in the New York market for Lone Ranger Disguise Kits.

KING-TRENDLE BROADCASTING CORPORATION

GEO. W. TRENDLE, *President*   JOHN H. KING, *Vice-President*
HOWARD O. PIERCE, *Secretary*   H. ALLEN CAMPBELL, *Treas. and Gen'l Mgr.*

EXECUTIVE OFFICES: SEVENTEENTH FLOOR, STROH BUILDING, DETROIT, MICHIGAN

Electrical Transcription License

AGREEMENT made this   day of   , 19   , between KING-TRENDLE

BROADCASTING CORPORATION, a Michigan corporation, of Detroit, Wayne County, Michigan, (hereinafter called

LICENSOR), and_____(hereinafter called LICENSEE).

NAME OF PROGRAM:_____

COPYRIGHT OWNER:_____

SPONSOR:_____

   ADDRESS:_____

   MANUFACTURERS OF:_____

Programs to be broadcast over Radio Station_____, City of_____, State of_____,

on the following days of each week_____and,_____

from_____(A.M.—P.M.), to_____(A.M.—P.M.).

TERMS: Licensee agrees to pay Licensor $_____Per program, payable_____.

DEPOSIT:

PERIOD: This license shall be for_____consecutive weeks, commencing the_____day of_____, 19_____.

Any programs furnished before written acceptance hereof, shall not be construed as an approval or acceptance by licensor of this contract.

THE WITHIN CONTRACT SHALL NOT BE BINDING UPON LICENSOR UNLESS AND UNTIL ACCEPTED IN WRITING HEREUNDER BY AN OFFICER OF LICENSOR CORPORATION.

ACCEPTED:

KING-TRENDLE BROADCASTING CORPORATION.

	Licensee
	BY_____
	ACCEPTED AND AGREED TO:
BY_____	
	Sponsor
DATED:_____	BY_____

(Subject to CONDITIONS on Reverse Side)

Contract for sponsors who wanted to lease the transcription discs.

Rentals of the transcription discs would continue through 1954. To maintain control of his property, it was required under contract that the discs be returned, to ensure the station did not continue further use beyond the initial playback. With the popularity of the cliffhanger serial, and the newspaper comic strip which premiered in September 1938, additional stations sought interest in the program. The Pfaff Baking Company of Fort Dodge, Mason City, and Estherville, Iowa, began sponsoring *The Lone Ranger* over KGLO on Monday, September 12. Up until this time Pfaff Baking was sponsoring *Junior Music Hall* over the same station and in the same time slot.

The year 1938 also marked the golden year for Chicago radio broadcasting, historically speaking. While Chicago was considered the central hub of network origination throughout the years, the number of original programs to succeed through national coverage from Chicago faded over time. With the growing dominance of programming from New York and Hollywood, drama production was declining from other regions. According to Erik Barnouw's *The Golden Web*, "During 1936-37 San Francisco, once the chief West Coast radio center, saw an exodus of talent bound for Hollywood. Chicago continued as a drama center, but with a shrinking roster of programs. Detroit survived by syndicating recorded drama series, mainly *The Lone Ranger* and *The Green Hornet*, both produced by station WXYZ."

The Lone Ranger cliffhanger serial premiered in local theaters in Menasha, Wisconsin, in September 1938, prompting the Gear Dairy Company, and the Pankratz Ice and Fuel Company, to sponsor the radio program for a brief time. (The radio program was picked up in Menasha through WGN in Chicago.) A Lone Ranger Club Question Quiz was printed in the September 8 issue of *The Menasha Record*, offering 70 free tickets to the Saturday matinee at the Brin Theatre, a pair given to the first 35 children who gave the correct answers. The Lone Ranger Question Quiz was run in conjunction with The Lone Ranger Club, meetings of which were held at the Brin Theatre every Saturday matinee. A grand prize of five boy or girl bicycles were among the prizes that amounted to approximately $350. The opening meeting of the club was held on Saturday, September 10 and as an added treat, each child received a large bottle of Bireley's Grape-ade.

Beginning November 11, 1938, *The Lone Ranger* program was heard over KGU in Honolulu, Hawaii, broadcast twice weekly, sponsored by the Honolulu Dairymen's Association, promoting Taroco Milk. * The serial would premiere in theaters towards the end of the same month. For a perfect example of how the radio adventures varied across the country with the use of transcription discs, the broadcast dates on the left correspond to the Hawaiian broadcast and the dates on the right are the original WXYZ broadcast dates. **

---

* (The final broadcast for the Dairymen's Association was on Thursday, August 8, 1940. *The Lone Ranger* would be sponsored by the Nehi Beverage Company of Hawaii beginning Tuesday, August 13, 1940.)

** Press releases accompanied the transcription discs shipped to radio stations, with three brief plot summaries on each page, matching the episode numbers on the disc labels. This was for the benefit of the radio stations, to send to local newspapers in the area for the purpose of publicity in the newspapers. One-sentence plot summaries rarely appeared in radio listings across the country but, for the Hawaiian newspapers, this was not uncommon and thus the source for the plots to be matched up with WXYZ dates.

KGU Broadcast Date	WXYZ Broadcast Date
Tuesday, December 6, 1938	February 4, 1938
Friday, December 9, 1938	February 7, 1938
Tuesday, February 28, 1939	March 30, 1938
Tuesday, March 14, 1939	April 6, 1938
Thursday, March 16, 1939	April 11, 1938
Tuesday, April 25, 1939	May 6, 1938
Thursday, April 27, 1939	May 9, 1938
Tuesday, May 9, 1939	May 16, 1938
Thursday, May 11, 1939	May 18, 1938
Tuesday, May 23, 1939	May 25, 1938
Thursday, May 25, 1939	May 27, 1938
Tuesday, July 18, 1939	July 1, 1938
Tuesday, August 1, 1939	July 11, 1938
Thursday, August 3, 1939	July 13, 1938
Sunday, March 10, 1940	December 2, 1938

Beginning August 1, 1938, *The Lone Ranger* was broadcast over stations KVOA, Tucson, and KTAR in Phoenix, three times a week, sponsored by Holsum Bakery. Not only did the ads promote the time slot, but also the bakery.

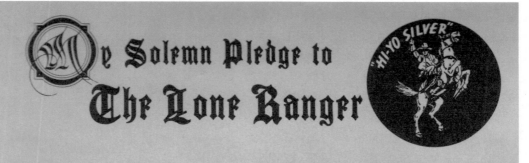

My Solemn Pledge to The Lone Ranger

1. I promise not to cross any street except at regular crossings and first to look both ways.

2. I promise not to play in the streets.

3. I promise not to cross any street against signal lights.

4. I promise to obey Junior Traffic Police at all schools and help younger children to avoid danger.

5. I promise not to ride on running boards or fenders or hook rides.

6. I promise not to hold onto the rear of automobiles or street cars when on a bicycle, scooter or skates.

7. I promise not to ride a bicycle on the wrong side of the street, or make turns without signalling, or ride on the sidewalk or in any playground where others are playing.

8. I promise not to hitch-hike or ask strangers for rides and to discourage younger children from this dangerous practice.

9. I promise to promote safety at all times and encourage others to join this safety movement.

10. I promise to obey my parents or guardians always.

> It is the duty of every Safety Ranger to memorize and observe these rules at all times.

SIGNED _____

MEMBER LONE RANGER SAFETY CLUB

This safety movement, for the happiness and well-being of all boys and girls, is sponsored by Merita Bread and Cakes in celebration of Merita's Silver Anniversary.

When *The Lone Ranger* premiered over KGKO in Fort Worth, Texas, November 1938, Monday, Wednesday, and Friday, management at the Texas radio station attempted to convince the sponsor to carry two programs. Tuesday, Thursday, and Saturday evenings were reserved for the popular Universal Cowboys, a singing troupe that the radio station pushed heavily since the cost for *Lone Ranger* transcriptions was much more than the cost of singing cowboys. When a free 4 x 6 photograph was distributed to anyone who wrote in for the Universal Cowboys, though, one week after the premiere of *The Lone Ranger*, the response was dismal. The station eventually dropped the Universal Cowboys from its roster in December. The sponsor was convinced that *The Lone Ranger* was all they needed.

When The Lone Ranger Safety Club was announced on Monday, November 28, over WNOX in Knoxville, Tennessee, by The Lone Ranger himself during a commercial break, the station received a record-breaking number of entries. Before Christmas it was discovered that Mayor Mynatt, Safety Director Otto Roehl and Traffic Chief Delbert Jenkins were charter members.

Beginning December 1938, *The Lone Ranger* was heard over KGKO three days a week, in Waxahachie, Texas, sponsored by the Cliff-Golman Baking Company, selling Golman Bread.

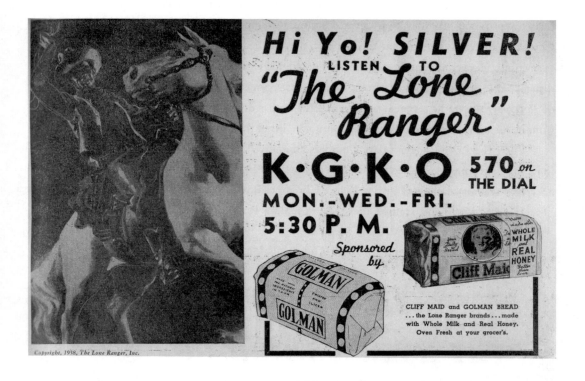

From Butter-Nut *The Lone Ranger News*, Des Moines, Iowa, May 1938.

The majority of the recordings that exist today originate from the transcription discs recorded at NBC in Chicago, duplicated and sent to King-Trendle in weekly batches. Trendle kept a set of discs in the station's inventory. The commercial breaks were replaced with musical interludes lasting a minimum of one minute. (Each broadcast carried an average of four minutes of commercial time.) When the program was sponsored in regional areas, to ensure accurate timing, the station never lifted the needle playing the transcription disc. The engineer simply faded the music level down so the local announcer would deliver the sponsor's message, and when the commercial concluded, the music would fade back in. On a technical side, the transcription disc never stopped playing so *The Lone Ranger* always concluded within the same time frame required for the broadcast schedule. For stations airing the program sustained, the station had two options: promotion of other radio programming heard in place of what would have been a local sponsor message or allow the music to play through uninterrupted. This is why the recordings that exist today have music interludes.

Today, the relatively few recordings with the original commercials intact are defined as "air checks" because they were recordings taken directly off the air. It should be noted that the commercial copy was always different broadcast-after-broadcast, even if the product, verbatim and catchphrases (sponsor's slogan) were similar. * Most of the commercial spots were designed to promote the wholesome goodness of the products; the only thing more valued to the companies than the sales of products was company image. While pitchmen were prone to asking children to ask their mothers to buy that loaf of bread or cereal box, the commercial copy primarily promoted the benefits of the product itself.

Commercial spokesmen varied from one radio station to another. When the Seven-Up Bottling Co. sponsored *The Lone Ranger* over WFIL in Philadelphia, Dave Tyson did the commercials until April 19, 1938, when he was replaced by a different staff announcer working at the same radio station. In San Francisco, commercial announcements were delivered by Tobe Reed for Kilpatrick Bread. When *The Lone Ranger* snagged a new sponsor over WGN in Chicago, Horlick's Malted Milk, beginning with the broadcast of June 5, 1939, the pitchman for the milk company was different than the one heard during sponsorship of the V-Bev Beverage Company as it was felt that the prior announcer was too closely associated with the earlier product.

In late 1938 and early 1939, when WTAG in Worcester was searching for a 12-year-old's voice for commercials for *The Lone Ranger* program, which aired over the Yankee-Colonial Network, studio officials walked down a couple of flights to the editorial rooms of the *Telegram and Gazette*, owner of the station, and found what they were looking for in the women's department of the newspaper. Marion Rogers, who wrote the social column and was somewhat of a mimic on the side. (Massachusetts law forbid 12-year-olds appearing on commercial programs.)

When the Supplee-Wills-Jones Milk Company began sponsorship over WFIL in Philadelphia in 1939, the sponsor requested the ad agency, N.W. Ayer & Son, to conduct a survey on *The Lone Ranger* program. WOR in New York, which could be heard as far south as Philadelphia, also carried the program and the agency feared that inasmuch as the show was heard on WOR, listeners might

* Circa 2006, when a collector began cutting and pasting the same commercial over and over into extant *Lone Ranger* radio broadcasts, believing he was "restoring" the recordings, he was unaware that the commercials would have different wordage from one broadcast to another.

Through an unusual arrangement, beginning January 1938, *The Lone Ranger* began airing over WHB in Kansas City, Missouri, with no sponsor. The station signed an agreement with H. Allen Campbell to record the program on transcription disc through closed circuit, three days a week, and would air the program at 12 noon on Saturday and Sunday. In June, when the Plaza began screening the cliffhanger serial, cross-promotion was made with announcements regarding new day and time for the radio program. It was in June that the program was heard over WHB on Tuesday, Thursday and Sunday at 4:30 p.m. The program gained a sponsor, General Baking, which paid the tab beginning with the broadcast of Monday, February 13, 1939, when the program moved to 5:30 Monday, Wednesday, and Friday. The general manager at WHB, John Schilling, along with Don Davis of the same station, signed an affidavit stating that the discs would be destroyed after playback. In the long run, the unusual arrangement paid off with a sponsor.

still be tuning to the original station. The survey, conducted in March and April 1939, concluded that conflict of interest arose in the cost of airing the program regionally when WOR and WJZ could be heard 90 miles away. The milk company ultimately dropped sponsorship for that reason.

The fame of *The Lone Ranger* was never more significantly demonstrated than during the FCC's so-called network-monopoly inquiry. On the afternoon of March 2, 1939, George W. Trendle and Horace Allen Campbell interrupted a vacation in Florida to testify before the FCC Committee investigating broadcasting and monopoly, to explain and justify the costs involved with networks in connection with Michigan Radio Network affairs. Much interest was shown by the Commission on the King-Trendle programs, *The Green Hornet* and *The Lone Ranger*, with Judge Sykes admitting that his two grandsons were faithful listeners of the *The Lone Ranger*, and that he occasionally cocked an attentive ear. The success of these programs originated in an NBC affiliated station and carried almost all over the country by the Mutual Broadcasting System, intrigued Judge Sykes and Judge Walker who presided over the hearing. *The Lone Ranger* program, Trendle explained, was broadcast twice from the Detroit studio, but during the major portion of the year, three daily broadcasts were necessary to feed the program to various parts of the country at acceptable hours.

In September 1939, KTOK held a Lone Ranger Pet Show in the radio station's backyard, inviting all Oklahoma City youngsters to attend and bring their pets. Prizes were given for the cutest, smartest, and most unusual. Entertainment was furnished, as was ice cream to all the kids, and doughnuts by the sponsor, the Bond Bread Company. Prizes were presented over the air in a special program, with station manager Kenyon M. Douglas interviewing a local veterinarian about the care of pets.

In October 1939, *The Lone Ranger* program lost a sponsor, McCormicks, Ltd., a big Canadian biscuit firm, over CHNS in Halifax, Canada, due to wartime conditions. The bakery was using transcription discs but found the company's entire output sold out to the Army and Navy, which meant the bakery had no need to promote their product to the youngsters. *The Lone Ranger* was still heard over other areas of Canada through different sponsors including over CFCF for Charles Gurd & Company, makers of soda beverages including Gurd's Ginger Ale, which began sponsorship on March 3. The same radio station was also broadcasting transcribed programs such as *Secret Agent K-7* for B. Houde Tobacco, and *House of Dreams* for Snap. By the end of the calendar year *The Lone Ranger* was heard in Canada, Australia, and New Zealand by means of transcriptions.

HI-YO
SUPPLEE LONE RANGERS

ANNIVERSARY ISSUE   JUNE, 1940

COLONEL BILL BRINGS AN INSPIRING BIRTHDAY MESSAGE!

This is our birthday. One year ago we sent you the first copy of the HI-YO BULLETIN! Many things have happened in that year. During that twelve months we have added twenty-three thousand new members, and we have organized over two hundred Troops. I am glad our birthday comes at this time of the year. In a very few days the whole Nation will be celebrating a birthday—a birthday that means so much to all of us. It will be the birthday of the United States of America—July 4th.

If being a Supplee Lone Ranger means anything, it means that you are an American through and through — it means that you love America.

We have gotten along pretty well this year but this is not the final goal. What we have in mind is to enroll so many boys and girls in our Supplee Lone Ranger Club this year that it will mean something in the life of this America we love. And, Rangers, we can do it. We can do it so long as you keep your courage and be guided by the banner that flutters so proudly at the head of forty thousand Rangers — LOYALTY, KINDNESS, COURTESY!

This is your Club. You have made it.

(Continued on Page 4, Column 2)

THE LONE RANGER SENDS BIRTHDAY GIFT TO EVERY RANGER (SUPPLEE)

We're sure there's nothing you could wish for, that would give you more pleasure than to have the congratulations, best wishes and even a picture from the Lone Ranger, himself.

Hundreds of Supplee Lone Rangers have asked for this very thing—so here you are, right inside your BULLETIN, a picture of the Lone Ranger with a personal message to bring you good wishes for future success.

Hi-Yo Silver!

*   *   *   *

SUPPLEE RANGERS PROVE TO BE REAL WORD BUILDERS
May Contest Huge Success!

If you would follow an Indian Chief through the streets of Apache, Oklahoma, you would never hear him say a word unless you asked him a question and then he would very likely say "Uh." But, if you would follow him to the corral where they trade horses you would hear him start talking and telling every person around what a fine horse he had.

(Continued on Page 2, Column 1)

Lone Ranger newsletter for the Supplee-Wills-Jones Milk Company, from June 1940.

In January 1940, *The Lone Ranger* became the central figure of two new advertising campaigns. The first was a continued story, "How the Lone Ranger Captured Silver," printed in serial format over an extended period of time, closely tied in with *The Lone Ranger* radio broadcasts. Seven chapters told of the wonder horse, Silver, wild king of the prairie, and how the "fiery horse with the speed of light" became The Lone Ranger's silent partner. A daring holdup by bandits; a battle for life between Silver and the king of the buffaloes; The Lone Ranger's rescue of the wounded Silver; his single-handed fight against five outlaws; and the final event that made the noble horse and The Lone Ranger partners for life. Each chapter was illustrated. Each full-page advertisement also contained a brief Merita commercial, telling of an outstanding feature for Merita Bread, such as "How Merita Captured Quality."

On Friday evening, January 19, 1940, in San Francisco, California, KFRC's switchboard was clogged for several minutes and some indignant people were on the other ends of the hot lines. They demanded, and in no uncertain terms, *The Lone Ranger* air as scheduled. The program was late that evening, held up by a speaker, and many of the masked rider's loyal followers were very much disturbed. The speaker was President Franklin D. Roosevelt. *

It was about the same time that Harry Morris, local manager of American Bakeries, which underwrote *The Lone Ranger* on WNOX and other southern outlets, was on a committee appointed to help a church lift a $15,000 mortgage. Morris wrote to the station manager of WNOX in Tennessee, asking if they had a *Lone Ranger* episode in which a church figured. There were none, but the Atlanta headquarters of the baking outfit contacted King-Trendle, Inc., requesting the masked rider come to the rescue with a specially-written and produced episode in which The Lone Ranger could help save a church in the Old West. The request was forwarded to Fran Striker, who wrote a script focusing on the church at Argus Falls, and Reverend Matthew Whitcomb, who required aid from The Lone Ranger. The episode was broadcast over WXYZ on the evening of February 5, 1940 as episode #1097 and the transcription disc was airmailed to Fred Shepherd, salesman of the account for American Bakeries, to air late that same month over WNOX. The episode was also played back at a church party which Morris and his committee put on as part of their fund-raising program. Thanks to The Lone Ranger, the First Methodist Church of Knoxville was assisted with the ease of pressure of a heavy mortgage.

In March of 1940, the Weber Baking Company celebrated its fourth year on the air as sponsor of *The Lone Ranger*. (Weber was not broadcasting the series through transcription.) "Because the Lone Ranger symbolizes truth, courage and helpfulness," said H.W. Costello, president of the Weber Baking company, "it is very gratifying that this dashing character has become the idol of several hundred thousand boys and girls here in Southern California. This same spirit of helpfulness which the Lone Ranger typifies inspired the organization of Weber's Lone Ranger Safety club, which organization has been widely endorsed by countless public officials, women's clubs, parent-teacher groups, etc."

Effective August 2, 1940, the Nehi Bottling Company took over sponsorship of *The Lone Ranger* over KWK, pitching Royal Crown Cola. The transcription series was under sponsorship of Bond Bread at the time. Both accounts were handled by the B.B.D.&O. advertising agency and newspaper copy was tied in with *The Lone Ranger* radio program. Trendle insisted no images of the masked vigilante be used in newspaper copy if the sponsor's product was mentioned, but station identification and broadcast time was acceptable.

Producers of radio programs via transcription disc had little – if any – clout regarding sponsorship. Any restrictions would handicap the potential rental of the discs. But George W. Trendle wanted to ensure his properties remained consistent with parental expectation. In the spring of 1939, for example, H. Allen Campbell would not agree to furnish *The Green Hornet* for a major network hookup (and perhaps the largest financial deal to ever be rejected by King-Trendle in the history of the program) because the sponsor that sought interest was the R.J. Reynolds Tobacco Company and they wanted to pitch Camel Cigarettes. Cigarette sponsorship was not at all uncommon for radio detective fare at the time but Trendle felt the promotion would influence youngsters and lead them one step closer to juvenile delinquency.

* Kilpatrick's Marvel Bakery, promoting loaves of bread, was the sponsor thrice weekly over KFRC, and KQW in San Jose.

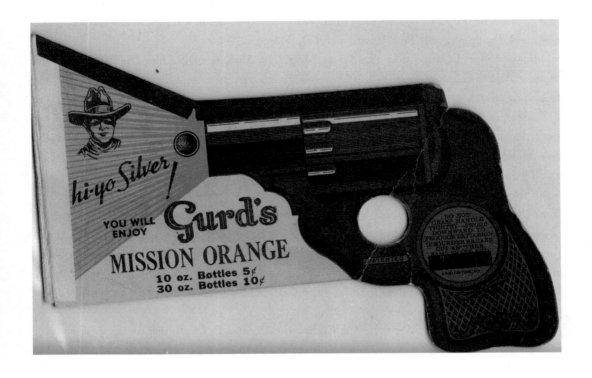

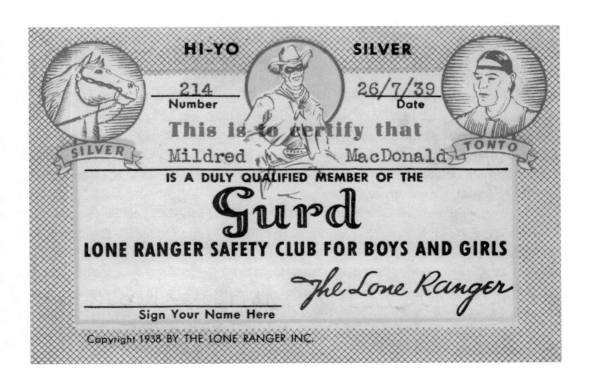

In December of 1939, the radio program received extra promotion.

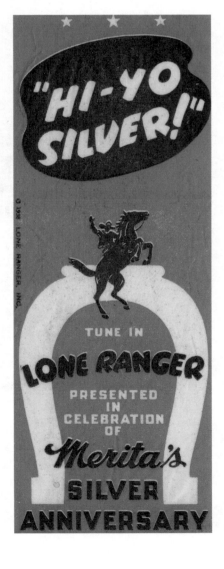

CHAPTER 1 — HOW THE LONE RANGER CAPTURED "SILVER"

Copyright 1940, The Lone Ranger, Inc.

HOW MERITA CAPTURED QUALITY

Bite into your first slice of Merita Bread; let its smooth goodness melt to a memory in your mouth. Up go your eyebrows . . . your taste has run across something *special!* You're too busy enjoying your discovery to take apart this exquisite new experience, so we'll *tell* you why Merita Bread is so satisfying. Merita gets its head start on all other breads—first—by using only the finest ingredients that good money can buy. These are skill-fully mixed and reverently baked—tenderly wrapped and speedily delivered—so that your grocer hands you *more* than a loaf of bread. Here's a package of delicious, healthful, fresh-made *quality*—quality you can touch, slice, toast, serve to your delighted family with unqualified assurance. Switch to Merita — The Lone Ranger's favorite bread. One loaf will explain forever why Merita is the South's fastest-selling bread.

Merita BREAD

TUNE IN
"The Lone Ranger"
Station WIOD
6:30 to 7:00 P. M.
Every Tuesday,
Thursday and Saturday

AB-1381

Bandits Shoot Sheriff

A man dismounted before a large frame building on which hung a sign reading "Jack's Saloon." Unnoticed, he entered through the swinging doors and sat at a table in the shadow cast by a pillar.

Although not late, the bar-room was already filled with the usual Saturday night crowd of men—of every description. A lucky strike had been made by one of the townsfolk, and the prospector, because of his good fortune, was making it a general holiday. Free drinks for all were on him.

He stood at the bar with a rough-looking stranger, telling just how he did it. Though the stranger was listening attentively, his shifty eyes closely surveyed the prospector, seeking for a hidden gun.

With a strident laugh, the stranger asked, "What're you going to do with your dust?"

The unsuspecting prospector confided. "Well, I reckon I'll see the world soon as I get it changed into regular United States money. Present it's deep down in mother earth. No thieves will get it there," he boasted. The prospector laughed until his knee-caps shook in merriment at the thought of where he had his dust.

The other's eyes glinted. Underneath his beard, his lips curled into a sneer as his mind formed a sinister plan. He looked down the bar at five hard-faced characters, drinking at one end of the bar. Simple indeed! All they had to do was demand the dust and if the prospector refused to give it to them—shoot.

"Easy," he murmured as he winked at one of his gang and walked to a table where his pal soon joined him. The rest, later taking the cue, drifted there. Under camouflage of a poker game, the chief laid his plans before his followers, who readily fell in with them.

SURPRISE ATTACK

Half an hour later, the six men rose and started for the door. The leader, who had talked before with the prospector, dropped back, drew his gun and, jerking the drunken prospector after him, started for the door.

The sheriff, seeing the outlaw's movement, drew his guns and shouted, "Hands up, you coyote. Hands off that man!"

For reply, the five men, who had reached the swinging doors, drew guns and opened fire at the men nearest, while their leader pulled the prospector before him across the floor to his gang.

The sheriff's gun flew to the floor as the chief outlaw shot him in the arm, and, as he prepared to finish off the sheriff, he himself fell, beneath the silver bullets coming from the guns of the man who, up to now, had been quietly sitting unnoticed, at his table.

The five outlaws, seeing their leader fall wounded, turned and fled. Grabbing the nearest horses, they headed for the great open spaces, as behind them a volley of shots was fired.

For hours they urged their horses along at top speed. The five half-dead horses with their human cargo made their way to a rocky hollow, where they prepared camp. The five bandits did not talk much, but rested for a hard night's ride they contemplated taking, to reach the border before they were too well known.

FLYING HOOFBEATS

In the middle of the afternoon, one man arose and left the enclosure. An hour later he staggered back, carrying a baby buffalo on his shoulder. "Killed him about twenty minutes ago," he announced to his grinning companions.

"How come we never heard the shot?" asked one bandit.

"Never needed to shoot. He broke his front legs in a rut and all I had to do was give him a couple of jabs with my knife," chuckled Joe, as he skinned the dead animal. He licked his chops as he cut luscious strips of bison steak and laid them over a hot stone, beneath which another had built a fire.

Dusk shaded the heavens and twilight faded quickly into night. The outlaws were saddling up when they heard the flying hoofs of a horse coming closer and closer. Within a hundred feet of them it passed, and the keenest eyes among the outlaws could just make out the form of a man on a horse as he swept by.

"The way that man's riding, he must be scared of ghosts," softly laughed one.

"Yeah? He probably got the scent of your hide going the other way," sneered one of his companions.

(Continued in this paper next Tuesday. Cut out each ad for your Lone Ranger scrapbook.)

1940 contest from the Weber Baking Company for the San Francisco Fair.

THE YANKEE NETWORK

STATION WEAN
CROWN HOTEL
PROVIDENCE, R. I.

May 17, 1938

Mr. Charles C. Hicks
King-Trendle Broadcasting Corp.
Detroit, Mich.

Dear Mr. Hicks:

Your letter to Mr. Richard Voynow has been
referred to me. On three programs of "The
Lone Ranger" we made an offer of the picture, which would be sent to the first five
thousand responding and enclosing a three
cent stamp to cover postage. We received
5,842 responses.

This response is very large indeed comparing it to similar offers made in recent
years. It seems that New England reticence
keeps the radio population of this area from
replying in large volume to give-away propositions, so that any offer which brings
nearly 6,000 requests can be attributed definitely to a very great popularity of the
program involved.

Very sincerely yours,

James S. Jennison
Supervisor WEAN

JSJ:RP

GORDON BAKING COMPANY

EXECUTIVE AND ACCOUNTING DEPT'S.
2303 VERNOR HIGHWAY EAST
DETROIT, MICHIGAN

WEST SIDE PLANT
6175 VERMONT AVENUE
DETROIT, MICHIGAN

DETROIT, MICHIGAN

November 29, 1935

CHICAGO PLANT
9324 FEDERAL STREET
CHICAGO, ILLINOIS

NEW YORK PLANT
42-25 - 147 STREET
LONG ISLAND CITY, N. Y.

Mr H Allen Campbell
General Manager
Station WXYZ
Detroit, Michigan

Dear Mr Campbell:

Two years ago when we decided to use WXYZ exclusively for increasing sales of Silvercup Bread in the Detroit market; we were apprehensive of successful results. The decision practically meant 'putting all our eggs in one basket'.

This month we started our third renewal of 52 weeks' contract for three half hour periods weekly of WXYZ's LONE RANGER Western Dramas, and it gives me great pleasure to cite the unusually satisfactory results; and to praise the powerful influence of WXYZ in the Greater Detroit market.

Just now we have counted 92,097 mailing pieces received from one complete broadcast of a month ago, with very brief follow-up mention in subsequent programs. Such huge response from boys and girls seems more remarkable when you consider that each respondent was invited to join a newly-formed Lone Ranger Safety Club by going to any Silvercup Bread dealer and securing a membership card and information.

This is added proof of WXYZ's showmanship in building entertainment that in turn builds station popularity; and in consequence has made our radio investment with you profitable from the standpoint of constantly increasing sales for Silvercup, The World's Finest Bread.

Sincerely yours,

E. Wilsher

President

EAWilsher
MW

TRADE MARK REG. U. S. PAT. OFF.

EMIL REINHARDT

- Advertising -

324 THIRTEENTH STREET
OAKLAND, CALIFORNIA
April 20, 1938

Mr. Charles C. Hicks
Radio Station WXYZ
Madison Theatre Building
Detroit, Michigan

Dear Mr. Hicks:

In answer to your wire received today, we now have 76,000 Kilpatrick Lone Ranger Safety Club members in the San Francisco area, which includes the following counties: Alameda, San Francisco, San Mateo, Santa Clara, Solano, Sonoma, Stanislaus, Contra Costa and Marin, with members also scattered throughout the remainder of Northern California.

Results The first 60 days

We have no information concerning Weber's Safe Club in Los Angeles. We suggest that you get in touch with Mr. William G. Scholts, Scholts Advertising Service, 1201 West Fourth Street, Los Angeles, regarding this.

After your tabulation is complete, would you please give us a report on the number of safety club members in the nation? We could use this information to very good advantage.

Very truly yours,

Emil Reinhardt

Emil Reinhardt/McM

RECOGNITION, A. N. P. A., A. P. A

BUTTE, MONTANA

April 25, 1938

Mr. Chas. C. Hicks,
King-Trendle Broadcasting Corp.,
3rd floor Madison Theatre Bldg.,
Detroit, Mich.

Dear Mr. Hicks:

Thank you for your letter of April 20th. From time to time we
check up on various different times of the day and programs that
we have on the air. On April 13th we made an announcement just
preceding the "Lone Ranger", which is on the air from 5:00 to
5:30. We had fifty premiums to give away to the first fifty
people writing in letters and after the announcement received a
total of 270 letters from this single announcement which is a
very good indication of the audience building quality of the
Lone Ranger. The Lone Ranger Safety Club has not been started.

Results the first 60 days

Respectfully yours,

K G I R, Inc.,

E. B. Craney

E. B. Craney

EBC:MLO

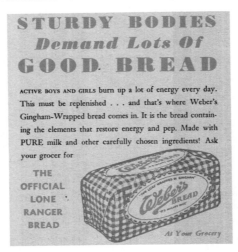

Cost of Recording Transcriptions

King-Trendle paid NBC $110 for the master and $3.75 for each pressing. If 74 stations across the country carried the program via transcription, Trendle paid 74 x $3.75 for each episode. For many years the masters would be stored at NBC but later the masters would be shipped to Michigan, thus splitting the location of the discs for a number of years. The transcriptions were sold by King-Trendle in the major markets but another sales contract gave NBC the exclusive right to distribute the program in secondary markets, an instance being High Point, North Carolina. The usual price for *Lone Ranger* and *Green Hornet*, to which Trendle testified to the FCC on March 1, 1939, was 50 percent of the purchasing station's highest half-hour rate.

Trendle further explained that the *Ranger* was taken from his station and transcribed at NBC Chicago headquarters for the master recordings and the necessary pressings. The usual price for *The Lone Ranger* and *The Green Hornet*, he declared, was 50 percent of the purchasing station's highest half-hour rate. He explained that WXYZ maintained a considerable talent list and that the prices for the program were to defray the talent cost. The transcribed programs were usually broadcast 30 days later (on average) by other stations which did not take the show off the Mutual line. *

The cost had gone down over time as both technology and equipment upgraded for ease of production. It should be noted that because of the small number of stations requesting transcriptions in 1938 and 1939, there were acetates made, not masters. Reproductions of those acetates, which were a little more expensive than pressings of the masters, was estimated to cost $2.10 per pressing and a minimum of 100 programs were required. For this reason, Trendle made a business decision: After 1940, when stations wanted to broadcast *The Lone Ranger* via transcription, the early broadcasts (circa 1938 to 1939) were no longer included in syndication packages. Summed up neatly, when a station decided to broadcast *The Lone Ranger*, they received discs pertaining to whatever recently aired just a month prior. ** By 1948, the cost of recording a sixteen-inch master at RCA in Chicago was $25 per half-hour episode.

* In a telegram from NBC dated January 14, 1944, the cost of having *Ned Jordan* or *Challenge of the Yukon* transcribed in Chicago was the same price as *The Lone Ranger*, $75 for each 30-minute program including lacquer masters, timing and checking test pressings, preparation and distribution cue sheets. Rate would be $49 per program without service of timing and distributing cue sheets. Duplicate records in quantities 25 to 49 were $1.55 each, and 50 to 99 were $1.45 each, and 100 to 249 were $1.40 each.

** By 1943, this policy was revised not to include pre-May 1941 broadcasts in syndication packages to ensure Earle Graser's voice was never mixed with recordings of Brace Beemer.

TELEPHONE
ROSEDALE 3210

Thomas Patrick, Inc.

ASSOCIATED WITH THE NATIONAL BROADCASTING CO.

ROBERT THOMAS CONVEY
PRESIDENT

HOTEL CHASE · ST. LOUIS

April 21, 1938

Mr. Charles C. Hicks, Manager
Sales Promotion Department
King-Trendle Broadcasting Corporation
Detroit, Michigan,

Dear Mr. Hicks:

This is in reply to your letter of April 20th.

Due to the fact that the Bakers Association of
which our client is a member, does not permit
any type of merchandising to be tied in with
their advertising campaigns, it is impossible
for us to furnish you with the type of information you desire, however, the client has assured
us that this program is producing results for
him inasmuch as the sale of Bread has increased
noticeably in St. Louis since he started using
the "Lone Ranger" feature.

Very cordially yours,
RADIO STATION KWK
THOMAS PATRICK, INC

Clarence G. Cosby
General Manager,

CGC:JB

Results The first 60 days

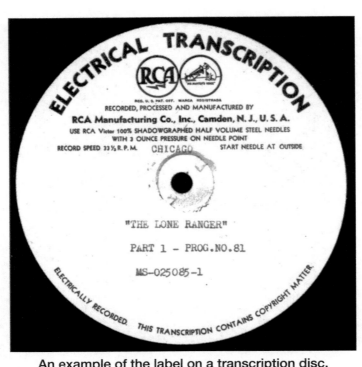

An example of the label on a transcription disc.
This one represents the broadcast of July 22, 1938.

An example of the label on a transcription disc.
This one represents the broadcast of December 31, 1948.

Chapter Two
The Story Behind the Music

RECOGNIZING THE VALUE OF A MYSTERY, Trendle withheld any information requested by radio listeners when they submitted a general inquiry regarding the identities of the musical compositions used on the program. His staff was instructed not to reveal the titles of the musical pieces, and only on rare occasion did Trendle himself reluctantly provide the information. The standard rejection read: "...we consider this music as part of our trade production secrets." Today, the theme music remains the least kept secret of the trade. Gioachino Rossini's overture to his 1829 opera, *William Tell*, was his last of 39 operas before he went into semi-retirement. The entire overture consists of four parts and the triumphant theme best known today as the Ranger's signature music was the fourth and final part. But while George W. Trendle attempted to withhold this information, the reason was more than likely just another business decision.

The job of assembling the original inventory of musical excerpts for use on *The Lone Ranger* program fell to Bert Djerkiss, a young man who was working at WXYZ as a turntable operator and sound effects man. He was followed by Ted Robertson, a chief sound technician who would go on to become the assistant director for James Jewell. Fred Flowerday, who was hired by George W. Trendle in 1934, was also responsible for the music cues. It was Flowerday who later admitted that the men who handled music and sound effects were also assisting the director; the name of the position was simply an official title. All of the men in the booth were considered an assistant to the director.

The radio station had a large collection of 78 records used for music on the program, including Toscanini's rendition of "The Sorcerer's Apprentice" (Victor 7021), Victor Arden and Phil Ohman at the piano for the "Maple Leaf Rag" (Victor 22608), Stokowski's rendition of "Danse Macabre" (Victor 6505), Leo Blech and the Berlin State Opera Orchestra's rendition of "The Flying Dutchman Overture" (Victor 9275), and Albert Coates conducting "Ride of the Valkyries" (Victrola 9163 – note the "Victrola"), among others. Of amusement was the use of "Omphale's Spinning Wheel" to creating a menacing mood for a number of scenes. The piece would be dropped from use on the program circa late

1938 after it was discovered the same rendition, Willem Mengelberg conducting the Philharmonic-Symphony Orchestra of New York (Victor 7006), was being used for the theme of another radio program, *The Shadow*. The last time the piece was heard on the program was during the intermission of a few consecutive radio broadcasts beginning with the broadcast of November 11, 1938.

Throughout early 1938, the sound men and director experimented with different musical compositions for the intermission music, including "Scotch Poem" by MacDowell (broadcast of April 6, 1938). Eventually "Les Preludes" would become the standard intermission beginning with the broadcast of December 23, 1940.

Scott Joplin's "Maple Leaf Rag" can be heard in the background during the opening scene of the broadcast of December 9, 1938, when The Lone Ranger strides purposefully into the Six-Gun Café.

For anyone hoping to find the exact rendition of the "William Tell Overture" used for the early *Lone Ranger* radio broadcasts, that would be two 10-inch 78s labeled Victor 20606 and 20607, with the Victor Symphony Orchestra, under the direction of Rosario Bourdon. The station had all four sections of the piece, which was released in stores during the summer of 1927.

Victor 20606, Side A, recorded on the afternoon of April 11, 1927.
Victor 20606, Side B, recorded on the afternoon of July 15, 1926.
Victor 20607, Side A, recorded on the afternoon of July 16, 1926.
Victor 20607, Side B, recorded on the afternoon of March 14, 1927.

It was Side B of 20607, which featured "The Finale" segment, that was used as the radio theme.

The radio station's library was so extensive that technicians at WXYZ were able to provide music for late hours at minimum overhead cost. The library contained commercial 78s from Columbia and Brunswick, as well as other releases.

Once every episode of *The Lone Ranger* began to be syndicated by recordings to stations not on the network, Trendle evidently became concerned with the problem of using recorded music owned by other companies. Trendle's worry coincided with the production of Republic Pictures' *Lone Ranger* movie serial, and that production used custom-recorded cues that did not rely on commercial 78 rpm records.

On February 5, 1938, George W. Trendle wrote to Al Adams in the New York City based publicity department of Republic Pictures: "Confirming our conversation, if you will have a print made of the soundtrack that is being used on *The Lone Ranger* serial, I will be glad to pay for it, and may I ask that you ship it as quickly as possible… so that we can take from this track certain portions of the musical background that would be best fitted for our radio programs, as I would like our radio music to conform with that used in the feature. As soon as we select that, I will have NBC make their best type recordings and then furnish you with the necessary supply of records to obtain complete releases to this organization so that we will not be running into the Copyright laws."

On February 19, Harry Grey at Republic in Hollywood, California, wrote the following letter. "I should like to call your attention to the fact that in our music track you will notice that the mood will vary at times. This music was originally recorded to conform with the action on the screen. In our *Lone Ranger* serial there have been times when only parts of the composition were required, but we felt it best to send the complete recorded composition on to you to have additional material to choose from. All of this music is the property of Republic Productions, Inc., and while, as is the custom, we have to assign the music material to a music publisher for reproduction and performance collections all over the world, we now have in our possession written confirmation from the music publisher as well as composer, a waiver and clearance, which permits *The Lone Ranger* radio broadcasts to use and reproduce, in part or whole, all musical compositions as used in the motion picture, *The Lone Ranger*."

The soundtrack for *The Lone Ranger* serial consisted of 62 separate pieces of music that were used in the first six chapters alone. After additional music cues were forwarded at Trendle's request, WXYZ selected an arrangement of the "William Tell Overture Finale" plus 27 interludes. More music would eventually be sent to Trendle. Of the 89 different compositions used in the movie serial, 50 were by Alberto Colombo, 18 by Karl Hajos, eight by Hugo Riesenfeld, four by Arthur Kay, three by Leon Rosebrook, two by William Lava, and one each by Rossini, Von Gluck, Liszt, and the ever-popular Public Domain. On-screen credit was given to Alberto Colombo, who more than likely composed a few new pieces and was responsible for assembling the music.

The reason multiple numbers were credited to others was because some of the music pieces in *The Lone Ranger* were recycled from other films produced and released through Republic. Some of the music of Karl Hajos was originally composed and conducted for *Robinson Crusoe of Clipper Island* (1936), *Riders of the Whistling Skull* (1937), *Dick Tracy* (1937), *S.O.S. Coastguard* (1937), and *Zorro Rides Again* (1937). His music score for *The Bold Caballero* (1936), Republic's first color feature, visually emphasizes how the music was used for similar action sequences on radio's *Lone Ranger*. Music of Hugo Riesenfeld was recycled from other Republic Pictures cliffhanger serials including *Undersea Kingdom* (1936), *The Vigilantes Are Coming* (1937), and *The Painted Stallion* (1937).

Adding to the mix was a shipment of music tracks that originated not from *The Lone Ranger* cliffhanger serial, but also from other Republic movies and serials. Some of these were used for *The Lone Ranger* radio program. Riesenfeld's tracks from *Dick Tracy Returns* (1938) and Arthur Kay's tracks from *The Fighting Devil Dogs* (1938)

Like WXYZ for their radio broadcasts, the movie studio sought to establish a music library of their own and for budgetary purposes reused many of the cues for motion pictures and cliffhanger serials. All of which makes us wonder how many children would watch a serial in movie theaters in the 1940s and not recognize the same music cue in an action-packed scene that they heard routinely on *The Lone Ranger* radio program?

The rapid displacement of the commercial 78 rpm classical selections by Republic soundtrack material became evident during the month of April 1938. By late April of 1938, two pieces titled "Turmoil/Calm" and "The Revolt" were heard. By transcription #47 (broadcast of May 4, 1938), "Turmoil/Calm" had settled into the intermission slot where it would not be dislodged for several years.

By the summer of 1938, music cues from the Republic Pictures serial would become the dominant source of music heard on the program. As time went on, the Republic Pictures rendition of the "William Tell Overture Finale" would not be used on the radio program. The Victor record used for years would continue to be a staple on the program. No one knows the reason why but Alberto Colombo had to rearrange the "Finale" to meet the needs of the movie serial, cutting out approximately one-third of the Rossini score. His version is only two minutes and nine seconds long. Alternate renditions of the "William Tell Overture Finale" can be heard on at least two radio broadcasts: transcription #20 (broadcast of March 2, 1938) and transcription #34 (broadcast of April 4, 1938). For those renditions, also conducted by Rosario Bourdon, band A of NBC's Thesaurus transcription record #112 was used.

"Fred [Flowerday] was happy and appreciative of the music we received from Republic," Charles Livingstone later recalled. "I greeted [the soundtrack cuts] with open arms… they had a Western flavor. They fit the Western biographies we were portraying. Our disappointment was that we needed more."

The reason why George W. Trendle sought soundtrack recordings from the Republic Pictures cliffhanger serial was to acquire as much recorded music as he could before a pending ruling by the Musicians Union became effective. James Caesar Petrillo, soon to be appointed the president of the American Federation of Musicians (AFM), was leading the charge against the use of recorded music over the radio airwaves, fearing the practice was becoming too common and posed a serious threat to the continued welfare and employment of musicians.

James C. Petrillo

Radio station WPEN in Philadelphia was the first to come under attack, in February 1940 when Local 77 of the AFM went to court for an injunction against the station from using phonograph recordings. The nationwide drive spread across the country and plagued many radio stations who attempted to defend their right to use recordings instead of live performers. This culminated in 1942 in a ban on the making of all musical recordings by union musicians in the United States.

Of equal concern to the broadcast industry was another frigid situation which was building up between them and the New York based American Society of Composers, Authors and Publishers (ASCAP). Founded in 1914 to protect composers, authors and publishers from having their works performed without authorization, ASCAP ensured royalties were promptly paid and distributed. In 1939, ASCAP bragged it paid out $5 million per year in royalties – making the organization a power player in the field. By June 1940, the situation between radio stations and the union escalated to a threat from ASCAP, promising a nationwide boycott of ASCAP music to take effect at midnight on New Year's Eve, December 31, 1940.

Corporate records indicate that by 1939, *The Lone Ranger* radio program could be heard over 140 stations throughout the world courtesy of the transcription discs. This setup was rewarding the company with impressive profits but that would come to a halt because the Republic Pictures music cues were protected by ASCAP. The programs could not be broadcast across the country without music so Raymond Meurer met with James C. Petrillo in Chicago to ask for advice on how WXYZ could get out of the tight musical corner into which it was fast being pushed. Petrillo explained that one loophole was to have WXYZ choose music that was free of copyright and all recorded music cues be performed and recorded by non-union members. A conference between Meurer and Trendle established a new business decision: making arrangements for selected musical arrangements to be recorded in Mexico, for use after the ASCAP ban took effect.

During late spring and early summer of 1940, there were discussions about having Rosario Bourdon record new compositions in New York City, with a 26-piece union orchestra. That idea was now scrapped. Consultation with C. Lloyd Enger, chief of NBC's Radio Recording Division, led to the engineer traveling down to Mexico City to make arrangements with Sr. Emilio Azcárraga, owner of station XEW, to make his staff of conductors available, and ensure a sufficient number of qualified musicians would be on hand to record new renditions of the pieces Trendle wanted. XEW was considered at the time the most modern and powerful station in the country.

From July to August, 50 separate cuts of mood music, consisting of public domain pieces and new arrangements of copyrighted Republic music, were recorded on nine single-sided 16-inch records, including the themes from *The Lone Ranger* and *The Green Hornet*. The first radio broadcast to feature the Maestro Castañeda recordings made in Mexico was transcription #416 (broadcast September 20, 1940). Beginning with that broadcast, the curtain was brought down on the Republic Pictures soundtrack music. *

Additional arrangements and revised renditions were recorded in Mexico on October 23, adding six more music cues to the existing 50.

NBC notified George W. Trendle that music from Republic Pictures, even if tweaked or re-scored with a new rendition, as had been done with some of the Mexican recordings, could not air if a strike was to become imminent. Beginning with the broadcast of December 23, 1940, "Peace Comes to the Frontier," the Republic arrangements were shelved and only public domain classical excerpts from the library were used. "Turmoil/Calm," which had been used as the intermission slot it had occupied since May of 1938, was replaced with excerpt 3 – the "Strife and Victory" sequence – from Liszt's *Les Preludes*. Once in place, it was there to stay.

Trendle quickly dispatched Raymond Meurer to New York City where, on December 27, he picked out a fresh set of interludes to help carry *The Lone Ranger* program through the current crisis. Enger sifted through a number of earlier Thesaurus releases plus the stacks of Mexican recordings which had been stockpiled for later release on that label. Out of this wealth of material, he identified 26 separate musical passages which he believed would avoid the ASCAP strike.

Among these new recordings were renditions of Hellmesberger's "Storm Scene," Schubert's "The Devil's Castle," Nicolai's "Merry Wives of Windsor Overture," and two waltzes from Johann Strauss, Jr., "Die Fledermaus Overture" and "One Night in Venice Overture." On a humorous note, a band arrangement of Tchaikovsky's "1812 Overture" was among them, and first featured on the broadcast of December 30, 1940, following the intermission. This piece would become a major staple on the radio broadcasts for more than a decade. "Storm Scene" was used three times during that broadcast, to accompany Silver when he raced to the rescue.

ASCAP fulfilled their promise when they began a nationwide boycott on Jan. 1, 1941, upset because a number of radio stations refused to pay some or all of the royalties due. ASCAP served as a clearinghouse between the music creators and the music users but the fees were too much for smaller stations. ASCAP was demanding radio stations pay a fixed percentage regardless of how frequently or infrequently their music was used.

* A couple of the new Bonnell arrangements were used on the September 16 broadcast, despite the fact that they were used regularly beginning September 20.

Trendle began building a library of mood music, pieces used as themes for his programs, and pieces that could be used throughout the dramas to heighten the scenarios and bridge a number of scenes. This proved to be quite an undertaking considering an average of 20 music cues were used for each program.

In February, Meurer and Enger were able to secure an additional 11 selections for use on the radio dramas. These included Beethoven's "Leonore Prohaska – Funeral March," Wagner's "The Flying Dutchman," Schubert's "Symphony No. 5 – 4th movement," Mendelssohn's "Symphony No. 3," and Reznicek's "Donna Diana Overture." That last one would become synonymous with *Challenge of the Yukon* as its theme.

A familiar cut of ASCAP-controlled music being used during the boycott without being noticed was not uncommon. Part 2 of Alberto Colombo's "The Getaway" from the Republic Pictures score was used on two broadcasts in a row: the broadcast of April 9, 1941, the day following Earle Graser's tragic death in an auto accident, and the broadcast of April 11, 1941.

As early as May 13, 1941, the Mutual Broadcasting System had reached an accord with ASCAP that permitted its music to once again be played on the air. NBC and CBS had not yet reached an agreement -- and would not -- until Oct. 29, 1941, ending the ten-month-old row. Throughout November 1941, phone calls, terse telegrams, and cryptic letters flew back and forth between Detroit and New York as Trendle, Meurer, and Enger worked out what could be done for the return of the Republic arrangements. By December 16, the details were settled and WXYZ was in a position to play with a full musical library again. (Five of the Republic music cues were temporarily unavailable for use.) Beginning with the broadcast of December 22, 1941, "Remember the Alamo," the Republic music score drought ended for good.

What remains remarkable is the fact that all the music cues in the stock library would be used for more than a decade and a little more than 2,000 radio broadcasts. With full understanding of the types of music cues used on the program, additional entertainment value as well as deeper historical appreciation can be found when listening to the extant radio broadcasts. William Lava's colleague, Jim King, conducted a professional studio orchestra in a festival of soundtrack cues using the original scores. The stereo recording was released commercially through the Cinédisc label in 1992, and can easily be found among collectors who want to familiarize themselves with those scores.

In 1987, Scarecrow Press, Inc., published a 220-page book extensively documenting the history of the music used on *The Lone Ranger* radio program. Researched and authored by Reginald M. Jones, Jr., *The Mystery of the Masked Man's Music: A Search for the Music Used on "The Lone Ranger" Radio Program, 1933-1954* is highly recommended for any fan of *The Lone Ranger*.

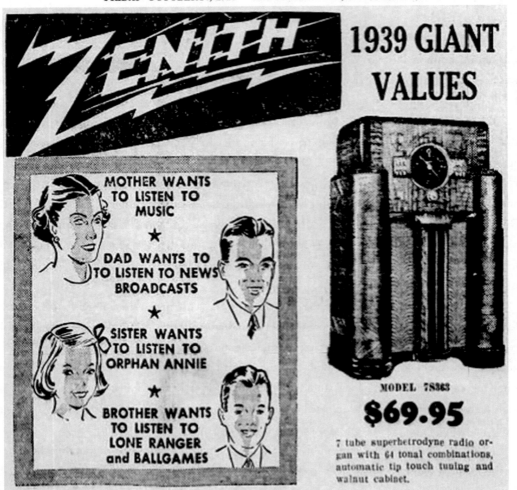

Advertisement in *The Daily Notes* from Canonsburg, Pennsylvania,
from October 14, 1938, promoting the Zenith radio.

Chapter Three
The Changing of the Guard

In May of 1938, Jim Jewell had a run-in with George W. Trendle, in the same manner and for the same reasons as they discussed twice before. "Jewell wanted to be paid a salary commensurate with the success of the show. Trendle was not inclined to do so and the parting took place under a cloud of bad feeling," Ted Robertson recounted to author David Rothel. With *The Lone Ranger* now being transcribed and aired over additional radio stations, and word that a newspaper comic strip and a filmed serial were in the works, Jewell felt his salary needed a boost to compensate. All of the growing profits left a sour taste in the mouth of James Jewell, who was directing multiple programs over the Michigan Radio Network, the Don Lee Network, and the Mutual Broadcasting System.

Jewell's assertion was founded by an executive at WWJ, a competing radio station in Detroit, who offered Jewell a job at four times the money he was making at WXYZ. Trendle mistakenly believed Jewell was bluffing. After all, more than once over the years Jewell threatened to leave when he was not promised a raise. Trendle considered Jim Jewell a valued employee, but merely as "work for hire." Trendle would not relinquish part ownership in the property to Jewell.

On May 17, 1938, Jewell addressed a letter to Trendle with a reminder that his contract would expire on the first of June and notified his employer he would not exercise the option of renewal. Trendle sent the director a confirmation of receipt in writing. Later, Trendle was surprised to discover Jewell had not been bluffing and had accepted another job at competing station WWJ as "program manager." Jewell offered to train anyone Trendle would pick to be his successor, with a firm departure date of July 1. His exodus came after nine years with the King-Trendle organization, and as WXYZ's dramatic director, writing, producing, casting, and directing.

George W. Trendle at his desk

Jewell was undecided about his future but knew there was no future at WXYZ. With permission from Trendle, he parted ways around June 15 for a long-deserved vacation. As a parting gesture to 60 children of the station's *Children's Theatre of the Air*, which he founded several years prior as the groundwork for building talent from the ground up, Jewell was granting numerous children a free two-week sojourn at his "Lone Ranger" camp near Detroit, which he had founded a couple years prior.

Besides *The Lone Ranger* and juvenile talent school, Jewell was producer-director of *The Green Hornet*, *Ann Worth, Housewife*, *Kiddie Karnival*, *Radio Schoolhouse*, and *Junior Matinee* in what amounted to a total of about 10,000 radio broadcasts in less than a decade. It remains difficult to fathom how Jewell was able to start out in 1929 with an acting company of three and a weekly budget of $30, and leave in 1938 with 45 players on payroll and a weekly budget of well over $2,500.

Remote broadcasts for James Jewell's *Radio Showcase*.

Two men were up for consideration as Jewell's successor: Charles D. Livingstone, who had been the assistant dramatic director for some time, and Al Hodge, the actor who played the title role of The Green Hornet. There has been nothing found to verify why Livingstone was chosen over Hodge, though an educated guess was that Hodge could not star on the same radio program twice weekly and handle the directing chores at the same time. (But to be fair, Livingstone was also playing supporting roles on the same radio programs where he assisted.)

It was during his tenure at the University of Michigan that Charles Daniel Livingstone discovered he was more interested in theater than law. He was president of the Comedy Club, the all-campus drama organization, and Mimes, which was the men's dramatic honorary society. This was during the era of silent movies and he was partial to actor Gilbert "Broncho Billy" Anderson. By the time he graduated he had the acting bug so hard that he gave up his potential law career and began touring with the illustrious actress, Jessie Bonstelle, making $30 a week, good pay during the depression. In 1930 he went to New York and joined William Brady Productions, appearing in *After*

Dark and other plays. During this time, he also performed with the Charlan Players Stock Company, then joined Shubert Productions to appear in *If I Were You*, *Bloody Laughter* and *Wolves*. In November of 1930 he married an actress he had met on tour named Harriet Russell. Together they worked on Broadway and for two summers with the Detroit Players. It was in Detroit that Livingstone looked up Adams Rice who was preparing his tent show for its summer tour. Rice hired Livingstone as a member of his stock company. It was when the tent show set up camp at Utica, Michigan, that he met, separately, Ted Robertson, Earle Graser, and Jim Jewell. (Jewell was doing a puppet act in the tent show.) After a brief stint in 1932 playing minor supporting roles in two Hollywood motion pictures, the Livingstones had their fill of traveling and Charles looked up Jim Jewell.

Having learned that Jewell was directing radio programs at WXYZ, he inquired about the possibility of performing for "The Jim Jewell Players." He even auditioned as an announcer for station manager Brace Beemer but wasn't hired.

Settling down in Detroit, though, Livingstone kept busy working in local theaters and industrial film companies for short subjects. In August 1933, Wynn Wright, director of drama at station WWJ, had been recruited by all the radio stations to do a combined radio broadcast for a special occasion. Livingstone gave a performance noteworthy enough to interest Jewell, who hired Livingstone occasionally to recite poetry, deliver the news, assist with production, and to play bit parts on *Warner Lester, Manhunter* and heavies on *The Lone Ranger*. As an actor he was soon rewarded with a contract, playing the male lead in *Thrills of the Secret Service* opposite actress Martha Scott, then a student at the University of Michigan.

According to Livingstone, James Jewell knew nothing about timing. If the script came up short, he simply walked into the studio and began ad-libbing for a moment or two. If the show was running behind, he would wait until music bridged a scene and tell the actors which pages to skip. Because actors varied the pace between rehearsals and performance, marking time for each scene proved futile.

Years later writer/actor Tom Dougall recalled similarly, "We never had a time rehearsal when James Jewell was doing the show. He was doing so much directing during the show that we just never knew how long the script would last. When we were on the air, he'd realize it was running much too long, and he'd come into the studio, take our scripts from us and cross out a scene. But his best method of 'on-the-air' editing was to clap his hand over an actor's mouth so he couldn't continue at the same time cueing the bridge music to be brought up loud and clear."

Livingstone receives credit for marking his script every fifteen seconds and using the markings as a guide to signal actors to either speed up delivery or slow down. "From that time on," said Livingstone, "we never ran over or under." (This has been verified when consulting the radio scripts that bore Livingstone's name.)

"He did introduce exact timing to WXYZ dramas," said writer Dick Osgood. "Before, they used to just, at the last minute, omit a scene or play it faster or slower. Livingstone was a perfectionist as a director. He was quite a serious man. His lip would curl if somebody did something funny. He was on the edge of mirth."

Jewell was a perfectionist who supposedly wrote scripts when Fran Striker was late with delivery, filled in for an actor who was late or drunk, and handled many of the other tasks that required the program to finish three times a week with a shine and polish that could only be accomplished by an efficient director.

Brace Beemer was the station manager, also doubling as announcer/narrator for *The Lone Ranger* and was directing *The Crimson Fang*, a spin-off focusing on the arch-villain from *Manhunters*, patterned after Sax Rohmer's yellow peril Fu Manchu novels. Because the program aired late in the evening, Beemer assigned the task of directing to Livingstone, who proved he was capable of handling the assignment. Jim Jewell assigned Livingstone the title of assistant director and would allow Livingstone to handle the timing during rehearsal, after the initial reading. (Charles Livingstone also played numerous roles on the radio programs.)

Charles Livingstone

"When Jewell left WXYZ, there was a decision to be made about who was to take over. I had been working as Jewell's assistant director and had been doing a good job, so I was selected," Livingstone recalled to author David Rothel. "Things had been running smoothly on the program, so I didn't make too many changes in the routine of things when I took over."

Charles Livingstone assumed the directing chores (with a raise in salary when his contract came to term) and would continue handling the task for more than a decade. Livingstone never took credit for having a hand in the creation of *The Lone Ranger*, *The Green Hornet*, or *Challenge of the Yukon*. The programs he directed from the beginning and thus had a hand in the dramatic presentation of were *Ned Jordan, Secret Agent* and *Bob Barclay, American Agent*. Livingstone would later serve as director on *Challenge of the Yukon* when that program premiered in January 1939. In late 1938, Beemer wanted to play the lead for *Challenge of the Yukon*, and Livingstone suggested the casting to Trendle. Livingstone compared Beemer as "a John Wayne type," known for charisma and the center of attention at any gathering. Trendle disagreed and instructed Livingstone to hire a different actor for the role.

Howard Pierce

Professionally, Jim Jewell was not well-liked by the cast and crew. Personally, he was well-respected over the years, evident by the many recollections of those at WXYZ recalling that the going-away party for Jewell rivaled that for any other employee leaving the station. Fred Flowerday took up a collection and had a set of miniature gold plungers (representing the sound effect for horse hoofs), along with a plaque made up inscribed to Jewell with all the actors' names engraved on it along with a farewell message.

No one from the executive offices was present at the party, but Jewell received a handsome watch bearing the inscription: "To James Jewell, a token of friendship and appreciation." It was signed with the names of George W. Trendle, John H. King, H. Allen Campbell, and Howard Pierce.

"He was an absolutely dedicated man. He had no sense of humor whatsoever, and he used to drive us to distraction because he made demands upon us," Ted Robertson later recollected. "He was an absolute perfectionist. I want to say I have met a lot of people, but I have never known a genius like Jewell."

Following his departure from WXYZ, Jewell's stay at WWJ was comparatively brief, but during his tenure there he created *The Black Ace* series. The aviation series was a blend of elements borrowed from *The Lone Ranger*, *The Green Hornet*, and *Captain Midnight*. As the announcer described: "Out of the night skies looms the shrouded form of a black super-plane with a hooded figure at the controls. The plane is a miracle of advanced aviation science with rocket power for super speed and embodies new and secret developments which permit amazing maneuvers. The hooded flyer is a mysterious crusader of the skies who, with his speechless ally, the 'Whistler,' makes his own laws in pursuing the wrongdoers who slip through the dragnet of justice. Known only as 'The Black Ace,' this daring adventurer baffles all efforts to reveal his identity."

The Black Ace series generated a number of giveaways including a comic sheet for dealers and a whistle, and one announcement without a giveaway generated 5,100 letters from listeners. This was over the concern and welfare of The Black Ace and The Whistler, who fell into a trap. The announcer suggested the listeners write in with a means of escape.

In the fall of 1939, when James Jewell attempted to expand coverage of *The Black Ace* nationally, it was promoted that he was the original producer or such programs as *The Lone Ranger*, *The Green Hornet*, *Ann Worth, Housewife*, and *The Children's Theatre of the Air*. This generated a letter from George W. Trendle dated November 1, to James Jewell, venting frustration: "We keep getting information regularly regarding your claim of authorship to *The Lone Ranger*… Today, I received a letter from New York to the effect that a company known as the General Amusement Corporation has been circulating the Advertising Agencies in reference to your piece of property known as *The Black Ace*, on which you are scheduled as the author, and that the circular states definitely that you are the author of *The Lone Ranger*. It is about time, I think, that we settle this matter definitely even if it becomes necessary that we take court proceedings to do so."

Cast of *Ann Worth, Housewife* in the Winter of 1937, the same actors who played supporting roles on radio's *The Lone Ranger*. Standing left to right: Ted Robertson, Ruth Dean Rickaby, Malcolm McCoy, John Todd, unknown, Harry Golder, Tom Dougall, Beatrice Leiblee, unknown, Fred Reto, Fred Flowerday, Lee Allman, and Jack Petruzzi. Seated are Joan Vitez (Ann Worth) and Gillie Shea.

With *The Lone Ranger*, *The Green Hornet*, and other radio programs on his résumé, Jewell found no difficulty moving on to Chicago soon afterward, where he ultimately took on the assignment in the spring of 1945 of writing and directing *Jack Armstrong, the All-American Boy*. By spring of 1951 he would create *The Silver Eagle*, featuring the fictional Jim West of the Canadian Mounties, a radio adventure program that would ultimately air on alternate weekdays with *The Lone Ranger* over the ABC network, also under the sponsorship of General Mills. Both financially and career-wise, Jewell fared better after leaving WXYZ.

With denial a defense mechanism, an unconscious form of self-deception used to avoid anxiety and emotional pain, Jewell's departure was a bitter pill for Trendle to swallow. While James Jewell deserves credit for creating and establishing many of the key elements of *The Lone Ranger*, his name never appeared in Mary Bickel's 1971 biography of George W. Trendle, which was personally supervised by Trendle himself. On rare occasion when a newspaper cited James Jewell being responsible for the formation of *The Lone Ranger*, the author of that article was sure to receive a poison pen letter from Trendle insisting James Jewell had nothing to do with the radio program other than directing the program *after* the radio program was already created. On one occasion, Trendle claimed *The Lone Ranger* was created before Jewell was even hired by the station!

As the new director of *The Lone Ranger*, Charles Livingstone ensured the job was handled to Trendle's satisfaction. "Chuck was a no-nonsense director," Dave Parker recalled. "No time to be social or anything not directly related to the job at hand, which was to get a quality show on and off the air at 29:30. I don't recall Chuck ever thanking anyone for a good job though compliments between the actors were occasions for pride. But that was Chuck's style."

"Once the show got started, Chuck was very intense about what he was doing, and when this carried over to the actors in the studio it could create animosities," announcer Fred Foy later recalled, adding, "but that was Chuck's manner of directing."

Livingstone was a man of medium size and dark complexion. He wore glasses with large black frames, which made him look angry much of the time, a fact well-noted by the actors over the years. Under Livingstone's direction, there was first a read-through to set the characters and for the actors to understand their roles. Then a timing rehearsal involving Livingstone noting script length every 15 seconds; followed by a production rehearsal to integrate the dialog, sound effects and music. Then came the dress rehearsal with no interruptions; followed by the actual show. Total rehearsal time was around three hours. Rehearsals were always on the same day as the broadcast.

"The whole technique of radio was to read and sound as if you were not reading," Livingstone later explained to author David Rothel. "We had to do *The Lone Ranger* and *The Green Hornet* with three hours rehearsal. While *The Lone Ranger* was on the air, every once in a while some stage actor would come to Detroit in a play. Occasionally I'd cast them in a program with the regular stock company of radio actors we had. Pretty soon in the script we'd get to a stagecoach robbery or a fight with the Indians. The actors new to radio techniques many times couldn't follow it on the script because the tempo was so fast. They would suddenly find themselves two pages behind. They couldn't follow it on the sheet of script as fast as the regular cast. The regular cast, of course, was part of the reason why the shows were so great. The stock company of actors on the program was melded together into such a team that they could handle the most difficult of scenes with little rehearsal and pull it off beautifully. Even though the audience recognized the same voices playing different roles on the programs week after week, they didn't seem to mind. It was important to keep this company together because you only had three hours of rehearsal for each program." *

Livingstone himself continued playing minor roles on *The Lone Ranger* and other programs, even while he was handling the directing assignment. It was not uncommon for radio actors to play more than one role, usually secondary bit parts such as townsmen in the crowd sequence to a ranch hand with just one line to deliver. For the three-part "Black Caballero" sequence in February 1939, the notorious outlaw known as "The Black Caballero," wearing black mask and cape, riding the midnight stallion known as El Diablo, mocked both the law and those settlers who lived within the law. When he first read the scripts, Livingstone personally took the lead of the masked villain for all three consecutive broadcasts.

"Outlaw on Lone Ranger Dramas"
Compliments of Cobakco
The bread that brings you the Lone Ranger

Compliments of Cobakco
The bread that brings you the Lone Ranger

As for sound man Ted Robertson, he was promoted to Charles Livingstone's assistant in February 1939, handing over the plungers to Fred Flowerday. A year and a half later Robertson left Detroit to further his career at WBBM in Chicago. "The reason for my departure was an ideological difference I had with Brace Beemer – a story of little importance to anyone but me," Robertson recalled to author David Rothel. "In Chicago I was hired almost immediately to fly to St. Louis and handle the radio campaign of a man aspiring to become the mayor of that city. The campaign was won and I joined the production staff of WBBM, Chicago, the key Midwest CBS station."

---

* Livingstone also recalled how many of the cast went into service during World War II and on one occasion went to New York City to audition actors and bring them back to Detroit.

Challenge of the Yukon and Silver Queen

Thomas Dougall, who began scripting at WXYZ in 1935, was responsible for creating the soap opera known as *Ann Worth, Housewife.* It was the second program to be transcribed for syndication but Campbell and Trendle soon discovered that it was a more difficult sell. Soap operas were cheap to produce so every radio station had their own daytime serial. In Campbell's office one morning, the two men theorized a greater demand for adventure programs because those required more skill and expense to produce – and because it was evident that a program catering to children was easier to sell than a program catering to housewives.

Tom Dougall

On July 16, 1935, Dougall sold all rights to his soap opera to Trendle for $10, in return for steady employment at the station. * In 1938, after the departure of James Jewell, Dougall was promoted to assistant director under Livingstone. Dougall also understood radio production so he was the perfect choice to create what would become *Challenge of the Yukon.*

With the financial success of *The Lone Ranger* transcriptions, George W. Trendle sought to expand his operation. If a children's western was popular enough to sell coast-to-coast, why not a series similar to *Blair of the Mounties* and *Renfrew of the Mounted*? Trendle asked Tom Dougall to create a Canadian Mountie program. *Renfrew of the Mounted* was already established over CBS, he explained, and a 15-minute program would be easier to sell than a half-hour. (Fran Striker had his

---

* Steady employment means $75 per week for scripting programs, $100 if the program was sponsored. According to Dougall's contract, drafted before the premiere of *Challenge of the Yukon,* the proposed title was "Call of the Yukon."

hands busy with two programs and five scripts a week.) The *Renfrew* program was dramatized in serialized format with lengthy story arcs that extended for months. Trendle asked that *Challenge of the Yukon*, like *The Lone Ranger* and *The Green Hornet*, have self-contained adventures that conclude at the close of every broadcast.

The Canadian Mountie hero (Sergeant Preston) rode no horse like *The Lone Ranger*, drove no automobile like *The Green Hornet*, rode no train like the later *Ned Jordan* but chose to travel behind a team of huskies on a sleigh. The program premiered in January 1939 and aired twice a week as a 15-minute adventure program. Charles Livingstone handled direction while Jay Michael took the lead. The program, as promoted by a press release from WXYZ, "glorifies the band of 20 police officers who were sent into the Yukon territory of Canada when the first great Klondike gold strike was made in 1895."

Inspired by the Jack London novel, *Call of the Yukon*, Tom Dougall attempted to replicate the adventures of the north country. Like The Lone Ranger and his aide, Tonto, Preston sledded over the icy wasteland with Pierre, his trusted French-Canadian guide, and King, his capable dog team leader, to bring justice to the north. The stories were more adult in appeal. Whereas The Lone Ranger shot a gun out of someone's hand, Sergeant Preston shot to wound the arm.

In the earliest of his adventures, Preston's lead sled dog was Mogo. Shot and killed by the criminal element, Mogo was replaced by King, wolf-like in description. Preston's initial sidekick, Terry Shea, was wounded and left for dead by a criminal element. Terry Shea was sent to Vancouver to recover and replaced by Pierre. (Pierre would be dropped from the series after a couple years.)

After failing to convince a sponsor to back the twice-a-week 15-minute series during the first year and a half, H. Allen Campbell proposed in the summer of 1940 to expand *Challenge of the Yukon* to 30-minutes as a weekly program. The *Renfrew of the Mounted* program went off CBS in 1938 and returned as a weekly half-hour program in 1939 on NBC. By the summer of 1940, it was announced in the trades that the program was going off the air for good. National commercial spread was "going slow," Campbell explained to Trendle. "Sponsors want a weekly half-hour program. Multiple 15-minute broadcasts every week is too expensive." Trendle would not relent. He hoped the series would sell to a dog food sponsor but those were few and far between.

Having read that producer Frank Melford of Century Pictures was finishing pre-production of *Silver Queen*, the story of a gambling lady of the Old West, with Claire Trevor signed to play the lead, Trendle flew to California during the last week of August 1940 to confer with Melford on securing a deal for the radio rights to the movie. Wanda Tuchock and Frank Melford, who co-wrote the story and screenplay, agreed to license the rights for radio but Trendle insisted that Claire Trevor play the lead – which would require her to move to Detroit to commit. According to the actress, who turned down the job offer, Trendle's proposition was "chickenfeed" compared to what she made in Hollywood. The movie was scheduled to go into production in October but plans fell through and the movie was never made. * Trendle's plans to replace *Challenge of the Yukon* with *Silver Queen* never happened so Sergeant Preston and his trusty husky continued their crusade across the Yukon.

---

* In 1942, United Artists released a movie of the same name with Priscilla Lane as Coralie Adams, a well-known and confident young woman from the Barbary Coast who decided to give up her chance at love in order to succeed in card games. Based on an original story by William Allen Johnston and Forrest Halsey, the premise was extremely similar to Tuchock and Melford's proposed motion picture.

In June of 1941, Campbell made arrangements to syndicate *Challenge of the Yukon* by wire to other areas of the country, similar to *The Lone Ranger* and *Ned Jordan*. The Canadian Mountie program, however, never exceeded the Michigan Radio Network (but could be heard in Ontario, Canada, for residents who could pick up one of the Michigan stations).

When extended coverage failed, Campbell proposed recording the series via transcription discs and syndicating the program that way in the same manner as *The Lone Ranger* and *The Green Hornet*. Trendle relented and, beginning in May of 1943, the twice-a-week 15-minute adventures were recorded on a regular basis.

Unlike Fran Striker back in January and February 1933, Tom Dougall had the advantage of being in the studio to assist the director with the formation of *Challenge of the Yukon* as it evolved during rehearsals. His direct input helped shape the series into an exciting Canadian Mountie adventure program that would ultimately become a half-hour program in 1947 and re-titled to *Sergeant Preston of the Yukon* in 1951.

Variety, **April 24, 1935**

"Charles Livingstone, of the WXYZ *Lone Ranger* cast, is shooting film scenario of the same play, for his home projector."

When Dougall left for the service in 1942, he was replaced by Striker, who knew little about Canadian Mountie fiction. Betty Joyce was a female scriptwriter who was at that time learning the craft. Under the guidance of Fran Striker, she was instructed to read *Lone Ranger* radio scripts and adapt and recycle them into *Challenge of the Yukon* scripts. While the plots were fairly similar in nature, the names were changed: References to The Lone Ranger were replaced with Sergeant Preston, San Antonio became Dawson City, etc. Today, many productions from the extant *Challenge of the Yukon* radio recordings from 1943 can easily be recognized as *Lone Ranger* plots, sans the masked man.

What's in a Name?

In 1934, almost a year after The Lone Ranger's personal appearance at Belle Isle and many months after the stage shows at the Fisher Theater, the Woodward Grand Theater in Highland Park advertised a personal appearance of "Silver, Star of the Lone Ranger Broadcast." According to Raymond Meurer, the station personnel knew nothing of this until an advertisement appeared in a Detroit newspaper, and a huge sign on display in front of the theater. Meurer immediately filed an action claiming that this was not Silver of *The Lone Ranger* broadcasts and the plaintiff had no right to claim any connection. "We did not use a horse on the radio show," Meurer later recalled, "but we once rented a white horse for a personal appearance… I walked out of the studio one day and saw a huge sign in front of a theater announcing the personal appearance of Silver. We had to stop such things once and for all or be confronted with phony Lone Rangers, Silvers, Tontos and everything else." Meurer tried to get an injunction against the theater and pleaded his case before Circuit Court Judge Alan Campbell (no relation to H. Allen Campbell), who listened unsympathetically.

The judge, with no knowledge of how radio broadcasts operated, could not comprehend how the theater was using a real horse when Meurer admitted the radio station did not own a horse of its own. This, the judge explained, would be the equivalent of a restaurant accusing the competition of stealing their recipe, but admitting they had no printed recipes to work from. After the noon recess, Meurer got an inspiration. He returned to court carrying two boxes and asked Judge Campbell if he could approach the bench. The judge watched in amusement as Meurer withdrew two toilet plungers.

"This is Silver," Meurer said. "There is no Silver on the radio show. The plungers are used for sound effects of beating hoofs." The amazed judge, having watched the demonstration, understood the complaint fully and granted the injunction. Later, Meurer established a successful track record for winning every case involving infringements of the *Lone Ranger* property and thus established a number of legal precedents.

**The sound effects men using plungers to replicate Silver and Scout's hoofs.
Left to right: Fred Fry, Ernie Winstanley and Jim Fletcher.**

It was this court case that caused Meurer to make an appointment with Trendle and propose they incorporate *The Lone Ranger*. "This time you were lucky," the attorney explained to his employer. "I claimed infringement but infringement in law implies some kind of patent or trademark or copyright. Having the program incorporated would put you (and your business partners) into a safer position." Trendle hesitated for some time, bearing the expense factor. Meurer, against Trendle's judgment, advanced the costs and billed Trendle later. As far as the law was concerned, *The Lone Ranger* would legally be a separate entity from the radio station. The Lone Ranger, Inc. was made official in January 1935.

For business purposes, the radio station was a separate entity of its own, known as King-Trendle, Inc. Going forward, each of the radio programs, as they gained popularity and potential coast-to-coast coverage, would be individually incorporated, and an artist commissioned to create a program logo which could be trademarked – a logo with the main characters incorporated into the artwork.*

Throughout the 1930s, the radio programs that originated out of WXYZ in Detroit were the property of the King-Trendle Broadcasting firm, and the shareholders of that station. By late 1939, all of the radio programs had become incorporated, each becoming a separate business entity. These included Ann Worth-Housewife, Inc.; Challenge of the Yukon, Inc.; The Fact Finder, Inc.; The Green Hornet, Inc.; and Ned Jordan-Secret Agent, Inc. Legally, if a lawsuit was filed against the radio station or King-Trendle, attorney Raymond Meurer would remind the plaintiff's attorney that a suit against the program was necessary when the grievance was against an aspect of the program – not the owners of the radio station.

It was in late 1938 that a Brooklyn resident named Silver demanded reparations from the Gordon Baking Company for the mental pain caused him as the result of *The Lone Ranger* broadcasts. His friends, he complained, had made life miserable for him by addressing him as "Hi-Yo Silver." The radio station's insurance policy never paid out to the Brooklyn resident and the threat of a lawsuit would eventually be dropped. But it was in that same calendar year that it became apparent some form of protection was to be established regarding the radio programs that originated out of Detroit.

Beginning in May 1939, insurance protection was offered to radio comedians who spoke out of turn on the air, a special policy underwritten by the Preferred Accident Insurance Company. The contract indemnified an account and its agency in the manner of suits for libel, slander, plagiarism, and piracy. This was referred to as an "errors and omissions policy." Most of the claims had to do with violation of dramatic script copyrights, allegedly unlawful use of photographs and statements made by a news commentator. The King-Trendle operation carried this insurance policy but it was Raymond Meurer who proposed – and implemented – the procedure to incorporate each radio program as a separate business entity.

For Trendle, he faced temporary damage control when the Gordon Baking Company expressed displeasure of the potential lawsuit; nothing could hurt business more than a sponsor optioning not to renew a program if faced with a lawsuit, or threat of a lawsuit. (Gordon Baking would drop sponsorship in March of 1939 but nothing has been found to verify that the resident from Brooklyn, and his threat of a lawsuit, was directly responsible.)

The situation regarding "Silver" prompted concern for names of fictional characters to avoid legal issues – after all, the Brooklyn resident was lodging complaint about the name of a horse. It was only a matter of time before the name of a fictional character fell victim of the same. During a meeting between Trendle, Campbell, Striker and Meurer, in November 1939, a solution was drawn up; a system was established.

Fran Striker had a habit of recycling names over the years and confessed to in the early years using the dictionary or encyclopedia for names of favorable characters. He was quickly convinced by Meurer and Trendle that the Atlas was better form. A system was devised on December 8, 1939, which ensured names used unfavorably would not be interchanged. Names like Scar would remain a villain, not a hero, even if reused multiple times over the years. Sometime around Thanksgiving 1939,

---

*Trademarked logos are documented in the first volume of this series, *The Lone Ranger: The Early Years, 1933-1937.*)

some 100 names were taken from the Atlas for use of favorable characters, in addition to 21 executed releases for names taken from various employees for designing unfavorable characters. "I believe the system as we have finally worked it out will prove satisfactory." This meant such names signed off for use on the radio broadcasts, for example, Francis Hamilton Striker, granted permission for "Francis Hamilton," "Francis Striker," or "Hamilton Striker."

In January 1940, a file of blue and white index cards was created. The white cards included the names taken from *The Rand McNally World Atlas*, with the following information: name, card number, and location in the Atlas. * *The Rand McNally World Atlas* was used by the Quaker Oats Company in prior radio productions and this tip was passed on to Trendle's office from a representative of that company. The blue cards listed names for which the studio had legal releases, secured through Meurer's office, and paid for at the rate of one dollar a name. (By law, one dollar was the minimal required in legal contracts to ensure payment for permission and clearances.) These cards included the following information: name, number (corresponding to the affidavit number), address of the individual, and the number of the check which paid for the release. The cards were arranged alphabetically, with a cross-file arranged numerically. When a name was used, the date and number of the script were noted on the card, to avoid frequent repetition of the same name. On the cast sheet of each radio script, starting in January 1940, next to each character's name was the file number. Eventually this was revised to the page and column in the Atlas for which the name was selected.

Fran Striker had a policy not to refer to characters in radio plays with both first and last name unless it was essential. Hence, the name Barbara Potter could be used once, but simply as "Barbara" throughout the rest of the script. If a reference to Barbara as the daughter of Francis Potter was made, no last name would be required. The less names used, the less confusion was the general thinking. Nicknames such as "Legs," "The Dope," "Mut," "Scar," etc., could be used but never coupled with any last name.

---

* This meant if the state of South Dakota shows the county of Codington containing the town of Henry, in the Atlas, the name of Henry Codington was used in a script.

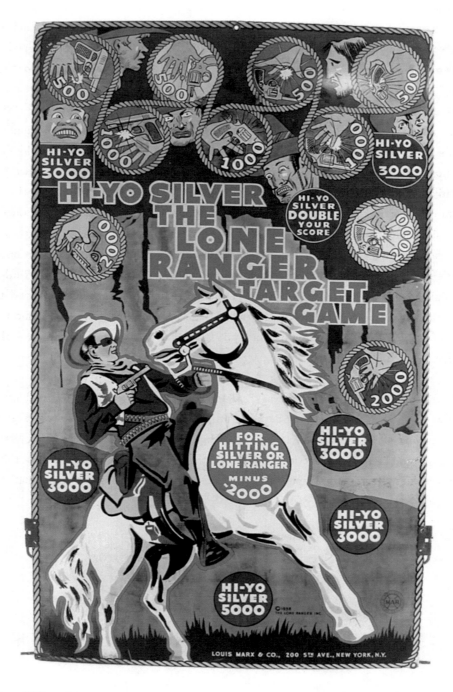

Fluffs and Bloopers

It was not uncommon for radio broadcasts to have bloopers go out live over the air, and if that blooper occurred during the broadcast that was transcribed, it was recorded for posterity. With three performances per evening, each for a different network (Mutual, Don Lee, and the Michigan), a blooper was only preserved when it occurred during the broadcast that was transcribed. Thus, many bloopers still exist in extant recordings.

For example, in one early broadcast (circa 1934 to 1935), John Todd, in the character of Tonto, remarked: "Hark! I hear a white horse coming!" In another episode, Todd doubled as an Englishman. The scene was that of riding across the prairies on a stagecoach. Todd had his script marked in such a way that he knew which part he was to be speaking and he would hold his place, which was marked "cue," with his finger. He would look up from time to time to check the program director for the signal to speak his lines. The first words of the line that he was to say were, "Ah, a hit…" Above that line he had written "cue" so that he would know to watch the director. As Brace Beemer recalled, when the signal came, "John came out in a beautiful English accent and said, 'Ah, a cue.'"

For one particular broadcast, Chuck Webster had difficulty pronouncing "Redskin," saying "Redskwin" instead. Charles Livingstone would say, "You better change that. Change that to 'Injun.'" But Webster insisted he was only kidding. During the second rehearsal, it came out "Redskwin." Dress rehearsal came out "Redskwin, too." Livingstone said, "Change it to 'Injun.'" First airshow it came out as "Redskwin," but the repeat show it was "Injun."

It was Fred Flowerday who, as chief sound technician, was responsible for constructing a large box on wheels which contained an automobile storage battery. This was connected to several car horns mounted in the box which were activated by buttons on the outside rear of the box. This gadget was used for contemporary dramas such as *Ned Jordan* and *The Green Hornet*. Short of storage space, the box was kept in the corner of the studio and the battery deactivated when not in use. On the evening of December 9, 1938, the sound crew forgot to unhook the battery. During a broadcast dramatizing the origin of how The Lone Ranger met Tonto as part of a sixth anniversary celebration, Tonto was sent to watch the horses as The Lone Ranger crept up on a cabin where a young girl was held captive. John Todd, tired after a long day at the microphone, retreated to the rear of the studio, sat on a chair and went to rest his feet on the horn box. Suddenly a klaxon horn honked across the prairie, drowning out the sound of crickets. Thankfully, that snafu did not occur during the broadcast that was recorded! From that day forward, though, the storage battery was removed from the horn box.

One of the prize fluffs happened after 1937 when the program was being transcribed from Chicago. Harry Golder, the announcer and narrator, received his cue for the familiar opening lines: "A fiery horse with the speed of light… a cloud of dust… and a *farty* Hi Yo Silver! The Lone Ranger!"

After that broadcast, the director received a wire from Chicago which read: "Have deleted windy portion of show."

"On one particular show, Dewey Cole was doing manual effects," recalled Tony Caminita. "The scene finds the Ranger and Tonto in the middle of the desert. They're crawling along, their horses suffering from thirst in the arid wasteland. Dewey was carrying a large sheet of glass from one studio to the other for use in the next scene, in which the sound of breaking glass was needed. In the middle of the scene, as Dewey was crossing the studio, he dropped the glass and the audience heard this tremendous glass crash in the middle of the desert which you must admit was strange as hell. But like everything else that ever occurred on the show, they kept going without so much as a fluff, and I'm sure the audience at home must have said, 'Hey, something went wrong with my ears!'"

In the role of a sheriff on one show, Frank Russell had a line in the script that read: "Every man that can ride a horse and shoot a gun follow me!" Well, on the air he got the line twisted and it came out: "Every man that can ride a gun and shoot a horse follow me!"

On another radio broadcast, the sound of chopping wood was effected by a sound man with a small hatchet and an old log. For the 10:30 p.m. show, Ernie Winstanley became involved with horseplay with Jim Fletcher. Distracted for a fraction of a second, the miscalculation drove the hatchet into Fletcher's shin. A spurt of blood gave Ernie reason to hustle Fletcher out of the studio and to a nearby doctor. For the remainder of the broadcast, the sounds of horses' hooves, wood chopping, and other sound effects, were mute.

For the broadcast of August 19, 1938, Earle Graser was on vacation and never heard during the broadcast. The signature closing, however, "Hi-Yo, Silver" was pre-recorded and at the conclusion of the episode, the signature Lone Ranger call skipped a track.

Another humorous blooper worth pointing out was on the broadcast of June 15, 1942, where a crook shouted an exclamation to his underhanded employer that The Lone Ranger "shot the hand out of my gun."

Fran Striker was cranking out so many scripts a week that the mix-up of names was not at all uncommon but during rehearsals the cast and crew generally caught any mix-ups and made the proper adjustments. One of them, however, slipped through the cracks. On the broadcast of June 28, 1940, observant listeners questioned why the name of the villainous suspect, "Breed Potter," was re-named "Breed Martin" during the second half of the program.

A few more: On the broadcast of January 7, 1942, Brace Beemer said "After the Black Arrow" by mistake when he was not supposed to speak, forgetting the microphone was still live. At the beginning of the July 3, 1944, broadcast, the narrator made an error and instead of dating the events of 1864, instead referenced 1964. On the broadcast of October 18, 1946, Jeb Martin greets the sheriff after there was a knock at the door… but his greeting occurred before the sound man had a chance to open the door. During the broadcast of August 30, 1948, Fred Foy narrated with "two days later" when he meant to say "two hours later." On the broadcast of April 20, 1949, Fred Foy mispronounced the word "drama" at the close of Act One.

Brace Beemer himself fluffed lines. "This was a time when we used to carry those messages for the kids," Beemer recalled. "Things like 'Mind your mom and dad and do what your teachers tell you.' Somewhere earlier in the show I tripped over a word in one of the announcements. In live radio, you just don't make mistakes and more especially, The Lone Ranger just doesn't make mistakes. After having fluffed over a word, when I got to the message for the kids, I ended after 'Do what your teachers tell you' with 'and never, never fluff.' When I looked into the broadcast booth I saw the program director's face." Beemer recalled the director's glowering expression.

"We did some crazy things back in those days," Ernie Winstanley recalled. "When we were in the Maccabees on Woodward Avenue in Detroit our broadcast studios were on the 15th floor. We had a stuffed dummy in the sound effects department that was used for creating the sound of a body falling to the floor. One afternoon, along with a fellow actor Jim Fletcher and sound effects technician Dewey Cole, we hung this stuffed dummy out of the 15th floor window, and from the street it looked as if someone had hung himself. It scared the hell out of passersby and caused quite a furor, along with a traffic jam at Woodward Avenue."

"John Todd, a marvelous actor who played Tonto, was a charming, witty and virile Irishman who was quite attractive to women," Ted Robertson later recalled to author David Rothel. "During my tenure as assistant director under Chuck Livingstone we did three broadcasts a night… the time between 8:00 and 10:30 p.m. was usually devoted to poker, Ping-Pong, snooker, or pool at the local pool parlor, or, for those of a romantic nature, it was an opportunity for a little hanky-panky. One memorable night we began the final broadcast and I failed to check the personnel. The first scene concerned a meeting between The Lone Ranger, Tonto, and the local sheriff. When Tonto's first line came up there was a horrifying silence… John Todd was nowhere to be seen (or heard). Earle Graser and the actor playing the sheriff somehow stumbled through the scene improvising as they went along to cover the absence of the (un)faithful Indian companion. Todd arrived shortly thereafter in a state of complete dishevelment and with his prominent bald spot covered with lipstick. The loveable bachelor had been dallying with a damsel in a nearby hotel and had lost all sense of time. John never revealed the identity of the lady friend, and I learned to count noses five minutes before the final broadcast."

"John always arrived early and sat in the same chair in the studio in Detroit's Mendelssohn Mansion on E. Jefferson Street. He was always friendly but seldom involved in the jocular fun of the other actors off-mike," recalled actor Dave Parker. "But John was greatly respected. In his 60s he was the oldest actor on the show and with far more theatrical experience than anyone else in the cast. In fact, when he wasn't playing Tonto, he was teaching acting in his own school in downtown Detroit. So there he was, John Todd, about five-foot-six, a bit stout, bald-headed, witty, charming, and virile and looking nothing like an Indian. In fact, his appearance was the reason no children were ever allowed in the studio. For that matter neither was anyone else. Just the actors, director, engineer, and sound effects guys – the Hengstebeck brothers and Tony Caminita – all regarded as the best in the business."

In fact, while *The Lone Ranger* radio program never had a studio audience, there was a little sponsor's section which could seat as many as ten people and sometimes there would be visitors – but as noted, never any children because it would shatter all of their illusions.

"As the show grew in popularity, the producers realized that with Tonto they had a character who could teach tolerance to the huge audience of children," Parker continued. "John Todd told me once that, 'Tonto doesn't aspire to be a hero in his own right, and The Lone Ranger accepts him just the way he is, including his mangled English. With Tonto you have the epitome of abject hero-worship. He has no expensive equipment like silver on his saddle but he loves The Lone Ranger.'"

For the record, Fran Striker was once asked to write a prospectus on the character of Tonto and, according to Striker, Tonto was the son of a chieftain of the Potawatomi tribe of Indians. He was about 26 years of age, spoke English brokenly and was usually serious, though he loved a good joke on an amusing situation. He lived to serve The Lone Ranger. He spoke most of the Indian languages, knew all of the lore of the woods, the fields, and streams. The Lone Ranger wore two silver six-shooters (in the 1930s they were ivory handled) specially made for him. When necessary, he used a rifle, though the rifle was carried by Tonto. Tonto also carried a knife, which he could throw with deadly aim, a bow with arrows, and the rifle, carried in a saddle scabbard, usually called a "boot."

Brace Beemer

On a number of occasions, Rollon Parker substituted for John Todd when the latter went on two-week vacations. One such example can be found in the broadcasts of August 14, 1939 through August 25, 1939. "During one vacation period, somehow or another, Chuck put me in as Tonto for a couple of weeks. I was lousy. There was a phone call that Chuck told me about. I can't use the word, but the lady said, 'That's a ------- Indian!'"

Few encyclopedias reference Hollywood actor John Hodiak as a cast member at Detroit, but the actor was regarded as the top pin man at the station beginning sometime in 1938 and lasting through 1939. Hodiak worked at Chevrolet and one day he came in the studio to see Jim Jewell, who was still directing the program. Hodiak would sit in the viewing booth to watch the program and get a feel for what was required for the job. He watched the program for three to four weeks until the day actor Fred Reto had a heart attack before airtime. Reto only had about six or seven lines of dialogue and Jewell grabbed John in the viewing booth and told him to take the part. Hodiak became a regular from that day on.

The earliest documentation on radio scripts to reference Hodiak in the cast was as an extra voice on the broadcasts of August 8, 10, and 12, 1938. Such a small and inconsequential role suggests he was in training about this time on the program. In one episode, John Hodiak was the hero protagonist and had a line to deliver: "I'm off to the execution." At that time, Hodiak was taking voice lessons so during the radio broadcast he accidentally said, "I'm off to the elocution."

On Wednesday evenings, after staff members completed their 11 p.m. *Lone Ranger* performance for the benefit of the West Coast, they engaged in weekly bouts at a nearby bowling alley that stayed open late for them. Having formed a bowling league of six teams, Chuck Dougherty, first trumpet, and John Hodiak, actor, were considered the best of the league.

For one episode, Frank Russell, who played character parts, was assigned the role of sheriff. He and his posse had located the gang of crooks. It was at night and they had their little camp in a circle surrounded by a forest. The sheriff deployed his men all around, and on a certain signal they were all to come in and he would say, "All right, gents, get your guns up." But when the time came to deliver the line, Russell said, "All right, junts, get your gens up; Gens, get your junts up. Oh, shoot 'em!"

There was once a letter from a young listener who commented on the two clicks of The Lone Ranger's pistol being cocked. According to the youth, during The Lone Ranger's time they only had single action revolvers which made four clicks when cocked, rather than two clicks of the more modern double-action pistols. The soundmen took note to be more accurate in future broadcasts.

During one of the radio adventures, The Lone Ranger made an overnight ride from his camp near the supposedly fictitious town of Medicine Mound and arriving by dawn at the Rio Grande. A youngster who lived in the real Medicine Mound wrote in, pointing out that his home was 600 miles from the Rio. "Not even Silver," he said, "could make that trip overnight."

Perhaps the most notorious of the bloopers, however, took place on the broadcast of May 30, 1949, titled "The Cattle Buyer." During that adventure, The Lone Ranger poses as a rich cattle buyer from St. Louis trying to smoke out whoever is tipping off a ruthless gang of robbers. When the guilty banker takes the Ranger's marked money, it is easy to trail him and have the sheriff overhear the confession. During one particular scene, The Lone Ranger and Tonto were supposed to be searching a hotel room on the second floor. They heard footsteps coming down the hall and the lines that were to follow went something like this: "Come on, Tonto, let's get out of here," and then they were to climb out of the second-floor window and drop to the ground. But John Todd dozed off and when nudged to wake up and deliver his lines, walked to the microphone hearing Brace Beemer's line, unaware his character was still in the hotel on the second floor, and remarked, "Ugh, Kemo Sabay. Get 'em up Scout!"

"*The Lone Ranger* recently celebrated its 700th consecutive broadcast on Mutual, and has just been signed for 52 weeks. First broadcast was heard in January 1933, over WXYZ in Detroit. It has continued to produce there. During that time author Fran Striker has written over 3,000,000 words or the equivalent of 30 novels of 100,000 words each. The drama has filled over 350 hours of airtime. Republic Pictures have purchased the serial screen rights and will run it in 15 installments. And now on the newsstands, so help us, is *The Lone Ranger* magazine. The serial has established two radio records. First, it has for the past three years garnered top fan mail response; secondly, no radio editor or listener has ever seen a picture of the hero unmasked. That, according to Mutual executives, would spoil everything."

– *Screen and Radio Weekly*, February 13, 1938

"The following story appeared in *Radio Daily* about KSO's *Lone Ranger* broadcast: 'San Francisco – Old couple driving slowly along East Bay highway suddenly hit it up to 60 going through new Broadway tunnel. Stopped by cop, they explained radio was tuned to *Lone Ranger*, there was no reception in tunnel, so they had to speed up in order not to miss too much of action. Case was dismissed.'"

– *Des Moines Tribune*, September 27, 1938

"Only two of the so-called 'children's programs' make the first ten in a radio popularity poll recently conducted among 14-year-old boys and girls by *Young America*, national youth paper. According to the nationwide survey of junior high schools, young America's favorite program is the adult *Gang Busters*, which has a slight but perceptible margin over Edgar Bergen's Charlie McCarthy hour. *The Lone Ranger* ranks third, followed by *Lux Radio Theatre*, Jack Benny, Eddie Cantor, *Maxwell House Coffee Hour*, *One Man's Family*, Fred Allen and *Dick Tracy*. In all, 49 different programs were mentioned by the boys and girls answering the question, 'What's Your Favorite Radio Program?' Of particular interest was the wide popularity of adult programs as compared with the strictly 'juvenile' features."

– Lowell, MA, *Evening Leader*, September 28, 1938

"When Jimmy Puntain and his friends get together on Saturday mornings in the future for a session of 'cowboy and Indian,' little Jimmy is almost certain to be chosen for the role of 'mysterious rider.' Every cowboy and Indian game must have a masked man. The reason for Jimmy's new honors is his ability to shout 'Hi-Yo, Silver' almost as well as The Lone Ranger himself. And The Lone Ranger, everybody knows, is the popular masked man who appears each Sunday in the *News-Sentinel*. Last week the *News-Sentinel* sponsored a contest over WISN in which boys and girls imitated the yell of the famous Lone Ranger. Listeners cast more 3,000 votes and Jimmy, who lives at 2426 N. Farwell Avenue, placed first with 323 votes, and will receive $25 cash. Second prize and $15 goes to Howard Kneip, 2523 N. 17th Street, who collected 319 votes. A little girl, Geraldine Mae Spicer, 1514 N. 50th Street, was third and will receive $15. She had 238 votes."

– *Roanoke (VA) News*, September 9, 1938

"LONE RANGER" DESIRES TO GET IN touch with refined young lady; object matrimony. Box 238, Tribune.

Newspaper advertisement from *The Winnipeg Tribune*, Manitoba, Canada, from December 31, 1941.

Chapter Four
Sponsorship and Premiums

"Citation of *The Lone Ranger* program of the Gordon Baking Company as one
of the most effective programs on the air is made in the August 1 issue of *Sales
Management*... So well has *The Lone Ranger* been received that it is being used by
many bakers in non-competitive territories as well as by companies in other fields. The
rapidly growing list of users now totals 42."
– *Baker's Helper*, August 20, 1938

DURING THE FIRST WEEK OF MAY 1937, a radio celebrity was surrounded by a group of about
40 young autograph seekers at radio station KFRC in San Francisco, found himself late for an
appointment, and desperately sought a polite way out. Spying KFRC sales representative Ray Baker
in the next studio, the celebrity suggested to the kids: "Why don't you get his signature? He's The
Lone Ranger!" Baker was soon surrounded by young admirers. According to *Variety*, "Unwilling to
disappoint the youngsters, Baker battled with his conscience, lost, admitted that he was not the real
Lone Ranger, but only the salesman for the show. But this did not make a bit of difference to the
young Lone Rangers. Baker was near enough to the real thing." The popularity of the radio program
was so immense that even the salesman for a potential sponsor was looked up to with youthful
adoration.

On June 14, 1938, there was an opening meeting of the Sales Managers Division of the National
Association of Broadcasters held at the Hotel Statler in Detroit, in connection with the Advertising
Federation convention. Among the guest speakers was Charles Hicks, sales promotional manager of
WXYZ, with a presentation titled "The Inside Story of The Lone Ranger." Of the presentations that
day, Hicks' address was considered the highlight of the meeting. The Lone Ranger craze regarding
merchandising and transcription disc rentals jumped that same month.

As we've noted, prior to the electrical transcriptions, *The Lone Ranger* was broadcast via remote hook-up over three major networks: The Michigan Radio Network, the Mutual Broadcasting System, and the Don Lee Network. Because of the time difference, three shows were performed nightly with the same cast. Once for WXYZ, MRN, WGN, and WSPD (i.e. Michigan) at 6:30 p.m.; another for WOR in Newark/New York (i.e. Mutual), and the Colonial and Yankee Networks at 7:30 p.m., and a third performance later in the evening at 9:30 p.m. for the west coast over Don Lee. Kilpatrick Bakeries, headquartered in San Francisco, and Western Bakeries, headquartered in Los Angeles (four stations and six, respectively), sponsored the program over Don Lee. (Gingham Bread was the product pitched.)

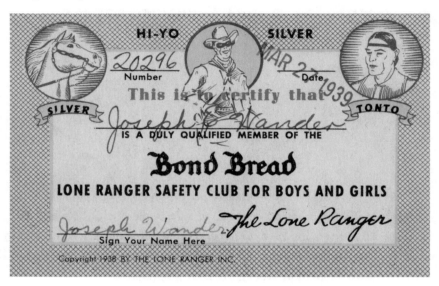

The Gordon Baking Company sponsored the broadcasts over Mutual through March 24, 1939, when Bond Bread replaced Gordon as the underwriter (except for Chicago where Bond Bread was not distributed). The withdrawal of Gordon was done on the recommendation of the advertising agency, Young & Rubicam, the new agency on the account. Bond's tie-up with the western was identified in five Mutual stop-offs for some time, including WOL in Washington, D.C., since September 26, 1938. The expansion gave Bond 19 spots on the Mutual Broadcast System. There was a week's interval of broadcasts on a sustaining basis so that the changeover in bread brand cajoling would not be too abrupt for the kid listeners. Bond's expansion began with the broadcast of April 3. One exception to that was over WXYZ, which began March 27.

Bond Bread would only sponsor *The Lone Ranger* until July 24, 1940, for a total of five billing cycles. For ten months the program was without a sponsor in the major markets of the east and middle west. H. Allen Campbell applied all his affable magnetism, persuasive charm, and great sales ability to the capturing of General Mills and eventually succeeded.

While many radio programs (*The Lone Ranger* included) are listed in reference guides as being on networks with specific start dates and end dates, many affiliates of those networks had prior contracted programming for the same time slot and were initially unable to carry the program via hook-up right away until arrangements could be made to move the time slot for the existing program, or cancel at the end of the next billing cycle. So, while many reference guides and websites claim *The Lone Ranger* premiered over Mutual on November 29, 1933 (others cite January 18, 1934), this is not reflective of all the network affiliates. As an example, below is an accurate list of the Mutual affiliates that began broadcasting *The Lone Ranger*.

Station	Beginning Broadcast Date	Station	Beginning Broadcast Date
WGN	November 29, 1933	WKBW	October 21, 1938
WOR	January 18, 1934	KTUL	January 4, 1939
WNBF	October 11, 1937	WHIO	January 23, 1939
WSYR	October 18, 1937	WDEL	January 30, 1939
WCKY	February 21, 1938	WORK	January 30, 1939
WCBS	February 21, 1938	CKCO	February 1, 1939
KSO	February 23, 1938	CKCL	February 1, 1939
KOIL	February 23, 1938	CHML	February 1, 1939
KGIR	March 14, 1938	WAAB	February 3, 1939
KFJM	March 28, 1938	WEAN	February 3, 1939
KUMA	July 18, 1938	WMAS	February 13, 1939
WFIL	September 5, 1938	WLLH	February 13, 1939
WESG	September 12, 1938	WHKC	February 13, 1939
KGLO	September 12, 1938	WHB	February 13, 1939
KXYZ	September 26, 1938	KTOK	February 13, 1939
WOL	September 26, 1938	KCRC	February 13, 1939
WMC	September 26, 1938	WABY	February 13, 1939
KWTO	September 26, 1938	WAVE	February 13, 1939
WGBF	September 26, 1938	WHEC	February 13, 1939
WBAL	September 27, 1938	WCLE	February 27, 1939
KARK	September 27, 1938		

While reference guides and websites report *The Lone Ranger* premiering over the Don Lee Broadcasting System on January 18, 1937, Kilpatrick Bakeries sponsored on the following stations over these corresponding start dates and affiliates.

Station	Beginning Broadcast Date
KHJ, KPMC, KXO, KFXM, KGB, KVOE, KDB, and KVEC	January 18, 1937
KFRC, KDON, KQW, and KGDM	February 15, 1937
KALE	October 11, 1937
KORE	January 7, 1938 *
KIT	May 2, 1938
KMO	September 12, 1938
KOL	October 3, 1938

* Sponsored by Williams Bakery in Eugene and Portland, Oregon, over KORE.

One of the largest sponsors for *The Lone Ranger* program was American Bakeries (producers of Merita Bread), who brought The Lone Ranger with his stirring radio adventures to the Southeast for the first time on September 25, 1938. The broadcasts were presented three times each week, over 28 stations. (Over the next few years, coverage would expand to 77 radio stations.)

On December 23, 1938, a representative of the James A. Green & Company advertising agency wrote a letter to H. Allen Campbell regarding Merita's progress with *The Lone Ranger* campaign. "Despite the fact the Government is giving away a vast amount of free flour in our territory, sales are holding up and last week we had a $10,000 increase over the same week last year, last year being the company's banner year. Sales for this week should show a similar increase… We feel that *The Lone Ranger* is doing a fine job for Merita and we look forward to 1939 with confidence."

With a sponsor covering as vast a territory as Merita Bread, it goes without saying that a number of *Lone Ranger* premiums would be offered with the Merita seal of approval. Beginning in the summer of 1937, *The Lone Ranger News* was printed. This miniature newspaper, printed in two colors, was distributed free through grocery stores, serving as a clearing house for the listeners of *The Lone Ranger* program. The newspapers contained one entire page of photographs of members of the Lone Ranger Safety Club in various midwestern cities. There were also numerous letters from fans, together with original poems and couplets. There were also instructions on how to make your own Tonto pouch, how to tie three different knots, and stories such as how the Cherokee alphabet was invented. (Some of these features were also included in the Lone Ranger Safety Club Official Manual distributed throughout the 1930s.)

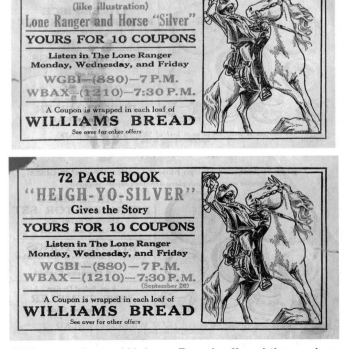

The Williams Bakery, makers of Holsum Bread, offered these giveaways if radio listeners collected ten coupons, one in each loaf of bread sold in the stores.

Today, these miniature newspapers are sought-after collectibles because while the contents can remain the same, the variants include regional sponsorships. They were printed in mass quantities and with different sponsors depending on the territory. The Cramer Baking Company, for example, prominently featured their Butter-Cream Bread in the newspaper. Merita Bread, on the other hand, featured an illustration for loaves of bread in their issues.

In the summer of 1938, another series of *Lone Ranger News* was published, with inclusion of similar features to the 1937 issues. These included secret codes such as "Ta-I-Kee-Mo-Sah-Bee" (Hello, Loyal Ranger), photos from the cliffhanger serial, and original art depicting The Lone Ranger and his horse Silver.

Lone Ranger News Published and Ready

FANS who follow the adventures of the Lone Ranger each week are receiving a miniature newspaper, the LONE RANGER NEWS this week. This tabloid, printed in two colors, is the second issue of the publication—and is distributed free through grocery stores. The paper made its appearance today.

The Lone Ranger News is a clearing house for the listeners of the Lone Ranger program. It contains one entire page of photographs of members of the Lone Ranger Safety club in various middlewestern cities. There are also numerous letters from these fans, together with original poems and couplets.

Membership in the Lone Ranger Safety Club has reached a new high, with thousands of young members in all parts of the city and surrounding territory. The purpose of the club is to promote and teach safety among youngsters—and special emphasis is now being placed on a safe and sane Fourth of July.

CITY AND SAFETY COUNCIL OFFICIALS have placed their stamp of approval on the work of the Lone Ranger Safety Club. The current Lone Ranger News also prints letters from mothers who enthusiastically indorse the club as a means of teaching safety to children.

The Lone Ranger program, popular from coast to coast, is sponsored here by the bakers of Butter-Nut Bread and Dolly Madison Cakes. It will be heard every Wednesday, Friday and Sunday at 5:30 p. m. over KSO.

Note: The program shifts from KRNT to KSO Wednesday.)

July 1938

Sponsorship was again featured prominently on the front page, and inside the newspaper, which varied from region to region. In Des Moines, Iowa, for example, where Schulze was the sponsor, Butter-Nut Bread and Dolly Madison Cakes were featured. When the V-Bev Beverage Company sponsored regionally, their vitamin health drink was promoted. Among the many features included in these newspapers were suggestions on how to form a Lone Ranger club, mentions of the upcoming theatrical serial, and praise from mayors and police chiefs for the safety club. In the Franz Bakery Lone Ranger News, for example, Dr. E.B. McDaniel, Oregon president of the nationwide organization of automobile owners, delivered the following message: "I want every member of the Safety Club to know that national highway safety leaders appreciate the work they are doing and will watch their progress with much interest. The organization work by the Franz Bakery, too, is worthy of commendation."

Brief script excerpts from a number of radio broadcasts, were also featured in some of *The Lone Ranger News*.

This is to Certify that

The Bearer

is a Duly Qualified Safety Ranger in
Eddy's Lone Ranger Safety Club

(Member Must Sign Here)

DR. WEST'S
LONE RANGER CLUB

This is to certify that

RANGER .... Allen Schendel

is a member in good standing, and entitled to all the
rights and privileges of The Lone Ranger Club.

The Lone Ranger

MEMBERSHIP CARD

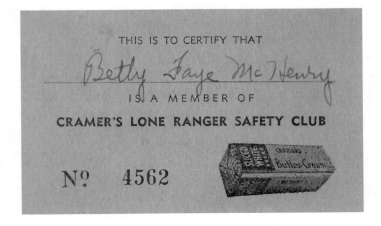

THIS IS TO CERTIFY THAT

Betty Faye McHenry

IS A MEMBER OF

CRAMER'S LONE RANGER SAFETY CLUB

No 4562

This is to Certify That

The Bearer

is a Duly Qualified Safety Ranger in

Hart's Lone Ranger Safety Club

Dorothy Knebel
(Member Must Sign Here)

In 1938, a Safety Contest encouraged children to write and mail submissions with a $25 cash prize for First Place. The producers of the radio program were shocked to discover one of the submissions came from none other than actress Shirley Temple.

Shirley Temple Ties With Harold E'Golf

Because Shirley Temple's entry in the Safety Contest was as fine as any one submitted, it was decided to award TWO First Prizes—one to Shirley and one to Harold E'Golf. Each of them will receive the full $25.00 First Prize money.

Shirley Temple was one of the first to join the Lone Ranger Safety Club and her membership number is 227. Besides being the best-known Safety Club member in the United States, Shirley is without doubt the most popular little girl in all the world.

In 1939 and 1940, another newspaper was distributed, now re-christened *The Lone Ranger Round-Up*, containing such features as a page devoted to famous Americans, puzzles, jokes, and an advertisement for the "Pilot Lone Ranger Radio." The May 1940 issue offered a contest for children to enter and win a free "Pilot Lone Ranger Radio" by rearranging the letters to the title of a Christmas song. (This was more than likely subliminal advertising as there would be no future issues beyond May 1940 and children who did not win the contest would certainly know before the holiday and instead ask Santa Claus for one.)

The miniature newspapers were designed by the advertising agency, Batten, Barton, Durstine, and Osborn, with content authored by C.D. Morris. The newspapers were printed by Arrow Press in New York City.

THE LONE RANGER NEWS

May 1938, first issue

July 1938, second issue

September 1938, third issue

THE LONE RANGER ROUND-UP

August 1939, Issue #1

October 1939, Issue #2

December 1939, Issue #3

Volume Two, Issue #1, February 1940

Volume Two, Issue #2, April 1940

Volume Two, Issue #3, May 1940

"TONTO HIM KNOW
YOU KEEP 'EM
PLEDGE TO LONE
RANGER"

The
LONE RANGER
SAFETY SCOUTS

are sponsored by the makers
of SILVERCUP, The
World's Finest Bread, for
the purpose of preventing
injury to children, and
building up the character
of youth.

build up with
SILVERCUP
the world's finest
BREAD

● Listen for "HI YO, SILVER!" the cry of the
Lone Ranger, over WGN every Monday,
Wednesday, and Friday evening at 7 o'clock.

Children dressed like The Lone Ranger in *The Lone Ranger News*, circa 1938.

THE LONE RANGER 1940 BUBBLEGUM CARDS

A collection of 48 bubblegum cards was produced in 1940, given away in packs of bubblegum, featuring the artwork of Charles H. Steinbacher. Produced by Gum, Inc., the candy and card combo was sold for a penny. The original concept was to consist of 60 different cards so that fans of the radio program could buy the candy with the intent of collecting all 60. Children who mailed in five of their wrappers could also receive an 8 x 10 inch photo from the series. Children who sent in 25 wrappers would receive a complete set of those five photos. Those large prints are today considered among the rarest of *Lone Ranger* premiums.

In the early-to-mid 1990s, the art for all 60 cards was discovered in the personal safe of the late Steinbacher, so the cards were reproduced by Dart Flipcards, Inc., in 1997, not just with all 48 original cards, but also with the dozen that had never been produced.

Steinbacher was the art director for the George Moll Advertising Agency, which handled the Gum, Inc., account. Steinbacher became a bit of a legend in the field of non-sports cards for producing the art for the *Horrors of War* set for Gum, Inc., which was marketed in 1938. Steinbacher's watercolor-on-board paintings, 7 x 6 inches, has been sold over the decades that followed for sums even larger than the cost of the original bubble gum cards.

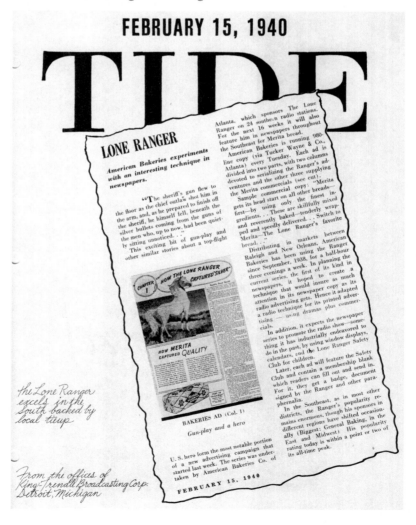

How The Lone Ranger Captured Silver

This was not the first printed premium from *The Lone Ranger* to cross-promote a sponsor's product. In 1936, executives at Silvercup Bread agreed to include a premium story booklet along with bread distribution. The small color paper cover and eight unbound pages contained a printed photo of John Todd as Tonto, and another with an illustration of Tonto standing full figure wearing a headdress with a teepee in the background. The photo of John Todd as Tonto in costume was in sharp contrast to the actor who appeared at the studio in a suit and tie.

Also included were seven chapters, each one distributed weekly as a premium with loaves of Silvercup Bread, telling the story of how The Lone Ranger captured and tamed Silver, involving King Sylvan and the fight with the buffalo. This was an adaptation of the August 26, 1935, radio broadcast by Fran Striker, but authorship was credited on the printed page by David Arnsan, whom the inside of the cover explained was a 16-year-old boy. Naturally, the booklet contained an advertisement for Silvercup Bread on the back cover.

It should be noted that while the 1935 radio broadcast claimed The Lone Ranger's horse was Dusty, before he met Silver, this rendition had The Lone Ranger's horse called "Nellie."

The same story was also printed in The Lone Ranger Safety Club Official Manuals, and would again be released as a premium, also in installments, in loaves of bread during the winter of 1939-1940. Based on feedback, the public clamored for so many copies of the story it was impossible to meet the demand. The story was then printed in serial format, beginning February 1940, but was actually a series of paid advertisements.

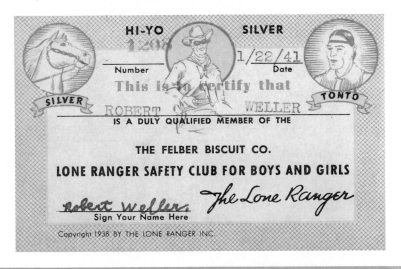

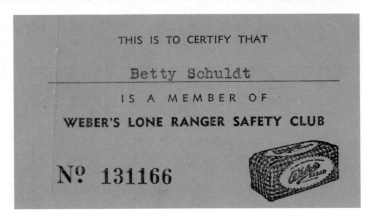

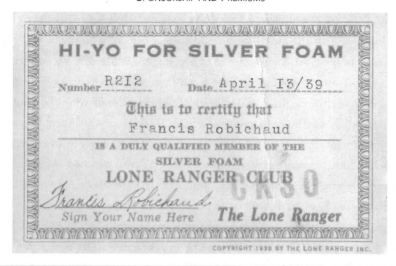

The newspaper serial brought thousands of unsolicited letters, which made it plain that the public wanted Merita to publish another Lone Ranger story. Comments, questions, and suggestions showed a particular interest in Tonto. Accordingly, in answer to public demand, a representative of the ad agency for Merita contacted George W. Trendle to ask if they could furnish another story. Fran Striker agreed to the assignment and furnished a 15-chapter story titled "The Life of Tonto." The majority of the novel focused on Tonto's childhood, tested for courage and endurance. Stubborn in an effort to prove himself to the tribe, the Indian boy ventured out alone one evening to kill a mountain cougar. After finding his prey and facing off against the beast, which clawed at his chest, an arrow plunged in the correct spot, killing the animal. Tonto, instead, learned that his father was not proud, but upset at the reckless act. Tonto insisted he alone become part of the "Vigil," a test that was anticipated by Indian boys with mixed feelings of delight and trepidation. If he passed the Vigil, he would be looked upon as a Brave of the tribe and allowed to ride with the hunters and fight with the warriors. Penalty for failure was death.

Taken by the hunters to an isolated spot where no moonlight could penetrate, they proceeded to disarm the boy. Tonto was then unclothed. The eagle feather robe was taken from him. With no weapon of any sort, he was to survive one week on his own. When they returned seven days later, if they found him in the same spot alive, he would be greeted with wild cries of joy. Using ingenuity and cunning, Tonto survived the ordeal for seven days, and became a hunter.

Upon returning to the tribe, Tonto learned of war, a fierce battle that would end only when the last fighter on one side or the other had gone down in death. The Apaches had use of the fertile valley, horses, and food. Tonto, the son of the chief, armed himself with the strongest bow and horse and prepared defense. The massacre was certain, however, as the Apaches were armed with rifles, which were stronger than any of the swiftest arrows. Dawn brought the first wild war cry of the savage Apaches. Shrill screams of rage rent the air and Tonto watched as his father fell, gravely wounded. "In you, my son," the good chief feebly muttered, "I am reborn. You must leave this valley and savage Indians who have come to take possession of it. You must go far away, where you can be taught new things. A new age is coming and you must be part of it. There are things that white men teach that you must learn. You must be a leader in peace, that white men and Indians may live together in harmony. You will find a friend who will be good. Trust this friend and help him." As the Apaches took possession of the valley, Tonto's tribe was eviscerated from the earth. Tonto was the only member of his tribe who still lived, and only because he was knocked unconscious in the fray.

The story closed years later as Tonto had grown to manhood. For several years he had been quite alone, traveling from town to town, doing what he could to help the white settlers. He served as guide for countless immigrants, showing them where the best trails were and how to ford the many streams. He drifted from Oklahoma as far north as South Dakota, then as far south as Texas. After hearing shots coming from a nearby canyon, he rode out to investigate and found the bodies of six Texas Rangers. Five of them were dead. The survivor lay on the brink of death. Loss of blood and shock kept him from moving. Dragging the body to the entrance of a cave, Tonto took heed of the grim situation that the man was in and began nursing him back to health.

As the wounded man began to recover, the two struck up a friendship. Tonto explained how he had buried the bodies of the Texas Rangers, plus one extra grave to simulate the appearance of death for the survivor. "You free to get revenge now," Tonto explained. "No one know that you live."

The white man nodded grimly. "So," he said, "the others were all killed."

Tonto nodded.

"While I was left alive. The only survivor, the lone Texas Ranger to capture those killers."

"You," said Tonto, "You Lone Ranger."

Photos were taken during the summer of 1940. Allen W. Palmer did the artwork for "The Life of Tonto" campaign. Actors for the photographs were Hank Corley, Louis Panaco, Dave Roberts, Morris Mofsie, Blue Mountain, Joe Wilson, shot in New York City, arranged by the Tucker-Mayne Advertising Agency. Photo permissions: Patricia Uline Hill (September 1942), Marjorie Barnes, (July 1940), and remainder July 1940: Tonto's father (Morris Mofsie), Indian on horse with Tom-Tom (Blue Mountain), Warrior with young Tonto (Joe Wilson), Old Lone Ranger (Hank Corley), Young Lone Ranger (Louis Panaco), young Tonto (Dave Roberts) Allen W. Palmer was the illustrator.

The photos on the next two pages are from Photographer Lejaren Hiller of Underwood & Underwood, who created these photographs for the serialized newspaper story. Merita Bread distributed almost 4,000,000 folders telling "The Life of Tonto" in loaves of bread, as well as running the story in selected newspapers across the country.

Fran Striker copyrighted the 15-chapter story on June 12, 1940. The story itself was published in 11 installments in a small number of newspapers across the southern states where Merita Bread could cross-promote their product. Merita also released one chapter weekly, made handy in convenient pocket size and included in loaves of bread, available to the public a few days in advance of the same chapter appearing in Merita's newspaper advertising. Folders with Chapter 1 of the Tonto story would be in stores the weekend of September 6. The newspaper advertisement would be on September 10. These newspapers in the South included the *Orlando Evening Star*, *The Miami Herald*, *The Macon Evening News*, *The Birmingham News*, *The Knoxville-News Sentinel*, *The Charlotte Observer*, and *The Atlanta Constitution*. Fran Striker registered his story for copyright in serial chapters rather than one single manuscript, from September to November 1940.

In September of 1940, on the occasion of the second year of Merita sponsorship, mayors of many leading Southern cities appeared on the radio program in person to broadcast proclamations declaring the popular hero's birthday as a time for the entire community to rally to the cause of safety. Among them were:

- Mayor G. Cullen Sullivan, Anderson, South Carolina
- Mayor O.A. Kirkman, High Point, North Carolina
- Mayor Graham H. Andrews, Raleigh, North Carolina
- Mayor Henry Lockwood, Charleston, South Carolina
- Mayor-pro-tem W.N. (Bub) Hovis, Charlotte, North Carolina
- Judge Robert P. Williams, Knoxville, Tennessee
- Judge Harris S. Birchfield, Roanoke, Virginia
- First Commissioner H.H. Keel, Rome, Georgia
- Commissioner of Public Works J.E.L. Wade, Wilmington, North Carolina
- Capt. E. Fleming Mason, State of South Carolina Highway Department
- Captain Daniel Reynolds, Police Department, Miami, Florida
- H.H. Treleaven, Manager of the Automobile Club of Louisiana, in New Orleans

"I congratulate Merita Bakers for their public-spirited action in enabling The Lone Ranger to enlist our young people in this splendid safety crusade."
– Mayor Ben E. Douglas, Charlotte, North Carolina

"This beloved hero and inspiring leader of American youth, The Lone Ranger, has built up in Merita's Lone Ranger Safety Club a tremendous force for safety, especially among our boys and girls. A vast number of them all over the South… many thousands in our own community and state… are pledged to his ten safety rules. Led by The Lone Ranger, they help make this a better, safer world to live in."
– Mayor William B. Hartsfield, Atlanta, Georgia

"All honor to The Lone Ranger for his example, in courage, clean living, bravery and honor, and for his safety leadership. I congratulate Merita, too, for enabling The Lone

Ranger to lead young people to safety, and for bringing us his splendid radio programs."
– Mayor George Blume, Jacksonville, Florida

The long-term relationship between American Bakeries (makers of Merita Bread), and King-Trendle, would celebrate the tenth anniversary of the program's appearance in the south, with a special broadcast over station WCON at 7:30 on September 13, 1948. *The Lone Ranger* had been heard over the station three days a week without interruption since September 1938. Years later, a column in the September 1953 issue of the company newsletter, *Merita Family Magazine* said: "In their daily service to dealers and consumers, all Merita salesmen strive to carry out the same ideals of character and enterprise The Lone Ranger stands for." At the end of each eight-week cycle, American Bakeries and *Merita Family Magazine* honored those salesmen with the highest records by placing them on The Lone Ranger Salesman's Club Honor Roll.

The other sponsor best associated with *The Lone Ranger* radio program was General Mills. In late 1940, H. Allen Campbell believed that *The Lone Ranger* was a good buy for General Mills, having had conversations with Howard "Mix" Dancer of the Blackett, Sample & Hummert advertising agency. Dancer sent young John Sample to Detroit to talk a deal. Campbell took him to Al Green's popular restaurant on the edge of Grosse Pointe for dinner. The talk went round and round as Campbell worked his guest gently toward the deal in dead center. The next day John Sample met again with Campbell and they talked with George Trendle. The sale was set. But there was a catch.

"There is one thing you cannot do," said Sample. "We won't want you to do anything to take Gingham Bread off the air."

It was Campbell's desire to simplify the whole set-up, having a single sponsor in all major markets coast-to-coast. It was explained to Campbell that General Mills made Gold Medal Flour. Gingham bought the flour, as did American Bakeries (producing and promoting Merita Bread). They were major General Mills customers. "We would like to have the whole country, south and west coast as well as the rest of it," Sample explained, "but we do not want you to do anything to take our customers off *The Lone Ranger*." Campbell agreed and American Bakeries was allowed to retain sponsorship in the southern states while General Mills would have the rest of the country. This is why *The Lone Ranger* was sponsored by American Bakeries in the southeastern states, and General Mills through the rest of the country during the nationwide hookup.

On May 4, 1941, General Mills assumed sponsorship of *The Lone Ranger* in every state except Alabama, Tennessee, Georgia, Florida, Virginia, Louisiana, and North and South Carolina. In those states, American Bakeries' Merita Bread continued to sponsor the program.

On February 23, 1941, General Mills folded its *Beat the Band* quiz with Ted Weems and his band, completing a year's run for the account. That program, which plugged Kix cereal, was a quiz which required the band's personnel to demonstrate a wide acquaintance with pop musical lore. The cereal company felt a children's program would generate more sales than a weekly musical quiz program. The initial set-up included not just 46 stations over the Mutual Broadcasting System, but Colonial stations WTHT, WELI, WSPR, WNBH, WHAI, WBRK, WSYB, WLLH, WSAR, WNLC, WCOU, WATR, and WLNH, Monday, Wednesday and Friday from May 5, 1941 to May 1, 1942, renewed annually. As time was contractually available over the months, additional stations were added to the lineup including WFBR in September 1941.

H. Allen Campbell provided the potential sponsor with a case history and study, with statistics and copies of letters from prior sponsors, regarding the sales success of the program. A business model to verify the property's reach was necessary to convince executives at General Mills to sponsor the program with a price tag into the millions.

"Trendle's impetus for extending *The Lone Ranger*'s radio reach was partly motivated by Republic Studios' refusal to release the 1937 *Lone Ranger* movie serial in cities where the radio series was unavailable. Trendle sold potential radio stations and local sponsors on the added exposure they would gain by tying the program to the impending film release," wrote Raymond Meurer, who handled the contract negotiations between The Lone Ranger, Inc. and Republic Pictures.

The general public today thinks of merchandising as a profitable secondary market – a way to extract as much profit as possible from a popular media figure or text. In both economic and cultural terms, *The Lone Ranger*, along with Hopalong Cassidy in the 1950s, became the primary text, supported by radio, motion pictures, television programs, and other adaptations. The right of publicity has been criticized by many over the years as George W. Trendle maintained an iron grasp on the way *The Lone Ranger* would be portrayed in newspapers, comics, and magazines. This served as a conceptual bridge between the basic protection of intellectual property in literary and the performance media, and the protection of the property in merchandising.

The emergence of consumer society by the end of the century saw a transitional struggle between the valuation of character versus personality, whereby the former stressed moral qualities, while the newer culture insisted on "personality," which emphasized being liked and admired. With so many children – and enterprising adults – falling in love with the property, Raymond Meurer strongly insisted to George W. Trendle that selection of merchandise was only one facet of protection.

"The first line of legal defense was the precise drafting of the licensing agreements," Meurer explained. "The second was the tough posture reflected in the language. To assert copyright and trademark infringement in court meant it was necessary to bring those very licensing agreements to the stand to verify our claims. Fran Striker was required to save all correspondence between any merchandising firm, including Republic Pictures, to affirm our ownership as it pertained to the trademarks of The Lone Ranger and Tonto."

Screen cowboys, along with their radio counterparts, were important civic discourse throughout the 1930s, '40s and '50s – Hopalong Cassidy, Gene Autry, and Roy Rogers, "whose own identities were virtually synonymous with the brands they sold and therefore embodied the formulas better than any particular text could." Historians speculate that George W. Trendle maintained an obsessive control over *The Lone Ranger* property in fear that various actors playing the character in public at county fairs and circuses and the like might usurp his own position. As this gave way in later years, imposters did, in fact, begin making the rounds across the country at rodeos and circuses.

"Limit deviations from a successful formula" was Trendle's articulation of *The Lone Ranger* and *The Green Hornet* programs, and he felt this played an important role in the success of each series. With financials gauging the success of merchandising, Trendle's gross receipts from *The Lone Ranger* in 1939 exceeded $1,000,000, according to Jim Harmon's *The Great Radio Heroes*, revised edition, 2001.

A number of reference books, however, charged George W. Trendle with only one lapse, connected to his dealings with Republic Pictures, despite a reputation for business acumen and protectiveness. In reality, Trendle, Striker, and Meurer had considerable oversight with the two serials, ensuring consistence with the radio material.

Lone Ranger Acclaimed In Tewksbury, Wilmington

THE LONE RANGER'S SCHEDULE TUESDAY

	THE TIME	NO OF GUNS	NO. OF MASKS
Littleton Center	11.30 a. m.	100	50
Chelmsford Center	12.45 p. m.	200	100
North Billerica Kohlrausch Playrounds	3.30 p. m.	250	125

Well rested after his long jaunt on Saturday, the Lone Ranger and Silver were out at the crack of dawn today. Leaning on his supply of guns and masks, which he gathered yesterday, the wild west buckaroo headed in the direction of Tewksbury, where he had an appointment with youngsters at the town hall.

So great was the reception there, that the boys would not allow the Lone Ranger to leave and made him stay for dinner. Shortly after that he broke away, but only after leaving 200 guns and masks. His trail then took him to Wilmington, where he gave away another large supply. Cutting across country, he arrived in Pinehurst on schedule and then headed back towards Lowell by the way of Billerica Center.

Tomorrow the Ranger will go to Littleton, Chelmsford Center and North Billerica. The youngsters in these towns have been shouting for this idol of adventure for weeks. So, you young buckaroos, hold everything until tomorrow.

Ancient naturalists believed that sloths lived on air.

Unknown actor playing The Lone Ranger, according to a newspaper article from Lowell, Massachusetts, October 10, 1938.

Another unknown actor masquerading as The Lone Ranger, at a local movie theater in Racine, Wisconsin, early January 1937.

Chapter Five
The Cliffhanger Serials

"For the past four years, *The Lone Ranger* has been one of the most widely listened-to programs in the country. The shrill cry of 'Heigh-Yo, Silver' is familiar to millions of listeners, young and old, all over the United States. The dashing and mysterious 'Lone Ranger' has become practically a member of thousands of households though his nightly visits by way of the radio. Now he is coming to the screen! Republic Studios are starring in the most expensive and exciting serial ever produced – *The Lone Ranger*. Just as his identity has been kept unknown on the air, so will it be on the screen. Always marked, the star of this remarkable serial will be known only as *The Lone Ranger*. His features will not be shown until the final chapter. The story of The Lone Ranger is laid during the reclamation of Texas immediately following the Civil War and is said to be excellent screen-fare for the entire family."
– *The Lone Ranger* publicity, Republic Studios, 1938

THE DATE WAS JUNE 22, 1937, seven months before The Lone Ranger, Inc. decided to transcribe the radio broadcasts for syndication across the country and an entire year before Trendle agreed to license the property for merchandise on an immeasurable scale. It was on that date, fixed on a contract between The Lone Ranger, Inc., and Republic Productions, Inc. that an agreement between both parties for a 15-chapter cliffhanger movie serial was finalized. The movie studio shelled out a licensing fee of $18,750 plus ten percent of Republic's share of the gross receipts. * George W. Trendle signed into agreement, along with M.J. Siegel, president of Republic Productions, Inc. the serial, fittingly titled *The Lone Ranger*, that would landmark a significant achievement in the history of Republic Pictures, and spawn more legend and lore in fanzines than almost any other serial in the studio's history.

* Because of the flat rate licensing fee, The Lone Ranger, Inc. received ten percent of the gross after $390,000 had been reached.

The story, with elements borrowed from a number of *Lone Ranger* radio plots, was one for the history books, an epic best described as bravery and action on the American Frontier. An outlaw leader named Captain Smith, planning to take control of Texas after the Civil War, kills Colonel Jeffries, a man empowered by the U.S. Government to levy taxes, and assumes his identity. Determined to succeed, and to avoid exposure, Smith (a.k.a. Jeffries) orders his men to murder a troop of Texas Rangers. A short time following, Tonto, an American Indian, stumbles upon the scene of the massacre and finds one of the Rangers still alive and breathing – but just barely. After nursing the Ranger back to health, Tonto agrees to aid the lone survivor in a vendetta to wipe out criminal activity and avenge his fellow brothers. As The Lone Ranger races to numerous sites to rescue the meek and apprehend the outlaws, it is here that the tradition of the cliffhanger serial becomes evident – the masked man manages to evade one trap after another. While The Lone Ranger quickly becomes a thorn in the side of Jeffries, a Jeffries spy named Snead narrows down five suspects who could potentially be the masked man. During the course of these adventures, Tonto is whipped and tortured, and The Lone Ranger is almost blown to pieces by a keg of gunpowder. Toward the end of the epic, Colonel Jeffries and his men get wise to the secret cave where Tonto and The Lone Ranger often hide from Jeffries' henchmen. Justice prevails in the end and the hero is unmasked for all to decree joyous celebration.

Evident of the radio program's popularity in California, executives at Republic were determined to cash in on an established fanbase. Negotiations went back and forth between both parties for weeks. It was standard practice among film producers and Hollywood studios to negotiate terms long before a contract was drawn up. Statistically, more than 90 percent of properties negotiated never even reached contract stage. Trendle held firm with his principal terms and relied on Raymond Meurer to handle the details.

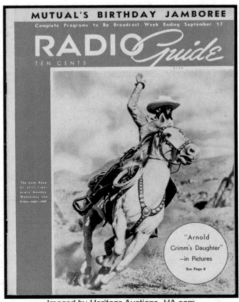

Imaged by Heritage Auctions, HA.com

**September 1938 issue of *Radio Guide*,
promoting the movie serial on the cover.**

Among the many clauses of the contract was a provision for excluding television rights, which Trendle firmly insisted be integrated. By the late 1930s, most of the movie studios were optioning television in their contracts, a prophetic strategy that would pay off in the long run. Trendle insisted that he did not want to revisit the contract and learn he already surrendered such rights or had given Republic first option. Television rights remained exclusive to the arrangement. "There will never be such a thing as television in your lifetime," said an executive at Republic.

"Then why worry about it and sign," smiled attorney Raymond Meurer, representing the radio interest. Republic signed.

The most significant stipulation in the contract emphasized Trendle's insistence on complete oversight regarding story and content. The production itself would be left to the hands of more experienced and talented individuals who worked for the movie studio. Two pages of the contract went into detail regarding The Lone Ranger and Tonto, descriptions regarding height, mannerisms, and clothing, descriptions Trendle and Meurer enforced to ensure trademark property enforcement. After all, The Lone Ranger was visual incarnate for radio listeners and the serial would maintain future trademarks that differentiated the masked rider of the plains from other screen cowboys. Included among the many bullet points: "Well groomed, does not wear chaps, wears high-heeled cowboy boots with trousers tucked into the tops. Wears a white Stetson hat. Smokes only if story plot demands, does not drink or swear." With the radio program lucrative to multiple parties, Trendle considered the thrice-a-week broadcasts more valuable than a filmed production, and therefore left no chance for anything going into the picture which would be detrimental to the radio program or the sponsor.

To maintain continuity between radio and film property, Fran Striker had a telephone call arrangement with the script department of Republic Pictures every Thursday, wherein any changes in the script were discussed. After a couple weeks, Oliver Drake at Republic proposed exchanging telegrams to save money – Striker agreed. (It should be noted that Oliver Drake was disappointed he did not get any credit for his brief but pivotal work on the serial. Since it was such a big success, he felt that being able to put it on his resumé would have helped his career.)

Dear Mr. Trendle:

Our delay in answering your letter of March 5th is due to the fact that we had to obtain from our studio in Hollywood the scripts which you requested.

We find that we have , and are sending you under separate cover, manuscripts received from you on which appear the following numbers: 368, 369, 370, 371, 372, 373, 401, 416, 454, 620, 621, 638, 638, 640, 650, 651, 647, 648, 649, 684, 683, 685, 624, 616, 614, 627, 628, 629, 630, 634, 635, 636, 637, 642, 644, 646, 645, 652, 654, 658, 659, 661, 663, 666, 670, 671, 668, 674, 675, 676, 677, 680, 681.

We are also sending you under the same separate cover the final shooting scripts entitled "Cutting Continuity" for each of the two serials and the feature version of the first serial.

Excerpt of a letter from Republic Pictures to George W. Trendle, returning specific radio scripts that were lent to the studio for consultation to create the screenplay. This letter verifies which radio scripts were consulted and therefore which various elements might have been utilized in the filmed serial from the radio series.

Striker chose 55 radio scripts to send to the studio, which he felt was more than enough material for the scriptwriters in Hollywood to fashion something feasible for the silver screen. Among the scripts submitted included the origin of Silver, the origin of White Feller, stories about the railroad, lumber camps, and a Frontier Day stagecoach race. Cactus Pete was in a number of the radio scripts, and the Lawyer Abercrombie story arc was included. Neither Cactus Pete or the crooked lawyer would be used for the chapters. The character of Black Taggart may have originated from radio script # 675, which featured Sheriff Taggart. The discussion between Snead and Jefferies in the first chapter of the serial mimics the discussion between Dunlop and Smokey in the radio broadcast of January 20, 1937.

It remains questionable whether any of the scriptwriters at Republic borrowed story elements from the radio scripts, as none of the characters or story plots were recycled for use on the big screen. Tonto signaling the Rangers with sign language, The Lone Ranger masquerading as an outlaw to infiltrate the gang of outlaws, settlers taking refuge from outlaws in the fort, and Tonto following the trail of a broken horseshoe were common elements found on any western program in general. The only aspects the writers truly borrowed for the serial was the characteristics of The Lone Ranger and Tonto, provided separately by Trendle as part of the contract with the studio. If anyone borrowed anything, it was Fran Striker who recycled two plot devices from the Republic serial. In the radio broadcast of December 8, 1937, two horse thieves robbed a federal government man who was out and about collecting taxes for the state of Texas. After murdering and disposing of the body, they use his identification papers to masquerade as an official tax collector, victimizing the citizens in the town of Cactus Bend. The other plot device would be the canyon ambush sequence for a later retelling of the origin of The Lone Ranger. Prior to the film serial, Striker never established an origin of the masked man on radio. He loved the rendition that originated from the filmed production and would later dramatize that origin on the radio program multiple times, each with slight variations.

"It was like the way comedy writers would work today," Oliver Drake later recalled to author Dave Holland. "A bunch of us would sit around, throwing ideas back and forth. We'd probably spend four or five days just discussing it… Generally, what we'd do would be to talk about a particular episode, everyone throwing in stuff, working it all out, then the head writer – in this case, it was Barry Shipman – would single out one guy and say, 'You seem to have a handle on this one. Go home and write it up. And Ollie, you take episode such-and-such. You bring that one in tomorrow.' And so on. We'd talk about an episode, smooth it out, then do an outline or treatment on it, bounce that around and work out the kinks, then go off again and do a shooting script."

The first chapter, however, proved to be the most difficult. The radio scripts provided a number of exciting adventures, but never an origin for the character. Just how do you begin an epic? Most of the serials established the origin for the hero in the first chapter. The writers had trouble justifying the adjective "lone" in the hero's nickname, and since he had an Indian companion riding alongside him throughout the serial, an origin was needed to support the title of the serial. One of the discarded treatments involved Abraham Lincoln assigning someone the task of going to Texas to clean up the west. "You must work alone, you will be alone, upon you alone rests this burden," the President remarked.

A reference was also made that the title character had once been a Texas Ranger, of the original Ranger force, and only five including the stranger remain alive. Another draft involved the leader of the Rangers, Captain Rance, found the only survivor from a massacre. The five heroes who were away on assignment swear an oath to their captain to finish their assignment since they were all that was left of the Texas Rangers… to defend Texas.

Finally, someone came up with the idea of The Lone Ranger being the sole survivor of an ambush at Grant's Pass. He would be found by an Indian. "Other all die," said Tonto. "You only Ranger Tonto find alive." Oliver Drake typed it up in outline form, dated October 18, 1937. The first chapter was reportedly shelved, with the writers coming back to it every few days, even as they hashed out the other episodes, which were written concurrently. *

This book, published by Whitman in 1938, was more of a pulp format, consisting of text with black and white illustrations by Robert Weisman.

* Striker used the ambush angle twice prior, *The Lone Ranger and the Mystery Ranch* (1938, Grosset & Dunlap) which involved The Night Legion instead of Butch Cavendish at Bryant's Gap, and Whitman's (No.710) Black and White No. 3, *Heigh-Yo Silver!* (1938). Striker also adapted the origin story from the serial for *The Lone Ranger and the Texas Renegades*, illustrated by Ted Horn (a pseudonym of Fred Harman), published in May of 1939. Striker retold the story again in a chapter in *The Lone Ranger Rides* (1941, Putnam) and it was there that Grant's Pass would become Bryant's Gap.

As the 15 screenplays were being mapped out and first drafts composed by Franklin Adreon, Ronald Davidson, Oliver Drake, Lois Eby, and George Worthing Yates, under supervision of Barry Shipman, the latter notified Striker via telegram that by contrast, two white horses in a black and white picture were not acceptable. For pictorial reasons and to avoid confusion, they wanted Tonto to ride a paint horse so that when a white horse was on the screen at any time, the audience knew it was Silver.

As indicated in the prior volume (covering the years 1933-1937), on the radio program Tonto originally rode a wagon with two jackasses, then later rode double with The Lone Ranger.

Subsequently, a white horse was provided for Tonto with the broadcast of September 30, 1935, and the Indian eventually referred to his horse by name as "White Feller." The telegram led to a phone call for clarification.

In Striker's own handwriting, the following explained how an assistant director phoned from Hollywood to tell the author of the radio scripts that they had a horse of the wrong color.

"Been reading your radio scripts," he said. "Tonto's got a white horse – like Silver. Right?"

"Right," Striker confirmed. "We call it White Feller."

"Two white horses. That's bad camera. No contrast."

"Yeah?"

"Yeah. Besides, in pictures only the hero rides a white horse. I'll make Tonto's horse a paint."

"A what?"

"A paint. Pinto – piebald – calico. Mottled, y'know. Black and white. We'll handle it at this end. Don't worry about it."

"Don't worry about it! Indeed! How could Tonto ride a white horse on the airways and a paint on the screen?" Striker asked. The solution would require a change of saddle on the radio program, Striker reasoned, and would have to be approved by his boss.

"I was at the farm at the time," recalled Fran Striker. "Mr. Trendle called and said to work out a fast series of scripts…the studio heads felt that two white horses would be confusing, whereupon Trendle instructed me to work in a paint horse for Tonto and on Trendle's suggestion, a story was written where Tonto left his white horse with friends to recuperate. Tonto borrows, buys, or otherwise gets himself a Paint. That's what we did. He got the paint and we called it Scout. I think the boss and everyone else submitted name suggestions. I don't know who suggested Scout but that was the name we used."

The transition began with the broadcast of August 5, 1938. There was a gathering of the most influential members of the tribe in the great lodge of Chief Thundercloud. They were debating the policy of going on the warpath and Thundercloud had summoned Tonto, the faithful Indian companion of The Lone Ranger, to advise him. The masked man waited outside the lodge while the meeting was in progress. The chief's intention is to take the braves on the warpath to gain more influence with the tribe. If he leads them successfully, he may remain as chief of the tribe. Thundercloud agrees to send a message to Grey Wolf, asking him to give up two of Thundercloud's braves that killed Standing Bear, to ensure peace between tribes. If there is no surrender, there will be war. The Lone Ranger, knowing Grey Wolf has a lot of pride, will not surrender a couple of Thundercloud's braves. The deadline will be two weeks from today. Red Crow, a member of Thundercloud's tribe and eager to lead the braves into war, wants to move up into the position of chief, and agrees to the two-week parlay.

Two white men, Bart Daly, bearded and powerful, and the other, his partner, Shorty Crane, a small man with shifty eyes, knew that Red Crow's ambition would never be satisfied until he became chief, and they used this knowledge to further their own ends.

The Lone Ranger, carrying the message from Chief Thundercloud to Grey Wolf, discovered that the outlaws themselves had shot Standing Bear, but that he was not dead, having been rescued by Grey Wolf. With this news, The Lone Ranger knew that war would not be necessary. The Lone

TONTO SAVES THE LONE RANGER

TONTO FIGHTS OFF THE TROOPERS

THE LONE RANGER RESCUES JOAN AT THE PIT

THE LONE RANGER FOILS AN AMBUSH

Ranger and Tonto had four days through treacherous country to reach Chief Thundercloud and deliver the good news. All that day the three men rode, and far into the night, pausing only to refresh their weary horses. At the first sight of dawn, they were in the saddle again. Standing Bear was well enough to make the travel, and at times gave the appearance of better strength than the horses. Soon they approached the White Rapids River which tumbled down from the mountains at express-train speed, its volumes swollen by the melting spring snows. The three horses plunged into the swirling waters while the current fought to drag them under. Silver, his powerful limbs working like pistons, took the lead, responding valiantly to the masked man's shouts of encouragement. Almost exhausted, the three men reached the far bank at last. There they rested until their trembling horses regained their strength.

The further they penetrated into the mountains, the more rugged and dangerous became the trail. They skirted precipices where a misstep would have plunged them to certain death. Again, they found their way blocked where landslides had piled great mounds of shale and loose boulders. Once, when Standing Bear's horse stumbled, its master's life was saved only by the quick action of White Feller, whose powerful shoulders pushed the wiry little Indian pony back to safety. Another time, a threatening rumble far above them warned of a landslide tearing a jagged furrow down the face of the mountain. As though sensing the danger, the three horses plunged forward, muzzles outstretched, hoofs striking a frantic tattoo against the uncertain footing. For a moment at long as eternity it seemed as though they must be buried under tons of hurtling rocks and earth, but with a final burst of speed, the faithful animals carried their riders to safety while behind them the trail over which they had just passed was torn from its granite foundations and ground to dust.

The third day found them face to face with their greatest hazard. A canyon split the trail in two, a canyon so deep that the sun penetrated its depths for less than an hour each day, a canyon whose sides were so steep that the masked man and his companions were forced to dismount and lead their horses down the perilous descent. At times their path fell away so abruptly they were unable to keep their balance and went slipping and sliding downward, the men grasping at the stunted vegetation to check their speed, the horses digging into the crumbling earth with straining hoofs. They forced their way upward slowly, foot by foot, their bodies scarred and bruised, their breath coming in tortured gasps.

At the top, after hours of climbing when every step seemed as though it were the last they could possibly achieve, they threw themselves, panting, on the cool grass. Their horses stood beside them with bent heads, completely exhausted.

In Chief Thundercloud's village, preparations for war went on while the deadline drew closer. On the afternoon of the last day, certain that the masked man could not arrive in time, the tribal drums began beating out their primitive challenge, while the warriors circled and stamped the earth in the frenzy of their war dance. But in the midst of this, Red Crow caught a glimpse of the approaching riders from a distance. The masked man did not know that still another obstacle, the most dangerous of all, faced his party. But as they raced toward the narrow pass through which their trail led, a tense band of Indian braves, members of Red Crow's following, waited for them with levelled weapons. Rifle fire burst through the plains and one of the bullets hit a mark – White Feller was wounded.

In the village, Thundercloud had not noticed the secret departure of those braves friendly to Red Crow. The old chief sat on his splendid paint horse, watching the war dance, while Bart and Shorty stood close to Red Crow. Tonto quickly approached from behind and roped Bart and Shorty. Red Crow was forced to admit defeat. But imagine his surprise when The Lone Ranger brought Standing Bear to the village, alive and well.

"Bart and Shorty stole some gold from Grey Wolf," The Lone Ranger explained to Chief Thundercloud. "They thought Standing Bear was after them and tried to kill him. They came here, and when they discovered Red Crow wanted to be chief in your place, they said Grey Wolf had shot Standing Bear. They believed if there was war, the guilt would never be discovered."

THUNDERCLOUD: What matter White Feller?

RANGER: He was wounded, Thundercloud.

THUNDERCLOUD: You wait… (SHOUT) Tonapah melpay laht!

VOICE: (BACK) Leetch!

SOUND: One horse approach

RANGER: Isn't that your horse, Thundercloud?

THUNDERCLOUD: Ugh. Him fine horse!

RANGER: But what are you doing?

THUNDERCLOUD: You findum out… Tonto!

TONTO: (APPROACH) What you wantum, Thundercloud?

THUNDERCLOUD: You heap good friend, Thundercloud. You helpum Thundercloud plenty!

TONTO: Me glad do!

THUNDERCLOUD: Me keepum White Feller here. Take-um good care White Feller. Make-um him strong like before!

RANGER: You'll take care of White Feller for us until he's well again?

THUNDERCLOUD: Ugh! That right!

RANGER: But…

THUNDERCLOUD: You listen… Tonto take-um horse Thundercloud. Him bets horse in tribe. Tonto take-um him for all time!

TONTO: Tonto thankum you!

BART: Blast it! Thundercloud's givin' Tonto the hoss I wanted fer myself!

RANGER: Bart, where you're going, you won't need a horse!

TONTO: Him make-um friends with Tonto!

RANGER: He likes you, Kemo Sabay! Look at him! Except for Silver, I've never seen a better horse anywhere!

The Lone Ranger and Tonto accept Chief Thundercloud's offer of hospitality and stay overnight, so Silver could rest up from the long trip. Then, in the morning, Tonto and the masked man started for town with their prisoners, Bart and Shorty. They had stolen from Grey Wolf, shot Standing Bear, and tried to start a war between the two tribes. But when the law got through with them, they would do no more harm for a long time to come. *

There has been some debate among fans of the radio program that the name of the horse was not "White Feller," but rather Tonto's primitive method of description of his horse, "a white feller." The name of the horse can be found in some of the early print renditions before the name was changed on the radio program such as the novel, "Heritage of the Plains," featured in the September 1937 issue of *The Lone Ranger Magazine*.

When Tonto first received White Feller on the radio program in 1935, the horse was without a name. "I was told not to name this white horse because the agency had ideas of a name contest, not to be confused with a later contest for the naming of Dan's horse," Fran Striker later recalled. "Well, while marking time and waiting for the agency to get going I had Tonto refer to his horse only as a white feller. It was 'Whoa, white feller,' and 'Gittum up white feller.' The agency dawdled too long. Before they knew it all the kids had accepted the name White Feller for Tonto's horse."

For the 1938 transition, the new paint horse underwent a similar situation. Fran Striker again suggested a name-the-horse contest but once again, like the 1935 proposal, no contest was launched and Striker eventually decided to give the horse a name.

Beginning with the broadcast of September 2, 1938, Tonto was inspired to christen his horse with the name of "Scout." (Fans of the radio program seeking closure to this continuity can feel assured that "White Feller" was still somewhere among the Indians waiting to be called for by Tonto.) From the September 2 broadcast:

VOICE 2: Stranger, that injun's hoss has sure saved us! If it hadn't a been fer him…

TONTO: Paint hoss plenty good!

---

* Because Fran Striker wrote his scripts days in advance, Tonto's horse in the August 10 broadcast was still named White Feller, but because of this transition, the name was scratched out to be described as a "paint horse."

VOICE 3: Injun, he's sure nuff won HIS spurs. By thunder, that hoss is a sure enough good scout!

TONTO: Good Scout! THAT GOOD! TONTO LIKE UM SCOUT!

RANGER: HI YO SILVER!

TONTO: GITTUM UP...SCOUT...

RANGER: AWAY!

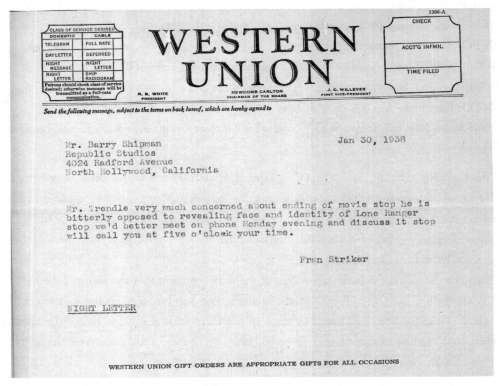

Having read all 15 chapter plays, Fran Striker discovered that The Lone Ranger was unmasked in the final chapter. Striker had no objection to a few of the men getting killed through the serial, but the mystery of the masked man had to remain a mystery. Striker even sent a telegram to Barry Shipman, requesting a phone call to discuss his concern. Trendle backed Striker. Barry Shipman flew into Detroit a few days before Thanksgiving to have a conference with George W. Trendle and Fran Striker, regarding the drafts and revisions applied to the screenplays. *

Multiple telegrams and letters had been exchanged regarding The Lone Ranger's dialogue to his mannerisms. Shipman insisted that the audience would be clamoring to know which of the surviving Rangers was The Lone Ranger. "You cannot provide a mystery without a solution," Shipman explained. Ultimately, Shipman assured Trendle and Striker that the unmasking aspect would be revised by his crew so that a reasonable resolution would be provided.

This did not stop *Variety* magazine from giving away the ending to the serial in the November 26 issue, no doubt due to a press release from a representative at Republic Pictures: "There are five

---

* Republic would later issue a press release promoting the cliffhanger serial, claiming (and exaggerating) they "sent four writers to Detroit, Michigan, to confer with Fran Striker, originator of the popular air program, *The Lone Ranger*, before attempting to write a script for the motion picture serial, *The Lone Ranger*."

masked mystery men in Republic's 15 episode, *The Lone Ranger*, one of which will emerge at the end of the chapter play as The Lone Ranger himself. Identity will not be revealed until the final few feet of the last episode. The five masked men are played by Lee Powell, Lane Chandler, Herman Brix, Hal Taliaffero and George Letz. One of the hooded gentries will be revealed as having played the title role for 15 installments without getting a nod from the audiences."

On the evening of December 22, Striker expressed displeasure to Shipman over the phone regarding the ending, requesting a different outcome, proposing a Mexican stand-off – the mask could be removed but only the back of The Lone Ranger's head be facing the camera until the mask was put back on. But his suggestion was too late. The studio was on the fourth week of production.

Two days before the serial went into production in Lone Pine, industry trades reported record expenses to produce the serial. Shooting at the Lone Pine location was set to begin November 28 but failed to get underway owing to illness of several members of the cast. Most seriously ill were director John English and actor Lee Powell. Initially the first seven days were devoted to the Lone Pine location and dealt mostly with sweeping horse action, chases, and run-throughs. Following Lone Pine, the company would return to Hollywood where the rest of the serial was shot at the studio and nearby locations including the studio backlot, Stage #8, Stage #5, and the tin shed.

Sol Siegel, producer, investigated the source of the epidemic which hit the company and figured that polluted water may have been the cause, since most of the unit suffered from a type of dysentery. The cast and crew would later jokingly refer to the illness as "the Lone Pine pip." Second unit, working only a few miles away, was not hit by the epidemic so that company, with Bill Witney in charge, commenced with the scheduled scenes. The first scene shot on location at Lone Pine was the night storm scene with The Lone Ranger on Silver, riding in past the camera, shouting "Hi-Yo, Silver," as a lightning flash comes on and he rides off into the background, followed by the scenes with The Lone Ranger leaping on three troopers.

Previously, Republic Pictures had commissioned filming on location for such cliffhangers as *The Painted Stallion* and *Zorro Rides Again*, but those were shot at Mission San Luis Rey, Kernville, Beal's Cut, Bronson Canyon and the Iverson Ranch. (The Iverson Ranch would be used many years later for *The Lone Ranger* television program). Until *The Lone Ranger*, Republic never commissioned John English and Bill Witney to film at the vast expanse of Lone Pine. Amongst that California community was the Alabama Hills, high desert country with snow-capped Sierra Nevada Mountains. Located three hours north of Los Angeles, legendary screen cowboys filmed many westerns there on location including Tom Mix, Roy Rogers, and Hopalong Cassidy. No amount of projection and backdrops could provide such majestic views.

Supposedly 14 stuntmen were on location and both directors, known for filming kinetic fights and chase scenes, succeeded by filming fight scenes continuously from start to finish. This procedure, however, may not have been artistic by choice, but rather to catch up to the schedule as a result of the unexpected delay caused by the temporary illness. The flaw, however, showed on camera as the stuntmen showed obvious exhaustion by the end of those sequences. Breaking down the fights to shorter segments would begin with 1939's *Daredevils of the Red Circle*, filmed immediately after the conclusion of the second Lone Ranger serial. By changing methodology, the stuntmen and actors were able to maintain a high energy level throughout the fight sequence. In the studio, props from

Zorro Rides Again were recycled for use on *The Lone Ranger* in an effort to keep the budget down. The cast and crew worked almost every day, completing production on December 31, but took a two-day break on December 25 and 26.

THURSDAY, NOV. 3, 1938.

"Lone Ranger" Brings Serials Back To Movies

THE Lone Ranger has torn off his mask.

He has left his faithful horse Silver and his mysterious mask at the top of a page in the November issue of Good Housekeeping Magazine and walked right down into print so that his thousands of devoted fans can see what he looks like.

He is Lee Powell and he was chosen as the "Lone Ranger" for the movies after studio scouts had surveyed the radio program's audience and blueprinted the exact appearance and character of the famous and romantic protector of the law: "The Lone Ranger must be 5 feet, 11 inches tall, weigh approximately 170 pounds, have no mustache or beard, never wear chaps, always wear a white hat, and constantly carry two guns."

"He smokes only if the story absolutely demands it," the blueprint specified, "and he does not drink or swear. He fires his pistol only in self-defense, and is allowed no romantic entanglements. Sad but true, he may not even kiss the girl in his adventures because youngsters would think the Ranger a sissy if he became serious about a girl."

And the Lone Ranger's faithful steed Silver wasn't so easy to find, either. Just as they tested and worried to find the right hero, so were they careful about the hero's horse. Thirty-five of the most beautiful white stallions in Holly-

The Lone Ranger

wood were brought to the studio. They were all given a screen test, put through their paces, and found wanting in appeal. Then somebody heard of an unusual white horse —but it was in El Paso, Texas. They flew the horse by airplane from El Paso to Hollywood. Silver arrived safely and he got the job.

"I have often wondered why the Lone Ranger made such a great hit," says Lee Powell. "The mysterious hero with his mask was a major reason. The cry 'Hi-Yo, Silver' was another. But whatever the reason for the Lone Ranger's popularity, the fact remains that today you'll hear small fry hail other small fry with a lusty 'Hi-Yo, Silver!' and in New York's swanky East Side theatres the serial was as popular as in Clinton Corners."

Right now Powell is working on the first full-length Lone Ranger picture. "What happens after that I don't know," he writes in the November Good Housekeeping. "How long the Ranger's popularity is going to last I can't guess. Soon enough another hero will capture the affection of the movie fans. Soon enough 'Hi-Yo, Silver!' may be as out-dated as '23 skidoo.' But while it lasts, it's fun."

"The Lone Ranger"

Rialto's New Serial Opens Saturday 10 a.m.

The Rialto Theatre starts tomorrow with the first episode of "THE LONE RANGER." It is adapted from the Radio Serial of the same name which has been tremendously successful over the air waves in the United States. The screen transcription brings out more vividly and concretely the thrilling adventures of the leading any mysterious actor. Against outdoor scenes splendidly photographed and with action from beginning to end, this is a Serial that will please old and young alike.

The first episode is in three reels and will be shown Saturday morning and afternoon, as well as Monday and Tuesday Matinees only. Don't miss any of the episodes.

Doors open 9:30 a.m. Show starts 10 a.m. every Saturday morning.

On December 23, 1937, Striker wrote to Shipman, stating that he was mailing a transcription of "last night's *Lone Ranger* program," together with a script, "in case you want to audition the actors trying out for the voice role by having them read the same lines as are transcribed. Another idea came to mind, if it will be of any help to you. I can have our Lone Ranger cut a record, reading the lines as in the scenario, and send this." Again, Striker's proposal came too late. Production was to be completed in a week and post-production, which involved looping voices into the soundtrack, was time-sensitive.

Regardless of what reference books and Internet websites claim, Earle Graser did not record his voice for use in the cliffhanger. A January 18, 1938 letter from Barry Shipman to Fran Striker states, "You and Mr. Trendle will be glad to hear *The Lone Ranger* came in with flying colors – set a pace in organization and production that will hard press this company or any other to live up to. Episode One was shown to the staff before it was shipped, and the reactions to it were extremely favorable. Of course, the real answer will come from the box office, but I have few misgivings in that direction. I believe everything you and Mr. Trendle had in mind concerning treatment of the Ranger has been taken care of. We have dubbed a voice over his dialogue that startlingly resembles the voice of the radio character, and in all of his action The Lone Ranger stands out in heroic proportions." The actor whose voice was used was Billy Bletcher, a little guy with a big voice, who ironically, started his film career during the silent era.

December 23, 1937

Mr. Barry Shipman
Republic Studios
North Hollywood, California

Dear Barry:

I am sending you today a transcription of last night's Lone Ranger program together with a script, in case you want to audition the actors trying our for the voice role by having them read the same lines as are transcribed.

Another idea came to my mind, if it will be of any help to you. I can have our Lome Ranger cut a record, reading the lines as in the scenario, and send this. If you think it will be necessary, let me know.

I mentioned the hand-book to Mr. Trendle again, and he said to wait until after the first of the year when I had my desk cleared of other things, and then get going on it.

With best wishes for a happy New Year, I remain

Very truly yours,

Fran Striker

FS:bh

Pausing for a moment to provide this side note: Billy Bletcher not only voiced The Lone Ranger in the serial, but for a while was a supporting cast member on the radio program. Circa 1950, he was in Detroit and found himself hired to play roles on *The Green Hornet*, *Challenge of the Yukon*, and *The Lone Ranger*. He was even Brace Beemer's understudy for a short time. (Supposedly Trendle brought him out from Hollywood.) Contrary to what has been set to print elsewhere, Bletcher never played the title role on radio. Fred Foy became Beemer's understudy following Bletcher's supposed eight-to-nine-month employment.

Proving valuable assistance to The Lone Ranger in the cliffhanger was Father McKim (played by actor William Farnum), and a little boy named "Sammy" (played by child actor Sammy McKim, the

last name a coincidence to the fictional Father McKim). Fans of the radio program could theorize that the two characters were the prototype to the recurring characters known as The Padre and young Dan Reid, both of whom would make their first appearance on the radio program in 1942.

Publicity went all-out for the serial including news of a supposed "casting call" for horses, reported in newspapers across the country: "Thirty-five of the most beautiful white stallions in Hollywood were brought to the studio. They were all put through their paces and judged on ability to obey commands and beauty. None of them would do. Robert Beche, in charge of this unusual job, heard of a white stallion that would be perfect for the role of Silver. But the horse was in El Paso, Texas. Beche was shown pictures of the animal and was so impressed he immediately made arrangements with American Airlines for the horse to be flown from El Paso to Hollywood in a special transport airplane. Silver arrived safely and was exactly the type of animal Beche demanded. He got the part."

Advance publicity reported that *The Lone Ranger* was the first time that the movies had made use of a fictional character created for and popularized by radio, but this was incorrect. Numerous movies had been produced in the early thirties with the intent of capitalizing on popular coast-to-coast radio programs. Amongst the earliest was Amos n' Andy who were the stars of their own picture, *Check and Double Check*, in 1930, and some of the *Seth Parker* radio cast reprised their roles for *Way Back Home* in 1931.

A chewing gun tie-in, which began with the radio broadcast of February 4, 1938, opened as a bally stunt simultaneously with the release of *The Lone Ranger* film serial, which opened at George W. Trendle's Palms-State first-run house starting February 11, as well as the Criterion in New York City the same day. *The Lone Ranger* gum was given away to patrons at those two theaters, with the King-Trendle Broadcasting Corp. to get royalties on all gum sold locally in stores near those theaters, and The Lone Ranger, Inc. received no cash on the line for the exploitation use of its 'Lone Ranger' tag but was in on royalties on all the gum sales after a certain figure was reached. It was reported that the gum firm put aside $50,000 strictly for the exploitation of its new product, which was expected to hit the street sometime in March. There was also a possible tie-up with a cookie company, though the details are vague, and it appears that deal never went through.

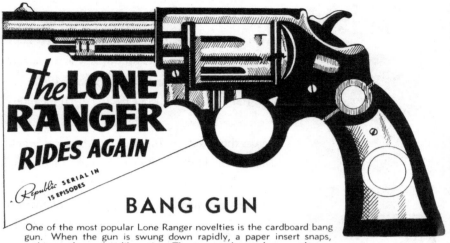

BANG GUN

One of the most popular Lone Ranger novelties is the cardboard bang gun. When the gun is swung down rapidly, a paper insert snaps, making a sharp, shot-like noise. The gun can be used over and over, and is a tricky and attractive "teaser" in getting children to attend the serial's opening episode. Space on one side of the gun carries theatre imprint and playdate, while the back is left blank for local tie-up ad. Prices, including theatre imprint and playdate: **$6.00 per 250; $10.00 per 500; $18.00 per thousand; $17.00 per thousand over 3000 and $16.00 per thousand over 5000. Order from Economy Novelty & Printing Co., 225 W. 39th Street, New York City.**

In the form of a rewards program, these type of cards were distributed to theatre patrons who could have their card hole punched for every week they came to see the next thrilling chapter. Not all movie theaters offered rewards programs like these, and the cards and the rewards varied depending on the theaters.

Trendle and company were privy to an advance screening of the first chapter on the morning of January 26, 1938. The next day, Striker wrote to Al Adams, Director of Advertising and Publicity at Republic: "We've just seen the first episode of *The Lone Ranger*, and I thoroughly agree with you that it is a 'wow.' If the remaining episodes are on a par with the first, public demand should keep The Lone Ranger and Tonto on the screen for quite some time… I'll bet you Tonto steals the show."

The Lone Ranger serial played across the country in good company (depending on the theater) alongside Tex Ritter westerns, a Three Mesquiteers entry, or an Andy Hardy movie. In some parts of the country the serial opened for *Snow White and the Seven Dwarfs* and *The Adventures of Robin Hood* with Errol Flynn. *The Lone Ranger*, like all serials, was merely a device meant to attract the audience back on a weekly basis. The serial aptly exploited the primal need for a satisfying closure of an unresolved chapter ending. Romantically, fans of the radio program falsely assume the serial as the sole reason for people going to the movie theaters weekly, but serial chapters were often bookmarked with cartoons, newsreels and movie trailers – the motion picture, heavily promoted in newspapers, was the main attraction. *The Lone Ranger* cliffhanger did receive equal amount of sideline promotion in the newspapers, as did most serials, alongside promotion of the major motion pictures.

In California, the demand for *The Lone Ranger* was so strong that Republic faced a shortage of prints. Reels of the cliffhanger serial were motorcycled between the Golden State Theatre at Riverside and the Sunkist Theatre at Pomona in February and March of 1938, and similar treatment between the Egyptian and Fairmont in San Diego.

In June of 1938, as *The Lone Ranger* radio program aired over WKBW in Buffalo, New York, a series of paid advertisements in the city newspapers promoted the sustaining program. You read that correctly. The radio program had no sponsor while *The Lone Ranger* was running thrice weekly and it was not the radio station paying for the advertisements, but the local movie theater who wanted to grow public interest pending release of the cliffhanger serial soon to be included among the summer's theatrical offerings.

In North Carolina, some members of Lone Ranger fan clubs theorized Buck Jones, Tim McCoy, or Ray Corrigan was the masked man himself… courtesy of publicity from Republic Pictures. In October 1938, columnist Mary Little of the *Des Moines Tribune*, remarked, "The Lone Ranger has torn off his mask. For months the Robin Hood of the air, along with his faithful horse Silver, has been traveling the air-lanes 'annoy.' But the hero of the 6:30 p.m. KSO show has been unmasked. He is Lee Powell."

It was not until late May 1938 that George W. Trendle viewed the last chapter of the cliffhanger serial. Trendle may have been privy to an advance screening of the first chapter, but he went to the theater on a weekly basis to watch the weekly installments like the rest of the citizens in and around Detroit. Up until the last moments of the final chapter, he was extremely satisfied with the production.

The first serial was produced by Republic in close cooperation with The Lone Ranger, Inc., production men calling Trendle's organization almost nightly as the film was being shot. However, contrary to Trendle's idea, The Lone Ranger character in the film was not unmasked to the characters in the film, with his back facing the camera, but also to the audience. Joan Blanchard even prompted the unmasking in the serial, then proclaimed the character of "Allen King" by name. Trendle walked out of the theater and back to his office, fuming and composing in his head the letter that he was to send to the movie studio.

Trendle strenuously objected both by letter and in person to the officials of Republic, believing that it would not only injure that picture and future pictures, but that it might also injure his proprietary interest in the theory and story of *The Lone Ranger* being a masked character at all times. His letter of complaint was lodged officially but the damage, in Trendle's view, had already been done.

The relationship between Republic Pictures and George W. Trendle may have been strained through an exchange of letters, but the two certainly maintained business relations. On July 11, 1938, Republic informed The Lone Ranger, Inc., in writing that per agreement dated June 22, 1937, the studio had the right to produce one serial and one feature ("of approximately 6,000 feet"). Complications, however, required the studio to ask for a 30-day extension from September 1, 1938 to October 1, 1938, as the producers wanted an additional month to make more money on the serial in second run theaters. Trendle agreed. Behind the scenes, filming a movie was complicated, and the studio, in reality, wanted time to edit the first serial into a movie before the expiration date.

In July, Republic Pictures considered filming the next batch of *Three Mesquiteers* westerns with Ray Corrigan, Big Boy Williams and Max Terhune, and the July 19 issue of *Variety* reported: "John Wayne is set for the lead in *The Lone Ranger Returns*, at Republic, a feature which Armand Schaefer will produce within three weeks. Script is in hands of Gerald Geraghty, formerly titled *Return of the Ranger*." The contract between The Lone Ranger, Inc. and Republic Pictures did not stipulate that the feature had to be a cut-down of the serial, and the film studio was trying to create an original screenplay for a motion picture. John Wayne was up for the lead.

THE COMPANY WILL APPRECIATE SUGGESTIONS FROM ITS PATRONS CONCERNING ITS SERVICE

1201-S

WESTERN UNION (25)

CLASS OF SERVICE		SYMBOLS
This is a full-rate Telegram or Cablegram unless its deferred character is indicated by a suitable symbol above or preceding the address.	R. B. WHITE PRESIDENT NEWCOMB CARLTON CHAIRMAN OF THE BOARD J. C. WILLEVER FIRST VICE-PRESIDENT	DL = Day Letter NM = Night Message NL = Night Letter LC = Deferred Cable NLT = Cable Night Letter Ship Radiogram

The filing time shown in the date line on telegrams and day letters is STANDARD TIME at point of origin. Time of receipt is STANDARD TIME at point of destination.

Received at Corner Congress and Shelby Sts., Detroit, Mich. ALWAYS OPEN   1938 FEB 14 PM 1 26

CDU115 26 DL=WUX NRK NEWYORK NY 14 1223P

H ALLEN CAMPBELL, KING TRENDLE BROADCASTING CORP=

 MADISON THEATRE BLDG DET=

LONE RANGER BROKE ALL HOUSE RECORDS CRITERION FRIDAY SATURDAY.
STOP. FIRST TIME SINCE THEATRE OPENED LINES AROUND BLOCK.
STOP. I SHOULD REALLY SEND THIS TELEGRAM COLLECT=

 RAY.

Repeated Attendance Second week on hold-over of First Episode

THERE IS NO DEPENDABLE SUBSTITUTE FOR WESTERN UNION TIME

John Wayne joined Republic Pictures officially on June 1, 1938, after completing his one-year contract with Trem Carr at Universal Studios, where he made 11 movies. Wayne signed a one-year pact for the lead in the studio's *The Three Mesquiteers* series. He was no stranger at the studio, having made *Westward Ho* for Republic in 1935. Wayne signed the contract in April, but in May the studio discovered their player acquisitions included one too many actors for the *Mesquiteers*. In acquiring Guinn (Big Boy) Williams as an intended member of the trio, with intentions of replacing Ray Corrigan, the studio discovered that Corrigan was draw appeal for the westerns and it was necessary to keep him in the series. In June, Robert Livingston was filming his last *Mesquiteers* entry, stepping out of the saddle to play featured parts at Republic, with Max Terhune amongst the cast in limbo regarding leaving the studio for what he felt was more promising roles.

Wayne's contract, dated May 7, 1938, stipulated that he would not be forced to appear in serials, which — The Lone Ranger's success notwithstanding — were considered to be inferior to features and potentially harmful to a rising star's appeal. The actor's flat refusal to play the Ranger in either feature or serial effectively killed any chance of *The Lone Ranger Returns* being produced as written by Gerald Geraghty. With Wayne out of the running, Robert Beche told the studio brass that he didn't have a prayer of finishing the feature by September 1, as stipulated by the terms of the contract. There was just not enough time to go through an extensive casting process for the leading man. That was why Republic applied to Trendle for the 30-day extension, so they could hastily edit a feature from the first serial as their only alternative.

Meanwhile, Robert Beche, producer, approached Trendle about getting a head start in producing the second serial as drafts and rewrites were common and, as exemplified with the first cliffhanger serial, took a few months. A new contract for a second serial was required and discussion between Trendle and Sol Shor, who acted as an agent and liaison man for Herbert Yates, the president of Republic, was a tad heated in the beginning.

Trendle agreed to permit Republic to film one additional serial (no additional movie) which, unlike the first, could not be released as a feature, on the express condition that the "refusal clause" be eliminated. The contract for the first serial, dated June 22, 1937, provided for the making of one serial of 15 episodes, and the making of one movie, and for the release and distribution of both serial and the feature, but featured a provision that worked against Trendle. In Article 2, clause (d) of the contract, there appeared a covenant on the part of The Lone Ranger, Inc. to Republic to give Republic first refusal on new licenses for production, distribution, and exhibition of motion pictures based on *The Lone Ranger*, prior to February 3, 1939. This meant until February 3, Republic had the option of first refusal for any sequels.

During the summer of 1938, Trendle was negotiating with Universal in respect to the making of serials not only for *The Green Hornet*, but also for the production of one serial and one feature of *The Lone Ranger*. These negotiations had virtually reached a state of verbal understanding but it was expressly understood by the parties that this understanding was to be embodied in a written contract before it would be binding.

Before such contract was made for *The Lone Ranger* with Universal, Republic, in some manner or other, obtained information about these negotiations and wrote Universal advising them that under Republic's contract for *The Lone Ranger*, Republic had the right of first refusal, and that Universal was not at liberty to enter into a contract with The Lone Ranger, Inc. Trendle stated his position, denying the claims of Republic on the right of first refusal. Raymond Meurer reviewed the contract and discovered Republic was correct… but only until February 3. Hence why Republic was fleshing out a story for the second cliffhanger serial and necessary casting considerations.

Trendle then advised Republic by letter that in view of the position taken by Republic, even though he, Trendle, was not bound to stop negotiations, he had the right to make a license for the filming of *The Lone Ranger* after February 3, 1939. Summed up simply, Trendle felt he had the right to negotiate, just not sign any contract dated prior to February 3, 1939. Universal, however, insisted to Trendle that they discuss and negotiate for *The Green Hornet* and revisit *The Lone Ranger* after August 31, 1939. For official purposes, to avoid any potential lawsuits, Universal acknowledged by letter that there was no binding undertaking between Universal and The Lone Ranger, Inc. If anything, their discussions were merely verbal proposals.

Trendle, while ultimately signing contracts for *The Green Hornet*, was merely using the terms offered by Universal for *The Lone Ranger* to negotiate financials against Republic. While Franklin Adreon, Ronald Davidson, and Sol Shor were rushing to complete a final draft of the second serial, now titled *Return of the Lone Ranger*, and Robert Beche, Republic associate producer, rushing preparations in order to make the release date, the studio was forced to pay $25,000 for the yarn as compared to $18,750 for its predecessor, *The Lone Ranger*, because of interim build-up via radio and newspaper strips. The contract was dated September 2, 1938.

Sol Shor, a scriptwriter in the serial department, got the head writing job for the second serial because he was Sol Siegel's brother-in-law. Shor was temporarily assigned to deal with Trendle because head writer Barry Shipman, who dealt with WXYZ during the first serial, was working on *Hawk of the Wilderness*, which was still in production and required partial rewrites while cast and crew were on location in Big Bear.

During the production of the second serial, Republic did not consult with Fran Striker or anyone with Trendle's organization regarding the script. Although there was no express prohibition in the amendatory contract about the unmasking of The Lone Ranger character, Sol Shor verbally assured Trendle that this would not be done a second time. Contrary to this understanding, The Lone Ranger was forced to remove the mask and operate under the name of "Bill Andrews" at times in order to successfully protect the homesteaders.

Meanwhile, in another part of the studio, the first cliffhanger serial was still being cut down into a feature-length motion picture. In July, Armand Schaefer was assigned to the project, as well as the proposed cliffhanger sequel. By August, he had a working script for additional prolog shots for the movie version. Schaefer approached producer Harry Sherman with the request to borrow George "Gabby" Hayes, then a regular in the Hopalong Cassidy movies, to play the brief role of Smokey who, at the Lazy U Dude Ranch, recounts the adventure to a little boy. Sherman declined. On October 26, 1938, Republic signed Raymond Hatton and Dickie Jones for the prolog shots. The movie version, titled *Hi-Yo-Silver*, would be released in theaters beginning in April of 1940.

As the first serial wound up its domestic run, it was then getting heavy play in South America, and preparing to open in England. With Armand Schaefer handling the motion picture rendition, Robert Beche was assigned to produce and guide *The Lone Ranger Returns* into production by the first week of December. *

---

* The sequel bounced back and forth between proposed titles but would ultimately be titled *The Lone Ranger Rides Again*.

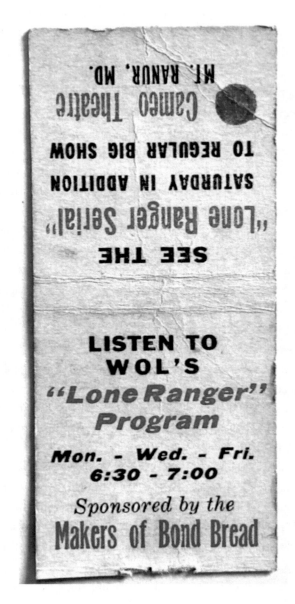

Matchbook promoting both the radio program, and the cliffhanger serial being shown at the Cameo Theater in Mount Rainier, Maryland.

On November 17, 1938, Robert Livingston was assigned by the studio to play the lead in the cliffhanger, replacing Lee Powell, who left for the East Coast for personal appearances in a circus in which he was partially invested. Powell had finished co-starring in *Trigger Pals* for Grand National, what was planned to be the first in a series of Westerns to compete against Republic's *Three Mesquiteers* series. Had *Trigger Pals* proven successful enough to warrant sequels, Powell would have departed the circus and returned to the silver screen, but the movie profited just enough to cover the cost of production and negatives.

Beginning Friday, December 9, 1938, Bill Witney and John English returned to co-direct *The Lone Ranger Returns*, with 70 players and technicians out to Mesa, Arizona for exterior shots. Republic briefly considered using stock footage from the first serial to avoid the cost of filming on location, but during the scriptwriting stage it was determined that new location shoots would be required – especially since the sequel had more exterior scenes than the first serial. The troupe returned to the studio for interior scenes on January 12, 1939, including filming on the Iverson Ranch.

The first serial cost Republic a total of $168,117 to produce including negative cost; the budget for the second serial came to $214,000 – a significant overage that made it Republic's most expensive serial to date. Principal photography of the second serial did not wrap until January 20, and editing was not completed until the first week in February. Republic screened the first three chapters in its New York City corporate headquarters on February 9. The serial premiered that month in numerous theaters across the country.

Over in Detroit, George W. Trendle sued actor Lee Powell, who was then performing in the traveling circus as "The Lone Ranger" and billing himself as the movie rendition to lure children to the circus. Republic found themselves in an awkward position. An attorney for Republic informed Trendle that the studio could not control the actions of an actor who might want to make personal appearances as The Lone Ranger, following completion and release of the chapter play. This went double for actors like Lee Powell who promoted himself as "the movie rendition." In discussing the matter with attorneys, Herbert Yates believed the best course of action would be to hire solely for the purpose of the feature, and not a so-called contract player, with a stipulation regarding personal appearances outside of the studio. Instead, Livingston himself came up with the solution by signing a one-page agreement not to play the role of The Lone Ranger for the purpose of public exhibition, even for studio publicity, without the express permission of The Lone Ranger, Inc.

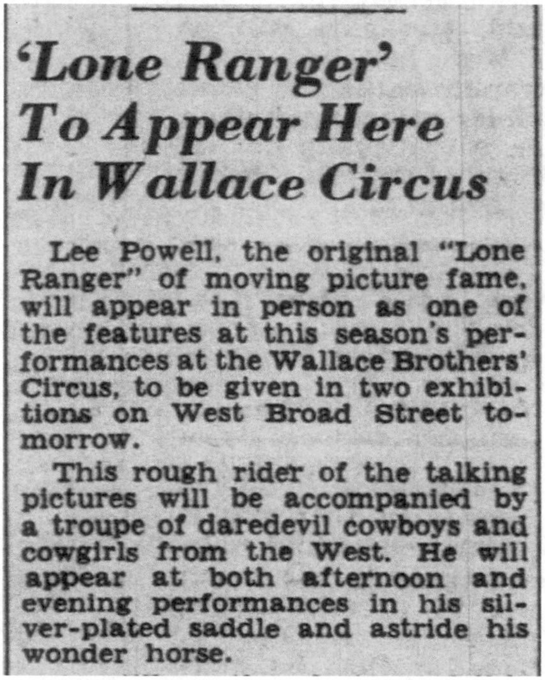

'Lone Ranger' To Appear Here In Wallace Circus

Lee Powell, the original "Lone Ranger" of moving picture fame, will appear in person as one of the features at this season's performances at the Wallace Brothers' Circus, to be given in two exhibitions on West Broad Street tomorrow.

This rough rider of the talking pictures will be accompanied by a troupe of daredevil cowboys and cowgirls from the West. He will appear at both afternoon and evening performances in his silver-plated saddle and astride his wonder horse.

Newspaper article from Richmond, Virginia, August 28, 1940.

Trendle was not fully satisfied so on the evening of January 5, 1939, Robert Livingston took time out of filming to place a long-distance call to Trendle to personally assure the radio producer that he had no intentions of playing the fictional hero in public. This apparently satisfied Trendle. Trendle's concern was short-sighted when, a month later, it was discovered that The Rialto in West Palm Beach, Florida, was screening the first serial and broke taboo by arranging for The Lone Ranger, a costumed employee, to appear in person to hand out Valentines cards on Saturday, February 11.

Trendle hesitated to give approval when movie theaters wanted to apply a gimmick to lure children to the movie theaters. Given the choice of a costumed impersonator or gimmicks, Trendle relented for the latter. Perry Spencer, director of publicity for Republic Pictures in the south, inaugurated a new service whereby exhibitors playing *The Lone Ranger Rides Again* were furnished with several thousand copies of *Lone Ranger* comic books. Some theaters even furnished Lone Ranger ice cream cones during kid matinees. Eph Charninsky, who owned the Harlandale movie theater chain in San Antonio, Texas, worked an arrangement with the local baker that sponsored the radio program to defray the cost of display set pieces in his theater, along with four sets of Lone Ranger outfits for each of his theaters, for the 15-week period covering the serial's run.

Variety reviewed the second serial in their February 15, 1939, issue: "Pic oversteps the mark and becomes almost unintelligible in the interests of action; but this should not thwart its popularity with the kids. Fearing to slow down long enough to explain what's happening, or to flash back, writers have woven all of their explanatory material into the dialog. It doesn't work, at least during the early episodes. The mix-up is further complicated by the presence of not only one 'Lone Ranger,' but two, one being an imposter who later gets his due."

With the "refusal clause" removed from the second contract, Trendle revisited negotiations with Universal for them to produce what would have been a third cliffhanger serial. This time Republic did not interfere with negotiations between Trendle and executives at Universal, but Republic was making plans for a third western serial that closely mimicked *The Lone Ranger* property. In June 1939, Republic executives went on the theory that a trade is a trade and let the ablest wranglers win. At least that was the attitude they assumed when Universal sent out a feeler for the loan of Robert Livingston for their forthcoming Lone Ranger serial (which never happened, of course).

"Sure, we'll let you have him on a player swap," was Republic's reply.

"Great," shot back Universal. "Whom do you want in return?"

"Deanna Durbin!" retorted the Republic spokesman. The deal was never made.

What Republic gained from this however was verification that Universal was indeed striking a deal with Trendle for a third *Lone Ranger* serial. Even today it is not uncommon in business for negotiations with a third party to be used as leverage for a contract with a second party. Such negotiations would result in a bidding war regarding initial deposit and royalties – either way, Trendle would win. Staffers at Republic spent the summer and fall of 1939 drafting a new cliffhanger serial that, with tweaks and minor adjustments, could be a third *Lone Ranger* serial or a similar facsimile. As verified in the April 8, 1939, issue of the *Motion Picture Herald*, Republic reported future serials to go into production such as *The Drums of Fu Manchu* and *"The Lone Texas Ranger."* The April 8, 1939, issue of *Showmen's Trade Review* reported *"The Lone Texas Ranger"* as "a follow-up to the popular *Lone Ranger* series."

But it was from a reference in the November 13, 1939, issue of *Variety* that Trendle caught wind of the studio's plans for its 1940-1941 season of cliffhangers. The news brief reported Republic Studio currently employed 18 writers working on ten stories slated for the cameras during the next few months. "Two serials are in preparation, *Drums of Fu Manchu* and *The Lone Texas Ranger*. Sol Shor, Franklin Adreon, Barney Sarecky and Norman Hall are scripting former and Ron Davidson and Morgan Cox are working out treatment on latter."

**Display in the lobby of the Marlow Theater in Helena, Montana,
with the local radio sponsor, circa 1939.**

On Tuesday, November 28, 1939, Lone Ranger, Inc. filed a $10,000 suit in federal court against Republic Productions, at the same time asking for an injunction to restrain further production of a serial that Republic was promoting in advance, not yet filmed, titled "The Lone Texas Ranger." Trendle charged the film outfit breached its license contract by exposing the identity of the Ranger in the first and second serial, and sought permission to examine the defendant's books as, under contract, the plaintiff was to receive ten percent of the gross of the serial after $390,000 was reached. Republic claimed the profits from the first serial never grossed $390,000, but the fact that the studio was planning to make a third serial using a similar name and formula suggested otherwise.

Republic, meanwhile, returned Robert Livingston to the top role in *The Three Mesquiteers* westerns, replacing John Wayne who vacated after eight movies in the series. This would legally

secure Livingston's employment for an additional year and eliminate any chance of him playing The Lone Ranger for another studio. Livingston's return to the series was *The Kansas Terrors* in which Livingston's character, Stoney, who normally wears a dark outfit, switches to one resembling the serial's Lone Ranger outfit, wearing the same Lone Ranger mask (sans mesh), whisked away on a white horse that could easily have resembled Silver; and referred to himself as "The Masked Rider." This was Republic's obvious attempt to capitalize on the second Lone Ranger serial. Trendle did not take kindly to the studio's attempt to incorporate a masked rider into the film series. After strong protest from someone at WXYZ, Livingston continued to masquerade as "The Masked Rider" for a handful of additional entries in *The Three Mesquiteers* series but now wore a dark outfit instead of light, a different black domino mask, and rode a palomino when masked (rather than the white horse).

On January 15, 1940, Federal Judge Alfred C. Coxe issued an injunction restraining Republic Productions, Inc., from interfering with negotiations for the sale of *The Lone Ranger* radio series for motion picture production. Trendle believed negotiations with Universal Pictures for the sale of a *Lone Ranger* serial were handicapped, alleging Republic had interfered with that transaction by promoting their new serial of a similar name. At the same time, Judge Coxe restrained Republic from advertising its upcoming "The Lone Texas Ranger" in a manner which would create confusion in the minds of consumers. The Court in its decision, however, denied an application of the plaintiff, The Lone Ranger, Inc., to prevent Republic from releasing their western serial, as long as the studio avoided any trademarks related to *The Lone Ranger*. The question would be what constituted a trademark as it related to *The Lone Ranger* property. Action sought $10,000 damages and a declaration from the court that the "Lone Ranger" title and serial belonged to the plaintiff.

Republic Pictures Corp. filed an appeal from the decision but as the weeks passed by it became apparent to executives at Republic that they were not going to win the case. The injunction would expire in March, but the terms still held. In New York City, on July 15, the suit was settled out of U.S. District court by payment of $15,000 from Republic to The Lone Ranger, Inc. and in return the studio promised not to produce a third *Lone Ranger* serial, or any western serial that would deceive the public into believing it was based on the radio program, and promised not to interfere with the plaintiff in selling the rights to another studio. (The settlement was officially dated June 27, 1940.) Amongst the negotiations was a stipulation that the studio could follow their format (utilized in such serials as *The Masked Marvel*) where the hero is allowed to unmask during the final episode, since that aspect was not a trademark of *The Lone Ranger*. The proposed serial was temporarily shelved, replaced with one titled *The Adventures of Red Ryder*. The intended script, "The Lone Texas Ranger," was never produced.

Once Republic lost their defense, Universal Studios realized George W. Trendle had no leverage regarding price and informed the radio mogul that the asking price was too high. Trendle would not budge and, as a result, Universal never produced a *Lone Ranger* serial. The movie studio, however, did succeed with producing two *Green Hornet* serials in 1940, starring Gordon Jones and Warren Hull in the leads.

Pride being the longest distance between two parties, George W. Trendle confessed his position in the form of a letter dated October 1941, to Freddie Fralick, who was commissioned to secure licensing to a movie studio for either a series of movies or another serial. Trendle wrote: "The longer I fool around with *The Lone Ranger* the more I have come to the conclusion that if Republic would behave themselves, it wouldn't be a bad idea to have another serial made by them on one of our long form contracts with sufficient protection so nothing could go wrong. They seem to gross more money on serials than anybody else."

The only exchange of communication Trendle had with the studio afterwards was on March 5, 1942, when Trendle wrote to Republic Pictures to remind them that under contract the distribution and exhibition rights of the first serial, *The Lone Ranger*, and feature photoplay, *Hi-Yo, Silver*, expired on March 1, 1941, and the same for *The Lone Ranger Rides Again*, which expired on February 26, 1942, and so requested the studio transfer all copyrights for the films to The Lone Ranger, Inc., and forward all copies of the final shooting scripts to the Detroit office. On March 31, the studio transferred the copyrights of two serials and one film to The Lone Ranger, Inc.

According to *Liberty* magazine, the two serials were among the highest grossing for the studio. For the U.S., profits for the first serial was $594,137 and for the second, $523,026. There was additional income from cuts of the first serial to turn out the *Hi-Yo, Silver* feature, which did a credible business. Rumors circulated for years regarding Republic destroying all prints of the cliffhanger, as a mode of protection to ensure the company did not re-release the serial in later years through oversight.

In July 1939, poverty row studio Spectrum Pictures released *Two Gun Troubador*, starring Fred Scott in the lead, a tale of a cattle-rustling gang that murdered the hero's father 20 years before. While it rings in numerous familiar western episodes, the identity of the swift-riding, black-cloaked daredevil was carefully concealed until the high spot of the picture. His mad marauding served as a coverup in his unraveling the mystery of his father's strange death. Whether this was deliberate to cash in on the pulp magazine, *The Masked Rider*, or Republic's *The Lone Ranger* serial, remains unknown but there were certainly enough cactus calls to suggest deliberate imitation. But such was almost any western that had a cowboy who shot from the hip, rode a horse, or made friends with Indians that could provide assistance from the side. Such comparisons make novel amusement, but it's just self-obsessed fanboy folly for anyone to take time to even suggest such westerns were deliberate imitations, or vice versa.

In the same letter, Trendle admitted bad blood between he and Republic and if Fralick knew how to approach the film studio with the idea of a third serial without "embarrassing" himself (Trendle wanted to maintain his pride and position), he would pay Fralick a commission. Fralick did contact Republic, in a manner that did not appear to be an interest on Trendle's part, as "representation with commission" but assured Trendle that the reason he was not succeeding in getting *The Lone Ranger* back to theaters was (based on his discussions with an executive at Republic) that "your contract is pretty tough and producers are very reluctant about going into the deal under those circumstances."

The January 12, 1940 issue of *Variety* reported: "It was more than a little startling to read in the Monday papers that 'The Lone Ranger Weds' and then to read on Tuesday that 'The Lone Ranger Now is Father of a Girl.' To clarify momentary confusion, Lee Powell, 31, who played The Lone Ranger in the movies, was married in Chicago on Sunday. Earle Graser, the voice of the radio counterpart, was the one who became a father in Detroit on Tuesday."

LEE POWELL—The famous Lone Ranger and his horse, Silver, playing host to children from Home for the Friendless Orphanage as Wallace Broth- ers Circus opened yesterday for a two-day run at the North Side Exposition Grounds. About 400 orphans were treated to a matinee show.

May 18, 1940 issue of *The Pittsburgh Sun Telegraph*

Children Picketing 'Hamlet' Film Will Get 'Lone Ranger'

LARKSPUR, Cal., Oct. 31 (AP)— Children who picketed the film work of Shakespeare today were assured of victory.

A score of youngsters threw the picket line around the Lark Theater protesting the showing of Hamlet instead of the usual Saturday cartoons and "Lone Ranger."

The pickets denounced the theater's plan to show classical films. They bannered: "Unfair to kids— we learn history in school." The line dispersed on the promise the Lone Ranger and Mickey Mouse will return to the Saturday screen.

Newspaper article regarding the cliffhanger serial, November 1, 1949

SCREEN COWBOY CIRCUS FEATURE

First 'Lone Ranger' To Head Performances Monday

Led by that dashing buckaroo, Lee Powell, the original "Lone Ranger" of the movies, dozens of fast riding and rope twirling cowboys and cowgirls will provide the western feature of Wallace Brothers trained animal circus when it appears here next Monday.

The circus—the first this season in East Liverpool—will make camp in Columbian park, East End, for an afternoon and night performances for benefit of the East Liverpool Elks lodge Christmas fund.

Will Ride Masked

Powell will be seen several times during the circus proper, riding into the arena upon his horse with a clarion call—and masked.

Then, later he reappears and will remove his mask just as in the final episode of the thrilling saga of the golden west.

There will also be a galaxy of prominent circus celebrities including the internationally renowned Marvello troupe of aerialists; the great Eno-Hai Chaik troupe of oriental equilibristic marvels; the Riding Royal Ladonas, in a superb display of equestrianism; Col. Bill Woodcock with three herds of performing elephants; Capt. Eddie Allen, premier equestrienne trainer with a vast display of thoroughbred horses and pretty riders, and an army of mirth provoking funsters, in fact every sort of imaginable feature possible to present.

500 Principals Listed

A colorful musical extravagaze will be offered with over 500 men, women, elephants, horses, camels, zebras, ponies, and a vertible maze of big top splendor prior to the circus performance.

ORIGINAL LONE RANGER. Lee Powell, the original talking picture "Lone Ranger", who is this season appearing personally with his congress of rough riders in the Wallace Brothers Circus.

East Liverpool, Ohio, May 4, 1940

Chapter Six
The Buck Jones Lawsuit

SOMETIME CIRCA 1935, RALPH BINGE AND JOE GENTILE on Station CKLW in Windsor, Ontario, across the river from Detroit, performed short skits and bits for their morning program, *Dawn Patrol*, entertaining the masses beyond small talk and reading news copy. After burlesquing The Lone Ranger and using the "William Tell Overture," the radio hosts received the wrath of Raymond Meurer, who threatened suit on grounds of copyright infringement for playing the overture as part of their spoof. Ted Campeau, the manager, was out of town at the time and Dick Jones, commercial manager then, received the call and reminded Meurer the overture had been in the public domain for years... and that a spoof or parody was not entitled to an infringement case. If anything, the parody served as promotion for *The Lone Ranger* radio program. From that day forward, Raymond Meurer exercised caution as he weighed potential lawsuits against prospective exposure from which the station would benefit. Satire, it seemed, was an earnest form of adulation. But Ralph Binge and Joe Gentile were not the only ones who chose to pay tribute to *The Lone Ranger* in comedic form.

The popularity of *The Lone Ranger* was evident when national primetime radio broadcasts paid tribute to the children's western including Jack Benny and his cast who, on the evening of April 24, 1938 featured a satire on *Snow White and the Seven Dwarfs* on Benny's weekly *Jell-O Program*. The ethnic stereotype character Schlepperman, who played the role of Prince Charming, called to his horse, "Hi-Ho Silverstein!" The laughter originating from the audience momentarily stopped the show. Less than a year later, on January 8, 1939, Benny's cast repeated the spoof, this time with gravel-voiced Andy Devine as the prince, calling to his skinny horse, "Hi-Ho Sliver!"

By 1939, The Lone Ranger was spoofed in cartoon form such as the Warner Bros. classic, *The Lone Stranger and Porky* (1939). When The Lone Stranger's faithful Indian scout observes stagecoach driver Porky Pig being robbed by a villain, the masked man rides to the rescue. Numerous jokes abound but the cartoon ends with Silver, having an encounter with the villain's horse, returns to his master with several little colts. Later that same year, Walt Disney presented *The Autograph Hound*, in which Donald Duck visits a Hollywood Studio in an attempt to collect autographs from screen idols, only to discover everyone wants *his* autograph, including The Lone Ranger's horse, Silver. From the MGM studio came an entry of their Happy Harmonies series titled *The Lonesome Stranger* (1940), the title character who arrives in town to discover the sheriff has been shot by the Killer Diller Boys, wanted dead or alive, and attempts to apprehend the desperadoes. Cornered in the local saloon and about to be shot, The Lonesome Stranger pleads for his life, stating, "after all, this is just a cartoon."

Lone Ranger parodies can also be found in Tex Avery's *Cinderella Meets Fella* (1938), a parody of the "Masked Marvel" in another Porky Pig cartoon titled *The Film Fan* (1939), the Katzenjammer Kids reference The Lone Ranger in *Buried Treasure* (1938) and *The Captain's Christmas* (1938), a Lone Ranger reference is in the Popeye, the Sailor cartoon, *Stealin' Ain't Honest* (1940), and when a gang of bank robbers find themselves distracted when listening to radio's *Lone Ranger* in the cartoon *Thugs With Dirty Mugs* (1939). In the Donald Duck cartoon, *Commando Duck* (1944), one of the Japanese snipers mentions The Lone Ranger. Additional cartoons featuring references to *The Lone Ranger* radio program included *Porky in Egypt* (1938), *You're an Education* (1938), *Holiday Highlights* (1940), *The Daffy Duckaroo* (1942), *Lost and Founding* (1942), *The Mouse-Merized Cat* (1946) and *A Horse Fly Fleas* (1948).

In 1943, Columbia Pictures released *They Stooge to Conga*, starring The Three Stooges. Curly shouts the line, "Quit that double talk! I want to hear *The Lone Ranger!*" In another Three Stooges short, *Yes, We Have No Bonanza* (1939), Curly orders his bicycle to come to a standstill remarking, "Whoa, Silver!" In the movie *Straight, Place and Show* (1938), the Ritz Brothers yell "Hi-Yo, Silver" when they hear the "William Tell Overture." And the catch phrase can be heard in the beginning of *The Philadelphia Story* (1940).

With so many spoofs and tributes, Raymond Meurer and George W. Trendle created a policy whereby they would question each other regarding any potential infringements before filing complaints at the courthouse. This dual process would also ensure, according to an inter-office memo from Trendle, that the public did not view The Lone Ranger, Inc. as an entity other than benevolent. So, it came as a surprise that the financial success of Republic's *The Lone Ranger* would spawn a lawsuit against the movie studio... and by default, The Lone Ranger, Inc.

On May 13, 1938, action was filed in Superior Court by actor Buck Jones against Republic Pictures raising new legal questions in the motion picture industry. Can a studio adopt mannerisms, costumes and other acting tricks used by an actor, for a picture in which that actor does not appear? Can a studio adopt an actor's style of calling his horse, and adopt that horse's name for use in connection with a mount almost identical in appearance? These points were raised by Buck Jones in his action asking $250,000 in damages and a restraining order to prevent exhibition of *The Lone Ranger* chapters. Republic was charged with causing Jones' mannerisms, costumes, and voice inflections to be used by Lee Powell doing filming of the chapter film. The icing on his cake, Jones contested, was the name of the horse, Silver, which was the same name as the horse Jones rode on the silver screen, and was the same coloring – white.

Buck Jones

The general public was led to believe that Jones was appearing in the serial, the western star's complaint alleged, because the lead character remained masked throughout the film. Jones asserted this led to numerous inquiries from his fans as to whether he played the masked lead in the serial. Use of characteristics developed by Jones during his 15 years as a western star, such as riding style, tone and quality of voice, manner of calling his horse, are all duplicated in the serial. The cliffhanger serial was also an imitation of former westerns made by Jones, according to the complaint.

By the end of the month, Republic petitioned the superior court to have the $250,000 damage action brought against studio by Buck Jones, transferred to U.S. District Court. The hearing on the motion took place on May 31, before Superior Judge Robert W. Kenney, and the case was transferred at the studio's request. By then, George W. Trendle was notified of the lawsuit and, according to a clause in their contract, any copyright infringements as it related to the property they licensed that resulted in a court case, would be financially reimbursed by The Lone Ranger, Inc.

On August 1, Republic filed their answer in federal court, declaring Jones' objections to the horse being called Silver and addressed with the call "Hi-Yo, Silver" were rather belated. "*The Lone Ranger* program has been broadcast from Detroit for several years," an attorney for the studio explained. The movie studio explained how they purchased picture rights from the owners of the radio program, providing a copy of the contract, along with the two pages of trademarks that Trendle insisted be incorporated to ensure The Lone Ranger and Tonto would be portrayed as depicted on the radio program and with no deviations. The attorney representing Buck Jones attempted to have the case sent back to superior court but this was overruled by Federal Judge Harry A. Hollzer.

The court case was scheduled for February, later rescheduled for March 31, 1939. Trendle paid for half of the attorney fees for the trial, with Republic initially believing that all costs and expenses in connection with the deposition was to be charged to The Lone Ranger, Inc., even though Trendle's organization was not party to the action. Republic put up a first affirmative defense, and in order to obtain evidence in support of this defense depositions from Detroit seemed essential. Added to the cost of $250, which Meurer paid on July 21, 1939, was $156.09 for reporting depositions taken for the three days (March 31, April 4, and April 5, 1939).

The case returned to the courtroom on May 12, 1939. On that morning, Jones explained how the studio system worked back in the silent era. According to his testimony, a star's contract, calling for $500 per picture (per serial chapter), insurance against accident and illness to total value of the production, and first-class trailer transportation were always provided for Silver, Buck Jones' motion picture horse.

During the trial, very little emphasis was put upon the connection between the motion picture serial and the radio program, but the course of the case was decided on the basis of Jones' evidence presented only, which did not give a complete picture of the relationship between the radio program and the motion picture, although Republic publicity which was offered in evidence by Jones very clearly tied up the two.

As far as the case itself was concerned, the evidence consisted of Jones' testimony and very brief testimony from John English, the co-director of *The Lone Ranger* serial. Attorneys Norman Newmark and Donald Hamblin, for Republic Pictures, argued that Buck Jones was not entitled to the sole use of the name Silver for a white horse in Western films. On the second day of the trial the court viewed five episodes of *The Phantom Rider*, a 15-episode cliffhanger serial starring Buck Jones, produced in 1936 at Universal Studios, eight episodes of *The Lone Ranger* serial – from which the defendant's attorneys brought out certain points deemed important – and a Buck Jones picture entitled, *The Overland Express*. The rest of the evidence consisted of photographs, newspaper clippings and pressbooks relating to Buck Jones and his horse, Silver, two Republic pressbooks in connection with *The Lone Ranger* serial, and a letter of Harry Sherman's to Republic dated December 21, 1937.

Following material evidence presented, and the contentions and arguments of both parties, on May 16, 1939, Judge Harry A. Hollzer declared a non-suit in Buck Jones' $250,000 damage suit. Jones was quoted by the press as saying he had "just begun to fight. We're going right on with the battle." His attorney, Austin Sherman, spent the summer preparing to take the resolution to a higher court, even though Judge Hollzer ruled that the cowboy star had failed to introduce sufficient evidence to support his claim that the Republic production of *The Lone Ranger* serial was an attempt to imitate him and his horse Silver.

The court further held in effort that "The Lone Ranger" could continue to shout his famous calls, "Hi-Yo, Silver" and "Hi-Yo, Silver, Away!" The court declared, after reviewing the films, that no one viewing *The Lone Ranger* cliffhanger serial would be led to believe that Jones played the title role or any other character in the film version. "While there is mystery as to the identity of 'The Lone Ranger' until the end of the serial," Judge Hollzer said, "it is clearly demonstrated that Jones as an individual is not being held out as one portraying the character of 'The Lone Ranger' or any other character in the picture."

On September 5, Jones filed for an appeal and Loeb & Loeb, attorneys in Los Angeles, represented Republic Pictures. On October 20, 1939, the appeal went to the United States Circuit Court from the Los Angeles District Court, where Jones' plea for a suit was denied, based on Hollzer's verdict. There, Buck Jones climbed off his horse, shoved his six-gun back in the holster and called in a lip reader to fight the battle of "Hi-Yo, Silver." The old cry, which Jones used in his equine pictures back in the 1920s, was the same, he claimed, as the one voiced in the Republic serial, *The Lone Ranger*. In those days there were no soundtracks to prove it, but Jones dug up a strip of 1927 film and declared he would prove his case through lip-reading testimony. Jones asserted that he used his horse Silver in more than 100 films and always addressed his steed with "Hi-Ho Silver, away" as The Lone Ranger did in the chapter-play. The appeal was denied.

Months later, on June 16, 1940, the way was paved for reopening of Buck Jones' suit for an accounting of profits from the film serial, *The Lone Ranger*, when U.S. Circuit Court of Appeals in San Francisco reversed the federal court ruling dismissing the action. Finally, the matter between Buck Jones and Republic Pictures was settled officially on September 2, 1942, in Los Angeles, California, when Jones signed a release, with prejudice, that he no longer owned the rights to a horse named "Silver," and was dismissing his case against Republic. (Official paperwork was dated July 30, 1942.) His wife, Odille D. Jones, signed off as well as she was representation/agent for her husband.

As for Silver, the horse that took the spotlight in the two serials, he continued trotting along through Hollywood, making an appearance in *Ziegfeld Follies* (1944) and what's more, instead of a rip-snortin' cowboy astride him, he had the glamorous Lucille Ball for a rider. Silver, with his tail braided and tied with six pink satin bows, and a pink ostrich feather between his ears, was featured in the merry-go-round number with ten other white horses.

Lucille Ball on Silver in *Ziegfeld Follies* (1945).

In August of 1941, RKO Studios attempted to get into the act by aiming for a distaff switch on *The Lone Ranger* radio show when the studio staked claim to the label "Mrs. Lone Ranger" for an upcoming movie. After an exchange of letters with Raymond Meurer in February 1942, the studio changed the name of the movie to "Mrs. Trail Blazer." The script was revised multiple times and ultimately went into production a year later, February 1943, as *A Lady Takes a Chance*, co-starring Jean Arthur and John Wayne. The film dramatized the story of a New York City working girl who travels to the American West on a bus tour, where she meets and falls in love with a handsome rodeo cowboy.

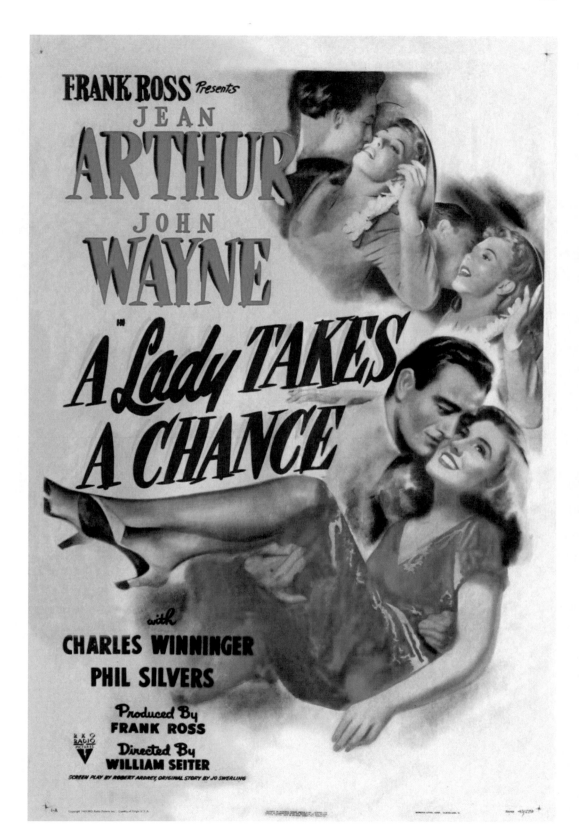

Chapter Seven
Raymond Meurer
& Merchandising

WHEN PHILLIP NOWLAN CREATED BUCK ROGERS as a pulp novel, eventually extended into a newspaper comic strip, the popularity of the fictional character cried out for mass merchandising. A radio program soon developed and John Dille, owner of the National Newspaper Service Syndicate, recognized that greater profits lay in merchandising. Buck Rogers ray guns and toy spaceships were prominent on store shelves while young children acted out the adventures of Buck, Wilma, and Dr. Huer within the confines of their front yard. *

Walt Disney licensed Mickey Mouse merchandise solely to fund his animation projects, which were not as profitable as those of his contemporaries. Disney would rethink his business model and eventually coordinate the release of Mickey Mouse toys with storylines appearing in the daily comic strips, and exhibitions at various markets across the country. Disney may have been one the first to recognize the importance of merchandising when he began licensing *Snow White and the Seven Dwarfs* merchandise before the theatrical release of his motion picture.

When it came to merchandising, George W. Trendle had that rare distinction of owning the property with little to no sponsor entitlement. The standard procedure in the 1930s was for a sponsor to hire an advertising agency to work for and represent the company. Executives at the ad agency would create a number of proposals. If the sponsor warmed to the idea of a specific proposal, they signed on the bottom line. The agency was responsible for leasing airtime, hiring the producer,

* In 1940, dividends from The Lone Ranger, Inc. came to $46,000, King-Trendle Broadcasting Corp. for $16,000, and The Green Hornet, Inc. paid out $160 in dividends.

director and scriptwriter(s). The producer would be responsible for hiring the cast and crew and assembling the program. Everything from fan mail, legal concerns, promotion, and marketing ran through the agency which in most cases called the shots. The sponsor was billed on a monthly basis, based on production costs and station coverage.

General Mills, for example, owned *Jack Armstrong, the All-American Boy*, which was created solely as a means of marketing breakfast cereal. The radio program was created by an advertising agency, hired by the cereal firm, and therefore the property of General Mills. The fictional character's exclusive association with Wheaties prevented Jack Armstrong from fully becoming a national icon because General Mills restricted the use of the boy hero beyond their marketing budget. *The Lone Ranger*, on the other hand, was not branded with any particular product since day one, which allowed for a wide range of marketing potentials regarding merchandising and sponsor tie-ins.

Reportedly, Trendle never accepted sponsorship of the program by distillers or cigarette firms, nor would he allow a license for Lone Ranger matches, knives, bows and arrows, or anything that could create harm to a child. The sponsors of *The Lone Ranger* had been primarily food companies and bakeries, although one sponsor in the West was an oil company.

For clarification, contracts for the many novelties and premiums were all made by or handled by Raymond J. Meurer. "Ray was a brilliant contract lawyer and very efficiently handled these contracts during the entire life of the show," Trendle later recalled. When negotiating for the licensing of many shows originating from WXYZ, whether for radio, television or motion pictures, pulp magazines, books, novelties, or premiums, there was always a three-corner conference: Allen Campbell, who did the active selling; Raymond Meurer, who handled the contracts; and Trendle, who handled the administrative department of the corporation. "Each of us handled his own department," Trendle later recalled, "and the combined results were very satisfactory." It was Meurer who stopped at least a dozen would-be imitators who wanted to hitch onto the glory of *The Lone Ranger*, or any of the other programs.

Today, Raymond J. Meurer is best known to radio historians as the legal counsel for George W. Trendle and radio station WXYZ. Raymond Meurer's career could fill a book all its own, ranging from his campaigns to have a World's Fair held in Detroit in 1940 to joining a Cleanup Committee for scrap paper drives. (For the sake of brevity, this section contains only a brief biographical summary, leaving his involvement as it pertains to *The Lone Ranger* throughout these four volumes. A lengthy biography of Raymond J. Meurer can be found in the first volume of this series, *The Lone Ranger: The Early Years, 1933-1937*.)

Before law, Meurer sought a career in the medical field. In September 1925, he enrolled in the Detroit College of Medicine and Surgery. After changing course, Meurer became a practicing attorney in the State of Michigan, having been admitted by the Michigan State Supreme Court in October 1931, duly licensed to practice in all courts within the state, including the United States District Courts. He was also a member of the Detroit and American Bar associations as well as a member of the bar of the Supreme Court of the United States of America. For 22 years, Raymond Meurer served as General Counsel, officer and Director of The Lone Ranger, Inc. He was an officer, director, shareholder, and general counsel of Trendle-Campbell-Meurer, Inc., The Green Hornet, Inc., Sergeant Preston of the Yukon, Inc., and The American Agent, Inc.

Grosset & Dunlap Novels

Beginning in 1936, a series of 18 *Lone Ranger* novels were published through Grosset & Dunlap. (The origins of these books, and details about some of those novels, are documented in the first volume of this series, *The Lone Ranger: The Early Years, 1933-1937*.) Covering the years of 1938 to 1942, six novels were published by Grosset & Dunlap, and one published by Putnam Books which is not considered part of the "official" line of 18 novels. The Putnam publication provided a retelling of The Lone Ranger's origin. For the books that were documented at length in the prior volume, we will avoid repetition and provide only the trivial details.

Book #2   *The Lone Ranger and the Mystery Ranch* (1938)

Book #3   *The Lone Ranger and the Gold Robbery* (1939)

Book #4   *The Lone Ranger and the Outlaw Stronghold* (1939)

Book #5   *The Lone Ranger and Tonto* (1940)

Book #6   *The Lone Ranger at the Haunted Gulch* (1941)

Book #7   *The Lone Ranger Traps the Smugglers* (1941)

The Lone Ranger and the Mystery Ranch (1938) was loosely based on the radio broadcast of November 2, 1933. In the novel, The Lone Ranger and Tonto are on the trail of the Night Legion, the notorious, ruthless gang of criminals responsible for an untold number of crimes across the States and territories, and responsible for the Texas Ranger massacre that forced the sole survivor to don a mask and set out to seek justice. The Lone Ranger and Tonto stumble on the dying testimony of Joe Frisby, overhearing a plot complicated by two halves of a treasure map. After rescuing two young women arriving from the East, Sally and Marge Whitcomb, from an ambush plotted by members of the Night Legion, The Lone Ranger deposits the girls at the ranch owned by their uncle, a known recluse whom they haven't seen in more than a decade. After discovering that Uncle Whitcomb's place is also nicknamed The Hoodoo Ranch, and someone working at the ranch leaked information to the leader of the notorious gang, The Lone Ranger and Tonto agree to keep an eye on the ranch for the girls' safety.

Meanwhile, a council of war is gathered in the office of Sheriff Cook, who recruits a number of deputies to help purge the notorious gang from the town of Sundown. The horrors of the Night Legion have swept across the countryside, but with The Lone Ranger in the area, the Sheriff is certain the gang will be apprehended. When Sally finds a blue vest worn by one of the men who killed Joe Frisby, she sneaks off the ranch to alert the Sheriff. Marge, attempting to cover for her sister, is escorted off the ranch by her uncle and soon learns that he is not really her uncle but, in fact, the hooded leader that has masterminded numerous crimes across the plains. He plans to eliminate the girl after he discovers where she and her sister had hidden the remaining half of the map. Without possession of their piece, Joe Frisby's half of the map is worthless. Upon learning where it was hidden in the house, he returns to the ranch.

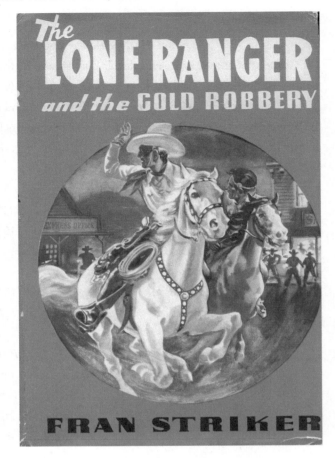

The Lone Ranger, while Marge and the fake uncle were away, discovered a cellar underneath the house where he finds an old man is being starved to death. He is the real uncle and the girls—and The Lone Ranger and Tonto—had fallen for the masquerade. The leader of the outlaw gang returns alone, and The Lone Ranger shoots the killer's gun out of his hand during their confrontation and beats a confession out of the criminal as to the whereabouts of Marge. The much-feared boss becomes a sniveling coward, begging and pleading for mercy. After learning that Marge is being kept against her will in Flynn's Cave, the law races out to apprehend the gang members and rescue the girl.

In this novel, Tonto was described as smaller than The Lone Ranger, with a bronzed, high cheek-boned face. His long, black hair was parted in the center of his head and drawn back tightly to be fashioned in a war-knot at the back of the neck. As for The Lone Ranger, Striker described him not physically, but as only others saw him in the West.

"His daring acts of courage in the name of Justice made him known throughout the West," wrote Striker. "To many of the pioneers he existed as an almost legendary character. Only a small portion of those who knew of him had seen him, and none of these had ever seen his face unmasked. Many times, his safety had depended upon his knowledge of a cave or other place of hiding. Many outlaws had sworn to kill the masked rider for his work in bringing countless desperadoes to justice and breaking up untold rustling gangs and outlaw bands. Even lawmen wanted the Lone Ranger. Only a few had been convinced that this strange figure was not an outlaw, and those few thanked God for the man who had no thought of personal glory or reward… for the man whose only purpose in life seemed to be to help the deserving and punish the lawless in a region where laws were few and those few, seldom enforced."

After burying a man Tonto and the masked man found hanging from a tree, The Lone Ranger pays his respects in an unusual way: "The shallow grave was finally prepared, and the body, wrapped in one of the Lone Ranger's blankets, was gently lowered to its final resting place. Then, hat in hand, the Lone Ranger did a rare thing. In the darkness, he removed his mask. For an instant, while his clean-cut face was lifted toward the sky in silent prayer for the departed soul, and while Tonto's head was bowed, the moon again broke through the clouds. Tonto echoed the white man's 'Amen.'"

Chapter five revealed Tonto's friendship with the Lone Ranger: "Tonto's hand showed white across the knuckles from the way he'd gripped the branch in tension! Though the Indian had yet to kill his first man, and though he knew it was against the principals of The Lone Ranger, his companion, to shoot to kill even the most evil of outlaws, he had been ready to shoot the Boss, if his masked friend has been killed."

Chapter 17 revealed the Lone Ranger's eyes were grey in color. Chapter 19 revealed the Lone Ranger was right-handed.

The final chapter in the book revealed the Lone Ranger's anger towards the man responsible for the massacre of his close friends. While a ruthless gang of Mexican bandits was not gunned down in cold blood, as had happened on the radio program, the scene in which The Lone Ranger beat the Boss into a corner to reveal the criminal as a sniveling coward, begging and pleading for mercy, revealed the darker side of the masked man. "The Lone Ranger had no place in his heart for mercy of sympathy. Hanging would follow in due course, but first, there was an unholy satisfaction in feeling his fists punish the hateful creature whose sadistic nature brought torture and death to so many fine men of the West."

The closing of the chapter reveals the Lone Ranger's intent to continue the good work accomplished from this adventure. "We have the Night Legion," the masked man told his Indian companion, "but there are so many countless other outlaws to be run down and there are so many people who need Justice, that… well, good friend, I think as long as we've made the name Lone Ranger mean something, we can continue to help people!" Tonto nodded, agreeable to anything his tall white friend suggested. "I'll not unmask just yet! I want to carry on, just as the Texas Rangers would, if the Night Legion hadn't wiped them out."

The Lone Ranger and the Gold Robbery (1939) opened with a brief summary of the events from the prior novel, and a basic introduction to the origin of The Lone Ranger for those who never heard the radio program or read the prior novel.

"Tonto had traveled with the Lone Ranger ever since that day long past, when the white man was the sole survivor of an attack which wiped out an entire band of Texas Rangers. The Lone Ranger, a member of the band, was badly wounded. His injuries would probably have killed him if it hadn't been for Tonto. For it was Tonto, a wandering Indian, who found him and nursed the faint spark of life back to a glowing flame of vigorous health."

"Then, so the killers would not know him as a survivor of the band of Texas Rangers, the white man masked his face. With Tonto at his side, he fought the marauders to avenge the death of his friends and rid the state of Texas of a choking yoke of outlawry. Time after time, he rode down on the killers. He captured some of them himself, as they skirmished away from the main band. Others, he brought the lawmen to arrest. Each time, when his hard riding and thrilling courage brought others of the outlaw band to justice, he rode away without awaiting thanks, or reward. His identity was never learned. Finally, the last of those who had battles and killed the Lone Ranger's partners, was lodged in jail to await a trial, and ultimately to hang."

"Then, his work in Texas finished, he found himself known only as the Lone Ranger and recognized as a power of strength in the name of justice... a grim nemesis to outlaws, however daring. The stories of his exploits spread throughout the West, and he became an almost legendary character with a mighty stallion, said to be the most powerful horse in seven states."

Soon after The Lone Ranger and Tonto rescue the twisted form of old man Ben Jenkins from the quicksand of The Devil's Bog, they uncover a plot involving outlaws and the theft of $100,000 worth of gold bullion at the express office in the town of Black River. After burying the old man who was shot by the outlaws (apparently Jenkins possessed the plans for shipment), the masked man and his Indian companion visit the express office only to find themselves minutes too late and forced to flee and hide out in the Devil's Bog to evade the sheriff and his posse, who believe the heroes were the guilty culprits of the gold theft.

After evading the pursuit of Sheriff Potter and Jack Bannerman, the manager of the express office, The Lone Ranger returns to Black River, during the annual three-day Frontier Day festivities, in disguise in the hopes of learning who was responsible for the murder and the gold robbery. Even with a superb disguise, The Lone Ranger is suspected of being the stranger who fled the express office the other day and is put to a test. During a sharpshooting contest, he finds himself competing against the best shooters in the county, in order to cover for his presence. The Lone Ranger wins the contest and flees the scene thanks to the speed of Silver and the assistance of Judge Bellows, who recalls a masked man in El Paso who once sought justice in a similar manner as depicted in Black River.

Bellows is placed under arrest on suspicion of aiding the men responsible for the gold robbery while Tonto creates the illusion that Captain Skinner snuck out of town late one night, along with the hundred thousand dollars of gold. His associates, Vinton and Brady, fear the worst and set out with spades and shovels after midnight to visit the local graveyard. Digging up the grave of their good friend Dick Tuttle, who had recently died, they remove the six-foot-long coffin to examine the contents. The gold still remains. The crooks are caught red-handed with the goods by Sheriff Potter, Jack Bannerman and a posse.

Captain Skinner, it is revealed, is Dick Tuttle in disguise and never really died. His premature death was an excuse to hide the gold bars that were stolen from the express office and an attempt to throw blame on the masked man who came snooping around at the time of the robbery. The Lone Ranger and Tonto had sought out the Sheriff and rationally explained the situation, proving they did not commit the murder or the robbery. Vinton and Brady make excuse after excuse, but to no avail. Skinner, alias Tuttle, tells the Sheriff that he'll confess his part in the robbery and tell a jury the part his two associates committed – including murder – under one condition. When all three hang for their crimes, he wants to be the last so he can see the two yellow skunks get theirs first.

In this novel, it was said that The Lone Ranger had gray-blue eyes, wore a white sombrero, dark trousers and a fawn-colored shirt. Tonto's moccasined feet allowed for him to walk silently. Both vigilantes stood over six feet tall. In chapter seven, his guns were described in the following manner: "Removing his bandanna, the masked man wiped away the blotches of greenish scum that had spattered his face and mask. This done, he gave his attention to the two ivory-handled weapons. The working parts, protected as they had been by the holsters, were quite dry. For a time he studied them, then jammed one back in leather. The other he broke, spilling the cartridges in the palm of his hand. Those cartridges were made of solid silver! Many times, the silver bullets had identified the Lone Ranger. People tried to trace him, by trying to learn where they were made, but they were never successful. Tonto alone knew where and how those silver slugs were cast, and the masked man's secret was quite safe with Tonto."

During the contest involving marksmanship, The Lone Ranger, disguised, fires five shots from the hip, in the space of two seconds. "He didn't aim, he shot by instinct. He didn't need to ask where those shots went, he knew! This was accuracy, seen only when the gods of thunder send their lightning bolts to crash to the earth."

The Lone Ranger and The Outlaw Stronghold (1939) plays more like a murder mystery than a Western, including the manner in which The Lone Ranger allows Spade to reveal all the details of his master plot. David Carling seeks to avenge the death of his father, Tom Carling, who was shot and killed while riding back home. The principal suspect is Flint Greggson, because of a long-standing feud between the families. It seems there was a disagreement over Tom Carling's right to a silver claim. Flint Greggson quarreled about the claim, and the law ruled it belonged to Carling. Then a short time later, Carling's wife was found dead, and the same court judged that the murderers were Indians, unknown. The murder was never solved. Thus, David suspects old Flint Greggson hired someone to shoot and kill his father.

After Tonto and The Lone Ranger find the body of Tom Carling, and a demented old hermit named Old Long Hair, they stumble upon a plot where someone attempted to have Old Long Hair blamed for the murder. When The Lone Ranger pays a late-night visit to Flint's stronghold in the San Juan Mountain region, he suspects that Flint was not involved. Hoping to prevent young David from making a fateful decision, The Lone Ranger is forced to run down David, injuring the young man. While Tonto tends to the boy's wounds, the Masked Man investigates. During a confrontation in Flint's homestead, Spade Beasley, an outlaw in Flint's gang, shoots Harve Greggson, Flint's nephew, dead.

After piecing together most of the puzzle, The Lone Ranger creates a set-up whereby David confronts Spade Beasley to discover the identity of the real murderer. It seems Spade was in love with Betty, Flint's adopted daughter. Knowing she had feelings for David, Spade committed a couple murders in an effort to eliminate those who stood in his way. Exposed, Flint and David help apprehend Spade Beasley and the sheriff takes him in. Flint and David have a heart-to-heart discussion and their differences are tossed aside for the romantic future of Betty and David.

Like the novels before this one, there is a reference to The Lone Ranger's guns having ivory handles. Chapter two reveals The Lone Ranger uses heavy .44s. Chapter five provides the following description of The Lone Ranger: "Above the mask she saw the large white Stetson, beneath it, a finely chiseled chin, a firm mouth, and a broad, strong-looking pair of shoulders." A later chapter mentions he has grey eyes.

As Fran Striker laid the groundwork regarding their method of vigilantism: "All things pertaining to trailing and woodcraft, camp craft and first-aid, were left to Tonto. The Lone Ranger's part in the strange combination was to plan the downfall of outlaws and desperadoes; deal with lawmen; and map out campaigns of justice. The two were equally adept at gunplay or roping. Each seemed to be a complement of the other, and together they made an ideal combination."

Adding to the mythology was this statement in chapter six: "Let those who have asked so many times, what the Lone Ranger and Tonto used for food, traveling as they did, be answered at this time. They fared far better than many a city dweller, as far as food was concerned. When there was time, Tonto went hunting and came back with wild turkey, or grouse! From time to time one of the two would drop a deer, and after taking the choicest of steaks for themselves, would swap what was too bulky to carry, for staples such as flour, salt, or bacon and sugar. There was beef-steak, of course, and frequently a plentiful supply of rich milk. Tonto knew all the edible berries and fruits, and from time to time returned from a foraging expedition with a supply of honey that a bear had overlooked. What their diet lacked in variety, it more than made up in quality. On the other hand, both men were able to go for days at a time, when the trail was hot, or the chase was a close one, with little more than water and hardtack. They had likewise accustomed themselves to going long periods without sleep and had been known to spend days at a time in the saddle; dozing as they rode, but ready at an instant's notice, to be wide awake, and ready for whatever Fate might have in store for them."

The story for *The Lone Ranger and Tonto* (1940) was the most simplistic of the 19 novels written. Dave Walters is falsely accused of robbery and the Lone Ranger breaks the youth out of jail. While Tonto keeps the boy hidden from the posse, the Lone Ranger learns the identity of the real guilty party -- Steve Delaney. A gambler by trade, Delaney owns most of the mortgages in town, making him a very powerful man in Snake River. Alone in Delaney's private residence, The Lone Ranger ties and gags the gambler so he can use his makeup kit to impersonate the crook and uncover enough facts to prove Walters' innocence. While Tonto comes to the aid of The Lone Ranger, the sheriff and his men find Dave held up in a cave and bring the boy back to town. Upon their return, the Ranger has uncovered enough evidence to prove Delaney stole the jewels from the old widow who was brutally murdered. Throwing the blame on Dave Walters, Delaney then attempts to double-cross his own comrades. Angry for the betrayal and hold-out of funds, the men reveal the truth to the sheriff. Dave Walters is reunited with his parents whom he was seeking before stepping foot in Snake River.

The Lone Ranger not only applied a makeup kit to disguise his appearance during this adventure, but there were numerous references to his mask. *"It took but an instant to remove the mask and hide it beneath his shirt. The Lone Ranger took a small bottle from a saddlebag and poured a few drops of fluid it contained into the palm of one hand. He replaced the bottle and rubbed his palms briskly together, then rubbed them over his face and neck. The fluid was a stain that Tonto made from roots. It darkened the Lone Ranger's complexion by several degrees. He hung his white sombrero on the saddle horn and replaced it with a battered old black felt that had seen far better days. Next, he changed his black silk neckerchief for one of brilliant hue. This was his disguise. It wasn't much, but past experience had proved it to be all that was required."*

Further detail was provided in chapter two: *"Dave watched the masked man, wondering if he would sleep with the mask in place. He did not know that the Lone Ranger wore the mask, habitually, whether there was need of it or not. It has become a part of him, and because of that it did not hamper him in action."*

At one point in time The Lone Ranger sends a message on paper via horseback. Tonto receives the message and reads it clearly, but Dave Walters is puzzled. In short, stilted sentences the Indian made Walters understand that the Lone Ranger's message was a combination of the white man's way of writing and the Indian's picture writing. Many of the masked man's thoughts and suggestions had been abbreviated in a way that only Tonto would understand. If anyone had intercepted the message it would have been totally without meaning.

The Lone Ranger's silver bullets were explored twice in this novel. Once when Tonto makes reference that he received cash from a silver mine toward the North. There were silver-bearing claims in the country to the north and many of these claims had been on land controlled by Indians. As Striker explained in chapter ten, "There were, at the time, instances where white men had made a deal with the Indians to work the land and sell the ore at ridiculously low prices. But those low prices represented vast wealth to the Indians." In chapter sixteen, Dave Walters looks over The Lone Ranger and Tonto's reserve supplies and finds extra blankets, countless cans of food, boxes of cartridges, clothing, saddle equipment, a couple of short rifles of the finest manufacture, a keg of gunpowder, a supply of rope, materials for reshoeing the hooves of the great horse Silver, and molds for making the Lone Ranger's silver bullets.

For the 1941 Grosset & Dunlap novel, *The Lone Ranger at the Haunted Gulch*, Fran Striker recycled the recurring character of C. Thorndyke Abercrombie of Placerville, who appeared in four radio episodes from 1935 to 1936, to become Luther Abercrombie of Haunted Gulch. In the novel, The Lone Ranger was described as wearing high-heel boots, a shirt that was the color of soft buckskin, a neckerchief, hat, and "clean black trousers that fitted closely to his calves and thighs and made it easier to ride and fight." But the most amusing entry in the book was a direct reference to the silver bullets that became a trademark of the masked man: "People thought the solid silver bullets The Lone Ranger used were sheer extravagance, but there was a definite reason for them. The Lone Ranger had pledged himself never to take a life. When he fired, it was in defense of his own life or the life of someone else. At these times he fired to wound – not to kill. He fired to blast away the gun of an opponent. Lead bullets striking the tempered steel of another man's gun might spatter and send dangerous fragments flying. Bullets of silver would not do this."

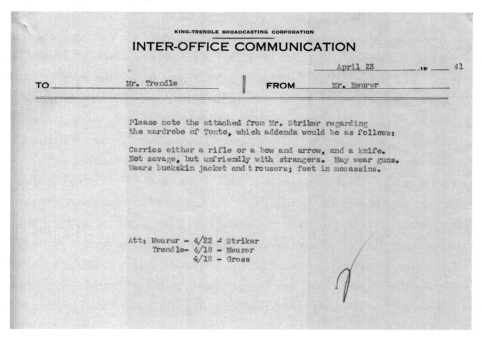

In *The Lone Ranger Traps the Smugglers* (1941), The Lone Ranger comes to the aid of young Patricia Knowlton when he learns she foolheartedly plans to take the law into her own hands. Sam Slake, with an unmistakable scar that starts from one side of his nose and goes all the way down to his jaw from an old knife wound that did not heal, is the leader of the pack of smugglers who killed her father. His genius for organization had built a gang of smugglers that extended from the purchasers of goods as far south as Mexico City, to the salesmen in Kansas. The same gang is to blame for many murders near the Rio Grande. Slake has many men working for him south of the border in addition to men who work north, smuggling guns and liquor to the Indians. Almost too powerful for the law to handle unless air-tight evidence can be found, Slake also has a number of people opposing him including Bart Beldon, a government man who ties up the masked man so he can infiltrate the cabin on Slake's ranch.

Beldon has no evidence against Sam Slake but he is determined to make a bold play in the hope that fortune will favor him and put him in possession of evidence when he makes an arrest. Luther Ponsby is a stool pigeon who is willing to sell out Slake, and Ponsby has the evidence sought by Bart Beldon and The Lone Ranger. Inside that cabin, however, Beldon falls victim to Slake's upper hand when Slake sees past his ruse and he discovers his cover is blown. Patricia Knowlton, who has been living on the same ranch under an assumed identity, discovers her cover is also blown, courtesy of Beldon's carelessness. Slake attempts to force Beldon to reveal the location of the ex-gang member. Thanks to The Lone Ranger and Tonto, Patricia and Beldon are rescued before Slake can perform fatal acts of torture.

Tonto returns to the ranch house to investigate. In a hidden basement in the barn, he finds the dead body of Luther Ponsby. Before he can retrieve the Slake papers that Ponsby stole, Tonto is knocked out from behind. His assailant steals the papers, sets the barn on fire, and flees. The Lone Ranger, who has captured Slake and left him tied up at his camp, races inside the burning barn to rescue his friend, only learning afterwards of the grisly demise of Ponsby.

Lefty, one of Sam Slake's gang, was responsible for the murder and the theft of the papers. Racing to Eagle Pass, he checks himself into a hotel in the hopes of selling the papers to either Slake or Beldon for a large sum of money. The Lone Ranger and Tonto trail Lefty to town and the masked man gets the upper hand by shooting the lights out and stealing the papers that Lefty had on his person. Racing back to the campfire where he has Slake tied up, The Lone Ranger verifies the validity of the papers. Overnight, Slake breaks free of his bonds, steals the papers and tosses them into the fire. After he races away, The Lone Ranger wakes to discover the ruse worked – and gives chase. Tonto, meanwhile, asks Beldon to follow him where all would be revealed.

Back at the ranch house, Patricia pays Sam Slake and his men a visit to avenge the death of her father. Slake gets the advantage of her, taking the small pistol she had concealed on her person. The Lone Ranger jumps into the room to intervene, having been in a secluded and hidden spot inside the room for a few hours. The Lone Ranger informs Slake that he burned an empty wallet – the papers that incriminate him never went up in flames. Tonto arrives with Beldon and his men to place Slake under arrest. Before riding away, The Lone Ranger suggests to Beldon that the reward money go to Patricia. It was her father who first learned that Sam Slake could be convicted. His daughter carried on where he left off.

The Lone Ranger Rides (1941)

Like most of the Grosset & Dunlap novels, Fran Striker took the time to make references to the characters of The Lone Ranger and Tonto that would have been inconsequential as narrative on radio. After mapping out a plot on notepad, Striker would write each chapter (usually consisting of three pages on a typewriter) and then retype a second draft with polished prose. It was usually the second draft that he submitted to the publishing company. But on one occasion his time was so limited that he never had a chance to go back and retype the second draft or polish the prose… nor did an employee at Putnam take time to polish the manuscript before production. *The Lone Ranger Rides*, published in 1941 by Putnam, sold on store shelves for $2.00.

The story concerns The Lone Ranger's efforts to smash a gang of cattle rustlers, known as the Cavendish clan. Bryant Cavendish was a bitter old man whose age had caught up to him, confining him to his homestead while his kin, whom he disliked, operated like outlaws. A number of Texas Rangers were ambushed in Bryant's Gap, with one sole survivor who was nursed back to health by an Indian named Tonto. The origin of Silver, the white stallion, was recounted from Striker's radio rendition. It was not until chapter ten that the wounded Ranger, fully recovered, knew he would fight the commandment, "Thou Shalt Not Kill," in his efforts to exact revenge against the men responsible for the massacre. "I'll see them made to pay in full," The Lone Ranger told Tonto.

 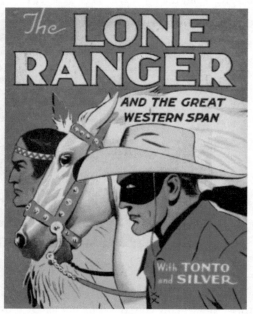

The Lone Ranger and the Dead Men's Mine (1939) was recycled from "Death's Head Vengeance," from the November 1937 issue of *The Lone Ranger Magazine*. *The Lone Ranger and the Great Western Span* (1942) was recycled from "Heritage of the Plains" from the September 1937 issue of *The Lone Ranger Magazine.*

Although not a Whitman Big Little Book, *The Lone Ranger and the Lost Valley* (1938) is considered by collectors chronologically as the fifth Lone Ranger BLB. This 1938 Dell Fast Action book (a different size than a standard BLB), involves The Lone Ranger and a wounded Tonto

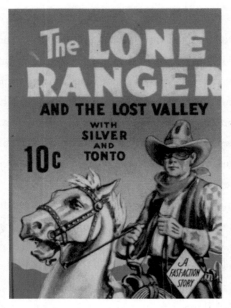

being pursued by a villain named the Cherub and his outlaw gang. Trapped in a cave, the two heroes find a lush, hidden valley accessed through a narrow cleft in sandstone. The friendly Indians inhabiting the paradise believe The Lone Ranger is the foretold Great Spirit and join with him to vanquish the intruding outlaw gang. The Lone Ranger and Tonto depart and then dynamite the entrance to ensure the valley remains hidden and peaceful.

The Lone Ranger and the Lost Valley reverts back to The Lone Ranger and Tonto riding together on top of Silver. It was not until the next Big Little Book, *The Lone Ranger and the Red Renegades* (1939, by Fran Striker), that Tonto rode a paint horse named Scout. Of the latter, the cover of the book is almost identical to the cover of the second *Lone Ranger Magazine* pulp (February 1937). The plot, involving Geronimo (a.k.a. The Red Fox) gathering his warriors to attack Fort Wade, was also adapted from the broadcast of November 25, 1933.

The Lone Ranger and the Black Shirt Highwayman (1939) was adapted from the radio broadcast of November 13, 1935 and told the story of a black-shirted outlaw named Killer Grimes, wanted throughout many counties. His numerous crimes captured the attention of The Lone Ranger and Tonto, who rode into the town of Little Rock to investigate. There, they meet with honest Sheriff Tuttle who has strict rules for the saloon and gambling hall run by Butch Beasley. Needless to say, these rules do not sit well with Butch. Late one night, as part of a plan, The Lone Ranger and Tonto attempt a robbery of the local Wells Fargo office. Tonto drops the loot when a man in a black shirt fires shots at them and they barely escape. The man, who gives his name as Bart Jones, becomes the town hero. The Lone Ranger and Tonto, still in their guise as outlaws, visit Beasley, where the masked man convinces him that "Bart Jones" is really Killer Grimes, and had told them about the money in the express office in the first place. Beasley sees opportunity and makes plans to use the young gunman to replace the old sheriff at the upcoming election. He uses the fact that Bart is supposedly Killer Grimes to blackmail him to do his bidding.

After Bart Jones is easily elected sheriff, he joins The Lone Ranger and Tonto and Beasley and his gang to hold up a stagecoach. Afterwards, Beasley leads everyone to his hideout, where The Lone Ranger and Tonto capture the entire gang. Arriving back in town, the old sheriff explains how he had followed The Lone Ranger's plan to capture the outlaws responsible for attributing more crimes to Killer Grimes, who, as is revealed, The Lone Ranger had found dead before ever even coming to Little Rock. Bart Jones turned out to be the lone survivor of a shootout with the "real" Killer Grimes. The Lone Ranger and Tonto had nursed him back to health and he had agreed to help them clean up the town. In one last twist, Bart Jones also turns out to be Tom Tuttle, the sheriff's son!

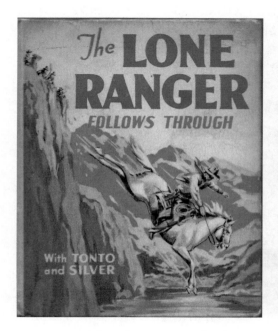 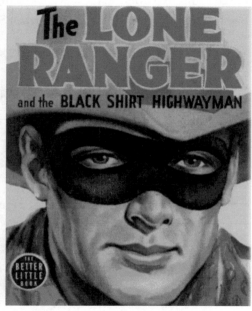

The Lone Ranger Follows Through (1941) appears to be an original story. The town of Gunstock is in need of law and order because of a murderous gang known as The Black Hat Gang. Tex Livingstone, a former Texas Ranger living in retirement outside of town, hung up his guns for ranching and raising a family. When he agrees to take up the badge again, he is shot outside his home before he can act. The Padre, a close friend of The Lone Ranger and Tonto, sends word for assistance. Tex's informant, a cow puncher who wanted to provide information to the retired lawman in return for a piece of the $500 reward, is killed before he can help. Tonto removes the bullets from Tex and saves his life, nursing the wounds. The Lone Ranger investigates, discovering no one knows who the gang members are but some in town speculate Pete Humphrey, a store owner, and Harvey Greer, a clerk in the local bank. Sheriff McCoy arrests Pete as a gang member because unsold weapons from his store were used in several killings. When The Lone Ranger learns that Jeff Gordon was involved, he arranges for the crook to be placed under arrest. Tonto secures his escape from jail and Gordon is unaware when he leads the law to a secret hideaway. The Black Hat Gang is promptly captured and the leader turns out to be Harvey Greer, the bank clerk. Potentially possible the story (or story elements) was recycled for use on "The Sheriff of Gunstock" (October 19, 1949) or "Retired Ranger" (February 22, 1950).

The Comic Strip

Following the licensing of Grosset & Dunlap hardcover novels, eight pulp magazines, and contracts for *Lone Ranger* transcription discs, Raymond Meurer reviewed and negotiated the terms with King Features Syndicate, Inc., in New York City, for newspaper comic strips. The contract was dated June 30, 1938. First drawn by Ed Kressy, he was replaced by Charles Flanders as of the newspaper strip of March 6, 1939. Flanders stayed with the strip until it ended in December 1971. The storylines for the comic strip were adapted from prior radio broadcasts and came courtesy of Fran Striker, who received authorship byline in the newspapers. In late 1943, when Striker went on strike, Bob Green replaced him, only to vacate the position when Striker returned.

1938 advertisement for the Chicago *Herald and Examiner*.

Contest in a local Reading, Pennsylvania, newspaper
from September 20, 1938.

Hi-Yo Silver! Here Comes That Daring 'Lone Ranger'

ADVENTURE! Romance! Action! Mystery! Thrills! Here comes "The Lone Ranger," riding lickety-split into Sunday's Akron Beacon Journal!

"The Lone Ranger," man of mystery, masked idol of millions, modern Robin Hood, hard-riding, fast-shooting hero of the Western Plains. Follow him in his thrilling rescues, in daring exploits, in feats of courage and grit. He'll be here with Tonto, his Indian-chief friend, and with Silver, his snow-white horse. Hi-Yo Silver!

"The Lone Ranger" is just one of the new comics to appear in the new 16-page—full size, not tabloid—color comic section of the Sunday Beacon Journal. There also will be Flash Gordon, Dixie Dugan, Off the Record, Ace Drummond, Mickey Finn, Ned Brant and Mickey Mouse.

And these favorites, too—Dick Tracy, L'il Abner, Tarzan, Big Chief Wahoo, Our Boarding House, the Curious World, Smoky Stover, Alley Oop, Boots and Her Buddies, Fritzi Ritz, Annibelle, Smilin' Jack, Dan Dunn, The Gumps, Out Our Way, Moon Mullins, Freckles and His Friends, Sweeney and Son, Captain Easy, Phil Fumble and the Katzenjammer Kids.

Sixteen full pages of the best comics available—in the Sunday Beacon Journal. You can't afford to miss them!

Promotion for the comic strip in a local Akron, Ohio, newspaper
from November 11, 1938.

Under contract, The Lone Ranger, Inc. would remain the exclusive copyright proprietor of the comic strip serial, for publications in newspapers. The Lone Ranger, Inc. would prepare, furnish, and deliver exclusively for King, story plots containing continuity, descriptive matter and other depictions for the artists to work from. It was agreed that such plots would not be the same done on radio within 90 days of delivery to King, to avoid readers recognizing the plot they may have heard in recent months, with King's artists and/or authors permission to revise, alter, and change the serial delivered to them to fit the format. Any revisions had to be approved within 36 hours of receiving the initial concept and with no response by 36 hours, it would be deemed to have been approved by The Lone Ranger, Inc. King had to provide on the first day of every fourth week a detailed itemized statement of receipts showing the amount collected, any deductible expenses, and pay The Lone Ranger, Inc. 50 percent.

The initial deal between The Lone Ranger, Inc. and Hearst was to have the strip used in conjunction with the broadcast, and the sponsor's ad appear in the final box. When it was explained by a representative at Hearst why the radio sponsor's advertisement could not be promoted in the final panel, a counteroffer was made whereby the sponsor would pay space rates. Ultimately it was agreed that local newspapers across the country could promote the radio serial in the byline section above the panels instead. Thus, many newspapers listed the local station and broadcast time alongside the strip byline. When the cliffhanger serial premiered in regional areas, a similar plug was referenced above the strip.

The newspaper strip was successful enough to warrant an extension of two years when the one-year contract came to term and was renewed for many years. As the months passed, additional newspapers signed up for printing the comic strip, providing additional income to Trendle, not to mention cross-promotion that would have cost Trendle and his business associates. After the first year, The Lone Ranger, Inc. was to receive $400 a week under the new terms. By 1945, the terms had been revised so that The Lone Ranger, Inc. was receiving 25 percent of gross receipts.

From its first appearance, September 11, 1938, in the *New York Journal American,* and many other newspapers nationwide, the Lone Ranger strip increased coverage so by 1948 it appeared through license arrangements with King Features Syndicate, that the strip appeared in 82 United States and 22 foreign countries' Sunday papers, and in 129 United States and 14 foreign countries' daily papers.

As newspapers replaced an existing comic strip for one with more potential popularity, there were some surprising results. The *Daily Dispatch* newspaper, for example, in Moline, Illinois, began carrying *The Lone Ranger* comic strip on Monday, August 13, 1951, replacing Mickey Mouse as a result of a readership survey conducted to determine the relative popularity of *Dispatch* features. Like most newspapers that decided to publish the already running *Lone Ranger* comic strip, the newspaper chose to wait until August 13 specifically because a new sequence in the story began.

Newspaper comic strips came in two different formats: daily strips and Sunday strips. The daily strip appeared in newspapers on weekdays, Monday through Saturday, and were usually printed in black and white. The Sunday strips were usually in color. The Sunday strip was also a separate story versus the one that appeared in the dailies. The comic strip artists never read the radio scripts. Fran Striker would compose a plot summary to submit to the artists, who would devise a multi-week story arc for the newspapers. A few examples can be found below.

"Mystery at Pine River" (published September 12 to October 15, 1938)
Adapted from the radio broadcast of February 9, 1938.

"The Evil Spirit" (published October 17 to November 19, 1938)
Adapted from the radio broadcast of January 21, 1938.

"Bad Men Amuck" (published November 21 to December 24, 1938)
Adapted from the radio broadcast of May 6, 1936.

"Six-Gun Saga" (published December 26, 1938 to January 28, 1939)
Adapted from the radio broadcast of April 29, 1938.

Soon after *The Lone Ranger* newspaper strip premiered in the *New York Journal American* on September 11, 1938, a doctoral dissertation was written at the University of Chicago by John J. De Boer entitled *The Emotional Responses of Children to Radio*. This dissertation is significant to the present study because it represented the first academic research to touch upon the popularity of the *Lone Ranger* series. De Boer's records, which were secured from 738 Chicago elementary school children in all grades, showed that 66 percent of the boys listened regularly to *The Lone Ranger* and ranked it first among 174 programs. Fifty-nine percent of the girls listened regularly to *The Lone Ranger* and ranked it second among 174 programs. Said De Boer: "Few radio programs possess such universality of appeal as to appear on the lists of preferences of a large number of children. It is interesting to note that only thirteen of the 174 programs listed in this study were mentioned by more than 10 percent of the children." De Boer further observed: "Boys and girls of all ages expressed enthusiastic preference for the adult adventure series, *The Lone Ranger*."

Writing earlier that same year in *The San Francisco Examiner*, columnist Darrell Donnell said, "Phantom Pilots have been roaring, Lone Rangers shooting, Renfrew riding the falls – and all to no purpose," according to John J. De Boer, important pedagogue of the Chicago Normal College. 'Noisy radio acts,' he declared in a report to the American Association for the Advancement of Science, 'do not in themselves create strong emotional responses in children. But the youngsters pay great attention to the radio announcer, to commercial announcements, to offers of gifts, and to straight narration, or stories.' When we contemplate the number of adults who have been pounding on sheet steel to create the illusion of thunder, jumping on apple boxes to simulate the breaking down of a door, howling like coyotes, and laughing like fiends, and otherwise making themselves ludicrous in the eyes of children just to advance commerce, we may be forgiven for weeping. And to think that a simple, dignified appeal to the youth of the land to urge that mother purchase a package of Tweetums breakfast food would have served the purpose adequately."

In 1939, another dissertation, *The Radio as a Factor in the Lives of Sixth Grade Children* by J.P. McKay, touched upon the popularity of *The Lone Ranger*. Attempting to discover the amount of time sixth graders in St. Louis, Missouri listened to the radio at home for a period of two weeks' duration, and what programs were the most popular, McKay concluded that *The Lone Ranger* ranked seventh in popularity with 1,233 and a half listening hours as compared with 2,021 listening hours for the *Lux Radio Theatre*, the program in first place. It is interesting to note that when McKay ranked the 25 most popular programs on a "percentage of time" basis (comparison of actual listening hours with number of possible listening hours), *The Lone Ranger* did not appear on the list.

Meanwhile, *Variety* was conducting its own poll to discover the extent to which parents approved or disapproved of the radio programs to which their children were listening. In the summary findings printed on June 28, 1939, it was discovered that *The Lone Ranger* ranked higher in terms of parental approval than any of the other shows rated. The approval sequence was as follows: (1) *The Lone Ranger*, (2) *Little Orphan Annie*, (3) *Jack Armstrong*, (4) *Dick Tracy*, (5) *Don Winslow*, (6) *Gang Busters*, (7) *Howie King* and (8) *The Green Hornet*.

In July 1939, *Radio Guide* magazine gave their annual award for the best children's program to *The Lone Ranger*. Although it was not explained on what basis the points were given, *The Lone Ranger* was first with 23.6 points. By comparison, *Little Orphan Annie* had 5.2 points and *Dick Tracy* had 4.3 points.

Also in July 1939, George W. Trendle resigned as President of the United Detroit Theatres to devote more of his time to his radio empire, including *The Lone Ranger*, which was well on its way to becoming a million-dollar property. J. Bryan III in the *Saturday Evening Post* cited King-Trendle's gross income from the newspaper cartoon strip as being $100,000; from assorted merchandise, $100,000; miscellaneous income, $50,000. "Add to these the income from the radio and The Lone Ranger, Incorporated's net for 1938 probably tops $400,000. For 1939, it will probably top half a million."

Shapiro, Bernstein & Co. registered the title "Hi-Yo Silver" with the Music Publishers Protective Association on April 5, 1939, which arrangement gave that firm, under ordinary conditions, a peremptory right to publish a tune with that title within six months. Since the words "Hi-Yo Silver" were associated in the public mind with *The Lone Ranger* radio program, the legal question arose as to whether their use commercially did not come with the provisions of unfair competition. The song written around the radio expression, "Hi-Yo Silver," taken by Chappell Music via license arrangement with Lone Ranger, Inc., was published in the first week of June 1938. Singer/songwriter Vaughn de Leath ("Are You Lonesome Tonight?") wrote the tune with Jack Erikson. It was intended to be plugged on *The Lone Ranger* radio program, but supposedly limited stations across the country played the song.

Released on 78 RPM shellac records, multiple performers recorded their own renditions including Jan Savitt and His Top Hatters, with vocals from Bon Bon and Harry Roberts, as a fox trot titled "Hi-Yo Silver," for Bluebird Records (#B-7666-A). Soloist Dick Todd sang the song with Larry Clinton and his orchestra, also for Bluebird Records (#BS-024022-1). Todd secured regular radio work on NBC in New York that same year. The same song, with Earle Graser's immortal cry launching the musical notes, was performed by Dick Robertson and his orchestra for Decca Records (#1914-64240). It was also recorded by Roy Rogers (Vocalian 04190) and Kay Kyser (Brunswick 8165) for release on 78 RPM. The sales department at the American Tobacco Company, sponsor of Kay Kyser's radio program, sent out a letter in August of 1938 suggesting the song would make the popular "Hit Parade" list – which it did not.

When Republic Pictures released the cliffhanger serials, it was suggested in the press books that theater managers play one or two of these phonograph records over the PA system to attract attention of passersby. Sheet music for "Hi-Yo, Silver" and *The Lone Ranger's Song Book: A Collection of His 50 Favorite Songs,* were also published.

Other *Lone Ranger* collectibles included clothing, toys and school supplies. A number of licensing agreements are listed below.

Norwich Knitting Co. of Norwich, New York. Sweat shorts, polo shirts of all types, knitted cotton underwear, and shorts. Contract dated June 25, 1938. Contract expired June 24, 1955.

Parker Bros, Inc. of Salem, Massachusetts. Board games, dice, and spinner, also card game. Contract dated July 19, 1938. Contract expired July 18, 1955.

Acme Plastics, Inc of Miami, Florida. A Lone Ranger movie viewer to project 16mm film, not to exceed two feet in length and a Lone Ranger Stereopticon. Contract dated June 4, 1940. Expired December 31, 1954.

Western Printing & Lithographing, Co. of Racine, Wisconsin. Books to retail at not more than 50 cents. Contract dated December 31, 1941, with new contract dated August 27, 1942. Expired December 31, 1954.

September 1938

By February 13, 1939, The Lone Ranger, Inc. had issued licensing agreements to 62 manufacturers to producer Lone Ranger items. (Most of them listed in Appendix C). By May 26, 1954, when the final contract was signed by The Lone Ranger, Inc. for Lone Ranger merchandise (for the manufacturing of The Lone Ranger Stuffed Rocking Horse to be produced by the Protection Prod. Company of Chicago, Illinois) Trendle had negotiated a total of 186 contracts since 1938. To gauge the popularity of *The Lone Ranger* in that one year alone (keeping in mind licensing did not begin until the summer of 1938), let us admire the ingenuity of department stores during that upcoming holiday.

Beginning July 1938, George W. Trendle entertained licensing agreements for *Lone Ranger* merchandise – provided the toys and accessories were wholesome products. When a number of department stores in New York City began advertising the latest of Lone Ranger apparel, the results surprised even George W. Trendle. When Abraham & Strauss paid for an ad in a November 1938 issue of the New York *Daily Mirror* to promote Lone Ranger sweatshirts, within one week the department store sold over 9,300. Another store, W.T. Grant, put 72 pairs of Lone Ranger shoes in each of ten stores on a Monday morning (which was considered not a particularly good sales day) and by the end of the day not one of the stores had a single pair of Lone Ranger shoes left. And when Gimbel Brothers of New York ran an advertisement in one New York City newspaper and sold over 6,000 *Lone Ranger* sun suits in a two-day period, they realized the potential for holiday sales required a major display.

An up-to-the-minute concern calling itself General Promotions, Inc., made a statement in December 1938 that Santa Claus was passé and about to yield in favor of a man with a mask and a horse named Silver – The Lone Ranger himself. Predating by two years both Superman and *The Shadow* becoming the highlight of a Christmas display in New York City department stores, an ad in a newspaper proclaimed: "*The Lone Ranger comes to Gimbel's! See The Lone Ranger's helper at work at his forge, casting his silver bullets. See 'Hi-Yo Silver Away' – our hero riding off in a cloud of dust!*" Sure enough, on Gimbel's seventh floor, there was a display featuring a nine-foot wooden Lone Ranger astride Silver (also wooden) and rearing dangerously. With Trendle insisting no person mimic The Lone Ranger in costume, masked or unmasked, Tonto, the loyal Indian, was also wooden. It was this display that made one newspaper columnist question whether an overabundance of Santa Clause impersonators throughout multiple department stores almost disillusioned the youngsters. According to a representative of General Promotions, "Santa Claus – he's through," he told a reporter for *The Windsor Star*. "Today it's The Lone Ranger, the biggest thing in America." To support this claim, he reeled off a list of perhaps a hundred Lone Ranger products that were available for purchase that holiday season.

It was estimated the paper mâché caves and lifelike depictions of events cost the department store $15,000 to reproduce, but Gimbels was not the only store to offer a Lone Ranger exhibit for the holidays. In Brooklyn, New York, The Lone Ranger took up quarters in a cave in Loeser's Toyland, eager to chat and shake hands with his youthful admirers and thrill them with his ringing call. With the stalwart Indian, Tonto, standing guard outside, visitors to the cave had no fear of

On the seventh floor of the Gimbels department store, children could have their photo taken alongside The Lone Ranger and Silver, for 25 cents. This photo was taken December 18, 1938.

prowling desperadoes as they heard the fearless, mysterious rider of the fleet Silver talk of the Far West in the glow of cheery log fire. Grown-ups were not allowed to enter the cave, furnished in real Western fashion with a varied assortment of animal skins, guns, pottery and cactus plants, and were therefore unable to receive any of the surprise packages handed out by The Lone Ranger and his friendly cowgirl assistant. But they could share in the excitement and enjoy the wide-eyed interest of the children by peering into a "magic mirror" that depicted the goings-on inside the cave in images about the size of a postcard. When the time came to bid The Lone Ranger farewell, the diminutive guests had little cause to be forlorn – the exit led them directly to the throne of none other than Santa Claus himself. Had George W. Trendle learned that Loeser's Toyland was breaking a taboo rule of having a man impersonate The Lone Ranger (and another impersonating Tonto), the store would have received a cease-and-desist letter from The Lone Ranger, Inc. The Lone Ranger and Tonto were not the only costumed characters at Loeser's. The fifth floor Toyland also included a clown and Donald Duck.

Gimbels department store did so well selling photos with The Lone Ranger and Silver that the store restaged the same for December of 1939.

On Christmas Eve 1938, the Senator, Illinois, *Daily Times-Press* reprinted "Dear Santa" letters from children in the community. Among the wish list items were dolls, typewriters, erector sets, Chinese checkers, a Sonja Heinie hood, and other requests. Almost ten percent of the requests were for Lone Ranger apparel and accessories, including gun and holsters, and The Lone Ranger cowboy suits. It was evident that the most popular items for Christmas that year were all Lone Ranger merchandise. In Paterson, New Jersey, more than ten percent of requests from children in the Dear

Santa letters were asking for Lone Ranger products. All of this can be summarized with the simple fact that the transcriptions helped boost popularity for *The Lone Ranger* program to a level which the prior hookup feeds were unable to accomplish.

The Lone Ranger doll available for sale in stores in December 1938.

A promotional photo distributed to visitors of the merchandising display at the Toy Mart in New York City.

This 16-page activity and coloring book was sold at The May Company during Christmas 1939. Besides the fact this book contained illustrations in both black and white and full color, the first three pages were devoted to The Lone Ranger and Tonto with text and three panels of art. The remainder of the book consisted of games and puzzles, mostly related to Christmas and Santa Claus, although one has a baseball theme. Back cover with text including "Santa Claus-The Lone Ranger-Toyland-The May Co.-Santa Claus and The Lone Ranger-7th Floor-Toyland-5th Floor."

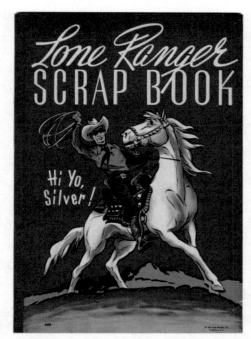

The 1938 Whitman Lone Ranger Scrap Book.

The 1938 Whitman Lone Ranger Paint Book.

The 1941 Whitman Lone Ranger Paint Book.

Among the rarest of *Lone Ranger* collectibles is the prototype calendar, created circa April 1940, with *The Green Hornet*, *Challenge of the Yukon*, *Ned Jordan, Secret Agent*, and *The Lone Ranger* portrayed, for distribution to clients but not created for retail. There was intention to include advertising matter printed inside in addition to the calendar itself.

By the end of 1940, *The Lone Ranger* was firmly established in five separate and distinct media; radio (1933), novels (1935), motion pictures (1938), comic strips (1938), and comic books (1940). That the writing of such a quantity of *Lone Ranger* adventures tended to work something of a hardship on Fran Striker was observed in a *Saturday Evening Post* article by J. Bryan III: "Edward Z.C. Judson, who wrote the Buffalo Bill stories under the name of Ned Buntline, once turned out a 600-page novel in 62 hours. Col. Prentiss Ingraham who took up the series when Judson left off, wrote a 35,000-word novel in a day. There are 773,746 words in the Bible; Gilbert Patten, author of the 776 Frank Merriwell books, wrote an equivalent wordage every four months. His total for 17 years was 35,000,000 words. Striker leads them all. He writes 60,000 words a week, every week – the equivalent of the Bible every three months… His 156 *Lone Ranger* radio scripts a year, plus 365 Lone Ranger cartoon strips, plus 12 Lone Ranger novels, plus editing the movie versions, plus his tremendous correspondence, account for two-thirds of his output. He also writes 104 *Green Hornet* scripts and 52 *Ned Jordan, Secret Agent* scripts a year for WXYZ. His working day is 14 hours; his return, $10,000 a year, or around a third of a cent a word."

By 1941, *The Lone Ranger* radio program added two more to the response statistics. From Detroit, a Detroit commercial surveying concern in November 1941, Commercial Services, conducted a survey in the public schools of Detroit for a client. The question was: "What one man would you like to hear on a radio program?" Each of the 250 youngsters interviewed, ages between seven and fifteen years, was given first, second, third, and fourth choices. The rated index of popularity (allowing four points for first, three for second, etc.) revealed that *The Lone Ranger* led the pack with a rating of 13.1 (over 14, when Tonto's rating was included). From New York, a giveaway was conducted in connection with *The Lone Ranger* program by Raymond Spector and a limited number of announcements produced over 60,000 requests from listeners in the New York market for *Lone Ranger* disguise kits.

See Appendix E for another case study of *The Lone Ranger*'s popularity.

Date _____

The King-Trendle Broadcasting Corporation
Detroit, Michigan

Gentlemen:

For and in consideration of the sum of One Dollar ($1.00), and other good and valuable considerations, receipt of which is hereby acknowledged, I hereby grant to you, your successors, transferees, licensees, and assigns (hereafter collectively designated "assignees"), for a period of ten (10) years from the date hereof, the absolute right to make whatever use of my name, initials or nickname in conjunction with any literary composition as assignee in any manner shall do, including but not restricting the same to radio broadcasting, television, recordings of all types, comic strip adaptation, advertising, merchandising, books, magazines, periodicals, motion pictures (silent or with sound), dramas, stage plays, including the right to copyright or otherwise protect the same in accordance with any statute made and provided.

It is understood and agreed that my name or any part thereof may be used as the name of any character even though the character bearing my name may be depicted or portrayed as a desperate and hardened criminal, who has committed or does commit numerous serious and loathesome crimes, who is being sought by law enforcement authorities, who is a fugitive from Justice and whose acts and speech may arouse the hatred, contempt and scorn of law abiding citizens, or may be depicted or portrayed as an object of pity or ridicule.

It is also understood that any literary composition or adaptations thereof which mentions or depicts any character bearing my name will not be submitted to me for any approval whatsoever.

I hereby expressly release assignee of and from any and all liability under any Slander, Libel, and so-called Right of Privacy laws growing out of any use of my name as herein authorized.

_____ (SEAL)

WITNESS:

_____

Disclosure statement cast and crew had to sign to allow their likeness and image to appear in magazines and newspapers for publicity purposes.

June 1938

August 1938

September 1938

September 1938

October 1938   November 1938

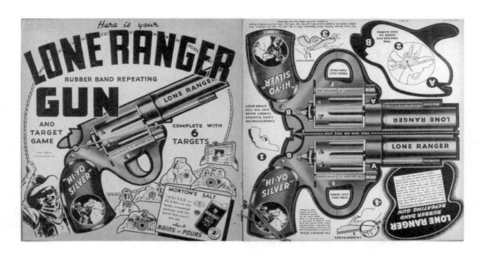

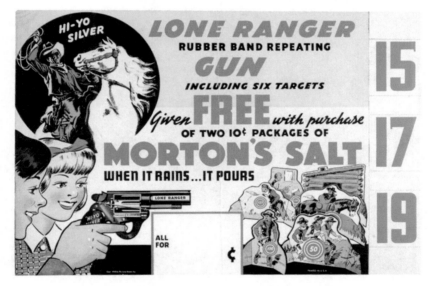

Morton Salt offered a rubber band gun and dart game in late 1938.

THE LONE RANGER AND SILVER

Chapter Eight
The Mythology

ANNOUNCER: *When the masked rider of the plains first started his fight for law and order in the early western United States, many people believed him to be an outlaw. It was not until later when Silver and his faithful Indian companion, Tonto, became familiar figures, that they recognized the masked rider as the greatest champion of justice that the west ever knew.*

ALMOST IMMEDIATELY AFTER TRENDLE commissioned transcriptions of *The Lone Ranger* beginning in February 1938, the recurring character of Cactus Pete was dropped from the long-running radio program. No longer would Cactus and his Ranch Revelers be heard on the thrice-a-week western. Thankfully, the character of Cactus Pete was preserved on transcription disc – twice – after the transcriptions commenced, providing us today with an example of how the character was portrayed prior.

For the broadcast of February 7, 1938, a crooked sheriff and a crooked border patrol agent conspire to protect their liquor smuggling by framing Cactus Pete for the crimes, unaware that he is a friend of The Lone Ranger, who would ride to his rescue. Cactus Pete's other appearance was for a special broadcast on December 7, 1938.

It was during that week in December 1938, commemorating the radio program's fifth anniversary, that a week-long celebration consisted of three special radio broadcasts. On the evening of December 5, 1938, the cast recreated a performance of the very first radio script from January 31, 1933… with one notable difference. In the original broadcast, the masked vigilante rode up to the lynching party, shot the villain dead, and proved that Logan was the real claim jumper by revealing Ezra's proof of ownership pre-dating the crooks. As Ezra tells his wife Millie later that evening: "Wal, the Sheriff, he ain't given tuh lyin' Millie, an' he says he never seen such shootin' as that feller done. Each an' every one of the men was shot clean thru the forehead, an' he says that the bullets were made of solid silver." For the December 5, 1938, broadcast, however, the ending was changed as The Lone Ranger shot the gun out of the villain's hand and held a gun against the remaining seven of the outlaws until the sheriff arrived to take control of the situation.

Newspaper advertisement from April 1937.

For the broadcast of December 7, 1938, Cactus Pete recounts the legend of how The Lone Ranger first met Tonto, his faithful Indian companion. Cactus Pete acts in the capacity of a narrator and not a character. The story concerned two miners who, having set off a blast, hear a faint voice calling for help. Buried in the landslide was the half-breed known as Tonto. One of the miners wanted to kill him immediately, rather than have him recover and scalp them in their sleep, but The Lone Ranger happened to be riding along (having heard the sound of the blast) and at gunpoint forced them to spare the half-breed's life. This script was a repeat of episode #12 of the radio program, broadcast February 25, 1933, and while the opening was added to incorporate Cactus Pete, the fact that the series was not recorded on a regular basis until early 1938 makes the extant recording from 1938 (and the other two broadcasts that week) all the more valuable for *Lone Ranger* fans.

ANNOUNCER: *There have been countless requests for information regarding Silver, the famous horse of the Lone Ranger. People have written asking what kind of horse it was, where it came from, whence came its tremendous strength, tireless energy, and lightning speed. Of course, the greatest mystery surrounds the origin of both the Lone Ranger and Silver, but there is a legendary story concerning the beautiful milk-white stallion, and tonight, in one of the most unusual of the Lone Ranger dramas, we are going to tell you the legend as it has been handed down through generations. The Lone Ranger did not always ride Silver. Before the fame of the mystery rider spread throughout the length and breadth of seven states, there was another horse. One called Dusty. It is this chestnut mare that is being ridden to a hitchrack outside the Six-Gun Café.*

Newspaper advertisement from August 1938.

The third and final anniversary tribute was on the evening of December 9, 1938, recounting the origin of Silver, the trusted stallion of The Lone Ranger, originally broadcast on the evening of August 26, 1935. The mythology of The Lone Ranger as it related to his origin, and the origin of Tonto, would be revised over the years, each with variations, verifying that the characters were developed over time and not created overnight. Such development requires deconstructing the continuity in a meticulous manner, but with understanding that assembling a list for consistent chronology is futile due to the number of variations. During the early years, from 1933 through 1941, Fran Striker wrote the majority of the radio scripts and therefore maintained what continuity he could. By 1942, George Waller and Tom Dougall were writing scripts, each with their own distinct style and rendition of the characters.

As an example, in the episode "Cattleman Cash," broadcast July 24, 1942, The Lone Ranger describes the villain Meecham with "his ugly face." In the episode "Murder Masters," broadcast on November 4, 1942, The Lone Ranger has an argument with Tonto, punches him and knocks him out, to ensure if anyone gets shot from ambush, it would be him and not his Indian friend. In the episode "Sign of the Swastika," broadcast December 7, 1942, The Lone Ranger wings someone with a bullet, instead of shooting the criminal's gun out of their hand.

The episode "Stagecoach to Blue River," broadcast July 31, 1942, was clearly not written by Fran Striker. The story provides a major public service message for the plight of juvenile delinquency and a rare moment when a sheriff, in an act of cowardice, turns in his badge and fails to uphold the law. The unusual story premise and execution, including top-notch dialogue, might make this arguably the best episode of the calendar year. With other writers that followed in 1943, continuity would – on occasion – be disregarded.

As an example, in radio broadcasts from 1938 through 1942, the following is a list of direct references to the wardrobe of The Lone Ranger and Tonto:

September 5, 1938 – Tonto claims he does not smoke.

May 22, 1939 – The Lone Ranger wore a white sombrero.

August 18, 1939 –The Lone Ranger wore a bandana.

November 6, 1940 – The Lone Ranger wore a sombrero.

December 4, 1940 – The sheriff says The Lone Ranger's sombrero hung so low it hid his mask.

March 7, 1941 – The Lone Ranger wore a wide-brimmed Stetson.

March 12, 1941 – The Lone Ranger wore a Stetson.

February 27, 1942 – The Lone Ranger wore a white hat.

September 2, 1942 – The Lone Ranger dressed in black.

September 18, 1942 –The Lone Ranger wears a dark shirt.

On the broadcasts of September 23, October 16 and 21, November 6, 9, 20, and 30, 1942, it was referenced that Tonto wore buckskin. On the broadcasts of October 21, November 6, 9, 11, 18, 30, and December 7, 1942, it was referenced that The Lone Ranger wore a white hat (which would clash if he was dressed in black). *

Tonto's medicinal gifts for healing wounds and tending the ill were demonstrated numerous times on the program, but some of his other talents were explored, too, courtesy of other scriptwriters. On the broadcast of May 30, 1941, Tonto was able to tell the time by looking at the stars. On the broadcast of June 30, 1941, The Lone Ranger mentions that "Tonto has many friends among the tribes."

As for The Lone Ranger, his sharpshooting skills and acts of bravery were demonstrated in almost every episode, often disarming the criminal. The masked man's character was explored a number of times, such as the episode, "The Pony Express Agent," broadcast January 17, 1941, when a shady politician named Sealy, attempting to line his own pockets, confronts The Lone Ranger.

SEALY: You speak like an Easterner.

RANGER: Perhaps I was. Perhaps I found the east too full of politics and corruption in public offices. Perhaps I sought a country where there wasn't such internal conspiracy. Isn't that quite possible?

---

* The continuity would continue to waver over the next few years but listed above covers only 1938 through 1942 as it pertains to the years covered in this book and will be explored again in the next volume beginning with 1943.

In the episode, "Little Rose," broadcast September 3, 1941, an angry mob of hundreds feared they might be evicted from their land if their property was turned over to Rosita, as a result of the De Leon land grant, so The Lone Ranger raced through the mob to rescue the girl. Later, the masked man had to justify his reasons to a judge.

JUDGE: I believe you're the man who kidnapped the De Leon girl.

RANGER: It wasn't a kidnapping.

JUDGE: They say you're The Lone Ranger, but if that's true I can't understand it at all. I thought you always worked on the side of the law.

RANGER: I work for justice.

The mysterious past of The Lone Ranger, before the massacre that made him launch his career of vigilante justice, was explored in a number of episodes. In "Mistaken for an Easterner" (May 13, 1942), a crooked lawyer named Big Daniel, who is also the owner of the local bank, hires Dirk and Blackie to drive a stage line owner out of business by robbing the mail and burning the stages. The Lone Ranger, disguised as an Easterner in town, attempts to encourage ol' Fighting Jim to grow the backbone he once had by preparing for a fight.

RANGER: Remember that time when you warned the Texas Rangers about an ambush? You told them about 50 men that were ahead of them? And then you fought side by side with six Rangers and cleaned out the gang?

On the broadcast of January 18, 1939, The Lone Ranger's past was revealed in part with a surprising revelation: the famed General Armstrong Custer knew the identity of the masked man. In the turbulent days when the Civil War had ended, and it was the desire of the President to conquer the savage Indian tribes of the west and make the country safe for white pioneers, men who knew the country were highly valued as scouts. When a solitary rider in a tattered Army uniform made his way through the broken country beneath a pale moon, he found The Lone Ranger, to whom he was to deliver an important message.

RANGER: You were to bring an important message for me.

MESSENGER: Important, stranger, the hull future of the west… may count… on you. The… the General… wants help.

RANGER: He may have anything I can give him. The General who sent you, is the one man on earth who knows my identity.

MESSENGER: General Custer?

RANGER: Yes. Where is the message?

The message was addressed to The Lone Ranger's real name, a promise General Custer made to ensure he would only use unless his life depended on it. The Indians have rifles and are using them against the white men. Colonel Williams does not know the Indians acquired the rifles, which is why Custer fears a massacre. He needs The Lone Ranger to show Williams the pass through the hills to Little Bear River, else he will face Blackfeet and his tribe. Custer learned of the news through Indian scouts, and figured the only person who could help was The Lone Ranger. After making the messenger comfortable, The Lone Ranger and Tonto packed their horses and started on the ride toward the garrison commanded by Colonel Williams. But Colonel Williams was stubborn and insisted the masked man was leading him on to a trap. For an unknown reason, news from Custer never reached the garrison so Williams still believed he and his men would face bows and arrows. The Lone Ranger promised to lead them around the Blackfeet, so they could move into Little Bear River without being wiped out in a battle against them.

COLONEL: And why do you choose to conceal your identity?

RANGER: I've found that I can accomplish more in helping to build the west, if I am an unknown.

The Colonel explains to The Lone Ranger that he received no message. No doubt because General Custer is dead. Word comes during the night that he died into a trap, and, in the words of the colonel, "perhaps just as you're trying to lead me into one." Custer met 6,000 Indians and every one of his own men was wiped out. The Lone Ranger defies the request to hand over his guns and be placed under arrest, choosing instead to flee away as fast as he could.

The Colonel was suspicious of his every move, even though his ten-year-old son recounted the tales he had heard of The Lone Ranger, and suspected someone may have even been masquerading as the legendary figure. When The Lone Ranger rode away, escaping capture by the troops, the Colonel gave no order to follow. The day was spent preparing for the march at midnight, the march that would, unless the masked mystery rider could act, become a death march for every soldier under Colonel Williams. At the stroke of midnight, the bugle was sounded, and men and horses fell into the ranks, ready to ride toward Little Bear, and the Indian trap ahead. Meanwhile, darkness covered The Lone Ranger and Tonto riding near the fort. The masked man know if the Colonel learned the Indians were waiting in ambush and knew they were armed with rifles, before he led his men into the area, he would have time to sound a retreat. He might be able to find his way through the mountain trail, and get past the savages, if he was warned. The Lone Ranger decided to ride a half a mile ahead of the troops. When they got close to the Indians, the masked man would charge the camp, the Indians would have to start firing, and that would warn the army men. Tonto would remain behind to act as a guide for the troops.

RANGER: Tonto, you and I have ridden a long trail together, and shared everything. This is one thing I'll not share with you.

TONTO: Tonto ride-um to Indian!

RANGER: There is one thing that can never be changed. You were born an Indian. It isn't justice that you should be the one to be killed by your own people, to help the white man.

TONTO: Those bad Indian!

RANGER: Not bad, Tonto, not always! They just haven't learned to think, and live, and understand things, as white folks do. They must be taught.

TONTO: Army find-up way through trail, alone! We go-um, together! Only few red man, get-um chance, die-um to save army!

RANGER: I understand, Kemo Sabay.

TONTO: Long time, we ride-um same trail. Now get-um to end at same time!

RANGER: There's just one way that I could stop you, Tonto, but I can't tie you up and leave you. If you want it so, we'll attack the savages… together.

Two strong men, The Lone Ranger and Tonto, waited in the saddle, firmly convinced that this would be their last night on earth, and ready to meet the end, with the same western courage they had shown throughout all their travels and adventures. One hour brought the troops in hearing, and then for another hour, the two were nothing but an occasional shadow, far ahead of Colonel Williams. Then The Lone Ranger rode to the troops and gave another warning. He explained how the Indians were armed with rifles and had plenty of ammunition. He gave instructions that if the troops were to circle to the south, and take the trail through the mountains, they could get past the redskins and reach Little Bear in safety. He then provided very specific instructions along the mountain trail that provided landmarks indicating a specific Northwest course, necessary for their safety. To prove his sincerity, he explained the desperate action both he and Tonto would take to verify the story.

Newspaper advertisement from September 1938.

The Lone Ranger and Tonto raced into the valley to put up a good fight, exchanging fast shots amidst the war cries and shouting from the Indians. Amidst the battle, furious rifle fire echoed through the valley and the army was taken by surprise. The Indians, routed from their hiding places, were compelled to attack The Lone Ranger and Tonto, but were taken so greatly by surprise, that they barely had a chance to leap to their horses before the mighty Silver was among them. The white horse reared high, then whirled, side-stepped and spun, using all the tricks the masked man had taught him, as hard a target as possible. The sharp, silver-shod hoofs rose high, then lashed down at the enemies who clamored close. In such close quarters, the Indians had difficulty bringing their rifles to bear, and not used to the weapons, many of their shots brought down their own men. The intruders surrounded, the savages drew knives and tomahawks, and fought close to the masked man and Tonto. The heroes had several wounds, but none of them serious. And then, when the end seemed close at hand, a new sound split the night. The clear tones of a bugle. A new burst of firing, accompanied by a thunder of 600 horses' hoofs, announced the coming of the troops. Colonel Williams commanded the charge. But this was no army taken by surprise. It was an army of grim men, plunging to the attack, and to the rescue.

"He's The Lone Ranger!" shouted the Colonel. "All my boy said was true! Get that man out of there alive! Get to him, use those swords! Club your rifles! Men, men save the life of that man! He's a friend of General Custer! He's The Lone Ranger!"

Slashing, hacking, fighting their way to The Lone Ranger and Tonto, cavalrymen half-carried him, while others did the same for Tonto. Then the fight was short. The Indians saw hopeless defeat, and those who survived, took flight. After the noise and commotion ceased, Colonel Williams offered his apologies. They could not leave him to die, thinking the army of the nation he loved would let him down. The Colonel was about to send a messenger back to the garrison to report to his wife and son, but The Lone Ranger knew he needed to rest for a spell and the garrison would be best. This would also allow him, the masked man, to deliver the message that the troops met and conquered the Indians. Such a tale told from the lips of The Lone Ranger himself would be a rare treat to the boy.

"Tonto, we've kept faith with General Custer," The Lone Ranger remarked to his comrade, "and our President's confidence in us has been justified." Little did the masked man know at the time that the President of the United States had more than confidence in him and would demonstrate it later in a lengthy story arc known as "The Legion of the Black Arrow." (More about that later in this chapter.)

While monumental events were not restricted to single-broadcast adventures, the larger challenges for The Lone Ranger and Tonto were dramatized in multi-part adventures that spanned multiple episodes. While fans of the program today have the advantage of knowing how long a particular story arc ran, courtesy of broadcast logs and reference guides (such as this book), radio listeners during the 1930s, '40s, and '50s did not have the same benefit. A story arc was only established for the listener towards the end of the broadcast, and it was never revealed when the story arc would be concluded until the final adventure. On many story arcs, every broadcast had a conclusion to the story, but the villain would be sure to return on the next broadcast.

Beginning with the broadcast of April 4, 1938, The Lone Ranger went up against the much sought-for character known as The Red, who had recently fled from the town of Fargo. No one knows the motives for his crimes. As an example, the other night in town, The Red stole $500 from the banker named Simms, but deliberately left behind the other $500 that he could have easily stolen.

The next day, a local named Jones paid a visit to Banker Simms to pay off his mortgage -- $500 – but the banker could not verify it was the same bills stolen the night before. As word got around, The Red was referred to as a modern-day Robin Hood and providing a service to the community.

Despite the fact that he did not have red hair, the masked Lone Ranger was mistaken for The Red as he and Tonto rode into town. Tonto was wounded and captured by the law, suspected of being an accomplice to "The Red." The only way the Lone Ranger could free his injured friend, was to bring back Dave Tuttle alive. In truth, Dave Tuttle was merely trying to help some old folks in Fargo by committing a robbery while wearing a red-haired wig. He immediately became known to lawmen, as "The Red." When circumstances made it appear that Dave was guilty of countless unsolved crimes, he had to flee the town of Fargo to save himself.

"The Red" was accused of thefts until the killing of a crooked gambler named Abe Darwin. Deputized men went out in search of The Red but they returned to Fargo without picking up any sign of his trail. There was one man who kept close to the outlaw, however. Throughout the day and most of the night, The Lone Ranger followed the faint trail left by Dave Tuttle. He rested only as long as necessary, and then continued on his way with the first faint light of dawn. The sides of the rocky hills over which the trail led, were covered with shale, which made uncertain footing for the strong white horse, but the masked man pressed on.

Meanwhile, Dave met with his friend Buck Barton and while riding through the hills, discussed how Dave wanted to pay a visit to Abe Darwin, only to discover him dead on the floor. It was lawmen who mistakenly believed "The Red" committed the crime. Buck, wanting to help assist with his friend, set up a few kegs of powder to explode and create a rockslide, blocking the trail and the masked man who was following them. When the rocks slid downhill, Silver slipped with them, his four hoofs pawing frantically in space while The Lone Ranger freed himself from the saddle. From a distance, Dave Tuttle watched with horror in his eyes as The Lone Ranger was buried in sand and shale up to his armpits. Dave and Buck observed how the great horse Silver went over to his master to help him get out of the trap. Catching up to their pursuer, Buck, Dave's friend, roped the neck of Silver and quickly tied it to a tree to prevent the beast from aiding. The Lone Ranger insisted on apprehending and bringing Dave back to Fargo. Without Dave, Tonto would face a hangman's noose.

Buck accused the masked man of being The Red. Realizing the name of the horse was Silver, and his Indian friend was Tonto, Dave realized the masked man was not The Red, but The Lone Ranger. Dave drew his gun and threatened to shoot Buck if he made a move against the vigilante. Dave turned to The Lone Ranger and promised to get him out of the shale in return for an hour's start.

"I won't promise that, Dave!" The Lone Ranger remarked. "If it were simply to take you to Fargo for trial, I would, but that's not the case. Tonto's wounded. The lawmen will try and make him tell things that he doesn't know. The only way to help him, is to take you back, and that is what I'm going to do, unless you kill me."

Using a knife and cutting the rope that held Silver, Dave watched as The Lone Ranger was pulled out of the shale thanks to his steed. Dave voluntarily lowered his guns to the ground while Buck reluctantly lowered his. Buck warns Dave that the young man will find himself swinging at the end of a rope in no time, but Dave believes otherwise. "I ain't figurin' on hangin'," he remarked. "The Lone Ranger is on my side!"

In the second episode, broadcast April 6, with so many unsolved crimes, and an election around the corner, the sheriff insists Dave Tuttle is guilty, and the young man firmly believes he will be hung within two days after he is brought into town. The Lone Ranger firmly believes Dave is innocent, having saved his life from the rockslide and could have taken advantage of the chance to kill the masked man and make an escape. On the ride back to Fargo, The Lone Ranger asks Dave how Buck became a friend. Dave explained that he hauled Buck out of a bed of quicksand when he first came to Fargo, and figured Buck wanted to return the favor and save Dave from the hangman's rope. It had been Buck's idea to set the fuse and plant the blasting powder, not Dave's. The Lone Ranger, however, had his suspicions.

At a waterhole a few hours out of Fargo, The Lone Ranger waters his horse and then asks Dave to remain behind and set up camp. The masked man wants to return to town to scout out the scenario there. He trusts Dave to remain until he returns. Late that evening, Deputy Kurt Forsythe and his deputies are meeting in the lawman's office. Tonto is still imprisoned in an adjoining room, with a barred door. Though the Indian's wound causes him a lot of pain, he ignores it in his eagerness to hear and remember all the lawmen said. One of the men informs the sheriff that they believe Abe Darwin might have dropped dead from a heart attack, because there were no external wounds and the local doctor could not find any evidence of murder. Outside the office window, The Lone Ranger overhears the entire discussion.

Confronting The Lone Ranger, the sheriff insists on charging Dave Tuttle with murder. "I was going to turn Dave Tuttle over to you, but I thought I'd come to town first and find out if he'd get an honest deal. I find he won't," the masked man remarks. "But instead of bringing Tuttle here to prove that Tonto isn't guilty of the things you've charged him with, I'm calling on the United States Marshal."

The Lone Ranger rode away to rejoin Dave Tuttle and take him to the United States Marshal. Buck had, in the meantime, found the camp and insisted on helping Dave flee the scene and get as far away from Fargo as possible. But during an exchange of Dave's stubbornness to remain, Buck accidentally gives himself away. He confesses to the robbery of an express office and the murder of the clerk, the robbery at Mort Bevan's house, and half a dozen other crimes in town. His goal was to have Dave continue being hunted so no one from Fargo would be looking for someone else.

The Lone Ranger was urging his great horse Silver to his utmost speed, dashing toward the town of Meredith, where the U.S. Marshal was stationed. While explaining the scenario to the lawman, The Lone Ranger was aware that the sheriff and his men followed the tracks of the masked rider of the great white horse. At noon they left Meredith, after learning that the Marshal had ridden away with The Lone Ranger. The tracks of the two were clear across the plain toward the distant hills.

Later the next afternoon brought Buck Barton and Dave Tuttle to the shack where Barton lived. Forced at gunpoint from the camp, Dave found himself dismounting his horse and ordered to saddle a fresh mount. Then he was ordered to pick up a sack formerly owned by the express office with some of the stolen goods. Buck planned to shoot Dave in the back and play the role of the hero. Before the crime could be committed, however, the gun in Buck's hand was shattered. The Lone Ranger had aimed carefully, and the U.S. Marshal informs the outlaw that he overheard the entire conversation, clearing the names of Dave Tuttle… and Tonto.

While Dave will be found guilty of small petty thefts, the reward for the capture of Buck, who committed the express robbery, will repay what he took from Banker Simms.

In the third episode of the trilogy, broadcast April 8, the sheriff placed Dave Tuttle in jail for the crime of stealing cash from the banker, even though the equivalent was returned to Banker Simms. The latter was downright powerful in town and prodded the sheriff to give Dave all that he could – including a ten-year jail sentence. While Dave and Buck sat in jail, Buck laughed. He firmly believed there was not enough evidence for him to be found guilty in a court of law. Tonto, having had a fresh bandage applied to his wound, returned to the camp of The Lone Ranger where he would remain for a few days until he was fully healed. The Lone Ranger realized that the only way Buck Barton could be convicted was to get the crook to reveal his hiding place where all of the stolen goods could be found. As long as he kept his secret, there would be a question about his guilt.

That evening, a stranger drifted into the café at Fargo. His tall form stood in the doorway for a moment, while he studied the assembled men. Then he sauntered casually to the bar and took his place next to one of the sheriff's deputies, whose hand was bandaged. Kurt and the sheriff were determined to find Dave Tuttle guilty of Buck Barton's crimes, and then the U.S. Marshal arrived, demanding the arrest of the stranger, who was in reality, The Lone Ranger. *

Arrested on suspicion of being The Frisco Kid, The Lone Ranger is taken to the sheriff's office where our hero witnesses the sheriff taking Buck out of the jail. In a back room, the lawman strikes a deal with the crooks. If Dave, not Buck, is found guilty of the crimes, Buck would be a free man. But such an arrangement would come at a price and the stolen cash Buck had hidden was worth a tidy sum even after splitting the goods. Buck would not trust the lawman, however, insisting he take them personally to the hiding place.

Later that same night, while Kurt watches the prison from the sheriff's office and another guard is posted outside, The Lone Ranger, still disguised, wakes Dave Tuttle. Shortly before the sun comes up, Tonto quietly gags the guard and ropes him. After removing the bars from the window, the disguised Lone Ranger explains to Dave that he must remain in jail until he is proven not guilty. Outside, The Lone Ranger removed his makeup, placed his gun belt back on, then his mask. Riding together across the plains on their great white horses, from the other side, came riders to join them… led by the United States Marshal.

After arresting Buck and the sheriff, the marshal and his men begin close inspection of the rocks, where they find the stolen cash. The sheriff, looking at a serious charge in the face of a superior, quickly insists that Buck was the masked killer, the man they want. The marshal laughs, revealing there was no Frisco Kid at all. The Lone Ranger insists that to right such a mistake would be to make sure Dave Tuttle has a chance to repay Banker Simms and square himself and be allowed to go free. "And at the same time, see that Benton pays in full for what he's done."

The sheriff is crooked, but now has to play straight until the trial is over; otherwise, he proves himself to be what Benton would call him… a crook. Because the sheriff has to let Dave go free, the banker makes sure the sheriff is replaced by someone else, so everyone will get what they deserve.

---

* The name Barton actually changed to Benton by the third episode of the trilogy, a continuity error that was never caught during rehearsals.

In February 1939, The Lone Ranger encountered another foe whose criminal exploits would be dramatized over three trilogies: "The Black Caballero." Each of the three Black Caballero story arcs aired over the course of one week, Monday, Wednesday, and Friday, with director Charles Livingstone playing the recurring role of a daring, Zorro-like swashbuckler. Each of the story arcs aired a few months apart, the first of the three running from February 13 to 17, 1939.

Suddenly, without warning, there appeared in the border country the most spectacular outlaw ever known to the West. Wearing a black mask and cape, riding the midnight stallion known as El Diablo, this mysterious figure called himself The Black Caballero. When he struck, it was with the blinding speed of lightning. He mocked both the law and those settlers who lived within the law. Within a month of his first appearance, his name had become a dreaded byword. When The Black Caballero challenged The Lone Ranger to be present when he planned to rob the bank at River City, the masked rider of justice accepted. When news of the coming contest became generally known, word spread through town and bets were placed as to who would be the victor. But the masked man soon discovered the plot: the outlaw's men were to create a distraction in River City while The Black Caballero was really robbing a bank in White Springs. The Black Caballero was surprised and his scheme foiled. As he was escorted to the law he swore, "No jail built can hold me!"

In the second chapter of the saga, true to the boast he had made at the time, The Black Caballero had been behind bars scarcely two weeks when one morning it was discovered that he had escaped from the jail at White Springs during the night. He did not leave the district, however, and instead continued his spree of crime. Sheriff Ramsey, campaigning for re-election, found himself accused of freeing The Black Caballero when some of the outlaw's money found its way into his pockets. After Deputy Steve Hanley resigned from his post and left town, he teamed with The Lone Ranger to help prove that the sheriff was employed by the outlaw. Pedro, who also worked for the notorious outlaw, is trailed by Tonto to the outlaw's camp. A U.S. Marshal makes an arrest of both the sheriff and The Black Caballero.

The Black Caballero was like no other outlaw the Lone Ranger had ever met. Courageous, clever, and gallant, the man challenged the law far less for bragging rights than for adventure. Twice already he had met the masked man and had been twice defeated. It was his conviction, however, that in a clear-cut contest he could yet prove himself The Lone Ranger's master. In the third part of the three-part story arc, though confined to jail in White Springs, awaiting trial, he sets his active mind to plotting another escape. Sharing his cell was the former sheriff, against whom had been filed charges of conspiracy with The Black Caballero. Members of the outlaw's gang break them both out of jail, then plan to rob the Whitfield Stage. The Black Caballero masquerades as a passenger to gain the upper hand during the robbery. To ensure escape, blasting powder was placed under a bridge to prevent the law from following. Tonto, spotting the outlaw's camp, warns The Lone Ranger, who races back to scare all the horses away so the outlaws would be stranded and picked up by the law. The Black Caballero, realizing his scheme is foiled, grabs one horse and attempts to flee but his steed is no match for Silver in the chase.

The second of the three trilogies aired from May 29 to June 2, 1939. In a private meeting between Major Winthrop of the U.S. and Captain Lopez of Mexico, a discussion took place to determine what could be done about a recent rash of escapades that had built tension between the two countries. Along the country's borders on the Rio Grande there represented a scene of 15 raids, each resulting in a score of men killed, cattle and money stolen. The situation built up and was ready to explode in a manner that neither government could control. It was recently learned through spies that the raids were not only organized, but led by two men representing both nationalities, working together to stir up trouble: J.B. Bronson and Miguel "Pancho" Chavez, both traitors to their countries. Both governments were not only friendly but wished to remain that way. Bronson and Chavez, however, were doing everything in their power disturb those relations. Bronson was staging raids hoping that both governments would be forced into a quarrel. Such a quarrel, developing into armed fighting, would not be popular with Mexico. It might even lead to the election of a new government. That is where Chavez would step in as he led the opposition and he could assume power. Bronson would also profit. Without proof, neither man could be arrested for the crimes. The army was powerless to stop the raids because any interference could result in lighting a fuse.

The Lone Ranger agrees to step in and take control of the situation, granted authority from both the U.S. and the Mexican armies to cross the border and thwart the schemes of Bronson and Chavez. In order to outnumber the cunning criminals, The Lone Ranger requests the release of the man known as The Black Caballero, who was presently behind bars at a district penitentiary. The masked man knows that The Black Caballero will agree to his particular methods and knows the country south of the border better than he.

"He broke the law, but he was never a criminal at heart," The Lone Ranger explains. "He loved adventure. He broke the law not for gain but for the excitement it gave him. I can honestly say he is one of the few men I thoroughly respect." Major Winthrop hesitates to this request, but in desperation to thwart a war, he approves it.

Early the next morning, The Black Caballero is being escorted to the dungeon to face what inmates refer to as the black hole, punishment served by the sadistic Warden Hogan to force prisoners to reveal the location of their stashed money. The black hole is a hole in the ground with no light, no room to sit or lay down. The prisoners receive grub once every three days which is a long way apart when prisoners suffering in the black hole could not tell when the days and nights passed. Before he could become the next victim to Hogan's crooked method of torture, The Lone Ranger, who had snuck into the penitentiary under cover of night, rescues the Zorro-like inmate. Bull, the prison guard, is forced to temporarily suffer the same fate he was about to exercise on The Black Caballero.

CABALLERO: [laughs] Ah, this is a great day my friend! Already I am once more a happy man. To think of my good friend, the guard, in the same pit where he would have put me? [laughs] That is a pleasure indeed!

RANGER: I've come here for a purpose Black Caballero. You know we were once enemies…

CABALLERO: But never were there enemies like us, amigo. We did not hate. It was only for sport that we opposed each other.

RANGER: I'm going to free you.

CABALLERO: Free me?

RANGER: Yes?

CABALLERO: But amigo, that I do not understand. Is it that you are no longer on the side of the law?

RANGER: No. I'm going to free you because you are needed.

CABALLERO: Needed?

RANGER: There's danger along the border, Black Caballero. Danger brought about by traitors to your country and mine. These traitors hope to involve our countries in war. The army cannot act. I've promised our aid.

CABALLERO: Whatever you say, that I will do.

RANGER: I think that together we can bring those traitors to justice.

While Tonto fetched the horses, including El Diablo, the horse owned by The Black Caballero, The Lone Ranger and The Black Caballero paid a visit to the warden in his office. Hogan, having enforced graft and abuse against the inmates, was ordered to sign a confession. The warden opposed. The Lone Ranger ensured that great harm would beset him by the hands of the inmates if a confession was not written out and signed by 10 o'clock. The warden believed his captors were bluffing. The clock ticked off by the second. But at 10 o'clock, the gates were flung open, and the inmates were free. Naturally, their first inclination is to make for the warden's office. Panicking, Hogan confesses to profiting from the criminals. After getting the confession, The Lone Ranger orders the men back to their cells, assuring them that Hogan would soon join them as he will be tried and found guilty. With no escape route ensured, the prisoners slowly returned to their cells.

Hogan laughs, certain that his forced confession would not be believed in a court of law, only to be shocked when Major Winthrop reveals he was within listening distance of the confession as it happened and ensures Hogan that he would indeed be found guilty. Laughing at how justice turned against the unlawful who thought he was above the law, The Black Caballero jumped on top of El Diablo and rode off with Tonto and The Lone Ranger side by side.

In the second episode, word spread of The Lone Ranger and The Black Caballero riding the border country. Pancho Chavez, meanwhile, is conspiring with Bronson to run for office so they can expand their operation. The whereabouts of the criminals are not a secret. The Lone Ranger and his partner enter their hideout to get the advantage. With The Black Caballero backing his play, The Lone Ranger enforces his authority. "You're a traitor to your country, Bronson. You and every man who works for you. We know your game. We know you've hired outlaws from the north to stir up trouble. You have stolen uniforms. Your men strike across the Rio masquerading as soldiers from the south. You are trying to arouse the people of Texas and to start a war if possible. You have paved the way for the election of your crooked friend, Pancho Chavez… I think their relations will improve if you clear out. I said clear out, go north cross the Rio, and stay there!"

Bronson, however, does not heed the warning and plots an act against the masked men. Days later, Bronson and his gang take off on another raid in defiance of The Lone Ranger's warning. Under strict instructions from Tonto, Major Winthrop and Captain Lopez wait for word to take action. Several hours later, The Lone Ranger and Tonto silently climb the steps of the ranch house where Bronson makes his headquarters and through a ruse Bronson's men mistakenly believe they were being sold out. Through a falling out among thieves, Bronson's guilt is cinched. Major Winthrop arrives and places the crook under arrest.

In the third episode, with only Chavez left to deal with, The Lone Ranger and The Black Caballero set out to smash the organized raids that rode north of the border. Burke, a messenger who worked for Bronson, rides steadfastly to Chavez to report the news that his partner was taken away in iron cuffs. Out of desperation, Chavez decides he should consult a woman who lives in a deserted mission referred to by the locals as a spooky mansion. The old woman is said to be a witch who could not only cast spells but also ensure the disappearance of certain individuals when the price was right. She was nicknamed "Bride of the Spider." In truth, the witch is not sane, and she uses secret underground rooms in tunnels underneath the mission to trap her victims and allow them to starve to death.

The Lone Ranger and The Black Caballero pay a visit to the mission, unaware that the wine being offered them is poisoned, but Tonto has the foresight to smash the canister before the masked men fall victim to the elixir. Cackling, the old woman asks The Lone Ranger and The Black Caballero to follow her down into the cellar, where they can find the man they're looking for.

As The Lone Ranger travels into the mysterious depths below, The Black Caballero remains behind. Five minutes pass. Ten, then twenty. And still the masked man has not returned. The Black Caballero slowly follows but falls into the trap when he does not notice the movement as the door of the cellar begins to swing shut. The Black Caballero tries in vain to force open the door. The Lone Ranger and Tonto, meanwhile, are following their elderly guide through an elaborate network of ancient storerooms and passageways that honeycombed the earth in a dozen directions. It was through a main corridor that they made their way lit by a lamp held by the masked man. It was through observation that The Lone Ranger was able to spot enough evidence to know that Burke and Chavez were hiding out in the tunnels.

In the cellar at the end of the passage, The Lone Ranger and Tonto observe the bed of the river flowing just beyond. This gives the masked man an idea. After freeing The Black Caballero, The Lone Ranger flees the passageways and rides out to the fort to retrieve Major Winthrop. Five hours later, the U.S. Army arrives at the old woman's abode to hear a thundering blast and a roar. Water starts to rise inside the tunnels after Tonto blasts a wall between the river and the tunnels. Burke and Chavez, who were hiding out in secret rooms, quickly discover what happened and flee like rats from a flood. Outside the tunnel entrance, the men are quickly apprehended and placed under arrest. Bronson and his men already met with a firing squad, Major Winthrop informed them… and Burke and Chavez would soon join them. As for the old woman, The Lone Ranger requests she receive treatment as she is not entirely sane. The Major agrees to use what influence he has to give The Black Caballero a full pardon for his past transgressions.

The third and last of The Black Caballero trilogies was broadcast from September 18 to 22, 1939, and occurred during Mexico's war for independence. When The Lone Ranger crossed the border to join forces with The Black Caballero, he aided the men of Juarez in their fight for liberty. As the Lone Ranger explained to Tonto: "(An emperor in Mexico) is one thing our country won't stand for. No nation in Europe has the right to interfere in any way with any country this side of the Atlantic. Each nation will decide for itself the kind of government it wishes." The vigilantes rode south of the border to investigate the recent theft of arms and supplies that might fall into the wrong hands. Juarez was at that time leading the fight for freedom against the emperor, Maximilian.

Santa Marta was a tiny, strolling village whose only distinctive feature was a fort on its western side. This was built generations before but was now occupied by troops brought into Mexico to uphold the illegal rule of the emperor Maximilian. The garrison was under the command of Major La Fête. Two crooked Americans, Duke and Squint, were hired by La Fête to steal the wagons and deliver them. The Black Caballero, meanwhile, insisted Mexico remain a republic and committed an act of sabotage to one of the wagons, throwing off the guards and soldiers of the Foreign Legion, led by the Major.

The Black Caballero recruits about twenty men to help assist in a ruse where La Fête and his men race out to apprehend the saboteurs, believing they have the advantage when sneaking up to the figures keeping warm at the campfire. Only after it is too late, under the cover of darkness, do the soldiers discover the figures were dummies. During this ruse, The Black Caballero, The Lone Ranger, and Tonto visit Santa Marta to confiscate the stolen munitions and supplies and return them to Juarez.

In the second chapter, the residents of Santa Marta are thrown into sudden terror when foreign legionnaires from the fort at the edge of town enter more than a dozen homes, forcibly seizing their occupants. No one is spared. The aged, the very young, even the women, all find themselves placed under arrest. Major La Fête, not a man of honor, finds it easy to figure which men are missing from town and no doubt assisting with The Black Caballero's scheme to steal back the munitions. Their families will be held hostage until the guilty parties surrender. In reality, this was La Fête's scheme to learn the whereabouts of The Black Caballero from one of the men. But no vigilante turned himself in and the women and children held captive sang in jubilation when they word reached them that they would soon be free.

The Black Caballero, The Lone Ranger, Tonto, and the 20 men, hid out in a cave in the mountainside, the entrance obscured by the grandeur of the rocky slope. There, they make plans with valuable stakes above the necessary risk. Dirk catches a glimpse of The Lone Ranger and follows the masked man's trail, leading his conspirators along the way, unaware that their approach is anticipated. Captain LeSueur, who followed the trail alongside Dirk, never returned, making Major La Fête nervous. It is soon evident that a trap has been sprung, similar to the manner applied the other day that led the crooks away from the unguarded munitions. With the army fort deserted, The Lone Ranger and The Black Caballero trap the Major and his men, forcing La Fête to free the families in exchange for his own men.

In the third and final episode… Poorly armed, disorganized, overwhelmed by the strength of the foreign troops imported into the country by Maximilian, the Mexicans in the territory around Santa Marta at first were able to do little to defend their freedom. But when twice The Lone Ranger and The Black Caballero, leading a small but determined band of men, struck successfully at the invaders, volunteers by the hundreds flocked to join them. With the wearing of the mask drawing unwanted attention, The Lone Ranger decided to go incognito for a spell, promising The Black Caballero that he would be within the area.

Dirk, meanwhile, is sent on an errand to La Rosa which has the largest fort of armed troops within a few days' travel. It is the hope of Major La Fête that with reinforcements, he can tip the armed rebellion in Maximilian's favor. When The Lone Ranger learns of this strategic maneuver, he alerts The Black Caballero. The vigilantes have no chance of winning the fight because the men are poorly armed. The Lone Ranger and Tonto decide it would buy them time to capture Dirk, tie him up to a tree, and hold him captive.

Meanwhile, Major La Fête is tricked into believing the supposed whereabouts of The Black Caballero and leads his own men on the hunt. La Fête's column is confident of apprehending the enemy, unaware that The Black Caballero is actually behind, not in front of the foreign soldiers. After two days, the soldiers make camp only to discover they're surrounded on all sides, and now on defense. The men open fire and while many of their bullets are unerring in their marks, La Fête is unaware that the men he's shooting and killing are under the command of Colonel Corbay, who was sent from the fort to support La Fête. The Lone Ranger merely waited for the right timing to arrange the set-up. As a result, the foreign legionnaires lost their foothold in the territory and The Black Caballero shouted with triumphant celebration. The Lone Ranger and Tonto, realizing their mission is accomplished, ride north back to the United States.

While The Black Caballero would not appear in character on any future adventures, he would be referenced by name in a few episodes. On the broadcast of June 3, 1940, for example, The Lone Ranger and Tonto rode out to the Crawford Ranch to investigate claims that Pablo Vegas was being paid unfairly for his labor. The masked man made a reference that he was sent by The Black Caballero to investigate.

Amongst their adventures, The Lone Ranger and Tonto made friends with a number of individuals who would make recurring appearances on the radio program. Among them were Bolivar Bates and Hacksaw Hastings, two cheerful but irresponsible veterans of the Civil War, who appeared on the radio program for a total of five different adventures between 1938 and 1944. Their first appearance was on the broadcast of May 20, 1938. Bolivar Bates and Hacksaw Hastings had drifted westward at the conclusion of the Civil War with little to show for their labors in the cause other than a saddle bag stuffed with worthless Confederate paper money. Ordinarily of a cheerful nature, the two old cronies were thoroughly disgusted by the depths to which their fortunes had sunk. They were mounted on a pair of sway-backed horses on the road leading to the capitol of the territory. (Bolivar's horse was named General Sherman, referenced many times on the program.) Their uniforms are ragged, their belts tightened to the last notch.

After meeting with The Lone Ranger, the two pals were motivated to get jobs as official tax collectors, but soon found themselves overcome by temptation and substitute worthless Confederate money for silver and gold. At every ranch where Bolivar and Hacksaw stopped, the masked mystery rider was ahead of them, posing as an outlaw to help aid the men in their task. Men who had held guns on former tax collectors, not only paid in full, but in many cases, paid in advance and thanked the two old timers to taking the money. When nearly a thousand dollars in silver was in the old men's saddle bags, they decided to turn an equal sum in Confederate money over to the government, keeping the silver for themselves.

Because The Lone Ranger helped them (unknowingly) collect, and knowing the two men were not thieves at heart, he interceded to teach them a lesson. "They made a mistake, but it isn't too late to correct it," the masked man explained to Mr. Bradley, the federal man in charge of the collection of taxes. "I want to show them that they'll gain nothing by what they did, and make use of them in collecting the rest of the Los Palmas county taxes."

After several days, old Bolivar and Hacksaw finished the list of names supplied by Bradley. They went to their former camp and counted the gold and silver coins into the box that held their former loot. Then taking more of the Confederate currency from their saddle bags, they prepared to return to Los Palmas and to Bradley, the tax collector. This time Bradley insisted they stay the night before leaving, allowing Tonto to secretly find their camp and dig up the silver that belonged to the Government. The next morning, after the men are paid their percentage (in Confederate money) and before the men leave, they find Tonto arriving with loads of silver – and no explanation. At the camp, the men discover the silver was dug up and stolen. Before the old men choose to report the theft, The Lone Ranger arrives to suggest some men turn crooked and try to pull one over on the U.S. Government.

"There are several kinds of men in the world," he explains. "Sometimes men turn crooked, without being crooks at heart. Those men can be made to see their mistake and changed into worthwhile citizens. The west needs those kind of men. Other men are naturally bad. They don't take advantage of the second chance that is given them to make good. They are the kind who spend all their lives in jail or end up at the end of a rope. You men were tax collectors. I hope you were good ones, because I got you that job. If you fell down on it, you would betray the trust I put in you." The Lone Ranger rides off, leaving the men time to realize the error of their ways, and how the masked man and Tonto gave them a second chance. Whenever Bolivar and Hacksaw appeared on the program in later episodes, this particular adventure would be referenced.

Fred Reto played the role of Hacksaw Hastings. Herschel Mayall played the role of Bolivar Bates. The two old men would return for the broadcasts of June 3, 1938, June 15, 1938, August 10, 1938, and March 8, 1944 – during the latter of which they would meet Dan Reid for the first and only time.

More prominent of the recurring characters were Mustang Mag and Old Missouri, who would appear on the radio program more than 30 times from 1939 through 1945. Both provided aid to The Lone Ranger in numerous ways and contributed greatly to the saga and mythology of The Lone Ranger and Tonto. As it was revealed on the broadcast of March 20, 1939, when Mustang Mag and Old Missouri first appeared on the radio program, Mustang Mag's spread was one of the choice ranches in the western part of Pecos County, Texas, protected from high winds by the surrounding hills and watered by many streams. Her land was known for having the best water in the region. She inherited the ranch from her late fiancé, who died before they could get married. Everyone around the territory called the owner of the Lazy Jay ranch "Mustang Mag." Years of struggle against drought and famine, schemers and Indians, gave Mag the aggression of a man. She had to fight to hold her small valley ranch against the schemes of the land-grabbing Lem Morton, yet Mustang Mag's rough ways concealed a soft heart. Her foreman, "Old Missouri," held his job because Mag didn't have the heart to fire him.

Morton attempted to add Mustang Mag's land to his already vast empire by claiming Slocum left a new will claiming the property would go to him. Mag protested, insisting the new will must be a fake, but the sheriff was placed into an uncomfortable position to enforce the eviction issued by a judge. After giving hospitality to Tonto, who was riding through the area, Mag discovers the redskin returned the favor by reporting what he overheard to The Lone Ranger. The masked man took pity on Mustang Mag, and Old Missouri, who could not defend themselves against someone who bent the law to fit their plans. The Lone Ranger, too, suspected the newly-discovered will was counterfeit, so he asked Mag and Missouri to follow specific instructions and vacate the premises as required by law. (This would prevent the fire-eater and her foreman from exchanging unnecessary gunfire.)

In the meantime, The Lone Ranger rode out to meet The Padre at the mission. There, the man of God verifies the deathbed confession of the villainous Cordova, who was recently executed for his crimes. The Lone Ranger also verifies that Cordova was the man responsible for creating the fake will and signing Slocum's name on the paper to perfection. Later, the will was brought to court where Mustang Mag could examine it for herself, within the presence of a judge. The Lone Ranger arrived with The Padre, who testified in court that Cordova cleared his conscience before he died, confessing that he himself faked the will. With The Padre's testimony, the judge reprimanded Lem Morton, who left the courtroom in disgrace.

This same episode introduced radio audiences to another recurring character, The Padre, a man of God, who would also become a recurring character on the program. (More about him later in this chapter.)

In the next broadcast, March 22, Mag refocused her time planning a cattle drive to ship her stock to the market. The critters need to travel through a narrow valley, surrounded by rocks, through an area known as Grant's Pass. With Morton's plans to steal the land thwarted, the crook now schemed to disrupt the cattle drive. Without a sale, Mag would be forced to default and sell the ranch for pennies on the dollar. The sale of cattle was essential for her livelihood.

Morton schemes with Butch, his foreman, to prevent the Lazy Jay cattle from traveling through the pass. The Lone Ranger, masquerading as a traveling ranch hand, applies for a job at Morton's ranch, to learn details of the plot. Although The Lone Ranger tips off Mustang Mag of Morton's plan, she laments that there is no other way to reach the railroad so the cattle drive will have to proceed as planned. Morton attempts to avoid suspicion by offering to split the cost of the cattle cars with her, thus burying the hatchet. She knows he can't go back on his word with the cattle cars, so she informs her men to be prepared for gunplay during the cattle drive.

The Lone Ranger, realizing the only way she could put up a strong defense is to have soldiers at a nearby army post back her play, rides out to alert Colonel Andrews. Knowing the army will not interfere with domestic issues, with their sole job to extinguish Indian uprisings, Tonto, outside the army post, steals a number of horses while The Lone Ranger pleads with the stubborn Colonel. Not wanting the theft to place a black mark on his career, the colonel races out and leads his men in pursuit of the Indian who stole the horses. Back at Grant's Pass, Mustang Mag and her men are reaching the valley. Moments before gunplay from an unfair advantage was about to begin, Morton's men witness the approaching soldiers. Not wanting to open fire at the uniformed men, the men quickly drop their weapons. Mag races her cattle through the valley and successfully reaches the railroad.

On the broadcast of March 24, 1939, Morton creates another scheme to acquire the land owned by Mustang Mag. A sheepman named Higgins is in town, looking to sell the animals that are despised by cattlemen because sheep are known to graze beyond the survival of cattle. Having sold her cattle to the East, Mag follows instructions from The Lone Ranger to purchase the sheep, against the protests of Old Missouri. Mag stands defiant. Higgins, hoping to double deal, pays a visit to Morton with the proposal to poison the waterholes so the sheep will become sick. The animals would not die, he assures Morton, and would later recover, but the situation will cause Mustang Mag to be run out in fear the "disease" will spread. Morton will not pay Higgins, insisting he would not play dirty, and orders the man out. In private with Blackie, Morton explains how the idea was sound enough for him to do the job himself without having to pay someone a share. What Morton does not know is that The Lone Ranger had ordered Higgins to propose the scheme to Lem Morton, so he could finish Morton once and for all.

A few days later, Lem Morton pays Mustang Mag a visit to make another offer on her ranch. He tells her he's heard stories of the sheep taking ill and that disease may finish them off. She confirms the rumors but holds stubborn. She insists on waiting it out, but Morton insists his price will drop after the sheep die. Mag extends her usual hospitality to anyone who visits the ranch and watches as Lem Morton drinks a glass of water. Observing the funny aftertaste, Morton discovers the water came from the same watering hole that the sheep drank from. Panicking, the crook begs for her to fetch the doctor, ultimately confessing his part in the plan to poison the sheep. The sheriff and a number of witnesses were within earshot, overhear the confession, and makes an arrest. Lem Morton is angry when he discovers the water he drank had salt added, not poison. Now that Morton is out of the picture, Old Missouri proposes marriage to Mag and she accepts.

Throughout future broadcasts, we discover more details about the two characters such as the fact that Missouri was toothless (broadcast of May 26, 1939), and that Mag had a reputation with using a rifle better than Calamity Jane (April 11, 1941).

Among the highlights of the Mustang Mag adventures was the broadcast of November 15, 1939. Reverend Jasper Kane, an Easterner, attempts to tame the rough settlers through honesty and The Good Book. Mustang Mag agrees with his preaching against cussing and smoking, which happens far too often on her ranch, but takes offense to Kane when he discloses to the sheriff that Mag is hiding Rod Sampson on her premises. Rod was accused of cattle rustling. Young Rod Sampson had been popular in the district while Seward, the rancher who swore out the warrant for his arrest, was despised by everyone. Prompted by the sheriff's arrest of Rod, the townsfolk start up a lynch mob to hang Seward. Seward, in self-defense, shoots and wounds one man in making an escape. The Lone Ranger rescues Seward from the cowboys hellbent on hanging him and takes him to the home of Mustang Mag for protection. Reverend Kane believes he did good but is shocked when a masked man defends Seward. But just as the crooked rancher begins to cheer, The Lone Ranger put him in his place.

RANGER: (To Seward) You misunderstood me. What I meant to say is that I am not your friend. I have good reasons for saying that. I came to your aid as I would have helped anyone else, no matter who or what he was. But I will tell you something before you leave, so there'll be no further misunderstandings. One of these days you'll end behind bars. And I hope I am the man who puts you there.

RANGER: (To Reverend Kane) From the little Mag and Missouri have told me I've gathered that you're trying to force a point of view you gained in the East upon the people bred here in the

West. We'll put it this way. There's law and there's justice. In the East the emphasis is upon the first. In the West, upon the latter. There have been cases where the one didn't follow the other. For instance, Rod Sampson. A warrant was sworn out for his arrest and the law said that warrant had to be served. But everyone in this district is aware that Rod's arrest was unjust.

KANE: It isn't for us to judge in these matters.

RANGER: That's the Easterner speaking. Where you come from you scarcely know your next-door neighbors. Here, people know everyone from miles around. Mag probably is acquainted with everyone within a 500-mile radius of her ranch. When you know people that well, Kane, you're qualified to judge from their characters whether or not an accusation of this nature is true. In the East, you wouldn't be so qualified, and your only course would be to depend upon the letter of the law and hope that it served justice. When you realize that difference, I think you'll understand the people of this country better and have more success in your work.

Kane, however, feels this is "a barbarous theory" and walks off, uncomfortable with the notion that he, a preacher, was preached to. Tonto, meanwhile, discovers two of Seward's ranch hands, Blake and Shaw, are guilty of cattle rustling and it was their attempt to blame Rod for the crime. They do not know Tonto means no harm to them, and thus they become badly frightened men. On the evening of the next day, there is a gathering of sober-faced men in Mustang Mag's parlor arranged by both the sheriff and The Lone Ranger. Seward was brought inside to face a trial of his peers, with the townsfolk acting as both judge and jury. With an innocent man in jail, The Lone Ranger insists justice be meted out. Kane, however, draws a gun to free Seward and give him a chance to flee. The Lone Ranger scolds the sky pilot by explaining how, as an Easterner, he followed the letter of the law and let a guilty man free. Kane insists this is not justice until two witnesses in the other room are brought in. Blake and Shaw, with the threat of being turned over to Tonto, confess how their employer was responsible for the cattle rustling. Kane, realizing he has helped a guilty man go free, feels ashamed for his actions – until it is verified that Tonto was outside the ranch house with the sheriff to catch Seward. The Reverend is man enough to admit he was wrong, and Mustang Mag displays Christian empathy but welcoming him to the community – and promising to visit his church every Sunday.

The broadcast of March 15, 1940 planted a seed in Old Missouri's head that would eventually set in motion a series of events leading to him being elected as sheriff of Trigger Bend in Pecos County. Missouri, Mustang Mag's foreman, had always been convinced that he was a fighting man and a person of consequence although he had never been able to get anyone to share that conviction. When two strangers, Abbott and Cooper, flatter him into believing he might easily be elected sheriff, he is ready to believe it and, more importantly, willing to sign what is represented to be a written statement of his views on law-and-order without reading the statement first. Later, to his horror, he discovers that he has signed away valuable timberland belonging to Mustang Mag, and that it is probably legal, as long as he cannot prove fraud, because Mag had given him her power of attorney. When The Lone Ranger appears on the scene, his very first act is to prevent Mag filing an injunction restraining Abbott and Cooper from cutting her timber. The timber has increased in value because of the railroad building west and needing it for construction. Mag had hoped to sell the timber to them, but now Abbott and Cooper made a deal in her place. They are not interfered with by the masked man when they cut the timber and send it to the railroad camp, but, in the meantime, The Lone Ranger sends Tonto to get in touch with their old friend, Chief Thundercloud, to call in a favor. When the two swindlers go to collect the money owed them by the railroad after delivering Mag's timber, they run into Mag and then scores of surrounding, unhappy Indians led by Chief Thundercloud, all claiming the timber to be their own. The two crooks discover too late that a ruse by The Lone Ranger has led to their doing the hard work for Mustang Mag and Mag ending up with all the money, as well as establishing her right to the land beyond any question of doubt.

Later, in "Mustang Mag in Politics" (September 18, 1940), a crooked mayor, sheriff, and gangster conspire to sabotage the election of Old Missouri as sheriff at Trigger Bend. Mayor Bushwhack, Sheriff Brent, and Jack Tolliver rig the upcoming election by having the townsfolk vote on a proposition that states no one can run for office unless they are a resident for at least one year. Brent knows an honest sheriff would send him to jail in no time, and such a law would put Old Missouri out of the running. The next day, everyone in town sees the notice tacked to the wall of the meeting house. When Mustang Mag learns the news, she sends for The Lone Ranger. When two of Tolliver's gunmen spot the great horse Silver outside Mustang Mag's home, they shoot bullets into the back of a figure, thinking they've killed the masked man – unaware it was merely a dummy. The Lone Ranger quickly forces confessions from the shooters, to verify the guilty culprits and the plot. During the meeting, Old Missouri instructs his friends to remain inside "no matter what happens." Moments after the meeting is called to order, shooting occurs outside, courtesy of Tonto and The Lone Ranger. Men race out to face the excitement, but Missouri and his friends remain to vote against the new law. Everyone opposed and the scheme fails.

In the episode "Missouri is the Law" (broadcast September 27, 1940), Missouri, now elected Sheriff of Trigger Bend, makes it his first duty to arrest his predecessor, Sheriff Brent, but he finds the former sheriff dead on the floor, and an innocent man named Ascension Jones is framed for his murder. Jones claims he was knocked unconscious from behind. Further investigation reveals a distinctive cigarette butt that suggests the gambler, Tolliver, committed the crime. In truth, Tolliver and Bushwhack, fearing Brent would testify against them, wanted the former sheriff dead and framed the crime on Jones – with plans to shoot and kill Jones when the prisoner tries to escape jail. Their almost-perfect plot is thwarted, however, when The Lone Ranger masterminds a jailbreak of his own to save Jones. Missouri follows instructions from the masked man, leaking information in town that he had found the cigarette butt at the scene, and that it was being kept at Mustang Mag's ranch for safekeeping. Tolliver pays a visit to Mag's ranch, unaware he is exposing his guilt, even threatening the life of Missouri in exchange for the evidence. Before Missouri can be shot, The Lone Ranger's bullet is unerring in disarming the killer.

In the episode "Dead Man Imposter" (broadcast January 10, 1941), Missouri must serve papers against his former employer, Mustang Mag, with a mortgage loan for ten times what she borrowed. Once again, The Lone Ranger happens to be riding through the area and, upon learning of her plight, assists them in revealing a crooked judge and faked papers.

When Silver begins to act unusual, The Lone Ranger and Tonto pay their friends a visit to stay over for a spell... only to discover Silver wanted to see his two-year-old colt. That colt would be raised on Mustang Mag's ranch, broken in by The Lone Ranger, and in early 1942 given as a gift to Dan Reid, The Lone Ranger's nephew. By 1942, Missouri was no longer the sheriff and had returned to the ranch as foreman.

The first woman to play the recurring role of Mustang Mag was Ruth Dean Rickaby. The actress was known for mimicking screen actress Marjorie Main and she played the role with Main in mind. Rather than act the part, she merely impersonated the character. A number of references claim Fran Striker may have been inspired to create the characters of Mustang Mag and Old Missouri from the Marjorie Main/Wallace Beery movies, for which the two teamed in more than half a dozen films at MGM. The radio characters, however, were established a year prior to the first Main/Beery team-up.

The second woman to play the recurring role of Mustang Mag was Mary Barrett Healy, sister of John Barrett, the man who had played a prototype Lone Ranger for Striker in Buffalo. Back in 1928, Striker had been an announcer at Buffalo's WEBR as well as the station's dramatic director and writer. Mary Healy came into the picture when she applied for a part in one of the five dramatic stories Striker was writing and sending out weekly over the local airwaves. One of the most successful series was entitled *Covered Wagon Days*. Healy won a major part in the show. When Striker later left Buffalo and WEBR to work under contract to WXYZ in Detroit, Healy continued on in Buffalo, becoming dramatic director for WEBR and appearing in numerous radio and theatrical roles.

"When I met and married my husband, Philip, in September 1938, I was ready to concentrate on housework," the actress recalled for the Buffalo *Courier-Express*. But in February 1939, she received a call from Striker in Detroit. *The Lone Ranger* needed a tough Marie Dressler type of woman who "specialized in shootin' irons and could rattle off a string of western cuss words." Remembering her past performances on *Covered Wagon Days*, particularly a recurring character she played on that program in the same manner, Striker invited Mary Healy and her WEBR announcer-husband to join the Detroit cast. Healy began playing the role of Mustang Mag by August of 1942.

Mrs. Healy returned to Buffalo in late 1943 when Mr. Healy was called into the service. It was there she played leading roles at the Studio Theater and the Island Playhouse, both where she had performed prior to her stint in Detroit.

Missouri was the foreman of the ranch owned by Mustang Mag, but listeners often assumed the two were married by the casual way they bickered. The characters were patterned off Fran Striker's radio program, *Hank and Honey*, broadcast over WEBR beginning in 1929. The program concerned a bickering couple who in each episode had an argument about something so ridiculous that the audience could only shake their heads in amusement.

Playing the role of Old Missouri was actor Fred Reto, who had what was probably the most distinctive voice among the repertory company at radio station WXYZ. John Fred Reto, known to fans of the radio program as the gravel-throated "bad man" on *The Lone Ranger* for seven years, and as "Fred" to his co-workers, was in show business for many years prior, in stock, repertoire and vaudeville alongside his wife. In 1932 they settled in Detroit for a career on the stage for potential job security. Among his notable performances was an excitable doctor to whom the life and death of a patient was nothing compared to a bridge date in Doris Dalton's *The Green Hat*, in 1932 at the Lafayette Theatre in Detroit.

In May 1933, Reto played a bombastic uncle in George Seaton's comedy of modern life, *Purely Platonic*, at the Comedy Theater. Seaton (the first Lone Ranger on radio) had by then already turned in his notice at the radio station so he could go to New York City to try his hand with comedy writing for the stage. By no means unknown in local theatrical circles, Seaton also assumed the leading male role. James Jewell went to the theater on opening night, May 15, 1933, to watch Seaton's play come to life on stage, and admired the "gravelly voice" of Reto. Within a few days, Fred Reto was hired by the radio station to play roles, chiefly that of a flustered sheriff. After a quarter of a century of trouping with stock companies in the East and Midwest, Reto joked to a cast member that radio was a bigger stage – but no one could see him. Jewell may have lost Seaton, but he gained Reto.

There is no record of Eva Smith, Fred Reto's wife, working at the radio station. But it was Fred's declining health and Eva's persuasion that convinced him that retirement would not be out of line. Sometime in early 1942, Fred Reto and his wife Eva retired and moved to Butler, Pennsylvania, for a long rest. For reasons unknown, they chose to go back to Detroit for a week or two to meet with friends, despite the fact that Fred's health was in decline. Following a five-week illness, at the age of 87, Fred Reto died in Harper Hospital in Detroit, on March 28, 1942. He was buried in Butler, Pennsylvania.

Although he played a variety of roles on *The Lone Ranger* program, Fred Reto played the role of a sheriff on more episodes than any actor up until the time he retired. Perhaps no better tribute to Fred Reto can be found than the radio script for the broadcast of May 2, 1941, which instructed the director to cast the sheriff to be "about Reto's type." His final performance as Old Missouri was on the broadcast of December 12, 1941, and it was because of his retirement that Fran Striker chose to drop the character of Old Missouri from the program. Eight months later, Fran Striker decided to revive the characters of Mustang Mag and Old Missouri, but this time Rollie Parker played the role of Old Missouri.

The final appearance of Mustang Mag and Old Missouri would be the episode "Missouri Goes to Town," broadcast on February 12, 1945. That episode was a decent whodunit plot in which two murdered men were found clutching a silver bullet. After Missouri is questioned by the suspicious sheriff, he chooses to go to jail rather than give details about the murder suspect – The Lone Ranger. Mustang Mag fetches the masked man to come to town to investigate and uncover who was responsible for the murder. Before the end of the calendar year, the characters of Mustang Mag and Old Missouri would return in the form of two new characters.*

While the characters of Mustang Mag and Old Missouri would not return to the program, a different rendition began with "Thunder's Mules," broadcast November 9, 1945. Thunder Martin, the same mule skinner who helped the Lone Ranger drive the camel brigade from San Antonio

---

* Following the final episode with Mustang Mag and Old Missouri, Mary Healy Barrett played a widowed, nearly broke ranch owner with two loyal hands, in "By Weight of Numbers," broadcast December 19, 1945, almost replicating the Mustang Mag voice. Stopping for water, The Lone Ranger and Tonto learn that a neighboring rancher is intent on acquiring her ranch (named the "Many Waters" ranch) to control water rights to other spreads to the south. When the woman's cattle were blocked from being driven to market, the masked man enlisted the aid of the other ranchers.

to California in a previous episode, was escorting a flock of mules to Clarabelle Hornblow, the female owner of The Rafter H. Lem Sherman, a land-grabbing schemer, made attempts to prevent delivery of her cattle in Kansas City to pay the mortgage, so he could acquire her land. This was a plot recycled from the broadcast of March 22, 1939, with Mustang Mag now referred to as Clarabelle Hornblow, and Old Missouri now referred to as Thunder Martin. Even the radio script instructed the actress playing the role of Clarabelle Hornblow as "the Marjorie Main type," just like Ruth Dean Rickaby was instructed to play the Mustang Mag character. Clarabelle and Thunder would appear on the program numerous times from 1946 through 1954, with many of the radio scripts recycled from the Mustang Mag adventures, sometimes with the names of other characters changed to avoid recognition.

As indicated earlier in this chapter, the March 20, 1939, broadcast not only introduced radio listeners to Mustang Mag and Old Missouri, but also The Padre. The man of God who ran a mission for those who sought guidance would be referred to as one of The Lone Ranger's best friends. In succeeding broadcasts, The Padre offered The Lone Ranger advice, provided tips regarding the whereabouts of the oppressed, and on many occasions notified the masked man of an injustice that he might want to play a hand in. For Fran Striker, this last bullet point was a fresh take: The Lone Ranger and Tonto could only discover injustice so many times through happenstance or Tonto overhearing a discussion outside a window or in a local café. On the broadcast of July 19, 1939, for example, The Padre sends The Lone Ranger and Tonto to the town of Oak Ridge, where Ma Garland and her son, Ted, are victims of townsfolk harassment. On other occasions, The Padre was referenced only by name.

On the broadcast of October 31, 1941, radio listeners learned that The Padre's mission is located in Kansas. (Continuity was thrown aside when the broadcasts of January 10, 1949 and March 15, 1950, revealed the Padre's mission is located in New Mexico.) On the broadcast of May 12, 1943, the Padre meets Dan Reid for the first time and while no one in the West knew of the connection between Dan Reid and The Lone Ranger, the masked man confides to the Padre that "we haven't told anyone that he is my nephew." On the broadcast of September 13, 1944, Dan's safety was in jeopardy so the young man hid at the Padre's mission. Outlaws Treg and Breed rode to the Mission, captured Dan and the Padre, and schemed to plant false evidence for the murder of the Padre, and evidence suggesting an illegal gun-running operation was masterminded by the Padre and The Lone Ranger. On that same broadcast, we learn that the Padre's Indian servant is named Juan.

Fran Striker, hoping to establish some form of continuity, wrote: "The Lone Ranger is shown not to be a member of any specific church, but he is definitely a respecter of all creeds. He is generally visualized as a Protestant, but one of his most beloved friends – in fact the only man aside from Tonto in whom he puts complete confidence is the Catholic Padre of a Mission. He shows respect for preachers and worshippers of every denomination, including the Indians' veneration of their own Great Spirits. The Lone Ranger believes that our sacred American Heritage provides that every individual has the right to worship God as he desires."

Prior, there was a reference to a Padre in the broadcast of January 22, 1937. The San Gabriel mission was referred to by name as Sara reminds Jim that they passed it during their travels. Jim responded, "We was mighty discouraged then, after failin' in the search for gold. They gave us a new lease on life, an' sent us south. An' the things they told us there. Sara, them Padre's saved our life. They gave us things we needed, an' started us out fresh. I promised 'em I'd spread the gospel." The Lone Ranger made a reference to The Padre, but it can only be "assumed" this was the same Padre that would later make recurring appearances on the radio program.

On the broadcast of April 3, 1939, we are introduced to another recurring character, Arizona Lawson, a good friend to The Padre and a professional bounty hunter who roams the West with his pet dog, hunting down killers wanted by the law. The Padre introduces Arizona to The Lone Ranger hours before The Lone Ranger races to stop a runaway stagecoach that was robbed by a highwayman. This broadcast opened with a conversation between The Lone Ranger and The Padre, making reference to the events from the broadcast of March 20, 1939.

Arizona Lawson's role on the program was just as valuable as that of his dog, Wolf, that could sniff out the scent and hunt down the criminals. On the broadcast of May 1, 1939, Arizona's dog picked up the trail of the outlaws into a valley and a camp in the hills. On the broadcast of July 17, 1939, Arizona Lawson's canine races into a back room to reveal Lamont, alive and well, a crook who was supposedly murdered for whom an innocent man was framed.

Arizona Lawson would be referenced by name on the broadcast of August 4, 1939, but never appeared in character. On the broadcast of August 28, 1939, Arizona finds himself accused of attempted murder when Clem Owens is attacked by a dog. No one in town owns a dog except Arizona, which gives the sheriff justification to jail the innocent man. The Lone Ranger and Tonto sets out to find the guilty party and expose the culprit.

Arizona Lawson's largest contribution to the saga comes during the Spanish Flats story arc (July 1940), in which The Lone Ranger is shot and wounded. During his recovery, which lasts for six consecutive episodes, Arizona serves as a faithful companion to Tonto as they foil multiple schemes of an outlaw army masterminded by the notorious – and mysterious – Graham. Arizona Lawson never appeared on the program after the Spanish Flats story arc, though, but another friend of The Lone Ranger and Tonto's came into the picture – with the same first name.

On the broadcast of January 5, 1942, The Lone Ranger meets up with his old friend Arizona Pete (not Arizona Lawson), who expresses concern that going up against the villainous Daremos, who pockets the taxes and sends men to jail if they don't follow his orders, may prove to be a challenge for his friend. Daremos is also leading an outlaw gang. Arizona Pete assists the masked man in apprehending the gang by exploding a keg of gunpowder, trapping the outlaws inside a cave long enough for the U.S. Army to make arrests. Whether the name change was by accident or intentional remains unknown, but it is assumed the character is the same, just with a continuity oversight. *

The Lone Ranger and Tonto also befriended two Mexicans, Pete and Pedro, who would make multiple appearances on the radio program. The duo's first appearance was in the episode "Fire in the Sky," broadcast January 27, 1941. The Lone Ranger and Tonto were riding across the country when a volley of shots rang out through the stillness of the afternoon. Instead of a gunfight, they found two Mexicans, Pete and Pedro, in a shooting contest. Pete is considered the best bronco buster in the West, and Pedro the best man with a lariat in the state of Texas, but from the Mississippi to the Pacific the two are the worst hands at holding a job. The Lone Ranger and Tonto were on their way to the Carter Ranch, to investigate trouble on the spread. Someone is trying to put Ellen Carter out of business. Ellen has been trying to run the ranch ever since her father's death. She is inexperienced, but has a good foreman. The Lone Ranger suggests Pete and Pedro apply for jobs at the ranch, to double as spies, and so she won't have to sell out to Grant, a rival rancher. Tonto gets a job at Grant's ranch as a cook, to act as a spy from the other side. When Grant sends his right-hand man, Red, to the ranch to encourage Pete and Pedro to leave, Red returns with a black eye and his guns stolen. Grant, furious, believes they are working too slow at closing in. Grant decides to set fire to the ranch house late that night, taking the life of Ellen Carter, her foreman Bill Morgan, and the ranch hands. The Lone Ranger and Tonto, overhearing the scheme, are surprised from behind and captured, bound and thrown into an old shack. As they struggle to free themselves, they discover the shack has been set afire and could hear the shouts of Grant and his men as they prepared to raid the Carter ranch. Silver races to the shack to smash open the door so the heroes can roll out. Meanwhile, over at the Carter ranch, Grant, Red, Faro and 20 men overpower Pete and Pedro, who make a desperate effort to free Ellen and break loose from Grant's crew in an unequal struggle. Ellen, Bill, Pete, and Pedro are tied hand and foot and left on the floor of the ranch house living room. The fire is set and the marauders flee back to Grant's ranch. The Lone Ranger arrives to aid in rescue, while Tonto races into town to fetch the sheriff and a posse. With all the evidence needed, the sheriff and his men visit Grant to place him under arrest and round up his gang. Pete and Pedro promise the masked man to remain at the ranch for a spell to help her rebuild.

Their full names were Pete Lacey and Pedro Martinez de Solvado y Runega, and they would appear on the radio program at least nine times, as well as one appearance in 1949 on the television rendition. In their seventh appearance on the radio program, "West of Dodge," broadcast May 15, 1942, Pete Lacey and Pedro Martinez were hired to go to Dodge and pick up the coaches and buy nearly a hundred horses for their new employer, Bill Harriman. Harriman was given the contract to carry the mail between Central City and Morganville, but with one stipulation: he must get his new stage line in operation before July first. If he does not, he pays the government a $500-per-day penalty. This involves building way stations. It means buying plenty of horses and at least half a dozen coaches. Harriman has enemies and if they delay him long enough, they can break him.

* The name "Arizona Pete" was recycled from the first episode of the series back in 1933, and used at least twice afterwards for the leader of an outlaw gang.

The Lone Ranger and Tonto ride along with their friends for added protection and their reasoning proves justified considering the multiple confrontations that followed. Cavell, an outlaw leader, leads an attack on the Malcolm ranch where the horses are to be purchased, but The Lone Ranger thwarts the scheme. Defeated but determined, Cavell warns most cowboys in the region against Pete and Pedro, preventing the hiring of men to assist with the trail herd.

CAVELL: As for the little half breed…
PEDRO: What is that you call me?
CAVELL: You heard me.
PETE: Careful, Pedro.
PEDRO: I am Pedro Martinez de Solvado y Runega. It is the blood of the conquistadores that runs in my veins.

Cavell attempts to shoot Pedro during an exchange, but The Lone Ranger shoots Cavell's gun from his hand, preventing bloodshed. This gives the masked man a chance to apprehend the Cavell gang. Then a caravan of coaches headed West and in each of them rode one of Cavell's men, a prisoner, but The Lone Ranger knew that more trouble could be expected. Rough trails, dangerous country, and many rivers lay ahead. Knowing Cavell and the last of his gang would wait until evening to attack the camp, just one night out from their destination, The Lone Ranger encourages Pete, Pedro, and the hired guns to circle back and use the cover of night to surround Cavell and his men. Arriving in Central City the following night, Pete, Pedro, Tonto, and the masked man surprise Bill Harriman with the stagecoaches – and the first passengers of the new stage line who will be taken to the sheriff's jail.

During the opening scene of the broadcast, Tonto refers to the two Mexicans as "them fire in air," a direct reference to the 1941 broadcast. The phrase "fire in the air" refers to shooting guns into the air as a demonstration of force to be reckoned with.

A number of story arcs on *The Lone Ranger* program were created out of necessity when the actors went on one and two-week vacations. John Todd's vacations never coincided with Earle Graser's or Brace Beemer's, so in many of those instances, the characters of Tonto or The Lone Ranger would be wounded, in hiding or (as indicated prior) replaced with another recurring character such as Arizona Lawson.

For "The Stage Line Challenge" story arc, broadcast from Friday, June 30 to Monday, July 17, 1939, Earle Graser went on a two-week vacation. To assist a stage line threatened by a notorious outlaw gang, The Lone Ranger would handle the reins of a stagecoach and ride incognito, masquerading as "Wild Bill Riley." For this example, the masked man was barely heard from and, on the rare occasion he called out to the team, his voice was heard only faintly from a far distance, played by a different actor.

In the first episode, which aired on that Friday, from Cooperstown to Washoe City, the trail used by the express coaches of the great Transcontinental and Pacific Stage-Line clung to vertical cliffs overlooking dizzy precipices. For ages, however, the granite of the mountains had been slowly crumbling before the assault of the elements. One day the masked man and his Indian friend, following the trail, make a startling discovery. Black Bart wants a contract bad enough to call in a bank loan on equipment to prevent Jim Plummer from succeeding in the Gold Flats stage line. Wild Bill Riley is scheduled to be the stage driver but Black Bart arranges for Riley to be shot and wounded. The Lone Ranger assumes the identity of Wild Bill, using makeup, to ensure Jim's stage reaches Gold Flats before the first of the month. Happy Joe, Riley's friend, agrees to ride shotgun. On the following day, the crowd gathers to see the stage lines take off in a race that will determine who receives the contract.

Through the next few episodes in the story arc, two full weeks to be exact, Black Bart makes multiple attempts to intercept the stagecoach by destroying a bridge, tricking a sheriff into locking up Wild Bill Riley, and giving liquor to the Indians so they would attack the stage line, among other nefarious acts. By the final episode, which aired on a Monday, actor Earle Graser had returned from his two-week vacation so The Lone Ranger once again resumed his vigilante identity to clear the name of the real Wild Bill Riley, who was falsely accused of setting a hotel on fire and killing a man.

One year later, Earle Graser went on vacation again, for two consecutive weeks. Beginning with the broadcast of Friday, July 12, 1940, the aforementioned "Spanish Flats" story arc involved another reason why The Lone Ranger was not heard from for two weeks – the masked man was injured and could not speak.

The Rio Grande country near Spanish Flats was a land of vast canyons, towering hills, and lonely plateaus where a horseman might ride for days without sighting another human being. The wild border town of Spanish Flats marked almost the exact center of a district extending for hundreds of miles in every direction that lay under the complete domination of a group of organized gangs. Smugglers crossed and recrossed the Rio Grande at will. Rustlers struck at undefended cattle. Merciless highwaymen roamed every trail. The reign of lawlessness demoralized not only the honest citizens of the district but the forces of law as well. Resistance was beaten down with such brutal disregard for human rights that when the first attempts ended in tragic failure, few were left to carry on the fight for decency. Resignation seemed the safer course… until at last only one man remained to dare raise his voice against a government of cutthroats and thieves. That man was Graham, an influential rancher.

Many days journey distant from Spanish Flats, and almost a month later, two men were camped where a small spring bubbled from the rocky wall of a narrow canyon. They were The Lone Ranger and Tonto. After meeting up with their friend Arizona Lawson, whom they have not seen for months, they learn of the rancher named Graham and his plea for assistance. Lawson, who grubbed out a living hunting wolves and collecting the bounty on them, and who traveled with a dog named Wolf, hopes his friends can help Graham combat the lawlessness.

Graham explains to the masked man how someone has organized criminals into at least half a dozen bands, each with its own captain, and each with its own specialty. One gang steals cattle, another carries out hold-ups, while another engages in smuggling. Not even the crooks who work for "the boss" know his identity. "The boss" has a go-between who transmits orders and collects his share of the loot. The only thing Graham has been able to unearth was the name of every leader of every gang that is employed. Turk Rigby, Red Kemp, Laramie, Big Bill Nolan, Pedro Mendoza, and the man Graham says is called the Buzzard. There is also Gunner, who serves as a right-hand man to "the boss" and takes care of people who oppose him.

When Gunner and another outlaw, Stub, figure out the hidden camp of The Lone Ranger, they set a trap and succeed in shooting and wounding the masked man. Tonto and Arizona, frantic with fear, kneel beside the fallen body of the masked man, lying horribly wounded, unconscious, unable to respond when they spoke. During that dreadful moment there was no thought of the cowardly marksman who had struck without warning. Their only concern was to do all in their power to keep the spark of life that flickered still burning. Tonto cut away the masked man's shirt, dressed his wounds, and showed Arizona how to prepare a healing broth of herbs. Realizing their camp had been found, they all had to move. Arizona proposed one of the caves along the Rio Grande. With hundreds of them in the region, he theorized, it should be almost impossible to be found. Gunner, meanwhile, cheers, for it was he who shot The Lone Ranger and, he believed, succeeded in killing the masked vigilante where many had not.

Later, Arizona happened to cross paths with Gunner, and an exchange of fisticuffs would have gotten deadly if it was not for Arizona's dog taking a hand in the fight. But the struggle with Wolf was too much for Gunner and when Arizona returned to Graham's ranch, he explained how Gunner took a fall down to the bottom of the canyon. "There's no denyin' he had it comin'," Arizona remarked. "He only got what he'd figured tuh do with me." But Arizona reports The Lone Ranger is in hiding and will remain in hiding for a spell as he recovers from his wounds, and they will have to wait until they hear from Tonto. "One o' them crooks has cashed in his chips, Mister Graham. An' whether The Lone Ranger lives or dies, Tonto an' me'll fight on yore side till the last o' them skunks're hung.

Advertisement from September 1937 when The Lone Ranger was "missing,"
and Tonto and Arizona Pete set out to find their friend.
This type of publicity was never used for the Spanish Flats story arc.

For the next six broadcasts, the masked man lay wounded and in hiding, as Arizona Lawson and Tonto worked side-by-side, meticulously smashing one criminal operation after another, and each time checking off one of the men on Graham's list. In the second episode, broadcast July 15, 1940, Graham and Arizona had what was a recurring discussion regarding the status of The Lone Ranger's slow – and life-threatening – recovery.

GRAHAM: Then you don't know whether The Lone Ranger's living or dead?

ARIZONA: Nope. Don't know a thing.

GRAHAM: D'you think they reached the caves?

ARIZONA: Don't know even that. Maybe the masked man didn't even live to get there.

GRAHAM: Them murdering skunks…

ARIZONA: They've done for the finest fellow the West ever seen… if he is gone, Graham.

GRAHAM: Gunner paid for it of course…

ARIZONA: That don't even the score.

GRAHAM: No, it doesn't.

ARIZONA: It ain't Gunner that's really to blame, you know Graham? It's the polecat that's hidin' behind Gunner and all them other crooks like him.

GRAHAM: I know that.

ARIZONA: It's the skunk that gives them their orders.

GRAHAM: I've thought about that Arizona.

ARIZONA: What do you mean?

GRAHAM: I've got an idea the only way we'll ever be able to learn who he is and bring him to justice, is to first destroy his organization.

ARIZONA: Uh-huh?

GRAHAM: If you jail the outlaws he rules, take away his power, then he'll be defenseless.

ARIZONA: Well, you know what I told you. Whether the masked man is living or dead, you can bank on me to do what I can. I reckon that's what the masked man would want me to do. It'd be, well… kind of like carrying on his work!

GRAHAM: You really mean that don't you?

ARIZONA: You can just bet I do.

In the fourth chapter, a strange and demoralizing rumor began to circulate throughout the territory surrounding the town of Spanish Flats… "The Lone Ranger is dead." This rumor spread with the speed of a wildfire. But when the rumor got to The Lone Ranger's faithful Indian companion, and Arizona, they assured Graham that the rumor was not true. Townsfolk may be demoralized but Graham, knowing the truth, continued to aid in the fight against the organized gangs of outlaws. One of the leaders was named Laramie and it did not take long for him to figure out the location of the cave and, along with an associate named Mendoza, to ride out to kill the masked man. Only in the end of the chase, Tonto, Arizona, and the sheriff laugh – The Lone Ranger was well enough to leave the cave, but not before setting up a trap that helped apprehend Laramie and Mendoza. Afterwards, The Lone Ranger would continue to keep low in an effort to continue to mend from his wounds, with the Padre tending to his care.

In the final chapter, broadcast on Monday, July 29, 1940, titled "The Return of the Masked Man," Arizona and Tonto conspire with the sheriff to leak word that one of the men in the gang, the go-between, would testify who the big guy is in return for charges being dropped. Late that night, as Stub, who stood behind bars, strikes the deal with Arizona and the sheriff to reveal the name of the boss of the outlaw gang, a window breaks and gunshots are fired, missing Stub. Arizona and the sheriff race out to apprehend the assailant, while Graham remains behind to finish the job.

GRAHAM: You were going to turn me in!

STUB: No, honest I wasn't, Graham! Wait!

GRAHAM: You were going to tell Arizona I was the man behind those gangs!

STUB: Please…

GRAHAM: Shut up! (BRIEF PAUSE) Hear them outside, Stub? (CHUCKLE) They're looking for Boylan. Don't know what he's got to do with this, but anyhow they're out there trying to find him. They've forgotten all about you and me!

STUB: Boss, wha… what're you gonna do?

Before Graham could shoot Stub, however, a gunshot rang out and his weapon dropped to the floor. The Lone Ranger appeared, having shot the weapon from Graham's hand. Standing behind the masked man was Arizona, who confessed that the masked man knew all along that Graham was behind the outlaw gangs. "You had to be the man, Graham, because when I first arrived in this section your men made an attack on my life," The Lone Ranger explained. "And you were the only one outside of Tonto and Arizona who even knew I was around. You called us in to round up those outlaws for exactly the reason you just mentioned to Stub. You planned to make us your tools to rid yourself of the organization for which you had no further use! But I played your own game, Graham. I let you betray your men while I stayed out of sight. As long as you turned them over to the law, you were doing what I wanted. Once they'd all been captured, however, you were finished, whether you knew it or not."

The longest story arc in the series was "The Legion of the Black Arrow," which launched on the evening of October 13, 1941, and would not conclude until March 9, 1942. After the mastermind behind the crimes was apprehended, the story did not end there. Five leaders of organized crime who were members of the Black Arrow escaped and The Lone Ranger and Tonto raced out to apprehend each of them, one by one, each dramatized in separate story arcs.

In the first chapter, titled "A New Mission" (October 13, 1941), the President of the United States (played by actor Paul Hughes) calls upon The Lone Ranger to help aid in a mission of vital importance. In Washington, D.C., the U.S. Government has information about a plot to overthrow that part of the government which applies to the states west of the Mississippi, a plot to form a new nation; a nation opposed to those principles upon which the country was formed. Behind that movement is greed and ambition. One man, unknown to all, who would make himself an emperor in a free land, threatens to destroy all things that brave men and women have fought to save. An increased frequency in Indian uprisings, armed with rifles, has been blamed on the schemers.

No living members of the gang are known. It is believed that some of them hold important posts in the government. There is no doubt that many have become influential in communities in the west. They seem to work from the inside, boring into the confidence of the people they plan to ruin. They are trying to gain control of scattered communities until they are ready to merge all these into a new nation – or empire. Such reliable men as Wild Bill Hickok and Buffalo Bill Cody agree with the secretary of the President that there is one man they can trust – The Lone Ranger – and all agree to spread word that the masked man is needed.

The greatest western scouts in the history of the nation ride far and wide in an effort to find The Lone Ranger. Far and wide, the horsemen range, pausing only to snatch a bit of food and rest. Those westerners race on across the plains and valleys, swapping horses with friendly ranchers when their mounts became exhausted. Tirelessly they push across the mountains and through ravines, carrying the word – knowing that each time they stop the message would be spread in an ever-increasing circle from that place. No one knew where The Lone Ranger could be reached, yet every man felt sure that somewhere, sooner or later, the famous masked rider would learn that he was needed.

Only when Tonto went into town to fetch supplies one afternoon did they receive the news. The Lone Ranger mounted and rode off. The Panhandle was behind him. He dashed on a northeast slant across the narrow western strip of Oklahoma. The Kansas border. One more short rest and then an all-day ride toward Dodge City and its lawlessness. Halfway between the border and the city, the tired man and exhausted horse came to the little mission where the Padre waited. From his good friend, the Padre, and through a message via telegraph, The Lone Ranger was instructed to ride to St. Louis, where the East met the West, where several cars of one train were shunted to a siding on the outskirts of the city. There, in private, The Lone Ranger met the President of the United States.

PRESIDENT: Upon the recommendation of men whom I can trust, I've come all the way from Washington to hear what you have to say. But I don't propose to listen to anyone who won't show me his face!

RANGER: Mr. President, I'll tell you exactly why I wear this mask. Some time ago, there was a massacre of some Texas Rangers. Six men were ambushed and shot. (START FADING OUT) There were six graves, but only five of those men actually died…

MUSIC: CRESCENDO THEN FADE

RANGER: (FADING IN) So you see, sir. Since then, I have worn this mask. If my identity were known, my usefulness would be finished.

PRESIDENT: (MOLLIFIED) I understand.

RANGER: Here, before you, I want to remove my mask.

PRESIDENT: Thank you.

MUSIC: SLIGHT LIFT THEN CUT

RANGER: There.

PRESIDENT: Um-m, you know, your face is just what I thought it would be. What I hoped it would be.

RANGER: Thank you, sir. Mr. President, I understand that the future of our country is in danger.

PRESIDENT: The next few weeks may determine whether the United States will stand, or fall. But let me point this out to you before we go further. From the moment you leave here, your life will be in danger. You will have to work alone, without the aid of our soldiers. If you, at any time, find yourself in difficulty or danger… and you will… you will have to fight your way out single-handedly. Do you understand that?

RANGER: Yes, Mr. President.

For the next 20 chapters, The Lone Ranger and Tonto lead a manhunt for the villainous Torlock, whom they quickly identify as a member of the Black Arrow – and a member of high regard. With each scheme foiled and another agent of the Black Arrow arrested, The Lone Ranger and Tonto discover not one man willing to exchange information about what they knew of the traitorous gang. Throughout the story arc, the announcer emphasized the dire importance of The Lone Ranger's mission and challenge.

ANNOUNCER: During the years of unrest that followed the Civil War, a powerful secret organization called the Legion of the Black Arrow sprang up in the Western United States. Its members were to be found everywhere – defying the law or using the law for their own purposes – working toward the ultimate goal of revolt and the foundation of a despotic empire. It was the masked rider of the plains who led the fight against this band of outlaws and traitors – and for once his great strength and courage – his daring and resourcefulness were taxed to the utmost in the cause of democracy.

The stronghold of the Black Arrow was a valley hidden high up in the remote vastness of the Sierra Mountains. The leader of the legion, at one time referring to himself as an emperor, worked at all times to undermine the government and strike terror into the hearts of settlers. With dramatic flair, the criminal empire was depicted.

ANNOUNCER: Lightning flashed and thunder rolled across the valley high in the Sierras. The rain poured down, but the great cavern at the far end of the valley gave shelter to hundreds of men. The Legion of the Black Arrow had gathered to receive the orders of their leader! He stood before them on the stone dais. The lower half of his face was covered by a black cloth. His eyes reflected the light of the two fires that leaped toward the roof of the cavern on either side of him. His hands met above his head. Behind him appeared the sinister shadow – the shadow of the Black Arrow!

SOUND: Cave Effect

TORLOCK: The Legion of the Black Arrow shall triumph!

SOUND: Ad Lib Cheer

TORLOCK: The West shall be ours!

SOUND: Cheer

TORLOCK: Death to our enemies! You have been summoned here from all parts of the West! So far you have done your work well, but the time has come for even greater efforts in the cause of our glorious destiny!

"Death to our enemies!" was the catch phrase used by members of the Black Arrow, much like members of the Nazi party saluting Der Fuhrer at the time.

In the episode titled "Torlock's End," broadcast of November 28, 1941, The Lone Ranger rides into Bennett City to meet Stephen Hayden, the newspaper editor, and his daughter Mary. Torlock has been on the run for so long, hiding his trail like a polecat, desperate to avoid the masked man. By placing an ad in the newspaper for witnesses, The Lone Ranger tricks Torlock's henchmen, Sam and Jake, into revealing Torlock's present hideout (a hunter's cabin) and, as a result, Torlock is finally surrounded and captured.

The Lone Ranger judges Torlock as "yellow," a sound judgment as Torlock panics, promising to tell all he knows about the Black Arrow, pleading not to be sent to Washington – a first compared to all of the other agents of the Black Arrow who were apprehended. Torlock was not afraid of what would happen in Washington, but rather how the gang members would murder him to maintain his silence during transportation. Before he can be taken east by private railway car, Torlock is poisoned by a secret ally of The Black Arrow, effectively sealing his lips.

The Lone Ranger and Tonto thought that when they got Torlock, they had reached the end of their fight against the Black Arrow. The news of Torlock's death spread rapidly throughout the region. It was obvious that not one man could be solely responsible in the outrageous plot against the government. There must be other leaders. Not only in the West, but in Washington as well.

This would lead to another rendezvous with the President of the United States, rejoining in St. Louis where they had met before. In "A Girl to Aid," a pivotal episode of the Black Arrow series, broadcast December 1, 1941, the President of the United States meets with a woman who has been working in government service for eight years. He commends her work, saying she has been invaluable to the United States on several occasions, showing great ingenuity in carrying out certain missions to which she was assigned. Some of the diplomatic work she did, he informs her, was worthy of an ambassador.

PRESIDENT: Tell me this, my dear, have you ever heard of The Lone Ranger?

GIRL: Yes.

PRESIDENT: You have heard of his work in connection with the Legion of the Black Arrow?

GIRL: Against the Legion, yes. I have heard of it.

PRESIDENT: Please read this message. It came this morning by the electric telegraph.

GIRL: (AFTER PAUSE) Torlock captured. Poisoned. Yes, sir, I've read it.

PRESIDENT: Have you no reaction to it? No thoughts?

GIRL: You want to hear them? Yes, I have thoughts. I didn't think Torlock could live long enough to tell anything to involve the men above him.

PRESIDENT: Your position has made it possible for you to follow the events in the West, especially those in connection with the Black Arrow. Now why did you think Torlock would be killed, before he could talk?

GIRL: Because Torlock was not the leader of the Black Arrow. He was just following orders.

PRESIDENT: And now what will happen?

GIRL: Someone else undoubtedly will take his place, to follow orders.

PRESIDENT: Exactly, and that is why I want you to go to Texas.

GIRL: I... I'm to go to Texas?

PRESIDENT: Yes. And without letting The Lone Ranger, or anyone else, know who you are, you're to learn all you can. You're to mingle with the people, renew old acquaintances, pick up the threads of the life you left ten years ago. Give what aid you can, to The Lone Ranger, but above all... learn who takes Torlock's place and who, here in Washington, sends that man instructions.

But the girl hesitates – protests even. Not even to help The Lone Ranger. She used to love the state, the whole West, with the plains and mountains, the valleys and the endless stretch of land. But now she hates it. She wakes in the middle of the night in the torture of dreams that re-live an awful day in Texas. It was then that she related the incident to the President.

GIRL: Several years ago, I was riding toward Grant's Pass one afternoon. It was one of those glorious days – it seemed that one could see for miles in every direction. I knew that my brother, a Texas Ranger, and some of his friends would come through Grant's Pass that day and I was riding, hoping to meet them. I hadn't seen Bob for some time. Then, suddenly...

SOUND: Distant shots, a regular pitched battle in the distance. Hoofs clatter to halt.

GIRL: There were gunshots! I reined up – listened with an increasing feeling of something clutching at my heart and throat. I couldn't be sure, but the gunfire seemed to come from Grant's Pass. And then, as suddenly as it began, it stopped. There was nothing but silence.

SOUND: Gunfire stops.

GIRL: I strained my ears. I thought I heard hoofbeats going away but I couldn't be sure. I spurred my horse and started toward Grant's Pass.

SOUND: Hoofs start hard and sustain

GIRL: A little way into Grant's Pass, with steep walls on both sides of the narrow canyon, I saw – (CATCH VOICE) – well, there were six of them. All Texas Rangers.

SOUND: Hoofs clattering to halt

GIRL: My brother was among them. Even the horses those men had been riding were shot down by the vicious killers from the protection of the rocks at the top of the cliff. There was no sign of life in the Pass. I realized that none of those men could be alive and yet I had to be sure. I examined them, they were dead. All but one. There was one man, terribly wounded, and unconscious of course, in whom there was still a spark of life. I tried to dress his wounds. I tried to force water from a canteen between his lips. I even tried to get him on my horse, but he – he was too heavy. I couldn't lift him. He too must have died soon after I left to try to send help to him. Texas had suddenly become a place I couldn't stand. The hills, the rocks, the valleys, which I had so loved, I now saw only as a hiding place for murderers. The ranches had become the lure for cattle thieves. The very streams and springs of good water had changed to things I hated, because they gave refreshment to men like those who had killed my brother and his friends. I – I can never return to Texas... to any part of the West.

PRESIDENT: The story you've told is a strange one.

GIRL: Strange? There's nothing strange about it, Mr. President. I'm only one of the countless people who've had an experience like that.

PRESIDENT: But the others have stayed to fight the things that aren't right.

GIRL: Well, perhaps that's because they didn't love the country as I did. My hatred of it became as deep as my love had been.

PRESIDENT: You said you rode away to get help for the men who still lived. Did you find that help?

GIRL: Not in time.

PRESIDENT: Then he did die?

GIRL: I don't know. The men who shot him must have returned to finish their work. It wasn't until the next day that men could get back to Grant's Pass. They found that graves had been dug, the dead men buried.

The President relaxed for a moment and told the girl of another story. The story the masked man had related to him all too recently on the train in St. Louis was similar to the one told by the mysterious woman. He, too, was a member of a small band of Texas Rangers, that was ambushed. The bullets did not kill him, but he recovered consciousness in a cave, with food and water beside him. While he lay on the ground, trying to remember what had happened, an Indian came into the cave.

TONTO: Me Tonto.

RANGER: Tonto? Tonto, did you say?

TONTO: That right!

RANGER: When I was a boy, I knew an Indian boy named Tonto.

TONTO: Me Tonto!

RANGER: You, the same one! I – you brought me here to this cave?

TONTO: That right! Me find you hurt bad. Wound plenty bad, but you get well. Get strong again. Someone bandage your wound. Stop bleeding. Save your life.

RANGER: Tonto, there were others – friends of mine – five of them. Did they survive?

TONTO: All other Ranger – dead.

RANGER: All of them?

TONTO: That right.

RANGER: Then I –

TONTO: You only Ranger left now. You alone.

RANGER: Lone… ranger… Tonto, I'm going to get those men who ambushed us.

TONTO: Um. You get strong first. Take long time. You unconscious all night.

RANGER: The others, what did you do with them?

TONTO: Me make grave. Make six grave.

RANGER: Six graves?

TONTO: Ugh. Let outlaw think you dead, too! But you not dead. You wear mask. You not let outlaw know you not dead. Then…you catch outlaw!

RANGER: I'll do it, Tonto! I'll wear a mask. No one will know who I am. Let them think all six of those Rangers have gone West! There'll be one who's still riding! I'll have no name! My name is beneath the mound of earth you built beside the graves of my friends. I'll just be… The Lone Ranger!

MUSIC: Start theme song very soft

PRESIDENT: (FADING IN) That man recovered his health and strength. He rode from out of nowhere, his face covered by a mask. He carried out the pledge he made and ran every last one of those outlaws to earth. He kept Tonto at his side, riding to where he could serve justice, relentlessly pursuing criminals in all parts of the West. People began to talk about his deeds of daring. He called his white horse Silver, and his thrilling cry of….

RANGER: (FILTER) Hi-Yo, Silver, Awayyyyy!

MUSIC: Slight lift then down

PRESIDENT: He became known from border to border and from the Mississippi to the Ocean. And The Lone Ranger is still riding!

It was then that the girl realized that The Lone Ranger was a friend of her brother. She was the one who saved his life.

GIRL: I DO ACCEPT! I want to go back to Texas! I want to help the Lone Ranger!

She was now dispatched by the President from Washington to secretly help track down the remaining members of the Black Arrow. Her ingenuity, and her ability to put apparently unrelated facts together, was to prove of great help to The Lone Ranger. But The Lone Ranger and Tonto knew nothing of this girl. As The Lone Ranger and Tonto continued their two-man crusade against the Black Arrow, the mystery of learning the identities of those in command was stacked upon an additional mystery: the identity of the mystery girl. After the Legion of the Black Arrow was officially smashed, it was learned that some of the members in prominent positions fled to avoid capture. This led to a number of story arcs in which The Lone Ranger and Tonto hunted down and apprehended former members of the Black Arrow. It was not until he brought Sydney Drake to justice that the Legion was officially broken. But the masked man's Presidential mission had not yet come to a close. In a new story arc beginning with the broadcast of February 13, 1942, The Lone Ranger was assigned one more mission and this one was appropriately titled "First of the Five."

A letter reaches the President of the United States with the names of the five members of the Black Arrow who were given wealth and position, all of whom came as a shock to everyone in his office. They know the vile organization is destroyed, but their attempts to cover their crimes and guilt will prove a challenge to convict. The mysterious girl suggests each of the five have business interests in the west and perhaps they can be proven guilty for other crimes to ensure their arrest and conviction. Both the President and the mysterious girl agree that The Lone Ranger is best suited for this task. Thus, when the Presidential car is parked in St. Louis, the masked man pays another visit to the President. His new assignment is to apprehend the five men and provide proof against them.

The story arc centered on the masked man's multiple attempts to expose Matt Kimberly for a number of crimes. He ultimately succeeds in getting a written confession out of Kimberly before turning him over to the law. During this story arc, The Lone Ranger has a lucky ring which was used to identify him when the law questioned the masked man's motives, and used as a messenger to convince soldiers to ride out under orders of The Lone Ranger. The ring was a premium giveaway during that story arc. Former members of the Black Arrow hunted down in succeeding story arcs included Clark Drexel, who ran a mining syndicate; Benjamin Steele, known as "The Cattle King," Jacob Webster of the Webster Warehouse Company, and Bronson Page, the inside man in Washington.

Along the way, the mysterious girl assists the masked man and his faithful Indian companion in a number of adventures, including the "Tomahawk" story arc from March 11 to March 25, 1942, "The Mountain City" story arc from March 27 to April 8, 1942, and "The Iron Spur" story arc from May 25 to July 6, 1942. Of all these adventures, the most revealing of the episodes to involve the mysterious woman was "The Vulture's Nest," broadcast February 23, 1942. Soon after The Lone Ranger leaves the Padre's mission, there is a poignant and highly emotional exchange between the Padre and the girl about what might have been.

PADRE: My child, I do not understand you.

GIRL: You…don't?

PADRE: You hide from a man you so greatly admire. He has never seen your face.

GIRL: No, Padre. You see, he knew my brother. They were friends. He might remember me, or he might guess that I am the sister of his friend. I look like my brother who was killed.

PADRE: But what of that?

GIRL: The Lone Ranger has closed that part of his life, Padre. He buried his identity in the graves of his companions. His life is dedicated to something fine and great. If he saw me, he might recall other days, happier days, where he didn't know loneliness.

PADRE: You think it would make him unhappy to recall those days? Before he became The Lone Ranger?

GIRL: Why risk making him unhappy?

PADRE: Or risk having him desire the love that can never be part of his life? You would say that but for your modesty?

GIRL: I wouldn't want The Lone Ranger to change. He must never be anything but what he is.

The Legion of the Black Arrow arc finally came to a close with "The End of Page," broadcast on April 17, 1942. The title referred to the capture of Bronson Page, the last of the five leaders who fled when The Lone Ranger managed to smash the Legion's operations.

But it would be the first episode of "The Iron Spur" story arc that would provide the solution to the mystery that radio listeners longed for. It was in that pivotal episode, broadcast May 25, 1942, that the name of the mysterious girl would be revealed!

Once again, The Lone Ranger had a private meeting with the President on his private train on the siding on the outskirts of St. Louis, almost in the heart of the forest. It was nightfall and the guards were posted, and the secretary waited with the ones farthest from the train. The masked man snuck inside to discuss a situation that threatened the development of the West.

To unite the East and the West, a transcontinental railroad is necessary. In three whole years only 40 miles of railroad has been built. The delay was caused by human nature; self-interest is – and has been – a driving force that is difficult to defeat. There has been a triple alliance against the railroad as cattlemen feel it would be the end of the open range, while the shipping companies and stage lines fear it would mean the end of their businesses. The newspapers call the alliance "the triangle." Behind the scenes, these interests have organized and pooled their resources and, with Henry Wilson in Congress, successfully fought it to a standstill. But, in spite of everything they could do, the triangle was ultimately beaten, and Henry Wilson left Washington.

Just as the President and others believed the railroad would be going through, they discovered shocking news. When Wilson left Washington, he never accepted defeat. Opposition would come in the form of brute force and – if need be – involvement from the red men. The President of the United States called upon The Lone Ranger to assist both the mysterious woman and Colonel Parkman, the engineer assigned to the task of completing the railroad. Evidence of sabotage has already begun, it is reported, with accidents including death and murder, and other mishaps that have only handicapped production.

To assist The Lone Ranger with his task, the mysterious woman entered the Presidential box car sans makeup. This was the first time the masked man had seen her without a disguise yet he recognizes her almost instantly, and with complete understanding he knows why she chose to remain in the shadows all these weeks. Her name is Joan Barclay and her brother, Jim, was one of the fallen Texas Rangers. *

The Lone Ranger's first task is to set out and find Philip Bradley, one of six surveyors who mysteriously vanished somewhere near Fort Kearney. After spending a few days following one dead end after another, The Lone Ranger and Tonto wander into a canyon and meet an old prospector who works for a notorious gang of outlaws. The prospector attempts to lead the masked man and Indian into an ambush, but the Lone Ranger suspects foul play and quickly gains the upper hand. After rescuing the other prospectors, and arming the men to help him apprehend most of the outlaws, The Lone Ranger prevails. The leader of the outlaws, Duke, manages to flee the region. Bradley informs The Lone Ranger that a man named Wilson was heading up the band of outlaws known as "The Iron Spur." The Lone Ranger assures Bradley that he and his men are going to have full military escort because numerous outlaw gangs are always seeking jobs for money and those who oppose the railroad construction have plenty of it.

The fact that Joan's last name was Barclay and her brother's first name was Bob (in the May 1, 1941, broadcast) adds amusement to what fans often refer to as the "WXYZ Universe" for in 1950, a new radio program was created and broadcast, a modern-day espionage series titled *Bob Barclay – American Agent*. To add, during the early thirties, *Thrills of the Secret Service* aired over WXYZ with the lead hero, Patricia Dare, combatting crime with the assistance of her boyfriend, Bob Barcley (note the spelling difference on that series).

* On the broadcast of December 1, 1941, Joan's brother was named Bob and was murdered in Grant's Pass. For the broadcast of May 25, 1942, her brother's name was Jim and was murdered in a valley. This was indeed a continuity error on the part of Fran Striker.

In later retellings, Joan's involvement would be dropped from the narrative and the name of Grant's Pass would be revised on future retellings to Bryant's Gap. Joan's last appearance on the radio program would be heard in "Surprise at Sunrise," broadcast July 3, 1942, which was the second-to-last episode of "The Iron Spur" story arc. According to an inter-office memo, the inclusion of Joan Barclay had become cumbersome. It was Striker's belief that precious dramatic time would be wasted explaining her presence in future broadcasts, so the character fell by the creative wayside. But, oh, a footnote to *Lone Ranger* history she became!

The ambush was originally set in Grant's Pass in both the serial and the 1941 radio rendition. When Fran Striker recycled much of that origin for use in his novel, *The Lone Ranger Rides* (1941), he changed the locale from Grant's Pass to Bryant's Gap. As revealed in the novel, "In a remote basin in the western part of Texas, a bitter old rancher named Bryant Cavendish" had carved himself an empire. He wielded such influence that the huge basin where he ran his cattle was called Bryant's Basin and the northern entrance to his valley, a winding narrow gap slashed by Nature in solid rock, was called Bryant's Gap. Rheumatism so severely tortured the old man's legs, by the way, that he stayed pretty much at the ranch house, not knowing fully all that went on in the valley he once rode each day. Meanwhile, the Texas Rangers had heard that certain outlaws were hiding in the secluded reaches of that vast domain. As the Texas Rangers had to ride through Bryant's Gap to get to the outlaws, Striker chose to eliminate Joan Barclay and the President of the United States from the narrative.

In the episode "A Nephew is Found," broadcast December 25, 1942, the origin was explored a second time on the radio program, and in more detail, when Grandma Frisbee, who is slowly dying from a weak heart, confesses that she is going away on a long trip, alone. Before her death, she shares with The Lone Ranger a box of personal items that recounts her trip from Council Bluffs. It was more than a decade earlier when she was among a wagon train of pioneers who ventured west, sharing a wagon with Linda Reid and her six-month-old son named Daniel. Just a night before reaching Fort Laramie, the wagon train was attacked by a marauding band of Cheyenne Indians. Linda was killed during the onslaught, so Grandma Frisbee took the babe under her wing. At the fort, two days later, she learned a letter awaited Linda informing her that Jim, her husband, was killed during an ambush at Bryant's Gap. In private, The Lone Ranger unmasks to get a closer look at the small photos in a locket that once belonged to Linda, verifying Dan's father was The Lone Ranger's brother. The Lone Ranger recounts the events as they happened at Bryant's Gap and promises the old woman on her death bed that he would raise Dan as if he was his own son. Later that evening, The Lone Ranger reveals the truth to Dan... as the dying Mrs. Frisbee remarks, "Ride on Lone Ranger... forever!"

In many of the Grosset & Dunlap hardcover novels that followed, a recap of the Texas Rangers massacre and origin of The Lone Ranger can be found with another rendition. As an example, from *The Lone Ranger on Powder Horn Trail* (1949): "Six Texas Rangers had been running down a band of outlaws. They had been ambushed in a canyon and five of their number had been killed. The sixth had been left for dead. Tonto had reached the scene of the massacre several hours after the outlaws had departed. He had carried the sole survivor to a cave and there had applied his Indian lore to fan the faint spark of life into a flame. For many days the wounded Ranger had lingered at the threshold of death. His wounds had become infected, and there were times during the days and nights of raging fever when Tonto thought his task was hopeless. But in the end, he had won the war with death."

"Then had come days of convalescence in the cave while the Texan slowly regained his strength. During those days, Tonto and the man whose life he had saved made plans to avenge the death of those fallen comrades and bring the Cavendish gang to justice. The surviving Ranger was known to every member of Butch Cavendish's outlaw army. He would be shot on sight by any man in the gang who learned that he was still alive. To forestall this and convince the gang that the canyon massacre had been complete, Tonto fashioned six wooden crosses to mark six graves. Beneath five of those mounds rested the bodies of Texas Rangers. The man who had come so close to being number six concealed his identity with a mask, and, his strength fully restored, thanks to Tonto's tireless ministrations, started on the long trail of justice."

"The secret of his identity was known only to Tonto and to an old man in whom the Ranger had implicit faith. This old friend lived in a small shack that concealed the entrance to a secret silver mine in far-off mountains. He worked the Ranger's silver mine alone – digging and refining only enough ore to meet the masked man's simple needs and to provide silver for The Lone Ranger's bullets."

> "I'm masked and you're an Indian. No matter what we know to be the truth, our testimony would never be accepted by people unacquainted with us."
> – The Lone Ranger speaking to Tonto in the broadcast of May 8, 1939

The drawing of The Lone Ranger, conceived by Gordon L. Erickson, age 16, was published in the September 11, 1938, issue of *The Buffalo Times*, the same day the newspaper strip premiered. This was a local contest and Erickson received the $1.00 cash prize.

"THE LONE RANGER, TONTO, SILVER AND SCOUT"

KING-TRENDLE BROADCASTING CORPORATION

INTER-OFFICE COMMUNICATION

April 30, 193 8

TO Fran Striker   FROM   Mr. Jewell

   The attached script is badly plotted. Kill first scene
indicating suicide. Story doesn't start until Jason and the
Sheriff visit Baldy. You could then have a short scene between
Cole and banker checking on shortages in his account books.
Young man cannot explain but promises to make up shortage.
He awkwardly attempts to hold up Ranger and Tonto, which gives
us the same result we have in the first scene. Point to
tobacco jar in scene where Ranger and Tonto visit Baldy.

Memo from Jewell to Striker regarding the first draft
of the radio script.

James Jewell at microphone with cast.
Charles Livingstone on the far right.

RIDING LIKE THE WIND

The dramatic staff at WXYZ in Detroit. Back Row (left to right): unknown, unknown, Jim Fletcher, Bob Liggett, Gillie Shea, unknown, unknown, Malcolm McCoy, Fred Fry, Earle Graser, Ted Johnson, and Harold Russell. Middle Row (left to right): Tom Dougall, John Todd, Harold True, unknown, Rollon Parker, Herschel Mayall, John Hodiak, Larry Kelley, Dick Osgood, Klock Ryder, unknown, Jay Michael, Fred Reto, John Barrett, unknown, unknown, Ernie Winstanley, Al Hodge, Dewey Cole, unknown, unknown, Ted Robertson, and Chuck Livingstone. Front Row (left to right): unknown, Lee Allman, unknown, unknown, Gwynne Fermin, unknown, Bernadine Ryan, unknown, Nancy Osgood, Beatrice Leiblee, Mary Barrett Healy, Bertha Forman, and Marjorie Svela.

Joan Evans was not only a student and cast member on radio's *Radio Schoolhouse*, hosted by Dick Osgood, but also made a few appearances on radio's *Lone Ranger.*

"One after another, the followers of Cavendish were tracked down – captured and turned over to the law by the relentless masked rider and his Indian companion. When his mission had been accomplished, The Lone Ranger continued his fight against the lawless in a crusade to make the West he loved a good place to live. The masked man's matchless skill with horse and gun, his sense of justice, and his deeds of daring made him an almost legendary character. His great horse Silver became equally well known, and so did Tonto."

On radio, the origin would not be dramatized again until the 15th anniversary program on the evening of June 30, 1948. That rendition, by most accounts, is considered the finest rendition, with Striker in an early draft of the script describing how the sole survivor of the Bryant's Gap massacre "seemed to be transformed by some strange alchemy into a composite of all six Rangers."

The Son of Silver

Another chapter in *The Lone Ranger* mythology came in August of 1941 with the "Son of Silver" story arc. On the broadcast of Friday, August 8, Tonto and The Lone Ranger find themselves accused of being part of a gang of renegade Indians, led by Breed Conway. Tonto is captured and it is about the same time that Silver begins acting bizarre – a minor reference that would lead into the three-part saga that began with the broadcast of August 11. While trying to prevent an outlaw from being rescued by his gang while he is being kept prisoner on a stagecoach, The Lone Ranger finds himself stranded when Silver runs away. The masked man is puzzled as he reunites with Mustang Mag and Old Missouri, scratching his head and theorizing what could have made Silver act that way. On the broadcast of August 13, Missouri is arrested for bank robbery and falsely charged with the crime of murder. The Ranger and Tonto break him out of jail, track down the Varley gang, and prove Missouri's innocence. In the process, they also track down the whereabouts of Silver. As they discover, Silver's mate bore a son and Silver simply wanted to meet the young colt that was by then only two years old. In the third episode of the saga, broadcast August 15, Missouri is shot while a gang of outlaws steals the son of Silver. The wound is not fatal, thankfully, and The Lone Ranger and Silver ride to the rescue.

The son of Silver would be referenced in a number of radio broadcasts that followed, such as August 27, when Tonto is in town buying supplies. The masked man teaches the son of Silver what is expected of him when his rider uses a lariat. A young woman named Sally later rides the colt and jumps over a ravine. On the broadcast of August 29, The Lone Ranger and Tonto complete the training for the young colt and wonder what name they should give him, only to discover that the colt has been poisoned. Thankfully, the young horse recovers and is left to the care of Mustang Mag and Missouri, while The Lone Ranger and Tonto rode off to new adventures.

TONTO: Colt him plenty happy, eh?

RANGER: He's the best colt I ever saw, Tonto. Someday he'll be almost as great a horse as Silver, his father!

TONTO: There Mustang Mag's ranch, now.

RANGER: Missouri will be glad to see his colt.

TONTO: You not change mind? You still give colt to Missouri?

RANGER: Missouri sacrificed his horse to save my life, Tonto. I promised him the colt and I keep my promises.

(later)

RANGER: Out here in the west there's one animal that walks beside us as a companion. Our land is long and broad and the prairies stretch as far as the eye can see. And wherever a man is, there you'll find his horse. He helped us build the frontier and he'll help us keep it, and anyone who would willingly hurt a horse is no true westerner. Why, I'd give my life to save Silver from danger as Tonto would give his to save Scout. And the same goes for every one of you, including Missouri and his colt, the son of Silver.

They had many more deeds to perform but promised to return and pick up the colt when he was grown in size. A name-the-colt contest began in September, encouraging young listeners to write in with proposed names.

RANGER: We must find a name for Silver's son. Can't let as fine a horse as that go unnamed.
TONTO: Mebbe call-um name about Black Star…
RANGER: I don't know. This calls for lots of thinking. When we take the little fellow back to Missouri, we not only want to have him well-trained, we want him named.

It would not be until a year and a half later, in February of 1943, that Dan Reid attempted to ride the new stallion, the son of Silver, and on the broadcast of March 1, 1943, the horse was officially christened "Victor."

It was the multi-part story arcs, regardless of their length, that provided The Lone Ranger with a number of villains and overarching antagonists. Inspired by the cliffhanger serials produced by Republic Pictures, Fran Striker wrote a number of story arcs in which a series of crimes were being committed by a number of antagonists whose plot devices created obstructions for The Lone Ranger and Tonto. (In the serials, such antagonists were referred to as henchmen.) Meanwhile, off to the side, it was the villain who carried out his schemes with malicious intent. Whenever The Lone Ranger apprehended an antagonist, the villain remained at large to command orders to another antagonist. Like a game of chess, The Lone Ranger would remove pieces off the board until what remained was the villain, who would then be exposed. Whether flawed, impetus, a bully or simply evil at heart, it was the villain who remained a challenging foe for the masked man and his faithful Indian companion. It was in 1942 that Fran Striker began to assign colorful names for the villains, adding a layer of intrigue for the listeners. Among the more challenging was The Tarantula, who menaced our heroes for a total of four consecutive episodes, beginning with the broadcast of September 7, 1942.

MINNEAPOLIS, MINN.

September 22, 1941

Dear Friend:

Hearty congratulations! Silver and I sure were mighty pleased with all that fine bunch of names that came in for Silver's colt. The name you sent in was so good that the judges have told General Mills you should be sent one of the prize flashlights that are being awarded in this contest. So your Eveready flashlight will be along in about ten days, and I know you are going to enjoy using it.

Silver and I want to congratulate you, and join with the makers of KIX in thanking you for that fine name you sent in. It was one of the 1,051 prize winners - and that's good riding, pardner ... 'cause you were up against thousands of mighty fine names in this colt-naming rodeo!

And, by the way, keep listening, because we're planning some pretty great times for you on The Lone Ranger in coming weeks. Don't let anything interfere with your regular dates with . . .

Your masked pal,

The Lone Ranger

Letter sent out to children who submitted possible names
for Silver's colt.

With three dark green plastic leaves surrounding a gardenia flower was three inches in diameter, and glowed in the dark. This 1941 General Mills premium was offered in the Lone Ranger National Defenders portfolio from Kix Cereals as "Something for Mother," along with matching earring set. The premium was also offered on soap operas sponsored by General Mills and in southeastern states as a *Whistling Jim* radio premium.

Five men have been murdered in Border City, located a few miles from the Rio Grande, and The Lone Ranger and Tonto pay a visit to Texas Jack's hotel and café, to question Sheriff Dan Martin, who may have a lead on the notorious Tarantula gang. It seems no one knows the identity of The Tarantula, but he leaves his mark with the symbol of the spider on the murder weapons found at the scenes of the crime. Assisting Sheriff Martin and The Lone Ranger is the beautiful café singer, Lolita. Soon after Texas Jack receives an Ace of Spades with a picture of a tarantula on it, the ominous warning comes true as someone throws a knife into the sheriff's back, killing him. The handle of the knife has the symbol of a tarantula. The Lone Ranger quickly sets out to apprehend Buzz Handford, the man who threw the knife and was clearly a member of the outlaw gang, to learn the next person to be targeted was Don Ricardo Terrero, an American matador who is performing in the arena south of the border. Don Ricardo is also the son of the late Dan Martin. Buzz also dies from a knife in the back, but not before he reveals the outlaws' plan to the masked man.

Two members of the gang, Scanlon and Red, are ordered to kill Don Ricardo before he visits the governor of Mexico to alert him of the presence of the outlaw gang – including singling out Scanlon and Red. During the Mexican bullfight, The Lone Ranger and Tonto keep an eye on the crowd, not just the events in the arena. Lolita collapses from poison meant for Don Ricardo, but The Lone Ranger realizes the outlaws would not resort to just one method of murder. Scanlon, desperate, decides to use a crossbow that could be aimed accurately into the heart of his victim. At the close of the bullfight, just as the matador begins to face the governor to reveal knowledge of the Tarantula's gang, the crossbow is brought out and aimed. The Lone Ranger races out on top of Silver to rope the two killers, revealing the crossbow in their hands, proof of their guilt.

On the second episode of the saga, there is trouble in the town of Border City. A vicious gang of cutthroats and trail robbers banded under the sign of the Tarantula were spreading terror everywhere. Texas Jack, keeper of the hotel and café in Border City, swears to avenge the murder of his friend, Sheriff Dan Martin. Richard Martin, Dan's son, also known as Don Ricardo, is a good friend of Lolita, who recovers from the poison she drank. Meanwhile, a belt that "shines like coal fire in the night," owned by Chief Thundercloud, is the object of desire by a tribe of Apache savages living in Hawk River Valley. The savage redskins suspect the belt is magic and, led by the notorious Tarantula, wage war against Chief Thundercloud and his tribe. The Lone Ranger sends Tonto to meet Thundercloud while the masked man races out to catch up to Richard who sought vengeance against the death of his father and brings him back.

Tonto returns with his masked friend to hold a counsel of war at Barton's Pass in order to explain how two white men took advantage of Thundercloud's hospitality, sneaking out of the village late one night with the belt that glowed in the dark. It seems the Tarantula now wears the belt and lives in a large wigwam in the middle of the Apache village. The masked man sneaks into the Apache village and kidnaps the man who claims to be the Tarantula, complete with magic belt. After handing the outlaw over to Richard to escort to the sheriff's jail, Tonto splits the magic belt in two, wrapping one as a head band while The Lone Ranger wears the other as a hat band. The Apache savages, giving chase, followed the glowing light in what was a trap to lead them into Thundercloud's warrior tribe. The Apache outfit was quickly divided and conquered.

In the third chapter, it is discovered that the captured crook sitting in the jail cell at the sheriff's office is not the Tarantula. His name is Dirk and he quickly confesses all he knows about the Tarantula. All of the outlaws who worked for The Tarantula were promised a split of the combined spoils, delivering the stolen goods to a cave and taking orders only by letters left behind for them. Only outlaws wanted by the law were recruited to the fold. Dirk does not know the identity of any other outlaws because they always wore masks.

Tonto and The Lone Ranger ride out to the cave ahead of the law to explore the numerous tunnels. Inside the cave, they find a note in an empty box that was supposed to contain cash, with instructions for one of the gang members to haunt a particular house on the Sand Flats. Lem Frisby and his wife, Martha, are settlers who took up residence of a cabin on the Texas side. A crook named Summers shows up one night and spooks them by claiming no one alive ever slept in the house. The Frisbys were not normally superstitious, but the sounds of creaks and noises from outside suggest the place really is haunted. A shadowy white encounter outside suggests a ghost. The Lone Ranger and Tonto ride out to investigate and apprehend Summers, who was outside, on the roof, trying to frighten the old couple, using a stone on a string and knocking on the door. The Lone Ranger explains how the cabin was used for outlaws to smuggle drugs across the border. The old couple taking residence was a minor inconvenience. Summers was meant to scare the couple away so he could use the place like a lighthouse and provide a signal to the smugglers with a lantern. The Lone Ranger forces Summers to create the signal so the outlaws will be fooled into visiting the cabin. Not only are the drugs found in saddle bags draped over the mules, but the new sheriff and his deputies now had additional prisoners to bring in. Still, The Lone Ranger and Tonto were no closer to learning of the Tarantula's identity.

In the fourth and final chapter of the saga, broadcast September 14, 1942, Texas Jack, having served a number of prominent citizens in his café, receives a tip that a gold claim out in the hills known as The Last Chance Mine is being operated by Larkspur, a known member of the outlaw gang. When Bart Billings is found dead, his body left in the arroyo, The Lone Ranger questions Jane, the dead man's daughter. Having struck gold, Jane explains, the men working the mine cannot be seen taking the gold out so they worked at night, but brought out worthless ore by day, so no one in town would know they struck paydirt. Her father tipped her off to the scheme, only to pay with his life as a result.

Larkspur, meanwhile, receives a message from the Tarantula, asking him to bury a knife in the back of The Lone Ranger – a knife with the image of a spider on the handle. Larkspur rides into town to investigate and learn more about the masked man who was on his trail, learning from Jane that the masked man is camped at a large overhang rock.

Late that night, while camping along the arroyo, The Lone Ranger confides to Tonto that he suspects Texas Jack of being the notorious Tarantula. The Lone Ranger gets the better of Larkspur, apprehending him, then explaining how the Tarantula's scheme was to have the outlaws deposit the stolen goods in the secret cave, including gold from the Last Chance Mine, then allow The Lone Ranger to seek out each of the crooks one by one, eliminating them from the equation, so the Tarantula would not have to split the wealth. Larkspur, realizing the truth in the logic, agrees to assist The Lone Ranger in smoking out the Tarantula.

Lured to the Last Chance Mine by Jane, Texas Jack attempts to eliminate The Lone Ranger and

Tonto by setting explosives in the mine to kill them – unaware the glowing head bands were not being worn by the vigilantes. The sheriff arrives and the killer, a.k.a. The Tarantula, is apprehended. Texas Jack claims there is no proof against him, but The Lone Ranger claims Sheriff Dan Martin was killed in Texas Jack's own hotel, after the Tarantula learned of the information the law had against him. Falling for the bluff, the Tarantula spews hatred and incriminates himself. The Lone Ranger and Tonto, having smashed the outlaw operation, realize that they need to return the magic headbands. Tonto questions whether the headbands really are magic, but chuckles before they ride out.

Giveaway premiums would be incorporated on a number of *Lone Ranger* radio broadcasts so that the sponsor's announcement could lure the listeners with a promise of having the same premium emphasized in the adventures. For the Tarantula story arc, a glow-in-the-dark headband that could also double as a belt was emphasized. Immediately following the conclusion of the Tarantula story arc, the broadcast of September 16 focused once more on the magic belt.

The Lone Ranger and Tonto set out to return Chief Thundercloud's magic belt, considered a good luck charm to members of his tribe. When our heroes stumble upon a dead man who was sent to deliver kegs of gunpowder and boxes of ammunition to Chief Thundercloud, they discover a band of Apache has infested the region. Should Thundercloud lose, the marauding Indians would move south and reach the white settlers. Thundercloud's scout reports back that they are at the mercy of the attackers, fully surrounded. If only the magic belt, handed down through generations, could be returned, they could defeat the enemy. The Apache, meanwhile, demand guns, the magic belt, and the surrender of Chief Thundercloud in return for his people's safety. Unable to get to Thundercloud's camp without going through the Apache, The Lone Ranger and Tonto create short fuses and connect them to bags of powder to create explosions and clear the way. The masked man and Tonto rescue Thundercloud and race away. The Apache scurry aside as a result of the explosions. Despite the fact that Chief Thundercloud is wounded, the Apache stampede with fear. The Lone Ranger gives the magic belt to Yiota, the next in command, and orders him to lead every brave of Thundercloud's tribe in a fight to the finish, armed with tomahawks, spears, and knives. Wigwams are set ablaze, war cries split the night, and the masked man and Tonto join in the fight against the Apache. With ammunition from the wagon, Thundercloud's men gain the advantage, turning the tide of the battle. In the end, the Apache are defeated but while Chief Thundercloud knows the magic belt was anything but magic, the tribesmen insist the belt brought them both good fortune and victory.

Patty Hill, who plays Gail Manning in "The Green Hornet" and a part in the "Lone Ranger" sketch, was "Miss Michigan" in the national beauty contest of a few weeks ago. She was in the final five.

*   *   *

San Diego, May 14. Jim Dillon, KGB program director on a bus, sat behind two Negro boys just out of Sunday school. "What," asked the smallest, "is God?" The other reflected a moment, then earnestly answered, "Well, God is something like 'The Lone Ranger.'"

– *Variety*, May 15, 1940

Chapter Nine
The Death of the Lone Ranger

On December 1, 1937, the annual radio showmanship awards of *Variety* magazine awarded kudos to radio station WXYZ. To its studios went the plaque for program origination, denoting that in the field of planning and marketing entertainment, the station excelled for the calendar year of 1937.

"Its success derives from the joint efforts of shrewd managers and a hard-working staff," quoted a journalist for *Life Magazine*. It was the December 23 issue that revealed publicly for the first time who was responsible for the role of The Lone Ranger. His name was Earle Graser and according to *Life Magazine*, "The enthusiastic idolatry of Detroit children forces him to wear a black mask to work." Graser was costumed and masked for the photo in *Life* and since the station did not permit audiences during broadcasts, this meant Graser was first revealed to the public. (It was later reported that Trendle was irate at the revelation of Graser's identity at that time.)

The story for the article was promoted by Felix Holt, the publicity chief at WXYZ, who was responsible for stories in multiple trade journals including "Making the Radio Drama" for the December 15, 1936, issue of *Broadcasting* magazine, solely praising George W. Trendle for strict "story conferences" and oversight in the formation of the radio programs that originated from WXYZ. That article painted a portrait of Trendle not as creator of the programs or author, but solely as oversight and final decision maker. Trendle was livid at Holt for the revelation and photo spread of Earle Graser in *Life* magazine.

Graser never held a gun in his life, but he held three college degrees – A.B., M.A., and LL.B. – he was also a lawyer. It was estimated that 20 million radio listeners had become familiar with his voice thanks to the radio program yet, in the manner of the character he portrayed, Graser made no effort to make known his identity. His intimate acquaintances were limited, and the station took precautions to see that Graser was never publicized by name – especially in Detroit newspapers.

Earle Graser

Earle Graser was born in Canada and came to the United States when he was a young boy. A graduate of the Wayne University Law School, Graser joined the radio station dramatic staff to finance part of his way through college. Following graduation from law school, he was admitted to the bar but never practiced law. Instead, he rode the plains three nights a week and demonstrated law and order through use of the six-gun. James Jewell later recalled how Graser was an expert with timing – better than some of the actors employed at the station.

According to a press release reprinted in the November 23, 1938, issue of a Des Moines, Iowa, newspaper: "The originator of the program looked high and low before he found a man with a voice capable of emoting that high pitched and catchy phrase of 'Hi-Yo Silver.' The idea to date, due to this catchy phrase, has netted a fortune to its owner. Recently he was offered a contract of $10,000 a week for 20 weeks if he would take The Lone Ranger on tour. But he turned it down. The reason is the owner of that Hi-Yo Silver's voice is short, fat and bald, and to take him on a personal appearance tour would do things to the romantic illusion now created by The Lone Ranger."

In contrast to his adventures on the air, Graser in private life was quiet and studious – even standoffish – but only to carry through the aura of mystery which surrounded his employment. Always wanting to own a farm in Connecticut, not a ranch in Wyoming, he bought a farm in suburban Farmington, Michigan, and began to raise horses as a sideline and hobby. The quaint farmhouse he lived in was built in 1842, was amply furnished with his wife and one-year-old daughter. Earle Graser was content to play the role of the masked rider because of the steady income the radio program provided. On Tuesdays and Thursdays, Graser tended the fields on his little farm.

"Success of The Lone Ranger which originated with our broadcasting company, illustrates a point I wish could be made with every station in the country. That is, more stations should be program builders," remarked H. Allen Campbell in the February 25, 1940, issue of *The Miami News*.

"They should do less tapping in of national network programs. There are lots of radio stations right now running local programs I believe are as good as *The Lone Ranger*. But these stations don't know how to expand. Regional stations will say all the talent for air shows is in big cities, but that isn't true. Everybody who plays roles in *The Lone Ranger* show is an unknown. If our present Lone Ranger were laid up in the hospital, I could go out and get somebody else to take his place tomorrow." Campbell was neither a soothsayer nor reading tea leaves when he made that comment, but a little more than a year later the producers of *The Lone Ranger* had to face that very dilemma.

It came as a shock to the cast and crew when word reached them that Earle Walter Graser died on the morning of Tuesday, April 8, 1941, on U.S. Route 16 in front of the Farmington Methodist Church in suburban Detroit, when his automobile hurtled out of control into the rear of a parked trailer. It was assumed that he fell asleep behind the wheel of his car. He was within two blocks of his home when the mishap occurred. Caution while driving was frequently urged on *The Lone Ranger* programs, during the commercial breaks where the announcer promoted the Lone Ranger Safety Club. One little irony during the week of his death: the station was still mailing out hundreds of requested "Lone Ranger Lucky Coins" and it was only Friday night, April 18, that the station formally ended the contest for which they had struck off Lone Ranger souvenir coins, the good luck pieces which, strangely, brought no luck to The Lone Ranger himself.

Earl W. Graser, 32, was killed early Monday when his automobile hurtled into a parked trailer. And so—the voice of the "Lone Ranger," a hero to countless thousands of radio listeners, was stilled by the very hazard he sought to curb, highway traffic.

—Associated Press Wirephoto.

Earle Graser

King-Trendle Broadcasting Corporation and
The Lone Ranger, Inc.
Stroh Building
Detroit, Michigan

Gentlemen:

Pursuant to my employment contract wherein I am employed
as an actor in the cast of THE LONE RANGER radio dramatic
serial kindly be advised that I hereby agree that I will
refrain from in any way during the term of my contract or
thereafter using my name, image or photographs of me directly
or indirectly in connection with any literary, property,
advertising or exploitation wherein the title "The Lone
Ranger" shall be used.

It is my understanding that I am merely depicting a fictional
character and in no way shall I ever represent myself as
THE LONE RANGER nor will I permit any person, firm or corporation without your written permission having first been obtained to so do.

Trusting that I have made it clear that I realize I am merely
depicting a role and am not the character THE LONE RANGER,
I am

                    Yours very truly,

                 BY *Earle Graser*
                    Earle Graser

Statement signed by Earle Graser indicating that he would never permit his name to go public, if possible, as The Lone Ranger.

"*The Lone Ranger* was at the height of its popularity," recalled Raymond Meurer, "when one night we heard the tragic news that Graser had been killed in an automobile-truck accident. We visualized tomorrow's newspaper headlines saying The Lone Ranger was dead. It could kill the show." The situation was worse than imagined when Trendle phoned Meurer late that evening, April 8. Meurer quickly dressed and rushed out to the accident scene and there he learned that a boy had rushed home to fetch a camera and returned to take a photo of the death scene. Meurer spent hours finding the youngster and then having to negotiate with the parents who knew that no amount of legal intimidation could warrant surrender of the film. Meurer ultimately purchased the film (the actual funds undisclosed) and made sure it was destroyed. (Reportedly, Meurer burned the negative with his cigarette lighter and smeared the ashes with the sole of his shoe into the grass on their front yard before leaving.)

"We never wanted the identity of the actor to overshadow The Lone Ranger," Trendle issued a formal statement answering why the radio rajahs never gave Graser billing. An actor's identity (unless the element of mystery is involved) was usually withheld from publicity because the producers were afraid that if the actor became too well publicized, he or she would ask for more money.

It was at the time of his death that someone at the radio station attempted to take into account the number of times Earle Graser appeared before the microphone as the masked man, including repeat performances. The official count was 1,330 times. At the time of his tragic death in an automobile accident in 1941, he was only 32 years old, had never been west of Michigan, had never ridden a horse, and had shot a pistol only once in his life. Graser was considered a homebody and somewhat standoffish by his neighbors but at his death was considered, by all those who truly knew him, as one of the immortals of radio. Even his neighbors never knew until the time of his death that he was The Lone Ranger.

"I was with him the night it happened," recalled Ernie Winstanley. "We had a bowling team, and after the game went over to the 'Alcove' – the old watering hole – and from there we went down to the London Chop House and we were down there until 12 midnight – and, Earl, y'know, never drank anything but beer – he was a very sober guy. He left there about 12:30 and, of course, he was killed about four blocks away from his home in Farmington on Grand River Avenue. Just ran right into the back end of a big Fruehauf trailer. He was driving a 1941 Packard – the trailer was parked – apparently, he fell asleep and ran right under this thing. It was a terrible accident. And Earl was a very fine actor – he really was."

Funeral services were held on Thursday, April 10, in the German Evangelical Church in Farmington. During his funeral services, the prosaic musical numbers were omitted, and the organist instead played "The Last Roundup." Paying a last tribute, nearly 1,000 people daily, over half of them children, passed the bier of Earle W. Graser, whose secret identity was carefully guarded before then, and was now public knowledge as a result of newspaper accounts in Detroit. All were avid Lone Ranger fans, children and the parents. Children broke into tears when they learned of The Lone Ranger's death, and more tears upon viewing the body. One father brought his six children, in response to their pleas. Members of the Farmington Girl Scout troop paid tribute by attending the church services. Pupils of the Clarenceville School, located at Eight-Mile Road and Grand River Avenue, launched so many pleas to honor The Lone Ranger that their superintendent excused the fourth, fifth and sixth grades early that day. When the funeral cortege passed, 105 of these students were standing tribute at the Grand River Avenue roadside. Probably none of them realized that among the mourners was The Lone Ranger's great ally Tonto, John Todd, not wearing an Indian costume but a suit of mourning.

Brace Beemer, who would carry on in The Lone Ranger's saddle, was also present. Marguerite Werner, organist, and Cyril Wezemael, singer, both WXYZ staff, furnished the music. Pallbearers included Dr. Stuart Lottier, Kappa Chi fraternity brother of Graser at Wayne University, Dr. P.W. Portz, and the following WXYZ fellow workers: Delbrige Carter, Charles Livingstone, Felix Holt, and Harold True. George W. Trendle was an honorary pallbearer.

Perhaps nothing could have testified so eloquently to the extent to which *The Lone Ranger* had entered the national consciousness as did the amount and character of the publicity which attended Graser's death. Specifically, *The New York Times* who reported: "Death lifted The Lone Ranger's mask at daybreak today. He died at five o'clock when his car zigzagged into a parked trailer in front of the Methodist Church. None of his estimated fifteen million devoted radio listeners would have recognized their stern-voiced, hard-riding hero in the figure that lay in the wreck. He was a mild-mannered, chubby man of thirty-two, an inch or so short of six feet. Away from the microphone and remote from Silver, his snow-white horse, he was Earle W. Graser. In the eight years that breathless children have thrilled to his 'Hi-Yo Silver, Awaaaay' he lived in a white Colonial house here with his wife Jeanne. His daughter Gabrielle, is fifteen months old."

Trendle was consulted about the possibility of announcing the death of Graser on the children's program; the decision was nixed. In conformity with the long-time policy of anonymity for the cast of the show, the casting change was not announced. The radio station issued a formal statement, that it was their hope few youngsters would hear of the wreck outside Farmington Church. According to a station official: "We have to do it that way. The Lone Ranger could never die. Every kid knows that in his heart."

In an effort to ensure newspaper reporters published a photo of his choice, Meurer supplied *Times Wide World* a photograph of Earle Graser with a statuette of Silver. The wired photo made the rounds among newspapers across the country.

The next day, April 10, *The New York Times* printed a minor retraction in support of the immortal Ranger, possibly compensating for concerned parents who wanted something to prove to their discontented children. "Earle W. Graser was killed in an automobile wreck early Tuesday morning, but the rumor that The Lone Ranger is dead is unfounded. It was a man who died – a man with a silver voice, a modest, pleasant personality, several college degrees and, it was said, an ambition to act Hamlet. His death, like the deaths he tried to prevent in his radio campaign for safety, was pitifully unnecessary. But he didn't take The Lone Ranger with him. The Lone Ranger doesn't die, and Silver, his horse, will never get broken-winded."

Graser passed away on Tuesday morning. The decision to promote Brace Beemer from narrator to the title role was made before the end of the day and he was properly prepared when he arrived at the station for rehearsals on April 9. Felix Holt issued a press release regarding Graser's replacement, mentioning Brace Beemer was the original voice of The Lone Ranger and the program's current narrator. Holt was mistaken about Beemer being the original Ranger, but his statement would be reprinted all over the country in newspapers. Over the decades a misconception that Brace Beemer was the original Lone Ranger was reprinted in multiple magazine articles and reference guides. *

Graser was buried in Grand Lawn Cemetery, after services in the Salem Evangelical and Reformed Church in Farmington.

According to Dick Osgood, Al Hodge (*The Green Hornet*), Jack McCarthy (*Ned Jordan, Secret Agent*), and Jay Michael (*Challenge of the Yukon*) were too well identified with the starring roles to carry a second program.

"Beemer, a giant of a man with a deep voice, was the answer," recalled Raymond Meurer. "Beemer was a narrator on the show but left to start an ad agency, then returned to WXYZ and once again became the narrator for the program. When Earle Graser died, Beemer was hired to play The Lone Ranger. After a few scripts Tonto brought The Lone Ranger back to perfect health and the powerful voice of Beemer shouted the famous 'Hi-Yo, Silver.'"

The April 9 issue of *The New York Morning Telegraph* reported: "Officials of WXYZ said yesterday in Detroit that there would be no interruption of the series. Graser's place as The Lone Ranger will be taken by Brace Beemer... Some doubt was expressed, however, as to whether the millions of children who tune in on the program will go for the change in voice."

Myron Wallace, a student at Michigan University, began his radio career playing supporting roles and doubling as an announcer at radio stations WXYZ and WOOD. Having devoted four years, beginning in 1937, to being behind the microphone, it was briefly suggested that Wallace replace Graser as The Lone Ranger. "He had the right voice but Trendle didn't think he could act and turned down the suggestion," Dick Osgood later recalled. Wallace continued as an announcer for *Ned Jordan, Secret Agent* and *The Green Hornet*, among other assignments. (Some reference guides state 1937, but the earliest verification that Myron Wallace was on *The Lone Ranger* was in the role of Bob, a 15-year-old who lost his father as a result of two killers, in "The Letter Steals a Murder," broadcast September 20, 1940. Thanks to extant recordings, today you can also hear Wallace as the announcer for *The Lone Ranger* on the broadcast of December 16, 1940.

"I left WXYZ in September of 1941 because I had a chance to go to Chicago and that seemed to be the Big Time," Wallace later recalled, but confirmed his decision to leave had nothing to do with being turned down for the role of The Lone Ranger. "I felt later on that I should probably have stayed in Detroit a little longer, rather than going into Chicago insufficiently prepared. I probably would have done better and been happier."

In Chicago, Wallace served as both announcer and/or commercial spokesman for numerous radio programs including *Vic and Sade*, *The Road to Life*, *Curtain Time*, *Meet the Meeks* and *Sky King*. By 1948 it was decided by more than one advertising agency to give Wallace a chance to star in his own weekly crime program, through various pilot auditions and short-lived series including *The Crime Files of Flamond*, *Crime on the Waterfront*, *Security Agent*, *USA*, and *A Life in Your Hands* (based on the creation of Erle Stanley Gardner). Sometime in 1951 he changed his name to Mike Wallace

---

* While a number of historians insist that Brace Beemer never appeared as a cast member on *The Green Hornet* because his voice became familiar to faithful radio listeners of *The Lone Ranger*, he did play a number of supporting roles on *The Green Hornet* including "The Money in the Meter" (broadcast Aug. 15, 1939) and "Speed Traps a Lawbreaker" (broadcast Oct. 12, 1939).

Cast of *The Green Hornet* in a promotional photo.

and in 1953 made the move to New York City where he would advance to both radio and television broadcasting at CBS and become the imposing figure probing interviewees on the television program, *Nightbeat*. Wallace would, years later, become synonymous with the long-running CBS television program, *60 Minutes*.

With Brace Beemer set to replace Earle Graser, Fran Striker came across a solution to help the radio audience avoid noticing the change in voice. Back in July 1940, Earle Graser wanted to go on vacation for two weeks so Striker wrote a story arc in which the masked man, lying wounded in a cave, was being nursed back to health by his Indian companion. Tonto assisted a new friend, Arizona, in tracking down the location of gold robbers in the Spanish Flats, and helped the sheriff apprehend them. The Lone Ranger slept in a cave, recovering from his wounds. Brace Beemer played the role of The Lone Ranger for a brief line or two but only as whispers, a short distance from the microphone, attempting to mimic the voice of Earle Graser. For the broadcast of April 9, 1941, Striker decided to utilize a similar premise.

Following with the sound effects of a gunshot and a grunt, the illusion was created that The Lone Ranger had been shot. Trendle and the crew hoped that when the newspapers reported Graser's death in the newspapers, children would react by listening to the broadcast and remark, "Oh no, he's not dead. He's only wounded." That was the broadcast of April 9 and The Lone Ranger, while trying to prevent a range war, was shot and badly wounded. Beemer's first assignment for the program was to whisper a few words as The Lone Ranger, weak from the near-fatal bullet wound. Tonto looked after him, mending the wounds and treating his friend with herbs and medicinal soup, while his masked friend lay in a bed at Mustang Mag's ranch.

"With great agility, Striker, who wrote more than 2,000 *Lone Ranger* scripts, dreamed up a scene in which The Lone Ranger was shot," recalled Meurer. "Tonto, played by John Todd, a Shakespearean actor also from the old Bonstelle Playhouse, would start nursing him back to health." For the next several radio scripts, the only sound to be heard from The Lone Ranger were grunts and groans, and a voice whispering to his Indian companion. "Brace was not the easiest man to get along with and his ego sometimes got in the way," recalled Meurer. "For years he would tell varied stories of how he took over the role from Graser, including a legend that he beat out multiple people auditioning for the role. I heard a story of a third party that Brace got down on his knees and begged for the role. The truth is, it was decided he would fill in for the late Earle Graser before the first broadcast aired following the accident." Meurer's recollection affirms what is evident when listening to the extant recordings – Brace Beemer is whispering The Lone Ranger's lines so the radio audience would slowly adjust to the new voice. It was also during these particular broadcasts that the trademark "Hi-Yo, Silver" opening was never used. After all, the masked man is supposed to be wounded in a cave.

Mustang Mag lights three fires to call on Tonto, who rides to her ranch to receive news that the masked man was recently wounded in a range war. The homesteaders are building fences, and cattlemen and ranchers are upset. Both sides are justified, both have rights. With the masked man shot and wounded, Tonto must pick up where he left off. Meanwhile, in a café in town, Sam Collins, Bevin, and Miller, cattlemen, meet to mastermind a plot against the homesteaders. Dan Farnsworth, in charge of the homesteaders, represents the opposing side. The Lone Ranger, resting at the home of Mustang Mag, provides instructions in writing, which Tonto delivers to Betty Farnsworth, Dan's daughter. Putting implicit faith in Tonto and following instructions from The Lone Ranger, Betty visits Miller to trick him into thinking Bevin arranged for a tax to have cattle cross the land. Miller quickly deduces that he is being stabbed in the back. She then rides to another ranch house and tricks Collins into believing the same. During a late-night rendezvous, the cattlemen meet to find themselves facing the homesteaders. Each of the three men, not wanting to be implicated in back-stabbing the other, signs an agreement with Dan Farnsworth to avert further war.

For the broadcast of April 11, The Lone Ranger is still lying wounded at Mustang Mag's ranch but two killers named Kincaid and Trigger crave vengeance against the masked man since their arrest in Albuquerque. Because they learn where The Lone Ranger is recovering from his wounds, Mag and Missouri move the masked man, still weak from exhaustion, to a nearby cave. Once again, Beemer whispered only a few words.

At the cave, Mag and Missouri work desperately to revive the masked man's failing strength. Mustang Mag knows that if Kincaid and Trigger learn the whereabouts of The Lone Ranger, they will make for the cave to get the masked man while he lay vulnerable and she will be outnumbered. The killers, meanwhile, break into her ranch house and ransack the rooms in search of their prey. While the duly elected sheriff, Missouri, creates a distraction, Tonto sets out to fetch the U.S. Marshal.

Back at the cave, Mustang Mag nurses the wounds and changes the bandages and damp cloths. For a moment she confesses that she has the rare opportunity to take off the mask that her patient wears even when sleeping, and he would never know. But even though she had the chance to learn who the masked man was, she decided against it. "I'm not gonna touch that mask, no Sir," she remarks. "Because that's part of The Lone Ranger." She then scolded herself for being sentimental.

Kincaid has a total of 10 to 12 men backing his play. After discovering the cave, he and the men make plans to attack at dawn. He suspects the law will soon arrive, but he knows he has the advantage. At the earliest light, Kincaid and Trigger lead the men to the cave, armed and hellbent to kill, only to find the cave empty. Just as they realize it was a ruse, a trap, a landslide blocks the entrance, trapping all of the men inside. A couple hours prior, under the cover of darkness, The Lone Ranger and Mustang Mag had vacated the cave and made sure the landslide would not seal the men totally. A few potshots from outside keep the crooks inside trapped long enough for the Marshal and his deputies to arrive and take control of the gophers.

For the broadcast of April 14, the homesteaders are bringing wagons through the territory and the cattlemen once again have a beef against the intruders, fearing their own cattle will be stolen. The immigrants are headed to the Santa Clara Valley which is almost 300 miles to the west. The government has just opened that land to the settlers and Jim Carson leads the 150 wagons to the valley. The Lone Ranger, still wounded and being cared for by Mustang Mag, uses notes to communicate with Tonto, providing instructions to Jim. While the ranchers and settlers combine to fight against the oncoming immigrants, a great flood begins. Wind, rain, and storm clouds from the mountains create the worst-case scenario. Flood waters threaten ranchers, homesteads, and settlers alike.

The immigrants, realizing the peril to all involved, start filling canvas bags with dirt and create a levee. A race to provide materials in strategic areas proves challenging. Shortly after dark, the bridge is carried away but the materials have already been divided between the two banks. The great timbers crash against the earthworks.

It is a little past midnight when a final crash of thunder and a last jagged spark of lightning spread across the sky. The rain stops but the river continues to rise, minute by minute, hour by hour. If the levee breaks, a great wall of water will sweep across the valley. The Lone Ranger refuses to be evacuated and insists on being taken to the river to see the men and women working to save the valley. His appearance there has the desired effect, inspiring everyone to pull together, regardless of whether they are cattlemen, immigrants, homesteaders, or ranchers. All of them work frantically. Haggard and weary, but without any thought of rest, the men fight desperately but still the river keeps rising. In the end, the gathering of many hands saves the valley and everyone cheers.

For the broadcast of April 16, Tonto gets down on his knees and prays that the Ranger will live, but The Lone Ranger's condition does not improve until the broadcast of April 18, when, at the end of the show, The Lone Ranger sounds normal and helps Tonto rescue two prospectors guarding a shipment of gold. After two weeks of being nursed back to health in a cave, the period of inactivity was utilized in order that the new Lone Ranger's slightly different voice quality would not be noticed by the younger audience.

For the broadcast of April 16, two gunslingers and notorious outlaws, Jake Smith and Cleve, learn from the Western Union office the news of The Lone Ranger, who was being called upon by Washington. The government paper tells all about plans of renegade armies over the border. The Lone Ranger was supposed to turn it over to Colonel Blake, but he was shot before he could deliver. Baldy Hanover, meanwhile, makes plans with Jake and Cleve to steal those government papers and hold The Lone Ranger for ransom. The good men of the community know that if the masked man's life was in jeopardy, they would pay handsomely. The bartender in town overhears Baldy's scheme and races to Mustang Mag's ranch to alert her of the plot. To back his play, Baldy pays a visit to the local tribesmen to have a tribe of Apache make war on Mustang Mag. Tonto, meanwhile, confesses he has never seen a wound that he could not heal until now. Sick with worry, Tonto assures Mustang Mag that The Lone Ranger, now back at her ranch, cannot be moved again. From this viewpoint, The Lone Ranger is threatened by both criminals and savages as well as the serious infection from his wounds.

Meanwhile, the Indians a few miles away shout and dance with wild leaps about their council fires. The townsmen bring their weapons to Mustang Mag's as each group of pioneers arrive in the course of the night. Tonto meets with the men and tells them the unpleasant news; it was The Lone Ranger's desire not to have any life lost. The sun rises the next morning with about 50 men in place in Mustang Mag's house and barn, ready to defend the life of The Lone Ranger, whose face is drawn by weakness and saddened by the sight of so many friends who stand ready to lay down their lives in his defense. The masked man is on a bunk in the center of the house, barricaded by upturned tables and trunks.

Then the Indians set fire in the area, ready to shoot arrows with flame. They face off against open gunfire. Despite the townspeople and ranchers determined to repel the siege at Mustang Mag's ranch, The Lone Ranger decides to give himself up. Just as everything looks bleak, a bugle call from the distance is heard. With guns firing, Colonel Blake in the large body of troops first intervened. The Indians know better than to face those hard riding soldiers. The Indians flee and the troops pursue. The Lone Ranger walks outside the house and races into the open to watch the thrilling spectacle of flags and banners flying above the riders' heads. Colonel Blake himself rides to the house and dismounts. He steps inside to shake the hand of the masked man, assuring him protection in the future and a prominent doctor as the U.S. Government wants to repay The Lone Ranger for all that he has done. For the first time, Tonto sheds tears of joy.

On the broadcast of April 18, in the desolate Shawnee country, a heavily laden freight wagon for Wells Fargo falls into the hands of Lance and Donner, two crooks who murder an express agent and lay siege to the wagon loaded with gold. The Lone Ranger, still weak but now well enough to leave Mustang Mag's ranch, teams with Tonto and Missouri to outwit the band of crooks. The wagon wheels are smashed with an axe to prevent further movement and The Lone Ranger knows the crooks have little options to move the ore. It would take many men and many horses. The two surviving prospectors, Shorty and Jasper, are stuck in the foxhole with no method of escape. Following orders from The Lone Ranger, courtesy of a note delivered by Tonto's arrow, the prospectors work their way downstream. The Lone Ranger's years of healthy living gave him a vitality that brought strength back rapidly once he started on the road to full recovery. With the assistance of Old Missouri, the men created a prairie schooner far upstream. This was the means of escape for the men who lay hidden in ambush. Their escape tricks Lance and Donner and their men into believing the escape would also mean they lose the gold – which proves to be their undoing when they find themselves trapped and surrounded. The adventure closed with the masked man mounting on his great White Horse for a brief moment, as Silver gave a mighty cry of happiness.

It was at the close of this broadcast that Beemer's first rendition of "Hi Yo, Silver, Awaaay!" was first delivered. This was also Brace Beemer's first appearance as The Lone Ranger in full voice.

During the broadcast of April 21, Brace Beemer attempted to play the role using mannerisms remnant of Earle Graser, but it was quickly evident that he should play the role in his own distinct style. (Depending on varied recollections of cast and crew, Beemer attempted to mimic Graser at the request of director Charles Livingstone, but afterwards informed the director that it was proven not to work and moving forward he would play the role as he felt it should be played.)

The April 21, 1941, issue of *Newsweek* reviewed the new Ranger and described Beemer as "the direct antithesis of Graser for the part." *Time* magazine went so far as to feature a photo of Brace Beemer, commenting "His voice is so much like Graser's that his substitute version of the Ranger's famed cry to his horse, 'Hi Yo Silver, Away' will scarcely be noticed by all the nation's moppets."

But not all young listeners were duped into believing the same actor was playing the role. In a dissertation by Irving Robbins titled, *Teaching Radio Program Discrimination in the Public Schools*, Ohio State, 1942, remarked: "One day the students were talking about the Lone Ranger. They knew that the real Lone Ranger had been killed in an automobile accident. The new Lone Ranger had a different voice. Jack said, 'He talks like he had a bad cold.'"

On the afternoon of May 5, the Robin Hood on Horseback returned to WGN in Chicago, which had been off that station since the start of the baseball season because no afternoon time was available for the games. *The Lone Ranger* was heard at a new time, 7:30 pm, and it was on May 5 that Chicago listeners were first hearing the new voice, Brace Beemer, in the lead, having never heard the transition broadcasts of April. There is nothing found to verify whether radio listeners in Chicago noticed the voice difference.

By the first week of May 1941, a photo of Brace Beemer posing as The Lone Ranger with hands on hips and dressed all in black, was circulating for publicity purposes. It would be this photo that Trendle would use repeatedly for members of the press, and perhaps the most reprinted and seen photo of Beemer as The Lone Ranger.

Uncertain how long to maintain the story arc of a wounded Ranger, Fran Striker wrote one script more than was needed, titled "The Silver Dollar." The story concerned Sheriff Morton of Greggsville who lost four deputies due to a notorious gang of stage robbers, and Tonto delivering a message from The Lone Ranger that helps assist the sheriff create a set-up meant to trick the outlaws to ride out to Potter's Cave where the masked man was supposedly hiding. The trap works as the sheriff and his posse catch the outlaws by surprise, surrounding them at gunpoint. The radio script would be tweaked (minorly) and eventually broadcast on September 4, 1942, with no reference of The Lone Ranger being wounded and Brace Beemer's voice as The Lone Ranger is never heard on the program.

On April 13, 1941, a letter was mailed to station KFRC in San Francisco, which was promptly forwarded to Fran Striker. According to the letter, on the afternoon of April 7, a little boy who faithfully listened to *The Lone Ranger* adventures was also killed in an automobile accident. That little boy was a fan of *The Lone Ranger* program. "Our minister said it was very beautiful in the funeral services Thursday morning at the Little

Chapel of the Flowers when he said The Lone Ranger, 'took him by the hand and they went away together.' This strange coincidence is touching to me. We would like to get a more definite account of The Lone Ranger's death and also a few facts about his life to add to the memoirs of our dear little boy. Could you supply us with these please?" Striker answered the letter by sharing a newspaper clipping from a Detroit newspaper.

Brace Beemer

Whenever H. Allen Campbell went out of state for business, he made it a policy to listen to the radio. While sitting in his Indianapolis hotel room, he listened to a program of poetry. The man delivering it had an exceptional voice, Campbell thought. After calling the station and asking to speak to Brace Beemer, he invited the actor to the hotel for dinner. During the course of the meal, Campbell offered Beemer a job in Detroit for a four-week basis (which was standard procedure in those days). A short time afterward, Beemer migrated to Motor City and auditioned for both Trendle and Howard Pierce. The men did not pretend to be talent experts and throughout the entire audition, they chatted businesses. After Beemer completed his assignment, which was heard over the speaker in the boardroom, Campbell asked them of their opinion. Neither were impressed. Campbell did his best to restrain from anger.

"Gentlemen," Campbell said, "I hope that you will not feel that I am too much out of order, but I'm having a difficult time controlling my temper. I hired this man. I believe he has one of the finest voices I've ever heard but for one half-hour you men have sat there yakkin' – to the extent that I couldn't even hear the audition. I didn't need to because I've already heard him. But – this is no way to judge a man." According to Dick Osgood, neither Trendle nor Pierce spoke; Trendle got up and returned to his office; and Beemer stayed at the station, almost permanently.

Born in Mt. Carmel, Illinois, December 9, 1902, the son of Mr. and Mrs. Joseph David Beemer of Connerville, Indiana, Brace Beemer was a rambunctious young man who would one day become an iconic symbol to millions. (One source reported he was born in Kentucky and raised on his father's stock farm in Mount Carmel, Illinois, but the Kentucky reference is incorrect.) Contrary to legend, Brace was indeed a family surname, not a stage handle invented to match the brace of silver and ivory Colt .45-caliber "peace-makers" the Ranger always carried. When he was in the ninth grade Beemer found it hard to accept a teacher who he said lectured continually on the merits of Kaiser Wilhelm II's Germany. No longer willing to tolerate what his teacher was saying, Brace one afternoon stood up and said, "You shouldn't talk about the United States that way." Apparently, a few blows followed, and after Brace's father had a talk with the school principal it was decided that there was nothing that the school could do with him.

At the age of 14 years, four months, and 12 days, Beemer enlisted in the 150th Field Artillery and was attached to Colonel Douglas MacArthur's Rainbow Division of the American Expeditionary Force. There was another man who also joined the Army because of the same school incident and when the two of them found themselves in France near the front lines his friend said that he was going back home. "Not me," replied Brace, "This is why I came over here. To fight." At the time he became the youngest soldier to serve in the American Expeditionary Forces during World War I and the youngest soldier to serve under General Douglas MacArthur.

Overseas, he served 111 consecutive days in the trenches in France. He saw action at Argonne and Luneville with the Rainbow Division, 150th Field Artillery, Battery E. He was gassed and twice wounded, for which stout-hearted Beemer won the military order of the Purple Heart. He received the Victory medal with battle bars, and an accolade from President Wilson. He came out of the war as the division's youngest survivor after seeing action at Belleau Wood, St. Mihiel, and Chateau Thierry. Though wounded twice, and decorated for valor, he never made it to high school until after his discharge. Despite his height, teachers thought he was still a boy, but the Army had made a man out of him. *

The Beemer family owned a chain of music stores in Southern Indiana and Illinois. In 1922, Beemer's father brought home a radio set. "It was one of those 14 dial affairs, you know," Brace later recalled. "It was then I told my dad that I was going to work in radio." He shortly quit horse raising and set out to see the world. It was that same year on station WKBF in Indianapolis that Beemer was hired as a singer, known as "The Mystery Baritone."

As Beemer recalled, "I was a fairly fair singer and I used to have a daily show where I sang a few songs… One day, for some reason, the announcer didn't show up. What else could I do? I picked up the commercial and read it. Later the guy who had bought the time came into the station and asked who read the commercial." When the station manager apologized, explaining why the regular announcer could not make it that day, Beemer was assigned the full-time job of program announcer. Beemer was on his way with a career in radio.

* His military record was rarely brought up in newspapers during his tenure at WXYZ because of a strict policy by George W. Trendle that Brace Beemer not bring up his military past during interviews, even when he was not in The Lone Ranger costume. In later years, during one interview with a newspaper reporter, Beemer was scratching at one of his legs when shrapnel came out. (He still carried some of the shrapnel in his legs until the day he died.)

Among the news copy, announcing, and spot announcements, he was also featured on a poetic-narrative show with Russell Neff, the "Silver-Voiced Tenor." This show, called the *Wandering Vagabond*, was broadcast in the early evening. One newspaper critic agreed with Campbell's view and claimed Beemer was "a fine poetic reader and oral interpreter." This comment was in reference to Beemer reading poetry on a program entitled, *The Night Shall Be Filled with Music*.

By the summer of 1931, Beemer was also moonlighting on the stage at the Detroit Laboratory Theater. By 1932, Beemer was the station's chief announcer and studio manager. A year later, following the departure of George Stenius in the title role of The Lone Ranger, Brace Beemer asked to play the lead. According to Jim Jewell, in an interview with author David Rothel, "He practically got down on his hands and knees to ask me to allow him to play The Lone Ranger when Jack Deeds went into the program. I refused him… I would never allow him to play the part." Later, Beemer became the announcer and narrator for the program. Inter-office memos and historical documents verify Beemer was the narrator for *The Lone Ranger* program from June to October 1934, and again from November 1938 through April 1941, but on and off with Al Chance, Myron Wallace and John Slagle occasionally as the announcer. (For a brief spell, Beemer was also the announcer on *Challenge of the Yukon* in 1939.) When Beemer took over the role of The Lone Ranger, Harry Golder became the new announcer, an almost permanent position until Fred Foy in 1948.

Replacing Earle Graser as The Lone Ranger, Brace Beemer signed a new employment contract, dated April 28, 1941, stipulating that beginning May 5, he would receive $150 per week on a non-commercial basis and $200 if sponsored on a national basis comparable to the General Mills-Lone Ranger sponsorship. Beginning May 5, 1944, Beemer received a raise but under specific stipulations. Beemer would be paid $300 a week when the radio program was sponsored in all three territories, $250 if sponsored only in two of those territories, and $200 under alternative sponsorship or non-sponsorship.

Territory #1 – General Mills, National, East and Midwest
Territory #2 – Merita, Regional, South
Territory #3 – Don Lee, Regional, West Coast

When Beemer first took over the role of The Lone Ranger on radio, he mastered "Hi-Yo Silver" but had difficulty getting "Away" with the proper inflection. This happened so many times that for a spell a recording of Earle Graser's signature was used at the close of the program. Later, when Beemer was able to pull it off at least once for recording, the new sound bite replaced Graser's.

Months after the changing of the guard, the November 19, 1941 broadcast of *The Lone Ranger* was reviewed by *Variety*: "Plenty of gunplay and lots of hard riding in each installment. Brace Beemer, who has replaced the late Earle Graser, is properly robust and direct as Ranger, while the supporting parts are all played without attempts at unnecessary subtlety... It's obviously a belt-line production job, but adequate for adventure dialers."

By coincidence, Grosset & Dunlap published a hardcover novel that same month and year (April 1941), from the pen of Fran Striker, *The Lone Ranger Rides*, in which the masked man fought 20 to 1 odds against an outlaw gang, wounded and beaten, having held them at bay long enough for rancher vigilantes to arrive and apprehend. The fight was brutal, resulting in The Lone Ranger collapsing from beatings, lacerations and physical abuse no man should endure. For the last third of the novel, Tonto devoted his time nursing The Lone Ranger back to health, searching the innermost recesses of his memory for treatments that had been handed down from generation to generation. The Lone Ranger, although weakened, recovered due to the miraculous healing and nursing proficiencies of Tonto. Meanwhile, during the weeks The Lone Ranger worked to regain his strength, Ace Cardigan regained his corrupt – and criminal – hold on Beacon City. Only in the last chapter was a wounded and weakened Lone Ranger well enough to leave his bed and seek vengeance. Only then did The Lone Ranger reappear, swinging a punch and dragging Ace Cardigan by the lapel of his coat, with the gambler's hand holding the point of his chin in a way that indicated where the blow had landed. Throwing the crook out into the streets to be judged for his crimes against society, justice was meted out.

"As a man, Brace was one of the finest individuals I've ever had the good fortune to know and to work with," recalled Charles Livingstone. "He had a heart as big as he was. He was a man's man, let's say. He was opinionated. He definitely had his own ideas on how certain things should be done,

WAIVER AND RELEASE

KNOW ALL MEN BY THESE PRESENTS that I, *Brace Beemer*,
of Detroit, Michigan, an employee of the King-Trendle Broadcasting Corporation, a Michigan Corporation of Detroit, Wayne County, Michigan, for
and in consideration of the sum of one dollar ($1.00) and other good and
valuable considerations, including my present employment, do by these
presents expressly and forever give, grant, bargain, transfer, assign
and surrender to the said King-Trendle Broadcasting Corporation, its
successors and assigns, all of my right, title and interest in and to any
services which may be rendered by me for, on account of, or to said
corporation, including services as a member of the cast of various radio
playlets and broadcasts, recordings, electrical transcriptions, television
and any and all mechanical reproductions of sound, together with the right
to said corporation to do with my services as it will and to give, sell or
license any and all uses to others and to do any and all other and/or
manner of things incidental thereto as said corporation may desire.

I expressly and forever do grant, set over, assign and surrender to
said corporation any and all of my right, title and interest in and to any
pictures, photographs, images, resemblances or personal likenesses made by
any process now known or which may hereafter be known, including drawings,
sketches and any and all other reproductions which shall be made of me at
the expense of said corporation during the period of my employment with
said corporation, and said corporation thereafter shall be entitled to the
sole use of any or all of the matters and things in this paragraph contained, to copyright the same, including renewals of any such copyrights,
and to use and license the use to others for any and all legitimate
purposes.

Dated, Detroit, Michigan *April 8*   ,1941

                                        Brace Beemer (L.S.)

Witness:

        Raymond Meurer

April 8, 1941 contract signed by Beemer waiving all rights to name and image.

and, naturally, in the stress of rehearsals we used to come to differences of ideas, but Brace's ideas were entirely set on what The Lone Ranger would say and do. He was the man physically, he was the man mentally, and he was The Lone Ranger in his heart."

The June 1943 issue of *Tune In* magazine described Beemer as being "every inch the Lone Ranger that he plays. Never drinks, smokes, chews or uses a cuss word, either as The Lone Ranger or as Beemer." Under contract, Beemer was never allowed to smoke where children were present or when appearing in costume as The Lone Ranger, with the added stipulation that "The Lone Ranger character is to be kept strictly mysterious."

Brace Beemer believed in the ideals of The Lone Ranger and he carried them through in his life outside of the studio. When asked where Beemer stopped and The Lone Ranger started, and vice versa, the actor told people that only when he arrived home, he was no longer The Lone Ranger. But everyone who worked with him and lived with him claimed he was The Lone Ranger, always.

The Beemer family eventually moved to Oxford, Michigan, a suburb north of the city of Detroit. Along with his wife Leta (married in 1937), they raised three sons, Robert, Richard and J.D., and one daughter, Barbara, who were born during Brace's prior marriage to Evelyn (Coovert) Lilley. During his tenure at WXYZ, he bred and trained paints and palominos at his 300-acre estate near Oxford, Michigan, which boasted a couple of lakes and a swift trout stream. He owned two white stallions, named Silver's Pride and Sundust, both of which were taken on the road. Together they were used many times when Beemer made personal appearances as The Lone Ranger. Silver's Pride was the horse Brace liked the best and used often. Tourists were always trying to track him down at his home and things got so bad that he eventually had to have a high picket fence erected around his estate to insure him a little privacy in his unmasked hours.

Included among the honors The Lone Ranger received were his induction into the Pawnee, Sioux and Seminole Indian tribes. He went through a four-day ritual of rites making him a Pawnee Chief given by Chief Young Eagle. His name was Nesaro-Kitti-puk-ki, Chief of all young people. In Montreal he was bestowed a lifetime membership in the Legion of Frontiersmen (a British worldwide military and police organization); in Houston, an honorary Texas Ranger; in many counties across the nation, a deputy sheriff; and all over the nation since 1943 he was welcomed and feted in public appearances by crowds into the millions. *

One day a long-distance call was received from the president of Colt Arms asking for an autographed picture of The Lone Ranger. He sent such a picture and after a short time he received a letter thanking him. It went on to say that there was a package being sent and it was hoped that Brace would accept the gift. When the package did arrive, it turned out to contain a matched pair of pearl-handled Colt .45 Peacemakers. As it turned out, these pistols were the last ones of this particular model, valued at $2,500. Other gifts over the years included a pair of silver spurs worth $1,000.

---

* By an unusual series of events, the Rainbow Division got hooked up with the famous radio feature. While Leland L. Whitney of Cleveland was national president, he decided the Rainbow Hour on February 22, 1937, should be a dramatization of Rainbow battle experiences in France. The Michigan Chapter went to bat in Detroit and the manager of Station WXYZ of that city agreed to furnish a cast and make WXYZ the key station for a nationwide NBC hookup that included about 70 stations. The script for the broadcast was written by Jack Henry of Marysville and the manager of the Detroit station assigned the continuity job to a chap named Fran Striker.

The Lone Ranger at the White House with Johnny Boettiger.

The Lone Ranger at the White House.

Security present, The Lone Ranger may have been the first to go into the Senate building with guns strapped, and possibly the first visitor on White House grounds to carry guns. On the morning of October 23, masked and in full western regalia, Brace Beemer was a guest at the White House to see Mrs. Anna Roosevelt Boettiger and her son, Johnny. Mrs. Roosevelt asked him to give an exhibition on the back lawn of the White House. He and his fiery steed went through their routine. Afterwards, President Roosevelt's five-year-old grandson became the envy of millions of young Americans when he mounted Silver, with The Lone Ranger holding firm, taking the child around the White House grounds. A couple photos from that morning made it to the newspapers in the days that followed.

At one point during the ride, Johnny wanted to handle and fire one of The Lone Ranger's guns. With all the Secret Service men looking on, Beemer took his .45 revolver from its holster and put it in John's small hand. The gun was loaded with blanks. Upon leaving late that afternoon, the Secret Service agent admitted, with obvious embarrassment, that no one had ever entered the President's home while armed with a gun. The Lone Ranger spent the entire afternoon on the grounds and none of the agents or security guards ever thought of disarming him or examining the weapons.

Harry Golder

With Beemer moving into the top spot, Harry Golder became the successor as both announcer and narrator for *The Lone Ranger*. Golder was a master at delivery, having reigned above most of his classmates in the debates held at the College of the City of Detroit. Among his earliest contributions at WXYZ was delivering the play-by-play for local baseball games in 1934, host of the early morning *Breakfast Club* throughout 1936, and a series regular on the daily *Farm Market Reporter* program. Golder was regarded by Trendle as the best newscaster at the station for more than a decade. Golder continued with his daily news assignments while he served as an announcer for *The Lone Ranger*, reportedly never attending rehearsals for the children's program fifty percent of the time after 1944. Golder's last contribution would be the broadcast of June 28, 1948, stepping aside for Fred Foy. *

Earle Graser's passing was the first of what would become a migratory shift in staffing for *The Lone Ranger* radio program, and not always for the best of reasons. Up until 1941 the radio program consisted of a stock company – voices both familiar and distinct to the faithful listener that recognition could not be avoided when the same actor who played the old miner on Monday's program was heard playing the sheriff on Wednesday's broadcast and the drunk townsman on Friday.

On Tuesday, June 10, 1941, Herschel Mayall, pioneer picture player, brought into silent films

_____

* Throughout the years announcers for the program included Bob Hite, Harold True, Charles Wood, Hal Neal, and Fred Foy.

by the legendary Thomas H. Ince, died in St. Mary's hospital at Detroit, after being stricken several days prior with a cerebral hemorrhage. He was 78 years old and left no known relatives. At the time of his death, Mayall had been playing character roles for nine years on, among others, *The Lone Ranger* and *The Green Hornet*. Mayall left Detroit a few times for professional commitments, but always returned. One such example was October through December 1938 to perform on stage in Cincinnati, playing heavies in *Queen of Liars* and as Svengali in Du Maurier's *Trilby*. He returned to Cincinnati again in April 1939 to play the villain in Richard Mansfield's *Baron Chevrial*. (Even when he was playing roles on radio at WXYZ, he was moonlighting on the Detroit stage.)

happy way.

Maurice Freeman is a born villain on the stage, and his acting as Legree far outclasses anything he has yet attempted. Herschell Mayall, Hudson Liston and J. J. Collins did well, Mr. Liston, as usual, furnishing the comedy. Louis Le Bey and Basil Burwell were fair.

Reference of Mayall in the cast of *Uncle Tom's Cabin* in the June 19, 1894, issue of *The Saint Paul Globe* (Saint Paul, Minnesota).

A screen contemporary of Dustin and William Farnum, Theda Bara and William S. Hart, Mayall was born in Kentucky. It was while attending school in Minneapolis that he took a minor role in an Edwin Booth road show. It was Booth's advice that continued him in theatre. He once boasted he still would have been playing Frisco if the earthquake hadn't toppled the theatre in which he played stock for six straight years. He was amongst the cast of Hall Caine's *The Christian*, founded upon his novel of the same name, at the Alhambra Theater, playing the role of John Storm when the earthquake hit. Immediately after the tragedy he left for Salt Lake City to perform on stage, intent on avoiding California for the rest of his life. His first Broadway appearance was in *The Garden of Allah*. Thomas Ince signed him and took him into films shortly after the 1906 earthquake. Mayall performed with most of the early stars, being Theda Bara's leading man in a score of pictures. He played the king in Thomas Ince's *Civilization*. He appeared in motion pictures for 18 years.

At WXYZ, on *The Lone Ranger*, he commonly played a senator, banker or the heroine's father. He became ill on June 6, 1941, dropping his script three times during the performance of *The Lone Ranger*, but like any dedicated stage actor who lived by the motto "the show must go on," continued through to the end of the broadcast. The cast knew something was wrong but he insisted he could finish playing the part. He never returned to the studio after that performance, though, and four days later passed away. He left a widow and one son.

Chapter Ten
The Victory Corps and Dan Reid

THE LONE RANGER BECAME THE CENTER of attention for a WXYZ special broadcast in 1941. Built at a cost of approximately $100,000, a new 5,000-watt transmitting plant was officially dedicated on Thanksgiving Day, November 23, 1939. Authorized by the FCC to increase its daytime power from 1,000 to 5,000 watts, the station built the new facility on 18-acre plot six or seven miles from Detroit. The power increase, reported *Radio Daily*, would substantially improve the radius of the station and intensify its signal throughout its service area. NBC devoted its *Club Matinee* program to WXYZ the afternoon of the dedication. But Trendle himself had a greater goal — increased power at night, which would provide coverage throughout Michigan, Ohio, and Indiana.

A campaign, high-powered itself, announced WXYZ's boost to 5,000 watts at night, starting Friday, February 21, 1941, at 7 p.m. The highlight of the promotional campaign was the presentation of a special 30-minute dedicatory program, which began a half hour later, aired only over the Michigan Radio Network.

The station bought space in business journals, daily newspapers in Detroit and the metropolitan area, weekly newspapers throughout Michigan, Ohio, and Indiana, and in Detroit neighborhood periodicals. To ensure comprehensive listener attention, special counter cards were placed in 5,500 retail stores located within the general scope of the new 5,000-watt coverage. More than 1,600 cards were distributed inside and outside of Detroit to passengers on suburban streetcars and buses. A total of 80 motion picture theaters in Detroit and surrounding cities carried special trailers for 10 days and, a direct mail campaign to time buyers and sponsors was conducted.

According to the February 17, 1941, issue of *Radio Daily*, cash awards totaling $300 and 10,000 special Lone Ranger good luck emblems were to be given away. Sixty cash prizes in all were awarded for the best 25-word letters describing the program, with $100 for first place, $50 for second and

$25 for third. Cash prizes were paid in silver dollars coined from 1860 to 1880, the period during which The Lone Ranger was supposed to have ridden the western plains. Trendle also tossed a dilly into the lap of Fran Striker since one of the highlights of the exploitation campaign was a half-hour dedicatory program, with the request to prepare a composite of three of the station's dramatic shows, *The Lone Ranger*, *The Green Hornet* and *Ned Jordan, Secret Agent*, which meant tossing together action of 1860 and 1941. This offered a unique one-time opportunity for radio listeners to hear Ned Jordan, Britt Reid, Tonto and The Lone Ranger in the same radio broadcast. After the "William Tell Overture," Charles Hicks offered an introductory announcement for the special broadcast and, later, a brief message during the intermission.

In the drama, Britt Reid meets up with Ned Jordan on board the club car of the Consolidated American Railroad, bound for Texas. Each given a mission of vital importance through Washington channels, the two team up to find Jim Grant, an old man hiding in a cave in a remote part of the Texas hills behind Boothill River. When the men give the password, "Silver," the old man reveals the secret of their mission. Since he was a small boy, Grant has held on to a treasure chest containing silver dollars and a note handwritten by The Lone Ranger himself. The silver dollars are to be used to the best advantage according to the judgment of the man who opens the letter. The Lone Ranger's message is addressed to the "Boys and Girls of America," asking them to remember the brave fight made by their forefathers and to be aware of the enemies that threatened to destroy the United States today. Britt Reid agrees with Ned that the Ranger's message should be delivered on the radio.

The radio cast reprised their roles for the broadcast: Al Hodge as Britt Reid; Jack McCarthy as Ned Jordan; Lee Allman as Judy Medwick, Jordan's personal

The cast of *Ned Jordan, Secret Agent,* who also played roles on radio's *The Lone Ranger.* Seated left to right: Malcolm McCoy, Gwen Firmen and unidentified. Standing left to right: Gillie Shea, Bob Liggett, John Hodiak, unknown, John Todd, Shirley Squires, Fred Reto, Jack McCarthy (Ned Jordan), unknown actress, and Herschel Mayall. Sound men on floor left to right: Jim Fletcher and Ernie Winstanley.

assistant; John Todd as Tonto; and Earle Graser as The Lone Ranger. Historically, this program also revealed what would become the first hint of a family relationship between Britt Reid and the masked man of the western plains. A congressman in Washington had contacted Reid and asked him to deliver the secret word, "Silver." As Reid explains, "The Texas Representative who communicated with me is one of my closest friends. He happens to know things about me that... well... that my own father doesn't know."

It would not be until December 1942 on The Lone Ranger program that the second connection would be made — the introduction of Dan Reid as a teenager, who rode the plains with the masked man.

Jim Grant confesses to Britt Reid that his own father worked in the same cave decades previous, serving The Lone Ranger on occasion. "Every so often The Lone Ranger would come ridin' in from somewhere on the plains," he explained, "an' need new shoes for his hoss, or bullets for his guns." The origin of the silver for the horseshoes and bullets wasn't generally known, it was explained, but it was revealed The Lone Ranger owned the silver mine from which he took what he needed. Jim was also tending to a white horse that was a descendant of the great horse Silver. In later radio broadcasts, Jim Grant's father would be portrayed on the radio program as The Lone Ranger and Tonto rode up to retrieve the silver needed for horseshoes and bullets.

It was then that The Lone Ranger stepped up to the microphone as Reid read the patriotic letter to the men. His reminder of the importance of freedom and the right to vote for the men who make the laws was emphasized for a full minute on the program.

RANGER: Boys and girls of America, these are days when you must remember the brave fight that was made by your forefathers. A fight for freedom. A fight against the hardships of the wilderness to settle the little villages that grew to be great cities. Fights against starvation, and bitter cold and fights against wild beasts and savage Indians. It has been a long, hard fight to make America the country that it is, the greatest country in the world. Now it is our duty to guard and protect America.

We in America are free people. We can speak openly and fearlessly. We are not compelled to do without the luxuries of life. We are free to work at anything we choose. We are allowed to spend our money as we please. It is possible in America as in no other country on earth, for the poorest of us to rise as high as our ambition and ability will take us. We have all these privileges because we fought for them and won them. Other countries envy us. Our enemies would like to destroy us. They may try to do this. Not by war. No nation could make a successful war on us, but we must always be on guard against the enemies who try to destroy America by talk. Be alert, be on guard. Remember that America is your country and that the laws are made by those who are selected by the vote of the people.

Remember that the code of America is based upon the things that are best for the greatest number. Keep your faith and your confidence in God and the United States and let nothing you read or hear destroy that faith. Boys and girls, be proud you are Americans.

The broadcast ended with Britt Reid offering a closing statement.

BRITT: The Lone Ranger, years ago, did not foresee the present war. He did, however, realize that a time would come when his message would be vital. Right now, we are surrounded by a world at war, with great nations fighting for their lives. This is war without glory. A needless and unjustified war in which a multitude must suffer for the greed of the few. But war will pass, like all things, and in the peace that comes the worried, hungry people of the world will look to us. To you. The Lone Ranger wanted you to have his message. And WXYZ would like the privilege of sending it to you, as a part of this special broadcast which dedicates our new high-power facilities. This message is neatly printed and ready for you. Let me know your name and address, won't you?

Not only was The Lone Ranger's message sent free of charge to those who wrote in, the station also offered a chance to share in the prizes that were to be given away. Silver dollars were offered, as well as Lone Ranger lucky charms. The announcer explained to the radio audience how to enter to win the prizes and signed off the broadcast.

Today fans of old-time radio think of *The Lone Ranger*, *The Green Hornet* and *Sergeant Preston of the Yukon* as the Big Three to originate from WXYZ. The Detroit radio station was actually responsible for a number of long-running and successful radio programs but with a minimum number of recordings existing today of such programs as *Bob Barclay, American Agent*, *Ann Worth, House Wife*, and *Ned Jordan, Secret Agent*, few consider those programs among the success stories. With very few recordings of *Ned Jordan* existing to best summarize the program's five-year history, the following is a brief summary.

With America leading in the development and research of atomic power, jet propulsion, and the atom bomb, spies were more active than ever before. Friendly nations, as well as potential enemies, had secret agents working tirelessly to probe secrets while agents of another type strived ceaselessly to create internal strife and sabotage economic policies, labor relations, and our relationship with other nations. This was the motive behind the enemies that preoccupied *Ned Jordan, Secret Agent*.

J.B. Medwick, President of the Consolidated American Railroads, had an important part in the war effort. Eager to continue his patriotic services, he approached a certain individual high in government circles with the suggestion that a carefully-chosen man, unhampered by governmental red tape who could work secretly and with unlimited financial backing, might uncover many plots hatched against the government by foreign agents traveling on railroad trains. Medwick selected Ned Jordan, a law school graduate who served as a newspaperman, then traveled extensively as a free-lance writer. He became affiliated with the claims department of Medwick's railroad. During the war he took a position with the Office of Strategic Services and was concerned mainly with combating enemy agents who sought various forms of sabotage.

After the war he returned to Medwick's employ and resumed his work in the claims department. His contact is a government man named Proctor. It was Proctor who would step in with official authority to make arrests while Jordan, having developed the case unofficially, stayed out of the spotlight. The stories were fictitious, but the issues were timely. Pre-dating the reported efforts of Matt Cvetic (*I Was a Communist for the FBI*) and Herbert A. Philbrick (*I Led Three Lives*), the *Ned Jordan* radio program was ahead of its time. Perhaps lacking the fears of Communist infiltration was the only reason why Trendle and Campbell had difficulty selling the program on a larger scale. Had the program continued into the

1950s, historians speculate that the series could have gained national popularity.

A slightly romantic counterplot prevailed throughout the series. It involved Ned Jordan and Judy Medwick. Judy learned of Jordan's secret work. She longs to aid him, but Ned tries to discourage this because of the dangers involved. His own life was in constant danger and because of this, he could not permit himself to fall in love with Judy.

Ned Jordan, Secret Agent * went on the air in the fall of 1938, joining *The Lone Ranger, The Green Hornet,* and *Challenge of the Yukon* as the big four dramatic programs originating from WXYZ. It was the least successful of the four. A product of its times, Jordan is today remembered as routine detective fare notable for expressing villains with Fifth Column memberships in the Axis of evil. Jack McCarthy played the role of Ned Jordan, who always delivered his man at the end of each broadcast, to the FBI. The theme was somewhat along the lines of *Gang Busters,* being written in flashback form, with several characters explaining the action to others, then fading while it was worked out or proceeding from where the narrator left off. Whether it was eliminating a printing press responsible for printing propaganda or foiling the scheme to steal airplane plans, each episode concluded with a crime-does-not-pay reminder that "The FBI wants you," or the announcer calling: "All aboard for Leavenworth!"

During the first week of January 1942, radio station WXYZ produced an hour-long musical and variety show which plugged the idea to "Buy a Bond – Tonight – Right Now." Putting its own flourish on the Treasury Department programs which promoted the sale of defense stamps and bonds, WXYZ asked for telephone pledges on its own special broadcast to get a sample of the public response to this kind of an appeal. The result was a jam up of the studio switchboard which, despite lost calls, resulted in the pledging of $158,835 following the hour program.

Talent on the program included Edgar A. Guest, Detroit poet and philosopher; Mayor Edward J. Jeffries; The Lone Ranger; a Joe Doe typical of the masses; the St. Paul's Cathedral choir; studio orchestra and featured singers. Calls persisted two and a half hours beyond the regular broadcast and hundreds were reportedly lost in the jam. A bulk of the pledges came from big donors, the top announcements being $50,000 from the Detroit Fireman's Fund Association; $25,000 from George W. Trendle himself and $10,000 pledges from the Detroit Federation of Musicians, Motion Picture Operators Union and John H. King, co-owner of the station. Latter was driving to Detroit from his home up-state when he caught the program, unaware that it was going to be put on, and stopped in a town on route to call in his $10,000 pledge.

Giles Kavanaugh, coordinator of defense savings, accepted the pledges on behalf of the internal revenue department. Bulk of the pledges were large ones including $5,000 ones from private individuals, but upward of $16,000 worth came from the small contributors. Carried away by his enthusiasm, Harry Golder, announcer on the show, pledged $100.

Three months later, during the first week of April 1942, the General Mills renewal on *The Lone Ranger* came to term and the affiliates of the Mutual Network were faced with a ticklish problem.

* The Ned Jordan series was originally titled *Secret Agent* for the first two broadcasts (November 26 and December 3, 1938). Beginning with episode three (December 10) the series was titled *Ned Jordan, Secret Agent.* Beginning with the broadcast of May 19, 1942, the series was titled *Ned Jordan, The Federal Ace.* Beginning with the broadcast of July 1, 1943, it was titled *Federal Ace.* The final broadcast was October 28, 1943.

The Blue Network had made a pitch for the General Mills business, and the question that Mutual had to put its affiliates was whether they were agreeable to meeting the Blue's rate proposition. The Blue offered to schedule the radio program nationwide at 6 p.m. Eastern at a daytime rate, which was cheaper than the primetime rate, with the proviso that if any affiliates could not clear the show at that time, it would be taken off locally on records and broadcast at a later period that same evening – the daytime rate would not be affected by those delayed broadcasts. In putting the proposition up to its affiliates, Mutual pointed out that if the same arrangement offered by the Blue was accepted by all, the cost per broadcast would be dropped and for many affiliates that meant less profit per broadcast. Every affiliate had a financial stake in the game. Mutual had, for several years, cleared *The Lone Ranger* in the East at 7:30 p.m.

The system was pretty much routine at the time. The advertising agencies leased airtime from the networks at a price, dictated by the number of affiliates that carried the program, and coverage per station. The sponsors were billed monthly based on the total, which flexed from one broadcast to another since some local stations were forced to pre-empt the children's program due to special broadcasts of local interest. For executives at General Mills, switching to a new network meant less money spent per month under this new proposal, but how extensive the coverage was always of concern.

On April 28, General Mills signed on the bottom line, turning *The Lone Ranger* and *Jack Armstrong* serials over to the Blue Network. The transition, however, would not happen overnight with the flip of a switch. The *Lone Ranger* started over the Blue Network with a hookup of 70-odd stations beginning May 4, while *Jack Armstrong* would follow in the fall. *

By October, the total number of stations would be between 90 and 100. Not all of the Blue affiliates were able to broadcast *The Lone Ranger* at 6 p.m. so those particular stations recorded the broadcast off the line onto disc and rebroadcast the program later at 7:30 p.m. It was reported that the network had experienced difficulty in getting right of way in several towns, including Cleveland, Ohio. *Jack Armstrong* would ultimately air on Blue at 5:30 to 5:45 p.m., with *Captain Midnight* intended for 5:45 to 6 p.m., eventually giving General Mills a full hour to promote Kix and Wheaties. Blue denied accusations that the 6:00 to 6:30 p.m. slot was being sold on a daytime basis, and reaffirmed its assurance that the terms given General Mills would be available to any other advertiser. Internal records, however, verify the daytime pricing. With *The Lone Ranger* so closely identified with the early struggles of the Mutual Broadcasting System, and credited in the trades with cementing the network's nucleus, which eventually spread to a chain of 202 stations, the April 1942 deal was Mutual's loss.

While the deal with General Mills may have saved the cereal company money in the long run, branding-competition may have played a minor role. "Kid listeners in the New York and other areas must have found things confusing Monday evening when they tuned in for their thrice weekly installment of *The Lone Ranger*," reported *Variety* (May 6, 1942). "If out of habit they dialed a Mutual station they got a horse opera strange to their ears, namely *Red Ryder*, and

---

* At first, a large number of stations on the Blue network on the west coast could not broadcast *Jack Armstrong* until September 14, so General Mills agreed to plug Kix cereal on the *Lightning Jim* program during the summer.

if, having read in the papers about General Mills switch of *Lone Ranger* from the Mutual to the Blue Network, they [would have] found themselves treated to tango music. Mutual, aware of the mixed *Lone Ranger* schedule and set on saving its kid audiences, pitched a fast curve Monday. It got in touch with the producers of *Red Ryder* and made a deal for an exclusive use of the cowboy strip's radio version... *Ryder* offers a double feature in an equine way. Whereas in *Ranger* there is but one horse, Silver, the Mutual opera touts two quadrupeds, Thunder and a pinto pony."

More amazing is the fact that Mutual was so desperate to replace *The Lone Ranger* with another cowboy western that the contract details were not completely consummated until about an hour before *The Adventures of Red Ryder* went on the air. As it was, Mutual had to broadcast a recorded installment across the country. The live program of *Ryder* did not start until Friday, May 8. *Ryder* would, in most instances, parallel the schedule of *The Lone Ranger* running Monday, Wednesday, and Friday.

According to a report in *Time* magazine, the Mutual Network's child audience became immediately attached to the *Red Ryder* program with the consequence that the first program ratings favored *Red Ryder* over *The Lone Ranger*. "Mutual, with a million young listeners who have the cowboy-and-Indians habit, had to have a substitute for *The Lone Ranger*," reported a columnist for *Time* (June 8, 1942). "Just in time, the forsaken network remembered *Red Ryder*, 'six foot of redheaded trigger lightning' famed in boys' books, NEA syndicated comic strips, cinema serials, and oddly enough, first serialized by the Blue, 16 weeks ago on the Pacific Coast." According to The Hooper ratings, *Red Ryder* had a rating of 4.8 against *The Lone Ranger*'s tally of 3.3.

The Lone Ranger radio program would remain with its new network until 1956, even when the Blue Network would officially change its name to the American Broadcasting Company in 1946.

Switching from one network to another was not the only change to *The Lone Ranger* program that year. Instead of endorsing a Lone Ranger Safety Club, the masked man promoted the new Lone Ranger Victory Corps.

Two months following the U.S. entry into World War II, attractive gold-simulated rings and pins bearing the insignias of all four of the armed services were offered to listeners who tuned in to *The Lone Ranger* on the evening of February 11, 1942. The offer was extended until March 2. Recalling the distribution of luminous belts the previous fall, which elicited the enthusiastic response of *Lone Ranger* fans, the present offer maintained the General Mills policy of devising attractive and useful gifts in keeping with the spirit of the times. The Lone Ranger Ring had as its outstanding feature a secret compartment. The insignia plate, which was inscribed with the insignia of either the Army, Navy, Marines or Air Corps, according to the listener's preference, slid back and disclosed a picture of The Lone Ranger. Adults could replace The Lone Ranger photograph with one of a friend or relative in one of the armed services. The pin, designed for women, had a hand-tinted laurel leaf shaped to form a graceful bowknot. This part of the pin was made of white metal plated in 24-karat gold.

The ring is known to have been designed by the famous radio premium creator, Orin Armstrong, working for the Robbins Manufacturing Company, in 1940. The firm specialized in premiums. The ring was initially designed in 1939 but rejected and never put into production because it could not be worn with the prongs, which held the top cover to the base, considered uncomfortable to the wearer's finger. The design problem was eventually resolved for the 1942 Victory Corps promotion, and later with slight revisions for The Lone Ranger National Defenders look-around ring.

One month later, beginning with the broadcast of March 11, 1942, The Lone Ranger Victory Corps was launched. Hundreds of thousands of *Lone Ranger* fans were enrolled, enlisting the services of youngsters from coast to coast for collecting needed war materials and assisting in air raids. Membership in the Victory Corps was granted to all boys and girls who sent in a three-cent stamp or three pennies. For this contribution, the children received a colorful membership card and a lapel button, certifying to their affiliation with The Lone Ranger Victory Corps. Alongside The Lone Ranger as a guest speaker for that broadcast was Lessing Rosenwald, director of the Bureau of Industrial Conservation in the War Production Board.

The Lone Ranger himself would, over a period of months, instruct the Victory Corps members in their duties from time to time, according to instructions he received from government officials. Members were told exactly what they could do to help their country in the war effort. These tasks included the collection of wastepaper, rubber, and metals. They gardened. They were instructed in air raid precautions.

On the broadcast of June 15, 1942, The Lone Ranger was officially designated the Corps Commander for the Lone Ranger Victory Corps. One month later, on July 15, Buchan Baking bought *The American Commando* as a weekly half-hour show on KOL. Scripts for the show were by Roy Grandey, station's program director, and the adventure strip was pointed chiefly at kids with Buchan's building a "Commando Club" a la *The Lone Ranger* club idea. Throughout the summer, the War Manpower Department was observing the results from the Lone Ranger Victory Club and considering establishing one of their own on a national level.

It should be noted that while the origins for Tonto, Silver, and Scout had been dramatized in past broadcasts, it was not until the "Legion of the Black Arrow" story arc that an origin for The Lone Ranger was first explored on the radio program. It should be noted that Fran Striker chose not to dramatize the origin in the form of a flashback, but rather as an explanation during an exchange of dialogue between two parties. Legally, the origin concept belonged to Republic Pictures, but since the property itself was licensed from Trendle, clarification was required. It was in 1941 that Fran Striker received a memo from an executive at Republic, granting him permission to use the origin as it was conceived for the cliffhanger serial, in full use, with any revision he wanted to make, and in perpetuity.

In connection with this public service, prominent figureheads appeared on The Lone Ranger radio broadcasts. For the syndicated transcriptions, the commercials were never included in the recordings, as well as the promotional giveaways or the guest speakers. Thus fans of the radio program may have copies of these radio broadcasts but not the guest speakers.

For the broadcast of July 24, for example, Coxswain John Cullen, the young Coast Guardsman who surprised four Nazi saboteurs when they landed on a Long Island beach recently, was interviewed. He related the part he played in bringing the enemy agents to justice and, in a special message to the youth of America, he encouraged them to buy War Stamps and to do their share for victory through salvage collection and other home front activities. For the broadcast of August 26, 1942, a 19-year-old sailor who fought with the cruiser Marblehead in the battle of Macassar Straits and who sailed with the battered ship on a 13,000-mile voyage home will be interviewed. His name is First Class Seaman Robert A. Healy.

Service heroes that were guests on the program for brief interviews are listed below.

July 17, 1942, Lieutenant Elliott Vandevanter, American war hero who led a successful bomber attack on Jap warships. Describing his sensations during combat, he said that while in the air, one is so busy that he has no time to think.

July 22, 1942, Ensign Donald Mason was the recipient of the Distinguished Flying Cross and the Silver Star for his heroic exploits and won national fame for his terse message to his Navy commander: "Sighted Sub, Sank Same."

July 24, 1942, Coxswain John Cullen, a young Coast Guardsman who surprised four Nazi saboteurs when they landed on a Long Island beach.

July 27, 1942, Lieutenant William C. Carrithers did that job so well on bombings of Japanese troops and

installations in the South Pacific that he won a citation from the Government. He tells the boys and girls of the nation about his war experiences.

August 5, 1942, Lieutenant Emmet F. Gibson, wounded survivor of the battle of Bataan, is the fourth guest to be interviewed on *The Lone Ranger*. (Newspapers reported third guest but, apparently, he was the fourth.)

August 12, 1942, Lieutenant George Welch, young Army flier who shot down four Jap planes during the December 7 attack on Pearl Harbor.

August 19, 1942, Interview with Ensign Francis Pinter, U.S. Navy hero, who rescued 17 from a life raft, was recently awarded the Distinguished Flying Cross for his daring rescue while on patrol duty at sea. He brought his big PBY flying boat down in a rough sea, took sixteen men and one woman off a tiny life raft and flew them to safety. (Some newspapers cite August 17, others August 19.)

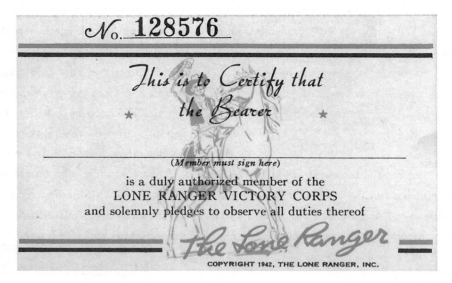

August 26, 1942, First Class Seaman Robert A. Healy, a 19-year-old sailor who was on the cruiser Marblehead when the Japs bombed it in the Battle of Makassar Strait and who sailed on the rudderless ship during its memorable 13,000-mile voyage home. Healy was on duty in the ship's fire control tower for 72 hours during the historic battle.

September 2, 1942, Lieutenant Irvin McPherson, who piloted a Navy plane through the rain of anti-aircraft fire in the Midway battle and urged the youth of America to help fight the war on the home front.

September 7, 1942, Technical Sergeant Robert Golay of the United States Bomber Command, stationed in the British Isles. Golay took part in the first American raid on occupied Europe, pounding German airdromes on July 4. On that first flight his plane was hit by antiaircraft fire which knocked off one propeller and part of the tall sections, also starting a fire in the plane. Roaring along at 270 miles an hour, it struck the ground, bounded up into the air and then miraculously kept rising. On the way back to base headquarters the pilot dived and put an antiaircraft tower out of commission. Golay received the Distinguished Service Cross for his share in the adventure.

September 9, 1942, A special letter from Donald Nelson to the members of the Lone Ranger

Victory Corps will be heard. Nelson was director of war production and pleaded for all boys and girls to participate in the scrap metal drive. His official letter was also printed in newspapers all across the country a week prior.

October 14, 1942, Sergeant William Sampson spoke on the army's glider training program, a little-publicized phase of the war effort.

Another indication that the mysterious woman was in love with The Lone Ranger, though depicted subtly, can be found in "Gold Rush That Failed," broadcast June 1, 1942.

October 21, 1942, Paul Frillman, the chaplain of the Flying Tigers, told of the bravery of the Tigers, their faith in God and appealed to youngsters to help in the war effort.

During the broadcast of September 11, 1942, a special message from the children of Hull, England, to the children of America, pointing the way to greater productive effort among young folks on the home front, was presented on *The Lone Ranger*. The message described some of the ways in which the children of oft-bombed Hull are helping to win the war on their side of the Atlantic. The message was directed particularly to the members of the Lone Ranger Victory Corps, the nation-wide group of boys and girls who were already making an impressive contribution to victory through the purchase of War Stamps, the collection of scrap and other home front activities. This marked the first of a series of messages from children of the United Nations to be brought to Lone Ranger listeners.

The final guest speaker on *The Lone Ranger* program was on the broadcast of October 21, the chaplain of the Flying Tigers, Paul Frillman, told of the Tigers and appeal to young Americans to help in the war effort. (The dates listed with the guest speakers may have varied across the country. Frillman, for example, was on *The Lone Ranger* program in Rochester, New York, on October 28.)

The first radio broadcast to mention the blackout kit was September 16, 1942. The kit contained five fabric materials plus a paper membership leaflet. Among the materials was a 2.5 inch diameter patch reading "Lone Ranger Volunteers," another with "Pledge to The Flag," a headband reading "Lone Ranger Volunteers" and a "V" pattern on either side of the Lone Ranger image. The kit was distributed through October 1942.

© 1941, T. L. R., INC.

Step forward one at a time and let me "Swear You In" as a trusted member of the NATIONAL DEFENDERS!

★ Welcome, stranger! But you won't remain a stranger long in the friendly ranks of the National Defenders! We're mighty glad to have you as a member! Because your writing in tells me that you're a real true-blue American through and through! Now first thing you want to do is read every word of this Secret Portfolio! Then turn to the big Membership Certificate. And if you can promise *on your honor* to abide by the National Defender's Creed printed on that certificate, sign your name and you automatically become a full-fledged member! Then, the next time you hear me give my well-known "battle-cry" on the radio, just try to feel that I'm talking to *you personally,* and what I really mean is, "Hi-yo *Member!*"

The Lone Ranger

HOW TO USE YOUR WARNING SIREN!

Illustrated below is the official warning siren of the Lone Ranger National Defenders. It's one of the most remarkable scientific sound devices you may ever have seen! Every Defender must know exactly how to use it in case of emergency, and for dozens of different club activities! It's really three instruments in one! (1) A bird-call whistle! (2) A musical instrument! (3) A Warning Siren! Practice until you can play it perfectly all three ways!

1 **TONTO'S BIRD-CALL SIGNAL —** To give Tonto's famous bird-call that you've heard over the radio so often, blow softly. Hold the plunger fairly close to the "bell" at the end of the whistle, and move it back and forth rapidly to produce the wavering tone of a night-bird calling to its mate. Then, while still vibrating the plunger, move it out further to make the lower tone at the end of the call.

2 **MUSICAL INSTRUMENT —** With little practice and a certain amount of musical ability, you can soon be playing real music on this amazing instrument. You can play more than an octave of clear flute-like tones. Don't try to blow too hard. Start out with simple tunes like "Home Sweet Home" and "America", and you'll soon learn to play harder ones.

3 **WARNING SIREN —** When used as a warning siren, your Defender's Siren is really a noise-maker! And every National Defender knows it isn't good citizenship to torment the neighbors! So use it wisely . . . and not too often! You'll have loads of fun with it when you're out playing . . . and it may really be very valuable at times to warn others of danger. It will imitate almost any kind of siren you ever heard!

WH-O-O-O-O!

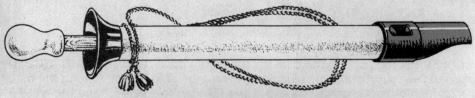

Dear Victory Ranger:

I'm sorry to keep you waiting for the Tonto headdress you sent for, but they have been in great demand and are all used up. I have arranged to get more of them, for you and other members of my club, but there has been a delay because of the war emergency. We all know war goods must come first, so I'm sure you'll understand the delay. I hope to have more Tonto headdresses very soon, and *I'll send yours to you just as soon as I get them.* Meanwhile, keep working for Victory, and listen to my radio programs. There are more surprises ahead for Victory Rangers. Thank you for your patience.

Your friend,

THE LONE RANGER.

This 1941 pamphlet offered a silver bullet for a Kix box top
and ten cents in coin.

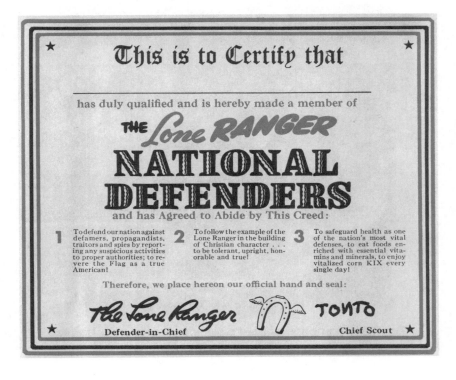

UNITED STATES TREASURY DEPARTMENT

For distinguished services rendered in behalf of the War Savings Program this citation is awarded to

George W. Trendle

Given under my hand and seal on January 6th 1943

Henry Morgenthau Jr.
SECRETARY OF THE TREASURY

UNITED STATES TREASURY DEPARTMENT

For distinguished services rendered in behalf of the National War Savings Program this citation is awarded to

George Trendle

Given under my hand and seal on August 28, 1942

Henry Morgenthau Jr.
Secretary of the Treasury

Following the success of The Lone Ranger Victory Corps, General Mills participated in the marketing of the Lone Ranger National Defenders, which included a toy siren that children could use to play birdcalls, imitate animals, play popular tunes, call for their friends, or create secret whistles. The Lone Ranger's "National Defenders" was a new club for red-blooded American boys and girls who received a membership booklet and list of valuable premiums.

The reason for the switch from Victory Corps to National Defenders first came about in September 1942 when Chief Paul V. McNutt of the War Manpower Commission, announced the creation of a war-inspired "High School Victory Corps" open to all of the 6.5 million students in the nation's 28,000 schools. The program was established to give "every high school student in the United States the opportunity to take a definite place in the national war effort through a voluntary enrollment plan." The National Victory Corps was headed by Captain Eddie Rickenbacker, aviation leader and flying ace of the first World War. The High School Victory Corps was to be a voluntary organization designed to mobilize secondary school students for more effective preparation for and participation in war service. Trendle wanted to maintain distance from a government-sponsored program and requested his staff to change the name.

With approval of the advertising agency representing General Mills, patriotic messages continued, sans guest speakers, under the National Defenders program starting in November. Throughout the winter, The Lone Ranger stepped up to the microphone to deliver a 60 second speech meant to motivate the listeners into doing their part to aid the Allies in their fight for freedom. This included volunteer efforts, participating in scrap drives, purchasing war bonds and volunteer duties in their local community.

Because The Lone Ranger program took place on the American Frontier decades before the war, it was up to The Green Hornet and Ned Jordan to fight against the axis of evil. But The Lone Ranger was not simply restricted to patriotic messages during the commercial breaks. The masked man and his faithful Indian companion's adventures provided subliminal themes of local activism, bravery, and speaking out when something suspicious was evident. Patriotism came not in the form of thwarting sabotage in American factories, or of Germans/Japanese attacking naval bases, but from thwarting outlaws from stealing an army payroll to deterring Indians from attacking frontier forts.

The damage from cattle rustlers was emphasized when locals cried out against a meat shortage, the Iron Spur story arc strongly symbolized the potential sabotage of American transportation under wartime conditions, and throughout the spring of 1942, the theft of fox pelts and furs was so commonplace that listeners could associate the furs to the value of war bonds. Patriotism became an underlying theme as The Lone Ranger reduced ugly rumors, maintained civilian morale and promoted the efficiency necessary for farms and backyard gardens (i.e. Victory Gardens). But none could be so more obvious than the broadcast of December 7, 1942, marking one year since the Japanese attack on Pearl Harbor. In that broadcast, "Sign of the Swastika," a band of savage Indians has been running amok, branding their victims with an "ancient Indian symbol." Though the word "Swastika" is not mentioned, the premise of the story was not without modern-day analogy.

Introduction of Dan Reid

Later that same month, December 1942, more than a year after the birth of Victor, the son of Silver, Fran Striker introduced a new recurring character to the radio program, Dan Reid – the nephew of The Lone Ranger. Broadcast from December 14 to December 25, the six-part saga involved The Lone Ranger and Tonto riding north into territory of Montana. While the majority of the adventures took place in Oklahoma or Texas, The Lone Ranger's adventures would on rare occasion take place in other territories. (For example, The Lone Ranger rode into Montana to deliver a ransom and rescue a kidnapped Tonto in "A Pitfall for Crime," broadcast August 12, 1940.)

10 by 15 inches, 1940 Whitman book #965, Stiff cardboard cover and four single-sided pages, all with beautiful color punch-outs of The Lone Ranger, Tonto, Silver, Scout, boy pal "Bud," Indians, outlaws, horses, and other animals. Could Bud have been a prototype of Dan Reid?

The plots for the six radio broadcasts can be found in the episode guide in this book. The plot that follows was taken directly from the 1946 novel, *The Lone Ranger Rides North*, published by Grosset & Dunlap. There were considerable revisions to the story in the novelization, not to mention the unusual fact that George Waller's radio scripts were adapted while Fran Striker received authorship on the dust jacket and title page of the book.

In the border town of Martinsville, a few miles from the Canadian border, Bart Gregg and Snake Arnold plot to deceive young Dan Frisby and his grandmother into purchasing a plot of land from Mason P. Martin, so they can legally gain control of the copper mines. To fool the boy into participating, Gregg masquerades as The Lone Ranger. When Dan meets the fake Ranger, he tries desperately to like the masked stranger who rode into town, but finds this challenging as he feels the masked man was trying too hard to be friendly, and did so awkwardly. Still, the boy pays a visit to the trustworthy Mr. Martin, who agrees to sell a plot of ground that appears to be useless, unaware of true motives. Gregg and Arnold alter the contract, making it appear as if Mr. Martin sold the copper mines instead of the useless plot of ground, and chuckle as they foresee no hindrance to their plan. Arnold was wanted by Canadian authorities but remains south of the border because the law dictates that he can not be arrested for his crimes if dragged across the border against his will.

When The Lone Ranger and Tonto arrive in town, they are ambushed by Red and Fenner, former members of Snake Arnold's gang who feel Gregg has double-crossed them. After shooting and wounding Silver, the men discover they mistook the real Ranger for the fake one. The Lone Ranger is pleased to learn Bart Gregg is in town; Gregg had led a band of lawless terrorists who preyed on ranches and ranchers, spreading poverty and fear through many counties in Texas. The Lone Ranger was responsible for smashing Gregg's marauding band, but not until Gregg had shot a Texas Ranger in the back. The masked man and Indian had been tracking Gregg's whereabouts.

Meanwhile, Snake Arnold and his associate trick Mr. Martin and his bookkeeper into visiting Grandma Frisby's home, where they are securely tied to a chair. The house is set on fire while the guilty culprits, Gregg and Arnold, are making their presence known at the local saloon to create an alibi at the time of the murder. The Lone Ranger and Tonto, seeing the flames engulf the house, race into action. After saving the four innocents, the masked man visits the saloon only to find himself minutes too late. In an act of vengeance Red and Fenner had shot Bart Gregg in the back and killed him. Justice would now be served to the two crooks.

Snake Arnold, however, found a way to evade the law by claiming innocence of the whole affair, of which nothing could be proven against him. Martin was upset because the string of lies held together, but The Lone Ranger decided to play a game with Arnold. Under disguise, The Lone Ranger paid a late-night visit to Arnold to convince him that he had evidence of a prior offence that, once handed to the law, would ensure a hanging. Setting up a trap near the lake, The Lone Ranger sets himself up as bait for Arnold, who takes off in pursuit. After Arnold stabs the sleeping figure multiple times, he discovers the real men standing behind him. Arnold, disgusted, discovers he was tricked. Tonto did some digging earlier in the afternoon to change the course of the creek, which generally ran along the border. Arnold, on his own choice and accord, was now standing in Canada. A Mountie took Arnold into custody as the guilty party mumbled incoherently, fell to his knees, and begged in abject misery.

It is the sixth and final episode of the saga that Dan's grandmother tells how she came to raise Dan Reid... including a re-enactment of the ambush of the six Texas Rangers by the Cavendish gang.

Back in Martinsville, The Lone Ranger discovered that Grandma Frisby, amidst the excitement, had taken a toll for the worse. Her heart had given out and the doctor revealed the sad news: she had only a few hours left. At her request, Dan seated himself along the edge of the bed. The Lone Ranger kept her company in the room. After asking Dan to retrieve a small box from the bottom drawer of a chest, she explained her story.

Grandma Frisby was one of two survivors of an Indian massacre which took place a few years ago. On route to Fort Laramie*, she befriended a woman named Linda Reid, from Virginia, who had recently given birth to a new baby boy, Dan. A day's travel from their destination, Indians attacked and the men had put up a good fight. Forced to defend the camp, Grandma Frisby soon discovered Linda had been shot dead. With no other choice, she hid with the small baby until the Indians were gone. Later at the fort, she discovered that Dan Reid, Linda's husband and the baby's father, was reported dead. She raised the infant like he was her own and moved north where she remained today.

The Lone Ranger pieced together the remainder of the story. Dan Reid was his brother, one of the Texas Rangers who died in the ambush at Bryant's Gap, of

---

* Her destination, Fort Laramie, was also told in the 1951 Decca record and the 1946 novel, *The Lone Ranger Rides North*.

which The Lone Ranger was the sole survivor. Dan Frisby's real name is Dan Reid, and he is the nephew of The Lone Ranger. The masked man explains to young Dan his code – to do what was best for the greatest number. Unwilling to take back his name, he chose to help the law fight crime throughout the West. With a just cause, he wanted to continue the good fight. Dan understood and exited the room. Moments before she passes on, Grandma Frisby, asks The Lone Ranger to take care of young Dan. The Ranger unmasks for the old woman and promises he will carry on the traditions of the brave souls who ventured west for a new frontier. A moving and significant episode... as the dying Mrs. Frisby says, "Ride on Lone Ranger... forever!"

The 1946 novel adapted episodes one, five and six of the radio story arc, dismissing the events that took place in episodes two, three and four.

To properly detail the timeline, the "Reid" surname began in 1936 with *The Green Hornet* program, establishing Britt Reid and his father Dan Reid. John Todd played the role of the latter, a recurring character who only appeared on *The Green Hornet* program infrequently. It was not until the 5,000-Watt dedicatory broadcast of February 21, 1941, that any connection (although indirect) was made between The Lone Ranger and The Green Hornet, and only as a suggestive remark. The next connection (and a direct connection) was the December 1942 story arc in which Dan's last name was revealed. Up until the Christmas broadcast of 1942, neither a first nor last name was provided for the masked man on *The Lone Ranger* program. And never would a first name ever be given on the radio program (or any of the novels written by Fran Striker).

This might sound contradictory when compared to the numerous reference guides that claim The Lone Ranger's first name is John, but the fact can also be substantiated by Striker and Trendle's insistence that the masked man remain a mystery and therefore his first name never given. The appellation "John" was never referenced on the radio program, television program, comic books, pulps, or novels during Striker and Trendle's lifetime.

The legend and lore regarding "John" began with *Radio's Golden Age* (Eastern Valley Press), an encyclopedia of old-time radio co-written by Frank Buxton and Bill Owen for publication in 1966, later reprinted under the new title, *The Big Broadcast*, in 1972. Charles J. Stumpf reprinted the error in his 1973 book, *Ma Perkins, Little Orphan Annie and Heigh Ho, Silver!* John Dunning reprinted the error in his book *Tune in Yesterday*, published in 1976, and both Stumpf and Dunning reprinted the error only because it was listed in *The Big Broadcast*.

As is the case of any fiction, what appears in print oftentimes will become the gospel and be reprinted so often that eventually, without due diligence, a myth is mistaken for fact. Both Buxton and Owen were consulted about the source of the error, but as that was decades long past, neither could remember. If anything, a newspaper article containing an interview with Raymond Meurer in the 1960s may have been their source, with Meurer's memory admittingly faded by then.

It would not be until the 1981 motion picture, *The Legend of the Lone Ranger*, that the name "John" would be used for the first time in any officially licensed product bearing the name of *The Lone Ranger*. Today, fans continue to debate whether The Lone Ranger's first name should be John. Historians of broadcast media and pop culture have universally agreed that "John" was lore added after the death of the creators and therefore not valid. As an applied analogy, this would be the equivalent to fan fiction written today where the author would create their own origin and by referring to The Lone Ranger as "James" or "Matthew."

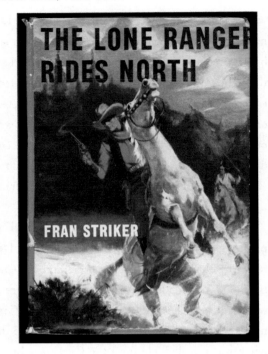

Fans of the program who consider themselves purists firmly believe that if Striker, Jewell, Trendle, and anyone else involved with the program were the only people with complete oversight in both creation and formation of the property, they alone had sole rights to insist and maintain a mystery as they strongly insisted many times over the years. (Remember, Trendle was against the names "Allen King" and "Bill Andrews" in the Republic Pictures cliffhangers, and fans today strongly dismiss the Republic renditions for the very same reason they claim John Reid is official.) Debating from the other side is the concept of an "artistic viewpoint" whereupon any licensed merchandise ranging from comic books, motion pictures and novels are free to provide their own artistic take, with variations that the author deems an improvement from the original source material, even if those authors decide to assign The Lone Ranger with the name "William Foster," "Thomas Grant," or "John Smith."

When the December 1942 saga was later adapted into a 1946 novel by Fran Striker titled *The Lone Ranger Rides North*, primarily consisting of material from the first and last chapter of the radio saga. Like the radio counterpart, the name of John was never provided.

The novel did explore the background of The Lone Ranger, including two unique aspects revealed in chapters 22 and 24.

"He thought of his own boyhood in the East and the friends he had made there. He thought and thought, but nowhere in the archives of his recollection could he find anyone whom Dan resembled." (Chapter 22)

"The thing that was best for everybody – for the greatest number! That, in a few words, was the whole code of The Lone Ranger. It was his scheme of things, the standard upon which all his actions were based. He was eternally asking himself what would be best for the greatest number. If the greatest number would benefit at the cost of a few, the cost had to be met. If sacrifice by some meant benefit for many, there must be sacrifice." (Chapter 24)

Chapters 27 and 28 retold the origin of The Lone Ranger, as told by the Ranger himself, including a direct reference to Captain Hargaves, who gave the orders to the Texas Rangers to inspect Bryant's Gap and look around, since it was generally known that every outlaw in that part of the country ventured into Bryant's Gap to elude capture. In the beginning of Chapter 29, The Lone Ranger explained to young Dan that the reason he did not work his silver mine was because he would have to appear as himself.

"The silver is still there, and Tonto and I take what we need," he explained. All of these chapters climaxed with young Dan confronting the death of his grandmother and the revelation that he is related to the legendary masked rider of the plains.

"There's nothing to cry about, Dan," The Lone Ranger provided comfort. "Your grandmother is the happiest woman in the universe. She hasn't gone. People like that never leave us. They're put here on earth to do a great good work and when their work is finished, they simply move on to greater work in another world."

Dan blew his nose and swallowed hard, but his eyes were dry. "I – I guess you're right," he said.

"There's something I want to tell you, Dan."

"What's that?"

"Your father and I were brothers."

"You mean –" gasped the boy, "You mean you're my uncle?"

"I want to be more than that. I want to be a father to you."

Dan stood for fully a minute without speaking. Such astounding news was more than he could register closely.

"I'm going to stay here for a little while until everything is settled. Then Tonto and you and I are going to travel together."

"I'm to ride with you? Ride with The Lone Ranger?"

"Yes, Dan."

The boy looked up at the strong man beside him. Now there were tears in his eyes – tears of pride and gratitude. He saw himself in all the future years riding with Tonto, the stalwart Indian, and the masked rider of the white horse. How he would be a part of the cry that was known from border to border – that cry of "Hi-Yo, Silver -- away-y-y!"

The radio saga was promptly adapted into the newspaper comic strip, to ensure continuity since Dan would become a recurring character on the radio program. In the comic strip rendition, the dying Grandma Frisby began telling her story on Friday, February 26, 1943, which followed the origin of The Lone Ranger, with Tonto presenting The Lone Ranger his mask in the strip of Thursday, March 4.

The purpose for adding Dan Reid to the radio program was to provide young listeners with association. Whether it be the request of the advertising agency representing General Mills, who was sponsoring *Jack Armstrong, the All-American Boy*, or the request of George W. Trendle to incorporate a youngster for a similar purpose remains unknown. * Dan never spoke with slang or western drawl (i.e. "gee willikers"), never fumbled with his assignments, worked hard for long hours, and at one time during the radio program it was referenced that Dan went East to college to further his education. Years later, in 1947, when Fran Striker later wrote a series of Tom Quest novels, one has to wonder if he did not pattern the character of Tom Quest after the established Dan Reid.

On radio Dan Reid was first played by Ernie Winstanley, who was attending Wayne State University at the time and worked at the studio assisting the sound men with the sound effects. He often doubled for supporting roles such as the character of Joan's young brother in "Joan of

* Executives at the advertising agency representing General Mills were responsible in arranging for The Lone Ranger to make a guest appearance on the January 18, 1943, broadcast of the *Jack Armstrong* program.

Clarksville" (broadcast March 10, 1941), the role of Bud in "Danger Landing" (broadcast July 4, 1941) and as "Jack" in "Flameup's Kickback" (broadcast August 21, 1942). In was this latter episode that served as a prototype of what would later become Dan Reid on the radio program. For historians, the name "Jack" may have been used to replicate the sponsor's other program, *Jack Armstrong, the All-American Boy.*

Episode Guide

May 1, 1939, to September 22, 1939, Monday, Wednesday and Friday, 6:30 p.m.

September 25, 1939, to April 26, 1940, Monday, Wednesday and Friday, 7:30 p.m.

April 29, 1940, to September 27, 1940, Monday, Wednesday and Friday, 6:30 p.m.

September 30, 1940, to April 25, 1941, Monday, Wednesday and Friday, 7:30 p.m.

April 28, 1941, to September 26, 1941, Monday, Wednesday and Friday, 6:30 p.m.

September 29, 1941, to May 1, 1942, Monday, Wednesday and Friday, 7:30 p.m.

Chicago, Illinois, WGN (Mutual Broadcasting System) Central Time

January 3, 1938, to May 8, 1940, Monday, Wednesday and Friday, 7:30 p.m.

July 1, 1940, to September 27, 1940, Monday, Wednesday and Friday, 7:30 p.m.

September 30, 1940, Monday, 7:45 p.m.

January 3, 1941, to April 9, 1941, Monday, Wednesday and Friday, 4:30 p.m. *

May 5, 1941, to September 24, 1941, Monday, Wednesday and Friday, 7:30 p.m.

September 29, 1941, to October 24, 1941, Monday, Wednesday and Friday, 8:30 p.m.

October 27, 1941, to May 1, 1942, Monday, Wednesday and Friday, 7:30 p.m.

The cover page for many of the radio scripts from 1938 and 1939 indicate three times for performances, 7:30 p.m., 8:30 p.m. and 10:30 p.m. This changed over the months and years to accommodate multiple networks and stations, until the transcription discs assisted with assorted time slots.

Sponsorship

Beginning with the broadcast of Monday, September 26, 1938, American Bakeries, located in Atlanta, Georgia, began sponsoring *The Lone Ranger* in southern states. Their commercials pitched Merita Bread. Among the stations for additional coverage that afternoon were WAPI in Birmingham, Alabama, at 5:30 p.m.; WIOD in Miami, Florida, at 4:45 p.m.; WNOX in Knoxville, Tennessee, at 5:30 p.m.; and WMC in Memphis, Tennessee, at 5:00 p.m.; among others. The radio broadcasts aired courtesy of transcription discs and were not the same episodes that aired over the Mutual Broadcasting System (and later the Blue Network), with a different local announcer providing the commercial at each station.

The final radio broadcast sponsored by General Baking was on June 28, 1940. General Baking advertised Bond Bread. The radio program would air over the Mutual Broadcasting System, coast-to-coast, without a sponsor. (The only exceptions were in the Southeastern states where Merita Bread was pitched, and Gingham Bread along the West Coast.)

Beginning with the broadcast of May 2, 1941, General Mills would take over sponsorship of the program over Mutual (except for the southern states where Merita Bread was a sponsor, and Gingham Bread, which continued sponsorship for the West Coast but for only a few more months.

The evening of May 1, 1942, marked the end of *The Lone Ranger* broadcasts over the Mutual Broadcasting System, and the start of the NBC Blue Network (soon to be ABC) radio broadcasts, beginning with the broadcast of May 4, 1942.

New York City, WJZ (Blue Network) Eastern Time

May 4, 1942, to December 30, 1942, Monday, Wednesday and Friday, 7:30 p.m.

* Sporadic dates as the afternoons were reserved for baseball games (White Sox, Cubs, etc.) and the time slot reserved for *The Lone Ranger* was reserved in the event of a game cancellation or if a game concluded early.

Washington, D.C. WMAL (Blue Network) Eastern Time
May 4, 1942, to December 30, 1942, Monday, Wednesday and Friday, 7:30 p.m.

Chicago, Illinois, various stations (Blue Network) Central Time
May 8, 1942, to June 5, 1942 WLS (Blue), Fridays only, 7:00 p.m.
May 25, 1942, to June 10, 1942, WENR (Blue), Monday and Wednesday, 8:00 p.m.
June 12 to September 23, 1942, WENR (Blue), Monday, Wednesday and Friday, 8:00 p.m.
Sept. 25, 1942, to Oct. 26, 1942, WCFL (Blue), Monday, Wednesday and Friday, 6:30 p.m.
October 28, 1942, to December 30, 1942, WCFL and/or WLS
(both Blue Network), 6:30 p.m. *

NOTES

The spelling of fictional characters in the plot summaries originate from the radio scripts. Therefore, "Wallie" is the proper spelling of the character on the broadcast of April 13, 1938, versus the universally accepted "Wally." The character of "Luke Smead" in the broadcast of October 18, 1939, is spelled that way throughout the entire script, not "Luke Snead" as one might assume by listening to the extant recording. There was a character named "Denis" on the broadcasts of August 2, 1940, and May 6, 1942, not Dennis as one would expect. The drunkard on the broadcast of August 2, 1940, is spelled "Jug," not Jud. The same verification is also applied for the spelling of towns and ranches such as the "Diamond Jay Ranch" on the broadcast of February 23, 1940, not the Diamond J Ranch. The name of the town is Bordertown, not Border Town, for the broadcast of May 12, 1941. Fran Striker never assigned script titles for the early years of *The Lone Ranger*. Over the years, fans of the radio program assigned "collector titles" to the recordings in their collection. Script titles were assigned on a regular basis beginning with the broadcast of June 10, 1940. To avoid confusion, the authors decided not to list collector titles in the episode guide. To ensure accuracy, only the script titles are referenced.

Authorship for the radio scripts were not assigned on the script covers on a regular basis until 1942. Fran Striker still wrote the majority of the radio scripts so episodes listed without authorship credit might have been from the typewriter of Fran Striker, but subject to revision.

Announcers:

January 31, 1938 to August 12, 1938 – Al Chance
August 15, 1938 to November 18, 1938 – John Slagle
(except for November 9, 1938 – *unknown*)
November 21, 1938 to July 28, 1939 – Brace Beemer
July 31, 1939 to August 18, 1939 – John Slagle
August 21, 1939 to December 29, 1939 – Brace Beemer
January 1, 1940 – *unknown*
January 5, 1940 to January 8, 1940 – Brace Beemer
January 15, 1940 to January 26, 1940 – John Slagle
January 29, 1940 to July 26, 1940 – Brace Beemer
July 29, 1940 to August 9, 1940 – John Slagle
August 12, 1940 to September 23, 1940 – Brace Beemer
September 25, 1940 – John Slagle

* The program bounced back and forth irregularly, and sometimes on both stations at the same time.

September 27, 1940 to October 30, 1940 – Brace Beemer

November 1, 1940 – John Slagle

November 6, 1940 to December 13, 1940 – Brace Beemer

December 16, 1940 – Myron Wallace

December 18, 1940 – Brace Beemer

December 20, 1940 to January 3, 1941 – John Slagle

January 6, 1941 to January 17, 1941 – *unknown*

January 20, 1941 to April 4, 1941 – Brace Beemer

April 7, 1941 to June 13, 1941 – *unknown*

Harry Golder was assigned the regular position of announcer beginning with the broadcast of June 16, 1941, and would remain in that position through 1948. There would be exceptions such as the broadcast of November 5, 1941, when Harry Golder had a cold and a different announcer provided duties for the Intermission Break.

Episode #770, Broadcast January 3, 1938

Copyright Registration #54,274, script received at Registration Office January 4, 1938.

Plot: Deputy Bob Forsyth enjoys spending time with Sally Granger, against stiff competition from young Bert Allen, who works hard at the Box Kay ranch and is saving up enough to buy himself a home. When Sally's father vents over losing cattle, he starts to suspect someone is borrowing from his stock, with all eyes against Bert. Windy Darwin, wanted for robbery and murder back in Abilene, is blackmailed by the crooked Sheriff Burley to rebrand the Box Kay stock and make it appear Bert was stealing cattle. Bob catches Bert with evidence in hand, not Windy, a perfect frame-up that puts Bob under arrest on charges of cattle stealing. Late the next evening Sheriff Burley displays heart by letting Bert out of jail to spend a few hours with Sally, if the prisoner promises to be back in the morning, and "suggesting" he put a gun to Bob's ribs and force a confession while Bob himself is making a play for Sally. Bert is unaware that the generosity is a trap in disguise – Windy is off the trail waiting to ambush Bert. The Lone Ranger keeps close tabs on the proceedings and intervenes, saving Bert's life. The sheriff rides out to order Windy to leave town quickly, before the ruse is discovered, only to be apprehended by a U.S. marshal who is witness to the discussion. Bob Forsyth, angry at the sheriff for trying to pin the crime on him, incriminates the lawman with proof of guilt.

Notes: Cactus Pete introduces an actor friend named Hamilton to the Grangers. Hamilton was Fran Striker's middle name.

Episode #771, Broadcast January 5, 1938

Copyright Registration #54,434, script received at Registration Office January 7, 1938.

Plot: El Paso is in an uproar as a herd of Longhorns stampedes through Main Street. The distraction provides ample time for three outlaws, Lefty Riggs, Smokey Brown, and Mush Barton, to rob the bank. The Lone Ranger and Tonto, riding east towards El Paso, find the body of Jack Lovejoy – shot in the back. Lovejoy's father, emotionally distraught for his son turning into a stagecoach outlaw, shoots and kills Lefty, but not before the old man takes a bullet himself. Smokey and Mush, in town to avoid suspicion since the posse rode out of town in search of the bank robbers, allow The Lone Ranger to take Lefty's place, after the masked man uses a letter of credentials found on Lovejoy's body. The bank robbers mistakenly assume The Lone Ranger is Jack Lovejoy. Aware that convincing the robbers to grab the cash and flee to the border would not prove guilt of crime, just possession, with the possibility of throwing blame on Lefty, The Lone Ranger devises a scheme to create a falling out among thieves. Mush ultimately exchanges gunfire with Smokey, killing is partner in crime.

The Lone Ranger shoots the gun out of Mush's hand and wounds the shooting arm, giving him the advantage of turning him over to Sheriff Wilson… especially since the sheriff was their next intended victim.

Episode #772, Broadcast January 7, 1938

Copyright Registration #54,435, script received at Registration Office January 7, 1938.

Plot: Sheriff Prior and an outlaw named Sawtell plan to blow up the bridge over Powder River, forcing the stage to ford the river, where it can easily be robbed. Mabel Frisby, riding to warn her father of the attempted robbery of the stagecoach, is captured by the Sawtell gang. At the same time, Dave Winters, seeking the aid of the sheriff, is thrown in jail. With no one to come to the rescue, The Lone Ranger initiates a plan of action. Convincing Sam Trout, owner of the general store, to load barrels of oil into the back of a wagon, The Lone Ranger smashes the barrels and dumps the crude into the river, then starts a fire. This creates a distraction that prevents the horses and stagecoach from crossing the river. Mabel, meanwhile, is bound hand and foot in the camp of the outlaws, not far from the river. She feels confident Dave will ride to her rescue and round up the outlaws before her father's stagecoach is to cross the broken bridge. She defies Sawtell when he tries to make her talk, then smiles when she hears of the river on fire, saving her father's life. The U.S. marshal is then brought to town by The Lone Ranger to place Sheriff Prior under arrest and release Dave.

Notes: The name Sawtell originated from a character in the Zane Grey novel, *West of the Pecos*, first published in serial form in 1931 in *American Magazine*, but it was more than likely the 1937 publication in book form where Striker might have come across the name.

Episode #773, Broadcast January 10, 1938

Copyright Registration #54,436, script received at Registration Office January 7, 1938.

Plot: In the local café in the town of Butterworth, hard-faced Ben Bronson orders his two men, Zeke Potts and Tom Lazard, to track down and kill The Lone Ranger and bring back the white horse as his prize. Bronson knows the masked man will interfere with his plans, but is unaware that The Lone Ranger, disguised, overhears the entire plot. After waiting patiently for over two hours, Zeke and Tom creep through the woods toward the small camp made by The Lone Ranger and Tonto. From a short distance, the men fire the single rifle shot, making sure their aim is without error. The men quickly grab the rope tied to Silver, then return to town to rejoice with Bronson, who orders the boys to make him a mask while he tries on new clothes. Early the next evening, men race into the sheriff's office to report being robbed by The Lone Ranger. Late that same night, Bronson plans to rob the express office while masquerading as the vigilante. Thanks to a tip-off, a group of Sheriff Turner's men are stationed in the express office ready to trap The Lone Ranger, unaware that this was fake news. Bronson, in disguise, is across town at the time robbing the bank. What the criminal didn't suspect was the fact that his men shot a dummy that was carefully arranged near the campfire. The real Lone Ranger appears in person to catch them in the act and unmask them in the presence of the sheriff. The horse they brought back to town and rode was Tonto's horse, White Feller, the only reason they were able to pull off their ruse. Silver would never have allowed them to ride him.

Episode #774, Broadcast January 12, 1938

Copyright Registration #54,437, script received at Registration Office January 7, 1938.

Plot: Colonel Steve Tucker, confidence man, professional gambler, and four-flusher, grasps an opportunity when he sees an innocent looking youngster heading west. John Wood from St. Louis (everyone calls him Jack) is coming to take over a gold mine, the Esmeralda Mine, left to him by his late uncle, Cliff, who had fallen victim to Sitting Bull and his redskins because they believed the Wood family mistreated them. The Indians would kill Jack, too, if they find out who he is. At the next stage stop, Tucker chances upon Tonto and pays the

Indian to take a message to Josh Billings in Carson City. Instead of going straight to his hired destination, the Indian pulls into the woods a few miles from town and hands the note to The Lone Ranger. According to the note, using the crooked Lawyer Squibbs, Tucker, and Billings need only kill Wood for control of the mine. The grim fate which threatened Jack Wood, however, came sooner than The Lone Ranger thought, but at break-neck speed he raced out to the mine to prevent an "accident." Steve Tucker represented himself as Jack Wood to get control of the mine, but the masked man apprehended the guilty parties by forcing them out of the mine and into the hands of the law, moments before they were to kill Jack. The Lone Ranger explains to the youth that Indians never killed his uncle; – they are friendly in this part of the territory.

Notes: The script called for the character of Colonel Steve Tucker to be played like W.C. Fields.

Episode #775, Broadcast January 14, 1938
Copyright Registration #54,639, script received at Registration Office January 17, 1938.

Plot: Jeff Baker rides to the Bar Kay Ranch where his partner, Dan Snyder, has built up a first-class operation, with the biggest stock of cattle in the state, and the two get set to be respectable cow men. Mark Stratton, a third partner, turned honest and wrote a confession for Sheriff Burley, much to the chagrin of Jeff and Dan. During a bar brawl between partners, the confession is torn in half. The sheriff retrieves half, but Stratton and his half with the signature is nowhere to be found. The Lone Ranger and Tonto, riding along a trail, stumble across the dead body of Stratton, and the half paper grasped in tight fist. The crooks decide to frame the sheriff for the murder of a man named Sloane, forcing Deputy Jack Burley, the son of the sheriff, to take his father in to custody. The chiselers then blackmail the young man into forgetting they witnessed the murder if Jack finds and retrieves his father's half of the paper. The Lone Ranger hears enough to understand that Jack Burley robbed his own father and that lawmen were pursuing. Urging Silver to his greatest speed, the masked man saves the lad from an ambush. Jack returns to town to find Sloane alive and well. Jack pretends to have the paper Baker and Snyder were looking for, giving the men reason to confess their involvement so The Lone Ranger would overhear the entire confession.

Episode #776-1, Broadcast January 17, 1938
Copyright Registration #54,640, script received at Registration Office January 17, 1938.

Plot: Amos Larriby is upset because cattle keep disappearing every day, with no trail, cut fence, or clue left behind. Brother Fred says Amos is going loco in his old age, with ranch hands Pete and Sam, in agreement with Fred… but only to save their jobs do they agree with Amos. With approval of Matilda Larriby, Amos's wife, Sheriff Grant takes the old man away to a rest home. Tonto gets caught stealing something from the general store and is thrown into jail where, from the inside, he can help manage a jail break late that night for Amos. The town is in an uproar the next morning, while the sheriff forms a posse. Tonto quietly returns in the morning and forces the sheriff to return to the Larriby ranch, where Amos and Fred count cattle. The Lone Ranger arrives with more cattle and explains how Sam and Pete were herding cattle into a swamp to alter the head count, then returning them in good time to make Amos think he was going insane. The entire plot was an attempt for Fred to take over the ranch. Pete is tied to a tree stump with dried grass alongside him set in flames to force a confession in the presence of the sheriff, and convict him.

Episode #777-2, Broadcast January 19, 1938
Copyright Registration #54,688, script received at Registration Office January 21, 1938.

Plot: Sheriff Pete Crowley of Hawkins County is in the pocket of Ben Bush, wealthiest man in town. Soon after The Lone Ranger breaks Steve Larson from jail, a man falsely accused of murdering Sam Turner, the masked man explains the scheme. Bush steals money that people put in his bank, then before the money can be claimed, arranges for the owner to get into trouble. Steve Larson is the third innocent The Lone Ranger rescues. Several days pass while the sheriff's men search for the three whom The Lone Ranger rescued. With Tonto playing dead, The Lone Ranger makes it look like another innocent, Markheim, committed murder in the streets. The masked man whisks the body of Tonto away before anyone can discover the ruse and waits until the trial comes up to surprise Ben Bush and the jurors. One witness after another takes the stand, paid by Bush, witness to the shooting of an Indian. Markheim has no chance of escaping the hangman's rope. When Tonto reveals himself alive and well, and a copy of the deposit receipt is provided in court – courtesy of The Lone Ranger – Ben Bush's scheme goes awry as a United States marshal reveals himself to take charge of the irregularities as the sheriff starts pointing fingers toward Bush.

Notes: Episodes three and four of the transcriptions are listed otherwise in Chapter One, but the first six episodes in this episode guide are based on the numbers listed on the physical scripts. Naturally, they do not match, but script continuity is documented for the sake of historical continuity.

Episode #778-3, Broadcast January 21, 1938

Copyright Registration #54,690, script received at Registration Office January 21, 1938.

Plot: In one of the most desolate parts of the country, two partly civilized Indians find copper. Their education by missionaries is just enough to give them greed for money and a knowledge that a week of hard travel over rock-strewn land will bring good prices for the ore they take from the ground. Their big problem, however, is labor. They cannot afford to hire the necessary help, but they find another means. Big Crow and his partner, Jim Fox, send an old man into town to fetch "slaves" to work the mine. The Lone Ranger and Tonto, having been led by Fate to the headquarters of the Indian slave masters, learn of the cruel scheme of Big Fox. The old man masquerades as a medicine man and performs feats of magic to convince members of Chief Thundercloud's tribe to visit the cave – to appease the evil spirits, only to be tricked into slavery. The Lone Ranger intervenes. Convinced by the sincere manner of the masked man and the ringing shouts of Tonto in their native tongue, every member of Chief Thundercloud's tribe arms themselves and follows commands. Surrounding Big Crow, Jim Fox, and the old man, The Lone Ranger orders them to put on the chains – else face a death at the hands of the entire tribe.

Episode #779-4, Broadcast January 24, 1938

Copyright Registration #54,689, script received at Registration Office January 21, 1938.

Plot: Geronimo, the craftiest of all Indian leaders, is also the most terrible and most feared. He was utterly ruthless in his cruelty, and many times had escaped from carefully prepared traps. Butch Reed is an outlawed white man who has done considerable raiding in his own name. Slim Purdy, Butch's partner, provides details of a new town that popped up almost overnight. But Geronimo prefers not to side with anyone. After disposing of the white outlaws who brought him the information upon which he based an attack, Geronimo rallies his hundreds of Indian savages and makes ready to stage an attack on Snake River, a small town backed by soldiers. Tonto has no trouble in joining Geronimo's band. He sees a look of cunning cross the face of the leader when commanded to join the sacrifice battalion moving south into the town, men who were to be mowed down by the rifles of the Army when they made what would surely be a futile attack. As the red men move in, the cavalry dashes to the attack, with matchless firing making quick work of the band of Indians. Most of the redskins are shot down, but a handful escape. The rest are made prisoners, and the town is saved, for the moment. Tonto is among the prisoners.

Colonel Turner, learning the Indians took the local fort while the town was under attack, and are making plans toward the town, orders every man who can use a gun to assemble. Turner's scheme is to race out and wipe out the Indians before they can move toward Snake River, but the town folk fear they will be unshielded from protection. Riding like the wind, the masked mystery rider goes in pursuit of the Army. Catching up with the soldiers, The Lone Ranger asks why they march into a suicide mission when they outnumber the Indians. After all, as Tonto points out, the Indians that survived the futile attack were pawns in the scheme of Geronimo and seek vengeance in their hearts. Adding to the head count, The Lone Ranger races to town to encourage the men to arm themselves. At daybreak, the Indians inside the fort are awake, ready for the expected Army attack. The Indians to whom Tonto had talked raced for the garrison, supposedly pursued by three of the Army men. Geronimo orders the gates of the fort thrown wide but as soon as the members of his band whom he sent out to be killed are inside, begins striking down the savages near the gate. A blast of bugle sounds the charge, and the cavalrymen come forward with guns blazing. Augmented by the townsmen, the soldiers have nearly as many on their side as Geronimo, and the white men are fighting for their lives, their homes, and their families. Rifles are thrown aside when the fighters come together. Six-guns are emptied, then thrown down, but fists and knives replace them. For a brief time, it is a furious battle but the Indians at heart are cowards, eager to surrender that their lives might be spared. Geronimo himself is roped as The Lone Ranger and Tonto ride away.

Episode #780-5, Broadcast January 26, 1938

Copyright Registration #54,691, script received at Registration Office January 21, 1938.

Plot: Over a two-month period in the southwest, many stagecoaches are robbed of gold and mail by masked bandits, and no one has a clue by which to plan a search for the desperadoes. The leader, Butch Sellers, had all the loot taken to a cave, the location of which is known only to him and members of his band. He and his lieutenant, Lefty Gorman, stay in the cave to guard the gold dust and the sacks of stolen mail, while the other members of the band are forced to camp outside the mouth of the cavern. Firing gold dust into the wall, Butch heads to the nearest assay office, then awaits the results that would fool anyone into believing he found a real gold mine. Thus, the men could spend the money without suspicion. Steve, a gang member who overheard the scheme, is shot by Lefty Gorman. Badly wounded, Steve is roped to a saddle and headed south. The Lone Ranger finds Steve, who confesses the men's scheme and attempted murder, unaware that Butch plans to split the gold two ways – not eight – by double-crossing the rest of the gang. He plans on calling them into the cave one by one, roping them and setting a blast to throw down lots of loose rock. Tonto trails Lefty Gorman to the cave, overhearing the conversation from his place of concealment. The masked man and Indian companion plot to give Lefty the impression that Butch is going to double-cross him too, switching gold for pyrite. The falling out among thieves, in the presence of the sheriff, ensures they face a trial for their crimes.

Episode #781-6, Broadcast January 28, 1938

Copyright Registration #55,321, script received at Registration Office February 18, 1938.

Plot: The Kirk Newcomb gang terrorizes the entire region of Pecks. Newcomb himself would hang for murder if caught, but he seems to always have a means of escape when the law brushes by. Newcomb shoots and kills Widow Prindle, and steals her cash in retribution for her husband putting the scar on his cheek with a near-fatal bullet. Miles southwest of Pecos, The Lone Ranger and Tonto momentarily rest their horses when paying a visit to Ma Burton, whose ranch was saved by the masked man when her husband died. When the posse approaches, led by Sheriff Dave Anderson, The Lone Ranger and Tonto quickly outdistance them and sweep toward the trail of Kirk Newcomb and his three companions. Tonto, with all his skill and cunning, studies the outlaws' trail. After tracking them to their hideout, the masked man and Indian find themselves up against opposition. Jane Anderson, daughter of the sheriff, is being held hostage. Unseen by Newcomb and the lawmen, The Lone Ranger rides in a wide circle to come back to the vicinity of the outlaws' shack. In the small grove of cottonwoods he waits, knowing Tonto will soon return with Ma Burton's two dogs. Tame as they can be, the canines appear vicious at first glance and Tonto uses the four-legged animals to outwit and apprehend the criminals.

Episode #782-7, January 31, 1938

Copyright Registration #55,322, script received at Registration Office February 18, 1938.

Plot: The sheriff of Abilene is unable to solve the mysterious thefts of many high-bred horses from numerous ranches in the county. He finally agrees to the demands of Cal Cummings, most prominent of the ranchers, to send for the Texas Rangers. Zeke Skinner, secretly paid by Cummings to not deliver the letter to the Texas Rangers, is held up in the streets by The Lone Ranger. Cummings is the leader of the horse thieves and plans to throw people off by recommending the Texas Rangers. Among his current plans is to steal the famous Silver, even though he has heard that he could not ride him. In attempting to borrow another horse to take after the thieves, Cummings accuses The Lone Ranger and Tonto of being the horse thieves themselves. The Lone Ranger knows he would have no chance to recover his great horse if he goes to jail. Furthermore, in jail his mask would be stripped off. He takes a chance on Tonto's daring plan and makes his escape on Tonto's horse while the Indian is taken into custody. The Lone Ranger sneaks onto Cummings' ranch to investigate, learning that the Texas Rangers arriving in town will be Cummings' men in disguise. Ben and Dave, masquerading, are exposed by The Lone Ranger in the presence of witnesses. They attempt to cover their crime by naming Cummings as their employer. The sheriff, wondering where the real Texas Rangers are, learns from The Lone Ranger that Zeke was paid not to deliver the letter summoning them. When Zeke denies the claim, The Lone Ranger pulls out the letter, convincing the sheriff to arrest Cal Cummings.

Episode #783-8, Broadcast February 2, 1938

Copyright Registration #55,323, script received at Registration Office February 18, 1938.

Plot: When Jim Palmer dies suddenly, his daughter Alice isn't convinced that his death is an accident, and yet there is nothing she can do to prove otherwise. After a crude burial, the girl is consoled by Mrs. Carroway from a neighboring ranch. The old woman assures Alice that her father's horse missed its footing on the edge of the ravine; even Sheriff Tucker insists it could have happened to anyone. Alice suspects otherwise. John Shipman, however, had tried a dozen times to buy Jim's ranch but Jim would not sell. Shipman claims he did not need to commit murder because he already owned the ranch through a signed deed, but Alice insists the deed is fake. After Alice Palmer moves into the Carroway home, she rides alongside The Lone Ranger and shows him the place where her father fell to his death. In truth, Gus and Pete were hired by Shipman to commit murder. In the nearby town of Mud Flats, Tonto suggests he was along the ravine and witnessed the crime, provoking the men into following the Indian out of town with the hopes another murder will cover their tracks. John Shipman rides alongside the two killers to ensure the job is done completely this time, then held at gunpoint by The Lone Ranger and Tonto, unaware that his confession was being overheard by the sheriff and his men, who surrounded the camp. Shipman's confession about a forged signature ensures clear motive.

Episode #784-9, Broadcast February 4, 1938

Copyright Registration #55,324, script received at Registration Office February 18, 1938.

Plot: While the cattle of many ranches were mixed freely on the open rangeland, each owner was able to identify his own stock by the brand and earmark. Then, as many more men settled and went into cattle raising, Blackie Stanton moved into the territory with his fast guns and shrewd brain. Together with Vince Lawton, they created a register and when new settlers came by, they would be told that the brand was already taken and a provided with a suggestion for another (such as the letter S could be rebranded as the number eight). After years of scheming, Blackie stole numerous cattle with no one able to prove otherwise. The Lone Ranger and Tonto are riding the plains under moonlight when they witness a burial, the body of Vince Lawton. Blackie tells a U.S. marshal that Vince ran off with all the cash in his house and exposes the branding scheme with Blackie the victim. A dividing up of the cattle will ensure Blackie can ride out with more steers than he started out with, thus avoiding suspicion. After kidnapping Two-Gun Smead, The Lone Ranger leads a posse of ranchers to Blackie's place where he exposes the unmarked grave of Lawton, and with Two-Gun missing, Blackie blames him for the murder. Two-Gun was, in reality, within ear shot and with anger from betrayal exposes Blackie's scheme.

Episode #785-10, Broadcast February 7, 1938
Copyright Registration #55,326, script received at Registration Office February 18, 1938.
Plot: Steve Brady of the border patrol knows alcohol is being brought over from south of the border but whenever he questions a potential suspect (such as the owner of a café), those who could testify are gunned down. When he finds the rats responsible for smuggling contraband liquor, he will also get them on two charges of murder. A crooked sheriff and a crooked border patrol agent are responsible for the crime and when the heat is up, they conspire to protect their liquor smuggling by framing a friend of The Lone Ranger, Pete Hawkins, also known as Cactus Pete. Public sentiment runs high against Cactus Pete, lodged in jail, and there is talk of organizing a lynch mob, which Sheriff Perkins quickly subdues. While The Lone Ranger races out to create a frame, Tonto heads north to overtake the man who made Pete changes clothes with him to verify the wrong man was jailed. Sheriff Perkins and Steve Brady are provided a note for a secret meeting rendezvous, unaware that the letter is coded so only the guilty parties would show. In the presence of the U.S. marshal, the conversation exchanged between the two cinches their guilt and ensures arrest. Cactus Pete is released from jail promptly.

Episode #786-11, Broadcast February 9, 1938
Copyright Registration #55,327, script received at Registration Office February 18, 1938.
Plot: A weird mystery surrounds the stagecoach route between Pine River and the station at Calhoun. Somewhere in the arid stretch of prairie, death strikes at the driver and guard. It happened twice in the past month and Bert Sawtell, the district superintendent, could find no cause of death. Four men had been drawn into Calhoun by the unguided horses, and there was not a mark on any of them to show the cause of death. David Ligget, an 18-year-old a.k.a. The Kansas Kid, a stage driver who sought a job with Sawtell, finds himself instead jailed by Sheriff Jack Beardsley, suspected of committing the crimes. When the Pine River stage arrives at Calhoun for the third time, with men mysteriously dead and the passengers on the stage unable to account for the crime, The Lone Ranger and Tonto free The Kansas Kid. Days later, The Lone Ranger fetches the sheriff and his deputies to ride like the wind along the trail to meet the westbound stage. Reaching their destination, they find The Kansas Kid holding three men at bay with guns. The criminals, it is explained, have been using a poison used for killing crop destroying inspects, to kill men. They poisoned a water hole and after the guards and drivers drink the water, they would die before reaching Calhoun. The killer would stop the horses and steal the cargo and send the horses on their way to Calhoun. The men will not drink the water, cinching their guilt, and The Kansas Kid finds himself employed by the stage line.

Episode #787-12, Broadcast February 11, 1938
Copyright Registration #55,328, script received at Registration Office February 18, 1938.
Plot: With Tonto, his faithful Indian companion, The Lone Ranger travels over fifty miles in record-breaking time to deliver a message to the governor. Then, with a man's freedom, and perhaps his life at stake, the masked mystery rider continues on his way with a governors' pardon for Jim Loomis. Loomis spent ten years of his life in prison, innocent of a crime to which Butch Vinton recently confessed. For the first five years, Loomis protested his innocence but with the death of his wife, the only person who believed in him, he gave up. After being released with the good news, ten years of unfair punishment and bitterness in his heart suggested vengeance on his mind as he set out to find and murder Vinton's wife. The Lone Ranger knew his only hope of saving her lay in getting her to move away from Buckthorne so Jim Loomis could not find her. Through the

window outside her home, the sheriff and The Lone Ranger witness what might be an attempted murder by Loomis as he confronts the widow, but when nine-year-old Ruth enters the room of her adopted aunt, Loomis immediately realized it was his daughter, whom he had never laid eyes on before. Loomis breaks down with forgiveness in his heart and together they leave to start a new life. The Lone Ranger later tells the sheriff that earlier in the day Tonto switched the bullets in the gun for blanks and that murder never could have happened.

Episode #788-13, Broadcast February 14, 1938

Copyright Registration #55,325, script received at Registration Office February 18, 1938.

Plot: When Texas becomes a part of the union, there is a small strip of land which neither Mexico nor the United States can claim. In the early days of the west, it furnishes a safe hideout for one of the most terrible bands of outlaws ever to strike at a settler. Under the ruthless leadership of Trig Schuyler, these murderers and raiders charged on a ranch, shot all who offered resistance, then made their escape with cattle to the country that had no flag. Too powerful for the law and too organized, The Lone Ranger decides to ride into Mexico and talk with Gonzales Rancho, whose grandfather was the Spanish governor of Texas, for help. Then racing for the huge Hank Wilson Ranch, to get help and prove support from Gonzales, the masked man shows the sword of Wilson's grandfather that until now was two inches deep in the wall of Gonzales home, placed there by one of the early governors of Texas as an I.O.U. voucher for a debt yet unpaid. Gonzales herds together all of the strongest cattle, the wildest, the most ferocious, and drives them to the Rio. Hard riding cowboys of the Wilson ranch concealed behind high rocks and boulders, ride out under specific orders of The Lone Ranger. Jose, foreman of the Gonzales ranch, creates a stampede that ultimately hems the outlaws in on both sides, while the Schuyler gang is forced to mount the frightened horses and race towards the huge rocks north of their hideout… only to be outnumbered by Wilson's men, fully armed. With no choice but to surrender or face death, cornered from all sides, Trig Schuyler and his men surrender.

Episode #789-14, Broadcast February 16, 1938

Copyright Registration #55,395, script received at Registration Office February 23, 1938.

Plot: Bill Brady is too level-headed to start a fight with bellowing bull-like Yank Jordan, twice his size, that might lead to a shooting and perhaps a death. Joshua Potter, father of the girl Bill Brady plans to marry, orders Bill not to visit anymore. Potter will not allow a yellow streak in the family. Sally, madly in love with Bill, understands his point of view and defies her father by defending her love. Tonto and The Lone Ranger, purchasing supplies in the general store, witness the incident and privately amongst themselves agree Bill Brady made the right choice. A week goes by and Bill Brady joined the wild horse hunters, while the masked man and Indian rode throughout the country surrounding Morgan's Gap, keeping a constant watch for signs of an uprising among the Indians. Small bands of natives have raided communities south of the Gap and seem to be working toward a main objective. The Lone Ranger rides into town and warns the townspeople that savage Indians are coming to attack them. Brady, meanwhile, talks with the masked man and agrees to cooperate in a scheme to aid the oblivious folks at Morgan's Gap. Soon the savages arrive, and a dozen buildings blazed in Morgan's Gap. As each man's house takes fire from the flaming arrows of the savages, the besieged occupants race for the nearest place that's still intact. Brady, leading the settlers in defense, and catching a glimpse of the Indians ahead, sees only the men they thought had stolen their horses and rush on the offensive to conquer them. It is really The Lone Ranger and Tonto who temporarily stole the horses, a necessary act to encourage the settlers to pick up arms. The savages flee but not before Bill's actions win the respect of his future father-in-law.

Episode #790-15, Broadcast of February 18, 1938

Copyright Registration #55,330, script received at Registration Office February 18, 1938.

Plot: Bob Frawley, the young sheriff of Needlepoint, has vowed to avenge his father's killing by a man known only as "Wildcat." When it turns out the reclusive father of the girl the young man wants to marry owns a gun with that name engraved on it, it looks like he will have to put duty ahead of love. The Lone Ranger, having ridden many miles, with his horse Silver tired, is badly in need of water. He stops at the home of Amy Holcomb, which exposes him to the scenario in which he decides to intervene. Panamint Nash, her uncle, decides the easiest way to hide his past transgressions is to lock Amy in her room and marry her off to a cousin (thrice removed), Morgan. For several days after Tonto goes to work as a cook on the big ranch where different members of the Nash family have their homes, Linda stays in her room as a prisoner. Tonto leaks word of a shotgun wedding to The Lone Ranger. A week later, before the shotgun wedding, the young sheriff arrives at the Nash homestead to rescue Linda, only to witness Panamint shoot and kill the vile Morgan. Panamint explains that the gun was once owned by a good friend who has since passed away.

Episode #791-16, Broadcast February 21, 1938
Copyright Registration #55,477, script received at Registration Office February 26, 1938.
Plot: This was the same script from the broadcast of April 30, 1934.

Episode #792-17, Broadcast February 23, 1938
Copyright Registration #55,478, script received at Registration Office February 26, 1938.
Plot: This was the same script from the broadcast of April 18, 1934, with one revision: the Eastern Gold Company was changed to the Eastern Mining Syndicate.

Episode #793-18, Broadcast February 25, 1938
Copyright Registration #55,479, script received at Registration Office February 26, 1938.
Plot: This was the same script from the broadcast of May 7, 1934. The only revisions were Lige's last name changed from Twombley to Trembly, and Tessie was now shortened to Tess.

Episode #794-19, Broadcast February 28, 1938
Copyright Registration #55,636, script received at Registration Office March 5, 1938.
Plot: Red Rock Valley stages a great celebration when the big irrigation system turns arid land into fertile fields. Bart Boswell is the one responsible for the undertaking, and no one resents the fact that he stands to make a fortune on his project. The Lone Ranger, learning of the reason for the celebration, knows Boswell took the water from the Indians. He also knows that Chief White Eagle is not the type of man who will do nothing while seeing his people dying of thirst. Fearing Boswell plans to claim the land he mortgaged after the citizens cultivate the land, Dan Hawks, U.S. marshal in the territory, approaches him. The marshal is aware that Boswell was a wanted man in another territory and threatens him with exposure if he does not remain on the straight path. On the other side of the valley, water holes have dried up and the streams are nothing but parched depressions in the ground. In desperation, the natives perform a rain dance. Approaching Chief White Eagle in private, Boswell tricks the Indian into believing the U.S. marshal is responsible for the lack of water and suggests murdering the lawman and damming the stream to change the course of the water and rectify the problem. A rancher named Tad Sloan, meanwhile, figures Boswell's scheme. With the water reverting to the other side of the valley, the farmland would dry up and mortgages would be foreclosed. The Lone Ranger rides out to inform the marshal of the death trap while Tonto discusses the situation with the Chief, with a plan to expose Boswell. The Indians show up at Boswell's place when the marshal arrives, tricking Boswell into staying inside the main room long enough to face the approaching Indians. Boswell, realizing the Indians are not mistaking the marshal for him, confesses his scheme out of fear. The Indians and farmers outside the house overhear the confession. Threatened with jail, Boswell agrees to The Lone Ranger's proposition to live at the w

ater divide. Boswell is to fix a lock on the water so it will be sent both to the Indians and to the white men. There is enough water for both if divided and Boswell agrees to handle the division.

Episode #795-20, Broadcast March 2, 1938

Copyright Registration #55,795, script received at Registration Office March 12, 1938.

Plot: The history of the southwest during the time of the Lone Ranger is filled with accounts of the Apache Kid. He was fully as savage and cruel as the great Indian leader, Geronimo, but where Geronimo led a huge Army of savages, the Apache Kid traveled alone. Raised by an agency after the murder of his father, the Apache Kid spoke English as well as the average white man, though he was a full-blooded Indian. He started his career of crime by becoming an outlaw with the murder of the man who killed his father. From then on, his trail was blazed with countless murders of lawmen who tried to capture him. When The Lone Ranger and Tonto come across the body of Tom Reynolds, a deputy, they learn that The Apache Kid was his murderer. Tom vowed revenge against the Indian for the death of his son. The masked man pays a visit to Sheriff Burns of Calloway County to inform him of the death of his deputy, then masterminds a plan to capture the notorious killer. Masquerading as the deputy, The Lone Ranger creates the illusion that The Apache Kid never shot clean, luring him back to finish the job. Tonto tracks the camp of The Apache Kid and informs him that Reynolds was left for dead – but survived and placed a $10,000 reward on him. The trap lures The Apache Kid to an abandoned cabin where The Lone Ranger gets the advantage and exchanges fisticuffs with the killer. After throwing down the badge once owned by the late deputy, The Lone Ranger insists on bringing in The Apache Kid alive. The Indian laughs, claiming they have no proof, but Tonto already spoke to The Apache Kid's wife to get a confession and she will testify against him in return for his jail time instead of a hangman's noose.

Episode #796-21, Broadcast March 4, 1938

Copyright Registration #55,796, script received at Registration Office March 12, 1938.

Plot: Jeb Norton never missed a chance to get hold of easy cash. When he finds a girl traveling alone toward Dodge City, he makes it a point to make the last part of the trip with her to win her confidence. His latest target is Betty Sawyer, on the westbound stagecoach, on the way to Dodge City to live at the ranch of her uncle, Nick Sawyer. While her uncle learns about her father's recent illness and death, she learns about Sawyer's recent brush with the notorious outlaw, Gopher Gage. Only when Betty arrives at the ranch and unpacks does she learn that her leather bag had been cut and all the money she inherited from her late father stolen. Her uncle sends his ranch hands out to Dodge to find Jeb Norton, unaware that The Lone Ranger and Tonto stumbled upon the dead body of the thief, mysteriously slain and robbed. The cowboys from Nick Sawyer's ranch give chase, only to lose the masked man and Indian. Now accused of murder and theft, The Lone Ranger masterminds a way to smoke out Gopher Gage. With assistance of Sawyer and Sheriff Jenks, word gets around that the dead body on the prairie was the notorious outlaw and the reward money was due to Betty for killing the criminal. In town that evening, a big celebration for the death of Gopher Gage was held. When Gopher pays a late-night visit to Betty and her uncle, he is surprised from behind by The Lone Ranger. Tonto ties the outlaw up. The Lone Ranger chuckles as the celebration in town started a little early, but now is held in earnest. For using herself as bait, the reward money given to Betty will be more than what was stolen from her.

Notes: Jeb makes reference to Billy the Kid, The Apache Kid and Geronimo in this episode. They were all villains The Lone Ranger had faced off against in past radio adventures, including the previous broadcast.

Episode #797-22, Broadcast March 7, 1938

Copyright Registration #55,797, script received at Registration Office March 12, 1938.

Plot: Jim Murdock lives alone in the big house he'd built on the edge of Grant's canyon with the profits from half ownership of a gold mine. His partner, Abe Jenkins, is disgruntled because the two own the mine between them, then split it into two sections. Sore because Jim's half panned out first rate and his was not, and with a wife and kid starving, Jenkins threatens a showdown. Murdock offers the hand of friendship and loads Abe's mule with provisions and supplies to take back home. Barney Boxer, meanwhile, races back into town to report Murdock's body at the bottom of a ravine. With Abe's house stocked with provisions from his partner, it stood to reason that the sheriff would suspect Abe of the crime. Abe Jenkins is placed under arrest and held until morning when the lawmen could investigate the supposed death of Jim Murdock. The Lone Ranger suspects Boxer framed Abe and sets up a frame himself whereupon Boxer's vest button and a promissory note suggest Boxer committed the act – not Abe. Panicking, Boxer confesses that Murdock planned to disappear while Abe Jenkins takes the fall, in the hopes that his partner did not find out how he had a survey of the gold mine before they split the property in half. After the confession, Boxer discovers Murdock is not dead – just roped and gagged outside. Having received a visit prior from the masked man, the sheriff played along with the scheme.

Episode #798-23, Broadcast March 9, 1938

Copyright Registration #55,863, script received at Registration Office March 16, 1938.

Plot: When, in the years shortly after 1870, the railroads expanded into the west in excess of traffic needs, there were many obstacles to overcome. Schemers saw a new means of getting easy money, savage Indians made work on the tracks a hazardous occupation, and the men who were to benefit most by the railroads were among those who fought hardest against them. Big Bill Cummings, with ulterior motives in the town of Cherokee, maneuvers a number of prominent and influential cattlemen into combatting the approaching construction of the railroad. Believing the iron horse will bring folks in from the East to settle down, thus diminishing the grazing land, the cattlemen agree to combat the threat. With the aid of an Easterner named Sanders, Big Bill Cummings writes a letter to the head of the railroad whose tracks are already stretched across the region. All the other ranchers in the region sign their names to the letter, then Sanders takes it to mail from the nearest stagecoach station. Cummings hires a con-man named Vinton to pose as a government man sent in advance to survey the land, to help convince the cattlemen of the validity to the imposed threat. Cummins, Sanders, and Vinton scheme to rob all the cash from the train—half a million dollars—knowing the cattlemen would take the blame. Later, the cattlemen dig holes to set blasts for an approaching train and The Lone Ranger, riding onto the scene, carries Big Bill Cummings, leader of the cattlemen, away with him on the back of his powerful horse. This does not prevent explosive charges to be set off, creating enough noise for Vinton to attempt to shoot Cummings in the back. Vinton and Sanders planned a double-cross against Cummings, to split the loot in half instead of thirds. Realizing one more explosion would wreck the train, The Lone Ranger gets the better of Vinton and ties him up. Cummings, realizing he already lost, agrees to help the masked man keep the cattlemen at bay while the masked man races like the wind to catch up to the approaching train and alert them to the impending disaster. The conductor, realizing there was foul play, stops the train in time.

Episode #799-24, Broadcast March 11, 1938

Copyright Registration #55,864, script received at Registration Office March 16, 1938.

Plot: Andy Beecham struck his gold claim after many hard years of prospecting. With assistance from a crook known as Black Mike, and financial fronting from Mark Goldman, a professional gambler and shady loan operator, Andy brought his recent samples to town – unaware the two schemed to defraud him of the rich mine that finally started paying out. Under contract of mortgage, Goldman exercises a clause that stipulates he can collect the debt on demand, and in cash – which Andy would not have because it takes weeks to have the gold converted into cash. Tonto overhears the schemers' plan and reports to his tall, masked friend. The next day, with Sheriff Purdy as witness, Goldman demands he be paid the full amount of the loan – in cash. The Lone Ranger takes up the cause with help from a reformed gambler, Rodney Ramsey, a man whose life he saved in the past. Ramsey pays a late-night visit to Goldman, tricking him into revealing the location of the note that had to be handed back to Andy upon payment. A bullet from outside the window shoots the lights out and a masked intruder races in to steal the note. Goldman rushes to the sheriff to report the theft, claiming Andy was the culprit, but the sheriff shakes his head. Andy has been with him during the past hour. The old skinflint discovers that the sheriff backed the law – without the papers to be handed over, he himself cannot accept paper money. And Tonto makes the suggestion, as Ramsey chuckles, that the stolen promissory note will more than likely be returned in about a week… the earliest it would take for Andy to have his gold converted into cash.

Episode #800-25, Broadcast March 14, 1938
Copyright Registration #55,329, script received at Registration Office March 21, 1938.
Plot: When California was opened for homesteading, the government little realized the complications that would ensue. It seems that the Spanish governors had granted huge tracts of land to noblemen and grandees before the U.S. took possession. When the homesteaders, having staked their all on the future in the far west arrived to take up their land, they found it held by others. Among the victims was Jeb and Martha, who will not raise a hand or kill the men who work for Manuel Ortega, the land baron claiming to own the property they own. Ortega stands firm with the only language he knows – a six-gun and a rifle. The homesteaders plan to wait for reinforcements but starting a war only means many deaths. The Lone Ranger and Tonto ride from the southern Sierra Nevada's into California in sight of the Ortega ranch and the camp of Easterners to verify the things Jeb Martin told them. The U.S. marshal explains how Ortega held land by an old Spanish grant, which was bounded on the south and west by a river and on the north by a marker line. The Lone Ranger realizes selfish Ortega would find his land and the deed to it of little value. For the best part of an hour, The Lone Ranger, Tonto, the local sheriff, and many of the Easterners all dug steadily, a row of holes extending from an arroyo to a section of the river boundary of Ortega's land. Thanks to kegs of gunpowder, an explosion blasts. Many years ago, the river flowed through a different bed. The river changed its course to its original bed and Ortega's 10,000 acres was reduced to less than 1,000 acres.

Episode #801-26, Broadcast March 16, 1938
Copyright Registration #56,029, script received at Registration Office March 21, 1938.
Plot: The thousands of acres surrounding the town of Mariposa, were the subject of much argument between the cattlemen and the sheep herders. Amos Franklin, a sheepman, believed that cattlemen were out to kill his stock and ruin him. In an effort to hold his land, he hired an outlaw named Scar Gordon and a dozen of the killers who traveled with him. This was part of a carefully laid plan by Gordon. He intended to attack and wipe out all of the cattlemen, then take their cows and ranches. He knew their pride would prohibit their seeking army aid to defeat a much-despised sheepherder. Scar schemed alongside Vince Bennet, knowing a range war would result in lots of deaths – and vacancies for the taking. Tonto overhears part of the plan, so The Lone Ranger fakes a murder to put the sheepman in jail and thwart the plans. He made his move tonight because every cowman would be in town, celebrating pay day, and all their guns checked with the sheriff, The Lone Ranger hoped to catch the cattlemen unprepared. Under the leadership of Scar Gordon, the outlaws move into town, keeping themselves in the dark as much as possible, attracting little attention. Their attempt to break Amos from jail so their plot will not go defeated was thwarted when they meet Tonto, the Indian that Amos supposedly shot and killed. The outlaws soon discover they are surrounded by the sheriff, a big cattleman named Bull McPherson, and his ranch hands.

Episode #802-27, Broadcast March 18, 1938
Copyright Registration #56,030, script received at Registration Office March 21, 1938.

Plot: The town of Flatbush was in the grip of outlaws. Sheriff Parsons seemed to shut his eyes to the activities of certain men, and there was a suspicion that a great deal of the stolen money in the region found its way to Sheriff Parson's pockets. His new deputy, Jack Garrett, is a straight-shooter so the sheriff arranges for a hired gun, Ben Wilson from the Panamint region, to eliminate Garrett. But the deputy is faster on the draw and soon charged with murder. Garrett flees, stumbling onto the camp of The Lone Ranger and Tonto, who mastermind a scheme to expose the crooked sheriff. When Sheriff Parsons finds that he is looked on with disfavor by many of the townsmen for his one-sided attitude toward Garrett, he is annoyed and determined to take further steps to convince the people that he was justified in what he did. His intentions to steal money from Zeke Merrill, the wealthiest man in these parts, and kill old Merrill to frame Garrett, would have succeeded if The Lone Ranger had not thwarted the crime and chased down Buck Beasley, the hired murderer. Facing a hangman's noose for the crime, Buck agrees to testify against that the sheriff planned the crimes.

Episode #803-28, Broadcast March 21, 1938

Copyright Registration #56,120, script received at Registration Office March 30, 1938.

Plot: Jim Burton ruled a county in the southwest with an iron fist. Everyone who wished to live in peace was forced to pay him for protection. Otherwise, his ruthless gang would sack and rob their homes, set fire to buildings, poison cattle, and ever go as far as murder. When The Lone Ranger arrives, he finds that half a dozen of Jim Burton's men, including his lieutenant, Bat Jordon, were wanted by the law in other parts of the state. In a series of daring captures, the masked man carried off those he knew to be outlaws. Meanwhile, Burton tried desperately to locate The Lone Ranger and put an end to the man who'd caused him so much trouble. Tyler, an old man who could not afford to pay for Burton's protection, offered the schemer a proposition – where he can locate Tonto and The Lone Ranger. Tyler explains how the two have been friendly with him, having been to his place several times already. Jim Burton eventually discovers, however, that Tonto is bait, and the entire scheme was meant to trap the remaining outlaws. Their confessions during their ruse to lay and wait to ambush the masked man was overheard by the sheriff, moments before they found themselves trapped in a pitfall, clinching their guilt for the court.

Episode #804-29, Broadcast March 23, 1938

Copyright Registration #56,121, script received at Registration Office March 30, 1938.

Plot: Zeke Salter, an old schemer, tricks people into believing that a masked man wearing a white hat, along with a young boy, spilled coal oil on his house and threatened to set it on fire if he did not give them all his money. Claiming he was knocked unconscious at the time, Zeke said he woke to find his house burned to the ground. Silver is drinking from a creek outside Osage and the Lone Ranger is sheltered at a high bank when he overhears the discussion that lawmen are out looking for him. An Easterner named Grant, found in the hotel tied up and wearing a white hat and a mask, is mistaken for the masked man who burned down Zeke's house and is arrested and taken into custody. At Grant's trial he explains he is an attorney for Nancy's deceased father and has tried to get an accounting of the estate left to Nancy, from Zeke, who has no cooperated. The judge demands an accounting of Nancy's money since Uncle Zeke was made her legal guardian upon the death of her mother. Without the necessary paperwork to vouch for her age, though, which supposedly went up in smoke, Zeke would continue to manager her money. The judge, using a family Bible given him by The Lone Ranger, verifies the birthdate of the family members including Nancy, proving she is of age to inherit her father's estate.

Episode #805-30, Broadcast March 25, 1938

Copyright Registration #56,122, script received at Registration Office March 30, 1938.

Plot: This was the same script from the broadcast of August 17, 1936. This same story would later be recycled again for the episode entitled "Texas Justice," broadcast July 23, 1945. The 1936 and 1938 versions were both more violent than the later version.

Episode #806-31, Broadcast March 28, 1938

Copyright Registration #56,296, script received at Registration Office April 6, 1938.

Plot: Jed Cramer, the most despised man in Big Bend, is a scheming money lender at the local bank who strikes a deal with Abe Turner, whose mortgage he ruthlessly holds. Abe robs Jed of $10,000 and flees the scene. The Lone Ranger and Tonto, having stabled their horses in town, realize that Abe could not have passed their way as Jed claimed. Firmly convinced that Abe committed his act, only because of the absolute despair of his starving family, he tries to aid the man, but Abe, suddenly frenzied, strikes the masked man down, then leaves with assurance to his wife that she and the baby would be cared for. Goaded, both by a desire to find a thief, and the urging of Jane Turner, the sheriff's men spend many days scouring the country in search of Abe Turner, but without success. After discovering the mortgage in the cash box was blank, Abe follows the advice of The Lone Ranger to pay Jed Cramer a visit. Abe accuses Jed of how he was being double-crossed. Jed embezzled money from the bank and wanted the insurance to cover the loss, with the promise that Abe's wife and son would be provided and the mortgage free and clear. During the confrontation, Jed confesses his part in the scheme, claiming he kept his word, unaware the sheriff and witnesses were listening outside. The Lone Ranger confesses the mortgage was inside and he merely switched papers to convince Abe to help convict the greedy banker.

Episode #807-32, Broadcast March 30, 1938
Copyright Registration #56,297, script received at Registration Office April 6, 1938.
Plot: Buck Newton, having made a promise to The Lone Ranger and Tonto to go straight, kept his word. He got a job as a stage driver and now has plans to settle down with Betty Stevens, whose father owns the general store in Dalton. Along the back country trail just north of the Rio Grande and east of El Paso, though, Black Mike and his gang of outlaws lay in ambush near the quicksand ford at Solter's Creek. Having switched the sign so the night stage from the town of Paso Doble would be misdirected into a quicksand bog, the outlaws stand to profit from a major theft of gold. Riding shotgun as a stage guard was Butch Larson, a member of the gang. Riding along the road to Dalton, The Lone Ranger and Tonto discover the signpost and the arrow pointing in the wrong direction. They work to pull the stagecoach out of the quicksand while the outlaws are celebrating the success of their venture. Buck, bound and gagged, is framed for the crime when Jake, one of the outlaws, rides into Dalton and claims to be a cowhand who witnessed the crime perpetrated by Buck. Because the gold was government property, the U.S. marshal arrives to take over the investigation. The Lone Ranger convinces the marshal to allow a second stage to run through the same trail, surrounding the real outlaws as they attempt to make the same play twice. Buck, cleared of the false accusation, fears he might lose his job but the marshal suggests the stage driver will get a raise… as a wedding present.

Episode #808-33, Broadcast April 1, 1938
Copyright Registration #56,298, script received at Registration Office April 6, 1938.
Plot: People are coming to El Dorado every day from all parts of the country to try their luck in the gold hills, including Hawk Vincent, an outlaw who has never been charged for a crime. Jack Bates, who has never committed a crime, is a fugitive from justice with a price on his head. The Lone Ranger masquerades as a bounty hunter to lure Hawk Vincent into believing Jack Bates is in town, and how a criminal with a price on his head would be willing to pay for a swift escape. Jack Bates, meanwhile, had done well in El Dorado. He, and a friend of his father's, were joint owners of a paying mine in the hills not far distant. and Jack Looked forward to the day when he could speak to Nancy Fawcett about marriage. Vincent, having learned a tip about Jack's whereabouts from Tonto, robbed a man, got away, and shouted Jack's name, roping him into the crime. The Lone Ranger arrives to take Jack away, disappointing Hawk who believed the masked man was pulling the same stunt. Hawk Vincent and his friend Sam rode ahead, confident that they would overtake Jack Bates and the masked man before the two reached Kansas. Over a campfire, Jack is surprised by the criminals, but not as surprised as Hawk and Sam when they discover they crossed the state line. Wanted by the law in Kansas, the men quickly discover they are surrounded by the sheriff and his deputies who are in their rights by territory. Jack Bates was working with The Lone Ranger to lure the criminals across the state line.

Episode #809-34, Broadcast April 4, 1938 [PART ONE OF THREE]
Copyright Registration #56,313, script received at Registration Office April 11, 1938.
Plot: See pages 230 to 232. The element where The Lone Ranger pursues a wanted man and falls victim to a rock landslide and rescued by the man he pursued, with a discussion about possibly giving him a head start was recycled from the broadcast of March 12, 1937.

Episode #810-35, Broadcast April 6, 1938 [PART TWO OF THREE]
Copyright Registration #56,314, script received at Registration Office April 11, 1938.
Plot: See pages 232 and 233.

Episode #811-36, Broadcast April 8, 1938 [PART THREE OF THREE]

Copyright Registration #56,315, script received at Registration Office April 11, 1938.

Plot: See pages 233 to 235.

Episode #812-37, Broadcast April 11, 1938

Copyright Registration #56,502, script received at Registration Office April 20, 1938.

Plot: This was the same script broadcast on April 24, 1936.

Episode #813-38, Broadcast April 13, 1938

Copyright Registration #56,503, script received at Registration Office April 20, 1938.

Plot: Jake Caldwell and Lem Purdy had quite a sum of money saved and hidden in their two-room shack. In the dead of night, one of the old men hears a noise and wakes his partner, only to find themselves shot and wounded, and their cash box stolen. Robbed of their life savings, the old men find a footprint left behind outside the shack, suggesting the sneak thief was Wallie Burke. Wallie has come into money suddenly, which looks suspicious, but The Lone Ranger knows personally that Wallie was given reward money and is innocent of the crime. Wallie, an overgrown but simple-minded fellow, was charged with being the thief who was recently responsible for a rash of night robberies in town. On the strength of the charge that the shot was fired with the intention of killing, the sheriff intends to hang Wallie. In reality, the crooked sheriff has been letting a man charged with cattle rustling, Simon Boswell, out of jail on selected evenings to commit the crimes and return before sunrise to ensure an alibi. The next night, the sheriff scares Willie with the threat of hanging and allows the simpleton to flee. Boswell was also set free to commit another crime as the two plotted to frame Wallie for another robbery. But with the assistance of Mary, Wallie's wife, the boots used to frame Wallie were stolen and Tonto locks the sheriff into his own jail. When Boswell returns a few hours later, his conversation with the sheriff cinches their guilt with The Lone Ranger and Mary as witnesses.

Episode #814-39, Broadcast April 15, 1938

Copyright Registration #56,504, script received at Registration Office April 20, 1938.

Plot: Ever since Grant Thorndyke opened the bank in San Carlos, the community has prospered. Men were taught to save instead of squander, and there was capital available for those who wanted to run an honest business in an honest way. The Lone Ranger whisks away the bartender to have a private chat, verifying the bartender is responsible for the scuttlebutt that is circulating about town about how the bank is not a safe place, dissatisfied because the men did not have money to spend in the café. The masked man explains how the deposits are used to pay for the mortgages on the homes, and the calamity that would befall the town should multiple parties start closing their accounts and withdrawing hefty funds. When appealing to the bartender's loyalty fails, the masked man breaks into the home of Abe Forman, the wealthiest man in town, to deposit his money into the bank. Meanwhile, the bartender continues to try to convince all the men in town that the bank is not a safe place for their money. Soon, nearly everyone plans to withdraw their savings as soon as the bank opens in the morning. Knowing all of the men have withdrawn their funds from the institution, Scar and his gang, camped outside town, spend the next evening cleaning houses – literally. One house after another is attacked by the outlaws, and in every case the men and women were robbed of their savings. Tonto apprehends the outlaws and ropes them, guarding them in the woods while The Lone Ranger returns the money with stern advice: the security of San Carlos depends on everyone trusting Grant Thorndyke and his bank. Having seen the error of their ways, all of the men are glad to see their money returned and promptly make deposits.

Episode #815-40, Broadcast April 18, 1938

Copyright Registration #56,505, script received at Registration Office April 20, 1938.

Written by Tom Dougall.

Plot: Zeke Parsons is the largest land and cattle owner in San Tuas County. He is also the town's most prominent citizen, holding the job of postmaster as well as that of sheriff. His headquarters is the general store, which he also owns, while hired hands run his extensive ranch. There is not a worse string of mudholes in the country than what are called roads in San Tuas County. Evoking an old law with a custom writ, he can serve the paper on all the able-bodied citizens in San Tuas to work on the roads for no wages. As postmaster and store keep, he witnesses the very paper he draws up as sheriff. Beyond the certain number of days working on county roads, Sheriff Parsons made slaves of the men, compelling them to work on his own property. With poor men hard pressed to earn a living, The Lone Ranger fears the citizens will likely rebel and kill the sheriff. The Lone Ranger and Tonto race out to stop the eastbound stage and steal the letter before it can arrive. Then The Lone Ranger pays a visit to the sheriff to inform him that his scheme will result in Federal prosecution – the U.S. marshal will be alerted of the abuse of power. Zeke agrees to pay the men for their time and hard work to repair the roads, then resigns from his positions as postmaster and as sheriff to manage his general store. Ben, the deputy, is promoted to sheriff and nothing can be charged against Zeke Parsons… who promises to go straight from now on.

Episode #816-41, Broadcast April 20, 1938

Copyright Registration #56,610, script received at Registration Office April 27, 1938.

Plot: Maggie Martin is the idol of all men around Cripple Creek. She is a dominant force among sheep herders and cattlemen, and it is only through the way in which old Maggie managed to control the situation that both types of herders lived without bloodshed. The cattlemen, led by Pete Prindle, one of the biggest cowmen in the region, scheme to trick sheep ranchers into selling their wool below market, intending to use their leverage to force them to move out, The Lone Ranger intervenes. A cattlemen organization would start trouble with the sheep-herders, causing bloodshed. It is the ranchers who should move, The Lone Ranger believes, and he switches envelopes to trick the cattlemen. Lem, working for the cattlemen, accomplishes his purpose when he gave Maggie the idea of selling wool to cattlemen. She comes to that decision, only when she feels they can be persuaded to pay the right place for it. The real price from the East is expected to be 20 cents a pound but the cattlemen offered six. Tonto overheard what Pete Prindle masterminded and reported back to The Lone Ranger. Intercepting two letters from the pony express, the masked man tricked Pete Prindle into believing the cost of wool would be 20 cents but in reality, it would be 15. Prindle signs a deal for 16 cents per pound moments before learning the truth. The Lone Ranger proposed Maggie and the sheepherders release him from their bargain if he and the other cattlemen head south for cattle country.

Notes: This script was originally slated for broadcast on Monday, May 2, 1938.

Episode #817-42, Broadcast April 22, 1938

Copyright Registration #56,611, script received at Registration Office April 27, 1938.

Plot: Cavalry troops are stationed not far from the border where rugged hills make perfect hiding places for countless outlaws. Colonel Dawson, in charge of the troops, frequently leaves the camp to see his daughter, Sally, in the nearby town of Greenville. Everyone in town is aroused over the recent attack of murderous brigands from the hills. Colonel Dawson did not dare violate his Federal Instructions by attacking outlaws in the hills without the sanction of the men above him. The outlaws send two of their gang to murder the pony express rider bringing the orders to Colonel Dawson. When The Lone Ranger and Tonto hear the rifle fire, they find the dead mail carrier and read the half-burned orders. In the battle with the killers, the important paper falls into a fire and is destroyed. "Sometimes a man can carry his military tactics too far," the masked man warns the Colonel, who will not believe in orders he cannot see with his own eyes. "There are times when a good soldier will throw aside regulations if he knows he is right." When the Colonel remains obstinate, The Lone Ranger knows something desperate will have to be done. Late that night, The Lone Ranger and Tonto break the two killers out of jail. The sheriff races to the nearby fort to alert the Colonel, explaining the killers also took Sally. If they get the girl into the hills, they know the Colonel would not dare to make an attack on them. Angrily, the Colonel orders his men to race out to apprehend the outlaws. Every man in the fort knows exactly why he was bring called to action. The men needed no command to ride in pursuit of the fast white horse on which a masked man carried the Colonel's daughter. Orders were barked, and the cavalry raced after the fugitive as the white horse broke into the timber at the foot of the hills. The fight was short and sharp, and the outlaws have no chance to conquer the well-trained, sharp-shooting army troops. As the soldiers ride in on the camp, they circle it and surround the gang to cut them down from all sides. When the outlaws throw down their guns in surrender, Colonel Dawson takes command only to discover the ruse. Tonto was disguised in woman's clothing to trick the cavalry into believing it was Sally who was kidnapped by the outlaws.

Episode #818-43, Broadcast April 25, 1938
Copyright Registration #56,612, script received at Registration Office April 27, 1938.
Plot: Eagle Pass is a narrow outlet between two sheer cliffs of solid rock. It's the only outlet from the fertile fields of lush grass where the finest cattle graze to the nearest shipping point toward the East. The ranchers, in driving their stock for shipment, make it a point to stop at old Pop Carter's general store and hotel at Eagle Pass. There, they buy supplies and rest before resuming their trip toward the East. Clem Peabody, leading his huge herd toward the pass, soon discovers Big Bill Lawson bullied Eagle Pass owners to sell out, now charging a toll of $25 a head from cattlemen to drive cattle through the narrow gap to deliver their cows to the buyer from the East. After Clem meets and talks to The Lone Ranger in the town of Longhorn, he returns to the gap and pays Lawson's toll in cattle instead of in cash. Lawson, suspecting that he was the victim of a frame-up, accepts the cattle in accordance with terms of an agreement, unaware that The Lone Ranger beats him at his own swindle. Two weeks later, Lawson finds himself with cattle that need to be fed – and cannot be sold in fear every lawman in the country wants to frame him for cattle theft. After all, there are cattle with fifty assorted brands registered in other names. Clem Peabody strikes a deal with Lawson to allow the cattle to graze on his land for $1,000 cash but during the trek to Clem's spread, Lawson finds himself paying a toll for the animals to cross land owned by other ranchers. One by one the tolls add up, and the sheriff backs their play to ensure the transactions were legal. Only when they reach Clem's spread does Lawson discover there is no water – which will cost money or the schemer can give the cows back to the ranchers and leave Clem with the $1,000 and clear out. With no other option, Big Bill Lawson gives in.

Episode #819-44, Broadcast April 27, 1938
Copyright Registration #56,814, script received at Registration Office May 4, 1938.
Plot: In all of the west, the worst town for gambling was Mud Flats. Though smaller than Dodge City, it was infested with gamblers and crooks of every description, and honest people had small chance of living a decent, normal life. After saving the life of Bart Goodwin from a crooked cardsharp named Harve Riggs, The Lone Ranger discovers the outlaws and gamblers chose their own crooked sheriff, Andy Bline. Bart is the former sheriff who hoped to someday make Mud Flats the decent town it used to be. Bart is jailed on a trumped-up charge while the masked man employs Henry Parker, a gambler turned straight, to come to town to clean out the establishments. From one joint to another, one crooked card play after another, Parker cleans out the gamblers – even gaining ownership of two gambling halls. Parker knows how the crooks cheat and plays the game on mathematics, avoiding the tricks that would have been used against him. The climax of the week is when the defeated gamblers follow

Henry Parker as he goes to Harve Riggs' huge establishment. They see him enter carrying a heavy bag in each hand and approach Riggs' favorite table in the corner. Pretending to be working in conspiracy with Riggs, Parker hands the bags of money over to the crook and confesses the con was slick and flawless, even slipping fixed cards in advance in all the places. With the conversation overheard, the infuriated gamblers go to work to smash Riggs' place beyond repair. Guns blaze and furniture is thrown about. A fire starts in one corner from an overturned lamp, and the flames leap up the dry walls. While the fire is more than The Lone Ranger figured, it was just as well. The men would get out all right, but all of Riggs' equipment would be destroyed. And thanks to a tip-off, The Texas Rangers arrive in time to help clean up the streets.

Notes: The opening scene involving fifteen-year-old Tommy Goodwin being conned by the crooked gambler, and his father attempting to seek justice by exposing the crook, is recycled from a scene from the broadcast of December 21, 1934. The name "Harve Riggs" was recycled from the broadcast of April 18, 1934.

Episode #820-45, Broadcast April 29, 1938
Copyright Registration #56,815, script received at Registration Office May 4, 1938.
Plot: The town of Broken Bow grew up around the railroad station and a telegraph office. On one particular evening, Mike Murphy, the engineer of the westbound train that halted for the night, finds himself facing a dilemma. Snake Lofgren, along with Meers, threatened the life of Betty Caulkins, the daughter of the telegraph operator and steady girlfriend of Mike, if he does not cooperate in wrecking a train carrying a large shipment of gold. Timing their threat and the distance between locomotives, the wreck is planned to happen out in the desert. Leaving Tonto to follow Snake Lofgren and his companion, The Lone Ranger rides out to the small cottage where Jim Caulkins lives with his daughter and discovers she is safe and unsuspecting. The kidnapping charge is merely a bluff. Sometime later, the heavy train is ready to move. Mike Murphy instructs Meers in shoveling the fuel, and the necessary switches are thrown to permit the train to run from the siding to the single track that spans the western state. The Lone Ranger, meanwhile, pays another visit to Jim Caulkins and tricks him into revealing Betty is safe and unharmed. It is her father who was working with the Lofgren Gang, taking advantage of Mike Murphy's love for his daughter, and leaking the info about the gold shipment to the outlaws. While The Lone Ranger takes care of Jim, Tonto races to the sheriff to explain the scenario. Backed with a posse, the sheriff takes control of the situation to arrest Snake and his men.

Notes: Actor Fred Reto played the role of Snake Lofgren by impersonating the Warner Brothers gangster screen persona of Edward G. Robinson. Gilbert Shea plays the role of Mike Murphy, an Irishman, in the same manner he played the recurring role of Michael Axford on *The Green Hornet*.

Blooper! The character of Jim Caulkins is referred to as Sam Caulkins by the narrator during the opening of the second act.

Episode #821-46, Broadcast May 2, 1938
Copyright Registration #56,816, script received at Registration Office May 4, 1938.
Plot: The Lone Ranger, unmasked but disguised, watches the crowd of miners in a cafe in Bixby, where Lem Purvis is celebrating the sale of his gold mine. When the miner discovers his mine is worthless, The Lone Ranger investigates and discovers a rep from an Eastern mining syndicate, Carter Dodson, plots with a crooked assayer named Tom Gordon to sell his gold mine to Dodson for $200. The scheme had been attempted against Jeff Salters, too, who was also unaware that his mine was really worth a small fortune. After overhearing the plot, The Lone Ranger and Tonto tip off Salters, who later turns down the offer from the two schemers. Dodson and Gordon hire Tonto to kill the stubborn miner, then fake his signature on the claim so they can

gain possession. Later, just as the two crooks feel confident of themselves, and the townsfolk take it for granted that Jeff Salters had put a deal over on the eastern representative, Dodson attempts to put one over on the local sheriff by claiming he was defrauded in the mine scheme, hoping the town will feel he truly owns the rights to the mine. Arriving at the Salters mine, they find Tonto at the scene, who plays a key factor incriminating Tom Gordon in double-crossing his partner. The two crooks have a falling out between them, incriminating themselves – and facing a surprise when Jeff Salters put in an appearance – alive and well.

Episode #822-47, Broadcast May 4, 1938

Copyright Registration #56,817, script received at Registration Office May 4, 1938.

Plot: The Lone Ranger is determined to apprehend and capture Bart Colt's gang, including Jim and Blacky. Colt's gang rides into the county seat town of Brown's Crossing, attacks Zach Andrews' ranch, and allows Dave Sanders, one of Zach's men, to hear them plan a raid on the town of Silver Springs. Dave informs his brother, Sheriff Andy. A posse is organized in Brown's Crossing, which rides to Silver Springs, but as soon as the sheriff leaves the crossing, the outlaws raid the unprotected town. When news of the attack reaches the posse, they accuse the sheriff and Dave of being crooked. They would have lynched them had they not been saved by The Lone Ranger. The masked man and his Indian companion once more pick up the trail of the crooks. Lem Moody, the new sheriff, is skeptical of any decoy, so Tonto pays a visit to warn the law that Bart Colt and his gang will be raiding the Briggs ranch. But Moody won't be fooled and instead follows the Indian back to camp, where The Lone Ranger and his friend play the role of crooks and laugh at how the law would never figure that the gang hides out at the Yellow King gold mine. The scheme works as the sheriff returns to town to deputize a number of men who then ride out to the Yellow King to apprehend the gang. There, Sheriff Andy and his brother assist in the apprehension and the ruse is revealed – excused by the two sheriffs for the ends justified the means.

Episode #823-48, Broadcast May 6, 1938

Copyright Registration #56,833, script received at Registration Office May 9, 1938.

Plot: Steve Garrett is the wealthiest rancher in the country and popular with the men in town. When he comes to town to stock up on supplies, he brings along his seven-year-old son, Billy. The Black Jack Martin Gang assemble in a wooded area not far from Garret's extensive ranch, then mastermind the successful kidnapping of young Billy, to be held for ransom. Sheriff Wilson, despite Steve Garrett's pleas for non-interference, leads a posse following a trail which brings him to The Lone Ranger's camp. He accuses the masked man and Tonto of the kidnapping. The Lone Ranger, seeking freedom so he can act on Billy's behalf, calls on his great white horse Silver to aid in lighting away from the lawmen. A U.S. marshal is brought in on the case, but just like the sheriff, his method to retrieve the youth would only result in Billy's death. The Lone Ranger, learning how the ransom is to be placed into a trunk and delivered at a specific spot, and how the trunk will be dragged along the water to avoid leaving a trail to follow, rigs a can of oil spilled inside. When fire is set to the coal oil, it delivers a trail leading back to the kidnappers. While the crooks are busy putting the fire out, The Lone Ranger races into their camp and rescues the boy.

Episode #824-49, Broadcast May 9, 1938

Copyright Registration #56,834, script received at Registration Office May 9, 1938.

Plot: Mort Leeds, a stage driver, reports that White Bear, the Indian chief, has attacked his stage and taken the arms it contained. The Lone Ranger and Tonto, having come across the empty stagecoach that was abandoned five miles away from the regular stage road leading from the town of Redwood to Fort Pearson, suspect his story. Later, the masked man's suspicions are confirmed when he overhears a plot between Mort and the army quartermaster Cramer to permit a second load of ammunition to fall into the hands of the Indians. The Lone

Ranger immediately suggests a plan to Captain Meadows that would prove the guilt of the two plotters, Mort and Erik Cramer. Leading the band of troops toward the hills, The Lone Ranger hopes to ambush the crooks with military. Somewhere on that road is the Willow Creek Bridge, where White Bear's braves await the approaching stagecoach, but when the chief discovers the stagecoach is filled with rocks and not guns, he feels betrayed. Before the renegade Indians can kill Mort and Cramer, the troops, summoned by Tonto when the stage was first attacked by the Indians, come pouring down from the hills, sweeping the ranks of the Indians with their concentrated fire. Their charge takes the Indians completely by surprise. Chief White Bear, though an enemy of the whites, is no coward. He fights with a fierce courage, time after time rallying his discouraged tribesmen. The superior training of the soldiers, though, is not to be denied, and at length they compel the Indians' complete surrender. With the fighting over, Captain Meadows and The Lone Ranger are satisfied with the proof of Leeds and Cramer's guilt.

Episode #825-50, Broadcast May 11, 1938
Copyright Registration #57,080, script received at Registration Office May 16, 1938.
Plot: When the Lone Ranger and his faithful Indian companion, Tonto, ride into the town of Potsdam, they find the streets deserted, despite the fact that it's mid-afternoon. The reason proves to be an important murder trial, with practically everyone jammed inside the courthouse to learn the fate of Bob McAllister. Bob is accused of robbery and the murder of Joe Findley. He has no alibi for the night Joe was knifed and is known to have had a row with Joe a couple hours previous, so Sheriff Greene called on him at the express office where he worked… and found the murder weapon in Joe's desk. Found guilty and sentenced to hang the following morning, Joe wished to send his savings to his mother, but felt that no one could be trusted on such an errand. The Lone Ranger, having been given reason to believe that Bob might be innocent, planned to release the young man long enough to carry the money himself but at the last minute, learning that Bob felt that Deputy Larson might be trusted, he returns him to his cell with the advice to follow his judgment. Fifteen minutes after The Lone Ranger puts Bob back in jail, the deputy recovers consciousness and finds himself ungagged and free to move. Bob informs Larson where money was hidden in a hollow tree stump in the front yard of his house. Larson keeps his word and as soon as he is relieved of guard duty at the jail, he rides toward the McAllister home. What Larson is not aware of, however, is that the entire scheme is a put-up job to trick him into stealing the cash and burying it where he hid the stolen loot – which only the real robber who killed Joe Findlay would know.

Episode #826-51, Broadcast May 13, 1938
Copyright Registration #57,081, script received at Registration Office May 16, 1938.
Plot: Slim Carter, whose elopement with Nancy Merrill was prevented by Sheriff Steve Tucker, agrees to face Nancy's father the next morning. But that same night he makes a secret trip to Merrill's mine, meeting Tonto on the way and firing at him in the dark. The following morning, when the sheriff calls for Slim, the young man pretends to be too ill to make the journey. While the two men talk, Tonto enters and, when the sheriff leaves, remains behind to threaten Slim for the attempt upon his life. In private, the Indian informs the sheriff that Slim attempted murder the other night, thwarted by the redskin. The next day, the sheriff and his Deputy, Sam, ride out to meet Zeke Merrill. They force Slim along, who miraculously looked and sounds better from supposedly being sick. At the cabin, The Lone Ranger exposes Slim's crooked scheme. Slim planned to have Zeke Merrill and the sheriff murdered so he could convince the daughter of the wealthy miner that her father gave him her hand in marriage. He even planted an explosive log in the man's firewood so he would not survive and tell anyone that he opposed the marriage. Having put a log on the fire, Slim starts to panic, fearing he might fall victim to the same trap. He filled a log with blasting powder, unaware that The Lone Ranger removed that log the night before. The trap was sprung for the man who incriminated himself before witnesses. The new U.S. marshal in the area, Dan Calloway, having overheard the confession from outside the homestead, places Slim Carter under arrest.

Episode #827-52, Broadcast May 16, 1938

Copyright Registration #57,135, script received at Registration Office May 23, 1938.

Plot: As the Lone Ranger flashes by on Silver, we hear him say that a band of outlaws was attacking wagon trains. The wagon train led by old Peter Ridley had been suffering increasing difficulties. Amos Carver, once Ridley's firm friend, quarreled with him until the two men were scarcely speaking. The entire party took sides and dissatisfaction grew daily. But when they reached the point where the Oregon Trail and the Santa Fe Trail divided, the trouble reached a crisis and the two went separate ways. Sam Dougall, an outlaw, was hired by Peter Ridley, the leader of the wagon train, as a scout. Sam, to weaken the party, brought about the quarrel between Ridley and Carver, another member of the wagon train, which led to the party dividing. Tonto, scouting near the camp of the outlaws, is captured. Later, when the outlaws have departed to make their first attack, he is freed by The Lone Ranger. The masked man rides out to alert Ridley, explaining how the outlaws will attack the other party somewhere beyond Saddle Pass. Under the direction of The Lone Ranger, the men in Ridley's party are organized to ride to the rescue of their friends. Then, with the masked man in the lead, they race toward Saddle Pass. In the meantime, the outlaws' attack is progressing smoothly. The greater part of the band proceeds to wear down the resistance of the emigrants at their leisure. The remainder, including Rick Logan and Sam Dougall, hold their positions at the pass. Amongst the volley of shots is the sound of thundering hoofbeats. A frenzied herd of buffalo, urged on by The Lone Ranger and Ridley's men, thunders through the pass with the force of an avalanche, sweeping all before it. Those animals that might have hesitated before the guns of the outlaws were instead pressed forward by the weight of the herd behind them. The buffalo, once through the pass, spread wide and lose the force of their momentum but the outlaws are completely demoralized. They turn and run in terror before the charge of the rescuing horsemen. When Amos Carver, seeing the turn of events, orders his own men to mount and attack, the outlaws hastily surrender. After apprehension of the outlaws is assured, Peter Ridley and Amos Carver patch up their differences and continue on their journey west – together.

Notes: The name Sam Dougall was a tip-of-the-hat to scriptwriter Tom Dougall.

Episode #828-53, Broadcast May 18, 1938

Copyright Registration #57,136, script received at Registration Office May 23, 1938.

Plot: There have been a number of petty thefts in town of Greentree, and no one knows who is to blame. In an effort to learn the identity of a sneak thief in the town, Baldy Bronson, former sheriff whose legs were paralyzed, outlines a scheme to the present sheriff and the banker, Jason Rudd. Cole Williams, a suspect who worked for Rudd in the bank, was allowed to know where bank funds were to be hidden, supposedly to be safe from bank robbers working in the vicinity. When the money was gone the next morning, Cole was accused of the theft. Definite proof was found against him when the empty cash box was found beneath the steps of his porch. The Lone Ranger and Tonto, who were friendly with Williams, were already convinced of his innocence. While Cole is taken to jail, Tonto holds a few of the sheriff's men at bay, tied to a tree, while The Lone Ranger pays a late-night visit to the banker. With the banker as witness, The Lone Ranger arranges for a showdown. Tonto sets fire to the house of Baldy Bronson. That is how he knew who drew cash out because he lived next door to the bank. When the house is set on fire, Baldy runs in to fetch and retrieve the stolen loot – giving himself away as the sneak thief. The ex-sheriff, in all the excitement, "regained" the use of his legs and revealed himself as the real culprit.

Notes: As an example of how much James Jewell was involved in the plotting of the radio scripts, reviewing the first draft of the script, he wrote the following inter-office memo (dated April 30, 1938) to Fran Striker: "The attached script is badly plotted. Kill first scene indicating suicide. Story doesn't start until Jason and the sheriff visit Baldy. You could then have a short scene between Cole and banker checking on shortages in his account books. Young man cannot explain but promises to make up shortage. He awkwardly attempts to hold-up Ranger and Tonto, which gives us the same result we have in the first scene. Point to tobacco jar in scene where (sic) Ranger and Tonto visit Baldy."

Episode #829-54, Broadcast May 20, 1938
Copyright Registration #57,137, script received at Registration Office May 23, 1938.
Plot: See pages 242 and 243.

Episode #830-55, Broadcast May 23, 1938
Copyright Registration #57,217, script received at Registration Office May 28, 1938.
Plot: Rain had fallen for many days on the town of Cottonwood and the hills surrounding it. Old riverbeds were filled to overflowing and water gushed through countless streams and rivulets to gather in a lake, made by damming a river in the hills north of town. Now the town is threatened by a flood when the dam that holds the mountain lake is likely to burst. To hasten the flood, so they could loot the town, the Slick Dalton gang plan a blast. Meanwhile, the townsmen need blasting powder to release a natural dam on the south side of the lake, to let the water flow harmlessly away. The only powder is in the hands of the outlaws and when The Lone Ranger leads the lawmen to their hideout, they accuse him of being an escaped criminal, while they pose as Federal officers. The Lone Ranger knows that their leader and a man named Kelso, are on their way to the dam with the blasting powder. In a daring escape, the masked man races toward the threatened dam. Meanwhile, the townsmen crowd hip-deep in fast-rushing water struggling bravely to keep their footing as they try to move the huge rocks. While the townsmen struggle in vain to move the boulders, Kelso and the boss, Slick Dalton, set the keg of blasting powder at the base of the dam to flood the valley. Thanks to The Lone Ranger's bravery, and assistance from Tonto, the thieves are disarmed and placed under arrest, while Tonto races the kegs of powder to the south side of the lake where they are sorely needed. Back in the sheriff's office, one of the thieves in jail, Malone, attempts to claim he really was a Federal man, even showing his badge to prove it, but the sheriff explains how, when Dalton escaped a few days prior, he had stolen a badge from the man he shot… cinching the crooks' guilt.

Episode #831-56, Broadcast May 25, 1938
Copyright Registration #57,218, script received at Registration Office May 28, 1938.
Plot: Old Colonel Marberry retired from Army duty to take up ranching, and in the latter years of his life, old wounds robbed him of the ability to go far from the house. His chief interest was his daughter Betty, and his main hope, to see her marry the right man. When Bart Benson arrives with credentials showing an Army record, and claiming to be the son of one of the Colonel's friends in the east, he is made welcome. As the weeks go on, Benson takes over more and more of the duties of running the ranch. Benson, in complete charge, due to Marberry's inability to get around easily, plots the murder of the foreman, then reveals his plan to marry Betty, that he might become sole owner of the ranch on the colonel's death. Betty chooses to escape rather than face the conditions Benson had brought about at the ranch, and when Benson's men have almost overtaken her, The Lone Ranger snatches her to the back of his own horse and carries her to the safety of his camp. There, she explains her problem. The masked man convinces the girl into returning and promises to investigate the unscrupulous drifter who impersonates a dead Army officer. The Lone Ranger races through the night, heading east towards an army post to gather evidence against the imposter. The next few days are uneventful as Tonto remains concealed from everyone but Betty who supplies him with food, knowing he will be on hand to help her, if he was needed. Bart Benson is highly pleased with the more friendly manner of the girl, until she put up a fight when he wanted her to go away with him. Tonto comes out of hiding and a fight occurs. The Lone Ranger arrives in time, with the sheriff alongside. The sheriff orders his deputy to place the imposter under arrest for the

murder of private Simmons in effecting his escape from military prison. The imposter, panicking, confesses he is not the real Benson, who he found dead on the plains and stole his credentials. His real name is Bill Slade. The sheriff knew the imposter would confess rather than face a murder trial… but Slade had a surprise. Chiquita, the house servant, was witness to the murder of Lem, the foreman, and the sheriff also had confessions from both Butch and Steve, who were hired to commit the crime. Bill Slade was placed under arrest.

Episode #832-57, Broadcast May 27, 1938

Copyright Registration #57,301, script received at Registration Office June 2, 1938.

Plot: Rustlers have been stealing cattle from the ranchers in Blackhawk Valley, driving the stolen herds through the hills and across the Mexican border by way of rocky canyons where the cattle left no trail. Most of these hills were covered with what is known in the Southwest as malpaís – that is, hardened lava, spilled there by volcanic disturbances ages before. Their rough floors, too flint-like to receive the marks of hoofs, serve the purpose of rustlers moving their stolen cattle. The Lone Ranger, however, camped beside one of these canyons, hears rustlers driving across southward and secretly follows them to their destination. In the meantime, many of the ranchers have decided they can no longer remain in the valley while the rustlers are operating. Only Clay Ramsen, the largest of the cattle-owners, expresses his willingness to continue the fight against the thieves. The leader of the gang of cattle thieves is being secretly paid by Ramsen so he can buy up all the remaining cattle from the desperate neighboring ranchers for a song. The Lone Ranger, keeping vigilant watch on the secret location, intercepts the courier who is delivering cash payment to Buck, the head of the outlaw gang. Delivering the payment himself, The Lone Ranger pretends to represent Clay Ramsen, paying only a fraction of the promised payment, and insisting he and Ramsen are keeping the profits for themselves. This causes Buck to race out and force Clay to pay what he was promised. His threats take place in the presence of other ranchers who are about to sell the remainder of their stock – and the sheriff, who happens to be there. The Lone Ranger disarms Buck before the outlaw can inflict death on his partner-in-crime, leaving the sheriff to handle the clean-up.

Episode #833-58, Broadcast May 30, 1938

Copyright Registration #57,302, script received at Registration Office June 2, 1938.

Plot: Abe Chetwick leaves his own home to go to Medicine Flats where his daughter lives. He brings his cash, determined to use it to hire gunmen who would confront Ned Flavin, a wealthy mine owner. Abe hopes to force Flavin to admit jumping the Rosalinda claim, stealing it from his son-in-law, and later murdering the rightful owner. To prevent bloodshed, The Lone Ranger sends Tonto to take the old man's cash, so he will be unable to hire the killers. A disguised Lone Ranger pays a visit to Flavin to seek a job at the Rosalinda mine. Flavin, meanwhile, keeps Dave tied and bound deep inside the mine, in the hopes of convincing the young man to reveal where he staked his claim, proving he was there before Flavin. Later that afternoon, a blast, planned by The Lone Ranger and Tonto, fills the mouth of the tunnel with rock and dirt and traps the miners inside. Flavin is inside with the others. The explosion causes a stream of water to flow into the tunnel, adding to the peril of those trapped. There was stark fear in every voice as the frenzied men saw their predicament. Outside the caved-in tunnel, many people had gathered, among them Sheriff Perkins and a group of deputies, Molly Chetwick, and her father. All of these amazed people were being held at bay by two heavy guns in the hands of a tall, masked man on a white horse. The Lone Ranger shouts from outside for Flavin to confess if he wanted to be rescued. Flavin denies the accusation that Dave is alive and being kept a prisoner inside. The men working the mine, however, panic and confess Flavin's guilt. After the sheriff admits he has heard enough of a confession, and also hears Dave's voice from within, The Lone Ranger orders everyone to stand back as another explosion beneath the rock that held the captives grants daylight to the men inside. The deputies place all of the men – except Dave – under arrest.

Episode #834-59, Broadcast June 1, 1938

Copyright Registration #57,346, script received at Registration Office June 4, 1938.

Plot: Oil was found in Texas. Vast fortunes were made in the fields. Ranch owners forgot their cattle, farmers forgot their crops, and everyone turned his attention to the new wealth an ocean of liquid gold beneath the surface of the ground. Cal Godfrey started his Wishbone Café in one of those boom towns. With the carefree wasting of the newly rich men, eager to spend their fortunes as soon as they were made, jammed the place to celebrate and Cal was the moving spirit behind the festivities. Stonewall Gregory is offered $10,000 for an oil lease on the north hundred acres of his ranch. He refuses the offer and drives away the two Easterners who made it at the point of a rifle. Tonto and The Lone Ranger learn that Bentley and Shane are planning a swindle but, believing that Gregory should sell the lease on his property, The Lone Ranger offers his help to the Easterners. As they ride close to Gregory's ranch, The Lone Ranger and Tonto pretended to attack them and Gregory, influenced by the frantic pleading of his wife, agrees to give them shelter for the night. In the morning, the men gave Stonewall a statement to sign, verifying they tried their best to lease the land and were turned down, so they can assure their jobs when they return to Pennsylvania. But The Lone Ranger steals Stonewall's copy and verifies that if the top part of the letter was torn off, it would serve as permission to drill on Stonewall's land… with the employees keeping the $10,000 in payment for themselves. The Lone Ranger muscles in and the two mavericks are arrested by the sheriff… but not before Stonewall Gregory receives the money and is told by The Lone Ranger to allow the drilling.

Notes: This episode contains recycled elements from the broadcasts of August 10, 1933, and August 11, 1937. Of historical note, oil was not discovered in Texas until 1901, at a well near Beaumont, called "Spindletop."

Episode #835-60, Broadcast June 3, 1938

Copyright Registration #57,347, script received at Registration Office June 4, 1938.

Plot: Bolivar Bates and Hacksaw Hastings, two cheerful but irresponsible veterans of the Civil War, have collected the taxes in Los Palmas County with the aid of the masked man. Then, with their commission in their pockets, they ride westward to the Catamount Hills where they decide to make their home in an abandoned cabin until another profitable enterprise comes their way. In the Acme Restaurant, Bensonville's leading eating establishment, Hacksaw boasts of his recent adventures, suffering from his usual inability to remain strictly within the facts. This leads to a fight in the café when Pete Greer, its proprietor, slaps the face of Aggie McGuire, his flirtatious waitress. The Lone Ranger intervenes and stops the fight and Hacksaw accompanies Aggie home to her mother. In the meantime, Pete informed Bolivar Bates of what happened, and Bolivar rides hurriedly to town in search of his partner. Aggie attempts to set one against the other in order to steal the money they claim they have. The Lone Ranger, unseen by anyone, is just beyond a half-open window and overhears her plot. Realizing Aggie is married to Pete, and the entire setup is to con the old men, The Lone Ranger shows up at a late-night rendezvous with Hacksaw, to reveal the approaching Bolivar is also being conned with the same sob story. The old men soon discover the female maverick was attempting a con, but not before The Lone Ranger saves Hacksaw's life from bullets fired from a house some distance away. The sheriff, within listening distance, takes Pete and Bart Sidney, a friend of Pete's, in for attempted murder.

Notes: Script marked as "Child Appeal Only," probably referring to the public service announcement during commercial break. The final page of the script, listing all the characters in the play, mistakenly refers to Bart Sidney as Bart Snyder.

Episode #836-61, Broadcast June 6, 1938

Copyright Registration #57,465, script received at Registration Office June 10, 1938.

Plot: Almost everyone in Pendleton gathers at the station when the stage is due. It's an important day, because popular young Sandy Tyndale is due to be on board. The sheriff, Bert Gordon, is especially watchful, not only for the stage, but for the sake of his daughter, Lenore, who was stuck on Tyndale. Two years ago, Sandy shot it out with an ornery polecat that tried to run a crooked game of poker. No one in town thought Sandy would get jailed but there was a cantankerous coyote on the jury, Banker Pottle. Having squared himself with the world by serving a two-year term in prison, Sandy was a reformed man. But when he came out, instead of returning to the town where his friends were waiting for him, including Lenore, he went into hiding, ashamed to face the world. Meanwhile, the stage was robbed and the driver killed. A fancy spur, known to be one from Sandy's boots, was found in the stage. The Lone Ranger sought the young man and convinced him to return to town and prove his innocence. When Pottle seems too anxious to see Sandy jailed, The Lone Ranger investigates. Upon learning that Lenore waited for him for two years and agreed to marry Pottle if he called off the search for him, Sandy agrees to a scheme masterminded by The Lone Ranger. Late at night, The Lone Ranger, the sheriff and Sandy pay a visit to Pottle with Sandy confessing he never robbed the stage, or killed the driver, but met a man who gave him some of the money and told him to keep quiet. After Sandy was taken away by the sheriff, Pottle dressed and raced out to the filthy shack in his back yard to wake a crook named Martin, accusing him of giving some of the money to the boy. Martin thinks Pottle went loco but the conversation between the two men gives away their guilt in the crime, with the sheriff outside listening to every word.

Notes: The script repeatedly refers to Pottle as Potter by accident, interchangeably throughout the radio script. The error was caught during rehearsals and remained consistent with Pottle throughout the entire broadcast.

Episode #837-62, Broadcast June 8, 1938

Copyright Registration #57,466, script received at Registration Office June 10, 1938.

Plot: The Lone Ranger learns of an outlaw scheme to capture the army captain and compel him to send for secret plans of the army which an unknown party is willing to buy. The Lone Ranger and Tonto intercept Captain Carter, and the masked man changes clothes with him, puts on a false beard, and goes to be captured in his place. In a cave headquarters, he finds that Carter's daughter Sally has also been captured. He writes a note for Snake Anson who leaves with it for the garrison. If Snake does not return with the dispatch case in two hours, Sally will be horribly tortured. Snake, however, is intercepted by Captain Carter, masquerading as a masked highwayman, and Tonto. Cleverly switching the note with a different one Carter wrote earlier in the day, he sends Snake on his way as he pretends to steer clear of army affairs. Back in the cave, Nate Merton, along with Steve and Butch, threaten to use the branding iron on Sally if there is any sign of soldiers following when Snake returns. When Snake returns with the dispatch box, they discover the lock requires a key. The Lone Ranger's hands are untied so he can crack open the box. Instead of army papers, which the outlaws wanted in exchange for the safe return of Sally, the box contains guns which The Lone Ranger quickly removes and uses to disarm the outlaws. Thanks to Tonto, the real Captain Carter arrives to take the culprits into custody.

Notes: The name of Snake Anson was recycled from a prior episode, the broadcast of September 17, 1937.

Episode #838-63, Broadcast June 10, 1938

Copyright Registration #57,515, script received at Registration Office June 17, 1938.

Plot: About a dozen miles from the town of Cranston, two men are hidden in a gully, watching the approach of a single horseman. The older of the two hidden men, Ed Scott, is in his middle forties, with a face that showed many years of crime. The younger, Lefty Cullen, is under thirty, but his features are thin and cruel, while the stock of the rifle he holds to his shoulder is marked with notches representing a dozen killings. They stare at the approaching rider until he comes within range, then fire. The man, Jim Bayer, is killed by the two outlaws, who wished to gain possession of the ranch Bayer had inherited 20 years before but had not seen since the day he claimed it. The outlaws steal the papers that identified Bayer and ride to Texas where Scott poses as the rightful owner of the Lazy Y Ranch and the father of Katherine Bayer, the murdered man's daughter. The Lone Ranger and Tonto, finding a note written by Bayer just before he died, learn enough to set them on the trail of the outlaws. The Lone Ranger rides to the sheriff of Butler City, to inform him of his findings. Early the next morning, Ed Scott saddles his horse and rides on a tour of inspection over the rich grazing land of the ranch he had stolen. By evening he had seen enough to convince him that the Lazy Y was even more valuable than he had expected. Desperate to file the paperwork in Denver to claim full and legal ownership of the property, the men force Katherine Bayer to go with them by train. Led by The Lone Ranger, the three men race across country in an effort to reach the railroad by a shorter route than that of the stage. The masked man holds Silver back to suit the pace of the two slower horses. When, topping a hill, they see smoke puffing from the stack of an engine ahead as it slowly gathers speed, The Lone Ranger speeds his great horse Silver to stop the train. After he succeeds, the sheriff boards the locomotive to place Scott, still pretending to be Jim Bayer, under arrest, claiming he has a reward notice for $5,000 for the capture of Jim Bayer, dead or alive, wanted for murder. Scott panics and confesses he is not the wanted man, only to discover he has been tricked into confessing his true identity. With the papers on his possession that were originally in Jim Bayer's hands, meant to file a claim on the inheritance, not a judge in the country would disbelieve that Ed and Lefty committed a murder.

Episode #839-64, Broadcast June 13, 1938
Copyright Registration #57,516, script received at Registration Office June 17, 1938.
Plot: In the town of Dawson, Doctor Stubbs is providing a musical show with minstrel singers and selling his famous "Snake Oil" tonic. Cowboys have come from miles around to provide shouts of encouragement to the small stage on the rear of a large wagon. The wealthy owner of the Bar K Ranch, Jim Kendall, purchases the tonic and returns to his ranch house, unaware the snake oil will make he and his wife sleep more soundly than they have slept for many years. Stealthy figures move through the night and Stubbs is joined by Snead, who slips inside the house and commits a robbery. In the morning, the wealthy ranchers in the surrounding area discover themselves all victims of robberies and Stubbs claims he himself has been robbed. He blames a banjo player among his troupe, but Tonto is arrested and accused of the crime. When Kendall's wife reports her husband dead from poison, Stubbs is jailed. Later, The Lone Ranger forces Stubbs to try a taste of his own medicine, proving how the effect of the drug puts people into a deep sleep. With the townsfolk convinced who the guilty party is, Kendall shows up alive and well and the sheriff acknowledges the ruse was meant to trick Stubbs into taking his own medicine.

Notes: This radio script was recycled from the broadcast of December 12, 1934, with a number of differences. Doctor Asa Stubbs was referred to as Doctor Stubbs, Triangle K Ranch was changed to the Bar K Ranch, the character of Doraldina was replaced by Snead, Stubbs blamed a banjo player for the crime instead of one of the black minstrel boys, and the second act was greatly revised to eliminate The Lone Ranger and Tonto breaking into the wagon to reveal the stolen loot to a ruse involving Jim Kendall being supposedly "poisoned." In the first draft of the script, Kendall was replaced with Kennedy, but during the second draft the name reverted back to Kendall again.

Episode #840-65, Broadcast June 15, 1938
Copyright Registration #57,542, script received at Registration Office June 20, 1938.
Plot: Martin Gates holds mortgages on almost every home in Three Corners. A poor cattle year makes it impossible for landowners to meet the payments and Gates forecloses in a heartless, ruthless manner. Hoping to find some way of aiding the poverty-stricken people, The Lone Ranger and Tonto head toward the community. Meanwhile, Bolivar Bates, with Hacksaw Hastings, plans to use a certain scheme to win at poker from the

wealthy, greedy banker. The Lone Ranger, knowing that the townspeople were all thrown from their land when Gates foreclosed the mortgages, waited outside and watched the progress of the game. Gates finally loses money – and his temper – and draws his gun, firing point black at old Bolivar Bates. The sheriff promptly threw Gates into jail, in spite of his angry protests, to await trial for the shooting of Bates. The banker could learn nothing of what had happened in town since his arrest and when he saw, from the window of the jail, The Lone Ranger passing by, he called to him. The masked man explained to Gates, from outside the window, that he took their homes, their ranches, their cattle… everything they worked hard to earn. Twelve men will be chosen for the jury, and there would certainly be a majority of the jury, of people whose land he took, or would soon. The charge is murder and Gates knows he is entitled to a fair trial, even with an impartial jury. Gates insists on being released so he can talk to people. The sheriff chuckles to himself and arranged for Gates to be released from prison under guard to call on those whom he had driven from their homes. With his pockets bulging with legal papers, and well-guarded to ensure he does not flee the community, Gates hurries from one homestead to another, leaving dumbfounded people with new mortgages behind him. The news spread through the town like wildfire and those who had already left their homes rushed to meet the banker to get their land back. After the banker has reformed, he discovers Bolivar is not dead. Hacksaw had placed blank cartridges in the gun in advance for a set-up that was masterminded by The Lone Ranger.

Episode #841-66, Broadcast June 17, 1938
Copyright Registration #57,543, script received at Registration Office June 20, 1938.
Plot: There's trouble in the town of Winford, the county seat. The sheriff, Greg Morgan, is known as a stern manhunter, a terror to outlaws who attempt to defy the law in his district. Dan Cooley, arrested on circumstantial evidence for the killing of a rancher named Bailey, and Wolf Brandt, an outlaw with both cunning and cruelty in his features, escape from jail with the aid of another outlaw, Red Brill. A posse is immediately formed, and the three men pursued into the hills. The fleeter horses of the fugitives soon make good their escape. The Lone Ranger, knowing that Dan had sworn the death of the sheriff, guards the lawman by day (Tonto by night) until he meets Dan. When Dan would have called the sheriff out for a gunfight, the masked man prevents him, permitting him, however, to escape. Wolf, in the meantime, laughs with Red. Wolf's real name is Clem Rabe and he killed Bailey and framed Dan, hoping Dan will eliminate the sheriff so there will not be a witness against him on the cattle-stealing charge. With cooperation from Sheriff Morgan, The Lone Ranger forms a plan. The next morning, the outlaws wake before dawn. Dan Cooley, under the watchful eyes of his companions, straps on his gun-belt, saddles his horse, and makes ready for the gunfight ahead. The sheriff faces off against him in the street. Dan shoots first and the sheriff drops. Dan returns to the outlaws' camp a few hours later with regrets for having done what he felt he had to do. The Lone Ranger, Tonto and the still alive sheriff, having followed Dan, catch the outlaws by surprise and apprehend them. The sheriff explains how overnight the bullets in Dan's gun were replaced with blanks. The real outlaws responsible for the crime are taken into custody.

Episode #842-67, Broadcast June 20, 1938
Copyright Registration #57,733, script received at Registration Office June 27, 1938.
Plot: Melting snow and flood waters imperil several communities around the Army post at Northfield. The government sends food and supplies for distribution to those in need. Captain Curtis, the fort's commandant, is absent at the time and the scheming Lieutenant Spade Calhoun, sees a chance to make some money with the aid of a civilian partner, Squint Merkle. Together the two make a profit out of charging people for food. The Lone Ranger and Tonto, in an effort to reveal their game, conceive a plan. Del Sturgis, from Valley Center, a community out of the jurisdiction of the army, pay Squint for food for the entire town. Squint takes the money and divides it with Calhoun, then leaves the fort so that nothing could be proven. Days later, Captain Curtis returns to his command, and receives the report of his lieutenant. Curtis managed to secure more food

at Red Bluff and would need to send a detachment of men – enough food to help everyone through the crisis. Lieutenant Calhoun is sent to fetch the wagons of provisions. On the return trip, fifty Indians pursue the wagons, without closing the gap that separated them. The muleskinners lashed the small strong beasts to frantic speed, with the heavily loaded wagons bouncing along the uneven ground. The army wagons are able to reach Valley Center, and as the townsmen crowd around, the Indians retreat. Calhoun orders the men and women to stand down, including the sheriff, insisting this was not their food. Valley Center, he explained, was out of his jurisdiction. The sheriff found this curious – the town bought and paid for food and gave Squint Merkle the cash the other day. Squint agreed to have Calhoun bring the food. At that point in time The Lone Ranger brings Squint Merkle into town to verify the sheriff's claim. The truth comes out during an exchange of words, with Captain Curtis standing off the side long enough to hear all that was said. The captain places the crooks under arrest and promises the sheriff that the money would be returned to those who paid it. Calhoun would soon face a court martial. As for the Indian threat outside of town, The Lone Ranger assures everyone that the Indians are friendly and they were, in fact, summoned by the masked man.

Notes: Beginning with broadcast #842-67, the copyright registration switched from the Madison Theater Building in Detroit to the Stroh Building in Detroit.

Episode #843-68, Broadcast June 22, 1938
Copyright Registration #57,734, script received at Registration Office June 27, 1938.
Plot: Chet Goulding plans to marry Patricia Mayfair, the daughter of one of the biggest ranchers in the territory, for the money her father would leave her. Mr. Mayfair, learning through The Lone Ranger of Goulding's criminal background, orders him out of the house by the next morning. Patricia, however, does not learn the truth. Goulding leads the girl to believe that her father has agreed to the marriage and when the next morning comes, he announces that Mr. Mayfair had been killed during the night. Patricia at once suspects the masked man with whom her father had spoken the previous day. Hank, the impetuous foreman, would have shot and killed The Lone Ranger at Chet's insistence had it not been for Tonto arriving to save the day. The Lone Ranger tells Patricia her boyfriend is really Dan Chester, wanted in many states for stagecoach hold-ups, murder, and robbery. The deputy from Eagle Pass arrives, finding the masked man tied to a chair in the house, as every person tells their version of the story – with The Lone Ranger's accusation the only one conflicting. The Lone Ranger explains that the protective guard dog, Sandy, was rigged with a booby trap that would shoot the man who released the dog. He suggests releasing the dog to see who he goes after. Scared of the vicious animal, Chet panics as The Lone Ranger forces a confession in front of witnesses. To cinch his story, The Lone Ranger reveals a surprise – Mr. Mayfair is alive and well, but he would have been dead from the trap had the dog's barking not attracted the masked man who kept watch on the house the previous night.

Notes: This episode was recycled from the broadcast of January 24, 1936, with but subtle changes such as the addition of the deputy and foreman Hank, and "Colonel Mayfair" in the 1936 version was murdered. For the most part, the remainder of the script, including dialogue and names of characters, remained the same.

Episode #844-69, Broadcast June 24, 1938
Copyright Registration #57,735, script received at Registration Office June 27, 1938.
Plot: This was the same script from the broadcast of November 26, 1934.

Episode #845-70, Broadcast June 27, 1938
Copyright Registration #57,841, script received at Registration Office July 2, 1938.
Plot: Bull Kremer steals $40,000 in gold from its army escort and captures Lieutenant Jack Harris, escaping

just before the arrival of The Lone Ranger on the scene. The outlaws, however, cannot reach the badlands and safety because of their wounded. The trail crossing into the Blackfoot Hills involves more than three miles of dangerous ledge with a drop of hundreds of feet below and a sheer granite wall rising above. With no other options, they make camp in the hills facing the Birch River. They tell the masked man who had followed them that they will not make terms for the release of their prisoner until all the soldiers from Fort Paxton had first been brought to the spot so he can be assured his escape would not be thwarted. With a hijacked Army payroll and a captured Army officer held hostage to prevent the gang's capture, The Lone Ranger convinces the post command to accept the outlaws' terms, with a plan in mind. The soldiers, led by Captain Brent and The Lone Ranger, race to the hills near Birch River where they join the small squad, under the command of Sergeant Murphy. The captain manages to buy them an hour, long enough for The Lone Ranger and Tonto to ride out far enough in front of the outlaws. After the hostage was freed, the outlaws decide to split the gold amongst themselves and start for the other side of the Blackfoot Hills. Before they can depart, however, they discover a prairie fire was started in front of them. The entire valley is ablaze and the wind is blowing the flame toward them. The outlaws, preferring to deal with the soldiers than the fire, approach reluctantly. The captain gives the orders to shoot the varmints down, but Jack Harris wants Bull Kremer for himself. The outlaws quickly surrender, with Bull swearing and fuming at the ruse against him.

Episode #846-71, Broadcast June 29, 1938

Copyright Registration #57,842, script received at Registration Office July 2, 1938.

Plot: This was the same script from the broadcast of January 20, 1936, with one revision: Chief Tacoma was replaced with Geronimo.

Episode #847-72, Broadcast July 1, 1938

Copyright Registration #57,816, script received at Registration Office July 5, 1938.

Plot: This was the same script from the broadcast of December 10, 1934, with one revision: Granville Fybush was replaced with the name Tom Granville.

Episode #848-73, Broadcast July 4, 1938

Copyright Registration #57,817, script received at Registration Office July 5, 1938.

Plot: Trouble threatens in the vicinity of the town of Big Bend when an eastern company, basing its claim on an old land grant, attempts to take over the homes and property of settlers in the disputed territory. The government decides in favor of the settlers and sends a representative to announce the decision in person. But Phillip Randolph, the agent of the syndicate, learns of the decision and arranges for the representative to be kidnapped and held while he buys up the settlers' land before they learn they had won their case. Seeking a place where a man might be hidden safely, The Lone Ranger turns to Sam Lennox, a blind ex-stage driver who knows the country better than anyone. Against the protests of John Perry, the manager of the stage line, The Lone Ranger asks Sam to drive the stage and lead him to where all the good hideouts could be along the stage trail. Although blind, Sam handles the heavy stage with perfect understanding between him and the horses and, while the masked man and Tonto ride on either side, he races down the trail to Kenwood. Twice, however, he stops and points out a possible hiding place to The Lone Ranger, but both times they are disappointed. When Sam remembers there is an old trail off to the side, Tonto checks for tracks and proves the third time to be the charm. Hours later, in Big Bend, Randolph calls a meeting to offer a dollar an acre… but fails to succeed when The Lone Ranger arrives with Mr. Bennett, the representative from the U.S. Government. The crooked stage driver responsible for the kidnapping, Joe Leiber, and the shrewd Easterner named Phillip Randolph, find themselves facing jail sentences.

Episode #849-74, Broadcast July 6, 1938

Copyright Registration #57,901, script received at Registration Office July 11, 1938.

Plot: On the outskirts of the western frontier, people living around the town of Clayville cultivate land handed down from pioneers and settlers who had lived under the Spanish Crown, before the territory had become part of the United States. The Lone Ranger and Tonto are keeping tabs on recently released John Wesley, sent to prison five years prior for stealing money. Judge Barrow, who helps the community with little to no pay for his services, was Wesley's accomplice and upon learning Wesley is in town, fears retribution. Under the Homestead Act, Wesley forces the Judge to grant him land which contains salt deposits, with plans to fence it in, guard it with armed men, and charge settlers for access. The Judge, threatened with exposure of his past, reluctantly agrees. After a few weeks a mob is formed, led by Jeb Morgan and Dave Kilbourne, men working themselves into a high pitch of excitement and shouts of defiance. Deciding to do the right thing, encouraged by the masked man, the judge cuts the wire and tells everyone that the salt is free. Angry, Wesley tells everyone that the judge stole money and was sentenced to jail, escaped and came here to pose as an honest man. Before the judge can return to prison, The Lone Ranger rides up with a full pardon from the governor – courtesy of The Lone Ranger who felt an honest man should always receive a second chance.

Episode #850-75, Broadcast July 8, 1938

Copyright Registration #57,900, script received at Registration Office July 11, 1938.

Plot: This was the same script from the broadcast of October 17, 1933.

Episode #851-76, Broadcast July 11, 1938

Copyright Registration #57,899, script received at Registration Office July 11, 1938.

Plot: Sheriff Snead of Carson City leads a posse to catch the man who just killed a banker and made off with cash. Andy Feldon, who said he witnessed the crime, identified notorious outlaw Pete Lorenzo to the sheriff. The posse catches up to a man who claims his name is Pete Atwill, even though he fits the description of Lorenzo as given by Feldon. Too late in the day to return to town, the sheriff orders the posse to make camp for the night while their prisoner remains tied until they decide what to do with him. After dark, Pete is freed by Feldon, hoping to cinch the stranger's guilt when he escapes. The Lone Ranger and Tonto explain things to the prisoner and Tonto takes his place, coming into conflict with the awakened members of the posse. The Lone Ranger verifies Pete never fled the scene and that the gun he had left for the escaped man was loaded with blanks. Realizing his guilt has been exposed, Andy Feldon shoots the masked man, unaware he is firing blanks, too, as The Lone Ranger took his idea and filled Feldon's guns with blanks, too. The posse admit they have the wrong person and seek justice against the true murderer, Andy Feldon aka Pete Lorenzo.

Notes: This radio script was recycled from the broadcast of October 28, 1933, with two changes. Andy Daiglish was changed to Andy Feldon, and the sheriff was not killed in the 1938 version.

Episode #852-77, Broadcast July 13, 1938

Copyright Registration #57,980, script received at Registration Office July 15, 1938.

Plot: When old Lafe Catlett, owner of the Box B, outside River City, dies, he wills the ranch to his son, Larry but within a week Larry is framed for the murder of Bill Sweeney. Jake Brimmer, Larry's uncle, framed his nephew for the crime, and conspired with the sheriff, Walt Travis. Jake wished to gain possession of the ranch and when Larry fled the district, he took over the management. When Larry returns, he is jailed, then tricked into attempting to escape. The Lone Ranger saves the young man before he can be shot down. At the well-concealed camp of The Lone Ranger, the masked man and his Indian companion learn that Jake does not like the sheriff because he is afraid what the lawman will do with evidence that could be used against him for another crime. The sheriff thinks Jake is holding out on his share of the ranch. The Lone Ranger plays off the crooks' suspicions of each other and sets a trap to get confessions. This includes a late-night break-in of the sheriff's office, leaving the place ransacked, and dropping a bandana that was owned by Jake. The sheriff and his deputy, Clegg, are furious at what they believe to be Jake's treachery and race over to the Box B Ranch. An exchange of gunfire elevates the conflict, and a further exchange of dispute is overheard by a U.S. marshal waiting just outside a window.

Episode #853-78, Broadcast July 15, 1938

Copyright Registration #58,031, script received at Registration Office July 18, 1938.

Plot: This episode recycled the same radio script from the broadcast of December 4, 1933, with slight variations: Doctor Fairfield was now Doc Seeley, The Box B Ranch was now the Cross Jay Ranch, and Sheriff Tubbs was now referred to simply as "sheriff."

Episode #854-79, Broadcast July 18, 1938

Copyright Registration #58,032, script received at Registration Office July 18, 1938.

Plot: The Crawford girls have a long hard trip from the civilization of Louisiana into the West, by rail and stage. Molly, the older of the two girls, is rather dignified and stately, while the younger girl, Betty, is full of life and vigor, and thrilled with the cowboys she had seen in traveling into the great state of Texas. When the girls arrive at the Bar Square Ranch, owned by their uncle, Dan Crawford, they are told Dan had been shot and killed but that he had deeded the ranch to Pablo Venado just before his death. The Lone Ranger, investigating the circumstances surrounding Dan's disappearance, inspects the deed produced by Pablo and warns the girls not to give up the ranch before they hear from him again. The Lone Ranger is not convinced the new deed is genuine, so he arranges for Tonto to trick Juan into believing old Dan has escaped, leading the masked man to the whereabouts of the kidnapped rancher. As Pablo brings the sheriff to the ranch to exercise his rights of ownership, The Lone Ranger and Tonto arrive with Uncle Dan, alive and well and proving the plot against the girls. Tonto ropes Pablo before he can shoot and flee.

Notes: This episode recycled the plot from the broadcast of November 2, 1933, which was adapted into the novel, *The Lone Ranger and the Mystery Ranch* (1938). For the 1938 radio rendition, some of the names were changed, The Lone Ranger never barges into the ranch house to gun down the Mexicans, and the women express appreciation for The Lone Ranger instead of expressing romance for the masked man.

Episode #855-80, Broadcast July 20, 1938

Copyright Registration #58,365, script received at Registration Office August 8, 1938.

Plot: The town of Wellsville was founded by Zeb Wells, an Easterner. Its citizens were old neighbors and friends of Zeb from the East and it had been Zeb's money that had made it possible for them to create new homes in the new country. Old Zeb stubbornly refused to adopt Western customers or make Western friends, so the other inhabitants of Wellsville were forced to obey his wishes. When two outlaws, Doff Layton and Monty Meegan, discover that no one in town carries a gun except the marshal, they plan to loot Zeb's safe where all the cash in town is kept. With assistance from other outlaws, loud commotion and noise is meant to distract the town citizens, including the marshal, while Doff and Monty rob the safe. While a band of mounted men are whooping and firing their guns in the manner common to cowboys celebrating their arrival in town, the townspeople are aroused by the extraordinary tumult and run to aid the town marshal to still the outburst and collect the guns. The Lone Ranger and Tonto intervene with the robbery, allowing Cliff Dolan, a young rancher, to get the drop on the crooks. The Lone Ranger assures Zeb that the men would never have tried a trick like this if they had thought they were going against armed men. Cliff has eyes for Rita, Zeb's daughter, and proved to her father that he is more than man enough to handle the situation with a loaded gun – the Western way.

Episode #856-81, Broadcast July 22, 1938

Copyright Registration #58,366, script received at Registration Office August 8, 1938.

Plot: This was the same script from the broadcast of March 2, 1934, with two changes. Cephus Pettingill was changed to Cephus Cooper, and the "center of the Oklahoma strip" was changed to the town of Graceville.

Episode #857-82, Broadcast July 25, 1938

Copyright Registration #58,367, script received at Registration Office August 8, 1938.

Plot: Steve Drago, a powerful and ruthless rancher, drove Lee Taylor's cattle from the range, stole his water hole, and finally ordered Lee himself to leave. Young Taylor, in spite of the urging of his wife, gives in to Steve, believing that he himself is a coward because his father had been one before him. The Lone Ranger learns of the situation and, at the point of his gun, carries Lee away from the café in town. In private, The Lone Ranger recounts a story of Lee's father to suggest that cowardice is not something that carries over to the next generation, and that his father was indeed a brave man. Spurred, Lee Taylor rides off with The Lone Ranger toward his former homestead. It is almost evening when they arrive, but the gathering darkness does not conceal their arrival from Buck, who had been stationed nearby to warn Steve Drago if Lee should attempt to return. While The Lone Ranger holds Buck at bay with his six-gun, Lee Taylor exchanges fisticuffs with Drago. Lee's wife, Ruth, and the local sheriff, overhear Steve call out for Buck to shoot and kill, a charge that the two bullies will have to face in court after a short jail sentence. In private, later, The Lone Ranger thanks Tonto for fetching Ruth and the sheriff and confesses the story about Lee's father was fake... but it was best for Lee for "as long as he believes it, he will keep his courage."

Notes: The story The Lone Ranger recounts to Lee Taylor in this adventure involves two men, Jim and Fletcher, a tip-of-the-hat to radio actor Jim Fletcher.

Episode #858-83, Broadcast July 27, 1938

Copyright Registration #58,368, script received at Registration Office August 8, 1938.

Plot: This was the same script from the broadcast of March 7, 1934, with minor revisions. Clay City was changed to Jackson City. The leader of the crooks, Scar Mulvay, was changed to Duke Reevers.

Notes: The closing commentary exchanged between The Lone Ranger and Tonto, regarding the masked man's inability to tell Mrs. Kent that her son Dan had fallen in with outlaws, was considerably revised during rehearsals from what Striker had typed in the script. Instead of suggesting Dan deserved consideration and was "probably killed" because he learned that his mother was to be an intended victim of Duke, The Lone Ranger insisted an act of humility would be more in line by leaving her to believe her son "as being honest and upright."

Episode #859-84, Broadcast July 29, 1938

Copyright Registration #58,369, script received at Registration Office August 8, 1938.

Plot: The end of the Civil War and the passage of more liberal homestead laws saw the tide of emigration to the newly opened Western territories reach its greatest height. Thousands of covered wagons carried hopeful families from the crowded Eastern states into what they trusted would be a land of limitless opportunity. A wagon train led by Grant Elder has become increasingly disheartened by the excess of hardships with which it had met. Along the celebrated Oregon Trail, Silas Digby stubbornly urges that the party should return to their homes in the East. Though the women objected, even Grant is forced to agree when the wagon train is first struck by a herd of stampeding buffalo, then threatened by renegade Indians. The Lone Ranger attempts to persuade the emigrants to continue, but when he learns of the Indians, he and Tonto leave to investigate. Returning to the camp, The Lone Ranger turns to the women who voice resentment at what they consider the men's lack of resolution. In the morning, The Lone Ranger and Tonto arrive with their captives, backed by the women holding rifles. There are just five Indians, not a large band, and when the red men discovered they were surrounded, they surrendered. "You'll find all kinds of hardship on the trail ahead," The Lone Ranger shames the men into continuing their trek west. "Perhaps some of them will be worse than those you've already met. But this should prove that none are as bad as your imagination makes them."

Episode #860-85, Broadcast August 1, 1938

Copyright Registration #58,539, script received at Registration Office August 18, 1938.

Plot: Gold had been discovered near Danville and the region boasted more than a dozen rich mines. But though the yellow metal brought prosperity, it also brought trouble. Outlaws began to hold up the stages carrying gold to Mill City, and the thieves continued in the face of every effort to stamp them out. Matt Cline, leader of the outlaws, along with Squint Porter, receives his information from a mysterious source. During his last hold-up, he had one of his men wear a mask and ride a white horse, hoping to place blame on The Lone Ranger. While the gang is in camp, they are fired upon by Tonto, and they immediately take out in pursuit. When The Lone Ranger discovers several of the town newspapers with a portion torn out, papers that were being burned at the vacant campfire, he realizes that Jake Faust, the stage-line manager, newspaper editor, and horse-raiser, operates the Mill City Bugle and his advertisements offering horses for sale were leaking the information to the outlaws. By changing the date of a coming story in the next paper, a trap is set. When the sheriff and a Wells Fargo agent urge deputized lawmen to race after the masked man, they come face to face with the outlaws, who discover they were tricked into showing up at a particular rendezvous.

Notes: This was the first of two consecutive episodes in which Tonto was referenced by name and action, but his voice is never heard on this broadcast.

Episode #861-86, Broadcast August 3, 1938

Copyright Registration #58,540, script received at Registration Office August 18, 1938.

Plot: Eric Wagner, a wealthy rancher in Texas, is murdered and his body discovered by Al Cook, the U.S. marshal for the district, and The Lone Ranger. The lawman insists that Eric had no enemies so, in exchange for a promise from the marshal to keep Eric's death a secret for the time being, the masked man agrees to ride to Arizona to inform Helen Wagner, Eric's niece, of her uncle's death. Upon his arrival, he finds that the hoofprints of the horse of Greg Spencer, a suitor for Helen's hand, correspond to broken horseshoe prints found near the scene of the murder. The masked man takes Tom Forbes, Helen's one ranch hand, away for questioning. Greg frames Tom for theft of her valuable jewelry, then mounts up and rides to town for the sheriff despite Helen's pleas. Helen, believing her valuable foreman was stealing from her, agrees to Greg's proposal of marriage. Two weeks go by rapidly while preparations for the wedding are carried out. Everyone for miles around is invited and, although the Wagner ranch is poverty-stricken, nothing was spared to make the occasion one to be long-remembered. On the wedding day, with everyone arriving at the Wagner ranch, The Lone Ranger rides in to deliver a letter from Helen's uncle, asking that the ceremony be held off a couple hours to give time for her uncle to arrive. The letter verifies that he is on his way to the ranch, Greg knows this could never happen and insists that the wedding go on without delay because her uncle is dead. Thus, he reveals his guilt. Tom explains that Greg killed her uncle and came back to the ranch to marry her, knowing he would get the ranch. When the sheriff notes the broken horseshoe on Greg's horse, the crook draws his gun to make an escape – thwarted by the quick shot of The Lone Ranger's gun, disarming Greg so the sheriff could take him in. Tom proposes with a ring on Helen's finger and, not wanting to lose the opportunity built up and decorated, agree to face the alter.

Episode #862-87, Broadcast August 5, 1938
Copyright Registration #58,541, script received at Registration Office August 18, 1938.
Plot: See page 129.

Episode #863-88, Broadcast August 8, 1938
Copyright Registration #58,542, script received at Registration Office August 18, 1938.
Plot: The café in the town of Rushville is crowded with the usual Saturday night gathering of ranchers and townspeople. There, Tonto witnesses a confrontation between Dan Adams, a rancher, and Mel Nugent, recently released after two years spent in jail for rustling Dan's cattle. A gunfight challenge is halted by the sheriff. Jack Dietz, Dan's foreman, had a grudge against Dan and his son-in-law, Clayt Summers, and suggested to Mel that they work together for revenge. After returning to camp to share what he witnessed with The Lone Ranger, Tonto follows the masked man's suggestion to keep an eye on the Adams Ranch. When Tonto applies for a job as cook on the ranch, Jake arrives with news that more of Dan's cows have been stolen from the corrals. They are trailed to Clayt's range, where Dan threatens his son-in-law, telling him that if another theft should occur, gunplay would settle the matter. The scenario was a frame-up, naturally, from the two schemers, with Jack eyeing Dan's daughter as the prize. Mel later convinced Jake that a bullet in Clayt would mean Dan being blamed for the crime. Once again cattle are stolen, the tracks headed east, and Dan urges his ranch hands to ride alongside. A confrontation with Clayt almost results in shooting until Tonto intervenes and offers to show Dan where his cattle are. Clayt, hoping to prove himself not a cattle rustler, insists they follow the Indian. Tonto leads the group to the place where Clayt's herd had been bedded down the night before, then points out that the tracks of the stolen cows circle the herd and continue onward still further eastward. The trail leads to Mel Nugent's tumbledown spread. Mel, realizing the scheme is about to be exposed, attempts to make a break for it but Tonto ropes the crook. Jake, in self-defense, incriminates himself and Mel during a quick falling-out among thieves.

Notes: Earle Graser went on a two-week vacation, so this was the first of six consecutive episodes in which The Lone Ranger is referenced by name and action but is never heard except in the opening and close, via recording.

Episode #864-89, Broadcast August 10, 1938
Copyright Registration #58,543, script received at Registration Office August 18, 1938.
Plot: When Bolivar Bates and Hacksaw Hastings stop at the Lazy N Ranch, they discover that its young manager, Steve Manners, had written an incriminating letter in his younger days which was held by the outlaw, Morgan Hanley, to force Steve to steal his employer's cattle. The two old ex-soldiers immediately depart to find The Lone Ranger. In the meantime, Morgan gives Steve a week to decide whether or not to obey his demands. On the sixth day, the two men quarrel and that evening Morgan goes to the café in town. Under instructions of The Lone Ranger and with the assistance of Tonto, the two old timers cleverly convince Morgan that Steve would be more cooperative if he was asked to steal 50 head of cattle instead of a thousand. They offer a letter far more incriminating than the one he already has. This establishes a set up against Morgan, who pays a visit to Steve to blackmail him with the other letter, unaware that Jane Colfax (the ranch owner's daughter) and the sheriff are around the corner of the ranch house listening to the entire conversation. The new letter would not incriminate Steve because the sheriff had been with him yesterday when the masked man told Steve what to write.

Episode #865-90, Broadcast August 12, 1938
Copyright Registration #58,544, script received at Registration Office August 18, 1938.
Plot: Old Ben Battle has been known for years as one of the unluckiest prospectors in the West. He has spent his life searching for gold and silver that he's never found. Though unsuccessful and advanced in years, he remains cheerful and active, his courage giving him youthful strength and hope. One day the citizens of the

town of Five Corners are startled to see old Ben ride down their main street, shouting with all the strength of his leathery lungs that he finally struck gold. To be precise, he had found a clue to Jake Adler's shipment of gold bullion that had disappeared five decades earlier. News of Ben's discovery spread like wildfire, attracting the attention not only of honest men but of outlaws as well. The Lone Ranger and Tonto also hear the reports and want to help Ben if they can. An outlaw named Smokey Joe makes Ben Battle his prisoner, hoping to force him to talk. Before he can succeed, Ben is rescued by a trick of the masked man. In desperation, Smokey hires Black Wolf to trail the old prospector. Believing Ben is blasting kegs of powder for unearthing the gold, the crooks wait at a distance for the explosion before moving in but they quickly discover Ben fled before the explosion, sending great masses of rock and earth from the side of the hill, blocking the narrow pass. The crooks, now trapped, find themselves in the hands of the sheriff who explains how The Lone Ranger already found the gold and convinced Ben to pretend to be blasting for it so they could be caught.

Episode #866-91, Broadcast August 15, 1938
Copyright Registration #58,545, script received at Registration Office August 18, 1938.
Plot: Limpy Davis leads one of the most daring bands of outlaws known to the West. Himself brutal and without fear, the men that follow him are of the same breed. Davis and his gang capture young Ridge Stevens, the nephew of a wealthy rancher, kidnapped from a locomotive. They plan to hold him until his uncle, Jake Stevens, who has never seen Ridge, pays $10,000 for his safe return. During his capture, Ridge received a severe blow on the head, and when he recovered consciousness, his memory was gone. In the meantime, The Lone Ranger and Tonto learn of the capture and develop a plan to outwit the kidnappers into giving up their hostage. Following the plan, Jake Stevens laughs when the boy is being returned, claiming the kidnappers grabbed the wrong person and that Ridge is safe at home. Limpy rages at the new development but figures they needed to kidnap the real nephew, then hide at the ranch until the young man claiming to be the real Ridge is alone. The outlaws plan well, but didn't know they would be pursued by the great horses ridden by The Lone Ranger and Tonto. A confrontation between the kidnappers and the masked man leads to a visit from the sheriff and Jake Stevens, leading a posse to complete the capture. Limpy spews hatred when he discovers that he did have the correct nephew all along and that the fake (Bill, a U.S. marshal) was at the ranch meant to lure them into giving away their hideout.

Episode #867-92, Broadcast August 17, 1938
Copyright Registration #58,546, script received at Registration Office August 18, 1938.
Plot: Buffalo Point, the county seat of Buffalo County, is the center of a stirring election campaign. Pete Samson, ex-rancher, is leading a determined drive to win the office of sheriff from its present occupant, Charlie Wilson. Ace Dolan, a powerful and dishonest rancher, controls the sheriff and, through him, has been able to break the law without fear. Samson ran for office in an effort to beak Ace's power and the election was only a few days off. It seems impossible for him to win, however, until The Lone Ranger enters the contest on his side. Later, Ace is told that his young brother is in danger of arrest in the town of Harmony, and the crooked rancher rides at once to protect him. Doctor Gideon Wells starts a clever story that would quickly be told and retold through the community until it reached the ears of every voter in the county. Soon the rumors of Ace's death struck Sheriff Wilson. Excitement in Buffalo Point runs high the next day during the casting of the ballots. Everyone knows that whichever candidate carries Buffalo Point will also carry the county. With the new sheriff, law and order will be restored and Charlie Wilson threatened with jail time. When Ace Dolan shows up in town to discover his stooge was not re-elected, the ruse comes out. The doctor follows orders from the masked man while The Lone Ranger and Tonto are out on the plains picking up every crooked ranch hand who attempted to flee town after learning of the false news of Ace Dolan's death. Dolan, furious, grabs a gun and attempts to shoot the new sheriff, only to be quickly disarmed by The Lone Ranger before he can pull the trigger.

Episode #868-93, Broadcast August 19, 1938

Copyright Registration #58,673, script received at Registration Office August 24, 1938.

Plot: When the Bar X trail herd, led by Walt Benson, reaches Big Horn County, they are halted by the scheming sheriff. They are close to the halfway mark of their lengthy journey. The lawman tells Walt that he has his choice of three alternatives: remain in the county for weeks until the herd is tested for Texas fever; avoid the county by taking the

Newspaper advertisement in *The Atlanta Journal* from August 22, 1938.

dangerous route through the Sioux Hills and across the Whitewater River; or pay the sheriff one-fifth of the herd for the privilege of passing through the county without an examination. Walt, following the advice of Tonto, tells the sheriff he will have his answer in the morning. Tonto outlines the masked man's plan to get the herd across the river safely but repeats all that they had learned about the tactics of the sheriff and his men. When the sheriff learns the Bar X is taking their stock through the Sioux Hills, the crooks mask up to part the herd and make a profit, regardless. Later, the sheriff and his men, hidden near the river awaiting the arrival of the Bar X herd, are astonished to find the riverbed dry. A keg of blasting powder was used to dam the river so the cattle could get through. Then the blasting powder is used again to release the water that pours in a great flood from the hills, sweeping along irresistibly with the speed and force of an express train. The group led by the sheriff is caught in its rush, carried helplessly along, then flung aside, bruised and battered, as the initial torrent subsides. Backed by the U.S. marshal, Tonto, Walt and the cowhands apprehend the crooks.

Episode #869-94, Broadcast August 22, 1938
Copyright Registration #58,674, script received at Registration Office August 24, 1938.
Plot: Lame Bear and Running Cloud are the chiefs of two Indian tribes that have lived in the same territory in peace for many years. They have long been friends but Black Fox, the medicine man of Running Cloud's tribe, envies the riches of Lame Bear and hopes to bring about war between the two tribes. He hires the outlaws led by Max Yeager to paint themselves like Indians and, during the night, seize Nokomis, Lame Bear's daughter. Just as Black Fox had planned, Lame Bear believed his former friend, Running Cloud, is responsible and immediately calls his braves together to go on the warpath. But one of those braves, Swift Eagle, suspects that the raiders had been white men, and he calls upon The Lone Ranger and Tonto to help him prove it. Facing off against Black Fox, the masked man sets out to prove that his white man's magic is stronger than Black Fox. The Lone Ranger challenges Black Fox to a contest. Black Fox has the advantage as they will use his rifle. The two men in turn will shoot at each other. The man whose medicine is stringer will be protected as the bullet turns. The Indians gather on a great plain outside the village and raise their voices in a ceremonial chant. Black Fox shoots but is not aware that a mud bullet was substituted so the Lone Ranger is not hurt when shot. When it comes to The Lone Ranger's turn, the medicine man panics and admits he was a coward. The Lone Ranger agrees to give the medicine man his life if he tells them where Nokomis is hidden. The girl is held captive in Black Fox's teepee, revealing to Running Cloud that the medicine man hired Max Yeager and his men to paint themselves like Indians so that Lame Bear would start a war.

Notes: Beginning with this broadcast, Earle Graser returns from his two-week vacation.

Episode #870-95, Broadcast August 24, 1938
Copyright Registration #58,675, script received at Registration Office August 24, 1938.
Plot: For months there have been rumors of a threatened Indian uprising under the leadership of Chief Little Bear. When Major Carson, in command of Fort Mason, divides his troops, sending half under Captain Stuart to track down Chief Little Bear and his braves, the Indians avoid Stuart and attack the fort in his absence. The weakened garrison is short of supplies and its rescue can be affected only by the return of Captain Stuart. But the Captain has been given instructions to return only if so ordered and, though he suspects the fort might be in danger, he dare not give the command to go back. The Lone Ranger, however, volunteers to learn the situation. With Tonto, he breaks through the Indians' lines and enters the fort under fire. Safe inside, the masked man chatted with the major and learns that someone in the fort has been supplying information to the Indians. Suspicion falls on Lieutenant Price. The Lone Ranger suggests sending the lieutenant out to deliver a message to Captain Stuart, then sending Tonto to follow. The scheme works flawlessly as Lieutenant Price rides from the fort and approaches the lines of the red-skinned besiegers, identifying himself. The message is relayed to Chief Little Bear, then the lieutenant rides out to meet Captain Stuart and relay the same: return to the fort

and approach by way of Buffalo Pass. In the meantime, at Fort Mason, the encircling Indians had kept up a sporadic fire designed to tempt the soldiers into wasting their ammunition. Major Carson, however, has given the command to fire only in case of necessity. The lack of food inside the fort's walls is the greatest problem. The men have been put on half rations and already they are beginning to feel the pinch of starvation. When Captain Stuart and his men arrive, The Lone Ranger suggests the major send out his men and engage the rebellious tribesmen from the other side. The sound of battle outside increases as Captain Stuart leads his men forward. Major Carson shouts a command, the gates are thrown open, and with the masked man heading the charge, the troopers charge forward. Attacked from both sides, the Indians fall back in confusion. With most of the braves at Buffalo Pass, the remainder put up little effective opposition. At the end of less than 20 minutes of hard fighting, the Indians begin to throw down their arms. The crooked lieutenant is arrested, having delivered his orders verbally to Captain Stuart, unaware that Tonto had arrived ahead of him to inform him the real orders would be in writing under the lieutenant's saddle.

Episode #871-96, Broadcast August 26, 1938

Copyright Registration #58,676, script received at Registration Office August 24, 1938.

Plot: Nestled at the foot of the High Ridge Mountains, Crow Valley is large and fertile enough to support a half dozen prosperous ranches. One of these ranches, the Lazy M, is owned by Bill Owens, an old-time cattleman who had been the first to settle in the region. The Lone Ranger and Tonto are riding through the rich rangeland skirts of Crow Valley, having heard about the stolen cattle and rustlers who remain elusive. Bill Owens suspects Nate Finch of the thefts, as does the sheriff and the other ranchers. When cows belonging to Mike Pearson, another rancher, are found on Bill's range, the sheriff arrests Bill and his foreman, Utah Simpson, who had been in Bill's employ for more than 20 years. With assistance of the sheriff, a posse is hastily formed and, with the masked man in the lead, races out of town toward the Pearson ranch. There, The Lone Ranger pauses until he makes out a dim glow in the distance toward the hills and gives the command to ride again. To blaze a trail at night, Tonto lights small fires that lead the posse to the culprits. Nate Finch and his men, driving Mike Pearson's purebred cattle ahead of them, follow a winding, confusing trail that leads them ever deeper into the mountains but, at last, they reach a broad valley where several thousand head of cattle are already settled peacefully. There, the posse exchanges gunfire until Nate and his men are roped and their slickest method of rebranding cattle is exposed.

Episode #872-97, Broadcast August 29, 1938

Copyright Registration #58,902, script received at Registration Office September 6, 1938.

Plot: The masked man and his faithful Indian companion, Tonto, pass a grove of trees less than a mile from Baker City and Tonto's horse whinnies nervously for no apparent reason. Investigation at the scene suggests someone is trying to cover up a crime from a shooting beneath a grove of trees. Entering town, it's discovered that Jason York, a jeweler from San Francisco, has been found dead in his hotel room. A valuable diamond is missing and a note beneath the dead man's hand accuses Dick Leonard, his bodyguard, of the crime. Dick is promptly arrested in spite of the fact that the masked man points out details which make the young man's guilt doubtful. Meanwhile, three men are standing before the bar of the café. One is Mort Prentice, a rancher with an outfit 15 miles from town; the second is Clem Sawyer, the town's domineering banker; and the third is Phil Tracy, a gambler who spends most of his time at the café's gaming tables. All three ride black horses, all three wanted to buy the diamond Jason brought with him, but not one of them could really have afforded the purchase. The western who-dun-it gives The Lone Ranger reason to trick one of the three suspects in the murder-robbery into giving himself away. Late that evening, after Tonto releases Dick from jail at the point of a gun, infuriating the sheriff, The Lone Ranger hands a note to all three suspects, individually. The note states he knows they committed the murder and if they meet at the scene of the crime, they could come to terms – else he reports what he knows to the sheriff. Under the cover of darkness, Mort shows up at the scene, giving away his guilt. During a verbal exchange between Mort and The Lone Ranger, the murderer confesses – unaware that Dick and the sheriff are hiding nearby to overhear the entire confession.

Episode #873-98, Broadcast August 31, 1938

Copyright Registration #58,903, script received at Registration Office September 6, 1938.

Plot: Old Zeke Hackett had once ranged cattle all the way from the town of Hinsdale through Cedar Valley and beyond. In the days of his prosperity, he had befriended numberless men and women who had come to him starving or sick or homeless. But with the end of the days of the open range, Zeke's prosperity has faded away... and with it, the fair-weather friends who had taken advantage of his generosity. In the end, he has been able to retain title only to Cedar Valley and a small strip of land to the west, where are grazed the shrunken remnants of his once vast herds. Duke Bradley, an unscrupulous rancher, poisons the waterholes in Cedar Valley that he might buy the land cheaply from old Zeke, then in turn resell it to the railroad for an exorbitant price, depriving the man of his profits. The Lone Ranger learns of the transaction through young Jerry Duncan, a railroad surveyor and, with Tonto, immediately offers his services to Zeke that Bradley might be brought to justice. With assistance from the surveying crew, the crook believes he purchased the wrong land and Zeke, at the point of a gun, is forced to sign the papers which returned him Cedar Valley in exchange for the strip of land where the surveyors were active. This done, he accompanies Duke and his men to town where the papers are notarized. Later that evening, the crooks, Duke Bradley, Lem, and Sawbuck, discover that they were misled by the surveyor and the railroad superintendent, having sold back the land to Old Zeke so he could sell it to the railroad. The crooks not only get what they deserved, but with The Lone Ranger backing his play, the sheriff escorts the crooks to jail.

Episode #874-99, Broadcast September 2, 1938

Copyright Registration #58,960, script received at Registration Office September 8, 1938.

Plot: For six weeks, crooks have been bringing dope over the border, creating misery for Sheriff Peg-Leg Sanders, with the crooks laying false clues for him all the time. The sheriff is so named for having only one leg – the other a wooden replacement so he could walk about town. After his daughter Betty has a confrontation with The Lone Ranger and Tonto at her rambling house, and reports the news to her father, his foreman, Buck Wilson, hand-delivers a note he claims the masked man accidentally dropped. Plans of drug smuggling are detailed on the paper, framing The Lone Ranger for the recent rash of smuggling in the region. The Lone Ranger lures the deputies across the border to verify they were not involved with the smugglers, and then earns their confidence to help catch the guilty culprits. During a confrontation, it is discovered that the dope is being smuggled through the sheriff's hollow leg. Every night he slept in a hotel south of the border, Buck Wilson filled the leg so his employer would unknowingly sneak the contraband into the United States. The false leads were meant to lure him south of the border on a regular basis.

Notes: There are several scenes that shift in this episode without the use of transition musical cues. It is as if the director was experimenting to see how the story flowed or the music cues were removed due to time limitations.

Episode #875-100, Broadcast September 5, 1938

Copyright Registration #58,961, script received at Registration Office September 8, 1938.

Plot: In the little town of Springville near the eastern boarder of Texas, Judge Ezra Eccles and the local sheriff dig up old forgotten laws that force the indignant citizens to pay hefty fees they can barely afford. The Lone Ranger and Tonto ride into Springville and discover that strangers can become victims of the scheme, too. Tonto rides into town solo committing minor violations so he can be jailed for not paying the fines, to verify the judge's methods. With encouragement from the masked man, the town's citizens begin walking into town with guns strapped on, or riding cattle down the wrong street. Choosing jail time overpaying the fines, the citizens pile 'til the sheriff has no more room in jail and the judge finds himself with a problem. The citizens will not leave once ordered, choosing to serve the remainder of their jail time -- or the judge can pay them their money back. The Lone Ranger arrives to force the judge and the sheriff to return the money and leave town.

Episode #876-101, Broadcast September 7, 1938

Copyright Registration #59,047, script received at Registration Office September 12, 1938.

Plot: A feud between ranchers Silas Markheim and Jim Hudson is preventing a school being established for the newly arriving schoolteacher named Mary. Hudson arranges to have the schoolhouse built himself, but Markheim and his hands say otherwise. The stand-off annoys the teacher who cannot understand how male showmanship can possibly prevent an education. The Lone Ranger, realizing the ranchers just need to talk out their differences, forces a meeting between parties which results in a surprising truth: Hudson's vengeful ranch hand has been creating the friction between the two, using false claims and poisoning cattle. Faced with the truth, the men shake hands while justice is met with the ranch hand.

Episode #877-102, Broadcast September 9, 1938

Copyright Registration #59,048, script received at Registration Office September 12, 1938.

Plot: Trying to learn where the railroad is going to lay tracks, a crooked gambler named Zeke Slavin cheats the son of the surveying crew, Jack Shaw, and then blackmails another man who works with him, Harve Grant, to steal the information from the safe. Once Zeke learns where the railroad was going to run, he would race to grab all the options on that land. When The Lone Ranger decides to investigate Harvey, the assistant to the boss of the railroad crew, he learns that Harvey has been assigned the task of protecting the manager's son. But Harvey frames the boy with fake I.O.U.s from Zeke, and Jack finds himself looked down upon by his father who gets wise to Zeke's scheme. The Lone Ranger barges in the small temporary shack that serves as the office of the construction gang with Zeke held against the point of a gun, to prove to John Shaw that his son is being framed for a crooked scheme. The Lone Ranger explains that the night before he placed a powder known as "magenta" into the safe which, when dipped in water, would cause the hands of the guilty party to turn red. Jack's hands did not turn red but Harve's hands did and before he and Zeke could escape, the sheriff and his lawmen outside take them into custody.

Episode #878-103, Broadcast September 12, 1938

Copyright Registration #59,115, script received at Registration Office September 17, 1938.

Plot: A crooked eastern lawyer named Nick Kirby buys a large ranch near the town of Dalton, then hires two cowmen to work for him – Scar Larkin and Barney, the former wanted in Kansas. Kirby then proceeds to blackmail most of the townspeople who have previous scrapes on their record. Even Sheriff Allen considers Kirby ornery, but without an actual crime to charge him with, the lawman finds his hands tied behind his back. Figuring wherever Kirby hid the evidence he had against the men in town would not be far from the house, The Lone Ranger asks the sheriff to find a reward notice for an Indian and another of his build, without photos, so they can masquerade as outlaws and be hired on to Kirby's ranch. Kirby, however, blackmails them to work at his ranch with no pay, later decides they are worth more being turned in – dead or alive. The masked man and Indian flee from the ranch, dodging bullets as Nick offers extra cash to the man that drills them. Unknown to Kirby, however, the phantom rider of the plains races off in another direction undercover of the trees. Safely away, he later returns to the ranch. There, he watches as Nick goes to stash the reward notices. Later, the chase leads into the streets of Dalton where, in the presence of the sheriff, Nick, Scar, and Barney discover the notices were not for The Lone Ranger and Tonto. An explosion from a distance verifies that all of Nick's materials used to blackmail the townsfolk is destroyed. Nick discovers the mud puddle he walked through outside of his ranch house was really paint and the trail led to where he hid the papers, moments before he is led to jail.

Episode #879-104, Broadcast September 14, 1938

Copyright Registration #59,116, script received at Registration Office September 17, 1938.

Plot: A scheming deputy sheriff and crook pit stubborn ranchers against each other to their advantage of starting a range war between Bart Conway and his outfit, versus Big Bill Halstead's. The entire region is being torn up with the feuding of the two paying for hired guns to add muscle on both sides. Knowing there never yet was a range war that settled anything, The Lone Ranger nearly gets himself killed trying to make each side see the truth. It takes a lot of stealth for the masked man to pay a visit to each of the two men, separately, to emphasize how a third party was trying to make them feud. Supposedly Halstead dammed up one of the main streams and diverted water from Conway's place to his own, but the masked man later learns this was not true. Conway will not stop fighting until Halstead releases the water, and he will not release the water until Conway sends him the cattle he thought stolen. After Tonto dopes the food and drink to put Conway's men to sleep, The Lone Ranger convinces the sheriff to pay Halstead a visit so they can ride out without interference from Conway. At a secluded campfire between both ranches, a crook named Pete and the sheriff's crooked deputy are in the midst of rebranding steer to make it appear as if one ranch was stealing from another. Exposed, the men are taken to jail. Halstead later pays a visit to Conway to close down the range war.

Episode #880-105, Broadcast September 16, 1938

Copyright Registration #59,175, script received at Registration Office September 21, 1938.

Plot: Three orphaned children come west expecting to be taken by their uncle Barnaby Greer, unaware that their uncle and his crooked schemer, Stan Denton, have been taking the profits from the children's gold mine. A few days after the letter from a lawyer in St. Louis informs them of the children's arrival, Stan waits at the town of Flat Rock for the stagecoach to arrive, dropping off Tom (the oldest, 15 years old), Sally, and little Betty. Convincing the kids that a cave-in collapsed any chance of retrieving the gold, and that their uncle has been living penniless, Denton hands Tom money and recommends they return East and go to an orphanage. Tonto, having witnessed the events as they unfolded, leaves town to report to his masked friend. The Lone Ranger attempts to convince the children that their uncle is good, just motivated by bad people. To help the children, the masked man gave the false impression that Barnaby and Denton fought, and that Denton was killed, his body placed into the tunnel before the entrance was blasted in. The sheriff arrives with 30 men to help Barnaby shovel the entrance open, only to discover no body inside. The Lone Ranger captures Denton and holds him at camp for a spell until the entrance is re-opened. With the inheritance now available to the children, Barnaby is allowed to make good and take care of the children – while Stan Denton is taken to jail.

Episode #881-106, Broadcast September 19, 1938

Copyright Registration #59,176, script received at Registration Office September 21, 1938.

Plot: Dan Latham, a shiftless frequenter of the café in the mining town of Burnside, attempts to convince his niece, Mary Frisbee, that he never drinks or gambles but she knew her father, Ned Frisbee, broke partnership in a gold claim years ago because of Dan's sinful habits. After they split the mine, her father struck it rich with a new lode. Mary plans to ride through Eagle Pass to visit her Aunt Sally, and The Lone Ranger, thinking that Tonto should kept watch from a distance to ensure her safety, is unaware of the plot against her. Mary is kidnapped by Jim Brant, a schemer, and Tonto is shot when trying to aid her. The Lone Ranger, meanwhile, keeps watch on Dan Latham, who has made plans to capture the girl. While Jim keeps her hidden in a cave, Dan sets her ransom at $50,000. Upon learning the kidnapper got the upper hand on Tonto, The Lone Ranger rides like the wind into the hills, then to the treacherous Eagle Pass, but there was scant hope that he would be able to find the girl, and Tonto either dead or wounded. Thankfully, Tonto is not dead and when he was able to break free from the rope and bonds that held him captive alongside Mary in the cave, he gains the upper hand and defeats Jim. Later, The Lone Ranger insists that Sheriff Stan place Dan and Jim under arrest on the charge of kidnapping, the latter of whom would be found bound and tied in a cave some distance away, while Mary returns to town on horseback, unharmed. The Lone Ranger is certain Tonto's wounds would heal in a few days.

Blooper! The name Jim Brant was also referred to as Jim Grant interchangeably through the episode.

Episode #882-107, Broadcast September 21, 1938
Copyright Registration #59,258, script received at Registration Office September 26, 1938.
Written by Tom Dougall.
Plot: It was the chance of a lifetime when Jim Webster is put in charge of laying railroad tracks through Texas to Big Bend, but the railroad contract is at stake when a sudden attack of fever in the camp threatens completion on time. When Tonto happens near Green Flats, where the western office of the construction company is located, he agrees to administer help. Later, the Indian rides to meet The Lone Ranger and report his suspicions. Suspecting Felix Gibbons and a man named Snead working against Jim Webster, The Lone Ranger pays a late-night visit to Gibbons to trick him into believing Snead was squealing on him. Upon learning through this trick that Snead rushed ahead to thwart the midnight train, carrying needed supplies, The Lone Ranger dashes across the open country toward the bridge at Red Rock. There, Snead is busy cutting away the supports of the bridge and succeeds. The Lone Ranger's desperate ride was too late, and the train crashes into the ravine. As Snead passes out from a near-fatality in the wreckage, Chief Thundercloud and his tribe arrive to help thwart the crook's plan by getting the load of supplies to Big Bend.

Episode #883-108, Broadcast September 23, 1938
Copyright Registration #59,257, script received at Registration Office September 26, 1938.
Plot: The Lone Ranger and Tonto try desperately to save the life of an old man who was shot and ultimately dies from the hand of a mysterious killer who has struck four times. When discovered in the house by two deputy sheriffs, the masked man and Indian flee the scene of the murder, becoming the suspected killers. Sheriff Brealt, crippled and restrained in his rocking chair, dictates orders to his two deputies to hunt for the masked man. Tonto inadvertently finds himself caught and jailed, charged with four murders. The sheriff, confined to a chair, and Judge Parker, attempt to learn from the Indian where his friend is – unaware that Tonto is bait for a trap against the real killer. Talk through town, however, is fed with liquor and heated emotion, leading to a mob crying vengeance and demanding a public hanging. When the hour of hanging is at hand, they troop from the local café, a body of nearly 50 men, some carrying ropes, others with rifles to prevent interference with their plans. As The Lone Ranger rides closer to Tuttle's Pass, someone crouched behind a rock takes careful aim at the approaching masked rider. Before he can pull the trigger to ambush The Lone Ranger, the judge sneaks up from behind him to order the man to lower his rifle. The sheriff was not really crippled. The Lone Ranger explains how Tonto had to be jailed to trick the sheriff into believing the masked man would be riding through the pass. The sheriff had been robbing people and the town doctor killed because he discovered the truth, and the others died because they saw the sheriff and his secret during the robberies.

Episode #884-109, Broadcast September 26, 1938
Copyright Registration #59,256, script received at Registration Office September 26, 1938.
Plot: Two shifty miners, Jake and Bull, discover a gold vein in Steve Gardner's claim, and plot to take the mine for themselves. Steve supports an ailing father, so he works the mine only a few hours every day. The schemers hire Tonto to ride out to the Gardner residence and report of gold being found in Big Stone Canyon, even

handing the Indian a few nuggets to support the story. Tonto, aware that the sacred ground was the burial place of a famous Indian Chief, knows if Steve ventures out there, he may not return. After alerting The Lone Ranger of the trick meant to lure the unsuspecting victim into a death trap, the masked man intercedes and sets up a swindle of his own. Tonto, in the meantime, does what he was paid to do and Steve Gardner makes his way toward Big Stone Canyon, with the belief that he could find gold there. Three weeks later, the schemers pay old Andy a visit to report why Steve has not returned. They tricked the old man into selling the mine for $1,000, twice the amount Andy and Steve paid for a mine the con artists salted. A few days later, after backbreaking work, the miners strike paydirt – only to discover they did all the work for Steve and Andy. It seems they never looked closely at the papers they signed – they bought a mine, but it was the same one they salted and sold a couple years later. Steve still owns the mine that was fought and schemed over – and, to their surprise, Steve is alive and well. The sheriff, having overheard the conversation, takes Jake and Bull into custody.

Advertisement in *The Detroit News*, September 27, 1938.

Episode #885-110, Broadcast September 28, 1938

Copyright Registration #59,255, script received at Registration Office September 26, 1938.

Plot: Eager to repay the $5,000 mortgage he owes the bank in the small town of Prairie Grove, an elderly rancher named Clem Barton makes an evening date with the banker only to be shot from ambush and the money stolen. At first The Lone Ranger suspects Shaw, the banker, because Shaw held a mortgage on Clem's ranch. But Shaw's alibi was too strong to prove otherwise. Shaw accuses The Lone Ranger and Tonto of stealing the money and the vigilantes make their escape from town. Investigating the area where the rifle fire happened, Tonto discovers the shootist's horse had a broken shoe on the left forefoot. Later, a crooked gunman named Pete rides into town with a horse that had the same broken horseshoe. In private, the masked man muscles a confession out of the crook to verify he was hired by Fred, the town postmaster, who knew about Clem making good on his mortgage. The Lone Ranger creates a set-up tricking Fred into believing the land had gold or oil. Fred pays a visit to Shaw, offering to buy the property, even placing $5,000 on the table. Moments later, having overheard the discussion, The Lone Ranger and the sheriff step out from the back room to validate Pete and his confession.

Episode #886-111, Broadcast September 30, 1938
Copyright Registration #59,507, script received at Registration Office October 6, 1938.
Plot: The Lone Ranger and Tonto, on an official mission from Colonel Hughes, are asked to investigate the recent thefts of army rifles from Fort Gardner. The stolen arms are being sold to hostile Indians. Private Stan Keating secretly allows his best friend, Carl Jordan, to leave the fort and visit Redwood City to get married to Amy, knowing Amy had a lead on the recent thefts. The following morning a soldier was missing. Major Brandon makes a hurried investigation, discovering 20 rifles and a case of ammunition had been taken from the fort the night before. He then arranges for Stan to be unfairly discharged. Playing on a hunch, The Lone Ranger sends Tonto to pay a visit to Mike, the crooked café owner in town, and in private accuses the man of killing the soldier known as Carl. Blackmail backfires, however, as the bartender locks the door and makes Tonto a prisoner in the back room of his café. The Lone Ranger breaks Tonto free from captivity. Late the next night, Stan barges into a room and accuses Mike of killing his best friend, admitting he received his news from a redskin. The Lone Ranger shows up to save Mike's life, ordering Stan to leave, and earns enough of Mike's confidence to propose selling rifles and ammunition to him. Mike, however, plans to double-cross the masked man. Later, Mike meets with Major Brandon, a crooked Army officer, to question why Brandon was selling ammunition to the masked man instead of to Mike – unaware that Stan and Colonel Hughes overheard the exchange from a short distance away. Stan is re-instated into service and his first assignment is to ride out to the Sunrise Mine with a detachment of men to rescue the girl who was kidnapped the night Carl was killed.

Episode #887-112, Broadcast October 3, 1938
Copyright Registration #59,508, script received at Registration Office October 6, 1938.
Plot: This was the same script from the broadcast of January 22, 1936, with the names changed. Jack's wife Margie was now Mary, Sheriff Masterson was replaced with Sheriff Masters, and the town of Cactus Bend was referenced merely as Kansas. Instead of a telegram signed by the President of the United States asking for a pardon, and reference to Jack's father being one of the leaders of the Alamo, a telegram from the war department went to the governor of Kansas to request a pardon on behalf of Jack's superior war record.

Episode #888-113, Broadcast October 5, 1938
Copyright Registration #59,510, script received at Registration Office October 6, 1938.
Plot: This was the same script from the broadcast of January 29, 1936.

Episode #889-114, Broadcast October 7, 1938
Copyright Registration #59,511, script received at Registration Office October 6, 1938.
Plot: This was the same script from the broadcast of February 5, 1936.

Episode #890-115, Broadcast October 10, 1938

Copyright Registration #59,645, script received at Registration Office October 12, 1938.

Plot: Led by a flaming beacon from a distance, The Lone Ranger and Tonto quickly ride to the Barnes ranch to discover from young Davey that his father, Pete Barnes, has been shot dead. The fire started when Davey's mother, Mollie, accidentally bumped a table holding a lamp when she tried to escape the crooks who rode off taking her captive. Seeing the fire, the sheriff and posse soon come across the same scene of bloodshed and plunder, and many falsely assume the masked man and Indian were responsible. The sheriff, however, suspects Red Purvis and his gang were responsible. In reality, Joe Barnes wanted to inherit his brother's property and hired Red for an act of wholesale slaughter. The Lone Ranger and Tonto, following the trail, discover the bridge supports cut and their path momentarily thwarted. While Mollie is being stubborn against her kidnappers, The Lone Ranger attempts to cross the chasm and, daringly suspended from a rope, with only the strength of his hands to save him from the sharp rocks more than a thousand feet below, is discovered by the outlaws on the other side. Tonto shoots to keep the men from cutting the rope. After assisting Tonto to the other side, the masked man rescues Mollie while Tonto races Silver through the outlaws' camp to create a distraction. There is evidence that while the outlaws were kept preoccupied over the escaping Indian, Mollie and The Lone Ranger plunged to their deaths while trying to cross to the other side by rope. Red Purvis and his men hastily mount up and ride to the cabin where they had agreed to meet Joe Barnes. Joe is upset because his nephew is still alive. Riding into town the next day, Joe plays the victim, then agrees to take the nephew in as his own son. Tonto, having overheard his plan to poison the boy, lets The Lone Ranger know, so the masked man attempts to have Joe drink his own medicine. Panicking, the poison plot is revealed in the presence of the sheriff. The lawman sends his men out to apprehend Red Purvis and his gang while Davey steps outside to be reunited with his mother.

Episode #891-116, Broadcast October 12, 1938

Copyright Registration #59,646, script received at Registration Office October 12, 1938.

Plot: Wagon trains braving the long miles into the newly opened Western territories were often the prey not only of hostile Indians, but of vicious white outlaws as well. Such was the fate of the small group of covered wagons five years ago that carried Jack Larramie and his young wife, Edith. The outlaws mercilessly slaughtered their victims so that no word of their attack should reach the authorities. One, however, they overlooked – a four-year-old boy, Ted Larramie. Now nine-years-old, Ted has been raised by the Crow Indians and rechristened Little Beaver. His grandparents, Martin and Jennie Larramie, are in the region and The Lone Ranger deduces and verifies the boy's true identity. Duke, one of the sheriff's deputies, had secretly been a member of the outlaw gang and decides to kidnap the boy and hold him for a $10,000 ransom. Knowing the kidnapper already killed two Indians to gain possession of Ted, The Lone Ranger fears the kidnapper will not hesitate to kill again. In conference with the sheriff and the Larramies, The Lone Ranger encourages them to follow the instructions in the ransom letter. Realizing someone knew of the search before The Lone Ranger, it was rationalized that one of the sheriff's deputies is the kidnapper. With assistance from Grey Elk, the medicine man of the tribe that raised young Ted Larramie, the guilty individual is identified. Duke confesses where the boy is being held captive and is later shocked to discover the Indian never properly identified him – Duke panicked too soon and gave himself away.

Episode #892-117, Broadcast October 14, 1938

Copyright Registration #59,647, script received at Registration Office October 12, 1938.

Plot: The Lone Ranger, knowing that old Andy Clark had found gold, suspected something more than an accident when the old man failed to arrive home in Danville. The old man's mule showed up three days ago and search parties were unable to find the old man. His daughter, Peggy, is concerned. The Lone Ranger suspects

Vic Fletcher and Lige Brinker. With the assistance of a trapper named Mike Moody, the crooks waylaid the old man and kept him hostage in their cabin. Andy held out while Mike attempted to get information out of the old man regarding the location of his strike. Cliff Dolan, a friend of Peggy's, tells the sheriff that he found the cabin where he suspected Andy was being held captive. This caused Lige and Vic to race out and alert Mike, unaware Cliff was telling a fib… giving the sheriff, Tonto and The Lone Ranger a chance to trail the guilty culprits and take them in.

Episode #893-118, Broadcast October 17, 1938

Copyright Registration #59,717, script received at Registration Office October 19, 1938.

Plot: Having tried two other trails leading to Beaver Falls and forced to turn back at each one by armed men, The Lone Ranger and Tonto break through a third trail in the dead of night. The cattlemen in town have been plagued with rustling and cattle theft. The sheriff employed a desperate act to send deputies to lookouts to eliminate potential cattle rustling. In spite of the sheriff's precautions, however, more cattle are stolen. The ranchers, believing the sheriff to be behind the rustling of their stock, throw him in jail. The Lone Ranger and Tonto gallop into town to rescue the sheriff before the townsfolk take justice into their own hands. With the lawman's cooperation, the three ride off to catch the train and force the conductor to back the locomotive back into town. Back in town, The Lone Ranger explains how the scheme was pulled off. Lee Dixon, a local rancher who sought to increase his stock, supervised the loading of others' cattle into cars drawn up on a spur of the newly built railroad. Abe and Jed were hired by Dixon to commit the thefts. The cattle were not rustled from the fields as everyone suspected, but directly from the train that was stopped outside town. The guilty culprits quickly confess and Lee implicates himself by venting anger at Abe and Jed.

Notes: This script was originally slated to air on the evening of October 14, 1938.

Episode #894-119, Broadcast October 19, 1938

Copyright Registration #59,718, script received at Registration Office October 19, 1938.

Plot: This was the same script from the broadcast of July 17, 1936.

Episode #895-120, Broadcast October 21, 1938

Copyright Registration #59,719, script received at Registration Office October 19, 1938.

Plot: Just outside the town of Westwood, The Lone Ranger meets Dave Clemson, a man of about age 40 who took in two orphan children, Edith and Johnson, ages seven and ten. The sheriff in town informs Dave that numerous people are accusing the children of stealing valuables, but with no proof. Silas, an elderly rancher, and his wife, Becky, offer to take the children in to ensure they have a good home. The Lone Ranger suspects the children are innocent, but someone is clearly carrying on a systematic series of robberies. The guilty culprit is Dave, who was clever enough to use the children as a blind. "The man who would do a thing like that deserves the worst punishment the law can give him," the masked man tells Tonto. Further investigation leads to The Lone Ranger securing the arrest of Ben Nugent for the crimes. When Ben is thrown in jail, the townspeople, indignant that he should have permitted children to be thought guilty, utter threats against the imprisoned man. The Lone Ranger pays a visit to Dave and assures him that cash alone cannot prove Ben's guilt, but personal items such as necklaces and rings would. The Lone Ranger tells Dave where to search and, if those type of items are found, it would clinch Ben's guilt. Little does Dave know that while The Lone Ranger was thwarting a flash mob seeking vengeance, he was fetching evidence against him. At the attempting lynching, Dave's guilt was cinched, and Ben's innocence cleared. Because Silas and his wife have no children, The Lone Ranger leaves knowing Edith and Johnson would be adopted and have the chance they deserve.

Episode #896-121, Broadcast October 24, 1938

Copyright Registration #59,862, script received at Registration Office October 26, 1938.

Plot: Outside of the town of Westwood, there has been an argument between Canfield and Chief White Cloud. The U.S. Government has sent a man to help settle the dispute as, if Canfield is permitted to steal the land, White Cloud will make his braves start trouble. Canfield's land runs up to Bitter Creek on the south and the reservation starts on the other side of the creek but White Cloud claims land north of the creek. A landslide changed the course of the creek, but the way Judge Allen sees it, the north land is still owned by the Indians. Rufe Corby, one of Canfield's men, insists when the creek changed, so did the territorial boundary. Bert Buckman, Indian agent for White Cloud's reservation, conspires with Canfield to kill the judge on the trail and leave his body on the reservation to blame the Indians for the crime. When the masked man intercepts the stagecoach carrying the judge, and warns him of his danger, the judge refuses to listen. Later, The Lone Ranger, Tonto, and White Cloud discover the judge was kidnapped by Canfield himself, along with Eric and Frank, the crooked stage drivers. They race to save the life of the judge before it is too late. Canfield, following instructions from an Indian in White Cloud's tribe regarding a marked stone that leads the way through the right canyon onto the reservation, doesn't know that The Lone Ranger marked multiple stones to hold up Canfield and his men long enough until White Cloud came with reinforcements. The judge, relieved that he would not be put out to pasture, promises to settle the boundaries of their reservation in a manner that the Indians will have nothing to complain about.

Episode #897-122, Broadcast October 26, 1938

Copyright Registration #59,863, script received at Registration Office October 26, 1938.

Plot: It is mid-winter and a raging blizzard has swept out of the North to strike at the little town of Sterling. Jerry Crane, an army deserter who stole the army payroll, is saved from freezing to death by The Lone Ranger, who suggests a plan that might make up for Jerry's crime. Just as the young man agrees, the masked man's camp is discovered by troops from the local cavalry, and the masked man and Tonto are forced to flee. Max Daly, once a corporal at the local fort, is discovered stealing from the other troopers. He is confined to the guardhouse, pending trial and punishment, but with the help of several of his worthless friends, he escapes. It was Daly who brainwashed six troops into deserting – Jerry included. Captain Boyd insists on a court martial of the strictest manner. Jerry joins Max Daly's outlaw gang, even splitting up the $3,000 in payroll that he had stolen. The Lone Ranger, late at night, sneaks into the fort and wakes up the captain. His plan is set in motion. Max, meanwhile, is scolding one of his men for starting a fire to keep warm, only to discover it was Jerry who started the fire… to let the troops know where the deserters could be found. With The Lone Ranger leading the charge, the outlaws are quickly surrounded. Captain Boyd congratulates Jerry on a job well done in helping them track down and apprehend the outlaws.

Episode #898-123, Broadcast October 28, 1938

Copyright Registration #59,864, script received at Registration Office October 26, 1938.

Plot: A nester named Neil Brogan chose to raise crops instead of cattle, a black mark in the eyes of the cattlemen in town. The young farmer planned to elope with Kate, the daughter of Sam Heffner, a rancher, until the sheriff rode to Neil's farm to serve a warrant against him for fighting with Sam's foreman. The sheriff, however, is found dead – murdered – and Neil is accused of the crime. The Lone Ranger and Tonto, riding past the ranch, find Whitey, Sam's hired gun, tied and bound. They release the gunman to learn the facts of the case, then decide to intervene and prove who really killed the sheriff. The Lone Ranger, after rescuing Neil Brogan from the rancher, Sam Heffner, and his men, leaves Neil in his well-concealed camp while he and Tonto return to town to investigate the murder. Meanwhile a range war starts brewing between the farmers and the cattlemen. During a confrontation in the streets of town, The Lone Ranger and Tonto help rope Whitey, the crooked gunman in

Sam's employ. That night The Lone Ranger unties Whitey near Sam's ranch house and the first thing Whitey does is call Neil a killer. The Lone Ranger knows then who the murderer is because the sheriff's death had not yet been discovered. The farmers and ranchers shake hands and make amends while Sam acknowledges Kate was right about Neil after all.

Episode #899-124, Broadcast October 31, 1938

Copyright Registration #59,910, script received at Registration Office November 2, 1938.

Plot: In the courtroom at Eldorado, a crowd gathers to hear the trial of Jed Lynch. Josephus Kinney, an elderly man and the chief witness for the prosecution, is on the stand accusing Lem Mason of robbing the stagecoach. Ten days ago, Kinney was on a stage headed for Eldorado. The stage was held up, the guard and driver killed, and a cargo of gold stolen. There were two outlaws. Lem insists he was innocent. When the law at Eldorado is unable to find the partner of the outlaw, Jed Lynch, and unsuccessful in its efforts to make Lynch talk, The Lone Ranger, acting swiftly, seizes Jed from his cell and races to the well-hidden camp where Tonto and Lem Mason await. The Lone Ranger pays Judge Powell a visit and although Lem Mason was already found guilty of the crime, the masked man convinces him to reopen the trial and allow Lem to testify on the stand. In court, The Lone Ranger applies a trick to prove that Kinney was hard of hearing and Kinney makes the mistake of mishearing the name Lem Mason as Clem Wilson – the latter being the sheriff in town. The crooked lawman attempts to flee the courtroom but is halted by the deputy.

Episode #900-125, Broadcast November 2, 1938

Copyright Registration #59,911, script received at Registration Office November 2, 1938.

Plot: A series of daring raids brings terror to Morgan City. Joe Kiefer and his gang have stolen hundreds of head of cattle, as well as people's life savings. A criminal with a record, Slim Egan, joins the gang and learns that with the heat applied against the sheriff, Jake Miller will be replacing him at the next election – Jake is in Kiefer's pocket. Tonto overhears the conversation while relaxing in the local café, but Slim recognizes the Indian as a friend of The Lone Ranger – the same man who sent him to prison a few years ago. With Pete Samson sneaking up from behind, Tonto is disarmed and kidnapped. The outlaws, led by Joe Kiefer, make Tonto a prisoner and take him to their camp, hoping to trap The Lone Ranger when he attempts to rescue his faithful Indian friend. Only Tonto's shouted warning saves the masked man's life. The outlaws then discuss another means to capture their most dangerous enemy. The men make sure Tonto's ropes are not tied as tight so he can escape and lead them to the hidden camp of The Lone Ranger. There, the plan is to apprehend him and make it appear the masked man committed the rash of crimes. The Lone Ranger, however, overhears this new scheme and uses it against them. Jake Miller, the newly appointed sheriff, finds himself forced to switch clothes with The Lone Ranger and when the posse comes by, the old sheriff assumes his job again against the protests of Jake, who claims he was framed. Not wanting to be hung for the crimes, Jake starts accusing other members of the gang as leading the daring raids that brought terror to the region.

Notes: In the original radio script, the newly appointed sheriff was referred to as Jake Miller in the first act and as Lige Miller in the second act. Because a recording of this radio broadcast is not known to exist at the time this book is written, it's impossible to consult the recording to verify which name was used.

Episode #901-126, Broadcast November 4, 1938

Copyright Registration #60,128, script received at Registration Office November 14, 1938.

Plot: A construction company has a contract with the railroad and Ray Holbrook is promoted as the new engineer to assure a bridge is completed on time near the town of El Dorado. This proves to be a larger challenge than initially thought when word on the street is that Indians about 40 miles away are threatening to go on the warpath, which could delay construction. Afraid of the locomotive, the Indians discovered their arrows could not penetrate the iron horse, so they sent smoke signals to call for other Indians from all over the region. Stevens, the former foreman on the job, steals liquor from the local saloon and gives it to the Indians to ensure the job is never completed. Frenzied from the fiery liquor, the Indians know no fear or failure. A few days later, the Indians begin their raids and the town of Alpert falls before the advancing mass, as more of the fiery liquor is taken and consumed by the savage Indians. The Lone Ranger confesses that the horde of red men is too great in number to consider fighting against. People of Alpert join those of El Dorado in the retreat toward the west. To prevent completion of the bridge, Stevens kidnaps a little boy, and states the boy, Jackie, will be released if the bridge is torn down. Chief Thundercloud and his tribe show up to help finish completion of the bridge while The Lone Ranger explains to Jane, Ray's girlfriend, that the safest place to avoid the Indians is the iron-clad box cars on the train. Upon completion of the bridge, the locomotive crosses to safety on the other side, where Stevens and his men are hiding. Jackie is rescued and no sooner do all of the white settlers cross, The Lone Ranger gives the signal to blow up the bridge, preventing the Indians from reaching the other side of the ravine.

Episode #902-127, Broadcast November 7, 1938
Copyright Registration #60,046, script received at Registration Office November 5, 1938.
Plot: Steve Craig, a deputy sheriff, is riding near the ranch house of old Nate Cooley one morning when suddenly a riderless horse reveals a horrible scene: Lynn Bishop has been killed, shot through the back. Bishop was recently the victim of cattle rustling and blamed his neighbor, Nate Cooley. Doug, Nate's son, insists his father never shot anyone and confesses to the crime, claiming he was tired of being falsely accused of cattle rustling and "sort of lost my head." The killing of Lynn Bishop and Doug Cooley's confession were almost the only subjects discussed in town that day, with men demanding a justified hanging in the morning. The Lone Ranger and Tonto, having observed hoof prints at the scene of the murder, rationalize that the crime was committed elsewhere and the body planted to frame Nate Cooley. The next day, Nate enters the sheriff's office with the statement that he himself had committed the crime for which his son was to be hung. To delay the hanging, the masked man carries the protesting sheriff to the spot where the body of Lynn Bishop had been found, then again follows the backtrail as he had with Tonto to verify the body was dropped off strategically to frame the Cooleys. The sheriff agrees to delay the hanging for a few days, until The Lone Ranger rides into town to fetch a posse. The masked man and Tonto find where the stolen cattle are being held, and the men keeping guard are ranch hands of Lynn Bishop. Ted Dawson, the crooked ranch foreman, is caught rustling and it's revealed he was forced to kill his boss and frame Nate Cooley. The posse apprehends the gang of rustlers and in an act of self-preservation, one of the men verifies Ted as the killer.

Episode #903-128, Broadcast November 9, 1938
Copyright Registration #60,047, script received at Registration Office November 5, 1938.
Plot: Vic Adler, the sheriff in Carter City, fails to raise money for his wife, who is seriously ill. Wolf Corby and his lieutenant, Squint, wanted in Montana, offer the sheriff a bribe -- enough to pay the doctor bills -- if he turns his head after they commit a robbery. The sheriff rejects the offer but hours after the crime is committed, finds the money in his hands and is forced to blame the crime on a bearded stranger who wandered into town. The bearded man is none other than The Lone Ranger in disguise, hunting for Corby. The masked man rides out of town and sets out to find Corby and his gang. He convinces them that the sheriff is dying. Angry, Corby visits the sheriff and takes the money back, giving the lawman no reason to hesitate to arrest him. The Lone Ranger rides out of town as the guilty parties are placed behind bars, knowing Adler will soon receive the $3,000 reward money for the capture, which will come in handy for his wife's medical bills.

Episode #904-129, Broadcast November 11, 1938
Copyright Registration #60,048, script received at Registration Office November 5, 1938.

Plot: A gang of hooded vigilantes led by Mark Delaney, evict all the criminals out the area of Loganville. After accomplishing their deed, Delaney then plots with the gang members to force prosperous ranchers to leave town when falsely accused of crimes they did not commit, so they can buy up the ranches and land. Townsfolk do not question the motives of the vigilantes, as innocent ranchers are given orders, forced to sell out cheap. When The Lone Ranger learns of the scheme, he finds it too late to do anything because Delaney and his men quit their operation before the townsfolk suspected something amiss. The masked man, with the help of Tonto and a few ranchers who fell victim to the scheme, recruits assistance from honest citizens to stage a series of robberies, raiding, and thievery so the vigilantes will be accused of the crimes. When the gang gathers for an emergency meeting, they are quickly overpowered and framed for their own crimes as the law enters the picture and sends the hooded vigilantes, including Delaney, to jail.

Episode #905-130, Broadcast November 14, 1938

Copyright Registration #60,129, script received at Registration Office November 14, 1938.

Plot: The Lone Ranger, realizing Sheriff Zeke Fuller of Pinewood would attempt to arrest the outlaw band led by Nick Gage and keep the reward for himself, warns the outlaws of the posse's approach so they can escape in time. The posse, soon outdistanced by the fleet horses of the outlaws, gives up the chase and disbands. The masked man is forced to commit this act against the law to ensure that Bob, a young boy of about 16, earns the reward money. In trying to support his mother, Bob found the location of the gang's hideout and it is Bob who deserves the $2,000 reward money offered by the bank that was robbed by Gage and his gang. With assistance of The Lone Ranger and Tonto, Bob tricks the bank robbers into confiding in him long enough to lure them in a chase through a rocky canyon, a pass so narrow that the outlaws could only go through one at a time – making it easy to apprehend them one by one. In this instance, with witnesses to verify, the boy takes sole credit for the capture… and the reward.

Episode #906-131, Broadcast November 16, 1938

Copyright Registration #60,130, script received at Registration Office November 14, 1938.

Plot: The Rancho Sanchez, south of the Rio Grande, property of old Don Diego Sanchez, is famous for the splendid horses it raises… horses, however, which are inevitably a temptation to thieves. Don Diego's animals have been disappearing, a dozen or so at a time, for more than a month. To prevent more being stolen, and to catch the thieves, he calls his son, Antonio, and several of his men together to master a plan to thwart future thefts. When Don Diego discovers Antonio was involved with the gringo rustlers because Dirk, the notorious outlaw, threatened to expose the boy's secret (Antonio married a beautiful girl of the opposition), Don Diego disowns his son. The boy attempts to compensate for the thefts but, branded a traitor, is captured by Dirk and his men. The Lone Ranger kidnaps Don Diego and takes him to the rustlers' hideout, where he overhears his son defy Dirk. Against the outlaw's insistence, Antonio refuses to steal the most prized horse from his father's lot. Don Diego, realizing his prejudice blinded him in seeing how honest and loyal his son is, accepts him back, with forgiveness and pride. The rustlers are rounded up by The Lone Ranger and Don Diego's men, while the latter accepts the young girl into the family.

Episode #907-132, Broadcast November 18, 1938

Copyright Registration #60,131, script received at Registration Office November 14, 1938.

Plot: Through Ezra Pike, a wheat farmer near the small western town of Hillsdale, The Lone Ranger learns that cattlemen and farmers there do not get along and Thaddeus Gruber, the banker in town, uses this knowledge as a means to steal land from the farmers. The railroad company plans to come by in a few months and make an offer for the farmers' land, and Thaddeus will not give money to live on unless they sell at a tenth of the price, forcing a stalemate. When Thaddeus convinces his associate, Lem Nugent, and Tom Roberts, head of the ranchers, to drive the cattle through the wheat fields, an outbreak between the ranchers and farmers seems imminent – until the masked man convinces both sides of the debate to live together and prosper. This meant the money Gruber paid the cattlemen to drive their cows into the farmer's fields can be paid to the farmers for pasturing their cattle. This prevents Thaddeus from selling the land to outsiders for the new railroad. Tom orders the crooked banker to leave the territory because he would not find the climate very healthy for him in the future.

Episode #908-133, Broadcast November 21, 1938

Copyright Registration #60,328, script received at Registration Office November 21, 1938.

Plot: Having already served two prison sentences, Tinhorn Taylor and Slick, two confidence men from the East, trick Hank Dobbins into buying the Blue Star Mine from Carl Faber, knowing in advance that the mine is worthless. When their scheme is exposed, the confidence men have already left town and Dobbins is left holding the bag. The Lone Ranger intercepts mail delivery to Westwood, steals one single package, and races back to town. Carl Faber, persecuted by the townsfolk, attempts to flee but each time he tries, the masked man forces him to return. A week later, Taylor and Slick arrive back in town. Angry that they never got any money, they pay a visit to Carl. The confrontation is proof against all the crooks. Not surprisingly, the sheriff and his deputies arrive to catch them red-handed and get a confession out of them.

Episode #909-134, Broadcast November 23, 1938

Copyright Registration #60,329, script received at Registration Office November 21, 1938.

Plot: Utah Jennings and Mac Loomis are suspected of committing a series of stagecoach hold-ups, but every time they are searched, no evidence can be found on their possession. The drivers of the Ogden-Hampton Mills stage line cannot identify the hold-up men sufficiently and the robberies are so quick and clever that witnesses are unable to point to Jennings and Loomis. When Charlie, the newly appointed stagecoach driver, is kidnapped by the hold-up crooks, The Lone Ranger suspects the regular stage drivers of committing the crime, with the assistance of Jennings and Loomis. While the sheriff holds the suspects at bay, the masked man finds the hidden compartment on the stage that holds the stolen goods, which the guilty parties would later split in equal shares, exposing the scheme.

Episode #910-135, Broadcast November 25, 1938

Copyright Registration #60,330, script received at Registration Office November 21, 1938.

Plot: A notorious criminal known as "The Hawk" has recruited hundreds of criminals, amassing an army bent on terror and destruction. The Lone Ranger and Tonto follow The Hawk south of the border to Dover, where they discover a clever plot involving the raid of a munitions depot and an attempt to sabotage a locomotive filled with 500 soldiers armed to fight The Hawk and his men. The Lone Ranger recruits Dan Badger, a young engineer always longing to join the railroad, to jump into the cab and follow orders. Meanwhile, men and women in town take up arms to combat The Hawk and his outlaw army. Using the locomotive, Dan bumps into the cars speeding out of control and brakes to save the soldiers. The soldiers are brought back to the fort when The Hawk's Army is advancing. Attacked from both sides, the outlaw army is defeated.

Episode #911-136, Broadcast November 28, 1938

Copyright Registration #60,453, script received at Registration Office December 1, 1938.

Plot: In the small town of Booneville, Link Hamlin and Rusty Brennan plot to steal the money out of Ezra's safe. Ezra, the barkeep at the local saloon and best friend of Andy Clark, takes care of young Neil Clark like he was his own son. Against the advice of his father and Ezra, Neil sides with Link and Rusty for an adventure in crime and profits… unaware that the criminals plan to frame the boy and his father for the robbery. The Lone Ranger and Tonto, having learned the truth, discuss the situation with Ezra and Andy, who both believe they can cover for the boy and teach him a lesson at the same time… which ultimately gives the sheriff the chance to arrest Link and Rusty which is something he's been wanting to do for years.

Episode #912-137, Broadcast November 30, 1938
Copyright Registration #60,454, script received at Registration Office December 1, 1938.
Plot: This was the same script from the broadcast of April 20, 1936, with one variation: Jackie's name is spelled Jacky in the 1938 radio script.

Episode #913-138, Broadcast December 2, 1938
Copyright Registration #60,455, script received at Registration Office December 1, 1938.
Plot: The town of Arrowhead was the last stop for wagons trains before venturing into the wild and dangerous country further west. From morning until night, its muddy streets echoed to the sounds of wagons, horses, and the shouts of the busy pioneers. Amos Currie, the leader of a newly arrived wagon train from the East, discovers the hard way that Reno Roberts not only owns the town, but insists on charging excessive fees for provisions and guides. Those who will not pay his ransom prices, such as Amos, will be blacklisted. The Lone Ranger interferes and orders Amos to continue on his journey – the masked man will ensure they have everything they need. Reno cheats the emigrants, robs and kills and tries every trick to prey on the wagon trains and the masked man intends to put a stop to it.

For the better part of a week the wagon train toils through desolate mountain passes, across barren plateaus, up rugged and seldom-used trails that bring it to the crest of the hills. As though the difficulties of the trip were not enough, they are followed by a series of misfortunes that seem at first only the natural results of the hazards they face. Wagons break down, gear and supplies disappear – stolen, it's thought, by Indians – unexpected slides of earth and rock imperil their safety. But the truth is revealed one morning when, the hills conquered, the wagon train makes ready to venture out upon the miles of trackless prairie that stretched before it. Overnight, every last water barrel had been emptied and there was not a drop left. A note left behind states this was the last opportunity to meet Reno's terms – or the wagon train would be destroyed. Reno knew if the wagon train was to pull through, without an "accident" that took the life of every member in the train, word would spread throughout the land that Reno's stronghold could be avoided.

The members of the wagon train now face a choice between meeting Reno's demands, or risking destruction. Tonto persuades them to reserve their decision until he speaks to the masked man. The great horse, Silver, obeying the command of his masked rider, gallops eastward toward Arrowhead. His pounding hoofs, shod with silver, thunder over the very trail so recently followed by the wagon train. In Arrowhead, the masked man barges into the saloon and at gunpoint forces Reno and another outlaw, Woody, to leave town with him.

In the meantime, while the three days slowly passed, the emigrants' wagons remained in a circle on the far side of the hills. The days were spent in hunting game to replenish their supply of food but on the evening of the third day, most of the party gathered together. The masked man arrived and explains his plan, then leaves the wagon train and rides on ahead that same night, leaving his two captives kept guard with Tonto. In the morning, following The Lone Ranger's instructions, the horses are hitched to the wagons, the drivers take their seats, and the command is given to start out. But two men had watched their preparations, and when it was evident that the party had finally resumed its journey, they mounted and secretly stole ahead of the wagon train to take their position in advance of the approaching wagons. Pike and Duffy, outlaws in Reno's employ, await the approaching wagon train from a distance and start a fire, fanned by the wind, leaping across the prairie with the speed of a locomotive. Hungrily the flames devour the dry grass, then roar onward toward the wagons. But the emigrants, warned by the signal shots of the masked man, were prepared for the emergency. Hastily the wagons were drawn into a circle. Then, under the direction of Tonto, men, women, and children, take burning brands, start backfires, beating out the flames as they approach the wagons.

Working furiously against time, a clearing of charred grass is slowly completed around the wagons. The advancing prairie fire sought in vain to leap the barrier. Tongues of flame shot out and sparks carried by the wind nearly accomplish the purpose. But Tonto's alertness prevented disaster. Through Reno's confession, The Lone Ranger knew what was planned but there had been no way to find Pike and Duff until they started the fire. They were too clever at hiding their trail. The only thing the masked man could do was ride parallel to the wagons and keep watch. Pike, overhearing the explanation, asks if Reno squealed on him. "He had to save his own skin," Amos laughed, explaining how the polecats (Reno included) would not bother any more wagon trains, "because the first tree we come to, you're being hung!"

Episode #914-139, Broadcast December 5, 1938
Copyright Registration #60,575, script received at Registration Office December 7, 1938.
Plot: This was the same script from the broadcast of January 31, 1933.

Notes: This is the first of three consecutive broadcasts of special episodes as part of a week-long Anniversary Series. This was also the fifth anniversary of the program being carried over the Mutual network.

Episode #915-140, Broadcast December 7, 1938
Copyright Registration #60,576, script received at Registration Office December 7, 1938.
Plot: This was the same script from the broadcast of February 25, 1933. This rendition was revised slightly to incorporate Cactus Pete, a wandering musician, who recounts the legend of how The Lone Ranger first met Tonto, his faithful Indian companion.

Episode #916-141, Broadcast December 9, 1938
Copyright Registration #60,577, script received at Registration Office December 7, 1938.
Plot: This was the same script from the broadcast of August 26, 1935.

Episode #917-142, Broadcast December 12, 1938
Copyright Registration #60,774, script received at Registration Office December 17, 1938.
Plot: On the trail west of El Paso, Verne Jackson attempts to shoot The Lone Ranger for revenge, claiming the masked man was responsible for the murder of his good friend Walt. Jackson spent five years in prison and recently escaped to seek revenge. The Lone Ranger convinces Jackson to hide out at a trapper's cabin long enough for him to learn the identity of the guilty party -- and then forces the real murderer to don a mask similar to The Lone Ranger's and visit the same cabin. Punished by his own cowardice, in fear of his life, the murderer confesses to the deed and Jackson learns that the pardon issued by the governor was intercepted by the crook. Thanks to The Lone Ranger, a duplicate pardon is issued, and Jackson is allowed to go free... after he escorts the real murderer to town.

Episode #918-143, Broadcast December 14, 1938
Copyright Registration #60,775, script received at Registration Office December 17, 1938.
Plot: This was the same script from the broadcast of November 21, 1933.

Episode #919-144, Broadcast December 16, 1938
Copyright Registration #60,776, script received at Registration Office December 17, 1938.
Plot: Along the eastern bank of the Rojos River squats the century-old adobe huts of Oro Rico, home of the superstitious Zuni Indians. On the western bank of these same waters

Hi Yo Silver! **Tell Santa to Bring You a Lone Ranger Suit**

from Sears

And Be the Hero of the Neighborhood Christmas Morn!

$1.98 and $2.98

Sold Elsewhere for $2.49 and $3.49

Boys! They're honeys! And just what the famous Lone Ranger himself wears! See them at Sears . . . and ask Santa to bring you one Christmas! Sizes 4 to 14.

Set Includes . . .

Trousers	Shirt
Bandana	Kerchief
Vest	Mask
Gun	Holster
Belt	Lasso

Kiddies! Listen to the "Adventures in Christmas Tree Grove"
Over WGST at 5:30 every day except Saturday and Sunday!

In Boys' Department

Ride 'em Cowboy!

Sears 's Headquarters for Cowboy Suits!

10-Piece Ranger Suits
Includes . . . hat, plaid shirt, leather - trimmed chaps, 'kerchief, pistol, belt, holster, lasso. Sizes 4 to 14 . . . . **$1.98**

Buck Jones . . . With Fur-Trimmed Chaps
Includes 8 pieces. Sizes 4 to 14 . . . . **$2.98**
Other Cowboy Suits, 98c to $3.98

Sears Also Carries Indian Suits, Mounted Police Suits!

Hi-Yo Silver Shooting Games
Large, bright-colored board, gun and two darts. Has picture of Silver and Lone Ranger on board . . . and the goal is to shoot Hi-Yo Silver! **98c**

Hi-Yo Silver Mechanical Toy
Horse and rider . . . you wind it up and the Lone Ranger twirls a rope round and round. The horse dances. **39c**

In Toy Department

SEARS, ROEBUCK AND CO.

Newspaper advertisement from the December 14, 1938, issue of *The Atlanta Journal*.

settled General Store owner Dana Sturges and his small but determined band of pioneers. These men, with their families, had but a short time before founded a farming settlement where rich, untapped soil beckoned to their labors. The mysterious tribe supposedly knew about the "Seven Cities of Gold," a legend that had been passed on from Spanish explorers to an old prospector in the region. When a Zuni idol is stolen from an adobe temple, the Indians set out to attack. The Lone Ranger thwarts a war between the Indians and the white, then sets a plan in motion to save Dana Sturges, who was kidnapped, and at the same time weld a lasting peace between the whites and the Zunis. Four days later, while searching for a clue to the theft of the idol, The Lone Ranger and Tonto find the trail where the idol was carried away by sled. With four settlers assisting, the masked man leads the group into an Indian camp a few miles away. Overnight, while the natives are sleeping, the white men steal the idol and spend many hours trekking it back to the Zuni tribe. Yam-Po, the chief of the Zuni Indian tribe, is delighted to learn that the white men helped retrieve the stolen idol from the redskins and he agrees to make the white man his blood brother, releasing Dana from captive.

Episode #920-145, Broadcast December 19, 1938

Copyright Registration #60,777, script received at Registration Office December 17, 1938.

Plot: Hank Baxter and his three sons, Greg, the eldest, Phil, and Ray, are making their way through the mountains after a successful season of trapping. Their packhorses, burdened high with the pelts of beaver, are the prize of Reno Ryan's eye. Reno and his outlaw gang trap Baxter and order him to surrender the pelts or face a downpour of bullets. Baxter is defiant. The rifle fire exchanged between the two parties attracts The Lone Ranger and Tonto. Reno is the worst killer in the district and the trappers can expect no mercy from him. The Lone Ranger sends Tonto to the nearby fort to Colonel Lowry to fetch troopers. If they can reach the ambush within three days, the masked man will find a way for the trappers to hold out that long. On the hill where the outlaws are encamped, Hank Baxter's treacherous former partner, Chris Nugent, is satisfied with waiting it out… the beaver pelts are worth a small fortune. After racing through the outlaws' camp, The Lone Ranger explains a plan to Hank and his boys. Day darkened into dusk, dusk becomes night, and with nightfall Hank Baxter and his son, led by the masked man, tow the packhorses behind them, away from the hill and toward the arroyo. The outlaws, discovering the flight, quietly follow the four-legged beasts only to discover too late that they followed saddle horses with no riders – the Baxter clan led their pack horses in a circle and took over the outlaw camp – with the outlaws now facing little to no cover from their assailants above. Beside himself with rage, Reno, the outlaw leader, wheels at the head of his gang, to gallop back up the Arroyo for the hill stronghold. He will seek revenge, if nothing more, for being so cleverly and swiftly tricked from that natural vantage point. During the following two days and nights, the outlaws attack the trappers – and each time are sent back down the slope in retreat. With the dawn of the third day, a distant bugle pierces the morning air. From both sides, circling around the base of the hill fortress, ride Colonel Lowry's mounted troops and alongside them, Tonto. A cry for mercy rises from the throat of the outlaw leader…

Episode #921-146, Broadcast December 21, 1938

Copyright Registration #60,778, script received at Registration Office December 17, 1938.

Plot: With all their possessions piled in the prairie schooner which they had purchased, Dan Griffin and his wife, Bess, were anxious to reach their new home – a section of land in Mason County that they had bought some weeks earlier. When they arrive at their new homestead, however, they find out the land was misrepresented and cannot be used for raising crops. After Tonto learns from Dan firsthand that he was swindled by Paul Ludwig, he races to the well-hidden camp of The Lone Ranger to report of the elderly couple's misfortune. Ludwig has an office in Brunswick. Hoping to teach the schemer a lesson, Tonto follows instructions from his masked friend and creates a scenario that gives the appearance he was giving a sure thing tip to Luke Bagley, another of Ludwig's victims. Ludwig, however, orders his two men, Joe and Curly, to capture and guard Tonto and Bagley as prisoners, forced to answer questions under threat of being shot. Ludwig rides out for Mason County and five days later approaches Carlos Creek, a shallow meandering stream that represents all that was left of a once large river. Finding enough evidence to suggest oil under the land, Ludwig attempts to buy back all the land from the farmers in the area that he swindled. On the appointed hour, all had arrived and, after discussion and debate, the farmers agreed to sell back their land for more than they paid. Minutes after Ludwig signs all the necessary contracts and land deeds, Joe rushes in to warn his boss not to sign – but it is too late. The only oil on the land came from kegs. The Lone Ranger assures Ludwig that no one made any false claims; it was Ludwig who jumped to the wrong conclusions.

Notes: This radio script was recycled from the broadcast of April 1, 1933, with considerable re-writes including name changes. Burt Seeley was changed to Dan Griffin, and the arroyo property needed for the right of way for a railroad was removed entirely.

Episode #922-147, Broadcast December 23, 1938
Copyright Registration #60,779, script received at Registration Office December 17, 1938.
Plot: Red Smiley and Cliff Noble are busy working a claim along a lonely tributary of the Frazier River in early spring. A third partner, Clem Peterson, has taken advantage of the opening trails to go to town for supplies. Hoping to divide the spoils among two men instead of three, Red eliminates Cliff and attempts to blame it on thieving Indians. The Lone Ranger, suspecting foul play, informs Clem in private that Red killed Cliff and that the Indians were invented. After a promise to cooperate, Clem goes back to working the mine with Tonto off in the distance to ensure his safety. The Lone Ranger, meanwhile, rides out and Clem and Red work the claim as before except for the absence of the murdered man. Red remains unaware of Tonto's watching eyes, guarding against treachery. Clem, obeying the masked man, appeared to harbor no suspicion against the big red-headed man who works beside him. As the days pass, Red develops nervous unease and open apprehensiveness as Cliff starts observing what might have been a ghost – the ghost of a dead man. During the next few days, Red faces an almost hysterical fear. Visions of a ghostly figure with the face of Cliff and a message from the great beyond stating Red killed Cliff drive the murderer to confess in the presence of the sheriff, hidden in the shadows. The Lone Ranger, Clem, and the sheriff plotted to have a local resident, Reid Bradley, disguised with a facial scar just like the one Cliff had, to play the role of the ghost. With absolutely no evidence against Red that would have served to bring him to justice, there was only one person who could punish him… and that was Red himself.

Episode #923-148, Broadcast December 26, 1938
Copyright Registration #60,934, script received at Registration Office December 27, 1938.
Copyright Registration #60,933, script received at Registration Office December 27, 1938.
Plot: Poverty is common in the town where Bob Hamill lives, and little can be done about it, while Eric Flint thrives. Flint was rich, owned practically all of the town, and was hated and despised. When Flint learns a masked man is looking for him, he hires two bodyguards, Butch and Cooper, but a desperate Bob Hammil decides to rob him to buy Christmas presents for his son. Bob is going to lose his homestead to Flint, unable to pay the mortgage, so he figures what harm would it be to give his son a holiday to remember? Catching the outlaws in play for The Lone Ranger, Bob draws his gun and forces the men – including Eric Flint – into an old shack, tied and bound. The Lone Ranger, meanwhile, learns from Tonto about Flint. There are a lot of men in the West who came to escape unhappiness in the East, the masked man rationalizes. Flint was one of them but his faith in his fellow men was destroyed before he arrived. The West did something to him. He lost his sense of values, his sense of fair play. The Lone Ranger breaks inside to kidnap Flint, leaving Bob with the two gunmen. The masked man asks Flint if he remembers when he was young hearing the story about old Ebenezer Scrooge. When Flint says he has and says, "Bosh!" He reminds Flint of the visits by three ghosts at night and how Scrooge was a changed man in the morning. Throughout Christmas Eve, The Lone Ranger forces Flint to

call on a few of his customers, people he loaned money to, and people who could not pay off their debts. The first person they call on is Dan and Jane Dickerman.

RANGER: He's not going to take your house. Those papers he signed with you were illegal. I want you to sign this paper telling just what sort of an agreement he made with you.

JANE: Illegal?

RANGER: Then I want you to come with me to the sheriff's office and lodge a complaint against him. He's on his way to jail.

FLINT: No, no! Yuh can't put me in jail. Them papers is legal!

RANGER: You be quiet! How about it, Dan?

DAN: But we can't do it now…

RANGER: There's no time like the present. The sooner he gets to jail, the better the community will be. We may have a long ride to the county seat in this kind of weather, and I've got to get him there before the first of the year if I'm going to save your property. All I need is one complaint against him.

DAN: Well, can't you get somebody else?

RANGER: What for? He made an agreement with you, didn't he?

DAN: But… well, I don't know. Look, stranger, it's Christmas Eve. I can't send a man tuh jail on Christmas Eve.

RANGER: Not even Eric Flint?

JANE: He oughta be in jail… if he's dishonest, Dan…

RANGER: It might save your house. Don't you realize that?

DAN: I won't do it. That's all. Taint the spirit of the day. You get somebody else to send him to jail. If it was day after tomorrow or next day, any other day but Christmas…

RANGER: We'll find someone else. Come on, Flint.

The Lone Ranger takes Flint to another house, and then another, and in each homestead Flint notes with increasing amazement that the spirit of Christmas, the thought of peace on earth and good will, so imbues the men and women, that not one could be found who would agree to assume the responsibility for jailing a man on Christmas day.

Eric's backstory was not so cheerful. Eric Flint came out to the West 20 years ago, intending to send word to his wife when she could come out and join him after he got a foothold. He sent that word and waited, but she never answered his letter. When next he heard, he read her name in a paper ten years later, saying that she was on the stage. It soured him. He was mad. Mighty mad, to think she wouldn't join him after all the promises he made. But he did not know his letter was never delivered. He did not know she waited years to hear from him. She did not know where to reach him. The Lone Ranger finds the letter Eric Flint wrote. He finds it with a pack of other mail that had fallen into the hands of Indians when a stagecoach was wrecked. Then The Lone Ranger locates her. She came out West in an effort to try and find him. She was singing on the stage to get the money for the trip. She hunted years and finally settled down. The Lone Ranger knew of this and was determined to show Eric Flint that there were things far better than cheating customers out of their land.

As the night wears on, Mary Hammil sits by the window where a small candle gleams out into the night. She can't sleep. She worries about her husband, worries where he went, and remembering the expression of grim determination on his face when he left, is fearful of what might happen before he comes back. But when Bob returns, he has a smile on his face. He tells his wife all about Eric Flint being taken away and justice served against the vile banker.

The next day, early Christmas morning, Eric Flint arrives at the Hammil homestead to surprise young Donny, Bob, and Mary's little boy, with a Christmas tree. Over the night, while everyone was sleeping, Butch and Cooper cut down Christmas trees and followed orders from Flint to deliver them to everyone's houses.

Mary was shocked to discover the old Scrooge had a change of heart. He plans to visit everyone in town and deliver them a generous Christmas morning. Then he has to leave town. Mary asks for how long.

FLINT: How long? Sakes alive, I don't know. I'm goin' to meet my wife. I ain't seen her in twenty years. She's still waitin' for me. I won't be back next month. Mebbe not until spring. Mebbe I won't come back! And who cares? A merry Christmas everybody!

Notes: For the West Coast and transcription, this was the same radio script recycled from the broadcast of September 8, 1937, which was not a holiday story. For the Mutual Broadcasting System (not part of the transcription series), an original holiday offering was dramatized, as featured in the detailed plot above. The Christmas-themed adventure would later be recycled for use as "The Christmas Tree," broadcast on Christmas 25, 1950. The element involving Donny wanting a Christmas tree and the delivery of a huge tree on Christmas morning was borrowed from the broadcast of December 24, 1934.

Episode #924-149, Broadcast December 28, 1938
Copyright Registration #60,935, script received at Registration Office December 27, 1938.
Plot: Lefty is upset that another hundred head of sheep were driven over the Sweetwater Canyon. He accuses the cattlemen of attempting to drive the sheepmen out of the territory but Peggy Hammond, the daughter of the local general store owner, cannot imagine her boyfriend Pete Lambert, a cattleman, would be responsible for such a thing. The Lone Ranger, however, having caught Big Bill Neiberg and turned him over to the law, knows that Big Bill's gang may have been broken up, but Notch Hopkins escaped and came into the territory. Two of Hammond's own men drove his sheep over the cliff, a half breed called Pedro and a man called Fritz. The Lone Ranger suspects Notch Hopkins and Lefty Curtis are one and the same person. It's clear that Lefty has been building up the belief that the cattlemen were killing Hammond's sheep. So far, he had not implicated any particular rancher or group of ranchers, but hoped public feeling, even without proof, would finally force the cattlemen out. Tonto rides out to meet all the cattlemen in the area, while The Lone Ranger fetches the sheriff in the early hours before sunrise. With the early sun to light their way, the masked man and the sheriff send their mounts hurrying down the trail toward the distant Hammond ranch house. As all the cattlemen, including Hammond, his daughter, and the sheriff, hide in the barn for a number of hours at the request of the masked man, they form a tight alibi against Lefty's newest claim that his sheep were killed over Big Smokey Canyon. The sheriff now knows Lefty's accusations are false. Tonto rides in with a gun on Pedro and Fritz, and Lefty's true identity is exposed.

Episode #925-150, Broadcast December 30, 1938
Copyright Registration #60,936, script received at Registration Office December 27, 1938.
Plot: There has been a recent rash of horse stealing in and around the town of Cedarville, and the two suspects are Yah-keemah and Little Wolf. With Yah-keemah's saddle found on one of the stolen horses, Newt Burst, the sheriff, admits the accusations have some validity. The real culprit is Duff Seeley, the local harness maker, who conspired with Poke Peter and his gang. Buck Davis, a young boy, is forced to send a message to Poke, fearful of the crooked harness-maker's threats, unaware that in spite of the precautions he had taken, the masked man and Tonto trailed him to within a mile of his destination. The Lone Ranger captures the boy as he rides back to town, making sure Buck's horse returns, riderless, to the home corrals. When morning arrives, but not Buck Davis, Duff decides to turn even this misfortune to his own advantage. Claiming Little Wolf kidnapped the boy in retaliation for his friend's incarceration, Duff provides a convincing theory to the sheriff. Later, riding his horse toward Antelope Pass, Duff meets with Poke. A falling out among thieves almost happens, resulting in Duff riding back sore and angry. Late that evening, under the cover of darkness, the masked man and Indian sneak into the narrow-mouthed canyon at some distance from his camp where the stolen horses are kept. They

steal the horses, stampeding them back to town. Duff Seeley rises in the morning and starts to prepare his breakfast when a glance through the window at his corral reveals the stolen horses. Poke Peters, assuming his partner double-crossed him, rides to the Seeley homestead. The falling out gives Poke a reason to draw his gun, but The Lone Ranger shoots the weapon from his hand, disarming him. What the thieves are unaware of is the presence of the sheriff, who remained outside to overhear the conversation between the two. He now knows the two Indians were being framed for the crime.

Episode #926-151, Broadcast January 2, 1939

Copyright Registration #61,071, script received at Registration Office January 5, 1939.

Plot: U.S. Marshal Harry Miller's manhunt of Jet Grabo leads to a case of mistaken identity when the outlaw gets the drop on the marshal and forces him to switch clothes. In the town of Plainfield, the stubborn sheriff mistakes the lawman from Crystal Springs for the wanted man and jails him. Tonto delivers a description of the wanted outlaw to The Lone Ranger, who quickly discovers the mistake. While Tonto rides out to apprehend Grabo, The Lone Ranger rides into town, masquerading as a resident from Crystal Springs. In the presence of the sheriff, the disguised stranger watches as Tonto brings in Grabo. The sheriff is confused as to who he jailed but the stranger plays a risky game by asking questions about the marshal's accomplishments. Grabo quickly latches on and brags, unaware that the sheriff knew the stories told by the stranger were fake. After being exposed as the real outlaw, Grabo attempts to escape but is grabbed by Tonto. The stubborn sheriff admits his error and releases the real marshal.

Blooper! The actor playing the role of Jet Grabo stumbles over a couple lines.

Episode #927-152, Broadcast January 4, 1939

Copyright Registration #61,072, script received at Registration Office January 5, 1939.

Plot: Lafe Custer plans to sell his cattle in Abilene, unaware that his foreman, Nate Custer, has crooked plans to gain ownership of the ranch. Nate not only holds a mortgage on his brother's ranch, but also a personal grudge. When The Lone Ranger and Tonto ride into Ridgeville, they accidentally learn how Nate plans to sell the cattle in a different town and profit on top of preventing Lafe from making good on his mortgage. Lafe, too, discovers the scheme and asks Colonel Hogan at the nearby fort to assist by sending his men to Cheyenne to intercept the cattle herd before delivery. The Colonel, however, will not intercept over a domestic concern. The Lone Ranger and Tonto decide to masquerade as outlaws, infuriating the Colonel, who sends the cavalry in pursuit. The party searches frenziedly, consuming three days where The Lone Ranger and Tonto create delays by scaring away the horses and creating landslides, timed to ensure a confrontation between the cavalry and the guilty party, caught in possession of the cattle. Only Nate is frustrated when he discovers he was tricked into delivering cattle to Abilene, right where they were supposed to be delivered.

Episode #928-153, Broadcast January 6, 1939

Copyright Registration #61,073, script received at Registration Office January 5, 1939.

Plot: Through Lem Pike, the storekeeper at Red Bank, The Lone Ranger learns that the town is drying up. Indian trouble caused construction of the railroad to cease at Salisbury, having originally planned to reach Red Bank before winter set in. The Lone Ranger and Tonto pay a visit to Red Eagle, chief of the reservation Indians, to learn the white men broke the peace treaty, killing off the buffalo and only giving half of the beef rations promised. The chief knows that by seizing the food he needs for the upcoming winter will mean bloodshed, possibly hunted down, but getting killed by bullets is better than starving in a teepee. The chief agrees to prevent a war for a few days to allow the masked man to investigate. The railroad construction camp, meanwhile, faces a serious problem in obtaining food in sufficient quantities for the laborers who are stretching the glistening trail of steel across the continent. The buffalo had been dispersed and cattle were to be had only from widely separated ranches. Fred Bowen, in charge of the construction camp, assisted with a mass exodus of cattle to extinguish the beef shortage – cattle stolen from the nearby ranch. The commotion through town gave The Lone Ranger a platform to expose how Ed Scott, owner of the Cross M, conspired with Jake Duffy, Indian agent over at the reservation, to rebrand the Bar N steer. They falsely reported to the government that the Indians received their full quota, and the two shared in the stolen profit. Fred Bowen examines the money in Jake's wallet, to verify it as the same bills he paid to Ed Scott. With the culprits exposed, and beef delivered to the Indians, the railroad will now be completed as originally scheduled with no interference from Red Eagle.

Episode #929-154, Broadcast January 9, 1939
Copyright Registration #61,198, script received at Registration Office January 13, 1939.
Plot: A young cowpuncher named Jack Ross wanders into the town of Willow City a short time after he partners with a man about his same age, a crook known as the Panhandle Kid, unaware of the Kid's reputation. When the storekeeper is shot and wounded, the young men flee north. The posse got an early start after Jack and his companion, but The Lone Ranger and Tonto got the drop on them and, overhearing an exchange between the two, restrain the men until Sheriff Alva Fisher arrived. The sheriff is stubborn and won't agree to giving Jack a fair trial, firmly convinced that Ross was equally guilty in the hold-up and refusing to accept the fact that the young man was framed by his partner. The sheriff even believes the masked man to be one of a member of a gang of thieves. While Jack keeps guard over the Panhandle Kid in The Lone Ranger's well-concealed camp, the masked man sneaks into town and kidnaps the sheriff. It was much later that night when old Zeke Munson, the man the Panhandle Kid had planned to rob of his savings, is awakened from a light sleep by a noise in the room adjoining that where he had retired. A hurried examination of his cash box reveals that Zeke's entire fortune, which he saved over the years, has been taken. When Zeke races into town to report the crime, the sheriff looks guilty for not having an alibi, having been seen riding away with a masked bandit. In front of witnesses, The Lone Ranger hesitates to clear the sheriff's name. "You see, sheriff, they're convinced of your guilt, just as you were convinced of the guilt of Jack." The sheriff admits he was mistaken and then, through a confession of the Panhandle Kid, Jack's innocence was confirmed. It was Tonto who stole the cash, using the sheriff's stolen badge to look like the lawman broke into Zeke's shack. The money is promptly returned to Zeke.

Episode #930-155, Broadcast January 11, 1939
Copyright Registration #61,199, script received at Registration Office January 13, 1939.
Plot: An investigation which the Lone Ranger had been following for several weeks finally leads him to a cafe in the town of Stillwater where he overhears Sheriff Charley Dodd speaking about missing Chinese laborers who were working on the railroad. Dick McCleod from the railroad camp suspects the Chinamen have cleared out but Brad, the sheriff's deputy, believes they wandered into Apache Valley, lured with the promise of gold, and fell victims to the savages. Despite a warning from the Apaches, The Lone Ranger and Tonto press onward into the valley which becomes wild and foreboding the farther they ride. The valley is wide, but so high are the cliffs which hem it in that its bed is somberly shadowed for all but a few hours in the middle of the day. By the diminishing campfire late at night, strange characters attack the sleeping figures in bedrolls, only to discover the campfire was a trap – and The Lone Ranger and Tonto discover their would-be assailants are not Indians, but white men dressed like Apaches. During the ride back, The Lone Ranger feigns being shot. As the masked man planned, it did not take long for Rio and Windy to undo the ropes that bound them, and they immediately take to the saddle and spur their mounts northward, deeper into Apache Valley. The masked man and Indian trail the crooks to their hideout where two other crooks, Pete and Brady, the outlaw leader, have forced the Chinese into slave labor to mine for gold. A few days later, when The Lone Ranger interferes, Brady sets a match to a fuse to set off kegs of blasting powder, enough to blow out the side of a mountain and get rid of the evidence

– including the Chinese labor force. But The Lone Ranger, having fetched Sheriff Charley Dodd and his men, confesses that he rigged the kegs not to blow the mine, but to give a signal for Tonto to lead the charge. The Lone Ranger disarms the crooks and holds them at bay long enough for the sheriff to take charge.

Episode #931-156, Broadcast January 13, 1939

Copyright Registration #61,200, script received at Registration Office January 13, 1939.

Plot: Mort Bowman, a wealthy rancher, finds himself the victim when his adopted 16-year-old daughter, Nellie, is kidnapped by Wolf Cutler, an outlaw who demands $20,000 in ransom. Just beyond the southern boundaries of Bowman's ranch there exist what are known as the Great Salt Caves. Dark and mysterious, their caverns threaded by a swift underground river, it was seldom that anybody in the neighborhood ventured to enter them. After witnessing Nellie trying to break free of the Wolf Cutler gang, The Lone Ranger attempts a rescue but discovers that it is impossible to attack the outlaws alone. In an attempt to prevent Bowman from paying the ransom and thus giving Wolf a reason to kill the girl, the masked man whisked the rancher away to have a private discussion. An hour later, Bowman returns to the ranch alone and unharmed. Bowman had agreed to a scheme masterminded by the masked man, and later gathered his men together for the trip to the caves to keep Wolf and his partners, Spike Curtis and Bid Abby, occupied while The Lone Ranger and Tonto went inside and get to the underground river without being noticed. While Bowman throws the ransom money to the outlaws where they stood behind the protection of rocks, the masked man is slipping into the mysterious waters of the underground river. Having snuck up behind the outlaws that way, The Lone Ranger puts up a fight and overtakes the three crooks, saving the life of Nellie as well as Bowman's money.

Episode #932-157, Broadcast January 16, 1939

Copyright Registration #61,319, script received at Registration Office January 19, 1939.

Plot: Duke Austin and his partner, Shorty Fowler, pay a visit to the office of the sheriff in Pine City to have a private talk with Billings, claiming to have been victims of the outlaw and hoping they can learn the whereabouts of their stolen items. Billings had been apprehended by The Lone Ranger a few nights earlier in a café, and Duke and Shorty reason their outlaw friend might want a change of scenery. Having tricked the sheriff, the outlaws break Billings free from jail for $1,000 of the money that was stolen from the café and hidden afterwards. The sheriff's deputy soon hears the sheriff's shouts and a posse is formed immediately. Every trail is blocked while the town itself is searched thoroughly for the escaped outlaw. Even the wagon train camped just outside town was investigated, though with no result. The Lone Ranger and Tonto, however, take out on the trail of the wagon train they suspect might hide the fleeing crook. Billings could not be found, but Duke and Shorty are not dressed like emigrants, giving The Lone Ranger cause to suspect the crook is indeed hiding in one of the wagons. After passing two water holes and never replenishing, The Lone Ranger realizes the crook is hiding in an empty rain barrel. Duke and Shorty, hoping to dispose of their partner, have arranged for the barrel to go over a canyon – unaware the masked man has already removed Billings and replaced the barrel with a few large rocks for weight. Angry for the betrayal, Billings incriminates the two crooks.

Episode #933-158, Broadcast January 18, 1939

Copyright Registration #61,371, script received at Registration Office January 23, 1939.

Plot: See page2 226 to 230.

Episode #934-159, Broadcast January 20, 1939

Copyright Registration #61,321, script received at Registration Office January 19, 1939.

Plot: Eric Badger, the most powerful rancher in all the fertile region surrounding the town of Ashland, agrees to a private deal with Dirk Hawkins, to allow him the spread containing the water holes, in an effort to maintain a stronghold. One week from now the government will open the land for homesteaders. After the emigrants claim the surrounding property, Dirk will sell back the land to Eric for a small price. Eric knows he doesn't have enough men to scare the homesteaders off, nor even enough to send into town to file on the same land. The Lone Ranger, however, recognizes Dirk as the leader of an outlaw gang camped over in the flats. In the meantime, Dirk and his men, by force of arms, stake out the most desirable homesteads, and, when the first of the month arrives, file upon them. Then, on a day when the rush for land has died down, Eric summons his foreman to the ranch house and jubilantly makes ready to carry out the terms of the agreement made with Dirk. Only then does he learn Dirk plans on keeping the homesteads. He and his men filed on every piece of ground that had water on it. The confrontation became heated, momentarily, and when Dirk Hawkins and his gang of outlaws would have added robbery to their treachery, the masked man came to the aid of Eric Badger and, in the midst of gunfire, helped the rancher make his escape. Without access to the water holes, the ranch was useless. The Lone Ranger reminds Eric that while there is little to no law in this part of the country, there is one solution. Since the country was first opened, it was conceded that any rancher finding rustlers on his range can punish them himself. Dirk needs cattle to make use of their property, so The Lone Ranger proposed a scheme against Dirk. Disguising himself as an outlaw, The Lone Ranger rides onto Dirk's property in a scene that appeared as if Eric Badger's men were giving chase. Several days later, Eric, following The Lone Ranger's instructions, sends his men to the ranches of his neighbors, appealing for reinforcements. At length, he gathers a force sufficient to handle the outlaws. Late one night, through coaxing of the disguised Ranger, Dirk's men cut off more than a hundred head of Dot-in-a-Circle cattle in a lonely valley where the fire they had built in which to heat their running irons could not be seen from a distance. With The Lone Ranger amidst the rustlers, he has an advantage over them to allow Eric and his men to race in and smash the operation. Dirk is taken into custody as the head of the cattle rustlers, and The Lone Ranger suggests Eric waste no time getting his men to the land office first thing in the morning to file on the properties that are going to become vacant.

Episode #935-160, Broadcast January 23, 1939

Copyright Registration #61,473, script received at Registration Office January 26, 1939.

Plot: Six men are dead and the only survivor of an Indian ambush near Yellow Creek leaves behind a mysterious trail for The Lone Ranger and Tonto to follow as he walks to Springdale on foot. Dave Fulton, the man, arrives home worn and weary, explaining in detail how he played possum to fool the murdering heathens. Dave even returns with all the gold and paper money from the dead men so their families could get what properly belonged to them. Late one night when Dave goes into town, a crook named Garvey shows up and robs Edna, Dave's wife, then shoots and kills her. Their daughter, Virginia, mistakenly believes it was her father who committed the murder. When a neighbor rides to the sheriff to report the crime, Dave is arrested and charged. The Lone Ranger is certain that Dave Fulton is not guilty of murder, and at the first glimpse of dawn he and Tonto ride to the spot where Dave had been arrested. There they pick up the trail they sought, and Tonto's keen eyes trace it to its end. Later, The Lone Ranger pays a visit to the sheriff to suggest how Dave might have been framed by Garvey, leading to Garvey being placed behind bars until the matter can be straightened out. The sheriff, following a suggestion from the masked man, leaks word that both men remain jailed on suspicion of working together on the killing. The effect is immediate. The news spreads through town like wildfire. The brutality of the crime enrages everyone, and not a half hour after the first report, a mob gathers outside the café demanding justice. Urged on by the bolder spirits, the mob soon advances upon the jail, shouting for the sheriff's two prisoners. The mob cries outside the jail, then comes the sound of the splintering crash of the ram as it was swung by sturdy arms. Tonto, from behind the jail, uses a horse to break the bars from the window and free Dave and Garvey. While the lynch mob breaks into the jail only to find that their intended victims have escaped, Tonto swiftly leads Dave to a secluded spot where they find the masked man and the sheriff waiting. The direction of Garvey's flight has been noted and the crook does not realize he is being tracked. A few miles out, racing to the foot of a tree, Garvey digs up the stolen gold and paper money, but the sheriff, backed by The

Lone Ranger and Tonto, observes him dig up his guilt. Only the thief and the killer could know where the money was hidden.

Episode #936-161, Broadcast January 25, 1939

Copyright Registration #61,474, script received at Registration Office January 26, 1939.

Plot: The great Empire Trading Company has established trading posts throughout the West wherever furs were to be obtained. As the bulk of their trade is of necessity with the Indians, these posts are to be found in the wildest territories where neither rancher nor homesteader have yet penetrated. The Lone Ranger is riding in the district near the Sandy River Post on his way to join his faithful Indian companion, Tonto, at their camp. It's there that he meets Bull Eckert, a scheming trader who, in retaliation of Chief Lame Bear's influence to convince the other redskins to stop trade, kidnaps the chief's son. Despite the sound of war drums and the possible consequences of their actions, with Indians working themselves up to a pitch of revengeful fury, Bull reasserts his blustering bravado. An Easterner named Jim Atkins, having worked with the company for more than a decade, claims he handled the toughest posts, the toughest men, and Indians were nothing to be afraid of. But when the Indians kidnap Jim's son, the possible chance of a trade is stubbornly stalemated. Hoping to make amends between both parties, The Lone Ranger and Tonto try a scheme whereupon Tonto impersonates Lame Bear to the whites and The Lone Ranger impersonates Jim Atkins to the Indians, hoping to make the trade. Acting as a father-in-trade, The Lone Ranger, in disguise, replaces the boy, Dale, who understands the ruse and races back to the trading post to let them know they need to release the Indian boy, so the Indians do not kill his "father" and start a war. When Bull figures the scheme, however, he throws a monkey wrench into the trade – even though all he had to do was release the Indian boy and send him back to his father. Just as the sun seemed to balance on the rim of the horizon at the Indian camp, Tonto shows up with Jim Atkins and the Indian boy. Jim explains how Tonto took over the situation and beat the heck out of Bull to ensure the boy's release. Jim also states that he was sent to check on Bull Eckert, and now he can assure all parties concerned that Bull would be replaced by an honest, competent man as soon as he returned. More importantly, his company would keep the trade with the Indians – a sign of the beginning of real peace in the country.

Episode #937-162, Broadcast January 27, 1939

Copyright Registration #61,475, script received at Registration Office January 26, 1939.

Plot: The new railroad, slowly pushing its steel rails westward, encountered a score of difficulties. Nature itself provided many of the obstacles... but some were born of jealousies and rivalry, and these were not less troublesome than the others. Bruce Abbott, superintendent in charge of construction, would like to get proof against Mike Cavanaugh, owner of the largest fleet of wagon freighters, for supplies stolen, men hit from behind, grub poisoned, and machinery staved in. The Lone Ranger and Tonto observe the latest act of sabotage and blame Bruce Abbott, whose office is in Ogden, Utah. Paul Booth, whose father is general manager of the line, masterminded the acts of sabotage, hiring a crooked breed named Pedro to commit the acts. Paul's father said the minute he proved himself on the job, he would turn over the money that was left to him in his trust by his grandfather. With Abbott fired, Paul would get the job and the trouble would stop and Paul would get all the credit. His latest scheme is to hire Pedro to fix the trestle that was completed a month ago, over Big Pin Canyon, so the passenger train from the East would break through. Five days later and only an hour before the scheduled wreck, Paul receives a telegram stating his father is on that same locomotive. Paul rushes from the office and hurriedly finds several signal flares, then saddles his horse with trembling fingers in the hopes he can prevent the wreck. But Paul was in for a surprise. His actions revealed his guilt – in the presence of his father – because Pedro had been apprehended a couple days prior, and the breed panicked and was forced to tell of the scheme.

Episode #938-163, Broadcast January 30, 1939

Copyright Registration #61,598, script received at Registration Office February 2, 1939.

Plot: Steve Archer, a young man who drives the New London stage line, is known about town for having no more backbone than a rattlesnake. As a coward, he let outlaws hold up his stage without fighting back. The townsfolk shun Steve and will not even give him the time of day. Steve's boss, Barney Evans, assures Steve that the townsfolk will change their minds eventually. Steve is engaged to Barney's daughter, Jean. The Lone Ranger and Tonto, investigating in the area, discover Brick Newman, the owner of the café in town, is the road agent who was robbing the stage. Tonto finds where Brick hid the loot, but with all the evidence against him needed for a conviction, The Lone Ranger decides to help make a man out of Steve. The next evening, The Lone Ranger has a talk with Jean and escorts her up to the second floor of the café, explaining his plan. Tonto, meanwhile, pays a visit to Steve at his campfire, urging him not to leave town in disgrace and handing him a note that states Jean is being held captive in Brick's private office. Infuriated, Steve races back to town and beats up Brick, with The Lone Ranger and Tonto off the side to make sure the crooked café owner does not pull a gun. Steve hurries upstairs to rescue Jean, revealing the safe containing the stolen loot from the stagecoach robbery, and finally ends up earning respect in the eyes of the townsfolk.

Episode #939-164, Broadcast February 1, 1939

Copyright Registration #61,599, script received at Registration Office February 2, 1939.

Plot: A small group of sleek, well-fed businessmen in the East led by a man named Merrick hires a crook named Link Fisher to strike a deal with Fernando Perez, an outlaw referring to himself as a "liberator," who made his headquarters in the mountains beyond the Rio Grande. Perez gathers a band of half-breeds, peons, and crooks from north of the border. So far, he's stood off the troops of two governments. With enough money and arms supplied by the Eastern businessmen, he would have the strength to seize most of the southern basin of the Rio Grande. In exchange, the wealthy will gain control of the finest grazing lands on the continent, the right to develop mines for gold, silver, and mineral rights, and a promise not to interfere with the transportation of gold or cattle north of the border. With a threat to the good relations existing between the United States and Mexico, The Lone Ranger poses as Merrick, who was due to arrive in El Paso by stage. He pays a visit to Perez to verify where his abode is hidden in Spruce Canyon. After being exposed as a fraud, the disguised masked man flees to avoid capture and races to Captain Gonzales, captain of the Mexican dragoons, to report the whereabouts of the "liberators." Upon learning that the captain recently received old guns that would not shoot, as a result of grafting army contractors, the masked man schemes to steal the weapons due to arrive in two weeks for Perez and his outlaw band. Afterwards, The Lone Ranger leads the fierce charge upon the stronghold of the outlaws. Behind him comes Tonto, and behind the Indian, leading his shouting, exultant men, is Captain Gonzales. The battle is soon joined. Perez, desperate, terrified, unable to understand why his weapons did not arrive as scheduled, frantically urges his forces to resistance. For the better part of an hour the fighting rages between soldiers and outlaws. Whenever the need was the greatest, there was the masked man. With the battle won, Captain Gonzales gathered the leader of the conspiracy in the cabin that had belonged to Fernando Perez and faced the real Merrick, who was exposed as financing the outlaws. Gonzales assured the masked man that his government would act through Washington to ensure Merrick and his business associates receive the punishment they deserved.

Episode #940-165, Broadcast February 3, 1939

Copyright Registration #61,600, script received at Registration Office February 2, 1939.

Plot: In a newly created territory, the choosing of a permanent capital faces an unexpectedly vigorous opposition. Arcade, the site of the temporary capital, hoped to retain the honor but a crook named Blake knows if Dundee is voted as the state capital, he will make a fortune. The railroad will build there and his town property will double in value. Three men, influential enough to sway the deciding votes, could not be bought. These included Harry Palmer and Fred Ulrich, ranchers, and Carl Hutton, a banker. Blake hires two crooks, Rip and Max, to hire other outlaws and arrange to make Arcade one of the most lawless towns in the territory, so few would vote for it under any consideration. A crime wave of untold proportion catches the attention of The Lone Ranger and Tonto, who quickly deduce the scheme and go to great lengths to save the life of the sheriff, who was to become victim in the plot. After capturing Rip and Max, the masked man sets out to pay a visit to the influential men and, at the point of a gun, give the appearance that crooks did not want Arcade to be voted as the capital. With reverse psychology applied, the men agree not to vote for Dundee. When the legislature convened for the all-important vote the following day, Arcade won out. In the presence of the sheriff, Rip and Max, afraid of the repercussions from Blake because they were told to do anything and everything to sway the vote, names Blake as the man to whom they took orders from.

Episode #941-166, Broadcast February 6, 1939
Copyright Registration #61,777, script received at Registration Office February 8, 1939.
Plot: The threads of destiny are strangely tangled when a dying young prospector aboard a ship, Luke Ross, gives a map showing a hidden gold mine to young Johnny Thompson. A cockney sailor called Limey overhears the exchange. Later, on the trail to Osage, The Lone Ranger rescues Tonto from the clutches of outlaws Baldy Baker and Ike, but not before Tonto overhears Limey making a deal with those two to go after Johnny Thompson and the gold mine. The Lone Ranger tracks down Johnny and warns him. Johnny finds honest old-timer Silas Hanson, a prospector, and his attractive daughter, Linda. Silas agrees to help guide Johnny into the mountains. The Lone Ranger and Tonto, meanwhile, keep an eye on them from a distance to protect the young man from Limey and his friends. The crooks seize Linda and take her with them as they follow Silas and Johnny into the mountains. Deep into the mountains the two ride, following the clear markings of the map, unaware they are being tailed. After finding the cave of gold and verifying it to be loaded with untold wealth, the Johnny and Silas face off against Limey and Baker who reveal that Linda is in their possession. The Lone Ranger puts in an appearance though to verify that Linda has, in fact, been rescued. Furious that The Lone Ranger ruined their plans in one stroke, Baldy and Limey recklessly spur their mounts to the place where they had left Ike and Linda. Reaching the spot, however, they discover they have been tricked – and trailed by Tonto and The Lone Ranger to make good on Linda's rescue.

Episode #942-167, Broadcast February 8, 1939
Copyright Registration #61,778, script received at Registration Office February 8, 1939.
Plot: Timothy Jordan is being blackmailed for a crime he did not commit. A few years ago, he switched clothes with another man whom he strongly resembled, Hurley, in what he was told would be a practical joke, unaware Hurley robbed the folks in a big house a short time prior. Timothy, whose real name was Douglas Moore, fled the scene. He changed his name then and became a Texas Ranger, now residing outside the town of Fremont with the motherly Kate Rooney. Hurley is now blackmailing the young man because wanted posters for Douglas Moore are circulating. The Lone Ranger and Tonto ride out to catch the stagecoach bound for Excelsior. They meet Hurley and warn the Easterner that it would be advisable for him to return to the East as promptly as possible without putting into effect his plan to collect blackmail. The Lone Ranger also recognizes outlaw Spud Cooper traveling on the stage. The Lone Ranger assigns Tonto to make sure Hurley doesn't go to the Texas Ranger barracks at Excelsior to turn in Jordan. Later, Hurley's dead body is found, having been shot. Tonto tells The Lone Ranger the culprit was Spud Cooper and he had been too far back to prevent it. The masked man has Jordan bring him Hurley's blackmail letters. Following the lead of The Lone Ranger, Tonto rides to fetch Captain Bowers at the barracks in Excelsior, captain of the Texas Rangers. The lawman rides back with Tonto to examine Hurley's body, then meets with The Lone Ranger and Jordan to find the incriminating

letters in the dead man's pocket. The Lone Ranger, hoping to clear Timothy's reputation, claims the dead man was actually Douglas Moore, having assumed the identity of Hurley to hide from the law. Spud Cooper is apprehended and Timothy Jordan is hailed a hero for the actions expected of a Texas Ranger.

Episode #943-168, Broadcast February 10, 1939
Copyright Registration #61,779, script received at Registration Office February 8, 1939.
Plot: Many of the settlers in the Old West, abandoning the restraints of Eastern society, swung too far in the other direction. The town of Freeland was typical of this trend, and the Reverend Sylvester Lamb its chief victim. His meeting house stood virtually empty. His sermons condemning frontier violence were misconstrued to approve cowardice. He was the butt of everyone's jokes but his principal tormentor was young Vic Donlin, son of the wealthy retired rancher, Frank Donlin. The Lone Ranger conspires with Vic's parents to help boost the approval of the townsfolk for the preacher. The Indians nearby are celebrating their harvest ceremonies, banging the drums which oddly put fear into the men and women of town. Frightened by a ceremonial dance, and the attacking redskins (courtesy of the friendly tribe of Chief Thundercloud), men, women and children, urged by the masked man's shouts, scurry as speedily as they can for the Reverend Sylvester Lamb's meeting house. The Indians outnumber the white men three to one, but this does not stop Lamb from volunteering when Tonto, a representative of the Indian tribe, demands one white man come to discuss with the chief. No one else in town braved the trip except Lamb. The Lone Ranger condemned the folks in the meeting house. "There goes the man you said you couldn't respect. The man you sneered at because he preached against fighting. The man you said was a coward, who didn't belong in the West." The townsmen, shamed both by the action of the Reverence Sylvester Lamb and the words of the masked man, watch tamely as the minister rides boldly toward the lines of the assembled braves. The Indians clear out and, afterwards, Vic admits he was a fool for looking down on the preacher, and considers himself half the man Reverend Sylvester Lamb is today.

Episode #944-169, Broadcast February 13, 1939 [PART ONE OF THREE]
Copyright Registration #61,951, script received at Registration Office February 16, 1939.
Plot: See page 235.

Continuity Blooper! The villain is referenced as Miguel Chavez in this episode but referred to as Pancho Chavez throughout the entire next episode.

Episode #945-170, Broadcast February 15, 1939 [PART TWO OF THREE]
Copyright Registration #61,952, script received at Registration Office February 16, 1939.
Plot: See pages 235 and 236.

Episode #946-171, Broadcast February 17, 1939 [PART THREE OF THREE]
Copyright Registration #61,953, script received at Registration Office February 16, 1939.
Plot: See page 236.

Episode #947-172, Broadcast February 20, 1939
Copyright Registration #62,028, script received at Registration Office February 23, 1939.
Plot: At the opening of the Oklahoma territory for the homesteaders, Government troops guard the line over which none may step until the cannon on the morrow booms the signal that will start the great wagons thundering to drive their claim stake over their homestead. Homer Phelps and his wife Hester, emigrants from Illinois, follow Red's lead into Grizzly Valley, but the prime acres of real estate that were promised are already taken. Red's business associate, Bat, offers to sell what was staked for $1,000. The land is magnificent,

as promised, but Homer and Hester were about to be conned out of their money. The Lone Ranger and Tonto intervene, preventing the transaction of cash, and while Tonto keeps everyone at bay, the masked man races away to bring the marshal. Bat and Red insist they only heard of the property prior, but when The Lone Ranger reveals the location of a garden, the marshal realized Red and Bat were sooners in the territory, hoping to pocket extra cash in the process. After the marshal escorts his prisoners away, The Lone Ranger confesses the garden was not there prior, not planted – just transplanted – to give the sooners a position to incriminate themselves.

Notes: This episode opens with the narrator stating the year was 1889. This episode recycled the same radio plot from the broadcast of December 12, 1934.

Episode #948-173, Broadcast February 22, 1939
Copyright Registration #62,029, script received at Registration Office February 23, 1939.
Plot: Half a dozen times Glen Hilton, owner of the Rocking H Ranch, fell victim to cattle thieves, and again an additional hundred head of prime cattle stolen this week. Worse, the thieves shoot the cattle and skin them for hides, leaving the carcasses behind. A smooth crook named Corey assures Hilton that with beef prices the way they are right now, there is no future business except for land – offering $5,000 for Hilton's property that is valued at $50,000. Having stumbled onto two wagons loaded with hides, protected by two crooks dressed from the north, Hank and Wyoming, The Lone Ranger and Tonto suspect Glen Hilton is being squeezed out of his land by their crooked foreman, Brick Roberts, conspiring with Corey. They realize the raids were planned so the hides would have just enough time to reach Longhorn City by wagon and be shipped out from there by train. Following The Lone Ranger's instructions, Glen Hilton signs a $2,000 option from Corey with the promise of not selling the property to anyone else for four weeks. Three weeks later, The Lone Ranger and Tonto stages it so Corey's own cattle are stampeded into Lost Valley where Brick Roberts and his men assume they were stealing more of Hilton's cows. Furious that it was his own cattle and suspecting a double-cross, Corey exchanges words with Hank and Wyoming, clinching their guilt as the sheriff, alongside Hilton and The Lone Ranger, overhear the plot. Brick attempts to get the better of the lawman, but The Lone Ranger shoots the gun out of his hand and terrorizes the cattle to cause the cattle thieves to flee against the narrowing walls of Lost Valley, and be apprehended.

Episode #949-174, Broadcast February 24, 1939
Copyright Registration #62,030, script received at Registration Office February 23, 1939.
Plot: The travelling troupe of players calling themselves the Great Winston Repertoire Company was, in reality, a seedy group of third-rate old-time actors. As it made its way through the rich western mining towns on its journey to San Francisco, the miners, starved for amusement, paid lavishly to enjoy its mildewed plays. In Sumner, the troupe was beginning the second week of an indefinite engagement at the opera house. Carl Meade, a greedy, taciturn crook with a grip against the community, hopes to marry Nora Stevens, the actress who traveled west solely to find her runaway brother. Word on the street is that her brother struck it rich, having discovered a vein of gold ore less than two days journey from town, and Meade's intention is only for his financial convenience. Nora rejects his offer, while The Lone Ranger and Tonto ride out to Bob Stevens' mine and the shack he hastily erected beside its entrance. Young Nora, unaware that her brother, Bob, is in the vicinity, finds that each passing day it is more and more difficult to refuse Meade's offer of marriage. He promises to put his fortune at her disposal that she might locate Bob and her love for her brother tempts her to accept an offer of marriage she would otherwise have not considered. The Lone Ranger visits Nora to provide her with the info about her brother, and how almost everyone in Sumner knew where Bob could be reached, but Meade had threatened anyone who told her. Angry, Meade orders two crooks, Rafe and Smokey, to dry gulch her brother along White Rock Hill. Suspecting a trick, Tonto followed the crooks and learns of the scheme,

then gallops ahead and meets Bob so the two can turn the tables on Meade's hirelings. Back in the sheriff's office, Meade insists Bob met with death at the hands of the masked man – moments before The Lone Ranger introduces himself to the sheriff. Tonto and Bob appear, then, with the two criminals in custody, breaking down Meade's story. The sheriff arrests the three crooks.

Notes: Graser made his initials in a small drawing on the back of his radio script.

Episode #950-175, Broadcast February 27, 1939

Copyright Registration #62,179, script received at Registration Office March 1, 1939.

Plot: It's pure luck that The Lone Ranger and Tonto happen upon the Flynn brothers, Earl, Ted and Chuck, convicted of the murder of Sam Harper, and fled the law. Tonto investigates the crime scene and finds evidence to suggest the men are innocent. To find proof that Banker Kline of Fairmont was responsible for the crime, The Lone Ranger visits Clay Buhler, a former employee of Kline's, who lives with his wife and daughter on a small farm a good six hours' ride from Fairmont. Clay's daughter, Alice, is suffering from fever so The Lone Ranger, Tonto, and the Flynn brothers create a litter to carry the girl to Fairmont to see a doctor. The trip takes a few hours, but the men eventually reach the doctor. The sheriff wants to jail the Flynn brothers, but The Lone Ranger insists to Clay that the men are volunteers and never forced to oblige. Alice needs medical aid and, out of guilt, Clay confesses that he had a sense of loyalty at the time to his employer and lied under oath. Banker Kline had caught Clay stealing and held it over his head, threatening jail. With a dislike towards Sam, Kline committed the crime and forced Clay to lie under oath. During this testimony, Tonto goes out to apprehend, tie, and bind Banker Kline, leaving him on the doorstep for the sheriff.

Episode #951-176, Broadcast March 1, 1939

Copyright Registration #62,180, script received at Registration Office March 1, 1939.

Plot: Sending their horses over the treacherous footing, The Lone Ranger and Tonto race with Jed Barlow, an old-timer, and Anne Barlow, Jed's granddaughter, until they come to the shelter Tonto had found. The area is shielded from the storm by a broad, shelving rock formation, and shelter from a posse in pursuit. Anne's brother,

Dick, operates a wagon freighting company into Oak Grove. Scar Lathrop, a crooked rancher whose house is nestled in the broad valley at the base of the hill where the masked man and Tonto had found shelter, holds Dick captive. Scar and his gang have been selling liquor to the Indians. With the law suspicious of smuggling through the hills from Avoca, they want Dick to use the freighting company to bring in liquor to avoid suspicion. From outside the house, The Lone Ranger shoots the lamp out so he can climb through the window and free Dick from the clutches of Scar. Later, Scar attempts to convince the sheriff that Dick was dealing with a distillery, but the lawman does not believe the story. The Lone Ranger leads the law – and Scar – in a chase to the wagon loaded with alcohol, proving Blacky and Lem were moving it near the marsh to hide the evidence. Rip and Hank, the two crooks working alongside Scar, are also placed under arrest and escorted to the jailhouse.

Episode #952-177, Broadcast March 3, 1939
Copyright Registration #62,310, script received at Registration Office March 8, 1939.
Plot: For months, hundreds of men had been engaged in the construction of a huge dam designed to control the flood waters of the Snake River and divert them to the useful purpose of irrigation. Butler, the cooked superintendent of construction, conspired with Flash Perry, outlaw leader, who infuriated the ranchers into action against the dam. Captain Stanford and his troops had no choice but to abandon their post guarding the huge payroll (estimated $20,000) in order to protect the dam, giving Flash and his gang members, Red and Wolf, an advantage to rob the stagecoach. The men, obeying Flash Perry's commands, had done their work well. The ranchers, convinced that once the dam was built, their range would be flooded by homesteaders, had talked themselves into taking armed action and had appointed the home of one of their number, a rancher named Ed Greene, as a meeting-place. In the meantime, The Lone Ranger had heard of the gathering and accompanied by Tonto, hoped to avert bloodshed. After discussion with Greene fails to thwart the attack against the dam, The Lone Ranger pays a visit to Captain Stanford. The troopers form a line of defense at the dam, expecting hostile ranchers, and instead find themselves talking to the stage driver, who races over to tell them he was robbed by the Flash Perry gang not five minutes after the troopers deserted their protection of the stage. The masked man informs the captain that the margin of time allows for another two hours until the homesteaders arrive, suggesting the uniformed men race out to apprehend the gang heading for Bear Canyon. When the mob arrives, The Lone Ranger forces Butler to confess that the valley was never going to be thrown open to homesteaders by the government, just because the dam was completed. Over in Bear Canyon, Flash and his men realize only too late that the friends who were admitted into the canyon were soldiers in civilian clothes.

Episode #953-178, Broadcast March 6, 1939
Copyright Registration #62,311, script received at Registration Office March 8, 1939.
Plot: King, a crooked rancher in Grove Center, Texas, is the legal guardian of his nephew, Jerry, a young boy. King has been taking advantage of his position until the boy runs away, and the guardian then fears he has to give a full accounting, so he sends crooks Abe and Dell to hunt down the boy. The Lone Ranger and Tonto, riding towards Hillsboro, a small village not far from Grove Center, happen upon the cottage of well-spoken-of, childless, young Widow Martin. They see Jerry outside the cottage. It was obvious, upon introduction, that Jerry was running away from someone. Widow Martin takes Jerry in her care. Almost a week passed. King, Jerry's guardian, expanded the search for the boy but his impatience increased. Widow Martin, meanwhile, learned from Jerry that his crooked uncle killed his father and beat the boy to keep him from talking. Abe, King's henchman, finds and captures Jerry and the widow. Tonto tries to stop Abe but the outlaw knocked out the Indian. When King finally catches up with Jerry, he threatens to whip the boy if he confesses what he knew to anyone. King and Abe kidnap Martin and Jerry. While investigating at the widow's cottage, The Lone Ranger is discovered by the sheriff and posse who accuse the masked man of harming the widow. He escapes the sheriff's arrest by Silver's charge, and takes off to find King with the posse in hot pursuit. He wants the law on hand

when he confronts him, and holds Silver's pace to a speed that permit the lawmen to keep him in sight. The Lone Ranger finds King and Jerry and the posse arrives. During the confrontation, King plays ignorance of the accusation, until the masked man cracks the whip and threatens to use it against King to make him speak – in the same manner the crook used to keep Jerry silent. Tonto, meanwhile, trails Abe and rescues the widow, and testimony from the Widow Martin and Jerry ensures that King and his crooks will hang.

Notes: This episode featured no scene of violence against young Jerry, but there were numerous references to the boy being whipped by King. The suggestion of child abuse was borderline taboo for radio broadcasts, but such taboo was featured once prior – on the broadcast of July 31, 1936.

Episode #954-179, Broadcast March 8, 1939
Copyright Registration #62,312, script received at Registration Office March 8, 1939.
Plot: No sooner does young Bill Tyler return to his father's ranch in Richfield to a joyous reunion than his father assigns him to ride trail herd to Central City. It does not take long for Bill to realize his father is still feuding with the neighboring Wilsons. If the Tylers get their herd to market before the Wilsons, the latter will lose their property. Bill insists there is range enough for both outfits, and having fallen in love with Mary Wilson, Zeke Wilson's granddaughter, insists on helping the rivals. To prove his devotion, Bill offers Zeke to get his herd to Central City before the Tylers', or his services would be provided free. The Lone Ranger and Tonto, realizing the family feud has never come to actual gunfighting but has led to everything else to drive each other off the range, keep tabs on the events as they unfold. On learning his father has a two-day head start, Bill realizes he needs to gamble. One week on the trail, when they reached the point of decision made between the two regular trails, he insists on driving straight ahead into the hills. The men disagree, insisting on going through the canyon like the competition, and fire Bill, who was forced to leave. The Lone Ranger insists Bill is correct because Tonto knows a trail that a herd could follow. Overnight The Lone Ranger, Tonto, and Bill worked swiftly before the trail crew knows of the scheme, with Mary and Zeke bound and placed on their horses. The cowboys discover they are disarmed. Carrying out his part of the masked man's plan, Tonto conveys old Zeke and Mary back to their home under guard. One week later, Bill returns to the Wilson homestead to report that he succeeded in getting their cattle to the market before the Tylers' herd.

Episode #955-180, Broadcast March 10, 1939
Copyright Registration #62,313, script received at Registration Office March 8, 1939.
Plot: Clem Hardy is the proud owner of a fine large ranch house when fire strikes. Having already sold off his stock. he is unable to bank his money before two outlaws, Notch Parsons and Stag Tracy, arrive to steal the cash and set fire to his house. The outlaws flee into the desert but the posse, led by sheriff Jake Whipple, finds it difficult to trail them. Their mounts find it difficult going in the loose, sandy soil. The burning sun overhead reflects from the earth, making the heat doubly intense. After the posse is forced to turn back, The Lone Ranger and Tonto follow the tracks to discover the outlaws went in not on mules or cattle, but on camels. Almost three weeks go by after The Lone Ranger talked with the sheriff to plot a scheme to capture the outlaws. The masked man consults Clem to ask him to join them in their quest, promising the reward money would him afford a new home. Late that night, Simon Bates, the same man who was so loud in his denunciation of the sheriff at the time Clem Hardy had been robbed, works alongside the outlaws to map another robbery. But when the robbery goes off and the sheriff realizes he needs to apprehend them this time or face turning in his badge, the lawman takes off in pursuit. In the desert, The Lone Ranger, Tonto, the sheriff, and Clem apprehend the outlaws because The Lone Ranger knows of their secret. Having gotten to the camels beforehand, The Lone Ranger and his friends prevent the outlaws from making a successful escape across the desert.

Episode #956-181, Broadcast March 13, 1939

Copyright Registration #62,427, script received at Registration Office March 15, 1939.

Plot: The Lone Ranger, disguised, is present among others in the cafe at Aurora, a mining-town, when two young men, Jim Graves and Bob Holt, excitedly enter. Both give evidence of many days spent in the hills prospecting. They had struck gold in the hills of Painted Rocks. But when The Lone Ranger examines their sample, he assures the prospectors that they found silver, not gold. The fire assay suggested by the masked man proves to Bob and Jim the truth of his statements. The specimen of ore they had brought to town was rich in silver. When, on top of this, they learn that two crooks named Lucky and Hardrock have been seen on the trail to Turtle Creek, the last of their doubt disappeared. In a rage at the trick played upon them, the two young men hastened back to the district and started an intensive search for the ledge from which the ore had come. A week later, when young Jim Graves arrives at the office of the county clerk in the town of Aurora to file upon the claim discovered by himself and his partner he is met with the charge of murder. The sheriff, paying no attention to Jim's protests, takes the young man to the county jail. Hardrock has been killed and Lucky claims Jim pulled the trigger. When The Lone Ranger learns of Jim Graves' danger, he rejoins Tonto outside town and races toward the distant claim where Bob Holt, unaware of what all had happened, was awaiting Jim's return. Silver and Scout, urged on by their masters, rode out to meet Bob. This would not be the first time men have murdered for wealth, The Lone Ranger rationalizes. Bob quickly agrees to carry through with the masked man's plan. When the sheriff and Lucky arrive, Bob puts up no resistance and agrees to ride back to town. Overnight at the campfire, Bob and Lucky have a discussion and Lucky is tricked into confessing the crime, unaware The Lone Ranger and the sheriff are listening from a short distance away.

Episode #957-182, Broadcast March 15, 1939

Copyright Registration #62,428, script received at Registration Office March 15, 1939.

Plot: Baldy Gordon, and his gunmen, Trigger and Gus, sneak into Fort Stevens overnight, switching the gunpowder and ammunition for gravel and sand. Tonto, catching the men in the act, is ambushed from behind, bound, gagged, and taken away before sunrise. A cavalcade consisting of two wagons and an escort of a dozen troopers, leaves the town of Lake Falls and begins the ascent through the lesser foothills into the Pipestone Hills. Members of the United States Army ride beside the wagons. They make good time on their first day, and when they camp that night, they are already on the edge of that stretch most favored by the Apache for their attacks. Everyone in the party draws confidence from the fact that they are impregnable to attack. But attack was sure to come. After the first sudden burst of firing, the attackers seem satisfied to assume positions of safety behind the innumerable boulders of either hand and snipe at the party on the trail at their leisure. Only during the heat of the battle when the soldiers need to reload do they discover the ammunition is missing. Just as the soldiers were forced to club their attackers, the arriving cavalry could be seen from the distance. With numbers in their favor, our heroes know they will prevail. The Lone Ranger later explains that Baldy Gorman captured Tonto and took him prisoner. Tonto's horse led the masked man to the place where he had been caught, then it was simply a matter of trailing Tonto until he found him. Tonto informed his friend about the ammunition being stolen and it was clear what was being planned. Upon closer inspection of the prisoners, the Major discovered that the white men were made to look like redskins. The renegade whites discovered the hard way that when the firing squad went through its work, there was one band of outlaws that had ridden upon its last raid.

Episode #958-183, Broadcast March 17, 1939

Copyright Registration #62,429, script received at Registration Office March 15, 1939.

Plot: Deke Brady and Lobo Lawson, two outlaw leaders, have ganged up and rustled cattle three times and succeeded in making Mike Rafferty, the sheriff of Columbus County, look like a fool. Tonto, overhearing a conversation in the local café, is almost arrested by the sheriff who insists the redskin is wanted by the law. He's rescued by an outlaw named Fritz. Racing away from the law, Tonto follows his new friend across the country toward a distant line of hills whose approach is marked by a belt of forest. At the outlaws' camp, he meets the men responsible for the recent rash of rustling. Later, in the camp of The Lone Ranger, Tonto reveals to his friend how he became an honorary member of the gang, which gives the masked man an "inside" to helping apprehend the outlaws. A few days later, Lobo Lawson agrees with Deke Brady upon the time when the two gangs should again attack, this time to intercept the Brunswick stage. The Lone Ranger tempts Lobo with bigger game – every man is prepared to defend the stagecoach based on recent events, leaving the town bank unprotected. The Lone Ranger had told the truth when he assured Lobo Lawson that the sheriff had left Brunswick with every man he could muster. What he neglects to tell, however, is that the sheriff, after leading his party out of sight, has circled back. With his men, he has taken a position in a deep gully which, while hiding them, permits them to watch all who approach town. The ambush is swift and Deke, discovering he is not backed by strength in numbers, is also forced to surrender on his end. The sheriff laughs when he confesses that he knew of the masked man's plan, even falsely accusing Tonto of a crime he never committed so that the outlaws would believe Tonto was worthy of induction to their gang.

Episode #959-184, Broadcast March 20, 1939 [PART ONE OF THREE]
Copyright Registration #62,636, script received at Registration Office March 29, 1939.
Plot: See pages 244 and 245.

Episode #960-185, Broadcast March 22, 1939 [PART TWO OF THREE]
Copyright Registration #62,637, script received at Registration Office March 29, 1939.
Plot: See page 245.

Episode #961-186, Broadcast March 24, 1939 [PART THREE OF THREE]
Copyright Registration #62,638, script received at Registration Office March 29, 1939.
Plot: See page 246.

Notes: This script was originally slated for broadcast on March 27, 1939. This episode recycled material from the broadcast of April 30, 1937.

Episode #962-187, Broadcast March 27, 1939
Copyright Registration #62,639, script received at Registration Office March 29, 1939.
Plot: This was the same script from the broadcast of September 23, 1936.

Episode #963-188, Broadcast March 29, 1939 [PART ONE OF TWO]
Copyright Registration #62,811, script received at Registration Office April 6, 1939.
Plot: This was the same script from the broadcast of December 30, 1935, which was originally part of a four-part story arc from 1935 to 1936. The script was performed perhaps too verbatim, as The Lone Ranger makes reference to having ordered the lawyer, Jasper Wellington, to leave in a prior adventure, but that did not happen in this three-part story arc.

Episode #964-189, Broadcast March 31, 1939 [PART TWO OF TWO]
Copyright Registration #62,812, script received at Registration Office April 6, 1939.
Plot: This was the same script from the broadcast of January 31, 1936.

Episode #965-190, Broadcast April 3, 1939

Copyright Registration #62,813, script received at Registration Office April 6, 1939.

Plot: Arizona Lawson, a professional bounty hunter and good friend of The Padre, roams the west with his pet dog, hunting down killers wanted by the law. The Padre introduces Arizona to The Lone Ranger hours before The Lone Ranger races to stop a runaway stagecoach robbed by a highwayman. A passenger is shot dead during the holdup and his widow, Ms. Whipple, suspects her banker husband was the intended target – not the gold shipment on board. Her husband exchanged words with Sam Snead, Ben Hawkins, and Windy Holten, all of whom held grudges for various reasons. Lafe, the stage driver, could not identify the masked highwayman. Later, Arizona Lawson wanders into town and is quickly accused of the crime. The sheriff keeps the peace by jailing the traveling gunman, while The Lone Ranger sets out to learn the identity of the guilty man. During routine questioning of the prisoner, in the presence of witnesses, someone shoots Arizona from the window. A posse takes off after the shooter, unaware that they are being led to the scene of the crime. There, Tonto explains that he never really shot Lawson, and with a mob of witnesses present, suggests they allow Arizona's dog to sniff the area. After all, the canine can smell out the killer. Panicking, Windy gives himself away and attempts to climb a tree to evade the barking dog. The Lone Ranger and Tonto share a laugh as they reveal that it was the carcass of a wolf, not Windy, that the dog went after.

Episode #966-191, Broadcast April 5, 1939

Copyright Registration #62,814, script received at Registration Office April 6, 1939.

Plot: The Gold King Mine is one of the largest ore workings in the vicinity of Pine Bluffs. It employs an extensive crew and the mine itself is composed of a dozen tunnels radiating from a central shaft. The frustration of young Dave Muncie, the foreman, comes to a peak after an explosion occurs. One of the miners, Bart, has been a troublemaker ever since he was hired. He talks others in the crew into disobeying orders. Worse, the crew sides with Bart when Dave punches him to the ground and accuses him of setting the explosion. The Lone Ranger saves Dave's life from a retaliatory mob and Dave finds himself fired. Amos Potter, the owner of the mine, may have to sell as a result of the recent handicaps. Potter and Dave meet with Colby, an interested buyer. Hoping to prove Colby is a crook attempting to gain possession of Potter's mine, The Lone Ranger steals the money intended for purchase of the mine, then sends Dave to the sheriff with the cash to ask him to visit the mine to unearth the real culprit. Meanwhile, with the assistance of Tonto, the masked man arranges for Potter, Colby, and Wilkins to ride to the Gold Nugget Mine, under protest, of course. With a professional assayer to examine the gold, it is verified that Colby's mine was played out and he has been stealing ore from Potter's. Colby had arranged for the manager, Wilkins, to create acts of sabotage, along with Bart. Exposed, the sheriff takes Colby and Wilkins in while it is clearly understood the money in Colby's bank account belongs to Potter – it was his gold, after all. As for Dave, he is re-hired, now promoted to a manager.

Notes: The first few pages of this script recycled elements (including narration) from the broadcast of June 3, 1933.

Episode #967-192, Broadcast April 7, 1939

Copyright Registration #62,815, script received at Registration Office April 6, 1939.

Plot: Bruce Andrews, U.S. marshal for the district, enters the cafe at Long Prairie to question Ray Carter, whose brother recently bought the Arrowhead Ranch, north of Pike City. Ray recently arrived from the East to help his brother. It's through the marshal that Ray learns the sad news: his brother was robbed and murdered on route. Later that afternoon, when The Lone Ranger stops at Luke Dailey's ranch and boarding house for a meal, the masked man questions some of Dailey's unscrupulous tenants in the hopes of learning who might have killed Ray's brother. When the marshal arrives and finds the stolen money in a saddle bag draped over Silver, The Lone Ranger realizes he's been framed. After making a steadfast escape, The Lone Ranger discovers

Luke has been placed under arrest on suspicion of scheming with the masked man. It was Luke who, out of an act of self-preservation, implicated The Lone Ranger in the killing of Bat Carter. It's decided by the sheriff and the marshal that Luke's trial will be held in Pike City and that immediately afterward he would be taken away to the safety of Long Prairie. That night, however, the masked man puts his suspicions to the proof by capturing Ray. Several times he and Tonto barely avoid search parties on their way back. The next day, the jury, hastily drawn, listens to the swift presentation of evidence against Luke and The Lone Ranger, with minds already determined upon their guilt. Before a verdict can be delivered, The Lone Ranger barges in to the courtroom and, in the presence of Judge Lambert, brings in his proof that Luke conspired with the killer. Bat is alive and well and was masquerading as his brother Ray – only there never was a brother – except in name only.

Episode #968-193, Broadcast April 10, 1939 [PART ONE OF TWO]

Copyright Registration #62,918, script received at Registration Office April 12, 1939.

Plot: This was the same script from the broadcast of February 26, 1934, with a few revisions: Caleb Fussby was renamed Caleb Bixby, and his wife Annie was renamed Sara. In the 1934 rendition, The Lone Ranger sung a song with his guitar, which was not included in the 1939 version.

Notes: This was the first of a two-part story. The second part would air four days later, which would normally be unusual except for the fact that Striker considered the second adventure to be a continuation with a recurring character, not necessarily a cliffhanger that needed to be concluded on the very next broadcast.

Episode #969-194, Broadcast April 12, 1939

Copyright Registration #62,919, script received at Registration Office April 12, 1939.

Plot: This was the same script from the broadcast of March 16, 1933, with one change: the town of Sleep Creek was changed to Eagle Grove.

Episode #970-195, Broadcast April 14, 1939 [PART TWO OF TWO]

Copyright Registration #63,099, script received at Registration Office April 20, 1939.

Plot: Money lender Taylor, who holds the mortgage on Caleb Bixby's homestead, will not extend the loan and demands the $5,000 owed by six o'clock tomorrow or Caleb must vacate. Caleb calls on an old friend, Jim Barton, who lives in another town, to borrow the money in return for less interest than Taylor demands. Jim agrees, unaware that Squint plans to rob Caleb on the ride back. In the local café, Tonto overhears the plot between Squint and Taylor, and reports the news to The Lone Ranger. When the sheriff catches the masked man examining papers in the bank late one night, he realizes a plot against the crooked money lender and agrees to play along. While riding back home the next day, Caleb is robbed of the envelope he received from Jim Barton. At six o'clock promptly, Taylor shows up at Caleb's homestead insisting on payment or eviction. In the presence of the sheriff, Caleb makes good on payment, thanks to The Lone Ranger. It seems the masked man convinced Jim to switch envelopes earlier in the day. What Squint stole was not the money – cinching his guilt. Taylor, accused of hiring Squint, surrenders the mortgage to Taylor in return for full payment, to avoid being placed under arrest.

Notes: This episode recycled the plot featured in the broadcasts of March 21, 1933, and June 7, 1935, with The Padre incorporated in the beginning of this story.

Episode #971-196, Broadcast April 17, 1939

Copyright Registration #63,100, script received at Registration Office April 20, 1939.

Plot: It is almost midnight in Sioux Springs, but Wolf Snyder's Last Chance Café is still going at full blast when a rancher named Bert Walker claims in front of witnesses that Dan Bowman stampeded his trail herd before he could make delivery. The two share a government contract. Bowman denies the charges. An exchange of gunfire would have resulted in the death of one – or both – men, but The Lone Ranger shoots the lights out before blood can be shed. Thorne, who wants the same contract, conspires with Jake and Wolf. Later, The Lone Ranger pays a late-night visit to Thorne to rationalize a better proposal than the one Wolf had masterminded. Throwing a scare into the two cattlemen, driving them out by giving them the choice of giving up their contract or losing their lives, would be better. After all, Thorne is the only other person in the county who had a spread large enough to get the contract and suspicions would have fallen on him eventually. For the promised payment of $500 the masked man agrees to bring the two cattlemen to Eagle Rock, blindfolded, so the scare tactic can be applied. Thorne agrees but, later, in private with Wolf, Thorne confesses he knew the outlaw was none other than The Lone Ranger and more than likely the scheduled confrontation would lead to the law overhearing the conversation and placing them under arrest. Hoping to trick the masked man, Thorne plans to shoot and kill the two men in transit from The Lone Ranger's well-concealed camp to Eagle Rock… unaware the Indian he hired to track the masked man to his camp was none other than Tonto. Late that night the outlaw, Jake, leads a half dozen horsemen to the halfway rendezvous to commit the brutal act. But the two men Jake grabbed and beat up were none other than Thorne and Wolf. Earlier in the day, The Lone Ranger captured the crooks, switched them into rancher clothes, and put sacks over their heads. Jake apologizes, assuming they are Walker and Bowman, as in the original plan. The vocal exchange creates a fallout – long enough for a U.S. marshal to overhear the plot and take the guilty culprits into custody.

Episode #972-197, Broadcast April 19, 1939
Copyright Registration #63,101, script received at Registration Office April 20, 1939.
Plot: It is evening when old Silas Hoffman, sheriff of Kings County, drives into his yard to meet The Lone Ranger. Silas is thrown from a horse and injured, preventing him from fulfilling his duties. He is disappointed that his deputies have not been able to outwit Lynch, operating a crooked gambling hall. Yielding to the arguments of his wife Abby, and The Lone Ranger, the old sheriff grants the masked man permission to tell his son, Jerry, of his predicament. Cripple Creek is a long way from Kingston, the county seat of Kings County, but weeks later, Jerry is found dead in a gulch beside a trail. Breed, working for Lynch, falsely claims Bob Keller's knife and spur were found at the scene. Bob Keller files to run for sheriff in the upcoming election and Lynch hopes to convince Keller to work for him – in return for enough votes to sure up the election. Keller insists it was a fair fight and not murder, but his innocence would never be believed. Lynch is clever enough to realize that in spite of his power, the majority of the county's citizens dislike him. He realizes also that they would inevitably suspect whatever candidate for sheriff he endorses. Therefore, to swing public favor towards Bob Keller, Lynch openly speaks for the crippled Silas Hoffman. Never in the history of the county has an election aroused so much interest. Unknown to the crowd that later celebrated Bob Keller's victory, Lynch was to be foiled. The Lone Ranger ropes the crook while Bob Keller announces his first duty would be to arrest Lynch. In retaliation, Lynch announces he has evidence against Keller for the murder of Jerry Hoffman. But Lynch is in for a surprise. There was no murder – Lynch faked the evidence because Bob Keller is really Jerry Hoffman, who also saved family face by taking on the mantle his father had proudly held.

Episode #973-198, Broadcast April 21, 1939
Copyright Registration #63,102, script received at Registration Office April 20, 1939.
Plot: Young Frank Sturgis and his wife, Bess, are recent arrivals in Silver City, coming there from the East. One of Frank's first acquaintances is a man named Price who sells them valley property for $1,000. The Lone Ranger is in the café at the time and, witnessing Stag Wilder pretending to be under the influence of liquor, suspects foul play. Frank and his wife take possession of the property, an arid, sandy valley, worthless for either farming

or grazing, but the hills on both sides had yielded silver. At first Frank is certain a vein of the precious mineral must underlie his land. Hard work, however, coupled with certain remarks dropped in town, reveal to Frank that he has been swindled. Frank pays a visit to the two schemers but the confrontation only leads to Frank being beaten up and thrown into the streets. Several days pass and early one afternoon Lige, a known prospector, seeking shelter from the gradually rising wind that filled the air with dust, enters the café. Lige claims he wants liquid hospitality on the property but is ordered off at the point of a gun. Before he leaves, he witnesses crates of equipment being brought in. Later, in the café, Frank shows up and pays for everyone's drinks with $50 in gold. Frank leaves mysteriously enough to lure Stag and Price into the valley. The Lone Ranger orders them off the property. Stag insists he has a 30-day option to buy back the land, but it's clear the masked man cannot be bought. Stag and Price race back to town, believing Frank has struck oil. They get together enough money to exercise Stag's option. They even enlist the support of the sheriff. The next morning the men pay a visit to Frank's property and, in desperation to convince Frank to sell, offer $2,000. After the agreement is signed and legal, the truth is revealed. Frank had put guards around the property to make it look as though he had struck it rich – there is no gold or oil. The sheriff admits Price and Stag were outwitted.

Episode #974-199, Broadcast April 24, 1939

Copyright Registration #63,200, script received at Registration Office April 26, 1939.

Plot: Abe and Limpy, notorious gunmen who were led by Two-Gun Haley, send a false telegram to arrange for the Eastbound and Westbound to crash into each other. The former carries a gold shipment. The Lone Ranger and Tonto, arranging for an old woman to board one of the trains bound for Sierra City so she can visit a doctor, inadvertently discover Haley's ruse. With the trains due to collide on the other side of Valley Junction, The Lone Ranger races from Grantsburg in an attempt to intercept one of the trains. The sheriff in Grantsburg is unable to prevent the disaster from his end because Two-Gun cut the telegraph wires. With the guards firing at the masked man for assuming he was a gold robber, The Lone Ranger braves the terrain and the bullets to alert the conductor. When the train is finally halted, Two-Gun Haley boards to force the trains to wreck in despite of the new developments. In the meantime, Tonto returns to Grantsburg, alerting the sheriff, who calls on a group of men to race for the point where they feel a collision is inevitable. While the masked man and the train guards cut off the flight of Two-Gun and his men in the one direction, the sheriff sweeps down upon the outlaws from the other. The outlaws, turning in desperation, attempt to deal with this new threat. But, hopelessly outnumbered, it does not take them long to realize the futility of resistance. They throw down their arms and surrender.

Episode #975-200, Broadcast April 26, 1939

Copyright Registration #63,201, script received at Registration Office April 26, 1939.

Plot: When Sally Gardner's parents died, she was left penniless and forced to make her living in the only way open to her... as a singer in Bull Kirby's café in the town of Wheeler. A U.S. marshal named Bill and a young rancher named Ted vie for her hand. Sally is unable to decide between the two – even when Bill speaks ill of young Ted and assures Sally that her employer is behind a lot of criminal action in these parts. Figuring the marshal has evidence against him, Bull Kirby plots the lawman's murder – and that of young Ted. (Should Sally run off and marry Ted, Bull would lose a lot of business.) Bull tricks Ted into a heated exchange with the lawman, in the presence of witnesses, setting up what would be a viable murder of Bill, with Ted accused of the crime. Gunfights to settle disputes were common, but in this case a challenge is offered and accepted, and a definite time and place named for the event – eight o'clock in the morning, in the streets, where all can witness the exchange, and a restless gallery would gather from every direction, standing at a safe distance. Tonto, pretending to be asleep in the café, overhears Kirby's plan with Dirk – the latter of whom would hide from a distance and shoot both Ted and Bill at the same time the shootout takes place to ensure both are killed. Late that night, The Lone Ranger rides to Ted's ranch house and carries the young man away. He then whisks Bill away. Tied up and held captive at the secluded camp, The Lone Ranger substitutes the real bullets in their guns with blanks. Working alongside Judge Wilson, the masked man explains his plan and arrives promptly at eight o'clock. The Lone Ranger publicly explains how he kept both men prisoner overnight, how both men were convinced their gun held real bullets, and how blanks were cleverly substituted. The men would arrive a few minutes late, but the exchange will go on as planned. The judge agreed with the masked man that both the marshal and Ted were fine men, the kind of men the West needed. They should not be allowed to kill each other over a misunderstanding. After they shoot it out, and neither one is hurt, maybe they will come to their senses. The judge, however, is a tad perplexed when Bull Kirby changes his stance and insists the duel not be held. Bull flees the scene in an attempt to prevent Dirk from pulling the triggers, only to have his plot exposed in front of witnesses. Dirk, however, is furious. Dirk explains to his boss how Tonto took his gun away and prevented what would have been a shooting. Ted and Bill make up, agreeing that jealousy does not become them.

Episode #976-201, Broadcast April 28, 1939

Copyright Registration #63,202, script received at Registration Office April 26, 1939.

Plot: Sam Wheeler is one of those unfortunate men consistently pursued by bad luck. He and his wife, Bertha, and their crippled daughter, Molly, occupy a small shack on a poverty-stricken homestead. The day comes when Sam, brooding over the poverty from which there seemed no relief, makes an important decision. Having learned crooks committed a robbery and made off with a ton of cash, Sam covers his face with a crude mask, and puts on dirty clothes that would keep him from being identified, and robs storekeeper Jeff Higgins. The Lone Ranger, however, pays Sam a visit three days later, takes the money and promises to return it – with complete understanding that not everyone who steals is an evil person. Jeff figures out it was Sam Wheeler who robbed him. The sheriff quickly discovered to his distaste that his party had been swelled to the size of a posse when the news rapidly circulates through town that Sam Wheeler is to be arrested. The Lone Ranger calls on an old friend, Martin Whitby, a public figure in town who commanded respect. The posse, however, dies down moments after they arrive at the Wheeler homestead. Whitby hands Sam a check for $300 and informs him that they can pay it off with a job on one of his ranches. Such charity extinguishes the fire in the eyes of the posse members, especially when they learn at the same time that the money stolen from Jeff was returned. Sam had his punishment – the fear of punishment that he must have suffered since the day he stole.

Episode #977-202, Broadcast May 1, 1939

Copyright Registration #63,326, script received at Registration Office May 1, 1939.

Plot: Glen Jordan is found guilty of the murder of Asa Sampson, a wealthy resident of Santa Rosa who was recently murdered. While sweating behind bars, Jordan awaits the 10th of August where he will be hanged by the neck. The Lone Ranger asks him to have faith until he brings Tonto back with evidence that will clear him of the crime of which he was falsely accused. Two criminals, Turk (a redskin), and Sig, are hired by Lefty Sampson, son of Asa, to catch and kidnap Tonto, who has the evidence against the crooked Lefty. Arizona's dog picks up the trail of the outlaws into a valley and a camp in the hills. The sheriff follows and, during a confrontation, the masked man explains how Lefty killed his father, making it look as though Jordan was guilty. Pike Nugent was a witness to the crime. Pike is south of the border but Lefty wants him killed because to ensure his silence. Tonto is kidnapped because he knew this. The Indian is freed and verifies The Lone Ranger's story, with the promise to bring Pike back across the border to testify in person, clearing the name of Glen Jordan.

Notes: This script was originally scheduled for the broadcast of April 28, 1939.

Episode #978-203, Broadcast May 3, 1939

Copyright Registration #63,327, script received at Registration Office May 1, 1939.

Plot: Silver and Scout, guided by their masters, swerve from the trail and plunge towards a dim, flickering beacon from a cave in the distance. They are riding through the broken, hilly country in the vicinity of Spanish Springs. Before they arrived, a man flees the scene, leaving behind the body of a dead man, shot twice. Inside the cave, the masked man and Tonto discover a secret passageway built either by the Spaniards or the Aztecs. Promising to come back to investigate at a later time they head out to find the trail of the horseman who left the cave just before their arrival before it grows cold. Two crooks named Red and Nick show up at the cave and set up kegs of blasting powder to blow up the entrance when the masked man returns. In town, The Lone Ranger and Tonto meet Sheriff Kate Peters, both masculine and competent, because she insisted upon assuming her husband's office and finding his murderer after he was killed. When The Lone Ranger meets with Benson, described as the type to use his gun instead of his head, explaining how he trailed the killer back to town from the cave. He plays the role of an outlaw and promises to reveal to Benson the secret inside the cave in return for a percentage of the profits – otherwise he would report Benson to the sheriff. When The Lone Ranger and Benson arrive and enter the cave, Nick and Red set off the blast which shakes the tunnel. At this signal that their work was completed, the crooks take to the trail. Two hours on brought them to a group of century-old buildings originally constructed by a Spanish owner. There, the mastermind named Foley, who has been smuggling dope over the border, gleefully cheers when learning Benson was also killed or trapped in the cave. The Lone Ranger and Benson then appear, having followed their way through the secret tunnel which had been used to cover the tracks for the smuggling operation. The guard in the cave was killed to eliminate equal distribution of profits. Benson, believing he was betrayed by his employer, assists the masked man with the apprehension. Sheriff Kate shows up, thanks to Tonto, to place the men under arrest – the same men responsible for the murder of her husband.

Notes: This was the first time a female sheriff was featured on the radio program.

Episode #979-204, Broadcast May 5, 1939

Copyright Registration #63,328, script received at Registration Office May 1, 1939.

Plot: Eric Hyde, owner of the Half Circle C Ranch, lodges a complaint to Sheriff Matt Gorman in the small town of Delta. Suspicion falls on two men, Deke Bowers and Rusty Clemsen, when, every time there are cows stolen, Rusty is conveniently unavailable. Rusty is the brother of Brad Clemsen, a man who escaped from jail after being convicted of the murder of Enoch Kinsey. Deke was just no good. Through Tonto, the sheriff asks The Lone Ranger to help. Although puzzled, the sheriff and Eric obey the masked man to the letter and spread word that in 24 hours the cattle rustler would be apprehended. Soon Delta was buzzing with the news that The Lone Ranger would find the man responsible for the rustling of Half Circle C stock. Playing the role of detective, the masked man arranges for Deke to be arrested by the sheriff. This buys time for the masked man to figure out how someone else could have shot at him and escaped – unlike Deke who would have had a clear shot. Three days later, The Lone Ranger figures where the rustlers stole half of the Half Circle C Ranch, and this time they did not take the cattle through the hills to the south as they usually do. The sheriff later tells Rusty that Brad has been found, and Brad is bringing to town evidence that will clear him of the murder charge. When Rusty Clemsen left the sheriff's office so hurriedly, he speedily made his way to his own horse, mounted, and set it racing from town. He headed toward a rough, wild country that opened at last to a narrow clearing in which stood a sagging cabin. There, he questions Brad about the evidence, only to discover this was a lure for Eric, the real murderer, who wants the evidence for himself. Eric is not only the murderer of Enoch Kinsey, but also the rustler of his own cattle. He owned another ranch across the hills, the Circle O Ranch. The first ranch belongs to the bank, and he made only the first payment. In the meantime, he planned to strip the range of cattle, rebrand it with the Circle O, then give up the Half Circle C with the excuse rustlers had run him out of business. Eric Hyde made his mistake by stating $6,000 was stolen from Enoch even though no one knew how much money had been stolen.

Episode #980-205, Broadcast May 8, 1939

Copyright Registration #63,421, script received at Registration Office May 8, 1939.

Plot: Mac Macklin, a pony express rider spurring his fleet mount toward distant Leesberg, is shot from ambush. Attracted by the shot, The Lone Ranger and Tonto find the body – and the killer, Duffy. But without evidence that would cinch a conviction, the masked man plays dumb and asks Duffy to ride into town to alert the authorities of the murder. The Lone Ranger would assume responsibility for the pouch. Knowing their word would not convict him, The Lone Ranger and Tonto find a way to prove his guilt. Alone, Tonto confides that Mac is not dead – he lied to trick Duffy. Mac confesses that Martha Weaver and her bedridden husband, Fred, were told by Mr. Whitlock that they could work his mine in Leesburg, for the season, but Duffy claims Whitlock told him he could work the place. The letter from Sheriff Hicks contained an affidavit from Whitlock stating Duffy has no rights. The Lone Ranger promises to deliver the letter. The masked man finds no difficulty, however, in eluding Sheriff Hicks' hastily formed posse and the sheriff himself is convinced of the futility of the chase almost before he started. Days later, an eviction notice is read but The Lone Ranger steals it from the sheriff to buy time for Martha and Fred. In the meantime, Tonto moves the young Mac Macklin to a camp in the nearby woods. With infinite cautions he probes for the bullet, sterilizes the wound when the bullet was extracted, and skillfully applies bandages. Days later, Duffy and Sheriff Hicks reach Fred and Martha's home and once again attempt to issue an eviction. This time Duffy's plan fails when the masked man and Indian bring in Mac Macklin, alive and willing to testify against Duffy. At The Lone Ranger's suggestion, the sheriff jails the crook on a charge of attempted murder. Between now and the time of his trial, he can write to Whitlock and get a reply that will validate Martha and Fred's story.

Episode #981-206, Broadcast May 10, 1939

Copyright Registration #63,422, script received at Registration Office May 8, 1939.

Plot: Old Jason Courtney arrived in Texas as a young man and now, in his seventies, commands a rangeland empire. He counts his cattle not by the hundreds but by the thousands; estimates his land not by the acre but by the square mile. Now, however, and for several months past, his health was failing. Old Jason, overcome by the excitement of his elder son Jim's return home, is stricken by a heart attack from which he rallied only feebly upon the doctor's arrival. His one thought, when he knew his end was near, was to make a will in favor of Jim, through whom he hoped to perpetuate the family name. Blake, the younger of the two brothers, is sent to town to summon a lawyer for the purpose when he meets up with The Lone Ranger. Tonto and the masked man promise to return a young boy to his parents, aware that Jim was attempting to masquerade as a married man with a young son that really was not his. Once through a trick they are shot at and just miss being killed. Later they lose time when they find they have traded horses and were following the wrong men. This put Blake into a bizarre situation. Either he save the ranch for himself, and sadden his father while he is on his deathbed, or permit his father to believe he really has a grandchild and lose what is rightfully his. The crooked son discovers the hard way, though, that the printed will left the ranch to Blake. It seems Tonto sent for a different lawyer the other day to make sure the crooked son would not inherit.

Notes: The radio script indicated that the role of the elderly rancher, Jason Courtney, be played like "the Lionel Barrymore type."

Episode #982-207, Broadcast May 12, 1939

Copyright Registration #63,423, script received at Registration Office May 8, 1939.

Plot: When Bat Freeman, whose ranch is just outside Western Flats, learns that attacking Indians took everything from a freight company that was meant for the town, he panics, ordering his foreman Jake to visit all the general stores and buy up all the supplies before anyone else learns what happened. The Lone Ranger, in one of the general stores at the time of a major purchase, confesses to Tonto that while Freeman has a right to buy those provisions, and a legal right to demand whatever price he wants to ask for, he has a moral right not to ask for too high a price. The sheriff must back him up, but the people could start a riot and end up with bloodshed. The masked man did not overestimate the seriousness of the situation. Half the town, with the sheriff in the lead, rides to Bat's ranch house. There they dismount and gather before the front porch. Emotions become heated and The Lone Ranger intervenes, promising the mob that within two days wagons will reach Western Flats, with all the food they need. Later, Bat Freeman realizes the only wagons that could approach town would have to come from the East. With his plan momentarily foiled, he orders Jake to choose a half dozen men and prevent their arrival. When they attack, the masked criminals discover that the wagons are empty – decoys. The real wagons loaded with provisions took the hill trail, a different trail from the east. When Jake returns to report to his employer, Bat is furious. With no other option, the supplies are loaded on wagons and taken back to town. Bat claims he wants to make good on his attempt to profit and sell the goods back at the cost he paid, with no profit intended. But The Lone Ranger barges in to intervene. "Don't buy on his terms!" the masked man suggested. "He attempted to cheat you! The law can't punish him! But he would be fittingly punished if he were to take a loss!" Bat knew the provisions would rot before he could use them himself, so in desperation he offered to sell at half the asking price. The Lone Ranger ensured the sheriff was around to witness the bargain. Just after the deal was made, the impending wagon train arrived in town looking to buy some grub. Bat was confused. The Lone Ranger explained that he stated wagons would arrive and at the same time there would be food to be bought at a fair price. He never said those wagons would come from the east, nor would they be loaded. Wagons came by both trails, but both groups of wagons were empty.

Episode #983-208, Broadcast May 15, 1939
Copyright Registration #63,675, script received at Registration Office May 18, 1939.
Written by Tom Dougall.
Plot: The Lone Ranger and Tonto intervene in a hostile situation when two crooks, Spike and Chris, make a play against Mary Dawson, a young widow. Mary explains how her dictatorial mother-in-law, Abby Winters, hated her after she married her son. Bob was not dead a week before Abby ordered Mary to leave – but leave the baby behind. In desperation of keeping her baby from her vile mother-in-law, Mary secretly gives the baby to two loving Mexicans, Pablo Garcia and his wife, Conchita. Consulting with Abby, the masked man discovers the old woman believes Mary married only for money. Through The Padre, the masked man learns of the whereabouts of Pablo and his wife, only to learn they have been taken prisoner by two men and seen heading north across Crystal River. When it is discovered that the baby is now the victim of a kidnap plot, both Abby and Mary, wondering at Tonto's demand for secrecy, nevertheless are forced to accede to his terms and accompany him alone. In the meantime, Spike and Chris have made camp in a secluded glade not many miles distant. With them, his hands tied, was Pablo Garcia, and also Conchita with the baby. Chris and Spike masterminded the scheme with the hope of selling the baby to the wealthy spinster, in retribution for her firing them. The confrontation with Abby and Mary when they reach the camp reveals Mary's sincerity. Without looking back or hesitating, Mary rides directly toward the pointed guns of the outlaws. She does not hurry her horse nor attempt to slow its pace. Instead, she rides calmly and apparently unafraid, her head held high. Facing off against the kidnappers, Mary reclaims her baby. Abby, realizing the child is in safe hands, tears up the court order that claimed the baby as her possession. The Lone Ranger takes Chris and Spike into custody.

Episode #984-209, Broadcast May 17, 1939
Copyright Registration #63,676, script received at Registration Office May 18, 1939.
Plot: Fisheye Foster, a reprobate perpetually attempting to be jailed so that he may live off the county, claims to have committed the recent robbery of Lem's store, even though Sheriff Dan Lansing knows otherwise.

Jake Rabe, one of the largest ranchers in the country, was recently killed with no clue left behind. At first Fisheye attempts to lay claim until The Lone Ranger reminds him that his scheme could backfire – murder convictions result in hanging, not room and board. When the sheriff meets a man named Luke, a former prospecting partner of Fisheye, he gains additional facts. When Fisheye Foster is discovered by the sheriff to be Cal Hopkins, from Placer City, up Montana way, and with a legitimate grudge against Jake Rabe, the murdered rancher, he takes the man to jail and locks him in a cell. The Lone Ranger investigates and forces the indignant sheriff to accompany him to Jake Rabe's ranch house. Inside, the masked man shows how a piece of cord was fastened to the nail inside the door, drawn across a second nail at the rear, and from that attached to the hammer of a revolver. In that position, anyone opening the cupboard door would release the hammer, the cartridge would be exploded. At the request of The Lone Ranger, the sheriff releases Fisheye from jail. Back at the ranch house, the sheriff asks his deputies to fetch a pipe from the cupboard. Only the sheriff's newest deputy, Red Whipple, hesitates opening the cupboard, giving himself away. It seems Red had rigged up the identical murder trap to catch the sheriff that he had used successfully on Jake.

Episode #985-210, Broadcast May 19, 1939
Copyright Registration #63,677, script received at Registration Office May 18, 1939.
Plot: Three women and a child are kidnapped by Chief Red Fox and his tribe. Tonto finds their hidden trail and joins the war party in hopes of leaving signs that the cavalry can follow. The Lone Ranger, meanwhile, meets with Captain Grayson from the U.S. Army, to help assist. Recent raids too well planned suggest white men were behind the scheme. The rumor heard by The Lone Ranger was correct. Scar Morgan and Dade Billings, renegade whites, had shrewdly turned the unrest of the Indians to their own profit. Chief Red Fox, vicious and war-like, willingly followed their counsel while permitting them the pick of his loot. When The Lone Ranger attempts to meet up with Tonto, he is caught by Red Fox and Scar and taken into the center of the Indian encampment where he is bound firmly to the trunk of a stunted but sturdy tree. Before torture can be applied, Tonto rescues his friend and the two make a swift getaway. Captain Grayson had vigilantly kept awake throughout the night, hoping against hope that The Lone Ranger had somehow escaped death. Then suddenly, shortly after dawn, he leaps to his feet. The Lone Ranger races into camp and with the command to charge. The troops swept forward in a body, thundering through the recently deserted camp of the Indians, rapidly bearing down upon the fleeing savages. Disorganized, panic-stricken, almost wholly without effective leadership, the Indians nevertheless do their best to save themselves from the soldiers but their efforts are useless. Better armed, better trained, more courageous, the troopers' attack is irresistible. The red men throw down their weapons. Red Fox, Scar, and Dade surrendered. Only then did the soldiers cease their fire. The Indians that survive the battle quickly flee when they discover the woman and girl display signs of smallpox. Tonto made them up to look like they had the virus, to ensure the redskins won't be returning to the territory for some time.

Notes: The Lone Ranger, disguised, tells Captain Grayson, "The last time we met I wore a mask. It was during an Indian campaign. I brought your commanding officer a message from General Custer."

Episode #986-211, Broadcast May 22, 1939
Copyright Registration #63,805, script received at Registration Office May 26, 1939.
Plot: The Union Pacific, pride and joy of the West, was roaring across the open stretches where vast ranches separated the small cross-roads communities but when the great iron horse came near the town of Red Stone, it was robbed. There was a sizeable reward for the capture of the train robbers. Steve Logan, who owns a ranch outside of town, is responsible for the crime and wants to acquire the reward money on top by framing Bill Andrews, another rancher. Andrews' time behind bars is brief when Steve breaks his friend out late one night and hides him at his ranch, suggesting the two of them work together to find the real culprits. Steve hopes the

sheriff will find Andrews in hiding, resulting in the suspect being shot and killed. After a stranger overhears a conversation in the local café, The Lone Ranger suspects Steve as the mastermind. Following The Lone Ranger's instructions, Andrews takes two horses and a buckboard to visit Steve, asking for provisions to make a steady getaway. When Steve loads some of the stolen cash onto the buckboard to cinch the frame, he is surprised by the masked man and the sheriff, who were witnesses, verifying Steve as the guilty culprit.

Episode #987-212, Broadcast May 24, 1939

Copyright Registration #63,806, script received at Registration Office May 26, 1939.

Plot: Mary Thorne suspects her husband, Andy, ran out on her. In reality, Andy met with an accident and suffers from amnesia. He is now known as Fred Ames. In the striving cattle town of Staghorn, three crooks named Ted, Barney, and Gus realize Andy's dilemma and take advantage of the situation. Framing a crime on Max Cramer, a resident in town, the crooks trick Andy into believing Max was responsible for his dilemma and they hope Andy will shoot and kill Max, giving the sheriff reason to believe Max was involved in the crime. The Lone Ranger thwarts the crime. Then, when The Lone Ranger meets Ted, knowing him to be a crook, he plays the role of a masked criminal to take the crooks into his confidence. Ted races back to his conspirators with fake news that lures them to Gunshot Pass, where they hope to waylay and kill Max, using Andy as the triggerman. The killers are caught red-handed by the sheriff, their crimes verified. Mary arrives to help Andy get his memory back.

Episode #988-213, Broadcast May 26, 1939

Copyright Registration #63,807, script received at Registration Office May 26, 1939.

Plot: Mustang Mag threatens to waste buckshot on Old Missouri if he does not assist her in evicting a half a dozen families of nesters from a small grove on the edge of her property. After discovering an infant sick with fever, she agrees to allow them to stay for a short while. Three weeks pass and resentment grows among the ranchers in the territory. She was warned several times, but she paid no attention. Already fearful that the nesters might start killing off their cattle to feed themselves, when cattle start disappearing, a committee is formed to force eviction. The ranchers would not back down, and Mag expresses how she loves a good fight. Thanks to Tonto's superb tracking skills, it's determined that The Gila Kid was responsible for the stolen cattle. In the meantime, the ranchers tell all their friends of Mag's answer to their challenge. Hatred against the nesters is deep-seated among the cowmen and feelings against Mag's attitude run high. The ranchers agree to work together as vigilantes, complete with hoods covering their faces. While the hooded ranchers make a play against the nesters, The Gila Kid and his gang mastermind a plot to steal hundreds more head of cattle from the nearby ranches which were left unattended. With the assistance of The Lone Ranger, the nesters help thwart and capture The Gila Kid, earning respect from the men who wanted to vacate them from the territory.

Episode #989-214, Broadcast May 29, 1939 [PART ONE OF THREE]

Copyright Registration #63,933, script received at Registration Office May 31, 1939.

Plot: See pages 236 to 238.

Episode #990-215, Broadcast May 31, 1939 [PART TWO OF THREE]

Copyright Registration #63,934, script received at Registration Office May 31, 1939.

Plot: See pages 238 and 239.

Episode #991-216, Broadcast June 2, 1939 [PART THREE OF THREE]

Copyright Registration #63,935, script received at Registration Office May 31, 1939.

Plot: See pages 239 and 240.

Episode #992-217, Broadcast June 5, 1939

Copyright Registration #64,033, script received at Registration Office June 8, 1939.

Plot: A score of covered wagons make up the wagon train that, under the leadership of Asa Flinders, had left the middle west for homes in the newly opened territories. Because everyone in the party owed Asa money, which he loaned so they could buy necessary provisions, he aimed to collect, with everyone agreeing to settle temporarily and mine for gold. The unwilling emigrants whom old Asa had forced to labor for his profit made camp where a spring afforded water and the overhang of a cliff offered refuge from the unbearable heat of the sun. Inexperienced as they were, they had so far gathered little gold, but Asa would not listen to their pleas to move on. To spur approaching Indians away, The Lone Ranger arrives to help the emigrants perform a trick that will cause the red men to race madly back the way they had come. Only then did The Lone Ranger learn why the emigrants had started mining instead of going elsewhere to settle down. After consulting Tonto, The Lone Ranger decides to meet with their good friend Chief Thundercloud, whose village was two days away. The emigrants, now wholly aware of the hostility of the Indians, are on the alert. Later, Asa is kidnapped and hustled away by Indian captors in spite of his screams and protests and finds himself at last in a small camp some distance away, bound and left to meditate upon his predicament. Late that night, after a brief discussion with The Lone Ranger, who had snuck into camp, a deal is struck for Asa to clear out of the valley and go on to the district he was originally headed for if cut loose. Asa agrees, but to prove the worth of loyalty, The Lone Ranger brings a number of the emigrants to charge the camp and rescue Asa. The Indians flee, but it was all a ruse created with the assistance of the masked man and Chief Thundercloud.

Episode #993-218, Broadcast June 7, 1939

Copyright Registration #64,032, script received at Registration Office June 8, 1939.

Plot: A scheming rancher named Joel Greer offers to buy out the cattle of a Mrs. Loomis, a middle-aged woman who had carried on with the ranch when her brother died. Ever since Cottonwood Creek dried up, the spring-fed pool on Greer's property is the only source of water for the nearby ranchers. With the threat of gunplay, and a charge of trespassing in his favor, Greer hopes to buy out Mrs. Loomis's stock with financial backing from another rancher, Kurt Schafer, and a scheming banker named Squires. When Greer is informed that the ranchers have agreed to sell upon his terms, it does not take him long to summon Banker Squires and conclude the deal. Before the night was done, title to thousands of head of cattle had changed hands. The next day, though, when the water hole dried up, Joel and Kurt began scratching their heads. Leading the two mystified schemers, The Lone Ranger sends his great white stallion alone, westward, in the direction of the ranch owned by Mrs. Loomis. Long before they reach the buildings, however, Kurt and Joel note a group of cattlemen in the distance, and fresh water from the property owned by Mrs. Loomis. It seems an underground stream ran beneath her land and, when blocked, dried up Greer's water pool but created a new one on her own land. In defiance, Joel Greer races back to his ranch and offers his ranch hands $500 each to return with him to her land, guns blazing. When the men find themselves surrounded, courtesy of another plot by The Lone Ranger, Joel and Kurt are forced to sell back the cattle for more money than they paid, since, without the water, the cattle will die. The scheming ranchers have no other choice than to sell.

Episode #994-219, Broadcast June 9, 1939

Copyright Registration #64,031, script received at Registration Office June 8, 1939.

Plot: They say every time members of the Parsons family and the Healys meet, there is always a brawl. Just about everybody in the county, and in Clay City, has chosen sides. In the tradition of William Shakespeare's *Romeo and Juliet*, Mark Healy and Anne Parsons are in love – against the wishes of their elderly rancher fathers. Mark's father, Sam, and Anne's father, Eric, have been enemies ever since they broke up their partnership, years ago. Meanwhile, The Lone Ranger and Tonto mastermind a plan to rectify the relationship of the two ranchers.

At six o'clock the next evening, in a back room of old Crimmons' general store in Clay City, where meetings are sometimes held, Sam and Eric are tricked into paying a visit. The Lone Ranger recounts how both old men were at one time in love with a young dancer from the south of the border named Rosita. Tonto brings into the room an elderly woman, wearing what looks like a mustache, named Rosita. Surprised at her outwardly appearance, the men confess they would not live it down if word got out that they had a thing for the woman they remembered as once being beautiful. Sam confesses the scheme is blackmail but consents to his son's marriage to Anne. The old men find themselves shaking hands and becoming friends again, now aware that most fights start from things so small that the original cause is magnified a dozen times over the course of a few years.

Episode #995-220, Broadcast June 12, 1939

Copyright Registration #64,158, script received at Registration Office June 16, 1939.

Plot: Amos Todd is robbed late at night, then bound and gagged and left alone on the prairie. The Lone Ranger and Tonto happen upon the elderly retired rancher and cut his ropes, then learn that the only thing stole from his cabin was a ring. Judge Livingstone claims the ring was valuable and paid $5,000 in cash. The judge planned to pick up the ring on the way back from a trip but while he was away, two crooks named Michael and Shay stole the ring, Amos finds himself in a dilemma. The Lone Ranger knows the Judge has little patience, so the masked man forces the Judge to accompany him, and steals his horse. The Judge is forced to walk six hours back from where he came. Meanwhile, Tonto trails the crooks while The Lone Ranger makes a play to steal back the ring. After returning the valuable to Amos Todd at his cabin along Iron River trail, The Lone Ranger finds himself facing the crooks, who followed him. The masked man gets the better of them, however, as the Judge overhears the discussion and knows Amos Todd was a victim. With the ring returned, Amos is able to fulfill his end of the bargain.

Notes: Judge Livingstone was a tip-of-the-hat to director Charles Livingstone. The name Todd, Shay, and Michael were also references to the radio actors.

Episode #996-221, Broadcast June 14, 1939

Copyright Registration #64,159, script received at Registration Office June 16, 1939.

Plot: In the town of San Felice, Pedro, the breed who set fire to the stables of the Red Star Stage Line, is caught by The Lone Ranger moments after he was observed fleeing the scene. Pressured, he confesses he has no quarrel with the stage line owned by Joan Adams and her friend, Abby Tuttle, but that Rick Leonard of a competing stage line hired him to do the job. The Lone Ranger rescues Leonard and later at camp explains how they suspect Bull Madsen, an employee of the Red Star, was responsible. Madsen wanted to create enough problems to discourage the women into selling the business to him, even framing a crime on their competition. The Lone Ranger races into town to free Pedro from jail, then tricks his captive into believing he was hired to eliminate the breed so no one talks. Upset for the betrayal, Pedro vents anger against his employer – Bull Madsen – where witnesses including Rick Leonard and Joan Adams discover the truth. Before Madsen is taken away, Rick and Joan agree to combine their stage coaches and go partners.

Episode #997-222, Broadcast June 16, 1939

Copyright Registration #64,160, script received at Registration Office June 16, 1939.

Plot: The Fuller Ranch, located in the small western town of Oasis, is managed in equal partnership by Vic Fuller and his father, Matt Fuller. Frosty Kelso has in his possession a signed confession that would send him to jail, and blackmails Matt to pay for a theft Matt since paid back in full. Matt atoned for it by leading an honest life ever since. Matt's friend, Banker Nate Lambert, has a beautiful daughter named Madge, with whom Vic is in love, but Frosty blackmails Nate, who was also involved with Matt, into giving the hand of his daughter in exchange for the same silence. Intercepting the blackmail payment from Matt Fuller, The Lone Ranger and Tonto thwart Frosty's scheme. Angry, the blackmailer races back to his cabin to fetch the confession so he can deliver it to the sheriff, unaware that Nate, Matt and The Lone Ranger followed him. The masked man takes the paper and burns it and proves to Madge that Frosty was not suitable for her. Madge feels ashamed until her father assures her that Vic would make a fine son-in-law.

Episode #998-223, Broadcast June 19, 1939

Copyright Registration #64,197, script received at Registration Office June 21, 1939.

Plot: Lame Crow always blamed the white men for damaging the local irrigation. When Squint Maxim succeeds in wiping out an entire white settlement by blowing up the Lobo River dam with gunpowder, The Lone Ranger investigates. Suspecting white men were dressed as Indians to create friction between both sides, knowing it would draw soldiers out of Buffalo City to aid, leaving the smelter in Buffalo City unguarded and ripe for plucking, The Lone Ranger pays a visit to Lame Crow. Captain Martin offers the Indian chief an ultimatum, but the chief claims innocence. The masked man explains to the chief his suspicions and recommends the Indians surrender for two hours, long enough for Tonto to track down the guilty parties and bring them to the camp to provide proof. Avoiding bloodshed on both sides for two hours, The Lone Ranger is a guest at Lame Crow's camp. Two hours later, Tonto arrives with Squint Maxim. Captain Martin locks up Squint's entire gang in Dodge City. Squint laughs, believing he will be set free sooner than later, but the masked man assures him that if Squint is released due to any legal wrangling, he would certainly become a victim of Lame Crow's justice.

Episode #999-224, Broadcast June 21, 1939

Copyright Registration #64,198, script received at Registration Office June 21, 1939.

Plot: Captain Matthews escapes a court-martial and execution to seek revenge against the men responsible for framing him for a crime he did not commit. Found in possession of the plans of Fort Davis which could have been used by the villainous Geronimo, Matthews is found guilty when two military officers, Tracy and Garvin, give false testimony. Captain Lewis conspires with Tracy and Garvin, out of jealousy – Matthews was engaged to Sally Griffin, the daughter of Major Griffin. The Lone Ranger pretends to be a masked bandit to convince Tracy and Garvin to blackmail Lewis with their knowledge. Tonto makes a late-night visit to Lewis to deliver a message, then finds himself forced at gunpoint to lead the captain to the scheming blackmailers. Matthews, meanwhile, swears against The Lone Ranger for remaining tied up. When Lewis is led to the secret camp, he confronts the blackmailers and insists they get not one dollar of the $1,000 they asked for, incriminating their guilt. Hiding in the shadows is Major Griffin. Overhearing the conversation, he orders the men who accompanied him to place the guilty parties under arrest. Matthews is untied and assured by the Major that he would receive back his rank… and he would also find Sally waiting for him.

Episode #1000-225, Broadcast June 23, 1939

Copyright Registration #64,199, script received at Registration Office June 21, 1939.

Copyright Registration #64,364, script received at Registration Office July 1, 1939.

Plot: Escaped outlaw Pete Brogan fetches outlaws from as many as six states to build a criminal empire, holed up in the badlands in a fortified hideout surrounded by rocks at least 20 feet high. The outlaws leave no mystery as to their hideout, holed up like a fort where the law cannot reach them. Their recent pillage and rampage were conducted at Smith's Corners, creating a stampede of Longhorns in the main street, led by hard-riding two-gun men. The stampede was a decoy, giving the outlaws the advantage to rob the bank and express office. The town is in mourning late that night, with twelve people dead and hundreds wounded. The Lone Ranger investigates and learns Brogan is really Koslick, an Army deserter who sold out to the Indians and applies military tactics.

Through shrewd planning, the masked man captures five of the Pete Brogan gang, including Brogan himself, but as the big man sits in jail, Brogan promises his men would seek retribution if he is not set free. Fire and brimstone would reign down on Smith's Corners. The Lone Ranger never counted on the fear of the townsfolk who voted on the principle of self-preservation. The sheriff's arguments were useless and Brogan was set free. Ma Healey, owner of the express office, scolded the men and women. The Lone Ranger was furious when he learned the news. "Your town isn't fit to be saved," the masked man shouts. When only two people, one of them being an old lady, are willing to ride alongside the masked man to ride up to the hideout and attack the outlaws, The Lone Ranger rides out to a prison to discuss the situation with the Warden. Reinforcements come in the form of prisoners who agree to take up arms and storm the rocky fort in exchange for a pardon – some with personal grudges against Brogan. The army of convicts fights bravely, but many fall to their deaths. Just as it appears to be a win for the outlaws, The Lone Ranger waves a flag of Old Glory and insists he is going to lead the next charge and plant the flag in the outlaws' fort. This motivates a strength in numbers against the outlaws and a defeat against the Pete Brogan outfit.

Notes: This episode features an announcement of the *Radio Guide* award. There are two copies of this radio script registered for copyright. The difference between the two is that one has the script pages for the *Radio Guide* award announcement, the other script does not.

While the information contained within this book remains factual, the authors would like to deviate for a moment and share their opinion: this is perhaps one of the ten best episodes of the radio program. A recording of this broadcast does exist and the authors highly recommend that you listen to this episode.

Episode #1001-226, Broadcast June 26, 1939 [PART ONE OF TWO]
Copyright Registration #64,365, script received at Registration Office July 1, 1939.
Plot: Dave Williams of Arizona bumps into Rusty Bailer of Wyoming and while neither are related, never has there been such an uncanny resemblance. Rusty convinces Dave to help pull a practical joke, returning to his homestead as a prodigal son to meet Lige, his father, and Jenny, his sister, and deliver money to the family. But when the sheriff pulls Dave aside, he assures the young man that he has a wanted notice with his name on it for murder. Dave insists he is not Rusty, even when Jenny verifies his claim because of a birthmark Dave does not have on his left arm. But the sheriff believes Dave is the wanted man. The Lone Ranger meets the real Rusty to learn how the practical joke backfired. Rusty explains how a man named Rudd Mallory framed him for a murder he did not commit. Realizing Rusty remained in the area and brought money to his father for the sale of his ranch, The Lone Ranger suspected Rusty was innocent. Not wanting to see Dave convicted on a charge against him, Rusty pays a visit to the sheriff to verify Dave's story. The Lone Ranger and Tonto decide to ride out to Arizona to find evidence that would clear Rusty.

Episode #1002-227, Broadcast June 28, 1939 [PART TWO OF TWO]
Copyright Registration #64,366, script received at Registration Office July 1, 1939.
Plot: Riding to Apache Ridge, Arizona, The Lone Ranger and Tonto investigate Rudd Mallory, an influential figure in this part of the country who owns multiple ranches, a café in town, and other businesses. With Rusty brought to town to face trial, and because the outcome of the trial is uncertain, Mallory plans for a lynching. The Lone Ranger thwarts those plans by conducting a jailbreak. A posse is organized with instructions to "shoot to kill." While Rusty remains hidden in the masked man's secluded camp, The Lone Ranger pays a visit to Slick, a weasel-faced associate of Mallory's and the weak link of the bunch. Through Slick, the masked man learns what he needed to know. Rudd Mallory, Jay Sampson. and Bull Branigan are involved in a complicated cattle rustling scheme. Bull owns the ranch where the stolen cattle reside, and Mallory owns the mortgage on the ranch. Jay murders his uncle, Bull, to inherit the ranch, after Mallory promises to relinquish the ranch at full value.

Releasing Slick, The Lone Ranger forces the U.S. marshal to join him to Rudd Mallory's office where Slick incriminates Mallory. Jay Sampson, disappointed in learning he was paid off for the ranch at less than full value, creates a falling out among thieves. The U.S. marshal, overhears the conversation after The Lone Ranger disarms the guilty culprits and takes them into custody, promising Rusty will receive credit for the apprehension.

Episode #1003-228, Broadcast June 30, 1939 [PART ONE OF EIGHT]
Copyright Registration #64,367, script received at Registration Office July 1, 1939.
Plot: See pages 258 to 260.

Episode #1004-229, Broadcast July 3, 1939 [PART TWO OF EIGHT]
Copyright Registration #64,430, script received at Registration Office July 7, 1939.
Plot: The stagecoach jolted and careened over the rough trail leading from Cooperstown on the first leg of its journey to the distant town of Gold Flats. Happy Joe Monk, the shotgun messenger, who had been given his nickname because of his pessimistic outlook upon life, hung onto the box of the coach with difficulty. He does not suspect that the skillful driver beside him is the famous Lone Ranger who, for purposes of his own, has assumed the name and personality, even the speech, of Will Bill Riley, a well-known stage driver. Black Bart, meanwhile, races out to intercept The Lone Ranger by closing the gates of an outpost, preventing "Riley" and Happy Joe from exchanging fresh horses. Further down the springs, Black Bart and his men destroy the bridge. The Lone Ranger, however, meets up with the crooks and forces the men at gunpoint to lash the fallen logs together so the stagecoach can float across the river and continue on its journey.

Episode #1005-230, Broadcast July 5, 1939 [PART THREE OF EIGHT]
Copyright Registration #64,431, script received at Registration Office July 7, 1939.
Plot: Driven by the Lone Ranger, who not only had disguised himself to look like Wild Bill Riley, the famous stage driver, but had assumed the latter's identity as well, the first of the coaches owned by young Jim Plummer is making a valiant attempt to reach Gold Flats in time to win a government mail contract. At the end of the first leg of the journey, Black Bart notifies Curly, the deputy of Marysville, that a stagecoach is due to arrive, and someone is impersonating Wild Bill Riley by a means that could only be described as "foul play." The sheriff and his posse manage to stop the stage that night, forcing The Lone Ranger to surrender. Late that evening, alone with the sheriff, the disguised Ranger convinces the sheriff of his real identity, cinched when the lawman examines the gun belt and the silver bullets. The Lone Ranger reveals his motive for the masquerade and the lawman agrees that he had been tricked. The stagecoach is sent off to continue the race with Happy Joe and the fake Riley, while Black Bart and Curly find themselves locked in the jail cell.

Episode #1006-231, Broadcast July 7, 1939 [PART FOUR OF EIGHT]
Copyright Registration #64,432, script received at Registration Office July 7, 1939.
Plot: Everywhere excitement runs high as The Lone Ranger and Happy Joe arrive twelve hours before the deadline. Mr. Lamont, pleased with the job, fires Black Bart, who pleads for a second chance, begging for one additional month to prove he can handle the task. Meanwhile, smoke signals from a distance suggest Yellow Fox is leading an uprising. A week goes by, and all is peaceful. Then, in swift succession but at widely separated spots, tragedy strikes swiftly. Indians attack the stage, killing the driver, the messenger and all three passengers. Outside an Indian village the famous warrior, Yellow Fox, schemed alongside Black Bart, who had masterminded the attacks with liquor as payment. Tonto, however, managed to contaminate the liquor with poison. Not enough to kill, but enough to make the Indians who drink the liquor sick for a spell. Tonto later attempts to stop Black Bart from delivering the tainted alcohol, but Black Bart will not allow anyone to intervene. A few days later, word goes through the streets that Black Bart was killed by Indians. Jim Plummer, when he hears the news, displays empathy for Black Bart. "If it'd been Bart takin' liquor to the Indians, they

wouldn't have killed him, would they? That stands to reason," Plummer remarks. "At any rate, Jim, whatever the truth, Black Bart's dead. I think we'll leave it at that."

Episode #1007-232, Broadcast July 10, 1939 [PART FIVE OF EIGHT]

Copyright Registration #64,433, script received at Registration Office July 7, 1939.

Plot: Mr. Dowd of the local bank insists on payment in full for a loan that was not due for many weeks. Jim Plummer insists that the note would have been paid before if it was not for the recent Indian troubles. Lamont, general superintendent of the Transcontinental, confesses later during a confrontation that his company bought the bank and, naturally, was anxious to obtain the franchise Jim Plummer had to carry mail, so would scarcely give financial backing to a competitor. None of the neighboring banks would care to accommodate, forcing Plummer to sell the stage line to pay off the debt. After learning of the situation, The Lone Ranger heads north out of Cooperstown to consult with Tonto. Three hours later, Bat Clements, whipping and spurring his mount, shoot down the main street of Cooperstown, to report immediately to Lamont, assuring him how he overheard Wild Bill Riley plan to rob the bank to get hold of the note so Plummer would not have to pay. Before they could alert the sheriff, The Lone Ranger holds up the bank and steals the note, riding away. Lamont realizes a larger problem is in play. The reward notices for Bat Clements were with the promissory note, and if the masked man is caught and the note returned, so would be the reward notices. If the company knew Lamont was protecting a man wanted by the company he worked for, his job would be at risk. In the morning, Wild Bill Riley was back in town. It was almost noon when Jim Plummer reentered town and, with a rapidly growing crowd at his heels, rode towards the bank accompanied by a prisoner. Bat is bound tightly. The sheriff looks at the reward notices for Bat McCabe, reward notices put out by the Transcontinental and Pacific, and signed by Lamont as general superintendent. Angry, the hired gun confesses Lamont's part in the plot so Jim Plummer will receive the $6,000 reward money.

Episode #1008-233, Broadcast July 12, 1939 [PART SIX OF EIGHT]

Copyright Registration #64,434, script received at Registration Office July 7, 1939.

Plot: U.S. Marshal Matt explained that when old Yellow Fox attacked the stagecoaches, it stirred up plenty of trouble. It was not enough that the soldiers caught him. Folks in the region were upset about the Indians so they wrote to Washington to the Commissioner for Indian Affairs. It was decided that the Indians will be placed on a reservation, back in the Sandy Buttes country. This meant turning Big Fork River back into its old channel. Jim Plummer had asked for permission to divert the river, because it was not needed there in Marysville, and there was nobody in the Sandy Buttes sections to use it. Between Piute Springs and Marysville, all four of Jim's stage-stations received their water from the river. It cost money to dam the river and divert the water, a fraction of the cost to drill water wells, and will now cost more money to divert the water back. Plummer has enough money to handle diverting the water, but not to drill the wells. One week later, Wild Bill Riley pays a visit to Lamont, suggesting he would perform an act of sabotage for a fee. Lamont is untrusting but decides to put Wild Bill Riley to the test, with a man called Red assigned to accompany him. A few days later, Lamont laughs at the sad news delivered to Plummer, but Wild Bill Riley explains how the dam was destroyed and the Big Fork River is back in its old channel, the river following its original course. Jim pauses for a moment and chuckles, then thanks Lamont for the favor. "The river had to be turned back," Jim explains. "The government was going to do it and take over my stage-line till the job was paid for. But you beat them to it and saved me from going smash!"

Episode #1009-234, Broadcast July 14, 1939 [PART SEVEN OF EIGHT]

Copyright Registration #64,435, script received at Registration Office July 7, 1939.

Plot: In desperation, Lamont employs a hired gunman named Speed Fletcher to come to Cooperstown and pay Jim Plummer a visit. In the local café, Speed shoots and wounds Plummer, causing the latter to be taken to his mother's house and tended to by the local doctor and the medical wonderments of Tonto. The Lone Ranger, still disguised as Wild Bill Riley, shoots the gun out of Speed's hand but not before Jim suffers from the wound. Doc Bender, however, tells a few people in town that Jim Plummer cashed in. Publicly, the hired gun feel sympathetic over the gunplay and the results, but having been paid $500 by Lamont, the entire affair was an act. Early the following day Cooperstown is the scene of such sorrowful solemnity. Jim Plummer's friends both in town and the neighboring countryside were numerous and few failed to call upon Ma Plummer to express their sympathy... although it had been announced that the funeral itself would be private. The Lone Ranger, meanwhile, prevented Speed Fletcher from leaving town, making the gunman increasingly nervous. Lamont paid a visit to Ma Plummer to encourage her to sell the stage line at $30,000. Only after the sale is made and applied under contract does Wild Bill Riley bring a few of Jim's friends to her homestead as witnesses when Tonto reveals a wounded but healing Jim Plummer, alive and well, who claims Speed was hired by Lamont to kill him. The deed to the land Ma Plummer sold Lamont was a quitclaim deed, which means there is no guarantee that the seller held title. As for the bill of sale for the equipment, it was for everything Ma owned, but she never owned the company. Jim still owned the company. Thus, Lamont was cheated out of $30,000. Lamont protests, claiming he would take them to court, but Wild Bill assures Lamont he would be wise not to... else he would have to explain how Speed Fletcher was hired to commit an act of murder.

Episode #1010-235, Broadcast July 17, 1939 [PART EIGHT OF EIGHT]
Copyright Registration #64,583, script received at Registration Office July 19, 1939.
Plot: During a confrontation between Abe and Slim in the back room of a small frame hotel, Lamont is murdered, and the hotel set aflame. The two crooks falsely accuse Wild Bill Riley and mob justice results in a posse surrounding The Lone Ranger, still disguised as Wild Bill, who is captured and promptly jailed. To help his good friend, the real Wild Bill schemes to switch places with The Lone Ranger, so the masked man can resume his vigilante identity and prove who really committed the crime. Jim Plummer, defending the good name of Wild Bill Riley against a lynch mob, asks the sheriff to agree to a scheme that would help solve the mystery. Wild Bill is brought out of jail, kept under guard, and brought to the Phillips house where the posse discovers two men masquerading as Wild Bill Riley. Here, The Lone Ranger explains why the masquerade and then accused Abe and Slim of drygulching. Arizona Lawson arrives with his dog and the canine races into a back room to reveal Lamont, alive and well. Just as the crooks are being taken into custody, the head of the Transcontinental and Pacific Stage-Line admits he heard the entire story and made it understood that neither he or the company he works for would have hired anyone to employ such tactics. To make good on Jim Plummer's situation, he promises Jim a good position with the company.

Episode #1011-236, Broadcast July 19, 1939
Copyright Registration #64,584, script received at Registration Office July 19, 1939.
Plot: The Padre sends The Lone Ranger and Tonto to the town of Oak Ridge, where Ma Garland and her son, Ted, are the victims of townsfolk harassment. Her other son, Vance, is accused of desertion when 40 men and women are found dead from thirst in the desert Vance had been hired to guide them across. Ted reveals his brother's hiding place, a cave at Wild Horse Canyon, and The Lone Ranger rides out to meet Vance. The accused explains to the masked man how he was captured by Apaches and later made an escape. His attempt to alert the men and women where the water spring was located, with a bonfire as a signal, was verified by the ashes The Lone Ranger found in the sand. Cal and Slim, having unsuccessfully attempted to convince Vance that The Lone Ranger was gunning for him, are later exposed for having convinced the men and women of the wagon train that the smoke signal was that of the Apaches. In reality, the Indians were white men in disguise, after the gold and money contained amongst the settlers had. After learning that Vance recommended that they hide

their riches at the base of Needle Rock, Cal and Slim race out to dig up the money – verifying their guilt. With no proof against them, The Lone Ranger steals their horses and leaves them in the desert to suffer from thirst. After teasing them with a water canteen from a distance, Cal finally breaks down and confesses their scheme. The sheriff, tagging alongside with the masked man, overhears the confession and places the guilty under arrest.

Blooper! The actor playing the role of the Padre stumbles over the word "deed" and says it twice during the first act.

Episode #1012-237, Broadcast July 21, 1939

Copyright Registration #64,585, script received at Registration Office July 19, 1939.

Plot: After riding into the town of Red Run, it does not take long for The Lone Ranger to discover he is accused of murder and theft. Someone held up a stagecoach, a pony express rider, and a rancher, and stole the money they carried on them. The description matches that of The Lone Ranger, right down to the white horse. Meanwhile, when Frank Mason needs guards for a shipment to Granite Falls, no one is brave enough to offer protection. Polk Kincaid, who lives within earshot of Wolf Creek and the recent robbery of Frank's shipment, is shot and wounded in the shoulder. The sheriff insists a local resident must be responsible and The Lone Ranger schemes with the local banker, Duncan, and Sheriff Pete Davis. Duncan and the sheriff make it known of the shipment, then in private laugh as they share a joke with Polk Kincaid. The strong box is empty. The real shipment is being carried by Bull Wiggins, a prospector, and his small burro. Late that evening, the fake Lone Ranger attempts to rob Bull Wiggins until the real masked man, hiding in the willows with Tonto, the sheriff and his posse, jumps out and pursues the thief. After apprehending the masked bandit, The Lone Ranger reveals him to be Polk Kincaid, who had shot himself in the shoulder before to avoid suspicion. Tonto washes off the white clay from the horse to verify how Kincaid was able to be near the scene riding a horse of a different color. Kincaid protests at the top of his lungs, while The Lone Ranger and Tonto ride out leaving the sheriff and his posse to prepare a legal hanging.

Episode #1013-238, Broadcast July 24, 1939

Copyright Registration #64,673, script received at Registration Office July 24, 1939.

Plot: Twenty-five years ago, Mark Paulson was falsely accused of cattle rustling and lost everything he had, having to spend the next ten years as a cowhand drawing wages. Under an alias identity, having built a respectable ranch and financial empire, he uses evidence against the local ranchers to blackmail and ruin them. Laura, Mark's wife, and Ray, Mark's son of about 20, resent his decision to seek a 25-year-old vengeance, and leave him. Local ranchers Jud Chadwick, his son Carl, and Tom Bierly, with reputations, homes and fortunes threatened by Mark Paulson, reluctantly come to the decision that the only way in which they can defend themselves is to strike at Mark. Acting upon their decision, they retrace the trail to Mark's ranch house to commit a fatal crime and later alibi each other. The Lone Ranger, however, gets the drop on them and orders the men to leave. Back in Mark's home, The Lone Ranger steals the papers used to blackmail all three of his victims and throws them into the fire. Mark promises his wife that he is a changed man but Laura still will not return home. The minute he found it was impossible to maintain his revenge of blackmail, though, Mark realized a weight was lifted from his shoulders. Three hours later, Mark returns in the company of the three men and apologizes, asking for forgiveness.

Episode #1014-239, Broadcast July 26, 1939

Copyright Registration #64,674, script received at Registration Office July 24, 1939.

Plot: This was the same script from the broadcast of July 13, 1936.

Episode #1015-240, Broadcast July 28, 1939

Copyright Registration #64,675, script received at Registration Office July 24, 1939.

Plot: The town of Kirkwood is a roaring, lawless example of the Old West. It contains more cafés and gambling halls than it does all other places of business combined. In the largest café, the Gold Nugget, Carl Vaughn, owner of a small gold claim not far from town, is cheated out of $1,000 by a crooked gambler, Spark Webber. Tonto, witness to the events, reports back to The Lone Ranger who identifies all three card players as crooked gamblers, each with several killings to their credit. When the masked man and Indian pay a visit to Carl, they find him dead – shot through the heart. When everything has been replaced in Vaughn's cabin to The Lone Ranger's satisfaction, he and Tonto remount and head their great horses back toward Kirkwood. In the office of Sheriff Temple, the masked man explains how Vaughn planned to bring the lawman evidence proving either Spark Webber, George Marshall, or Tippy Phelps were running a crooked card game. With all three equally under suspicion, the sheriff follows a suggestion from The Lone Ranger and one by one convinces the gamblers to visit the prospector's cabin to verify the report of a murder. With each gambler returning from the trip to report of their findings, each was promptly jailed. Afterwards, The Lone Ranger explains how two of the men are innocent because they had to make the trip over the cliff trail in order to make an accurate report. The only man who did not have to make the trip in order to give a report was Carl's murderer. Spark already knew what was in the cabin and never had to make the trip. Panicking, Spark pulls a gun and attempts to flee but The Lone Ranger disarms him so the sheriff can make an official arrest.

Notes: This radio script was originally scheduled for broadcast on January 18, 1939.

Episode #1016-241, Broadcast July 31, 1939

Copyright Registration #65,162, script received at Registration Office August 2, 1939.

Plot: This was the same script from the broadcast of January 5, 1934, with a number of variations. Sheriff Calhoun became Sheriff Dan Reilly, The Laughing Kid (a.k.a. Dannie) was changed to The Smilin' Kid (a.k.a. Bob Jessup), and Kate was changed to May Williams.

Episode #1017-242, Broadcast August 2, 1939

Copyright Registration #65,163, script received at Registration Office August 2, 1939.

Plot: Sam Slocum and his family, like many another pioneer in the days of the early West, migrated into the newly opened territories with high hope. With all their possessions carried within the confines of a covered wagon, they planned to settle outside on a homestead north of Showdown, despite the advice given by others against such a notion. Showdown was among the most lawless in the territory. Abe and Lige Tobin, brothers, were masters and made no pretense to honesty. Their word was law and those who differed with them paid for the presumption. As a result, the citizens of Showdown were their henchmen. Hoping to clean up the town with one sweep, The Lone Ranger masquerades as Sam Slocum and rides into town, wagering both money and the deed to the Slocum land. After catching Abe cheating at cards, he takes the deed and the money back and flees. In the morning, Abe and Lige arrive at the homestead and demand the Slocum family leave. Soldiers from the nearby fort intervene and hear the Tobin brothers, only to chuckle. Sam could never have gone into town to gamble last night… the soldiers were camped with the Slocum family all night on the way back to their fort. The Army Lieutenant decides this is the perfect time to clean up the town by placing the Tobin brothers under arrest.

Episode #1018-243, Broadcast August 4, 1939

Copyright Registration #65,164, script received at Registration Office August 2, 1939.

Plot: For more than 30 years Asa Wiggs has prescribed for the aches and pains that afflicted the citizens of

Harmony and the surrounding territory. A widower with a grown daughter, Nancy, he is loved by those who know him for his wisdom and tolerance. He and Nancy make their home in a rambling frame house in town convenient to all who need him. Graham, a stiff-necked young doctor, takes offense when his patients are provided different treatment from Asa Wiggs, than what his medical school training taught him. Out of spite, Graham arranges for the state medical board to withdraw Asa Wiggs' license to practice medicine, which is an inconvenience when The Lone Ranger happens by with a wounded reformed outlaw who needs treatment. The Lone Ranger and Tonto have arranged to signal the border patrol regarding their campaign to smash a smuggling operation across the Mexican border. The wounded outlaw will provide testimony needed to identity the chief of the smugglers. Graham, however, almost throws a monkey wrench into the mix when he reports to the sheriff of his rival's attempt to heal a wounded outlaw without a license to practice. The confrontation leads to a stand-off at Asa Wiggs' place, only to reveal the chief of the smugglers, Sandy, the sheriff's crooked deputy, and the young doctor admits he was a fool to place his reputation above all others.

Episode #1019-244, Broadcast August 7, 1939

Copyright Registration #65,298, script received at Registration Office August 14, 1939.

Plot: Indians charge down upon the tiny group of cabins clustered at the base of the foothills just where a swift mountain stream, its source in the snow-covered slopes of Mount Crater, meets the plains. The settlers had warning of the attack, however, and take refuge in the sturdiest of their dwellings, soon to defeat and thwart the attack. The Lone Ranger, traveling through the area, explains the cause of the attacks is because a man who fits the description of Fritz Jensen, one of the settlers, has been prospecting on the east slope of the crater, in a valley the Indians refer to as the Valley of the Great Spirit. No Indian has stepped foot in the valley; for a white man it is considered sacrilege. Jensen insists he found gold and this only leads to defiance against the red men and an expedition to the valley. The Indians believe a sacrifice of the white men would appease the Great Spirit. The Lone Ranger and Tonto, determined to prevent trouble between the whites and the red men, pay a visit to the village of Chief Spotted Wolf to explain how futile it would be to seek red man's justice on all white men for the guilt of one. White Bear, Spotted Wolf's son, had gone to white man's school and understood the situation, insisting no punishment unless the white men trespass again. Although The Lone Ranger was not aware of it, Fritz Jensen had already led his party back to the valley on Mount Crater to point out to his companions the rich deposits of glacier gold. But after a few days of panning for gold, Fritz Jensen and another crooked settler, Hank, plan to set off a charge of dynamite to kill the settlers and profit with a 50-50 split on work done by the others. The night before the settlers planned to leave the valley, the masked man meets with Hank to learn the scheme. In the morning, The Lone Ranger, astride Silver, sweeps up Fritz and brings him to the settlers to explain the intended destruction and expose the plot. Tonto, meanwhile, obeying The Lone Ranger's orders, intercepts the Indians they knew would ride to the valley the moment they learned it had again been invaded by whites. Fritz manages to escape and the explosion goes off. The explosion has scarcely died away when Tonto leads White Bear to where the bewildered settlers sit their mounts, staring back at the result of the tremendous blast. Unfortunately for Fritz, he found himself too near the blast, unaware The Lone Ranger and Tonto changed the position of the powder so that the blast would close the valley for all time. Regrettably, Fritz's own actions meant he was killed by a device of his own means.

Episode #1020-245, Broadcast August 9, 1939

Copyright Registration #65,299, script received at Registration Office August 14, 1939.

Plot: The town of Scorpion Bend, like most others situated near the border, has a distinct Mexican section. Pancho Cardoza, despite his comparative youth, is commonly looked upon as its leader and there were few occasions when he showed himself to be other than light-hearted and friendly. When Pancho is accused of stealing a Palomino that was once owned by Big Steve Emmet, a crooked café owner, a lynch mob forms. The

Lone Ranger and Tonto rescue Pancho safely away from the mob, and listened to his story. The masked man admits there have been too many thefts, too many hold-ups in the district that have gone unpunished by the law. After disguising himself and re-entering the town, The Lone Ranger learns through questioning that the real culprit behind the rash of thefts and killings is a man named Emmet and his associate, Rip. The disguised Lone Ranger even makes a number of accusations publicly before riding out. Later, miles from town, The Lone Ranger and Tonto meet Pancho and his brave band of friends, who plan to retaliate against the townsfolk for the invalid claims against them, The Lone Ranger devises a plan. Rip, however, feels a stranger showing up in town and vanishing without a trace suggests he knows something, and sets out with Big Steve Emmet to silence the potential conspirator. At the campfire that evening, the disguised Lone Ranger is caught off guard and a discussion exchanged between the parties verifies Big Steve Emmet's guilt. Before The Lone Ranger can be silenced, Pancho and his friends, along with the sheriff, arrive to take the guilty parties into custody.

Episode #1021-246, Broadcast August 11, 1939

Copyright Registration #65,300, script received at Registration Office August 14, 1939.

Plot: Along a glade in a small, wooded region some miles to the east of Crow Ridge, The Lone Ranger and Tonto intervene in the attempted murder of middle-aged rancher Matt Rock by a gunman named Pecos. The latter was hired by Luke Smiley, a shady lawyer, who represents Abby Sanders in her claim to the Randolph Estate. The Lone Ranger investigates Matt's claim to discover the crooked lawyer is indeed hoping to gain possession of the estate, and wants Matt dead so he can eliminate the only person to inherit upon her death. Keeping Matt at their camp to ensure the illusion that he was killed, The Lone Ranger then recruits Pecos in return for Pecos to turn a new leaf and not face charges for his attempted crime. In a private meeting between Luke Smiley and Pecos, the truth comes out, revealing a confession that is overheard by Abby, who was brought to the scene by Tonto so she would overhear. Sending Abby, Tonto, and Pecos away, The Lone Ranger serves Luke Smiley with an ultimatum. Confess to Judge Greavy that he schemed to take over the Randolph Estate from Abby or face a murder charge. Luke reluctantly agrees and confesses to the judge – moments before Matt puts in an appearance and places the finger of attempted murder on him.

Episode #1022-247, Broadcast August 14, 1939

Copyright Registration #65,861, script received at Registration Office September 14, 1939.

Plot: The Lone Ranger suspects Amos Chandler and his wife, Nellie, are prisoners in their own home, but needs proof for the law to act. Meeting a man named Potluck Potter, and his donkey called Luther Jones, the masked man asks the prospector to visit the Chandler homestead and secretly deliver a letter to Nellie. Potluck falls victim to the trap and is held against his will, however, when he inadvertently discovers the Chandlers' foreman, Hook, is attempting to force Amos to sign over their gold mine. The ranch hands side with Hook, making the situation dangerous in numbers. When The Lone Ranger and Tonto find Luther Jones and an upturned cart, they suspect foul play. Setting fire to the bunkhouse to alert the neighbors, the distraction allows The Lone Ranger and Tonto to sneak inside the ranch house and free the captives. They barricade the doors to direct resistance against Hook's attacks, and use furniture to fortify as bullet resistance. As their ammunition runs low, The Lone Ranger plans to leave by a window to create the illusion of a getaway while the others flee from the back of the house. Before he can go through with the plan, neighbors and the sheriff arrive. The fire was a brilliant signal and leads to a swift roundup of the men who chose to exchange bullets with the law.

Notes: This was the first of six consecutive episodes in which another actor plays the role of Tonto for a vacationing John Todd.

Episode #1023-248, Broadcast August 16, 1939

Copyright Registration #65,862, script received at Registration Office September 14, 1939.

Plot: A posse led by Sheriff Hastings of Little Falls pursues The Lone Ranger and Tonto, accused of shooting and killing an express agent and stealing $7,000 in cash. The Lone Ranger turns the tables on the lawman when he kidnaps the sheriff and holds him long enough to prove the real culprit responsible. Suspicion falls on Harvey Black, manager of the bank, to whom rumors suggest his books were off and a scheduled audit was bound to discover that. The masked man returns to town to inform Harvey that the money not only belongs to Tom Ridgely of the Eastern Syndicate, but the bills were marked. It does not take long to realize Harvey did not steal the money to cover the loss. With assistance of Deputy Pinky and Harvey Black, the masked man creates a set-up that spreads a new rumor through the streets that the stolen money has been found and is due to be returned to the bank. The sheriff escapes from his temporary restraint only to discover too late that recovering the stolen cash verifies his guilt. The Lone Ranger explains that when they first met, the lawman said $7,000 had been stolen but no one knew how much was stolen – this is what tipped off the masked man to the real culprit. Deputy Pinky took the crooked sheriff into custody and placed him behind bars.

Episode #1024-249, Broadcast August 18, 1939

Copyright Registration #65,863, script received at Registration Office September 14, 1939.

Plot: Answering a call from Colonel Miles from a nearby fort, The Lone Ranger receives reports that something has frightened the Indians to a point where they will not trade or have business dealings with Burt Crockett, owner of a local trading post. Worse, this suggests an Indian uprising might happen soon. The only results from three days of hard riding through the territory were deepening the mystery. Big Wolf, a native from Chief Thundercloud's tribe, claims a great bird strikes from the sky. Tonto visits Chief Thundercloud to learn that the natives were informed by a white medicine man, forewarning impending danger if the redskins commune with white men. Later, the dead body of Big Wolf is found, stabbed to death. Following a rugged trail bordered on a cliff, The Lone Ranger and Tonto eventually discover the root cause: a trained eagle with needle-thin spikes attached to its talons. An old prospector, wanted by the law on a murder charge, had ventured into the wilderness and discovered he could use a horn to train an eagle to swoop towards any quarry who trespasses or gets too close. The old man, however, is mentally disturbed. Fanatical and out of his head, the old man screams in agony for fear of being taken back to civilization and races off a cliff to his death.

Notes: This episode was possibly the first time that the new sound effects of gun shots were applied rather than a stick hitting a box.

Episode #1025-250, Broadcast August 21, 1939

Copyright Registration #65,864, script received at Registration Office September 14, 1939.

Plot: The village of Cedar Grove, nestling at the base of a towering hill, owed its prosperity to the cattle industry, although recently an important gold strike had been made nearby. A prospector discovered a rich vein a little more than half-way up the hill's steep slope and sold his claim to an Eastern Syndicate. Bull Scanlon, named so for being bull-headed, has been imported by the syndicate to supervise the operation of the mine. When Saul Grayson arrives at the mine site, representing the townsfolk with the fear that explosions might bury the town with a landslide of earth and shale, Bull insists he is within his legal rights and orders the man to leave. A recent detonation resulted in a near-casualty when The Lone Ranger rushed into action to save a woman from becoming victim of such a landslide. The townsfolk, learning of the rescue, agree that while a fair and peaceful means failed, the next result would require clubs and guns. The Lone Ranger, hoping to avoid bloodshed, kidnaps Bull and gags him, racing back into town so the mob will turn around. Bob, whose wife was saved by The Lone Ranger, agrees to file a claim above the mine. Bull Scanlon is not a crooked man, just stubborn. When released from his bonds, it is explained how the town merely wants it put into writing that the Syndicate would compensate any damage resulting from the explosions. Bull does not agree until he witnesses Bob set off a blast of his own, burying the entrance of the mine. Bob is also within his legal rights and when explained through example, the gruff mine supervisor agrees to sign a paper, with witnesses, stating compensation would be given to any inconvenience.

Episode #1026-251, Broadcast August 23, 1939

Copyright Registration #65,865, script received at Registration Office September 14, 1939.

Plot: Luke Dailey was charged with a number of crimes but when Judge Fred Wilkie discovers that the prosecution is without evidence, having been stolen from Sheriff John's office the other night, he adjourns for one week. Lawyer Greg, working for Luke, destroyed the evidence and knows he gets a $1,000 bonus for getting his client off. Milt Collins, however, is the only risk. Milt decides he would indeed testify as a witness against Luke Dailey. The scheming lawyer blackmails the witness with papers proving Milt was guilty of a murder 15 years earlier but that fails to convince Milt to steer away. The Lone Ranger knows the lawyer will exact revenge, but only half as much as he wants Milt's silence. Hiding Milt at his camp for a week with Tonto standing guard, the masked man learns the details of the case and races back into town to gather more facts. One week later, in the courtroom, Lawyer Greg makes one last attempt to intimidate the witness until The Lone Ranger barges in to ask the sheriff to take the paper out of the lawyer's hand and verify. It seems the man Milt shot and killed in self-defense 15 years ago was an outlaw with a price on his head. The reward money is still waiting for him. The judge, frustrated by the events, charges the lawyer for contempt of court and intimidating a witness. Before the judge can charge The Lone Ranger for interrupting the proceedings, he discovers the masked man has already vacated the courtroom and raced out of town.

Episode #1027-252, Broadcast August 25, 1939

Copyright Registration #65,866, script received at Registration Office September 14, 1939.

Plot: When Buck Wheeler, notorious outlaw, masquerades as the sheriff from Millsburg, he plans to deal out gang punishment and death to a U.S. marshal. The trusting and unsuspecting Sheriff Sayer of Mesquite City is taken in by Buck's scheme, taking the jailed prisoner away with him. The Lone Ranger and Tonto, a few miles outside of town, find the real Sheriff Wilson and Deputy Chuck, who were stranded. Sheriff Wilson explains how Buck Wheeler and his men stole his badge and identification, as well as their horses. The Lone Ranger helps the lawmen into town, but Sheriff Sayer won't allow a fast one to be pulled on him and jails Wilson and Chuck. The Lone Ranger soon finds it necessary to break the real lawmen from jail. He then waits a few moments for Sheriff Sayer to form a posse and give chase. Tonto follows their trail in an effort to rescue Jacobs, the U.S. marshal who was at one time undercover in the Buck Wheeler gang but finds himself caught and tied to a tree alongside Jacobs. The sheriff's posse, never gaining and never losing ground, follows The Lone Ranger, Wilson, and Chuck, until they come upon Buck Wheeler's campfire. There, the truth is exposed and the real lawmen are identified, with Sheriff Sayer realizing he had made a mistake.

Episode #1028-253, Broadcast August 28, 1939

Copyright Registration #65,867, script received at Registration Office September 14, 1939.

Plot: Arizona Lawson finds himself accused of attempted murder when Clem Owens is attacked by a dog. No one in town owns a dog except Arizona, which gives the sheriff justification to jail the innocent man. Arizona, as a friend of The Lone Ranger, asks the masked man to help find the guilty party. A man named Forbes is in town spreading rumors that Clem had been seen across the border, gambling in the crooked gambling hall of Miguel. The Lone Ranger, knowing Arizona's dog was used to hunt wolves and not humans, suspects someone else in town owns a dog and has kept it a secret. After riding across the border to investigate, The Lone Ranger orders Miguel to ride back with him into Texas to help clear Arizona's good name. Miguel hesitates at first, but realizing he might be able to get the money owed from Clem Owens, consents. When everyone is confronted, Miguel identifies Forbes as the man he knows as Clem Owens, and within the presence of the sheriff, discovers Forbes was using an alias when gambling over the border. Forbes had a dog of his own and hoped Arizona would take the blame and Miguel would write off the gambling debts, believing Clem Owens to be dead. With the real culprit exposed, thanks to The Lone Ranger bringing both dogs into the street to battle against each other, Forbes is arrested, and Arizona Lawson is released from jail.

Episode #1029-254, Broadcast August 30, 1939

Copyright Registration #65,868, script received at Registration Office September 14, 1939.

Plot: Neither Lige Tuttle, the storekeeper at Comanche Corners, nor Ike Sims, an elderly prospector, guesses that the tall stranger looking on silently while Ike chooses an outfit is the famous Lone Ranger in disguise. It is on this particular afternoon that The Lone Ranger learns how Lige grubstaked prospectors with square deals, frustrating his competition, Pearson. Two months passes with no trouble until Ike strikes a rich vein. The townsfolk spread the news through main street faster than a telegraph could and publicly ridiculed Pearson, who never treated anyone fairly. In private, Pearson schemes with Joe to poison Ike with arsenic – only enough to make him sick, not kill him. When Ike recovers, he sets out to gun down Lige, who stands to gain possession of the mine upon the death of his partner. The masked man convinces Ike to remain in hiding and leaks another main street rumor— that Ike was found murdered. Lige is discredited, courtesy of Pearson's rants, suggesting anyone else grubstaked by Lige may fall victim to the same if they strike gold. After breaking up a lynch mob outside Lige's store, The Lone Ranger tricks Joe into believing Pearson wanted to eliminate the man who knew too much, especially since the murder of Ike meant a fall guy was needed. Joe, surviving the murder attempt, races out to Pearson's cabin and a falling out among thieves cinches their guilt. The sheriff and a number of townsfolk are outside to overhear the conversation. The Lone Ranger then reveals Ike is alive and well, much to the delight of the sheriff and townsfolk.

Episode #1030-255, Broadcast September 1, 1939

Copyright Registration #65,869, script received at Registration Office September 14, 1939.

Plot: U.S. Deputy Marshal Sandy Clifford is disgraced when his manacled prisoner, Slim Rafferty, escapes custody onboard a train from Colfax, before the locomotive can arrive at its destination, River Junction. Sandy is forced to turn in his badge, but he swears to apprehend Rafferty and earn his badge back, even if it takes him ten years. Stumbling upon The Lone Ranger's camp, Sandy is informed that Slim has never been found guilty in a court of law for any of the charges due to insufficient and coincidental evidence. When a forest fire breaks out, a stranger pleads for help – his wife and child are in the cabin and the fire is so wide that escape seems impossible. A quarter mile away is Slim Rafferty's hideout. Slim is shot and wounded by an assailant, when Slim chose to remain to save the woman and child. The Lone Ranger, Tonto, and Sandy arrive and between the men, underbrush is cut away and a backfire is started. The battle between man and nature is brutal and hot, but the cabin is saved, and the forest fire is destined to burn out when it reaches the hills. Slim admits Sandy got the better of him, but the former lawman cannot find himself arresting Slim. Perhaps, he realizes, there were false accusations against Slim Rafferty. The fire attracted the U.S. Marshal and men from the town. When Sandy uses his gun to hold back the law to let Slim ride off, the marshal chuckles. He knew the evidence was flimsy and Slim may truly be innocent. But Sandy earns back his deputy badge for understanding and demonstrating that honesty and integrity are necessary for the job.

Notes: It was instructed on the script that the character of Slim Rafferty be played like the gangster screen icon Edward G. Robinson for the first half of the episode.

Episode #1031-256, Broadcast September 4, 1939

Copyright Registration #65,870, script received at Registration Office September 14, 1939.

Plot: A rivalry between Jack Roberts and Deputy Sheriff Red Denton develops into a bitter feud when they both pay court to Jane Morgan. Her father is the richest man in town and Red seeks to win her hand by eliminating the only obstacle that stands in his way. Red conspires with a Mexican named Felipe to rob Morgan's general store and steal the gold, planting evidence to suggest Jack guilty of the crime. Felipe, however, double-crosses Red by stabbing him dead with Jack's knife and stealing the gold himself. The Lone Ranger and Tonto, after trailing Felipe to Pecos, discover what happened when Felipe tells the sheriff that he saw Jack Roberts racing away from the scene of the crime. A visit to Jack Roberts' house finds a knife missing and a small bag of gold in his bedroom. The sheriff returns to town with his man and meets a lynch mob. Jane defends Jack but she is restrained. The Lone Ranger steals laundry from a Chinaman named Sing Loy to ride into the center of the mob to prove Felipe was the guilty culprit. It was Felipe who stole Jack's knife and planted the gold and during the struggle with Red, the Mexican got cut. With the laundry, the masked man verifies Felipe is wearing Red's shirt, too short for him, and Felipe's blood-stained shirt is Red's wash. Panicking, the breed attempts to flee but is shot dead. Jack is set free to marry the woman who stood by him through thick and thin.

Episode #1032-257, Broadcast September 6, 1939

Copyright Registration #65,871, script received at Registration Office September 14, 1939.

Plot: An old prospector named Crawford, known as "Lonesome" to many, resides in a tumbledown shack outside town. Having struck gold, the eccentric prospector puts his claim down in a map. Everyone in town knows of the map, including Sheriff Rankin, who rides out to defend Lonesome against four hooded outlaws attempting to shoot and kill the old man. The Lone Ranger and Tonto, hearing the rifle fire, gallops in to scare the outlaws away. Curly Beckett, the owner of the local saloon in town, is furious when he learns that the hired outlaws, especially Blackie and Snake who had a head on their shoulders, had high tailed it away from the old man's abode. Blackie schemes to kidnap Lonesome's daughter-in-law, the widow Mary Crawford, and her son Ted, as the old prospector planned to give the map to them and once accomplished, the gold would go into a bank. Held hostage, they would be a perfect swap for the map. Once again, The Lone Ranger and Tonto thwart their scheme and Tonto takes the disarmed outlaws to the U.S. marshal. After delivering Mary and Ted safely to the tumbledown shack, The Lone Ranger discovers the house torn apart. The sheriff follows the masked man's orders to bring Curly Beckett to the shack to verify where the stolen map is located. Curly, however, does not have the map and when someone shoots the oil lamp from outside a window, starting a fire, everyone vacates the shack. The sheriff is the last to leave, having retrieved the map he stole but never had time to take away from the shack when he was interrupted by the arrival of Mary and Ted, giving himself away. The U.S. marshal arrives to take both the sheriff and Curly into custody. Lonesome agrees the ramshackle was not fitting for a woman or child and promises to use the gold to build a house in town.

Blooper! The engineers goofed with timing in the opening sequence/theme song for this episode.

Episode #1033-258, Broadcast September 8, 1939

Copyright Registration #65,872, script received at Registration Office September 14, 1939.

Plot: Sheriff Bart Sanders and deputy Greg Morton journey from White Rapids to Ten Strike Junction, a distance of many miles, part of which includes the broad Lost Hope Desert, to pick up the outlaws, Tex Seeley and Vern Keller. On their return trip, the outlaws get the advantage and steal the lawman's credentials and badge, stranding the sheriff and deputy to heat, exposure and certain death. Having overheard the sheriff's task prior, the crooks ride into the town of Littlefield, representing themselves as the real lawmen. A stagecoach to arrive in Littlefield will be carrying a gold shipment and the crooks plan to use their false credentials to steal it. Sheriff Lathrop of Littlefield falls for the scheme but The Lone Ranger conspires with the manager of the stage line, Clay, to set a trap and catch the crooks. When Clay insists the bank back at White Rapids gave the sheriff a letter of credentials and would not release the gold until the letter was presented, the fake lawmen race back to find the sheriff and deputy. Only when The Lone Ranger and Tonto follow the outlaws and disarms the crooks is the scheme revealed: there was no such letter from the bank and the real sheriff and deputy are rescued.

Episode #1034-259, Broadcast September 11, 1939

Copyright Registration #65,905, script received at Registration Office September 15, 1939.

Plot: Lem Tolliver had a stroke of good fortune when he came upon a $5,000 inheritance and celebrated in the Cedar Grove café. His promise to pay everyone back the money they had loaned him through the years goes awry when he discovers his money has been stolen. Someone in the café apparently snuck into his house and stole the wooden box where the cash was kept. While folks in town laughed at Lem, believing his wife hid the money so he would not spend it, The Lone Ranger and Tonto follow the trail from Lem's house to the location where the thief buried the cash box. The masked man verifies the stolen goods, then reburies the money and rides back to town where he discusses the matter with the sheriff. Injun Pete, in town with a traveling medicine show, agrees to assist by putting on an act and claiming he has learned an ancient mystic talent to find hidden money. Everyone in town knows about the stolen money so they find the performance amusing – especially when he describes the scene where the money is buried. The real culprits, two crooks, race out before everyone else to the location where they buried the money to make sure their loot was still there. The crooks are surprised when the law comes out of hiding to arrest the guilty culprits.

Episode #1035-260, Broadcast September 13, 1939

Copyright Registration #65,906, script received at Registration Office September 15, 1939.

Plot: The townsfolk lose respect for the sheriff of Buffalo Ridge when he is unable to tame the Bar W outfit, who ride into town every Saturday night raising a ruckus and causing damage. Such defiance meant criminals from all over the region are pouring into town. The deputies quit and outlaws begin using Buffalo Ridge as a base of operations. Worse, neighboring ranches have fallen victim to robbery and cattle rustling… but not the Bar W. The Lone Ranger, acting as a town tamer, masterminds the theft of cattle from the Bar W, prompting Sam and Smokey and their bunch to turn to the sheriff. It is then that they discover the damage caused by their Saturday night exploits. With The Lone Ranger present, the men from the Bar W agree to be deputized to ride out and clean up the region of outlaws. With the sheriff in the lead, and in whirlwind fashion, the known outlaws are apprehended and placed under arrest. Only after the scheme of stealing Bar W cattle is exposed and returned do Sam and Smokey agree to enjoy their Saturday nights with less hollering and gunplay. In fact, some of the men want to remain as deputies in case outlaws ride into town again and the sheriff needs backup.

Episode #1036-261, Broadcast September 15, 1939

Copyright Registration #65,907, script received at Registration Office September 15, 1939.

Plot: On the way to Meadville, an old trapper named Dade misleads Jason Baker into believing the Indians have been pushed out – traveling through the hills, instead of riding around the hills, is perfectly safe. Jason, however, is more stubborn than a mule. Against the advice of The Lone Ranger and others, Jason insists on traveling through the hills. In reality, Dade is a member of an outlaw gang who hopes to waylay the wagon train, allowing the Indians to attack and kill off the settlers, then ride down to scare the Indians away and steal the provisions – including Jason's $10,000. Tonto, having overheard the plot from the outlaws, is apprehended, but the cunning Indian breaks free from his bonds and escape with a $100 price on his head. When it is discovered that the outlaw white renegades planted blasting powder to cut off the pass from behind, preventing the wagon train from turning around and riding around the hills, The Lone Ranger and Tonto mastermind a clever plan. The next day, as the wagon train continues trekking forward, Indians ride down to attack and when it appears all the white settlers are dead, the outlaws ride down to scare the Indians away. Only the outlaws, Dade included, are surprised when they discover there was no Indian attack. Some of the settlers had disguised themselves as Indians and with everyone alive and well, and fully armed, the outlaws are surrounded.

Episode #1037-262, Broadcast September 18, 1939 [PART ONE OF THREE]

Copyright Registration #66,152, script received at Registration Office September 28, 1939.

Plot: See pages 240 to 241.

Episode #1038-263, Broadcast September 20, 1939 [PART TWO OF THREE]

Copyright Registration #66,153, script received at Registration Office September 28, 1939.

Plot: See page 241.

Episode #1039-264, Broadcast September 22, 1939 [PART THREE OF THREE]

Copyright Registration #66,154, script received at Registration Office September 28, 1939.

Plot: See pages 241 and 242.

Episode #1040-265, Broadcast September 25, 1939 [PART ONE OF THREE]

Copyright Registration #66,202, script received at Registration Office September 28, 1939.

Plot: At the ranch house of Mustang Mag, Missouri is recovering from wounds after being beaten up by Bull Nugent and his men. Mag's niece, meanwhile, is coming from the East to pay her a surprise visit. Bull Nugent somehow intercepts her letter, and later her stagecoach, making her a prisoner. Missouri reasons the lack of ransom is because the kidnapping involves a government land Mag leased for grazing. In order to exercise the option for another five years, she has to use it by the first of the month. Old Garrick of the Box G offered cash for her to let the option lapse. Seeing she did not need the land at all, she was going to wait until the last minute to make up her mind. Mag fetches The Lone Ranger and Tonto to locate Alice, unaware that Tonto would also be apprehended and held captive. With Mustang Mag and her ranch hands backing his play, The Lone Ranger trails Tonto's whereabouts to a tumbledown cabin. The Lone Ranger rescues his friend and ambushes Bull Nugent, while Mustang Mag meets up with Alice. The Lone Ranger assures Mag that he plans to stay around for a while to learn why Garrick wants her lease so badly.

Episode #1041-266, Broadcast September 27, 1939 [PART TWO OF THREE]

Copyright Registration #66,203, script received at Registration Office September 28, 1939.

Plot: The law cannot make Bull Nugent talk. He seems confident of protection, even though the law cannot figure out what he had to gain by the kidnapping. He was obviously hired for the job. Figuring he won't talk even when he goes to trial, The Lone Ranger masterminds a way to trick him into confessing on the stand. Hoping to make Bull believe

Garrick is not going to help him, and conviction is certain, The Lone Ranger masquerades as the notorious Scar Higgins and gets himself arrested. Sharing a cell with Nugent, the disguised Lone Ranger verifies Nugent was hired by Garrick and makes an escape in the morning when the deputy arrives to serve breakfast. Alerting the sheriff later, The Lone Ranger informs the lawman that he learned of an up-coming jailbreak, where Garrick will smuggle guns to the criminals in jail. With understanding of the plot, the sheriff allows the jailbreak to happen near midnight. The trail leads to a confrontation between Bull and Garrick, with the former believing he was being framed. Their confession is overheard by the sheriff and The Lone Ranger, who places both men under arrest for the crime.

Newspaper advertisement in *The Detroit News*, September 20, 1939.

Episode #1042-267, Broadcast September 29, 1939 [PART THREE OF THREE]
Copyright Registration #66,204, script received at Registration Office September 28, 1939.
Plot: Garrick, under the custody of the local sheriff, won't pass the option of grazing land to Mustang Mag, even though he is scheduled to hang. In an effort to learn the reason why Garrick won't loan the land to Mag, The Lone Ranger preys upon his greed and strikes a business deal whereby Garrick is selling out his friends for $500 profit. Garrick is released from jail momentarily to sign papers leasing the grazing land owned by the Government, while The Lone Ranger prevents Mag from renewing her option. Moments after Garrick signs the papers, Mag and Missouri show up and Garrick gloats. He explains how cattlemen from Colorado are coming with thousands of head of cattle and are willing to pay loads for grassing land. But The Lone Ranger surprises them when he confesses that he pushed the clock ahead an hour and it isn't really past noon, only a little past eleven. Mag still has first option of renewal.

Episode #1043-268, Broadcast October 2, 1939
Copyright Registration #66,348, script received at Registration Office October 5, 1939.
Plot: Sheriff Kurt Savage is not only custodian of the law for Wolfhead County but also one of its wealthiest ranchers. His wife had died years before, leaving him with two children, Sally, now aged twenty, and Philip, a young man of twenty-three. Both children were well-educated, having been sent to schools in the East, but whereas Sally, upon her return to the West, was liked and admired, Philip found himself heartily detested.

Philip's ideas do not align with his father, who believes his son has no gumption. Mace Franklin, with whom Sally was in love, was employed by Whip Tyber, who the sheriff suspects is an outlaw. When Philip helps Mace and Sally escape her father and the posse, the sheriff tells his men that Philip is no longer a son. "Forget he is my kin. If you meet, shoot him on sight," the sheriff orders. After The Lone Ranger meets the three young folks, he orders Mace to continue working undercover with the outlaw gang and trick Whip into his confidence. Mace seeks the killer of his brother and tells Whip that Phil's father has an envelope in his possession with evidence against the killer. Whip and his men pay the sheriff a visit to steal the "evidence," unaware it was only bait to lure Whip into the hands of the law and verify his guilt as the killer of Mace's brother. Philip acts as a deputy and takes Whip into custody. The Lone Ranger arrives to verify to the sheriff that Mace was indeed working undercover.

Episode #1044-269, Broadcast October 4, 1939
Copyright Registration #66,349, script received at Registration Office October 5, 1939.
Plot: Ward Dunlap leads the cattleman's association in a feud against the sheep herders, going so far as to force squatters away from the territory. Dave Randall and his wife Connie, Easterners who came west for Connie's health, are ordered by Ward to vacate by the end of the week or be buried six feet deep. Ward informs Dave that it took some lead three weeks ago to force the sheepman out of the territory, and it won't take that much to force Dave and Connie. Meanwhile, Adam Sawyer, the former leader of the cattleman's association, is sitting in jail in the neighboring town of Kinsville, known to others as a sheepman's town. Ward is in charge and unaware he is being motivated by sheepman who posed as cattlemen, stirring up a potential range war. The Lone Ranger prevents Ward and his right-hand man, Zack Whimple, from reaching Kinsville, taking their guns and horses, ordering them to walk back to town. This buys time for the masked man and Dave Randall to sneak into Kinsville and break Adam Sawyer from jail. Dave visits Adam and then surprises the sheriff of the town when Adam is gone. Dave claims he was knocked from behind and forced to switch places. Rather than face embarrassment, the sheriff releases Dave, who returns to town to find Ward Dunlap appreciative of the favor. Not only was a range war prevented, but Dave and Connie were allowed to stay.

Episode #1045-270, Broadcast October 6, 1939
Copyright Registration #66,350, script received at Registration Office October 5, 1939.
Plot: Four con artists are making their way to Maysville to meet with the wealthy Eben Stokes, and his wife Jennie, in the hopes of stealing his life savings. It doesn't take long for them to discover that Mark Loomis, a victim of their scheme in another town, is trailing them to prevent others from falling victim. At the only water hole within miles, the schemers empty the pool, hoping to thwart their pursuer. The Lone Ranger and Tonto, finding Loomis dried of thirst, offer their canteens and learn from Loomis what is happening. Two of the crooks, meanwhile, pay Eben Stokes a visit, claiming to be representing a major oil company, offering $20 per acre and $1 per acre up front to have first rights for 30 days. When one of the crooks witnesses Tonto and Loomis riding into town, they quickly ambush them and hold them at bay. The next day, the other two crooks arrive pretending to represent a rival oil company offering much more per acre and suggesting Eben refund the first pair. The Lone Ranger rescues Tonto and Loomis at the outlaw camp, then pays Eben a visit before he gives away his life savings. In front of witnesses, The Lone Ranger explains the scheme, an old trick, and that no oil company is interested in the property. Mark Loomis will not only testify to the sheriff but the crooks will also be tried for attempted murder on top of their crooked scheme.

Notes: This episode marks one of the rare times Tonto rides Silver.

Blooper! One of the con artists in the gang during the opening scene almost stumbles over his lines.

Episode #1046-271, Broadcast October 9, 1939

Copyright Registration #66,418, script received at Registration Office October 11, 1939.

Plot: Dick Slone and Rufe Plunket, orphans, find themselves drawn into a blackmail plot when they are tricked into delivering a note to Mrs. Endicott at her ranch. Her daughter, Betty, knows what the note means but Sheriff Quinn and his deputy, Slim Slade, are puzzled. The only possibility of a solution to the mystery is The Lone Ranger, seen outside the ranch house. In reality, an outlaw named Dutch and his two conspirators discover Mrs. Endicott holds a secret: her husband was a criminal and is sitting in a penitentiary. Mrs. Endicott, fearful of the townsfolk judging her, keeps up a charade that her husband was dead. The note demanded $2,000 to be left at a location outside Red Rock in return for their silence. The Lone Ranger encourages the woman to follow instructions to the letter, using the money as bait against the blackmailers. Mrs. Endicott takes on the two orphans as ranch hands, so they would stop wandering and instead have a new home. At the rendezvous, Dutch and his men arrive – as does The Lone Ranger, the sheriff and his deputy. Exposed, the blackmailers reveal the secret about her husband. Only then she is surprised to discover the blackmail letter was of no value as the townsfolk already know about her husband. As Sheriff Quinn explains, no one in the community thought the worst of her (or her daughter, Betty) as a result, and based on her actions with two orphan boys, she deserves the recognition.

Episode #1047-272, Broadcast October 11, 1939

Copyright Registration #66,419, script received at Registration Office October 11, 1939.

Plot: The Lone Ranger breaks up a brutal fight between Mort and Bill Graves, only to discover the feud is over the family ranch, the Circle K. Mort was the adopted brother and certainly contained not an ounce of empathy in the marrow of his bones. Bill was shocked to discover his father, Jud Graves, was disowning him because of the fight, trying not to favor one son over the other but, in his efforts, he misjudged Bill. The townsfolk – and The Lone Ranger – could see past Mort's insincerity. Mort, meanwhile, plotted to gain possession of the ranch. When Jud falls off a ladder and the windmill is caught on fire, The Lone Ranger rides out to Bill to fetch Doc Fletcher, the frontier doctor. Back on the ranch, the masked man orders the ranch hands to combat the fire and then orders Sarah, Jud's wife, to play along when Mort arrives at the ranch house. Mort claims the doctor is behind him but is caught off guard when Doc Fletcher appears – courtesy of Bill. Mort's story about fetching a doctor to save Jud was proven a lie. Tonto verifies a rung on the latter broke because it was partly cut through. The fire was started by Brazos, the crooked cowhand who conspired with Mort. The old man, realizing he trusted the wrong son, agrees to mend wounds when he himself is mended from the fall. As for Mort and Brazos, they are being taken to jail.

Blooper! The announcer in the first act refers to the Circle K as the Box K, but throughout the rest of the episode the ranch is referred to as the Circle K. As of the time this book was assembled, only the first half of the episode existed in recorded form. To add confusion, according to the radio script, the announcer referred to the same ranch as the Circle J and again as the Box K (but not known if this oversight was caught during rehearsals and corrected before the broadcast).

Episode #1048-273, Broadcast October 13, 1939

Copyright Registration #66,420, script received at Registration Office October 11, 1939.

Plot: Neil Butler has been haunted by the events of the past. As a stagecoach driver who was encouraged by his superintendent to make a harrowing trip with both money and valuable passengers, he took a risk during a brutal storm – causing the stage to flip over and costing the lives of the passengers. Neil knows the town citizens turn an accusatory eye against him, even though in judgment the accident was not his fault. The Lone Ranger and Tonto, enroute to Alvaredo, meet Butler and after learning what he has been going through, investigate the pass. There, they discover and reveal to Neil that the accident was not his fault – someone had dynamited part of the pass. After the masked man, Indian, and Neil dodge a trap sprung against them in the form of a landslide, Neil returns to Alvaredo to once again pick up the reins of a stagecoach. With Neil cracking the whip, and following the advice of the masked man, he forces Jensen to be on board as they race the same trail he took in that brutal storm. Between canyons the stagecoach careens over the trail and as they reach sight of the dangerous corner that was sabotaged, Jensen panics and admits it was he who dynamited the pass. He rigged the trail to rob the stage of the $15,000, regardless of the lives that were taken as a result. When the stage comes to a stop, Jensen is surprised to learn that the sheriff and Bart of the stage office are inside. The Lone Ranger and Tonto tied, gagged, and forced the men inside so they could hear the confession. Bart apologizes to Neil for the persecution and promises his old job back… as well as his innocence verified throughout town for everyone to know.

Episode #1049-274, Broadcast October 16, 1939
Copyright Registration #66,719, script received at Registration Office November 2, 1939.
Plot: The expected arrival of young Matt Crowley brings far more than the usual quota of visitors to the town of Plainsville. The grandson of a famous two-fisted hombre arrived from the East. Plainsville consisted of farmers, not cattlemen, and when the railroad – powerful, rich, employing thousands of men – desired to seize the land it needed for its right of way at prices scarcely representing a fraction of the land's true value, the homesteaders panicked. Boyle, a crooked railroad man, has built a reputation for sending two toughs, Hogger and Buck, when homesteaders reject his offer to buy their land. Without evidence, Boyle cannot be accused or found guilty. Matt Crowley, however, when he arrives, confesses he only came to settle his grandfather's estate. To the homesteaders in the district, his appearance meant an opportunity to make a successful fight to save their homes from the railroad, but in truth he never had a fight in his life. That is, until Boyle approaches him in the streets and during a confrontation, punches Matt Crowley. The Lone Ranger, witness to the events, jumps into action by getting the draw on Matt, knocking him unconscious, before the young Easterner could take a defensive course of action. The Lone Ranger asks Matt to take a hand in the fight and, in return, he will give Matt all the help he would need. This would require learning how to ride a horse and shoot a gun. The next day, The Lone Ranger and Tonto sneak onto the construction camp and takes Boyle away as a prisoner, blindfolded. Dragging Boyle into the office of the U.S. marshal, and keeping his blindfold on, they create the illusion of being placed into Fred Miller's barn, that will be set on fire. Panicking, Boyle confesses his involvement to his captives, unaware that the U.S. marshal is listening to every word. Matt Crowley, meanwhile, apprehends Hogger and Buck, and brings them to the lawman's office.

Episode #1050-275, Broadcast October 18, 1939
Copyright Registration #66,720, script received at Registration Office November 2, 1939.
Plot: Cattle grazing peacefully in Clearwater Canyon are suddenly startled out of their calm by a horseman who seems to appear abruptly from nowhere. While his mount rears and prances, he shouts at the top of his voice and rapidly fires two guns drawn from twin holsters. This creates a stampede that almost kills elderly rancher Asa Botts. Asa broke his leg but was rescued by The Lone Ranger from the Longhorns that charged his way. Asa accused his partner, Luke Smead, because if anything happened to one of them, the partnership ensured the other received his share of the ranch. Asa once caught Luke's brother in the act of rustling. He was hanged soon after and Luke never forgave his partner. Later, when Asa's son Bud is found murdered, the sheriff takes Luke into custody. The Lone Ranger and Tonto, meanwhile, are examining the ground to find the trail of the man responsible for the stampede. When Luke escapes, the sheriff takes up pursuit for a short time, then sends his deputies out to hunt for Luke Smead's trail. Late that evening, the shock following the news of his son's death, combined with the pain of his fractured leg, make sleep impossible for Asa Botts. The Lone Ranger

pays a visit to Asa and requests the following night he have three men besides himself in the room: His foreman Curly Macklin, the sheriff, and one of the deputies, Cal Munson. During that meeting the next evening, Asa pieces together the clues left behind at the scene of the crime and insists a stranger on the prairie witnessed the crime and write a note, placed in an envelope. The lamp falls to the floor and before the lamp it relit, the envelope goes missing. Curly Macklin didn't realize that while the clues formed the solution, the identity of the killer remained elusive until Curly gave himself away because there was chalk on the envelope and his hands had chalk on them.

Episode #1051-276, Broadcast October 20, 1939
Copyright Registration #66,721, script received at Registration Office November 2, 1939.
Plot: According to Lieutenant Wade, white men who would arm redskins with new army issue rifles deserve the firing squad. Major Clemson at Fort Wister works secretly with The Lone Ranger to learn the identity of the gun smugglers who are making this district their headquarters. The Lieutenant sends out scouting parties to look for signs of Indian war parties while The Lone Ranger, disguised, roams the fort at will, investigating what might be an inside source. Hogan, meanwhile, arrives in a freighter with a partial delivery of munitions, claiming the Indians attacked and stole some of his guns. Two days later Indians pour from the hills, sweeping down to the fort for attack. While the troopers, summoned by a call to arms, tumble out of their barracks, the panic-stricken settlers abandon their belongings to crowd within the walls of the fort. A seemingly irresistible horde, the red-skinned savages burst into view, howling like fury and charging the fort. Sooner or later the Indians are bound to take over. When the hoped-for reinforcement does not arrive, The Lone Ranger loads the settlers and soldiers into the freighters, concealed from sight by tarpaulins drawn over their heads. Behind each driver kneels a trooper, gun in hand, with The Lone Ranger himself watching over Hogan, whose wagon is the lead. During the escape, the Indians do not attack. The red men know Hogan personally, because he was their supplier, and thus do not attack the wagons. Hogan tells the Indians to stay outside the fort – the doors are left wide open as a scheme to give the false impression that the fort is empty. When the Indians leave, awaiting their next plan of attack, Hogan leads the wagons away as fast as they can… but knowing he will eventually be placed under arrest for supplying the enemy.

Episode #1052-277, Broadcast October 23, 1939
Copyright Registration #66,722, script received at Registration Office November 2, 1939.
Plot: An hour after the notorious outlaw known as The Hawk shows up at a café in Millford and robs the patrons, The Lone Ranger takes after him, suspecting The Hawk's hideout to be back in the Red River country. After confronting The Hawk and his men and stealing the cash away, The Lone Ranger and Tonto discover the hard way that the riverbed and canyon prove not to be the hoped-for haven of escape. The outlaws hold their positions and propose setting the underbrush on fire, smoking out the masked varmint. The outlaws lose no time putting their scheme into effect. Matches are hastily lit and applied to brush as ready to burst into flame as paper. The flames spread rapidly. As the breeze continues what they started, the outlaws wait tensely for The Lone Ranger to make his appearance. They stand with hands on holsters peering beyond the flames but in spite of the closeness of the watch they keep, the masked man does not appear. The fire marches steadily toward the river, and then, reaching its goal, slowly burns itself out. The puzzlement of the outlaws grows when they soon discover they are surrounded by a posse, lead from behind by The Lone Ranger. It seems the hollow log Tonto stepped into was used as a means of escape in broad daylight. Our heroes swam under the log courtesy of the rotted and hollowed out air passage inside. They escaped underneath the log and there was enough space in which they could breathe and were entirely concealed.

Episode #1053-278, Broadcast October 25, 1939
Copyright Registration #66,723, script received at Registration Office November 2, 1939.

Plot: Bart Walker, an elderly blind rancher, mysteriously disappeared as completely as if he had never existed. No one had seen his departure, no reason why he should have vanished ever came to light. Ten years passed while his daughter, Mary, grew into a beautiful young woman. His wife, broken by sorrow, became embittered and feeble. Meanwhile, in the town of San Pedro, a conman named Richmond was trying to sell to an Easterner named Gorman what he claimed was the Lost Bonanza. A blind man named Dan intervened, giving The Lone Ranger a reason to save Dan from the roughhousing of Richmond and Tom Craig, a young rancher. Later, The Lone Ranger theorizes the old blind man, burned and scarred from a bad fire, is really Bart Walker, who has spent the last decade wandering as a hobo. For 50 years, prospectors and speculators have been searching for the Lost Bonanza mine, but the masked man figures it was on the Flying W property. Later the next afternoon, against the protests of George Casey, loyal foreman of the Flying W, and Mary, the elderly Kate is willing to sign over the property to Richmond, who made an offer to buy. The Lone Ranger does not intervene with the sale. Richmond laughs when he confesses he wanted the property because he knew where the hidden mine was located – below the trail to Cedar Point, between a big oak that was blasted out by lightning, and a curve just ahead down below in the canyon. Richmond starts fuming, though, after he reveals the location and discovers he never really purchased the Flying W. He purchased Tom Craig's land. Tom prepared a deed to his place and substituted it when Richmond wasn't looking. After Richmond leaves, The Lone Ranger reveals the blind man's identity. His memory came back to him when he was caught in the fire. He came back not to tell who he was, but to learn how his family had gotten on without him.

Episode #1054-279, Broadcast October 27, 1939
Copyright Registration #66,724, script received at Registration Office November 2, 1939.
Plot: The worst reign of terror the district had ever known had come to Salina County. What had started as a minor quarrel between the heads of two great ranches had developed swiftly into a feud dividing the county into two armed camps. As a result of the Kimball and Bowman feud, business in Salina City, the county seat, was paralyzed. Few men dared to ride the open range without the protection of partisans. Normal life was wholly disrupted, and fear and hatred had ousted all other emotions. In the face of this, the law was helpless, so the sheriff turned in his badge. Brought to Salina County by news of the feud, The Lone Ranger and Tonto enter the district by the north trail. Kimball cannot control his men because Duke, Kimball's crooked nephew, has convinced them they are fighting as much for themselves as for the outfit that employed them. Steve Bowman confesses he has no control over his own men, especially after his son Clayt was shot and wounded in the shoulder. The Lone Ranger speaks to Steve to explain that if Kimball's outfit knew Duke was willing to commit murder to become owner of his uncle's ranch, the feud could be stopped. Late that night, Duke informs his uncle he is taking over the ranch and shoots his uncle down. Claiming Steve Bowman shot and killed Kimball from an open window, the enraged crew from the Kimball ranch, with Duke in the lead, thunders down upon the silent and darkened buildings belonging to the Bowman outfit. The ranch is vacant, though, and the Kimball ranch hands find themselves surrounded. The Lone Ranger reports the truth and the mob listens as Kimball himself shows up to verify the betrayal of his nephew. Kimball, it seems, had been shot by blanks thanks to The Lone Ranger's interference. The men agree to settle their differences and end the feud.

Episode #1055-279, Broadcast October 30, 1939 [PART ONE OF THREE]
Copyright Registration #66,725, script received at Registration Office November 2, 1939.
Plot: A man named Clemens is shot in the back and killed in Yellow Gulch. The man who committed the crime lives in Laramie. A young orphan boy named Billy had been adopted by a resident of Laramie, Blacky. The boy is unaware that his adoptive father is the Yellow Gulch killer. When word of Marshal Cleary and Sheriff Otis looking for the murderer reaches the homestead, Blacky confesses his crime. Billy is disheartened, but Blacky assures the lad that he was good and square to the youth. Billy, however, flees out of emotional impact. A

sheriff's posse, riding along the countryside in search of the killer, observes the boy from a far distance, wearing Blacky's coat. One of the bullets meant for the killer finds its mark. After it is discovered that Billy was shot in error, he is rushed to the town doctor. The Lone Ranger, however, tracks down Blacky and hands him over to the marshal. When word reaches of the boy's condition, the masked man races back to ask the marshal to return to Laramie. The boy may be on his death bed, and it could be psychosomatic medicine needed for Billy's recovery. The marshal will not oblige, forcing The Lone Ranger to kidnap Blacky. The marshal takes aim and shoots both The Lone Ranger and Blacky in the back as they flee. The masked man's wound would heal in due time. Blacky, however, knew the bullet that hit him would be fatal. This did not stop Blacky who, back in Laramie, sat by the boy's bedside to encourage him to get better. Blacky dies from the wound, fulfilling his promise to the boy that he would never hang.

Blooper! The confrontation between the U.S. marshal and The Lone Ranger results in an unexpected pause in an exchange of dialogue.

Episode #1056-280, Broadcast November 1, 1939 [PART TWO OF THREE]

Copyright Registration #66,726, script received at Registration Office November 2, 1939.

Plot: Saul Bulow, Laramie's banker, offers Billy, now recovered, a job at the local bank. Billy prefers to work on a ranch, but accepts the job nonetheless. The Lone Ranger and Tonto, true to the promise they had made Blacky when the outlaw lay dying, are camped in the vicinity of Laramie, and plan to remain there until Billy's future is assured. A couple weeks later, the safe in the bank is busted open, close to $50,000 goes missing, and all of the employees are accounted for except Billy, who was nowhere to be found. When it is reported that Billy was seen racing swiftly from town with a satchel under one arm, a posse hastily gathers. Upon learning of the bank robbery from Tonto, The Lone Ranger races out to find Billy before the sheriff and his posse. Billy, who has been familiar with every foot of the swamp since early childhood, spurs his laboring mount over the only trail within its treacherous area that offered solid footing. Tonto finds Billy first, suggesting he return to town and surrender, but the sheriff catches up with them and brings Billy back. Although the sheriff, assisted by Saul Bulow, questions Billy again after he has been confined to a cell, the boy still stubbornly maintains his silence. Moreover, the efforts of hunting parties to find the money in the swamp are met with failure. As a consequence, Bulow's bank is forced to close its door, numerous depositors having lost heavily, and feelings are running high. Only Billy's youth prevented lynch talk. Soon after Billy takes the stand in the courtroom, The Lone Ranger enters with Clem Place from Jonesville. It seems Bulow had told Billy he would use a letter written by Clem Place against his friend if Billy did not flee after the robbery. With Clem's testimony, the masked man verifies that no such letter was written by Clem, claiming The Lone Ranger would be accused of murder. Thus, Billy's innocence was validated.

Episode #1057-281, November 3, 1939 [PART THREE OF THREE]

Copyright Registration #66,727, script received at Registration Office November 2, 1939.

Plot: Weeks after the events in Laramie, Billy finds difficulty in the fact that people refuse to believe he can be involved in so much trouble without the fault being his at least in part. The Lone Ranger, sympathetic to Billy's plight, informs Tonto that if they could find the money Blacky hid away, and if it were Billy who voluntarily turned it over to the law, then no one could continue to suspect him of dishonesty. But while The Lone Ranger and Tonto are away seeking the hidden cache, Billy pays a visit to Walt to sell some vegetables. Walt's wife quickly discovers her grocery money missing and accuses Billy of stealing it. Without finding the money in Billy's possession, the sheriff cannot make an arrest but this sets off a chain of events whereupon the citizens of Laramie, instead of helping Billy, treat him like a convicted thief. Discovering Walt is willing to pay five times the amount of the property worth, The Lone Ranger and Billy watch as Walt digs up Blacky's hidden cache. It seems Walt once knew Blacky. Courtesy of a distraction led by the masked man, Billy steals the money and rides into town, where he returns the stolen cash to the sheriff. Walt's wife, meanwhile, finds her grocery money and confesses her mistake in judgment. The Lone Ranger, shaming the town citizens, point out how they were so ready to judge him before they knew the facts. "And perhaps you'll be ready to use charity instead of criticism."

Notes: It was referenced in this episode that Billy is age 14.

Episode #1058-282, Broadcast November 6, 1939

Copyright Registration #66,825, script received at Registration Office November 7, 1939.

Plot: Josh Haskins, along with his wife and children, ride onto the ranch of his brother, Paul, in the hopes they can earn their keep. Josh was never able to succeed in keeping a job back East, but Paul is a different story. With a house like a castle, and thousands of head of cattle, Paul holds onto his empire jealously and he turns down his prodigal brother in fear he would have to share the wealth. When The Lone Ranger learns from Josh what happened, he arranges room and board for the family at Mustang Mag's, while the masked man assists Josh with proving to his brother that he can earn his keep. Against the advice of his foreman, Steve Grady, Paul rides out with the villainous Kane into Spring Canyon, knowing the risk he is taking. Paul's double motive urges him on as his pride will not allow him to show fear and his conscience from turning his brother away was eating at him. Sure enough, the trap is sprung and Jempson, seeking revenge for five years in prison, ties Paul to a chair with ropes. Kegs of dynamite are planted to blow up the shack and the rancher but The Lone Ranger and Josh race inside. At the risk of their own lives, they cut the ropes and help Paul flee – racing away moments before the shack explodes. Tonto races out after and apprehends the culprits. Paul admits he was wrong and foolish and welcomes Josh and his family to the ranch.

Notes: The Lone Ranger reveals in this episode that "Kemo Sabay" means "good friend."

Mustang Mag was referenced by name, but never appears in the program.

Episode #1059-283, Broadcast November 8, 1939

Copyright Registration #66,826, script received at Registration Office November 7, 1939.

Plot: "Gamblin' always leads to trouble," was Laura's advice. Young Jimmy Lane and his wife, Laura, fall victim to the scheming gambler known as Clayton. Hoping to square a gambling debt, Clayton suggests Jimmy play a game of cards – or face exposure and lose his job as a clerk at the express office. But the game is rigged, and Jimmy loses his money – again. He quarrels with a man named Glen Tucker. The next day, the sheriff of Haleysberg arrests Jimmy on suspicion of murder when Glen Tucker is found murdered. Jimmy's quarrel with Glen over the crooked card game was enough for the sheriff to cinch Jimmy's guilt. Jimmy has no alibi, but Clayton does. The Lone Ranger, realizing Jimmy was with him at the time of the murder, disguises himself and rides into town to play detective and investigate the facts. Tonto, paying a visit to Clayton, claims to have witnessed the murder and offers to leave town and keep his mouth shut for $100. Clayton agrees to pay and suggests they meet at the icehouse in an hour. Clayton is surprised, however, when he discovers he stabbed a dummy, not the Indian, and within the presence of the sheriff. The Lone Ranger reveals the cardboard cutout that was used to create a shadow of Clayton by the window, which breaks down his alibi.

Notes: This episode concludes too sudden-like. Towards the end of the episode, The Lone Ranger pays a visit to Laura and explains a scheme he had in mind, but she never appears in the remainder of the episode, defeating the point of having the scene. There is no resolution within the presence of Jimmy. It is believed that there should have been a closing scene that followed, whereupon Jimmy was set free, his innocence established, and his promise to Laura that he would no longer gamble again.

Episode #1060-284, Broadcast November 10, 1939

Copyright Registration #66,827, script received at Registration Office November 7, 1939.

Plot: The loungers in the cafe at Big Pine are excited to learn of a bronc busting contest that wagers high stakes. A man named Palmer, from Montana, claims he is the only person who can ride a horse named Killer and wagers $1,000 to anyone who can break and ride his horse. Bill Stedman, considered the best bronc buster in town, agrees to take on the challenge. In reality, Palmer and two accomplices were setting up a scheme to lure the citizens out of town at 5 p.m. tomorrow, so his accomplices could rob the office of the stage line of gold bullion, kept there awaiting shipment. When Bill backs out, a skinny bum named Sam Limpy accepts the challenge. The townsfolk ridicule the bum, unaware that he is a better bronc buster than Bill. Thanks to the interference of The Lone Ranger, Limpy not only succeeds in breaking Killer, but rides him back into town where all of the men and women take off in pursuit. Back in town, everyone is shocked and surprised to see Tonto, who caught the two crooks. The Lone Ranger exposes Palmer for having performed this same stunt in other towns, under other aliases. Exposed, the crooks are due for a lynching at the demand of the crowd, but the sheriff intervenes and assures them a fair trial will happen first. As for Sam Limpy, he is offered a job at Jud's ranch… and the lawman in town has no objection to Limpy taking possession of Killer.

Episode #1061-285, Broadcast November 13, 1939

Copyright Registration #66,950, script received at Registration Office November 16, 1939.

Plot: At one time the Ranch of the Three Pines, as it had been named by its original Spanish owner, had been a place of lavish hospitality and much simple gayety. That time was long past, however, and with the flight of years the place had slowly gathered a sinister reputation. Fear kept natives of the region from approaching its low, sprawling buildings of thick adobe, and strangers seemed to avoid them by instinct. Whatever evil or tragic thing befell the neighborhood, the malign influence of the Ranch of the Three Pines (now christened "The Hacienda of El Diablo") was certain to be held at fault. When a drought came, the ranch was something to blame. Knowing The Lone Ranger had no faith in such superstitions, The Padre calls on his friend to investigate. The masked man and Tonto soon discover the ranch is owned by an old Spaniard named Don Pablo, whose wife died 20 years ago, after which he fled to Spain to start anew. Having returned to his abode, along with his daughter Carmen and her husband, Julian, who find themselves taking care of the aging father but longing for a joyous life outside. Meanwhile, Juan Rivero leads the locals to attack the ranch with rifles, pitchforks, and flaming clubs to burn out the evil that lives there. Tonto succeeds in getting Carmen and Julian away from the ranch, but only momentarily when Julian decides to return and defend the house, only to discover that The Lone Ranger has altered the course of events. Don Pablo has invited the mob in as his guests and new friends, providing love instead of resistance. The men realize that their superstitions were unjust and old Don Pablo learns that it is not wise for an old man to bury himself in the past, and unjust to ask the same sacrifice of young people.

Episode #1062-286, Broadcast November 15, 1939

Copyright Registration #66,951, script received at Registration Office November 16, 1939.
Plot: See pages 247 and 248.

Notes: The plot to his episode resembled the 1921 King Vidor silent, *The Sky Pilot*, in which a preacher (also referred to by the movie title) arrives in a small rough-and-tumble cattle town in Canada, intent on bringing religion to its tough residents. They reject him at first, but in time he wins the residents over with his prowess.

Blooper! Fred Reto has a problem delivering his lines in the beginning of this episode, choking on air.

Episode #1063-287, Broadcast November 17, 1939

Copyright Registration #66,952, script received at Registration Office November 16, 1939.
Plot: Elderly Job Turner, a respected leader for the local farmers, is part of a small group that gathers in Banker Gould's office. Upon the advice of his good friend, Tom Bevins, a respected lawyer, the offer to swap an acre for an acre from the Rainy Valley to the Wolf Creek Valley would benefit both the ranchers and the farmers, the latter of whom would receive far better land for farming, while the ranchers would get the land needed only for grazing. The deal on paper was legit, Bevins assures his friend, but a month after all the farmers relocated and built new homesteads, the truth came out. A syndicate led by Banker Gould applied through the state capitol to construct a dam and reservoir for irrigation purposes. The land Gould and his men acquired through the business swap, formerly owned by the farmers, would soon become far more valuable. On top of that, after Job Turner learns the news from The Lone Ranger and pays a visit to the crooks to verify the truth, he discovers Banker Gould forged his name to a deed of 1,000 acres that provides the outward appearance of a bribe. Tom Bevins, who discovered how bad it feels to sell out his friend, rides out alongside The Lone Ranger to the state capitol to explain the situation with the governor. Meanwhile, back in town, the farmers discover the news and mob justice is enforced outside the Turner homestead. Before death could be dealt, the U.S. marshal, The Lone Ranger, and Tom Bevins ride up to back Job's story that he was framed and the signature on the deed forged. The governor, having heard the story, cancels the permits needed for the dam project. Banker Gould, with the U.S. marshal willing to bring him in on a charge of forgery, agrees to give all of the farmers their land back and together everyone can build the dam and reservoir without the crook profiting from the venture.

Episode #1064-288, November 20, 1939 [PART ONE OF THREE]

Copyright Registration #67,022, script received at Registration Office November 20, 1939.
Plot: Sheriff Muncie of Mercer City finds it difficult to believe Beth Christie's story. She's a woman in her early

thirties who claims her husband disappeared four months ago but has been replaced by an imposter. Scheming with a smooth lawyer named Foster, an outlaw named Yank Billings is masquerading as Thomas Christie. Beth's husband had inherited the JX Ranch upon the death of his uncle and through the imposter, the lawyer now controls the ranch against her protests because she has no proof of the imposter. To add to the confusion, Sheriff Muncie writes to another sheriff in Texas to verify her story, only to discover via written response that Beth Christie is really Mrs. Johnson, who was at one time under observation, and with time they might effect a cure. Doc English even offered to take her into his home and look after her. Doc English, of course, was also crooked and involved in the scheme to help Foster take over the ranch. Sheriff Muncie sees no other possibility than the fact the woman is clinically insane. Late that night, as the doctor tries to offer Beth more medicine (a.k.a. poison), The Lone Ranger and the sheriff enter Foster's residence to thwart the crime. The Lone Ranger suggests the doctor and Foster try a taste of their medicine, since the doctor insists it was harmless. When the men will not drink the poison, the sheriff places them under arrest.

Episode #1065-289, November 22, 1939 [PART TWO OF THREE]
Copyright Registration #67,023, script received at Registration Office November 20, 1939.

Plot: The Lone Ranger and Tonto, having exposed Foster and Yank Billings and Doctor English, proving Beth Christie was not insane and that those three planned to kill her, now find themselves on the other end of the law. The sheriff is found murdered the next day and the masked man and Indian accused of the crime. Lem Shiley, formerly Muncie's chief deputy, but now acting sheriff, takes Mrs. Christie into his office to question her regarding the recent events. Lem will not believe her story, even when the doctor uses phrases that the lawman cannot understand. Foster, meanwhile, is busy stuffing clothes into a valise. He needs to reach Dodge City in Kansas before the masked man catches up to her real husband, to ensure the real Thomas Christie is hung as scheduled a week from today. "I won't feel safe until I know Tom's been hanged," Foster tells Yank. Foster is taking the stage to Windom and catching the train there. Through that, he can get to Dodge City ahead of the masked man and Indian. When Foster meets up with The Lone Ranger, the crooked lawyer is taken to the secret camp where Tonto applies enough makeup to disguise the lawyer as the prisoner. Later that night, Tonto is forced to knock the deputy unconscious while the men make the switch and free the real Thomas Christie. With Thomas Christie set free and reunited with his wife, Forster is forced to fend for himself in the jail… until the makeup can be washed off and he be set free.

Episode #1066-290, Broadcast November 24, 1939 [PART THREE OF THREE]
Broadcast November 24, 1939
Copyright Registration #67,024, script received at Registration Office November 20, 1939.

Plot: Yank Billings, known to the people of Mercer City as Thomas Christie, is approached by Foster to continue impersonating Thomas Christie for a little bit longer. A rancher named Larson wants to purchase the JX Ranch for $30,000. Despite the fact the men do not legally own the ranch to sell, Foster insists selling. The Lone Ranger whisks the imposter out of the window in the back room and rides away. No sale can go through without a signature and as long as Yank is the masked man's prisoner, he cannot sign his name to anything. Tonto is sent to San Carlos to fetch Sheriff Price, who knows the real Thomas Christie. The Lone Ranger orders his friend not to return without the sheriff. The entire trip should take a month so. Yank insists he cannot be held prisoner for a month. A little more than two weeks pass. The Lone Ranger feeds his prisoner and assures him that while he has an errand to do, he will be back shortly. Alone, tied and bound, Yank discovers his plight to be useless until Foster and Doc arrive, sneak into camp and cut the ropes that bind Yank. Back in town, Foster attempts to make the sale final and Yank's determination to steal the money instead of an exchange proves the adage "Once an outlaw, always an outlaw." Sheriff Price and The Lone Ranger overtake the criminals and disarm them. The masked man explains how, when he sent Tonto to fetch Sheriff Price from Texas, and indicated it would be four weeks round trip, Tonto really went only into the next town and used the telegraph to send a message to Sheriff Price. Larson chuckles, as he was involved in the scheme to catch the crooks red-handed, hence why he dangled the cash in front of them to reveal their hand.

Episode #1067-291, Broadcast November 27, 1939
Copyright Registration #67,138, script received at Registration Office November 30, 1939.

Plot: Old Abby Salem orders Mason off her ranch, after she hears the rat-faced crook suggest she run off the emigrants from the land she owned, which Mason's employer, Caleb Chandler, is willing to buy. Despite the fact that the emigrants only paid half of what they owe for the property, Mason proposed she cut off their water supply. Frank, Abby's weak and crooked grandson, schemes with Mason to have the settlers removed by framing them for theft and butchering Abby's cattle. In defiance, the old woman insists on cutting off the water supply from Jones Creek, which flows from her property. Frank stands to profit from a reward for helping Caleb Chandler get the same property which the settlers will soon have to vacate. Mason, in return, plans not only to defraud the settlers, but his employer as well. He will get the land for a fraction of what he was authorized to pay, pocketing the difference after he pays off Frank. Days later the settlers leave the property (at the suggestion of The Lone Ranger, who explained his plan). As her grandson guessed, old Abby Salem makes no further protests when Mason offered to buy the land formerly occupied by the settlers. She accepts the price Mason suggests. The next day, Tonto brings Caleb Chandler to Abby's ranch and, with the assistance of The Lone Ranger, reveals the plot. Chandler paid Mason more than the $1,000 purchase price. Even more of a surprise was Dan Reynolds, leader of the settlers, who paid off the remainder of his mortgage on the property that Abby thought the settlers deserted. It seems they had the legal right to pay before the end of the month and own the property. Abby judged too fast and sold before she was entitled to. After discovering her grandson, Frank, pocketed part of the difference with the land sale, scheming with Mason, she makes good on her promise. Caleb fires Mason and orders him to leave the state.

Episode #1068-292, Broadcast November 29, 1939
Copyright Registration #67,139, script received at Registration Office November 30, 1939.

Plot: With only a handful of men to protect settlers who are scattered over a thousand square miles, the U.S. Army tries to keep the peace, only to face confrontation with Lame Bull and his tribe when a crooked Indian agent named Kemp steals the beef rations meant for the natives. Captain Holbrook, attached to the post at Decatur, knows that Kemp's right-hand man, Shorty Fay, is doing all the dirty work while Kemp schemes with Madigan, a crooked rancher, to sell the beef and split the profits. After discussing the concern with The Lone Ranger, Holbrook sets a trap to catch Kemp in possession of the stolen beef, by claiming publicly that renegade rustlers were involved. Lame Bull, meanwhile, gets ready for the warpath, despite the week-long delay his friend Tonto advised. The Lone Ranger rides out to trick Madigan and his henchman, Jute, into believing Shorty is headed for a cabin beyond Stony River in the forest, along with the money he made from the sale of the beef. When Kemp shows up at the same cabin, a falling out among thieves occur, resulting in a confession between the guilty parties. They are each so afraid the other would sell him out that they can't wait to get their accusations in first.

Episode #1069-293, Broadcast December 1, 1939
Copyright Registration #67,140, script received at Registration Office November 30, 1939.

Plot: Old Jasper Leach, the bad-tempered editor of the Bell City Bugle, has not been going easy with his editorials, practically throwing verbal rocks. With a new state, the entire future depends upon decisions made during the next election. Tom McGraw, an honest candidate for legislature, is facing surmountable odds against Dakin, a crooked candidate who is in the pocket with Heath, a smooth schemer. If the people represented by

Heath and Dakin gets the upper hand, they will exploit the state and its resources for themselves, lining their pockets. The Lone Ranger and Tonto follow the trail of a crook name Fritz, and Pedro, known as a notorious breed. When the masked man learns that Pedro knows of Tom's past—having stolen money, served his time in jail, and then gone to the trouble of saving up enough to pay back what he stole afterwards—he beats Dakin and Heath's attempts to discredit Tom. After kidnapping Dakin, The Lone Ranger and Tonto use the bad-tempered editor to expose the truth and the good credit of Tom McGraw. Meanwhile, handbills attempting to discredit Tom, printed by Heath and Dakin, are spread across the territory. Three days later, Dakin is released and discovers that the citizens in town want to tar and feather him. The Lone Ranger applied reverse psychology to ensure that Dakin and Heath's attempts to harm Tom McGraw only helped him.

Episode #1070-294, Broadcast December 4, 1939

Copyright Registration #67,168, script received at Registration Office December 4, 1939.

Plot: John Barton, a young Easterner who made good in less than a year in the West, settles down with a ranch house fit enough for his mother and his fiancé, Claire Proctor. When Jackson, a young rancher, insists he was cheated out of a sale, John explains to his mother how, months ago, beef was cheap. He heard certain things in St. Louis and had a bill of sale drawn up before the cost of beef went up four times. Now Jackson fears he will profit little because John's title with the round-up will net very little profit while John will flip the same cattle for market at a profit. The Lone Ranger and Tonto, camped just outside the small western cattle town of Bluefield, learn from Jackson what John Barton did within the confines of the law, despite the underhanded trick he applied. Making money, it seems, caused John to lose all sense of values. The Lone Ranger pays him a visit to remind him of what is more important than money, giving John something to think about. Two weeks later, John succeeds in profiting despite the resentment of the local ranchers. His mother and his fiancé leave him. Even Sam, his jack-of-all-trades, leaves him. When a mob of angry ranchers starts forming outside the ranch house, John steps out on the front porch to explain he had a change of heart. Having sold all the cattle at a prime rate of $10,000, he is pro-rating the difference (sans his $1,000 commission) of $9,000 to each man with a share corresponding with the amount of beef they sold him. With this change of heart, Claire returns, along with John's mother.

Episode #1071-295, Broadcast December 6, 1939

Copyright Registration #67,169, script received at Registration Office December 4, 1939.

Plot: For several months there had occurred a series of efficiently executed stage robberies outside the town of Chatfield—more than a dozen within the last three months. Elliott, the owner of the stage line, confesses to Dan Crocker, the stage line manager, that he made good on the stolen shipments totaling more than $60,000. But the robberies are not hit-or-miss affairs. The bandits apparently know when gold or cash is being carried. Ace Devlin, special investigator for the stage line, suspects Gus Hastings, proprietor of the local café. When Ace Devlin is later shot and murdered, The Lone Ranger realizes the investigator was close on the heels of the guilty culprit. It doesn't take long for the masked man to realize that Hastings was not the man responsible for the recent rash of stagecoach robberies. With the assistance of Sheriff Markham, Dan Crocker, and Mister Elliott, The Lone Ranger and Tonto set a trap that exposes two outlaws, Spot and Idaho, along with Limpy, a crook posing as an odd jobs man, leaking information to them. Limpy was pretending to be a handyman with no spending money around town in order to avoid suspicion. It was Limpy who committed the murder, but his two friends who committed the roadside robberies, so Limpy had an alibi during the dozen crimes.

Episode #1072-296, Broadcast December 8, 1939

Copyright Registration #67,342, script received at Registration Office December 11, 1939.

Plot: The Lone Ranger and Tonto ride to the aid of crippled Old Nate Warren and his son, Matt, when a scheming money lender lacks compassion by holding them to the strict deadline on a promissory note. Mr. Thorn, in the town of Stockton, plans to bid on Matt's stock of horses to reclaim part of his debt, even though he knows Matt only needs a few days' extension until Captain Ives of the Army arrives on the Stockton stage to pay for cavalry remounts. Thorn plans to sell the stock to the same but Matt withholds the information to whom he plans to sell. While Judge Luther is unable to grant an exception in the courtroom, The Lone Ranger and Tonto steal Matt's horses and hide the stock where no one can find it. Parties of expert trackers, led by the sheriff and Matt, find all their efforts futile. Thorn publicly accuses Matt of stealing his own horses, and hires Fresno to find the horses before the law does. Four days later, Captain Ives arrives at the Warren homestead and before old Nate can explain what has happened, the sheriff and Matt arrive with the horses, the deputies leading them into the corral. Perfecting timing, not by coincidence, as Tonto leads them and Tonto is accused of being one of the thieves. Captain Ives prepares to make the sale and Thorn finds himself in a precarious situation when he knows he cannot bid against the Army. Worse, Fresno wants his $100 as promised. The Lone Ranger barges in to rescue Tonto and ride away, verifying Matt had nothing to do with the theft and leaving Thorn now facing a lawsuit. The scheming money lender knows when he is licked and backs down.

Episode #1073-297, Broadcast December 11, 1939
Copyright Registration #67,343, script received at Registration Office December 11, 1939.
Plot: The two daughters and three sons of old Sarah Yates are gathered together in the home of the eldest, Ezra, to discuss the possibility of selling the family property. The Red River Line needs their property in Salt Creek Valley to lay a short line, offering $5,000 plus 30 percent of the voting stock. But old Sarah Yates will not sell. Ben Yates, one of her sons, pays a visit to Miguel and Rosa, to offer them money to leave, but Miguel prefers to stay. Sarah allows them to live on her land as Miguel trades on a favor from her late husband 40 years ago. The Lone Ranger rides to the state capitol to investigate. Three days later, the family is again trying to persuade Sarah to sell, but the old woman would rather break her arm than break a promise. When the masked man returns, he discovers Miguel and his wife have cleared out, even cleaning the cabin they lived in, and have left behind a note explaining how they did not want to hold Sarah back from a good sale. Miguel, though, the masked man explains, cannot write. The Mexican is rescued and brought back to testify against Harvey, the owner of the Red River Line. Only the family is surprised to discover that the company exists only on paper. Harvey planned on purchasing the land fair and square, then controlling the water rights that would profit him greatly when he later "abandons" the rail line and instead makes money as a result of the water rights.

Episode #1074-298, Broadcast December 13, 1939
Copyright Registration #67,344, script received at Registration Office December 11, 1939.
Plot: "Don't ever forget or forgive," was the advice given by Miss Willis of Argus Falls, who blamed her no-good son, Bob, for the death of her husband. Following the funeral, Bob discovers he is unable to get a job in town – not with a tarnished image. Two years before, Bob had fallen into bad company and his father financially bailed him out, but according to Bob's mother, his father kept paying and the debt is now the reason the family has to vacate and move into a small cottage at the end of town. Offering assistance is a well-to-do rancher named Clayton, who proposes to Helen, Bob's sister. Helen is not in love with the rancher, but in the interest of having her mother and younger brother, Danny live comfortably, she agrees to a marriage of convenience. The Lone Ranger, meanwhile, breaks into the bank late one night to steal the account books – not the money – and discovers Clayton was the recipient of the money Bob's father kept paying. Suspecting blackmail, The Lone Ranger creates a scheme whereby the rancher inadvertently reveals the location of his "evidence." Weeks later, following the advice of The Lone Ranger, Bob prevents the wedding from being conducted, at gunpoint, long enough for the masked man to return from a lengthy trip to expose Clayton. A wounded man, Jessup, was supposedly killed by Bob and a deathbed confession on paper had been held against Bob's father, the cause of

the blackmail. Clayton denies the charges until Tonto forces Jessup into the church to reveal the wounded man never died – he was sent to Arizona. Bob's family, realizing they misjudged their son, cancels the wedding as Clayton is taken into custody.

Episode #1075-299, Broadcast December 15, 1939
Copyright Registration #67,345, script received at Registration Office December 11, 1939.
Plot: Mullins and his outlaw gang plot to steal $100,000 in gold from the mill. With escape to the north or south impossible, the escape to the west would only be thwarted as a result of the newly-constructed telegraph. For this reason, his men perform numerous acts of sabotage. Tex Morgan, the scout and safety inspector, manages to thwart those acts. For this reason, Mullins has one of his men lure Tex outside of the camp to kidnap and hold him for a ransom and halt construction. The Lone Ranger, passing through the region, is handed a note by a passing messenger and asked to deliver it to Tom Halstead, the engineer in charge of the Western Union construction. Valuing the life of another man, Halstead calls a halt to construction – not a single mile of wire until they find Tex Morgan. Halstead orders his men to scout the region, but they could find no clue to Tex's whereabouts, or the masked man who was falsely accused of kidnapping. Tonto follows the backtrail of the initial messenger to where the outlaws hide out at South Pass. After alerting The Lone Ranger to the whereabouts, the masked man races back to camp and lures the telegraph workers to form a posse and pursue. With the crooks caught, and Tex Morgan rescued and freed from his bonds, construction of the telegraph continues and two weeks later is the wires are connected. The first message is sent from coast to coast to strengthen the attachment that binds the Eastern and Western Territories.

Episode #1076-300, Broadcast December 18, 1939 [PART ONE OF THREE]
Copyright Registration #67,562, script received at Registration Office December 22, 1939.
Plot: The town of Kirkwood lost a good man when lawyer Martin Craig was shot to death by Brad Wallace, a homesteader. The real culprit, though, was Snyder who, with money, power, and influence, succeeded where few had with his influence by trickery, lies and murder. Snyder offered $10,000 to Brad, who witnessed the crime, if he would take the fall. Snyder promised to use his money and influence to ensure Brad never goes to jail but when Brad is found guilty in a court of law and sentenced to jail, he quickly discovers he was betrayed. The Lone Ranger pays a late-night visit to Judge Thornton, an elderly gent who agrees to a ploy that would prove Wallace is innocent and Snyder is the real killer. Following The Lone Ranger's instructions, the judge writes a letter demanding blackmail in return for his silence. Snyder, furious, decides to use gunplay instead to silence the judge. The masked man intervenes and saves the life of the judge, as well as the sheriff who stood alongside to overhear the conversation that will convict Snyder for the crime.

Episode #1077-301, Broadcast December 20, 1939 [PART TWO OF THREE]
Copyright Registration #67,563, script received at Registration Office December 22, 1939.
Plot: Behind bars days before his trial, Snyder threatens the life of Brad Wallace's daughter, Jean, unless Brad flees town. Figuring his confession could not be used in court, Snyder's only problem is the testimony from Brad. Molly, the daughter of Martin Craig, who was shot down two weeks ago, informs Brad that Snyder has a dozen men working for him – taking orders even if Snyder is behind bars. Before Brad can find The Lone Ranger, he discovers Jean has disappeared. Two days later, in Kirkwood, Snyder is on trial, his fate dependent upon Brad's testimony. Judge Condon is presiding instead of Thornton. With Brad Wallace unavailable, the prosecution has 24 hours to produce his witness, or the charges would be dropped. In a daring move, a disguised Lone Ranger barges into the courtroom and forces Snyder, at the point of a gun, out into the streets. Threatening to shoot and having pulled an act never before seen in a courtroom, The Lone Ranger forces a confession out of Snyder – Jean was being held captive at the old Matthews' place. Order is restored to the courtroom when Jean, Brad and the kidnappers appear. Brad agrees to testify, Jean verifies she was kidnapped and her assailants confess they were hired by Snyder.

Episode #1078-302, Broadcast December 22, 1939 [PART THREE OF THREE]

Copyright Registration #67,564, script received at Registration Office December 22, 1939.

Plot: The night before last, Ben Hoffman's place was busted open and robbed. An Indian was seen racing from the scene of the crime. During the day, Tonto is mistaken as the thief and promptly arrested by the sheriff. Meanwhile in Kirkwood, Brad Wallace proposes to Molly, but her mother will not give her consent. In her eyes, Brad is not financially stable enough for her daughter. The sheriff is forced to arrest Brad for the robbery when the young man confesses for a crime he did not commit, in an effort to cover for Tonto. When The Lone Ranger learns from Tonto what happened, he pays a visit to the sheriff's office, locking the lawman in his own jail while freeing Brad. Meanwhile, the authorities in Kiowa City have been as active in investigating the recent bank robbery there as The Lone Ranger has. Sheriff Hutson, pursuing all leads, at length called upon the sheriff at Kirkwood. The Lone Ranger brings in the notorious Bat Fletcher and accuses him of the bank robbery. Bat panics and insists he never committed the robbery but was hoping to plead guilty to a lesser offence, proving he was in Kirkwood at the time by producing the cash and watch stolen from Ben Hoffman. As for Brad, he puts in an appearance at the sheriff's office with Bud Lenox, also known as The Gila Kid, who was the guilty culprit for the bank robbery. Brad is informed he will receive the $5,000 reward for Bud Lenox– more than enough to ensure approval from Molly's mother.

Episode #1079, Broadcast December 24, 1939

Copyright Registration #67,651, script received at Registration Office December 29, 1939.

Plot: John Lambert is forced to take in his two grandsons, Bruce and Tim, when he learns that their mother is dying and needs someone to care for her. On Christmas Eve, separated from their mother, the boys are unable to spend a joyous holiday. To Lambert, the day is merely an inevitable nuisance. To Martha Lambert, though, John's wife, the approaching holiday ranks with those of her own son's childhood. During a blizzard, the boys learn the truth and run away in the hopes of rejoining their dying mother, who lives three days' travel south of the Lambert ranch. The two boys fight their way through the blizzard hand in hand. The snow blinds them and the fierce cold is agony. To keep Tim occupied, Bruce tells him the story of the Nativity. When the Lone Ranger discovers what has happened, he races to find and rescue the boys. John, meanwhile, feels sorry for the scornful way he treated his son when he married Laura, then despised Laura when his son died. The Ranger finds the boys and brings them back to the Ranch, where they discover their grandpa doesn't hate them. Unexpectedly, their mother is also at the ranch, thanks to Tonto and his wonderful methods of healing the sick!

Notes: Typed on script "Not for Transcription."

Episode #1080-303, Broadcast December 27, 1939

Copyright Registration #67,652, script received at Registration Office December 29, 1939.

Plot: Major Clark, commander of the Army post outside Deerfield, summons one of the Army's civilian scouts to his headquarters. Red Wolf needs to surrender, Captain Greer explains. Jack Smith, the scout, having been raised by Indians when he was young, insists his blood brother, Red Wolf, is friendly to white men. Not so, claims Big Mike, a hunter who tells a different story. In truth, Squint and Hank, friends of Big Mike, killed three Indian braves and stole their horses, causing the Indians to go on the warpath. Big Mike hopes his fake story would lead an army to rescue his friends. Both Jack and Tonto learn the truth from Red Wolf while The Lone Ranger sneaks into the Indian camp and frees the two captives. Pretending to be an outlaw, the masked man gains the confidence of Squint and Hank and ultimately learns the whereabouts of the stolen horses, in a small, well-concealed valley. Captain Greer and Major Clark, meanwhile, lead an attack in the arroyo against the Indians, but discover their mistake when The Lone Ranger and Tonto present the crooks and the stolen horses, revealing the truth about Big Mike. Captain Greer apologizes to Red Wolf and Jack Smith for misjudging them and promises to think twice before taking action against a potential foe.

Episode #1081-304, Broadcast December 29, 1939

Copyright Registration #67,653, script received at Registration Office December 29, 1939.

Plot: There is a range war outside of Reed's Ferry between Bart Frazer and the villainous Jorgan. When Bart gets sick and feeble, and despite the fact he is on the road to recovery, his men either quit or Jorgan hires them away. Jorgan would love to run Bart out of the district, while Sheriff Miller would love nothing more than to jail Jorgan. After The Lone Ranger and Tonto decline an invitation to come work for Jorgan, the Indian keeps an eye on Jorgan and his men while The Lone Ranger divides his time guarding the Frazer ranch house and Bart's valuable herd of purebreds. Jorgan, meanwhile, organizes his men to create a stampede and scatter the herd, leaving no trace of suspicion. Bart Frazer's only defense is a young boy who stood guard along the valley where the herd of shorthorns grazed. After Tonto alerts The Lone Ranger of the news, the masked man sends his friend to fetch the sheriff and the posse. The Lone Ranger, having discovered the young boy is really Betty, the Frazers' tomboy daughter who taught herself all the accomplishments that a boy could do, races to save her. The attack comes swiftly and, as Jorgan's men exchange gunfire with Betty, The Lone Ranger fears a bullet will soon find its mark. After convincing Betty that it's futile to fight off the attackers, The Lone Ranger encourages her to ride alongside him as they race away to safety, always keeping enough distance to ensure the outlaws continue to pursue. Fearful of exposure, the outlaws, led by Jorgan, are determined to kill The Lone Ranger and Betty, unaware the chase is circling back to the valley where Tonto and the law trapped the outlaws. Jorgan is shocked when his men quickly surrender, and he learns the young man he was trying to kill is a really a young woman.

Episode #1082-305, Broadcast January 1, 1940

Copyright Registration #67,724, script received at Registration Office January 4, 1940.

Plot: An Easterner named Mr. Harris purchases land in Wolf Prairie to start his own cattle ranch, unaware that a shady con man named Mannix, a large land-and-cattle owner of the district, already sold the range of land to Phillip Taylor, representing an Eastern Syndicate. The Lone Ranger attempts to warn Harris about Mannix, but the Easterner believes the masked man is working for the Syndicate and ignores his warnings. Mannix, meanwhile, attempts to poison Harris' cattle with Larkspur so he will be forced to sell the land back to him, knowing he tied up all his money in the stock. Buck, working for the con man, soon discovers that the task he was hired for might include a double-cross. After creating a stampede to save the cattle, The Lone Ranger is forced to kidnap Harris so he can overhear a discussion exchanged between the crooks, verifying the underhanded scheme. This also allows for the law to take over.

Episode #1083-306, Broadcast January 3, 1940

Copyright Registration #67,725, script received at Registration Office January 4, 1940.

Plot: Jeff Corwin was recently promoted to the position of sheriff at Gold Flats, both a mining and a cattle town, twice the attraction for crooks. Within a month he was good as his word in cleaning up the streets, and no town in the state was more law-abiding than Gold Flats. The Lone Ranger, however, disagrees with Corwin's methods, because the sheriff fails to apply mercy and quickly gained a dozen notches on his gun. The sheriff's resentment against the masked man grew over time, following a verbal confrontation. One year after Corwin was handed his badge, White Cloud was shot and killed. The sheriff promptly arrests a local named Ray for the crime, despite the fact that the body of White Cloud was carried away. Corwin was surprised when he discovered the man that he arrested was his brother, who he never saw since they were seven or eight years old. Touched, Jeff releases Ray from jail, an action that spurs a lynch mob demanding justice. Seizing Sheriff Corwin and placing him in the saddle of a horse they had brought for the purpose, the mob rode out from town toward the grove that more than once had seen hangings without benefit of trial. The Lone Ranger and Tonto race to the scene with White Cloud, to reveal there never was a murder. Tonto took White Cloud away, having arranged everything beforehand. The fake quarrel, the pretended shooting, the berry juice to use as a stain, all with witnesses to help teach Corwin a lesson. As one of the most efficient lawmen in the state, he never learned that there were occasions when men who have broken the law deserved mercy.

Episode #1084-307, Broadcast January 5, 1940

Copyright Registration #67,866, script received at Registration Office January 10, 1940.

Plot: Amos Foley and his wife receive a contract to deliver 1,000 head of cattle to a construction camp in Cedar Point. If he succeeds, he will be awarded another contract. His problem, however, is that ranch hands are needed for the cattle drive, and they are few and far between. Morley, a competing rancher, has cunningly hired every able-bodied man in the region. Morley also purchased Foley's mortgage from the bank, so his motive is to prevent Amos from delivering so he cannot pay the loan and be forced to legally surrender the land. When Amos sends for his boys, who have since grown up and moved away, he is shocked to discover none of them showed when the stage arrived. Desperate, Amos and his three hands decide to move the cattle themselves. When Morley learns of this desperate stunt, he and his hired men attempt to start a brawl on the trail, preventing Amos from succeeding in his task… until The Lone Ranger and Tonto arrive with Amos' sons. The boys each thought the other went to help their father and understanding the scenario, rode with The Lone Ranger to the rescue. Outnumbering Morley and his men, the brawl wins in Amos' favor.

Episode #1085-308, Broadcast January 8, 1940

Copyright Registration #67,867, script received at Registration Office January 10, 1940.

Plot: A man is killed at Westport and Herb tricks his younger brother, Ray, into covering for him while he makes his escape. When the sheriff comes calling, Ray discovers he is accused of the crime and Herb is long gone. The Lone Ranger, learning what happened to the innocent brother, rides out to Marshal Clearly from Stageville to ask for a favor. At The Lone Ranger's request, the marshal prints a fake reward poster for the dead man, $5,000, dead or alive. Ray is released from jail. Word soon spreads through town and the next day, moments before Ray is awarded the $5,000, Herb arrives to confess the crime. He cannot be jailed for killing a wanted fugitive. With Herb's confession overheard by witnesses, The Lone Ranger reveals the truth: the fugitive was indeed wanted but with no reward money. Shamed, Herb leaves town.

Episode #1086-309, Broadcast January 10, 1940

Copyright Registration #67,868, script received at Registration Office January 10, 1940.

Plot: Outside the town of Twin Falls, a young rancher from the East named Jerry Brennan settled to start a new life… along with Gail Foster, the Eastern ingénue who agreed to marry him. Gail, however, dislikes the savagery of the West and prefers to return back East. Mark Kenyon, realizing he has a chance to win the woman's heart, hires two outlaws named Slick and Chris to kidnap Gail. One afternoon as Mark and Gail are riding through Chimney Rock, The Lone Ranger and Tonto hear shots and race to find Mark wounded. The schemer claims there were half a dozen, and he never had a chance to fight them off. They were hiding behind the rocks and no sooner were Mark and Gail surrounded, they were right on top of him. The sheriff rides out with a posse to comb the hills in search of the kidnappers, while Mark tells his story to Gail's father. When a stranger appears outside of Jerry's cabin, a note is found. The men who have Gail Foster want $50,000 for her return.

Late that night, in their camp, the masked man and his faithful Indian companion discuss the mysterious tracks that ran into the hills toward the west. There were tracks for only three horses – not half a dozen – and they covered their trail by keeping to the bed of Willow Creek. To avoid being seen hundreds of feet from the outlaws' cabin, The Lone Ranger and Tonto ride around the outside of the canyon and lower themselves by rope into the canyon. The vigilantes manage to creep up on the cabin from behind and when they discover their attempt was short-sighted, and a standoff occurs, the masked man has an idea. Using a container of kerosene, The Lone Ranger pours the fluid under the front door and lights the liquid. The distraction keeps the outlaws from shooting Gail and instead act on the impulse of self-preservation. Tonto kicks the door down and races in to rescue Gail. Having observed the thick smoke of the burning cabin, the sheriff and his posse arrive, along with Gail's father. Slick and Chris attempt to get the masked man to throw in with them, but The Lone Ranger instead tricks them into believing that Mark tipped off their location. Certain things made the masked man suspect Mark knew more about the abduction than he had told, especially being more concerned for his flesh wound before relating the events of the kidnapping. As the sheriff takes the three crooks in, Gail assures Jerry that the excitement of the West was worth the trip and "maybe there's still a chance I'll decide for the West."

Episode #1087-310, Broadcast January 12, 1940
Copyright Registration #67,923, script received at Registration Office January 13, 1940.
Plot: A stranger had arrived in the small village of Eagle's Nest, beyond the Pecos River, and there had settled himself. He was the proprietor of a combination bar and general store, and he introduced himself to his new neighbors as Judge Roy Bean. Meanwhile, a gang of thieves led by Snake and Bull, profit from the attack upon parties of whites. Little Wolf's tribe of Apaches strike against a trail herd crossing through Castle Mountain Gap, leaving Bull and his men to gather up the scattered cattle, leaving the Indians to do their dirty work. As Tom Clark and his party approach the Pecos with his thirsty cattle forging ahead, he observes the far-off approach of Indians, courtesy of a warning from The Lone Ranger and Tonto. The band of outlaws waiting below to gather the scattered cattle, explained The Lone Ranger, have nothing to fear in this part of the country, but asks Tom to help clean up the territory. Tom pays a visit to Judge Roy Bean to ask the judge to come witness the crime and exercise justice against the outlaws. Following the advice of The Lone Ranger, Tom creates a set-up that tricks the outlaws into acting accordingly as they had in the past. The trap works and the outlaws, including Bull and Snake, are taken into custody. The outlaws heard there was no law west of the Pecos, but today they are going to meet up with the judge at Eagle's Nest. The crooks are found guilty and sentenced to hang… or leave this part of the territory.

Episode #1088-311, Broadcast January 15, 1940
Copyright Registration #68,125, script received at Registration Office January 24, 1940.
Plot: Old Sam Catlett, always too meek for his own good, had been imposed upon by his wife, his children, and his neighbors until he could scarcely call his soul his own. What he had suffered in part, however, was nothing compared to the indignities put upon him when his wife's brother arrived at the ranch for an indefinite stay. Homer Larkins, the brother, was a pompous, conceited, and inept fool. He was supremely contemptuous of Sam's ability to manage his own affairs and wholly confident of his own. At the very beginning of his stay, he assumed the management of the ranch, bulwarked by the approval of his sister, of whom Sam stood in mortal fear, and turned a deaf ear upon the advice prompted by Sam's misgivings. It seemed as though Sam had been thoroughly discredited as the directing head of his own ranch… until The Lone Ranger revealed to Sam that crooks (Ike Slater and Meade) were cleverly playing upon Homer's ego to further their own criminal schemes. Sam still hesitated to assert himself, although warned by the masked man. Sam had been used to giving way before the demands of his family for too many years, and what The Lone Ranger had told him, although coinciding with his own suspicions, was not immediately acceptable as proof. Without proof, he did not dare brave his wife's scorn, and he saw no way in which this proof could be obtained. The Lone Ranger, however, had made himself active on Sam's behalf. With Tonto, he gathered the evidence Sam needed. And, armed with this, Sam enjoyed a remarkable transformation. The indignation he had kept buried for so long boiled over. Homer was expelled from the ranch, Sam's wife put in her place, the crooks turned over to the law, and Sam himself restored to the position of respect he deserved.

Episode #1089-312, Broadcast January 17, 1940

Copyright Registration #68,126, script received at Registration Office January 24, 1940.

Plot: Jack Webster, examining certain old documents, had his curiosity aroused by one written in Spanish on parchment and accompanied by a map. Appealing to the local padre to translate these papers, Jack was met with the startling news that it was the record of an early Spanish explorer and contained meticulous instructions designed to reveal the location of a long-lost Aztec City, reputedly rich in gold. Jack, set afire by this information, refused to listen to the advice of either the padre or his wife, Alice, but set out with a companion, Rusty, to make the treasure his own. At first reconciled to his departure, Jack's wife was suddenly alarmed when she learned that Jack's uncle and aunt, for whom he was supposed to be managing their ranch in their absence, would soon return. She appealed to the padre for aid, and the padre in turn sent for The Lone Ranger, who promised to bring Jack back, by force if necessary. In the meantime, Jack and Rusty, penetrating a wild and barren country in their search for the treasure, aroused the suspicions of outlaws who suspected them of being lawmen. The outlaws, led by Baldy, spying upon their movements, overhead a conversation that they misunderstood… a conversation that convinced them their suspicions has been correct. To protect themselves, they decided Jack and Rusty must die. They reckoned without considering The Lone Ranger, however, who not only saved Jack and his companion, but made the outlaws prisoner as well. He persuaded Jack that his duty lies at the ranch he had deserted and, when Jack consented to return, revealed that the map and documents that has enticed him on the search were merely the forgeries of a swindler.

Episode #1090-313, Broadcast January 19, 1940

Copyright Registration #68,127, script received at Registration Office January 24, 1940.

Plot: The district centering around the town of Painted Wells was first alarmed, then terrified, by a series of abductions that seemed to have neither a pattern nor a motive. A wealthy member of the community had been abducted, and a town ne'er-do-well. A boy had disappeared, and an old man. The law, finding nothing to link these people together, confessed itself baffled. And when The Lone Ranger and Tonto arrived upon the scene, the sheriff was in no mind to object to the assistance of a masked man. In fact, hoping against hope that The Lone Ranger could solve the mystery, he willingly gave him access to such information as he had been able to gather. He carelessly let it be known, however, that The Lone Ranger had resolved to get to the bottom of the affair… and as a result The Lone Ranger's life was threatened and but narrowly saved. The masked man, persisting, at length came to the shrewd conclusion that these abductions were not the work of a madman, as common opinion maintained, but the actions of a man who knew every moment what he was doing and why. Putting this theory to the test, the masked man and Tonto carried out a plan arranged between them… and had the satisfaction of proving their suspicions correct. They safely returned the abducted people to their families and revealed that only one of the four had inspired the kidnappings. The other three had been seized to confuse the trail; the fact that no one was known to have grudges against them had effactually prevented suspicion being directed towards the guilty man who had wished to revenge himself upon the fourth.

Episode #1091-314, Broadcast January 22, 1940

Copyright Registration #68,128, script received at Registration Office January 24, 1940.

Plot: The Lone Ranger and Tonto attempt to prevent an Indian War around the Sawtooth Hills when Captain Fletcher, in charge of a cavalry troop, leads his men into Black Fox's camp in Snake Ridge because white women have been kidnapped by Black Fox. One of the women is Fletcher's wife and another is the wife of a brave lieutenant who fights off the spirit of his father-in-law. The case gets personal for Tonto because Black Fox once led a war party on Tonto's good friend, Chief Thundercloud. Tonto infiltrates the camp, assuming the character of an Indian anxious to make war upon the whites. Having no difficulty making himself a member of the chief's immediate party, he learns where the women are. The Lone Ranger convinces Fletcher to dress his men in women's clothing to perform a switcheroo in Black Fox's hideout below Snake Ridge, and thus get the advantage and defeat Black Fox.

Notes: The names of fictional characters in this episode include Private Tom Cole, Captain Fletcher, Mr. Todd, etc. These were named after the radio cast: Dewey Cole, Jim Fletcher, John Todd, etc.

Episode #1092-315, Broadcast January 24, 1940

Copyright Registration #68,129, script received at Registration Office January 24, 1940.

Plot: When a troubled orphan named Tommy is caught stealing by Job Hopkins, a store proprietor in the village of Sweetwater, The Lone Ranger insists that jail is not the solution. Instead, the masked man takes Tommy to Mustang Mag's ranch house for guidance. Two months later, under Mag's wing, Tommy is rehabilitated but two crooks, Spade and Jeb, pay the boy a visit. In fear of his past exposed, Tommy agrees to help them create a distraction that would allow the thieves to steal money from Hopkins' safe. Unaware The Lone Ranger and Tonto were trailing the two crooks, Tommy chooses an act of betrayal and shouts a warning to Job Hopkins that the crooks were waiting to rob him... at the risk of being shot by the crooks. The bullets miss Tommy by inches, but his warning alerts The Lone Ranger who apprehends the crooks. Hopkins agrees with the masked man that jailing the boy a couple months ago would not have been the solution.

Episode #1093-316, Broadcast January 26, 1940

Copyright Registration #68,130, script received at Registration Office January 24, 1940.

Plot: Outside the town of Pine Bluffs, The Lone Ranger and Tonto assist an Easterner named Taber in the apprehension of two brothers, Dave and Pete Gruber, who once framed Tabor for the murder and disappearance of an old man named Ben. Tabor went to the West when he learned that the Gruber brothers escaped prison and the killers blame him for their incarceration, now seeking vengeance in the worst way. The Gruber brothers scowl when captured, until Dave Gruber uses Tonto as a human shield to make an escape but fails to reckon on the cunning of The Lone Ranger when they reach the town of Pine Bluffs. Sheriff Maxwell and his deputy rode out with The Lone Ranger and Tabor, setting a trap that forces Gruber into revealing the location of Ben, and revealing the truth that Tabor did not commit the murder, hoping to play the role of a victim against the two men who were trailing him.

Episode #1094-317, Broadcast January 29, 1940

Copyright Registration #68,266, script received at Registration Office February 2, 1940.

Plot: When Matt Duncan, although still in the prime of life, found that he was losing his sight, he was convinced that his usefulness was ended. He had been the head of a firm of drovers organized and owned by ranchers who did not themselves assume the management. Upon his resignation his post went to Richman, once a trail foreman and later Matt's assistant, who had worked himself into the confidence of the owners. The moment he was secure in his position, however, he put into effect a scheme to defraud the company. He purchased cattle from Austin and Bixby, a pair of dishonest ranchers, with the firm's money. He paid them for prime steers... but accepted scrubs and yearlings for delivery, pocketing his share of the difference. Only Ezra Slocum, Matt's best friend, suspected that something was wrong, and he could have done nothing had not The Lone Ranger come to his aid. The masked man, passing herds sent by Richman up the trail to the markets at Wichita, had noted a circumstance that had aroused his suspicions. Enquiries convinced him of Richman's dishonesty. Once convinced, The Lone ranger called upon Matt, persuading him his blindness did not disqualify him for the work he had performed for the better part of his life, gaining Matt's promise to take back his position if Richman were discharged. Then, employing a young homesteader he had befriended, The Lone Ranger convinced Austin and Bixby that Richman faced exposure and was planning to shift the entire blame to them. At a meeting of the firm's owners, they furiously denied the charges… only to learn too late the charges had never been made and the masked man had tricked them into exposing themselves voluntarily.

Episode #1095-318, Broadcast January 31, 1940

Copyright Registration #68,267, script received at Registration Office February 2, 1940.

Plot: Old Zeke Prentiss had done more than any other single man to bring prosperity to the community of Painted Wells. He had administered the bank he owned as a public trust and, when the day came for him to die, he bequeathed the bank to his two sons, John and Ward, in the same spirit. The Lone Ranger, learning of Zeke's death, was dubious of the future, fearing that John and Ward would not work well together. John, the elder, educated in the East, was regarded by the ranchers who used the bank as an outsider. Ward, well-liked by then, was headstrong. The invisible friction between them came to a head when John refused to make loans to the ranchers for the purchase of cattle, insisting that all signs indicated the market would break. Ward, furious, withdrew from the bank entirely, taking with him his own personal funds, and loaning these funds to the ranchers while they lasted. But the masked man, convinced that John had gauged the market correctly, advised him to stay with his decision and promised him help in the event of trouble. Tonto was dispatched by The Lone ranger to Grove City, the nearest town boasting a telegraph, with orders to return to Painted Wells immediately if the market broke. In the meantime, Ward had retired to a ranch his father had owned, while John continued with his policy. To the ranchers he tried to explain that his refusal to loan them money for the purchase of cattle was as much in their interests as those of the bank. They could not see this, however, and certain John was preventing their doing business, they finally worked themselves up to a pitch of rage where it seemed they must drive John from town. The masked man brought Ward to John's aid, the mob was held off, and finally Tonto arrived with news that vindicated John's policy and reunited the brothers.

Episode #1096-319, Broadcast February 2, 1940

Copyright Registration #68,268, script received at Registration Office February 2, 1940.

Plot: The Lone Ranger learned in conversation with Dan Bowen that the elderly rancher nursed an almost fanatical devotion to the land. Beyond this, he was a happy and contented man, wanting but one thing he did not possess, a home in the small valley where he and his wife had always someday hoped to live. When The Lone Ranger suggested that he obtain the money he needed by prospecting in the hills behind his home, Dan informed him that he had known for years that gold was there but, fearing a gold rush and despising the type of men who engaged in them, he had resolved never to touch it. The masked man, knowing that a prospector had been in these same hills recently, said nothing, not wishing to alarm Dan, but when the feared gold rush developed, Dan blamed the masked man. A narrow pass, close to the place where Dan lived, served as a corridor to the hills where the gold-seekers hoped to find the precious metal. Dan, however, determined that no one should pass through it and, with his son Jim, guarded it during alternate watches. It was narrow enough for a single man to defend, except in the event of a concerted rush, and the prospectors at first held back in the hope that Dan would give in peacefully. When it became clear that he would not, they determined to make it through at any cost, and would have made the attempt had not the masked man first talked to their leader, Hardrock. The plan the masked man suggested met with Hardrock's enthusiastic approval. He, in turn, enlisted his men, and Dan's opposition melted away when he learned that the men he had hated had built him the home for which he had longed for so many years.

Episode #1097-320, Broadcast February 5, 1940

Copyright Registration #68,360, script received at Registration Office February 8, 1940.

Plot: The church at Argus Falls owed over $5,000 on its property and, although Dan the elderly rancher who held the mortgage did not wish to foreclose, Reverend Matthew Whitcomb realized that he could not afford to do otherwise without, in turn, losing his ranch. He promised Dan that the money would be forthcoming and immediately called upon the wealthier members of the community, seeking contributions. They refused him, however, on various flimsy pretexts, and that night he was utterly dejected until The Lone Ranger appeared and promised him his aid. Leaving the minister, the masked man joined Tonto and told him they had work to do, that he had a plan in mind to teach certain members of the community a badly needed lesson, but that first they must gather certain information. Later, when the information they had gained proved to fit the masked man's idea, he sent Tonto to call on Mustang Mag. Several weeks later, Jed Keith, Red Logan and Asa Flinders, the three men who because of their wealth and position, The Lone Ranger had singled out to be made examples, began to act strangely. Each called upon the sheriff, asked questions concerning Mustang Mag, then swore upon the sheriff to secrecy. In the meantime, the masked man had warned the minister that if these men attempted to purchase the church land, not to talk business with them unless all three were present. As the masked man forecast, Keith, Flinders and Logan arrived one after the other and angrily began bidding for the land. In the midst of the bidding, the minister learned they had been tricked into believing the land would be wanted by a railroad as a right of way. Refusing to profit from their mistake, he told them the truth. The Lone Ranger entered, compared their behavior to that of the minister, and awakening them to a sense of their shame, persuaded them to pay the mortgage themselves.

Episode #1098-321, Broadcast February 7, 1940
Copyright Registration #68,361, script received at Registration Office February 8, 1940.
Plot: The Lone Ranger and Tonto, watching from the top of a hill, were astonished to see an apparently sane rancher deliberately frighten the horse that drew his buggy into attempting to run away. Although they set out to halt the runaway, they were forestalled by the young rancher, Pete Marsden. Duffy, the driver of the buggy, appearing effusively grateful, promised to withdraw his objections to Pete, who had been courting his ward, Kate Freeman, and further insisted upon reimbursing Pete for damage done his clothing. The explanation for the act that had puzzled The Lone Ranger became apparent later, however, when Pete was arrested in Ward's Crossing upon Duffy's charge that he had held him up and stolen from him a $1,000 bill. Pete, when the bill had been given to him by Duffy, had assumed it to be a one-dollar bill and hadn't troubled to examine it. When the masked man contacted Pete, he learned that the young rancher suspected Duffy was looting his ward's estate and wished to prevent her marriage in order to save himself from being forced to give an accounting of his stewardship. The Lone Ranger knew that in order to free Pete, Duffy must be forced to betray himself. Capitalizing upon Kate's loyalty to the young rancher, in spite of the fact that he was under arrest, the masked man convinced Duffy that the young couple intended to get married anyhow. The masked man hid Kate so that she couldn't be the target for Duffy's anger. Then, aware that with Kate out of his reach, Duffy could halt the marriage only by murdering Pete, he laid a trap that brought the sheriff upon the scene in time to witness the murder attempt, arrest Duffy, and clear Pete of the charges against him.

Episode #1099-322, Broadcast February 9, 1940
Copyright Registration #68,362, script received at Registration Office February 8, 1940.
Plot: Carver, a crook with influence, had long grafted from both the Indians and ranchers in the great Indian Territory. When ranchers wished to rent rangeland from Chief Standing Elk and his tribe, they were forced to deal through Carver, who, getting the Indians intoxicated with rot gut, obtained the leases for practically nothing while charging the ranchers large sums ($25,000 to be exact), more than the leases were worth. Marsden, representing a group of Texas ranchers, refused to cooperate with Carver and insisted upon dealing with the Indians direct. Carver, threatening little, was understood by everyone to be twice as dangerous on that account. Bat, one of his men, breaks into the house and stole a letter that told when Marsden would deliver the rent money to the Indians, but upon the same occasion The Lone Ranger also learned when Marsden planned

to transport the gold. Fred Baker, Marsden's intermediary with the Indians, from whom the letter had been stolen, was worried for Marsden's safety and for the safety of the gold he and his party carried. He had reason to worry, because Carver and his men had every intention of halting Marsden's party and seizing the money. The Lone Ranger, however, had been cooperating with Major Willis and the army, which for long had been anxious to get something on Carver. So, when Carver and his followers, wearing hoods to conceal their features, rode out to Willow Gulch and halted the two wagons led by Marsden, they discovered that thanks to The Lone Ranger the wagons held full complements of soldiers, only too anxious to arrest them.

Notes: This radio script was originally planned for broadcast on January 29, 1940.

Episode #1100-323, Broadcast February 12, 1940
Copyright Registration #68,433, script received at Registration Office February 12, 1940.
Plot: The arrival of Dick's elder brother, Red, was unfortunate for Dick when it occurred just after the latter had quit his position with the stage line until he could decide whether or not it was wise to work for the father of the girl he intended to marry, Sally. Henry Warren, the stage line owner, wanted Dick badly, offered him a fine position and promised to keep it open. But Red's arrival worked a change in the young man. Red, a swashbuckling cowboy, typified everything Dick admired. Dick, imitating his brother, began drinking and gambling excessively and refused to heed the warnings of his friends. The Lone Ranger and Tonto, having trailed Red to Elk City, advised Red of the situation and learned that Red had not realized Dick was throwing away such excellent opportunities. Red, attempting to reason with Dick, was repulsed… Dick claiming he was old enough to do as he pleased. At this Red turned to the masked man for advice… and learned to his unpleasant surprise that The Lone Ranger had trailed him from Texas because of a hold-up he had committed there in the town of Hondo. The Lone Ranger told Red, however, that he thought it more important to awaken Dick to his foolishness than to turn Red over to the law immediately, and suggested a plan that Red could put into effect if he wished to make the sacrifice. Red agreed for this brother's sake, and not long afterwards Dick was horrified to learn that Red was accused of robbing a wealthy widow in town. Red, brought to the sheriff's office by The Lone Ranger, at first denied the crime, then confessed when it seemed that the evidence could not be ignored. Dick, horrified, turned from his brother with revulsion and told Warren he would take the position offered. After Dick leaves, The Lone Ranger revealed that Red's reward for accepting the blame for a crime he had not committed was pardoned for the one he had. In private and in the presence of the U.S. Marshal, to whom Tonto fetched, Red and the widow confess the scheme to the sheriff so the charges would be dropped – there was no such robbery and therefore, no charges could be brought against him. When the marshal discovers why the masquerade, he orders Red to flee the region so the masquerade would not be unveiled, for the betterment of Dick's future.

Episode #1101-324, Broadcast February 14, 1940
Copyright Registration #68,434, script received at Registration Office February 12, 1940.
Plot: When The Lone Ranger learned Tom Barker's foreman, young Fred Mason, was in reality the brother of a man Fred mistakenly believed his employer had murdered, the masked man informed Barker of Fred's identity, but convinced the rancher that if put to the test Fred would find that he had less desire for revenge than he imagined. In line with the masked man's plan, Barker pleaded illness as an excuse for a journey and a long vacation, which gave Fred a power of attorney to exercise in his absence. This power of attorney was to be used to affect the sale of a strip of Barker's land to the sheepman, Clay Loftus, as an alternative to Loftus' suggestion that Barker sell him his entire ranch. Making clear to Fred that the sale of the ranch at this time would ruin him, Barker left, supposedly on his journey. Shortly afterwards Fred was approached by a man claiming to be Loftus' representative. Fred refused a bribe to sell the entire ranch… but, refusing the bribe, consented to sell

anyhow, explaining to Siegel, the representative, that he wanted revenge, not profit. The sale was put through… and when the ranch was seemingly sold beyond recall, Fred awakened to the fact that Barker had treated him with an unusual kindness while Fred had been in his employ. For the first time realizing what he had done, he was in despair, and appealed to The Lone Ranger for aid. The masked man, explaining that with his power of attorney, Fred had sold the ranch legally, professed to believe that Fred could not be helped. Fred, rushing to town, tried to get Siegel to return the ranch, but without success. Seizing his gun to threaten Siegel, Fred found himself halted by The Lone Ranger, who suggested that Fred's one chance to restore the ranch to Barker was to confess everything to the sheriff. Fred, agreeing although it meant jail, found that his willingness to face the consequences had restrained him in the good graces of his employer, to whom the ranch still belonged.

Episode #1102-325, Broadcast February 16, 1940

Copyright Registration #68,435, script received at Registration Office February 12, 1940.

Plot: Ted Bennett, a young doctor having a reputation as a drunkard, was blamed for the death of a patient when he was not at fault. Nevertheless, he was ostracized by the community of Huntsville, and when The Lone Ranger prevented Bennett's attempt at suicide, he made it clear that Bennett deserved to lose the faith of the townspeople, although on this occasion they were mistaken. However, he encouraged Bennett to remain and fight to win back the place he had held, promising to return when he could to learn how Bennett was making out. Months elapsed before the masked man could keep his promise. And when he did, he returned not because of Bennett, but because he had received a mysterious message from one of the doctor's neighbors, calling for aid. The neighbor was Lem Decker, who explained to The Lone Ranger that although he knew the identity of the killer who had recently been terrorizing the district, he feared to go to the law and was appealing to the masked man to get independent evidence against the outlaw. Shots from outside interrupted Lem, however, when he would have named the killer. The masked man, returning from an unsuccessful chase, was met with the information that Tonto had been arrested for the murder and that Lem was unconscious, near death. The masked man immediately called upon Doctor Bennett, although he knew that if Bennett attended Lem, it would arouse the fury of the townspeople. But while Bennett operated, the masked man held off the mob that gathered. And when Bennett's efforts were successful, Lem cleared Tonto, named the mob's ringleader as the guilty man, and indirectly, by the fact of his recovery, restored Bennett to the esteem of his former friends.

Episode #1103-326, Broadcast February 19, 1940

Copyright Registration #68,723, script received at Registration Office February 28, 1940.

Plot: The Lone Ranger, drawn to the vicinity of the great Eureka Mines by rumors that workers in the mines were losing their lives because of the greediness of the owner, Meekin, is present when a young woman is told that her husband, Jim Edwards, had been killed in a cave-in on the very day he had intended to quit the mines for good. With actual tragedy brought close, the masked man resolved to force Meekin to take measures to make the mines safe. Riding to Meekin's home, he learns that young Dave Meekin disapproves strongly of his father's miserly policy… so strongly in fact that it leads him to break with his father, although Dave affords his father the one unselfish outlet for affection in his life. Taking advantage of the situation, the masked man persuades Dave to join him in a plot designed to force Meekin to turn the management of the mines over to his son. Successfully disguised by Tonto, Dave entered the employ of his father again without the latter's knowledge as a common miner. In the meantime, Meekin has instituted a frantic search for his son, whom he hopes to induce to return home. All efforts to find him fail, however… until the day another accident is reported in the mines and The Lone Ranger informs Meekin that the miner trapped in one of the tunnels is his own son. Meekin, horribly frightened, offered the men in his employ whatever sum they wished to rescue Dave, but the risk seemed too great to undertake and their resentment prevented sympathy. The masked man volunteered to enter the tunnel, but only on the condition that Meekin first agree to retire and let Dave manage the mines according to his own, more humane ideas. Faced with that or the supposed death of his son, Meekin agreed, never suspecting that Dave's danger had not been nearly as great as it appeared. Only after it was discovered that Dave survived because he was in another mine, the entire affair staged, the old man held true to his bargain, hoping his son will make good on his father's mistakes.

Episode #1104-327, Broadcast February 21, 1940

Copyright Registration #68,724, script received at Registration Office February 28, 1940.

Plot: Twenty-five years ago, there was a shooting accident that took the life of Saul Gilman. The tragedy of the old man's death was a shock for the community, and for his two sons, Mort and Hank Gilman. Later they learned that their father had been mortally wounded by a stray bullet and that it must have issued from either Mort's or Hank's gun. When it seems to have been established that Hank was the cause of the accident, Mort, in a revulsion of feelings, disowns his brother, leaves their home, and promises someday to pay Hank back. Years later, when Hank had a grown son, Neil, age 22, a mysterious stranger named Mr. Franklin bought the Black Arrow Café and encouraged Neil to get in his debt. Suddenly, when Neil, who was employed by the local bank, found himself far beyond his financial depth, the stranger insisted upon payment or exposure. In the meantime, miles distant, The Lone Ranger learned from the account of an eyewitness that Mort, not Hank, had accidentally killed their father. Neil, desperate, steals a part of the money he owes from the bank, but the greater amount he still cannot obtain. Finally, when Hank had questioned him, aroused by Neil's obvious worry, he confesses the truth. Hank, taking with him enough money to pay his son's debt, also takes with him his guns, intending to kill the gambler who had made his son a thief. Forcing his way into the gambler's presence, he is stunned to learn the man is Mort, his brother, who had chosen this means to revenge himself upon Hank. The tables are turned, however, when the arrival of The Lone Ranger reveals that Mort had actually been the killer. Both brothers, awakened to the futility of hatred, are reconciled and the desire for revenge that had lived for 25 years dies in a single evening.

Episode #1105-328, Broadcast February 23, 1940

Copyright Registration #68,725, script received at Registration Office February 28, 1940.

Plot: Outside the town of Redwood, several things happened to the crooked rancher Purvis, all at one and the same time. A distant kinsman, young Tim Perry, arrived to take over the large Diamond Jay Ranch Purvis felt should have been willed to him. Coincidentally, he gave sanctuary to a man fleeing from The Lone Ranger and Tonto, who introduced himself as the notorious killer, Flash Norris. The arrival of Flash seemed a godsend to Purvis. It solved the problem he had been pondering… where to obtain a gunman willing to murder Tim Perry, making the Diamond Jay Purvis's by right of inheritance. Flash agreed to the proposal and Purvis was exultant, although in the meantime The Lone Ranger had told Tim that he need not fear any effort Purvis might make upon his life. Purvis had been acting as a figurehead for the rustler chief, Scar, whose men put Purvis's brand upon the cattle they stole, marketed this stolen beef through Purvis, and shared with him their profits. Plans were laid by Scar for one big round-up and a quick sale, to be followed by Scar's withdraw from rustling. At the same time, Flash left to carry out his attempt upon Tim's life and returned shortly afterwards with the statement that Tim was dead. Purvis, checking on this, learned that the news of Tim's death was all over town. But too late he discovered that it had been a ruse of the masked man, that Tim was still alive, that Flash was in reality a U.S. Marshal, and that through The Lone Ranger the Texas Rangers had been enabled to round up Scar's entire gang.

Episode #1106-329, Broadcast February 26, 1940

Copyright Registration #68,726, script received at Registration Office February 28, 1940.

Plot: Matt Graham, learning that his son and granddaughter were reported dead after Indians had attacked a stagecoach, appealed to The Lone Ranger to investigate the truth of the account, and the masked man consented. However, when he started his search, he did not know that the granddaughter, a mere infant, had already been discovered by a young boy and taken from the hands of an Indian squaw. This boy, Billy Overman, was the son of Jim Overman, an impoverished prospector who had just bought the reputedly used-up Lucky Dollar Mine on time from Niles, a wealthy citizen of Cottonwood. Immediately after the sale Niles learned the mine was still rich and at once took steps to make it impossible for Jim to meet his payments. In the meantime, both Jim and his wife Bess secretly used their individual saving to purchase medicine for the ailing child, each in the belief that the savings of the other would be ample to meet the next payment. The Lone Ranger, carrying on his investigation, had learned from an employee of the stage line that everyone on the stagecoach had been killed and accounted for, with the single exception of a child, believed to have been taken away alive by the Indians, who had since disappeared. Tracing the Indians, Tonto learned that the child had been taken from a squaw by a white boy in the vicinity of Cottonwood. At Cottonwood, The Lone Ranger, describing the boy to Niles, was purposely misled by the latter, but the masked man, catching Niles in a lie, remained in the district to discover why Niles did not want him to know who had found the child. He discovered the reason when Niles insisted upon taking back the Lucky Dollar Mine when it appeared Jim could not pay him. Tonto, however, sent by The Lone Ranger, had brought Matt Graham on the scene in time to reward the Overman's financially and keep the mine in their possession.

Episode #1107-330, Broadcast February 28, 1940
Copyright Registration #68,727, script received at Registration Office February 28, 1940.
Plot: Outside the little town of Crown Butte, a stagecoach was held up, but not for robbery. The hold-up was the prelude to an act of vengeance when the hooded horseman who had halted the stage brutally murdered its single passenger, Banker Whipple, then disappeared. Three men were possible suspects, but the sheriff could obtain evidence against none of them until The Lone Ranger appeared on the scene and mentioned an inhabitant of the town whom he and Tonto were convinced had witnessed the murder and could tell the killer's identity. But when the sheriff visited the home of this witness, Wolf Larson, he found that the killer had arrived before him. The witness was dead. Furious at the trick fate had played upon him, the sheriff tried more desperately than ever to break down the alibis of his suspects… but with complete lack of success. In the meantime, The Lone Ranger, however, convinced that the same man had committed both murders, believed that the killer could be trapped by means of the second murder, if not the first. No direct evidence existed either against the killer, but the masked man cleverly played upon the killer's guilty knowledge of the murders to force a confession. Realizing Larson's dogs would seek out justice against the man they witnessed killed their master, the guilty culprit confesses -- unaware that the Lone Ranger used a wolf pelt to attract the dogs that would never have attacked the guilty party.

Episode #1108-331, Broadcast March 1, 1940
Copyright Registration #59,912, script received at Registration Office November 2, 1938.
Copyright Registration #68,728, script received at Registration Office February 28, 1940.
Plot: Torrential rains in the mountains, lasting for days, finally built up such a wall of water behind a dam that it burst. The waters rushed into the flooded channel of the Red River and, when the bridge was swept away, the citizens of the small town of Riverside were cut off from the mainland. In the meantime, a rancher named Munson, receiving a forewarning of what might happen, had cornered all the supplies in town before the townspeople awoke to their plight. The flood caught the community unprepared. The Lone Ranger, acquainted with the plight of the citizens, first suggested a means to communicate with Tonto, still on the far side of the river, and sends Tonto for supplies. A kite sailing across the flood was successful, and The Lone Ranger turned his attention to outwitting Munson. He made a deal with the rancher through the sheriff that gave

the townspeople immediate food but seemed to promise the rancher an immense profit in the end. The sheriff agreed to pay double the worth of the food if Munson could not be paid back in kind within a week… and as there seemed to be no likelihood of the river returning to normal within that time, Munson felt himself safe. He was thwarted, however, when The Lone Ranger showed the townspeople how to construct a pontoon bridge and Tonto arrived with supplies in time to keep the terms of the agreement.

Notes: This radio script was originally slated for the broadcast of November 4, 1938. For reasons unknown, it was never broadcast, and a different script was dramatized instead. Fran Striker sat on this script as a temporary backup in case he needed to come up with a script in a short period of time. As a result, the first draft, submitted for copyright in November of 1938, was also submitted again in February 1940. The only difference between the two versions is that the un-produced 1938 rendition, the crook known as Munson was instead named Abe Freeman.

Episode #1109-332, Broadcast March 4, 1940
Copyright Registration #68,890, script received at Registration Office March 6, 1940.
Plot: When young Dick Culver, a deputy sheriff, answered a mysterious summons to an abandoned line cabin, he was met by two crooks, Moose and Pete, who, knocking him unconscious, promptly made it appear that he had gone to sleep after an extended bout with whiskey and cards. Money had been stolen from the safe of the sheriff and when the latter, accompanied by a second deputy, Phil, discovered Dick in an apparently drunken state, it was immediately assumed that Dick had been the thief. Moose and Pete swore that the night before Dick had been at the cabin, gambling recklessly. In the meantime, The Lone Ranger, having faith in Dick, called upon the young man's mother for more details concerning the case… only to be arrested by Phil. The Lone Ranger and Tonto successfully made their escape, however, and returned to their camp, where later that day they learned that Mrs. Culver, Dick's mother, had been robbed of her savings. The masked man, knowing that he and Tonto would be blamed for the crime, promptly took steps to hunt down the real criminals and found them in the persons of Moose and Pete. It was then that he realized they must have learned of the money through Phil, which meant that Phil also was responsible for Dick's predicament, his motive being the office of sheriff, which Dick would have assumed on the sheriff's retirement had it not been for the charge lodged against him, but which now would go to Phil. News that Tonto had been seized by a posse and was in danger of his life, gave The Lone Ranger the incentive to force confessions from Moose and Pete that cleared Tonto and Dick while incriminating Phil.

Episode #1110-333, Broadcast March 6, 1940
Copyright Registration #68,891, script received at Registration Office March 6, 1940.
Plot: Andy Pickett, after spending years in the employ of the great Diamond X ranch, owned by absentee Eastern interests, found that his years of service meant nothing when he was abruptly discharged to make way for an egotistical Easterner named Mr. Shanks who had no previous experience in the cattle business, but possessed an unqualified belief in his own abilities. Andy, at first confident that his experience would soon get him employment, reached the nadir of despair when after six long months he had heard on all sides that he was past the age of usefulness. Only the arrival of The Lone Ranger, with a promise to secure Andy's old position for him, helped keep up his courage. In the meantime, the crew that had remained with the new manager of the Diamond X, Shanks, quit on a flimsy pretext just before the day set for the beginning of the spring round-up. The Lone Ranger explained to Andy that he had anticipated such a move and explained why, giving Andy certain instructions to carry out faithfully. Andy, obeying these instructions, gained a promise of cooperation from the sheriff. Butler, one of the ranch owners, arrived to witness the spring round-up, but to his anger and to the despair of Shanks, the anticipated tally was fifty percent below what it should have been. Shanks, receiving

a dressing down from Butler when the round-up was completed, was interrupted by the masked man who took the men outside the ranch house and pointed out old Andy Pickett, returning with most of the ranch's 25,000 head of stolen cattle. The very men Shanks hired, who stole from the ranch and had planned to leave the district before the round-up could disclose the truth, were foiled by the vigilance of the masked man… clinching Andy's re-employment and Mr. Shanks returning from where he came.

Notes: The name of the ranch for this episode was originally called the Diamond T in the script but changed to the Diamond X for the broadcast.

Episode #1111-334, Broadcast March 8, 1940

Copyright Registration #68,892, script received at Registration Office March 6, 1940.

Plot: The Lincoln County War, having been brought to an end, causes Billy the Kid to flee the district, being the only one concerned in the fighting who was not covered in the general amnesty when it was finished. His enemies still pursued him, however, and two of their men, Tobe and Charlie, made it appear that Billy had brutally murdered a Mexican, hoping in that manner not only to make the law redouble its efforts to effect Billy's capture, but to lose Billy the friendship of the Mexicans as well, who up to this time had been his staunch allies. Billy, accused of murder, was taking refuge in flight, when he met Lola Brent, who prevailed upon him to help her rescue her father, thrown by his horse into a canyon. Billy, keeping his identity a secret, rescued Jess Brant, only to find the delay had permitted the law to catch up with him. Lola was heart-broken to learn his capture was her fault, but The Lone Ranger's unexpected arrival brought Billy his freedom again. The Lone Ranger, having investigated Billy once more, knew that the reputation he had built up as a killer was largely undeserved. His first killing had been in defense of his mother, and since then enemies had never permitted him to lay down his guns. The masked man knew also that Billy would never have harmed a Mexican and suspected the truth, that Tobe and Charlie were the real murderers. He appealed to Lola Brent to help Billy prove his innocence, and she, grateful for what Billy had done to save her father, consented gladly. Billy and Tonto, following the masked man's orders, seized Charlie, while The Lone Ranger convinced Tobe that his partner had made a full confession to the law, implicating Tobe. Tobe afterwards realized it has been a trick, but not until concealed witnesses had heard the truth and Billy was absolved.

Episode #1112-335, Broadcast March 11, 1940

Copyright Registration #69,015, script received at Registration Office March 13, 1940.

Plot: When Sheriff Bob Landis trailed outlaws who had held up and robbed the Coronado stagecoach, he discovered that he had been anticipated by The Lone Ranger, who had already made three of the four outlaws into prisoners. The masked man attempted to keep the fourth outlaw from the sheriff's knowledge, but the sheriff, stubbornly insisting upon learning his identity, discovered to his horror that he was Sid Baldy, once a wealthy rancher who had given the sheriff his start in life. Baldy, because of his misfortune, was reduced to traveling with outlaws. The masked man, however, suggested a way in which the three outlaws could be sent to jail, while Baldy was taken to town and a prominent bank job secured for him by the sheriff without revealing Baldy's past. Four months later, the outlaws, Turk, Mace and Slash, are released and headed for Coronado again, having heard that Baldy was there, employed as a guard in a bank. Convinced that Baldy had obtained his favor with the sheriff by selling them out, Turk and his companions took pains when robbing the bank to let Baldy's employer know of Baldy's past, which led to the sheriff's resignation. Thanks to the masked man, Baldy and Landis apprehend the three crooks and bring them back into town with the stolen money. The town cheers as the mayor reinstates Landis to the position of sheriff and Badly gets his job back.

Episode #1113-336, Broadcast March 13, 1940

Copyright Registration #69,016, script received at Registration Office March 13, 1940.

Plot: Fred and Bud Vance, brothers, unjustly convicted of rustling cattle in Montana, had come to Wyoming to get a new start in a district where ignorance of their conviction would permit them to start with a clean slate. Unfortunately, however, the activity of rustlers in the district, led by Polk, had prompted a correspondence with sheriffs all over the West that finally revealed the prison term they had served. Ordered to leave the district, they refuse and make plans to forcibly resist any efforts to dislodge them. And so certain are they that they have only enemies in the district, that when The Lone Ranger and Tonto ride to aid them, they fire upon the two with the intention of killing them. Overpowering the two brothers, The Lone Ranger soon convinces them he is their friend and secures their consent to a dangerous plan that, if successful, will establish them in the confidence of their neighbors. With the masked man they enter the badlands, the locale of the rustlers' hideout, where the outlaws are holding Tom Patrick's young son until their own leader, Polk, captured and resting in jail, is released. Tricking the outlaws, the boy is freed, and the ranchers are left with a free hand to proceed against the rustlers without any fear that any of their own will be injured by it. The part Fred and Bud Vance had played in the exploit at the direction of The Lone Ranger earned the two boys the ranchers' sincere gratitude. Realizing he was wrong, the prominent rancher, Tom Patrick, apologies for his prejudice and offers to help the new ranchers.

Episode #1114-337, Broadcast March 15, 1940

Copyright Registration #69,017, script received at Registration Office March 13, 1940.

Plot: See pages 248 and 249.

Episode #1115-338, Broadcast March 18, 1940

Copyright Registration #69,069, script received at Registration Office March 18, 1940.

Plot: Mary Winthrop, newly arrived from the East for a visit at the ranch of her uncle, Ezra Larkins, was prepared to find the West a romantic territory, and when her life was saved by Swift Eagle, the son of an Indian chief, she was convinced that even her expectations had been exceeded. She found her Indian rescuer a young and picturesque figure and her gratitude for what he had done was expressed in a manner as sincere as it was ill-advised. When The Lone Ranger cautioned her, she was certain that his warning was prompted simply by envy of a character finer than his own… an envy accented by prejudices of blood and color. Therefore, when Swift Eagle, taking advantage of her inexperience, employed her trust in him to strike at her uncle, she was at once bewildered and horrified. Only the masked man's assurance that she could help undo the harm for which she was responsible gave her the courage to remain at the ranch in spite of the obvious scorn of her associates. Swift Eagle, in reality a renegade from his tribe even though the son of its chief, was a tool of rustlers who employed Swift Eagle and his renegade companions to steal the cattle they desired, knowing that the Indians' custom of helping themselves to the beef of their white neighbors in order to supplement their own meager rations would effectively hide the real reason for the frequent raids upon the district's herds. They were unaware, however, that The Lone Ranger had long suspected their activity… just as they were unaware of Mary Winthrop's resolve to redeem herself. And their ignorance of these things brought about their abrupt downfall when the masked man led Swift Eagle into a trap baited by his own vanity.

Episode #1116-339, Broadcast March 20, 1940

Copyright Registration #69,070, script received at Registration Office March 18, 1940.

Plot: Two powerful cattle outfits, the Circle Jay and the Lazy B, were engaged in a life and death struggle for control of the range. Sandwiched between these two ranches was cautious Ben Healey and his small Rocking H outfit that owned the approach to the only feasible crossing on the treacherous Yellow River. As the river had to be crossed by all three outfits whenever they sent trail herds to market, Ben occupied both a strategic and dangerous position. Both the Lazy B and the Circle Jay put every manner of pressure upon him to declare himself for one faction or the other. Although fully aware of the fact that he was thoroughly out of sympathy with the ruthless owners of the Lazy B, Ben refused to yield to the pressure of either, hoping to maintain his neutrality or, failing that, to finally join the group that seemed certain of success. When at least it seemed as if the Lazy B must win, Ben would have joined had not The Lone Ranger intervened. Ben, at first in despair because the masked man had tumbled him from his position of timid neutrality, abruptly discovered once the die had been cast that he rather enjoyed his new role of an active partisan, even though his own destruction threatened along with that of the Circle Jay. He entered into the struggle vigorously, denied the Lazy B the right to cross his property to ford the river as they had formerly done, and cheerfully prepared to face overwhelming odds in the effort to enforce his dictum. Only at the very last when defeat seemed certain, did his courage waver, and then he was rewarded when The Lone Ranger turned defeat into victory.

Episode #1117-340, Broadcast March 22, 1940
Copyright Registration #69,071, script received at Registration Office March 18, 1940.
Plot: A wagon train composed of emigrants from the East hired young Idaho Jones to guide them through the hills that lay in their path. Two men, Lindsay and Newlin, disagreed with the course Idaho chose, however, and although overruled by the leader of the company, Saul Daggett, they prophesied that when they reached it, the canyon trail through the hills would be wiped out by a landslide, and the entire party would have to retrace their steps to Sioux Valley, another pass, wasting several weeks in the process. Idaho, certain that the canyon trail could be traversed, nevertheless was pleased when he met The Lone Ranger and Tonto and learned from them that they had used the trail just two weeks before, finding it passable. With this assurance, the shock to Idaho was doubly great when, arriving in the hills, the canyon trail was discovered wiped out just as Lindsay and Newlin had said it would be. Daggett, disgusted with what he thought to be Idaho's incompetence, dismissed the young man. The Lone Ranger and Tonto forced Idaho to accompany them to their camp, and there the masked man pointed out to Idaho that this development meant that Lindsay and Newlin were crooks, possibly working with Scar Rankin and Scar's gang, whose trail had brought the masked man to this district. Only by this theory could it be explained why Lindsay and Newlin had been positive the trail would be wiped out even before the disaster had occurred. Trailing Scar further, The Lone Ranger soon discovered the rest of the answer to the puzzle. Scar wanted the emigrants to pass through Sioux Valley, bordering Sioux Lake, so that, when the outlaws dynamited the dam, the emigrants would be helpless, and the outlaws could loot the wagons at their leisure. They discovered too late, however, that the masked man had not only been able to vindicate Idaho but had made it possible to give them a taste of their own medicine.

Episode #1118-341, Broadcast March 25, 1940
Copyright Registration #69,281, script received at Registration Office March 27, 1940.
Plot: When Jack Fisher's father, owner of a short-line railroad, died unexpectedly, the young man found himself suddenly thrown into a position of responsibility for which he was totally unprepared. Bewildered by the complexity of the problem facing him, he made several mistakes of judgment that proved costly, and as a result he lost what little faith he had in himself. This suited Blake Atwood perfectly as he desired to gain control of the Fisher properties and saw an opportunity to do so cheaply. But it did not suit Jack's fiancé, Alice Blanchard, who wanted him to prove his manhood, nor did it please The Lone Ranger, who realized that Atwood desired the Fisher properties for selfish ends. He could do nothing to forestall Atwood, however, as long as Jack lacked faith in himself, therefore he planned to restore the young man's confidence by a ruse. He approached an old friend in the matter and, outlining his plan, gained the latter's promise of cooperation. This friend, Lem Dawson by name, had profited by one of Jack's previous mistakes. Now, however, following The Lone Ranger's instructions, he made it appear that Jack's earlier judgment had been correct, that he, an old hand at the intricacies of

business, had been bested by a tyro, and that he was filled with admiration for Jack's shrewdness. Jack, at first astonished by this development, did not take long to persuade himself that he had been in fact extraordinarily acute. Therefore, with his confidence thus given a new lease on life, he found the courage to defy Atwood, and Atwood, having staked everything upon Jack's willingness to sell, found that his scheming had brought him face to face with ruin.

Episode #1119-342, Broadcast March 27, 1940

Copyright Registration #69,282, script received at Registration Office March 27, 1940.

Plot: Tom Martin and Bart Hurley had been friends and partners for years – therefore when one day Tom was arrested and Bart himself furnished the evidence that seemed to prove Tom guilty of a recent stagecoach robbery, only three men in the entire district questioned his word. One was Tom Martin – and the others were The Lone Ranger and Tonto who had found signs pointing to the guilt of others and Tom's innocence. Determined to investigate, the masked man captured Bart and accused him of lying. Bart, goaded beyond endurance, finally confessed to the truth of the masked man's accusation, but pleaded with the masked man to do nothing about it because the men really at fault had taken his son prisoner and had threatened the boy's death unless Bart obeyed them. The Lone Ranger, sympathizing with Bart in his predicament, promised silence and advised Bart not to speak of their conversation. When Bart left them, The Lone Ranger informed Tonto that with Tom's case set for an early trial, everything depended upon their acting swiftly and surely, but that he had already determined upon the steps they must take. In the meantime, Tom Martin, not understanding what had prompted his partner's treachery, had convinced himself that he hated Bart and stubbornly refused all the latter's offers of financial aid for his defense. The trial arrived and the crooks congratulated themselves upon the success of their ruse when Bart took the stand to clinch the case against Tom. But in the middle of his testimony, he interrupted himself to accuse them, not his former partner, and the surprise of the criminals was resolved when it developed that The Lone Ranger had made it possible for Bart to tell the truth by freeing his son.

Episode #1120-343, Broadcast March 29, 1940

Copyright Registration #69,283, script received at Registration Office March 27, 1940.

Plot: When old Ezra Stokes, having made a fortune in the cattle business, decided to sell all that he owned and devote the proceeds to various benevolent enterprises in order to repay, before his death, the territory that had treated him so generously, swindlers found the occasion an ideal opportunity for the practice of their art. They gained Ezra's confidence, professing to share his ideals, and secured his acceptance of a project that, on the face of it, would contribute to the well-being of the entire district. This was a plan to build and endow an irrigation system, and Ezra became increasingly enthusiastic as he envisioned the good such a project would do… until that time when The Lone Ranger revealed that the men who had won his trust, having secretly purchased the property involved by means of proxies, were the individuals who stood to profit most by Sam's benevolence. Sam, furious at the trick played upon him and bitter in his disillusionment, would have abandoned all his charitable plans had not the masked man assured him that he could still carry out his original project while at the same time punishing those who would have taken advantage of him. The elderly rancher, now suspicious of everyone, would promise nothing but that he would defer his decision until the masked man had had time to prove the practicability of his suggestion. This was all The Lone Ranger required and, with Tonto, he immediately put his plan into effect. It was owing to him that the swindlers, convinced that Sam had altered his plans, frantically disposed of their property at a loss in order to invest according to what they believed would be Sam's next venture – only to discover too late that The Lone Ranger, taking a leaf from their book, had tricked them into investing their money in a profitless speculation while arranging for Sam's friends to buy the land of which they had so hastily rid themselves.

Episode #1121-344, Broadcast April 1, 1940

Copyright Registration #69,408, script received at Registration Office April 6, 1940.

Plot: Brant Huston and his father, Mort, temporarily incapable of working together, came to the parting of the ways when they quarreled over a detail that concerned the management of the Huston ranch, on which Brant had been foreman. Brant, making ready to leave with his wife, asked his father for enough money to put him into the cattle business for himself. Mort did this several years earlier for Brant's mother, Vera. Mort, however, angrily refused and Brant departed, although when he and his wife, established in a new home, received a check signed with Mort's name for the amount that Brant had requested, they were not surprised, Brant's father having acted in this eccentric manner on other occasions. But it was The Lone Ranger himself who, not long after, brought Brant word that the check had been a forgery and the sheriff, following Mort's orders, was even then on his way to Brant's place to arrest the young man. Brant, completely at a loss, swore to the masked man that he was innocent, and the latter was convinced by his behavior that this was true. He promised Brant that he would attempt to clear him, but warned him not to express surprise if, in the process, he seemed to be working not for but against him. Brant, encouraged, surrendered to the sheriff without protest, and when his father and his brother, Vern, visited him at the jail, he revealed nothing when The Lone Ranger, disguised, entered and pointed out that while there might be some doubt of Brant's guilt on the evidence of the check alone, it was almost certain that if Brant were the forger, he must have practiced his father's signature and a search of his home might show if this were true or not. Accordingly, the next morning, such a search was made, and evidence of the type indicated by The Lone Ranger found – but it was revealed that Vern, tempted by The Lone Ranger's suggestion, had himself prepared this additional evidence in order to clinch the case against his brother and make himself the sole heir to their father's ranch.

Episode #1122-345, Broadcast April 3, 1940

Copyright Registration #69,409, script received at Registration Office April 6, 1940.

Plot: The arrival of Jed Sampson, brother to the notorious outlaw, Poke Sampson, in the small western village of Titusville, immediately divided the hitherto peaceful community into two bitterly opposed camps. That party which was led by the banker wanted Jed run out of town on the strength of his brother's evil reputation, while the remainder of Titusville's citizens, unfortunately in the minority, demanded that Jed be judged solely according to his own behavior, not that of Poke. The schism created by this dispute became wider with each passing day and Jed, rather than see friends and neighbors divided on his account, would have left town voluntarily if The Lone Ranger had not urged him to remain, pointing out that wherever he went he was likely to be confronted with the same situation and, as long as he knew himself to be in the right, it was better to settle the issue once and for all where he was. Jed, seeing the logic of The Lone Ranger's advice, consented to stay – but he had reckoned without the banker and his friends who, prevailing upon the sheriff, had forced that officer to agree to order Jed on his way. A small mob accompanied the sheriff to see that the order was carried out, while another gathered to prevent it. But before hostilities could occur, a greater sensation interrupted them; it was announced that the wife of the banker had been forced from her home, supposedly by one of the banker's enemies. Out of the entire crowd, Jed was the only one to act promptly and courageously and, when he had returned her to her grateful husband, only she and The Lone Ranger knew that she had been in no danger but, acting upon the masked man's instructions, had taken this way to teach her husband tolerance.

Episode #1123-346, Broadcast April 5, 1940

Copyright Registration #69,410, script received at Registration Office April 6, 1940.

Plot: Dan Brewer, owner and founder of a prosperous stagecoach company while still comparatively young, had made his way to the top by a combination of hard work and resourcefulness but, once there, his character seemed to change. Although at heart amiable and decent, he convinced himself that he had won to his position by adopting the hard-boiled ethics of that school of business enterprise whose only credo was that of dog-eat-dog. The Lone Ranger, aware of this transformation, did not interfere as long as Dan's new policy affected only the men in his employ, for they both understood and respected him. But when Dan decided to run out of business young Bill Paulson, operator of a small feeder line and in no sense Dan's competitor, the masked man felt it was time to take a hand. He interviewed Dan, and when the latter refused to alter his tactics, the masked man warned him there would be retribution. In spite of the masked man's warning, Dan went ahead, sending his own coaches over the route formerly served by Paulson alone, and taking advantage of his superior resources literally to seize the whole of Paulson's traffic in passengers and express freight. Young Paulson was frantic, but The Lone Ranger told him what must be done in order to teach Dan a lesson. Paulson, going to Dan, made a frank confession of his firm's assets and liabilities and requested a bid. Dan, still playing the high-handed businessman offered an outrageously low price, and Paulson asked for time in which to consider it. At the end of that time, he accepted, and Dan paid without making a further investigation. He was brought up short immediately afterwards, however, when he discovered that, thanks to The Lone Ranger, the liabilities of Paulson's concern and apparently increased by thousands of dollars between the time that Dan had named his figure and Paulson had accepted. Faced by the prospect of a ruinous loss, Dan was forced to grant Paulson everything he demanded in order to persuade the latter to accept the return of his stage line.

Episode #1124-347, Broadcast April 8, 1940
Copyright Registration #69,444, script received at Registration Office April 10, 1940.
Plot: Dusty Liggett, the newest member of the crew at the X Bar X Ranch, threw his saddle on Satan, a powerful bay stallion with the reputation of a killer that had never been conquered, and rode the beast with the grace and ease of a master horseman. Mary, the daughter of his employer, Andy North, is sent to Sage City to make payment on cattle, carrying close to $10,000. When Dusty is sent alongside to accompany her, Ted Bassett, the foreman, gets jealous. The Lone Ranger and Tonto are in the area, on the trail for the Rio Kid, who could be masquerading under an alias. Confiding in Bassett, the masked man sets up a scheme that would expose the Rio Kid. Along the trail the next day, Mary suspects something off when Dusty leads her down the wrong trails. After confessing his real identity and demanding to take the money, the outlaw finds himself surrounded by Mary's father, Ted Bassett, the sheriff, Tonto and The Lone Ranger. The sheriff takes his prisoner in but laughs beforehand, acknowledging how the masked man wanted the outlaw to incriminate himself first.

Notes: The name of the ranch in this episode really is the X Bar X Ranch, as verified in the radio script.

Episode #1125-348, Broadcast April 10, 1940
Copyright Registration #69,445, script received at Registration Office April 10, 1940.
Plot: In a rich valley outside Mayville, homesteaders filed a claim and spent long months prospecting for gold – a fool's errand considering the rich soil underneath their feet that could be cultivated for farmland. Hoping to see the land become a prosperous community, oddly, two men who did not belong to the little undeveloped community, Spade Wylie and Jake, were interested in seeing the prospectors, whose hopes and dreams were shattered with no luck finding gold, return East from whence they came. The Lone Ranger and Tonto rode two miles out and silently approached the campfire to secretly listen to the conversation. The next morning, Zeke Cotter, his wife Martha, and other homesteaders such as Laura and Cal Munson, all departed for the East. Hours later, Spade and Jake returned to the community, now vacated, with a gang of a dozen men, a bearded and hard-bitten lot that quickly made themselves at home in the cabins. They spent the night with both drink and gambling and slept late during the day. The Lone Ranger and Tonto, meanwhile, convinced the homesteaders to turn around and return to their cabins – and it was there that the homesteaders discovered the ruse. It seems Spade knew that the railroad planned to build further west by way of the valley and by deliberately encouraging the people to leave, he could help himself. Spade called for assistance from his gang. The battle

that followed could have been heard for miles. Led by The Lone Ranger, Tonto, Zeke and the farmers hurled themselves at the gang led by Spade. Chairs were smashed, bottles thrown, men knocked to the floor and trampled. But finally, the courage of the outlaws broke. Spade was the first to cry for mercy.

Episode #1126-349, Broadcast April 12, 1940
Copyright Registration #69,446, script received at Registration Office April 10, 1940.
Plot: Young Buck Evans was an anomaly in the West, a lad who had been born and raised on a cattle ranch, but who was deathly afraid of horses. He had a sufficient excuse for his phobia, however, although this fact did not save him from the sneers and jibes of his neighbors. As a youngster he had been a horrified witness to the death of his older brother at the slashing hooves of a wild stallion, and years later he himself had been thrown by a bronc, suffering a serious concussion and narrowly escaping with his life. From that time on he could not have been forced into a saddle by any urgency, and even the contempt of those who could not understand his fear had no effect on him. This was his status when Bull Kohler, hunting for a place where there was food and shelter, after having led his men out of a trap prepared by The Lone Ranger, descended upon the ranch house owned by young Hank's mother. It was late in the fall in Walnut Grove, the crew had been dismissed for the season, and the occupants of the house could put up no resistance. The outlaws (Bull Kohler, Jug and Dirk) made themselves at home, reasoning that the Evans house would be the last place where they would be sought. But The Lone Ranger, knowing they must be in the district, halted there to enquire if they had been sighted. Mutual recognition led to gunfire, and The Lone Ranger and Tonto, accompanied by Hank who mistakenly thought his mother had escaped, took up positions outside the house. Their situation was serious, however. Mrs. Evans was still inside, and only constant vigilance could prevent the outlaws seizing her to use as a hostage for their escape. The law had to be summoned and only Hank, who feared horses, could be spared. But the boy, aware of the danger to his mother, and aided by The Lone Ranger, conquered his insane fear long enough to summon the sheriff – and discovered afterwards that the fear seemed to have vanished for good.

Episode #1127-350, Broadcast April 15, 1940
Copyright Registration #69,610, script received at Registration Office April 22, 1940.
Plot: It was late one afternoon when The Lone Ranger and Tonto were startled by the arrival of a rancher in the camp they had thought too well hidden for discovery. The rancher explained, however, that he had seen and recognized them earlier in the day, that he had followed over the route they had taken and had stumbled on their camp more by accident than calculation. He went on to appeal to the masked man, to keep his ranch house under surveillance that evening, that he was expecting visits from men who, though both his friends, were bitter enemies each toward the other, and that he feared gunplay when they met, perhaps even a killing. The Lone Ranger assented to his plea and, with Tonto, accompanied the rancher to his home, but when they arrived there, they discovered the warning had come too late. One of the two men was already dead, murdered, and the rancher offered to ride after the sheriff while the masked man held the other prisoner. Strangely enough, however, when the rancher had embarked on his errand, the masked man offered his prisoner a chance to escape. The prisoner, puzzled, asked for an explanation and learned that The Lone Ranger was satisfied that he was innocent. The man rejected the opportunity to flee but did consent to ride with Tonto to The Lone Ranger's camp and remain there until, as he had promised, The Lone Ranger revealed the guilt of the actual culprit. The rancher, returning with the sheriff, was furious at the disappearance of the man he claimed must be the murderer, and when The Lone Ranger calmly admitted he had let the man go, the rancher's fury was redoubled. But at the last minute The Lone Ranger revealed that his fury had ample cause – the rancher himself, was the murderer and had hoped to provide himself with an iron-clad alibi – with an alibi provided by the famous Lone Ranger.

Episode #1128-351, Broadcast April 17, 1940

Copyright Registration #69,611, script received at Registration Office April 22, 1940.

Plot: Who had been the murderer of Sheriff Dan Halstead was the exciting but baffling mystery that puzzled the citizens of San Juan County. Unaware that The Lone Ranger and Tonto were attempting to find the answer to this question, they naturally looked to young Don Halstead, the murdered man's son, to uncover the killer. Don desired to do this with all his heart, but rather than accept the position of sheriff, for which he was ideally fitted, and which San Juan's citizens wished him to fill, he chose instead to become the bodyguard of the districts wealthiest resident, a man named Fenton. This choice was determined by the fact that Fenton had offered him double what a sheriff could hope to make, and Don, planning marriage to Betty Thomas, wanted the additional income. To his surprise, however, he learned that Betty shared the opinion of the community as a whole concerning his decision; she believed that Don had permitted money to swerve him from his real duty. The Lone Ranger, too, shared this opinion, but he had faith that Don would awaken to his duty. When his investigation had made it possible for him to make a shrewd guess as to the identity of the killer, he approached Don and suggested a plan whereby his father's murderer could be brought to justice. Don agreed to this plan… although he did so in the belief that he was doing so in an effort to trap a suspect the masked man privately knew to be innocent. In fact, when the masked man's plan was successful, Don learned that his employer, Fenton himself, was guilty. But the masked man prevented whatever criticism of Don this revelation might have aroused by permitting the community to believe Don had accepted employment under Fenton simply to bring the man to justice.

Episode #1129-352, Broadcast April 19, 1940

Copyright Registration #69,612, script received at Registration Office April 22, 1940.

Plot: Emma Bailey did not learn until after her marriage that her husband had courted her simply because her parents owned one of the richest ranches in the district. But from the day that Emma had persuaded her father to turn all his property over to Tom Bailey, the latter went from bad to worse. He spent what money was in the bank, then began disposing of the cattle as his drinking and gambling demanded it. At length, even these resources exhausted, he turned to crime to bring him more money. Emma, learning that her husband and a man called Abe were plotting the hold-up of a train, threatened their exposure, but learned to her dismay that if she carried out her threat, she and her aged parents, dependent upon her, would be evicted and left to shift for themselves. She was desperate and her desperation was not relieved when, mistaking The Lone Ranger for one of her husband's accomplices, she discovered that she had revealed a part of the plot to a stranger. The Lone Ranger, in spite of the fact that she refused to give him all the information concerning the plot at her disposal was confident that she could be prevailed upon to do so when it became necessary. So, in the meantime, having convinced himself that her silence was indeed prompted by fear, and not because she was an accessory to the plot, he arranged a plan to prevent her having to suffer by delivering her husband and Abe to justice. He called on the ranchers of the district, let them know what sacrifice her action was demanding, and suggested a means by which they could repay her, a means they eagerly assented to. Therefore, when Tom Bailey and Abe learned that they had been reported to the law in spite of their threats, they learned at the same time that those same threats were valueless. The ranchers had conducted a round-up, branded all mavericks with Emma's brand, and presented her with a herd sufficient for a new start.

Notes: John Todd doubled for the role of the second voice.

Episode #1130-353, Broadcast April 22, 1940

Copyright Registration #69,806, script received at Registration Office May 2, 1940.

Plot: Ralph and Carl Walker, two young men in their early twenties recently orphaned by the death of their father, found that he left them little. Therefore, when Morley, a wealthy mine-owner, suggested that he might have a job for one of them, they were grateful. Their conversation with Morley took place in Tex Dolan's café after a meal for which Ralph paid. After Morley told Ralph he had been selected for the job, Ralph's pleasure was rudely shattered when Tex confronted him with a marked bill that had been part of the sum stolen from the rancher Velie a year before. Ralph, before learning the bill was marked, had identified it as the same bill with which he had settled accounts for their meal. The incident was not enough to secure Ralph's arrest, but it did raise suspicion in the minds of the townspeople, cause Morley to hesitate in the matter of the job and arouse the interest of The Lone Ranger when he learned of the affair. He did not believe in Ralph's guilt in spite of the fact that the young man's behavior was dubious. Ralph, although at first stated he could name the source of the money, had afterwards flatly declined to do so. Moreover, rather than challenge Tex for his insinuations, he seemed to prefer to let the matter drop. The masked man, investigating, discovered that Tex had good reason to hate Ralph, and began to consider the theory that Tex had framed the young man, in spite of the fact that Ralph's identification of the bill in question as his own seemed to preclude the possibility. Putting his theory to the test, The Lone Ranger played a trick upon Tex that sent him to the stolen hoard, thereby, by his knowledge of its location, proving his guilt. And Ralph's attitude, it was learned had been caused by the fact that he had feared, mistakenly, that if he spoke it would direct suspicion towards his dead father.

Episode #1131-354, Broadcast April 24, 1940
Copyright Registration #69,807, script received at Registration Office May 2, 1940.
Plot: For a number of years Lynn Fowler had led a useful life in the West, winning the respect of his neighbors by his good sense and industry. In fact, so capably had Lynn applied himself that he was on the point of becoming a comparatively wealthy man, the local banker having offered him money to increase his holdings to any desired amount. But disaster overtook Lynn on the very eve of this promised triumph. Douglas, once Lynn's partner in the East, arrived in the West, recognized Lynn, and had him arrested for absconding with funds that had been their firm's property. Douglas, admitting that Lynn had urgently needed the money at the time and that since then Lynn had fully repaid him, still was convinced that he should be returned to the East for prosecution. The Lone Ranger, learning that Douglas was on Lynn's trail, decided to come to Lynn's aid. The Lone Ranger knew the West needed Lynn's sort, that the rancher had amply proved his desire to go straight. Under the circumstances the masked man felt that no good purpose could be affected by Lynn's exposure, and he determined to resort to drastic means to alter Douglas' resolution. Therefore, while Lynn was being taken across the desert by Douglas and a U.S. Marshal, a seeming accident occurred that placed the lives of the marshal and Douglas at Lynn's mercy. Only Lynn could ride for aid, and Douglas was positive he would never return, but would go on to freedom, leaving them to die. Lynn, however, reacted as the masked man had known he would. He chose to save his companions rather than seek freedom, and Douglas – aware of the temptation Lynn must have conquered, but unaware of the role The Lone Ranger had played – was so impressed that he chose to drop all charges.

Episode #1132-355, Broadcast April 26, 1940
Copyright Registration #69,808, script received at Registration Office May 2, 1940.
Plot: Dan Riley, a young rancher, had a fiery temper that led him into a succession of brawls and finally into court where, if The Lone Ranger had not come to his aid, he would have received a severe sentence for assault and battery. He did not, however, go scot-free. He was placed under bond to keep the peace, threatened by the judge with jail if he appeared in court again, and was told by his fiancé that if he expected to marry her, he must learn to behave himself. This situation, a difficult one for Dan, struck a pair of blackmailers as ideal for their own profit. They forced Dan into a quarrel and, when Dan knocked down Whitey, one of the pair, the latter cleverly simulated paralysis as a result of the blow. Dan was horror-stricken both by what he had done and what

he knew must follow if the affair becomes public. Thus, when the swindlers guaranteed silence for a price, he agreed hastily. The swindlers did not know, of course, that The Lone Ranger, anxious to know how Dan was getting on, was on his way back to the district. In the meantime, Whitey and his partner Max bled Dan for all he was worth, demanding large sums of money from him and occupying a comfortable cabin he had purchased. Dan's fiancé realized that something was troubling him, but Dan refused to confide in anyone until The Lone Ranger appeared, whose discretion he knew could be depended upon. Investigation soon convinced the masked man that the situation did not ring true and, suspecting what had really happened, he determined to trick the swindlers into revealing the deception. Dan, he knew, did not dare to challenge them as long as there was a possibility Whitey was not shamming, but a dramatic ruse by the masked man exposed the swindlers in time to save Dan from stripping himself of all he owned.

Episode #1133-356, Broadcast April 29, 1940
Copyright Registration #69,809, script received at Registration Office May 2, 1940.
Plot: A wealthy rancher named Ashley sold property to Gil Heath and his wife, Mary, outside Freeport, a strip of land that looked promising and a bargain price. But when Gil later learned that Ashley owned the adjoining property and Gil had no water rights, Ashley offered to grant access at fifty cents per head as a toll. Worse, Gil realized his only way out was to sell the property he bought but only Ashley was willing to purchase and at a cost less than the initial purchase price. Gil needed water for the stock, so he raised the money only to learn Ashley lowered the price to buy. Ashley pulled this same scheme on the very same property multiple times, but always staying within the law to avoid jail. Gil and his wife, meanwhile, befriended and took in a wanderer named Lonesome Jones, who had a past of being a bad luck charm. When Lonesome learns of Gil's plight, he believes he is the man responsible for their dilemma. The Lone Ranger and Tonto, having scouted the region for weeks, seeking a man named Jason Lang, due to inherit a small fortune from his uncle, discover he changed his name to Lonesome Jones and did a good job disappearing and leaving barely a trace. The Lone Ranger kidnaps Lonesome, spurring Gil to believe Ashley was responsible and a confrontation almost leads to fisticuffs until the wanderer returns with the good news. Lonesome has an option to buy the adjoining property on the other side from Parkman, who agrees to defy Ashley, and the couple's friendship is not forgotten as they now have access to the river and can pay Lonesome off for the property whenever it is convenient. For once, Lonesome laughs, he gave someone else good luck.

Episode #1134-357, Broadcast May 1, 1940
Copyright Registration #69,810, script received at Registration Office May 2, 1940.
Plot: Tonto had been present when Si Bolton announced his loss to the sheriff of Claypool. Squint Barclay and his gang, hooded to mask their faces, robbed Si of the money he made from a recent cattle sale. Sheriff Spencer was unaware that he and his deputy, Shorty, had been put on a goose chase to keep them far away from the rancher's house so the crooks could commit the crime. Learning of the news from Tonto, The Lone Ranger investigates. But when a trail leaving the ranch is nowhere to be found, the masked man finds himself just as puzzled as the sheriff. Paying the lawman a visit, The Lone Ranger explains that he knew for certain Squint and his gang were sitting in a jail in Nebraska. The trail to the real crooks began with Pike and Spud, crooks who gave the sheriff the false lead. Tonto sets out to apprehend a member of the suspected gang, Fresno, and holds his prisoner at bay in the secluded camp of The Lone Ranger. When word gets leaked by the deputy, Sheriff Spencer receives a visit from Pike and Spud asking why their friend is in jail. Three days later, Spud overheard the lawmen discussing how Fresno finally broke and revealed the truth. Spud raced out meet his outlaw friends, the ranch hands who worked at Si Bolton's ranch, only to be apprehended by The Lone Ranger and Tonto. Brought to the sheriff's jail, Spud and Pike turn against each other with each accusing the other of details that would clinch a conviction.

Earle Graser's sketch on the page of his radio script,
depicting director James Jewell at the mike.

Episode #1135-358, Broadcast May 3, 1940

Copyright Registration #69,811, script received at Registration Office May 2, 1940.

Plot: A gangster known as Bat Klein has terrorized the prospering community of Cherokee Ridge. He hired outlaws to do his dirty work, killing the sheriff and then double-crossed the hired killers to prevent any witnesses. The ranchers are too small and too disorganized to fight back. Those that oppose Klein suffered at the hands of the outlaws. Bart Merrick, who attempted to organize an opposition, discovers this the hard way when his ranch is attacked later one night. Jimmy, his young son, sneaks out the back to fetch help, unaware that Logan, the U.S. Marshal, is a fake. The Lone Ranger, having already demonstrated Klein is a coward and ordered him to leave the region, rides out to the Merrick ranch when he learns that gunplay was involved. Learning from Ada about the rescue party, and aware the real marshal is named Keller, The Lone Ranger and Tonto follow the trail of the outlaws to a valley. The outlaws, observing the approach of the masked man, conceal themselves in the underbrush for ambush, laying a trap for the approaching vigilantes. The masked man and Indian, however, suspect the trap based on trail signs and decide to face off against the outlaws on their own terms. Hiding among a herd of steers, stolen by outlaws from other ranchers, The Lone Ranger and Tonto gain the element of surprise. Back in town, Bart Merrick drives the stolen cattle into main street, with the outlaws – including

Merrick – tied to the longhorns. The town citizens cheer and laugh at the crooks as they cut the ropes and lead the outlaws to jail. The humiliation of being laughed at, Bart explains, is the finish of any outlaw every time.

Episode #1136-359, Broadcast May 6, 1940

Copyright Registration #70,031, script received at Registration Office May 17, 1940.

Plot: Two old ranchers, Jake Sanders and Amos Buckner, had been feuding for years, although their feud luckily had never reached the point where either man ever felt called upon to go gunning for the other. Jake, however, had long sought for a way to legally bring about the ruin of Amos, but because of the fact that his means were strictly limited… he lived upon money sent him from time to time, presumably by his son… opportunity to affect his desire was limited. A situation arose that, if acted upon, would make his wish come true. Amos would be stripped of all he owned, and Jake gleefully looked forward to his impending triumph. The Lone Ranger gathered some startling information and, when accident revealed to him Jake's purpose, he determined to find out if the information he had was authentic or not. Amos refused to answer the masked man's questions on the score, and The Lone Ranger was forced to resort to a trick to get at the truth. His trick worked and he rode at once to prevent Jake taking action against Amos. Jake proved equally stubborn, but his stubbornness did not last long when the masked man dramatically revealed the truth about his feud with Amos. Amos, unknown to Jake, had long nursed a warm spot in his heart for his elderly antagonist and, years before, when he had seen Jake about go to the wall, he had started to send Jake money, making it appear that the money was coming from Jake's long absent son in order to save the old man's pride. Jake, learning the truth at last, pretended to be furious with Amos, but when the masked man rode away, he knew he had left the two old-timers firm friends.

Episode #1137-360, Broadcast May 8, 1940

Copyright Registration #70,032, script received at Registration Office May 17, 1940.

Plot: The Lone Ranger and Tonto, crossing the mountains to reach Crescent City, altered their course when it became apparent that the unusually deep snows of winter threatened a disastrous flood in Redwood Valley when the spring thaws finally set in. It was their purpose to warn Bert Ross, a rancher newly come from Texas, and his danger and to suggest adequate safeguards, but when they arrived, they learned from Bert's foreman, Lee Miller, that he had already warned his employer and had been discharged for his pains. Lee had suggested that the dam he was building in Boulder Creek be supplemented by a levee in the event of a flood of larger proportion than usual in the spring. Bert, protesting at the expense, had refused to admit that the ranch buildings could be in any danger, and Lee, a married man, had felt it impossible for him to remain where the life of his wife might be put in jeopardy. The masked man had scarcely learned this when the rains he had feared began. Knowing that Bert would not listen to reason, he immediately followed the only feasible plan that suggested itself. It was true that Lee has been discharged – but it was also true that no one knew of this as yet except Bert himself, Lee, Lee's wife Kate, and The Lone Ranger. The masked man, unknown to Lee, made Bert his prisoner, then returned, explained that Bert could not possibly return to the ranch within a week, and appealed to Lee to carry on in spite of his discharge. Lee, convinced that he had no alternative, did so, and as his quarrel with his employer was unknown, no one questioned his authority. Aware that the rains made a flood imminent, he took advantage of his position to carry on the construction he had originally advised. In the meantime, The Lone Ranger awakened Bert to the reality of the danger he had disregarded – then, when the rancher was convinced, revealed that his foreman, acting contrary to his orders, had saved his home and family.

Episode #1138-361, Broadcast May 10, 1940

Copyright Registration #70,033, script received at Registration Office May 17, 1940.

Plot: Kessler, who managed the great Box E Ranch for its absentee owner, Evans, found the influx of homesteaders into the county dangerous to his desire to be the political boss of the district. They filed upon no land either claimed by or necessary to the Box E, but he used the old antagonism between cattleman and homesteader as an excuse to justify his attempt to drive them away. The Lone Ranger came upon the scene when he arrived in time to force Kessler to pay a homesteader for a deliberate act of vandalism. Afterwards, knowing that the situation in the county was rapidly developing toward a tragic showdown, he left Tonto to keep an eye on events in the county while he took the long journey to Cheyenne to interview the Box E's owner. Evans, who had not visited the Box E for several years, protested that he had complete faith in Kessler's integrity and that he saw no reason for making an investigation – but the masked man, by cleverly insinuating that Evans was deliberately closing his eyes to the truth to maintain his own comfort, so angered him that he agreed to get to the bottom of the affair. It did not suit The Lone Ranger's purpose to have Evans himself visit the county, however. Instead, he suggested an alternative that appealed to Evans, and several weeks later a new homesteader arrived in the county – a young man who called himself by the odd name of Jim Snave. Kessler, not recognizing him, proceeded against the young fellow with the same tactics he had used upon the other homesteaders. When, however, the inevitable showdown between Kessler and the homesteaders finally arrived, the ranch manager learned to his consternation that Jim Snave was none other than Jim Evans, his employer's younger brother, and instead of the triumph he had anticipated, Kessler found himself abruptly dismissed from his lucrative position.

Episode #1139-362, Broadcast May 13, 1940
Copyright Registration #70,034, script received at Registration Office May 17, 1940.
Plot: Jed Pelkey learns from Doctor Rice that he will soon go blind – and without any warning. Years ago, unable to fulfill a contract due to Texas fever and cattle rustlers, Jed's livelihood was saved by Nate Irwin. Hoping to do a good turn for Nate before he goes blind, Jed spends a couple weeks constructing a gorgeous ranch house in a well sun-lit valley, far enough in isolation to avoid discovery until he can surprise Nate. Yank, a no-good of the community, discovers Jed's secret and threatens exposure unless he gets paid blackmail. The Lone Ranger, however, gallops by and orders Yank to leave – with a promise of threat if Yank tells anyone. Yank, however, gets revenge by later burning down the newly constructed ranch house. It was only then that Jed was struck down with blindness. With the help of Samantha, Jed's wife, the doctor and Nate, the masked man schemes to avoid heartbreak. Nate praises the construction of the ranch house and the craftsmanship, and Yank confesses he never burned the property to the ground – he was only lying. Jed is pleased that he was able to do one good turn before he was confined to his own home due to his handicap. Outside, Yank is once again threatened by the masked man – and Yank agrees to rebuild the ranch house at his expense to ensure the masquerade does not fail. The Lone Ranger promised to return in a few weeks and verify the construction, proving sometimes truth takes second place to a man's happiness.

Episode #1140-363, Broadcast May 15, 1940
Copyright Registration #70,035, script received at Registration Office May 17, 1940.
Plot: Two years ago, Sweeney arrived in San Pedro, living in the finest house and does nothing to generate an income. Sheriff Birch of Seminole County suspects Sweeney of leading cattle rustlers and outlaws in nighttime raids and would love nothing more than to jail the crook. But Sweeney is the big spender in town, gaining the love of the business owners who rely on his spending, and his crimes are always committed outside of the county. A series of mysterious crimes in town, including the robbery of the local saloon, suggests the masked man is a member of the notorious outlaws. The sheriff suspects otherwise when money is never stolen in the masked man's haste to flee the scene, but the succeeding crimes frustrates the townsfolk – especially when the masked man claims he has the protection of Sweeney. It doesn't take long for Fred, the sheriff's deputy, to figure out who the masked man is and encourages the sheriff to play along with the scheme. One evening as The Lone Ranger is being chased by a posse, the masked man rides onto Sweeney's homestead and pleads for sanctuary

by hiding out. Sweeney won't have any of this nonsense, but before he can throw the masked man out, the posse arrives. The Lone Ranger shoots the lamp out and sneaks outside the back door as the sheriff and his men arrive to take the crooks into custody. Sweeney claims he was framed but the sheriff insists on adhering to mob justice by jailing the crook long enough to find out from lawmen in other counties what evidence they have – enough, he knows, to clinch a conviction.

Episode #1141-364, Broadcast May 17, 1940

Copyright Registration #70,036, script received at Registration Office May 17, 1940.

Plot: Red Banning and Slim Thatcher escaped the penitentiary where they were serving a 20-year sentence, seeking vengeance against Judge Homer Ellis of Rim Rock Gap. Learning the judge will arrive in town in four days, on the stage from Logan's Port, they plot a clever "accident" with their friend, Bart. Planting blasting powder along the stage trail, about 20 miles out of town, a detonation would ensure a collapse of the road and a landslide, plunging the stage over the cliff and killing everyone inside – including the judge. The Lone Ranger pays a surprise visit to Bart, beating him into a confession. Tonto ties up Bart, leaving him for Sheriff Pierce. Racing wildly to Eagle Crest to prevent the stage from falling victim to sabotage, The Lone Ranger and Tonto fight against gale-force winds that were picking up throughout the day. Red and Slim, meanwhile, dropped a tree in the road knowing the stage would stop long enough for the lit fuse to reach the kegs of gunpowder without missing their mark. But the killers were never able to light the fuse before a tornado was formed from a distance. The Lone Ranger attempts to warn the men, but his voice was futile, drowned out by the winds. Red and Slim, too busy shouting at The Lone Ranger, never noticed the funnel racing towards them. As swiftly as the storm came, it passed. The criminals perished but the stage and its passengers were safe. The Lone Ranger turned to Tonto, questioning whether Red and Slim "were punished by a higher justice than the law."

Episode #1142-365, Broadcast May 20, 1940

Copyright Registration #70,149, script received at Registration Office May 24, 1940.

Plot: After a silence of 20 years, an old Indian superstition was revived when the sound of spirit drums could be heard coming from the valley. Ranchers in the region gave no stock to the superstition until Hugh Finch's reservoir breaks and his fields are flooded. Days later, when the drums sound again, Tom Brewster, another rancher, finds his barn burning to the ground. The Lone Ranger and Tonto, realizing neither Indians nor soldiers were responsible for the drums, investigate to find the imprints of cowman's boots and cigarette butts outside where the barn once stood. One week later, as a train approaches town with a delivery of $50,000 for Slocum's bank, the drums sound again. A crowd of men and women, including the sheriff, pour into the valley in excitement, hoping to find the source of the mysterious tom toms. Meanwhile, in town, two hooded figures rob the train and before fleeing the scene are stopped in their tracks. The Lone Ranger and Tonto figured out that the mysterious drums were nothing more than a decoy. The masked man shoots the boilers, spitting steam into the air, distracting the bandits long enough to get the advantage over them. The Lone Ranger and Tonto bring the crooks, now tied and bound, to the sheriff. Curly and Hank are taken into custody.

Episode #1143-365, Broadcast May 22, 1940

Copyright Registration #70,150, script received at Registration Office May 24, 1940.

Plot: In the time-worn conflict of cattlemen vs. homesteaders, the farmer's intrusion was resented by Jim Roberts, who led the cattlemen's association against the nesters. The Lone Ranger and Tonto dispel the momentary conflict but know both sides are legally obligated to protect their property. Lige Plummer fears the next attempt to lead a cattle drive through his fields of wheat will destroy what is left of his crops. No one in town expected, despite the involvement of The Lone Ranger, that the cattlemen would come in second place in their battle, spurring defiance against the cattlemen in town. The battle would have been futile in any case for hours later a dark cloud loomed in the horizon. A plague, millions of grasshoppers, flew through the area and ate all of the farmers' crops. The community was demolished – except the cattlemen who knew the bugs don't eat prairie grass and would prosper. The farmers, with no other alternative, started to pack their wagons for better ground. The Lone Ranger pleaded for Roberts to help the farmers, insisting they were his neighbors, but Roberts stood in defiance. With no other alternative, the masked man whisked the rancher away and gave him a guiding tour of the farmers' homes. There, Roberts saw newborn babies with no food, children wearing clothing that resembled rags. This is what human suffering looks like. Returning home, Roberts ordered his men to gather food and provisions. The stock of supplies would be distributed amongst the farmers to help them through the hard time. The Lone Ranger and Tonto left, knowing that peace was once again set in the region. After all, you can't hate a man you've done a favor.

Notes: Due to a clerical error, this episode and the one prior both have a recording suffix of 365.

Episode #1144-366, Broadcast May 24, 1940

Copyright Registration #70,151, script received at Registration Office May 24, 1940.

Plot: Stag Phelps, a stranger in the district, came upon a wagon recently attacked. A wagon train of emigrants was attacked over the trail from the Cumberland. The motive, no doubt, was robbery. Every member of the family massacred, and the wagon burned. This is not the first time this has happened by any means. Stag came upon the wagon while it was still in flames, dismounted and set upon a party of horsemen who mistook him for the one responsible. He was hit by bullets and escaped by river. Feelings ran high because of the suspicious holdups. The Lone Ranger and Reverend Matt Whitcomb knew Stag was innocent. As the minister tended to Stag's wounds and maintained secrecy by hiding the accused from an angry mob that set about with a manhunt. As the vigilante mob led by Rocky went from door to door, without asking permission, The Lone Ranger investigated to find the guilty culprit was too eager to see the accused hung for a crime he never committed. After word of a wealthy emigrant riding through the area reached Rocky, The Lone Ranger proved Rocky and his gang were the guilty culprits, as they took the bait within the presence of the sheriff.

Notes: This episode was a sequel to the broadcast of February 5, 1940, with the recurring character of Reverend Matt Whitcomb of Argus Falls making his second of two appearances on the program.

Episode #1145-367, Broadcast May 27, 1940

Copyright Registration #70,247, script received at Registration Office May 27, 1940.

Plot: When rancher Andy Mawson, owner of a small ranch near Millvale, discovered Lefty and Cliff running brands on stolen cattle, instead of turning them over to the law, he promised to remain silent about their rustling if they left the district, never to return. His leniency was caused by the fact that Cliff, a young man, was a distant relative of his. Cliff and Lefty both pretended to agree to his terms, but when Andy had departed, they decided instead to make an attempt on his life, for once murdered and unable to speak against them, Andy could not threaten their safety. They did not know that the entire incident had been witnessed by Tonto, who immediately reported it to The Lone Ranger. The masked man, riding to warn Andy of the rustler's duplicity, arrived in time to frustrate an attack upon the rancher's life. Both Cliff and Lefty made their escape, but the masked man, confident that Tonto could pick up their trail again the next morning whenever he liked, contented himself with showing Andy that his duty lay in reporting the entire affair to the sheriff. Leaving Andy to rejoin Tonto, the masked man was well on his way to his camp when he discovered that a second attempt had already been made upon Andy's life, one that this time promised to be successful. The two rustlers had started a raging prairie fire and Andy's home was directly in its path. Pinning his faith in Silver's ability to outrun the flames, The Lone Ranger raced through the conflagration, awakened Andy, and, sending Silver on alone, lived through the fire to capture the outlaws when a water well offered both him and the rancher sanctuary.

Episode #1146-368, Broadcast May 29, 1940

Copyright Registration #70,248, script received at Registration Office May 27, 1940.

Plot: Pecos, in common with many other towns in the West when the railroads first began to stretch out from the East, wanted a railroad above everything else. To secure the Pecos and Western, a short line whose president was named Blaggett, they voted bonds totaling $200,000 which, according to the contract entered into with Blaggett, would be turned over to him when the first train ran over the completed line. The Lone Ranger was suspicious of the entire enterprise, and particularly of Blaggett himself. Investigation only stretched his suspicions and, calling upon his old friends Mustang Mag and Missouri, he told them he planned to expose Blaggett if it developed that the man really was a swindler. Blaggett's scheme was to build the line cheaply and mostly on credit, to accept the bonds when the first train went into Pecos, then to convert them into cash and disappear. The Lone Ranger, becoming acquainted with the details of the scheme, determined to prevent this. There was no way in which he could reveal Blaggett's purpose until it would be too late for action, but he determined that he had been betrayed by an associate, Jake, and in turn led Jake to believe that Blaggett had betrayed him. As a result, on the very day that Pecos turned out en masse to celebrate the first train, they were treated to the spectacle of Jake and Blaggett mutually accusing each other and were saved the loss of their bond issue.

Episode #1147-369, Broadcast May 31, 1940

Copyright Registration #70,249, script received at Registration Office May 27, 1940.

Plot: When the West was first settled, one of the swindles employed to fleece Easterners was the sale of lots in non-existent towns. Everyone was eager to own land in the fabulous new Western cities they were sure were springing up everywhere. Two such swindlers were the men known as Deke and Richter. Representing Eureka Groves as a flourishing community on a river deep enough for navigation, they sold worthless lots to scores of emigrants, among them old Sam Hutchins, who gave them his entire savings. The Lone Ranger, learning of the transaction, and having never heard of any such community as Eureka Groves, rode to investigate. He quickly discovered that Eureka Groves was merely a barren expanse of prairie with not a single building on it. Returning to Junction City where the two swindlers made their headquarters, he was mistaken by them for an outlaw and fired upon. In spite of their resistance, The Lone Ranger and Tonto took them prisoner and raced from town. Later, the masked man returned for their money and records and, rejoining the swindlers, promised them that although they had operated within the law technically, they were not only going to return the money to their victims, but were going to do so willingly. The two swindlers scoffed at this and Richter, having surmised the masked man's identity, felt confident that The Lone Ranger would not keep their money for himself. His confidence and Deke's evaporated rapidly, however, when they learned that their destination was Eureka Groves, where the men and women they had defrauded awaited them. Arriving there, only the masked man's intervention and their own willingness to repay the emigrants saved their lives.

Episode #1148-370, Broadcast June 3, 1940

Copyright Registration #70,296, script received at Registration Office June 3, 1940.

Plot: Pablo Vegas, employed at the prosperous Crawford Ranch, plans to depart for the Rio Grande with his wife, Maria, after discovering he was scammed by Crawford, who built a reputation padding receipts and insisting he had justification for not paying wages to his Mexican ranch hands. Pablo, he claims, owes him $500 and must make good before he can leave – or be charged by law and jailed for attempting to skip out on him. Under the encouragement of The Lone Ranger, sent by The Black Caballero to investigate, Pablo steals two horses and flees overnight. Crawford's men race out to apprehend and lynch the Mexican, but The Lone Ranger saves him from a necktie party. While morally dishonest, Crawford's actions are not illegal, the masked man explains to Pablo. The only way they can resolve the problem is to have Crawford willingly destroy the receipt slips. Pablo and Tonto trick the ranch hands into being locked in the stable while Crawford and his foreman, Rufe, are trapped inside the ranch house while an angry mob of Mexicans stand outside demanding justice. The masked man sets fire to the home, using a can of kerosene, forcing Crawford and Rufe to flee through the window. All records and receipts went up in smoke, the masked man explains, and the fire will be certain to draw the sheriff and townsmen to the scene to investigate. Lest Crawford face an angry mob that will tear him apart, he will have to not say anything about the receipts to the sheriff and forego the debts he cleverly forced against his workers who want to leave – and now have no holds against them.

Episode #1149-371, Broadcast June 5, 1940

Copyright Registration #70,297, script received at Registration Office June 3, 1940.

Plot: The Lone Ranger and Tonto stumble upon a horse without a rider, a saddle with Matt Carpenter's initials, and bloodstains. Along the back trail they find in a wild deserted canyon the dead body of Matt, shot in the back and his guns still in the holsters. Matt Carpenter organized the front against the sheepmen who hired breeds and outnumbered the cattlemen two to one. The Lone Ranger, realizing he was the same build, could rob the sheepman of their victory by pretending to be Matt Carpenter for a spell. Hauser, who led the sheepmen, confided with Dirk his fear when the two find Manuel tied and gagged, claiming Matt Carpenter caught and ties him up. Yes, Manuel explains, Matt is still alive. Tonto, meanwhile, rides into town with a note for the cattlemen, from Matt Carpenter, explaining how someone tried to dry gulch him and asked the men to stand defiant. The Lone Ranger rode out to fetch the nearest U.S. Marshal, who resided in Cascade Falls. The haunting scheme of ghosting Matt Carpenter eventually leads to a deserted line cabin where Hauser, along with 12 of his men, were tied and tricked into confessing the crime. But with no one really shot dead, laughed Hauser, he could not be found guilty of a murder charge. Outside the cabin, overhearing the confession, was Tonto, the U.S. Marshal and a deputized posse. Matt Carpenter removed part of the stain on his face to reveal Matt was indeed dead. Hauser will, with assurance, be hung for the crime of murder.

Episode #1150-372, Broadcast June 7, 1940

Copyright Registration #70,298, script received at Registration Office June 3, 1940.

Plot: Two crooks named Vogel and Bowers mastermind a scheme to defraud the good citizens of not one town – but two. With the expansion of the West, banks were popping up all over the country and extending credit to settlers. With no regulations, men and women would fall victim to banks that had little strength and credit. Sans charter, Bowers opens the Clearwater Bank while Vogel opened a bank in the town of Desert Wells. When prospectors deposited gold, they received bank notes in exchange. To redeem them, the victims had to travel to the other bank where they only found themselves provided a runaround. Only when a victim threatens to go to the law do they get paid out in gold. For a few weeks the two banks profit greatly until The Lone Ranger investigates and borrows the assistance of an Easterner, Bob, to deliver a letter to Vogel, insisting the U.S. Marshal is due to arrive in town in a week to put them out of business. Panicking, Vogel rides to Clearwater so the two can grab all the gold they collected and ship it East by stage. The Lone Ranger and Tonto rob the stage, steal the strongboxes, and silently return them to the back room of the bank at Clearwater. Bob alerts the townsfolk who create a run on the bank. Bowers and Vogel insist their bank notes are good, but the mob demands gold. When the strongboxes are found in the back room, the mob insists payment on demand. The crooks, exposed, are taken into the streets as tar and feathers are prepared. Bob is instructed by The Lone Ranger to make sure everyone gets their gold back.

Episode #1151-373 "THE TRUMPET OF VICTORY"

Broadcast June 10, 1940

Copyright Registration #70,466, script received at Registration Office June 15, 1940.

Plot: Captain Howard of Fort Stanley has spent a good part of a year trying to apprehend Spotted Fox, one of the most cunning Indian chiefs to lead resistance against the white settlers. His latest scheme might work, luring Spotted Fox into a trap at Beaver Pass, using an Army patrol as bait. But Washington decided a year was too long and sends Captain Ransom to replace Howard, replacing lax for strict discipline. Ransom even believes Howard was taken in by Tonto, who was part of this newly proposed scheme. Jimmy Draper, the young bugler, assists Tonto in escaping at the risk of being court martialed. Meanwhile, Howard follows through with the scheme masterminded by The Lone Ranger, an ambush that was unprepared and a slaughter suspected. Just when Captain Ransom and Howard and the rest of the Army men believe all is lost, the sound of the charging cavalry approaches along with the sound of Jimmy's bugle. The Indians, discovering they are surrounded, surrender. Only after they throw down their arms did they discover there was no cavalry – just the stampeding empty wild horses, The Lone Ranger and Jimmy. Captain Ransom, realizing that sometimes an unorthodox method works, apologizes for misjudging the men under his command.

Notes: Beginning with this episode, the radio scripts were assigned script titles.

Episode #1152-374 "TRAILS END AT THE GALLOWS"
Broadcast June 12, 1940
Copyright Registration #70,467, script received at Registration Office June 15, 1940.
Plot: A train bound for Flat Rock slowed when the engineer discovered the trestles were missing, but the momentum of the train forced it to plunge into the gorge below. A band of hooded men ride onto the scene and steal $30,000 in gold. With four people dead and survivors given first aid, The Lone Ranger and Tonto are determined to seek out and apprehend Red Jensen and his cut-throats. When word got around that the masked man was after Red, the outlaws fled the territory. Six weeks later, one of the outlaws was careless, lighting a campfire that drew the masked man to their camp like a moth to flame. While The Lone Ranger rode off to fetch the law and reinforcements, Tonto quietly kept watch… only to be caught by the crooks. The sheriff and his posse made short work of the outlaws, but Red Jensen and his henchman, Brazos, escaped and the Indian was held for ransom in exchange for the outlaws to be released. The Lone Ranger arranged for a jailbreak. At the hideout, Tonto discovered he was rescued when The Lone Ranger and the sheriff and the posse arrived. The sheriff, having ridden Scout, was not aware at first that the horse would return to Tonto, giving away the location of the new camp. This time The Lone Ranger and the law were able to apprehend not just the gang of outlaws, but Red Jensen as well.

Episode #1153-375 "THE MAN WHO WOULD NOT DIE"
Broadcast June 14, 1940
Copyright Registration #70,468, script received at Registration Office June 15, 1940.
Plot: In the small town of Mason Corners, Milt Thompson holds prejudice against Paul Kerry and his father, Zeke Kerry. A little more than a month ago, Milt's son was killed and saddlebags containing $20,000 were missing. The culprit is Bat Tanner, who Milt insists is being hidden on the Kerry ranch. Milt Thompson hires an ex-Army scout, Travis, to find Bat and report back. Travis succeeds, discovering Paul is indeed hiding the killer in a shack almost hidden by vegetation in the swamp. Paul has been delivering grub to the man he is hiding out. Milt Thompson and his men race out to capture or kill Bat, unaware of the trap laid out before them. Jim, Milt's son, is alive and well and was bound and gagged in the shack about to be sprayed by bullets. The Lone Ranger and Tonto arrive in time to prevent gunplay, explaining how Jim was never killed – he merely lost money in a gambling scrape and refused to be blackmailed by Bat Tanner. Jim assumed once Tanner was apprehended and hung, he would take the blame. Travis, under the employ of Milt Thompson, was an alias for Bat Tanner. Tanner hoped to turn the tables on the situation by leaving Jim to be shot by the Thompson mob. With Tanner now in

custody, Milt agrees that his son's life is worth more than the money lost and was pleased to know his son was alive and well… and that Paul Kerry, who he misjudged, was looking out for his son.

Episode #1154-376 "THE LADY AND THE LAW"

Broadcast June 17, 1940

Copyright Registration #70,550, script received at Registration Office June 22, 1940.

Plot: In the little western town of Dry Lake, Sheriff Olson and Deputy Dusty are determined to apprehend Snake Walters, even willing to act on the advice of The Lone Ranger. The outlaw was to be a passenger on the stagecoach but when it came to a halt, only a woman was inside. Even The Lone Ranger is puzzled, certain his tip-off was from a reliable source. After three days of hunting for the masked man and Indian, the sheriff returned only to discover the bank was robbed of $5,000 and Banker Judson expressed indignation. The assailant was clearly Snake Walters, but the outlaw was nowhere to be seen after the robbery. When The Lone Ranger came by to offer another tip, the sheriff chooses to ignore him until the masked man steals the community cash box from the sheriff's office. The sheriff and his deputy race out in pursuit and find The Lone Ranger holding up the stage that departed the town. Once again, Mrs. Crumpet, was the only passenger on board the stage. This time the masked man placed the cash box on the stage and assured the sheriff that Snake Walters was present. Tonto removes the wig off Mrs. Crumpet to reveal Snake Walters in disguise – which is how the outlaw managed to perform the robberies and then masquerade as a woman to avoid capture.

Episode #1155-377 "JUSTICE AT SUNDANCE"

Broadcast June 19, 1940

Copyright Registration #70,551, script received at Registration Office June 22, 1940.

Written by Tom Dougall.

Plot: Soon after Drummond purchases a ranch with money of unknown origin or earnings, he blamed the death of a ranch hand named Sam Yates on Mark, a rival rancher. Seeking murder as revenge, Mark's intention is interrupted by The Lone Ranger. The only way of being cleared of the charges, the masked man explains, is to play the game without crossing the law. After visiting Clem of the local printing press, the Sundance Argus, The Lone Ranger uses a fake reward notice to smoke out the guilty culprit. Drummond's foreman, Tim, finds the notice and the rancher promptly visits the sheriff to confess killing Sam Yates. It seems the fake notice offers a $5,000 reward for the killer of Sam Yates, who was wanted by the law. With Mark no longer accused of a crime he did not commit, Drummond attempts to profit – only afterwards discovering the reward notice was fake. Under another name, Drummond was wanted in the state of California for claim jumping. The sheriff won't take Drummond's confession back and instead puts the killer behind bars, laughing, as this was the first time someone thought they could truly be paid to tell the truth.

Episode #1156-378 "SILVER: STALLION OF MYSTERY"

Broadcast June 21, 1940

Copyright Registration #70,552, script received at Registration Office June 22, 1940.

Plot: Someone attempted to engineer a raid against a trail herd moving from Abilene to Rawhide City, frustrating Jack McCain of the Circle M Ranch, and his foreman, Buck. The Lone Ranger and Tonto, attempting to trail the assailant, attempt a desperate measure by letting Silver run free range. Many caught sight of the magnificent white stallion and while hunting parties were organized, none were successful. No man in the region was able to apprehend the stallion but Buck Siebert recognized the horse as the property of The Lone Ranger. Realizing Buck was never seen in any area where the masked man roamed, The Lone Ranger and Tonto knew they had identified the cow thief. Buck, meanwhile, wants to flee and attempts to lure Alice, his employer's daughter, to run away and elope. Jack, however, locks his daughter in her room and only when Buck, in desperation, attempts to break Alice from the boarded-up window does he get caught by The Lone Ranger. Tonto tied the crook up while The Lone Ranger promised to take Buck to the law, explaining how no one in Cheyenne would have been responsible for the attempted cattle rustling unless they knew who the masked man was who was on their tail.

Episode #1157-379 "LONE RANGER TRAPS A HORSE THIEF"

Broadcast June 24, 1940

Copyright Registration #70,553, script received at Registration Office June 22, 1940.

Plot: It isn't often someone can steal Silver in front of a café without a racket, but for this story, The Lone Ranger must escape a charge of stealing a stallion left in place of Silver, then convinces the sheriff of the real thief's identity with the aid of a savvy old woman. This episode is recycled from the broadcast of September 25, 1935, with a female element added and minor revisions. This same story would later be dramatized as "Black Arab," for the broadcast of April 2, 1947.

Episode #1158-380 "GONE ARE THE GHOSTS"

Broadcast June 26, 1940

Copyright Registration #70,554, script received at Registration Office June 22, 1940.

Plot: Tormented by the memory of their partner's accidental drowning, two old fur trappers named Josh Carey and Cal are easy prey for a pair of thieves (Slag and Gunner) who pretend to be the ghost of the dead man. The Lone Ranger and Tonto, trailing the same thieves, find and rescue Cal from a bog of quicksand. Cal explains how he was lured into the deathtrap as a result of the ghostly voice. Josh, meanwhile, chooses a self-imposed life of solitude and loneliness away from a town he feels deserted him and a partner who is no longer alive. It takes intervention by The Lone Ranger to reveal the ghostly voice is that of Gunner, the son of the dead man, who was trying to trick Josh into revealing the location of his hidden furs. As for Cal, it is revealed that he is alive and well and Cal forces a confession out of the crooks to save the life of his partner.

sEpisode #1159-381 "HERMIT'S GOLD"

Broadcast June 28, 1940

Copyright Registration #70,555, script received at Registration Office June 22, 1940.

Written by Fran Striker.

Plot: This was the same script from the broadcast of August 23, 1935, with one difference: Jack Medwick was now changed to Jack Mason. (The name change was probably because Judy Medwick was a character on the *Ned Jordan, Secret Agent* radio program, also originating from the radio studio of WXYZ.) There is also a reference that "Silver isn't saddled," but this was not the case by 1940. This was a fact back in 1935, however, and carried over from the 1935 script.

Episode #1160-382 "HOLD-UP STAGECOACH"

Broadcast July 1, 1940

Copyright Registration #70,698, script received at Registration Office July 1, 1940.

Plot: An elderly couple named Edith and Caleb Saxon are on a stagecoach headed for Basin City to start anew, after Caleb was plagued by a false accusation of mishandling Ted Bellman's investments while managing his own fortune successfully. The courts found Caleb innocent but the court of public opinion, based on newspaper accounts from back East, charged the man intentionally squandered the sum entrusted to him by his best friend, left to benefit the man's son. An outlaw named Jet Bledsoe robs the stage and kidnaps the passengers, knowing full well who Caleb Saxon is and believed the old couple carried tens of thousands of dollars with him. The Lone Ranger and Tonto, meanwhile, befriend Ted, and discover the young man is on his way to Basin City in search of Caleb with intent of seeking justice outside the law. After learning of the stage hold-up, the masked man and Indian follow the trail that led to an appropriated and provisioned hide-out. Jet was pleasantly surprised to learn the couple carried $40,000 in cash, everything they had. The Lone Ranger sneaks inside when Jet was not present to hear the old man's story, then sneaks away to ask Tonto to keep tabs on them while he fetched Ted. It did not take long for the masked man to convince Ted to rush the hide-out and rescue the captives. After which, Ted found it difficult to dislike a man after he did him a favor and is taken under their wing as an adopted son.

Episode #1161-383 "GUNPOWDER BALLOTS"

Broadcast July 3, 1940

Copyright Registration #70,699, script received at Registration Office July 1, 1940.

Plot: After a bitterly contested election for sheriff in the town of Moss Springs, Putnam, the unsuccessful candidate with a powerful following, proves to be a sore loser. Reason stood if he cannot control the county with ballots, he would try it with bullets. One week later, Webb, the new sheriff, receives word that Putnam has men arriving at his place every day with many now camping on the grounds. Hoping to stoke the flames of hatred, Putnam launches a plan to drive off local Indians from their reservation, a fertile valley, with his army of followers leading the charge, believing everything wrong from massacres to bunions was the result of the red men, and driving the redskins into the badlands. After The Lone Ranger is unable to convince Putnam to see the error of his ways, the masked man rides for Chief Thundercloud to ask for a favor. Chief Thundercloud and his tribe have no connection with the reservation Indians, but at the suggestion of The Lone Ranger, arranges for his tribe to stage a fake attack on the town. Sheriff Webb was in on the scheme, instructing the faithful in town to not exchange any gunfire. The attack lures Putnam's raiders away from the reservation, and Thundercloud's tribe flees before any gunfire can be exchanged. The new sheriff looked superior in the eyes of Putnam's followers, who discovered their leader has a change of mind.

Episode #1162-384 "A SHEEP IN WOLF'S CLOTHING"

Broadcast July 5, 1940

Copyright Registration #70,783, script received at Registration Office July 11, 1940.

Plot: After rescuing whom they believe to be a young boy from a speeding train, The Lone Ranger and Tonto learn "he" is really a "she," Johnny, the 19-year-old niece of the local banker falsely accused of murder back in Lobo City. But after learning from the sheriff the details of the crime, The Lone Ranger and Tonto return to their camp to find the niece has fled the scene. They follow her secretly to the house of Chink Yarbo, the man who testified in the sheriff's office that he saw the murder. Overhearing the conversation and Johnny's disappointment for being accused of a crime she did not commit, it doesn't take long for The Lone Ranger to realize the real killer was Chink, the gardener and only person who was at the house during the crime. The Lone Ranger speeds away, but not before Chink's conscience gets the better of him, believing the sheriff was outside to overhear the conversation. The Lone Ranger makes a daring move to lure a posse out to the hideout, tricking Chink into a confrontation, without realizing the sheriff never heard the confession and thus giving himself away.

Episode #1163-385 "OUTLAW VALLEY"

Broadcast July 8, 1940

Copyright Registration #70,784, script received at Registration Office July 11, 1940.

Plot: A young man named Brad Whitman takes a job under a false name of Jack Burton with the boss of a gang of thieves operating from a large ranch. When the notorious Hawk Slade discovers he has a spy in the midst, he holds Brad prisoner. Jeff Whitman, Brad's grandfather, was the first rancher to enter the valley. For years his cattle had the entire valley to themselves. But when the homestead laws were passed, he did not believe they affected him, and the notorious Hawk Slade filed on the best parts of the valley. When Jeff tried to fight back, he found the law was against him. But Hawk was impatient and did not hesitate to step outside the law. Jeff knew it was a dangerous game allowing his grandson to go out and infiltrate the gang. When he discovers Brad's identity was discovered and now held prisoner in a shanty this side of Bullhide Creek, until sun-up when they plan to take the boy to Echo Canyon and make it look like his horse slipped and went over the side. Tonto creates a distraction while The Lone Ranger rides in to save Brad, only to discover he fell into a trap. After escaping, the masked man masterminds a means for Hawk to reveal where Brad is hidden while Jeff barred Hawk's gang inside their bunkhouses like pigs in a pen. Brad helps assist Tonto and The Lone Ranger to tie Hawk up and leave him for the law.

Episode #1164-386 "A DOUBLE MASQUERADE"
Broadcast July 10, 1940
Copyright Registration #70,785, script received at Registration Office July 11, 1940.
Plot: At the age of 19, Mark Weaver is bestowed a gift from his mother, Sarah – a pair of guns and holsters that once belonged to his father. She tells him the story of when the family first came from the East and the day he rode off with his father's bitterest enemy – never to be seen again. Of recent, she learned that the polecat, Job Clark, lives on a ranch, the Bar C Bar, outside Long Prairie, in Texas. Using his father's guns, Mark sets out to reap a family vendetta. The Lone Ranger and Tonto, meanwhile, meet up with Job to find out why he plans to sell the prosperous ranch. Job confides that many years ago a polecat named Job Clark, the same name he is using now, killed a feller in an argument. But the way it turned out, the law back there figured he was guilty. He still suffers a broken heart when he learned Indians attacked the wagon train crossing Nevada, and everyone including his wife and son killed. He left the wagon train when Job said the law was catching up to him, but now regrets having ridden out that evening. When the U.S. Marshal comes around with a letter from the East suggesting Job is really an alias, The Lone Ranger tricks the lawman into believing otherwise. Mark, however, wants to settle a score and thanks to The Lone Ranger's intervention, Tonto was able to ride out in time and bring back Sarah, who can identify Job as Mark's father and prevent a murder.

Episode #1165-387 "A RENDEZVOUS WITH DEATH" [PART ONE]
Broadcast July 12, 1940
Copyright Registration #70,786, script received at Registration Office July 11, 1940.
Plot: See pages 258 to 160.

Episode #1166-388 "TONTO RIDES ALONE" [PART TWO]
Broadcast July 15, 1940
Copyright Registration #70,938, script received at Registration Office July 18, 1940.
Plot: An outlaw named Turk Rigby, who worked for Gunner, orders his men to force the boss of the local mine to fulfill the next gold shipment so it can be stolen en route. When Arizona Lawson attempted to tell the Padre, that in spite of his fears, the masked man was still alive, he learned that Tonto had already told him the news. Even the Padre does not know where The Lone Ranger is hiding. While The Lone Ranger remained hidden in recovery, Tonto and Arizona work to ambush the gold robbers, using a ploy masterminded by the masked man by proxy. Tonto and Arizona hide in one of the boxes of gold with intent to surprise the robbers. Gary Collins, boss of the local mine, was scared when he learned of the scheme and ran off to tell Turk about the ambush plans. Turk laughs, believing he has the advantage. When the wagon is stopped at Willow Pass, Turk's gang robs the shipment of gold. Aware of the ambush, the men shoot into one of the boxes expecting to fill Tonto or Arizona with lead. But they are surprised when they discover Tonto captured Turk earlier in the day and threw the gang leader into the box. Turk, wounded, will survive the ordeal, but his lips are sealed about what he knows of the big boss.

Episode #1167-389 "OUTLAWS OF THE RIO GRANDE" [PART THREE]

Broadcast July 17, 1940

Copyright Registration #70,939, script received at Registration Office July 18, 1940.

Plot: With Turk Rigby and half his gang under arrest by the U.S. Marshal, waiting to hang, the rest of the outlaws ride out to meet Red Kemp, who masterminded a plot to shoot Arizona and kidnap Graham. Red leaves behind a trail for the posse to follow. The outlaws are too well organized and having punished any man who got in their way, knew the law would keep distance. Tonto, following orders from The Lone Ranger, pays a visit to the sheriff and hands him a map of where the outlaws were supposedly hiding. The local sheriff is reluctant to do his duty, leading a posse on a wild goose chase in the opposite direction. Believing the Indian was trying a stunt, the sheriff placed Tonto into handcuffs and forced the red man to ride along with him. The sheriff was unaware that his cowardly reputation was expected, and the map was to trick the lawman into riding out in the correct direction. Upon realizing he was coming face-to-face with the outlaws, the sheriff's astonishment was at first so great that all he could do was stare. Sweeping down upon the startled outlaws, the posse rode with desperation and fought like so many wildcats. The fact that he was handcuffed meant nothing to Tonto, who rode straight for Red when the latter, in his haste, realized the Indian was braver than he. The sheriff, unwilling to face the gang, realized his duty came first and struck up the courage to lead the charge, passing through the thick of the battle. If the numbers of the outlaws had been twice as great, the law would have had to acknowledge defeat. But soon the air was loud with shouts of surrender, ensuring that the law would prevail. In private, the sheriff removes the handcuffs from Tonto's wrists.

Episode #1168-390 "WHEN THIEVES FALL OUT" [PART FOUR]

Broadcast July 19, 1940

Copyright Registration #70,940, script received at Registration Office July 18, 1940.

Plot: See page 262.

Episode #1169-391 "A BULLET OF SILVER" [PART FIVE]

Broadcast July 22, 1940

Copyright Registration #71,083, script received at Registration Office August 7, 1940.

Plot: Dirk tells two outlaws, Nolan and Buzzard, that Gunner was supposed to have killed The Lone Ranger, but just before the law hung Mendoza, he swore up and down it was The Lone Ranger that tricked him into attacking Laramie when Laramie thought he and his gang had the sheriff cornered. Men and women who were terrified of the gangs were now starting to talk, motivated by the recent events that suggest a downfall in outlaw territory. Instead of grabbing all the money they can, the priority of the outlaws shifted to terrorism: raiding, burning and gunfire. Laramie cleverly worked out a scheme whereupon a false tip made Arizona, Tonto, the sheriff and his deputies hide at Mander's ranch, anticipating an attack that would never come. Meanwhile, the outlaw gang looted and plundered the town. An angry delegation of honest citizens led to a meeting and decision to leave Spanish Flats and build a new homestead elsewhere. Up in Roseville, about 40 miles northeast of Spanish Flats, Frank Larson was an operator and railroad agent. Dirk holds the operator at gunpoint, preventing the operator from pulling the approaching train to the side so the locomotive does not run into fifty dozen cattle cars. Eliminating any chance of transporting cattle out of the region by honest ranchers would demoralize the remaining townsfolk. Tonto and Arizona, following a tip from The Lone Ranger, prevented the crash. Buzzard and Nolan, caught off guard, were forced to drop their guns. Taken into custody, the outlaws were informed that the eastbound was loaded with every tough hombre on the railroad's payroll, to help aid the fight against the outlaws.

Episode #1170-392 "A DECOY TO DEATH" [PART SIX]

Broadcast July 24, 1940

Copyright Registration #71,084, script received at Registration Office August 7, 1940.

Plot: Tonto and Arizona Lawson ride to Molly Fletcher's aid, after she was frightened by some masked crooks who wanted to know where her father's money was. Her father was in Houston, recovering from a serious illness, and she confessed she knew nothing about where her father hid his money. Her father borrowed money from the bank in Spanish Flats with their ranch as security, and the money must be paid back in eight days or she loses everything. Manuel, who shows up once a year to do odd jobs about the ranch, knows where the money is hidden but she does not know where he is at the moment. One of Dirk's men, listening from a distance, overheard the conversation and rides out to report the news. A trap was set to catch and kill Tonto and Arizona Lawson but The Lone Ranger, still in hiding, shoots from afar to save the life of his friends. While Arizona races out to fetch the law, Tonto finds the cash and uses it as bait to lure the outlaws back across the border into the United States. The chase leads back to Molly's ranch house where the sheriff and Arizona await Tonto and the men giving chase. The law surrounds the outlaws – including Dirk – and takes the culprits in. Arizona hands the stolen cash to Molly, suggesting she hand over the payment in full to the bank.

Episode #1171-393 "AN OUTLAW MANHUNT" [PART SEVEN]

Broadcast July 26, 1940

Copyright Registration #71,085, script received at Registration Office August 7, 1940.

Plot: The remnants of the gang that terrorized the district have been depleted in numbers, now a fraction of their former strength. When gathered together, however, they still tallied a formidable force, and each member of that assembly was in a grimly vicious mood. Formerly they had answered to the commands of a dozen leaders, but now they were united into a single force under the outlaw known as Pawnee Pete. The outlaw expressed to Stub how he was fed up with taking orders from "the boss," and gave orders of his own. He would lead a search party to turn over every rock in the region until they find Arizona Lawson and Tonto and kill them. Pawnee Pete's scheme worked out sufficiently well, all things considered, when a day later they found the secret camp of Tonto and Arizona and gave chase. The pursuit consisted of narrow escapes, dodging bullets, and Arizona's horse too tired to continue without rest. Tonto, in desperation, led his friend to a dead-end canyon where the outlaws could not get to them except from where they rode in. They could hold off their pursuers for a spell, as they were equipped with plenty of ammunition – but no food. Pawnee Pete, realizing they have their prey holed up in a canyon, ordered the men to take cover and strategically maneuver to blast them or starve them. Three days passed until The Lone Ranger sent the Padre to alert Graham of the situation. The rancher rode to the sheriff and urged the lawman to action, insisting that so many outlaws have them cornered that a clean sweep of so many outlaws in one swoop would do the sheriff well in his already tarnished record. A posse is formed. From directly overhead the sun, burning white hot, poured down its searing rays into the canyon where Tonto and Arizona lay. When Pawnee Pete and another outlaw observe the sheriff and his posse from a distance, they set a decoy to lure them away from the outlaws… and a trap where the lawman and his deputized would be shot from ambush. Tonto and Arizona, mounting their horses, ride out to alert the sheriff. Although the outlaws, knowing that defeat meant hanging, fought desperately, they also fought on foot, having deserted their horses to hide themselves. The forces of the law were mounted and at length, seeing that further resistance was useless, Pawnee Pete himself led the rush to surrender.

Episode #1172-394 "THE RETURN OF THE MASKED MAN" [PART EIGHT]

Broadcast July 29, 1940

Copyright Registration #71,086, script received at Registration Office August 7, 1940.

Plot: See pages 262 and 263.

Episode #1173-395 "SETUP FOR MURDER"

Broadcast July 31, 1940

Copyright Registration #71,087, script received at Registration Office August 7, 1940.

Plot: Helen Barker is concerned when her husband Jack leaves mysteriously, in answer to a request from her father. Jack and her father have never talked since they got married. But when old man Sampson is found dead and Jack wakes with a head wound, he finds himself framed for a murder he did not commit. Tonto soon discovers the old man is not dead and begins nursing the wounds. While Jack remains behind bars in the sheriff's jail, Helen will not believe his story. The Lone Ranger, however, has reason to believe Jack's innocence and pays a visit to the sheriff to learn the names of men who held a grudge against Sampson. But rather than question all the suspects and verify alibis, the sheriff follows The Lone Ranger's instructions and visits the saloon at night to reveal Sampson was still alive and being nursed. The next day, the sheriff calls on the suspects to form a posse. At a specific spot on the trail, The Lone Ranger meets with the lawman to explain how one of their posse members, Carp, went off in a different direction – unnoticed. Tonto kept vigilance from a distance to follow. Exposed, Carp panics and threatens gunplay. The Lone Ranger explains how Sampson did in fact pass away and Carp, believing the old man would live to testify against him, attempted to make an escape.

Episode #1174-396 "A HORSE NAMED TOBY"

Broadcast August 2, 1940

Copyright Registration #71,088, script received at Registration Office August 7, 1940.

Plot: Nine-year-old Eric Blake and his twin sister, Celia, are upset when they discover their father Denis is selling off some of the horses to Blackman, a man with a reputation for being mean to horses. Worse, one of the horses being sold is Toby, one Eric considers his pet. Denis and his foreman, Zeke, agree that while the ranch could use the money, this also gives the opportunity to get rid of the scrubs. Denis was wanting to cull the horses out for quite a while. If he is going to raise horses, he has to start out with a good sound stock. When Eric and Celia visit the Blackman ranch to get their horseback, Blackman catches them in the act and uses his whip on the boy. The Lone Ranger and Tonto, taking shelter from a storm, witness the events and get the upper hand against Blackman. From Eric, the masked man learns what happened and orders Blackman to allow the horse to be returned. The Lone Ranger assured him that a refund would be applied, or the horse returned, after he talks to Eric's father. Meanwhile, back at the Blake ranch, Edna slipped and hit her head against a log. Denis orders Zeke to ride out as fast as he can to fetch a doctor. Angered, Denis vents his disgust until the masked man reminds him that the entire affair started because of Denis. "You refused to allow for the love children can hold for pets," he explained to Denis. "You were not only thoughtless, you were cruel when you sold Toby." Zeke returns to report the bridge is down and the river is raging a flood. The river cannot be crossed. The Lone Ranger races out on Silver to cross the raging river and fetch the doctor, only to find Eric on Toby, attempting the same. Both make it to the other side safely and fetch the doctor, who later confesses Edna will be all right. "But I wouldn't have answered for her if I'd been delayed another hour." When The Lone Ranger explains how Eric was equally responsible for fetching the doctor, Denis admits he was wrong and displays fatherly love to his children.

Notes: In a bizarre scene, John Todd played the role of Doctor Wheeler in this episode, but not as Tonto. As The Lone Ranger remarked when he realized someone needed to race out and fetch the doctor, "I'm sorry I told Tonto not to come with me…"

Episode #1175-397 "A NEW LIFE"

Broadcast August 5, 1940

Copyright Registration #71,207, script received at Registration Office August 14, 1940.

Plot: Jug Daggett and his wife Hettie lived in a squalid shack several miles from Concho City. Jug was a brutal, drunkard, petty thief who ruled the house with an iron fist. His wife and their son, a boy of 16 named Billy, lived in constant fear of Jug's bursts of temper. The Lone Ranger and Tonto, passing through, witness the drunkard cracking a whip on the boy so the masked man knocks the drunkard down with a stern warning not to abuse either of the two ever again. Observing how Billy did not resemble the mother or father, The Lone Ranger suspects Billy is not their natural child and rides into town to meet the sheriff and learn more. It does not take long for the masked man to suspect the boy is the sheriff's brother, kidnapped at birth by the vicious Jug. After an attempt on the boy's and wife's lives, the masked man has a showdown with the man and the sheriff. Jug, meanwhile, decides to silence Hettie and Billy by pouring kerosene throughout the shack and setting it on fire, locking them inside. A number of ranchers in this section suspected Jug has been butchering their beeves, and the sheriff has yet to find evidence. This did not stop the sheriff from frantically racing out to the shack when Jug showed up in town with a story about not being able to open the burning shack. Three hours later, with the shack burned to the ground, Sheriff Bob Roper gets testimony from Jug and has him sign a paper to attest. But Jug was in for a surprise when The Lone Ranger showed up with Hettie and Billy, who testify a completely different story, incriminating Jug. Now charged with attempted murder, Jug is placed behind bars while Billy and Hettie get a new home under the Roper home.

Episode #1176-398 "DESERT MURDER"

Broadcast August 7, 1940

Copyright Registration #71,208, script received at Registration Office August 14, 1940.

Plot: On the route through the desert to Cactus Gap, The Lone Ranger and Tonto find a dead man – a prospector shot and murdered. Two days later, after burying the body, The Lone Ranger, disguised, entered Cactus Gap hoping to find a clue to the identity of the dead man they found. After browsing a few cafés and general stores, he learned the identity of the dead man was Jake Bevins. His partner, Abel Billings, claims Jake went through the desert to a Sand City, a nearby town, to cash in their gold, but the masked man suspects otherwise and keeps news of the dead man from going public for a spell. Fritz Daly, with pockets full of cash, claims he took them tinhorn gamblers over at the Silver Star Café, but Abel, believing he found evidence against Fritz, left to seek out the sheriff to report his suspicions. The Lone Ranger schemes with Tonto to trick the killer into going directly to the spot where they found the body, it would be conclusive evidence against him. In the presence of the sheriff and both suspects, The Lone Ranger reports finding the dead man and a message left behind, scrawled on a rock by Jake. Where the body was found, however, was never revealed. Later that night, with the sheriff alongside the masked man, the killer shows up to inadvertently reveal his guilt – Abel Billings. Only Abel was not happy when he learned that there was no message left behind and his impetuous attempt to frame Fritz was what tipped off The Lone Ranger.

Blooper! Someone coughs twice into an open mike just as concluding music is brought up.

Episode #1177-399 "RANGELAND VENGEANCE"

Broadcast August 9, 1940

Copyright Registration #71,209, script received at Registration Office August 14, 1940.

Plot: Four men, wearing hoods, had entered the café in Canfield and seized the owner of the café, Gus Ziegler, only to have him taken from them by The Lone Ranger. Alone in their camp, The Lone Ranger asks Gus what the hooded men want of Judge Powers, Sheriff Nate Bender and Hawk Marlin, who they overheard were targets of a personal vendetta. Two years ago, the four cowboys held up the café and stole the valuables from the strongbox and the intended victims were responsible for the testimony that convicted them. The Lone Ranger and Tonto set off to investigate while Gus returned to town, only to be picked up by Bill Kindred, leader of the cowboys. Kindred, along with Jud Wayne, Tod Lang, and Pete Sibley, managed to kidnap the judge, sheriff and Hawk. To learn the truth and rescue the captives, the masked man stages a fake murder of the judge and the sheriff, to trick Hawk Marlin, the crooked gunman, into confessing. Hawk confessed his involvement with Gus to steal the goods that were in the strongbox that night. The judge and sheriff, having faked their death, take the guilty culprits into custody, clearing the name of the four cowboys who served an unjust two-year sentence.

Notes: The name Sibley might have originated from a character in Zane Grey's *Western Union* (1939). Zane Grey was Fran Striker's favorite author.

Episode #1178-400 "A PITFALL FOR CRIME"

Broadcast August 12, 1940

Copyright Registration #71,374, script received at Registration Office August 30, 1940.

Plot: Up high in the Montana country, at Martin's Point, Red Vickers was the biggest rancher in the region. Responsible for poisoning the cattle of competing ranches, murder and theft, Vickers reigned supreme because no one would come forth to testify. The sheriff agrees to work alongside The Lone Ranger when the masked man claims he knows of a witness in hiding who can testify to Red committing the act of murder, but needs a few days to find the witness and bring him in. Days later, when the sheriff rides out with The Lone Ranger to the masked man's camp to meet the witness they found, Bob Foster, Tonto and the witness are nowhere to be found. A $5,000 ransom note left behind threatened the life of Tonto, with an exchange at a rendezvous point in Big Moose Valley. Bob Peasley, with a grudge against Red Vickers, explains to the masked man how the valley was cut up with gullies and dry arroyos that could keep a man from getting out alive. After the money is raised, The Lone Ranger rides out to the appointed spot a day early to dig a pitfall that would be covered by fresh snow, trapping Red and his right-hand man as if they fell into a bear pit. The sheriff takes his prisoners in, knowing Red Vickers will soon hang for the crimes he was accused of, thanks to a witness who can verify a murder charge against him.

Episode #1179-401 "THE FLOATING STAGE-COACH"

Broadcast August 14, 1940

Copyright Registration #71,375, script received at Registration Office August 30, 1940.

Plot: Barney Titus, in spite of the fact that he was employed by a stagecoach line in Wolf Rock so small that it could afford to keep only one coach in operation, was the most famous driver in the entire state. Some years earlier an accident had robbed the old man of his sight, but to the surprise of everyone, blindness had not ended his usefulness. His two lead horses, Big Red and Dusty, knew the trail and understood their duties better than most humans, and with their aid Barney never missed a trip nor been so much as ten minutes off schedule from the time of the accident until the present. Running a stage line is not a woman's business, but when Jane's father is found shot straight through the heart, she finds herself having to decide whether or not to sell out to the crooked Thorpe. A notorious gunman named Hack Burgess shot and killed Jane's father, and it was Thorpe who hired the gunman and ordered him to flee far away as to never be seen again. Pending government contract, all Jane has to do is have Barney deliver the next shipment of mail on time and the franchise is theirs. The credit that comes with the franchise will carry enough cash for her to hire a dozen employees for use as guards. While Tonto sets off on Hack's trail to capture him, The Lone Ranger advises Jane not to sell. The next day, Barney sets off on the route to deliver the mail and an hour away from his destination, Thorpe halts the stage and steals the horses. The Lone Ranger happens by a short time later and discovers the calamity. Lashing logs onto the bottom of the stage, the masked man helps Barney ride the stagecoach, floating down the river. After delivering the mail in time, within the presence of Swanson, a government man, having fulfilled the provisions of the contract, horses or no horses, Barney won his employer's contract. Thorpe insists the theft of horses could not be proven, but Tonto arrives with Hack Burgess, who proves to be a coward and incriminates his employer.

Episode #1180-402 "BURIED TREASURE"

Broadcast August 16, 1940

Copyright Registration #71,376, script received at Registration Office August 30, 1940.

Plot: A young rancher named Don Dawson, and his sister Peggy, are both desperate to maintain the homestead that has been in their family for three generations. Having sold most of their belongings to keep the debts paid, they sat in their home wondering why thieves would bother to break in and steal their grandfather's rug. The Lone Ranger, hearing the legend that their grandfather hid $200,000 in gold somewhere, believed the old Indian rug was the key. The gold was hidden somewhere in a place referred to as "the City of the Dead," and all four of them followed the trail of the thieves. After riding into the ghost town after dark, Peggy mysteriously vanishes and Don, Tonto and The Lone Ranger meet the outlaws who agree to let Peggy go if the men leave in the morning after the sun rises. The Lone Ranger tricks the outlaws, revealing where they kept Peggy hostage in a cave. It just so happens the men were also digging in the cave and unearthed a chest filled with gold. The leader of the outlaws, Snapper, knew of the old Indian woman who sewed markings woven in the rug, a clear map of the caves. Don figures when they get Snapper back into town, they will put he and a rope together.

Episode #1181-403 "OUTLAW TRAIL"

Broadcast August 19, 1940

Copyright Registration #71,377, script received at Registration Office August 30, 1940.

Plot: A young rancher named Dan Marlin, cheated out of title to his spread by Gabe McMasters, a greedy banker, is approached by two former friends, Whitey Barrett and Sig, and decides to turn outlaw. But he draws the line at bank robbery, even when it was McMasters' bank, and is shot by the two outlaws and left for dead. The Lone Ranger and Tonto find the injured Dan and treat his wounds. Leaving Tonto to look after Dan, The Lone Ranger rides into town where the crooks commit the daring bank robbery as initially planned, then robs the outlaws of their cash. Sheriff Sim Wheaton gathers a posse to take off after the outlaws, only to catch up to Whitey and Sig outside of town. Dan hands the stolen cash to the sheriff, along with the guilty culprits. Dan receives the credit for apprehending the bank robbers and returning the money. The sheriff suggests Gabe McMasters give Dan his ranch back and time enough for him to pay off the loan. McMasters protests at first but changes his mind and agrees with the sheriff when the posse looks down on him for being (momentarily) heartless against the man who saved the day.

Episode #1182-404 "THE Easterner"

Broadcast August 21, 1940

Copyright Registration #71,378, script received at Registration Office August 30, 1940.

Plot: Jack Murdock, an Easterner who recently arrived in the small western town of Cottonwood, and trying to make a go of it, is seeking to secure a promised job at the express company. Mr. Thornton of the express is influenced, however, by the town bully, Job Munch, who puts Jack to shame. Job even dares to bully Jack's sister, Dot, in the streets. But Jack backed down when Job challenged him, giving Thornton reason to be too judgmental over the Easterner. Confiding in Dot, The Lone Ranger explains a plan that offers a hope of winning the respect of Thornton and the townspeople, for Jack. The plan requires the assistance of both Dot, and the Widow Ridgely, who Jack and Dot befriended earlier in the week. The scheme involves tricking Jack into believing the bully assaulted and kidnapped his sister, which results in an exchange of fisticuffs – complete with blows, grunts, and chairs knocked over. Thornton, witnessing the entire affair, admits he made a mistake about Jack and misjudged him as a coward. "I want a fighter in this office, Jack, and it certainly looks to me as if you're the man," Thornton remarks.

Episode #1183-405 "TWO BROTHERS"

Broadcast August 23, 1940

Copyright Registration #71,379, script received at Registration Office August 30, 1940.

Plot: Gil Stevens has plenty of provocation to sell the ranch and split the sale fifty-fifty with his lazy, younger brother, Lon. Without the necessary help and with Lon throwing money away at card games and alcohol, Gil has no other option. While Lon is spoiled and needs the discipline of work, The Lone Ranger recognizes Gil as stubborn, inclined to be dictatorial. Without treating his brother as an equal, Gil lost all influence with his brother. Lon, meanwhile, found himself a job with Hook Bascom, a crooked card sharp who Lon had met in the café. With understanding that Lon has the sweets for Marge Taylor, Hook asks Lon to purchase a particular spread from her father, acting as a secret agent for Hook, in a land grab that would – unbeknownst to Lon – cut off Taylor from getting his steers to the market. The Lone Ranger, pretending to be working for Hook, applies muscle against Lon. Infuriated, the lazy rancher renounces the deal by tearing the deed up and punching Hook to the floor. The Lone Ranger brought Taylor, his daughter Marge, and Gil to the café to witness the reformation of Lon, bringing harmony back to the family. As for Marge, who insisted Lon was not good for anything… she tells him he can call on her anytime.

Episode #1184-406 "A LIFE FOR SALE"

Broadcast August 26, 1940

Copyright Registration #71,491, script received at Registration Office September 7, 1940.

Written by Tom Dougall.

Plot: The Lone Ranger and Tonto are forced to stop over at the ranch house of Andy Drummond, an impoverished rancher. His wife Sarah helps tend to Tonto's superficial wounds by prescribing him with the same tonic Doctor Seitz gave her husband. When the doctor's prognosis of Andy's ailment gives him 30 days left to live, Andy accepts an offer from Hobe Chaplin, a crooked mine owner. In return for making sure Sarah and the kids are taken care of, Andy is to crawl into a mine shaft and light the fuse for blasting powder to uncover a lost vein from a recent cave-in. Andy has a one-in-a-thousand chance to get out before the explosion. Unknown to Andy and Hobe, The Lone Ranger was outside Hobe's office, listening to their conversation. Riding back to his camp, the masked man learns from Tonto that the so-called medicine given at the ranch house was poison. The doctor and Hobe Chaplin are working together in a scheme that persuades Andy to sacrifice his life. True to his word, Hobe pays Andy the $10,000 for the job but hired a crook named Buck to follow Andy to learn where the money is secretly hidden, so after Andy's death, Hobe can recover the cash. But after Andy crawls inside to plant the powder and the fuse is lit, the men are surprised to find Andy alive and well. Tonto had caught Buck, who cowardly testified against his employer. The sheriff, having witnessed the men attempt to shoot and kill Andy after their plot failed, are thwarted and taken into custody.

Episode #1185-407 "THE HOWLING DOG"

Broadcast August 28, 1940

Copyright Registration #71,492, script received at Registration Office September 7, 1940.

Written by Tom Dougall.

Plot: Zeb Crump and Charlie Teal have been bitter enemies and rivals for years, and a battle between their two hounds in the streets of Canyon City typified the hatred of their owners. Zeb's soul has been poisoned by hatred. He is as wealthy as Charlie, but despite his wealth and power, he has no real friend in the world. Charlie, on the other hand, secured respect with his neighbors. Late one evening, a few miles outside town, Zeb is shot and killed, and Charlie is the prime suspect. No one in town mourned for Zeb Crump but his black hound howled in the night, supposedly aware his master has passed on. Oddly, the murderer dragged off the body and, puzzled at first, The Lone ranger realizes the answer lies in the apparent need to kill the howling dog. Late at night, The

Lone Ranger and the sheriff hide behind large rocks in Splinter Ridge to await the killer, who would make a second attempt against the dog's life. The killer, as it turns out, is Zeb who faked his death in an effort to throw the blame against Charlie. But he needed to silence the dog who howled, and it was his attempt to kill the dog that tipped off The Lone Ranger.

Notes: The WXYZ sound crew is still experimenting with sound levels at the opening.

Episode #1186-408 "OUTCASTS AND OUTLAWS"

Broadcast August 30, 1940

Copyright Registration #71,493, script received at Registration Office September 7, 1940.

Plot: A crooked rancher named Ross owns the Western Land and Development Company, having sold all his holdings that included the land in Buffalo Basin. The farmers built the little community of New Hope and the courts ruled that he did not own the title to the basin. If the people living in the basin could be forced out, it would be the same as if they had admitted they are squatters. Ross hires an outlaw leader named Scalp to block Buffalo Creek, hoping the framers will leave when the much-needed waterway is closed off. The Lone Ranger, knowing the farmers are ill-prepared to battle the gang, enlists the aid of three drifting outcasts, Dick, Jake and Sandy, wanted for crimes they didn't commit, to fight for the farmers and thus earn their right to settle down and make an honest living. While The Lone Ranger exchanges fisticuffs with Scalp, the outcasts break the dam that prevented water from running through the valley. In desperation, Ross offers to pay the farmers if they leave, realizing his attempt at crooked means failed. The masked man advised the farmers to take the offer. They can move a hundred miles, find land as good as what they have, and bank money besides. The outcasts are rewarded homes and property as a result of their bravery.

Episode #1187-409 "COW THIEVES AT THE KAY SEE"

Broadcast September 2, 1940

Copyright Registration #71,494, script received at Registration Office September 7, 1940.

Plot: When the cattle from the Kay See ranch was the objective of a pack of predatory wolves in human form, the fight was sharp but short. The Hood Milford gang is rustling Kay See cattle, nearly bankrupting Betty and Janie, the two sisters who inherited the spread. Hood Milford cannot be arrested for the crimes without proof that he was the leader of the crooks and Milford paid for his protection. That made it almost impossible to prove that he was leader of a cattle-stealing gang that found an outlet for their stolen goods in Ceasar, the half-breed leader of a renegade army of revolutionists. The Kay See livestock was driven at a killing pace that wore important poundage off the well-fed beasts. Speed was the all-important factor to the cattle-stealers. To trap the thieves, The Lone Ranger "borrows" some Army cattle and with the assistance of the Kay See cowhands, race the cattle into the secluded renegade camp just north of the border. Ceasar, the leader, watched in some perplexity. He didn't notice that the masked mystery rider moved off in the darkness. With the soldiers following close behind to retrieve the stolen property, Hood and his gang are apprehended, while Ceasar panics and implicated Hood Milford.

Episode #1188-410 "SWAMP BOSS"

Broadcast September 4, 1940

Copyright Registration #71,495, script received at Registration Office September 7, 1940.

Plot: Until this year, the good folks of Mosquito Pass only had to contend with Boss McGruder. This year, however, there has been an epidemic of fever. No one seems to know how to treat it. The solution comes in the form of James Bates, a young doctor who comes from the East. The Lone Ranger and Tonto intercepted Bates, en route to Pecos and persuaded him to stop at Mosquito Pass to begin his career as a doctor. There used to be a fair-sized stream of water running through McGruder's farm, then North through the edge of town. McGruder had his men dig a new channel so that stream would water a new pasture he fixed up. When the stream was changed the old bed dried up except for one large low spot which remained stagnant – a swamp that had bred mosquitoes until they became a menace in the town. When the doctor confirms with his equipment that the mosquitoes are spreading the disease, The Lone Ranger knew that McGruder must be made to let the creek back in the old bed to wash away that swamp. Spreading falsehoods that the doctor was doping his patients, the townsmen, misled by McGruder's friend, the mayor and accompanied by the sheriff, used axes on the doctor's precious supplies. Bates was ridden on a rail, told that his cabin and his priceless supplies were to be burned, and given a mule at the town's edge and threatened with death if he returned. The Lone Ranger and Tonto use dynamite to blow up the swamp, but the fever continued to spread, and McGruder and his men saw to it that no one credited the suspicion that the insects spread the malady. Days later, when Boss McGruder himself comes down with the fever, the mayor begs for the good doctor's return, offering a sincere apology and promises to rectify the damages. Bates hesitates at first, but remembering his oath, he performs a minor operation that saves the life of McGruder and holds his head up proud as the doctor of Mosquito Pass.

Episode #1189-411 "PARTNERS AT PISTOL POINT"

Broadcast September 6, 1940

Copyright Registration #71,496, script received at Registration Office September 7, 1940.

Plot: In the Last Chance gambling hall in the town of Sagebrush, two lifelong friends, Spud and Brand, suddenly become enemies over a rigged card game. Garvey, a crooked gambler, made it appear as if one of the two partners was trying to cheat the other with a rigged deck. Brand and Spud own land which surrounds the only good water in town. Right now, it is open. But if Garvey gained control of the property, he would close that off and in cattle country that would become a nightmare scenario. Garvey hired a gunman named Creeper to fire two shots, the first into Spud's cabin. The second into Brand's cabin, but the second shot apparently hit The Lone Ranger by accident, wounding the masked man. Wounded, The Lone Ranger discourages the two men from exchanging gunplay long enough to prove Garvey was after their land. Following Creeper's trail back to town, The Lone Ranger tracks down the hired gun and brings him back to the gambling hall. There, in the presence of Spud and Brand, Garvey and Belle (the saloon gal) conspired to make two hot-headed fools shoot and kill each other. Creeper confesses his involvement and Spud and Brand, partners once again, grab Garvey by his legs to drag him to justice.

Episode #1190-412 "GRUBSTAKE LEADS THE WAY"

Broadcast September 9, 1940

Copyright Registration #71,777, script received at Registration Office September 28, 1940.

Plot: Shep Harper, an old timer, visits a lawyer named Lake in the town of San Salvo to execute a will leaving his big ranch to his granddaughter, Molly. The shyster lawyer, however, schemes with Brannigan, a crook, to plot the old man's demise and after bumping into Shep and knocking his glasses off, switch wills, so he inherits the ranch. The two schemers would later split ownership of the property. Later, when The Lone Ranger and Tonto discover old Shep has disappeared, they suspect he was stranded on the barren, hard, flat table rock outside of town known as Grogan's Bluff, which was isolated when the old bridge – the only means of ingress and egress – was blown up. The masked man and Indian encounter Grubstake, Shep's faithful dog, that leads them to Shep. There, they find Shep and verify the old man was lured to the remote mesa and left to die. By means of Tonto shooting arrows tied to fishing cord, Grubstake retrieves the arrows, and their lariats attached to the cord, then loop and fasten the ropes around large rocks enabling them to cross the chasm and rescue Shep. Later, when Lawyer Lake and Brannigan pay Molly a visit at her grandfather's homestead, with Ma Meggs, the house servant, as witness, the schemers attempt to lay claim to ownership of the ranch. Brannigan explains when he chatted with Shep before the bridge was destroyed, that the old man wanted to visit Grogan's Bluff, and would be dead by now. The Lone Ranger and Shep show up to break down Brannigan's story, and explains how the dog was the reason why the old man is still alive today. The sheriff was outside the house, ready to arrest the two schemers for attempted murder.

Episode #1191-413 "CHINOOK TOTEM POLE"

Broadcast September 11, 1940

Copyright Registration #71,778, script received at Registration Office September 28, 1940.

Plot: This was the same script from the broadcast of June 23, 1937. The plot and the names of characters remained the same. Only two slight revisions were made. In the beginning of the episode, instead of the crooks trying to frame The Lone Ranger and Tonto for the murder of the Chinook Indian, the masked man and Indian brought the body back to the Indian camp. At the end of the episode, with peace established, The Lone Ranger took Kay and Steve to jail. In the original version, the masked man ordered the crooks to leave and never return.

Episode #1192-414 "LEAP FROM AMBUSH"

Broadcast September 13, 1940

Copyright Registration #71,779, script received at Registration Office September 28, 1940.

Plot: It was sometimes cheaper to pay for it than fight for it. Chief Tawanda was agreeable to avoid bloodshed, but when it appeared the government did not keep its word and make payment for the land sold, the Indians sounded the war cry. The Lone Ranger stumbled upon the dead body of a courier named Clayton, who was supposed to bring the treaty money, but was apparently robbed and killed. The Lone Ranger asks Chief Tawanda to hold back the war paint for two days, promising to return with the money and prove the U.S. Government spoke straight. Tawanda and a crooked trader named Grunback, however, schemed to thwart the attempt. It was Tawanda who dry gulched the courier, handing the money over to Grunback. Tawanda prefers not to accept the money, but rather keep the land for the red man. Suspecting the masked man could not possibly return in time because it would take four days for delivery, Tawanda knew the masked man would be out of the way when they launch their next attack at sunrise on the third day. Captain Kilburn fears the masked man will not be back in time and the fort will be a smoking ruin. Thanks to a tip-off from Tonto, The Lone Ranger avoids an ambush on the return trip, catches Grunback and forces a confession out of him, then jumps a ravine to save three miles and reach the fort on time. Realizing Grunback failed in his ambush attempt, Tawanda confessed when The Lone Ranger reveals the plot. Chief Tawanda was not killed, but he was banished from his tribe.

Episode #1193-415 "FOOLS GOLD FOR THE DOCTOR"

Broadcast September 16, 1940

Copyright Registration #71,780, script received at Registration Office September 28, 1940.

Plot: Right outside of Gilpin County, The Lone Ranger and Tonto overhear rifle fire, the result of Captain Gabber, a confidence man, salting the earth with gold dust. The scheme fools Doc Withers, a local with enough liquid cash to afford the purchase price on land he did not realize was barren. The gullible doctor had gone west after serving many years during the Civil War back East. Gabber asked for $2,000 but sold the property for $600 and a mortgage on his home – against the wishes of Jessie, his wife. It doesn't take long for The Lone Ranger to explain to the doctor how he was swindled but assured him that it needn't be the finish. At the suggestion of the masked man, the doctor provided the names of the men he counted on as his friends, fixed up his house, and created a scenario that strongly suggested the claim was paying off in spades. Assuring Gabber that there was no gold underneath the land, the doctor suggested something more valuable was under the ground – and paying off. Only in the presence of the sheriff and pleading with the doctor to buy the land back for $4,000 and a return of the mortgage did Gabber learn the land is indeed worthless. Much of the dirt from the recent manual labor of Doc Withers' friends is to fill in a swamp with dirt to create a new road sorely needed – and all paid in cash courtesy of the $4,000 payment.

Notes: Only the first half of this plot was recycled from the broadcast of October 3, 1933, with different character names. The second half was an original concept.

Blooper! Captain Gabber is also referred to as Captain Gabby more than once. The inconsistency occurs in the script itself and was never caught and corrected during rehearsals.

Episode #1194-416 "MUSTANG MAG IN POLITICS"
Broadcast September 18, 1940
Copyright Registration #71,781, script received at Registration Office September 28, 1940.
Plot: See page 249.

Notes: This was the final episode to use music from the Republic Studios soundtrack of *The Lone Ranger* cliffhanger serial.

Episode #1195-417 "THE LETTER STEALS A MURDER"
Broadcast September 20, 1940
Copyright Registration #71,782, script received at Registration Office September 28, 1940.
Plot: Two crooks named Dacey and Lafe rob the stagecoach to steal the U.S. Mail, learning from one specific letter that there is gold on the Kuston homestead. Days later in Three Pines, the crooks shoot Josh Kuston when he steps out on the front porch one morning, making Sarah a grieving widow and giving 15-year-old Bob, their son, a sour spot in a vengeful and angry heart. Later, Dacey provides the suggestion to Sheriff Taylor that the murder was committed by redskins, eliminating any possible suspicion against him. When The Lone Ranger and Tonto ride into town to investigate, they quickly discover Tonto accused of the murder. At the suggestion of the masked man, Tonto permitted himself to be led to the local jail. After Sarah sold the land to Dacey for a decent price, she learned that the assay office reported gold. When Bob overhears a conversation exchanged between his mother and the masked man, he races into town to shoot Dacey and Lafe with his father's rifle. The confrontation leads to Dacey admitting to the scheme, including the stagecoach robbery. Dacey and Lafe decide to murder the boy and make it look like Tonto escaped and the two shot each other during an exchange of gunfire, "Both dead in a shootin' scrape." Only the scheme was foiled when The Lone Ranger and the sheriff overheard the conversation, and the masked man shoots the guns out of the hands of the crooks so they can replace Tonto. As for the purchase of the property, that becomes void with the arrest and conviction of Dacey and Lafe.

Notes: This was the first episode to use the new mood music library as documented in Chapter Two. This was the first occurrence of "Hi-Yo Silver" after the closing line or variation of "Who Was That masked man?"

Blooper! The Lone Ranger refers to the Bailey family, but throughout the rest of the episode their last name is Kuston.

Episode #1196-418 "HOOFMARKS TO NOWHERE"
Broadcast September 23, 1940
Copyright Registration #71,783, script received at Registration Office September 28, 1940.
Plot: Anne Beckwood, owner of the B Box ranch, has had cattle stolen. She and her husband took over the

ranch about two years ago. Her husband, Jimmy, followed the cattle trail through the valley that led into the canyon. Jimmy told Sheriff Bates about the trail but the lawman did not take him seriously. It may have been four head stolen, but if they cannot increase their cattle herd beyond 200 head, Anne's father will call them back East for not being able to succeed in the West. Her father was against them living in the West, so Anne and Jimmy struck a deal with him. Jimmy since went to Shelby to get the Texas Rangers to help find the cattle. But Jimmy never reached the town of Shelby. He was met on the trail by masked men, two of them, who took him to a cave in the canyon and held him there. It does not take long for Jimmy to realize Jenks and Hood, outlaws, were hired by the sheriff – the only person who knew where he was riding to fetch the Rangers. The Lone Ranger and Tonto take the law into their own hands, following the trail, get the better of the sheriff to learn the truth: the lawman was to be paid cash for a new courthouse and new sheriff's office for the town if he helped get the youngsters back East. After the scheme is exposed, the four longhorns are recovered, and everyone returns to town. The next morning, Anne's father, Mr. Stevens, arrives on the stage. As The Lone Ranger escorts the old man personally to the Beckwood ranch, he reminds Anne's father that they hang horse thieves – including those who hire horse thieves. His arrival at the Beckwood's abode verifies that he was wrong and that the youngsters were fit for the West.

Episode #1197-419 "THE VOICE FROM THE WATERFALL"

Broadcast September 25, 1940

Copyright Registration #71,784, script received at Registration Office September 28, 1940.

Plot: Where a great waterfall spilled its sparkling cascade into a deep pool set among huge trees, a drum suddenly sounded. Chief Thundercloud informed his tribe that there is no evil spirit of the water, but a young brave named Kadotah opposed him by substantiating a superstition. Kadotah convinces the tribe that "the spirit of the water" commands the exile of their chief, and Thundercloud soon finds himself cast out. When The Lone Ranger learns how the Indians are being led astray by two white men, Bashford and Luke, casting gold into the water, and how a wagon full of new rifles, with an unscrupulous leader to command them, could make trouble, he jumps into action. After preventing Kelvin's new Sharps repeaters from being stolen, saving the life of the trader who drove the wagon, the masked man and Tonto investigate. During a confrontation with Kadotah and the Indian tribe, The Lone Ranger on top of Silver jumped into the lake and disappeared. Later, after rescuing Tonto and Chief Thundercloud, the masked man forces Kadotah into the lake, revealing the underwater cave where Bashford and Luke are laughing over the scheme that tricked the Indians into giving up their valuables. Kadotah, having overheard the conversation, assists The Lone Ranger to bring the crooks to the surface and expose them as false spirits… resulting in the reinstatement of Chief Thundercloud with his tribe.

Episode #1198-420 "MISSOURI IS THE LAW"

Broadcast September 27, 1940

Copyright Registration #71,852, script received at Registration Office October 3, 1940.

Plot: See pages 249 and 250.

Notes: The last three lines delivered in this radio script were improvised during rehearsal. The script, as initially typed, featured a statement from Mustang Mag that "Yuh better hope that he don't ride too far from here!"

Blooper! Jack Tolliver is mistakenly referred to as John Tolliver in the beginning of this episode.

Episode #1199-421 "COWMEN PUSH A PLOW"

Broadcast September 30, 1940

Copyright Registration #72,036, script received at Registration Office October 11, 1940.

Plot: Lige Newsome cleared the country of redskins and made it safe for cattlemen, so he has no care for the government any more than he did for the Indians. His bravery is matched with an attempt to run Ben Bates and his family off their homestead. Bates had a fence built to border his rangeland, but Lige plans to tear it down because the fence keeps the cattle from the waterholes. Bates acquired the land from the government, legal, despite Lige's insistence that he has numbers in his favor and has to watch out for his own interests. The struggle comes to a climax when Ben is shot and wounded. Despite a warning from The Lone Ranger, Lige Newsome broke the law. The cattlemen resented Ben Bates, the homesteader. They tore down his fences, started a stampede onto his property and destroyed the crops. Bates was beaten, ready to quit and move away while he was still six feet above ground. Lige, however, did not laugh long. The sheriff delivered warrants against Lige Newsome, Bat Hanson, Bob Swan, Chickenfoot Jones, Fred Allen, Jeb Grant, Bob Hamilton, Newt Renfrew, Vince Hawkins, Jim Stevens, Hank Mills, and Pete Logan. The Lone Ranger rode out to fetch Judge Plumley to preside over a jury trial on the large number of complaints ranging from theft to attempted murder. The judge as a dignified figure who commanded respect and who brought with him five stalwart, heavily armed giants. His fame as a fair and impartial judge had spread throughout the west and it was well-known that his commands and judgements were always enforced in one way or another. At the conclusion of the court, the judge ordered the defendants to repair the Bates farm – and he will return in two weeks to verify. The men worked hard on the fence, and plowing the fields, and enjoyed the best tasting food they ever had during lunch at the Bates homestead… and by the end of the week the men stood by admiring what they accomplished. In the end, Tonto led a group of Indians to the Bates homestead where they needed to cross. The gate was lifted and the red men allowed to cross the property. Lige Newsome's men discovered that asking gets better results than force, especially when asking like Indians who respect another's rights and property.

Notes: Hamilton was Fran Striker's middle name. Bob was the name of his son. (Striker also used Bob Hamilton as a pen name for two Gene Autry novels.)

Episode #1200-422 "THE SHERIFF OF POWDER BEND"
Broadcast October 2, 1940
Copyright Registration #72,037, script received at Registration Office October 11, 1940.
Plot: The sheriff of Powder Bend has become another name on another tombstone in Boot Hill. The town was ruled by outlaw Rock and his gang of lawless badman. To any sheriff who tried to make his office mean something, who tried to uphold law and order, sooner or later came the same end. When the widow of the last sheriff arranges for a new lawman to come to town, the famous Bat Cordrey, she is unaware that a scheme was against her. Burgan and Placer, allies of Rock's, captured the real Cordrey with surprising ease. For a man with a reputation for gunfighting, Cordrey acted almost as if he were afraid. Placer changed clothes with Cordrey and masqueraded as the roving sheriff, for the widow's benefit. Tonto tracked down the location of Placer's cabin to rescue the real Cordrey. In town the next day, the widow insists the hired gun will send him and his allies into jail. Rock sneers and laughs until he sees from a distance the real Bat Cordrey walking down main street. The reason Cordrey would not defend himself prior was a case of rheumatism. He cannot hold his guns but that did not stop him from coming to stand up against lawlessness. Rock attempts to shoot Cordrey but quickly finds himself disarmed by The Lone Ranger, who is indeed quick on the draw. Widow Long had the privilege of opening the jail cell door herself but not before Cordrey orders all the townsfolk to disarm Rock's men.

Episode #1201-423 "CANYON BETRAYAL"
Broadcast October 4, 1940
Copyright Registration #72,038, script received at Registration Office October 11, 1940.
Plot: Knife Wound Canyon was so named because of its formation. A long, deep gash in the earth's surface,

the canyon made it necessary for both horsemen and stagecoaches to spend an extra day in crossing the state. One of the biggest engineering projects of the age was the bridge under construction across the gap. When an outlaw named Rawhide mistook The Lone Ranger for someone else, the masked man discovers a crooked foreman, Joe, plans to sabotage the construction of the bridge, kill the men on the construction crew and steal the payroll. The scheme involves having the Indians attack as soon as the bridge was completed, with Rawhide and his accomplice, Codgy, misinforming the Indians that the trains would not only drive all the game away, but would steal their horses and children. The Lone Ranger rides into the construction camp to alert Sam Barton, the Eastern Construction Engineer, and his men to hold off a few days' completion so he can bring army men to go up against the Indians, but being masked his warnings go unheeded. With no other options, the masked man himself blows up part of the bridge to delay the Indian attack. Racing out to the distant post, The Lone Ranger attempts to convince Captain Grimes, only to learn he left for another fort and Colonel Martin was now in charge. Grimes knew the masked man personally; Martin did not. The need remained the same. The engineers at Knife Wound Canyon were in need of help. Colonel Martin would not send out the Calvary until a fight has already broken out so in desperation, The Lone Ranger kidnaps the Colonel and raced away from the fort… with the entire detachment in fast pursuit. Just as the railroad men, laboring with all their strength and speed completed the bridge save for a few last ties and beams, the war-cries of the Indians could be plainly heard as the workmen spiked the last beams in place. It was then that the mighty Silver, carrying The Lone Ranger and Colonel Martin, were within sight and close on their heels rode the soldiers of the fort, their rifles pouring a withering fire into the frenzied ranks of the savages. And it was Colonel Martin, lowered from the horse, that charged up to the surprised outlaws with his guns.

Episode #1202-424 "RIFLES FOR REDSKINS"

Broadcast October 7, 1940

Copyright Registration #72,039, script received at Registration Office October 11, 1940.

Plot: The U.S. Marshal named Baldwin rode into Pine Flats searching for the outlaw gang that was selling contraband rifles to the redskins. When the sheriff's prisoner, Hank Lazarus, a prime suspect, is found dead from poison, blame falls on the jail hand named Trigger. At Baldwin's suggestion, Trigger is put behind bars for the time being until Sheriff Jim Grant can figure out when the food was poisoned. Tonto raced away from town to report the news to The Lone Ranger, who masterminds a plan to smoke out the man engaged in selling rifles to redskins. After convincing the sheriff and marshal to visit the café in the evening, Tonto pays a visit to Baldy Oliphant, who runs the café in town. The trail then leads to Baldy's one-room cabin, where he lifted three or four short carbines from a box in the corner. Before he could make his sale to Tonto, Baldy is interrupted by The Lone Ranger and Marshal Baldwin. The tables are turned, however, when it turns out Baldwin is not a U.S. Marshal and was scheming with Baldy to eliminate any possibility of suspicion by throwing the blame on Trigger. Sheriff Grant chuckles when he explains to Baldwin that blank cartridges were switched and his attempt to shoot and kill The Lone Ranger failed… but helped prove his guilt. As for Baldy, he was not guilty. He was handling rifles that were owned by men around town. Baldy was working alongside the sheriff and the masked man to help expose the culprit.

Episode #1203-425 "THE PONY RIDER"

Broadcast October 9, 1940

Copyright Registration #72,040, script received at Registration Office October 11, 1940.

Plot: This was the same script from the broadcast of January 2, 1935. The only difference between the 1935 version and the 1940 version are the names of the locations. Instead of taking place in the town of Stony Creek, this story takes place in San Pedro. Deadwood Forest was replaced with Bear Lake. All character names remained the same.

Episode #1204-426 "PLACER GOLD FOR PLUNDER"

Broadcast October 11, 1940

Copyright Registration #72,041, script received at Registration Office October 11, 1940.

Plot: Shiftless 17-year-old Chad Wilkins and his psalm-singing parents live comfortably in the valley that narrows into a canyon off sorts, backing up the whole creek to ensure irrigation and ditches. Pa managed to construct a dam which yields placer gold. Two schemers, a crooked storekeeper named Blackey Sherman, and Bull, his toadying aide, conspire to kill the family and get hold of the land. Gold is being spent by the shiftless son, Chad, who disagrees with his father, Lije, over which is more valuable: crops or gold. Chad errs in providing information to the crooks that can be used against him and by destroying the dam, they hope to kill all three and take over. The Lone Ranger and Tonto, riding into Roaring Branch and overhearing the conversation between Blackey and Bull, set out to thwart the scheme. The son has a change of heart when he learns that his parents will be killed when the dam blows, and helps The Lone Ranger and Tonto warn his parents and capture the crooks. In the process, Chad learns there are things more valuable than gold. The sheriff took the crooks into custody while Chad shows his parents, now homeless as a result of the flooding from the dam that was destroyed, how the water came down so hard that it scraped the rock walls clean – revealing a vein of solid gold that will provide them with more than enough to establish a new homestead.

Episode #1205-426 "THE LONE RANGER MAKES BIG MEDICINE"

Broadcast October 14, 1940

Copyright Registration #72,072, script received at Registration Office October 19, 1940.

Plot: Little Bear, a friend of The Lone Ranger's, backs the play of his father, Tomwando, who posted sentries to keep the settlers off their land. The words of Tomwando inflamed the frenzied braves who leaped about a fire that licked the sky with hungry red tongues. War drums thumped. But after risking his life to have a conference with Tomwando, The Lone Ranger discovered the cause of the trouble. A new rancher known as Buckeye who had terrorized the valley settlement with his gunmen. He controls the settlement, but he is not satisfied. He is trying to get the Indian land, and willing to risk war. Tonto pays a visit to Buckeye, a meeting arranged by The Lone Ranger. Buckeye mistook Tonto as Tomwando and from that meeting it is learned the ultimate goal is control of Black River, the only source of water in the valley needed for crops and cattle. Buckeye and his partner named Hank wanted land that the Indians held so they could control all the water that supplied the settlement. If the land couldn't be gained otherwise, they planned to stir up an attack by the Indians and benefit by the war that would follow. The Lone Ranger rides out to Slim, an honest settler, to seek assistance. With Slim's help, local ranchers jumped into action to divert the river into a new bed. The ranchers toiled for many hours in the gully. Then a mighty charge of blasting powder was set in the rocks. Its mighty roar echoed through the hills. Buckeye and Hawk neared the entrance of the gully – more worried with every moment they ventured east. They could not find the river that was the keystone of their plan to defraud the settlers. The Indians were forced to give Buckeye the land east of Hopkins Gully. The settlers dug a new channel and blasted a wall of rock across the gully so the river would follow the new course. The course of the river was changed until Black River runs west of the Gully. "There's no place in the valley for you anymore," The Lone Ranger told Buckeye, who would promptly leave, having misappropriated funds and sold his ranch the other day under the grand scheme of the masked man.

Notes: Due to a clerical error in the Detroit office, two consecutive episodes were labeled no. 426. (This is not a mistake on the part of the authors.) This type of clerical error in the numbering system occurred a few times over the years. This is a major reason why collectors should catalog their episodes using both episode and recording numbers, as listed in this episode guide.

Episode #1206-427 "THE BEST OF FRIENDS"

Broadcast October 16, 1940

Copyright Registration #72,073, script received at Registration Office October 19, 1940.

Plot: This was the same script from the broadcast of December 28, 1934. Everything remains the same including the names of fictional characters. The only difference is that the town of Gunsight is not mentioned by name and there is no reference to the Christmas holiday.

Episode #1207-428 "THE TRAIL TO NOWHERE"

Broadcast October 18, 1940

Copyright Registration #72,074, script received at Registration Office October 19, 1940.

Plot: Across the rolling barren country of the Midwest toiled a wagon train, covered wagon pioneers seeking the trail to Oregon. Led by the brave Ezra Crawford, the pioneers ventured west by day, and camped with guards for lookout by night. When two crooks named Shad Simmons and Turkey Wainwright arrange for Crawford to be shot, they frame the crime on the masked man and Indian who, moments prior, issued a stern warning that the wagon train was on the wrong trail. Having to flee the scene of accusation, The Lone Ranger and Tonto trailed the wagon train out across the waterless desert, taking care to remain unseen, while Simmons found himself promoted as the new guide. Each day the pioneers saw their water supply lessen, and the two schemers knew it was only a few days off the beaten track where they could hold up with their rations, leaving the wagon train in the desert to die of thirst. They had intention to return and plunder. Only when the wagon train wakes one morning to find the crooks ran off with the horses in the middle of the night do they discover the warnings from The Lone Ranger were sincere. The Lone Ranger returns and finally gains the confidence of the wagon train to lead them to a dried-up water hole, and encourages every man, woman and child to dig until they hit water. Later, the men and women agree to abandon the wagons and hide among the rocks to bait the crooks and apprehend them by surprise. After Simmons and Wainwright are tied and bound, The Lone Ranger advises the wagon train to head north fifty miles where they will hit the Oregon Trail, and where they will meet other pioneers and get a new guide.

Episode #1208-429 "THE THIRTEENTH NOTCH"

Broadcast October 21, 1940

Copyright Registration #72,113, script received at Registration Office October 23, 1940.

Plot: This was the same script from the broadcast of April 5, 1937, with only one revision: The name of Pete Jenkins was changed Poison Pete.

Episode #1209-430 "GUILTY OR NOT GUILTY"

Broadcast October 23, 1940

Copyright Registration #72,114, script received at Registration Office October 23, 1940.

Plot: This was the same script from the broadcast of April 2, 1937.

Episode #1210-431 "GULCH CREEK CROOKS"

Broadcast October 25, 1940

Copyright Registration #72,115, script received at Registration Office October 23, 1940.

Plot: This was the same script from the broadcast of November 25, 1935.

Episode #1211-431 "THE SILVER MINE THAT WAS STOLEN"

Broadcast October 28, 1940

Copyright Registration #72,441, script received at Registration Office November 12, 1940.

Plot: This was the same script from the broadcast of July 5, 1937.

Notes: Due to a clerical error in the Detroit office, two consecutive episodes were labeled 431. (This is not a mistake on the part of the authors.) This type of clerical error in the numbering system occurred a few times over the years. This is a major reason why collectors should catalog their episodes using both episode and recording numbers, as listed in this episode guide.

Episode #1212-432 "SILK BAIT'S A TRAP"

Broadcast October 30, 1940

Copyright Registration #72,442, script received at Registration Office November 12, 1940.

Plot: This was the same script from the broadcast of June 9, 1937, with two notable differences. The character of Sheriff Blandon was removed, and The Lone Ranger was not accused of the crime by the sheriff because he wore a mask.

Notes: Fran Striker reused this same plot from a prior *Green Hornet* radio broadcast of March 18, 1937, substituting valuable furs with cheap ones. For more information, please consult page 460 in *The Green Hornet: A History of Radio, Motion Pictures, Comics and Television* (2010, Grams and Salomonson).

Episode #1213-433 "THE SON OF A KILLER"

Broadcast November 1, 1940

Copyright Registration #72,443, script received at Registration Office November 12, 1940.

Plot: A bitter ex-convict named John Hawkins, freed after 15 years in Huntsville Prison, has intentions to exact revenge on the three men who framed him. He kills two of the men, then sets out to torment the third, Lanford Beasley. Beasley was the worst of them all, Hawkins contends, and death is not good enough for revenge. Upon leaning Beasley has a son, Jack, the ex-convict frames the 17-year-old for a bank robbery. While Hawkins laughs at Beasley's torment, Tonto follows the trail from the bank to learn who committed the crime. Later that evening, the town was awakened by a volley of shots, as The Lone Ranger masterminds a jailbreak. The posse sets out to apprehend Jack, now a wanted man. But when the masked man introduces Jack to the guilty culprit, the old man breaks down. Hawkins never knew that Beasley secretly raised his orphaned son after the convict's wife was killed by Indians. Seeing the error of his ways, Hawkins confesses to the crime to clear the name of his son.

Notes: Lanford Beasley was referred to as Lan a few times in this episode. Proper spelling originated from the radio script and his name is not Lem as one might suspect by listening to the recording.

Episode #1214-434 "PLOTTERS IN MURDER"

Broadcast November 4, 1940

Copyright Registration #72,444, script received at Registration Office November 12, 1940.

Plot: Tonto thwarts a scheme to set off dynamite meant to create a cave-in, trapping Jim Drennen, a young miner, inside a gold mine. Hank and Squint, the hired killers who set the charge, investigated what went wrong and discovered the fuse was merely cut short after Jim Drennen was warned and the young man fled. The blast started a slide, effectively sealing the entrance to the mine where two men died in the explosion of their making. The killers were hired by Paxton, a middle-aged schemer, who attempted to make the townsfolk believe the explosion and landslide was caused by Drennen's carelessness with his blasting powder. Drennen and his crooked partner, Snyder, hoped to re-assign the stock of the mine after it was proven the shareholders were dead. Susan, Jim's sister, was trapped in the mine but Jim, having been lured out by Tonto before the explosion, starts getting men to shovel the shale and soil away to rescue the girl. She survives, but not the two killers. After The Lone Ranger learned that two of the three owners of a gold claim plotted the death of their partner, he realized proof was lacking. Taking Snyder captive, the masked man forced the crook into a pitfall to become victim of a mountain lion. Then The Lone Ranger ties up Snyder and lights a candle to burn down to the fuse of a keg of gunpowder. Leaving enough for the men to be able to make an escape using their wits, The Lone Ranger rode out to persuade the sheriff to accompany him. This creates a falling out among the two thieves, resulting in as good as a confession within the presence of the sheriff.

Episode #1215-435 "BUZZARD BAIT BADMEN"
Broadcast November 6, 1940
Copyright Registration #72,445, script received at Registration Office November 12, 1940.
Plot: For reasons unknown, a gang of crooks led by Cactus Varden are trying to drive a rancher Bailey and his wife away from their homestead. After saving the life of Bailey from being given the buzzard treatment in the desert, The Lone Ranger rides out to eavesdrop on the outlaws. There, he learns of their plans to set fire to the dry prairie grass that would burn like wildfire. Under the cover of darkness, late at night, Varden and his men, including his closest aide, Purdy, would set a torch to it. The crooks plan to set a ring around the cabin so when the fire drives them out, they would fill Bailey and his wife with lead. And if The Lone Ranger and Tonto are among them, the trap would be set against them, too. The Lone Ranger, observed, was chased down by the crooks and an exchange of gunfire led to the masked man being shot and falling into the creek like a sack of potatoes. When Silver returns to the Bailey homestead with an empty saddle and a partially written message, the Indian instructs Bailey to plow a wide furrow around the cabin to create a firebreak. Varden and his men, having started the fire, observe Silver taking off with no one in the saddle and assume The Lone Ranger is dead. Varden goes after the horse for a bounty only to find the lure was a trap to apprehend the badman. Only then did Varden learn that it was indeed a sack of potatoes that fell into the creek. The furrow succeeded in stopping the flames that ultimately died down. Tonto apprehends the outlaws one by one.

Episode #1216-436 "TROUBLE FOR A DOUBLE"
Broadcast November 8, 1940
Copyright Registration #72,446, script received at Registration Office November 12, 1940.
Written by Tom Dougall.
Plot: Sagebrush and his gang have left a trail of robbery and murder, of highway banditry and crime, and they usually leave a victim to be blamed for their crimes. Ed Granger, charged with murder and found guilty in a court of law in Lead City, stood behind the barred door in the rear of the sheriff's office in protest. The Lone Ranger asked the sheriff to postpone the hanging for two weeks so he can prove Granger was innocent. Following a train robbery of a government gold shipment, Sagebrush and his men flee into the hills and set blasting powder underneath a bridge to thwart the masked man's pursuit. The Lone Ranger and Tonto urged their great horses forward just as the cask of blasting powder shook the flimsy bridge with its explosion. The force of the blast hurled the two riders into the dangerous whirlpools of Crazy River. With desperate strength the heroes clung to their mighty horses and struggled to the surface. One of the crooks, Slick, rides into town to buy an outfit near to that of The Lone Ranger and orders the others to scout around and find a white horse. In Dodeville, Slick masquerades as the famed lone rider of the plains to hold up an express office, hoping the law would set off after the masked man so the outlaw gang can continue their plunder without pursuit. The sheriff and his posse follow Tonto, hoping the Indian would lead him to The Lone Ranger so the law can make an arrest, unaware Tonto was leading them to a cave where Sagebrush, Slick, Red Ace and Fanner were hiding

out. The real Lone Ranger visits the cave for a showdown, exchanging verbs and pronouns with Sagebrush and his men, a confrontation that led to a confession of their crimes. The sheriff and his posse surround the outlaws and places them under arrest, clearing the name of The Lone Ranger and Ed Granger.

Episode #1217-436 "THE TRAIL LEADS TO RUSTLING"

Broadcast November 11, 1940

Copyright Registration #72,658, script received at Registration Office November 22, 1940.

Plot: Hank and Jed Sheperd, brothers, fail to heed their mother's warnings to stay away from Karney, who displays false joviality on his sleeve, and is in secret the leader of cattle rustlers. Ma Sheperd has a profitable stock of cattle, estimated 500 head, in a valley behind the cabin. The only way for the cattle to leave is past the canyon. When Hank, the oldest son, is kidnapped and forced to reveal the secret way out of the box canyon, Karney and his compadre, Fegler, master a plan to rustle the cattle to a railroad station two days away to fetch a fancy price. When The Lone Ranger is unable to track the gang, he leaves the task to Tonto while the masked man rides out to fetch the sheriff. Tonto, however, is shot and wounded in the shoulder, and falls out of the saddle moments after reporting where the hideout is. Reluctantly, the masked man rides out, turns the cattle in the dark and chases the rustlers back to the posse. Karney and Fegler are heading to jail on a charge of cattle rustling, with Hank able to testify against them. The Lone Ranger rides back to town to join his Indian partner.

Notes: Due to a clerical error in the Detroit office, two consecutive episodes were labeled 436. (This is not a mistake on the part of the authors.) This type of clerical error in the numbering system occurred a few times over the years. This is a major reason why collectors should catalog their episodes using both episode and recording numbers, as listed in this episode guide.

The script says Hank is a boy about 17 and Jed is a boy about 16, even though their ages are not referred to during the radio broadcast.

The episode ends with the assumption that Tonto will heal from his wounds as he was taken inside to mend, but no resolution was featured at the conclusion. Tonto appears to be fully mended at the beginning of the next episode, despite no reference to the prior adventure.

Blooper! One of the actors muffs the phrase "lock, stock and barrel" in the first act.

Episode #1218-437 "SOUTH OF THE BORDER"

Broadcast November 13, 1940

Copyright Registration #72,659, script received at Registration Office November 22, 1940.

Plot: Eben Case, a mean money lender, plans to foreclose on the Lazy T ranch of an elderly pioneering couple named Jim Titus, and his wife Martha. As friends of The Lone Ranger, Jim explains to the masked man how rustlers took all their stock so the couple cannot make payment by the deadline tomorrow. Jim suspects Eden Case was responsible for the rustling, but without proof the sheriff is forced to evict them tomorrow. The situation becomes complicated when Eden Case is found dead, shot to death, on the Titus ranch and Jim accused of the crime. Al Bristol, a known cattle thief, was suspected of being employed by Eden and the masked man and Indian rode off on a trail toward the Rio Grande to visit a military camp on the Mexican bank. Paying a visit to Captain Sancho, who has been frustrated by cattle rustling crossing the border, the two scheme a plan to expose Al Bristol. In town, disguised, The Lone Ranger finds himself apprehended and placed under arrest by the law, along with Al Bristol, for a trumped-up charge. Behind bars, he gains Bristol's confidence and when a jailbreak is accomplished, The Lone Ranger rides alongside Bristol to a getaway only Bristol knew. The soldiers grinned widely at Captain Sancho after the supposed escape of the prisoners. At the secret location, Tonto warms the branding iron in the fire as The Lone Ranger accused Bristol of working with the revolutionists. Panicking, Bristol confesses he makes his money stealing cattle, unaware the details he provided was being overheard by the sheriff and his men. The sheriff takes the cash from Bristol, who had already sold the stolen cattle, and promises to hand it to Jim when he is released from jail so he can pay off the mortgage and save his home.

Episode #1219-438 "THE BEAR THAT WOULDN'T DANCE"
Broadcast November 15, 1940
Copyright Registration #72,660, script received at Registration Office November 22, 1940.
Plot: In the town of Ridgeville, a clever thief named Leech uses a trained grizzly bear to distract townspeople as a cover for robbery. The tame bear escapes and people flee, unaware the bear was trained to act ferocious while Leech stepped inside the express office and committed a hold-up. The Lone Ranger and Tonto, trailing Leech, arrive in town to learn the Wells Fargo office was robbed of $50,000 in gold. Outside of town, Leech and his pet grizzly show up at the camp where his associate in crime, Bayley, discuss their next move. The Lone Ranger and Tonto ride into town, only to find themselves jailed as suspected accomplices of Leech. The grizzly bear, however, went berserk, broke its chain and rushed into the darkness. Leech was terrified, certain that the bear would return and repay him for his cruelty with the whip. The masked man and Indian get the better of Deputy Johnson and escape from jail. The sheriff and his deputy take off in pursuit. Back at the camp of the crooks, The Lone Ranger uses Leech's fear of the bear to get him to waste his ammo while Tonto held the chain on the bear that was as tame as a sheep dog. The confrontation leads to a confession while the sheriff and his deputy were listening.

Notes: The radio script indicates that the title of this episode was courtesy of someone named "R. Swan."

Episode #1220-439 "IN THE FACE OF FIRE"
Broadcast November 18, 1940
Copyright Registration #72,661, script received at Registration Office November 22, 1940.
Plot: A raw army soldier named Brandon panics during an outlaw skirmish and soon after The Lone Ranger and Tonto flank the Gerry gang away, they learn Brandon deserted moments after the ambush concluded. The Lone Ranger figured John Brandon needed a little guidance, especially since he was sure to face a court martial and with a wife back at the fort to witness the disgrace. While Tonto picks up Gerry's trail before it gets cold, The Lone Ranger attempts to track down the coward. Found in Brandon's home by the captain, The Lone Ranger is placed in jail, suspecting of aiding in Brandon's escape. Meanwhile the deserter rides toward the west, away from the army post. Tonto returns to the fort to break his friend out of jail. The jailbreak does not go unnoticed, and Captain Kinnard orders his men to take pursuit. Before fleeing the post, The Lone Ranger left a note on the captain's desk, giving the exact location of Gerry's band, courtesy of Tonto's excellent tracking skills. Racing out to an arroyo, The Lone Ranger meets Brandon, whose horse took lame. "The first time a man's under fire he may break and run. Many do," the masked man explains. But when they see the regiment marching west, with the wrong idea of Gerry's position, and would march straight into an ambush, Brandon gets the courage to ride alongside The Lone Ranger and Tonto to save the regiment. During the exchange, the bugler sounded the charge and the uniformed officers fired when they saw a target. Brandon fought like a wildcat and while he deserted, he made up for it by his gallant conduct. The captain admits they should forget all about the desertion, for the army needs such bravery and courage.

Notes: Names of military officers are Hodge, MacAfee, and Shertliff. Hodge might have been a tip-of-the-hat to actor Al Hodge, who played minor roles on *The Lone Ranger* and the title role of *The Green Hornet.*

Episode #1221-440 "THE SCARLET ARROW"

Broadcast November 20, 1940

Copyright Registration #72,662, script received at Registration Office November 22, 1940.

Plot: There is an old Indian superstition in the Texas Panhandle of a lost silver claim that nobody has ever seen. Years ago, Indians killed anyone who was in the mine and killed them with scarlet arrows. The Lone Ranger witnesses a scarlet-colored arrow from tip to tip, suggesting someone was trying to play on people's fears, and a man named Johnson panicking in fright. Finding a shack with an old couple in their sixties, Sary (nickname for Sarah) and Marty, The Lone Ranger meets a number of men who are assisting them with their recent silver discovery. A map to their claim was stolen from Johnson. The Lone Ranger suspects Purvis and Hank, and sets up a trick to expose the real crook. After telling Sary and Marty that he knows who stole the map and would return with proof, The Lone Ranger and Tonto return to their camp. The two create dummies by the campfire to lure the crooks. Hank and Purvis hoped to frighten the old couple, so they pull up stakes and leave, deserting their claim. Late that night, the crooks take shots into the dummies and ride off. Tonto captures Hank and ties him up, then follows the trail left behind by Purvis to give The Lone Ranger the advantage to apprehending the crook, leading everyone who followed to the hiding place in an old, abandoned mine.

Episode #1222-441 "A DEAL IN REAL ESTATE"

Broadcast November 22, 1940

Copyright Registration #72,663, script received at Registration Office November 22, 1940.

Plot: During a thunderstorm, The Lone Ranger and Tonto come across a girl named Jane Milbury who was fleeing from kidnappers who planned to force her father to deed them his land as ransom. She planned to ride to her aunt in Pine Flats, but the masked man explained how her attempt to thwart Dart Danning's scheme only backfired. The next morning Grant Milbury was worried. There was no sign of his daughter in the big ranch house. Before Dart could fulfill his ransom scheme, promising Jane would not be returned home safely unless the Milbury land was signed over, Tonto roped Dart while The Lone Ranger kidnapped Grant Milbury. Milbury did not know that Dart himself was the schemer. He though Dart was simply the one who was to handle the negotiations. The Lone Ranger took Grant to meet his daughter and explain how Dart Danning would never be brought to justice and would continue as a menace. Dart will finish Grant off as soon as the land is registered to him; the death has to look accidental. The next day, Dart Danning and Jenks, his associate, visit Pine Flats to register the land in his name. But after the registration was accomplished, Jane and Grant show up and Dart Danning gloats of his success – giving the sheriff evidence to arrest him. Dart claims he still owns the land, even if he is behind bars, but Jane explains how the crook lost. The title transfer could not be valid because Grant transferred the title to her earlier in the day. Nothing Grant made out had any bearing.

Episode #1223-442 "JUSTICE FOR ALL"

Broadcast November 25, 1940

Copyright Registration #72,955, script received at Registration Office December 13, 1940.

Written by Tom Dougall.

Plot: Outside the little town of Split Rock, a Mexican rancher named Estaban is being harassed by a vicious crook named Kelter, who is trying to drive him off his land. After Estaban is temporarily disabled by a rigged rodeo accident, Kelter and his aides, Duke and Blackie, drive away the ranch hands with threats. The Lone Ranger and Tonto happen to be passing by the ranch and Cito, Estaban's wife, follows the advice of her foreman, Watrus, to hire new hands who do not know anything about Kelter. Suspecting the woman needed help as her husband remained bedridden, The Lone Ranger and Tonto become ranch hands. One month later, Kelter visits the ranch and attempts to muscle the masked man and Indian away from the ranch, only to leave Estaban's ranch under the menace of the Ranger's guns. Back in town, Kelter schemes with his aides to visit the ranch late at night and attack with a vengeance. Cito makes sure all the rifles are loaded while Estaban, Watrus, The Lone Ranger and Tonto take to their posts to fend off the attack. What the crooks never counted on was Watrus bringing reinforcements – armed townspeople who help corner the attackers. Kelter escaped and, despite his broken leg, Estaban took after him. The Lone Ranger pursues and prevents Estaban from exacting justice with a six-gun, so that Kelter would join his men in a fair trial.

Episode #1224-443 "THE TOWN THAT FELL ASLEEP"

Broadcast November 27, 1940

Copyright Registration #72,956, script received at Registration Office December 13, 1940.

Plot: The small mining town of Brownsville was shrouded in a mystery. All twenty men and women of the town have mysteriously vanished and all of the dogs in town lie in a mysterious coma. There were signs of recent occupancy, but no signs of a hasty departure. Private possessions were in order; nothing was disturbed. After discovering the only residents who remained are Jim Lansing and his sister Betty, the solution starts to become clear. Their father placed Tom Tully under arrest, but the lunatic escaped and inadvertently dropped a package of dope into the only water well in town. Everyone in town was now trapped in the tunnel of the mine except the half-mad Tully who used drugs and explosives to get them there. Senior Lansing, the owner of the mine, meets his children along with The Lone Ranger and Tonto when they discover an explosive blew tons of rock, almost sealing the tunnel's mouth. The townsfolk are trapped inside and while a few start blaming others for their situation, Miller offers the ration of water to maintain their posture. The Lone Ranger quickly figures the canteen was filled with poison and Miller wanted to gain control of the mine if the present owners of the land were put out of the way. Tully was merely a willing tool in the hands of the real killer – Miller. When the masked man insisted Miller try a taste of his own medicine, and there was hesitation, the citizens discovered the truth. Using a keg of powder and a fuse, Tonto and The Lone Ranger figure a way to clear open the tunnel without a cave-in. Miller laughs because they had nothing on him after the blast killed Tully – but not before the crook provided a confession.

Episode #1225-444 "AT THE END OF THE ROPE"

Broadcast November 29, 1940

Copyright Registration #72,957, script received at Registration Office December 13, 1940.

Plot: Cliff Doran showed the sheriff his amazing discovery: Sam Dobbs' stolen cattle on the range land of Chick Brown, with the brands altered. Sally, Sam's daughter, was courting Chick and insists the young man had no reason to rustle cattle. In the Prairie Rose Café, meanwhile, Cliff Doran and his accomplice, Sid, stirred up the townsfolk who look a disliking to cattle rustlers, instigating a lynch mob. Tonto slipped out of the café to alert The Lone Ranger of what he discovered. The masked man and Indian race into Sheriff Martin's office to break Chick out of jail, saving him from an unjust lynch mob, unaware it also gave the sheriff the idea that Chick was working with masked outlaws. Paying a visit to Sam Dobbs, the masked man explained how the real rustler expected the rancher to turn against Chick on the flimsy evidence of finding his own cows on Chick's land. The real crook knew that was mighty thin evidence to stand up in a trial. He wanted to dispose of the whole case with a lynching. Sam agrees to assist the masked man to find the evidence that would convict Cliff Doran. In town, the disappointed mob, infuriated by Chick's escape, was stirred by Cliff Doran to take action against the sheriff, with the suggestion that the sheriff was crooked. The crowd, half-crazed by the inciting words of Cliff Doran, mauled the sheriff. They tore off his badge and dragged him out of the office despite his protests. Over at Doran's ranch, Sam, Chick and The Lone Ranger search the barn and eventually find branding irons. Racing back into town, the masked man prevents the hanging of the sheriff and reveals the proof needed to convict Cliff Doran as the cattle rustler.

Episode #1226-445 "CHIPS CATCH THE GAMBLER"

Broadcast December 2, 1940

Copyright Registration #72,958, script received at Registration Office December 13, 1940.

Plot: Among the rugged country of the Sierras, The Lone Ranger and Tonto prevent a railroad supply convoy from being blown up and capture the two crooks, Kirby and Buck, who were hired to ambush the mule train carrying blasting powder for the new railroad. Ace Murdock, a professional gambler, found the cards stacked against him when the ambush was foiled and the possibility that Kirby and Buck might shoot off their mouths. In private, Ace schemes with the sheriff to allow a jailbreak or be exposed for his gambling debt. Tonto overhears the discussion and reports back to The Lone Ranger. Without consent of the jailor, Ace Murdock got the two gunmen out of jail. When the crowd of railroad men who filled the town rushed to the jail, they found The Lone Ranger and Tonto inside, trapped as they came to prevent the jailbreak. The vigilantes managed to escape, but not without a tell-tale poker chip incriminating Ace as the mastermind, and evidence to suggest Daisy, the saloon gal, conspired in the scheme. Ace, as it happens, placed a wager that the railroad would not get to Sacramento in two months, otherwise the builders lose their backing. Sabotage on the railroad would ensure he wins the bet – despite that the destruction of the train would mean many deaths. Sheriff Gordon, not wanting death on his hands, was discovered by The Lone Ranger, courtesy of a poker chip, and learned from the lawman what Ace Murdock's scheme was. Daisy and Ace were out on Two Feathers Pass to blow up the supply train. The Lone Ranger raced out and shot his gun while riding through the center of town to encourage the posse to pursue. After racing into danger and exchanging gunshots, The Lone Ranger and Tonto prevent the train from being blown up and led the posse to the real crooks.

Episode #1227-446 "LAW FOR A LAWMAN"

Broadcast December 4, 1940

Copyright Registration #72,959, script received at Registration Office December 13, 1940.

Plot: A crooked sheriff guns down a gambler, then accuses an innocent settler of the murder, pursuing him in his wagon. Dan Cowdry and his wife Sary (nickname for Sarah) attempted to flee and succeeded after The Lone Ranger and Tonto trick the sheriff and his posse into going on the long trail. During the masked man's and Indian's attempt to help Dan Crowdy, they were surprised to learn from Dan's own lips that he was guilty of murder – and he threatened to give them the same treatment. Further investigation verifies that the lone wolf was with his wife's brother the night a crooked gambler named Jenkins died. Dan's story, however, is broken down by The Lone Ranger and he quickly discovers Dan is trying to protect his wife's brother, Clem, already in jail. Dodging the sheriff's posse, The Lone Ranger and Tonto apply an old Indian trick by submerging themselves under water and breathing through hollow reeds. Dan, however, is ultimately captured by the law and sent to jail to join his brother-in-law. While hiding, the masked man and Indian overheard a discussion between the sheriff and Jeff, the sheriff's sycophant, that the lawman shot Jenkins in the back. The sheriff had I.O.U. notes with the gambler and the deputy was later caught going through Jenkins' strongbox with the notes. All of this comes out in a trial and Jeff, panicking, confesses he knew the sheriff killed Jenkins.

Episode #1228-447 "THE RACE TO VICTORY"

Broadcast December 6, 1940

Copyright Registration #72,960, script received at Registration Office December 13, 1940.

Plot: In the little western town of Sawtooth, covered with a blanket of heavy snow, a bitter, bullying blacksmith named Wolf Murchison pushes his young apprentice around. Jerry Saunders, a boy of 14, wants to learn the trade but Wolf's only scheme is to marry Jerry's sister, Peggy, a young woman of 18, whom he fancies. Travers, the driver of the stagecoach, works for her father and won her favor in a marriage proposal, which frustrated the blacksmith even more. Two crooks, Clawson and Blaney, conspire to wrestle the stage franchise from the girl's father by challenging them to a race. If the stage line was out of business, Travers would be out of a job and her old man would be broke, adding more appeal to the blacksmith for Peggy's hand in marriage. If the blacksmith could set it so Clawson and Blaney win an important race, they would steal the franchise away from Saunders. Jerry overheard the discussion and fled from the crooks, dodged Clawson's bullets and was saved by the masked man. Days later, the stagecoach race between Sawtooth and Brazos starts off with great excitement, but Travers quickly discovers his horses are lame. The Lone Ranger rides up to find the horseshoes were filed down. The delay was only momentary when Scout and Silver are hitched to the stagecoach and used to participate in the race. In Sawtooth, The Lone Ranger accused Wolf of the crime and the bully confesses with no hesitation. His attempt to start a fight is quickly thwarted when The Lone Ranger beats Wolf Murchison in a fight fair and square, freeing the townsfolk of the bully and Jerry away from a brutal employee.

Episode #1229-448 "LAND GRABBER'S MASQUERADE"

Broadcast December 9, 1940

Copyright Registration #72,961, script received at Registration Office December 13, 1940.

Plot: Several days after the abduction of Jane Dale and the Easterner named Brooks, from a westbound stagecoach, The Lone Ranger and Tonto rode up to the Lazy D Ranch. The Virginia ingénue inherited the ranch from her uncle, unaware that much of the cattle has been sold off at low prices and the foreman, Jake Cyphers, was responsible. In place of the kidnapped Jane was a girl named Madge, who schemed with Pete and Jake to take the role of Jane so they could sell the ranch, collect and vacate. But the masked man insists the sheriff from Calhoun needs to come by and have her sign the last of the papers – which he knew the imposter's signature would not match. It was Madge's speech and tan that struck him as odd and caused the masked man to suspect an imposter. The captives were under the ranch house and realizing they needed the real Jane Dale to complete their masquerade, Pete and Jake force Jane at the point of a gun to play along when the sheriff arrives. But when the sheriff attempts to escort Jane from the house by placing her under arrest on charges he withholds, his rescue attempt goes afoul. Pete pulls a gun on the lawman and The Lone Ranger intervenes. A shootout causes both the sheriff and the masked man to get shot. But the ruse tricked Jake and Pete into believing they got away with their crime until Vince, the deputy, and Tonto unveiled the ruse so the law could take the crooks into custody, Brooks be rescued from the basement and Jane give the crooks a piece of her mind.

Notes: John Todd doubles as the stagecoach driver.

Episode #1230-449 "THE DOG THAT HOWLED"

Broadcast December 11, 1940

Copyright Registration #72,962, script received at Registration Office December 13, 1940.

Plot: It was late in the afternoon when The Lone Ranger and Tonto were guiding their horses along the sandy bank of a western stream, near the towering peaks of the distant Rocky Mountains. When they witness a howling dog in a canoe, drifting along with the current, they rescue the canine. A note for help under the collar leads upstream to the remains of a campfire, but no trail to follow. The canine's sense of smell followed the trail that Tonto could not find with his eyes. Mary, a wildcat of about 20, was endangered by two outlaws, Dirk and Sagebrush, who were closing in on the whereabouts of her father, who they had already shot and wounded. But as the dog gets closer to the camp, the outlaws threaten to shoot the dog until Mary confesses her father was holed up at Sawtooth Canyon. The Lone Ranger and Tonto raced into the camp and rescued the girl. Rather than push on, The Lone Ranger decided to make camp and the two badmen were bound and the dog left to guard them. Her father, Brady, struck it rich and the crooks were after the gold dust. Escaping late that evening, the crooks race out to find the old man before The Lone Ranger and Tonto catch up to them. They raced through the hills during a storm, with two or three hours ahead of the masked man, but they failed to reckon with Brady and the odds were against them.

Episode #1231-450 "LYNCH LAW LOSES OUT"

Broadcast December 13, 1940

Copyright Registration #72,963, script received at Registration Office December 13, 1940.

Plot: Josh Craddock, a windy, harmless stooge, attempts to rile the citizens of River Gap against Shad Burley, who was recently appointed to drive the stagecoach to and from Parsons Corner. Since taking over the position, Burley has survived a number of shooting scrapes and robberies. Keno, the crooked guard on the stage, substantiates Craddock's suspicions of who is mastermind behind the recent stagecoach hold-ups. When young Burley is pursued by a lynch mob, The Lone Ranger rescues him. When a young woman named Mary arrived in the town of River Gap from the East, she learns the man she was to marry had to be rescued from a lynch mob. The masked man kidnapped Craddock to find out why he was so insistent on stringing a man up without a chance for a fair trial, only to learn he was talked into it. Before Craddock could talk, someone shot him from ambush. To clear Burley's name and expose the real crooks, The Lone Ranger and Tonto set up a trap by luring Keno and his compadre Durkee, their prime suspects, to Burley's house where the redskin claimed he saw them gathering. Keno figured it was a stroke of good luck that he learned the whereabouts and barked orders for a lynch mob to form. But when the mob shows up, The Lone Ranger holds the men back to reveal how Burley was made to appear guilty so that the real hold-up men could escape unpunished. Craddock, now recovering from his wounds, was able to reveal how Keno convinced him to spiel talk about town. Tonto showed up, having been to Keno's house during the distraction, with the stolen express box and a handkerchief with eyeholes cut in it. The townsfolk, angry for the betrayal, take Keno and Durkee to the jailhouse. Mary, who stood by Shad Burley the entire time, was pleased with the outcome and knows the entire town, in an effort to beg for forgiveness, will attend the wedding.

Episode #1232-451 "THE DEPUTY FACES TROUBLE"

Broadcast December 16, 1940

Copyright Registration #73,061, script received at Registration Office January 7, 1941.

Plot: Not wanting to ride into the border town of Cara Grande without generating some excitement because of his mask, The Lone Ranger arranges for Tonto to ride into town and at a point of a gun force Sheriff Harkness to pay him a visit. At their hidden camp, the masked man explains how he has been trailing a killer named Scar Seely and the sheriff claims he knows nothing of the gunman until he hears the description: black hair and dark complexion and a scar on his right cheek that is shaped like the letter "L." The sheriff declares he knows the man as Smokey, who was clever enough to break out of his jail and flee the countryside. His deputy, Randy Jackson, went out searching for Smokey, unaware that the minor criminal described as a "chicken stealer" is, in reality, a notorious gunman. Meanwhile, the deputy walked right into Seely's hands, was apprehended, and forced against his will by Scar and his crooked pal, Manuel, in a mesquite clump. After ambushing the sheriff and a posse member, the outlaws backtrack to town where The Lone Ranger and Tonto race to rescue the deputy. Seely hopes to shoot the badge off Jackson's chest and leave him at the sheriff's office but is momentarily restrained at the point of a gun by Marybelle, the sheriff's daughter and Jackson's girlfriend. Her spunky nature was a distraction long enough to keep Manuel and Seely preoccupied for the masked man to arrive and shoot the gun out of the killer's hand. Tonto leads the criminals into the jail and locks them inside.

Notes: The chicken stealer named Smokey was originally Durkee in the first draft of the script.

Episode #1233-452 "TOLL BRIDGE"

Broadcast December 18, 1940

Copyright Registration #73,062, script received at Registration Office January 7, 1941.

Plot: Cattlemen throughout the area depended on Black River Bridge to get their cattle to the market. Jack Harper and his two companions, Moose and Breed, dug around the supports to destroy the bridge, which came down into the roaring rapids of the river. Harper worked under orders from Jasper Turner, of the T Bar Ranch, which bordered on Black River. It was one of the largest ranches in the vicinity and Turner was one of the county's meanest and stingiest men. With Turner owning a private bridge and the only means of cattle crossing, he now charges per head for the privilege. At a meeting in town hall, the local ranchers contemplate forcing Turner to allow the local ranchers to cross the bridge without a toll, possibly with the Texas Rangers to enforce. By eavesdropping, The Lone Ranger learns that Turner arranged for the public bridge to be destroyed and his profit-making scheme. The masked man paid a visit to Ben Carvell, an honest rancher, to mastermind a scheme whereupon Carvel drove his cowhands to roundup the cattle for market and prepare for a cattle drive to the railroad north of Black River. But after Turner is paid $600 for the toll, Tonto rides up to falsely represent Harper, demanding his half for the work done on the bridge, as agreed upon. When Harper later visits Turner to get his half of the money, he will not believe Turner's story about an Indian. The falling out among thieves causes Harper to remind Turner of the destruction of the bridge, which is overheard by Bates, the deputy sheriff, and The Lone Ranger. The masked man disarms the crooks to avoid bloodshed and the sheriff forces Turner to rebuild the bridge or go to jail.

Episode #1234-453 "THE TRAIL OF THE TIMBERLINE"
Broadcast December 20, 1940
Copyright Registration #73,063, script received at Registration Office January 7, 1941.
Plot: After a few years of prospecting, Jed Baker and his wife Deborah finally discovered placer gold along the stream near their house. Moments after the old couple were elated with the discovery, The Lone Ranger and Tonto rode fast to rescue them from a rockslide. The masked man later explains how he and Tonto saw two men high up on the cliff and started an avalanche that was meant to bury them under tons of rock. The two crooks from the town of Navarro, Cactus and Sneed, discovered a richer deposit of gold nearby and wanted to eliminate the old couple before they learned there was more to prospect on the claims they filed in town years ago. Tonto trails the two, only to be knocked unconscious from behind and taken prisoner. Setting up a trap, Jed and The Lone Ranger put blankets on branches with their sombreros to create an illusion and trick the two crooks into believing they shot and killed their quarry. Tonto escaped and started a fire to help create the illusion of the men sleeping, luring the crooks to the campsite and dry gulch. Deborah discovered the rich vein that was sought after by the crooks and The Lone Ranger recommended she and her husband go into town to register their claim while he took his two prisoners to deliver to the law.

Episode #1235-454 "PEACE COMES TO THE FRONTIER"
Broadcast December 23, 1940
Copyright Registration #73,064, script received at Registration Office January 7, 1941.
Plot: When a settlement is attacked and burned to the ground, the stubborn Lieutenant Carter refuses to believe that a white man named Burkley has turned renegade and is inciting young braves to war. The Lone Ranger and Tonto, having trailed the war party, insists the Indians are no worse than any other man who is misled. But Burkley, an Indian Scout for the army, already spoke to the army colonel of the nearby fort and assured him that the masked man and Indian must be mistaken. With no other option, The Lone Ranger and Tonto flee from the fort to meet Chief War Cloud of the Sioux, only to discover he lost control of his young braves who choose to listen to Burkley instead, unaware that the white renegade wants control of the territory. Whipped up by the badman, the young braves seized The Lone Ranger and Tonto and tied them to stakes at the council fire. It took the bravery of Chief War Cloud and The Lone Ranger to rationalize to the Indians that a burning at the stake would go against generations of what was taught to them, and the masked man and Tonto are set free. With the settlement of Painted Rock the next target, The Lone Ranger races to the fort to prove his story – and fetch a cavalry that would find the Sioux raiding party being led by Burkley. The Lone Ranger's

bravery and Burkley displaying a sense of cowardice, reveals to the young braves the errors of their ways and return to Chief War Cloud.

Episode #1236 "CHRISTMAS COMES TO THE BAR CIRCLE"

Broadcast December 25, 1940

Copyright Registration #73,065, script received at Registration Office January 7, 1941.

Plot: A bitter old ranch owner named Josh Cartwright, of the Bar Circle Ranch west of Painted Arroya, stops his hands from preparing for Christmas, believing "on this hear Bar Circle ranch Christmas ain't no different from no other day." On the night of a blizzard, he turns a woman and child away from his door, infuriating his ranch hands – including the foreman, Shorty – even more. On the trail into town, The Lone Ranger and Tonto track down the woman only to find the wagon empty. The woman and child fell out when the horse pulling the wagon broke off and ran away. While Tonto tends to the woman and child, The Lone Ranger rides out a long way and pushes through the deepening snowdrifts. Eventually the masked man arrives at a ramshackle sod cabin to meet Danforth, accused of a crime he did not commit and was recently released. Danforth sent a letter to his wife and son, suggesting they ride to the Bar Circle to escape the persecution of the town. One week later, Shorty is giving Cartwright the verbal treatment when The Lone Ranger arrives to join in the persecution. Ten years ago, just before Christmas, the old man ordered his son from the ranch because of an argument. He's regretted it ever since – and regrets it again when he discovers the woman and boy (named Tommy) he turned down was his daughter-in-law and grandson. Because Christmas is the season of forgiving, the family reunion included forgiveness from both sides and rekindles the spark of Christmas in an old man's heart.

Notes: This episode was never recorded. Trendle felt that a special holiday offering aired on a different calendar month due to syndicated transcriptions would not be acceptable.

Episode #1237-455 "CASH FOR CATTLE"

Broadcast December 27, 1940

Copyright Registration #73,066, script received at Registration Office January 7, 1941.

Plot: In the small town of Sagebrush, at the head of the Red River Valley, Dan Parsons, the local banker, buys longhorns for $10 each, more than they are worth, to help two marginal ranchers who are at odds against each other. Brady and Carstairs have a rivalry that might end in gunfire, but not as long as they are not undercutting each other in the sale of cattle, which is the type of violence Parsons is hoping to avoid. After overhearing the banker's predicament outside the window of his home, The Lone Ranger schemes with Tonto to save the banker from a debt for which he does not have enough money to pay. The next morning as the two rival ranchers show up to receive payment, the masked man barges into the bank to steal the money and rides away. This gave Parsons a breathing spell, but The Lone Ranger wants to let Brady and Carstairs realize how much they are indebted to him. After exploring the mountains where water once flowed down to Red River Valley, The Lone Ranger and Tonto visit Parsons to explain their plan and arrange for him to ride a wagon up north, filled with kegs of dynamite. A confrontation with all parties after the explosion reveals a dam should have been built long ago, that would have provided the dried-up valley with all the water they needed – if only Brady and Carstairs had worked together. The two ranchers, discovering how much of a friend the banker was, agreed to let bygones be bygones and instead work together so the valley will prosper.

Episode #1238-456 "SILVER TO THE RESCUE"

Broadcast December 30, 1940

Copyright Registration #73,175, script received at Registration Office January 15, 1941.

Plot: Mitch Travis runs Snake Creek, promising citizens a Garden of Eden but instead he runs the general store and gambling hall. The citizens decide to pull up stakes and move out, seeking a better community to raise their families. Realizing the stories they tell could discourage new travelers from passing through town, Travis arranges with Trigger, Shorty, Gunsight and a Mexican breed named Sebastian to attack the wagon train and wipe them out. There is more than 150 miles to the nearest fort and it would take the wagon train a week to arrive. Tonto, overhearing the crooks' scheme in the general store, races out to reveal how Travis planned to ambush the wagon train before word could be spread that the town of Snake Creek was nothing but a scheme for making money out of newcomers. Just as the heroes catch up with the wagon train in Needle Pass, the pioneers are besieged by the attackers and find themselves in a fix. With The Lone Ranger and Tonto's warning of the ambush just in time, it is almost certain that Tonto and the pioneers holding off Travis and his men for five days was ensured. The Lone Ranger raced off to the nearest fort. Silver, his giant muscles bouncing beneath his shimmering skin, raced across the land toward the distant fort, fighting natural obstacles, with swift hoofs cutting into the miles. Two hundred miles round trip and five days later, the pioneers were running out of ammunition and pondering whether they would succeed. Suddenly the sound of an Army bugle could be heard from a distance and some of the soldiers from the fort raced in to apprehend Travis and his men to take them back for a trial, while the rest of the cavalry escorted the wagon train to the fort.

Blooper! Music is cut in the second half of this episode. It has a "skip" and is quickly lifted off.

Episode #1239-457 "TRAP FOR A FUR THIEF"
Broadcast January 1, 1941
Copyright Registration #73,176, script received at Registration Office January 15, 1941.
Written by Tom Dougall.
Plot: High in the snow-covered trail cutting through the heavy trees of the Sierras, The Lone Ranger and Tonto meet Henry Duchamp, a fur trapper who discovers his girl, Sally Benson, was robbed of his valuable pelts, and she was taken captive. Before the masked man and Indian can follow the back trail from her riderless horse, in search of the girl, they discover Duchamp snuck out overnight on his own to seek Sally. Wolf and Burly, who stole the furs, try to decide what their next course of action is during a fierce winter storm. Duchamp becomes distraught when he finds himself caught in a bear trap and the crooks leave him to die in the cold. After rescuing the trapper, The Lone Ranger rationalizes the crooks' cabin is closer than Duchamp's and follows the trail to the hideout of Wolf and Burly. There, they find Sally alone as the fur robbers fled the region. Wolf and Burley, making haste in their escape, happen to meet the sheriff and trick the lawman into believing their pursuers, The Lone Ranger and Tonto, are outlaws. The masked man shoots and disarms the crooks and explains that it is they who are the crooks. The Lone Ranger suggests jailing them until they can bring Duchamp to verify it was he who was victimized. To make everything official, Tonto lodges the complaint. The sheriff, with complete understanding and common sense, agrees to hold the crooks until The Lone Ranger brings Duchamp into town to testify. Wolf and Burley are surprised to learn that the old man was rescued from the bear trap in time and is already in recovery.

Episode #1240-458 "CUSTER RIDES WITH THE LONE RANGER"
Broadcast January 3, 1941
Copyright Registration #73,177, script received at Registration Office January 15, 1941.
Plot: The "Lizard Warriors" are outlaw Indians, so vicious that their own tribes turned them away, and are "bad medicine," says Tonto. They make war parties, kill, burn and steal. Even other Indians seek to capture them and stop their crimes. When The Lone Ranger pays a visit to Fort Johnson to ask General Custer to help the settlers and ranchers at Stony Creek, who will soon be under attack, he discovers the Army garrison is short-staffed with Custer confined to base. With no possible chance of reinforcements, The Lone Ranger raced out to warn the ranchers. Tonto scouted the movements of the renegade Indians, and was discovered. He soon finds himself

captured by the renegade Indians. The leader of the savages, as it turns out, was a white man and one of the worst in the entire West. As the renegades prepared to burn Tonto at the stake, General Custer sneaks into the camp, cuts the ponies loose to create a distraction, and rescues Tonto. Back at Stony Forks, Tonto assists The Lone Ranger and the ranchers with digging trenches and preparing barrels of oil for a trap as the Lizard Warriors are certain to follow Tonto's trail. Setting fire to the oil, a wall of flame distracts the charging Lizard Warriors, long enough for the cavalry to arrive with General Custer leading the charge. Most of the horses were tied and forced to race after the renegade Indians, creating the illusion of a cavalry, complete with bugler. By the time the Lizard Warriors get ready to attack again, the soldiers will be back from the north. But with the leader of the outlaw Indians shot and killed, chances are success will be ensured.

Episode #1241-459 "RUSTLERS AT THE RIO GRANDE"

Broadcast January 6, 1941

Copyright Registration #73,178, script received at Registration Office January 15, 1941.

Plot: Sam Kurdey's cattle were grazing peacefully on the buffalo grass that covered the rangeland. They were Texas longhorns, sleek and well-fed. During a cattle drive, wolf scent created a stampede. The Lone Ranger and Tonto, witnessing the stampede, race to save Regan, a young cowhand whose horse hit a gopher hole. Sam is not happy, however, when his men get the cattle under control, and it is discovered the head looks a heap smaller than it ought to be. The cattle might have smelled wolf, but Sam smells cattle rustlers. The trail leads to Rock Gulch, which leads right to the ford across the Rio Grande and right smack into Mexico, where they watch rustlers at work changing the brand on Sam Kurdey's cattle. It does not take long for The Lone Ranger to discover Jeff, the crooked foreman, of conspiring with Wooster, a badman from Mexico. With the assistance of Regan, the masked man and Indian arrange for the stolen cattle to be reined into Wooster's ranch, where Regan fetches the law and Sam's posse, to find the stolen longhorns not alone on the prairie in Mexico, but in the custody of the thief. Jeff and Wooster, sharing a laugh at the latter's ranch, are shocked when the stolen cattle show up on the ranch and not across the border in Mexico, out of reach of the law. The Lone Ranger disarms Jeff as the law arrives to catch the crooks with possession of the goods.

Episode #1242-460 "INVISIBLE TRIGGER FINGERS"

Broadcast January 8, 1941

Copyright Registration #73,179, script received at Registration Office January 15, 1941.

Plot: Eliza Shanley writes a letter, addressed to The Lone Ranger, pleading for help. The envelope traveled all over the panhandle, from Albuquerque and back, and is finally passed on to the masked man courtesy of a stagecoach driver. Her husband, Hank, is being driven insane by ghosts of his past. The Lone Ranger and Tonto investigate outside the Shanley cabin, are shot at, and discover the assailant vanished in mid-air. The only clue to the mystery is the screams from jackdaw birds up on a bluff, moments before the gun shots. Shanley disappears and miles away, across the plains, Jeff Bruder and his associate, Purdey, drove their horses with the limp form of Hank Shanley across Bruder's saddle. The Lone Ranger and Tonto find an old tunnel underground that was used as a means of escape for the shooters, vindictive scoundrels who plotted to drive Hank Shanley insane. After the masked man rescued Hank and explained the truth about the affair, he asks Hank to hitch a plow to his horse and work the fields under moonlight to masquerade as a lunatic to bait the killers. With the sheriff by their side, and hiding from sight, our heroes and the law witness Bruder planning to shoot at Hank with his buffalo gun. Exposed, the crooks are taken into custody.

Episode #1243-461 "DEAD MAN IMPOSTER"

Broadcast January 10, 1941

Copyright Registration #73,180, script received at Registration Office January 15, 1941.

Plot: The Lone Ranger and Tonto, camped in an arroyo, stood beside their horses, watchful and waiting, and remained silent as they overhear a plot exchanged between two crooks. The crooks mentioned the name of Irwin, with the suggestion that he could send them to jail for past crimes. Meanwhile, Old Missouri, the recently elected sheriff, must serve Mustang Mag with a mortgage loan for ten times what she had borrowed. It seems Irwin lent her $200 but the paper claims she owes him $2,000. When Missouri goes to confront the lender, he finds him dead with a knife in the back and Missouri is blamed for the murder. The Lone Ranger and Tonto investigate and quickly deduce Irwin faked his death. The judge who wrote up the papers to be served against Mag was kidnapped and taken to a cave. Hoping to cash in on her ranch (or the $2,000), the crooks, Sid and Bat, shaved the judge's head and planned to murder him so it would appear an unrecognizable stranger died in the desert, eliminating anyone who could swear against them. The Lone Ranger followed the tracks from Irwin's house to rescue the judge and verify the crooks killed their boss and sided with Irwin, who was alive and well.

Episode #1244-462 "HEIR TO A RANCH"

Broadcast January 13, 1941

Copyright Registration #73,181, script received at Registration Office January 15, 1941.

Plot: Brock is an unscrupulous heir to a large ranch, taking desperate action to get hold of his future inheritance. The Wells Fargo stage from Pecos to Saddle Bow was held up so he could kidnap the grandson of the ranch owners, hoping the elderly couple will die of sadness. For two weeks old Dave Brenners and his wife, Beth, were heartbroken as no sign of the seven-year-old boy, Robert, was found. The search is taking a toll on the old man's heart. The Lone Ranger and Tonto learn of the kidnapping and follow the trail starting from the scene of the crime, only to be shot at from an assailant up on a cliff. Robert was being kept at the Indian camp of Eagle Feather, whose squaw falls in love with the child because her own died a few years ago. After learning from the town doctor that Brock would stand to inherit if something happened to the boy, The Lone Ranger pays a visit to Brock's uncle to find the black handkerchief used to mask his face during the kidnapping, confirming who was responsible. But Brock escapes and flees. Following the trail, The Lone Ranger explains to Eagle Feather that he was misled – the boy's parents were killed but he was going to his grandparents to be cared for. The masked man is forced to exchange fisticuffs to win the argument with Brock and in the morning the boy is returned. As for Brock, The Lone Ranger explains to old man Brenners that their nephew went to California and "I don't think he'll be back."

Notes: A chance meeting between the town doctor and The Lone Ranger led to the rescue of the boy and a happy reunion. The doctor made reference to the time back when The Lone Ranger and Tonto helped assist him with that epidemic back in Powder Gulch, which was in reference to the episode "Swamp Boss," broadcast September 4, 1940 (only the town was named Mosquito Pass in the 1940 broadcast).

The ending is unusual as it leaves the radio audience to decide for themselves what happened to Brock.

Episode #1245-463 "THE HAUNTED BUNKHOUSE"

Broadcast January 15, 1941

Copyright Registration #73,182, script received at Registration Office January 15, 1941.

Plot: The Lone Ranger and Tonto found their curiosity aroused as they approached an extensive ranch that had once been a prosperous outfit, but which showed neglect on every side. A peddler named Sidney Fairchild invites them to share dinner inside with the Collins sisters, Agatha and Bessie, to reveal the curse of Lyman Durick, a foreman on the ranch. One night when all of the hands were in town on a spree, he stole some fine old jewelry worth a fortune. Durick was later caught and hung, but not before he placed a curse on the property. The Lone Ranger was surprised when John Barton, who spent the night in the bunkhouse to investigate the strange sounds heard by Agatha and Bessie Collins, was found in the morning, dead. The sisters suspected the ghost of Lyman Durick was responsible, but the masked man took no stock in the supernatural manifestations. Even Silver was nervous, as Tonto observed. Late that next evening, with the Collins sisters staying in town, the sheriff, Fairchild, The Lone Ranger and Tonto hid in the bunkhouse and waited in the shadows for the real killer to show up – a horse that was once owned by Lyman Durick. The horse returned every night to paw outside the building, inadvertently killing Barton the other night. Tonto pries open the floorboards to find the dead body of Lyman Durick and the stolen jewelry. It was Fairchild that killed Durick and had intentions someday to return and get the stolen goods. He created the curse and the story to scare the Collins sisters away so he could finish his task. Fairchild attempted to kill the three men but discovered quickly that his gun was unloaded – courtesy of The Lone Ranger.

Episode #1246-464 "THE PONY EXPRESS AGENT"

Broadcast January 17, 1941

Copyright Registration #73,183, script received at Registration Office January 15, 1941.

Plot: Dan Slade, an ex-gunfighter, is now a pony express agent in the town of Julesburg and promised a full pardon for his past crimes by Sealy, a shady politician out to line his own pockets. But Sealy withholds the pardon and attempts to hold out unless Slade switches an envelope being carried through the Pony Express, containing false results of an election. When Henry Jenkins, a friend of Sealy's, is shot and killed, The Lone Ranger rides out to apprehend the killer, Slotkin. Through Slotkin, he learns of a plan from a number of schemers in Washington to tamper with the election results. If new officials move into power in Washington, the grafters who are in office in the west will have to cover their tracks and then get out. They need time to do that, hence the substitution of the fake election reports. In Sealy's hotel room, The Lone Ranger and Slade have a private conversation whereby the politician is frightened when he learns the dinner that was served is meant as a last meal – provided the Pony Express is not delivering the pardon because Sealy intercepted the pardon and has it in his possession. Realizing he has no other option, Sealy hands over the pardon to Slade. But his confession is overheard by the U.S. Marshal and his deputies outside the door and Sealy is taken into custody.

Notes: The radio script describes the character of Dan Slade as an "Edmund Lowe type."

At one point Dan Slade claims the pony express office has a 14-year-old working for him, and "the best rider that comes through here. His name is Cody, Bill Cody. You'll hear of him some day."

The original draft of this script had the town of Julesburg, but changed to Jonesburg, Henry Jordan was changed to Henry Jenkins, and Wheeler was changed to Sealy.

Episode #1247-465 "BLIND JUSTICE"

Broadcast January 20, 1941

Copyright Registration #73,471, script received at Registration Office February 3, 1941.

Plot: The Lone Ranger and Tonto ride into Porter's Gap and come to the aid of Sheriff Jim Bradley who is losing his sight. Bradley is trying to hang on until his missing son, on a return trip back home, arrives to take over. The townsfolk know of the sheriff's situation, but they have no real need for a sheriff anyway. No bad Indians and Bradley drove the outlaws out of the district years ago. When two outlaws, Buck Winters and Ed Ransom, shoot and wound the sheriff by ambush one evening, The Lone Ranger and Tonto are quickly accused of the crime and hunted as outlaws. Befriending the sheriff after mending his shoulder wound and bringing him back to his ranch house, The Lone Ranger explains how he plans to ride to San Merino for a plan against the crooks. But Buck is leading the posse, and he will probably try to seize the reins of government by getting himself appointed sheriff in Bradley's place. If he succeeds, he will bring in his own deputies and the town will have to fight to get rid of him. Finding Bob, Bradley's son, The Lone Ranger convinces the young man to ride back to Porter's Gap to identify the two crooks he knew as Buck Winters and Ed Ransom. In town, Bob finds himself appointed the new sheriff, but Bob insists he was in bad company for a month on a false charge... but when he sees what happened to his father and the two men who were responsible – the same two men who framed him back in San Merino, Bob takes the badge and the position. The Lone Ranger assists Bob in shooting the gun out of Buck's hand, so the town gets a new sheriff.

Episode #1248-466 "HANGED BUT NOT DEAD"

Broadcast January 22, 1941

Copyright Registration #73,472, script received at Registration Office February 3, 1941.

Plot: Thanks to The Lone Ranger, Sheriff Standish had one prisoner as a result of his intensive efforts to clean up a ruthless gang of cattle thieves that worked in the vicinity. Dan Jagger, the leader of the gang, was found guilty of murder in the first degree and before the criminal is hung, he swears to come back from the grave to get even with Sid, the cowardly crook who testified against him. Hours after the execution, Sid, behind bars and under protective custody, is knifed from the window. Dan Jagger was both seen and heard from outside, before riding off. The Lone Ranger and Tonto, as well as the sheriff, were at a loss to account for the weird manifestation. Meanwhile, those who served on the Jagger jury felt that there was no power on earth to combat the thing that had killed Sid. The next day, Tonto volunteers his services to trail the supposed ghost and the sheriff fetches his posse. Through the rocks and brush the Indian follows the trail outside of town until he comes upon a stranger who, they suspect, is the guilty party that masqueraded as a ghost and killed Sid. The stranger is none other than The Lone Ranger in disguise. Led by Deputy Beldon and several others to a place beneath a noose, the strong, lean body of The Lone Ranger dropped and swung in the grey light of dawn. After he was cut down and Doc Potter moved in to verify did The Lone Ranger rise and order the sheriff to arrest the deputy and the doctor. Beldon fixed the rope around his chest beneath his arms, instead of around the neck, and the doctor was in on the scheme. The sheriff was in on The Lone Ranger's scheme to expose the killer's accomplices and Beldon confesses to where Dan Jagger is hiding out.

Episode #1249-467 "ALONG THE EL PASO TRAIL"

Broadcast January 24, 1941

Copyright Registration #73,473, script received at Registration Office February 3, 1941.

Plot: Shad Rankin had a growing freight business in the Texas Panhandle. In spite of Indians, floods and trouble, he was beginning to bear dividends. When two crooks, Bulger and Sawtel, ambush the young driver, they hope to take over his profitable business and skin the customers for plenty. The Lone Ranger and Tonto happen to be riding along to find the horses and wagon, and the wounded Shad. After rushing the wounded man back to the doctor, The Lone Ranger discovers Shad's wife decides to take up the reins while her husband recovers. Egged on by Sawtel and Bulger, the local settlers believe The Lone Ranger and Tonto did the shooting. On a fool's notion, the crooks plan to ambush the wife, believing the masked man will get the blame. As night fell across the plains, the moon casting shadows from the giant cactus and mesquite that dotted the trail to El Paso, the woman was heading east for El Paso, handling her husband's wagon. In a dramatic race, The Lone Ranger and Tonto ride out to save the woman's life and trap the crooks, shooting the gun out of the hands of both Sawtel and Bulger.

Notes: Tonto uses the word "I" in act two, a no-no according to Fran Striker.

Episode #1250-467 "FIRE IN THE SKY"

Broadcast January 27, 1941

Copyright Registration #73,474, script received at Registration Office February 3, 1941.

Plot: The Lone Ranger and Tonto were riding across the country when a volley of shots rang out through the stillness of the afternoon. Instead of a gunfight, they find two friends, Pete and Pedro, in a shooting contest. Pete Lacey is considered the best broncho buster in the West, and Pedro Martinez de Solvado y Runega is the best man with a lariat in the state of Texas. But the two are the worst hands at holding a job from the Mississippi to the Pacific. The Lone Ranger and Tonto were on their way to the Carter Ranch, to investigate trouble on the spread. Someone is trying to put her out of business. Ellen has been trying to run the ranch ever since her father's death. She is inexperienced, but she has a good foreman. The Lone Ranger suggests Pete and Pedro apply for jobs at the ranch, to double as spies, and so she won't have to sell out to Grant, a rival rancher. Tonto gets a job at Grant's ranch as a cook, to act as a spy from the other side. When Grant sends his right-hand man, Red, to the ranch to encourage Pete and Pedro to leave, Red returns with a black eye and his guns stolen. Grant, furious, believes they are working too slow at closing in. Grant decides to set fire to the ranch house late that night, taking the life of Ellen Carter, her foreman Bill Morgan, and the ranch hands. The Lone Ranger and Tonto, overhearing the scheme, are surprised from behind and captured, bound and thrown into an old shack. As they struggled to free themselves, they discover the shack was set on fire and could hear the shouts of Grant and his men as they prepared to raid the Carter ranch. Silver races to the shack to smash open the door so the heroes can roll out. Meanwhile, over at the Carter ranch, Grant, Red, Faro and twenty men overpower Pete and Pedro, who made a desperate effort to free Ellen and break loose from Grant's crew in an unequal struggle. Ellen, Bill, Pete and Pedro were tied hand and foot and left on the floor of the ranch house living room. The fire is set, and the marauders flee back to Grant's ranch. The Lone Ranger arrives to aid in rescue, while Tonto raced into town to fetch the sheriff and a posse. With all the evidence needed, the sheriff and his men visit Grant to place him under arrest and round up his gang. Pete and Pedro promise the masked man to remain at the ranch for a spell to help her rebuild.

Notes: The villain, Grant, was originally named Grainger in the initial draft.

Episode #1251-468 "AMBUSHED AMBUSHERS"

Broadcast January 29, 1941
Copyright Registration #73,475, script received at Registration Office February 3, 1941.
Written by Tom Dougall.

Plot: The Lone Ranger and Tonto happen upon a woman named Sadie Grant, wounded and dying, partially out of her mind and suggesting a crime was soon going to happen. Tonto remained behind to tend to her wounds while The Lone Ranger rode into town to fetch a doctor and the sheriff. But when the party returns, Tonto has vanished, and the woman is found dead – The Lone Ranger is accused of murder. Tonto, meanwhile, in one of the very few of his unguarded moments, was taken captive by two men. They forced him to go with them to a camp where other men were waiting. Scar Lefever and Lefty apply torture on the Indian to make him confess, as they were puzzled how the woman learned of their plans and what she might have told Tonto... even threatening a branding iron on him. Tonto escaped and alerted The Lone Ranger of the westbound stagecoach that not only held a fortune in paper money, but a man of national importance as a passenger. Andrew Taggert, a congressman from Washington, was traveling west with his daughter, Joan, unaware that the bridge ahead was sabotaged, support beams weakened. With no time to alert the law, the stage had to be halted at all costs. The plan was to abduct the congressman and his daughter. But when the masked man fails to convince the law and the congressman about the sabotaged bridge up ahead, he rides through the night like the wind, leading a mad chase toward the bridge. Close behind him came the sheriff and his deputy. The Lone Ranger raced to the bridge, the hoofs of the mighty Silver thundered on the boards, and then collapsed beneath the weight. Silver dove into the water in a spectacular sight as the outlaws were revealed and the law took them into custody. The Lone Ranger surfaced to meet Tonto and ride away.

Episode #1252-469 "THE LONE RANGER'S PROTEGEE"

Broadcast January 31, 1941

Copyright Registration #73,476, script received at Registration Office February 3, 1941.

Plot: Jim Hawkins is unable to get a job in town, unable to prove he is not a crook. His father was a member of a drug smuggling gang, and the family name was now tarnished. When Jim gets a call from The Lone Ranger, who proposes a plan to trap the rest of the gang and recover the stolen loot, the 16-year-old agrees to assist. Jim's father went to the hangman's rope without ever squealing on the rest of the gang, but also went without telling the gang members where the cash was hidden. The masked man convinced the brave lad to get in with the gang and let it be known that he suspects the location of the hidden cache. Martin Manners (Mart for short), leader of the gang of dope smugglers, and his right-hand man, Bat, do not suspect the entire set-up was bait to lure them into the open. The Lone Ranger, Jim, Manners and Bat ride into town to visit the small general store, where in the back room the masked man gets into an argument and shoots Jim Hawkins. Realizing the kid was squealing on the gang, Manners, Bat and The Lone Ranger race out of town. Manners lost no time in putting his gang to work. While two dug in the ground near the house that served as a hideout, others ripped up floorboards. The contraband was loaded into saddlebags for a swift getaway. But the gang of smugglers are surprised when they find themselves surrounded by army troopers, led by Jim Hawkins, who is alive and well. Jim will be hailed a hero by the townsfolk, and how he was a protégé of The Lone Ranger.

Episode #1253-470 "SET A THIEF"

Broadcast February 3, 1941

Copyright Registration #73,805, script received at Registration Office February 26, 1941.

Plot: When the Stockman's Bank in Claymore is robbed by Bat Benson and his ruthless gang of crooks, the town's entire savings was depleted. The sheriff threatened, begged and reasoned with the outlaw, Two-Gun, who was wounded and left behind for the law to pick up. When banker Sam Cramer gave away certain facts, people drew their own conclusions that Tom Craig, the young banker, arranged the robbery. After questioning Tom to discover he is innocent of the accusations, The Lone Ranger sets out to retrieve the stolen money. Because Bat Benson has never been trailed or apprehended, The Lone Ranger walks intothe sheriff's office and at the point of a gun he forces the lawman to free Two-Gun. With the outlaw, the masked man swept from town, cut away from the trail, and told Two-Gun that he wanted to join the gang and in three days they will meet again. Two-Gun fled for the hideout but kept a wary eye out on his backtrail for a sign of a white horse, which he never saw. Two-gun failed to note the Indian who, on his paint horse, moved as stealthy and as silently through the night as a ghost. It doesn't take long for Bat to realize who the masked man really is, and the motive to find their secluded hideout. The sheriff, meanwhile, forms a posse to pursue The Lone Ranger. Bat's attempt to lure the masked man inside the pass where he could be outnumbered, out-gunned and unmasked, is foiled when the masked man quick-draws to disarm the gunmen and give Tonto and the law the edge to enter the fortified hideout. The Lone Ranger leaves before the sheriff and his men find the stolen loot, clearing any suspicion against Tom Craig.

Episode #1254-471 "FOOL'S GOLD"

Broadcast February 5, 1941

Copyright Registration #73,806, script received at Registration Office February 26, 1941.

Plot: Young Jimmy and his friend Dixie are prospecting in secret, hoping to surprise his mother with a load of gold that they extract. Dixie files the claim (Jimmy is too young) and after removing bags of the ore, pays a visit to the assay office. Only then does Jimmy discover the ore is iron pyrite, also known as fool's gold. The old timers in town laugh at the young man forgetting they, too, at one time made the same mistake. The Lone Ranger, realizing Jimmy had the best of intentions, visits old Silas Fawcett, a retired prospector and owner of a general store. Silas agrees to help the masked man by allowing The Lone Ranger and Tonto to prospect from Silas' claim, extracting real gold. The extra money will help Jimmy and his mother's situation, an act of kindness no one in town would expect from Silas, known as a cantankerous old man who deliberately wants people to think he is callous, even though he has a heart of gold. The Lone Ranger and Tonto create a scenario whereupon they switch the bags of ore and make it look like someone was trying to steal the real gold and leave behind fool's gold. After the masked man and Indian flee town, the sheriff tells Silas that he suspects the scheme and chuckles, leaving his posse to take pursuit in what he knows is a futile chase… but necessary to ensure the ruse pulls through.

Episode #0000-000 [TITLE NOT KNOWN]

Plot: The town of Big Bend was a lawless as any in the West. Its citizens, quick to anger and with no thought for consequences, were more than ready to settle their differences with six-guns. Of them all, however, Sheriff Windy Conners was probably the hardest and roughest. He and his two deputies, Sampson and Weaver, were men to be feared and even the most desperate outlaws to enter their district hesitated to cross them. The Lone Ranger, startled to see the breed, Jose, calmly riding toward Ben Macy's ranch when he was supposed to be in town as a prisoner of the sheriff, was determined to investigate. After all, it was The Lone Ranger who apprehended and brought in Jose. In the meantime, Ben was convinced he had killed the sheriff, and could scarcely conceal his agitation. Ben was unaware his gun's cartridges were replaced with blanks and Jose took advantage of the opportunity to shoot and kill Sheriff Windy Conners, figuring no one would be aware of a second shot. Further investigation revealed a startling surprise. In the local saloon the next day, staged with the assistance of Ben, The Lone Ranger arranges for lemon juice to be used on Jose, wiping off the stain. After the wig is removed, it is verified Jose was the one who was shot – the sheriff was masquerading as Jose. His deputies were not in on the scheme as otherwise they would have recognized their employer. In the presence of the U.S. Marshal, the plot is exposed. The blackmail attempt against Ben, tricked into believing he shot and murdered the sheriff, would have given the crooked lawman ownership of the ranch. After a quick sale he would have disappeared.

Notes: This plot summary originates from an unproduced (and untitled) radio script originally slated for the broadcast of February 5, 1941.

Episode #1255-472 "UNLUCKY STRIKE"

Broadcast February 7, 1941
Copyright Registration #73,807, script received at Registration Office February 26, 1941.
Plot: No one saw the thief leave Ma Harvey's cottage late that night, just as no one but Ma herself had seen him enter. The next morning, in Bart Salem's general store, Sheriff Pearson of the town of Prospect mistook Jim Thornton, a young prospector, for a wanted criminal when he begins spending his hard-earned gold dust. Jim is accused of being Whitey Conklin and the sheriff was inspired by two distinct motives. In the first place, he was an honest sheriff with a sincere desire to enforce the law efficiently. But in the second place, nothing pleased him more than to arrest a citizen of Wabash County, whose Sheriff Stevens was his most bitter rival. The Lone Ranger, disguised, watched the events in the general store and rode out to consult with Tonto. The Indian rides into town to verify Jim Thornton is not Whitey, because Whitey has a small scar under his chin and Jim does not, so the masked man raced out to Wabash County to meet with Sheriff Stevens. Late that evening and the following day there ran an undercurrent of lynch talk throughout the town. It rapidly gained popular support, though the sheriff was unaware of what was being planned. The Lone Ranger returned and, upon hearing of the recent developments, masterminded a jailbreak to save the life of young Jim. The angry sheriff gave his posse no rest as they followed the trail throughout the night. Once safely across the county line, The Lone Ranger clears

the good name of Jim Thornton. Sheriff Stevens explains to the posse members that he already hung Whitey Conklin. Whitey stole the gold, found on his possession, which was returned to Ma Harvey the other day.

Episode #1256-473 "ON THE TRAIL"
Broadcast February 10, 1941
Copyright Registration #73,808, script received at Registration Office February 26, 1941.
Plot: This was the same script from the broadcast of January 19, 1934, with some of the names changed. Lige Bascom was now Jeff Munson, Nancy was changed to Nellie, Buck Hennessey was now Slick Hennessey, and the Gunsmoke River was changed to Comanche River.

Episode #1257-474 "HANGMAN'S TREE"
Broadcast February 12, 1941
Copyright Registration #73,809, script received at Registration Office February 26, 1941.
Plot: Death at the end of a rope is the penalty for not paying tribute to a ruthless gang of extortionists led by a man who called himself "Rattlesnake." After The Lone Ranger and Tonto save the life of a rancher named Jed Grover, from the Hangman's Tree, having been tipped off by his wife, Lydia, they learn the locals are fearful of the repercussions if they talk. The outlaws demand money from all the honest folk and threaten to kill if they are not paid. People like Jed who stand up to the outlaws find themselves hanging by the noose. Working on a plan schemed by The Lone Ranger, Tonto rode up to the hills and allowed himself to be captured so he can admit Jed Grover was rescued, and that the plans of the outlaws could be learned. Then, the masked man rescued his friend and galloped full tilt out of the hills. Riding back to the Grover homestead, The Lone Ranger asks Lydia to call on all the settlers in the valley to meet near the Hangman's Tree before dawn. Jed is to remain so when the Rattlesnake and his men arrive, they will again take him back to the Hangman's Tree. Moments before Jed is about to be hung, The Lone Ranger gives the signal and the settlers come out of hiding and surround the outlaws. Pedro, the right-hand man of Rattlesnake, is disarmed when The Lone Ranger shoots the gun out of his hand. Rattlesnake fled on his horse, named Poison, and the masked man took off in pursuit. Like a grey ghost in the darkness before dawn, the great horse Silver streaked after the racing badman. The Lone Ranger drags the body of the outlaw leader back to watch as the Hangman's Tree is chopped down and the settlers cheer as they successfully rallied against the tyranny.

Notes: The tree in this episode was provided a name, not a designation, much like the name of a town or ranch, which is why Hangman's Tree was capitalized in the radio script.

Episode #1258-475 "THE ROUNDUP AT CORONADO"
Broadcast February 14, 1941
Copyright Registration #73,810, script received at Registration Office February 26, 1941.
Plot: In the tiny western hamlet of Coronado, Bart Kimball, an Easterner-turned-cattleman, stands between the sheep ranchers of Coronado Valley and cattlemen to the west. Three crooked ranchers plot to take over the entire valley: Deke Quigley with a spread over by Willow Crossing, Brophy of the Bar B, and Sam Cotter who owns the Hashknife outfit. The court upheld the rangeland for sheep herders and the sheepman's association will put up a fight unless the crooks gain possession of the entire territory. Deke Quigley and his friends elected the sheriff to office, so Bart cannot depend upon the law for protection. Bart holds firm, despite the drought, and most of the cattlemen follow his lead. Bart is lured away from his house and kidnapped, ordered by Deke to vacate and advise the rest of the men in the valley to move on. After Bart was rescued by The Lone Ranger from the crooked ranchers, Deke orders his gunmen to sweep through and clean out the valley. To prevent a range war, news of the attack upon Bart Kimball circulated throughout the valley and the already disheartened settlers

found little reason to defend what land they were convinced was worthless. Slowly, one by one, the cattlemen rounded up what was left of their stock, loaded their household goods in wagons and began the dispirited trek to a more hospitable country. The Lone Ranger shows the men how to feed and water their cattle during the drought, courtesy of the cactus, and convinces them their homes are worth protecting. The settlers, their despair suddenly changed by the masked man to top, frantically prepared for the coming battle. Applied strategy, the men would trick and surround Deke, Brophy and Sam and their ranch hands. The men are forced to leave, and The Lone Ranger assures them, moments before the rain comes into the valley, that their kind fight only when they think their opposition is frightened and won't return.

Episode #1259-476 "JUSTICE WEARS A MASK"

Broadcast February 17, 1941

Copyright Registration #73,811, script received at Registration Office February 26, 1941.

Plot: Jerry, a young rancher in town, is engaged to Ann, who seeks another job than singing in the local saloon. The two planned on getting married in Jonesville so when she leaves Greenwood, she will never return. Bart Sterling, a crooked sheriff who is also in love with Ann, frames the young man for the murder of Joe Williams. Judge Rolfe, a Judge Roy Bean type, has run the town for the last two years, alongside Bart Sterling, and will side with a dead man's word against Jerry. The Lone Ranger rides out to Horseshoe Valley to fetch old Jonathan Greenwood, a lawyer by profession, dignified but spirited, for whom the town was named after. Jerry was with Ann at the time of the murder, and her testimony will convince the jury. But they need someone to help them who is not afraid of Bart Sterling. The sheriff and the judge will not let the girl testify on the stand, and when the stage arrived in town, neither Jonathan Greenwood nor the guard were on board. The Lone Ranger suspected the sheriff had some connection with the lawyer's disappearance. Pete Atkins, the stagecoach driver, tied the old man up and left him in an old cabin. Following the stagecoach driver, The Lone Ranger and Tonto track the whereabouts of Jonathan Greenwood and rescue him. The Lone Ranger arrived in the courtroom to interrupt the proceedings, then at the point of a gun takes the place of the judge and orders Ann on the stand. When Pete was put on the stand, the stagecoach driver was tricked into revealing the sheriff was responsible for the murder. Special officers took charge of the sheriff and his deputies, and the judge, until new law is established.

Episode #1260-477 "THE LAW'S DELAY"

Broadcast February 19, 1941

Copyright Registration #73,812, script received at Registration Office February 26, 1941.

Plot: This was the same script from the broadcast of October 3, 1933, with one name change: the judge named Jim Hurley was changed to Jim Carter.

Episode #1261-478 "SWORDS DEFEAT A DUELLIST"

Broadcast February 21, 1941

Copyright Registration #73,813, script received at Registration Office February 26, 1941.

Plot: When the masked rider of the plains goes to a lonely ranchero to seek the eccentric Mexican Don Rivera, located in a lonely section of the Panhandle, who has been missing for two months. No one in Prairie Bend has seen the Don and it seemed strange since he never failed to get into town from time to time. He lived alone with his daughter, Diosa, and The Lone Ranger and Tonto have Indian medicine in case the old man was sick. When turned down at the hacienda, there was enough evidence to suggest foul play. Tonto gets shivers up the spine when he and The Lone Ranger decide to explore the "haunted hacienda" when darkness falls. The masked man learned from Diosa that her father needed to be saved from the villainous Murdock and his associate, Slim. They are attempting to steal the gold from the Don's hidden dungeons of the ranchero. Upon learning the masked man and Indian are on their trail, rather than face a fight, the badmen hit the trail with Don Rivera, heading for the Sawtooth Mountains. The crooks attempt to make the Don sign a paper willing his money to them in the event of his death, but Don Rivera chooses to fight back with a rapier, to fight as his ancestors did. Murdock laughs and holsters his guns and uses a saber on the wall to duel. The Lone Ranger arrives in time to disarm Murdock and tear the paper into pieces. The Lone Ranger holsters his guns and orders Murdock to draw first, but the crook chooses not to so the masked man attempts to even the odds but dueling against the crook with a saber against a rapier. The Lone Ranger combats and disarms his opponent, moments before he and Tonto decide to take the crooks to jail where they belong.

Episode #1262-479 "MEDICINE MAN"
Broadcast February 24, 1941
Copyright Registration #74,173, script received at Registration Office March 21, 1941.
Plot: This was the same script from the broadcast of December 29, 1933. The name of Potluck's wife was changed from Bessie to Martha, Doctor Mulcahy was changed to Doc Evans, and the Indians were changed from Apache to Kiowas.

Episode #1263-480 "A RANCHLAND FRAME UP"
Broadcast February 26, 1941
Copyright Registration #74,174, script received at Registration Office March 21, 1941.
Plot: This was the same script from the broadcast of April 29, 1935, with one change: The name of the beautiful Josie was changed to Nellie.

Episode #1264-481 "DOCTOR BUCKAROO"
Broadcast February 28, 1941
Copyright Registration #74,175, script received at Registration Office March 21, 1941.
Plot: Outside the town of Hopeville, Jud Walton, a hard-as-nails rancher, has a beef against homesteaders. When a middle-aged homesteader named Lige Perkins needs a doctor, Bob Langdon takes a hand. Bob had recently returned to the valley where he helped cattle after completing a few years of medical school in Chicago. But his assistance throws him in between a bitter feud between the cattlemen and the farmers. Weeks later, after a debilitating illness, Mary Perkins was finally back to walking again and the homesteaders were mighty grateful. The ranchers, meanwhile, started hiring outlaws to get ready for a war. The homesteaders, they believed, meant the end of the open range. Jud Walton and his outlaw men were breaking down the fences and getting ready to drive a herd through the fields of crops. The sheriff was too far away. There were no troops within a hundred miles. When Jud was thrown from his horse and knocked unconscious, he was carried into his ranch house. Despite the fact that Doc Langdon tended to his wounds, the range war was bound to occur, but not until Jud, the leader of the rancher, gets better. Lige Perkins, one of the ranchers, is ready for the signal to join in the combat until a tribe of Indians ride down from the hills and kidnaps the doctor. The Lone Ranger races onto the ranches to alert the cattlemen, to seek volunteers for a rescue party. Then he raced to the farmers for the same. The men forgot their grudges to fight together. With The Lone Ranger and Tonto in the lead, the ranchers and the farmers raced for the hills. But just as the trail neared the end, the ruse is disclosed. Chief Thundercloud and his men volunteered to dress like Apache at the request of the masked man. "Supposed that had been a war party of Apache," The Lone Ranger explained. Together they had strength in numbers. Split up, they would have lost. In other words, as the men agreed, there was plenty of room for both farmers and ranchers in the valley.

Episode #1265-482 "AUTUMN TORRENT"

Broadcast March 3, 1941

Copyright Registration #74,176, script received at Registration Office March 21, 1941.

Plot: The Lone Ranger and Tonto happen across Bill Corrigan, a ranch hand shot and wounded, a victim of rustlers who exchanged gunfire with Brand and his outlaw gang. Maria Garrison is disappointed that none of her ranch hands are willing to take after the outlaws, despite the fact that the crooks stole a hundred head of the Bar G herd. Slade, her foreman, insists that there are over a hundred canyons cutting into the foothills, and no amount of cattle can leave a trail on rock. A reformed gambler at the Bar G named Calhoun proposes finding a second entrance to the valley where stolen cattle would graze, and further searching ultimately finds the whereabouts of Brand and his gang. Calhoun uses his profession to get in with the gang, working as an inside man for the law. From a distance, The Lone Ranger saw the rancher, Slade, ride into the outlaw's valley. The sheriff formed a posse and raced out to apprehend the outlaw gang. With The Lone Ranger and Tonto in the lead, the posse raced across the storm-swept plain. The rain beat against the slickers of the men. Lighting flashed. A raging torrent of a band of outlaws meant gunplay. Sudden death behind and desperate men ahead. The valley was just ahead, but now a wall of water raced toward them. As the outlaws raced out of the valley, through the entrance to the canyon, they were apprehended by the sheriff and his men. Slade attempted to claim he was taken prisoner, but Calhoun insisted the renegade was as crooked as Brand himself. Calhoun agrees to become one of the sheriff's deputies and gets sworn in.

Episode #1263-483 "A NEW LEAF"

Broadcast March 5, 1941

Copyright Registration #74,177, script received at Registration Office March 21, 1941.

Plot: This was the same script from the broadcast of May 17, 1935.

Episode #1267-484 "FLAG IN THE WEST"

Broadcast March 7, 1941

Copyright Registration #74,178, script received at Registration Office March 21, 1941.

Plot: Using a clever ruse, an Army outpost, deep in the lonely Kansas territory, is taken over by an outlaw gang led by Larkin and Bulger. An army lieutenant's wife managed to escape and fled for help, meeting The Lone Ranger and Tonto. She explained how Larkin and his gang disarmed the sentries and locked everyone into the guardhouse. During this time of year, the fur trappers come out of the northwest, heading for the Mississippi, to sell their fur skins at Big River. They pass right by that army outpost. Larkin plans to dress his men in uniforms and take the trappers by surprise. The furs are worth plenty of cash. But visiting another fort for reinforcements, The Lone Ranger discovers the captain is out with his troop on an expedition against the Cripple Creek Sioux Indians. The Lone Ranger and Tonto visit the army outpost on the Little Osage and scale the stockade at night to speak to the few remaining soldiers imprisoned in their own guardhouse, to learn when the fur trappers are due, then sneaks back out before being caught. The next day, when the fur trappers are close by, the gates are flung open, and Larkin and his men give the appearance all is normal at the outpost. The Lone Ranger and Tonto sneak back inside while Larkin orders the men in the guardhouse to remove their uniforms. With the guardhouse door open, The Lone Ranger and Tonto create a distraction giving the army men a chance to fight back against the outlaws. Larkin, Bulger and the rest of the outlaws now find themselves jailed. The Lone Ranger and Tonto ride away as the stars and stripes flag keeps on waving in the breeze.

Episode #1268-485 "JOAN OF CLARKSVILLE"

Broadcast March 10, 1941

Copyright Registration #74,179, script received at Registration Office March 21, 1941.

Plot: With the coming of the railroad Clarksville had achieved its destiny. A sleepy village became a booming cattle market, but it still retained many of the characteristics of a small town. Ben Forbes, the mayor, took offense to an editorial about him, and arranged for his outlaw gang to murder the crusading newspaper editor. Joan, a girl of 18, and her brother Johnny, took up their father's crusade and managed The Clarion newspaper. While the big press was broken up, they still had the small one to use. Bob Sherman, the sheriff, called for a vigilante committee, consisting of men who had their property destroyed by Ben Forbes. During the meeting, The Lone Ranger explains how the majority of the taxpayers were in attendance and therefore could hold an election to elect a new mayor and a new sheriff. With a sheriff and a posse, the law would be on their side. A Scottish storekeeper named MacKenzie was nominated. But this was only the first step. Getting the honest men to brave up and arm themselves was another matter altogether. Later, The Lone Ranger discovers the newspaper office is being targeted (to be burned to the ground) because of Joan and Johnny's intent to print the facts. When The Lone Ranger was discovered outside the Golden Slipper café, he shot out the lamp in Forbes' office and then slipped away into the darkness before the outlaw's men had swarmed out of the café after him. The Lone Ranger races to save Johnny, and as soon as the firing starts, the town wakes up. The honest men in town think that Johnny is holding off the gang by himself and it was all that was needed to make them stand up and fight. The newspaper is burned to the ground by torches and by all appearances, Johnny was killed in the fire. The next afternoon, Sheriff Bob Sherman awaited the signal for attack as Joan spoke from the window of the newspaper office, in full view, urging the men and women in the crowded streets to defend their homes against Ben Forbes and his gang. She revealed how Johnny never died while defending his office. While the men revolt against the outlaw gang, The Lone Ranger pays a visit to Ben Forbes in his office. An exchange of blows between the two results in the masked man forcing the outlaw leader down the hallway to the entrance of the café. At first Ben won't tell his men to surrender, but in fear of being killed by a vigilante mob, he orders the gang members to throw down their guns and surrender to the sheriff. The crooks are led to jail where a trial will no doubt ensure a conviction and execution for the men responsible for the murder of Joan and Johnny's father.

Episode #1269-486 "ROBBERS ON THE RAILROAD"

Broadcast March 12, 1941

Copyright Registration #74,180, script received at Registration Office March 21, 1941.

Plot: The town called Railhead changed its location every day, moving westward with the new railroad under construction. Brad Carter, head scout for the railroad, gets into a scuffle with Sloan, a crook who takes it personally when he receives his walking papers. The Lone Ranger and Tonto, riding into the area, are tracking Sloan for a bank robbery back near Saint Joseph. When Brad is shot and wounded from ambush, the masked man was falsely accused of the crime. The Lone Ranger and Tonto made good their escape and trail the ambushers. Carter, suffering a shoulder wound, later clears the masked man of the shooting. During an attack on the end of the railroad track, a solitary rider galloped into Railhead, alerting the rest of the men who quickly take arms and race off as reinforcements. Sloan, always wearing a striped shirt, was not among the attackers and the masked man realized the plan to attack the construction gang was a diversion to steal the company payroll. With the town almost deserted, the payroll was ripe for plucking. Molly, meanwhile, was still nursing Brad Carter when Sloan snuck inside to finish the job and kill Carter. She was unable to defend the attack, but The Lone Ranger arrived in the nick of time to disarm the crook and save the lives of Molly and Carter.

Notes: The outlaw named Trent was originally listed as Preston in the radio script but changed during rehearsal, to avoid using the name of another fictional radio character, *Sergeant Preston of the Yukon*.

Episode #1270-487 "BLIND LEADER"

Broadcast March 14, 1941

Copyright Registration #74,181, script received at Registration Office March 21, 1941.

Plot: Fort Casper, deep in a district where hostile Apaches were constantly on the warpath, was nervously alert for any sign of the savage enemy. Recently an Apache bullet wounded the post commander himself, Major Davis. When Doctor Parrish, the post surgeon, informs the Major that he is officially blind, the obstinate post commander is reluctant to turn command over to Captain Faust, a vigorous officer. Faust believes in decisive engagements. Running Wolf, meanwhile, is gathering Indians in such numbers that it was obvious the intent would not do the settlers or the soldiers any good. Paying a visit to Fort Casper, The Lone Ranger made his way to the quarters of Major Davis. After learning of the situation, the masked man orders Tonto to keep tabs on the Indians, from a distance, and send smoke signals when he learns what they plan. At the advice of The Lone Ranger, Major Davis passed command over to Captain Faust to let him ride out with troops in search of Running Wolf. Afterwards, the Major rides out with The Lone Ranger to assume command again before the troops go so far that they could not return to the fort in case of an attack. Courtesy of a clever ploy by the masked man, and quick shooting, everyone is fooled into believing the Major's eyesight was perfectly fine. Thanks to Tonto's smoke signals, and with the Major leading the charge, a desperately charging battalion of uniformed figures thrust directly at Running Wolf's bewildered braves. The Indians wavered, broke, and panic-stricken urged their mounts in flight toward the security of the hills. They discovered, too late, that they had been cut off. One by one, targets for the aim of the troopers, the red men slid from their mounts, fell to the ground. Running Wolf himself was hit and mortally wounded. The remnants of the marauding band threw down their arms in token of surrender. Only afterwards does the truth come out and Major Davis had his last ride as he passed on command to Captain Faust.

Episode #1271-488 "THE STOREKEEPER STANDS UP"

Broadcast March 17, 1941

Copyright Registration #74,182, script received at Registration Office March 21, 1941.

Plot: Sam Birdwell ran the general store in Rainbow Bend, the only store in over 400 square miles of rangeland and every settler and rancher bought supplies from him… except Dirk Kincaid, the man who owned the Lazy K, the biggest spread in the section. Birdwell accuses Kincaid of rustling cattle, stealing horses, and poisoning water holes. The Lone Ranger and Tonto thwart a physical confrontation between the two parties, but the dominating rancher takes it personally and orders his men to ride out to every rancher, settler and townsman with orders never to buy from Birdwell again. The boycott in trade put Birdwell in a tight spot. Out of desperation, he strapped on a gun belt and rode out to see Kincaid. The Lone Ranger and Tonto learn from Birdwell's wife of the recent events and with Birdwell in danger of losing his business and his life, the masked man rides out to rescue. After preventing an exchange of gunplay, The Lone Ranger takes a hand, making it look like the storekeeper met with foul play to rally his friends. Deborah, Sam's wife, soon discovered people supporting her business – it is the least they could do. With their plan foiled, Kincaid, along with his top hand, Gonzales, ride out to The Lone Ranger's camp to dry-gulch the masked man and Indian. Tonto fetches friends of Sam Birdwell to the camp to hide and witness the murder attempt. Sam Birdwell, the masked man explains in front of witnesses, did what every one of them wanted to do – he stood up against oppression. Luckily, Sam Birdwell was alive and well – which could not be said for Kincaid and Gonzales, who are taken into custody for an attempted murder charge.

Episode #1272-489 "ONE NATION INDIVISIBLE"

Broadcast March 19, 1941

Copyright Registration #74,183, script received at Registration Office March 21, 1941.

Plot: On the way to Malpas, The Lone Ranger and Tonto observe a dangerous prairie fire that even a herd of buffalo race away from. After noticing two cabins in the path of destruction, the two race to rescue two ex-soldiers and their niece, Sally. Josh Brandon, an old northerner, accuses Carter of setting the fire. Carter Engells, an old southerner, accuses Josh. When Denver, a crook scheming to acquire the land owned by the two old men, discovers his scheme failed, he and Scar set out to poison the old men against each other. Tonto investigates the area and discovers a spur which proves neither of the two old men started the prairie fire, even though the crooks are trying to force them to believe the other was responsible. The scheme almost works, tricking the old men to considering signing their property over to Denver for pennies. When Carter learns the truth, and the motive of the crooks, he follows the advice of The Lone Ranger and pretends to be shot when Denver attempts to murder him. Josh apologizes and makes good with Carter, as the arsonists trying to swindle the feuding uncles out of their land are exposed.

Notes: This episode bears no relation to the episode of the same title broadcast on May 19, 1941.

Episode #1273-490 "THE TAX COLLECTOR"
Broadcast March 21, 1941
Copyright Registration #74,191, script received at Registration Office March 21, 1941.
Plot: A crooked schemer named Larson owns the sheriff and all the deputies, and ranchers in the region are losing cattle, blaming the Indians. Larson's latest scheme is to raise taxes on those who opposed him and collect on them. When Jack Wilson attempts to organize men to fight Larson, Jack finds himself accused of murder and placed under arrest. The way some of the ranchers are getting out of line, the sheriff fears the next person who tries to collect taxes will be shot. The Lone Ranger, in disguise, takes a job collecting taxes. Naturally, this results in The Lone Ranger being deputized, and being handed a list of only the men who resented the way things were being run. Realizing Jack Wilson will not be found guilty in a court of law, due to lack of evidence, the sheriff and Larson schemes a jail break so Wilson will be shot while trying to escape. The Lone Ranger, now masked again, arranges for Tonto to visit those ranchers and call on a meeting outside the jail to arrange for the sheriff to retire and Jack Wilson act as a deputy sheriff in charge of the office until the next election. In the woods, Jack Wilson held a gun on the sheriff until The Lone Ranger brought Larson, kidnapped from his own home. The sheriff was tied to a tree while The Lone Ranger explained how the Texas Rangers are outside of town, under orders of the governor, awaiting the request of the man in charge of the law office – now Jack Wilson. With the ranchers attesting to Wilson as the sheriff, a higher law intervenes… especially when Larson is forced into Jack Wilson's clothes and ordered to leave the office, where his men await to shoot and kill the escaping prisoner. Larson, in desperation, confessed to the crime.

Episode #1274-491 "RUSTLER AND SON"
Broadcast March 24, 1941
Copyright Registration #74,749, script received at Registration Office May 2, 1941.
Plot: Laura finds her past catching up to her when Dan, an ex-convict and father of her son, Buddy, pays her a visit at the Circle H, owned by her father, the old Jud Harrigan. If her son discovered his father was a worthless crook, it would break his heart. With blackmail assured, Dan stays at the Harrigan homestead long enough for the cattle to be driven to market and cash is paid. The Lone Ranger and Tonto, happening upon old Jud who broke a leg in an accident, brought him back to the ranch house and put his leg into a splint. This left Dan in charge of the roundup and not content over the $1,000, schemes with a rustler named Trigger and a breed named Manuel, to drive the whole herd through the pass and sell them to Garcia across the border. But Dan will need to get rid of the crew. The rumor of a band of rustlers near the border had brought The Lone Ranger and Tonto to the Circle H spread and on the day the trail herd was starting for market, Manuel kidnapped

Buddy and rode out in the hopes the trail hands take pursuit. Using the boy as a decoy while Trigger sets out to accomplish his mission, almost succeeds but The Lone Ranger and Tonto intercept Manuel and rescues the boy. When the masked man and Buddy create noise to stop or slow down the cattle drive, and Dan breaks off from the trigger-happy Trigger to handle the situation. Siding with the protection of his own son, Dan agrees to assist The Lone Ranger while Tonto leads the charge with the Circle H crew. With the outlaws apprehended, Dan redeems himself in the eyes of his son.

Episode #1275-492 "A HORSE CHANGES BRANDS"
Broadcast March 26, 1941

Copyright Registration #74,750, script received at Registration Office May 2, 1941.

Plot: A crooked sheriff named Drukker and his deputy, Jubel, steal a horse and plants it in the corral of Tex Hanlon, a young horse wrangler he intends to charge with theft. The sheriff hopes to gain possession of the wrangler's string of horses. Ma Hasty of the Lazy Y ranch falls for the sheriff's scheme, especially when she sees Tex's brand on top of hers, and she discovers she was the victim of a horse thief. The Lone Ranger would not have believed a lawman would pull such a stunt if it was not for the fact that Tonto overheard the plan and reported back to the masked man. Property of the prisoner becomes the property of the county and as the duly elected officer of the county, the sheriff gains possession. The Lone Ranger took advantage of a scenario and had himself jailed alongside Tex. At night, Tonto went to the jail and released The Lone Ranger and took his place so that he could have a head start towards solving the problem. Riding out to Carson's Gap, The Lone Ranger encourages Marshal Raddigan to ride with him back to town where the trial against Tex Hanlon was soon to begin. After disarming the deputy, the masked man exposes the true identity of Sheriff Drukker as a wanted man named Benzer. Jubel confesses to the horse thieving but not murder, incriminating the crooked sheriff.

Episode #1276-493 "SLOW FREIGHT"
Broadcast March 28, 1941

Copyright Registration #74,751, script received at Registration Office May 2, 1941.

Plot: A spur line ran from the mining camp on Rainbow Creek down through the hills to the Junction. While the largest shipment of gold ever sent out from Rainbow Creek was being loaded on board, The Lone Ranger and Tonto were keeping an eye out for Scar, an outlaw leader. Along the route and on board are Wild Bill Garrison, a gambler, Linda, a dance hall singer, Checkers, a cattle rancher and Sally Mason, a young widow with a baby whose husband was recently killed by the gang and whose ranch was burned down. As The Lone Ranger expected, Scar and his gang attempt to hijack the train. Bill and Checkers were taken prisoner by Scar just as the train left Springville. By the time The Lone Ranger returns with the posse, the outlaws boarded the train, and the caboose has been set loose to crash and kill four innocent people. Scar wanted no one to survive and tell the tale as they flee with the gold. Linda conspired in secret to work with the outlaws, but she revealed herself as Harvey Ashland's sister, seeking revenge against Scar who killed her brother. Linda was overpowered and thrown into the caboose. From a distance The Lone Ranger and Tonto observe the uncoupling and ride onto the car to cut the ropes that bound the intended victims and rescue them. The masked man and Indian jump off the train to pursue Scar, shooting the gun out of his hand and tie him up with the same rope that was used against the four, and takes him into custody alongside his outlaw gang.

Episode #1277-494 "TRAP FOR A SAFE ROBBER"
Broadcast March 31, 1941

Copyright Registration #74,752, script received at Registration Office May 2, 1941.

Plot: After seeking overnight shelter in a cave, The Lone Ranger and Tonto hear a mysterious gunshot and set out to investigate. The next afternoon in the town of Land's End, ten miles west of where the masked man was camped, Mr. Barton sought out Jimmy Stevens, the youthful manager of the express office. Jimmy hoped to show the Wells Fargo people that he and his sister Molly could handle the office so the job would be permanent, and the company not send a man to replace Old Abe. Barton claims to be a Wells Fargo detective and warns them how the Wells Fargo station is in danger of being robbed by an outlaw named Durkin. To prevent the theft of the railroad payroll, Barton arranges with a young temporary Wells Fargo employee to trap the notorious thief. Late that night, Barton tricks Jimmy into unlocking the safe and through a clever ruse robs the safe and attempts to blame it on an intruder. The Lone Ranger intervenes moments after the robbery as Tonto disarms Barton. The masked man explains how last night he and Tonto discovered the dead body of the real Barton, washed ashore downstream. It was Durkin who killed the Wells Fargo detective and stole Barton's horse and credentials. Jimmy checks Barton to find a hat stuffed inside his vest filled with cash. Jimmy and Molly's father, who sided with the masked man earlier in the day and tipped him off to the proceedings in town, assures the two that Durkin will hang for the murder, and The Lone Ranger assures them there was reward money for his capture.

Episode #1278-495 "BUYERS BEWARE"
Broadcast April 2, 1941
Copyright Registration #74,753, script received at Registration Office May 2, 1941.
Plot: Pedro Martinez and Pete Lacey are hired by Fraser, a crooked café owner in San Marco and the leader of a gang of rustlers, to buy some land in a scheme to cheat the ranchers. Fraser hires the men to act as his agent, to avoid the locals from holding him up for more money. He offers a bonus of $100 for every deed they acquire. Specifically, he wants the strip on the south shore along the river, in a valley where the Circle Bar, the Lazy D and the Bar N reside. The Lone Ranger, in the district to investigate Fraser, suspected of rustling, meets Pete and Pedro to learn of their new job. Further investigation finds a young railroad man named Jim Bryan tied to a tree, who claims half a dozen men led by Fraser forced information out of him. The Lone Ranger realizes the only way to turn the tables on the crooks is to make them purchase worthless property. Back in town, the ranchers are angry, having felt cheated after they learned the railroad changed its plans and was coming through the valley. The railroad would have given three times as much as Pete and Pedro. Fraser, revealed to be the purchaser, denies hiring Pete and Pedro, then discovers the railroad had changed their plans and wanted the north side, not the south side. Fraser's right-hand man, Joe, was found at a secluded hideout where hides and stolen cattle were also found. Pete and Pedro, not wanting to be ranchers and settle down, gives the land back to the ranchers.

Episode #1279-496 "LANDGRABBERS' LOSS"
Broadcast April 4, 1941
Copyright Registration #74,754, script received at Registration Office May 2, 1941.
Plot: The U.S. Government is going to open Comanche territory to homesteaders and Tonto, overhearing the plans of Barber, a café owner and crook, reports back to The Lone Ranger. The crooked landgrabber hires Lefty to play gunman in a plan to cheat Hank Carson out of a prime choice by thwarting the settler from ambush. Carson has what he considers the fastest horse in the territory, named Blizzard, but that would be no match if rifle fire from ambush occurs. At the edge of the Comanche territory a crowd milled through the night, waiting for dawn and the gun that would send them pouring across to claim new land. Horses, wagons, every type of conveyance added to the confusion so that The Lone Ranger and Tonto, who had gotten away from Barber after he was caught listening to his men plotting, was unable to locate any of his men afterwards. Taking a gamble, Barber's men got a four-hour start ahead of everyone. The Lone Ranger alerts the local Colonel who promises the only thing he can offer is a few army men to ride after Barber. After the start of the race commences, The Lone Ranger took off like a shot with Silver, proving to be the fastest horse, and catches up with Barber and Lefty to prevent them from selecting the choice land that Hank Carson wanted. With the soldiers right behind him, the masked man watches as the crooks are taken into custody and Hank Caron can stake his claim.

Notes: During rehearsals, the character of Shifty was changed to Lefty and Hank Cactus was changed to Hank Carson.

Episode #1280-497 "SIXTY DAYS FOR LIFE"

Broadcast April 7, 1941

Copyright Registration #74,755, script received at Registration Office May 2, 1941.

Plot: Jeff Ritter, although known to be guilty of several murders, has been jailed on a minor charge. Then, with his short sentence almost completed, he surprised everyone by breaking out of jail. He only had one week left but when caught he would need to serve his 60 days sentence again. Jeff kidnaps lawyer Abner Cricket to learn the whereabouts of a large cache of unrefined gold, owned by Betty Carlson, an inheritance from her late uncle. The moment Abner Cricket revealed the hiding place of the Carson gold, Jeff Ritter changed his tactics and ordered him down the cellar stairs of the ranch house to hold him at bay. Her uncle had the gold hidden away in the mountains quite a distance from the nearest town, never daring to bring it in from his hiding place and put it in the bank because of Jeff Ritter. It would have been a difficult job to transport the gold through the mountains. There were a dozen places where men could ambush, and it would take at least a half a dozen horses to move the load. When the sheriff approaches the crooks, he finds himself outnumbered by Jeff Ritter and his men. The Lone Ranger creates a ploy where the crooks not only succeed in stealing the gold, but inadvertently transport the ore to town for Betty. Nearly 100 men raced down from the hills on all sides of the ranch house and closed in on the outlaws without a shot being fired, before rendering his gang incapable of transporting the gold any further and rescuing the sheriff. Caught by surprise, they found themselves surrounded.

Episode #1281-498 "HOMESTEADER'S RUSE" [PART ONE OF FIVE]

Broadcast April 9, 1941

Copyright Registration #74,756, script received at Registration Office May 2, 1941.

Plot: See pages 300 and 301.

Episode #1282-499 "HIDEOUT FROM BADMEN" [PART TWO OF FIVE]

Broadcast April 11, 1941

Copyright Registration #74,757, script received at Registration Office May 2, 1941.

Plot: See pages 301 and 302.

Episode #1283-500 "WORK AND WIN" [PART THREE OF FIVE]

Broadcast April 14, 1941

Copyright Registration #74,758, script received at Registration Office May 2, 1941.

Plot: See pages 302 and 303.

Notes: This was the same script from the broadcast of April 23, 1937, with variations to accommodate the wounded Lone Ranger.

Episode #1284-501 "UNITED WE STAND" [PART FOUR OF FIVE]

Broadcast April 16, 1941

Copyright Registration #74,759, script received at Registration Office May 2, 1941.

Plot: See pages 303 and 304.

Episode #1285-502 "LONE RANGER MOVES" [PART FIVE OF FIVE]

Broadcast April 18, 1941

Copyright Registration #74,760, script received at Registration Office May 2, 1941.

Plot: See pages 304 and 305.

Episode #1286-503 "OUTPOST IN THE DESERT"

Broadcast April 21, 1941

Copyright Registration #74,761, script received at Registration Office May 2, 1941.

Plot: The Overland Stage from Frisco to Saint Joseph raced across the desolate stretch of land but none was more lonely or more barren than the desert section known as Rattlesnake Run. In the whole section of 100 miles, the only sign of civilization was the stagecoach station set in the middle of the desert, owned and operated by Jed and Beth. Two men schemed to rob the stage, Choctaw Pete and Purdy. The former rode as a passenger, waiting for the stage to pick up the gold dust from the Lost Gopher Mine. Upon discovering the plot, The Lone Ranger and Tonto followed the coach trail in the darkness, riding to catch up to the bad men before the driver is shot and killed, and the robbery. The masked man and his faithful Indian companion take a shortcut. But at the stagecoach post, Jed and Beth are forced to take up defense. The villains set fire to the post, keeping the couple busy while the crooks change a fresh new set of horses. No horse alive could catch up to the stage but Silver was the exception. The stage robbers thought they succeeded when, a mile from the border, The Lone Ranger catches up to them and shoots the guns from their hands. Ordering them back to the burned-down post, the crooks find themselves facing no other alternative. Back at the post, Jed and Beth are hailed as heroes for helping assist with the stand-off, and everyone cheers as the gold is delivered to secure hands and the thieves tied up.

Episode #1287-504 "MUSTANG MAG GROWS GRAIN"

Broadcast April 23, 1941

Copyright Registration #74,762, script received at Registration Office May 2, 1941.

Plot: Mustang Mag had a feeling of suspicion when she found Timothy Simmons, the influential banker, far more agreeable than usual. She was aware that she mortgaged her ranch for the cash advance but unaware that the syndicate wanted to buy the land she owned. Banker Tim Simmons, aware that she plans to pay back the loan when she sells a fodder crop, schemes with a breed name Manuel to perform an act of sabotage. Mustang Mag knew nothing of the banker's scheme to have her grain fields set on fire so she would be unable to repay the mortgage, but The Lone Ranger and Tonto, curious to know where the breed got his newfound money, kept tabs on him. The masked man left town and raced across the valley to where he knew an army detachment was encamped. He convinced Captain Foster to ride out with him to view a place where the army horses could find winter range, and natural protection from savages. The same place where crops of grain and straw are being grown. Arriving just in time, The Lone Ranger witnessed the field on fire and raced to help Mag and Missouri load their wagon with scythes, reapers and tools of every sort to cut grain and cut off from the burning section. Mustang Mag was appreciative of the army men who helped assist. Back in town, the sheriff visits banker Simmons to verify how Tonto captured Manuel after the breed set fire to the fields, and Tonto is witness. Manuel panics and claims Simmons paid him for the job. In the presence of army witnesses, she paid off the mortgage courtesy of a down payment by the army, tore up the mortgage papers, and orders the banker to get out of town by the end of the week... or else.

Episode #1288-505 "DODGE CITY OR BUST"

Broadcast April 25, 1941

Copyright Registration #74,763, script received at Registration Office May 2, 1941.

Plot: The Lone Ranger and Tonto catch up to Tex Cameron, a young cowboy who shot and killed a man in Bennett City. The Lone Ranger knows Tex shot in self-defense and the town was glad to get rid of the bully, but the masked man wanted to know if Tex was going to live it down or get himself a bigger reputation. It was

The Lone Ranger's suggestion that Tex go to work for Borneo Smith, a rancher with one of the biggest spreads around San Jose, who needs gunmen to protect his range from rustlers. Borneo, however, lent Peggy Andrews $5,000 and if she does not pay by September, she loses her ranch. Borneo saw to it that he hired all the able-bodied men to prevent her from a cattle drive to Dodge City… except for Tex who chooses to go to work for her. Two thousand longhorns and fifty head of horses is a monumental task, as Tex discovered. Along the Chisholm trail, the herd drove north and always faced the threat of violence. Borneo's men, led by the notorious gunman Dirk Reynolds, tried to stampede the herd, tried to drive off the horses, then shot rifles through the night. The Lone Ranger rides into camp to help thwart Black Crow and his men, then helps combat a herd of buffalo that was so large the cattle could never be driven through. Knowing the water was higher on the Canadian than any other river, Borneo masterminded a scheme to strike when the cattle drive camps on the bank for a night. This meant a man-made stampede of buffalo that would become deadly if the camp remained. At the suggestion of the masked man, the cowboys shouted, the six-guns barked. The longhorns stopped grazing and broke into a run. An approaching storm and roaring thunder helped startle the terror-stricken cattle, which ran towards the river and by mid-stream the cattle were forced to swim. As the cattle made it across the river, the race was clearly over, and the victory was theirs. In Dodge City, Borneo and Dirk were disappointed. Perseverance rewarded Peggy $30,000 in the sale of cattle and the schemers decided to rob her in the streets – after all, no one pays attention to gun shots in Dodge City. Peggy, meanwhile, offers Tex a job as foreman of her ranch. Before she can get on the stage to return to San Jose with the money, Dirk takes aim. The Lone Ranger shoots the gun out of the gunman's hand and the sheriff takes him and Borneo in. The law was watching the sidewinder for the last hour and heard Borneo give the order to shoot.

Episode #1289-506 "WILD HORSES UNTAMED"

Broadcast April 28, 1941

Copyright Registration #74,764, script received at Registration Office May 2, 1941.

Plot: Horse rancher Jud Tobias, owner of the Bar T ranch, mistreats his half wild mustangs, believing he needs to break their spirits. When a young wrangler named Dan Springer jumps in to prevent Tobias from abusing the animals, the confrontation gets personal. The Lone Ranger prevents an exchange of gunplay, then lets Springer know that Lazy Jones, owner of the Rippling River outfit, is looking for a good bronco buster and horse wrangler. Despite the new job, Springer is lured out when he gets word that Tobias was in town bragging about his abusive means against the mustangs, and the suggestion to free the mustangs in Tobias's corral. Purdy, a weaselly drifter, schemes with Tobias to shoot and kill Springer. With no moon, there would be nobody who would blame him for shooting what looks like a horse thief. Tonto, having overheard the conversation in the town of Tawanda, reported back to The Lone Ranger, who takes a shortcut and races out to save Springer from an ambush. To get close to the ranch, Tonto and The Lone Ranger muffle the horses' hoofs with cloth, so they won't make any sound. Sneaking up to the corral without being noticed, the heroes sneak up to Tobias and disarm him before he could pull a trigger. Placing Tobias into the corral with Silver, the masked man makes him face off against the white stallion, and minutes later Tobias begs to be let out of the corral… convincing the rancher that cruelty doesn't pay.

Episode #1290-507 "DEAD MEN PAY NO BLACKMAIL"

Broadcast April 30, 1941

Copyright Registration #74,765, script received at Registration Office May 2, 1941.

Plot: Pete Lacey, Pedro Martinez and a middle-aged widow named Mary Lawrence, of the Diamond L, rode into the little town of Glenville, where the two assist as witnesses to an exchange between Red Bannister and Mary. She does not believe her husband ever borrowed any money from Bannister and while he cannot provide the paperwork, he claims the sheriff has seen it. Pete and Pedro, hired by her husband to thwart potential rustlers, also suspect it was not rustlers that killed her husband. But Red was shot and wounded in the confrontation and Pedro raced out of town, heading straight for the Padre, to call for help from The Lone Ranger. Pete, meanwhile, sat in jail with a charge of murder against him. The Lone Ranger pays a visit to the sheriff to set in motion a series of events, including a chase outside of town where the masked man and Indian circle back to question Pete and Pedro regarding the details of the murder. Later, riding out to the Lazy Y, a ranch south of town owned by Bannister, our heroes discover the crook is not really dead. The sheriff conspired to frame Pedro so that Bannister could assume a new identity in San Francisco and escape a blackmailer who was after him. Meeting up with Jose, a breed employed by Bannister, Pete and Pedro explains how his employer is dead and Jose now has a price on his head on suspicion of murdering Mary's husband. Jose confesses that he saw Bannister shoot and kill her husband, moments before Red was brought to the fold, alive and well. The confrontation led Jose to point an incriminating finger, having never been paid in full for keeping his mouth quiet and referring to the supposed dead man as a "double crosser."

Episode #1291-508 "TRAIL OF THE BROKEN HORSESHOE"
Broadcast May 2, 1941
Copyright Registration #74,766, script received at Registration Office May 2, 1941.
Plot: An old stagecoach driver named Williams is shot from ambush while driving a stage and manages to live long enough to reach Brad Carnell's ranch, a young homesteader residing halfway between Wolf Run and Bardo. Filling in for Williams, Brad brings the stage into Wolf Run. But with the express boxes of silver and cash missing from the stagecoach, he finds himself accused of murder and robbery. The Lone Ranger and Tonto, meanwhile, follow the trail of a broken horseshoe, the left hind shoe with a break across the toe, to track down the man who shot and killed Williams. The trail led to Murdock and Drucker, stage line owners, who quickly try to throw the blame on the masked man. Moments before The Lone Ranger and Tonto flee town, they offer comfort to Brad's wife and explain that they know who did commit the crime and will save her husband from injustice. Further tracking of the broken horseshoe reveals the location of the stolen express box, and a trap is set to catch the murderer. The hint he left behind in the office of the stage line should lure the culprits. The Lone Ranger then breaks Brad free from jail, giving Sheriff Prout a trail to follow. Disarming the lawman when the sheriff arrives at Brad's homestead, The Lone Ranger explains how things have gotten too hot for the real gunman, so they plan to dig up the box and plant the evidence on Brad's property, believing the cabin is empty. The Lone Ranger was not sure if it was Murdock or Drucker, but the culprit turned out to be Drucker, who inadvertently gave himself away – and the broken horseshoe on his horse clinches the guilt.

Episode #1292-509 "THE GAMBLER DRAWS A BLANK"
Broadcast May 5, 1941
Copyright Registration #74,767, script received at Registration Office May 2, 1941.
Plot: Blue Chip, a gambler who was run out of town a month ago, faces down Sheriff Lige Blake of Washoe Flats, who's lost his nerve after killing the notorious Duster Gang. Jimmy Drake, his 13-year-old son, looks up to his father but is shocked when he discovers his old man has turned coward. The Lone Ranger and Tonto witness the events unfold in the Bear Knife Café. The masked man pays a visit to Blue Chip and pretends to be a bandit wanted by the law so he can learn from the gambler why he is so confident that the sheriff will not draw in a showdown. The sheriff mistakenly believes he never gave his victim time to reach for his holster, and that preyed on the lawman's mind until Drake was now gun-shy. Later, The Lone Ranger assures Jimmy that his father is not a coward, then kidnaps the boy and tells the sheriff if he wants his boy back, ask Blue Chip. The brazen act causes the sheriff to strap on his gun belt and race into town to face off against the gambler. Tonto, having loaded Blake's gun with blanks, gives The Lone Ranger the advantage from behind to shoot the gun from Blue Chip's hand. With the boy returned and an explanation provided, the sheriff realizes The Lone Ranger's trick worked… having arranged matters so that that sheriff regains his self-respect.

Episode #1293-510 "SPRING ROUNDUP"

Broadcast May 7, 1941

Copyright Registration #74,768, script received at Registration Office May 2, 1941.

Plot: Aware that two stubborn ranchers have been feuding for years, a rivalry between John Lorimer, owner of the Circle Dot ranch, and Bill Farrel, owner of the Diamond F spread, there was a period of truce on the range during the annual spring roundup, but the hard feelings between the two outfits put every man on his mettle and the work went fast. No one remembers when the rivalry in Wyoming began, but the long-standing feud comes to a crescendo when Chick, a crooked foreman hires an outlaw named Blacky to murder John Lorimer and pin the crime on Greg Farrel, Bill's son. After hearing the gun shot and finding John Lorimer shot in the back, Tonto takes the man to their camp and tends to the bullet wound. The Lone Ranger, meanwhile, investigates to discover Bea Lorimer and Greg Farrel have been quietly spending time together as lovers, but neither told their parents. Chick, eager to throw blame on Greg, attempts to blackmail Bea into marrying him or her lover will be turned over to the law. Bea insists Greg is innocent and prefers to wait until her father is found. Disappointed in the way things turned out, Chick holds the girl a prisoner in his camp. After The Lone Ranger has a discussion with Bill Farrel, the old man agrees to follow the masked man's lead and rescue the girl. Blacky and Chick soon find themselves surrounded with Blacky's gun shot out of his hand. John Lorimer, having witnessed his rival race to the rescue of his daughter, serves as a witness against Blacky and Chick… and agrees to let bygones be bygones. Both ranchers agree their children should be allowed to marry.

Episode #1294-511 "MOUNTAIN OF THE WIND"

Broadcast May 9, 1941

Copyright Registration #74,769, script received at Registration Office May 2, 1941.

Plot: When a well-outfitted wagon train heads over the Rockies bound for California, ten wagons and 20 head of oxen and horses, they fail to heed The Lone Ranger's warning. Even seasoned westerners have been trapped in those mountains, the masked man warns, and someone like Barber (the guide) is not to be trusted. But Wallace, the wagon master, insists on sending the masked man away and continuing the trek over the mountains. The wagon train crawled up the mountains like a giant centipede, up and up slowly and carefully. And with each incident and hazard, Barber showed himself to be as worthless as The Lone Ranger and Tonto warned. Barber, in shooting off his gun, started an avalanche, engulfing the wagon train in the mountain pass high in the Rockies. The Lone Ranger and Tonto rode straight into the storm, fighting their way up the steep incline. Seton and Barber were chosen to head for a rescue party, but Barber went loco. The Lone Ranger masterminds a trick to get the better of Barber, who stole much of the food, and help the train avoid starvation. Tonto, meanwhile, having gone down the mountainside, returned with two horses carrying food and provisions. As the men and women work their way down the mountainside, The Lone Ranger insists they keep Barber tied and bound and deliver him to the sheriff.

Episode #1295-512 "VALLEY IN THE HILLS"

Broadcast May 12, 1941

Copyright Registration #74,770, script received at Registration Office May 2, 1941.

Plot: When a blind, dying father in Bordertown named Ben Sherman tells his son Dart about "Paradise Valley," described as a true paradise with shady trees and water, hunting and fishing prospects, and grass as green as pond moss, The Lone Ranger fears his vision will ignite a land stampede on a wild goose chase toward dangerous territory. Despite the masked man's warnings that Paradise Valley was a mirage, and that happiness is not over the horizon someplace but rather to work for it, Dart uses a map his father left behind to guide him. A badman named Starmer, and his stooge, Brady, overhear a discussion between Dart and his girlfriend, Diana, and like timber wolves they take after the young man. The Lone Ranger and Tonto, learning of the recent developments from Diana, race out to rescue Dart before the badmen kill him. With Tonto applying his keen tracking skills, they find Dart's night camp, but the heavy rains washed away most of the trail. At the camp, they find a sketch of the map in the dirt, made by Dart, revealing the location of Paradise Valley. Just as the vigilantes are within sight distance, Starmer and Brady make for the pass where they know they can hold off an army. The Lone Ranger's quick shooting disarms the crooks and rescues Dart. Before they depart back to Bordertown, The Lone Ranger suggests everyone take a good look at their surroundings. Nothing but rocks. Ben Sherman imagined the whole thing. "Remember what I told you before," The Lone Ranger advises. "You have to work for happiness. Forget about Paradise Valley. Get back to Bordertown and build your own happiness."

Episode #1296-513 "BIG BEND"
Broadcast May 14, 1941
Copyright Registration #74,771, script received at Registration Office May 2, 1941.
Written by Tom Dougall.
Plot: Fort Benton was the head of navigation on the Missouri. During the gold rush to these diggings, most of the prospectors from the East traveled by steamboat and the village around the fort became a boom town overnight. In order for Colonel Barret to keep order in the mining camps and still have enough men to garrison the fort, he needed reinforcements. They were supposed to leave St. Joe on the Prairie Belle, but the crooked Gordon who got himself elected sheriff of Virginia City had plans to sabotage the boat and ambush the soldiers. On board the vessel was Virginia Barrett, the Colonel's daughter, so the Colonel had two reasons why he wanted The Lone Ranger to investigate the delay of the Prairie Belle, which was steaming slowly up the river. Gordon plans to wreck the boat and get rifles for the Indians, preventing the Colonel from getting reinforcements. After discussing the situation with the riverboat captain, and entrusting aid from Harry D'Arcy, the riverboat skipper, The Lone Ranger plots a scheme of counterattack against the Indians with a renegade white man for their leader, hell-bent on attacking the riverboat where the passengers have no retreat. Harry D'Arcy mounted a cannon on the forward deck to get the advantage, while The Lone Ranger leads a group of armed men to use the element of surprise to apprehend the two white men and Indian Chief, Black Eagle, to prevent bloodshed. Virginia, after the escapade concluded, discovered the persecuted D'Arcy has a history of bravery among the U.S. Army that deserves recognition.

Episode #1297-514 "BORDER QUEEN"
Broadcast May 16, 1941
Copyright Registration #74,772, script received at Registration Office May 2, 1941.
Written by Tom Dougall.
Plot: The little town of Alexandra on the north bank of the Rio Grande was dominated by the Border Queen café. The place was owned by Alexandra White and ever since it had opened two years before, the town had become a haven for outlaws from both sides of the border. With her café of dubious repute, she controlled the sheriff and harbored outlaws. But the recent election voted the crooked Van Gordon out of office and the former sheriff now seeks refuge. Alex insists her café was fitted with embrasures, thick wood and plenty of rifles and ammunition. The Border Queen is a fort and could stand off any posse that the new sheriff, Neal Chalmers, could raise. When Van Gordon learns that Roberts won big money in the café and used it to pay off the mortgage, a ranch Van Gordon was supposed to come into possession after it was foreclosed, he arranges with a breed named Manuel to commit a murder and prevent payment from being made. The new sheriff investigates and both Manuel and Van Gordon were identified by widow Roberts. The Lone Ranger and Tonto save the life of Sheriff Chalmers of Bennett City from an ambush outside the Border Queen. Desperate, Van Gordon and Breed hold Alex prisoner in her own café, while Manuel searches for her money, hidden away someplace. The Lone Ranger and Tonto sneak inside to create a distraction so the new sheriff can lead the charge with a posse to break in and apprehend the murderers.

Episode #1298-515 "ONE NATION INDIVISIBLE"
Broadcast May 19, 1941
Written by Tom Dougall.
Plot: Freight line owner Jeff Wilson is vocally anti-railroad, believing progress will put him out of business. He makes an open threat against Carney, the head engineer of the railroad, when he discovers his surveyor son, Jim, returned from schooling in the East to work for the railroad. When Warner schemes with Dan to create a number of "complications" to slow the crew down a mile a day, he figures this will discredit his boss and Warner can take over his job. Dan and his thugs perform a number of acts of sabotage, including tearing up the tracks and frames Jeff Wilson. When Carney had enough with the sabotage, he led his men to pay Jeff Wilson a visit. Warner believes his boss will be fired when, the camp unguarded, an attack is made on the railroad and a man is killed. The Lone Ranger and Tonto, friends of Jeff Wilson, help defend the freight line owner. Tonto fetches a posse from the local sheriff and The Lone Ranger leads the charge, circling around the outlaws to trap them. Warner is exposed by Dan, and the men are taken into custody. Jeff Wilson admits he was a fool for shooting off at the mouth and welcomes the railroad… and agrees the tracks laid from coast to coast will be what is best for the country.

Notes: This episode bears no relation to the episode of the same title broadcast on March 19, 1941.

Episode #1299-516 "TROUBLE ON THE RIO GRANDE"
Broadcast May 21, 1941
Written by Fran Striker.
Plot: While taking shelter from a storm late one night, near a cabin on the Rio Grande, The Lone Ranger and Tonto discover a girl, Abby Watkins, wandering alone in the dark. Thinking her in trouble because of gunshots he and Tonto heard, he follows her back to the hideout of Jud Bascomb, head of a large smuggling gang. The girl feigns a sprained ankle and is held captive in the back room, although Jud's wife, Martha, is fully aware the girl is not who she appears. The Lone Ranger pretends to be an outlaw to gain the confidence of Bascomb, and in doing so he reveals the girl's identity as the daughter of Sheriff John Watkins, who Jud shot and killed a short time ago. After learning from the girl that proof of the smuggling operation must be in the house, and the cyclone cellar underneath revealed nothing, The Lone Ranger and Tonto fix it to appear as if the cabin was on fire. The roaring flames crept closer as The Lone Ranger led the outlaws to the back door – unaware the masked man, during the confusion, disarmed them. Jud, fearing the fire would engulf the entire cabin, had raced over to the hiding place of the books – evidence that would guarantee the Bascom gang a jail sentence.

Episode #1300-517 [TITLE NOT KNOWN]
Broadcast May 23, 1941
Plot: The plot remains unknown for this broadcast.

Episode #1301-518 "STOLEN CLAIM PAPERS"
Broadcast May 26, 1941
Plot: While traveling east to Pecos, The Lone Ranger and Tonto witness a messenger, Rod Scott, shot from ambush. Before Bender and his right-hand man can retrieve the papers on Scott's possession, The Lone Ranger and Tonto intervene. Scott asks the masked man to deliver the papers to Sarah Collins, but the masked man is surprised to learn later that the papers are blank. Ben, Sarah's uncle, has been selling cattle off and claiming the steer had to be disposed of due to a virus plaguing the cattle, and did not want Sarah to get possession of the papers which he already stole. The Lone Ranger was quickly accused of stealing the map to a gold claim her late father left her, but the masked man figures out the plot and decides to trap the crooked uncle into revealing it was he who stole the papers. Arranging for a midnight rendezvous at Grover's Woods, The Lone Ranger meets

up with Sarah, only to be surprised by the two bandits – and a third hiding behind a bandana. The masked man reveals the masked bandit as her Uncle Ben who, during a verbal exchange, confesses his part of the crime including hiring the two gunmen. Before The Lone Ranger could be silenced from a bullet, the sheriff and his posse step out from their hiding places, having overheard the entire affair. Sarah is given the claim papers and map while her uncle is led away on a charge of murder.

Notes: This was the first in a series of consecutive episodes where Tonto whittles a stick of willow to create a whistle used to signal The Lone Ranger, in place of the Indian's night bird calls. A plug in the stick allows Tonto to create multiple sounds, used through a few consecutive episodes to alert The Lone Ranger of danger. This was connected to a premium whistle giveaway courtesy of General Mills.

Episode #1302-519 "AMBUSH AT WINDY RIVER"

Broadcast May 28, 1941

Plot: The Lone Ranger rescues a cattleman named Randy, trapped by restless longhorns, only to find himself and Tonto trapped in a deadly chess game by outlaws on the far side of Windy River. As Randy lay wounded and Tonto tends to him, The Lone Ranger learns that Travis, who makes his living trapping wolves, used wolf pelts to create the stampede. Travis and his henchman, Hurley, are out to steal the cattle and Randy's death must first be assured. Tonto and the masked man take the wounded Randy to a natural defense position where the Indian can fight off the rustlers while The Lone Ranger rides out to Stockton to fetch reinforcements. Under cover of night, the masked man encourages cattlemen to pick up their guns and follow his lead – but not before Randy's wife fears the worst. Throughout the night an exchange of gunfire holds back the rustlers who are hell-bent on making sure Randy never sees the sunrise. Just as the rustlers get wise and circle around to the other side of the river to get the advantage on Randy and Tonto, the posse arrives. After The Lone Ranger and his friends apprehend the rustlers, Randy's wife shows up to discover the masked man was not an outlaw – he was The Lone Ranger. Her fears were unwarranted. Randy's son, Jimmy, is handed a whistle that was given to him by Tonto. (Don't worry, Tonto has a spare.)

Episode #1303-520 "IN SEARCH OF A WITNESS"

Broadcast May 30, 1941

Plot: Alice Ames is worried when her boyfriend, Red, agrees to be the new sheriff of Seymour City. The shiny badge he wears is a target, or so she thinks. But Red insists he had to be appointed as the law when his good friend Bill Anderson was shot and killed. Red suspects Hy Roberts, owner of the local gambling hall, hired Slim Darrell of committing the crime and is determined to find proof. The men are at odds with one another, threatening the law of the gun, but Red prevents bloodshed. The Lone Ranger and Tonto, however, follow the trail of Pancho, and figures the breed witnessed the crime. Tonto, in turn, is shot and wounded when he got too close to the truth. Alice's uncle, Simon Porter, is not only the mayor but a brave soul in agreement with The Lone Ranger to set a trap for Anderson's killer. The mayor needs to ride to a nearby town with a lot of money on his possession. The sheriff and The Lone Ranger ride alongside the mayor to ensure safe delivery. The trap was sprung at midnight at the Witch's Garden when an attempt is made on Red's life, and the mayor is quickly disarmed. Pancho is forced to confess that it was Alice's uncle who wanted Bill Anderson dead. Hy Roberts and Slim Darrell, no longer suspects in the case, make peace with the new law officer and agree to be ready and able should Red need to call on a posse to back a play.

Blooper! The announcer flubs the opening.

Episode #1304-521 "THE SHERIFF OF CLAYBOURNE COUNTY"

Broadcast June 2, 1941

Plot: Sheriff John Harvey of Claybourne County is up for re-election. Jerry Blaine, the opposition, is dry-gulched out on the prairie and The Lone Ranger and Tonto find and rescue him. While Tonto remains at camp to tend to Jerry's wound, the masked man rode into town to discover a woman who owns a ranch, Agatha Monroe, is receiving letters meant to intimidate her into leaving. Doc Blackwood, who endorses Joe Harvey for re-election, is presently treating the good Colonel Stewart of a heart ailment. Everyone in town has respect for the doctor, almost ensuring Harvey's re-election. The Lone Ranger, suspecting foul play, asks the Colonel not to take the "medicine" that was prescribed by Blackwood until he returns, then rides out to fetch a real doctor. The masked man rides southeast to the Rio Grande, then south to Brownsville, and the night before the election Doctor Evans backs The Lone Ranger's play. The election at Redmond City had no opposition since Jerry Blaine was nowhere to be seen for the past week, but the masked man exposes the attempts on Jerry's life. Doctor Blackwood is exposed as a fraud, known to others in Brownsville as Cotter, and Jerry shows up to verify the attempt on his life. Blackwood, realizing the crooked sheriff was not backing him, pointed an accusatory finger on John Harvey – the leader of a posse by day and road agents by night. Harvey was not only a killer but the leader of the Night Riders. Despite the fact that the election is not scheduled until tomorrow, Jerry is quickly appointed sheriff to take Harvey and Blackwood into custody.

Episode #1305-522 "KOWALA INDIAN LAND SCHEME"

Broadcast June 4, 1941

Plot: An Indian woman named Bright Sky menaces The Lone Ranger and Tonto from a high prominence, Sentinel Rock, considered by many Indians as haunted. But after foiling both arrows and falling boulders, The Lone Ranger discovers the woman was merely trying to protect her tribe. Her husband, Bear Paw, is the chief of the Kowala, a tribe of the Pawnee. Scar Kraven and his friend, Hela, offered to buy the Indian ground for a price better than the U.S. Government and her husband went into town to finalize the deal. Soon after Bear Paw signs the deed, he discovers the paper money was counterfeit and gets shot and wounded for his trouble. Kraven and Hela flee town in a race to meet up with the government land agent and finalize the deal of selling the land to the government for a higher price. The Lone Ranger, Tonto and Bright Sky, upon discovering what happened in town, leave Bright Sky to tend to her husband. Racing out to prevent the sale, The Lone Ranger gets within sight distance of the crooks and the land agent. In desperation, Kraven and Hela exchange gunplay and try to steal the money they felt would have been theirs had they finished the sale. Kraven eventually surrenders and the land agent agrees to testify against them in court for attempting to defraud the U.S. Government.

Blooper! An actor stumbles over a line when exchanging dialogue with The Lone Ranger.

Episode #1306-523 "CHANGED CLAIM MARKERS"

Broadcast June 6, 1941

Plot: The east branch of the Chocose River was quiet and deserted until gold was discovered there. Word of the strike spread like wildfire and homesteaders, settlers and ranchers rushed into the region. All along the wooded shores, axes struck into trees, pickets dug into rock and shovels dug into soil as men searched for the precious metal. Among those men was Dan Jefferies, who plunged over a cliff and into the roaring rapids. The Lone Ranger and Tonto, following the trail of a notorious outlaw known as Turant, found themselves wandering into the region and quickly rescued Dan. Macklin, a bully among the gold camp, was responsible for Dan's dilemma, never having lifted a finger to rescue him. When the gold prospector discovers gold as a result of his fall into the creek, he stakes his claim. Dan's wife Linda and daughter Sal are joyous in the discovery but Macklin and his henchman, Wiley, attempt to steal the claim. When the government land agent arrives in camp, Macklin claims to have staked claim and insists the land agent verify with his own eyes. Dan was unaware that the crook switched stakes, but Tonto uses his whistle to alert The Lone Ranger. Macklin is surprised to discover the stakes were switched back. The masked man quickly deduces and verifies Macklin is none other than Turant, who changed his name when he left Pecos, a man wanted by the law and now taken into custody with a charge of claim jumping against him.

Notes: This was the last episode to feature Tonto's "danger whistle" until June 13.

Episode #1307-524 "SANTIAGO'S REVOLT"

Broadcast June 9, 1941

Plot: Charles Brandon, a crooked land schemer, tricks Don Santiago into thinking the governor of New Mexico Territory named Johnson is planning to impose onerous taxes once the territory becomes a state. When the Don masses men to ride against the governor, The Lone Ranger attempts to convince the land baron that he is being tricked. Instead, The Lone Ranger, Tonto, and a friend named Slim are bound hand and foot and thrown into a vault-like room under the Don's Hacienda. Thanks to Dolores, the Don's daughter, they escape. Brandon, meanwhile, attempts to send a telegram to Johnson to report the revolt and the Don's plans to destroy the Stony River Bridge so the governor won't be able to defend himself or call out the troops. Thanks to The Lone Ranger's interference, the telegram is not sent out and instead is used to convince the Don that Charles Brandon wanted the Don to become an outlaw so he could take the land and ranch from him.

Episode #1308-525 "DISAPPEARING STAGECOACH"

Broadcast June 11, 1941

Plot: Two crooks named Brady and Hawkins scheme to hi-jack a stagecoach and hide it in a cave, making off with the money being shipped in from Eastern banks. They use explosives to cover the entrance of the cave, thus giving the sheriff and his posse a mystery as to the whereabouts of a stagecoach, ward and driver that mysteriously disappeared in thin air. But a greedy hotel clerk named Claney complicates their plans by pretending to be The Lone Ranger and then offering to kill the masked man for a share of the loot. The disguised Lone Ranger, riding shotgun on the stage, was able to escape in time to throw the crooks off. When Tonto uses dynamite to uncover the stage in the same manner used to hide the entrance to the cave, The Lone Ranger reveals how the stage mysteriously vanished. The masked man explains to the sheriff, along with a number of men from town, that he met Claney in another town and the hotel clerk kept one of the silver bullets as a means of conning his business partners into believing he eliminated The Lone Ranger as a threat. Exposed, the men point accusatory fingers at each other, incriminating themselves.

Episode #1309-526 "SHERIFF OF MARSHVILLE"

Broadcast June 13, 1941

Plot: Lem Smiley and Ed Torrence have been leading road agents in thefts ranging from stagecoach robberies to cattle theft. When one of their associates, Blackey, fears exposure because The Lone Ranger was reported within the vicinity, the crooks kill Blackey and frames Sheriff Bailey for the murder, while scheming to tie The Lone Ranger and Tonto into the plot. The town, suspecting the crimes went unheeded because the sheriff was involved, turns into a lynch mob. To save the lawman's life, The Lone Ranger kidnaps the sheriff from his own jail cell. One week later, with the help of Magdelena, an old friend, The Lone Ranger learns details that helps set up a trap for the real culprits. A stagecoach passing through picks up two passengers, the sheriff and Tonto, while The Lone Ranger rides into town to convince the townsmen that the sheriff was framed, and the real outlaws are going to rob the stage. The posse follows the masked man's lead and the confrontation, with Sheriff Bailey and Tonto on the inside, get the upper hand on the outlaw gang taken into custody. Sheriff Bailey is vindicated of the crime.

Notes: After two consecutive episodes of Tonto not using his "danger whistle," he uses it again in this episode.

Episode #1310-527 "NO FAVORS"

Broadcast June 16, 1941

Copyright Registration #75,532, script received at Registration Office July 3, 1941.

Plot: Tom Hilton, a civilian who was in charge of the commissary at Fort Lincoln, conspired with Steve Randall, Hilton's assistant, to steal Army rifles and sell them to Chief Red Fox, leader of a band of renegade Indians. Since the cases were not marked, the men scheme to trick the slow-witted Big Ben Smith to handle delivery, telling him the wagon is loaded with canned goods. When The Lone Ranger rescues Ben from the Indians, only to discover Chip Roberts, Ben's partner, is sent to the guardhouse, charged with conspiracy against the United States government, as Hilton accuses him of stealing the rifles that the Colonel so desperately wants returned. With the rifles in Red Fox's possession, he is sure to go on the warpath. Every settlement around will be in danger. But The Lone Ranger knows without ammunition, the rifles are useless. With assistance from the Colonel, The Lone Ranger hatches a plan to expose the real weapons dealers and clear the man's name. Tom Hilton is informed that Fort Seward needs ammunition badly, and the Colonel cannot spare any of his men. The Colonel asks Steve and Hilton to drive the wagons to Fort Seward. Along the route, the two crooks plan for the wagon to be attacked along the trail, having the Indians wreck the wagon, then head west to enjoy the riches of the sale. The trap was sprung perfectly as the culprits were exposed and Red Fox was apprehended by the masked man.

Notes: With the "danger whistle" premium offer expired, The Lone Ranger emphasized the silver bullet as his calling card in every episode, a trademark of The Lone Ranger that was rarely given away to others for identification. In the Spanish episode prior, the female was given a silver bullet and she proclaimed this meant she was a friend of The Lone Ranger. In this episode, the silver bullet was given to Ben as a means of friendship. In the next episode, Tonto gives the bullet to Diana for the same reason. A silver bullet had become the next giveaway premium.

Episode #1311-528 "SUNSET HOUSE"

Broadcast June 18, 1941

Copyright Registration #75,533, script received at Registration Office July 3, 1941.

Plot: To the east of Sunset Ridge was the range country that stretched for miles. To the west was Nugget Valley, rich in gold and silver. On the crest of the ridge was Sunset House, owned and run by Stanford Moore where cattlemen and miners met every night. Stanford Moore runs the gambling parlor catering to miners and cowmen. On one particular evening, four men sat in a friendly game of chance. Eric Morrow and Brent Hayden, gold miners, and ranchers Jim Tolliver and Mike Riley. When his daughter, Diana, find a paper on the floor, accidentally dropped by one of four visitors, she discovers one of them is The Hawk, the worst killer in the whole West. Fearing The Hawk will return to clean her father out and won't stop to murder, she agrees to assist The Lone Ranger, who picked up the trail of the killer and lost it for nearly a year. No one has been able to catch a glimpse of The Hawk, but since evidence points to one of four men as the notorious Hawk, The Lone Ranger must trick the outlaw into an admission of his identity. With all of the men gathered a week later, Diana reveals the letter and a silver bullet, claiming the masked man was outside ready to apprehend the killer. Just then the door kicks open and the masked man shouted "Reach for the ceiling, Hawk!" Eric Morrow drew his gun and knocked the light out having realized he gave himself away. The Hawk fled by horse toward level rangeland, with unerring instinct. A thrilling chase across the plains heading east ended only because of the speed of Silver, who closed in on the killer. The apprehension concluded when the masked man got the better of Eric, who drew a large knife in defense and found his attempt at self-defense futile.

Episode #1312-529 "WILD HORSES"

Broadcast June 20, 1941

Copyright Registration #75,534, script received at Registration Office July 3, 1941.

Plot: Pete Lacey and Pedro Martinez intend to round up some wild mustangs after setting up a corral but find themselves accused of a crime they have no committed when Dan Miller, elderly rancher of the Circle M ranch, insists Pete and Pedro are planning to rustle his cattle and mustangs. The Lone Ranger and Tonto, finding a man-made fence at the opening of a canyon, turning it into a natural corral, investigate to discover someone has been rustling Circle M cattle and changing the brands. Miller's foreman, Red, conspired with Lance and Lefty to rustle the cattle and now schemes to kill the old man and fake a will leaving the entire spread to him. When found dead in the morning, Red planned to accuse Pete and Pedro of committing the crime. To cinch his plan, Red and his men visit Pete and Pedro's new homestead to bust up their corral and spur them to visit the Circle M with anger in their heart. When The Lone Ranger tips off his good friends, the confrontation does not lead to the dead of Dan, but rather the Mexicans defending Dan and his homestead. The odds are five against twenty, but as Dan fired on Red and Lance, the outlaws attacked in full force and the little band inside the house were faced with a fight for their lives. The siege continued for two hours and then The Lone Ranger realized the sheriff and his posse was their only true defense. But with no way to town without ambush, the masked man has his friend give the appearance they succeeded in getting a posse on the way to the ranch, so the outlaws had their choice of clearing out or finding some place where they could hold off in superior force. With a stampede of wild mustangs running wild, the crooks mistakenly believe a posse was heading toward them. The outlaws fled and with their whereabouts revealed, the sheriff and his posse were fetched where the sheriff admitted he never made a bigger haul of crooks in his life.

Blooper! In this story, The Lone Ranger inexplicably knows the crook's plans without previous explanation, a flaw in the script.

Episode #1313-530 "DEATH TRAIN"

Broadcast June 23, 1941

Copyright Registration #75,535, script received at Registration Office July 3, 1941.

Plot: The Lone Ranger and Tonto, unable to stop a train of half a dozen cars racing downhill at breakneck speed, investigate what becomes a railroad disaster that caused the death of multiple passengers. When a band of Indians approach to plunder and pillage, The Lone Ranger switches clothes with one of the dead men to listen to the Indians and see what they do with the wreckage. Mary Austin's father, the engineer, died on that train and she alerts Jeb Turner of the railroad that her father suspected someone employed by the railroad was stealing goods from the train and working in cahoots with the redskins. By mingling with the Apache, Tonto learned the name of two unscrupulous railroad men who are working with Indians. The Lone Ranger's scheme of playing possum verified the same. The masked man kidnapped Jake, an engineer, and the sheriff and his posse doubled their efforts to locate the missing railroad man, but without success. A few days later, with everyone including Mary Austin, convinced that Jake was the one to blame for the crash of the train, a new locomotive arrived. On board, The Lone Ranger held the sheriff, Mary, Baldy and a few passengers found themselves held hostage as the box cars started drifting downhill – a repeat "runaway" created to extract a confession. Baldy, panicking, confessed that he and Jeb Turner conspired. The stolen loot was under the floor of the station, a percentage of the plunder courtesy of the Indians. Jake was also on board, who applied the brakes after he overheard the confession, clearing suspicion from him.

Episode #1314-531 "CATTLE CODE"

Broadcast June 25, 1941

Copyright Registration #75,536, script received at Registration Office July 3, 1941.

Plot: Bart Gates and Maggie, an old couple in charge of a prosperous ranch in Texas, learn from their foreman, Sam, that the cattle drive was momentarily halted. Kester, a neighboring rancher of the Bar Kay outfit, had agreed to allow the cattle to cross his property but the barbed wire and a fifty-cents-head toll says different. Overhearing the conversation between Sam and his employer, The Lone Ranger digs into the case and discovers the old couple are also illiterate and being taken advantage of. Sam calls back the cattle until Bart can figure a solution to his problem. Kester, meanwhile, chuckles when Sam delivers the news. Realizing there is not enough to graze on by the end of the month, the cattle will starve, and Kester theorizes he might be able to buy the steer up for whatever price he offers. In the meantime, Kester will make use of the cattle cars that his neighbor has no use for. What Bart Gates is not aware of is the new spur of tracks. The Lone Ranger, outside the window, heard Kester scheming and then rides off to explain to Fields of the railroad what happened. The cars are then directed down the spur toward the Gates outfit. Sam, during a confrontation with The Lone Ranger, is ordered to leave town if he knows what is best for him. Kesler races out to discover his cattle, already loaded onto the box cars believing Gates was not going to use them, now must have his steer unloaded. Gates offers to do the job, seeing Kester's ranch hands fled town, at a price per head. Realizing he was licked Kester agrees to be neighborly in the future as this is a country where men have to depend on each other.

Episode #1315-532 "DESERT WATER"

Broadcast June 27, 1941

Copyright Registration #75,537, script received at Registration Office July 3, 1941.

Plot: In the great Western desert, water was the most important thing on earth. Waterholes were few and far between, sought after by animals and human beings alike. Dave and Abby Danvers, pioneers traveling in a covered wagon, cross paths with two outlaws on the run, Staner and Kelso, who misdirect them away from water, to ensure the old couple don't run into any lawmen. The Lone Ranger and Tonto, observing fresh wagon tracks going the wrong direction, ride out to save the weak and feeble pioneers. After giving them water from their canteens, the heroes agree to lead them to the nearest waterhole. Kelso and Staner, making for San Francisco, defend the waterhole by shooting from a distance, even clipping The Lone Ranger's hat. The standoff comes to a parlay when The Lone Ranger gives his word that he will not apprehend the outlaws in return for Dave and Abby to gain access to the waterhole. After they get their fill of water, horses refreshed and canteens replenished, Abby is taken as a human shield, forcing Dave and The Lone Ranger to surrender their guns. All three are to be tied up like beef and left to be barbecued. A short time later, under the guise of moonlight, Tonto arrives to sneak up behind the crooks and overtake them. The Indian used his horse as a distraction to make the crooks think he was coming from the other direction, and the nightbird sound was Tonto's signal.

Episode #1316-533 "THE TWO EMPTY GRAVES"

Broadcast June 30, 1941

Copyright Registration #75,538, script received at Registration Office July 3, 1941.

Plot: In the town of Burkeville, Dan Mason explains to The Lone Ranger how a bully named Ritchie wants his land and won't pay a third of what the land is worth. Ritchie has failed in a number of attempts to frame him into jail, so he could buy the land from his wife. The situation gets complicated when Sheriff Doyle takes Dan in for the murder of Ritchie, and the masked man and Indian holds up the sheriff and kidnaps the prisoner before Dan could be thrown into jail. One week after Dan's escape, the stage from the east arrived in Burkeville and Ritchie's twin brother is furious to learn the news. The Lone Ranger, however, agrees to lead the sheriff to the hideout where Dan is being kept, with Abby and Ritchie's brother tagging along. But the masked man takes them into Indian territory, and it does not take long for a tribe to take everyone as prisoner. Several days went by, during which the sheriff, Abby, Ritchie's brother and The Lone Ranger were held captives by a tribe of Indians under the leadership of Tonto. The Lone Ranger and the sheriff, overhearing the crook trying to convince Abby to sell her land, expose the truth: the railroad plans to buy the land through there. Tonto's friends, as part of the scheme, are preparing to burn Doc Sykes at the stake. Doc was a friend of Ritchie's and was the man who pronounced the crook dead, but in his haste to pay the Indians a ransom for his life, Doc reveals Ritchie's brother is Ritchie himself who faked his own death. Dan, now cleared of a crime he did not commit, agrees to avoid fighting – which got him into this scrape in the first place.

Episode #1317-534 "BIRD FLYING HOME"
Broadcast July 2, 1941
Copyright Registration #75,539, script received at Registration Office July 3, 1941.
Plot: The town of Painted Forks lay right in the path of two migrations. It served as a way station of the Oregon Trail, and a layover for great flocks of carrier pigeons. Bad men like Smeby and Purvis are responsible for the wholesale slaughter of such birds, believing the buffalo can never be wiped out, either. A conflict between Jasper Brandon, a local settler, and the two bad men, is all a matter of differences between the protection of wildlife and the right to hunt game. The man who tried to save the bird, Jasper, and his young son of 14, Tod, ride out one morning to save the birds and finds themselves ambushed. When their pet pigeon returns to the coop, Smeby inadvertently gives away the location of the Pasco Trail. Purvis and another of his henchmen, Mogor, went to drygulch the two. The Lone Ranger and Tonto race out, rescue the father and son, and take the crooks into custody for the law to take over.

Episode #1318-535 "DANGER LANDING"
Broadcast July 4, 1941
Copyright Registration #75,540, script received at Registration Office July 3, 1941.
Plot: The steamboats that carried the miners to the Montana diggings used wood for fuel. Slim Goodrich, with his son, Bud, had built a cabin on the upper reaches of the Missouri and had gone into the business of supplying the boats with logs. Rio and his gang of outlaws take possession of Goodrich Landing, a lumber station on the upper Missouri, where riverboats frequently refuel. Their intent is to hijack the first gold shipment of the spring from Fort Benton, which is loaded on a steamer. But the up-river steamer lets off Ann, the wife of the station's owner, who escapes and is found by The Lone Ranger. Tonto sneaks into the camp and sets fire to the logs piled along the riverbank, drawing the outlaws from the cabin so the masked man can sneak inside and rescue Slim and Bud. Back at camp, The Lone Ranger and Tonto discover Ann ran off to carry out the rest of his plan, learning that it was easier to face a real danger than the kind one imagines. Hoping to alert the riverboat captain, The Lone Ranger races up the river and onto a sandbar where he swims out in the center the channel. The riverboat had to either stop or run him down, because the captain would not be able to hear the masked man until he got on board. The captain was grateful of the warning but since soldiers are 300 miles away, The Lone Ranger insisted the men on the boat vote to arm themselves and help deliver both law and justice. Gunfire erupted from both sides as the outlaws, organized by Rio and Spur, who thought they had the element of surprise, discovered the tables turned against them. While Tonto drives the outlaws' horses away, the men from the boat closed in, led by The Lone Ranger. With the gang captured, the outlaws were placed in irons.

Episode #1319-536 "AN ALIBI CRACKED"
Broadcast July 7, 1941
Copyright Registration #75,541, script received at Registration Office July 3, 1941.
Plot: Sheriff Doyle came to his office in the early morning to learn about one more in a long series of robberies.

Suspicion falls on Sam Parker, a wealthy rancher who is also the leader of the gang of crooks, but Deputy Brady sat outside their ranch house and saw no one leave despite the fact someone robbed the bank in town last night. March, owner of the express office, is worried because of all the gold he has stored up for the next eastbound stage to arrive tomorrow. Parker, discussing the situation with his henchman, Butch, schemes to make another robbery tonight – and again with an airtight alibi. With a masked man seen in town, Parker figures on throwing blame on the outlaw, unaware he schemes against The Lone Ranger. Tonto, however, figures out where the trap door is in the floor of the ranch house, which descended to a cellar and a tunnel under the ground, which gives Brady's men the ability to leave the ranch unnoticed. Back in the express office, The Lone Ranger fixes it with the sheriff, March, and Dolly (March's daughter) to stack wooden cases that look like the ones that gold might be shipped in. Late that night the robbery goes off without complication, but with the cases locked tight, the bandits agree to open them back inside the tunnel. The Lone Ranger follows them, exposing them for the robbery, and assures them the trap door in the house has been closed with the sheriff and his deputy on the other side. As for the boxes, they are filled with lead and hornet nests. The trap door, it is explained, will be open only when the outlaws confess their crooked alibi scheme. The Lone Ranger shoots the locks open, and the hornets fly out of the boxes. Commotion and panic ensued as the men confess to the express robbery, the bank robbery, the Sam Jergens robbery and other crimes.

Episode #1320-537 "MURDER AT THE SCHOOLHOUSE"

Broadcast July 9, 1941

Copyright Registration #75,542, script received at Registration Office July 3, 1941.

Plot: Jim Ashland returns to his father's ranch seeking help because he shot a man in self-defense over at Abbotsville. His sister reluctantly hides him in the schoolhouse until she can learn more about the incident. The Lone Ranger and Tonto, following Jim's trail, figures out where the young man is hiding out. When someone attempts to shoot and kill Jim from a window, The Lone Ranger and an undercover U.S. Marshal suspect there was more behind the mystery of the shooting at the schoolhouse. Red Weatherby, foreman of Jud Ashland's ranch, conspired with Tex Chalmers, a U.S. Marshal, fixing it up with Scar to start a fight over in Abbotsville. Jim was supposed to shoot and kill the Scar. But the outlaw was only wounded and escaped. After Tex escapes jail, with the assistance of Red, the sheriff takes off in pursuit. Outside a canyon, the truth is exposed. Tex has been working with the masked man to find the location of cattle rustlers and it was Red who attempted to shoot and kill Jim Ashland, who was back in Tonto's camp on the mend. Red was the leader of a band of cattle rustlers and the crooked foreman overplayed his hand… now with an extra charge brought against him, attempted murder.

Episode #1321-538 "ROAD AGENTS GO WRONG"

Broadcast July 11, 1941

Copyright Registration #75,543, script received at Registration Office July 3, 1941.

Plot: Jebediah Peters, who called himself Professor Peters and travelled from town to town with partner, Meecham, who dresses as an Indian, performing a medicine show, made a living selling their Magic Root patent medicine. One evening they are held up by two road agents, Grundy and his friend, who wore kerchiefs instead of masks. When The Lone Ranger and Tonto hear shots in the night and find a medicine show man wounded and Meecham dead, they cover the body with a blanket and promise to return after tending to Meecham. But the body mysteriously disappears, and money found in a trunk in the medicine show wagon, so the sheriff of Red River puts Peters into jail on the charge of murder. Later that night, after Tonto was jailed alongside Peters when Tonto claims to be the dead man, the sheriff pays a visit with Grundy to find out what the body disappeared, and the money tossed into the wagon. Grundy's 17-year-old partner, Bob, insisted the dead man receive a Christian burial and the money should not have been stolen. The crooked sheriff, meanwhile, follow

Grundy's suggestion and leaves the jail door unlocked so he can shoot and kill his prisoners as they tried to make an escape. Bob arrives to save the lives of Tonto and Peters, explaining how Grundy is supposed to be a rancher but is really a road agent by night. Bob explains that he teamed up with Grundy but never realized he was a road agent until last night. Before the three of them can flee and be shot, The Lone Ranger gets the better of Grundy and the crooked sheriff. Bob has a surprise for Jebediah Peters – he is Meecham's younger brother.

Episode #1322-539 "THUNDER FROM THE PLAIN"

Broadcast July 14, 1941

Copyright Registration #75,930, script received at Registration Office August 6, 1941.

Plot: Government land out on the Flats by Stony Creek, just ten minutes of out Sagebrush, is open to homesteaders. But Tom Winters of the Flying W considers Sagebrush a cattle town and the Flats belong to the Flying W graze. Homesteaders were not welcome, and he makes this obvious to Jonathan Merrill and his daughter, Rose, who were in the midst of completing their cabin. Tom even discourages the local general store from selling supplies to the homesteaders. Instead, Tonto delivered supplies under the cover of night, infuriating Tom and Hank. A letter from the marshal at Circle City reminds the ranchers that threatening Jonathan Merrill with bodily injury opened themselves to criminal charges and if anything happens to the homesteader, they would be held accountable. This, however, did not prevent them from interfering with the homesteaders' rights on the Flats. The evil rancher orders his gang of roughnecks to stampede the cattle during a terrible thunderstorm, and a herd that size would level the newly constructed cabin to the ground. Worse, the destruction would lead to the death of Jonathan and his daughter, and no one would ever know it was not an accident. The Lone Ranger races to wake Jonathan, Rose, and their friend, Larry Dexter, to convince them to race away from certain destruction. With the storm driving them on, the little band races south for the rimrock, but always behind them, closer and closer, came the stampeding herd. The thunder in the sky was echoed by thunder from the plain and The Lone Ranger urged Silver onward. Hours later the storm had spent its fury and Tom Winters waited in his ranch house for his men to return. Later that evening, The Lone Ranger forces Tom to leave his residence and ride out to a valley that is good range but is not good farming land. He will never be bothered by homesteaders again. His men, captured by the masked man and his friends, will face jail time or follow the advice that leads to eventual reconciliation. "The West needs all of you," The Lone Ranger explains, "cattlemen and farmers. Just remember that the future of the country depends on your working together."

Notes: Jonathan Merrill was originally Jonathan Edwards in the first draft of this script.

Episode #1323-540 "REVENGE RIDES THE WAGONTRAIN"

Broadcast July 16, 1941

Copyright Registration #75,931, script received at Registration Office August 6, 1941.

Plot: Just west of Saint Jo, Missouri, old John Dawson joined a wagon train, at the behest of his daughter, Charity, age 20, who wanted to travel west since her mother died. Dan a young man of 21, trails the wagon train and explains to Charity, who he befriended, that he is gunning for the man who murdered his brother. The Lone Ranger, stumbling upon a dead body recently shot, sets out on Dan's trail to solve the mystery. Day after day the wagon train crept westward across the great plains, the white canvas tops strung out like sails in the wind. The Lone Ranger and Tonto catches up to the wagon train and introduces themselves to Barlow, the wagon master, explaining Dan's motives. Dan's brother, Joe, was a gambler, a card sharp and a cheat. Barlow suggests the same, advising Dan to avoid keeping his troubles bottled up inside lest they turn sour. "Yuh can't be a lone wolf without goin' loco," Barlow adds. Tonto alerts The Lone Ranger that the dead man was identified as Joe Sawtell, who got into a quarrel with a man named Dawson. When Sawtell accidentally shot himself, Dawson believed he would have been accused and fled. Charity's father, John Dawson, was hoping to flee from trouble and The Lone Ranger races back to the wagon train to prevent Dan from making a deadly mistake. The masked man arrived just in the nick of time, shooting the gun out of Dan's hand. The masked man explained how there was a witness and the sheriff learned about it later – after Dan bolted. The old man demonstrated forgiveness, pleased to know he was vindicated, and offers Dan a ride in his wagon as they continue to ride west.

Episode #1324-541 "GOLD IS WHERE YOU FIND IT"

Broadcast July 18, 1941

Copyright Registration #75,932, script received at Registration Office August 6, 1941.

Plot: The little town of Banksville sprung up in the Rockies and pay dirt had been found in many of the canyons and gulches that surrounded the valley. Riding through the area, The Lone Ranger and Tonto help two old prospectors, Ezra and Jeremy, escape a band of bad Indians. Later that same afternoon, they rescue Tommy, a young boy who was a captive of the Indians for almost a year. The boy was the sole survivor of an Indian ambush. The prospectors of the Colorado gold fields, who just struck it rich, agree in unison to adopt the boy. All would say this was a happy ending to an action-packed story if it was not for two scheming crooks, Rance Jordan and Larkins, who discover the old men struck it rich when they return to town to buy all new tools to replace those stolen from the marauding Indians. While Tonto rides out to fetch the U.S. Marshal, The Lone Ranger explains the man who practically runs the town, Rance Jordan, is wanted for a hold up and a murder. But when Larkin follows the old men and boy out of town to learn the whereabouts of the mine, he underestimated the folks he was pursuing and was surprised from ambush and roped. Rance hires about fifty men to back his play, set Larkins free, and throw a noose around Ezra's neck. The fear of a hanging is meant to force Tommy and Jeremy to reveal the whereabouts of the mine, but The Lone Ranger, Tonto and the marshal are soon to arrive. Rance, panicking, uses Tommy as a human shield in an attempt to get away. Rance, exchanging fisticuffs, attempts to force The Lone Ranger over the cliff until the masked man punches Rance to the ground, knocking him unconscious. The mob, hoping to vindicate themselves, apprehend Larkin for the approaching law. The mob, wanting a piece of the action, was not a bad proposal, The Lone Ranger tells Ezra. With bad Indians in the territory, a little extra company in the region would be welcome.

Episode #1325-542 "GENTLEMAN OF HONOR"

Broadcast July 21, 1941

Copyright Registration #75,933, script received at Registration Office August 6, 1941.

Plot: Clark Sumner, a notorious gunman who built a reputation of being a "gentleman of honor" by allowing the other guy to draw first is, in reality, a cold-blooded killer who shoots to kill and uses his reputation to avoid the law. Clark extorts a half-interest in the business of Dave Gray, the largest cattle buyer in Clarksville, who has a shady business reputation among the ranchers. Their opposition is young Bill Gordon, who buys cattle in large volume. Clark joins forces with an outlaw gang led by Joe to run Gordon out of business, to stage a fake hold-up to gain the young man's confidence. The Lone Ranger intervenes and rescues Gordon, explaining how the outlaws were working for Clark. Gordon will not believe the masked man, however, so The Lone Ranger and Tonto are forced to prove Clark is not an ally. Visiting Ben Milan, owner of the Bar M whose cattle are being transported to the region for Gordon to purchase, The Lone Ranger asks him not to sell until they get to town. Clark, believing Bill Gordon bought the cattle, shows his true colors when he makes a desperate play to keep the cattle reaching town. In a showdown between The Lone Ranger and Clark, the masked man proves the gunman was a coward and all talk. In his confession, he also admitted to going into partnership with Dave Gray.

Episode #1326-543 "STAGECOACH"

Broadcast July 23, 1941

Copyright Registration #75,934, script received at Registration Office August 6, 1941.

Plot: Abner is old and stove in, worn out as much as his old horses. Even the stagecoach he drove in the good old days is in better shape than Abner. He told his wife Martha that he was about to hang up his hat when Tonto was in town and overheard Abner talking to the men in the office of the Deadwood stage line. Minutes after Abner left town, thieves went to the Deadwood office and stole a fortune in gold that was ready for shipment. There is a big reward for the capture of Red Brogan and his gang. Brogan knows that the sheriff will have a posse searching in the three directions out of town that provide a good chance of escaping. But Brogan is smart and will choose the trail over the Powder River bridge, the most dangerous of the escape routes. Red Brogan and his men stop over at Charley Bates' house, near the bridge, to change fresh horses. Charley married Abner's daughter, Jane. As Tonto raced to fetch Charley and rifles in pursuit of the outlaws, The Lone Ranger raced back to Abner's house to encourage the old timer to ride his stagecoach one last time – not to rekindle his love of driving the stage but to help catch the outlaws. With Silver among the horses hitched to the stage, old Abner felt thrills of another day returning to him as he sat once again on the high, jouncing seat of the aged stagecoach. The Powder River bridge, narrower than the wheels of the stage, is blocked so the outlaws cannot cross. Guns bark from both sides, but the outlaws are quickly disarmed by the quick shooting of The Lone Ranger, and Abner is told by the masked man that the reward money will ensure he lives comfortable for quite a spell.

Episode #1327-544 "NO FURY"

Broadcast July 25, 1941

Copyright Registration #75,935, script received at Registration Office August 6, 1941.

Plot: A crowd gathered in town on the day the stage arrived in Centerville, bringing the town's first schoolteacher, Susan Blaine. Sheriff Jim Faraday finds the woman strikingly beautiful and hopes to court her… against the wishes of Meg Anderson, who already confessed she had a thing for the sheriff. The Lone Ranger and Tonto, riding into town in search of the Christopher gang, figures where the outlaws plan to kidnap Billy Anderson, Meg's 14-year-old brother, in Sweetwater Canyon. The ransom for Billy was not the end game – the sheriff would be instructed to deliver the money alone so the gang could kill the law officer. Meg is entrusted with the information, and she promptly instructs Sheriff Faraday to organize a posse of 20 men to meet the masked man south of the canyon at daybreak. Jealous over the schoolteacher, Meg suggests to Susan that she see the sunrise from the canyon, and to wake an hour before dawn to be there in time. The schoolteacher is kidnapped instead of Billy and a ransom note requests $1,000 be delivered by the sheriff, alone, at Big Bear Cave by tomorrow night or the girl dies. Steve Farley, a smooth crook, plans to replace Jim as marshal of Centerville when Jim is out of the way. After realizing what she did, and learning from The Lone Ranger that the trap was meant for Jim, Meg chose to show up with the money. Tied and bound in the cave alongside Susan, Meg learns how the misunderstanding between the two of them was not to vie over the affection of Jim, but of a surprise birthday present. The Lone Ranger and Jim led a posse from outside the cave, knowing Meg would be a distraction long enough for the law to apprehend Christopher and his gang, including Steve.

Notes: This was Elaine Alpert's first appearance on the series. The role of Meg Anderson was instructed in the script to be played with a "touch of Calamity Jane."

Episode #1328-545 "RUSTLERS AT BREAKNECK CANYON"

Broadcast July 28, 1941

Copyright Registration #75,936, script received at Registration Office August 6, 1941.

Plot: A gang of cattle rustlers led by Leach, a crooked ranch owner, and his companion, Madden, stampeded the Circle Y herd down Breakneck Canyon, shooting and wounding Shorty Long, a young cowhand. While Tonto took Shorty to the ranch to mend his wounds, The Lone Ranger attempted to trail the gang of rustlers. A torrential rainstorm, however, poured in buckets and the trail was washed away. Back at the ranch house of Dan Forrester and his wife, Bertha, The Lone Ranger and Tonto are pleased to see Shorty recover. Leach, however, pays a visit to the Forresters, expressing sorrow for the death of Shorty, unaware he gave himself away as the man who shot their ranch hand. Later, The Lone Ranger and Tonto set out on Leach's trail, unaware the rustler plans to rustle more cattle while last night's booty was rebranded and already on the way to Abilene for sale. After all, who would suspect rustlers would hit the herd two nights in a row? Soon after the second rustling, The Lone Ranger and Tonto discover blankets dragged behind the horses to rub out the hoofprints and cover the trail. It does not take long to discover the secret of Breakneck Canyon – a hidden mine tunnel used by the rustlers to disappear. The Lone Ranger holds the crooks at bay long enough for Forrester and Shorty to arrive and effect capture.

Notes: The Circle Y was originally the Cross Y in the first draft of the script.

Episode #1329-546 "THE LINE THROUGH RED ROCK"

Broadcast July 30, 1941

Copyright Registration #75,937, script received at Registration Office August 6, 1941.

Plot: Walter Keen, head engineer and crooked railroad surveyor, is extorting money from towns competing for the projected railroad, including River City, Valley Center and Gainesboro. When The Lone Ranger meets Don Williams, an engineer who was fired by the crooked surveyor and shot and wounded from ambush, the masked man decides to help trap the men. Rita Manning, witness to the shooting, mistakes The Lone Ranger and Tonto for the shooters and alerts her father, the sheriff of Red Rock. The posse was unable to pick up their trail and the sheriff was forced to admit defeat, despite the fact that he knows Walter Keen is attempting to extort from the town. In the meantime, the masked man sets a trap and rounds up not one crook – but three. When Rita pays the $10,000 bribe, Don shows up with a gun in hand to take the money about to be paid to Walter Keen, who is surprised to discover the engineer is not dead. Keen insists Don not run off with the money, but assist him and Al, as they can collect $10,000 in every county they pass through from here to the coast. Keen was unaware, however, that Don was working alongside the law and Keen confessed to his crime. The sheriff, overhearing the confession, and with testimony from a gunman named Butch Wheeler to whom Tonto apprehended the night before, the men are taken into custody. Wheeler pointed a finger against Keen as the man who hired him to pull the trigger the other night, while Don feels confident that he will ultimately be promoted to the job Keen had.

Notes: The character Rita Manning and Sheriff Manning were originally Rita Manners and Sheriff Manners in the first draft of this script.

Episode #1330-547 "VALLEY OF THE CLIFF DWELLERS"

Broadcast August 1, 1941

Copyright Registration #75,938, script received at Registration Office August 6, 1941.

Plot: Two crooks named Ferris and Kelsey prey on the superstitions of the local Indians by making themselves to look like spirits of the ancient cliff dwellers in the valley. Buffalo Horn was the first to notice the evil spirits, glowing in the dark, and alerted his father, Eagle Feather, the head of the tribe. Hoping to induce the Indians to give the spirits gold, silver and furs, the crooks inadvertently stir up the settlers when the Indians who used to come into town to trade at Widow Blake's general store, no longer purchase anything. With their tribal wealth exhausted, the Indians now steal and rob anything made of gold and silver, and furs that were on display. A local settler named Carlisle hopes to ride out and alert the soldiers at the nearby fort, causing the crooks to plan a drygulch. When The Lone Ranger hears what's happening, he risks his life to prove the spirits are only crooked white men. Because the crooks paint only one side of their horses with material from matches that glowed in the dark when it was wet, the masked man uses the same material to reveal to Eagle Feather how the ruse was accomplished. After a chase into the valley, the masked man proves how the superstition was just a story and Carlisle takes the two crooks into custody and Eagle Feather promises his tribe will return the stolen goods.

Episode #1331-548 "LAST LAUGH"

Broadcast August 4, 1941

Copyright Registration #75,939, script received at Registration Office August 6, 1941.

Written by Tom Dougall.

Plot: The sheriff of River City, on the Rio Grande, and a seemingly harmless old-timer who owns a freight line, play a prank on the new U.S. Marshal, the young Bill Collier, who was sent to the region to locate a band of smugglers who are running guns into Mexico for a rebel army, camped south near Monterey. The old-timer, Ringo, happens to be a member of the gang and he conspires with the crooked Sheriff Morgan to keep tabs on the new marshal. To eliminate suspicion, Ringo and the sheriff plan to have the marshal ride with them as protection with the next shipment... only Bill Collier will meet with an accident and not return. The Lone Ranger masquerades as an outlaw in an attempt to get in with the gang's leader, Butch, only to be discovered and forced to flee before the outlaws got the better of him. With information about the wagon full of rifles on the way to Rocky Ford, the masked man races out to bring the troops from Fort Cameron in time to round up the crooks. While The Lone Ranger leads half of the troops charging up stream after the outlaws, Tonto led the other half from the lower trail, surrounding the smugglers. The outlaws reined up before the deadly fire of the soldiers and with all hope of escape gone, Butch took the lead in shouting his surrender, saving the life of the U.S. Marshal, moments before he was to meet with an "accident" and his body disposed.

Episode #1332-549 "BEST LAID PLANS"

Broadcast August 6, 1941

Copyright Registration #75,940, script received at Registration Office August 6, 1941.

Plot: Harvey Eldredge, a smooth gambler and owner of the Last Chance café in Sagebrush, schemes with Jack McGowan, crooked deputy sheriff of Mason County, to frame a rancher named Ed Scott, in order to obtain ownership of Scott's property. As long as Sheriff Barton is sick, the crooked deputy grants Eldredge leeway to perform a crooked scheme. As owner of the Circle E spread to the South, Eldredge purchased the cattle of Maria Daniels, owner of the Lazy D over by Ransom Pass, for which her son was to sell and return home with the money. But her son, Larry, lost the money playing faro and she claims Ed Scott rustled her cattle, unaware Larry was promised the money back if he agreed to lay low long enough for Scott to take the blame for cattle rustling. The Lone Ranger and Tonto investigate, saving the life of Larry by getting him out of town. During a confrontation with the crooked deputies, The Lone Ranger learns Sheriff Barton is not sick – he is dead. The crooked deputy insisted Larry was responsible for the murder, then accused of the murder of Scott's brother, Andy. Panicking, the deputy accused Eldredge of killing Andy. Ed Scott, however, has a surprise for the crooks when he reveals his badge – he is the new sheriff and his first duty is to take the crooked gambler and deputy to jail.

Episode #1333-550 "THUNDER RIDES THE FLOOD"

Broadcast August 8, 1941

Copyright Registration #75,941, script received at Registration Office August 6, 1941.

Plot: Silver is acting strangely, wanting to ride west instead of east, but The Lone Ranger and Tonto dismiss the stallion's peculiarities as they trail a band of renegade Apache outside the town of Wildfern. Blackhawk and his tribe are being led by an outlaw named Breed Conway, pillaging the town while the citizens are forced to defend themselves against fire arrows. A posse, led by the impetuous Bates, mistakes The Lone Ranger for the white man who led the renegade Indians. Tonto, meanwhile, attempts to trail the crooks and is captured. Soon after The Lone Ranger's identity is verified, and Bates and the posse agree to follow the masked man, Tonto tricks the outlaws into believing his treasure map reveals a hidden location of gold. When interrogations do not work, Breed and Blackhawk build a bonfire in the hopes that the threat of burning alive will force the Indian to talk. Tonto tells the story of an outlaw with a price on his head, slowly and meticulously, buying time until The Lone Ranger arrives with backup. The bonfire attracted the law like moths to a flame and only when Breed Conway discovers his mistake, and that the story of the outlaw was about him, does the masked man ride into camp to disarm the crooks and rescue his friend. The posse surrounds the outlaws and takes them into custody.

Episode #1334-550A "SILVER'S ESCAPE" [PART ONE]

Broadcast August 11, 1941

Copyright Registration #77,049, script received at Registration Office August 15, 1941.

Plot: The Lone Ranger and Tonto, noticing increasing restlessness in Silver, decided that the big stallion needed a rest. Silver has, of recent, been restless and the masked man was afraid the stallion will bolt and run away at the first opportunity. They hope a stayover at the ranch of Mustang Mag would help, but their trip was interrupted at the station when a stagecoach arrived and Matty, the station agent, held a gun on the masked man and Indian, fearing they might interfere with the stagecoach as fresh horses are exchanged. The passenger was an outlaw named Fleck, who was being escorted by a U.S. Marshal. Later, Silver's restlessness had increased to a point where the big stallion broke from The Lone Ranger and raced away, riderless, toward the west. The runaway came at a time when the masked man and Tonto were trying to capture outlaws who were waiting in ambush for the westbound stage. Two crooks, Whacker and Steve, plan to rescue Fleck from the approaching stagecoach, despite the fact that such a daring move would mean the death of the U.S. Marshal and the woman passenger who rode alongside. The Lone Ranger dropped as if he had been poisoned or taken suddenly and violently ill. Feigning helplessness, he asked the two to lift him into the stage and speak for Fleck's benefit about the sudden illness. The ruse worked as the stage was indeed held up further down the trail. Young Jean was held hostage momentarily as the marshal was disarmed. Before Fleck could be taken away by his two friends, The Lone Ranger disarmed the crooks by shooting the guns out of their hands.

The stage driver agrees to give The Lone Ranger one of his horses, then commenting: "I noted another hoss that was a mighty lot like him. That was a good ways' west of here. It couldn't have been yours because you was with Silver, then. This one wasn't pure white, Neither. It was almost white. Just one black spot, a star in the middle of the forehead. By crickity, it was the purtiest lookin' horse I ever seen in all my life. Youngish one, too. Bout a two-year-old. Wild as they come. I had a notion of tryin' tuh catch that hoss, but when I seen it run… well, I thought at that time that there was a hoss that come closest to anything I'd ever seen tuh bein' like The Lone Ranger's Silver hoss." Having observed Silver nuzzling a colt earlier in the day, The Lone Ranger has an idea what took Silver away from him. When Tonto returned, the masked man informs his friend that he suspects Silver has a son. Perhaps the colt is back in Wild Horse Valley where they left Silver's mate a long time back. "Yes," The Lone Ranger told Tonto. "The colt would have grown by this time so it would be about two years old."

Episode #1335-551 "THE SON OF SILVER" [PART TWO]

Broadcast August 13, 1941

Copyright Registration #77,050, script received at Registration Office August 15, 1941.

Plot: A daring bank robbery in town resulted in the death of banker Haskel, shot during the hold-up. Jasper Sneed, a man with much influence and secretly linked with an outlaw gang led by Varley, insists Old Missouri was the culprit. When some of the stolen cash was found, incriminating Missouri, The Lone Ranger and Tonto break their good friend from jail. Forced to borrow a stagecoach horse to pursue Silver, our heroes track the real killers to Wild Horse Canyon, where Silver's two-year-old offspring is discovered. Varley, however, discovers he was being trailed and arranges for an ambush that traps The Lone Ranger, Tonto and Missouri. All day and all night the men maintain their position, but without food and water, Missouri insists his mouth is becoming as dry as Death Valley. Worse, the crooks shot Thunderbolt, Missouri's trusted horse, so a steadfast escape was not possible. Under moonlight, in giant strides the great horse Silver, who rode in to rescue his master. Riding away to fetch help, The Lone Ranger luckily dodged bullets as the outlaws fired desperately. The masked man returned quickly with a posse to round up the outlaws, including Varley and Jasper Sneed. Finding the son of Silver, The Lone Ranger bestows the two-year-old colt to Missouri as a replacement for Thunderbolt... under two conditions. The masked man reserved the right to name the colt, and if something should ever happen to Silver, he reserves the right to take the colt back.

Episode #1336-552 "THE BREAKING" [PART THREE]
Broadcast August 15, 1941
Copyright Registration #77,051, script received at Registration Office August 15, 1941.
Plot: Dan Brogan, leader of an outlaw gang, sets his sights on the young colt housed at Mustang Mag's ranch. With assistance of his outlaw gang, the colt is stolen. The crooks left no trail a posse could follow, but Tonto finds enough signs to trail them. At the outlaw ranch outside Crystal Springs, Dan Brogan attempts to break in the colt using spurs and a whip. Eddy Grayson, a member of the gang, displays resentment at the treatment the outlaws plan to use to break the animal. Eddy quits and flees, with determination to thwart Dan's plan by fetching the law. The young colt, however, breaks free and rides away for safety. After learning from Eddy of the outlaws' plan to trap the U.S. Marshal and his posse, The Lone Ranger uses their plan against them. Tonto fetches the law while the masked man ensures Silver and his son are reunited. The posse surrounds the crooks, Eddy will get a second chance, and Missouri takes the young colt back home.

Episode #1337-553 "WATER MAKES TROUBLE" [PART FOUR]
Broadcast August 18, 1941
Copyright Registration #77,262, script received at Registration Office September 4, 1941.
Plot: A settler from Pine Canyon named Bradlow pays a visit to the ranch of Mustang Mag to implore assistance from The Lone Ranger. Land grabbers aim to thirst out a dozen families so they can take over the property. The settlers worked and sweated to build their homesteads, plowing and planting and now there is no water for the crops and the settlers. There used to be a good-sized stream that ran through Pine Canyon, taking care of all their needs, but crooks dammed up the stream above the lip of the canyon. They are too small a group to have any law and order yet, and with no marshal or sheriff within 300 miles, The Lone Ranger and Tonto agree to investigate. Cogswell, discovering that what he was doing was against the law, offers to compromise on account he paid large sums of money for the construction of the dam. Through The Lone Ranger, he organizes a meeting with all the settlers at eight in the morning, to discuss a proposition. But when the settlers begin to arrive at Jim Bradlow's homestead for the meeting, The Lone Ranger and Tonto rode out to discover why Cogswell and his associate, Kale, rode out in the middle of the night. After witnessing the men lighting a fuse and racing away before the dam blew up, a flood of water raced down to the bottom of the canyon where the cabins were clustered. The Lone Ranger took off like the wind across the prairie to warn the men and women to get up on higher ground. The masked man raced out to save young Dan Bradlow, while Tonto raced out to capture the crooks and bring them back, roped and bound, to be turned over to the law for attempted murder.

Notes: Odd that Bradlow claims there is no law within 300 miles when Mustang Mag had received visits from the law many times in the past, and Missouri was a lawman himself.

Episode #1338-554 "YELLOW BOSS" [PART FIVE]

Broadcast August 20, 1941

Copyright Registration #77,263, script received at Registration Office September 4, 1941.

Plot: The ranch of Jennie Crawford and her mother, Abigail, have fallen victim to a gang of crooks who cleaned them out, took all their livestock and the deed to a couple other ranches that Ben Crawford bought up. They even took Pa hostage. Jennie and Abigail would not enlist the law to aid in the recovery of the cattle, in fear of Ben's life. Tonto, having found one of the crooks hiding in the hay loft, knocks Red Beeler out momentarily before questioning him about the gang. After The Lone Ranger let Beeler go, the crook ran into the town café to talk to another crook, Scar, who would ride off to report to the leader of the gang. The boss is keeping Ben alive because he needs his signature on some papers before turning the deeds into cash. Back in town, the masked man worked alongside the sheriff to uncover the identity of the boss. Discovering the clerk at the local hotel moved Beeler to a new room, the masked man recalled an outlaw that found it easier to kill off his men, rather than pay them their share. A killer would be planted in a hotel room and the clerk bribed to change the victim to that room. When The Lone Ranger tips off Beeler to the death trap, Beeler pays a visit to Sawtell, the man who was the boss of the outlaws, leading the law and The Lone Ranger to the man responsible for the kidnapping. After disarming the crooks, the masked man rescued Ben Crawford and Tonto returned to town to report where he found the stolen cattle.

Episode #1339-555 "THE RACE" [PART SIX]

Broadcast August 22, 1941

Copyright Registration #77,264, script received at Registration Office September 4, 1941.

Plot: By now the son of Silver had become used to the saddle and bridle, and now took command from the reins. When The Lone Ranger and Tonto heard a gunshot from the direction of the McLean spread, they raced out to discover Jim McLean, rancher, ordering Brad Rockwell, another rancher, off his land. It seems Rockwell gained the $1,000 note on McLean's land and wants the money by Monday – or he loses the ranch. His only chance to make the money is to win the big race scheduled for Saturday. Two gamblers, Ace Burnett and Eddy Powell, surprise Jim McLean on his way to the corral and knocked him out, giving the rancher the suggestion that they were hired by Rockwell. When Jim rides out to face off against Rockwell, The Lone Ranger intervenes to learn how Jim's fast horse, with even odds against him, was stolen. A confrontation verifies Rockwell's innocence and how someone was trying to frame him. When Jim's horse is mysteriously returned and with a lame leg, The Lone Ranger enters the son of Silver in the race for Jim. The sheriff agrees as the switch does not violate any rules of the race. Ace and Eddy are asked to be judges at the finish line, seeing they are strangers in town, only to find themselves trapped and handcuffed for sabotaging Jim's horse so they could profit from the money they wagered on Rockwell. The race was neck and neck, but the son of Silver won the race, and the masked man rode off after witnessing the sheriff signal that the crooks were under arrest.

Episode #1340-556 "ELECTION DAY AT PLACER"

Broadcast August 25, 1941

Copyright Registration #77,265, script received at Registration Office September 4, 1941.

Plot: This was the same script from the broadcast of October 2, 1935. The only difference is The Lone Ranger making a reference to finding a stable for the son of Silver before venturing into town.

Episode #1341-557 "THE ESCAPE"

Broadcast August 27, 1941

Copyright Registration #77,266, script received at Registration Office September 4, 1941.

Plot: Jonathan Garde, Sally's father, calls himself the sheriff and the judge of Garde County, practically taking the law into his own hands. Garde owns so much land that his fences stretch for miles and posted a guard at each of the 20 gates. For many, this was Garde County and Del, the foreman of the Bar G, was considered the deputy. Del longs to marry Sally, the daughter of his employer, but she does not share the same affection. Tonto rides into the camp of The Lone Ranger, having gone into the town of Osage to get supplies, to report of his sighting of Wild Bill Palmer, Old Brent Palmer's son from Wyoming. Wild Bill's uncle was a sheriff in Claton County, Texas, and his grandfather was the judge. Jonathan Garde believed his father was framed for cattle rustling and when Wild Bill applies for a job at the Bar G, he finds himself condemned to a hanging at daybreak. The Lone Ranger rescues the young man from the vindictive rancher, only to learn Sally is in love with Wild Bill. The lovebirds have to cross the badlands to be married at Fort Cameron, and the race involved Sally riding the son of Silver and jumping over a ravine to take a shortcut. But when Jonathan Garde and a few of his ranch hands arrive outside the fort, they watch as their quarry walked out of the front gates. Del hoped to shoot The Lone Ranger for taking the girl away from him, but Jonathan Garde knocked the foreman off his horse. He won't have anyone trying to commit murder – especially since his daughter went in and out of the fort willingly. The Lone Ranger informs Jonathan Garde that Del was selling the colonel a hundred head of cattle every month. Jonathan wants to perform a hanging but instead the masked man insists the old man has no territorial law and suggested he lodge his complaint to the colonel inside.

Episode #1342-558 "A MAN AND HIS HORSE"
Broadcast August 29, 1941
Copyright Registration #77,267, script received at Registration Office September 4, 1941.
Plot: The Lone Ranger and Tonto had completed the training of the two-year old son of Silver. They went back to Mustang Mag's ranch to return the colt to Missouri. Snake Dawson and Tracy, having finished serving a 30-day jail sentence, schemes to get revenge against the sheriff by poisoning the colt, after witnessing Missouri being gifted the magnificent animal. Late that night they sneak into Mustang Mag's corral and feed the horses cubes of sugar – and the colt gets sugar with poison in it. Roused by Silver's frantic whinnies, Tonto and Mag tended the sick colt while The Lone Ranger and Missouri raced to town for a doctor. While the medic examined the colt, The Lone Ranger and Tonto pressed on northward, on the trail of the badmen, their keen eyes searching out every mark in the sand, every crushed and trampled shrub, every scrape of steel-shod hoofs on barren rock. In confidence, Tracy felt bad about the coward's trick played on Missouri, and admitted he was ashamed. During the dispute, Snake attempted to shoot and kill Tracy, but the masked man arrived in time to disarm him and be forced back to Mustang Mag's ranch. Tracy revealed the bottle of poison Snake administered, assisting the doctor in treating the colt and making sure the son of silver would recover. The crooks are sent to court where The Lone Ranger speaks on behalf of Tracy, moments before the judge pronounces sentencing. The Lone Ranger rides away as Missouri remarks, "Colt, you an' me are pardners from now on, just like th' masked man says! An' whatever name he picks out for yuh, it's goin' tuh be a jim dandy! Yes, sirree!"

Episode #1343-559 "WAGONS ROUND THE MOUNTAIN"
Broadcast September 1, 1941
Copyright Registration #77,268, script received at Registration Office September 4, 1941.
Plot: Outside of the little frontier town of Coyote Run, a town on the overland trail, a freighter named Curley Brewster, known for being a crack shot with his bullwhip, hopes to take away the telegraph contract owned by Rockwell with a newly formed gang. The Lone Ranger, acting on a tip from Tonto who overheard Brewster's plans, raced out to meet Stevens, the engineer, and explain how the outlaws plan to wreck the freight wagons making for the advance camp on the other side of Iron Mountain will meet with sabotage. Stevens explains that if Rockwell does not meet the deadline, anyone – including Brewster – can get the business. Brewster and his men plan to ride down at night like redskins, shooting the horses and burning the wagons and fleeing

before Rockwell and his men know what hit them. Dan, in charge of the freighter, insists that savages, floods or high water, the freight goes through, despite the warnings from the masked man. To ensure reinforcements, The Lone Ranger encourages men from Stevens' camp to ride over the top of the mountain, a necessary and daring shortcut to make it to Dan's freighter in time to put up a defense. The attack was short-lived as Brewster underestimated the number of men ready to defend, or that they would be prepared in advance. The Lone Ranger and Tonto rode from behind to surround the outlaws.

Notes: This script was originally slated for the broadcast of Monday, August 18, but temporarily shelved to make room for the "Son of Silver" story arc.

Episode #1344-560 "LITTLE ROSE"

Broadcast September 3, 1941

Copyright Registration #77,269, script received at Registration Office September 4, 1941.

Plot: While in Sante Fe, Pete Lacey and Pedro Martinez meet a 17-year-old Spanish girl named Rosita Vegas who stands to inherit a valuable land claim, based on evidence held by her scheming guardian. By birthright she is Rosita de Leon and will claim all the land that the King of Spain gave to her family – all of New Mexico. Pete and Pedro send for The Lone Ranger, who then learns a crooked lawyer named John Carter had a judge make him her legal guardian and took her to a big house out of town, making her a prisoner. When an angry mob of hundreds fears they might be evicted from their land if the property is turned over to Rosita as a result of the De Leon land grant, The Lone Ranger races through the mob to rescue the girl. After learning Rosita was adopted, The Lone Ranger asks Judge Moreland to postpone a decision for a month so he can ride all the way to California to find Senora Vegas, who can testify her daughter was killed by Indians and Rosita was merely adopted. One month later, in the courtroom, the crooked lawyer finds his plans thwarted when the old woman testifies that Rosita is not heir to the land grant. The lawyer will be taken into custody for his attempted fraud and Rosita will be free to marry the man she loves without the burden of a land grant on her shoulders.

Notes: This episode was originally slated for the broadcast of August 20.

Episode #1345-561 "TWO SHERIFFS ARE BETTER THAN ONE"

Broadcast September 5, 1941

Copyright Registration #77,270, script received at Registration Office September 4, 1941.

Plot: The western town of Blue Rock was in the grip of a lawless element – a badman named Kelvin, best described as an outlaw, a gambler and a killer all-in-one. The Lone Ranger saves Sheriff Shannon from an ambush, during a showdown in the streets, where Kelvin had his men off the side ready to shoot the lawman in the back. The first two sheriffs were shot and killed in a similar manner. The third, Lem Douglas, quit his job on account of his wife. When Kelvin pays Douglas a visit to state no one sits on the fence, he encourages the former lawman to help burn out a group of settlers from the East who chose a section of free land below the dry wash. The Lone Ranger and Tonto, meanwhile, scouted the region to get familiar with the territory, knowing a direct attack against Kelvin would not be possible – the outlaw has too many men on his side. But the scheme Kelvin has in mind is nothing but a trap to kill the men who opposed him, destroying the dam to send a wall of water pouring through the dry wash like a stampede of buffalo. After the dam blows, The Lone Ranger and Tonto race to warn Shannon and Douglas, then races out to warn the settlers to escape. With the men and women backing in numbers, The Lone Ranger turns the tide against Kelvin and his men who find themselves unexpectedly surrounded. The quick shooting of the masked man disarms the outlaws, and the Kelvin and his gang are taken to jail.

Notes: This episode was originally slated for August 8, then rescheduled for August 15.

Episode #1346-562 "TWO MEN FOR ONE CRIME"

Broadcast September 8, 1941

Copyright Registration #77,271, script received at Registration Office September 4, 1941.

Plot: Someone last night held up Pete Dekler and stole his monthly cowhand payroll. The sheriff and his deputies, having trailed the thief along the Chisholm Trail, came across two men in possession of the money. Jack Crayton, an unsuspecting cowboy, insists he is innocent and the other man, Winters, handed him the stolen cash. The sheriff decides to put both in jail until he can figure out which is the real culprit. For several days the sheriff and his deputies tried to discover which of the two men was the outlaw, but they learned nothing further. Winters, a deadly outlaw, was really named Storm and his gang forms a jailbreak, murdering the sheriff and taking Crayton prisoner, conveying the innocent man was guilty. Having trailed the outlaws to their hideout, The Lone Ranger asks Tonto to join the gang so he can keep an eye on Crayton and make sure he does not get killed. The masked man, meanwhile, rides into town and when Deputy Malden insists the masked man is part of the outlaw gang, they take pursuit, unaware they are being led to the outlaws' camp. Crayton is cleared of any wrongdoing, who was tied and bound alongside Tonto.

Episode #1347-563 "BAIT FOR THE TRAP"

Broadcast September 10, 1941

Copyright Registration #77,272, script received at Registration Office September 4, 1941.

Plot: A feisty old-timer named Higgens was a passenger when the stagecoach was stopped. With the guard and driver shot, he alone fights off a gang of stage robbers until The Lone Ranger and Tonto arrive to back his play. Higgens, however, takes the money that the crooks failed to get so the crooks would take the blame. The Lone Ranger visits town to question the local sheriff and discovers the old timer is really setting himself up as bait in a dangerous trap, with the hope the thieves would hunt him down to get it and give him a chance to shoot it out with them. The Lone Ranger arranges for Tonto to rope the old man so they can save his life and create a trap of their own. The sheriff and his deputy, meanwhile, saw the tracks at the scene of the attack and theorize an Indian that wore moccasins was responsible for the stagecoach robbery. When word leaks through the streets that Higgens was killed by an Indian – and probably the same sought by the sheriff, Tonto is apprehended and jailed for a hanging in the morning. Believing Higgens is dead, Steve and Norton, the crooks responsible for the attempted stagecoach robbery, visit the old man's house in search of the money... giving themselves away when The Lone Ranger places them into custody. In the morning, before the scheduled hanging, the masked man brought the crooks into town, along with Higgens. The charge of murder was promptly dropped against Tonto. The crooks plead for their innocence until The Lone Ranger reveals the stolen cash in their possession.

Episode #1348-564 "THE FENCE"

Broadcast September 12, 1941

Copyright Registration #77,273, script received at Registration Office September 4, 1941.

Written by Tom Dougall.

Plot: In and around the town of Buffalo Pass, the days of the open range are over, and it will be difficult to make the ranchers face the future. The Circle Bar is the biggest outfit and when a young rancher named Ray Gordon faces the end of the open range and prepares to fence his land, he meets violent opposition from his fellow cattleman. On top of which, Sunshine, a pessimistic old timer and one of the ranch hands, almost becomes the victim of drygulchers, led by the crooked Sheriff Bill Kendall. It doesn't take long for the men of the Circle Bar to discover the sheriff leads a gang of night riders. But when Ray is taken prisoner, Sunshine follows instructions from The Lone Ranger to organize a posse. Thanks to Tonto's tracking skills, the outlaws' camp is discovered and revealed, the crooks, including the crooked sheriff and the outlaw leader named Bat, are taken into custody. Tex, one of the ranch hands of the Circle Bar, is promoted to the role of sheriff and the masked man suggests everyone listen to Ray as he tells the story of what happened in Spring Valley some time ago, when the ranchers would not lease out the property to the farmers – explaining why the fence is needed.

Episode #1349-565 "TRAVELERS SPRING"

Broadcast September 15, 1941

Copyright Registration #77,505, script received at Registration Office September 24, 1941.

Plot: The Lone Ranger and Tonto, having made their camp in a grove of cottonwoods near Eagle Point, receive a visit from young Bob Blake, who just turned 21 and longs for action and excitement. Bob, having left his parents' homestead outside the town of Meadville, inadvertently joins a gang of outlaws led by the notorious Mike Ward. The masked man and Indian sneak into the outlaws' camp late one night to rescue Bob, in the hopes of saving the young man from the first step on the road to crime, repeating the same mistake his father made many years back. Mike Ward, and his associate, Joe, organize the gang into attacking a wagon train. When the masked man learns the wagon train features the Blake family, he arranges for Bob to discover the news, convincing the young man to race in the face of gunfire to warn the wagon train. The men and women from the wagon train, having been tipped off, joined the masked man in a secret ambush, getting the upper hand against the outlaws. His father, having held a long-kept secret that he was once a criminal himself, understood the boy's wild oats and forgave him for leaving.

Notes: This episode was originally slated for broadcast on Friday, September 19, 1941.

Episode #1350-566 "THE RANGER BEATS THE ROPE"

Broadcast September 17, 1941

Copyright Registration #77,506, script received at Registration Office September 24, 1941.

Plot: A young man named Tod Graham is framed for a killing, found guilty in a court of law and sentenced to hang on Tuesday. The Lone Ranger, having found evidence that verifies he was framed, prevails on the local sheriff of Buffalo Gap to send for a stay of execution from the local governor in order to aid the condemned prisoner. Clench, the real killer, hopes the case is closed shut after the hanging but upon learning of the news, arranges with his accomplice, Spider, to waylay Dudley, a friend of Tod's who happens to be the pony express rider carrying the stay of execution. The crooks ride toward Osage to ambush the young man when Dudley heads back to town. The crooks trip the pony express rider, leaving Dudley unconscious long enough to steal the official papers and leave, making Dudley think his horse stepped into a gopher hole and tripped. The Lone Ranger and Tonto, figuring the trick the outlaws used to cover their tracks, caught up with them moments after they stole the pardon. After shooting and disarming the crooks, the masked man races back in time to deliver the pardon just moments before the hanging.

Episode #1351-567 "TONTO TAKES CHARGE"

Broadcast September 19, 1941

Copyright Registration #77,507, script received at Registration Office September 24, 1941.

Plot: A notorious smuggling ring led by "Black Jack," struck terror to the hearts of many pioneers. Black Jack was also known in town as Jim Jackson, the assistant to the U.S. Marshal. An outlaw named Blake was Black Jack's associate; he and other members of the smuggler band made a pretense of ranching to cover their real activities. The Lone Ranger hoped to trap the leader of the gang of smugglers with evidence that would convict. He allowed himself to be captured (while in disguise), but not before he gave instructions for Tonto and Missouri to be captured by the rest of the gang. The letter in Tonto's pocket revealed to the outlaw gang the true identity of Black Jack, which Jim Jackson strongly insisted to Blake never be learned. Back in Black Jack's cabin on Sandwich Hill, The Lone Ranger was questioned endlessly by Black Jack, whose rage and fury mounted with the continued refusal of the mystery man to give any information. The outlaws, eager to verify the identity of Black Jack, race up to Sandwich Hill. After seeking a masked man at the cabin, the outlaws shoot and kill the man they thought was The Lone Ranger. With the U.S. Marshal and a posse on one side and The Lone Ranger on the other, with Tonto and Missouri in the middle, the outlaws are rounded up and taken into custody. Missouri, glad to know The Lone Ranger was not shot and killed, rides back to his ranch on the Son of Silver, to meet with Mustang Mag and tell her of his adventure.

Notes: It sounds as if Brace Beemer was not in the studio during the broadcast; possibly a recording. Brace Beemer has little to do or say in this script, about four lines total.

Episode #1352-568 "IT'S A FREE COUNTRY"

Broadcast September 22, 1941

Copyright Registration #77,508, script received at Registration Office September 24, 1941.

Plot: The Lone Ranger and Tonto were riding the range in the middle of the night when they see a lighted cabin and shots indicating a shooting scrape. A gang of hooded riders, ranchers with a disposition against nesters, threaten to drive Jim Fletcher and his wife away. Jim's wife, Caroline, insists this is a free country but not according to the hooded riders who wounded Jim. After Tonto mended the wounds and assured Caroline that Jim would survive, one of the hooded men returns the next day to finish Jim off – only to face the wrath of The Lone Ranger. The men are cowards, according to the masked man, because they believe in mob violence – but are apt to be more dangerous than a den of rattlesnakes. The Lone Ranger and Tonto follow the trail of the hooded men and learn the identity of the mod leaders, Sharell and Jasper, tough and influential ranchers. The masked man kidnaps Sharell to have a conversation with him and convince the rancher to see the side of the homesteaders. They have rights, too. This is America, the masked man explains, where every man has rights. Meanwhile, Jasper arranges for the cattlemen to create a stampede that would ride through the canyon leaving a trail of destruction so there would not be enough left of the cabin to take notice. The Lone Ranger and Tonto race to the rescue and help apprehend Jasper and Crowder who schemed the stampede, with their hands tied behind their back, headed for jail. Sharell apologizes to the homesteaders and assures them that they can stay on the land they chose.

Notes: The name of Jim Fletcher is a tip-of-the-hat to the radio actor of the same name.

Episode #1353-569 "WINTER RESCUE"

Broadcast September 24, 1941

Copyright Registration #77,509, script received at Registration Office September 24, 1941.

Written by Tom Dougall.

Plot: Soon after the cabins were built in White River Valley, just south of the ridge, the Circle Bar trail herds reached Grantville. Half were driven onto the Ed Norton range, while half were held in a sheltered valley nearer the town. Then every week Thundercloud received his ration of beef, but only half enough to feed his people. With the first snowfall of the winter, the game disappeared from the north side of the ridge and the Indian camp was faced with slow starvation, unaware a crooked Indian agent named Lew Grady was cheating the tribe out of their winter ration of beef. It only takes a few weeks for Bill Connors, the foreman on the ranch, to discover the crooked scheme and quit Ed Norton, Grady's confederate. When the Indians surround the cabin in search of vengeance, especially after Ed Norton shot and wounded an Indian, The Lone Ranger intervenes and asks Chief Thundercloud for a temporary parlay so he could fetch the law. The Indian chief agrees for 24 hours, and the masked man fetches Walters, a U.S. Marshal. When the threat of facing the Indians appears worse than jail time, Ed Norton and Lew Grady confess their crime. Sharon Day, Norton's stepdaughter, was to inherit the ranch when she marries and Bill Connors, who stood up against Ed Norton when he learned of the crooked scheme, will remain not just as foreman, but as her husband.

Notes: This script was originally titled "Winter Siege," changed during rehearsals.

Episode #1354-570 "A NEW RECORD"

Broadcast September 26, 1941

Copyright Registration #77,510, script received at Registration Office September 24, 1941.

Plot: The Lone Ranger dons a disguise to ride shotgun on the stage carrying gold to Rapids City. The same stage has been held up two or three times a month, like clockwork, and the insurance company is causing the premiums to go high. Bob Sherman, the old timer who drove the stage, is innocent but when the disguised Lone Ranger is introduced to Link Carey, the crooked express agent, the truth becomes known. Their new compatriot is instructed on how to be a hero on the next stage run, gaining confidence of the passengers and once folks start shipping valuables again, they will go on to a big job. The Lone Ranger, claiming to be bad man Lefty Collins, almost gets in with the gang to get evidence against the band of road agents until the real Lefty shows up. Thanks to Tonto, The Lone Ranger made a swift escape and outran the posse. Armed with the info he acquired, and assistance of the sheriff, The Lone Ranger employs honest Bob Sherman to help trap and capture the road agents. Three days later the gold was loaded onto the stage at Deerfield and Bob was tipped off to the ambush. As the outlaws raced through the pass, the sheriff and his men closed in from both sides of the trail with their guns blazing. Completely taken by surprise, the gang was unable to put up any resistance, and five minutes later the sheriff ripped the bandana from the leader's face… Link Carey.

Episode #1355-571 "THE TRAIN ROBBERY"

Broadcast September 29, 1941

Copyright Registration #77,511, script received at Registration Office September 24, 1941.

Plot: Dan Jagger and Rod Cummings, outlaws, tricked Red Crow and his murderous tribe into attacking a locomotive and stealing a cannon that was being sent to Fort Galloway. The passengers were slaughtered during the pillage, leaving the cash on board ripe for the two outlaws. Despite The Lone Ranger's attempt to prevent the train from being wrecked and the passengers slaughtered, his efforts only succeeded in rescuing two survivors: Jack Rogers, a young lieutenant, and his fiancé, Mary. Leaving Tonto behind to scout over the scene, The Lone Ranger attempts to warn the soldiers at Fort Galloway before the Indians besiege. But the fort has little powder to waste and outside, the Indians are trying to learn how to work the cannon to smash the fort to bits. Jack fetches the only dry keg of powder and delivers it to The Lone Ranger, then races to the fort to deliver plans. Following the suggestion of the masked man, at dawn the gate opens and the bugle sounds as the soldiers ride out to attack. Using the keg of gunpowder, The Lone Ranger and Tonto blow up the gunpowder so the Indians could not use the cannon, and the soldiers capture the warriors without firing a single shot.

Episode #1356-572 "HOUSE AND HOME"

Broadcast October 1, 1941

Copyright Registration #77,512, script received at Registration Office September 24, 1941.

Plot: When Jeff Carruthers got his section of land proved up and homesteaded, the first thing he did was arrange to build a decent-sized house in place of the cabin he'd lived in for a year. The community house-raising is interrupted, however, when a crook named Dawson arrives with the sheriff, to claim he homesteaded three years prior – and has the law to back him. It turns out the crooked land agent named Sully was involved in the scheme and when The Lone Ranger learns of the news, he suspects this is the same Sully up near Pecos who once was suspected of using his office to grab land for himself. The Lone Ranger and Tonto allow the sheriff to arrest them and put them into the jailhouse to be used as bait. Sully, aware that there was gold on the property, wanted the masked man and Indian out of the way to prevent them from spilling the info. Moments after Sully fired and shot at The Lone Ranger and Tonto, he discovered he shot up bundled up bed clothes in the jail cell. The masked man races off to rescue the sheriff from Dawson, who planned to leave the lawman's body on the Canyon trail. Moments after The Lone Ranger rescues the sheriff, the posse arrives to take Dawson back to town.

Episode #1357-573 "RELIEF TRAIN"
Broadcast October 3, 1941
Copyright Registration #77,513, script received at Registration Office September 24, 1941.
Plot: The Lone Ranger asks Jim Sheridan of Nebraska City to help lead a wagon train loaded with relief supplies for a starvation camp that has (at best) one month to live. Just as the frost is getting out of the ground and the creeks becoming raging torrents, Jim and his assistant, Bill Rogers, were up for the challenge… especially as The Lone Ranger and Tonto promise to act as advance scouts for the train. With 28 wagons, 300 oxen and 50 horses, no finer outfit ever left Nebraska City. Conspiring with an outlaw named Marty, the commissary chief, Joe Corby, arranges for a fake message to be delivered to the relief train from The Lone Ranger, misdirecting the train from the Platte, cutting south and heading for St. Francis, where they would ultimately fall victim to Red Fox and his Comanche tribe. Marty would profit from the gold; Red Fox just wants the ammunition. When the masked man learns of what happened, he sends Tonto to warn Sheridan while The Lone Ranger rides out to fetch the cavalry from St. Francis. The Indian drew a tight circle around the train as the men and women put up a good fight to hold off the attacking Comanches. Soon after the colonel arrived with The Lone Ranger, Red Fox and his tribe found themselves caught between two fires. The Indians were forced to throw down their arms and the soldiers made Corby, Red Fox and Marty prisoners.

Blooper! One of the actors mispronounced Kearney, Nebraska.

Episode #1358-574 "LOSER TAKE ALL"
Broadcast October 6, 1941
Copyright Registration #77,514, script received at Registration Office September 24, 1941.
Plot: A young man named Jerry Leigh seeks The Lone Ranger's advice on trying to mine for gold in Virginia City, especially when he strikes it rich on Lookout Hill. Having kept tabs on a slick confidence man named Karl Miller, the masked man encourages Jerry to strike a partnership with the crook, with Jerry insisting on 50 percent ownership of stock of Nugget Mountain and complete charge of the mining operations. Miller, behind Jerry's back, begins to sell bogus stock to unsuspecting investors, a half interest to six different people. Later, when the mine starts to pan out, Miller finds himself in a situation. His first attempt was to hire his confederate, Al Norton, to create an accident with dynamite – but the accident unearths a larger vein of gold. Desperate, Miller orders Al to hire a gunman named Lefty Dawson to shoot and kill Jerry. The Lone Ranger takes matters into his own hands by placing Miller into the marksman's fold, causing Miller to sweat it out and confess in order to save his own life. Only Miller was shocked to learn afterwards that Lefty was merely Sheriff Parks, lurking in the shadows, who orders his men to arrest the two crooks for attempted murder.

Episode #1359-575 "WIRES AND HOOFS"
Broadcast October 8, 1941
Copyright Registration #77,786, script received at Registration Office October 17, 1941.
Plot: Old Jared Danbury owned a ranch that stretched straight across Antelope Valley. In spite of the fact that the valley was the most direct route between Carson City and the west, Jared forced travelers to go the

long way around, letting nobody use his property for a thoroughfare. When young Bill Slater, field engineer in charge of stringing up the new telegraph line, learns of this fact the hard way, he finds himself putting in a complaint and a court order to go through the land. But when his daughter, Marybelle, runs out of life-saving medicine, the old man discovers only the telegraph, and the strength of the great horse Silver can save her. If it was not for the telegraph, news of her needing medicine would have taken an additional day – and one day too late. Onward across the plains flashed the great horse, his silver-shod hoofs pounding the prairie as The Lone Ranger urged him forward, from Carson City toward the ranch in the distant valley. Old Jared, grateful for the telegraph getting the message through, orders the men to string up the wire through his land – even offering to help do it himself.

Episode #1360-576 "THE KNIFE"

Broadcast October 10, 1941

Copyright Registration #77,787, script received at Registration Office October 17, 1941.

Plot: Sheriff Collier of Deadwood Gulch murders a man in a card game to further plans to cheat a mine owner out of his property by withholding water rights. Tom Hamlin, who supplied the miners on the bench land with water, was knifed to death. Larry Lawler, a young miner who made the biggest strike in the last six months, was accused of the crime. When Tonto is arrested and accused of murder, The Lone Ranger helps him escape from jail and then circles back to investigate papers in the sheriff's office to discover how Blacky Leonard, a gambler, Matt Sheldon, a political boss, and the sheriff conspired together. When Tonto recognizes carvings on the knife handle as that from Kiowa country, The Lone Ranger rides out to that part of the country to fetch a Federal Marshal from the office of the U.S. at San Fernando. After browsing wanted circulars in the marshal's office, The Lone Ranger verifies the sheriff is Bat Connor, wanted in San Fernando for a murder and a bank robbery. A confrontation in Deadwood Gulch reveals the guilt of all three men, saving Larry's life from a hangman's noose.

Episode #1361-577 "A NEW MISSION" [PART ONE]

Broadcast October 13, 1941

Copyright Registration #77,788, script received at Registration Office October 17, 1941.

Plot: See pages 263 to 265.

Notes: The front page of this radio script states: "The first of a new series which deals in 'long-range' plots."

Episode #1362-578 "OUTLAWS PLAN AN EMPIRE" [PART TWO]

Broadcast October 15, 1941

Copyright Registration #77,789, script received at Registration Office October 17, 1941.

Plot: Major Connel tells of a secret legion of badmen who plot revolt against the United States. The President puts his trust in The Lone Ranger, who is ordered to smoke out the "Legion of the Black Arrow." Army intelligence staff sent out four men, secretly and separately. The last one to go forth was Major Connel, who posed as a gunfighter. He meant to start out from Fort Laramie. He disappeared and like his predecessors, was never heard from again. Tonto managed to find Connel, crawling on the ground, barely on the fringe of life. With the aid of Tonto's Indian medicine and food, the exhausted major regained some of his strength. When he was well enough, he revealed what he learned from his investigation, having been kidnapped and blindfolded to the secret lair, and managed to escape. Armed with a secret commission from the President of the United States, The Lone Ranger raced across the plains to the west of St. Louis; his faithful Indian companion, Tonto, rode at his side. On and on they rode, on toward the hidden stronghold of the Legion of the Black Arrow. The stronghold was supposedly in a cave somewhere hidden in the mountains. Knowing every member of the Legion carried the mark of a black arrow on his wrist, The Lone Ranger theorized that members of the Black

Arrow must have to report to headquarters from time to time. If they could find one of those members and follow them, the hideout would be revealed.

Episode #1363-579 "FIRST ENCOUNTER" [PART THREE]

Broadcast October 17, 1941

Copyright Registration #77,790, script received at Registration Office October 17, 1941.

Plot: An outlaw named Flint reported to Torlock that the President of the United States sent out word to locate The Lone Ranger and two months prior they met in St. Louis. The government did not know much about The Legion of the Black Arrow in Washington, just their name and what they stood for. But The Lone Ranger has been assigned the task to locate their hideout and smash their operations. Torlock and Flint hatch a scheme to have General Cartwright at Fort Lincoln disgraced and recalled to Washington. A crook named Flint managed to have himself recruited under the name of Everett, then helped Torlock mastermind the robbery of a gold shipment. The great covered wagon started out with a detachment of soldiers riding alongside but was called back when The Lone Ranger and Tonto thwarted the outlaws. During the courtroom trial, Flint claimed he was acting under orders from the General. Before charges could be filed against the innocent General of Fort Lincoln, The Lone Ranger schemes a fake note to Flint asking him to recall his testimony and Flint retracts his statement, maintaining the General's innocence. The next morning Flint was found dead in his cell, poisoned from the drink in a flask that was handed to him through cell bars the night before. Torlock, the most important member of the gang, escapes.

Episode #1364-580 "THE BRIDGE" [PART FOUR]

Broadcast October 20, 1941

Copyright Registration #77,791, script received at Registration Office October 17, 1941.

Plot: The Lone Ranger became convinced that a man named Torlock was one of the more important members of the Legion of the Black Arrow so he and Tonto followed his trail from Fort Lincoln. It led them to Phillipsburg, where they paid a visit to Sheriff Brady who confirms and a man fitting Torlock's description (tall and dark, with a black mustache and black eyes),

arrived the other day but referred to himself as an engineer, going to Cottonwood Canyon to take a look at the railroad bridge that was built across it. The Lone Ranger and Tonto followed the trail and stepped into the clearing at the foot of Eagle Point, where the railroad bridge spanned Cottonwood Canyon at its narrowest point. It was just a month after its completion and Torlock planned for the destruction of the bridge to thwart officials who were to be passengers on a train from Meredith. Racing out to the bridge late at night, The Lone Ranger, Tonto and the sheriff witness a number of men working under the light of torches, planting kegs of gunpowder under the bridge. The posse closed in as the outlaws were driven out on the bridge. They could see the train charging toward them and finally in desperation threw down their guns and with their hands held high, ran toward the posse and the canyon's rim to escape the oncoming locomotive. But The Lone Ranger saw one man disappear below the rim and he leaped from Silver to follow him. But the sheriff pulls a gun on The Lone Ranger… even if The Lone Ranger saves the bridge, Sheriff Brady has his orders because he was a member of the Legion of the Black Arrow.

Notes: Torlock told the sheriff his name was Cavendish, an alias to hide his real name.

Episode #1365-581 "UNITED WE STAND" [PART FIVE]

Broadcast October 22, 1941

Copyright Registration #77,792, script received at Registration Office October 17, 1941.

Plot: Before he could have The Lone Ranger shot and unmasked, the sheriff was forced to flee because of

Tonto coming to the rescue. When dawn came, The Lone Ranger and Tonto discovered one of their horses was wounded and pursuit would have to wait a few days until the wound heals. Meanwhile, Torlock ordered Sheriff Brady to Virginia City, Montana, where certain delegates of the territory plan to make Montana a state of the union. Montana is ripe for the Legion, and to prevent statehood, Brady is sent to assist Craddock, another member of the Legion, to intimidate some of the seven men in town (in particular, Donald and Hanson) who were scheduled to vote on whether Montana should apply for admission to the union as a state. When Brady and Craddock realize Tonto overheard their plans, they let the masked man assume they were going through with their scheme and instead kidnapped two other men, Moreland and Petrie. The whole gang headed along Needle Trail. At breakneck speed the great stallion and the paint horse raced through the darkness, cutting across the country to Needle Trail, catching the outlaws by surprise and rescuing the two delegates who arrive in time to place their votes.

Notes: Montana did not become a state until 1889.

Episode #1366-582 "HEADLINES ON THE FRONTIER" [PART SIX]
Broadcast October 24, 1941
Copyright Registration #77,793, script received at Registration Office October 17, 1941.
Plot: Stephen Hayden, a newspaper editor in St. Louis, is coming west to Bennett City. The Black Arrow disapproves of his progressive ideas in the Frontier Times, which reports in his editorials that if the Indians were treated fairly, the white men would have no further trouble with them. Torlock and Craddock kidnap Hayden and his daughter, Mary, so Craddock can masquerade as the new editor of the paper in Bennett City, with Judith (a member of his gang) impersonating the role of Mary. News of the Indian unrest brought The Lone Ranger and Tonto riding south from Helena on the trail of Torlock and Craddock, then on to Bennett City. The crooks plan to use the Frontier Times to start an Indian war with Chief Thundercloud and his tribe. Linda tries to convince the townsfolk that she was attacked by Thundercloud's tribe and Craddock prints an extra edition to call on every decent man to ride against Thundercloud's tribe and wipe them out. The Lone Ranger and Tonto rescues Stephen and his daughter from the camp where the Black Arrow was holding them prisoners. With assistance from the local sheriff, the imposters are called out and apprehended. The Lone Ranger and Tonto, riding out of town, discover their efforts to prevent a war may have been futile when a man falls victim to having his ranch burned to the ground, claiming Torlock and Chief Thundercloud were responsible.

Notes: It is referenced that the leader of the Black Arrow refers to Judith as "The Flame," and it was not a compliment, because when she flares up, she was apt to lose her good judgment and act on impulse.

Episode #1367-583 "THE MAGIC BELT" [PART SEVEN]
Broadcast October 27, 1941
Copyright Registration #78,197, script received at Registration Office November 7, 1941.
Plot: Running Wolf, a brave loyal to Chief Thundercloud, gets word to The Lone Ranger. Thundercloud's tribe has been taken over by Tomahawk, a bad Indian who is in reality working with the Black Arrow. Thundercloud knew Tomahawk was a fool, being led astray by the men outside of their tribe. But Thundercloud's men turned against him, forcing The Lone Ranger and Tonto to sneak into the Indian village and conduct a daring rescue of the Indian Chief. Miles away from the village, Thundercloud tells the masked man that the only way to thwart Tomahawk is to retrieve the magic belt which is the symbol of his authority over the warriors. "With the belt, my braves will once more respect me as their chief," Thundercloud explains, "for the belt is mighty medicine, respected and revered by every red man." The magic belt was given to a medicine man for safekeeping so they must venture to Finger Mountain and seek out Kadotah, the medicine man, keeper of the belt.

Notes: The radio script labels this was Number 7 in the Black Arrow series and Number 1 in the Magic Belt series.

Episode #1368-584 "SENTINEL ROCK" [PART EIGHT]

Broadcast October 29, 1941

Copyright Registration #78,198, script received at Registration Office November 7, 1941.

Plot: As The Lone Ranger, Tonto and Chief Thundercloud headed for Finger Mountain to find the magic belt and regain the leadership of the tribe for Thundercloud, they were unaware that the Black Arrow knew of their mission. It was on the third day of their journey when they came across the homestead of Jim Blaine, a trapper, and learned that Torlock, Turner and other members of the Black Arrow are ahead of them in a race to get to Finger Mountain first. Torlock arranged for Linda to be bound to a tree in the forest, subjected to the potential threat of a mountain lion, momentarily slowing down his pursuers. Meanwhile, Torlock and Turner find the tepee of Kadotah, friend of Chief Thundercloud, only to discover they are unable to trick him into revealing the hiding place of the magic belt. With the life of Chief Thundercloud threatened, Kadotah is forced to reveal the hiding place of the magic belt. As Torlock and his men rode on toward Finger Mountain, confident that The Lone Ranger, Tonto and Chief Thundercloud were killed by the falling rock and the avalanche that follows in its wake, after having lit a fuse and blew up kegs of dynamite in a trap set for The Lone Ranger, he was unaware that the heroes hid under the overhang of a cliff that gave protection.

Episode #1369-585 "FIRE IN THE NIGHT" [PART NINE]

Broadcast October 31, 1941

Copyright Registration #78,199, script received at Registration Office November 7, 1941.

Plot: Having located the medicine man of Finger Mountain and saved him from a gang of outlaws, only to discover that he had already been forced to reveal the hiding place of Chief Thundercloud's magic belt, The Lone Ranger raced against the group of outlaws who were already halfway up Finger Mountain to get the belt. On top of Silver, the masked man jumped across the Black Gorge to beat the outlaws to the magic belt. After returning the belt to Chief Thundercloud, The Lone Ranger and Tonto observe Kadotah's choice to remain home on Finger Mountain. The outlaws will trouble him no more. Rationalizing that the Indians have never seen the magic belt, Torlock's only remaining chance for widespread Indian revolt was to use a false belt in place of the real one. Regardless of the fact that the magic belt was returned to Chief Thundercloud, but Torlock creates an imitation belt from decaying wood known as foxfire, fastened to a strap of leather. In the darkness, Tomahawk puts it on and tricks the assembled Indian braves into launching an attack on Fort Lariat. Once started, it will be too late to stop and the war against the white man will spread throughout the whole west.

Notes: The announcer described the magic belt, a giveaway premium, with dramatic appeal. "His groping hand touched the heavy belt, secure in its hiding place. He drew it forth. Even with beads of water clinging to it, the stones in the ancient belt glowed and sparkled with a magic shine! …(later)… As the old chief rode off, he turned once more toward the masked man and Tonto. In the darkness, the magic belt glowed and sparkled with a secret light, shining like the stars in the sky above them!" Chief Thundercloud's magic belt would later become the temporary property of The Lone Ranger again in September of 1942 for another story arc.

Episode #1370-586 "DARK OF THE MOON" [PART TEN]

Broadcast November 3, 1941

Copyright Registration #78,200, script received at Registration Office November 7, 1941.

Plot: The Lone Ranger and Tonto, realizing that only Chief Thundercloud and the real belt can prevent the Indian uprising, raced across the badlands in the direction of Thundercloud's village. Captured by soldiers on the prairie, the masked man and Tonto are taken to the Colonel who at first will not listen to their pleas. Only after The Lone Ranger shows his letter from President Grant to verify his story and seek cooperation will the Colonel assist them. Knowing the Indians will not attack for three days, not until the dark of the moon, The Lone Ranger hatches a desperate plan to use Thundercloud and the real belt. The Indians, meanwhile, followed the instructions of the renegade, Red Fox, as they watched the imposter and the fake belt glow in the dark. But during the stampede of Indians toward the Fort, The Lone Ranger arranges for Chief Thundercloud to be seen from a distance and the charade exposed. The fact that Thundercloud's belt was much brighter was enough to convince the Indians that they were misled. The Colonel, having followed The Lone Ranger's orders, verified he held a pipe of peace in his hands, not a gun, verifying the white men were friends and not enemies.

Notes: According to the radio script, this would serve as the fourth and final chapter in the Magic Belt series, but also the tenth episode of the Black Arrow series.

Episode #1371-587 "WRONG PARTNERS" [PART ELEVEN]

Broadcast November 5, 1941

Copyright Registration #78,201, script received at Registration Office November 7, 1941.

Plot: When The Lone Ranger and Tonto interrupt a quarrel between a testy prospector named Chandler, and two crooked prospectors named Trench and Slagle, it initially appeared to be a simple argument over a gold claim. But soon the situation develops that two of the three men planned to sell the claim to Torlock, an agent for the Black Arrow, who wants to gain control of the gold strike in the hills. No sooner was The Lone Ranger in the town of Brazos and in an empty room at the Longhorn Café to find the man to whom Trench gave the map of the location of the gold strike, Torlock raised the cry of "outlaw" and every man below rushed up the stairs, guns drawn and ready. The Lone Ranger narrowly escaped with his life. Assisting Chandler from losing his claim, The Lone Ranger circles behind the crooks while Chandler sets off a volley of shots as a distraction. With Trench and Slagle apprehended, tied up and taken to the law in Brazos, The Lone Ranger and Tonto set out to apprehend Torlock.

Episode #1372-588 "RICHMOND STAGE" [PART TWELVE]

Broadcast November 7, 1941

Copyright Registration #78,202, script received at Registration Office November 7, 1941.

Plot: Making camp outside of Richmond City, The Lone Ranger observes a woman named Karen taking on a job singing at the local saloon – the same woman who was working for the Black Arrow in Bennett City. In private, Karen discusses with a crooked rancher named Bart Rivers how he can become the new sheriff in town. Torlock schemed to have Maria, the wife of Silas Mason, threatened to make the man lease his grazing land to an agent of the Black Arrow. Bob Crawford of the Bar C was also the sheriff and his lease with Silas was coming up for renewal in a few days. Without a renewal, he would be forced to sell his stock at a dead loss or drive it farther west where there was open range… opening the position of sheriff for Bart. With promise for assistance in the kidnapping, Bart must pledge allegiance to the Black Arrow. After rescuing Silas Mason, The Lone Ranger learns of the news and rides out with Bob Crawford and a posse to intercept the stagecoach carrying Maria. With Maria's horse alongside them, the men explain what happened and encourage her to ride alongside them so the intended robbery up ahead along the trail would not succeed. The unexpected attack from the stage took the outlaws by surprise. The Lone Ranger opened fire and once more the outlaws were forced to rein up. As the posse closed in, the outlaws knew their last chance for escape was gone. One of the masked bandits was Trench, so another member of the Black Arrow was taken into custody.

Episode #1373-589 "SETTLERS FOR BUFFALO VALLEY" [PART THIRTEEN]

Broadcast November 10, 1941

Copyright Registration #78,203, script received at Registration Office November 7, 1941.

Plot: Torlock explains to Dekker, another member of the Black Arrow, that he wants to destroy the Buffalo Valley wagon train. The government just opened up the valley and the first wagon train left Culver City. Torlock wants to prevent the valley from getting settled. All day long The Lone Ranger and Tonto rode around the floor of the ravine looking for a possible way out, but they could see none. The outlaws would be able to destroy the wagon train unhindered. After sunset, using a lariat, our heroes manage to find a way out of the ravine. After threatening the guard who fell asleep by the campfire, The Lone Ranger learns that the outlaws plan to attack the wagon train when it makes camp at Blue Run, with a wagon full of kerosene and an open flame. The Lone Ranger and Tonto race out to aid in rescue, arriving before Torlock's men could strike, and snuck into camp to explain the situation with Bill, one of the settlers in the wagon train. Bill quietly wakes every man in the wagon train who take up arms and wait as Tonto and The Lone Ranger approach the outlaws from a different direction. Desperately the outlaws tried to defend themselves, but they were outlined against the flames – easy targets for the men from the wagon train led by The Lone Ranger. In a few minutes the outlaws saw how useless it was and the fight was over.

Episode #1374-590 "DODGE CITY ROUND UP" [PART FOURTEEN]

Broadcast November 12, 1941

Copyright Registration #78,204, script received at Registration Office November 7, 1941.

Plot: Hoping to escape The Lone Ranger, Torlock takes cover with a trail crew headed for Dodge City. Torlock traveled with Jed Fulton and his trail crew as far as Dodge City, but even before the herd had been bedded down, he said goodbye to Fulton and rode into the roaring, booming market town by himself. Having witnessed 4,000 head of cattle in the drive, Torlock visits Al Brent, a crooked cattle buyer in town, to break the market for steers and purchase the cattle at a steal. To arrange for false quotations to be posted, the men scheme to eliminate Johnny Day, a young telegraph operator. With livestock quotations coming through from Chicago, it was Johnny's job to write them out and post them on the bulletin board first thing in the morning. Johnny was shot and wounded. It was Ann Everett who had seen The Lone Ranger and Tonto ride off with Johnny Day. Unaware the vigilantes were rescuing Johnny, her cries for help brought a hundred men from the cafes and Brent rounded up a posse. After questioning Johnny to learn what the motive of the murder attempt was, Tonto applied medical treatment and then rides out to let Ann know her boyfriend was safe and sound. Fulton, meanwhile, is not happy to learn cattle is sold at $5 a head when yesterday the prices were $12. Alone at night in the telegraph office, Ann uses what trade she picked up from Johnny to ask Chicago what the prices were and learned the price went up to $20 a head. Figuring it was all a scheme to get Fulton's herd, The Lone Ranger arranged for Tonto to lead Fulton's cowboys into town to drive Brent's men from their cover. The round-up was quickly completed and Ann publicly verifies the true price for cattle. The gang is sent off to the sheriff's office and The Lone Ranger checked Al Brent's wrist to find a tattoo of a Black Arrow and Brent is taken into custody.

Episode #1375-591 "FALSE DISPATCHES" [PART FIFTEEN]

Broadcast November 14, 1941

Copyright Registration #78,205, script received at Registration Office November 7, 1941.

Plot: The Lone Ranger and Tonto come across a riderless army horse and in the saddlebag a note with a single word scrawled in desperate haste on the paper: "Help!" An army courier named Robert Vance with a bag full of dispatches went out of his way to see the beautiful Maria, only to be robbed, shot and wounded. The latest scheme by the Black Arrow was to forge some of the dispatches in place of those stolen. The new dispatch states that a new captain would take over the garrison at Buzzard Gap. Churlon, a member of the Black Arrow, was to masquerade as a Captain who, under orders, was to relieve the present captain from Buzzard Gap. As an ex-army man, Churlon would be able to masquerade without suspicion. After being healed from his wounds, Private Vance returns to the garrison to report the theft only to discover a new Captain is in charge and Vance was found guilty and sentenced to a firing squad in the morning. When Maria tells The Lone Ranger that she noticed a tattoo of a black arrow on the wrist of the new captain, The Lone Ranger suspected foul play. The masked man snuck into the army garrison and broke Vance out of jail to save his life. Captain Churlon, meanwhile, makes arrangements for the theft of rifles and ammunition. The Lone Ranger then rides out to fetch Captain Lacey, the man previously responsible for the garrison, and explains how forged papers misled the military. Hoping to bring the column behind him at all possible speed, The Lone Ranger led the charge as Captain Lacey and his men arrived. It was too late when Churlon saw who had arrived with the masked man. Before he could signal the outlaws outside the fort to rush forward and seize the stacked rifles, The Lone Ranger and Tonto were on him. The soldiers reached the rifles first and under Lacey's command, the outlaws faced sixty armed men where they had expected to get sixty rifles.

Episode #1376-592 "THE NIGHT WATCH" [PART SIXTEEN]
Broadcast November 17, 1941
Copyright Registration #78,582, script received at Registration Office December 6, 1941.
Plot: The Lone Ranger and Tonto were riding along the banks of the Missouri when they rescued a man from a cabin fire. What the men do not know is that Kurt schemed the fire to lure the steamer into rescue and pick-up. Captain Weston of the Missouri steamer plans to quit and report all he knows about the Black Arrow to the commander at the fort downstream. Kurt was ordered to kill the captain before he makes it to the fort. Kurt threw Betty, the captain's daughter, overboard to ease his mission. After The Lone Ranger rescues Betty, he finds a way back on the steamer to save the captain before Kurt could fulfill his mission. The captain, however, was not able to survive the death trap. Before he passed away, he reveals to The Lone Ranger his suspicion that Judd Calvert, a rancher in Wyoming, is the leader of the Black Arrow. He also reveals to the masked man that the Black Arrow knows The Lone Ranger was sent by the President himself to smash the gang. Jerry Knight, a young ensign on board, comforts the mourning Betty, reminding her what The Lone Ranger said: her father died for his country.

Episode #1377-593 "WAR IN WYOMING" [PART SEVENTEEN]
Broadcast November 19, 1941
Copyright Registration #78,583, script received at Registration Office December 6, 1941.
Plot: Sent into the green hills of Wyoming by the dying captain, The Lone Ranger hopes to infiltrate the gang of a large and powerful rancher named Judd Calvert. When Red Dixon, foreman of the Bar C, forgot his manners with Ann Davis, cowhand Bob Turner defended her honor – losing his job in the process. The Lone Ranger, having lost his inside spy at the Calvert ranch, works his way into Calvert's employ. Calvert plans to take the Davis ranch without payment and marry their daughter, against her will. The Lone Ranger raced out to get the Flying W crew as reinforcements to fight against the Bar C. Red's plan is to set fire to the barn and as people raced out, be shot down. But little did Red and his men realize that the honest ranchers swept down the hillside to surround the crooks. Red and his men were taken into custody and Judd Calvert will be taken to St. Louis since he was a member of the Black Arrow. The sheriff, in the payroll of Calvert, is helpless to do anything when it is revealed that Bob Turner was appointed the role of a Federal Marshal. Torlock, the suspected leader of the Black Arrow, was recently in the region and The Lone Ranger and Tonto ride out to follow the trail.

Episode #1378-594 "DANGER AT BREAKNECK RAPIDS" [PART EIGHTEEN]

Broadcast November 21, 1941

Copyright Registration #78,584, script received at Registration Office December 6, 1941.

Plot: Rack Torrence attempts to kill his nephew, Jed Parker, by pushing him into a geyser, but his plan is foiled by the approaching Lone Ranger and Tonto. Suspecting something foul, the vigilantes ride out to the Flying W to investigate, discovering a plot where Rack wants to inherit his stepbrother's ranch by eliminating the only kin to stand in his way. With assistance of Snake, Rack arranges for Jed to fall into Breakneck Rapids, which is so violent that no man could survive. It was an understatement that Phil Parker was saddened by the loss of his son, unaware that The Lone Ranger quickly raced to the rescue – despite the fact that Rack and Snake testify a masked man on a white horse pushed Jed into the rapids. As a result, The Lone Ranger is taken into custody by the sheriff and scheduled for a trial. The masked man breaks out of jail and leads a posse to discover Jed was rescued from the rapids and Jed verifies Rack and Snake pushed him in, and Rack wanted to inherit the ranch. Phil, angry, orders the sheriff to take the crooks to jail. As The Lone Ranger and Tonto ride away, they find a glove that was owned by Torlock.

Episode #1379-595 "THE OUTLAW WEARS A MASK" [PART NINETEEN]

Broadcast November 24, 1941

Copyright Registration #78,585, script received at Registration Office December 6, 1941.

Plot: The Lone Ranger and Tonto manage to escape Torlock's clever trap and manage to thwart the Black Arrow one more time. An outlaw named Snavely, under orders of Torlock, disguises himself as The Lone Ranger in order to bilk an unsuspecting new Indian Agent, John Morrell, out of his identification. Abby, John's wife, proves female intuition was not to be questioned when they later discover the scheme after meeting the real Lone Ranger. Late at night, Snavely discovers he never stole the real papers and returns to get the identification so he can dupe the Kiowa chiefs. The Lone Ranger and Tonto surprise the crooks from behind and rope them up. The masked man questions Snavely where they can find Torlock and they learn the man they are hunting went to Sioux City.

Episode #1380-596 "THE GOLD BEYOND THE RIVER" [PART TWENTY]

Broadcast November 26, 1941

Copyright Registration #78,586, script received at Registration Office December 6, 1941.

Plot: While looking for Torlock in Sioux City, where he delivered their prisoners, The Lone Ranger pays a visit to the sheriff only to find himself assisting the law. Ben Johnson, a guard on board a stagecoach, was shot and killed. $50,000 in gold was stolen during the robbery and the surviving stage guard, Nick Mason, claimed Dan Hardy was the culprit. But when The Lone Ranger uses Dan's twin brother, Dave, and Dan's girlfriend, Jane, to track down the accused, he questions the suspect to discover Dan is innocent of the crime. Riding into Windy Ridge, the masked man follows the trail like a standard detective and the guilty party is revealed: Nick Mason, who shot the guard and stole the gold. Nick planned to shoot and kill Dan and tell the sheriff that he trailed the thief and shot him. Nick discovered getting rid of the gold was difficult and would rather be content with the reward money. But Tonto arrived with the sheriff to take the advantage over Nick and the real culprit is handcuffed.

Episode #1381-597 "TORLOCK'S END" [PART TWENTY-ONE]

Broadcast November 28, 1941

Copyright Registration #78,587, script received at Registration Office December 6, 1941.

Plot: See page 266.

Episode #1382-598 "A GIRL TO AID" [PART TWENTY-TWO]

Broadcast December 1, 1941

Copyright Registration #78,588, script received at Registration Office December 6, 1941.

Plot: The mysterious girl who assisted The Lone Ranger and Tonto during the past few weeks, either in disguise or lurking in the shadows to avoid recognition, was called upon by the President of the United States to help assist in the masked man's crusade against outlaw members of the Legion of the Black Arrow, who fled after the apprehension of Torlock. Meanwhile, The Lone Ranger and Tonto ride onto Mustang Mag's ranch to check up on the young colt. Mag and Missouri explain how an Easterner named Leach arrived in town and was asking to see The Lone Ranger. In town, the masked man learned from the bartender that Leach was getting weaker all the time, something mysterious-like. No one can tell what is ailing him, but he was (by all accounts) hanging on to life long enough to talk to The Lone Ranger. But when The Lone Ranger and Tonto paid a visit to Leach at his abode, they discovered they were trapped inside. Leach and his men planned to kill them with an explosion of blasting powder. The Lone Ranger turns the tables by keeping Leach inside, knowing he would not want to die from the same fate, and Tonto extinguished the lit fuse. After escaping, the men realize that Leach has proved himself a cunning schemer who would go to great lengths to carry out his plots.

Notes: For more information about this episode, see page 266 to 270.

Episode #1383-599 "DEATH AND TAXES" [PART TWENTY-THREE]

Broadcast December 3, 1941

Written by George Waller.

Copyright Registration #78,589, script received at Registration Office December 6, 1941.

Plot: Having tried – and failed – to kill The Lone Ranger and Tonto, Jedediah Leach found himself pursued by the masked man. Before they can turn Jedediah Leach over to the law, the masked man learns Leach was being used as a pawn in a bigger scheme to fund the Black Arrow. Andrew Thompson, a government agent, sent out from Washington three months ago, is in charge of the land office and the collection of taxes in the region. In the town of Riverdale, The Lone Ranger learns that Thompson has been pocketing the money and blaming the tax collector, Leach. The masked man follows a lead from a note left behind by the mysterious girl, while the sheriff leads a posse in search of Leach. During a confrontation between all parties, The Lone Ranger arrives with a Federal Marshal to arrest Thompson for murder. It seems The Legion of the Black Arrow arranged for the murder of Andy Thompson and the man in front of everyone is an imposter. The fake Thompson attempts to throw the blame on Leach, but the tattoo on Thompson's wrist cinches his guilt.

Episode #1384-600 "HE WOULDN'T STAY DEAD" [PART TWENTY-FOUR]

Broadcast December 5, 1941

Copyright Registration #78,590, script received at Registration Office December 6, 1941.

Plot: Acting on another tip from the mysterious girl, The Lone Ranger acts just in time to prevent a frame-up which would lead to the freeing of two Legion of the Black Arrow agents. Simon Bates, a member of the Black Arrow, attempts to frame Jack Collins, owner of the Bar C Ranch, for a murder he never committed. In return for his silence, Simon asks the sheriff to release his friends from jail. But the sheriff will not give in to the blackmail. Uncertain why Simon was so eager to get the men out of jail, The Lone Ranger played a game at the risk of his own life to learn how and why the Black Arrow was involved. With the sheriff and his men riding in, The Lone Ranger finished the fight against Simon who admits The Lone Ranger's fists are more dangerous than his six-shooters. Naturally, Jack's wife, Jane, is relieved that her husband is no longer accused of a crime he did not commit.

Episode #1385-601 "STAGECOACH TO DEADWOOD" [PART TWENTY-FIVE]

Broadcast December 8, 1941

Copyright Registration #78,591, script received at Registration Office December 6, 1941.

Plot: Sheriff Harper of Hawksville is tipped off by Chattering Clawson that the recent stage hold-up and shooting of Elgin was committed by a masked man and an Indian. Thanks to a letter from the mysterious woman, assisting The Lone Ranger in his battle against The Legion of the Black Arrow, the masked man convinces the sheriff that Clawson may be the guilty man. After all, why would he falsely accuse The Lone Ranger of a crime? Clawson is a member of the Black Arrow and the organization's scheme is to put the stage line out of business. With the six-horse stage leaving for Deadwood, The Lone Ranger works alongside Robert Scott, the driver, to surprise the stage robbers and catch them off guard and unmask Clawson within the presence of the approaching sheriff and his posse.

Notes: The network broadcast of this program was pre-empted, due to news coverage of the attack on Pearl Harbor. The local broadcast in Detroit did air as scheduled.

Episode #1386-602 "THE PARSON OF FAIRFIELD" [PART TWENTY-SIX]

Broadcast December 10, 1941

Copyright Registration #78,861, script received at Registration Office January 9, 1942.

Plot: An itinerant preacher named Matthew Bartlett decides to build a church in the lawless Fairfield, where "there's no Sunday west of Junction City." But when the parson succeeds in establishing decency in the community, despite the lack of community involvement, he finds himself the pawn of a larger scheme. Dirk Snider, Black Arrow member, plans to steal an entire trail herd and with outlaws Nate Bragg and Al, schemes to set fire to the church to create a distraction. It only takes a few moments for The Lone Ranger to discover 3,000 head were stolen while men from the community, including those of the trail herd, raced to the rescue. With the assistance of Sheriff Lige, the masked man arranged for a large number of cowboys to back his play and create a stampede of longhorns to capture the outlaws. Dirk was caught off guard and apprehended as a result of the round-up. The Lone Ranger assured the parson that when the church is rebuilt, he will now have a community assisting him.

Episode #1387-603 "THE IRON BOX" [PART TWENTY-SEVEN]

Broadcast December 12, 1941

Copyright Registration #78,862, script received at Registration Office January 9, 1942.

Plot: Just about everything goes wrong for The Lone Ranger as he tries to trap the mysterious girl, and instead winds up with the wrong instructions and a bullet wound. Following her instructions, The Lone Ranger holds up a stagecoach to steal a heavy iron box. The driver managed to shoot and wound the masked man. Under her instructions, he was to impersonate a drummer and live in a hotel in the nearby town of Clarksville. Without questioning orders, The Lone Ranger – despite the pain from the wound – fulfills his obligation. Old Missouri warns the masked man that word in town is that a masked man and Indian stole the box from the stage. The stage was set as Bart Nevill and his men pay a visit to the hotel and find the drummer in his room and steal the iron box. Inside the box, when opened, was not money but valuable plans from the Government. The Lone Ranger started a brawl and punched a few men, then fled down the hallway and jumped through a window to escape with the plans. The sheriff arrived and catching the men with the stolen iron box, takes Nevill and the gang to jail.

Episode #1388-604 "FOR THOSE WHO FAIL" [PART TWENTY-EIGHT]

Broadcast December 15, 1941

Copyright Registration #78,863, script received at Registration Office January 9, 1942.

Plot: After rescuing a girl from a raging torrent, during a brutal storm, The Lone Ranger discovers Nell Carthage was seeking evidence against the man responsible for her father's murder. Duncan Powers wanted Judson Carthage to finance the Southern Railroad, as an investment opportunity. Soon after the old man rejected the offer, he was found dead, shot in the back. Further digging reveals Nell's father was working for an agent of the Black Arrow. The masked man convinces Johnny and Emily to use the papers, placed into a box, as bait to lure the killer who would need to retrieve the papers. The trap was sprung at 4 o'clock in the morning as the killer showed up to retrieve the box: Deputy Jim Trueman. Jim laughs as men of the Black Arrow have surrounded the Carthage home, but The Lone Ranger smiles as Tonto left some time ago and got the advantage over the men outside. Jim attempts to shoot The Lone Ranger, only to have the gun shot from his hand. The Lone Ranger knew he could force Trueman into a confession for honest Sheriff Mike Sawyer. Later, the crooks are delivered to the colonel of a nearby fort for transport to Washington. Before leaving, The Lone Ranger learns that Breed Latham and his gang is in the region and on the trail of a small detail of soldiers unaware of potential ambush.

Episode #1389-605 "THE MASKED MAN'S FISTS" [PART TWENTY-NINE]

Broadcast December 17, 1941

Copyright Registration #78,864, script received at Registration Office January 9, 1942.

Plot: Breed Latham, outlaw leader of a notorious gang, slaughters a band of army hunters and steals their uniforms. Plotting the masquerade as members of the U.S. military, with Breed masquerading as Captain Conway, they steal a shipment of gold that was meant for payment to all the soldiers out in the West. After the crime is committed, Latham attempts to convince the local sheriff that not only did the cooks get away with the money, but The Lone Ranger and Tonto fell for the trap in the baggage car of the train and were killed. Latham was in for a surprise, however, when the masked man and Indian turn out to be alive and The Lone Ranger uses his fists to punish the criminals. One by one the men stood up after being knocked down but found themselves knocked to the ground again until they gave in, and The Lone Ranger and Tonto tied them up hand and foot. The tattoo on his wrist proved Latham was a member of The Legion of the Black Arrow. In fear of further beatings, Vince Williams and Hank, the men responsible for the trap in the baggage car, quickly turned over the location of the Black Arrow's hideout.

Notes: The Lone Ranger, when using his fists on Latham, remarks how he is going to beat the criminal with a thrashing that he deserves.

Episode #1390-606 "AMBUSH IN THE DESERT" [PART THIRTY]

Broadcast December 19, 1941

Copyright Registration #78,865, script received at Registration Office January 9, 1942.

Plot: Led by a whimpering dog, The Lone Ranger and Tonto find two men dying of thirst on the desert, lying at the base of a cactus. Tonto gave the men water. The sun set and darkness spread over the desolate desert. In place of the heat, the air turned cold and biting. But among the chill air the masked man learned the two men, Jed Hawkins and Sam, were from the town of Arrowhead. Their dog, Lop Ear, saved their lives… but the water from their well, for which they filled their canteen, was poisoned. Two gunmen, Shaler and Brand, attempted to shoot The Lone Ranger, Tonto and their two friends from ambush, only to discover the men played dead. The gunmen fled, unaware they were being trailed by the masked man. Through a trap of their own, The Lone Ranger and Tonto learn that Shaler and Brand were hired by the local storekeeper, Lem Beardsley, to commit murder. Beardsley found a rich vein behind the mine owned by the prospectors and wanted them out of the way so he could cash in. In order to get a confession from the storekeeper, The Lone Ranger threatens to force the tainted water in the canteen down Beardsley's throat, counting to three. Beardsley, panicking, confesses to the scheme.

Episode #1391-607 "REMEMBER THE ALAMO" [PART THIRTY-ONE]

Broadcast December 22, 1941

Copyright Registration #78,866, script received at Registration Office January 9, 1942.

Plot: When The Lone Ranger and Tonto learned that the mysterious girl who had given them so much information had ridden North in the direction of Tamarack, they hit the trail at once. There, they discover an army of outlaws, working for the Black Arrow, attacking the town. The Black Arrow plans to take over the gold mines that made the town so prosperous and operate it themselves. When Black Bart and his outlaw gang arrive to take over the town, the women and children flee into the Rainbow Mine while the men hold fort against the murderous outlaws. The defense of the town turns bloody as men on both sides are shot and killed. With the American flag raised above them, the townsfolk remember another band of courageous men fighting for freedom at the Alamo. During the battle, when all hope has failed, and The Lone Ranger in the position of losing the battle, Tonto arrives in time with the Colonel and the Calvary from a nearby fort to even the odds. The scars of the battle would be felt for months, but the price of freedom outweighed any wounds the town suffered that day.

Notes: The year is referenced as 1876.

The long musical hiatus for the musical arrangements of Republic Pictures ends with this broadcast.

Episode #1392-608 "THE THREE WISE HOMBRES" [PART THIRTY-TWO]

Broadcast December 24, 1941

Copyright Registration #78,867, script received at Registration Office January 9, 1942.

Plot: The Lone Ranger and Tonto ride into the Valley of the Magi, also known as the Valley of the Three Wise Men, for it was magi who years ago followed a star to Bethlehem. In the snow-covered valley, three cattlemen, Slaughter, Kelsey and Davis, were at odds with Henry Baker, a sheepherder, and his young son Jack. The cattlemen create a stampede, scattering the sheep like chaff from the wheat. The snow, meanwhile, whirled heavier and thicker from the heavens, but unerringly The Lone Ranger guided the great white stallion towards the figures of Jack and his ailing father. Tonto quickly deduces Baker has pneumonia, and the two get the family to their cabin to take shelter from the storm.

It was just four days until Christmas and as Tonto tended to Baker by the fire, Baker's wife felt helpless in not knowing how to treat pneumonia… but was grateful for the two strangers who came to their rescue. Young Jack prayed by the bedside for his father to be healed in place of the Christmas toys he asked for on prior evenings. On Christmas Eve, The Lone Ranger rode out to find Kelsey and Davis, then forced them at gunpoint to visit Slaughter. Of the three, Slaughter displayed no remorse over Baker's condition. Baker has a wife and children and was trying to build a home. Yet, Slaughter led the charge to persecute and hound the sheepherder and close in on him like hounds after a rabbit. The Lone Ranger provides a perspective regarding how the land was there before them, would remain after, and how there was more land than the cattle required. In the spirit of Christmas, they were too focused on taking and forgot about giving. The Lone Ranger fled, knowing he could not change their hearts – they have to do that themselves.

The quick winter twilight darkened the sky. Inside the crude cabin, a single kerosene lamp flickered in the wind that carried flakes of snow through the chinks in the log walls. The yellow flame cast a soft glow over the interior, over the man whose labored breathing filled the single room and the kneeling figures beside the bunk.

As the soft murmurs of prayer rose and fell, occasionally the lamplight was mirrored in the eyes of the dog or of the small lamp lying on the side near the fireplace. All night long, until the sky lightened outside the cabin and the strong, clear shine of the rising sun heralded the dawn of Christmas, Henry Baker starts to feel better and it is clear that he is past the worst of pneumonia.

The Bakers then receive a visit from three men who were wiser than they were. Davis delivered a pair of snowshoes for young Jack. Slaughter delivered food, but not before admitting he and Kelsey and Davis were "mighty ornery, mighty bullheaded. We wuz three dumb hombres if ever there was any. But now we're different, we been set wise." The promise of no more fighting included evidence that there was room enough for cattlemen and sheepherders alike.

Episode #1393-609 "THE MASKED MAN'S DEDUCTIONS" [PART THIRTY-THREE]

Broadcast December 26, 1941

Copyright Registration #78,868, script received at Registration Office January 9, 1942.

Plot: "There is untold worry and misery in Calabash!" was the way the note began. It was the latest of so many messages that The Lone Ranger had received from the same mysterious woman. Following instructions, he took a package from a saloon singer named Mazie, avoiding being shot at by Sheriff Collins, and returned to camp. In the presence of Tonto, he found the package contained thousands of dollars. The mysterious girl plays detective to learn that members of the Black Arrow are threatening to disfigure women in town, with hot branding irons to their faces, unless their husbands sell off their land to pay blackmail. After paying a visit to Grant Dundee and his wife, The Lone Ranger and Tonto questioned the victims to unearth more clues as to who was blackmailing the women in town. Through deductions, the masked man figured out how to trip up the guilty man, Jack, falsely claiming the money was marked with ink. Jack attempts to flee but is apprehended. The tattoo of the Black Arrow was on his wrist, but his fund raising comes to an end as the money is returned, and Jack is sent to Washington under guard.

Episode #1394-610 "A PAGE FROM MR. LINCOLN" [PART THIRTY-FOUR]

Broadcast December 29, 1941

Copyright Registration #78,869, script received at Registration Office January 9, 1942.

Plot: Pete Lacey and Pedro Martinez return in an episode in which title refers to Lincoln's defense of a man convicted by the light of the full moon. Jake was killed in the back of the Lucky Dollar. A witness named Bates identifies "a big hombre with yellow hair," thus identifying Pete as the murderer. Pedro insists Pete was nowhere near the Lucky Dollar. The mysterious girl handed Pedro a note to deliver to The Lone Ranger, which reveals Jake was working for the government. After discovering a witness named Jed Scott was fleeing town, The Lone Ranger rides out and boards a train to force the witness back to Rockford and testify at the trial. Thankfully, while there was two hours' distance between towns, the circuit judge had taken care of a number of minor cases that morning in Rockford and declared a recess before Pete's case was called. The Lone Ranger arrived in time to break down the testimony of the witness, proving he could not have seen the killer because there was no full moon on the night of the murder – an almanac in the courtroom verified this. With the witness discredited, the real criminal was exposed: the sheriff who had the mark of the Black Arrow tattooed on his wrist. Jed Scott saw the crime and in fear of the law, confessed to the crime – temporarily – until the sheriff's guilt was exposed in the courtroom.

Episode #1395-611 "DRUMS AT DUSK" [PART THIRTY-FIVE]

Broadcast December 31, 1941

Copyright Registration #78,870, script received at Registration Office January 9, 1942.

Plot: The Lone Ranger and Tonto arrive outside the town of Palmersville to warn the men and women that the

Indians have left the reservation. The red men have camped out in the hills, and they mean to attack. The war dance has started. The masked man suggests John Colton, the Indian agent, pay a visit to find out what their grievance is and settle without bloodshed. The Indians are so large in number that they could wipe out the town if they attacked. Colton has been operating the Circle Bar Ranch, which young Kay Palmer owns. Colton was in cahoots with a shady lawyer named Larry Gage, to steal cattle meant for the Indians, and used the Circle Bar to stock the beef. The lawyer altered the papers to ensure 500 head from Pothook were delivered to the Indians, instead of the full 5,000. The Lone Ranger sneaks into Gage's office to compare papers, then gallops out to the ranch to talk to Greg Forbes, the hot-headed foreman of the Circle Bar. Together with ranch hands and The Lone Ranger and Tonto alongside, Forbes arranges for the stolen cattle to be rounded up and returned. John Colton and Larry Gage had guessed The Lone Ranger might pay the ranch a visit and had persuaded the sheriff and his posse to ride out there. They caught sight of the cowboys south of Rocky Canyon. The Lone Ranger shows the two forms, one saying 500 head and another saying 5,000 head, to prove his story against Gage's. With proof against him, and The Lone Ranger's quick shooting to disarm him, Gage is taken into custody alongside John Colton. The Lone Ranger and Tonto receive another note from the mysterious woman stating a judge is in danger and they must ride like the wind to Santos.

Episode #1396-612 "THE MASKED MAN AND THE LAW" [PART THIRTY-SIX]
Broadcast January 2, 1942
Copyright Registration #78,871, script received at Registration Office January 9, 1942.
Plot: The Lone Ranger comes to the aid of Judge Davis of the county of Santos, who was about to be subjected to tar and feathers by a mob led by two Black Arrow members, Raiden and Spur. The judge ruled in favor of Lem Wilkens, local rancher who reserved the right to cut off water. The town contributed to Wilkens' man-made stream but without a written agreement, Wilkens reserves the right to dam the water and restrict other ranchers to access. Tonto paid a visit to Hannah, Davis' wife, and brought her to The Lone Ranger's camp for safety. The Black Arrow men, who misguided Wilkens to dam the water, are exposed in the presence of a mob and Wilkens admits he was wrong. The judge insists Raiden and Spur be tried in a fair court of law as the ranchers cheer, knowing the problem over water rights is now resolved. Before The Lone Ranger can read the letter that Tonto received from Hannah, a bearded stranger pulls a gun and orders the masked man to surrender the letter.

Episode #1397-613 "THE MASKED MAN'S FRIEND" [PART THIRTY-SEVEN]
Broadcast January 5, 1942
Copyright Registration #78,872, script received at Registration Office January 9, 1942.
Plot: The Lone Ranger removes the fake beard from the stranger and discovers he is his old friend Arizona Pete, the man holding him up for the letter. The Lone Ranger learns that Arizona Pete is afraid that this may prove to be a challenge for his friend. Daremos runs the town, pockets the taxes, sends men to jail if they don't follow his orders, and discovered the mysterious girl was from the government. But when the mysterious girl discovers Daremos is an old woman and not a man, she tries to alert The Lone Ranger. Meanwhile, with the masked man on the trail, the old woman arranges for a gang of outlaws to set a trap. When The Lone Ranger and Tonto enter the cave, they will be caught off guard and roped from behind. The outlaws planned to use a keg of dynamite to seal off the cave and trap the masked man. But when Arizona Pete sneaks into the cave in advance and the outlaws mistake him for The Lone Ranger, the outlaws find themselves surprised from behind by the masked man and his faithful Indian companion. When the keg explodes, the outlaws are trapped inside... and The Lone Ranger rides off to get the Army who can arrive and arrest the outlaws and Daremos.

Episode #1398-614 "HOUSE OF STONE" [PART THIRTY-EIGHT]

Broadcast January 7, 1942

Copyright Registration #78,873, script received at Registration Office January 9, 1942.

Plot: The Lone Ranger and Tonto discover a small, one-story stone house on a mountain, used as a message center for the Black Arrow. Reading Morse code originating from the house, The Lone Ranger discovers an outlaw gang of 50, led by Mercer and his associate Red, plan to master a jail break, disguised as pioneers, some of them in women's clothing, riding prairie schooners. The Lone Ranger rode out to the jail to alert the warden, who in turn strikes a deal with the prisoners. If they promise to vacate so the approaching outlaws discover their efforts are in vain, their sentence would be commuted down. But the outlaws instead took over the warden's office and raced out masquerading as Indians to combat the outlaws without concern for returning to the prison. As the confrontation between two outlaw gang gets started, the cavalry arrives, led by The Lone Ranger, to make a huge sweep of two outlaw gangs and place them under arrest… except for Mercer and Red, who will be transported to Washington, D.C. to face crimes far more serious.

Episode #1399-615 "ADVENTURE OF THE YELLOW DOG" [PART THIRTY-NINE]

Broadcast January 9, 1942

Copyright Registration #78,874, script received at Registration Office January 9, 1942.

Plot: The Lone Ranger and Tonto happen to find the dead body of Purdy, a member of the Black Arrow, who drew a map in the ground before he passed, revealing the location of stolen Army payroll. Slater, another member of the gang and the man who committed the murder, conspired with Dekker, an Army soldier who revealed the details of the payroll's intended delivery, races out to find his outlaw gang. The stolen payroll was buried near the edge of the Yellow Dog River. The Lone Ranger, having learned that the outlaws also plan to burn the blockhouse to the ground, races out to prevent the disaster. The masked man convinced Captain Wainwright to return to his post to fight off the outlaws and retrieve the stolen army payroll that the outlaws had retrieved from the burial spot. Captain Wainwright was appreciative of the masked man's help, giving him a full salute before returning to his post, and handing The Lone Ranger a note from the mysterious girl. The note read "Ghost Canyon."

Episode #1400-616 "GHOST CANYON" [PART FORTY]

Broadcast January 12, 1942

Copyright Registration #78,875, script received at Registration Office January 9, 1942.

Written by Fran Striker.

Plot: This story has nothing to do with the Black Arrow. The Lone Ranger helps trip up outlaws working an abandoned gold mine and trying to scare everyone away. Ned Rockwell, hoping to take over where his uncle left off, begins prospecting in the canyon. Mary Hamilton, postmistress of Prairie Bend, warns strangers not to go into Ghost Canyon, but that did not stop her brother, Jim, from investigating himself. Ned Rockwell discovers he will lose possession of the mine in a month if he does not work it, according to the provision of his uncle's will. Having stumbled onto the outlaws, and the fact they struck a gold vein, he is caught off guard and tied and bound. The Lone Ranger and Tonto ride into the canyon to investigate, meet Jim, and together they use a torch in the mine to create a distraction and get the advantage over the outlaws. Mary, believing her brother was an outlaw, discovers instead that he is a U.S. Marshal. The Lone Ranger leaves knowing Ned and Jim will ensure the outlaws are tied and bound and taken into custody.

Notes: Hamilton was Fran Striker's middle name.

Episode #1401-617 "A DEADFALL BRINGS TROUBLE" [PART FORTY-ONE]

Broadcast January 14, 1942

Copyright Registration #78,876, script received at Registration Office January 9, 1942.

Plot: Riding from Prairie Bend and heading west to the Sawtooth range, The Lone Ranger and Tonto discover two badmen named Slade and Dorgan are members of the Black Arrow. The two crooks try to prevent a hot-tempered young cowboy named Gary Reynolds from marrying Sally Blake. They try to arrange an "accident" with a deadfall and a family tree but were saved by The Lone Ranger and Tonto. Then, they frame Reynolds as a cattle rustler with a branding iron and pair of gloves, but even the masked man knew this was not sufficient proof. In the hopes of disgracing Reynolds, the two take desperate action by arranging for the young man to exchange gunfire with The Lone Ranger. At first everyone believes the masked man was shot dead, but thanks to Tonto tending a minor wound, The Lone Ranger returns to help apprehend the two crooks, prove Reynolds was not responsible for the crime accused, and on Clawhammer Mountain he and Tonto prove it was the crooks who were cattle rustling. Sally tells Reynolds that anyone who puts their faith in The Lone Ranger can only benefit.

Episode #1402-618 "VIA PONY EXPRESS" [PART FORTY-TWO]

Broadcast January 16, 1942

Copyright Registration #79,148, script received at Registration Office February 4, 1942.

Plot: The Lone Ranger and Tonto circled Majorville along the Overland Trail when they come across a Pony Express rider who fell from his horse. With a sprained ankle and a broken arm, Johnny is brought to the Two Sisters Ranch, owned by Brad Wilson, where Brad's daughters, June and Clair, looked after him. The Lone Ranger doubles as a Pony Express rider to help keep valuable dispatches out of the hands of the Black Arrow, with assistance of Johnny. Bill Lacey and the rest of the outlaws who attempted to get their hands on the papers discovered how they were caught off guard as they attempted to waylay the honest mail carriers. The Lone Ranger leaves with his prisoners forced to ride in front of him.

Notes: The story ends with a rather strange and prophetic foreshadowing by Clair, who remarks: "It's hard to say. He's cleaned up the outlaws around here so even if Pa, you or Larry are hurt, we'll feel safe. But him, I'll never feel he's safe. He'll take those crooks to Majorville but he won't stop there. He'll go on and on, fightin' for justice, facin' danger until he... until he reaches the end of the trail."

Episode #1403-619 "OLD WOMAN'S CALL" [PART FORTY-THREE]

Broadcast January 19, 1942

Copyright Registration #79,149, script received at Registration Office February 4, 1942.

Plot: Having figured out that a mysterious girl was working alongside The Lone Ranger, members of the Black Arrow, led by Curly, set a trap to catch the masked man. After sending out a message to the outlaws for a ten o'clock meeting, they knew The Lone Ranger would visit and the sweet-smelling liquid on the floor would stick to The Lone Ranger's boots. Curly's scheme is to use a bloodhound to trail the masked man to his cave hideout. The masked man fell for the scheme, despite a warning from a young man named Jack, sent by the mysterious girl (disguised as an old woman), and fled from the outlaws when he realized he was considerably outnumbered. With The Lone Ranger, Tonto and Jack trapped inside the cave, the outlaws attempted to smoke them out. The mysterious girl, disguised as an old woman, paid a visit to the site and convinced the outlaws to let her go inside and bring them out, under orders from "the big guy." By clever means the masked man and his friends escape from the cave and race into town. After discovering the bloodhound belonged to a lawyer named Bill Tatum, The Lone Ranger brought evidence to the sheriff to make sure "the big guy" was put behind bars.

Episode #1404-620 "MURDER WEARS SKIRTS" [PART FORTY-FOUR]

Broadcast January 21, 1942

Copyright Registration #79,150, script received at Registration Office February 4, 1942.

Plot: In another attempt to trap The Lone Ranger, two Black Arrow members named Butch Williams and Truckston visit the town of Clifton, where lawyer Bill Tatum is presently in jail awaiting trial. The outlaws murder the lawyer and frame the mysterious girl by planting her bonnet in the cell. Ma Penny, the old woman who provided room and board for the girl, attempted to cover her crime, but The Lone Ranger turns the tables on them. Arranging for a secret rendezvous, the masked man discussed the proof he had that tripped Butch into confessing he framed an innocent girl for a crime she did not commit. The sheriff and his men, a short distance away, overheard the entire confession and took the outlaw to jail.

Episode #1405-621 "CRYSTAL CANYON" [PART FORTY-FIVE]

Broadcast January 23, 1942

Copyright Registration #79,151, script received at Registration Office February 4, 1942.

Plot: Jeff Penrose, leader of a wagon train, falls victim to a gang of Apache Indians only to discover later from The Lone Ranger that the Indians were nothing more than outlaw renegade whites. Among the victims was Chalmers' boy, kidnapped and held for ransom. The Lone Ranger and Tonto ride out to Crystal Canyon to rescue the boy and in the midst of the chase, drop the boy off with Tombstone, an old hermit, then lead the 20-man team of outlaws in further pursuit. While the masked man lures the outlaws down Rocky Ford to Laurel Pass, Tonto races to the wagon train to ask the men to act as a posse and, giving strict orders, arranges for an ambush. The outlaws quickly surrender when, surrounded from all sides, discover they are outnumbered. The outlaws will be turned over to the sheriff while Nick, the outlaw leader and member of the Black Arrow, will be turned over to the marshal. Nick laughs before taken away… The Lone Ranger was not aware that Tombstone is a madman who loves throwing people off a thousand-foot canyon rim. The masked man raced out in time… just as Tombstone had lured the boy to the edge of the cliff. The Lone Ranger roped the old man and promised to take him to Clarksville where someone can look after him. The hermit, with rationale, thanked the masked man for arriving in time…

Episode #1406-622 "LAST COMMAND" [PART FORTY-SIX]

Broadcast January 26, 1942

Copyright Registration #79,152, script received at Registration Office February 4, 1942.

Plot: Jim Miller and Jake Watson, local ranchers in Wyoming and members of the Black Arrow, trick a retired U.S. Army Colonel named Harcourt to build an impregnable fort. While the fort will cost the ranchers money, they rationalize that the expense will be necessary. Cleaning out the Indians in the area first; building their cattle empire second. The Lone Ranger, riding into the area, is spotted by one of the outlaws and ambushed from a far distance with a high-powered rifle. Three weeks later, with his wound mending thanks to Tonto, a disguised Lone Ranger attempts to infiltrate the construction site to unearth the facts, only to be jailed for being seen with an Indian. Despite the fact Tonto is a friendly native, Colonel Harcourt believes all Indians are the enemy. But when Harcourt discovers the truth about the construction of the fort, and that the 200 outlaws who take orders from the Black Arrow are due to arrive and take command of the fort, it takes the bravery of The Lone Ranger and the assistance of Harcourt to save the day. After breaking free from jail, the masked man schemes with the colonel to turn the tables as each outlaw is gagged and disarmed as they entered the fort, one by one. The fort will soon be turned over to the army. Colonel Harcourt laughs when he realizes his last command involved the apprehension of 200 outlaws without firing a single shot.

Episode #1407-623 "DOUBLE EXPOSURE" [PART FORTY-SEVEN]

Broadcast January 28, 1942

Written by George Waller.

Copyright Registration #79,153, script received at Registration Office February 4, 1942.

Plot: The Lone Ranger and Tonto were headed south of Sweetwater when, near Bitter Creek, they save the life of a young woman, Janet McClaine. It would be through Janet that they learn of a freight train that was raided by outlaws a week ago, taking the life of Johnny Donovan. Later, when Ted Donovan sells his cattle to fund the start of a freighting company of his own, the townsfolk are mystified until they discover Ted was a twin brother of Johnny. When Ted learns that his brother died because he would not concede to Mike Rafferty, a member of the Black Arrow, and Johnny would not smuggle rifles to the Indians, Ted decides to seek out Rafferty with vengeance in his heart. At this time Rafferty discovers Ted is a twin brother, The Lone Ranger races to Cheyenne to rescue Ted from what would be certain death. Thanks to The Lone Ranger interceding with the confrontation, Rafferty's guilt is exposed, and Ted's life is saved.

Episode #1408-624 "SCHOOL FOR RANCHERS" [PART FORTY-EIGHT]

Broadcast January 30, 1942

Copyright Registration #79,154, script received at Registration Office February 4, 1942.

Plot: The Lone Ranger must help a young couple escape the clutches of Black Arrow-led ranchers who are trying to get their own crooked sheriff elected with the unsuspecting aid of an honest young rancher. Ben Chalmers is trying to get Red Gorman to become voted in as the new sheriff and uses an influential rancher, Jake Thompson of the Circle T Ranch, to spread the word through the region, days before the election. None of the ranchers want any homesteaders in the area, and at the suggestion of Chalmers, Jake uses this to influence the locals' decision. But when a new schoolteacher arrives in Bryantsville and befriends Jake Thompson, The Lone Ranger intervenes and employs the woman to help expose the scheme and create peace in the valley. A note left in Red Gorman's home lures him to the home of the new schoolteacher, unaware that his guilt would be exposed within the presence of witnesses, as a plot was masterminded against Jake. Moments after Chalmers and Gorman are taken into custody, it is discovered Red Gorman has a tattoo of a black arrow on his wrist. Jake Thompson, meanwhile, assures that the homesteaders will be given a fair chance to settle in the valley. Before The Lone Ranger can question Red, Tonto arrives with an urgent message from The Padre and the two ride off.

Episode #1409-622M "A SILVER SUMMONS" [PART FORTY-NINE]

Broadcast February 2, 1942

Copyright Registration #79,411, script received at Registration Office February 28, 1942.

Plot: The mysterious girl finally gets captured but manages to enlist the aid of a telegraph operator named Lefty to send for help. In desperation, the girl asked Lefty to carry her brother's ring and a message to the Padre. The Lone Ranger and Tonto, having been alerted by The Padre, realizes her danger when he sees the gold ring with the U.S. emblem on it, the ring once owned by her husband and his late brother. A member of the Black Arrow named Dorn fears their regional scheme is going to be exposed, knowing she was an informant for The Lone Ranger. So, Dorn orders his outlaw gang to hold off The Lone Ranger and the cavalry that was due to arrive, while he, Jake and Red make ready to ride off with the girl and Lefty. The Lone Ranger and Tonto arrive at Dorn's hideout when Dorn least expects, and rescue Lefty. The mysterious girl, however, fled to pursue her mission. Before Dorn could name the leaders of the Black Arrow, he died of a heart attack.

Episode #1410-623M "MOFFET'S MOVE" [PART FIFTY]

Broadcast February 4, 1942

Copyright Registration #79,412, script received at Registration Office February 28, 1942.

Plot: A reluctant Army captain, newly promoted, will soon fall victim to an attack from a sizeable band of outlaws. When The Lone Ranger delivers the warning, the captain believes the masked man is an outlaw himself. The Lone Ranger is forced to pull both of his guns to make a swift escape from the fort, when he fails to convince the captain to attack a Black Arrow encampment. All this follows the mysterious girl's abortive attempt to enlist an old ex-trooper named Amos as a go-between, who was the man responsible for tipping off the masked man, then being ordered by the girl to return and utter a new warning about the new Army captain. But Amos was held back by the outlaws, thus the reason why The Lone Ranger faced the obstacle. The Army captain ordered his men to race out in pursuit and during the chase, they discovered The Lone Ranger's story was accurate and instead of chasing the masked man, the captain redirected his men to attack the outlaws who were caught off guard... and rescue Amos.

Notes: The Lone Ranger's ring, referenced in prior episodes, was disclosed as having a hidden compartment inside where a thin piece of paper could be hidden. This was a premium giveaway during the commercial breaks. It is not known what the letter M stands for with the recording number but many theorize it has something to do with the premium giveaway.

Episode #1411-624M "THE FIFTH CONDEMNED MAN" [PART FIFTY-ONE]

Broadcast February 6, 1942

Copyright Registration #79,413, script received at Registration Office February 28, 1942.

Plot: The Lone Ranger arranges with a U.S. Marshal to be placed under arrest and jailed alongside the four prisoners who were known to be members of the Black Arrow. Sentenced to hang and believing they would be rescued by members of the gang, none of the men would name names. It was the hope of the masked man, in disguise, to gain the confidence of the prisoners. But when Marshal Cody dies from the collapse of a sabotaged bridge over Arrow Creek, and the law arrives to take the men to San Lamay for their scheduled execution, The Lone Ranger realizes he is stuck in a complex position. The mysterious girl races to Tonto to alert him that Sydney Drake somehow knew of The Lone Ranger's scheme and arranged for the death of the marshal. When Tonto finds the lawman, alive but weak and wounded, he creates a makeshift harness for Scout and Silver to take the marshal to San Lamay in time to reveal the truth about the fifth condemned man. Hours later, as the men were ushered up to the top of the gallows, Tonto rides in with the U.S. Marshal in time to reveal the identity of fifth man. The hanging postponed for an hour as the four men were jailed, The Lone Ranger reveals to Tonto and the marshal that the entire affair was not in vain... They learned that Sydney Drake was a high official of the Black Arrow.

Notes: John Todd doubles for one line as a member of the imprisoned Black Arrow gang.

Episode #1412-625 "TRAIL'S END" [PART FIFTY-TWO]

Broadcast February 9, 1942

Copyright Registration #79,414, script received at Registration Office February 28, 1942.

Plot: The U.S. Marshal is furious when he learns that Sydney Drake, a high Black Arrow official, escapes before The Lone Ranger could learn the whereabouts of the secret Black Arrow cave. The Lone Ranger has a general idea where the headquarters is located, a high cliff north of the forest. Drake, however, anticipates being discovered so he and his outlaw army set up an ambush. Soon thereafter the masked man employed the services of Bill Cody, Wild Bill Hickok and others who were willing to lay down their life for the security of the nation. Tonto alerted Chief Thundercloud and his tribe to join the cavalry. The mysterious girl learns of the ambush plans and sends a warning to The Lone Ranger that Drake is a master of disguise. The masked man, however, has enough doubt in mind to figure out the scheme – the outlaws want the posse to enter the cave so they can be killed from within, while the outlaws hid outside. So The Lone Ranger orders great fires to be built and smoke sent into the cave to smoke out the outlaws. Angry, one of the outlaws names the five men who were among leadership of the Black Arrow.

Episode #1413-626 "SILVER RACES STEAM" [PART FIFTY-THREE]
Broadcast February 11, 1942
Copyright Registration #79,415, script received at Registration Office February 28, 1942.

Plot: Sydney Drake may be in jail again, but he does not give up easily. He manages to send a coded message, arranging for the Washington-bound train carrying the names of the Black Arrow members to be wrecked and robbed. Jake and his men drop trees on the tracks. The mysterious girl learns of the plot and warns The Lone Ranger and Tonto, who race out to stop the train in time. The Lone Ranger was forced to throw his ring into the locomotive so that the engineer and conductor find a message inside warning them of the foul plot ahead. After the train is stopped, the crooks are taken into custody.

Notes: While fans of the program cite The Legion of the Black Arrow story arc lasting 64 episodes, the radio scripts cease numbering sequence at no. 53, and then pick up with a new numbering sequence. Technically the characters from the story arc became the primary focus in a series of additional story arcs that were interconnected. The numbering sequence reflected in this episode guide originates from the radio scripts.

Episode #1414-627 "FIRST OF THE FIVE" [PART ONE]
Broadcast February 13, 1942
Copyright Registration #79,416, script received at Registration Office February 28, 1942.

Plot: Hoping to corner the five members of the Black Arrow that avoided capture, who were attempting to cover all evidence of their crimes, The Lone Ranger first sets his sights on railroad man John Kimberly, who is trying to sabotage the completion of the construction of the railway line by preventing a shipment of lumber from reaching Omaha. But Kimberly proves an elusive prey when his right-hand man, Bill Haywood, has his sights on The Lone Ranger and attempts to shoot the masked man from a distance. An old trapper against the pillage of the lumber assists the masked man, but Kimberly's guilt is not ensured and only Bill Haywood goes to jail. The Lone Ranger, having returned to get the ring he left behind at the old trapper's house, suspects the ring is a good luck charm.

Episode #1415-628 "THE OUTLAW GUARD" [PART TWO]
Broadcast February 16, 1942
Copyright Registration #79,417, script received at Registration Office February 28, 1942.

Plot: Warren City grew in size from a junction to a town now facing a boom of railroad workers, and Mr. Warren himself believes there might be trouble, including a fight in the streets, as a number of thefts have been made on the town's supplies. The Lone Ranger suspects another attack on the train and warns Matt Kirby to make sure the train is well-guarded. Matt Kirby, in charge of the general store and town's supplies, is sweet on Mary Hamilton, singer at the Silver Trail café, who appears to know too much about the impending act of sabotage plotted against the railroad. Kirby wants to ensure that the supplies reach their destination and hires fifty men to board the train to act as guards. But John Kimberly and Ross Chalmers plot to use the fifty men against The Lone Ranger, all of whom are misinformed about the masked man, who is forced to walk car by car shooting the guns out of the hands of the misinformed guards. Chalmers arranged for a few rails to be torn out at Lookout Hill. It was fifty against two as The Lone Ranger commandeered the train in Ross' attempt to delay the Southern & Western Railroad. The Lone Ranger is eventually saved as soldiers from the nearby fort arrive in time to stop the locomotive before reaching the act of destruction.

Episode #1416-629 "KAHWAYGO CANYON" [PART THREE]

Broadcast February 18, 1942

Copyright Registration #79,418, script received at Registration Office February 28, 1942.

Plot: The advance construction camp, located fifty miles outside of Warren City, is working full speed ahead to reach completion of the railroad by October 1. Just fifty miles north of the camp was Kahwaygo Canyon where the railroad men were constructing a bridge. Jim Herold was in charge of construction, along with his son Bob, and were tipped off by The Lone Ranger that Kimberly wants to own the Southern and Western and having failed to prevent supplies reaching their destination from Warren City, plans to sabotage the bridge. Butch Rankin is paid by Kimberly $100 a day to ensure the construction job is held up, and after he wounds Jim Herold, the lead engineer, Bob takes over. As Herold remains into a coma, The Lone Ranger inadvertently receives the blame (and a gunshot, though not seriously wounded). After thwarting the scheme and preventing the bridge from being sabotaged, Butch stands defiant not to confess who hired him for the job… leaving The Lone Ranger to find another means of proving Kimberly was the mastermind.

Episode #1417-630 "BROTHERS OF THE WEST" [PART FOUR]

Broadcast February 20, 1942

Copyright Registration #79,419, script received at Registration Office February 28, 1942.

Plot: Hot on Matt Kimberly's trail back to Warren City, the masked man and Tonto ride into town just as dissatisfaction with the current sheriff, Bob Dixon, because he's a former Rebel, is reaching a fever pitch. Before Kimberly can goad gambler Ace Johnson into taking over the town, The Lone Ranger kidnaps the sheriff to prevent bloodshed and with permission from the sheriff, begins a series of hold ups on various businesses (promising not to kill or wound anyone) until the townsmen rebel. The masked man is mistaken as an outlaw as the sheriff, Sol Gardner, is unable to perform his duties to the satisfaction of the men and women in town. Eventually, after a few days of crimes, the masked man returns the stolen money and stolen goods and explains to the townsfolk how their prejudice gave them cause to support a man who was not capable of holding the position. "United we stand," the masked man reminded them. After proving no harm was done, the townsfolk realize that it was their prejudice that made them lose the best lawman they had and agreed to allow Bob Dixon his old post back.

Episode #1418-631 "THE VULTURE'S NEST" [PART FIVE]

Broadcast February 23, 1942

Copyright Registration #79,420, script received at Registration Office February 28, 1942.

Plot: In desperation to halt the production of the railroad by October 1, John Kimberly brought an unscrupulous doctor in from the East to poison two key railroad men and make their deaths mimic heart failure. Matt Kimberly blackmails Doctor Manson to do his bidding. Returning to Warren City, The Lone Ranger learns of the doctor's arrival and investigates… even stealing some of his toxic powder. After learning of Kimberly's scheme, the masked man and Tonto plot to foil the scheme. Soon after Jim Warren and Harry Miles are chased by outlaws in a vast desert known as vulture country, where poisonous waterholes are the only source of water, they put up a good fight. Eventually captured and taken to a shack, the two men are almost forced to drink "bad water" and left in the desert to appear as if they drank from one of the waterholes. The Lone Ranger, having followed the outlaws, showed up to prevent the men from drinking and reveal he has possession of the same white powder, and that the outlaws all drank from the same water. In return for the antidote, the outlaws forced Kimberly to sign a confession and the men signed as a witness. Only after the confession is acquired does the masked man reveal the truth. Tonto replaced the poison with harmless salt and Jim and Harry agree to hold the criminals at bay until the law arrives with Tonto.

Notes: Tonto replacing poison for ordinary table salt was recycled from the broadcast of May 31, 1937.

Episode #1419-632 "THREE GENERATIONS" [PART ONE]

Broadcast February 25, 1942

Copyright Registration #79,421, script received at Registration Office February 28, 1942.

Plot: When gold was found in the Black Hills, new communities sprung up almost overnight. Each day brought men with families who staked all they had and whose goal it was to be among the lucky ones to strike it rich. Flimsy houses were assembled, gambling houses flourished and prices for commodities went sky high, and everyone talked in millions. Lone Ranger and Tonto arrived in the Black Hills after a trip of many days from the south, heading to Deadwood. Having turned in Matt Kimberly to the Federal Marshals, the masked man now set his sights for Clark Drexel, who ran a mining syndicate. They knew Drexel was one of the founders of the Black Arrow, but without proof they knew their mission was to find whatever crooked scheme he was pulling so they could get him convicted. There, they became involved in a plan to take over Eli Crane's gold mine by Grant after Eli's son, Jim, dies in an accident. Eli Crane, to whom the town was named after, owned the most profitable mine and the largest home in the territory. The guilty parties, Rodney Grant and Lige, accuse The Lone Ranger of riding up to them and stealing the body of the dead man, giving the sheriff reason to hunt the masked man down. The Lone Ranger, learning from Eli what he needed to know about Rodney Grant, the masked man created a scenario whereas the law thought The Lone Ranger shot and killed Eli, sending the law on a goose chase that led to Rodney and Lige, who were forced to confess under circumstances that would have meant a worse fate. Lige confessed he and his partner schemed to steal Eli's gold mine, and their mistake was tipping off where they saw Jim, when it was the masked man who found the dead body elsewhere.

Notes: Certain elements from this episode would later be recycled for use on the December 23, 1954, broadcast of *Sergeant Preston of the Yukon*, including some of the opening narration and the names of Crane, Jim and Sally.

Episode #1420-633 "BLAST AND DOUBLE BLAST" [PART TWO]

Broadcast February 27, 1942

Copyright Registration #79,422, script received at Registration Office February 28, 1942.

Plot: Drexel Syndicate agent Beasley is trying to buy up all the mines near Deadwood and arranges accidents for the mine owners who won't sell. Moreover, Drexel has posted a $10,000 reward for The Lone Ranger, forcing the masked man to don a disguise to trap Beasley and help the mine owners. The Lone Ranger, after having a discussion with one of the victimized mine owners, Verne Gardner and his wife Sarah, dons a disguise as a hired gun and pays Beasley a visit. With Tonto outside mimicking The Lone Ranger, the real Ranger manages to convince Beasley to hire him to kill the masked man. Using the money paid, the masked man pays Verne the money he needed to operate his mine and hit paydirt. After Verne's mine becomes active again, despite the strongarm tactics applied against him, Beasley gets desperate enough to hire the disguised Lone Ranger to set off a blast in Verne's tunnel. The payment and the agreement were overheard by the sheriff and his posse, cinching his guilt. Sheriff Potter agrees that since his posse is turning over the real Lone Ranger, who was now revealed to Beasley, the Drexel Syndicate is to pay the $10,000 reward. Beasley, realizing he could be facing jail time, relents.

Episode #1421-634 "DOUBLE TROUBLE" [PART THREE]

Broadcast March 2, 1942

Written by George Waller.

Copyright Registration #79,712, script received at Registration Office March 30, 1942.

Plot: Problem for the miners near Deadwood continues as Beasley, one of Drexel's agents, orders a survey of claim boundaries, then hires a lookalike gunslinger to impersonate the surveyor and alter the claims. His attempt to falsify a young surveyor's report in an effort to cheat the miners out of their land almost works if it was not for The Lone Ranger. The masked man locates the real surveyor, Ted Lawson, and attempts to convince a skeptical sheriff which of the two is the real crook. Meanwhile, landowners Hank Oliver and his wife Martha discover the boundaries changed and their mines in the Black Hills being taken as property of the Drexel Mining Company. When the outlaw gunslinger named Dan Carradine is exposed, the sheriff finds himself disappointed in Beasley's scheme and jails both Carradine and Beasley.

Episode #1422-635 "DIAMOND TRAIL" [PART FOUR]

Broadcast March 4, 1942

Copyright Registration #79,713, script received at Registration Office March 30, 1942.

Written by Tom Dougall.

Plot: Clark Drexel comes to Deadwood and with Rance hatches a scheme with Rita, a waitress in his café, to frame The Lone Ranger for holding up the stagecoach and robbing the lady of her diamonds. The sheriff arrests the masked man and his companion, but Tonto managed to escape, later returning to jail and frees The Lone Ranger. Rita, in the meantime, visits Rance to alert him of a new development... she wore one of the stolen diamonds (the "Rockwell" diamond) after the robbery and then misplaced it. Tonto pays a visit to the crooks and at gunpoint orders them to ride out to into the woods. Meeting The Lone Ranger, Rita attempts to strike a bargain. She promises to tell the sheriff it was a frame-up in return for the strongbox that contains the stolen diamonds. The confrontation was overheard by the sheriff who was hiding inside the cave entrance. The Lone Ranger promises protection if they provide evidence against Clark Drexel, but neither Rance nor Rita would testify against Drexel.

Episode #1423-636 "MASKED MAN'S DUAL ROLE" [PART FIVE]

Broadcast March 6, 1942

Copyright Registration #79,714, script received at Registration Office March 30, 1942.

Plot: With Beasley in jail, Clark Drexel orders his banker accomplice to help him scheme to hold-up miners bringing gold into town to be deposited. Deadwood City was a boomtown and the Drexel Mining Syndicate, having established the bank Jeff Turner owned and operated, forced the banker to participate in the scheme. Gold thieves struck and miners with fresh hue and cry began talk of forming a vigilante committee. A disguised Lone Ranger, wandering town, was framed for the robberies, so he went on the offensive, trailing the robbers to their camp. The Lone Ranger tricks the crooks in a manner to lure them to a rendezvous where the confrontation creates a confession that incriminates both the banker and his associate... and names Drexel as the man responsible for the scheme. The miners who were victimized, hidden outside the house, overheard the criminals who in turn will soon face an unsympathetic jury.

Episode #1424-637 "DREXEL'S END" [PART SIX]

Broadcast March 9, 1942

Copyright Registration #79,715, script received at Registration Office March 30, 1942.

Plot: Clark Drexel was the subject of discussion at every café as a result of his recent arrest, courtesy of The Lone Ranger. But before Drexel can be hung for his crimes, he escapes jail and circles back and sneaks into Deadwood City in order to burn down his offices, attempting to destroy the evidence against him. By the time The Lone Ranger arrived, there was nothing but a pile of embers. Witnesses claim Clark Drexel died in the fire, but the masked man suspected the crook faked his death, and someone had to help assist Drexel. The masked man sets up a trap for Buck, Drexel's accomplice, which leads the sheriff and his deputies back to Drexel's hiding place and Drexel's final stand. Buck, panicking, takes the men to the hunter's cabin where the posse closes in. Drexel flees from a window off the side, but the lawmen open fire and Drexel pays for his crimes with his life.

Episode #1425-638 "STAMPEDE IN THE DARK" [PART ONE]

Broadcast March 11, 1942

Copyright Registration #79,716, script received at Registration Office March 30, 1942.

Written by Sheldon Stark.

Plot: Five men of the Black Arrow were able to walk because there was no evidence against them. On the trail of those five men, The Lone Ranger and Tonto focused on the trail for Benjamin Steel, and evidence against him. The scene shifts back to Texas and the Tomahawk Basin where Benjamin Steel has amassed a huge cattle empire by rustling. After getting an angry rancher named Jeff Aldon out of a gunfight, The Lone Ranger learns that someone wants Jeff Aldon to sell his land after a series of mysterious incidents including a poisoned water hole, shots through the window and stolen cattle. The Lone Ranger, finding evidence that Jeff was dragged from his saddle, assumes Jeff was captured. Further investigation revealed Farro, hired by Steel, plans to spook a herd of Texas longhorn steers into a stampede toward Jeff's ranch house. Tonto races out to rescue Jeff's wife while The Lone Ranger thwarted the stampede into a circle. The posse arrived to apprehend the schemers, except for Farro, who died when his horse tripped from a gopher hole. With Steel's man killed, there was no evidence against Benjamin Steel.

Episode #1426-639 "CLOUDY WATERS" [PART TWO]

Broadcast March 13, 1942 .

Copyright Registration #79,717, script received at Registration Office March 30, 1942.

Written by Sheldon Stark.

Plot: Having made camp in Tomahawk Basin to find evidence against Benjamin Steel, king of the cattle country, The Lone Ranger and Tonto discover a local rancher named Jim Carey, and his daughter Abby, are victims of a poisoned water hole. Breed, Steel's henchman who escaped from the cattle rustling scheme in the last adventure, was responsible for the scheme. With the only water on his range poisoned, Carey must accept Steel's offer. The Lone Ranger, however, interrupts the purchase of the land and orders Steel to leave. Tonto insists Steel is worse than a rattlesnake because a rattlesnake gives warning before attacking. Meanwhile, Ted Bailey, who rides herd for Steel and with an eye for Abby, is ordered by Steel to inform Carey and Abby to use his waterhole at the cottonwood as a sign of good faith. Breed, having masqueraded as The Lone Ranger, throws a bag of poison into the waterhole, unsuspecting that the real masked man would ride after him and apprehend the crook. Forcing Breed back to the scene and ordering him to drink from the waterhole to force a confession, Carey and Abby learn the truth and agree to turn Breed over to the sheriff.

Episode #1427-640 "FIFTY THOUSAND HEAD" [PART THREE]

Broadcast March 16, 1942

Copyright Registration #79,718, script received at Registration Office March 30, 1942.

Written by Tom Dougall.

Plot: On the day Breed Gomez, the Tomahawk foreman, went to trial in Leadville, Benjamin Steel found a loophole that prevented Breed from a hangman's knot. But Jim Carey was not surprised and exposed Steel's scheme to the local ranchers, launching what will no doubt become a range war. The ranchers agree to start a cattle drive to get their longhorns to the market before Steel can depress the market, giving ranchers a reason why they should sell out. The Lone Ranger supervised the cattle drive on the way to Clarksville, doing his best to thwart Steel's schemes – except for a stampede which he was unable to prevent. But despite the schemes of Steel, The Lone Ranger managed to reach John Bennett first, the cattle buyer in Clarksville, and explained how the cattle ranchers were in jeopardy. Bennett understood the situation and sided with the local ranchers – which Steel discovered the hard way when he arrived with Breed and his 50,000 head.

Episode #1428-641 "FORCED SALE" [PART FOUR]

Broadcast March 18, 1942

Copyright Registration #79,719, script received at Registration Office March 30, 1942.

Written by Tom Dougall.

Plot: During a confrontation in Leadville, rancher Benjamin Steel of the Tomahawk fires Wolf Barrett and his men. Steel, having been a former member of the Black Arrow, arouses The Lone Ranger's suspicions. The scheme was to throw suspicion away from Steel when Wolf conspired with his employer to kidnap Abby and demand a ransom. Carey is unable to afford the ransom unless he is able to sell his ranch… much to the delight of Steel. Wolf and his men charged multiple times as The Lone Ranger and Tonto took careful aim to keep the men back in the pass long enough for the sheriff to arrive and apprehend the kidnappers. Abby arrives in time to prevent her father from signing over the ranch for $10,000, even when Carey suspects that Steel is going to pay some of the money to the kidnappers. But just as it looked like Wolf's testimony would finally be the evidence needed to convict Benjamin Steel, the masked man learns that Wolf was shot by his own men who were determined to get out of a sticky situation.

Episode #1429-642 "MEN WHO WON'T TALK" [PART FIVE]

Broadcast March 20, 1942

Copyright Registration #79,720, script received at Registration Office March 30, 1942.

Written by Fran Striker.

Plot: Departing from Tomahawk Basin for a spell to investigate a mystery, The Lone Ranger and Tonto ride out to Coldwater to learn why men disappear and return somehow changed. Body snatchers? No, only a gang of extortioners trying to gain control of the land in the region, attempting a scheme that even Benjamin Steel would find impressive. It was Betty Manning who called on The Lone Ranger to help investigate since her father returned a changed man. The masked man played the game back against the criminals and tricked the real culprit (the bartender in town who was the ringleader) into signing over the property he stole back to all the men he cheated. The sheriff was witness and he ordered the gang members to flee town before he starts making arrests.

Episode #1430-643 "WAR SWEEPS THE RANGE" [PART SIX]

Broadcast March 23, 1942

Copyright Registration #79,721, script received at Registration Office March 30, 1942.

Written by Sheldon Stark.

Plot: The whole vast region of Tomahawk Basin had become an armed camp, and the local ranchers know the truth about Benjamin Steel and his effort to take away their homestead. The ranchers decide to band together take up arms against Steel, starting a range war. Gunplay started in town when Breed put in an appearance, and when The Lone Ranger learns that a local rancher named Andrew Fergus has gone vigilante, he asks for a brief pause to intervene. Jeff Darrow, shot and wounded, is nursed back to health by Tonto. Jeff confesses that Benjamin Steel has become desperate and stole his land through foul means with a disregard for the law. When the local ranchers learn what happened to Jeff, they arm themselves. The Lone Ranger, aware that Fergus and the men are outnumbered against Steel's professional gunmen who are dead shots, rides out to fetch the sheriff. Just as the ill-conceived attack is to begin, the masked man shows up with "evidence" against Steel, convincing the ranchers to pause momentarily so they can all be deputized. The attack, led by the sheriff and The Lone Ranger, kept Steel's men busy with a simple trick – long enough for the posse to ride in and surround from behind. Steel, however, was able to flee with his top gunslinger, Breed Gomez.

Episode #1431-644 "SOUND AND FURY" [PART SEVEN]

Broadcast March 25, 1942

Copyright Registration #79,722, script received at Registration Office March 30, 1942.

Written by Tom Dougall.

Plot: The Tomahawk Series concludes as Benjamin Steel returns to the Tomahawk Basin and breaks his men (all 100) out of jail. They terrorize the ranchers who have ranchland in the basin, including burning the town to the ground, The Lone Ranger returns with Jim Casey, having sent Tonto to Fort Union for re-enforcements. Steel puts the word out to outlaws and gunmen across Texas, growing his outlaw army by the day. The sheriff insists that he and the ranchers are overwhelmed by the attacking bad men. The settlers are nearly over-whelmed by the attacking bad men until they are saved by the Army. Breed Gomez and Rusty, close associates of Steel, are taken into custody. The Lone Ranger races out to apprehend Steel and bring him back to face the men whose homes were burned to the ground… but in fear of mob justice Steel agrees to be turned over to the military instead. Steel will be taken to Washington to be put on trial for treason.

Episode #1432-645 "THE MARSHAL OF MOUNTAIN CITY" [PART ONE]

Broadcast March 27, 1942

Copyright Registration #79,723, script received at Registration Office March 30, 1942.

Plot: For years the fur trappers had come down from the mountains in summertime to Great Meadows. From there they sold their furs to the agents of the various companies and bought supplies for the coming winter. In time, a permanent settlement sprung up and Mountain City became the fur capitol of the West, center of the northwest fur trade. It boasted a post office, stores and cafes and the warehouses of the great Webster Company. The town slept through the winter and only came to life with the first stirring of spring. Then the tents of the trappers covered the meadow and Mountain City came into its own. Colorful, exciting and roaring with vitality of thousands of men released from their winter prisons. An election would be held for a new marshal and Johnny Maitland was convinced to run for office, especially since he was an impressive sharpshooter. There have been outlaws at work and only the Great Webster wagon trains have fallen victim. Johnny's intention to run for office is opposed by one of Jacob Webster's men, who attempts to lure Johnny to his doom with a fake note from his girl, Rose O'Brian. Knowing she lived too far away for such a note to have been delivered this early in the spring, The Lone Ranger and Tonto ride out to rescue. The vigilantes are too late, however, finding Johnny wounded from rifle fire. While Tonto mends the wound and treats the fever the masked man rides into town to inform the men suspected of committing the crime that a witness to the shooting will testify… unless they pay him off. Webster instructs Rance Corby, the man responsible for the shooting, to ride out with his associates to find out what the price for silence would be. Not only did this lure the shooter, but after The Lone Ranger shoots the gun out of Rance's hand, the outlaws discover they are surrounded. Rance, however, would not give the name of his boss… even though The Lone Ranger knows Jacob Webster is their leader.

Blooper! In the beginning of this episode, the actor playing the role of the bartender pauses in his delivery, momentarily, as he flips the page of his script.

Episode #1433-646 "FURS TRAP A BADMAN" [PART TWO]

Broadcast March 30, 1942

Copyright Registration #79,724, script received at Registration Office March 30, 1942.

Written by Sheldon Stark.

Plot: Johnny Maitland established himself as a sufficient marshal in the territory, but this does not stop one of Webster's henchmen, Harry Sedley, from hiring two crooks named Sorell and Burley to rob an Indian riding into Mountain City with two pack horses with pelts. The Lone Ranger and Tonto thwart the scheme only to learn that the Indian's winter cache of valuable black fox fur was stolen. Tonto, snooping outside the window of the Bearcat Café, overhears the conversation between the crooks and reports back to The Lone Ranger. When Maitland was called upon to act on this evidence, Sorell and Burley were jailed and Sedley, called out in public as a crook, missed a bullet that was initially meant for Maitland. The Lone Ranger, realizing the bullet was really meant for him, creates a trap to expose the crooks. The next day, Sorell and Burley are released from jail and ordered to leave town. Sedley, meanwhile, plans to make another theft as Running Fawn, wife of the Indian who had black fox pelts stolen, reveals how her husband Siskayu found the trail from his cabin and is tracking down the thief… with a scalping knife in hand. But when Sedley explains to the two crooks how he wants them to take the stolen black fox pelts to Portland to sell and send him the percentage, profits from stolen goods never appear on the company books. But as the stolen pelts are revealed, they are caught with the goods and Sedley keeps his mouth quiet – he takes the blame for the theft and won't name Jacob Webster as his boss.

Episode #1434-647 "WEBSTER'S BIG FIRE" [PART THREE]

Broadcast April 1, 1942

Copyright Registration #79,725, script received at Registration Office March 30, 1942.

Plot: Jim Blake, a bounty hunter, rode into town with a chip on his shoulder. A new law was put into effect that pelts cannot be paid for unless it was the entire pelt, ears and all. For folks like Blake, this hampers their assignment and places Webster's company into a strategic position. But Blake was misinformed and there is no such law. Such scheme cuts pricing to hurt the competition including the trading post owned and operated by Ma Collins and her daughter. Webster's new manager in Mountain City, Tom Turner, undertakes a scheme to buy worthless furs in order to substitute them for insured valuable ones. When Jim Blake and The Lone Ranger are knocked from behind and captured, he is left to burn in the warehouse fire. (Inexplicably, the crooks ignore The Lone Ranger's mask, while bound and gagged.) Tonto fights his way into the fire to rescue him. As the townsfolk arrive to witness the warehouse ablaze, The Lone Ranger puts in an appearance to explain how the new policies established by the Webster company was never meant to pay out with the warehouse scheme. Tom Turner was quickly incriminated, along with Sam Peters and Butch, who worked alongside him. Since the Webster Company would be in default for not providing a warehouse after the fire, but the goods found and retrieved, Ma Collins receives the credit and payments.

Notes: The character of Hank is doubled by John Todd. The premise of a warehouse fire with substitutes of cheap furs was done prior on the April 12, 1938, broadcast of *The Green Hornet*, and then recycled again (sans furs) on the March 11, 1940, broadcast of *The Green Hornet*.

Episode #1435-648 "A GIRL'S BONFIRE" [PART FOUR]

Broadcast April 3, 1942

Copyright Registration #79,726, script received at Registration Office March 30, 1942.

Plot: Ma Collins now manages the town's warehouse, despite the fact that Johnny Maitland confesses how Turner and Butch may walk from the crime for the only person who can bring charges against him is Jacob Webster, who owned the warehouse that was set on fire. Joan Barcley, having traveled down from Deadwood, returns as she poses as Webster's agent to press charges against Turner and Butch for burning the fur warehouse. This puts a streak of fear into Turner and Butch, despite the fact that Turner has evidence that Webster was his employer. Then she asks The Lone Ranger to break the two men out of jail so they will lead Marshal Maitland to evidence which might point to Webster's guilt. Late at night, someone attempted a jailbreak and there was no chance to overtake Turner and Butch as the crooks rode off before anyone could take pursuit. Following the trail of Turner and Butch, The Lone Ranger follows the trail and then arranges for Tonto to report back to Maitland so a posse will arrive to take over. With the assistance of the masked man, the crooks are overtaken at their hideout in the woods, and the evidence Turner sought to retrieve against his employer was confiscated by the law.

Episode #1436-649 "TURNABOUT" [PART FIVE]

Broadcast April 6, 1942

Copyright Registration #79,727, script received at Registration Office March 30, 1942.

Written by Tom Dougall and George Waller.

Plot: The warehouse of the Great Western Company, owned by Ma Collins, a battle axe, and whose daughter is going to marry Johnny Maitland, the marshal, fell victim to an attack. Webster instructs Walter Driscoll, his newest manager, to induce Ma Collins to file charges against Webster, with a charge of hiring outlaws to attack her warehouse. But Webster knew the laws of libel and slander and had a plan in mind. Tonto was in Mountain City when Webster was marched into town and placed into jail. After reporting the arrest to The Lone Ranger, the masked man wonders why the thieves even bothered to break into a warehouse so early in the evening… unbecoming of real thieves. Further investigation reveals Webster was not responsible and he makes it known he plans to sue Ma Collins for $50,000 for false arrest… and such a suit could help him gain possession of her fur business. Webster agrees to waive all his claims if she agrees to sell her business for $5,000. In the morning, Webster plans to travel to the county seat in Salt Lake City to file charges. Hoping to beat Webster at his own game, The Lone Ranger and Tonto ride out to stop the stagecoach and moments later the marshal arrives with a warrant to inspect Webster's carpet bag… where Tonto planted black fox pelts that were stolen from Ma's warehouse. Facing a charge against him, Webster agrees to drop the suit. Before returning to Mountain City, Webster exchanges words with The Lone Ranger.

Episode #1437-650 "SET A THIEF" [PART SIX]

Broadcast April 8, 1942

Copyright Registration #79,996, script received at Registration Office April 23, 1942.

Written by Tom Dougall.

Plot: Desperate, Jacob Webster decides to legally buy Ma Collins out for $100,000, twice the value of the business. To compensate for the purchase price, Jacob Webster knows he will own the only company that buys furs in the region and will purchase at half price. After consulting The Lone Ranger, Ma Collins agrees to sell with a revision to the non-compete clause… she cannot start another fur trading business within 100 miles of Mountain City. Soon after she signs the papers, Webster laughs as the price for furs will be dropped in half. Upset for the scheme, Ma Collins announces she will open a new post at Fort Haul. Trappers will have no problem traveling a further distance to make twice the money with their furs. As a result, Webster arranges for Curt Morgan and his outlaw gang to ambush Ma. Tonto overhears the plans and alerts The Lone Ranger, who races out to warn her in time. Having captured Driscoll, The Lone Ranger orders him to write a letter to Colonel Graham at the nearby fort… but the letter was never meant for the Colonel. Giving the false appearance that Webster was going to frame the recent crimes against Morgan, Morgan and his men ride out to the office of Jacob Webster to steal from their employer and fix it so Webster does not double-cross them. The marshal and his deputies show up to reveal they overheard the conversation – testimony against Webster proving all of his previous crimes. Morgan's men are already under arrest and Morgan, angry, reveals Webster was known under another name and wanted for a murder committed 20 years ago. The falling out among thieves is enough to clinch Webster going to the gallows.

Episode #1438-651 "ALONG THE OREGON TRAIL"

Broadcast April 10, 1942

Copyright Registration #79,997, script received at Registration Office April 23, 1942.

Written by Sheldon Stark.

Plot: The pioneer trail to Oregon was dangerous. Whoever rode it faced miles of lonely country, where marauding bands of Indians swept down from the barren hills, where badmen and buzzards waited to attack the weary traveler. Lance Kinnard, a smooth, deadly gunman who shot his way out of a posse, had more than 20 killings to his credit. When the gunman steals gold from Randy Davis and his wife, Martha, who were traveling to Oregon, he also steals their wagon because the gold was too heavy to take on horseback. The Lone Ranger and Tonto, meanwhile, observing buzzards circulating above, come across the body of a wolf bounty hunter named Graham, who was shot and left for dead the night before. Weak, he tells the masked man that he was shot by Lance Kinnard who, along with a badman named Welman, was making for the Oregon Trail. While Tonto remains to look after Graham, The Lone Ranger, hot on the killer's trail, overtakes the wagon and eventually comes face-to-face with the killer…in a fast-draw showdown. If the posse caught up and attacked, Kinnard and Welman would shoot it out. It was open country and honest men would be killed before the outlaws were caught. The Lone Ranger hoped to apprehend the killers. Against the odds, even knowing Kinnard has lightning fast on the draw, The Lone Ranger out-nerves and outshoots the badman to capture him for the approaching posse.

Episode #1439-652 "THE BROKEN SPUR"

Broadcast April 13, 1942

Copyright Registration #79,998, script received at Registration Office April 23, 1942.

Written by Tom Dougall.

Plot: The whole county celebrated the wedding of young Jerry Tolliver and Nancy Hayden. The lovers hoped the fighting between the Tollivers and the Haydens would end as a result of the marriage. But two weeks later, on the long trail to Birchville, riding through Two Bit Canyon, Jerry was shot from ambush. The Lone Ranger and Tonto, riding through the region, mends the wound and tends to Jerry, while finding a broken spur as the only clue to the shooter. Jerry's father, Sam, suspects Nancy fixed it up with her father to create the ambush. When Sam and The Lone Ranger ride out to the Hayden ranch to confront Nancy's father, Ben, they verify the broken spur is his – and Ben discovers his spurs are missing. The Lone Ranger took Ben to Birchville to prevent a murder by Sam and his men, but that would not stop him from being tried and convicted. Nancy later confesses to The Lone Ranger that her brother, Nick, was accused of taking money from a bank and the only man who could clear him is in Chicago. She sent her husband to Birchville to mail a letter to fetch the man who could clear him. But what Nancy did not know was that her brother, Nick, was in fact guilty. He did not want the letter mailed, shot Jerry, and framed it on his father so the feud between the two families would begin again. If Ben was not hung for the crime, he would surely die from the exchange in the feud, and Nick would inherit the Hayden ranch. Outside the sheriff's office in Birchville, Nick attempted to shoot his father from outside the window the jail, only to be thwarted by The Lone Ranger and Tonto.

Episode #1440-653 "DIVINING ROD"

Broadcast April 15, 1942

Copyright Registration #79,999, script received at Registration Office April 23, 1942.

Written by Fran Striker.

Plot: This was the same script from the broadcast of November 18, 1935, with two names changed. Black Burton was replaced with Butch Burton, and the old woman named Mag was replaced by an old Hermit.

Episode #1441-654 "THE END OF PAGE"

Broadcast April 17, 1942

Copyright Registration #80,000, script received at Registration Office April 23, 1942.

Written by Fran Striker.

Plot: Having left Mountain City and riding out for Plainville, The Lone Ranger and Tonto happen upon a primitive tribe, not savage, possessing what appears to be stolen Army rifles. After discussing an exchange with the chief, the masked man learned someone was exchanging "thunder sticks" for black fox pelts worth more than the guns on the open market. In Plainville, The Lone Ranger meets the mysterious girl, who aided him so often in his fight against the outlaw legion known as the Black Arrow. After learning that Bronson Page handled many purchases for the U.S. Government, and bought rifles for the army, the masked man could piece together the clues. Rifles and other supplies bought and paid for by the Government were swapped with Indians for furs. One of her operators in Washington found letters addressed to Bronson Page. Those letters came from Plainsville. A short time after, Bronson Page and his associate, Lefty, questioned The Lone Ranger (in town under a disguise) as to where he acquired the black fox pelts. The Lone Ranger explained how he found a camp of Indians who were willing to trade the pelts for cartridges, so he came to town to buy cartridges, go back and trade for furs, then return to sell the furs for a large profit.

Page wanted to purchase the furs, knowing he could profit from the deal, and struck a bargain with The Lone Ranger to supply cartridges that would fit the rifles. Setting the trap, knowing Bronson Page took the bait, The Lone Ranger explains his rendezvous with the Indian to pick up the furs is shortly after dark, tomorrow night, at Gopher Spring. In return for the cartridges, The Lone Ranger would divide the pelts in a partnership. Gopher Spring was in a clearing about half a mile from town. Surrounded by woods it was an ideal secret meeting place. Tonto went there shortly after sundown with the furs. He concealed them in a thicket and then sat on the ground beside the spring and waited. He did not wait long. The two crooks met with Tonto, believing he was a member of the Indian tribe outside of town. After showing the bags of ammunition, they attempted to strike a deal with Tonto for the pelts. After verifying the pelts were indeed waiting for trade, Lefty makes an attempt on Tonto's life and is almost immediately stopped in his tracks by The Lone Ranger. As the masked man disarmed Lefty, Tonto punched Page to the ground. The Lone Ranger reveals a secret to Bronson Page. The law was in hiding and within listening distance to overhear Page admit trading supplies that belonged to the army.

Notes: The script title is "The End of Page," referring to the character of Bronson Page, not "The End of a Page" like some collectors have listed in error.

Episode #1442-655 "GAMBLERS' END"

Broadcast April 20, 1942
Copyright Registration #80,001, script received at Registration Office April 23, 1942.
Written by Tom Dougall.
Plot: Two professional gamblers named Greg and Silk were thrown off a riverboat along the Missouri and find themselves working their way back to safety, preferably Plainsville. They happen to come across Martha Winton and her son, Jimmy, who were on their way to the diggings at Alder to meet her husband. Offering aid while traveling through Indian country, with understanding of safety in numbers, the four follow the advice of The Lone Ranger, to avoid a band of 20 Indians half a mile away. After thwarting a minor attack from the red savages, Jimmy drove the wagon out on the trail once more, with The Lone Ranger and the gamblers alongside. The masked man believes the gamblers are the kind of men the West needs and gives them an opportunity to make contributions. Ben Winton, Martha's husband, gambled away his claim to Ace Harding, a crooked card shark, and was ashamed to have done so. The Lone Ranger spoke to the gamblers and arranged for them to play against Ace Harding. During the late-night poker game in the Golden Nugget Café, the gamblers succeeded in winning the claim back for Ben Winton, who also allows the men to work the claim until Ben recovers from his illness.

Episode #1443-656 "THE DEPUTY FOR TUMBLEWEED"

Broadcast April 22, 1942

Copyright Registration #80,002, script received at Registration Office April 23, 1942.

Written by Fran Striker.

Plot: A crooked café owner named Ace Wills owns and operates a gang of outlaws for cattle rustling. Beacon City is a stopover place on the trail to the north country. Wills gets friendly with the herd drivers that come into his café. He learns where herds are being moved, then his men go and steal the longhorns. After the third sheriff was killed since the first of the year, shot in the back, Bob Turner, editor of the local paper, the Beacon City Star, exposed the racketeers and demanded townsfolk take back their town. When the newspaper office is ransacked and destroyed, The Lone Ranger visits Tumbleweed, an aged lawman who was appointed as a figurehead sheriff. The masked man convinces the old timer to deputize him so he can proceed to dispense real justice. With approval from an old cattleman named Lige, who was managing 1,200 head, The Lone Ranger masterminds with Tumbleweed the release of Bleak, one of the crooks responsible for breaking up the newspaper office. Bleak races to the hideout to report the news of the new deputy and how Ace Wills was also jailed… unaware he led The Lone Ranger and Tumbleweed to their hideout, caught with the goods as earlier in the day they stole Lige's 1,200 head of cattle. Bob Turner, who tagged along as backup for the law, gets the inside scoop and Tumbleweed gains respect in town as the new sheriff.

Notes: Bob Turner was originally Tom Turner in the initial draft of this radio script.

Episode #1444-657 "RAISING THE SEIGE"

Broadcast April 24, 1942

Copyright Registration #80,003, script received at Registration Office April 23, 1942.

Written by Sheldon Stark.

Plot: A small out-of-the-way prairie town known as Split Rock was a huddle of less than fifteen small shacks along one dusty street. The town was by-passed by the telegraph by seventy miles to a town called Crawford, and Mr. Dobey in town believes the new technology would be troublesome, despite the advantages. The Lone Ranger and Tonto, camped in the hills near Split Rock, discovers an outlaw band is coming down from the hills, intent on robbing the town of $50,000 in prospector gold. Warned ahead of time by The Lone Ranger, the men of Split Rock were ready when the attack came. They poured a withering fire back at the outlaws circling the little town. All day long they held them off, but toward dusk when the shooting slackened up, the defenders clustered in Dobey's general store. When The Lone Ranger makes a break under cover of darkness, he reaches the telegraph and, cutting the wire, touched them together to send a message, alerting the army stationed at the post 100 miles away. The Lone Ranger manages to return to fend the town off against the outlaw gang and, just as the townsfolk start running out of bullets, the army column swept down on the outlaws – in a few minutes they were prisoners. "I take back all I said about the telegraph," Dobey remarks. "It's a wonderful invention. Why, it saved our lives." The captain of the cavalry explained that they also have The Lone Ranger to thank.

Episode #1445-658 "FOR HIS SON'S SAKE"

Broadcast April 27, 1942

Copyright Registration #80,004, script received at Registration Office April 23, 1942.

Written by Fran Striker.

Plot: A prominent banker, Squire Tubbs, is blackmailed by a band of crooks, Steve Smith, Jake and Lefty, who threaten to expose his missing son as a cowardly deserter shot during the Civil War. The Lone Ranger, having picked up Lefty because the crook was masked, learned of the private meeting, and intercepted the proceedings to steal the papers Steve claimed verified his story about Jim Tubbs. Squire's wife and Jim's widow were holding to an ideal, and the banker would do almost anything to protect their happiness, including robbing the bank of

$20,000 to pay for blackmail. The masked man later paid a visit to the banker to ask him to stall the planned robbery for about a week while he played a few cards of his own to learn the truth of how Jim Tubbs really died. The Lone Ranger and Tonto, late one night, visited Steve's house and ransacked the place, giving the appearance that someone was searching for something. Steve quickly removed a rock from the fireplace to make sure the papers hiding there were undisturbed, unaware the masked man and Tonto watched from a window to see Steve reveal the hiding place. This comes in handy when The Lone Ranger invites the sheriff to join him as the crooks are exposed. The real letter (from a friend of Jim's in the army) verifies Jim was badly wounded in fighting and how he risked his life to save his captain. A hero revealed, Steve's scheme to blackmail the banker into robbing his brick-and-mortar employment failed, but not before Steve finds a loophole to claim he never robbed the bank – he never even touched the money. But Steve and his men are surprised when they are charged with robbing the United States Mail, an offence more serious than bank robbery.

Episode #1446-659 "THE CALL OF DUTY"

Broadcast April 29, 1942

Copyright Registration #80,005, script received at Registration Office April 23, 1942.

Written by Tom Dougall.

Plot: Morganville was the headquarters for all the sheep ranchers in the county. It was quieter than any cattle town and Sheriff Sam Blake had often complained that there was not enough action connected with his job. When Jim Dewey's flock of nearly 2,000 head were grazing in a valley, he notices smoke in a distance. The Lone Ranger and Tonto ride out to alert Jim that Ed Miller hired outlaws to start a fire, hoping to drive his flock to the south side. After The Lone Ranger diverts the fire and saves the flock, he tells Jim to beware of Ed Miller, who wants Jim to vacate the area. The next day, the sheriff arrives to investigate a claim that Jim's sheep dog, Laddie, was responsible for killing his lambs. With the dog missing, the sheriff starts a search for the animal. The Lone Ranger and Tonto were responsible for finding Laddie, wounded from a gunshot, and suspects a frame-up. After telling Jim's 12-year-old son, Buddy, to hide and look after Laddie, the masked man and Tonto went into town to arrange for a trial. The next day, with a judge, the sheriff and a jury, the dog known as Laddie was put on trial. During a daring exhibition with a wolf dog (courtesy of an old timer named Jake Summers), Laddie demonstrated he protects sheep, not kills them. The wound around the dog's neck and gunpowder on the dog's wounded foot suggested Ed Miller and Bragg chained the dog, stuck pieces of wool in his coat, shot him in the leg, and framed him for a crime so Jim Dewey would either kill or be killed in protecting him. With Jim either in jail or dead, there would be no one to stop them from using the north half of Jim's section. The court returns a verdict of not guilty, and Ed Miller is taken into custody by the sheriff.

Episode #1447-660 "GUNNER CREEK COW THIEVES"

Broadcast May 1, 1942

Copyright Registration #80,196, script received at Registration Office May 14, 1942.

Written by Fran Striker.

Plot: Ben Barton, one of the wealthiest ranchers in the region, has never been proven crooked because he had enough money to buy his way out of trouble. A young highwayman kept his face covered and his guns handy when he ordered a stage driver to surrender his passenger, Ben Barton. Sid Layton, the scheming crooked lawman who got himself elected as the sheriff of Gunner Creek, raced out with a posse to rescue. Before the stage robber, Dave Sanders, can exact revenge on the death of his father from the gang that was hired by Barton, the wealthy crook died of a heart attack. Having dropped to the ground, the last thing Barton did in his life was grab a gun and shoot and wound Dave Sanders. Tonto treats the wound while The Lone Ranger explains that the doctor in town is as crooked as the sheriff and wounds may be inflicted on the dead man to claim Barton was shot and killed. After the masked man established a plan to trap the crooked sheriff, his deputy

Frisby (who assists the bandits), Dave made sure to be caught and arrested so papers on his possession would lure the sheriff into the trap. Barton was responsible for the sale of stolen cattle and with no channels to sell the cattle, the papers provided a solution. The sheriff, his deputy and the bandits drove the cattle into a close-packed herd and then started on a long trip south. Towards sundown of the next day the herd reached Powder River, approaching the rancher who was willing to buy the cattle. Verifying the cattle was theirs, the rancher confirms the stolen goods and men from the cattlemen's association surround the cattle thieves – including the sheriff and his deputy.

Notes: During the beginning of the second act, The Lone Ranger identifies himself by name which is something he rarely ever did on the program – at least, in a script written by Fran Striker. (It was tradition that Tonto or someone else identified him by name.) The character of Sid Layton was originally Sid Abel in the first draft of this radio script.

Blooper! Near the end of the episode, the announcer accidentally refers to Sid Layton as Sid Abel.

Episode #1448-661 "ISLAND IN THE RIO"
Broadcast May 4, 1942
Copyright Registration #80,197, script received at Registration Office May 14, 1942.
Written by Fran Striker.
Plot: This was the same script from the broadcast of December 25, 1933, with only minor rewrites of dialogue.

Episode #1449-662 "OUTLAW POINT"
Broadcast May 6, 1942
Copyright Registration #80,198, script received at Registration Office May 14, 1942.
Written by Tom Dougall.
Plot: Brent Wylie, an Easterner and smooth crook, partners with an outlaw leader named John Macklin, who has been selling the Indians whiskey and guns. The latter would like to see Gordon Wylie out of the way because, as Indian commissioner, if he puts an end to the Indian trouble, it means money out of his pocket. Brent is Gordon's sole heir to a small fortune. When Mary O'Brien, the scout's daughter, learns of the scheme, she and Lt. Denis McCullough are kidnapped by Macklin to prevent his plan from failing. The Lone Ranger and Tonto, learning of the plot through Clare Sumner, the Colonel's daughter who had feelings for Brent, race to Brent Wylie's abode to release the captives. In his effort to thwart the renegade plans to murder the Indian commissioner and start a war, The Lone Ranger and Lt. McCullough race into a heavily wooded and blind canyon. Trapped, they hold off wasting their ammunition to buy time against Brent and Macklin's men. Desperately Macklin lunged at the masked man. Both men lost their footing and as they struggled, crashed down the steep slope of the canyon. The Lone Ranger tossed away his gun as the outlaw went for his throat on the level ground at the foot of the slope. Ultimately this led to Macklin falling into a trap as the Colonel and his men surrounded the culprit, unable to shoot from their present position until the men came down the slope. Only then Macklin learned that the cloaked figure he shot from a horse was not the Army's negotiator, but rather The Lone Ranger in disguise. Brent's uncle was never murdered, thanks to the masked man known as The Lone Ranger.

Episode #1450-663 "SMUGGLER'S BOSS"
Broadcast May 8, 1942
Copyright Registration #80,199, script received at Registration Office May 14, 1942.
Written by Fran Striker.

Plot: Lew Gorman was in jail in Amaranthe. The law intended to keep him there for at least 20 years, but Gorman had other plans and staged a clever jailbreak. The sheriff in a nearby town left with his deputies to hunt for Gorman. Sally Marker, whose father was the former sheriff and shot and killed by Gorman, believes she can be of help to the new sheriff and rides out to the cave that Gorman used to use as a hide-out. Widow Prindle, a friend of Sally's mother, was the boss of the drug smugglers, and tips off the gang members about the girl's impetuousness. The opening of the cave, a few miles from town, was hidden by dense underbrush. The Lone Ranger comes across Sally and when she mistakes him for Gorman, the masked man pretends to be the escaped con and ties Sally up. Through this masquerade he learns the names of the identities of the smugglers, including Scar Fenner, Red Tuffy, and Jenks. It doesn't take long for Sally to learn that Gorman was recaptured by the law, and another man was posing as Gorman. When she reports her findings to her mother, she inadvertently tips off Widow Prindle. Following instructions from The Lone Ranger, Sally fetches the sheriff and when the fake Lew Gorman leads the men into a trap, and thus identifying themselves as members of the smuggling gang, the law surrounds them. The sheriff and his deputies never left town after being informed by Tonto that they could apprehend the smugglers in one sweep in town.

Notes: The guard in the beginning of this episode remarked, "Yuh know doggone well, it is." The radio script called for the word "blamed" instead of "doggone," replaced during rehearsals to ensure young children did not pick up on the word and repeat it in the manner of a swear word.

Episode #1451-664 "TRAIL OF RED MUD"
Broadcast May 11, 1942
Copyright Registration #80,200, script received at Registration Office May 14, 1942.
Written by Fran Striker.
Plot: Andy Conway, who ran a general store in Hawksville, was willed a map to a valuable gold mine from his late brother. Before he can leave and stake his claim, the map was stolen by Lefty Carter. Members of the Carter gang created a stampede of longhorns through main street, creating a distraction so Lefty could steal the map. The Lone Ranger, a masked stranger in town, was accused of the crime. Lefty Carter, wanted by the law in several counties, joined his outlaw band not far from town. Because most of the town citizens were invested in the claim, grubstaking Andy, Lefty Carter knows filing a claim would result in jail time. But having the law dismiss the charges against him and his gang was worth the safe return of the map. Upon learning The Lone Ranger was nearby, the crooks kidnap Tonto as a means of keeping the masked man from interfering with their plans. The sheriff explains to The Lone Ranger that the U.S. Marshal is due soon, and if he is on hand, they will not be able to make any deal at all. After observing red clay on the hoofs of Butch's horse, as high as the fetlocks, it stood to reason that there was only one section in the area where there was red clay as deep as that… leading to the hideout of the crooks. With the sheriff and his deputies as backup, the crooks are rounded up by The Lone Ranger, the map recovered and Tonto rescued.

Episode #1452-665 "MISTAKEN FOR AN Easterner"
Broadcast May 13, 1942
Copyright Registration #80,201, script received at Registration Office May 14, 1942.
Written by Fran Striker.
Plot: When a crooked lawyer, Big Daniel, who is also the owner of the local bank, hires Dirk and Blackie to drive a stage line owner out of business by robbing the mail and burning the stages, The Lone Ranger investigates. Jim Mosely and his daughter, Gail, fear they will be out of business and suspect an Easterner named Mr. Tupping is responsible for the acts of sabotage. Big Daniel represents Mr. Tupping. The Lone Ranger, disguised as an Easterner in town, attempts to encourage ol' Fighting Jim to grow the backbone he once

had by preparing for a fight. With the cooperation of Sheriff Curly Bedford of Ranceville, The Lone Ranger plays a bandit to apprehend a stagecoach bound for town. Inside, they do not find Mr. Tupping, but Blackie masquerading as Mr. Tupping, to convince Jim Mosely to sign the papers that would transfer his business over to Tupping. Believing the stage robbers are members of the gang, Blackie inadvertently confesses how it was he and the gang that robbed and killed the men under Jim Mosely's employ, and the necessity of his arriving in town to complete the ruse. The sheriff takes Blackie into custody and then pays a visit to Big Daniel. The Lone Ranger quickly goes through the desk to find papers verifying there was no Mr. Tupping interested in the stage line, it was all a trick to convince Jim to sign over his company to Big Daniel.

Episode #1453-666 "WEST OF DODGE"

Broadcast May 15, 1942
Copyright Registration #80,202, script received at Registration Office May 14, 1942.
Written by Tom Dougall.
Plot: When Bill Harriman was given the contract to carry the mail between Central City and Morganville, there was one stipulation: he must get his new stage line in operation before July 1st. If he does not, he pays the government a $500-per-day penalty. This involves building way stations. It means buying plenty of horses and at least half a dozen coaches. Pete Lacey and Pedro Martinez, friends of The Lone Ranger, are hired to go to Dodge and pick up the coaches and buy nearly a hundred horses. But Harriman has enemies and if they delay him long enough, they can break him. The Lone Ranger and Tonto ride along with their friends, for added protection, and their reasoning was justified considering the multiple confrontations that followed. Cavell, an outlaw leader, led an attack on the Malcolm ranch where the horses were to be purchased, but The Lone Ranger thwarted the scheme. Defeated but determined, Cavell warns most cowboys in the region against Pete and Pedro, preventing the hiring of men to assist with the trail herd. Cavell attempts to shoot Pedro during an exchange, but The Lone Ranger shoots Cavell's gun from his hand, preventing bloodshed. This gave the masked man a chance to apprehend the Cavell gang. The caravan of coaches headed west and in each of them rode one of Cavell's men, a prisoner, but The Lone Ranger knew that more trouble could be expected. Rough trails, dangerous country, and many rivers lay ahead. Knowing Cavell and the last of his gang would wait until evening to attack the camp, just one night out from their destination, The Lone Ranger encourages Pete, Pedro and the hired guns to circle back and use the cover of night to surround Cavell and his men. Arriving in Central City the following night, Pete, Pedro, Tonto and the masked man surprise Bill Harriman with the stagecoaches – and the first passengers of the new stage line who will be taken to the sheriff's jail.

Episode #1454-667 [TITLE UNKNOWN]

Broadcast May 18, 1942
Copyright Registration #80,203, script received at Registration Office May 14, 1942.
Plot: A wandering cowpuncher named Jeff Drummond is framed for a Wells Fargo bank robbery, having been knocked unconscious when he passed by the bank at the time of the blast. A notorious crook named Slade Rankin, and his gang of eleven men, were responsible and Jeff was accused of being a member of the gang. The sheriff of Painted Rock, with no sympathy for outlaws, places the man in jail. The Lone Ranger, after hearing the facts of the case, breaks the innocent man out of jail. The masked man's actions lured the sheriff and his posse to the outlaw gang while Drummond, accompanied by Tonto, spies on the outlaw gang from afar. After hearing the bark from The Lone Ranger's guns, Tonto and Drummond create a rockslide, a thunderous sheet of shale that would trap the outlaws. Rankin's men were terrorized and quickly discovered the sheriff's posse was approaching. In desperation the outlaws exchanged gunfire but quickly realized they would be trapped regardless and surrendered. Drummond's innocence was verified, he was hailed as a hero, and the man who would receive the reward money for aiding in the capture.

Notes: Originally it was slated to recycle the same radio script broadcast on December 27, 1935, with two names changed. The crooked lawyer named C. Thorndyke Abercrombie was changed to Basil Thorndyke. The town of Placerville was changed to Bald Rock. But the recycled script was never used and instead the original plot of Slade Rankin and his gang was dramatized instead. The title of the intended script was "Thorndyke's Double Deal."

Episode #1455-668 "HANDS ACROSS THE PLAINS"

Broadcast May 20, 1942

Copyright Registration #80,204, script received at Registration Office May 14, 1942.

Plot: When a young Englishman named Larry Winton is framed for a bank robbery, The Lone Ranger trails him to another town, Valley Center, but – once he hears Larry's story, he is convinced of his innocence. Befriended by a rancher named Josh Brent, and his sister, Alice Brent, Larry Winton agrees to stay at the ranch while The Lone Ranger and Tonto scout the valley for the outlaws who are trying their hand at cattle rustling. The pass to the north leads to Bennett City, where they could sell cattle. When Josh Brent hires a new cowhand and Larry recognizes him as one of Smokey's gang members, Larry reports back to the masked man. The new cowhand alerts the local sheriff, in the hopes of incriminating Larry for the bank robbery, but The Lone Ranger intervenes and races off with Larry. Tonto rides out to track the rustlers and finds Smokey and his men hiding out in a cave in the canyons. Saving Josh and Alice's cattle from being stolen by the outlaw gang, The Lone Ranger rides onto the Brent ranch and convinces Alice to pretend she is being kidnapped, so the sheriff and his men, and her ranch hands, will pursue. The chase leads to the outlaw gang. Smokey and his men are rounded up and the stolen money from the bank robbery Larry Winton was accused of is also recovered, clearing Larry's name.

Notes: The Lone Ranger and Tonto make reference to knowing Larry Winton from a prior episode, but this was the first time the character was on the program.

Episode #1456-669 "GHOST TOWN"

Broadcast May 22, 1942

Copyright Registration #80,205, script received at Registration Office May 14, 1942.

Written by Fran Striker.

Plot: This was the same script from the broadcast of May 1, 1935. This script was originally slated for the broadcast of April 11, 1941, as registered for copyright at the Library of Congress. Because of the untimely death of actor Earle Graser, and the last-minute decision to change the radio scripts to reflect a new actor playing the title role, this script was shelved and eventually dramatized on May 22, 1942.

Episode #1457-670 "TOMORROW'S TRAIL" [PART ONE]

Broadcast May 25, 1942

Copyright Registration #80,206, script received at Registration Office May 14, 1942.

Plot: See pages 273 and 274.

Episode #1458-671 "STEAMBOAT ON THE RIVER" [PART TWO]

Broadcast May 27, 1942

Copyright Registration #80,207, script received at Registration Office May 14, 1942.

Plot: Omaha became a boom town when the construction of the railroad to the west got underway. It was the focal point for laborers in search of work, who came from all parts of the country. It was in Omaha that the construction supplies were brought together. Timber, blasting powder and other supplies. Colonel Parkman, the engineer who was in charge of this stupendous undertaking, lived for the time being in Omaha. Shipment of blasting powder was due to arrive any day. Both Joan Barcley and The Lone Ranger fear too many people know about the secret delivery. Henry Wilson put in an appearance at Colonel Parkman's office, offering assistance and a tip that a criminal named Lefty, working for the opposition, boarded the boat containing the explosives. Lefty boarded the riverboat at St. Joseph. In secret, two crooks named Red and Butch were hired by Henry Wilson to set fire to the riverboat and cause the explosives to blow up during transportation. After setting fuses to one of the kegs, the two men are apprehended as The Lone Ranger secretly extinguishes the fuse, knowing that Lefty was not the real criminal that Henry Wilson wanted the authorities to believe. Fearing the boat is about to blow up, the two criminals confessed to the deed in the hopes of saving their own lives and testified who hired them. The man who claimed to be Henry Wilson, however, turned out to be an imposter, hoping to trick the Colonel and Joan into arresting Lefty, who in reality was an undercover government man.

Blooper! The announcer stumbles over a couple words during the opening lines!

Episode #1459-672 "LONGHORNS' BACKTRAIL" [PART THREE]
Broadcast May 29, 1942
Copyright Registration #80,296, script received at Registration Office May 22, 1942.
Plot: Joan Barcley admits that she was a fool when she turned her back – even momentarily – on the impostor posing as Henry Wilson, as he took advantage of the opportunity and fled. The Lone Ranger and Tonto travel north to northwest from Omaha, searching for the imposter who called himself Henry Wilson. After introducing himself to Jim Blake, the construction supervisor for the railroad at the camp, the masked man discovers that the cattle being raised for food have been poisoned. Without food, the railroad employees will starve. When the imposter who referred to himself as Wilson arrives with cattle for sale, Jim Blake is forced to make the purchase… failing to recognize Blake's scheme until the local rancher shows up and claims that the cattle were stolen. The rancher, now against the railroad and the member of the opposition, threatens to use the law against Blake and draws his guns until The Lone Ranger arrives to extinguish the heated situation. The Lone Ranger and Tonto create a stampede, causing the angry rancher and his men to give chase… which led near the hideout where Wilson's men were caught off-guard. After listening to The Lone Ranger and how the railroad would benefit them (cattle could be transported to more prospective buyers), and how the opposition wanted to create a war between the local ranchers and the railroad, the rancher admits he was short-sighted. After releasing Blake and his men from their bonds, the local rancher promises to provide all the meat they need at a fair price. As for Wilson and his men, the rancher plans to take them into town to face the law.

Episode #1460-673 "GOLD RUSH THAT FAILED" [PART FOUR]
Broadcast June 1, 1942
Copyright Registration #80,297, script received at Registration Office May 22, 1942.
Written by Sheldon Stark.
Plot: The government was building a railroad straight from Omaha across the plains, the Rocky Mountains to the Pacific coast. A ribbon of steel to tie the country together. With the U.S. government and other business interests establishing rails from coast-to-coast, Dan Kincaid, a railroad agent, is hired to recruit men for the construction job. His efforts are momentarily thwarted by cowhands who appear from nowhere, shooting their guns into the air to validate their threats. The man responsible for the shootings is Dawson, and his right-hand man, Slade. Kincaid is not disillusioned, however, and sets out to recruit 200 men and bring them to the construction camp via steamboat from St. Joseph. The Lone Ranger arranges for the local sheriff to deputize 20 men and orders them to scrutinize every man boarding the steamboat. If a man has the mark of a spur, they are gang members and are to be taken into custody. The Lone Ranger, meanwhile, uses a branding iron in the shape

of a spur, to mark all of the shoes owned by the criminals while they sleep in camp. At the wharf, moments before the ship sets sail, the crooks show up attempting to convince people that there was gold found in the hills, and almost succeeds in causing the recruited to desert for empty promises… but The Lone Ranger verifies the claim was nothing but fool's gold. The crooks draw guns in desperation of preventing the steamboat from taking off but the deputies, having been tipped off, promptly arrest every man with the mark of a spur.

Episode #1461-674 "THIRST IS BETTER THAN WATER" [PART FIVE]

Broadcast June 3, 1942

Copyright Registration #80,298, script received at Registration Office May 22, 1942.

Written by Sheldon Stark.

Plot: The Lone Ranger and Tonto foil another scheme of the Iron Spur when Indians attacked the grading crew, who were laying railroad tracks – but the results left behind a dead body. Worse, it was discovered that recently escaped criminals were masquerading as Indians. Meanwhile, gang boss Ralph Killigrew, having discovered how The Lone Ranger was able to identify his men with the mark of a spur, quickly turns the tables on the scheme by using the mark of an iron spur as a sign of terror to reign down against the newly laid railroad tracks. A killer named Brazos was hired by Killigrew to kidnap Joan Barcley, and poison the waterhole being used by the railroad workers. The Lone Ranger and Tonto, discovering she was late for her rendezvous, follows the trail to an abandoned cabin in the mountains. Only after she is rescued does the masked man learn details of the intended act of sabotage. The Lone Ranger rides like the wind to save the men from being poisoned, succeeding only at the last minute by shooting a hole into the watering cans men were filling at the waterhole. When Joan Barcley and Tonto arrive at the scene, they observe all of the men, including The Lone Ranger, spread out on the ground as if they are dead. Brazos and other gang members arrive to examine their handiwork but, before Brazos can remove the mask off the dead man, all of the men playing possum come to life to apprehend the crooks, catching them off guard.

Episode #1462-675 "MOONRISE ON POWDER CREEK" [PART SIX]

Broadcast June 5, 1942

Copyright Registration #80,299, script received at Registration Office May 22, 1942.

Written by Sheldon Stark.

Plot: "End of Track," the name of the traveling town, was relocated fifty miles west of Powder Creek. Jeff Koster has been hired as a marshal to police the traveling gambling halls and liquor stores that continue to spring up along the regions where the tracks are being built. The appointed sheriff, under orders from the leader of the Iron Spur, plants a note on Tonto's saddlebag, providing a tip for The Lone Ranger where he can find and arrest members of the Iron Spur. Unaware that it is a trap, the masked man follows the trail. At Powder Creek, the leader of the Iron Spur arranges for a large number of men to mingle in with the crowd and start a massive exchange of gunfire and riots. His plan is to have as many employees of the railroad dead by morning, tracks pulled out of the ground, and work sheds and buildings set on fire. They appointed sheriff, meanwhile, plans to dry-gulch The Lone Ranger at the rendezvous point. The masked man, figuring this to be a trap, arranges for a trick to fool the killers into thinking The Lone Ranger and Tonto were shot. The masked man, meanwhile, alerts the railroad men who arrive to apprehend the outlaws. The appointed sheriff, now in the custody of the law, claims they may have him under guard, but they still have not gotten the leader of the Iron Spur.

Episode #1463-676A "LUMBER FOR THE RAILROAD" [PART SEVEN]

Broadcast June 8, 1942

Copyright Registration #80,554, script received at Registration Office June 17, 1942.

Plot: A Frenchman named Antoine Bourday is responsible for making sure all of the lumber cut down in the Northwoods successfully floats down the Missouri River to be made into railroad ties. The Great Central Railroad is under construction and its importance to the country is emphasized by the funding from the U.S. Government. But Colonel Parkman may lose the contract if the company does not meet a particular schedule. Metal was being shipped in from the East and men were recruited from all over the country. A gunman named Pollard, employed by the notorious Iron Spur gang, hires a number of lumberjacks to sabotage the next shipment of logs needed for railroad ties. If they can hold back the logs from getting into the river for another week, there will not be enough water in the river to ensure their safe passage without the logs splintering on the rocks. The motive for the Iron Spur is to maintain the stage line that spans across the countryside, fearful the locomotive will put them out of business. The Lone Ranger swims out to overhear the discussion between Pollard and his men, only to be shot and wounded by Waddel, Pollard's right-hand man. For three days Joan Barcley and Tonto fear the worst, but The Lone Ranger eventually surfaces and explains how he dressed his wounds. Thanks to a tip off, the saboteurs are surprised and ambushed from both sides by the honest lumberjacks and an armed military led by The Lone Ranger. Antoine, who cannot swim, falls into the roaring rapids and The Lone Ranger, on top of Silver, jumps into the water to rescue the lumber man.

Episode #1463-676 "FOOL'S GOLD" [NEVER BROADCAST]

Copyright Registration #80,300, script received at Registration Office May 22, 1942.

Plot: Killigrew, the leader of the undercover gang known as the Iron Spur, came into the gang's headquarters with a heavy sack which he threw on the floor. The sack is filled with iron pyrites, also known as fool's gold, and Killigrew believes that fool's gold is going to ruin the railroad. They have not gotten anywhere because The Lone Ranger has been in their way. Killigrew believes they have been fighting the railroad in the wrong way all along, and this new scheme is one he believes The Lone Ranger cannot fight against. Using the bag, they plan to make the railroad men believe there is a big gold strike up in the north country, causing them to desert their job for the promise of riches. Days later, Killigrew and his men dressed themselves carefully to give the appearance of prospectors. They drifted into one of the local communities, entered a café and sat at a table playing cards for fantastically high stakes, creating attention and ultimately leading to interest from others. Several days lapsed. The men in charge of construction on the railroad found the laborers working without the usual enthusiasm. As the men start deserting their positions, one by one, Joan Barcley realizes something foul and rushes out to alert The Lone Ranger.

When the masked man attempts to convince the men not to leave, that Killigrew attempted to lure them away with fool's gold, he finds his efforts stumped. Asking them to allow fifteen minutes to prove his case, Killigrew's cabin was on fire. The Lone Ranger understood men. He turned and hurried from the café, knowing that for the first time, the threat of a rush from the vicinity had been averted. The men would stick and see what the fire at Killigrew's place brought out. Every man in the café followed the masked man as he hurried on foot toward the flames that were leaping high into the air. Killigrew, along with crooks Red and Butch, were puzzled as to what could have started the fire. While everyone stood outside, away from the heat and smoke, The Lone Ranger dashed into the burning building, fumbled in the smoke a moment and then located the sack of fool's gold. Outside, the masked man proved the ore was not real gold when he explained how Killigrew never left the burning cabin with the gold. Had it been real, he would have rescued the valuable ore. Desperate, Red, Butch and Killigrew draw guns and attempt to make an escape. The men, angry, want to seek justice in their own hands. But The Lone Ranger suggests letting them get away. "If they show up around here again, you'll know how to handle them." The villains flee the region as Joan Barcley takes off in the locomotive for Omaha, with the letters to their wives from the men who work on the railroad. The Lone Ranger knows that while the men have been exposed, the railroad workers will keep an eye out for the saboteurs. One day there will be enough evidence found to jail them.

Notes: The plot featured above was never dramatized on *The Lone Ranger* program. While the radio script was initially meant to serve as the seventh episode of The Iron Spur story arc (labeled episode #676), it was shelved and replaced with episode #676A.

This radio script verified that the initial concept was "the Broken Spur."

Episode #1464-677 "THE WRONG REDSKIN" [PART EIGHT]

Broadcast June 10, 1942

Copyright Registration #80,555, script received at Registration Office June 17, 1942.

Plot: Killigrew and his men, working for the Iron Spur, ambush Tonto, mistaking him for a member of a native tribe living near the railroad. Killigrew hopes to spur the friendly Indians onto the warpath. The Lone Ranger finds his friend and nurses the wounds, then goes after Killigrew, forcing him to dress as an Indian and visit the camp. When the expected attack never comes, The Lone Ranger realizes the true scheme and races out to the railroad camp to prevent an attack from Killigrew's man. The Lone Ranger sets fire to coal oil to reveal the location of Killigrew's men, providing the railroad workers with a much-needed advantage.

Episode #1465-678 "OUTLAWS IN WAR PAINT" [PART NINE]

Broadcast June 12, 1942

Copyright Registration #80,556, script received at Registration Office June 17, 1942.

Plot: The outlaws of the Iron Spur gang, dressed as Indians, attack the train Joan Barcley is riding as a passenger, but quick-thinking Joan encourages the engineer and his crew to move full speed ahead to outrun the redskins. Tonto, having learned at Fort Kearney that Joan is on the train due to arrive soon, was attacked by Indians, suspects foul play after consulting The Lone Ranger. Indians in the region are friendly. Joan, revealing how a buffalo hunter named Stoney fired above the heads of the attacking Indians, also suspects one of the railroad's buffalo hunters is not trustworthy. But her suspicions are proven valid when she is captured because the gang members know who she is. Following the trail of the men who wrecked the railroad camp, The Lone Ranger rescued Joan. While freeing Joan from her bind, The Lone Ranger learns how the men plan to attack the other buffalo hunters to prevent the railroad workers from receiving the much-needed food. Slade, the Iron Spur crook, is caught off guard when The Lone Ranger arranges for reinforcements to help apprehend Slade, who was in charge of the recent act of sabotage.

Episode #1466-679 "RACE TO DRY CREEK" [PART TEN]

Broadcast June 15, 1942

Copyright Registration #80,557, script received at Registration Office June 17, 1942.

Plot: With a major route of rails completed, the tracks needed to be tested. The train was scheduled to make a trip from Wolf Bend to Dry Creek. When Billings, in charge of the locomotive, learns that a crook named Fisher took over the local stage line and The Lone Ranger learns that the crook is in with the Iron Spur, both he and Joan Barcley attempt to figure out the scheme. A wager is made to determine who would reach Dry Creek first. Side by side the racing stagecoach and the speeding train sped from Wolf Bend but on route the masked man rides alongside the train to alert Tonto, who rode on board, to stop the train. The Iron Spur planned to wreck the locomotive by sabotaging the bridge, knowing the iron horse would not cross with a weakened trestle. Having turned the train around, the railroad workers attack Fisher's employees and mete justice. Then, at the encouragement of The Lone Ranger, the railroad men race out to the bridge to fix the logs so the train could cross – and win the race, ahead of the stagecoach by half a mile.

Episode #1467-680 "AMBUSH AT BRIGHT RAINBOW" [PART ELEVEN]

Broadcast June 17, 1942

Copyright Registration #80,558, script received at Registration Office June 17, 1942.

Plot: The Iron Spur has a man on the inside telling them how the railroad payroll will be shipped. With this knowledge, they successfully hold-up a train with the pay cash. An honest employee of the railroad, Dave Clark, is suspected of being an outlaw when some of the stolen cash was found in his hotel room. The Lone Ranger tracks down the outlaw hideout, discovers another plot to waylay a train of pack mules carrying the replacement payroll, but before he can do anything, Santos catches The Lone Ranger and Tonto off guard and chains all three. The Lone Ranger uses a clever means to free himself and his friends and get the better of Santos. The Lone Ranger races to the office of Murdock, the paymaster and inside man, pretending to be a member of the Iron Spur to trick Murdock into revealing his participation and guilt. Fetching army troops to ambush the outlaws at Bright Rainbow, The Lone Ranger leads the charge.

Episode #1468-681 "MORTGAGES PAID OFF" [PART TWELVE]

Broadcast June 19, 1942

Copyright Registration #80,559, script received at Registration Office June 17, 1942.

Plot: Far west of the labor crews laying train tracks, in the town of Gregg's Corners, a number of homes are set afire. The founder, Gregg, is accused of the rash of arson because he owns the mortgage on those properties. Soon after the homesteaders start to migrate elsewhere, Tonto positions himself at the only waterhole outside of town to insist they remain for a few days. An unscrupulous rancher named Watson, meanwhile, schemes to buy up all the mortgages at cheap prices. Gregg, unable to fulfill his obligations when the settlers packed up and moved out, was eager to sell the worthless vacancies. When The Lone Ranger discovers the scheme, and how Watson plans to sell the land to the railroad for a profit, tricks the crook into thinking the railroad is steering south of town. Watson, in desperation, swaps worthless land that the homesteaders had just staked claim, with the homesteads they vacated back in Gregg's Corners... unaware the news where the railroad tracks were going to be laid was incorrect. The Lone Ranger rides up to report how Lefty overheard two railroad surveyors, a trick meant to convince Watson into buying up worthless land. The homesteaders, learning they will make a profit with their original land when the railroad comes through, apologizes to Gregg for falsely accusing him of trying to smoke them out.

Episode #1469-682 "BADLANDS FOR BADMEN" [PART THIRTEEN]

Broadcast June 22, 1942

Copyright Registration #80,560, script received at Registration Office June 17, 1942.

Plot: After hearing three distress shots, The Lone Ranger and Tonto discover evidence of a kidnapping (a messenger named Steve Henshaw) and find an important message that was meant for Colonel Parkman. The Lone Ranger rides out to the railroad to make sure the note gets delivered while Tonto remains behind to keep watch. But the Indian is captured by men of the Iron Spur, shot and wounded by a gunman named Raven. After The Lone Ranger met with Joan Barcley to deliver the letter and then raced back to rescue the messenger – and Tonto. Dexter and the Iron Spur men, realizing how valuable Tonto is, sets up a trap for The Lone Ranger. Into a hail of bullets, The Lone Ranger races in to whisk Tonto off the ground, then races away. After making Silver pretend to go lame, The Lone Ranger succeeds in leading the bandits on a chase... with deliberate intent so the outlaws ride up to a cavalry of armed troops.

Blooper! The narrator pauses unintentionally during the narration that opens the second act.

Episode #1470-683 "CLOUDS ACROSS THE MOON" [PART FOURTEEN]

Broadcast June 24, 1942

Copyright Registration #80,561, script received at Registration Office June 17, 1942.

Plot: Doc Barlow of the Iron Spur, along with Angel Face and Murphy (the latter dressed as a Cheyenne Indian), attempt to thwart the construction of the railroad tracks, having a giant rock come crashing down along the tracks, throwing blame on the redskins. One man was killed, and two flatcars were smashed. Tonto and The Lone Ranger meet with Chief Blackhawk to learn that white men captured a Cheyenne brave and cut his hair off. The masked man explains how this was the act of outlaws, not the railroad men, thwarting an attack of the Cheyenne tribe. But when Pete, the foreman on the construction, convinces the men not to halt construction, and Barlow discovers the Indian will not attack the construction crew, the crooks take desperate measures by starting a prairie fire. Tonto, looking up at the moon to observe the direction of the wind, realizes the railroad camp is not in danger of the flames – but the Cheyenne camp is. The Lone Ranger uses the steam cars to rescue the Indians before the fire takes away their camp. In the excitement, the crooks were captured and turned over to the law as the railroad men are assured that the Cheyenne Indians have nothing against the construction of the railroad.

Notes: One of the railroad workers in the opening scene was doubled by John Todd.

Episode #1471-684 "QUICKSAND FOR A GAMBLER" [PART FIFTEEN]

Broadcast June 26, 1942

Copyright Registration #80,562, script received at Registration Office June 17, 1942.

Plot: In the town called End of Track, a notorious gambler named Sid Barton plays a crooked card game in an effort to kill a railroad surveyor working for the Great Central Railroad. His scheme fails when The Lone Ranger shoots the lights out and rescues Vince Walters. The card shark, hired to thwart the construction of the railroad, then arranges for a fake note from Colonel Parkman, luring the surveyor out to a bog of quicksand. The Lone Ranger and Tonto race out in time to rescue Vince. Barton and his men, not realizing the strength of the great horse Silver, unaccounted for the speed of which rescue would arrive. The villains ultimately become victims of their own trap. Sinking in the quicksand and pleading for their lives, the crooks surrender as Tonto chuckles and throws a rope out to rescue… and to be taken to the sheriff.

Episode #1472-685 "TROUBLE AT THE CANYON" [PART SIXTEEN]

Broadcast June 29, 1942

Copyright Registration #80,563, script received at Registration Office June 17, 1942.

Plot: A crooked railroad surveyor named Travis, working for the Iron Spur, attempts to slow the construction of the railroad by proposing the tracks be laid around the valley, not through. To eliminate The Lone Ranger, Travis shoots his assistant, Ted Borden, and puts the blame on The Lone Ranger, who is made prisoner of the U.S. Army. A member of the Iron Spur gang, Custer, plans to wreck the dam the night after next, with the assistance of two dozen outlaws camped outside, pouring water into the valley with full force and wash the camp – and the men – away. To distract the railroad workers, Travis would set fire to a few of the tents. While Borden lay wounded and unconscious, Tonto overhears the plot and reports back to The Lone Ranger. Travis then attempts to murder Borden but gets caught in the act and disarmed. It seems the masked man was released from jail courtesy of the captain, who listened to the masked man's story. The army officers follow orders to ride out and apprehend Custer and his men before the dam was sabotaged with blasting powder. With Custer swearing disappointment, Colonel Parkman gives thanks to The Lone Ranger.

Episode #1473-686 "KIDNAPPED" [PART SEVENTEEN]

Broadcast July 1, 1942

Copyright Registration #80,564, script received at Registration Office June 17, 1942.

Plot: Foiled repeatedly in their attempts to halt the westward progress of the railroad construction, the Iron Spur takes desperate measures. Colonel Parkman, construction engineer, was on a supply train when outlaws released the coupling and sent the caboose speeding freely down Telegraph Hill. Parkman was thrown from the wreck, injured and kidnapped. The Lone Ranger, mistaken for an outlaw, is surprised from behind by Lefty, one of the men responsible for the wreck of the caboose. Captured and taken to the leader of the local outlaw gang, who doesn't recognize The Lone Ranger, the masked man gets in good with the outlaws. Cal, the outlaw leader, sends The Lone Ranger to deliver a $50,000 ransom message to Pete, the railroad foreman, held against the life of Parkman… and Tonto who is instructed to remain behind. Instead of delivering the ransom demand, the masked man sets a trap for the gang, so they get caught by the law.

Episode #1474-687 "SURPRISE AT SUNRISE" [PART EIGHTEEN]

Broadcast July 3, 1942

Copyright Registration #80,565, script received at Registration Office June 17, 1942.

Plot: A rancher named Grant plans to use the railroad to ship his cattle to market, despite the warnings of an Iron Spur gunman named Slaughter. It will take a week to drive the herd north to the stockyards. When Grant's foreman, Jeff Thomas, paid a visit to the construction camp to see if the soldiers would add protection, he finds his request turned down. Joan Barcley calls on the masked man to help the men of the Flying Y, at Red Basin, especially after learning Slaughter tossed an iron spur to Grant to show he meant business. While offering his services to Grant, Tonto was shot and wounded from ambush. Whitey, the gunman who was responsible for shooting the Indian, was captured and thrown into the shed in the backyard of Grant's ranch. When Whitey escapes and flees, he was unaware he provided a trail for The Lone Ranger and the law to follow. As the outlaws thought they were setting up an ambush against the Flying Y cattlemen, they discovered they were ambushed themselves. Outside the shed, Grant and his men revealed fake plans for the cattle drive and arranged for Whitey to escape and report.

Episode #1475-688 "END OF THE IRON SPUR" [PART NINETEEN]

Broadcast July 6, 1942

Copyright Registration #81,156, script received at Registration Office July 2, 1942.

Plot: The Transcontinental Railroad was almost completed. The tracks being laid from the west and the east were to join at the Promontory Point. Colonel Parkman, chief engineer of the railroad, learns that the President of the United States will soon arrive to hammer the golden spike that finishes completion. The Iron Spur, aware of the news, was determined to assassinate the President with a concealed charge of powder under the spike. When The Lone Ranger comes close to Hazzard, the leader of the Iron Spur, the masked man and Tonto fall into a trap. As they race into a mine to apprehend a member of the gang, Hazzard's right-hand man, Prentiss, sets off a keg of blasting powder to seal up the entrance like a tomb. It was only through sheer luck that our heroes were able to escape… kegs of dynamite were found deep within the tunnels and could be used to blow open the entrance. Racing by moonlight to Promontory Point, following the North Star, the men covered as much ground as possible to save the President. By daybreak the masked man arrived in time, seconds after the silver spike had been hammered into the ground, to warn Colonel Parkman of the danger to the railroad. and the President The gold spike was just being set into the rail above the hidden powder charge when the masked man arrived, leading the cavalry to round up the outlaws of the Iron Spur, and their leader.

Notes: Like a number of episodes in 1941, this episode makes use of the "Donna Diana Overture," the theme of radio's *Sergeant Preston of the Yukon*.

Episode #1476-689 "WAY OF THE TRANSGRESSOR"

Broadcast July 8, 1942

Copyright Registration #81,157, script received at Registration Office July 2, 1942.

Plot: In the little town of Benton, a young man named Loren Mitchell finds himself restless and want to leave home to either be The Lone Ranger or an outlaw. He dreams of a life of wild escapes and adventures. Flora Mitchell, concerned for her brother, confides to The Lone Ranger who promises to help out, especially when she explains how Loren Mitchell went and joined Bat Walter and his gang of murderers and thieves. Bat enjoys luring young men into a life of crime, and soon plans to rob a bank safe in Littlefield. Everyone knew somewhere among the twisted trails was the hideout, but few wanted to find out. The Lone Ranger, in disguise, rode out to face a challenge of courage in the form of an initiation to get in with the gang. The next night, in town, the bank robbery goes off without a hitch and while grabbing the money, The Lone Ranger makes sure Loren sees the mortgage on his father's property, paperwork for Loren's neighbors, money that belonged to the church. "Bank robbers take everything," the masked man explains. "Bank robbers either take money or lead bullets." Loren has a change of mind, and The Lone Ranger shakes his hand – proud of the boy's decision to stay on the straight and narrow. Loren kicks the lantern to extinguish the light and, during an exchange of gunplay, The Lone Ranger and Loren flee out the back. Tonto, having alerted the sheriff and waiting outside for a signal, leads the charge to apprehend Bat Walter and his gang.

Episode #1477-690 "BARCLEY BROTHERS DOWNFALL"

Broadcast July 10, 1942

Copyright Registration #81,158, script received at Registration Office July 2, 1942.

Plot: Everyone in Pine City is terrified of three Barcley brothers, Jake, Hank and Moe. Together, they have the town in a grip of fear as they rustle cattle and intimidate honest people. After discovering Cephus Gilroy's boy, Billy, is sick from fever and Cephus himself is beaten when he stands up to the crooks, The Lone Ranger takes a hand. After using his fists against the Barcley brothers, the masked man ordered them to deliver the stolen cattle from the Bar C (the Gilroy brand) back in the fences by sunrise – or else. Following the masked man's instructions, the sheriff orders his deputies to take down the fence to the Bar O spread, which housed the stolen cattle, and take them back to the Bar C and rebrand the steers. Despite the fact that their task was against the law, they hoped to rid the community of the scourge of the Barcleys, knowing a bigger scheme was afoot. In the morning, a rancher named Sam Grogan pays a visit to the Barcleys, upset that he paid for stolen cattle, only to wake and find the cattle stolen from him. With this frame-up, the man responsible for aiding and abetting the crooks was not only exposed but also an accessory to stolen cattle, and the sheriff and his men take all four into custody.

Episode #1478-691 "HIGH-GRADERS"

Broadcast July 13, 1942

Copyright Registration #81,159, script received at Registration Office July 2, 1942.

Plot: On route to the town of Red Stone, The Lone Ranger and Tonto come across a dead man, shot in the heart. Deputy Marshal Evans was ambushed in gold mining country and when the masked man pays a visit to the sheriff, he is quickly mistaken as the killer and jailed. Meanwhile, Nancy races into Sheriff Fred Boone's office to report the murder of her father, Jim Wallace, a miner who recently struck paydirt. The old man was murdered in the stamping mill by the waterfall and it does not take long for the sheriff to discover a golden cufflink that tipped him off to the identity of the killer, who old Jim caught in the act of stealing good ore from his abandoned mine. The Lone Ranger and Tonto escape jail to investigate the mine, and discover the investigating sheriff was caught off guard and being held captive by a rival miner named Bart McKee. After The Lone Ranger shoots the gun from Ed Craven's hand, Bart found himself without an armed backup and attempts to shoot it out with The Lone Ranger. Bart backs up and ultimately loses footing and plunges to his death. The sheriff explains how Bart and Ed planned to eliminate the Deputy Marshal to avoid further digging into their criminal acts.

Episode #1479-692 "BREAD UPON THE WATERS"
Broadcast July 15, 1942
Copyright Registration #81,160, script received at Registration Office July 2, 1942.
Plot: The Lone Ranger and Tonto, on the trail of two confidence men, ride into Coffin Corners where they meet Lije Perkins, owner of the General Store. Against the advice of Sara, Lije's wife, the store owner grubstaked the two confidence men – one of whom calls himself The Colonel. The two men fail to pay Lige back and leave town. Hoping to exact revenge against them, Lije rides into Tomahawk to face off against the crooks. The Lone Ranger races down main street to intervene and prevent bloodshed. The next day, Tonto wanders through the streets to report how the owners of a prosperous gold mine died and Lije is the man to inherit. The crooks, having discovered that Lije was not told the news yet, pays a visit to the store owner to apologize. The Colonel returns the $400 he cheated out of Lije and casting bread upon the waters, offers to pay $500 for a worthless plot of ground up at Buffalo Pass. Days later, the crooks named Weldron and Jason discover the land is worthless, tricked in a plot worthy of their own admission. But they also discover in doing so they crossed into Washoe County where the sheriff has a warrant for their arrest… which The Lone Ranger and Tonto are pleased to deliver to the law.

Episode #1480-693 "ONE WIDE RIVER"
Broadcast July 17, 1942
Copyright Registration #81,161, script received at Registration Office July 2, 1942.
Plot: Pioneers on the Oregon Trail are beset by tragedy. A prairie schooner is set on fire and a keg of blasting powder explodes, alerting The Lone Ranger and Tonto from a distance. Discovering oil on the outside of the burned wagon, the masked man and Indian realize the fire was deliberate. The ill-fated wagon train was bound for rack and ruin as a result of their destination, Unity Valley. In the event of death, the old Indian custom was to distribute the wealth of land equally among the others – and murder for sole ownership of the valley was bound to happen. For six days The Lone Ranger and Tonto keep watch, eventually figuring the scheme of wholesale murder would occur as the wagon train attempts to ford the strong current of Snake River. When the men and women are in the midst of crossing, The Lone Ranger shoots the axe out of the hand of Johnson, the leader hell-bent on sabotage, preventing the rope from being cut that would send the emigrants to their peril. The vigilantes take the criminals, Jasper and Burman, to the nearest jail while the wagon train continued their trek to Oregon.

Episode #1481-694 "SORREL-JACK OUTLAW HORSE"
Broadcast July 20, 1942
Copyright Registration #81,469, script received at Registration Office July 31, 1942.
Plot: Childhood sweethearts are thrown into turmoil when red-headed Danny Walsh is framed for the murder of a gambler, Paul Daggot. Mary Ashley, whose father is the sheriff in town, does not believe Danny is guilty but the young man is placed under arrest on a charge of murder. After being found guilty in a court of law, Danny is sent to a penitentiary while his wild horse named "Sorrel-Jack," tamed only by the hand of Danny, leads a pack of wild mustangs and causing havoc among the community, driving off other horses from neighboring spreads. The law even issues a warrant in the name of the horse! Discussing the situation with the sheriff, and discovering Danny escaped, the masked man conspires to prove the wild gunshot that killed Daggot never came from Danny's gun. The principal suspect, Fred, is tricked into a confrontation with Danny and an exchange of words inadvertently provides the confession the law needs to ensure Fred takes Danny's place behind bars. Danny and Mary ride off together on Sorrel-Jack, laughing, a fine pair they make.

Episode #1482-695 "DOUBLE IN MURDER"

Broadcast July 22, 1942

Copyright Registration #81,470, script received at Registration Office July 31, 1942.

Plot: Two men named Lou Russell and Pete escape prison and return to the town of Placer where one of them was falsely accused of rustling. Hoping to clear his name, Lou Russell, the former sheriff of town, attempts to face off against the elusive "Mr. Murdock," who supposedly owns the mortgages on most of the ranches and homes in town, represented by the banker known as Dan Cummings. It was Dan who arranged for Lou Russell's escape from prison, but it was also Dan who planted false evidence of cattle rustling that went up against the sheriff. Pete is shot and killed, but Lou Russell survives the ambush that was set for him and mends quickly thanks to Tonto's medicinal skills. Ethel Carter, the woman to whom Lou Russell was in love with, is kidnapped by Squint. Another trap is set for Russell, but The Lone Ranger arranges for a meeting with the local ranchers to rescue, while Murdock, demanding justice, is unmasked as the crooked banker.

Notes: John Todd doubles in the beginning of this episode as the warden of the territorial prison.

Episode #1483-696 "CATTLEMAN CASH"

Broadcast July 24, 1942

Copyright Registration #81,471, script received at Registration Office July 31, 1942.

Plot: On the trail of Meecham and his gang, The Lone Ranger is lured into an ambush in Blackwater. Meecham was stealing money from the Cattleman's Association and aware The Lone Ranger was on his trail, rigged an explosion that knocks the masked man unconscious. Initially mistaken for dead, the masked man is found to be unconscious and quickly revived by Tonto, who takes him away. Later, the vigilantes set on the outlaws' trail, while Jed Lanker, a member of the outlaw gang, deliberately leads the cattlemen of the region into an ambush. Having stolen all the gold, the outlaws need the horses of the cattlemen to help transport the stolen goods. The sheriff does not believe The Lone Ranger – initially – then suspects foul play and errs on the side of caution. The skeptical sheriff and his posse agree to work with The Lone Ranger and set up an ambush of their own, apprehending the outlaws when they least suspect.

Episode #1484-697 "HOMESTEAD PROVED UP"

Broadcast July 27, 1942

Copyright Registration #81,472, script received at Registration Office July 31, 1942.

Plot: A young man named Josh Cranfield must spend two more months on the Circle Square to claim title to the 160 acres of farmland. Having discovered silver ore on the side of a cliff on his 160 acres, two crooks named Bradley and Silas scheme to kidnap him so they can gain possession of the grasslands. Meanwhile, Sara Gordon, Josh's mail-order bride, arrives in town only to discover Josh is nowhere to be found and fears he deserted. While The Lone Ranger and Tonto rescues the young man and explain to Sara what happened, land agents agree to sign over the property to Bradley and Silas – provided Josh does not return to the land before the deadline. But the schemers are surprised when they find Josh on the property, mining for silver. Angry, an exchange of words reveals their guilt. The masked man disarms the crooks and turns them over to the law while Tonto arrives with Sara for a warm welcome.

Episode #1485-698 "HAUNTED ROCK"

Broadcast July 29, 1942

Copyright Registration #81,473, script received at Registration Office July 31, 1942.

Plot: Outside the town of Tamarack, a crooked banker named Crawford and his henchman, Jasper, scheme to buy valuable land near Haunted Rock. Carey Marsden owns the land and unlike Abby, his wife, is not spooked by the strange sounds coming from the "Indian Ghost" that wails down into the valley. When Carey disappears, Abby believes in the superstition and expresses her desire to return back East, and her willingness to sign over the land to the two crooks – unaware they were responsible for his kidnapping. For a week hunting parties scouted for Carey and The Lone Ranger asks Abby to allow some time to prove her husband is alive and well. To prove his theory, The Lone Ranger tricks Crawford and Jasper, along with Abby, up to the mountain top near Haunted Rock to reveal the honeycomb tunnels that creates the sound whenever wind blows through them. Carey Marsden, having been rescued by the masked man and Indian, reveals to Abby the schemers who plotted to take his property. Abby, no longer afraid, agrees to stay in the valley. Before The Lone Ranger and Tonto take their prisoners to jail, they blow a few kegs of powder to destroy the honeycomb passages, eliminating the ghostly sound once and for all.

Episode #1486-699 "STAGECOACH TO BLUE RIVER"
Broadcast July 31, 1942
Copyright Registration #81,474, script received at Registration Office July 31, 1942.
Plot: Four men named Johnny Pickett, Frank Wilson, Pete Marcus and Ed Ryan rob a bank in the town of Colbert. During the daring hold-up, Frank is killed and Johnny Pickett, in what was his first hold-up, holding the horses meant for escape, is captured. The town is in an uproar and by evening men were eager to seek justice. When a lynch mob forms outside, the sheriff resigns, and The Lone Ranger frees Johnny to prevent the lynching. The masked man plans to take the youth to a jail in Blue River, and on route his trust in Johnny is returned when the other two outlaws board the same stage for Blue River. Pete and Ed attempt to steal the gold shipment on board the stage, with The Lone Ranger and Johnny inside. Johnny gets the better of the crooks but not before he takes a bullet wound to the leg in the process. Before riding into Blue River to face the law, The Lone Ranger promises to put in a good word to the judge on Johnny's behalf, suggesting the sentence against him will not be so hard.

Episode #1487-700 "STAGECOACH STRIFE"
Broadcast August 3, 1942
Copyright Registration #81,475, script received at Registration Office July 31, 1942.
Plot: Two young men operating competing stage lines between Big Horn and Mesquite are set against each other by a scheming halfway house operator. Both Bob Nelson and Jim Jarvis have hair-trigger fingers and the scheming Topaz sabotages a wheel on Jim's stage in the hopes Bob takes the blame. The Lone Ranger, fixing the wheel and suspecting the rivalry was masterminded by a third party. Topaz arranges for Morris to set fire to Jim's stage, leaving an empty container of coal oil with Nelson's name on it, to ensure a perfect frame. The Lone Ranger prevents the confrontation by revealing the truth behind the act of sabotage, and the fallacy of the men's hatred for one another – including the love and affection of Nellie, who chose Jim Jarvis as her husband. As the two crooks are apprehended and taken away, Bob Nelson and Jim Jarvis agree to form a partnership in the business.

Episode #1488-701 "TURNABOUT IS FAIR PLAY"
Broadcast August 5, 1942
Copyright Registration #81,476, script received at Registration Office July 31, 1942.
Plot: The Lone Ranger and Tonto are trailing two crooks, Nevins and Mossback, to the town of High Valley, territory unfamiliar to the masked man. The crooks spread word that The Lone Ranger and Tonto are notorious criminals, hoping to frame them for the crime they were about to pull off. When The Lone Ranger learns of the scheme, he set a trap by suggesting that Randy Perkins, the Pony Express driver, is carrying valuable mail. Turnabout was fair play when the sheriff and the posse give chase, with the masked man leading them to the

robbery-in-progress. Moments after Mossbeck knocks Randy unconscious, the posse arrives to catch the crooks in the act. After The Lone Ranger explains the scheme to frame him for a crime he did not commit, the crooks are taken into custody.

Episode #1489-702 "THE SICK AND THE WELL"

Broadcast August 7, 1942

Copyright Registration #81,477, script received at Registration Office July 31, 1942.

Plot: In the town of Rio Santos, a political boss named Lem Brandt, armed with a gang of cutthroats, controls all aspects of law including the town judge. Doc Flenner, a medical quack, turns to Brandt in the hopes of striking a deal in return for the competition to be eliminated. As a result, John Baker, the honest doctor in town, soon finds himself on top of a horse and facing a hangman's knot. After The Lone Ranger interrupts proceedings and rescues the doctor, he rallies the poor citizens of town to the doctor's aid. Despite the fact that Baker's wife felt it was pointless to cure those who could not pay for her husband's services, the time had come to repay the doctor. The standoff at dawn proved the adage "United We Stand." In sheer numbers the outlaws were surrounded. Thanks to the bravery of The Lone Ranger, Lem Brandt's bullying came to an end while restoring law and order.

Episode #1490-703 "VOTES WON, VOTES LOST"

Broadcast August 10, 1942

Copyright Registration #81,478, script received at Registration Office July 31, 1942.

Plot: Caleb West, the beleaguered sheriff of Grant County, is about to lose an election to a crook named Zeke Ramsey, who imported a score of outlaws to town to add to the vote for him. The Lone Ranger faces off against Zeke two separate times, each attempting to size the man up. The first was in a local saloon resulting in Zeke being knocked unconscious. The second resulted in Zeke and his associate, Red, being dropped off miles away from town, forced to walk back without a horse. But the third time was the charm when the masked man created a scenario that created the illusion of gold found in Three Rivers, located outside of town. Gold fever spreads through town and within minutes all of the outlaws flee town in the hopes of cashing in big… outlaws who had not yet cast their vote.

Notes: The Lone Ranger applies the same trick used on the broadcast of July 12, 1935, creating gold fever to prevent a meddlesome gang of crooks from participating in an election.

Episode #1491-704 "TWINS TURNABOUT"

Broadcast August 12, 1942

Copyright Registration #81,479, script received at Registration Office July 31, 1942.

Plot: When The Lone Ranger visits the ranch of Buck Lundeen, he quickly discovers the ranch owner is an imposter. Worse, the "evil twin" has disposed of Buck and turned the Lundeen Ranch into an armed camp, flouting the law. The masked man sets out to Calabash to find a man named Baldy Smith, the real Buck Lundeen, before the men under the employ of the evil twin brother finds Buck. When Tom Grant, Buck's former foreman, discovers he was fired by an imposter and the severity of the situation, he assists the masked man in riding out to find the old, loyal ranch hands to amass an attack against the outlaw stronghold. The Lone Ranger, meanwhile, alerts the sheriff, who forms a posse to back the play and overthrow the evil twin brother's regime.

Episode #1492-705 "ACE OF CROOKS"

Broadcast August 14, 1942

Copyright Registration #81,817, script received at Registration Office September 12, 1942.

Plot: A crooked gambler named Ace Collins shows up in Deadwood City and The Lone Ranger knows something is aloft. Investigating, The Lone Ranger finds Collins dead with a knife in his back and false evidence suggesting Larry Grant, a stage driver, committed the crime. This after Collins and Grant had a public altercation in the saloon earlier that same evening. The stage driver was lured into a rigged card game, and nearly shot Ace with blanks before The Lone Ranger intervened. Unaware that the entire affair was a ruse and Ace was really alive and well, Larry is asked by Boss Barnacle to tip the stage with a full cargo of gold at the bridge over the ravine at Cripple Creek – even if there are passengers on board. Larry hesitates in spite of the frame-up job but is pleased he does not have to commit the act when the masked man once again intervenes. After forcing a confession out of the Barnacle's henchman, The Lone Ranger rides out to fetch Ace Collins and reveal his existence so Larry, realizing it was a frame, continues over the bridge without sabotage. The Lone Ranger tells Ace to choose between confessing his part in the plot to the sheriff, or face Larry when the stage driver returns to town. Ace chooses the former of the two.

Blooper! The narrator stumbles over the words "early dawn" in this episode.

Episode #1493-706 "MUSTANG MAG RETURNS"

Broadcast August 17, 1942

Copyright Registration #81,816, script received at Registration Office September 12, 1942.

Plot: Two old friends, Mustang Mag and Missouri, are swept up in a wheat buying scheme run by a crook named Morehouse, working under the alias of Lodeman. Missouri, the sheriff in town, suspects Lodeman is a crook but when The Lone Ranger and Tonto discover this was the alias of a man they were seeking, they race out to apprehend the killer. But they find themselves trapped in a box car of a train owned by Lodeman. To escape, the two have to shoot it out and got lucky to avoid bloodshed. The masked man sends Tonto out to Mustang Mag to sell her wheat to Lodeman and have it delivered to the train station for shipment, regardless of the price Lodeman offers. Without questioning his orders, Mag orders Missouri to help assist. The deal involved Lodeman does not pay until the wheat is shipped. In the meantime, The Lone Ranger rode out to get a lawman from a nearby county to help back his play. The wheat is stored in a warehouse and Lodeman assures the two that the train will ship it out in a week. But a fire breaks out in the warehouse and the flames grew too hot for anyone to get near the burning structure. The wheat is inside, and everyone loses money per terms of the contract. The Lone Ranger arrives to prevent mob justice, along with the sheriff of the nearby county, to verify the wheat was already loaded onto the train and shipped out, located elsewhere. Lodeman wanted to trick everyone to think the wheat went up in flames so he would not have to pay.

Episode #1494-707 "SPURS THAT JINGLE"

Broadcast August 19, 1942

Copyright Registration #81,815, script received at Registration Office September 12, 1942.

Written by George Waller.

Plot: A dying outlaw named Waco sends for The Lone Ranger and gives him a single silver spur which, with its mate, will give the owner title to valuable land in Custer County. Unknown to the masked man, the outlaw's daughter is wearing the mate and is in deadly danger from the man's former partner, John McCord. The Lone Ranger thwarts the attempt to kill Rusty Adams, the girl, who possessed the other silver spur. The masked man and Indian trailed John McCord to the half- completed dam at Boxwood Creek, a construction site supervised by McCord that is suspected by the town's newspaperman, Tommy Webb, of being crooked. McCord was the former partner of Waco. Known as the sheriff in skirts, Rusty was good for a laugh in town, but despite the warnings of The Lone Ranger, the woman was headstrong and rode out to face off against John McCord. The Lone Ranger eventually rode out to help even the odds against the crooks who figured badge or no badge, no woman would defeat them. After the crooks were taken into custody, The Lone Ranger explains how the land the dam was being built on was owned by her father, hence the reason why he was so desperate to acquire the two spurs.

Episode #1495-708 "FLAMEUP'S KICKBACK"

Broadcast August 21, 1942

Copyright Registration #81,814, script received at Registration Office September 12, 1942.

Plot: Terror rode through the night in Silver Creek, and no one knew where it would strike next. The town citizens insist on replacing the sheriff or fetching the Texas Rangers if the criminals are not apprehended. In desperation, the vicious gang decides to frame the first Indian they can find and leave enough evidence to convict. When young Jack overhears their plans, he warns Tonto, who he meets along the trail, but the hard-riding men grabbed the redskin and had him jailed. But when The Lone Ranger rides into town, he cleverly arranges for a jail break. In private with young Jack, Tonto and The Lone Ranger figure that despite the evidence against Tonto, the most important evidence was not found – the stolen money from recent robberies. Paying a visit to Mansfield, The Lone Ranger throws a scare into the outlaw leader so he will lead them to the stolen loot. The sheriff, working with The Lone Ranger, arranged to trail the outlaws as Mansfield and his associate, Badger, snuck off to uncover the stolen loot and make a getaway. Digging up the stolen loot ensured their guilt and cleared the name of Tonto.

Episode #1496-709 "GOOSE CREEK KILLER"

Broadcast August 24, 1942

Copyright Registration #81,813, script received at Registration Office September 12, 1942.

Written by Fran Striker.

Plot: The Lone Ranger and Tonto are riding by the region of Goose Creek and find a dead man, and a short distance away a prospector, ambushed and wounded, named Lambert. A woman named Mrs. Porter rode in from the East in search of her husband, Henry Porter, who disappeared and was reportedly last seen near Goose Creek. The sheriff, and his deputy named Jim Tucker, ride out to search for her husband, only to find The Lone Ranger and Tonto at the scene of the crime. The vigilantes are forced to flee when accused of the crime of murder. The masked man investigated the mystery which led to a hermit Indian, a wild man shooting in the hills, and exposing the crooked deputy as the man responsible for the murder and the attempted framing of an innocent man. Mrs. Porter agrees to settle down in the region as a widow, left off wealthy as a result of her loyal husband, knowing that while the region has crooks like the deputy, there are fine ones around like The Lone Ranger.

Notes: Fran Striker recycled the name "Goose Creek" from his radio script of June 29, 1936.

Episode #1497-710 "GREED DROWNS A TOWN"

Broadcast August 26, 1942

Copyright Registration #81,812, script received at Registration Office September 12, 1942.

Written by Fran Striker.

Plot: This was the same script from the broadcast of May 29, 1935, with the name of the man shot dead changed from Pete to Lefty, and the Indian named White Fawn was changed simply to "the chief."

Episode #1498-711 "GOLD AND CHIMNEY RANGE"

Broadcast August 28, 1942

Copyright Registration #81,811, script received at Registration Office September 12, 1942.

Plot: Riding through Chimney Range in Rainbow Valley, The Lone Ranger and Tonto find the body of a murdered deputy marshal, John Bart, who was sent to the town of Bristow to assist R.C. Coleman, a rancher, combat a ruthless gang of cattle rustlers. Taking the dead man's credentials, The Lone Ranger masquerades as the lawman to work alongside Coleman – but not before he finds out the local sheriff is crooked. When a local rancher named Frank Clemens is murdered, the masked man investigates and finds himself subject to a trap that knocks him unconscious for three days. When he wakes, nursed back to health by Barbara, Frank's daughter, the masked man rides out to assist her boyfriend, Brad Wilson, to learn that Coleman has a gold mine. Further investigation reveals the entire valley is filled with gold. The rustling was meant to convince the ranchers to leave, and the mine offers a trail where the rustlers can lead the cattle out of the valley without being found. Prisoners of the crooked sheriff are never shipped out of town – they are sent to the mine. The Lone Ranger and Tonto get the advantage of surprise by hiding in the box car to disarm the crooked sheriff and his compatriots.

Episode #1499-712 "EXTORTION GANG"

Broadcast August 31, 1942

Copyright Registration #81,810, script received at Registration Office September 12, 1942.

Plot: A brutal gang of extortionists is intimidating the good people of Twin Pines and so brazen as to flout the law. When the newspaper office of Pete Potter is smashed, because he would not agree to paying tribute to their messenger, Slim, The Lone Ranger steps in to help. The masked man persuades the publisher to press charges after Tonto gets his wife, Jane, safely away. When the gang presents a note signed by the woman saying she is a prisoner, The Lone Ranger verifies she is alive and well and in hiding with Tonto. This tips off the masked man who figure out who had access to and was able to copy her signature. Hours after Slim is arrested, he is found murdered. All the fight and determination ran out of Potter, but only momentarily when The Lone Ranger exposes the crooks, with Butch and Banker Timmons accusing each other, and the frightened town citizens who witness the fallout quickly reverse their position and swear against the extortionists.

Notes: John Todd doubles as the sheriff.

Episode #1500-713 "REVENGE FOR AN OUTLAW"

Broadcast September 2, 1942

Copyright Registration #81,809, script received at Registration Office September 12, 1942.

Written by Fran Striker.

Plot: A young boy named Bob Foster, orphaned when his outlaw father is killed in a robbery, grows up not knowing who was responsible for the murder. Having turned 18, he gets a job at the Drake Ranch, where he finds himself in love with Drake's daughter, Betty. But happiness comes with a price when two old friends,

Blackie and Slim, trick Bob into believing Drake bought the ranch with money he got for killing Bob's father. The young man, with vengeance in his heart, initially mistakes The Lone Ranger for his father's killer until Slim and Blackie provide their startling revelation. The masked man, having been tipped off due to his encounter with Bob, investigates. Soon after Drake sold the ranch for $50,000, accepting a $500 three-day option from Slim and Blackie, the young man was tricked into gunning after Drake so the crooks would legally own the ranch. After Drake is shot dead, the crooks ride over to the ranch to lay claim only to be surprised by The Lone Ranger and Drake – alive and well. It seems The Lone Ranger replaced the cartridges in Bob's gun for blanks and this helps explain how Sheriff Charles Drake shot Bob's father, at that time an outlaw, in the line of duty because he resisted arrest. Betty and her father knew the truth but held back revealing this to Bob for far too long. With the crooks' plan exposed, they are taken into custody as Drake insists Bob call him "Pa."

Episode #1501-714 "THE SILVER DOLLAR"
Broadcast September 4, 1942

Copyright Registration #81,808, script received at Registration Office September 12, 1942.

Written by Fran Striker.

Plot: Sheriff Morton of Greggsville lost four deputies since a notorious gang of stage robbers have plagued Grant County. All clues and tips have led to a dead end. Soon after someone broke into the back room of the sheriff's office to steal all the papers which the lawman had on the recent crimes, Colonel Jackson (from Washington) arrived to oversee the investigation. The sheriff's daughter, Betty, ever impetuous, shot and wounded Tonto, believing the Indian was a member of the outlaw gang. Thankfully the Indian received a mere flesh wound and in private, delivers a message to the sheriff from The Lone Ranger, stating the criminal mastermind not only hails from the East, but carries a unique silver dollar on his possession. The masked man also reports how Colonel Jackson was a passenger on the stage that was recently robbed. Jackson was killed and the head of the outlaw gang switched clothes and stole his credentials. Tonto, following instructions from The Lone Ranger, helped create a set-up meant to expose the fake Jackson, then tricks the outlaws to ride out to Potter's Cave where the masked man is supposedly hiding. The outlaws schemed to blow up the cave with a wagon full of gunpowder. Only after the outlaws arrive do they discover the entire affair was a trap and the sheriff and his posse surround the outlaws.

Episode #1502-715 "TORRERO AND TARANTULA" [PART ONE]
Broadcast September 7, 1942

Copyright Registration #81,807, script received at Registration Office September 12, 1942.

Plot: See page 286.

Episode #1503-716 "DIVIDE AND CONQUER" [PART TWO]
Broadcast September 9, 1942

Copyright Registration #81,806, script received at Registration Office September 12, 1942.

Plot: See pages 286 and 287.

Episode #1504-717 "BORDER SMUGGLERS" [PART THREE]
Broadcast September 11, 1942

Copyright Registration #81,805, script received at Registration Office September 12, 1942.

Plot: See pages 287 and 288.

Episode #1505-718 "THE BOSS OF THE TARANTULAS" [PART FOUR]

Broadcast September 14, 1942

Copyright Registration #81,909, script received at Registration Office September 24, 1942.

Plot: See page 288.

Episode #1506-719 "THE MAGIC BELT"

Broadcast September 16, 1942

Copyright Registration #81,910, script received at Registration Office September 24, 1942.

Plot: See page 289.

Episode #1507-720 "DOUBLE FOR AN OUTLAW"

Broadcast September 18, 1942

Copyright Registration #81,911, script received at Registration Office September 24, 1942.

Plot: Soon after the Mustang Café is held up by the Frank Slaughter gang, the sheriff of Cactus City organizes a posse to give chase. Despite the fact that the gang members shot and killed people during the rainstorm in the streets of town, Mr. Carver, who owns the biggest spread in the basin, implores the sheriff not to ride out, because his daughter, Cora, is being held hostage. Dan Mennick, foreman of the Carver ranch, insists on justice, but being sweet on Cora he agrees with his employer. Scheming with the sheriff, The Lone Ranger masquerades as Cal Fisher, the notorious train robber, and gains the confidence of those in jail. After a pre-arranged jail break, Sam Carp and Steve takes "Cal" with them to a shack three miles into the hill country. There, The Lone Ranger's masquerade is foiled when he discovers the man in charge of the outlaw gang is the real Cal Fisher. Carver, meanwhile, arranged for the $10,000 ransom from the East and Fisher orders Frank Slaughter and his gang to arrange for a train robbery – thus forcing Carver to get more money afterwards. The Lone Ranger quickly shoots his way out of the outlaw camp and races away from the hideout. Frank Slaughter dismissed the outlaw, unaware he is The Lone Ranger, believing an outlaw carries no harm to their plans. After tipping off Tonto and the sheriff where the hideout is, The Lone Ranger returns to Frank Slaughter and holds him at bay. As the time of the scheduled train robbery approaches, Frank fears a penalty for not fulfilling his orders, and convinces the masked man to join his gang. Together they ride out to join in the train robbery, which the sheriff and his posse foil and apprehend the gang. Cora is rescued and The Lone Ranger, observing a bullet wound on the back of Dan Mennick's hand, unmasks the Carver foreman as Cal Fisher in disguise.

Episode #1508-721 "SET A THIEF TO CATCH A THIEF"

Broadcast September 21, 1942

Copyright Registration #81,912, script received at Registration Office September 24, 1942.

Plot: Lance Arnold presided over the meeting with the gold miners outside Gold Canyon, hoping to lead a resistance against Tod Vain and his gang, who recently robbed the Overland Gold Express along the Old Sioux trail, shooting and killing the stage driver, Pop Foster. In secret, Lance is the big boss who leaks the necessary information regarding gold shipments to Tod Vain. Unbeknownst to anyone, Pop survives the attack, with Tonto tending to the wounds. In Pop's hand was a piece of clothing from Vain's shirt, which can ensure the outlaw goes to jail if matched with his present shirt. When Sheriff Dan Parker arrests Tod Vain, the outlaw gang, masked and led by Vance, kidnaps Mary, Pop's daughter, and is held ransom to prevent Vain from being tried and naming Vance as his boss. Leading up to the day of the trial, Vain sends Limpy to Lance Arnold to ask that he be released by any means necessary by midnight, or he talks. Limpy returns to the jail window to let Vain know he won't have anything to worry about because of the kidnapping. The Lone Ranger, keeping guard of Tod Vain in the sheriff's office, released Vain at midnight, providing shades of suspicion that Vance cared not a whim for Vain's concern. This leads to a confrontation whereupon the thieves accuse and incriminate each other. Vain discovers afterwards that the clock in the sheriff's office was set an hour and a half earlier to trick him into thinking he broke out at midnight. The abandoned mine in Gold Canyon, where Mary was held captive, is revealed and the law, along with The Lone Ranger, rescues her.

Episode #1509-722 "GUN ACROSS THE BORDER"
Broadcast September 23, 1942
Copyright Registration #81,913, script received at Registration Office September 24, 1942.
Written by George Waller.
Plot: A gang of cattle rustlers on the Texas-Mexico border act in a most unusual manner...with an owl hoot for a signal. Tonto claims the owl hoot is not only manmade, but a poor rendition. The Lone Ranger is more curious to know why the rustlers work under the light of a full moon. In disguise as a cowpuncher from the States, The Lone Ranger rides south of the border. Sam Peevey runs a Cantina for a hideout and overhearing a conversation between Sam and Butcher, the leader of the outlaws, he learns the crooks are running guns and stashing their supply in the El Diablo mine. After verifying what they learned, The Lone Ranger rides out to report to the Mexican authorities, but the police suspect the masked man of gunrunning. After handing over his guns to verify his claim, the masked man rode out with the law to prove his story, only to discover Tonto and the guns were missing. Taking his guns back and racing away from the Mexican police, the masked man follows the trail to another hideout where the crooks had Tonto bound and gagged. The Lone Ranger races in, frees Tonto and holds the outlaws at bay long enough for the law to catch up to him and take the crooks into custody.

Episode #1510-723 "MYSTERY OF THE NIGHT MARAUDERS"
Broadcast September 25, 1942
Copyright Registration #81,914, script received at Registration Office September 24, 1942.
Plot: The manner in which a band of Apache Indians raided wagon trains laden with gold dust as they moved along a certain region of Texas, spoke of intelligent planning and knowledge of the miners' intentions. Then the U.S. Cavalry took charge. Colonel Bragg thought he had a plan to apprehend the Apaches, led by Spotted Deer, only to discover the Indians vanished without a trace in a basin known as Indian Gulch. Following a lead, The Lone Ranger disguises himself as a gold prospector and visits a cantina named La Cucaracha in the town of Fernandez. Inside, he succeeds in getting Tonto and himself recruited to the outlaw gang. During a recent raid, the vigilantes discover a stash of gold behind a waterfall. After a showdown with Spotted Deer later that night, Tonto fetched the Cavalry while The Lone Ranger races in to block the exit by the waterfall.

Episode #1511-724 "LEGACY FOR A GHOST"
Broadcast September 28, 1942
Copyright Registration #81,915, script received at Registration Office September 24, 1942.
Plot: The bank in Dawson, Nevada, was held up. The robber was shot and killed by the sheriff, thanks to a tip-off from The Lone Ranger, and the dead man buried. Jack Potter, age 28, arrives in town to discover his name is on the gravestone. The Lone Ranger, questioning why anyone would contact the sheriff with a tip-off, using his name, meets Jack Potter and figures out how Cass Greenstreet, president of the bank, and Saul Conroy, the head teller, schemed to steal the land owned by jack Potter's uncle and throw the blame on a derelict. Potter was never shot and killed back in Pineville, however, an oversight in Greenstreet's scheme. The Lone Ranger arranges for Potter to send a letter to the crooks, dated the day prior, suggesting the ghost of the dead man is arriving in Pineville tomorrow. Saul travels out to meet Jack Potter, hoping to complete the part Greenstreet failed, but has jittery nerves because he believes the dead man's evil soul may not have found peace. The Lone Ranger, switching bullets for blanks in Saul's gun, watches off to the side as Saul shoots the sleeping figure, who screams in agony. The next day, Saul returns to Dawson to witness another letter being delivered from Jack

Potter, who claims he missed the train and will arrive by stage. Potter arrives and by this time Saul cracks and confesses to the "ghost," while Greenstreet draws a gun. The confrontation leads to a confession – the attempt to steal money from the estate of Jack Potter's uncle. Sheriff Tuttle, having overheard the confession, sides with The Lone Ranger who jumps in and disarms the killers.

Episode #1512-725 "DOUBLE COUNTERFEIT"

Broadcast September 30, 1942

Copyright Registration #81,916, script received at Registration Office September 24, 1942.

Written by George Waller.

Plot: Denby, the publisher of the ink-stained Prairie City Chronicle, is really a former counterfeiter, wanted back East by the U.S. Government. He ventured out West with his daughter, Mary, trying to make a new start and go straight. When his old accomplice, Ormond King, arrives in the growing boom town, Denby finds himself blackmailed into producing counterfeit $100 bills. King is not only a bad penny, but an accomplished actor by profession, who masquerades as an emigrant passing through town and passing the counterfeits. Outside of town, after King shoots and kills a Federal Agent, he swaps clothes and impersonates the agent, so he can falsely verify in the town bank the counterfeits are legit so he can continue to pass more counterfeits. The Lone Ranger and Tonto find the dead man and some counterfeit bank notes in his wallet and pay a visit to the bank to verify the masquerade. After verifying his suspicions with Denby, The Lone Ranger tricks the crook into thinking the Federal Agent is alive – just wounded – and resting in the local hotel. Late that night, King walks into the hotel and sneaks into the room, unaware his attempt at finishing off the federal agent was merely shooting bullets into rolled up blankets. Sheriff Bartlett takes the crook in for murder and a charge of counterfeiting, while Banker Holmes agrees to honor the masked man's request and sees to it that John Blake gets a good turn at the trial for helping to turn the tables against Ormond King.

Episode #1513-726 "MURDER STRIKES THRICE"

Broadcast October 2, 1942

Copyright Registration #82,176, script received at Registration Office October 12, 1942.

Written by George Waller.

Plot: In a hot, dusty town of Excalaber, a young vagrant named Paul Zenber is accused of murdering Zeke Martin. Paul's alibi is that he was playing poker at the Black Casino at the time of the murder, but the other card players deny playing cards with him. On Paul's birthday, he was found guilty and sentenced to the penitentiary. One year later, Cole Rankin was poisoned on his birthday. Lem Parsons was knifed in his sleep on his birthday, and Seth Hollands celebrated his birthday being shot to death in the streets. Sheriff Tim Runyon fears he will lose his job as a result of the birthday killer, agreeing to assist The Lone Ranger in his investigation, especially since he is romantically involved with the judge's daughter, Jane. Tonto, meanwhile, rode out to discover Paul is not only the judge's son, but was released four months ago on a pardon. Sneaking over to the cabin of Shane and Hook, the masked man and Indian overhear a conversation how Shane was a partner with the other three, left for dead ten years ago and attempted to take his share of the mine. Only now he can take over the company, with Hook ensuring the deal as the new sheriff, replacing Tim Runyon. But when The Lone Ranger apprehends Shane and Hook, and grabs the evidence, Sheriff Tim Runyon places them in jail. The judge, the next intended victim, is now saved when it was discovered his son, Paul Zenber, was shot and killed by Shane, meant to be another frame against him.

Episode #1514-727 "HORSE'S MASTER"

Broadcast October 5, 1942

Copyright Registration #82,177, script received at Registration Office October 12, 1942.

Plot: The sheriff was a troubled man, tortured by the complaints from the local ranchers who have been plagued by horse thieves. When Tonto rides into the region, the ranchers, having formed a vigilante meeting, attempt to frame and hang the Indian, accused of being a horse thief. Tonto, however, verifies his horse "Scout" is really his by mastering commands the others could not. Both Jim Jones and Red Talbot attempt to take blame for the rustling, knowing the Indian is innocent. Jim and Red were veterans of the Indian wars, willing to confess to a crime they did not commit to save the Indian from being hung without courtroom justice. In reality, Tate Raft, the sheriff's deputy, was the leader of the gang of rustlers for there was not a single robbery in three days since he left for Pine Flats. Thanks to a tip-off from the sheriff, the deputy believed the horses he recently stole was about to be sold to the man they were stolen from. In his effort to race out to stop his rustler gang from making a mistake, he ultimately gave away his guilt and revealed the location of the rustlers.

Episode #1515-728 "HOOFBEATS TO ARIZONA"
Broadcast October 7, 1942

Copyright Registration #82,178, script received at Registration Office October 12, 1942.

Plot: The Lone Ranger and Tonto, having wandered through one of the most rough and desolate stretches of the desert, seeking relief from the blazing sun, come across Cody Junction, a railroad station. There, they find the station agent dead, presumably so the crooks can rob the train. In truth, their goal was to shoot and kill Mr. Brewster, owner of the Bar F Ranch… and they succeed in dry-gulching. The Lone Ranger and Tonto are quickly accused of the crime and are forced to race away. Three days later, Millie Brewster sat about the ranch house of the Bar F, formerly owned by her late father, to discover Kurt Larkin, the foreman, will inherit the ranch tomorrow. Kurt claims Mr. Brewster had a will made up and a lawyer named Crawford will arrive from town tomorrow to execute the will. In desperation, Millie claims her father would never have given away the ranch to anyone but her, and her father's journal would verify. Only after two crooks, Red Colton and Brophy from the Circle T, hired by Kurt, steal the journal do they discover it was all a ruse – the book was nothing but a photo album. Sheriff Giles arrives to hear testimony from The Lone Ranger and Tonto, who overheard the confession between the crooks, saving the ranch from falling into the wrong hands. More importantly, Kurt Larkin's gun will convict him of the murder.

Episode #1516-729 "QUICKSAND TELLS A TALE"
Broadcast October 9, 1942

Copyright Registration #82,179, script received at Registration Office October 12, 1942.

Written by George Waller.

Plot: This was the same script from the broadcast of March 30, 1938, with a few names changed. Buck Newton was changed to Jim Lane, Betty Stevens was changed to Barbara Wilkins, Black Mike was changed to Vince Collins, Jake was changed to Lucky Peters, and the names of the towns the stagecoach traveled, Rio Grande to El Paso, was changed to Elbow Bend to Colby.

Episode #1517-730 "APACHE TRAP"
Broadcast October 12, 1942

Copyright Registration #82,180, script received at Registration Office October 12, 1942.

Plot: Bruised and battered, against the odds, The Lone Ranger and Tonto fought a small band of Apaches, armed with arrows and tomahawks, who succeeded in killing advance scouts from a wagon train. Coming across prairie schooners bound west, The Lone Ranger explains to the leader, Ezra, how a band of Apache Indians are slowly growing for an attack. Despite his warnings, Ezra follows the advice of Jake, the guide, who insists on going straight while the masked man suggests they go around Apache territory. But it doesn't take long for Ezra to decide otherwise and venture around the Indians. As more and more Apaches gathered for their war party,

Tonto suspected a white man was in charge. Later, the masked man discovers Jake's pets are carrier pigeons that will convey information on the wagon train's change of plans to the Apache war party leader. The Lone Ranger and Tonto shoot and kill a pigeon, intercept the letter, and return to the prairie schooners to reveal Jake's guilt. Jake planned to receive a percentage of the spoils in return for assisting the Indians in the raids. Rather than venture north to avoid the Indians, The Lone Ranger explains how they could use the carrier pigeons to get the advantage on the Apache Indians and the pioneers overtake the red men in a swift battle, making the West safer for white men. The word of six captured Indians, and the men and women of the wagon train are enough to clinch Jake's guilt in a court of law when they arrive at the next town.

Episode #1518-731 "THUNDER MORGAN'S FALL"

Broadcast October 14, 1942

Copyright Registration #82,181, script received at Registration Office October 12, 1942.

Plot: Big Thunder Morgan was a giant of a man. He stood head and shoulders above every man in town. His strength put him in the class of the legendary Paul Bunyan. The only person he was afraid of was Ma Pringle, who could verbally put him in his place. When Morgan is shot and wounded in the streets, Tonto is momentarily accused of the crime. But The Lone Ranger, having ridden into town following the trail of stage robbers back in Deadwood, discovers Thunder Morgan is accused of the crime when some of the stolen money is found on his possession. The Lone Ranger, suspecting the medicine being administered to Thunder Morgan was actually liquor and that he only faked being wounded, stays in the same room where Morgan was recovering, to warn him about the "medicine." Loftus masterminded the scheme as one of the stage robbers and hoped to frame Thunder for the crime. In the hopes of a jury showing mercy, Loftus confessed where the rest of the money was hiding and the names of the other robbers, but this was after Thunder pretended that he was going to beat Loftus to force the confession.

Episode #1519-732 "INDIAN TROUBLE"

Broadcast October 16, 1942

Copyright Registration #82,182, script received at Registration Office October 12, 1942.

Written by George Waller.

Plot: Trouble always brews when the Apache begin wearing war paint and shouting the cry of death to settlers. The Lone Ranger and Tonto, investigating a case of cattle rustling, find enough evidence to suggest a band of white men are masquerading as Indians, and their actions which might stir up relations between the red men and white men. The Indians, frustrated because the water hole was poisoned, resulting in the death of their cattle, now find themselves having to purchase new cattle. The ranchers, however, are blamed for the poison. The Lone Ranger pays a visit to Chief White Cloud to persuade him to wait a few days to prove two or three white men were responsible for the trouble. When Old Mack was shot and wounded during the latest cattle raid, Jeff Carson of the Bar Q forms a posse and prepares to ride out and attack the Indians. Blackie and Mace, having poisoned the water hole, then schemed to sell the stolen cattle to the Indians. Not only would they profit, but the Indians would take the blame for cattle rustling. Both the Indians and Jeff Carson gave the masked man until sundown to clear up the matter. During a confrontation with White Cloud and Carson, The Lone Ranger proves how Blackie and Mace were responsible – including money found on their possession from the sale of the stolen cattle and the water they drink they think is from the poisoned water hole, which makes them panic and give away their guilt for the poisoning.

Episode #1520-733 "BLUE PEBBLES"

Broadcast October 19, 1942

Copyright Registration #82,183, script received at Registration Office October 12, 1942.

Plot: John P. Cartwright, a prominent rancher, passed away and is apparently leaving everything to Nathan Black, who served as both range foreman and boss of the mine. Angered by the news, Jeff Thompson, serving time in a territorial penitentiary having been convicted on false evidence, breaks free and sets out to find his son and stop Nathan from inheriting the property. Jeff stumbled upon the camp of The Lone Ranger and stole Scout to make a swift getaway. After The Lone Ranger catches up with Jeff and his son, and learning of Jeff's motives, the masked man agrees to help assist and together they ride to Trinity Basin in Montana. It seems many years prior Jeff tried to raise cattle there, but the venture was doomed to failure, so he tried his hand at mining. The property should belong to his son, he figures, but Nathan Black was resolved to gain control for the vein he sought to profit. During the confrontation, The Lone Ranger spurred Silver to jump across a ledge as only the powerful stallion could, to get the advantage over the criminals who sought to kill Jeff and his son. As the crooks are being led into town for creating false evidence and attempted murder, and Jeff lays dying as a result of the exchange of gunplay, the "worthless blue pebbles" are revealed to be sapphires and Jeff's son will inherit what is rightfully his.

Notes: John Todd plays the prison guard in the opening scene.

Episode #1521-734 "DOUBLE EXPOSURE"
Broadcast October 21, 1942
Copyright Registration #82,184, script received at Registration Office October 12, 1942.
Written by George Waller.
Plot: The Lone Ranger and Tonto have been trailing an elusive group of cattle rustlers for weeks and in the process, stumble upon a notorious gang of stagecoach drivers operating just outside Pine Creek. Only when he discovers the strong boxes contained harnesses did The Lone Ranger investigate further. Pop Frisby, owner of the harness store, was especially not happy. He specifically had the payroll put inside the harness to foil the scheme of the stage robbers and somehow even this scheme failed. Not waiting for the boss to arrive, the stagecoach thieves open the wooden crates and discover the harness and then the money hidden inside. The Lone Ranger trailed the robbers and rode onto the camp, mistaken by the robbers as "the boss." The robbers insist on getting their cut and the masked man assures them that they will receive payment soon, asking them to remain in the boxed-in ravine for another day. Lefty and Ace, meanwhile, leaders of the cattle rustlers, were trailed by Tonto. When the masked man and Indian discover how they can expose twice the number of outlaws – two gangs with one stone. Spurred by Tonto's shots and the masked man's clever maneuvering, the stolen cattle were stampeded and made for the ravine. The cattle rustlers give chase for losing their plunder would be beyond embarrassing. But their struggle to slow the tide was futile. Back in the ravine, the stage robbers quickly surmised the situation and mounted horses to ride away from the longhorns that were sure to injure, if not kill. With the sheriff and his posse joining chase, both organized gangs were rounded up like cattle and disarmed.

Episode #1522-735 "STEEL RAILS AND GOLD"
Broadcast October 23, 1942
Copyright Registration #82,185, script received at Registration Office October 12, 1942.
Plot: Train robbers committed a brazen act at Beakman Junction, stealing the gold shipment and shooting the armed guard and engineer. This was the third train holdup in two months. John Peterson, superintendent of the Southwestern Railroad in Cold Springs, spent three days riding around the community in hopes of sending a message to The Lone Ranger. When the masked man pays Peterson a visit and learns that the mining payroll will be shipped on the next train, The Lone Ranger races out to ride on board as added security. What The Lone Ranger did not expect was two crooks who boarded the same train a few stations back and knocked the masked man out from behind. Knowing the outlaw gang planned to wreck the train with another, they tied their captive to the front of end of the steam engine. The Lone Ranger woke to hear the oncoming train that

would soon meet head on, and quickly tugged on his bounds. Thankfully, rawhide stretches when wet and the masked man escaped in time. Tonto tracked the hideout of the thieves and with The Lone Ranger overhearing the conversation from a distance, figures one of only three men could have been responsible for masterminding the recent train robbery. Back in Peterson's office, The Lone Ranger forces all three men to write the same letter instructing the gang to visit a special location, and each letter with a different location. Knowing the gang would believe the handwriting most recognized as their boss, Bart Keegan at the office panics and pulls a gun. Tonto shoots from a window to disarm the culprit. The sheriff organizes a posse to ride out to apprehend the crooks.

Notes: One of the train operators in the opening scene was played by John Todd.

Episode #1523-736 "TURNABOUT"

Broadcast October 26, 1942

Copyright Registration #82,186, script received at Registration Office October 12, 1942.

Written by George Waller, based on a story by Fran Striker.

Plot: Hunk Masters, a prospector to whom the sheriff of Blue Ridge suspects robbed a bank and shot a guard, has managed to stay outside the law. His recent robbery, however, netted paper money that happens to be rare in this part of the West. The bank teller recalls how a $100 bill was torn and taped on the back, which makes for easy identification. Wayne Cole, a con man posing as a wealthy Easterner interested in purchasing the land owned by Ben Hastings, uses some of the stolen money as payment, which Hunk agreed to front. Having panned for gold for some time, Masters discovers the gold specks he is finding originate from a vein located somewhere on the Hastings land. Ben Hastings and his bride, Tess, having discovered the hard way that the land is worthless for farming, agree to sell the land to Cole for $3,000, and accepts the $1,000 deposit, refundable if Cole's wife chooses not to homestead. The Lone Ranger and Tonto ride up to the Hastings homestead to steal the money, so Cole puts plain paper into an envelope and seals it, assuring them another $1,000. Late that night, a crook named Slim sneaked into the house to steal the envelope – hired by Cole and Masters – so the crooks will return the next day to decided not to buy and force the old couple to surrender the $1,000 or the property. Thanks to The Lone Ranger, the old couple learn the news and are satisfied with returning the envelope – surprising the crooks until they discover the stolen $1,000 was inside. When Masters verified it was the cash – including the recognizable $100 bill – the sheriff takes the crooks in. Angered by the trickery, Hunk, Cole and Slim accused each other for the crimes charged against them. As for the property, Ben and Tess Hastings will stay as they now know about the gold underneath the soil.

Notes: This episode was loosely adapted from the Fran Striker radio script broadcast on February 22, 1935.

Episode #1524-737 "THE GUNSMITH OF SAN BELLO"

Broadcast October 28, 1942

Copyright Registration #82,300, script received at Registration Office October 24, 1942.

Plot: San Bello was an old Spanish town and Caleb Sibley, the old gunsmith, believed this was a perfect place to hide from his criminal past – but discovered this was not the case when Darby forces him to sign over the shop to the crook, and then gets shot and killed. The Lone Ranger, visiting the gunsmith shop to have some rust filed away from his six-shooters, is accused of the murder. It doesn't take long for The Lone Ranger, who fled town, to realize what the scheme of Darby Hicks and Bart. Caleb's daughter, angered at the masked man for the death of her father, eventually discovers she was mistaken. It was she who delivered the letter from The Lone Ranger to Darby, stating he will ride through the south gate of the plaza tonight, in defiance of the crook. Meanwhile, the bank robbers are busy digging a tunnel to the bank. When The Lone Ranger discovers the woman is masquerading as the masked man to right a wrong, he races out not just to save her life, but defeat

Darby Hicks who planned to ambush the masked man using an Army carbine, proving his skill with the ivory-handled six-shooters.

Episode #1525-738 "BIRDS OF A FEATHER"

Broadcast October 30, 1942

Copyright Registration #82,301, script received at Registration Office October 24, 1942.

Plot: Hutch Larson and his gang was responsible for the stage robbery from Sutter's Gulch, the Adobe City bank robbery, and numerous cases of cattle rustling. With so many crimes, it comes as no surprise that Sheriff Carter was the object of an angry crowd. Jeb Carter, the sheriff's son, returned from schooling from the East to discover his father will lose his tin star if he doesn't find evidence against the gang, whose members keep getting jailed and then get released due to lack of evidence. Jeb visits the local Marshal Carey to propose being arrested and while in jail, gets in good with the gang to help gather evidence for the law. When the U.S. Marshal is dry-gulched, there is no one alive to verify Jeb was working undercover. The Lone Ranger, meanwhile, was in the midst of the same scheme and with the assistance of Tonto, masqueraded a jailbreak. While the lure of gold helps smoke the crooks out, The Lone Ranger quietly arranges for the sheriff and his posse to visit the same site to surround and apprehend the outlaw gang. Young Jeb is almost accused of being a member of the gang until The Lone Ranger explains that the U.S. Marshal is alive and being nursed back to health and will ensure Jeb – and his father's name – is not tarnished.

Episode #1526-739 "DEAD END"

Broadcast November 2, 1942

Copyright Registration #82,302, script received at Registration Office October 24, 1942.

Written by George Waller.

Plot: The Lone Ranger and Tonto happened to be riding through a canyon infested with outlaws when they come across the remnants of a stagecoach that was robbed, the driver and guard shot dead. The payroll for the troops at the fort was stolen. The newly elected Sheriff Flint and his deputy, Dutch, were the leaders of the outlaws that were responsible for a number of stage robberies that plagued the community. When Windy, an aged outlaw, wanted out, he was shot dead. While The Lone Ranger and Tonto investigate "Death Cavern," courtesy of a tip from the dying lips of Windy, the sheriff in town attempts to blame Jeff Young, the young dispatcher of the stage line – even planting evidence from the recent stage robbery. Flint wasted no time rushing the youth to trial, and even speedier to ensure a conviction and a hangman's noose. The verdict was guilty of murder in the first degree. The Lone Ranger and Tonto barge into the courtroom and kidnap Jeff Young, prompting a posse to give chase. Discovering there was poison gas coming from the cave, Tonto puts a large rock over the hole to smoke out the crooks, who flee outside and into the hands of the U.S. Marshal and his posse. The deputy was accused of murder; the outlaws swore the remnants of the stolen loot would be found inside, clearing the frame-up of Jeff Young. The crooked deputy, not wanting to take the blame for the murders, accused the crooked sheriff and the marshal took them into custody.

Notes: Todd doubles for the role of the judge for one line in the second act.

Blooper! John Todd stumbles over the first line he delivers in this episode.

Episode #1527-740 "MURDER MASTERS"

Broadcast November 4, 1942

Copyright Registration #82,303, script received at Registration Office October 24, 1942.

Plot: The Lone Ranger visits Sheriff Parmeley to deliver a full pardon from the governor for Steve Hawkins, who has been on the run and in hiding for months. His daughter, Betty, will not reveal the location of her father's hideout, so the masked man and Indian need to seek the old man and verify his freedom. But two crooks, Pete Maxim and Jake Whitcomb, two witnesses against Hawkins during the trial, are taking desperate measures to find Steve Hawkins before the masked man. This includes an ambush from the rocks above after The Lone Ranger and Tonto find Steve and attempt to ride back to town. After realizing the third witness was Mort, also known as the weasel, who worked in the state department where he would have learned about the pardon and leaked the info to Jake and Pete, the masked man rode out to abduct him and bring him to the sheriff. The confrontation leads to Mort being a witness to the crime itself, verifying where some of the stolen loot Steve Hawkins was accused of stealing, could still be found. A falling out among thieves verifies Hawkins' innocence and the three crooks are taken into custody.

Episode #1528-741 "THE PHANTOM KILLER"

Broadcast November 6, 1942

Copyright Registration #82,304, script received at Registration Office October 24, 1942.

Written by George Waller.

Plot: The Lone Ranger and Tonto stumble upon a deserted stagecoach from Prairie City to Adobe that has been robbed, the driver and guard found dead with no sign of injury. When the masked man brings the stage into town, he finds himself accused of the robbery and murder. There have now been six mysterious deaths, each with no mark on the bodies, and the stage robberies infuriate Ryan, the district superintendent of the stage line. Danny Kern, son of the recent stage driver found dead, hopes to take his father's place in an effort to help unmask the killer. As Danny drives the next stage, The Lone Ranger arranges for Tonto to lure the sheriff's deputies away so the killer and stage robber would not be prevented from making another attempt. When the stage comes to a stop at the only water hole within miles, The Lone Ranger orders Danny to hold the sheriff at bay as the masked man gets the advantage over Ryan, who hoped to rob the stage again. The district superintendent claims to be innocent until The Lone Ranger points out how the water hole was poisoned – not the kind that kills horses, but it will kill humans. Ryan won't drink the water, giving away his guilt.

Episode #1529-742 "THIEVES IN THE NIGHT"

Broadcast November 9, 1942

Copyright Registration #82,305, script received at Registration Office October 24, 1942.

Plot: Riding into the town of Greentree, The Lone Ranger and Tonto pay a visit to the general store only to discover that two crooks were robbing the place. Before The Lone Ranger realized the general store owner is not who he claims to be, the heroes are knocked unconscious from behind and fled the town. The sheriff and his men mistakenly believe the masked man and Indian are the robbers. What poses as a mystery is why the crooks stole only Indian beads and trinkets, not the money or gold. Meanwhile, the two crooks scheme with a tribe of Indians to rob the train that will ride into the region shortly, paid off in the trinkets. The Lone Ranger and Tonto trailed Fenton and Sig to find them in the process of planning to wreck and rob the train, with the assistance of the renegade Indians. The sheriff's posse arrives to stop the train and thus foil the scheme. The outlaw Indian leader, upset because he was betrayed on a promise, attempts to knife Sig but The Lone Ranger disarms the Indian.

Episode #1530-743 "THIEVES FALL OUT"

Broadcast November 11, 1942

Copyright Registration #82,306, script received at Registration Office October 24, 1942.

Written by George Waller.

Plot: Lud Dane, hired by Kansas Myers and Lance McCarey to retrieve a written confession from Dutch Collins, shoots the lights out in the café at Prairie Flat, in order to grab the paper and flee. The sheriff maintains half of the confession but without the other half, which is in The Lone Ranger's possession, each half is useless.

The outlaws, having established the Lazy B Ranch and a lot of cattle, would rather take drastic measures versus leaving the territory. When Dane is drilled and the murder weapon found to be the property of Larry Kirk, the son of the local sheriff, the murder accusation is used to blackmail the sheriff's son into surrendering his half of the confession. After The Lone Ranger visits the sheriff to hand him the half he and Tonto came across, they discover the sheriff's half was stolen – by his son. Out on the prairie, the vigilantes discovered Larry's situation and ordered him to deliver the paper as planned. During the confrontation between Larry and the outlaws, The Lone Ranger intercepts the exchange and with the assistance of the sheriff, verifies the scheme – and how Lud Dane was not killed but only faked his death.

Episode #1531-744 "WEST OF BIG RIDGE"

Broadcast November 13, 1942

Copyright Registration #82,307, script received at Registration Office October 24, 1942.

Plot: Dorothy Travis claimed her brother was hiding in a cave near a ridge, believing he committed a murder in Crawford Gap, but The Lone Ranger knows of no murder and the girl has no brother. Puzzled, the masked man investigates and riding toward the ravine, is shot and falls from his horse. In a cave where Tonto tends to The Lone Ranger's wounds, the Indian learns from Travis (not her brother but a man who coincidentally has the same last name) the story behind Dorothy's request. Mr. Hendricks owns half interest in a gold mine. The other half is split evenly with McDuffy and Travis, who must strike a vein by the end of the month or Hendricks will own the mine completely. When Hendricks is found dead, two men named Vic and Daggart claimed to be witness to the murder and finger Travis. In reality, McDuffy committed the crime and paid Vic and Daggart so he alone can inherit. Dorothy, conspiring with McDuffy, hoped The Lone Ranger would be shot by Travis, knowing he has an eagle eye with a rifle, clinching his guilt in the eyes of a jury. When Vic and Daggart are shot with an arrow, like Hendricks, McDuffy does not hesitate to claim Travis was responsible. Tonto uses a note and an arrow in a saddle bag to lure McDuffy out of town to see the bodies and make an adjustment – it seems the note from The Lone Ranger explained how someone used the Indian arrow as a murder weapon – not shooting it from a bow, but as an instrument of stabbing. McDuffy's with a broken hand, was never suspected until now… and his attempt to alter the wounds to verify the bow and arrow Travis was keen on using would be proof against him. Dorothy's guilt with McDuffy was also proven as the sheriff and his men caught McDuffy in the act.

Episode #1532-745 "DEVIL'S SINK"

Broadcast November 16, 1942

Copyright Registration #82,639, script received at Registration Office November 30, 1942.

Plot: The ranch of Jeb Anderson was located near the southwestern desert, but Jeb also owned a tiny gold mine at Mount Arroyo where, every day, he prospected. Jeb was confident that no one knew about his gold mine and the men and women of Kingsford merely tagged him as a rancher. A gang of crooks led by Duke Bandy, robbed Jeb of his gold, used coal oil to set fire to his cabin, and shot the man dead when he tried to escape the flames. Jimmy Hightower, son of the sheriff and nephew of the dead man, was quickly arrested for horse stealing. The Lone Ranger and Tonto, in the presence of the young man and the burnt remains of the Anderson cabin, were arrested for murder. Law moved swiftly in Kingsford, with The Lone Ranger and Tonto found guilty and sentenced to hang. In jail, The Lone Ranger learns from Jimmy, who longs to join Duke's gang, that they hide out in Devil's Sink. The masked man applied a trick to escape from jail, then races out to Devil's Sink, comprised of endless ravines, tunnels, and rocky crags made up of volcanic slag. At the rim of Devil's Sink, The Lone Ranger sends Tonto to the Governor's office to ask for a pardon for Jimmy. With handcuffs still on their wrists, The Lone Ranger uses this as a means of smoking out Duke and being led through the labyrinth to Duke's cabin. Pete escorted the cavalcade through switchbacks and to a subterranean spring. Their attempt to get in with the gang failed, however, when Duke observes the silver bullets and decides to have the two men staked to the ground to suffer the scorching sun. Half an hour later, a thunderstorm pours through providing relief from the torture and a means for The Lone Ranger to free a hand and break from his bonds. Duke's outlaw gang, however, was already on the way to town to commit a robbery when the masked man and Jimmy raced to the sheriff's house. With extra gunplay, the outlaws are apprehended, and The Lone Ranger testifies how he overheard Duke's confession of murdering Jeb Anderson. Tonto arrives with the pardon, and Jimmy is certain to stay on the clear and certain path now that he found himself combatting the outlaws.

Episode #1533-746 "THUNDERING HOOFS"
Broadcast November 18, 1942
Copyright Registration #82,640, script received at Registration Office November 30, 1942.
Written by George Waller.
Plot: Two outlaws named Spade and Barney cleverly start a prairie fire destined for a ranch house as a means of cattle rustling. As Lafe Stevens and his men seek aid to combat the flames, the rustlers make good time stampeding the longhorns. Sheltered from the dust storm in a cave, The Lone Ranger and Tonto observe the prairie fire from a distance and quickly ride out to help the ranchers. Tad Harrison, who was sent up for cattle rustling, happened to be riding through the region, recently released from the penitentiary. Tad quickly finds himself falling into a death trap as the stampeding longhorns race to him, but Lafe is killed. The Lone Ranger suspects Spade and Barney knew Tad was returning and hoped to blame the theft of the Bar Z brand on Tad. The Lone Ranger insists Tad remain outside of town while he rides in. The two crooks host a hastily conferred meeting with The Lone Ranger, who lets the men know Lafe is six feet under, victim of the stampede. The outlaws mistakenly believe the masked man was Tad Harrison who initially exacted revenge against Lafe. At the suggestion of The Lone Ranger, the rustlers agree to kidnap the sheriff's daughter and use her as hostage to hold back the law from interfering with their cattle drive escape. Tad, meanwhile, races out to alert Betty to stay outside of town where it is safe, while Barney and the masked man are outside the sheriff's house to catch Betty. The masked man, however, foils the scheme. Barney's ransom note meant to be left behind is found on his possession. Spade, meanwhile, is being apprehended elsewhere and the sheriff verifies the masked man is not Tad, a surprise to Barney.

Episode #1534-747 "THE AVENGER"
Broadcast November 20, 1942
Copyright Registration #82,641, script received at Registration Office November 30, 1942.
Written by George Waller.
Plot: Vince McNary, known as a quick shot, is willing to go to all ends to acquire access to the only water pond in miles, located on Grant's ranch. All attempts at intimidation failed, but that did not stop Grant from demanding a showdown. Vince, a coward at heart but with a bulldog bite, throws beer into Grant's face to get the advantage, shooting the man down. The townsfolk are at a loss to rule the gunfight fair, but his reputation succeeds in silencing the gossip. Days later, Vince schemes with Hawk, an outlaw, to intercept the stagecoach where Grant's brother, Jed, will soon arrive to inherit the ranch. Hawk will get a nice cut if he kidnaps Jed and uses the credentials to impersonate the brother. Tim, Grant's 12-year-old son, sought vengeance against Vince and his gunplay was intercepted by Tonto, who reports back to The Lone Ranger. Jed, meanwhile, is held hostage in a shack with two crooks, Lefty and Rufe, kept guard. Outside the shack, Tonto creates a fire as a distraction, rescuing Jed. Back in town, the lawyer observes Jed as a spitting image of the dead man, a twin brother, and Hawk's impersonation is called against. Hours after Hawk is thrown into jail for fraud, The Lone Ranger convinces the sheriff to let Hawk out to help expose Vince as a murderer. Following The Lone Ranger's instructions, Tonto delivers a note of challenge to Tim and then spreads word through town of the impending

fight. A gunfight in the streets is arranged and the while everyone knows the kid won't have a chance against Vince, The Lone Ranger knows the crook is a true coward and makes sure, in the presence of witnesses, Vince sweats as he cannot find an advantage and reveals himself as a coward. The sheriff tells Vince McNary to choose – stay and remain for the townsfolk who demand lynching or go to jail by confessing to the murder of Grant.

Episode #1535-748 "LENNIE'S LOCKET"

Broadcast November 23, 1942

Copyright Registration #82,642, script received at Registration Office November 30, 1942.

Plot: He was 240 pounds and stood over six feet, but the dark-haired giant named Lennie was more than a reliable top cowhand of his employer's ranch. He was personal bodyguard and oversight to Cal Gentry's motherless daughter, Barbara. Lennie wore a slender locket around his neck and while Barbara was always curious, he kept the contents of his locket a secret. Many years ago, an infant was dropped off at Cal Gentry's ranch and Barbara was raised like his own daughter. An outlaw named Bat Cummings killed a number of sheriffs and the result of his struggle against society led to a broken nose, which made him easy to identify with the law. Bat hid out in a small cabin in Blackstone Cavern, plotting the robbery of the Twin Forks bank, alongside his cronies, Pete and Flagg. Bat has been blackmailing Gentry with the knowledge of Barbara's adoption, and Gentry mortgaged his ranch to keep paying the blackmail. When Bat recognizes Lennie, he kidnaps the giant. Cal Gentry and The Lone Ranger race out to apprehend the outlaws, and during the exchange of gunfire, Lennie takes a bullet for Barbara, who raced onto the scene. After Bat and his men are apprehended, Lennie dies from his wound. The photos in the locket reveals Lennie was Barbara's father. Lennie was a former outlaw of the gang and after the baby was born, turned straight.

Episode #1536-749 "MURDER FOR PROFIT"

Broadcast November 25, 1942

Copyright Registration #82,643, script received at Registration Office November 30, 1942.

Written by George Waller, based on a story by Fran Striker.

Plot: Banker Steele and the dishonest Sheriff Carey plan to hang three innocent men, using fake evidence against them. When The Lone Ranger poses as a threat, Steele threatens to replace the sheriff if the masked man is not apprehended. Rather than wait for a trial, Steele orders the sheriff to ensure Harris, one of the three accused, is hung in his jail cell. The Lone Ranger and Tonto prevent the murder and after exchanging fisticuffs, race away with Jeff to their secret camp along the arroyo. After questioning Jeff and explaining how they rescued two other innocent men (Seth Holloway and Jeff Harris), The Lone Ranger realizes the only connection is that all three men made large deposits at the bank. Banker Steele hoped to profit with them no longer alive, with witnesses paid to falsely testify to a murder they never saw. The next day, a stranger arrived in town and paid a visit to the bank to make a deposit with $10,000 in bank bills. Outside the bank, the stranger got into a scuffle and murdered an Indian (a.k.a. Tonto) in the streets. During the trial, the dead body of the Indian is identified by the guilty culprits and only afterwards Tonto rises, proving he was never murdered and destroyed the testimony of the "witnesses." Offering to turn state's evidence, one of the three false witnesses claims to have been paid by Banker Steele. The stranger, the accused on the stand, turns out to be a U.S. Marshal who interrupts the judicial proceedings and takes the guilty in.

Notes: This episode was originally slated for November 20, 1942. This episode was also recycled from a script by Fran Striker, originally broadcast on January 19, 1938.

Episode #1537-750 "THE HORSEHAIR BRIDLE"

Broadcast November 27, 1942

Copyright Registration #82,644, script received at Registration Office November 30, 1942.

Plot: In the town of Mumford, Ed Galloway ran the café and general store, often buying and selling without concern of ownership. Among his recent acquisitions was the hand-woven bridles made at the territorial prison, including one made by John Carter, the former sheriff, who was falsely accused of robbing a bank. Carter never fired against the bank robbers and by outside appearance it was evident he allowed the crooks to flee with the money that was never recovered. It did not take long for the masked man to figure Sam Thorpe, the deputy, was not happy over losing the election to his boss and conspired with Ed Galloway to get Carter thrown in jail and Thorpe promoted. While Tonto rides out to visit the warden with a letter from The Lone Ranger, the masked man questions Jimmy Carter, the ex-sheriff's son, to learn why he wanted to buy the hand-woven bridle created by his father… and why the present sheriff wanted it more than the boy. John Carter sent a message to his son inside the bridle, explaining how he gave it long thought and figured out where the money was hidden – inside the coat now hanging in Jimmy's closet. The coat was owned by one of the three crooks and dropped at the scene. When Tonto returns with the U.S. Marshal, the lawman orders Sam Thorpe to remove his badge. The warden verifies John Carter will soon receive a full pardon from the governor. Carter is almost blind, verified by the prison physician, which is why he was unable to stop the bank robbers that night. Sam Thorpe, hoping to steal the unrecovered money, gave himself away as an accomplice to the crime. Jimmy plans to use the reward money coming to him for an operation that might help with the old man's eyesight.

Episode #1538-751 "RENEGADE"

Broadcast November 30, 1942

Copyright Registration #82,645, script received at Registration Office November 30, 1942.

Written by George Waller.

Plot: Disguising himself as an outlaw to try to get in with Tex Vinson and his gang, The Lone Ranger ventured south of the border to San Cosmo, where rich silver strikes in the hills have resulted in a boomtown attracting outlaws and prospectors from both sides of the border. Tex Vinson, responsible for numerous criminal acts in Texas, was trailed by the masked man and Indian. Jeff Hardy fled to San Cosmo, hunted by the Texas Rangers, falsely accused of a bank robbery and murder, agrees to assist The Lone Ranger with a scheme to apprehend Tex and clear his name. Inside the local café, Tonto pays for drinks with a large and impressive amount of silver ore. When forced to confess where he got the silver, the Indian suggests a stranger named Jeff has a lead on stolen loot. Tex visits Jeff and, verifying the man has a price on his head, insists on blackmail for his silence. Chaquita Martinez, a girl Jeff is in love with, defends her man against Tex, but plays her part well in the scheme. As Monk, one of Tex's men, follows Tonto to learn where the silver mine is, all of the cogs and sprockets in the scheme lure Tex and his gang across the border to Texas where the local sheriff, in hiding, overhears the confession. Tex framed Jeff for a crime and hopes to profit from blackmail, unaware that he put his own head in a noose.

Episode #1539-752 "HALF A LOAF"

Broadcast December 2, 1942

Copyright Registration #82,646, script received at Registration Office November 30, 1942.

Plot: In the town of Buena Vista, Sam Crawford, a widower, operated a bakery with his son Kip. When he receives a visit from Len Hackett and Jay, former gang members for which Sam fled from when he wanted to ride the straight path, Sam finds himself blackmailed to assist his old pards in a clever stagecoach robbery. Instead of placing loaves of bread in the window at 3 o'clock like he normally did, Sam put the loaves out earlier so a replacement for the stage driver can take hold of the stage – which happened to contain a cargo of $25,000. Naturally, the sheriff believes San Crawford was responsible for the caper and forms a posse to retrieve and apprehend the baker. In reality, Sam Crawford was kidnaped by the real bandits, who also killed and stole horses. Sam manages to get away from the crooks, but not before being shot and dies in front of his son, who will now inherit the bakery. The Lone Ranger and Tonto, on the trail to apprehend the crooks, are captured by the outlaws and later manage to break free of their bonds just as the sheriff and his posse arrive on the scene. The masked man quickly verifies the story Kip tells about his father not wanting to work with the outlaws, clearing the good name of Sam Crawford, even though he proved that everyone's past will catch up to them.

Episode #1540-753 "DYNASTY OF TERROR"

Broadcast December 4, 1942

Copyright Registration #82,647, script received at Registration Office November 30, 1942.

Written by George Waller.

Plot: Jim Blood is running a protection racket, ruling a small western town with an iron fist. His business code was blunt and profitable: Peace at a price. Law abiding citizens who wished to live unmolested were forced to pay him or suffer the consequences. Ruthless gunmen and masked riders came into the night to terrorize those who refused… and few dared to refuse them. Jim Blood gained power simply by disguising his position with a cloak of respectability. Hutch and Drake, leaders of the gunmen who performed the dirty work, reported to Jim Blood. When young Ted Loomis is shot for refusing to pay up, his bride, Jane, is kidnaped and held hostage for her life in exchange for her brother Ned's ranch. The last Jane saw her husband, the house was set on fire and Ted left inside, wounded, to die in in an oven. Ned, meanwhile, receives a ransom note of $10,000. Jim survives his ordeal and learns the news of his wife and the ransom from The Lone Ranger and Tonto who rescued him. The Lone Ranger encouraged Ned to move forward and pay the $10,000, and during the payoff Ned assured Jane that her husband is alive and well. The Lone Ranger and Tonto, meanwhile, allowed the ransom payoff as a distraction so they could plug the chimney to smoke out the outlaws. The distraction worked long enough for the sheriff and his deputies to apprehend and disarm the crooks, with Ned ready to swear to the confession he (and the deputies) heard – enough to ensure Jim Blood, Hutch and Drake face a guilty verdict in court.

Episode #1541-754 "SIGN OF THE SWASTIKA"

Broadcast December 7, 1942

Copyright Registration #82,648, script received at Registration Office November 30, 1942.

Written by George Waller.

Plot: Two years ago, a notorious criminal named Scar was branded with half an ear during his confrontation with the law, now hounded in every county. Hoping to exact revenge against the vigilante committee led by Carstairs, Scar conspires with Red Fox, to lead a band of hard-riding savages, renegades that combat white men who face useless defiance as fiery arrows burned down ranch houses and cabins. Carstairs is eventually captured and becomes the first victim to be scarred with a hot branding iron, an "ancient Indian symbol." In their search for the renegade Indians, the sheriff and his posse arrive in Sutter's Gap, mistaking Tonto and The Lone Ranger as outlaws. After evading the law, Tonto observes the tracks and discovers a mystery: the raiders vanish without a trace by the water's edge and the tracks are not Indian ponies. Hoping to find the secret of Sutter's Gap, The Lone Ranger dives into the water to finds an underwater cavern. The masked man is quickly overtaken by Scar and Red Fox, especially when the masked man takes a savage blow from a tomahawk to the head. Waking to find his hands and feet tightly bound, The Lone Ranger is rescued by Tonto, who dove in to rescue. With an idea in mind, The Lone Ranger sends Tonto to fetch kegs of gunpowder. With Tom Henshaw's ranch as the next target, The Lone Ranger orders the men and women to fill buckets with water to put out any fires that may be started. The war cries from the savages were rushing in from a distance and the ranch hands started firing back, standing their ground against the savage onslaught. Tonto, meanwhile, sets off kegs of gunpowder, draining the water from the basin, revealing the entrance of the cave where the outlaws hid out. The sheriff and his men race in and exchange gunfire, quickly overtaking the outlaws and renegade Indians by surprise. The sheriff assures Scar, now in custody, that he and the killers will hang for their crimes.

Episode #1542-755 "BADGE OF COURAGE"

Broadcast December 9, 1942

Copyright Registration #82,649, script received at Registration Office November 30, 1942.

Written by George Waller.

Plot: The sheriff of Sage City, along with a gunman named Todd Lang, allows outlaws a haven if they are willing to pay for it. Deputy Vic Colton, who was cleaning up the streets in an effort to prove himself a better man than the sheriff, was forced to shoot a breed named Gomez who was trying to rob the stagecoach. Despite Vic's shoulder wound by the knife thrown by the breed, Vic was accused of trying to hold up the stage since he was one of only two who knew it was carrying silver. The stage driver and guard also pointed an accusatory finger against the deputy. The Lone Ranger, realizing there was an injustice to frame the honest deputy for a crime he did not commit, rescues him from facing jail. The sheriff posts a wanted notice for Vic Colton, but the townsfolk express indignation and they themselves suspect foul play. To change the minds of the townsfolk, Todd Lang decides to rob the bank and murder the banker, wearing a mask and dressed in Vic's shirt and chaps, so that in the dark he would be mistaken for Vic. Todd Lang, believing he got away with the crime, is caught by Deputy Vic Colton who holds the gunman at bay with his six-shooter and sensitive trigger finger. Vic confesses he was in another town establishing an alibi, knowing full well Todd's and the sheriff's scheme. With Todd wearing Vic's clothing, the confrontation leads to Todd blaming the crooked sheriff, but The Lone Ranger already apprehended the sheriff. The town citizens, pleased to see justice cleared and enough to verify in a courtroom, cheer as honest Vic Colton will soon be elected the new sheriff.

Episode #1543-756 "NO MAN'S LAND"

Broadcast December 11, 1942

Copyright Registration #82,983, script received at Registration Office January 11, 1943.

Plot: A strip of land known today as Oklahoma was once considered no man's land, located between four states and not yet officially under jurisdiction of any state. It was during that short span of time that the Slater Gang escapes a sheriff's posse by crossing the border, where no one can arrest them. A judge in the nearby state of Texas hopes for a legal way to corral the outlaws. Jason, however, wants to use any means of apprehending the killers and thieves so he can return to his ranch in peace. Slater boldly makes a move to apprehend Jason, who led the posse many times against him, and held Jason prisoner. Tonto overhears the situation in town and races back to tell The Lone Ranger what he learned. Slater's larger scheme is to hold Jason hostage and make ranchers pay a tax per head of cattle, paying tribute, and kill Jason if they don't pay up. The Lone Ranger and Tonto boldly ride into the outlaws' camp, kidnaps Jason, and race out with the captive. The outlaws, having learned who the masked man was, take off in pursuit, unaware they crossed the border near Wild Horse Lake, running straight into a posse. The outlaws, taken by surprise, surrender quickly. Slater laughs until he learns that the posse was led by a U.S. Marshal and while the land was not under legal jurisdiction by any state, it was certainly covered under Federal law. The attempt to make ranchers pay taxes was a Federal violation and enough to ensure a conviction.

Episode #1544-757 "HEADING NORTH" [PART ONE]

Broadcast December 14, 1942

Copyright Registration #82,984, script received at Registration Office January 11, 1943.

Written by George Waller and Fran Striker.

Plot: Just south of the Canadian border, several hard-faced men, Snake Anson and Gregg have been thick as thieves for weeks as they plotted a means of stealing the valuable Martin copper mine. Knowing how Grandma Frisby tells stories of The Lone Ranger to Dan, a young man who is close friends with Martin, Gregg impersonates the masked man into believing he needs a specific strip of worthless property for the water rights to benefit local residents. Martin agrees to assist, but more for curiosity than the money he would be paid in the deal. The Lone Ranger, meanwhile, had made a pledge to a dead man that he would apprehend Gregg, and the trail led north to Dodge City in Kansas, then cold nights in Nebraska, and finally the grim wilderness of Montana. The Lone Ranger and Tonto were riding high in the border country on the trail of the outlaw. Back in the shack, Gregg and Slick laugh as they convinced Dan to bring Martin and his clerk to their abode to finalize the deal. In reality, they knew the deed, after being signed, would be fixed so the words could be revised, and Gregg would have complete ownership of the copper mine. Blasting powder was set about the place to create an "accident," to ensure they get away with the scheme. Martin, however, observed the scar on Snake's hand and identified him not as The Lone Ranger, but as a criminal wanted by the law. The two men and boy are bound hand and foot and would have died if it was not for The Lone Ranger who found the kegs of explosives and shot the fuse that was lit. As Tonto freed the men, The Lone Ranger raced out to apprehend Gregg.

Notes: The character of Frisby provided an unusual remark in this episode: "You're trying hard to be fair, Dan. I suppose you had The Lone Ranger pictured as a lot different. That's usually the way it is. You probably thought of him as a White Knight following the search for the Holy Grail. After all, Dan, even The Lone Ranger is a flesh and blood human."

Episode #1545-758 "DESIGN FOR MURDER" [PART TWO]
Broadcast December 16, 1942
Copyright Registration #82,985, script received at Registration Office January 11, 1943.
Written by George Waller.
Plot: Snake shoots Old Mac in the back to steal his prized possession, a silver bullet. Snake, realizing The Lone Ranger took a liking to the boy, realized if the kid was in danger, the masked man would ride to the rescue. The silver bullet could be used to verify a message from The Lone Ranger and lure the youth away as bait for a trap meant to be sprung on the masked man. The masked man chose to remain for a spell because of the lively, alert lad of 14 years. His qualities appealed strongly to the masked man. He showed courage and resourcefulness, and his resolve could not be shaken. Dan had heard about the Lone Ranger from his grandmother. The thrills of her many stories, told over a period of many years, were exceeded only by the recent action of the masked man. The Lone Ranger and Tonto paid a visit to Grandma Frisby to discover the ruse and raced back out to rescue Dan. The Lone Ranger's fear was that the kidnappers would cross the Canadian border and avoid capture. Sure enough, they crossed into Mountie country and when the masked man and Indian took pursuit, they found themselves trapped in a clever ambush, surrounded by boulders and gunmen from all directions. After finding a clever means of escaping, they raced for cover in a cave. Snake and Flint schemed to start a fire and smoke them out. There was no means of rescue by the sheriff since they were in Canadian territory. As the cave filled with smoke, our heroes discussed the possibility of holding out for as long as possible, then agreeing if they go, they go together. Dan, having broken free from his bonds, raced out to fetch the Mounties, who rode to the rescue in time to surround Snake and Flint. The Lone Ranger and Tonto assured Snake he would be taken back over the border to turn in to the sheriff for the murder of Old Mac.

Episode #1546-759 "ROPE'S END" [PART THREE]
Broadcast December 18, 1942
Copyright Registration #82,986, script received at Registration Office January 11, 1943.
Written by George Waller.
Plot: An old prospector named Joshua Lemp, known for spending many years up in the Yukon and never depositing much in the bank, is robbed by two outlaws, Buck and Fagan. After murdering the old man and stealing his gold, they laughed as they rode off. Not only were they successful in tipping off The Lone Ranger to visit the scene to be framed for the crime, but the sheriff of the county seat and his posse arrive as a result of

a similar tip. The Lone Ranger and Tonto exchanged fists with the posse as they worked their way through the crowd and outside the prospector's home. In private, Tonto confides to The Lone Ranger that he saw footprints and evidence that Dan was at the scene of the crime. Knowing the boy could not have committed murder or theft, The Lone Ranger paid a visit to the boy. After learning how Dan was offered a job to work at Joshua's cabin, due to his age, and discovering the old man was dead, The Lone Ranger gathers information from Dan that describes the supposed assailant who set up the frame. Tonto and Dan visit the cabin to investigate how the killers came and went without leaving tracks in the snow. They discovered a ladder leading to the roof and footprints in the snow on the roof, and a tree that afforded entrance and escape for the killers, thanks to the suggestion from the old man's dog, Prince. Only when the dog is used to frighten the killers was a confession quickly made before they could clear out of the region.

Episode #1547-760 "LAW OF THE APEX" [PART FOUR]
Broadcast December 21, 1942
Copyright Registration #82,987, script received at Registration Office January 11, 1943.
Written by Fran Striker.
Plot: The Lone Ranger and Tonto were in the copper mining region just south of the Canadian border when they observed smoke signals calling for "help." They discover young Dan was using Indian signals after finding a wounded Blackfoot Indian. Meanwhile, the sound of war drums verifies the local natives are preparing for an attack against the citizens of Copperville. Hoping to take advantage of the impending attack of the Blackfoot braves, two crooks named Al Currey and Jake Spode hope to gain possession of the Martin claim, a valuable copper claim, with "the law of the apex." Dan rides to alert the men and women of town to quickly vacate before the Indians arrive while Tonto tends to the wounded Indian. When The Lone Ranger faces off against Chief Running Bear, he reveals how two white men were responsible for the savage act, hoping to start a war between Indians and white men, and the wounded lost Indian verifies their story. The crooks are forced to choose justice at the hands of the Indians or be jailed by the sheriff – Al and Jake chose the latter of the two.

Notes: Law of the apex is a provision or term related to mining law. It refers to the principle that title to a given tract of mineral land, with defined mining rights, goes to the individual who locates the surface covering the outcrop or apex. Tonto makes a reference at the end of the episode when The Lone Ranger first rescued him and how, after his wounds were treated, he found a better way… this was in reference to episode #12 of the radio program, broadcast February 25, 1933.

Blooper! Al accidentally refers to his partner as "Spade" instead of "Spode" at one point in the episode.

Episode #1548-761 "DAN'S STRANGE BEHAVIOR" [PART FIVE]
Broadcast December 23, 1942
Copyright Registration #82,988, script received at Registration Office January 11, 1943.
Written by Fran Striker.
Plot: For reasons that puzzle The Lone Ranger, young Dan refuses to aid the masked man in a new adventure, moments after receiving a note from his grandmother. Having learned that a crook named Higgins is wanted by the law in Canada, having stabbed a woman in the back, The Lone Ranger masterminds a plan to trick the killer into turning himself in. As long as Higgins remains in U.S. Territory, south of Coon Creek, and unless he crosses into Canada on his own volition, the Northwest Mounted Police will not make an arrest. Using the contents of an envelope as bait to lure the killer to his camp outside of town, Higgins is shocked to learn afterwards that Tonto dug a channel in the snow to redirect the creek. With Higgins caught on Canadian soil, the Mounties take the killer into custody. The Lone Ranger returns to learn what caused Dan to run off

– Grandma Frisbee's heart is starting to give out and the doctor fears her time is coming to an end. On top of this, The Lone Ranger learns that Dan's last name is not Frisbee…

Episode #1549-762 "A NEPHEW IS FOUND" [PART SIX]

Broadcast December 25, 1942

Copyright Registration #82,989, script received at Registration Office January 11, 1943.

Written by Fran Striker.

Plot: Fourteen-year-old Dan lights three signal fires to fetch The Lone Ranger and Tonto, at the request of Grandma Frisbee, who is slowly dying from a weak heart. Grandma confesses that she is going on a long trip, alone, and shares with The Lone Ranger a box of personal items that recounts her trip from Council Bluffs. It was more than a decade ago when she was among a wagon train of pioneers who ventured west, sharing a wagon with Linda Reid and her six-month-old son named Daniel. Just a night before reaching Fort Laramie, the wagon train was attacked by a marauding band of Cheyenne Indians. Linda was killed during the onslaught, so Grandma Frisbee took the babe under her wing. At the fort, two days later, she learned a letter awaited Linda informing her that Jim, her husband, was killed during an ambush at Bryant's Gap. In private, The Lone Ranger unmasks to get a closer look at the small photos in a locket that once belonged to Linda, verifying Dan's father was The Lone Ranger's brother. The Lone Ranger recounts the events as they happened at Bryant's Gap and promises the old woman on her death bed that he will raise Dan as if he was his own son. Later that evening, The Lone Ranger reveals the truth to Dan… as the dying Mrs. Frisbee remarks, "Ride on Lone Ranger… forever!"

Episode #1550-763 "MURDER'S PAY-OFF"

Broadcast December 28, 1942

Copyright Registration #82,990, script received at Registration Office January 11, 1943.

Written by George Waller.

Plot: Twin Oaks was a peaceful patch of grass in the wooded border country near the town of Middleton and it was there that The Lone Ranger, Tonto and Dan come across the body of a wounded man. The killer confesses that Mark Sanders is innocent, but soon to be hanged for a murder that he and Ace Sheridan committed. The Lone Ranger attempts to talk sense to the sheriff, but the confession was not enough to set Mark free. Forced to take desperate measures, The Lone Ranger frees Mark from a hangman's knot and while Tonto and Dan keep Mark hidden from the law, the masked man sets out to prove his innocence. After taking Ace Sheridan into custody, The Lone Ranger suspects the sheriff was also involved and sets a trap to expose the two. After changing the details of a stage robbery to create a falling out among thieves, Ace and the sheriff incriminate each other moments before the sheriff attempts to eliminate his associate. After all, Ace can take the fall for the murder of the bank guard and who would doubt the word of the sheriff? Before Ace could be killed, however, a number of witnesses overhear the conversation… including a Federal Marshal who was brought to the scene. The Lone Ranger shoots the gun out of the sheriff's hand and Mark, now vindicated, knocks the lawman to the ground to ensure he does not escape.

Episode #1551-764 "MURDER WILL OUT"

Broadcast December 30, 1942

Copyright Registration #82,991, script received at Registration Office January 11, 1943.

Written by George Waller.

Plot: Still in a snow-tipped mountain scape of Montana's high border sky, the town of Miner's Gulch was facing an unseasonal fall season. Young Molly Thatcher went to her neighbor's house, under instructions of her father, who would later be found shot – an apparent suicide in the head. The Lone Ranger, Tonto and Dan, having paid a visit to the house, find the old man dead and the masked man rationalizes how Thatcher could not have shot himself. Realizing it was murder, Dan investigates to find the killer had a wooden leg. But when Molly and the neighbors arrive, they accuse The Lone Ranger of murdering him, forcing the vigilantes to flee the scene. The motive behind the murder was a map revealing a load of gold buried somewhere within the vicinity. Blackfeet's tribe buried gold on the land that Thatcher was unable to sign over to Pegleg, which resulted in a confrontation and a botched murder made to look like a suicide. Pegleg knew of Thatcher's past and insisted a tintype of his wanted poster for "The Montana Kid," to whom Thatcher was known as in years prior, would destroy his reputation. Realizing Molly will be the next targeted, The Lone Ranger, Tonto and Dan cleverly set a trap and replace Pegleg's cartridges to keep Molly from being shot and killed. The sheriff, having witnessed the murder attempt, gets a confession out of the killer.

Elinor Flynn, Radio and Stage Actress, Is Killed

Glens Falls, N. Y., July 5.—[Special.]—Elinor Flynn, 27 years old, a radio and stage actress, was injured fatally yesterday when the automobile in which she was riding ran off a highway near here. Miss Flynn, who was born in Chicago, had been rehersing for a part in a Broadway production. At one time she was a member of the Lone Ranger radio show cast. Donald O. Cunnion, sports editor of the Glens Falls Post-Star, who was driving the car, was injured seriously.

Elinor Flynn.

Appendix A
The Reid Family

FOUND AMONG FRAN STRIKER'S PAPERS were three biographical sketches, composed December 14, 1947, of Reid family members never actually featured on any radio broadcasts. but assumed to be part of Striker's intention to create further continuity on the programs. As two of the men were described as authors/journalists, it can only be assumed that this was a means of establishing the newspaper profession in their genes, since Dan Reid assumed editorship of *The Daily Sentinel*, followed by Britt Reid. Striker had informed Trendle that, "these might be mentioned sometime, as bearers of the name Reid, hinting that they are distinctly related – (or might be) to Britt. I think this could be handled in some way. Possibly by simply stating that under Britt Reid's name there may be found some other people whose name is the same, who did big things in the past." As stated, though, none of these were ever referenced on the radio programs.

THOMAS MAYNE REID – (April 4, 1818 – October 22, 1883) Novelist and writer of juvenile fiction. Born at Ballyroney, County Down, Ireland. Son of a Presbyterian clergyman. Studies directed toward ministry, but in his 20th year, desire to travel took him to America, landing at New Orleans. He explored Platte and Missouri rivers, and lived in forests – hunting, trapping, and trading with the Indians. In 1843, he went to Philadelphia and wrote, becoming friends with Edgar Allan Poe. Wrote poems, short stories, novels, plays. Became 2nd Lieutenant in Mexican War. Fought at Vera Cruz and several other engagements ending with Battle of Chapultepec. In 1849, went to Ohio and wrote of Mexican experience. Went to England in 1849, returned to America with a wife in 1867. In 1870 went back to England. Has some 90 titles to his credit.

WHITELAW REID – (October 27, 1837 – December 15, 1912) Journalist, diplomat. Born near Xenia, Ohio. Father, Robert Charlton Reid, a farmer in modest circumstances. Other – Marion Whitelaw Ronalds Reid of Scottish decent. Delicate in health, given to reading. Weny to Xenia Academy and Miami University. Began to write for country newspapers in 1856. Edited Xenia News. Supported Lincoln, influential in securing support for him among Ohio delegates. Wrote political dispatches, for Cleveland Herald and Cincinnati Gazette. Became city editor of Gazette. Writings won attention with their energy, vividness, independence. Became war correspondent in Civil War. Few journalists attracted more attention during conflict. In 1868, joined New York Tribune. Became second to Greeley. In 1869, made managing editor. Obtained writing services of Mark Twain, Bret Harte, etc. After Greeley's death, Reid became – at 35 – head of the most powerful newspaper in America. Reid performed valuable service in keeping journalism based on brains and character at time when Dana, Pulitzer, and Hearst were depending on sensationalism. Made special Ambassador to London. Died in London.

SAMUEL CHESTER REID – (August 26, 1783 – January 28, 1861) Sea Captain, designer of the present form of the American Flag. Born at Norwich, Connecticut.

Appendix B
Awards

**Trendle receives the 1940 C.I.T. Safety Foundation award,
handed to him in July 1941.**

January 1937 – C.I.T. Safety Foundation awarded their bronze plaque of Safety
Championship to *The Lone Ranger* for its complete organization of The Lone Ranger Safety Club.

Circa 1937 – WXYZ was honored with a place in the Hall of Champions of Detroit by
winning the 1937 Citation for Showmanship in Program Origination

April 1938 – *Variety* awarded its special plaque for Program Showmanship to *The Lone Ranger*.

1938 and 1939 – *The Exhibitor* awarded Republic Productions their bronze plaque for the "Best Serial of the Year" for both years, for both serials.

June 1939 –*Radio Guide* gave their annual award for the "Best Children's Program" to *The Lone Ranger*.

May 1940 – *Movie & Radio Guide* announced *The Lone Ranger* had again won the award for "Best Children's Show."

July 1941 – C.I.T. Safety Foundation awarded their bronze plaque of Safety Championship again to *The Lone Ranger*. It was voted the "most effective radio promotion of traffic safety for the year 1940."

December 1941 – *Radio Editor's Poll* rated *The Lone ranger* second in the United States.

January 1943 – *Radio Daily* rated *The Lone Ranger* first in the United States.

January 1943 – The National Safety Council announced their Award of Honor to *The Lone Ranger* for "Distinguished Service to Safety."

December 1943 – The Fifth Annual Poll of Radio Editors, known as the *Radio Editors' Poll*, found *The Lone Ranger* first among all children's programs.

January 1948 – The American Broadcasting Company presented *The Lone Ranger* with a scroll for Distinguished Achievement in Radio on the occasion of the 15th Anniversary of the first broadcast.

January 1951 – The Academy of Television Arts and Sciences nominated *The Lone Ranger* for first place in Children's Programs.

February 1951 – *TV Forecast Magazine* awarded their gold statuette to *The Lone Ranger* in their Annual Poll of readers who voted it the "Most Popular Network Western Television Program" for 1950.

April 1951 – *Radio Television Mirror* awarded *The Lone Ranger* as their favorite Western Television Program in their Annual Poll of American television audiences.

1953 – "Mike" Award to *The Lone Ranger* program for consistently outstanding children's programs of wholesome quality and highest inspirational, education and entertainment appeal, presented by the American Legion Auxiliary.

Congressional Record

■ *The Lone Ranger* was honored by A.S. Mike Monroney in the Congressional Record (January 24, 1950) as a result of *The Lone Ranger* broadcast, "The Banner of Virginia."

■ *The Lone Ranger* was honored by Senator Homer Ferguson of Michigan in the Congressional Record (January 29, 1953) on the occasion of the 20th anniversary of the program.

PROCLAMATIONS

■ July 15, 1943. In the city of Tulsa, Oklahoma, Brace Beemer (The Lone Ranger) was officially inducted into the Pawnee tribe and given the name of "Nesaro Kitti-Puh-Ki," translated as "Chief of All Young People."

■ June 13, 1948. The mayor of Cheyenne, Wyoming, changed the name of the city to the Lone Ranger Frontier Town for one day.

■ June 12, 1953. The Lone Ranger was made an honorary citizen of New Orleans, Louisiana.

■ (date unknown) The Muscular Dystrophy Associations of America, Inc., awarded a Citation of Merit to Brace Beemer in recognition of distinguished service in the search to find a cure and in giving comfort to patients with Muscular Dystrophy.

HOW THE LONE RANGER SAFETY CLUB PROTECTS YOUR CHILD

HOW *MERITA* PROTECTS *FRESHNESS*

First thing you think about when you taste Merita Bread is its astonishing freshness. You almost wonder why it isn't warm, so close to its recent home in the oven it still seems to be. Merita *is* fresh, with a lingering freshness that emphasizes its delicate flavor and tender texture. The goodness of Merita Bread grows on you—as it has grown on other thousands until it is today the fastest-selling bread in the South. Switch to Merita now—share the satisfaction of the many friends of Merita's fragrant freshness. It is your purchases of Merita Bread that make possible the Lone Ranger Safety Club.

TUNE IN
"The Lone Ranger"
WNOX
6:00-6:30 P. M.
Monday, Wednesday
and Friday

Copyright 1940, The Lone Ranger, Inc.

RULE 1

"I solemnly promise not to cross any street except at regular crossings and first to look both ways."

You can be sure the lads shown here who are having such a narrow escape aren't members of Merita's Lone Ranger Safety Club! Lone Ranger Safety Club Scouts cross streets carefully because they obey Rule 1 of the Lone Ranger's Safety Pledge.

There are nine additional rules to protect boys and girls from accidents. Led by America's most beloved hero, the Lone Ranger, hundreds of thousands of boys and girls all over the South are pledged to safety as members of Merita's Lone Ranger Safety Club — the club every boy and girl should join! Is your child a member? If not, ask your grocer for a club card or send in the one below.

Cut out and Mail to THE LONE RANGER
c/o Merita Bakers, Atlanta, Ga.

THE LONE RANGER
c/o Merita Bakers
Atlanta, Ga.

DEAR LONE RANGER:

I want to join your Lone Ranger Safety Club, sponsored by Merita Bread and Cakes. Please send me my FREE Membership Card and the key to your Secret Code. As a member of the Lone Ranger Safety Club, I solemnly promise:

1. Not to cross any street except at regular crossings and first to look both ways.
2. Not to play in the streets.
3. Not to cross the street against signal lights.
4. To obey and cooperate with school Traffic Patrols and to help other children avoid danger.
5. Not to ride on running boards or fenders or to hook rides.
6. Not to hold onto automobiles or street cars when on bicycle, scooter or skates.
7. Not to ride a bicycle on the wrong side of the street, on the sidewalk or in a playground where others are playing and not to make turns without signalling.
8. Not to hitch-hike or ask strangers for rides and to discourage other children from this dangerous practice.
9. To promote safety at all times and encourage others to join this safety movement.
10. To obey my parents or guardians always.

_____
(Name)

_____
(Street Address)

_____
(City)   (State)

_____
(Parent or Guardian sign here)

Appendix C
Manufacturers Licensed
to Produce Lone Ranger Articles

(as of February 13, 1939)

1. American Advertising and Research Corporation, Chicago, Illinois.

    Toy moving picture machine, toy puppet theatre, toy paddle, and toy pistol.

2. The Harmony Company, Chicago, Illinois.

    Musical string instruments, ukuleles.

3. Jacobson Company, New York City, New York.

   Cowboy hats and souvenir label hats.

4. Collegeville Flag and Manufacturing Company, Collegeville, Pennsylvania.

   Cowboy suits and neckerchiefs.

5. Louis Marx and Company, New York City, New York.

   Guns, target games, and mechanical toys.

6. Etched Products Corporation, Long Island City, New York.

   Badges, bracelets, pins, and metal buttons.

7. The New Haven Clock Company, New Haven, Connecticut.

   Watches

8. Pathegrams, Inc., New York City, New York.

   10, 25, 50, and 100-foot 16mm animated movie film of *The Lone Ranger* for home projectors.

9. Kenin, Gordon & Zimmerman, New York City, New York.

   Neckties, mufflers, necktie and handkerchief sets, and bow ties.

10. Gum, Incorporated, Philadelphia, Pennsylvania.

    Bubble gum, chewing gum, and candy.

11. Norwich Knitting Company, Norwich, New York.

    Sweatshirts, polo shirts of all types, knitted cotton underwear, and shorts.

12. H. Jacob & Sons, Brooklyn, New York.

    Shoes, boots, and slippers.

13. Dollcraft Novelty Company, New York City, New York.

    Dolls and doll figures depicting the characters of The Lone Ranger and Tonto.

14. Feinberg-Henry Company, New York City, New York.

    Holster sets (without Ranger guns), belts, wallets, school bags and brief cases, and cowboy gloves.

15. Salz Brothers, New York City, New York.

    Fountain pens, mechanical pencils, and combinations.

16. Whitman Publishing Company, Racine, Wisconsin.

    Books to retail at no more than 50 cents. Stationary tablets of blank or ruled sheets.

17. Graphic Arts Process Corp., Detroit, Michigan.

    Lithographed items to be used in connection with exploitation of Lone Ranger Safety Club. (Must be sold only to *Lone Ranger* radio sponsors.)

18. Art Textile Corporation, Highland, Illinois.

    Lone Ranger Health and Safety Masks. (Must be sold only to *Lone Ranger* sponsors.)

19. Chicago Show Printing Company, Chicago, Illinois.

    Dealer kits, including counter cards, window display material, window streamers. (Must be sold only to *Lone Ranger* licensees and sponsors.)

20. Kerk-Guild, Inc., Utica, New York.

    Novelty bars of soap and other soap novelties.

Newspaper advertisement from April 1937.

21. Whitman Publishing Company, Racine, Wisconsin.

   Box coloring sets for paints and/or crayons and jigsaw puzzles.

22. Kramer Bros., New York City, New York.

   Children's hosiery.

23. Process Manufacturing Company, Chicago, Illinois.

   Photographs and pictures, laminated and otherwise, mounted and unmounted.

24. New York Toy & Game Sales Company, New York City, New York.

   Toy fingerprint and secret writing sets.

25. The Superior Type Company, Chicago, Illinois.

   Rubber stamp sets

26. Barclay Knitwear Company, Inc., New York City, New York.

   Sweaters, exclusives of knitted sweatshirts and/or polo shirts.

27. Penn Novelty Embroidery Company, Philadelphia, Pennsylvania.

   Embroidered insignias on fabric, novelty skull caps, sailor hats, winter aviation hats, hockey and baseball caps.

28. American White Cross Lab, Inc., New Rochelle, New York.

   First Aid Kits and Bandages in every price range.

29. Sackman Bros Co., New York City.

   Overalls, coveralls, "Rangeralls," dungarees, slacks, and sun suits.

30. Basson's, New York City, New York.

   Animated displays for store windows, counters, and like locations, but excluding outdoor displays and billboard displays.

31. Chappel & Company, Inc., New York City, New York.

   Exclusive right to use the words "Hi-Yo Silver" in connection with a song published by them.

32. Kilgore Manufacturing Company, Westerville, Ohio.

   Tumblers, shaker tops for tumblers, rings, novelty items made of plastic materials, flashlights. Also, cast-iron plaques and figures and yo-yo tops.

33. American Lead Pencil Company, Hoboken, New Jersey.

   Pencils, pencil boxes, pencil sets, and lead pencils (other than automatic).

34. Maryland Baking Company, Baltimore, Maryland.

   Ice cream cones

35. Parker Bros., Inc., Salem, Massachusetts.

   Board games, dice and spinner for home use only. Also, a card game.

36. Zell Products Corp., New York City, New York.

   Novelty coin banks

Edmonton, Alberta, May 1, 1940

37. International Silver Company, Meriden, Connecticut.

   Silver plated spoons, cups, and knives.

38. Chappel & Company, Inc., New York City, New York.

   Song book titled, "Collection of The Lone Ranger's Favorite Songs"

39. Anchor Hocking Glass Corp., Lancaster, Pennsylvania.

   All types of children's table glassware and glass tumblers.

40. Fiatelle, Inc., New York City, New York.

   Cotton and rayon fabrics with "Lone Ranger" imprint.

41. Trojan Maic, Inc., New York City, New York.

   Children's dresses up to age 14. Playsuits for boys ages 1 to 8.

42. Knickerbocker Toy Company, Inc., New York City, New York.

   Toy stuffed horse depicting Silver.

43. Lakewood Manufacturing Company, Chicago, Illinois.

   Toy known as Silver Arabian Pony (a variation of a hobby horse).

44. Alpha Brush Company, Inc., New York City, New York.

   Combs and toothbrushes and brushes of all types.

45. Howe Baumann Balloon Company, Newark, New Jersey.

   Toy balloons and inflatable rubber toys.

46. Whitney Manufacturing Company, New York City, New York.

   Advertising and sales tags, factory and shipping tags, embossed labels, gummed labels, marking tags, and pin tickets. (Must be sold only to Lone Ranger licensees).

47. I. Jablow & Company, Philadelphia, Pennsylvania.

   Boys' pajamas and robes.

48. The Mengel Company, St. Louis, Missouri.

   Toy rocking horses.

49. Wovencraft, New York City, New York.

   Woven labels and buttons. (Must be sold only to *Lone Ranger* licensees.)

Compliments of Cobakco

Your Friendly Announcer of the Lone Ranger Program

Appendix D
Stations Carrying
The Lone Ranger

(As of October 30, 1940)

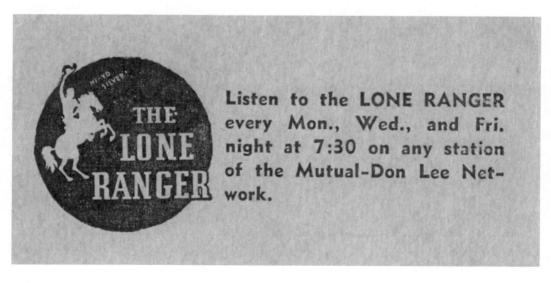

Listen to the LONE RANGER every Mon., Wed., and Fri. night at 7:30 on any station of the Mutual-Don Lee Network.

LIVE TALENT

Don Lee Broadcasting System

KHJ, Los Angeles, California	Western Bakeries	Scholts Agency, Los Angeles
KPMC, Bakersfield, California	Western Bakeries	Scholts Agency, Los Angeles

KXO, El Centro, California	Western Bakeries	Scholts Agency, Los Angeles
KFXM, San Bernardino, California	Western Bakeries	Scholts Agency, Los Angeles
KGB, San Diego, California	Western Bakeries	Scholts Agency, Los Angeles
KVOE, Santa Ana, California	Western Bakeries	Scholts Agency, Los Angeles
KDB, Santa Barbara, California	Western Bakeries	Scholts Agency, Los Angeles
KVEC, San Luis Obispo, California	Western Bakeries	Scholts Agency, Los Angeles
KFRC, San Francisco, California	Kilpatrick Bakeries	Emil Reinhardt, Oakland
KDON, Monterey, California	Kilpatrick Bakeries	Emil Reinhardt, Oakland
KQW, San Jose, California	Kilpatrick Bakeries	Emil Reinhardt, Oakland
KGDM, Stockton, California	Kilpatrick Bakeries	Emil Reinhardt, Oakland
KMO, Tacoma, Washington	Jordan Bakery	
KOL, Seattle, Washington	Buchan Baking Company	

Mutual Broadcasting System

WHKC, Columbus, Ohio	Felber Biscuit Comp.	Harry M. Miller, Inc.

TRANSCRIPTIONS

KFEL, Denver, Colorado	Old Homestead Bread	W.E. Long, Chicago
(beginning March 15, 1938, Tuesday and Thursday)		
KGHF, Pueblo, Colorado	Old Homestead Bread	W.E. Long, Chicago
WAPI, Birmingham, Alabama	American Bakeries	Tucker Wayne & Comp., Atlanta
WJBY, Gadsden, Alabama	American Bakeries	Tucker Wayne & Comp., Atlanta

WRUF, Gainesville, Florida	American Bakeries Tucker	Wayne & Comp., Atlanta
WJAX, Jacksonville, Florida	American Bakeries Tucker	Wayne & Comp., Atlanta
WIOD, Miami, Florida	American Bakeries Tucker	Wayne & Comp., Atlanta
WDBO, Orlando, Florida	American Bakeries Tucker	Wayne & Comp., Atlanta
WGST, Atlanta, Georgia	American Bakeries Tucker	Wayne & Comp., Atlanta
WMAZ, Macon, Georgia	American Bakeries Tucker	Wayne & Comp., Atlanta
WRGA, Rome, Georgia	American Bakeries Tucker	Wayne & Comp., Atlanta
WSMB, New Orleans, Louisiana	American Bakeries Tucker	Wayne & Comp., Atlanta
WBT, Charlotte, North Carolina	American Bakeries Tucker	Wayne & Comp., Atlanta
WBIG, Greensboro, North Carolina	American Bakeries Tucker	Wayne & Comp., Atlanta
WMFR, High Point, North Carolina	American Bakeries Tucker	Wayne & Comp., Atlanta
WAIR, Winston-Salem, N.C.	American Bakeries Tucker	Wayne & Comp., Atlanta
WMFD, Wilmington, N.C.	American Bakeries Tucker	Wayne & Comp., Atlanta
WPTF, Raleigh, North Carolina	American Bakeries Tucker	Wayne & Comp., Atlanta
WAIM, Anderson, South Carolina	American Bakeries Tucker	Wayne & Comp., Atlanta
WFBC, Greenville, South Carolina	American Bakeries Tucker	Wayne & Comp., Atlanta
WLAK, Lakeland, Florida	American Bakeries Tucker	Wayne & Comp., Atlanta
WCSC, Charleston, South Carolina	American Bakeries Tucker	Wayne & Comp., Atlanta
WIS, Columbia, South Carolina	American Bakeries Tucker	Wayne & Comp., Atlanta
WBTM, Danville, Virginia	American Bakeries Tucker	Wayne & Comp., Atlanta
WLVA, Lynchburg, Virginia	American Bakeries Tucker	Wayne & Comp., Atlanta
WDBJ, Roanoke, Virginia	American Bakeries Tucker	Wayne & Comp., Atlanta
KNOX, Knoxville, Tennessee	American Bakeries Tucker	Wayne & Comp., Atlanta
WGAL, Lancaster, Pennsylvania	Wright's Bakery	
WDEL, Wilmington, Delaware	Wright's Bakery	
WORK, York, Pennsylvania	Wright's Bakery	
KYUM, Yuma, Arizona	Western Bakeries	Scholts Agency, Los Angeles
KVOA, Tucson, Arizona	Holsum Bakery	
KTAR, Phoenix, Arizona	Holsum Bakery	
KTSA, San Antonio, Texas	Bohnet's Bakery	Wilhelm-Conroy-Wilson
KXYZ, Houston, Texas	Schott's Bakery	
KARK, Little Rock, Arkansas	Colonial Bakery	
WROK, Rockford, Illinois	Oil Refining Co.	
KGKO, Fort Worth-Dallas, TX	Bestyett Food Co.	Ray K. Glenn, Oklahoma City, OK
WJAC, Johnstown, Pennsylvania	The Harris-Boyer Co.	
KTSM, El Paso, Texas	Surebest Bakeries	
KFDM, Beaumont, Texas	Beaumont Broadcasting Company	
KANS, Wichita, Kansas	KANS Broadcasting Company	

Headquarters

BESTYETT SAFETY CLUB

Sponsored by the LONE RANGER

Jack Hoahi Jr.   Jack Hoahi Jr.

STATION K G K O
FORT WORTH, TEXAS

Dear Safety Club Member:

I am enclosing your membership card in the Bestyett Lone Ranger Safety Club
bearing your name and your membership number.

Your name and this number have been placed on the official rolls here at
headquarters, and you are now a fully qualified member of the Bestyett Lone
Ranger Safety Club, and entitled to all of it's privileges and participation in its activities.

Remember, it's mighty important that you keep this membership card in a
safe place so you will always be reminded of the Lone Ranger Safety Pledge
you will find printed on the back. Be sure to sign your name in the space
provided, and in doing so remember the promise you made to me when you applied
for membership. I know you will do your best to keep these promises and this
pledge <u>all the time</u>, thus making your community a safer, happier place in
which to live.

Now I have lots of surprises planned for every member of the Bestyett Lone
Ranger Safety Club, and I will tell you about them from time to time over
the radio, so be sure and don't miss a single program if you can help it.

In the meanwhile, don't forget to be careful and help others whenever you can.

Until we meet on the radio, then . . . Hi-yo Silver!

Your friend,

The Lone Ranger

The Lone Ranger

P. S. <u>IMPORTANT</u> <u>NOTICE</u>

Of course you will want an official Lone Ranger Safety Badge.
To earn this beautiful badge all you have to do is to have three
of your neighbors who have never used BESTYETT SALAD DRESSING
promise to buy BESTYETT on their next trip to the food store.

I am enclosing a card which I want you to return to me as soon as
it is filled out.

DOUBLY - WHIPPED...DOUBLE-DELICIOUS

SOLD WITH A DOUBLE-YOUR-MONEY-BACK GUARANTEE

Foreign

CKCL, Toronto, Ontario	Brown's Bread, Ltd.
CKOC, Hamilton, Ontario	Brown's Bread, Ltd.
CKCO, Ottawa, Ontario	Standard Bread Company
CFLC, Prescott, Ontario	Standard Bread Company
CFPL, London, Ontario	Parnell Baking Company
CJCS, Stratford, Ontario	T.V.B. Baking Company
CKY, Winnipeg, Manitoba	Bryce's Bakery
CKX, Brandon, Manitoba	Bryce's Bakery
CKSO, Sudbury, Ontario	Sudbury Brewing Company (soft drinks only)
CFCF, Montreal, Quebec	Gurds Ginger Ale
CHLT, Sherbrooke, Quebec	Gurds Ginger Ale
CFAC, Calgary, Alberta	Great Western Garment Co.
CJCA, Edmonton, Alberta	Great Western Garment Co.
CJOC, Lethbridge, Alberta	Great Western Garment Co.
CJAT, Trail, British Columbia	Great Western Garment Co.
CFGP, Grand Prairie, Alberta	Great Western Garment Co.

125,000 letters from boys and girls within listening reception of Sudbury, Canada, responding to a sales tie-in contest over CKSO in Sudbury, Ontario. From September 1 to October 31, 1939, for twelve Lone Ranger programs, announcements for a pony and saddle

CFQC, Saskatoon, Sask.	Great Western Garment Co.
CKCK, Regina, Sask.	Great Western Garment Co.
CJIC, Sault Ste Marie, Ontario	Great Western Garment Co.
CKPR, Fort William, Ontario	Kakabeka Falls Brewing (soft drinks only)
CJKL, Kirkland Lake, Ontario	McDonald & Son (soft drinks only)
CKGB, Timmins, Ontario	McDonald & Son (soft drinks only)
CHNS, Halifax, Nova Scotia	Ben's Bakery
CKY, Winnipeg, Manitoba	Modern Dairies

CFPL, London, Ontario	Marra Baking Company
CFCO, Chatham, Ontario	Marra Baking Company
CJCS, Stratford, Ontario	Marra Baking Company
VOCM, St. Johns, Newfoundland	Crosbie & Co., Ltd.
KGU, Honolulu, Hawaii& Sydney, Australia, New Zealand	Cadbury Fry Hudson, Ltd.

Sustaining

Michigan Radio Network

WXYZ, Detroit, Michigan	WIBM, Jackson, Michigan
WELL, Battle Creek, Michigan	WBCM, Bay City, Michigan
WFDF, Flint, Michigan	WJIM, Lansing, Michigan
WOOD, Grand Rapids, Michigan	

WSPD, Toledo, Ohio (special supplementary use via Michigan Radio Network)

Don Lee Broadcasting System

KXRO, Aberdeen, Washington	KGY, Olympia, Washington
KPQ, Wenatchee, Washington	KVOS, Bellingham, Washington
KIEM, Eureka, California	KSLM, Salem, Oregon
KOOS, Marshfield, Oregon	KRNR, Roseburg, Oregon

Yankee-Colonial Networks

WRDO, Augusta, Maine	WICC, Bridgeport, Connecticut
WLBZ, Bangor, Maine	WBRY, Waterbury, Connecticut
WTHT, Hartford, Connecticut	WEAN, Providence, Rhode Island
WLNH, Laconia, New Hampshire	WTAG, Worchester, Massachusetts
WAAB, Boston, Massachusetts	WNBH, New Bedford, Massachusetts
WCOU, Lewiston, Maine	WLLH, Lowell-Lawrence, Massachusetts
WSAR, Fall River, Massachusetts	WBRK, Pittsfield, Massachusetts

Mutual Broadcasting System

WSYR, Syracuse, New York	WOL, Washington, D.C.
WOR, New York City, New York	WABY, Albany, New York
WBAL, Baltimore, Maryland	WHK, Cleveland, Ohio
WHBC, Canton, Ohio	WKRC, Cincinnati, Ohio
WGR, Buffalo, New York	KADA, Ada, Oklahoma
WVSO, Ardmore, Oklahoma	WBBZ, Ponca City, Oklahoma
KGFF, Shawnee, Oklahoma	KCRC, Enid, Oklahoma
KGGF, Coffeyville, Kansas	

Texas State Network

KGKL, San Angelo, Texas	KFRO, Longview, Texas

WRR, Dallas, Texas

KGKB, Tyler, Texas

KRBC, Abilene, Texas

KNOW, Austin, Texas

KCMC, Texarkan, Texas

KTAT, Fort Worth, Texas

KFJZ, Fort Worth, Texas

KBST, Big Spring, Texas

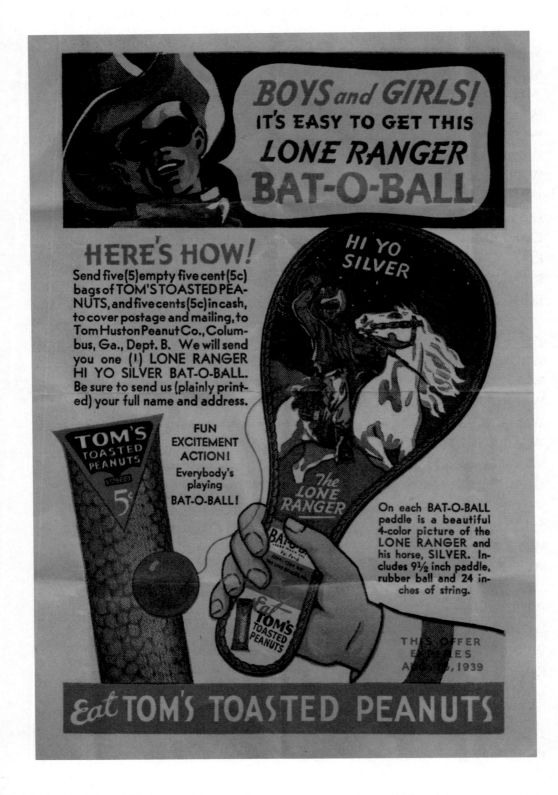

Appendix E
The Lone Ranger Case Study

HOOPER WAS COMMISSIONED BY THE Mutual Broadcasting System to do a study on *The Lone Ranger* Monday, Wednesday, and Friday, August 26, 28 and 30, 1940 in New York City, Philadelphia, and Washington, D.C. Employees of Hooper phoned a total of 5,821 homes during the period of 7:30 to 8:00 p.m., Eastern, asked the following questions:

. 1. Were you listening to the radio just now?

. 2. To what station were you listening?

. 3. What program is coming over that station?

. 4. What advertiser puts on that program?

The following additional questions were asked of all listeners who answered claimed to be listening to *The Lone Ranger* program:

. 1. Will you please tell me how many people in your home are listening to this program?

. 2. How many are adult men?

. 3. How many are adult women?

. 4. How many are children?

. 5. What are the ages of the children?

In New York City, 25.6 percent of the homes had the radio on. The total percentage of radio listeners tuned in to *The Lone Ranger* was 31 percent. Regarding sponsor identification:

55.1% named the sponsor "Bond Bread"

3.8% named the sponsor "safe driving"

2.6% named the sponsor "some insurance company"

2.6% named the sponsor "bread"

0.6% named the sponsor "Wonder Bread"

0.6% named the sponsor "Ward Bread"

0.6% named the sponsor "Silvercup Bread"

Of the people who were listening to *The Lone Ranger*, men made up 30.5 percent, women made up 31 percent and children made up 38.5 percent. The ages of youthful listeners were as follows:

Age	Percentage
0	58.8%
6	935.8%
10	1339%
14	1716.4%

In Philadelphia, 37.1 percent of the homes had the radio on. The total percentage of radio listeners tuned in to *The Lone Ranger* was 24.3 percent. Regarding sponsor identification:

46.6% named the sponsor "supplies"

40.2% named the sponsor "Bond bread"

2.0% named the sponsor "various milk products"

5.6% named the sponsor "bread"

Of the people who were listening to *The Lone Ranger*, men made up 36.2 percent, women made up 38 percent and children made up 25.8 percent. The ages of youthful listeners were as follows:

Age	Percentage
0	58.5%
6	934.2%
10	1336.6%
14	1720.7%

In Washington, D.C., 24.5 percent of the homes had the radio on. The total percentage of radio listeners tuned in to *The Lone Ranger* was 18.7 percent. Regarding sponsor identification:

28.8% named the sponsor "Bond Bread"

1.4% named the sponsor "bread"

1.4% named the sponsor "Wonder Bread"

Of the people who were listening to *The Lone Ranger*, men made up 25.3 percent, women made up 30.5 percent and children made up 44.2 percent. The ages of youthful listeners were as follows:

Age	Percentage
0	513.6%
6	933.9%
10	1340.7%
14	1711.8%

Appendix F
THE 5,000 WATT INAUGERAL Broadcast of February 21, 1941

MUSIC: LONE RANGER THEME

ANNOUNCER: Insert here by Mr. Hicks are the introductory announcements.

<u>SOUND: RARILROAD STATION ATMOSPHERE</u>

NARRATOR: Our first scene takes us to the Consolidated American Railroad Station where Ned Jordan stands with Judy Medwick, daughter of the railroad president.

JUDY: But, Ned, you've never been quite as secretive about anything before.

NED: Judy, honest to goodness... about all I can tell you is that I'm going to Texas.

JUDY: That's all you know?

NED: Practically!

JUDY: Well, how did it come about? Did father send you on this trip?

NED: Nope. It isn't even railroad business.

JUDY: Oh, then... foreign espionage?

NED: Not that either.

JUDY: Oh, you're exasperating! Don't you know anything about the trip?

NED: Only that I'm to look up an old man named Jim Grant. I've a couple of people's names here. I hope they'll be able to tell me where to find him.

JUDY: Jim Grant, and then what?

NED: Look, Judy, I'll tell you all I know about it. Have you ever heard of Britt Reid?

JUDY: Oh, of course! He runs the Daily Sentinal, that big eastern newspaper.

NED: That's right, and he has a lot of influence in getting to people, Britt Reid with all of his power of the press can reach a tremendous number of people.

JUDY: What has Britt Reid to do with this mysterious trip?

NED: Britt Reid is going to Texas, too.

JUDY: Oh.

NED: I had a phone call from a man in Washington. He asked me to go.

JUDY: But why?

NED: He said Britt Reid would meet me on the train.

JUDY: But Ned…

NED: All I know is that I'm to try and locate Jim Grant so Britt Reid can talk to him!

JUDY: I'd like to know Mr. Reid. I've heard so much.

NED: Well, you won't! This is one trip, my dear, that you are not taking.

VOICE: (BACK, ON SPEAKER) Train fourteen now leaving on track nine. (FADE BACK TO JUMBLE)

NED: That's my train. Wish me luck, dear.

JUDY: Luck! And Ned… be careful.

NED: Always.

VOICE: (COME IN AGAIN) All aboard!

SOUND: STATION NOISES UP. FADE INTO TRAIN GATHERING SPEED.

MUSIC: MATCH TO RAILROAD GATHERING SPEED, FULL UP, THEN FADE OUT.

SOUND: RAILROAD RUNNING FULL, THEN FADE UNDER LINES.

ANNOUNCER: On the train, Ned Jordan found a well-dressed man in the club car, reading *The Daily Sentinal*. He took an adjacent seat and…

NED: This is a long way from *The Daily Sentinal's* headquarters.

SOUND: RUSTLE OF NEWSPAPER

BRITT: Eh?

NED: I am supposed to meet the publisher of that paper on this train.

BRITT: You are Ned Jordan?

NED: That's right.

BRITT: My name is Reid. Britt Reid. I'm glad to know you, Jordan.

NED: And am I glad to know you. I've heard a lot about you, Reid. I often read your newspaper.

BRITT: Well, that's complimentary. (LAUGHS) Thanks. Have a bite of something?

NED: No, not now thanks. You're going to Texas?

BRITT: Yes.

NED: To talked to a man named Grant?

BRITT: If he can be found. I understand that you have a little information concerning his whereabouts.

NED: A couple of names, that's about all I have. Names of people who might be able to tell us where to find him. I'll tell you frankly, Reid, I'm at a loss to understand this trip. After all, I'm simply head of the Claim's Department of the Consolidated American Railroads. Why in the dickens, should I ---

BRITT: Is that all you are, Jordan?

NED: What do you mean?

BRITT: Exactly what I said. Have you no other affiliations? Are you nothing more than head of the Claims Department of the Railroad?

NED: I have no other official capacity.

BRITT: I see.

NED: And by the way, Reid…

BRITT: Yes?

NED: What about yourself? Have you any connection with the government?

BRITT: None whatsoever.

NED: You're simply the publisher of *The Daily Sentinal*?

BRITT: Publishing a newspaper can hardly be called a simple proposition, Jordan. As a matter of fact you'd be surprised at some of the difficulties I run into.

NED: I wonder if the same man in Washington called both of us?

BRITT: There is no particular secret about his identity. He's one of the representatives from the Southwest.

NED: The same one, I guess.

BRITT: It seems that a message was left with the father of Jim Grant. Now Jim, himself, is an old man. He is still guarding the message.

NED: Yes?

BRITT: Well, at the same time a Southwestern patriot was advised what the message was. Now a successor of the patriot is one of the Congressmen in Washington. He feels that this is the proper time to make the message public. What's why we're to find Jim Grant and get further information from him.

NED: Well, here's hoping we find him.

BRITT: That, Jordan, is your job.

NED: Yes, I know. Have you any idea why I was selected?

BRITT: Probably because of the ability you've shown in tracing claims, finding lost shipments and missing persons.

NED: Um-m-m.

BRITT: Unless you do happen to have another affiliation.

NED: Oh uh… Why were *you* chosen?

BRITT: The Texas Representative who communicated with me is one of my closest friends.

NED: I see.

BRITT: He happens to know things about me that… well… that my own father doesn't know.

NED: What sort of things?

BRITT: Oh… small perhaps, in themselves. On several occasions I have been able to suppress certain items. I have contacts…. er… a means of reaching the public… that he felt made me peculiarly suited for this assignment.

NED: So when I've located Grant, you'll take over, eh?

BRITT: When we find him, we are to use a code word. A sort of a countersign.

NED: You know the word?

BRITT: It's silver.

NED: Silver?

BRITT: Silver. Like a dollar. Like the name of The Lone Ranger's horse.

NED: That's all you know?

BRITT: There are a few further instructions that I've had trouble understanding. Perhaps when we've talked to Grant, I'll know more about what I'm supposed to do.

NED: Well, let's hope we succeed in whatever we're to do.

BRITT: Agreed.

NED: By the way, you mentioned The Lone Ranger.

BRITT: Yes?

NED: That brought to mind another character. One in whom you've been keenly interested.

BRITT: One in whom I have been interested?

NED: Well, at least *The Daily Sentinal* has published a lot about him. You've posted a reward for his capture.

MUSIC: FAINT HORNET THEME

NED: I refer to The Green Hornet.

BRITT: (PAUS) Oh…. The Green Hornet.

NED: You have been interested, haven't you?

BRITT: We have a few men on the staff of *The Daily Sentinal* who spend most of their time thinking about The Green Hornet.

NED: You know, Reid, I have had some curious notions about that character.

BRITT: How's that?

NED: Well, it doesn't seen to me that it is possible for one man to be engaged in as many rackets as The Green Hornet is supposed to be.

BRITT: Oh?

NED: Well, what do you think? The Hornet has been on the scene when at least a dozen rackets of major importance and countless minor rackets were broken up.

BRITT: On the scene?

NED: On or near. At any rate, he's been involved. Now it seems to me that he might not be as bad as the police and federal authorities seem to think.

BRITT: I'm advised that if The Green Hornet is ever captured, there is evidence to tie him into almost every crime in the book.

NED: Oh, sure, there might be evidence to do that, but is it the truth?

BRITT: Well, Jordan, as you know my paper has offered a reward for the capture of The Green Hornet.

NED: Yes.

BRITT: Frankly, I'm sometimes a little pleased that the reward hasn't been paid over.

NED: Exactly!

BRITT: The Green Hornet furnishes us with such splendid news stories.

NED: Umhum.

BRITT: Recently he has become more active than ever. I want to tell you, Jordan, The Green Hornet, as you say, may not be the real leader of the racketeers, but he certainly leads the police to plenty of them.

NED: Now that brings up another thing I've observed about him.

BRITT: (SOFT LAUGH) You have been following his work.

NED: In a great many cases, the people, the police capture through The Green Hornet, are people who thought they were just bending the law, not breaking it.

BRITT: There is no doubt about that.

NED: I have wondered, sometimes, if this Hornet wasn't strictly on the level. If perhaps he doesn't hate crime and criminals, and uses his role to trap them where the forces of the law are helpless.

BRITT: Do you know, Jordan, that same idea has occurred to me.

NED: Sometimes I think The Green Hornet is a lot like... well, like The Lone Ranger we mentioned a few moments ago. Now don't laugh at that notion!

BRITT: (PAUSE) No, Jordan. I won't laugh at that notion.

MUSIC: HORNET THEME FADES OUT.

SOUND: RAILROAD UP, THEN DOWN

BRITT: (THOUGHTFULLY) It's odd... mighty odd...

NED: Eh? What's odd, Reid?

BRITT: Your comparison between The Green Hornet and The Lone Ranger. Perhaps I ---

NED: The Hornet and The Lone Ranger wore masks. In an earlier day, The Lone Ranger had a horse called Silver. Today The Hornet has that mysterious black car.

BRITT: Jordan, I – I might not have mentioned it, but our trip to Texas... has something to do with... with The Lone Ranger.

SOUND: RAILROAD WHISTLE, RAILROAD UP FULL

MUSIC: INTERLUDE

SOUND: SMALL TOWN STATION BACKGROUND

ANNOUNCER: In due time Britt Reid and Ned Jordan arrived at their destination and left the train at a station in a small town in Texas.

SOUND: BACKGROUND OF RAILROAD STARTING, VOICES OF PEOPLE AD-LIB-BING, ETC.

BRITT: The two singled out one of the bystanders and asked about Jim Grant.

LIGE: Grant? Um-m… Jim Grant yuh say?

BRITT: Yes! Do you know where he is?

LIGE: Reckon I know where he is, stranger, same place he's been fer as long as anyone c'n remember.

BRITT: Well, how do we get there?

LIGE: Doggoned if I know. It's a hard trip. A mighty hard trip. You'll have tuh use hosses an' good ones at that. But say, what fer d'you want tuh see old Grant?

BRITT: It's rather personal.

NED: If you'll tell us how to get there, we'll see about getting horses.

LIGE: Wal, yuh start north from town here. It'll take a full day of good ridin', an' you'll have tuh go uphill fer the most part. You'll come tuh the Boothill River, which is plenty fast… (SUS-TAINED TALKING) Then you'll foller upstream to the falls. You'll be doggoned lucky if yuh ain't caught in a bad storm because it's brewin' up an' will hit about tomorrer… be thunder an' lightnin'… At the falls, cut due east an' head fer the cliff you'll be in sight of, an' there you'll find a cave.

MUSIC: TRANSITION

SOUND: CRACK OF THUNDER, RAIN, SLOW HOOFS OF TWO HORSES.

BRITT: When that old man said we'd hit rain, he knew what he was talking about.

NED: Yeah.

BRITT: Doesn't that look like a cave over there?

NED: Say, it does at that. Old Grant's cave!

SOUND: THUNDER

BRITT: Well, so far so good. Now if only Old Grant is there…

NED: The word… Silver… I wonder!

SOUND: DISTANT SHOT

BRITT: Hey! That was a shot!

NED: Yeah! From the cave! Look! There's the old man! He has a rifle!

SOUND: SHOT

GRANT: (BACK) Git back from here, yer on private land.

NED: Should we get back?

BRITT: After this trip> not on your life! Put down that rifle!

GRANT: (BACK) Clear out! I don't want strangers here!

NED: Hold your fire and listen to me! We've brought a special message to you.

GRANT: (BACK) What d'you mean by special message?

BRITT: A one word message!

GRANT: (BACK) Let's hear it!

BRITT: Silver!

SOUND: CRACK OF THUNDER, SUSTAIN RUMBLING

GRANT: (SOFT AND CLOSE AGAINST THUNDER) Silver! They've come at last. Oh, thank yhe good Lord for sendin' 'em here while I'm still on earth. I kept the trust. I kept the trust, all these years. (SHOUT) Hey there!

BRITT: (BACK) Yes?

GRANT: Say that word again!

BRITT: Silver!

SOUND: HORSE WHINNY, HOOFS CLATTER

GRANT: All right! All right! Come on, friends! Come on inside this cave out of the rain! I've been waitin' for a long, long time!

MUSIC: MINOR THEME

ANNOUNCER: Let us pause at this point. Before we learn the secret of Grant's cave; the strange mission that brought Ned Jordan and Britt Reid together in a remote part of the Texas hills; Mr. (_____) has a word for you. An important announcement.

COMMERCIAL PLUG

SOUND: THUNDER AND RAIN

ANNOUNCER: Inside the cave, the rain and thunder could barely be heard. It was a place that was large enough to hold many horses. A forge, long idle, stood at one side of the entrance. Jim Grant, white-haired and bright-eyed, welcomed his visitors.

GRANT: I supposed folks around town think I'm loco.

BRITT: We heard nothing of that sort, Mr. Grant.

GRANT: Well, maybe I am a little loco on one subject. I been here since Pa died. That was a long time ago. I been waitin' fer this day.

BRITT: This day?

GRANT: The day when someone would come with the password. You gave it to me.

BRITT: Silver?

GRANT: That's it. Oh, I ain't been a hermit exactly. I been in tuh the town when I need supplies yuh see, but I spent most of my time here.

NED: Look, Mr. Grant, we've come a good many miles to see you.

GRANT: I 'spect so.

NED: What for?

GRANT: Well... I'll tell yuh the hull story. First come back here... Come on, back tuh the recess in the cave. One of yuh fetch that lantern, I'll show yuh somethin'!

BRITT: I've got the light.

SOUND: Steps on shale.

GRANT: Right here.

SOUND: HOOFS PAWING

NED: Great Scott! Look at the size of that horse.

BRITT: (LOW WHISTLE) A beauty!

GRANT: Snow white! Take a look at those muscles! The set of the head.

SOUND: SLAP NECK

GRANT: Look at a horse that any man would give his eye teeth tuh own!

BRITT: Hello there boy!

SOUND: Soft whinny.

GRANT: That horse is descended from an even finer horse! The original horse was named Silver.

BRITT: Silver!

NED: You don't mean...

GRANT: I mean Silver! The horse that was ridden by The Lone Ranger!

BRITT: Great Scott! Jordan, we're seeing something not many people have had the chance to see.

NED: Don't I know it?

GRANT: I was just a kid. The Lone Ranger used tuh come here to my Pa. This is where the silver shoes for The Lone Ranger's horse were made.

BRITT: Here?

GRANT: Yes, sir! Right over yonder in that old forge! Every so often The Lone Ranger would come ridin' in from somewhere's on the plains, an' need new shoes for his hoss, or bullets for his guns.

BRITT: Where did the silver come from?

GRANT: Wal… it ain't generally known, friend, but The Lone Ranger had a silver mine that he took what he needed from.

NED: I never knew that.

GRANT: Oh, he could o' been a right rich man, if he'd wanted tuh be, but he figgered that there was things a lot more important than money.

NED: So this is where The Lone Ranger – and you say his own horse, Silver, was the ancestor of this one?

GRANT: Yep!

BRITT: Now about our coming here… what has this trip to do with The Lone Ranger?

GRANT: I'm getting' tuh that. The Lone Ranger felt that my Pa was a man that could be trusted, an' he must've felt the same about me, even though I was nothin' but a little shaver at the time. I guess I warn't more'n seven years old when he come in fer the last time.

BRITT: What did he do then?

GRANT: Dunno.

BRITT: Did you never hear from him again?

GRANT: Never. Never a word.

BRITT: You don't know where he died? Or how?

GRANT: Mister, I don't even know if he died.

BRITT: But he must ---

GRANT: There was somethin' about The Lone Ranger. I allus thought that maybe he was still alive somewhere's an' that when the time came an' he felt that he was needed… aw-w-w shucks, I'm just an ole fool that's talkin' through his hat.

BRITT: No, go on Grant.

GRANT: Humph – sounds silly.

NED: Please go on.

GRANT: Well… I – I had a notion, 'way back in my head, that maybe the time'd come when The Lone Ranger would ride again!

BRITT: (PAUSE) I wonder.

SOUND: INCREASE THUNDER A BIT, THEN DOWN.

GRANT: I'm glad yuh didn't laugh at me when I said that.

BRITT: Laugh? No, Grant, sincerity such as yours isn't to be laughed at.

GRANT: I'm glad tuh hear yuh say that. Mighty glad, it shows that you're the right man.

BRITT: What is to be done?

GRANT: Wal… I gotta git back tuh what I was tellin' you again. I was a youngster around seven or so the last time The Lone Ranger came here. Pa was over there, workin' at the forge, makin' extry silver shoes tuh have agin the time The Lone Ranger would need 'em. I was pumpin' the bellows fer him.

SOUND: FADE OUT RAIN AND THUNDER

SOUND: FADE IN BELLOWS AND HAMMER ON ANVIL

GRANT: He was workin' away… Pa hammerin' on the hot silver, me workin' the draft tuh kep the coals hot… it was after dark, but we was still a workin'. Outside we could hear the nightbirds from time tuh time an' the katydids an' once in a while the howl of a critter…

SOUND: KATYDIDS, BIRDS, HOWLS, ETC.

GRANT: Then Pa stopped.

SOUND: STOP HAMMERING. SUSTAIN BELLOWS.

BOY: Matter Pa? Did yuh hear somethin'?

PA: Wait, son. Stop the bellows.

SOUND: STOP BELLOWS

MUSIC: VERY FAINT STRAIN, (ONE TRUMPET) RANGER THEME. THEN STOP AFTER A FEW BARS.

BOY: What is it?

PA: Thought I heard somethin'.

BOY: I didn't hear it.

PA: Might o' been nothin' but an animal o' some sort. Listen a second.

RANGER: Come on, Silver!

MUSIC: REPEAT A TRIFLE NEARER

PA: There, did yuh hear that?

BOY: Heard somethin'. Couldn't tell what it was, though.

PA: Sounds like --- (PAUSE)

MUSIC: FULL BAND START THEME, VERY FAINT AND DISTANT.

RANGER: Hurry, old boy!

BOY: I hear it Pa!

PA: He's Comin'! I know the signs!

MUSIC: LOUDER

BOY: Yuh sure? Oh, gee, Pa! He ain't been here in a long time!

PA: He is! I know he is!

RANGER: (DISTANT) Come on, Silver!

SOUND: FAINT HOOFS, WITH MUSIC.

PA: He's comin' up the hill! That's him lad, that's him! The Lone Ranger!

MUSIC: FADE MUSIC AND HOOFS IN TOGETHER

RANGER: (NEARER) Come on, Silver!

SOUND: BRING HOOFS AND MUSIC IN GRADUALLY TO FULL VOLUME.

SOUND: HOOFS COME RIGHT IN CLOSE THEN CLATTER BROKENLY TO HALT.

SOUND: CUT MUSIC WITH HOOFS HALTED

MUSIC: IMMEDIATELY PIC UP THE LONE RANGER THEME ON SOFT STRINGS OR WOODWINDS AND SUSTAIN IN BACKGROUND OF THE SCENE.

RANGER: Hello there, Grant! It's good to see you again!

PA: Lone Ranger, it's good tuh see you!

RANGER: (DISMOUNTING) And the boy! You're getting big and strong, son,

BOY: I want to be as big an' strong as you... er... as Pa!

RANGER: (SOFT LAUGH) That's the right idea.

PA: Tonto with yuh?

RANGER: He's outside opening the saddle bag. I've brought something here Grant.

PA: Yere?

RANGER: Something for safe keeping.

PA: What about Silver? Need shoddin'?

RANGER: No, Grant. I don't think you'll need to do that this trip.

PA: No?

RANGER: As a matter of fact, I…

BOY: Here comes Tonto!

TONTO: (APPROACHNG) Me fetch um box!

RANGER: Here. Let me have it, Tonto. I'll just put it here for the time being.

TONTO: Ugh.

SOUND: SET DOWN BOX

BOY: What's in thar?

RANGER: Here, Grant, take a look. I'll open the box.

SOUND: OPENING

BOY: Golly! What're them?

RANGER: These are silver dollars. They are to be given away.

SOUND: DOLLARS JINGLING

PA: Given away?

RANGER: Not right now. Perhaps not for many years. I want this chest held here.

PA: Yere?

SOUND: CLOSE LID

RANGER: I'll lock the box, and leave they key with you. Tonto will you bring the letter from the other saddlebag.

TONTO: Ugh. (FADING) Tonto gettum.

SOUND: LOCKING BOX

RANGER: There! Here's the key, Grant. Take care of it. Hold it until the right man comes to claim it.

PA: But how'll I know the right man? Who owns that cash?

RANGER: It is my own money. I'm leaving it here… for the right man to distribute.

PA: How'll I know... I...

TONTO: Here letter.

RANGER: Very well, Kemo Sabay! Keep this letter, Grant. Keep it with the chest. It has instructions for the man who comes here. He'll give you the word --- "Silver!"

PA: That ain't much to go by. I...

RANGER: I'll tell you this, Grant. I'm going to leave it to the judgment of your Governor. He will decide when it is best for my message to the children of America to be made public.

PA: The Governor, eh?

RANGER: Yes. He's in a better position than I am to do this. Remember the word "Silver."

PA: "Silver."

RANGER: Come, Tonto, that's all for this time.

PA: When will you be back?

RANGER: (FADING) That, Grant, is hard to say. We'll meet again though. Goodbye!

PA: Goodbye, Lone Ranger.

RANGER: (BACK) Goodbye!

SOUND: CLATTER OF HOOFS BACK

RANGER: (OUTSIDE) Hi-Yo, Silver... Away!

SOUND: HOOFS START TO FADE

MUSIC: START STRONG FADE OUT WITH HOOFS

SOUND: FADE IN THE RAIN AND THUNDER, THEN SUBDUE BENEATH THE VOICES.

GRANT: (FADING IN) Well, the Governor went to a higher office in Washington. Then Pa died. I grew up and still nobody came for the letter or the chest. That was many a year ago. I thought about it plenty times and wondered if the letter'd ever be called for.

BRITT: It seems that the message of The Lone Ranger was passed from the Governor to men whom he could trust.

GRANT: Seems so. Well, I'll get the keys and open up the box and show you.

SOUND: STEPS

BRITT: Is this it?

GRANT: There's the box. (BLOW DUST) Mighty dusty. It's been here a good many years.

SOUND: UNLOCKING CHEST

GRANT: My hands are tremblin' so that I can't hardly hold the key.

BRITT: Let me try it.

GRANT: Yere. You – you try it.

SOUND: UNLOCKING CHEST

BRITT: The lock's mighty old. There we are.

GRANT: Got it, Reid?

BRITT: Yes.

SOUND: CREAKING OF HEAVY LID BEING OPENED ON RUSTY HINGES

GRANT: First time it's been opened since I see The Lone Ranger open it when I was a boy. There's the silver dollars just like he left 'em.

BRITT: Sure enough.

SOUND: JINGLE OF COINS

GRANT: Here's the letter he left.

BRITT: The letter – the letter from The Lone Ranger!

NED: Open it up, Britt. Let's see what he says about this cash.

SOUND: TEAR ENVELOPE AND RUSTLE PAPER

BRITT: There's another envelope inside this one.

NED: There's a message there, too.

BRITT: This message is apparently for… well, for me. The Lone Ranger states that the silver dollars are to be used to the best advantage according to the judgment of the one who opens this letter.

NED: I supposed that means charity or something of that sort. Don't you?

BRITT: No. I don't think so. This other envelope is The Lone Ranger's message.

GRANT: Open 'er up, lad. Open 'er up. See what The Lone Ranger's message is.

BRITT: Well, here goes.

SOUND: TEAR ENVELOPE. RAIN AND THUNDER FADED OUT.

MUSIC: FAINT LONE RANGER THEME IN BACKGROUND

GRANT: (SOFT AND CLOSE) It seems like I hear The Lone Ranger ridin' again. (PAUSE) Ridin' out o' the past. Ridin' out o' nowhere like he used tuh do when I was a little boy.

MUSIC: FADED OUT AGAIN

NED: (SOFT) The rain has stopped, Reid. It's clearing up outside the cave.

BRITT: Um. This letter, Jordan… it's strange…

NED: How's that?

BRITT: It is like listening to The Lone Ranger himself.

GRANT: (SOFT) The Lone Ranger… The Lone Ranger is ridin' again.

MUSIC: VERY SOFT STRAIN OF "DAWN" MOVEMENT FROM WILLIAM TELL

RANGER: Boys and girls of America, there are days when you must remember the brave fight that was made by your forefathers. A fight for freedom. A fight against the hardships of the wilderness to settle the little villages that grew to be great cities. Fights against starvation, and bitter cold and fights against wild beasts and savage Indians.

It has been a long, hard fight to make America the country that it is, the greatest country in the world. Now it is out duty to guard and protect America. We are in America as free people. We can speak openly and fearlessly. We are not compelled to do without the luxuries of life. We are free to work at anything we choose. We are allowed to spend our money as we please. It is possible in America as in no other country on earth, for the poorest of us to rise as high as our ambition and ability will take us.

We have all of these privileges because we fought for them and won them. Other countries envy us. Our enemies would like to destroy us. They may try to do this. Not by war. No nation could make a successful war on us, but we must always be on guard against the enemies who try to destroy American by talk.

Be alert, be on guard. Remember that America is your country and that the laws are made by those who are selected by the vote of the people. Remember that the code of America is based upon the things that are best for the greatest number. Keep your faith and your confidence in God and the United States and let nothing you read or hear destroy that faith. Boys and girls, be proud you are Americans.

MUSIC: CRESCENDO "DAWN" TO FINISH, TIMED SO FINISH COMES IN TWO OR THREE SECONDS. THEN GO INTO THE "FINALE" OF WILLIAM TELL. AFTER OPENING BARS OF THIS, FADE OUT.

GRANT: (ON CUE AFTER MUSIC IS FADED) I tell yuh I heard him! He was here! He was right here in this cave!

BRITT: Curious, but I felt that too, while I was reading the message from The Lone Ranger.

NED: Britt, somehow The Lone Ranger, years ago, must have known about the present war.

BRITT: Some day when his message would be needed, he wanted it to be given to the nation. Now I understand! I know what we're to do.

NED: What?

BRITT: Spread The Lone Ranger's message far and wide!

NED: Then let's do it!

BRITT: Just wait till we get back home! We'll go on the radio. We'll tell the world about the message of The Lone Ranger!

MUSIC: BREAK

ANNOUNCER: Ladies and Gentlemen, Boys and Girl, Britt Reid, the well-known publisher, is in the studios of WXYZ to bring a word of vital importance to everyone... Mr. Britt Reid...

BRITT: The Lone Ranger, years ago, did not foresee the present war. He did, however, realize that a time would come when his message would be vital. Right now, we are surrounded by a world at war with great nations fighting for their lives. This is war without glory. Needless, unjustified war, in which a multitude must suffer for the greed of the few. But war will pass, like all things, and in the peace that comes the worried, hungry people of the world will look to us. To you.

The Lone Ranger wanted you to have his message! And WXYZ would like the privilege of sending it to you, as a part of this special broadcast which dedicates our new high power facilities. This message is neatly printed and ready for you. Let me know your name and address, won't you? The message will be send to you free of charge. There is also a chance for you to share in the prizes that are to be given away. Some of you can win the silver dollars of The Lone Ranger. Some of you can also win The Lone Ranger lucky charms. A pocket piece to carry with you at all times. You'll all have an equal chance to win one of these prizes so listen carefully to the announcements that follow.

Appendix G
ANNIVERSARY PROGRAM
THE LONE RANGER
SATURDAY, January 23, 1943
10:15 to 10:45 p.m.

MUSIC: (FANFARE)

ANNOUNCER: Tonight marks the tenth anniversary of the beginning of radio's most famous story, The Lone Ranger. Here in Detroit, Michigan, we are proud to have with is America's best-known, best-loved poet and philosopher, whose typically American ideals and thoughts have brought daily inspiration to millions – the keynoter of our program, Edgar A. Guest. (PAUSE) Mr. Guest.

GUEST: Ten years have gone by since The Lone Ranger's hearty cry, Hi Yo Silver!, first rang out on the air. Ten years in which boys have grown to manhood. Ten years that have brought undreamed-of changes to the world. The year was 1933, the month was January...

MUSIC: "THERE SOMETHING ABOUT A SOLDIER"

GUEST: Yes, orchestras were playing "There's Something About a Soldier." And also...

MUSIC: "WHO'S AFRAID OF THE BIG BAD WOLF"

GUEST: And also "Who's Afraid of the Big Bad Wolf." Hmm, looking back, there's something ironical about those two song titles. For of all the people who were whistling the tunes in 1933, few had even heard of Adolf Schicklegruber Hitler. The world was reading the best-sellers, "One Hundred Million Guinea Pigs" and "Life Begins at Forty." President Hoover was in the White House. President Roosevelt had been elected but was not to take office of several weeks (he's still there). Ex-President Calvin Coolidge had recently passed away. The country hadn't yet heard of the N.R.A. The Prohibition Amendment had not yet been repealed. In a Detroit, Michigan, radio station, WXYZ, one of the announcers entered an office with a typewritten page in his hand...

SOUND: DOOR OPENS – CLOSES

RED: Say… they just handed me an announcement to go over. We're to run it at least twice this afternoon.

CHUCK: Okay. Let me look over the schedule and see where we can put it. What is the announcement about?

RED: It's a plug for a new show. That western program the dramatic group's been working on.

CHUCK: Oh! What did they finally decide to name it?

RED: The Lone Ranger.

CHUCK: That sounds good. The Lone Ranger, eh?

RED: Want to hear the announcement?

CHUCK: Yeah. Go over it.

RED: (READONG) Tonight at seven-thirty a brand-new program makes it bow on WXYZ. This is the first of a series of adventure stories dealing with the thrilling tales of the West of yesteryear. For action-packed drama, tune in tonight at seven-thirty and follow the adventures of The Lone Ranger.

MUSIC: STANDARD LONE RANGER OPENING – MUSIC UNDER (RECORDING)

GUEST: On that evening in January, 1933, The Lone Ranger was born.

MUSIC: UP AND FADE

MAN 1: Who is The Lone Ranger?

MAN 2: What is the purpose of The Lone Ranger?

ANNOUNCER: This program was dedicated to the Youth of America. Its purpose was to recreate the thrilling episodes of amazing courage, the pioneer spirit that carried American ideals of civilization beyond the Mississippi and on to the West – so that we of today might know what was endured to give us our heritage.

MAN 1: But who is The Lone Ranger?

ANNOUCNER: The Lone Ranger is Justice. Fair Play. Square dealing and straight shooting. He is the rule of "That which is best for the greatest number." He is a voice that rings with dauntless manhood – American manhood that has sought for the trail that is right and then followed that trail. Manhood that is proud of its position, yet humble in the sight of God. The Lone Ranger is the embodiment of clean living. He is the composite of Dave Crockett, Daniel Boone, Kit Carson, Wild Bill Hickok, Buffalo Bill, and all those other pioneers whose names bring a tingle to men's spines and make their hearts beat just a little faster. He is the voice that brings the fundamentals of Americanism out of the past to the boys and girls of today.

ANNOUNCER 2: Typical of the brilliant young leaders of our nation is America's youngest governor, Harols E. Stassen, of Minnesota. It has therefore seemed fitting that he be chosen to speak to this youthful nation tonight, in commemoration of the tenth anniversary of The Lone Ranger radio program. We are honored by a word from him. (PAUSE) Governor Stassen ---

TRANSCRIPTION FO STASSEN SPEECH

ANNOUNCER: Thank you, Governor Stassen. In a moment, we will hear more about the young Americans who are overseas in our armed forces. But now we will hear a musical tribute to The Lone Ranger in the mood of the West.

MUSIC: "CARRY ME BACK TO THE LONE PRAIRIE"

ANNOUNCER: Governor Stassen, in his talk a few moments ago, spoke of our soldiers. We are especially proud of the many who have gone into battle with the defiant, challenging cry of The Lone Ranger on their lips.

MUSIC: START "MARINE HYMN" – FADE ON CUE

ANNOUNCER: The Marines!

MUSIC: SUSTAIN "MARINE HYMN" IN BACKGROUND

MAN: I'm back home for a little while, but I'm going back. I was in the Philippines when it began –

SOUND: BOMB. ZOOM PLANE. BOMB

MAN: Those Jap Zero's came over fast and sudden. They got most of our planes on the ground, but that's old news now. I guess everyone knows how we were outnumbered. Soon we had only six P-40s left. Then we lost four of 'em. We were down to two. Two planes against everything the Japs could throw at us.

MAN 2: Better take our two planes and scramble. They're coming in again.

MAN: How many of 'em?

MAN 2: I don't know – but plenty.

MAN: Here's your plane.

MAN 2: Yeah, The Lone Ranger is set to go.

MAN: The what?

MAN 2: I call this baby The Lone Ranger.

SOUND: JAZZ MOTOR

MAN 2: Hi-Yo, Silver, Away-y-y-y!

SOUND: MOTOR ROARS, MACHINE GUNS, BOMBS, etc.

MUSIC: "MARINE HYMN" up, strain of "WILLIAM TELL" in the "MARINE HYMN," then full up to finish.

SOUND: WAVES UP AND DOWN

MUSIC: "ANCHORS AWEIGH" – FADE DOWN

MAN 3: I was on a convoy to Murmansk taking guns and planes and food and ammunition to the Russians. It was the stuff that's winning the war. The sugar and gasoline and butter and steel and rubber we're doing without. The stuff that's winning the war, made in America. Well, those sons of Shicklegruber had us spotted. They came over in a cloud.

SOUND: (SOUND… BOMBS)

MAN 3: The bombs fell as thick as hailstones. Before black oily smoke got too thick, I saw a couple of our ships hit. Then we had plenty of trouble of our own. Three dive bombers concentrated on us.

SOUND: DIVE BOMBERS, BOMBS and ACK ACK

MAN 3: We let 'em have it with our ack-ack. I don't know about the rest, but I was pretty sure we were done for. Then I saw a lifeboat in the water below our rail. It was capsized, riding along on the waves. There was a fellow from one of the other boats straddling it. He saw me looking at him. The waves were bouncing him up and down like he was riding a bronco. He waved to us, and yelled out…

MAN 4: (BACK) Hi-Yo, Silver!

MAN 3: (PAUSE) You can't lick guys with spirit like that. The Nazi planes got beaten off. Russia got that stuff to win the war.

MUSIC: UP FULL AND FINISH. CHANGE TO ARMY AIR CORPS, FADE DOWN

ANNOUNCER: A pilot in California…

PILOT: There were four of us at the start, in high school they called us The Four Horsemen. We all went over and joined up with the Eagle Squadron. We called our planes The Four Horsemen and had four white horses painted on each of 'em. Well, by the time the United States got into the scrap, three of us were gone. I came home to join Uncle Sam's air force. I want to get back there and take a crack at those rats that got my partners. (PAUSE) This? Oh, I'm just painting one horse on this plane. I – I'm calling it, The Lone Ranger.

MUSIC: ARMY AIR CORP, UP TO FINISH

MUSIC: FIELD ARTILLERY, FADE DOWN

VOICE: We were in Southern Tunisia, but hadn't yet met the enemy. We were waiting for the word to go.

MAN: (SOFT) How much longer?

VOICE: I dunno – we'll get the word strong enough. I wonder how many of us there are in this raiding party?

MAN: Enough! Remember, we're Yankees. You scared?

VOICE: Scared to death. How about you, Jim?

JIM: I wish I was out of this.

MAN: The top kick says to yell your head off when you wade in. It helps.

JIM: This'll really be the first time the Yanks have met the enemy over here. We gotta make it good. The folks back home will want some good news.

SOUND: WHISTLE

VOICE: Hey, the signal! Wait for the grenade, then go – and what I mean, GO! Take, em!

MAN: Remember, yell! Yell your head off!

SOUND: BOMB

JIM: That's it!

MAN: (YELLS) Hi-Yo, Silver! Yell!

SOUND: BOMBS AND FIRING

ALL: (AD LIB YELLS) Hi-Yo, Silver, Away-y-y-y!

MUSIC: BURST

ANNOUNCER: From Tunisia to Murmansk, from England to the Phillippines. The cry of The Lone Ranger has spread throughout the world. If, in some small measure, this cry gives a lift of courage to the heart of just one of our fighting men, we are proud to have helped. It is our hope and prayer that the young listeners of today will carry the fine fundamentals of Americanism to their jobs of the future, when they are given the task of maintaining a good peace throughout the world.

MUSIC: ORCHESTRA

ANNOUNCER: And now, Larry Paige and his orchestra, playing a short medley…

MUSIC: "OH, SUSANNA" AND "WHOOPITEE-I-O!"

ANNOUNCER: Edgar Guest now returns with words of his own.

GUEST: (_____*his own words*_____)

MUSIC: INTERLUDE

ANNOUNCER: And now we present, in person, The Lone Ranger and Tonto. The story tonight is a little fantasy in which we try to think of The Lone Ranger riding out of the past and into a boy's dreamland today.

MUSIC: PASTORAL

ANNOUNCER: A tall, stalwart Indian stands outside the window of a white frame house. He looks in at the bedroom of a little boy. There are tin soldiers on a shelf, a toy gun, and a teddy bear. On the dresser he sees a photograph of a soldier. Then he hears the boy sobbing into his pillow.

BOY: (FADE IN SOBBING)

MUSIC: FADE IN "MY BUDDY"

ANNOUNCER: The door opens, and…

SOUND: DOOR OPENS

MOTHER: Jimmy dear, why aren't you asleep?

BOY: (SOB) Mother...

MOTHER: What is the matter, dear?

BOY: I – I want my daddy...

MOTHER: There, now... let mother turn your pillow.

BOY: Daddy...

MOTHER: Daddy will be back as soon as he can, Jimmy. He told us that in his last letter.

BOY: why does Daddy have to fight?

MOTHER: I don't know, Jimmy. (SIGHS)

BOY: Why are there wars? Wh – why did Daddy have to go away from us?

MOTHER: (CATCH) Please, dear, you must go to sleep. Maybe tomorrow there will be a letter from Daddy – here, now, put this picture under your pillow and let Mommy tuck you in. (PAUSE) There. There now... sleep, Jimmy. Daddy will be home, some day.

BOY: (SOBS) I – I want my Daddy. (PAUSE FOR COUNT OF THREE) If – if The Lone Ranger was here, (SNIFFLE), I bet he'd bring him back.

TONTO: (OUTSIDE) Gittum up, Scout!

SOUND: HOOFS START AND SUSTAIN

MUSIC: WITH HOOFS, GALLOP

ANNOUNCER: An Indian astride a string paint horse, rode through the night. Through the years, through the generations.

MUSIC: AND SOUND UP, FINISH

SOUND: HOOFS STOPPING

TONTO: Whoa, Scout! Whoa, feller!

RANGER: Tonto!

TONTO: Me come fast.

RANGER: I can see that you've been riding hard.

TONTO: There new kind of trouble. Feller want you. You come!

RANGER: But Tonto, we weren't going to leave this camp.

TONTO: Where Silver?

RANGER: Silver is grazing over there.

TONTO: You call-um. Little feller need-um you.

RANGER: You're sure?

TONTO: Ugh! Me plenty sure!

RANGER: All right, then. (CALLS) Here, Silver!

SOUND: WHINNY, HOOFS APPROACH, CLATTER

RANGER: Steady there, Silver! Steady, now!

TONTO: Silver anxious to travel.

RANGER: All right, Silver old boy. We're going to ride again. Hi-Yo, Silver! Away!

SOUND: HOOFS

MUSIC: THEME – FINISH

BOY: (SOFTLY) Daddy, oh Daddy, when will you come back? You were going to show me how to make my soldiers drill. Y-you said we'd learn to swim this year. I – I haven't even shown you my school report. Daddy, when'll you be back? I – I want you.

MUSIC: THEME DIES DOWN

RANGER: Whoa, Silver!

SOUND: HOOFS STOPPING

RANGER: (SOFTLY) Jimmy… (PAUSE) Jimmy…

BOY: Wha – who –

RANGER: Your daddy is coming back to you, son.

BOY: Y-you're masked! Y-you're The Lone Ranger!

RANGER: That's what they call me.

BOY: Then you tell me, why did my Daddy have to go to war?

RANGER: Lie back there, Jimmy, and I'll tell you. Years and years ago, America was just a little nation of thirteen states, but the people of those states were men like your Daddy. Men who loved freedom and were willing to fight to keep their freedom. They were men who didn't believe in oppression. They fought and made America greater and greater. They fought for their freedom and then they fought to hold it. Time after time they had to fight. But, finally, men like your Daddy came along and got tired of seeing their sons go away to war. They decided that they're put an end to that sort of thing, and they'll do it. Your Daddy is fighting the last fight for America. After this fight is over, he will come home and say, "Son, we finished the job. You'll never have to go!"

BOY: Y-you're sure… he'll come back to Mommy and me?

RANGER: I'm sure of this much, Jimmy. One hundred and thirty million people are spending billions and billions of dollars to give your Daddy and those with him, the very best of everything. You'll go without butter and sugar, and maybe a lot of other things, but we're all going to make sure your Daddy has those things. Everyone in this country is working night and day to bring your Daddy back. And we're going to bring him back, just as soon as we can! That you may be sure of, son! Now – sleep!

SOUND: HOOFS TROT IN

RANGER: Steady, Silver. (MOUNTS) Come on, Silver!

SOUND: HOOFS UP – FADE

MUSIC

BOY: Daddy, wait, you look like him! He looks like you! My Daddy looks just like you, Mommy. Mommy, Daddy is here! Daddy is here!

SOUND: DOOR OPENS

MOTHER: Jimmy, Jimmy, what's the matter, dear?

BOY: He was here! And he looked like Daddy!

MOTHER: You've been dreaming, Jimmy. Now, let me tuck you in again.

BOY: But he was here! I saw him! And he told me not to be afraid! He said that Daddy would be back, and he'd say, "We finished the job."

MOTHER: Who, dear?

BOY: The Lone Ranger!

RANGER: (FAR BACK) Hi-Yo, Silver! Away!

MUSIC: THEME

ANNOUNCER: The next feature comes as a surprise to nearly everyone, including the members of The Lone Ranger cast. We take you to Chicago, for an important announcement by Paul Jones, director of Public Information for the National Safety Council. Mr. Jones, speaking from Chicago –

SIX SECOND BREAK

JONES: Thank you, Detroit. Every parent knows what The Lone Ranger means to Young America. In fact, I think I speak for a lot of parents when I admit that we envy The Lone Ranger and only wish our boys would listen to us with the same rapt attention they give him. I am sure it is a source of great satisfaction to parents everywhere that The Lone Ranger and the originators of his program recognize the opportunity he has for constructive leadership among the youth of America – and that he is using this opportunity to instill in our boys and girls a wholesome desire to become better citizens. An outstanding example of this is the Victory Lone Ranger Safety Club, which has enlisted four million boys and girls in a crusade against accidents. The fact that so many active American young people are following The Lone Ranger in this safety crusade and thus preventing untold tragedy and suffering, prompts the National Safety Council to bestow on The Lone Ranger program at this time, a special award for distinguished service to safety. It is our sincere hope that he will never stop this war against accidents.

SIX SECOND BREAK

GUEST: Thank you, Mr. Jones. George W. Trendle, president of WXYZ and The Lone Ranger corporation, asked me to accept this honor and to assure the National Safety Council that this splendid recognition of achievement will serve as a spur to greater efforts in the days to come. Mr. Trendle also asked me to observe that his conception of The Lone Ranger was just a beginning and that a great share of the honor is due Fran Striker, the author of the stories, Charles Livingstone, the director of the dramas, Brace Beemer and John Todd, who interpret the leading roles – and every member of the production staff, whose enthusiasm and loyalty have been important contributions to The Lone Ranger's success.

MUSIC: THEME

ANNOUNCER: This brings to a close the special program marking the tenth anniversary of the start of radio's best-known program, The Lone Ranger. Because of the difficulties of transportation, Governor Stassen's talk was transcribed. The authentic accounts of our boys overseas were taken from the books, *They Were Expendable* and *Convoy to Murmansk*, and from dispatches by the United Press and the Associated Press. This program came to you from Chicago and Detroit. This is the Blue Network.

Appendix H
The Lone Ranger
Special – Birthday Recording
Special Recording, originally intended for Friday, May 3, 1940.
"For Recording Only – No Date"

Fran Striker Summary:
Every year, on his birthday, it was the custom of The Lone Ranger to ride to the little mission near the Rio Grande where lived his friend, the padre, and there, within the tiny chapel, to pay tribute to his mother who had died years before. As his birthday approached on this occasion, however, the masked man anticipated trouble. Three years earlier he had been responsible for the arrest and conviction of two rustlers named Carter and Link. They had received two-year sentences, to be served in the jail at San Juan, a small town only a few miles from the mission. Now, the masked man knew they had been released, and upon their arrest they had promised vengeance if even the masked man returned to that territory when they were free. This, The Lone Ranger explained to Tonto as the latter departed on a mysterious journey whose purpose he declined to explain to his white friend. The Lone Ranger did not know that the padre had summoned Tonto to aid him in securing a gathering of the men and women who had been aided by The Lone Ranger… a gathering to pay him honor on his birthday.

All of those within riding distance of San Juan who owed the masked man so much were invited. Mustang Mag and Missouri; the Black Caballero; Chief Thundercloud; Cactus Pete; Arizona Lawson; ranchers he saved near Apache City, farmers and sheepmen, and the homesteaders over beyond Eagle Pass. They made their way swiftly to San Juan and in a huge army warehouse on the edge of town prepared for the party. Through the length and breadth of seven states of the early west, the pioneers gave thanks for the work of The Lone Ranger. They all benefited by his deeds of daring, but none had ever known the time when they could express his gratitude. Now in the San Juan region, Tonto had given the settlers their long-desired chance. At the mission, however, no hint of this activity was allowed to obtrude. Therefore when, on his birthday, The Lone Ranger put in his annual appearance, he suspected nothing. In fact, after his visit to the chapel, when shots seemingly were fired in his direction, he headed for town anticipating a showdown with the men he had jailed. To his surprise he discovered the shots had been fired to lure him there, and he was greeted with such a celebration as the West had never known before.

ANNOUNCER: At a camp cleverly concealed in a sunlit mountain valley far to the north of the border, The Lone Ranger stood beside the dying embers of a small campfire and watched the approach of Tonto, leading his great stallion, Scout…

SOUND: ONE HORSE APPROACHES TO STOP

ANNOUNCER: Not until his faithful Indian companion had halted before him did the masked man speak…

RANGER: You must make this journey, Tonto?

TONTO: Ugh.

RANGER: And you can't tell me where you're going, or why?

TONTO: Ugh.

RANGER: Kemo Sabay, if you feel you shouldn't speak, I'll not attempt to persuade you against your will. I'll ask only one thing… your word that you're not going where there's danger I should share.

TONTO: There no danger.

RANGER: I'll believe that, Tonto. In all the time we've been together, you've never spoken a word that hasn't been strictly true.

TONTO: You no worry.

RANGER: With your assurance, I won't. I hope you understand the only reason I asked is because I haven't another friend as loyal as you in the world.

TONTO: Ugh. Tonto savvy.

RANGER: There's still work for us to do, Kemo Sabay. And if anything happened that made it necessary for one of us to continue without the other, he'd have little chance. Injustice is strong even in the West. Justice needs every friend willing to fight on its side.

TONTO: That right.

RANGER: One thing more before you leave…

TONTO: What that?

RANGER: Something I hadn't intended to mention but find I must. You know, Tonto, that every year on a certain date I visit the mission of our friend, The Padre.

TONTO: Ugh.

RANGER: It will not be long until I must ride there again.

TONTO: It one month.

RANGER: Yes. I had hoped that I could always make that one journey in peace. Until now I have. But this year…

TONTO: There trouble?

RANGER: I can't say for sure. But trouble has been threatened.

TONTO: Tonto not knowum that!

RANGER: As I said, I didn't want you to know. I mention it now just so you'll realize why I wish you to return before I leave.

TONTO: Me gettum back. What trouble?

RANGER: Do you recall San Juan? That little town just to the west of the mission?

TONTO: Ugh.

RANGER: And do you remember the time almost three years ago when we exposed that pair that has been running stolen cattle across the border?

TONTO: Ugh. Sendum them jail.

RANGER: Yes. To the jail at San Juan. They received sentences of two years each. But now they're out again. They've been out since a month after my last trip to the mission.

TONTO: Them make-um trouble?

RANGER: Tonto, The Padre called on them just after they started to serve their terms.

TONTO: Ugh.

RANGER: One day he told me about that interview…

SOUND: SNEAK IN MUSIC BACKGROUND

RANGER: (SLOWLY FADING OUT) He had gone to them in the hope that they could be reconciled to their punishment. He offered them consolation. He wanted them to know that when they were given their freedom once more, their debt to society would have been paid. He wanted them to understand that no obstacle would be placed in their paths if they wished to lead honest lives.

SOUND: BRIEF PAUSE

PADRE: (SLOWLY FADING IN) My friends, come to me when your terms are finished. I shall do all that I can to help you. The Lone Ranger has spoken to me of this. It is his wish as it is mine. There was no hatred in his heart when he captured you. Let there be none in yours when you go free.

LINK: (SHORT LAUGH) Padre, yo're wastin' yore time!

CARTER: Why don't you go on back tuh yore mission an' leave us be? If me'n Link'd wanted a lecture, weed've sent fer yuh!

PADRE: Perhaps I have come too soon. You are still angry.

LINK: Angry? (SHORT LAUGH) Yuh hear that, Carter? Yuh hear what he said? Angry! Padre, you lissen tuh me!

PADRE: Si?

LINK: Carter an' me, we've got a message for you tuh give that masked hombre if you ever meet up with him agin. You tell him this. You tell him if we was rustlin', it wasn't none o' his business. You tell him me'n Carter allus stuck to our own affairs an' expected other folks tuh do the same!

PADRE: You took that which did not belong to you, my friends.

LINK: Yere? Wal, that ain't neither here nor there. It jest so happens weed've got along all right if that masked hombre hadn't butted in. he tricked us an' turned us over to the law. He got us sent up afore the judge. He's the feller tuh blame 'cause now we're lookin' out from behind bars!

PADRE: It is not good, my son, to blame another for the fault that is your own.

LINK: Aw, cut that! We're in the calaboose an' it was him that sent us here. So you tell him this fer the both of us. We ain't in jail fer life. One day we'll be out agin. An' when we are…

CARTER: An' when we are, Padre, we're blastin' that hombre the first time he comes back tuh this part o' the country!

LINK: You tell him we dare 'im tuh come back!

CARTER: We'll be ready an' waitin', an this time bein' lighnin' fast with them irons o' his ain't gonna save him!

LINK: Padre, we're makin' a promise. If he ever comes inside a hundred miles o' San Juan when we're loose, he'll never top a hoss agin or make another camp!

CARTER: No more than them pore hombres lyin' out in boothill!

LINK: An' fer the same reason!

PADRE: Amigos, you speak as men who are blind.

LINK: Bah!

PADRE: Yes, amigos… as men who are blind. (FADING OUT) But I shall obey you. I shall deliver your message to The Lone Ranger. And he shall act in this matter as he sees fit…

SOUND: MUSIC BACKGROUND UP AND OUT.

SOUND: BRIEF PAUSE

RANGER: (FADING IN) The Padre returned to them soon after, Tonto, but they only repeated what they had said. So now you understand.

TONTO: Me savvy.

RANGER: They are free! I must journey to the mission. What will happen, no one can tell. But when I head for the border, it would be good to have you riding at my side.

TONTO: Me not fail you!

RANGER: Thanks, Tonto. That's all. I won't keep you longer. If you must leave, you had better start.

TONTO: Ugh. (MOUNTS)

RANGER: I'll meet you at this same camp at the end of three weeks. And, Tonto, whatever your errand… good luck!

TONTO: Ugh… Gittum up, Scout!

SOUND: ONE HORSE STARTS AND SUSTAINS

TONTO: (AT MIKE) Gittum up, feller! Gittum up!

MUSIC: TONTO THEME, SUSTAIN

SOUND: SUSTAIN FAST HOOFS, ONE HORSE

ANNOUNCER: Tonto kept his strong paint horse at a steady, ground-covering gait that could be maintained for days with a minimum of time lost for rest and refreshment. His mysterious journey took him southward toward the Rio Grande, which he sighted after days of riding. Then the tired Indian saw the ancient mission, built many years before by the Spaniards.

SOUND: HOOFS

MUSIC: TONTO THEME SUSTAINED, THEN FADES

SOUND: MISSION BELLS INTO LAST PART OF TONTO THEME

ANNOUNCER: The Padre, informed of Tonto's approach, waited at the entrance to the patio to greet him.

TONTO: Whoa, whoa, Scout! Whoa, feller! Whoa, whoa!

SOUND: HOOFS STOPPING

PADRE: (APPROACH) Buenos dias, amigo!

TONTO: (DISMOUNT) How!

PADRE: I sent for you and you have come. Muy gracias! You have kept silence, yes? You have said nothing… not even to the Senor Lone Ranger?

TONTO: Me no talcum.

PADRE: Buenos! It is well! Now you must come within and rest and refresh yourself while we talk.

TONTO: Tonto not tired.

PADRE: Non! But soon you must ride again. You must ride far. And there is but little time.

TONTO: Where ride-um?

PADRE: That I shall explain quickly. But come… (RAISE VOICE) Pablo! Manuel! Here! See to my amigo's horse!

SOUND: MISSION BELLS UP AND OUT

ANNOUNCER: Tonto listened to The Padre while he rested. The tension in the Indians face relaxed until by the time the speaker finished, Tonto smiled. Rested and refreshed, the faithful Indian companion of The Lone Ranger once more took the saddle and rode. A week later, we find Mustang Mag in her house near Pecos. She stands just inside the kitchen door, her face stern as she hears footsteps cross the porch.

SOUND: DOOR OPENS

MAG: Missouri!

MISSOURI: (BACK) Huh? (CHUCKLE) Oh, howdy, Mag…

SOUND: CLOSE DOOR

MISSOURI: Gittin' a mite chilly outside. I…

MAG: You come here!

SOUND: STEPS APPROACH, ONE MAN

MISSOURI: (APPROACH) Mag, what's the matter?

MAG: You! You ornery, spavined, stove-in, perambulatin' vessel o' sin! You…

MISSOURI: What?

MAG: You story-tellin' old idjit!

MISSOURI: Me?

MAG: Yere, you!

MISSOURI: G-gosh, wh-what've I done now?

MAG: I found out what you was doin' yestidday at the time you told me you was ridin' fence!

MISSOURI: (GROAN)

MAG: I got it out o' Lefty!

MISSOURI: Now, Mag, wait! Jest lissen a second! What if I did take jest a taste o' Pete's likker? Warn't enough tuh do any harm! Finished my work, didn't I? Gosh…

MAG: Oh! So you was drinkin', too!

MISSOURI: Huh? Ain't that what Lefty told yuh?

MAG: No!

MISSOURI: But you said…

MAG: Shut up! (BRIEF PAUSE) Now then! How many more sins you got on yore conscience, huh? What else you been hidin' from me? (BRIEF PAUSE) Wal, don't stand there like the cat got yore tongue! Speak up!

MISSOURI: But you said tuh keep still! I was only tryin' tuh tell yuh that…

MAG: Shut up!

MISSOURI: There! Yuh see? How's a feller to explain anythin' when you won't let 'im?

MAG: Might as well keep still! You'd jest fix tuh lie agin anyhow! If you was drinkin', don't let it happen agin! Next time Ill fire yuh fer it! (BRIEF PAUSE) (CLEAR THROAT) Leastways… leastways, I hope I will. But that ain't what I started tuh ask yuh. Missouri, why didn't you tell me you seen Tonto yestidday? Why'd you keep it from me? Ain't he an' the masked man as much my friends as they are your'n?

MISSOURI: (GROAN) Oh, golly, Mag. I promised I'd tell yuh an' I clean fergot!

MAG: Heavenly Days! Missouri, don't you ever remember anythin' but mealtimes?

MISSOURI: Ain't nothin' else so important.

MAG: (SNORT) Not tuh you there ain't! Wal, git on with it. What'd Tonto want? Why didn't he come tuh see me?

MISSOURI: He didn't have time. He had a bunch o' other places he had tuh go.

MAG: What fer?

MISSOURI: Why… why, fer the masked man's birthday!

MAG: Huh?

MISSOURI: Shore. He's got a birthday. Didn't you know that?

MAG: Yuh fool, O' course I knowed it! Ain't everybody?

MISSOURI: Shore. He's got a birthday. Didn't you know that?

MAG: Yuh fool, O' course I knowed it! Ain't everybody?

MISSOURI: Huh? Everybody? Why… why, yere, I guess they have. Shore. Shore, o' course they have. (CHUCKLE) Ain't that funny? Never thought o' that afore!

MAG: Missouri, one o' these days you're gonna drive me clean daft!

MISSOURI: Honest?

MAG: What about the masked man's birthday?

MISSOURI: Oh. Reckon I was fergittin' agin…

MAG: (SNORT)

MISSOURI: Wal, Mag, it's like this. You know about how he allus goes to the mission each year when it comes his birthday, don't yuh?

MAG: Uh-huh.

MISSOURI: Wal, in a couple weeks he'll be there agin. Yuh see, it's on account of his mother. Gosh, he sets a lot o' store by her, Mag.

MAG: It does his credit.

MISSOURI: Uh-huh. I ain't denyin' it. An' it's one o' the things that make yuh like him. She died years ago, but he thinks jest as much of his birthday, no matter from how far away he had tuh ride, he goes to the mission jest in her honor. He goes in the chapel an' stays there alone so's he kin do a bit of rememberin'...

MAG: (SNIFFLES)

MISSOURI: Then after that he... (BREAKS OFF) Why, Mag, yo're cryin'!

MAG: Ain't either! It... it's jest from them onion I was peelin'...

MISSOURI: Inions?

MAG: Didn't I say so?

MISSOURI: But we ate the last o' them yestidday!

MAG: Awwww....

MISSOURI: An' them's taters you've been slicin' there!

MAG: Drat it, Missouri, you mind yore own business!

MISSOURI: But...

MAG: Never mind about me! You still ain't explained about Tonto. Yu tryin' tuh stand thar an' say Tonto rode clear over here jest tuh tell us somethin' we knew already?

MISSOURI: Oh, no, that warn't it!

MAG: Then why was it?

MISSOURI: It's fer the party!

MAG: Huh? Party?

MISSOURI: Shore. It was The Padre's idea, Mag. He told Tonto there's folks all over the West that wouldn't like nothin' better'n the chance tuh thank 'em fer the things he's done.

MAG: That's true enough. I could name a dozen like that.

MISSOURI: Uh-huh. So The Padre's gonna give them a chance!

MAG: Huh?

MISSOURI: 'Course, everybody the masked man's helped can't be there. Wouldn't be time tuh round 'em up nor a place tuh put 'em if there was. But The Padre sent Tonto out to invite all o' his special friends.

MAG: Glory be!

MISSOURI: There's gonna be youn me, Mag!

MAG: There'd jest better!

MISSOURI: An' Cactus Pete, an' Arizona Lawson! There's gonna be The Black Caballero, and' Chief Thundercloud!

MAG: Golly!

MISSOURI: Them homesteaders over beyond Eagle Pass an' the ranchers he saved near Apache City! Mag, there's gonna be farmers there, an' ranchers an' sheepmen! There's gonna be folks from town an' some that don't come down out o' the hills once in twelve months!

MAG: Land o' mercy!

MISSOURI: San Juan's gonna see such a blow-out as there never was before in the hull state o' Texas! An' The Lone Ranger ain't tuh know a thing about it till he gits there! (CHUCKLE) An' Mag…

MAG: Huh?

MISSOURI: He's gonna git another surprise…

MAG: On top of all that?

MISSOURI: Uh-huh. One that's gonna please him most of all!

MAG: Missouri, what is it?

MISSOURI: Can't tell yuh.

MAG: But…

MISSOURI: A man's got tuh keep somethin' to himself, don't he?

MAG: Missouri…

MISSOURI: What?

MAG: You can't do this tuh me! You can't git my curiosity up without explainin'!

MISSOURI: (CHUCKLE) You jest think I can't…

SOUND: STEPS FADING, ONE MAN

MISSOURI: (FADING) Wal, g'bye, Mag. I still got work tuh do.

MAG: (RAISE VOICE) Come back here! (EFFORT)

SOUND: SNATCH SKILLET FROM STOVE

MISSOURI: (BACK) (CHUCKLE) Nope, Mag….

SOUND: OPEN DOOR

MISSOURI: I have tuh… (BREAK OFF) (SCREAM) No, Mag! Mag! No, don't! Don't throw that skillet! (FADING FAST) Hey…

MAG: (EFFORT)

SOUND: DOOR SLAMS. SKILLET HITS DOOR.

MAG: Drat 'im! He got away! H'mph! I ever lay my hands on that man, I'll… I'll.. (CHUCKLE) Doggone the old fool!

ANNOUNCER: In the meantime, rejoined by Tonto, The Lone Ranger prepared for his journey. Tonto said nothing of his recent business and the masked mystery ride had no suspicion of the things that awaited him in San Juan. His face was more sober than suual as he mounted and said…

SOUND: CLATTERING HOOFS

RANGER: (MOUNTING) There! Ready, Tonto?

TONTO: (MOUNTING) Ugh. Me ready now.

RANGER: Tonto, forget what I told you about Link and Carter. I'll handle it alone.

TONTO: No. Me go-um.

RANGER: But you've ridden Scout far and hard. He looks tired. I'll not ask where you've been or what you've done, Kemo Sabay, but you yourself look tired. Why not rest here until I return?

TONTO: Me all right.

RANGER: You're sure?

TONTO: Ugh.

RANGER: Then listen to me, Tonto.

TONTO: Ugh.

RANGER: If things go wrong… if Link and Carter are able to keep their threat… promise me you'll save yourself. My trip to the mission is personal. It doesn't involve you. There's no reason why you should suffer because of me.

TONTO: Tonto not gettum hurt.

RANGER: Very well. It's time we started. Come.

TONTO: Ugh… Gittum up, Scout!

RANGER: Come on, Silver!

SOUND: TWO HORSES START AND FADE

RANGER: (FADING) Hi-Yo, Silver! Away!

MUSIC: INTERLUDE

ANNOUNCER: The curtain falls on the first act of out thrilling Lone Ranger drama. Before the next exciting scenes, please permit us to pause for just a few moments.

COMMERCIAL

ANNOUNCER: Now to continue our story. Through the length and breadth of seven states of the early west, the pioneers gave thanks for the work of The Lone Ranger. They all had benefited by his deeds of daring, but none had ever known he time when he could express his gratitude. Now in the San Juan region, Tonto had given the settlers their long-desired chance. They entered into the plans for The Lone Ranger's birthday celebration with unbounded enthusiasm. San Juan became a beehive of activity.

SOUND: CROWD NOISES

ANNOUNCER: Men talked of the plans, the legends of the masked rider were told and retold, but with all that went on, there was a shroud of mystery surrounding the town.

MUSIC: SHORT BREAK. FADE TO MISSION BELLS

ANNOUNCER: Finally, the great day came… the anniversary of The Lone Ranger's birth! Missouri was at the mission with The Padre… waiting… waiting impatiently.

SOUND: SLOWLY FADE OUT MISSION BELLS BEHIND DIALOGUE

SOUND: CLUMPS, ONE HORSE, SLIGHTLY BACK

MISSOURI: Gosh, Padre, why don't he come? Must be gittin' on tuh two. You figger somethin's happened tuh keep him away? Somethin' that'll keep him from gittin' here atall?

PADRE: He will come, Missouri.

MISSOURI: But…

PADRE: Always he has come, the Senor of the Mask. Nothing will ever prevent him. Dios! I remember once he arrived so weakened from a gunshot that he could scarcely sit his saddle. He swayed as he rode. His face was as pale as that white wall you see before you. It was a miracle that he reached this place alive. But in spite of all he came, my friend. And will again.

MISSOURI: (CHUCKLE) Padre, you sound like Mag!

PADRE: Si?

MISSOURI: You an' her both think there ain't nothin' or nobody this side o' glory that c'n stop that masked feller once he's set his mind tuh do a thing. Wal, I can't argue that. I agree with you. If I'd ever doubted it… which I never… I shore couldn't after hearin' some o' the stories o' them folks that've showed up in San Juan. Gosh! The things he's done. If I hadn't seen that hombre in action more'n once myself, I wouldn't believe 'em!

PADRE: It is so.

MISSOURI: Padre, there's one little old lady thar in town that wouldn't be walkin' tuhday if it warn't fer him. Yes, sir, that's a fact! One time she was silin' bad. The Lone Ranger found out about it, rode close to a thousand miles tuh fetch the best sawbones west o' the Mississippi... (CHUCKLE)... an' would yuh believe it? He made a miserly old skinflint back where she lives foot the bill!

PADRE: And that, Amigo, is but one of his good deeds among the many!

MISSOURI: Wal, I sh'ld smile! Oh, I could go on the rest o' the day jest tellin' what I heard since me an Mag got here. But that ain't the best of it. You should see the faces on them folks, thinkin' how they're gonna git the chance tuh thank 'im. Pleased as kids with candy. So that's why... (PAUSE)

PADRE: Si?

MISSOURI: Wal, Padre, that's why it'd be a terrible thing if he never showed up. The way they'd be disappointed. It'd be awful. (SIGH) I dunno as I'd care tuh see it...

PADRE: (SOFT LAUGH) You have a kind heart, my friend.

MISSOURI: (INDIGNANT) Who? Me? Now look here, Padre, you can't...

PADRE: (LAUGH) Missouri, listen.

MISSOURI: Huh?

PADRE: Is all prepared? Do these people understand what they must do?

MISSOURI: Oh, sure, don't you worry none about that. I told 'em. Everything's fixed. 'Course you know we're usin' that old warehouse fer the party.

PADRE: Si.

MISSOURI: It's where the army used tuh keep supplies. Dunno anyplace else that would've been near big enough. Everybody's been workin' day an' night tuh git it ready.

PADRE: That is good.

MISSOURI: An' as soon as I see he'll be here, I'll git back an' let 'em know. That's what they sent me fer... tuh warn 'em. Yere, an' that's somethin' I aimed tuh ask yuh about.

PADRE: What is that, Missouri?

MISSOURI: Fetchin' the masked man there. How's it gonna be done without makin' him suspicious? Reckon you don't need tuh be told he's a goshawful hard feller tuh fool.

PADRE: (CHUCKLE) That shall by my task.

MISSOURI: Sure, but...

PADRE: It shall be done, my friend. That is something you need not worry about. He shall suspect bothing.

MISSOURI: Well, if you say so…

PADRE: Si. I do.

MISSOURI: Then… (BREAK OFF)

RANGER: (DISTANT) Come on, Silver! Come on, old fellow!

MISSOURI: Padre! You hear that?

PADRE: The Lone Ranger!

MISSOURI: Oh, golly! What if he should see me here? How'd I explain it? Gosh, Padre, what'm I gonna do?

PADRE: Quick! To your horse!

SOUND: SEVERAL FAST STEPS ON BRICK. FADE IN CLUMPS.

MISSOURI: Yere!

PADRE: That gate you see open! That way, amigo! The wall shall hide you!

RANGER: (CLOSER) Come on, boy! Come on!

MISSOURI: (MOUNTS) Right!

PADRE: Tell all that he is here!

MISSOURI: I'll tell 'em, Padre! An' gosh! Won't tonight be a night tuh remember! Adios!

PADRE: Quickly, my friend! Quickly!

MISSOURI: Git up, boy!

SOUND: ONE HORSE STARTS AND FADES

PADRE: (AD LIBS TO HORSE, FADING OUT)

SOUND: SLOWLY FADE IN FAST HOOFS, TWO HORSES, THROUGH PAUSE.

RANGER: (ON CUE) (BACK) Hello! Hello! Hello!

PADRE: (RAISE VOICE) Amigo!

RANGER: (APPROACH) Whoa, whoa, Silver! Whoa, old fellow! Whoa, whoa!

TONTO: (APPROACH) Whoa, Scout! Whoa, whoa, feller! Whoa!

SOUND: TWO HORSES APPROACH TO STOP

RANGER: (DISMOUNT) Padre, it is good to see you again!

TONTO: (DISMOUNT) (CHUCKLE) Ugh!

PADRE: El gusto es mio!

RANGER: No, we're as glad as you. You're looking well. Nothing here has changed.

PADRE: Time lays a light hand upon those who are contented, amigo.

RANGER: Yes. As he rode up…

PADRE: Eh?

RANGER: I thought… Padre, didn't a horseman just ride through that gateway?

PADRE: But yes, my friend.

RANGER: From a distance there was something about him that seemed familiar. He put me in mind of someone I know near Pecos… Well, never mind. It couldn't have been him. If it had been, he would have known my horse and waited. Father, the chapel…"

PADRE: Is empty. You wish to enter now?

RANGER: Yes.

PADRE: Then you will be quite alone.

SOUND: SNEAK IN SOFT MUSIC

RANGER: Good.

PADRE: Amigo…

RANGER: Yes?

PADRE: During these months that you have been away, I too have said prayers for that kind lady, your mother.

RANGER: Thank you.

PADRE: But those of none other can be as welcome to her as yours…

SOUND: BEGIN BUILDING MUSIC

PADRE: (FADING) Go, my son. Enter the chapel. Tonto and I shall await you here…

SOUND: MUSIC UP AND DOWN, THEN SUSTAIN BEHIND ANNOUNCER

MUSIC: SUSTAINING CHORAL THEME

SOUND: BIRDS TWITTERING

ANNOUNCER: Coolness and peace pervaded the little chapel. The only sound came from the birds that lived just beyond the windows in the patio. One felt that some unseen choir might at any moment fill the air with divine music. Slanting beams of sunlight streamed through the windows to fall upon the bared head of The Lone Ranger. He knelt before the alter, and removed his mask. The Lone Ranger's fine face wore no covering of mask or disguise. He faced he alter as himself, just the son of a fine woman whose memory he cherished and honored on this day. Kneeling there, the lines of strain and tension that had marked the strong man's face relaxed. His head was bowed, eyes closed, for quite a while. When he lifted his head, a transformation had come over him. His face seemed to have become the face of a boy. In the twittering of the birds he seemed to hear a woman's voice say to him, "well done, my son," and then a moment later another voice seemed to say, "Ride on, Lone Ranger."

MUSIC: CRESCENDO TO FINISH AS BIRDS STOP

ANNOUNCER: It was sunset when The Lone Ranger came from the mission to join the Padre. The Padre was about to speak when suddenly ---

SOUND: TWO RIFLE SHOTS. AD LIB SURPRISE. LINK AND CARTER, BACK, AD LIB GIT-UPS. TWO HORSES, BACK, START AND FADE

TONTO: (APPROACH) You gettum down!

RANGER: No, Tonto! Wait! They're riding away!

TONTO: Ugh!

RANGER: Tonto, that's Link and Carter!

TONTO: That them all right!

RANGER: We're going after them! Silver! What have you done with Silver?

PADRE: Amigo, I am sorry! It was stupid of me, but how was I to know there would be trouble!

RANGER: What…

PADRE: Manuel has taken him. He was unsaddled by Tonto. Even now he is grazing.

RANGER: Then…

TONTO: (FADE SLIGHTLY) Me go-um! (MOUNTS)

RANGER: Tonto…

SOUND: COUPLE FAST STEPS. FADE IN CLATTER, ONE HORSE.

TONTO: (FADE IN) Ugh!

RANGER: I'll have to let you go! They're well mounted and if Scout carried double, they'd get away! There's no time to saddle Silver!

TONTO: That right!

RANGER: But don't do any more than follow the, do you hear me?

TONTO: Ugh.

RANGER: Just keep them in sight. Don't get within rifle range under any circumstances! You promise that?

TONTO: Me promise!

RANGER: Find where they're going, then report to me here. This is my fight. No one's going to face danger that's mine!

TONTO: Ugh!

RANGER: Then remember your promise… and on your way!

TONTO: Gittum up, Scout!

SOUND: ONE HORSE STARTS AND FADES

TONTO: (FADING) Gittum up! Gittum up!

PADRE: (PAUSE) My friend…

RANGER: Yes, Padre?

PARDE: Do not fear for Tonto… I give you my word, amigo, all will be well.

MUSIC: INTERLUDE

SOUND: FADE IN NIGHT NOISES

ANNOUNCER: The masked man waited anxiously for Tonto. He paid no attention to the Padre when he moved away. Then finally, he hurriedly located and saddled his great horse, Silver. Just about to mount, The Lone Ranger began the drumming hoofbeats of an approaching horse…

SOUND: SLOWLY FADE IN FAST HOOFS, ONE HORSE

RANGER: It's Tonto, Silver!

SOUND: WHINNY, CLUMPS

RANGER: (PAUSE) (SOFT) Riding fast… (PAUSE) (CALL) Tonto!

TONTO: (BACK) Tah-ee!

RANGER: Here!

TONTO: (APPROACH) Who, whoa, Scout! Whoa, feller, whoa!

SOUND: HOOFS APPROACH TO HALT

RANGER: You trailed them?

TONTO: Me trailum!

RANGER: And…?

TONTO: Then headum town!

RANGER: San Juan?

TONTO: Ugh.

RANGER: Then they've never left the district! Listen, Kemo Sabay! Did you see where they stopped?

TONTO: Ugh. Tonto take-um you there!

RANGER: Good! And did they see you?

TONTO: Me takeum care.

RANGER: Better yet! Steady boy! (MOUNTS) Well, Tonto, this is it. They told The Padre I'd never leave this district alive. They've already struck first. But now… (PAUSE)

TONTO: What thinkum?

RANGER: Only the last blow counts, Kemo Sabay. We'll see who strikes that! Let's go!

TONTO: Gittum up, Scout!

RANGER: Come on, Silver!

SOUND: TWO HORSES START AND SUSTAIN

RANGER: (AT MIKE) Come on, old fellow! Come on!

MUSIC: RANGER THEME, HIT HARD AND SUSTAIN

SOUND: SUSTAIN FAST HOOFS

ANNOUNCER: Away from the mission they raced and across the sunbaked earth of the plains now made dark and mysterious under the faint glow from the stars. San Juan, at first a mere pinpoint of light in the distance, came swiftly closer. But before they arrived at the town Tonto, pointing to an immense building looming greyly ahead, gave the signal to halt…

SOUND: RANGER THEME TO PEAK AND CUT

TONTO: Whoa, whoa, Scout! Whoa, feller! Whoa, whoa!

RANGER: Whoa, Silver! Whoa, old boy! Whoa, whoa, there!

SOUND: HOOFS STOPPING

TONTO: There place!

RANGER: That's the warehouse the soldiers used before they abandoned the fort!

TONTO: Ugh.

RANGER: They went inside?

TONTO: That right. You lookum. There hoss.

RANGER: Two horses!

TONTO: Ugh!

RANGER: They're still inside!

TONTO: Ugh. Not ride-um closer. Them hearum hoofs.

RANGER: Yes. (DISMOUNTS) I'm going in there, but I'm leaving the horses here with you. Guard them. Don't come after me unless you know there's trouble.

TONTO: Me not stay-um!

RANGER: But…

TONTO: Tonto go-um too!

RANGER: Do you realize that they may have heard us? Do you understand that right now they may be just waiting for us to get in range before they fire?

TONTO: Me savvy!

RANGER: And you still want to come?

TONTO: Ugh! (DISMOUNTS)

RANGER: All right then, Kemo Sabay, we're in this together. Follow me. (FADING) But stay in the shadows…

SOUND: SNEAK IN MUSIC BACKGROUND

ANNOUNCER: They moved cautiously but with no waste of time. Not a sound nor a ray of light met them when they reached the building. With the masked man leading the way, they circled it warily. They passed a pair a huge double doors without pausing. But shortly afterwards The Lone Ranger suddenly halted…

SOUND: SUSTAIN MUSIC BACKGROUND

SOUND: NIGHT NOISES

RANGER: (SOTTO) Tonto, there's a side door!

TONTO: Me see-um.

RANGER: We couldn't have opened the others without announcing ourselves. But if this is un-locked…

TONTO: Them not hearus.

RANGER: Right. Here. This way. And not a sound!

TONTO: Ugh.

RANGER: (PAUSE) I'll try the door. Stand aside.

TONTO: Ugh.

SOUND: BRIEF PAUSE. TRY DOOR. DOOR SLOWLY CREAKS OPEN.

RANGER: (PAUSE) Hear anything?

TONTO: Me no hearum.

RANGER: Then inside. Quickly. Leave the door open.

TONTO: Ugh.

SOUND: SEVERAL SOFT STEPS ON CREAKING BOARDS. CUT STEPS.

RANGER: (VERY SOFT) Tonto, someone's in here. I can feel it. I know there's someone here. Can you see?

TONTO: It plenty dark!

RANGER: Funny they don't strike…

TONTO: Ugh.

RANGER: Listen to me, Tonto.

TONTO: What do-um?

RANGER: I'm going farther in before I strike a light. Take my gun belt and hold on. Got it?

TONTO: Ugh.

RANGER: We'll not lose each other. Come.

SOUND: SLOW CREAKING STEPS THROUGG LONG PAUSE.

SOUND: BEGIN BUILDING MUSIC BACKGROUND.

SOUND: ONE CUE, DOOR IS SLAMMED AND LOCKED, BACK. SUDDENLY OUT STEPS.

RANGER: (CALL) Who's there? Who locked that door?

SOUND: HUSH

MISSOURI: (BACK) Masked man, we've locked the door!

RANGER: What?

MISSOURI: (APPROACH) Now jest try'n git away without bein' thanked! (SHOUTS) Folks, light up your lamps!

SOUND: AD LIB EXCITEMENT. CHEERS, LAUGHTER, SHOUTS. MUSIC UP AND OUT.

RANGER: Why… why, it's Missouri… Mustang Mag… There's Cactus Pete… Tonto, what does this mean?

TONTO: (CHUCKLE) There Padre. Him tellum!

PADRE: (APPROACH) (RAISE VOICE) Amigos! Quiet! Please!

SOUND: CROWD NOISES SUBSIDE

RANGER: Padre…

PADRE: My friend, do not be angry with is. Here are gathered just a few of those who owe you their lives, their happiness, their property. They wish to show you their gratitude. If you were tricked into coming here, senor, it was because there was no other way.

RANGER: Padre, I… I don't know what to say…

PADRE: And now, amigo, one thing further. (RAISE VOICE) Come, senors!

SOUND: STEPS APPROACH, TWO MEN

RANGER: Link! Carter!

PADRE: (SOFT LAUGH)

LINK: (APPROACH) Friend, that was us fired our rifles back there at the mission, all right, but we never meant you no harm. Fact is, we fired 'way over your head. It was The Padre's idea.

CARTER: We had tuh git you tuh come here some way that wouldn't make you suspicious.

LINK: An' listen…

RANGER: Yes?

LINK: Fergit them threats we made. That's all in the past. I'll admit it took us awhile tuh see things traight, mister, but after the Padre'd showed us what you were doin' fer the West an' why… wal, it made me'n Carter look like a pair o' prize idjits.

CARTER: We've got honest jobs an' we're goin' straight!

PADRE: You see, my friend?

RANGER: Padre, you knew that this would please me most of all…

PADRE: Yes, my son.

MISSOURI: (SLIGHTLY BACK) (SHOUT) All right, professor, strike up the music!

SOUND: TIN-PAN PIANO

MISSOURI: It's The Lone Ranger's birthday, folks! C'mon! Let's whoop 'er up!

SOUND: CROWD NOISES UP, HOLD FOR COUNT, THEN MUSIC TO COVER

ANNOUNCER: The events of that night became an occasion that was described over and over from one end of the West to the other. It was a demonstration of gratitude and affection such as the border country had never seen before and never saw again. But just before dawn, when the celebration was at its height, two figures silently stole away. A few moments later they were in the saddles of their great stallions, their eyes looking back at the scene of the party that was still at its height…

SOUND: MORNING SOUNDS. CLUMPS, TWO HORSES. DISTANT CELEBRATION

RANGER: Tonto…

TONTO: Ugh.

RANGER: We've had our hardships, Kemo Sabay. Yes, and danger and disappointments, too.

TONTO: That right.

RANGER: There are people who would say the lives we lead and the work we've chosen are barren, without rewards.

TONTO: Ugh.

RANGER: But they don't know, Tonto. Perhaps they'll never know, and it doesn't matter. For in the things that count we have wealth they never dreamed of.

TONTO: Ugh!

RANGER: We have friends. Tonto's let's take a pledge.

TONTO: What that?

RANGER: Never to fail them.

TONTO: Ugh!

RANGER: For our friends have never failed us! … Come, Silver!

SOUND: CLATTER

TONTO: Gittum up, Scout!

SOUND: TWO HORSES START AND FADE

RANGER: (FADING) Hi-yo, Silver! Away!

MUSIC THEME

SOUND: HOOFS

RANGER: Come on Silver, old fellow! We've still work to do! Hurry, old fellow, hurry! Hi-Yo, Silver! Away!

Earle Graser (left) and friend George B. Sherman (right) celebrating on New Year's Eve, at the Graser residence on December 31, 1937.

Appendix I
Radio Script of Wednesday, September 5, 1941 Never Broadcast, Intended for #1254-471

The following radio script was intended for the broadcast of September 5, 1941, to serve was episode #1254-471. For reasons unknown the script was tossed aside, and a different script was used for that broadcast date. This script was never broadcast at a later date. The script has been reprinted verbatim, with no alterations or corrections despite grammar in the original script, representing foreign accents.

ANNOUNCER: The town of Big Bend was as lawless as any in the West. Its citizens, quick to anger and with no thought for consequences, were more than ready to settle their differenced with six-guns. Of them all, however, Sheriff Windy Conners was probably the hardest and roughest. He and his two deputies, Sampson and Weaver, were men to be feared and even the most desperate outlaws to enter their district hesitated to cross them. It is evening as our story opens. The sheriff, Windy, is following the trail that leads northward from town. Riding beside him is an Indian on a powerfully muscled paint horse.

SOUND: NIGHT NOISES. SLOW HOOFS, TWO HORSES.

WINDY: So yuh say yore handle's Tonto, eh?

TONTO: Ugh. That right!

WINDY: If yo're up tuh some game then, Tonto, you can take it from me, you'll live tuh regret it!

TONTO: You see-um outlaw quick now!

WINDY: A breed, eh?

TONTO: Ugh.

WINDY: How'd yuh know he's the feller kilt the stage driver? You shore yuh got proof?

TONTO: Masked friend gottum proof!

WINDY: Wal, so that's why yore pard didn't want tuh bring the breed intuh town! He's sportin' a mask!

TONTO: That right.

WINDY: (CHUCKLE) One crook turnin' in another!

TONTO: Him not crook… him catchum crook!

WINDY: (CHUCKLE) Oh, shore! He wouldn't be a crook, oh, no! He jest wears a mask 'cause he thinks it's fun! (CHUCKLE) How much farther we got tuh go?

TONTO: There woods… them waitum there.

WINDY: Umm… Yere, think I see somethin' er somebody already. Ain't that a white hoss agin them trees?

TONTO: Ugh. That Silver.

WINDY: All right, Injun… before we git there, lemme remind yuh agin if this is a trap, I'm plenty fast on the draw, an' nobody's gonna down me without I take a couple o' you along with! Savvy?

TONTO: It not trap!

RANGER: (BACK) That you, Tonto?

TONTO: (CALL) Ugh! Here lawman!

RANGER: (CLOSER) Good!

JOSE: (CLOSER) I weel feex you for these, senor weeth ze mask! You wee pay!

RANGER: (FADE IN) Quiet, Jose!

TONTO: Whoa, Scout!

WINDY: Whoa, there!

SOUND: HOOFS STOP; CLUMPS, FOUR HORSES

RANGER: here's your prisoner, sheriff!

WINDY: Not so fast, there, stranger! First off, jest who're you?

RANGER: That doesn't concern you!

WINDY: Now look here! No masked feller c'n…

RANGER: Is it against the law to wear a mask?

WINDY: N-no... but...

RANGER: Is there a law that says I must give my name?

WINDY: If yo're gonna give evidence agin the breed here, yuh do!

RANGER: The evidence doesn't depend upon my testimony! Tonto and I came on the stage right after the hold-up. The driver was dead and one of the passengers. The other passenger, however, lived long enough to write an accusation!

WINDY: A dead feller's word ain't evidence!

RANGER: You should know the law better than that, sheriff! An accusation written by a dying man who states in the accusation that he knows he's dying will be accepted by any court!

JOSE: Diablo! Peeg! Dog!

RANGER: That'll be enough!

WINDY: An' you got a writin' like that, stranger?

RANGER: Right here. Take it...

SOUND: PAPER

RANGER: It's signed by the man who wrote it. If you doubt the signature, he's well known in Lava City. You can go there and compare the handwriting! There's no other evidence against Jose, but none is needed. He didn't get any loot, as you probably know. The fight the driver and passengers put up frightened him off!

WINDY: What's was the idea o' makin' me come out here? Why didn't yuh jest bring the breed intuh town?

RANGER: I think my mask answers that question.

WINDY: I reckon... All right, breed! Stick out your hands!

JOSE: You cannot do these to me, Jose! You weel...

WINDY: Shut yore mouth an' do like I told you!

JOSE: Si.

SOUND: HANDCUFFS

WINDY: There! I reckon them cuffs will hold yuh! Stranger, jest what was you figgerin' on gittin' out o' this? There ain't no reward, yuh know.

RANGER: I'm not interested in rewards. I simply wanted to see justice done.

WINDY: (CHUCKLE) Yere? Yuh needn't give me any smooth story like that, mister. Ain't no-body chases crooks fer nothin'. Even me, I do it jest fer what the county pays me. Most likely you'n the breed was enemies of one kind er another... but I reckon that ain't nothin' tuh me.

RANGER: You're taking this man to jail now?

WINDY: That's jest what I'm doin'... Git movin', breed! On yore way!

JOSE: Peeg! ... Get ooop!

WINDY: Git up, there! Git up!

SOUND: TWO HORSES START AND FADE. SUSTAIN CLUMPS AT MIKE.

TONTO: Go-um to camp now?

RANGER: Wait, Tonto... (LONG PAUSE)

TONTO: What matter?

RANGER: Just thinking... (PAUSE)

TONTO: There trouble?

RANGER: Tonto, I don't know why... I can't explain it... but I feel uneasy!

TONTO: Tonto no savvy.

RANGER: That sheriff... his eyes... the way he acted... I'd be less surprised to see him outside of the law, than working for it.

TONTO: Ugh!

RANGER: He's got the prisoner, the evidence he needs, and everything should be all right... and yet... (PAUSE)

TONTO: You actum heap strange!

RANGER: I know it, Tonto! And I can't understand it. We should be on our way. But something tells me we'd better stay around for a while. And we're going to!

TONTO: Ugh!

RANGER: Back to camp, Tonto! Come on, Silver!

TONTO: Gittum up, Scout!

SOUND: TWO HORSES START AND FADE

MUSIC: INTERLUDE

ANNOUNCER: Windy, strangely enough, entered town with his captive by a round-about way and made no announcement informing the townspeople that the badly wanted killer who had recently held up the stage had been apprehended. Instead, reaching his office, he called one of his deputies, Sampson, and sent him on an errand. Then he talked long and earnestly with the furtive half-breed.

WINDY: Remember, breed, if you got the notion yuh don't want tuh do like I say, this here writin' the masked feller give me will hang yuh just as shore as I'm a foot high!

JOSE: Si, si, I jabe...

WINDY: Ben Macy will be along in jest a minute now.

JOSE: Senor Macy, his reech hombre, eh?

WINDY: (CHUCKLE) Finest ranch around here, breed. Cash in the bank, a fine set o' buildin's, jest about everthin' a man'd like tuh have.

JOSE: Si!

WINDY: You git behind that door there, out o' sight, savvy?

JOSE: Senor Macy weel not see me!

WINDY: Yuh mean, not until it's time for him tuh see yuh, he won't.

JOSE: An' ze papaire ze marked hombre geeve you...

WINDY: Will be burnt up jest as soon as yuh've done all I've told yuh to... an' not a second sooner!

JOSE: Si, si!

WINDY: Now then, we'll...

SOUND: HOOFS STOPPING, OUTSIDE

JOSE: Somebody come!

WINDY: Quick! Mebbe that's Ben now! Behind that door with yuh!

SOUND: STEPS FADING

JOSE: (FADING) I go, amigo...

SOUND: RAP ON DOOR

WINDY: (LOW) All right, breed?

JOSE: (BACK) (LOW) I am ready!

SOUND: RAP ON DOOR

WINDY: (CALL) Come in!

SOUND: DOOR OPENS

BEN: (BACK) Evenin', sheriff...

SOUND: DOOR CLOSES; STEPS APPROACH

BEN: (APPROACH) Sampson jest rode by my place an' said as how you had somethin' tuh tell me that couldn't wait. How about it?

WINDY: Uh-huh. Sit down, Ben. That chair there... the one by the desk... No! Wait!

BEN: Huh?

WINDY: Before yuh set, Ben, mebbe you'd better hand me them there guns o' yores...

BEN: Guns? But what...

WINDY: Jest a precaution, Ben. I got somethin' tuh say that mebbe won't be sech good hearin'. An' I wouldn't hanker tuh have you fergit yourself an' start throwin' lead!

BEN: Are you loco, Windy? I ain't ever done nothin' tuh cross the law or anythin' like that!

WINDY: That bein' the case, you shouldn't have no objections tuh handin' me them irons then!

BEN: Wal, if yuh say so...

SOUND: GUN BELT

WINDY: Thanks. I'll jest set them over here on this table.

SOUND: LAY BELT AND GUNS ON TABLE

WINDY: Now you c'n set.

SOUND: CHAIR

BEN: Windy, I think mebbe you'd better start explainin' what this is all about!

WINDY: Shore. I don't mind. You got considerable cash in the bank, ain't yuh, Ben?

BEN: Some.

WINDY: How would yuh like tuh give me some... say about two thousand?

BEN: Gosh, Windy, I dunno if I c'n loan yuh that much jest now. I...

WINDY: This ain't no loan!

BEN: Huh?

WINDY: Mebbe you didn't hear me jest straight. I said give me two thousand... not loan me!

BEN: What in blazes are you gittin' at?

WINDY: Or would yuh rather be the guest o' honor at a lynchin' bee!

BEN: Hey, now…

WINDY: Take it easy, pard, take it easy… Mebbe y'ore surprised, but don't git the mistaken notion that I don't mean exactly what I said!

BEN: Windy, what's yore game?

WINDY: Think back a little, Ben. Recollect when Jake Calhoun got kilt?

BEN: By Injuns!

WINDY: You git hitched tuh Jake's wider, didn't yuh? That's how come you got sech a fine ranch, ain't it?

SOUND: SHOVE BACK CHAIR

BEN: You…

WINDY: Siddown!

SOUND: CHAIR

BEN: If y'ore hintin' that I kilt Jake…

WINDY: (CHUCKLE) Shucks, Ben, I know yuh didn't…

BEN: Gosh, fer a second there I thought…

WINDY: (HARD) I know yuh didn't kill Jake, Ben. But unless you hand over two thousand in cash, I'll shore make it look as though yuh did!

BEN: A frame-up!

WINDY: Right!

BEN: Yuh can't do it! Y'ore jest bluffin'!

WINDY: Think so? Recollect them Crow Injuns camped over south?

BEN: Wal?

WINDY: Recollect an old feller named Red Fox?

BEN: Allus drank on bad likker from the traders!

WINDY: Uh-huh. Wal, what if one day he come tuh town, seemed tuh git more likkered up than usual an' started blabbin' about how you paid him fer drillin' Jake?

BEN: It's a lie! I never done so sech thing!

WINDY: A-course yuh didn't! But it c'ld be made tuh look as though yuh did. If Red Fox told that story, then showed the watch yuh give him an' them blankets with yore name on them that he's got, I got a notion folks'd be doggone near convinced!

BEN: Blankets… watch… them things were stole from me!

WINDY: You'd have tuh hustle tuh prove it!

BEN: Red Fox'd never say a thing like that! He'd git lynched hisself!

WINDY: (CHUCKLE) Not if I seen to it he broke jail when nobody was around tuh stop him!

BEN: Of all the lowdown, dirty, sneakin' schemes!

WINDY: (CHUCKLE)

BEN: If you've been schemin' this, why didn't yuh never try it before?

WINDY: 'Cause somethin' jest happened tuhnight that makes the scheme about perfect!

BEN: But if I give yuh the two thousand, yuh won't frame me, is that it?

WINDY: Shore.

BEN: An' how about afterwards? How do I know you won't be after me fer still more cash?

WINDY: (CHUCKLE) Why, that's jest it, Ben… I never had no notion o' stoppin' at two thousand. I figgered you'd be glad tuh pay me a little somethin' more every now an' then!

BEN: Yo're serious about this?

WINDY: Wasn't never more so!

BEN: Then it's either me er you, eh?

WINDY: Uh-huh. An' it looks like it's gonna be you!

SOUND: SHOVE BACK CHAIR

BEN: That's jest where you made a mistake!

WINDY: (GASP) A gun!

BEN: Fergot there was one in the drawer of this desk, eh?

WINDY: Don't!

BEN: You asked fer it!

WINDY: No, wait!

BEN: Take this!

SOUND: SHOT

BEN: (GROAN) Drilled me… shot… (GROAN)

SOUND: SEVERAL STUMBLING STEPS; FALLING BODY

BEN: I... I kilt him... I've got tuh git out... someone'll see me... (FADE FAST)... got tuh clear out.

SOUND: SNATCH DOOR OPEN; FADE OUT RUNNING STEPS, CROSS PORCH, DOWN STEPS.

BEN: (DISTANT) Steady there, hoss! (MOUNTS) Git up! Git up!

SOUND: DISTANT HOOFS START AND FADE. PAUSE.

WINDY: (CHUCKLE) Is he gone, Jose?

JOSE: (APPROACH) (CHUCKLE) Senor Macy, he ride like ze posse ees after heem!

WINDY: (GETS UP) Better close the door.

JOSE: (FADE SLIGHTLY) Si, amigo...

WINDY: (CHUCKLE) I knew doggoned well he'd be too skeered tuh find out the gun was jest loaded with blanks!

JOSE: (APPROACH) (CHUCKLE) You are clevaire...

WINDY: Stand over there a second, breed.

JOSE: Eh? Wha --

WINDY: Go on! Git over there! Don't stand an' argue with me! Want tuh git me mad?

JOSE: (FADE BACK) But I do not understan'...

WINDY: (CHUCKLE) The gun Ben thought he drilled me with was loaded with blanks, breed.

JOSE: (BACK) Si, Si...

WINDY: (HARD) But this one ain't!

JOSE: (BACK) (SCREAM) W'at you do? No, no, Senor! Amigo! No! I beg you... (AD LIB PLEAS BEHIND LAUGHTER)

WINDY: (LAUGH AND BUILD UNTIL COVERED WITH MUSIC)

MUSIC: INTERLUDE

ANNOUNCER: The Lone Ranger and Tonto had made their camp in a heavy grove of trees not far from the trail that led to Ben Macy's ranch. In the morning, after they had partaken of breakfast, they began packing their equipment, making ready to break camp and move on.

SOUND: CLUMPS, BACK

RANGER: Do you need any help, Kemo Sabay?

TONTO: (SLIGHTLY BACK) Tonto packum.

RANGER: I'll cover these coals…

SOUND: SCRAPING EARTH

RANGER: (EFFORT) Can't take chances on sparks setting fire to grass or timber… (EFFORT)

TONTO: (APPROACH) Leave-um here for good?

RANGER: I think so, Tonto. I don't know why I was so suspicious last night.

TONTO: Tonto not know-um.

RANGER: Something seemed to tell me there was trouble in the air. It must have been nothing, however.

TONTO: Ugh.

RANGER: Probably just the reaction after the chase we had to trail and capture Jose.

TONTO: That right.

RANGER: Well, if everything's in our saddle-bags, we might as well be getting on.

TONTO: (SUDDEN) You wait!

RANGER: What is it, Tonto?

TONTO: There! Lookum!

RANGER: What… Oh, a horseman.

TONTO: Lookum hoss!

RANGER: I don't see… (BREAK) Tonto, what on earth?

TONTO: That hoss breed ride-um!

RANGER: Back, Tonto! Behind these trees! He'll pass by on the trail here!

TONTO: Ugh!

RANGER: This will do… Tonto, that's Jose!

TONTO: Ugh! Him hoss, him clothes… that breed all right!

RANGER: And free! Quiet!

TONTO: Ugh!

SOUND: HOOFS APPROACH TO PEAK IN BACKGROUND, THEN FADE OUT. (SLOW HOOFS)

RANGER: (ON CUE) (LOW) Heading towards Ben Macy's place!

TONTO: That right! Ride-um after him?

RANGER: No, Kemo Sabay! We've got to figure this out! Did you notice that he was taking his time? If he'd broken jail… if the law were after him… he'd never be riding like that! He'd be spurring his horse for all it was worth!

TONTO: Ugh!

RANGER: Instead, he acted like a man had nothing in the world to fear!

TONTO: Tonto no savvy!

RANGER: Nor do I! I wonder if he could have bribed the sheriff to let him go… bribed him to destroy the evidence we turned over! If that's gone, there's nothing on earth to connect him with those stage killings!

TONTO: That bad!

RANGER: But it doesn't seem possible that Jose could have bribed the sheriff! He had no cash on him!

TONTO: Ugh!

RANGER: We're going to find out about this!

TONTO: What do-um?

RANGER: Look! He's heading for the Macy place, all right!

TONTO: Ugh!

RANGER: I'm going to follow him!

TONTO: Tonto follow-um?

RANGER: No, Kemo Sabay! You'll ride into town! See if you can learn anything there! Find the sheriff! Get him to talk!

TONTO: Ugh! Tonto do!

RANGER: Ride now!

TONTO: (CALL) Here. Scout!

RANGER: (CALL) Here, Silver!

SOUND: TWO HORSES APPROACH

RANGER: We're not going to break camp after all! We'll meet right here!

TONTO: (MOUNTS) Ugh!

RANGER: (MOUNTS) I'm going to swing around and get to the ranch before Jose does! All right, Tonto! Head for town! I'll see you later!

TONTO: Ugh! Gittum up, Scout!

RANGER: Hi-Yo, Silver! Away!

SOUND: TWO HORSES START AND FADE

MUSIC: INTERLUDE

ANNOUNCER: The curtain falls on the first act of our thrilling Lone Ranger drama. Before the next exciting scenes, please permit us to paus for just a few moments.

COMMERCIAL CREDIT

ANNOUNCER: Now to continue our story. The Lone Ranger, startled to see the breed, Jose, calmly riding toward Ben Macy's ranch when he was supposed to be in town, a prisoner of the sheriff, determined to investigate. In the meantime, Ben, convinced he had killed the sheriff, could scarcely conceal his agitation. He was aware that the deputy, Sampson, knew of his call upon the sheriff the night before. And he could not be certain that his flight from the office had not been observed. His wife, Molly, studied her husband closely...

MOLLY: (APPROACH) Ben, there's somethin' on yore mind. Now why can't yuh tell me what it is? Lan' sakes, whenever there's somethin' worryin' me, I tell you, don't I?

BEN: It... it's nothin' honey...

MOLLY: Yo're goin' out to the bunkhouse, ain't yuh?

BEN: I reckon...

MOLLY: Wal, here's yore hat an' coat. I couldn't find yore gun-belt an' guns. I declare, the way you leave things around, then fergit 'em beats anythin' I ever seen!

BEN: Thankee, Molly. You... you c'n jest lay my things down fer now...

MOLLY: You mean you ain't goin' out right away?

BEN: Not fer a second...

MOLLY: Ben if there ain't somethin' on yore mind, then yo're ailin', that's what! I never seen the day you neglected yore work since we got married!

BEN: I... I don't feel so good, honey.

MOLLY: Then why couldn't you've said so at first, 'stead o' gittin' me all curious! Now you jest set there! I'll git you.

SOUND: RAP ON DOOR

BEN: Wh-who's that?

MOLLY: Most likely the foreman, comin' tuh find out why you ain't been around tuh give the orders fer the day! (FADING) I'll anser it...

SOUND: RAP ON DOOR

MOLLY: (BACK) Jest a second...

SOUND: OPEN DOOR

MOLLY: (BACK) Tex, this is the first time you... (BREAK) Oh! Oh, 'scuse me! I thought you was Tex, our foreman!

BEN: (CALL) Who is it, Molly?

MOLLY: (BACK) Why, I dunno...

WINDY: (BACK) Eef I could 'ave speech weeth Senor Macy...

MOLLY: (BACK) Someone fer you, Ben.

BEN: I don't feel like company. Tell him...

WINDY: (APPROACH) Senor, I would speak to you.. of las' night!

BEN: (GASP)

MOLLY: (APPROACH) Now you look here, breed, didn'y you hear Ben say he wasn't feelin' good? You git right...

BEN: No, no, honey! It... I'll talk tuh him...

MOLLY: But Ben, you said...

BEN: Th-that's all right, honey. Jest... jest closes the door then leave us alone, will yuh? This... this is somethin' real private.

MOLLY: Ben, you ain't actin' like yoreself!

BEN: Please, honey. Jest... jest leave us alone. I... I'll tell yuh all about it later.

MOLLY: (FADING BACK) You'd better! I'll see tuh that!

SOUND: DOOR CLOSES

MOLLY: (BACK AND FADING OUT) I'll be in the kitchen if you want me.

SOUND: DOOR OPENS AND CLOSES

WINDY: (CHUCKLE)

BEN: You... You wanted tuh see me about... last night?

WINDY: *CHUCKLE) Si, senor! (LOW) I was there w'en ze sheriff, he was keel!

BEN: (GASP) No! It can't be! You...

WINDY: I do not lie, senor! I 'eard eet all, yes! Ze sheriff, he try to blackmail you, no? He ask for dinero... two 'tousand een cash! You pull ze gun from ze desk! You fire! (CHUCKLE) He ees dead!

BEN: You... you can't prove it!

WINDY: No? (CHUCKLE) You leave in ze beeg hurree! Your guns, they are lef' behin'!

BEN: The sheriff wasn't kilt with one o' my guns!

WINDY: But who weel know z'st, senor? Several bullet 'ave been fire from ze chamber... who weel know wan did not kel ze senor of ze law?

BEN: Nobody'd take yore word fer it!

WINDY: Ze deputy... Senor Sampson... he know you are there! He suspect you... but he 'ave no proof. Weeth w'st I can tell heem, amigo, he weel no longer doubt! You weal be arrest!

BEN: Blackmailed first by one schemin' crook... an' now by another!

WINDY: (CHUCKLE) Only thees time you weel not keel, amigo! You 'ave no gun! An' eef you 'ave, I would not be caught napping like ze sheriff!

BEN: What... what do you want?

WINDY: Ze rancho, amigo!

BEN: Why, you...

WINDY: Eeet ees that... or death!

BEN: No! You can't... Id never be able to explain it to Molly... we'd have nothin'... nothin' left.

WINDY: You weel tell her you lose eet to me een ze game of pokaire!

BEN: Oh, Lord...

WINDY: Now, at w'ance, amigo... you weel take your pen an' write out ze I.O.U. Eeet weel say ze rancho ees mine!

BEN: No! I won't! I...

WINDY: Very well! I go to ze deputy!

BEN: You can't! You mustn't...

WINDY: Then you write, no?

BEN: (PAUSE) I... yes, I'll do as you say... my pen...

WINDY: Eet ees at yore hand. There ees ze papaire...

BEN: I... I've got to... no one must know...

<u>SOUND: PEN</u>

WINDY: (CHUCKLE)

BEN: There! You'll tell no one? You'd have no reason! There's nothing left. You can't blackmail me any more. You're got everything…

WINDY: Theese weel do quite well, amigo!

SOUND: PAPER

WINDY: An' for now, adios! You weel 'ave w'an week! Then you weel move out!

BEN: Yes… yes…

WINDY: (FADING) Again, amigo… adios! (CHUCKLES)

SOUND: DOOR OPENS AND CLOSES

BEN: (MUTTER) Everythin'… gone! Molly… what'll she say? She… she knows I was worried about somethin'. I… I'll tell her it was the I.O.U… I was afraid to say I'd gambled away the ranch… Yes, yes, I'll tell her that. I…

SOUND: DOOR BURSTS OPEN

BEN: Wha… masked!

SOUND: STEPS APPROACH

RANGER: (APPROACH) Jose told me to come in and keep an eye on you, Ben!

BEN: But he said…

RANGER: It doesn't matter what he said! I know everything!

BEN: He lied… he lied tuh me then…

RANGER: Yes?

BEN: But you can't blackmail me! What if I did kill the sheriff? He had it comin' to him, the rotten schemer! An' the breed… he's got the ranch! You… you'll have tuh split it between yuh! I've got nothin' more tuh buy yuh off with!

RANGER: So you killed the sheriff!

BEN: The breed… he must have told you.

RANGER: Ben, he told me nothing! All I knew was that something was up between you and I had to trick you into telling me what it was!

BEN: Tricked!

RANGER: Now you're going to tell me the whole story!

MUSIC INTERLUDE

ANNOUNCER: When The Lone Ranger had extracted the story of the shooting in the sheriff's office, he left the ranch and returned to the site of his camp, where he was to meet Tonto. When Tonto arrived, he told his masked friend wat he had learned in town...

SOUND: CLUMPS, BACK

RANGER: The sheriff has already been buried, eh?

TONTO: Ugh!

RANGER: There's one thing you've told me that needs explaining! You say several people recalled hearing two shots at the time of the killing...

TONTO: Ugh. That right.

RANGER: Why didn't they investigate at the time?

TONTO: Them thinkum cowboy fire-um shot for joke.

RANGER: That's logical. Cowboys riding into town and firing into the air would be perfect cover for a murderer. I've often wondered why killers haven't taken advantage of that before.

TONTO: Ugh.

RANGER: That, however, isn't the point I was getting at. I made Ben tell me everything about the killing. And he told me distinctly that only one shot had been fired!

TONTO: Mebbe him make-um mistake.

RANGER: No, he was certain. It remained in his memory because he was astonished that his first shot... fired in the heat of anger, when he scarcely had time to aim... hit a vital spot!

TONTO: Then him not tellum truth.

RANGER: That doens't make sense. He's confessed to the murder. What possible difference could it make to him whether or not two shots were fired? His punishment would be the same!

TONTO: Ugh!

RANGER: No, Kemo Sabay, there's something behind this that still hasn't been explained!

TONTO: What you thinkum?

RANGER: I've got an idea, Tonto.

TONTO: What that?

RANGER: You remember how confident Jose seemed.

TONTO: Ugh.

RANGER: The sheriff took him to jail. He must have been there when Ben fired at the sheriff. Perhaps Ben's shot didn't kill Windy. Ben would have been too excited... too panic-stricken to make sure.

TONTO: Ugh!

RANGER: But Jose would have seen his chance. Even with the handcuffs on, he could have fired a second shot, making sure of the sheriff's death!

TONTO: Mebbee that it!

RANGER: Then he could have got the keys from the sheriff's pocket, unlocked his own cuffs, and after that stolen the evidence against him and destroyed it!

TONTO: Tonto think him do-um that!

RANGER: Whether we're right about the killing, we can't be sure. However, Jose must have destroyed that evidence. Nothing else would explain the fact that he's not worried!

TONTO: Ugh!

RANGER: We can no longer get him on that stage-coach charge!

TONTO: Then what do-um?

RANGER: If he killed the sheriff, however... and we can prove it... that will do as well!

TONTO: Ugh!

RANGER: So it's up to us to prepare a trap that will catch him if he's guilty!

MUSIC: INTERLUDE

ANNOUNCER: Ben Macy, after the masked man's visit to his home, had been unable to fathom the role The Lone Ranger was playing in the skillfully devised plot which was leading the rancher to his ruin. The masked man had demanded no money... had made no threats... and the memory of that interview was in Ben's mind the next day as he rode alone across the rangeland...

SOUND" SLOW HOOFS, ONE HORSE

ANNOUNCER: Ben wished to take a last look at the range he was soon to lose. But, thinking of the masked man, he felt no real surprise when he heard a ringing shout...

RANGER: (DISTANT) Come on, Silver!

BEN: The masked man... agin!

RANGER: (CLOSER) Pull up, Ben!

BEN: Whoa, boy!

SOUND: HOOFS STOP. FADE IN FAST HOOFS TWO HORSES.

BEN: Wal, I'll be... There's a redskin with him!

RANGER: (CLOSER) We've got to talk to you, Ben!

BEN: (CALL) What's happened now?

RANGER: (APPROACH) Whoa, Silver! Whoa, boy! Whoa!

TONTO: Whoa, Scout! Whoa! Whoa!

SOUND: HOOFS STOP, CLUMP

RANGER: Ben listen to me! Have you told your wife yet about losing your ranch?

BEN: Stranger, I... I jest ain't had the nerve to yet.

RANGER: Then don't!

BEN: Huh? But...

RANGER: You're not going to lose it!

BEN: Not... Not lose the ranch? Wait... I, I don't git it! I can't savvy...

RANGER: Ben, I've discovered several interesting things. I've made discoveries that are going to clear up all your trouble!

BEN: You... you couldn't have...

RANGER: I still must prove what I know, however! And you'll have to help me!

BEN: Help yuh?

RANGER: I wear a mask, Ben, but I'm not an outlaw. You may think this is a trick. You'll have to trust me, however. You have no choice. It's your only chance! And you have nothing to lose by doing it! Nothing to lose... and everything to gain!

BEN: Stranger... friend... I'll do anything! Anythin'! If I thought there was a way out...

RANGER: There is!

BEN: An'... an' I should help?

RANGER: You promised Jose to get off the ranch at the end of the week.

BEN: That's right.

RANGER: Then find Jose! Tell him you want an extra week... you need it to straighten up your affairs.

BEN: He won't do it, stranger. I savvy his kind!

RANGER: The week doesn't matter. It will be just an excuse to get him to accept a sum of money. Could you raise a thousand dollars?

BEN: I... I've got jest about that in the bank.

RANGER: Then tell Jose you'll give him that thousand for an extra week. Tell him if he won't agree, you'll fix it so that when he does take over, it will be hard to lay his hands on the cash. He'll probably accept.

BEN: But… but what if he takes the cash, then double-crosses me… still makes me git out when he first said?

RANGER: I told you the time doesn't matter. Your request will just be an excuse to give him that money. He'll take it readily enough. If you can think of a better excuse, use it!

BEN: An' then…?

RANGER: And then we'll spring our trap! Will you do it?

BEN: I will! Like you said, I've got nothin' tuh lose. Anythin' at all that looks like a chance fer me, I'm grabbin'!

RANGER: Then it's settled! Tonto!

TONTO: Ugh! Me go-um now?

RANGER: Yes, and make the trip as fast as you can! When you get back, meet me at the place we've been using. I'll be waiting! Now hurry!

TONTO: Tonto do! … Gittum up, Scout!

SOUND: ONE HORSE STARTS AND FADES

BEN: The Injun! Where's he goin'? What's he got tuh do with this?

RANGER: Ben, get that money! Take it to your ranch! Then wait for me and you'll learn my plan!

BEN: But…

RANGER: That's all for now! Come on, Silver!

SOUND: ONE HORSE STARTS AND FADES

RANGER: (FADING) Stretch out those great legs of yours, old boy!

MUSIC: INTERLUDE

ANNOUNCER: Three days went by. Ben Macy secured the thousand dollars as instructed, had another talk with The Lone Ranger, then went into town and offered the cash to Jose. The Breed, only too eager to get his hands on money, promptly accepted and that night entered the café to celebrate…

SOUND: CAFÉ NOISES

WINDY: (CALL) Every w'an! Jose ees buying ze drinks for ze 'cuse! Step up to ze bar, amigos! Buy w'at you weel! Me, Jose, I weel pay! (LAUGH)

BARKEEP: (BACK) Step up, gents! Step up an' name youre pizon!

AD LIB: The breed's allright!
        He's shore free spendin'!
        Here's mud in yore eye, Jose!
        First free drink I've had in a coon's age!

WINDY: (LAUGH) Drink, amigos! Drink your fill an' be 'appy! There weel be plentee for all!

RANGER: (BACK) On moment!

SOUND: BRIEF HUSH, THEN AD LIB EXCITEMENT

RANGER: (APPROACH) Stand where you are, Jose

WINDY: W'at een…

RANGER: Slap leather and I'll outdraw you… Everyone! Stand back! Don't try to interfere!

SOUND: AD LIB EXCITEMENT

RANGER: And keep still!

SOUND: HUSH

RANGER: Tonto!

TONTO: (APPORACH) Ugh!

RANGER: Sampson and Weaver, the two deputies, are standing there at the bar! Bring them here! If they make any objection, handle them any way you wish!

TONTO: (FADE) (CHUCKLE) Ugh! Tonto do!

RANGER: Come here, marshal! I want you to see all of this! You too, Ben!

MARSAHL: I'm watchin', friend!

BEN: An' me too!

WINDY: Marshal! W'at you mean, senor? Ze U.S. Marshal?

RANGER: The U.S. Marshal!… Barkeep, you've got some lemon juice behind the bar there? Hand it to me!

BARKEEP: (FADE SLIGHTLY) J-jest a second, mister… (APPROACH) Here… here yuh are…

RANGER: Thanks!… All right, Jose! Stand still!

WINDY: Peeg! Take your hands from me, senor! Do not touch me! Carramba! You… (STRUG-GLE) Non, non!

RANGER: (EFFORT) Struggling won't do you any good! We'll see what effect lemon juice has on that dark complexion of yours!

WINDY: Non, non, sacre… (STRUGGLE) Diablo! I weel keel you! I weel…

RANGER: I think not!… There!

BARKEEP: Wal, I'll be hornswoggled! The breed's face was dyed! Look it… that lemon juice takes the color off!

SOUND: AD LIB SURPRISE

RANGER: Now for the wig! (EFFORT)

WINDY: Blast yore meddlin' hide!

RANGER: With that dark wig gone you don't look nearly as much like a breed… Sheriff!

SOUND: AD LIB SURPRISE

AD LIB: The sheriff!
   The breed was Windy all the time!
   He disguised hisself!
   What was he up to?

BARKEEP: But… but gosh! We buried the sheriff, stranger!

RANGER: No, you buried a breed named Jose! The sheriff killed him. And then the sheriff pretended to be Jose!

BARKEEP: But that ain't possible! The sheriff's deputies would've knowed it if there was any trick!

RANGER: You're right, barkeep! They did know it! They were in on the scheme from the first! You can get proof by looking at the man they buried int eh sheriff's place. You'll see he was really a breed. But there's other proof too! Got them, Tonto?

TONTO: (APPROACH) Ugh! Me gottum!

SAMPSON: (APPROACH) Leave us be! Doggone, you can't do this!

RANGER: Search them, marshal! You'll find the marked money on them that Ben gave to Windy here. Windy shared it with them!

SAMPSON: Doggone yuh!

MARSHALL: This is it!

RANGER: Then I believe that proves everything! You can put them under arrest!

MARSHAL: Which same, as U.S. Marshal for this district, I'm doing right now!

BEN: But… but stranger! How'd you git ontuh all this?

RANGER: I almost didn't Ben. The only thing that led me to it was the fact that you insisted only one shot had been fired in the sheriff's office, while others reported there had been two shots!

BEN: But I still don't see…

RANGER: Wait! Even then, I didn't know Windy was the breed. Until then, I hadn't had the opportunity to look closely at the man calling himself Jose!

BEN: Yere?

RANGER: When I did, however, I knew at once he wasn't Jose! Tonto and I had captured the breed and new him well!

BEN: Doggone, if that ain't the doggonedest thing!

RANGER: Windy must have had this scheme in mind for a long time! When he saw Jose was about his build, he saw his chance to go through with it. Then, if you had turned over your ranch to him, he would have made a quick sale and disappeared!

WINDY: Are you fellers gonna believe what a masked feller says? He's jest lyin'! There ain't none of it true!

MARSHAL: Then why did yuh pretend tuh be what yuh wasn't?

WINDY: It… it was jest a joke.

BEN: (LAUGH) Mighty thin, Windy! Mighty thin!

MARSHAL: Too thin tuh keep you from hangin' like yuh should! An' if yore deputies don't hang, the least they'll git is a good long term in jail! Which'll take keer o' their schemin' fer some time tuh come!

RANGER: (OUTSIDE) Hi-Yo, Silver! Away!

SOUND: HOOFS START, OUTSIDE.

MUSIC: THEME

Appendix J
Cast Sketches

**Sketches by actor Liggett on the back of his radio script,
featuring the cast and director James Jewell (dated December 1938).**

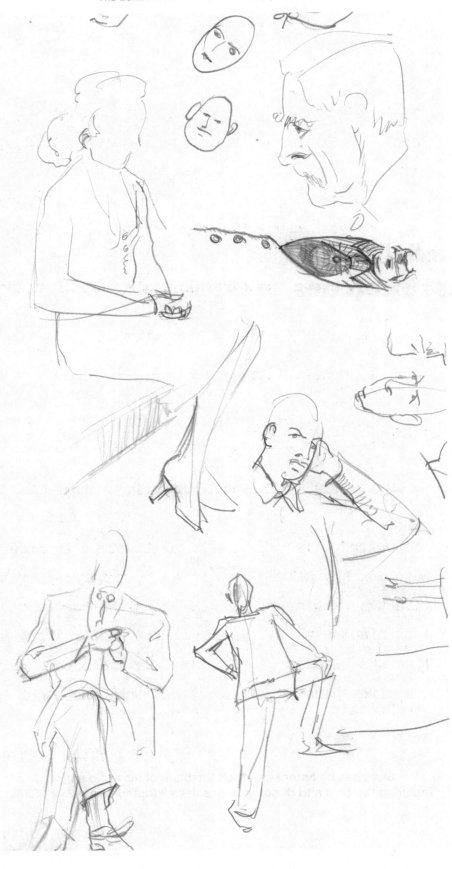

Index

Episode Titles

Also by Martin Grams, Jr.

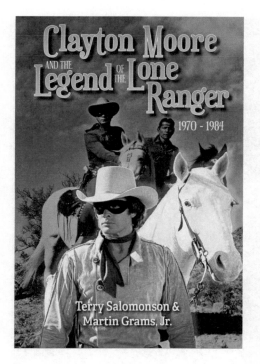

CLAYTON MOORE AND THE LEGEND OF THE LONE RANGER, 1970-1984

It was a new motion picture, told in the old Lone Ranger tradition... Numerous gun fights, satisfying explosions, and a dandy climatic fistfight. The production design was meticulous and elaborate. More than five people were credited for crafting the screenplay and some of the best talent in Hollywood was involved in all phases of production. The Lone Ranger was a name that brought back memories of radio serials and film matinees, and now he was back in a $15 million dollar movie. This book documents a day-by-day making of the 1981 motion picture and the true facts behind the minor battle between Clayton Moore and a corporation hell-bent on producing a top-notch movie.

THE LONE RANGER: The Early Years, 1933-1937

Regrettably, it was not until 1938 that the radio broadcasts were recorded on a regular basis, which means the first five years of radio broadcasts are not known to exist in recorded form. Consequently, very little has been documented about those first five years, herein referred to as "The Early Years." Historians Terry Salomonson and Martin Grams, each of whom devoted two decades researching the subject, present us with this 800-page book (technically culminating a total of four decades of research) presenting the true facts behind the origin of THE LONE RANGER program, verifying the character was not created overnight but rather developed over a period of time.

Also by Martin Grams, Jr.

THE GREEN HORNET: *A History of Radio, Motion Pictures, Comics and Television*

A complete history of the radio series from the creation to conception sketches, reprints from production files to the untold adventures, biographic details of the cast and the characters they played (including Mike Axford, Kato, Gunnigan, Lenore Case, Linda Travis, Ed Lowry, Clicker Binney, Commissioner Higgins, etc.) and background information is all provided under one cover. Also included are details of the two cliffhanger serials produced by Universal in the early forties, the unaired 1952 television pilot, the long-running popularity of the comic books and the William Dozier television series (1966-67) starring Van Williams and Bruce Lee. A complete episode guide documents every adventure including unproduced scripts and plot ideas.

THE SHADOW: *The History and Mystery of the Radio Program, 1930-1954*

"For Shadow and OTR fans, this tome will be one of the two indispensable volumes on the subject. Because it was co-written by Shadow creator Walter Gibson, The Shadow Scrapbook (1979) will remain the "bible" for many fans. But for a detailed, accurate, incisive history of The Shadow radio show and movies, it is hard to believe that there will ever be a better source than Martin Grams' definitive book."
— *Rob Farr, August 2011 issue of Radio Recall*

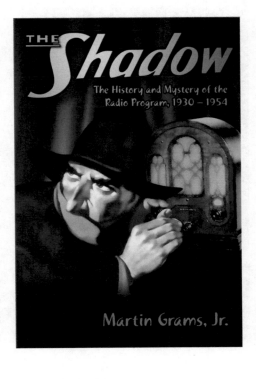

THE TWILIGHT ZONE: *Unlocking the Door to a Television Classic*

Very few television shows withstand the test of time, and Rod Serling's *The Twilight Zone* is one of the notable exceptions. Proven to be an important part of American culture since its debut on CBS in October 1959, many Hollywood producers, screenwriters and directors have been inspired and influenced by this series. Comic books, magazine articles, numerous television revivals, a major motion picture and even modern audio productions have been produced, showcasing the continuing popularity of this television classic. This definitive history presents a portrait of the beloved Rod Serling and his television program, recounting the major changes the show underwent in format and story selection, including censorship battles, production details, and exclusive memories from cast and crew. The complete episode guide recalls all 156 episodes of the series in detail that has never before been accomplished in any publication.

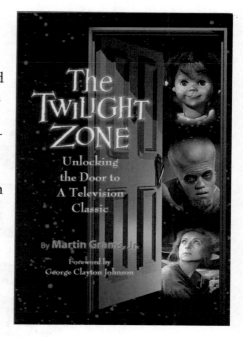

RENFREW OF THE MOUNTED: *A History of Laurie York Erskine's Canadian Mountie Franchise*

There can be no debate that his greatest success was Renfrew of the Mounted, the dramatic series of a Canadian Mountie who was more than a match for the wiliest and most hard-boiled of criminals. The cry known as the Renfrew call — which children all over America imitated, heard daily on the long-running radio program — echoed through city streets and alleys. In an era when brutality and bloodshed seemed to be exerting a baleful influence on young and old, Renfrew was unusual in that he dealt with his enemies without stooping to torture, dishonesty, and third-degree methods. In consequence, a greater strain was put on his courage and moral behavior, and he was respected, even revered, by the underworld. At the peak of his popularity, the followers of Erskine's stories, books, and radio programs could be counted in the millions.

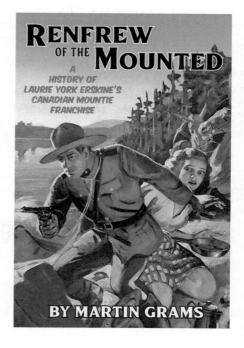

WANTED

LONE RANGER FANS

The Lone Ranger
Fan Club

Established in 2003, with a foundation dating back to 1988, The Lone Ranger Fan Club has brought together Lone Ranger fans for over two decades. With a mission of "Gathering enthusiasts to celebrate The Lone Ranger in the present, to preserve the past, and to dream for the future", The Lone Ranger Fan Club produces a quarterly e-publication, The Silver Bullet.

The Silver Bullet features historical information on The Lone Ranger, cosplayers keeping the legend alive, members' personal stories of The Lone Ranger, collections of Lone Ranger memorabilia, profiles of the cast and crews who brought *The Lone Ranger* to life, public appearance schedules of actors and artists from The Lone Ranger, along with opportunities to win Lone Ranger memorabilia.

For more information about The Lone Ranger Fan Club and to learn how to join, visit the website.

TheLRFC.org

Made in the USA
Thornton, CO
12/19/24 03:14:19

0c1322ab-7913-457b-8405-f747ab4f246aR01